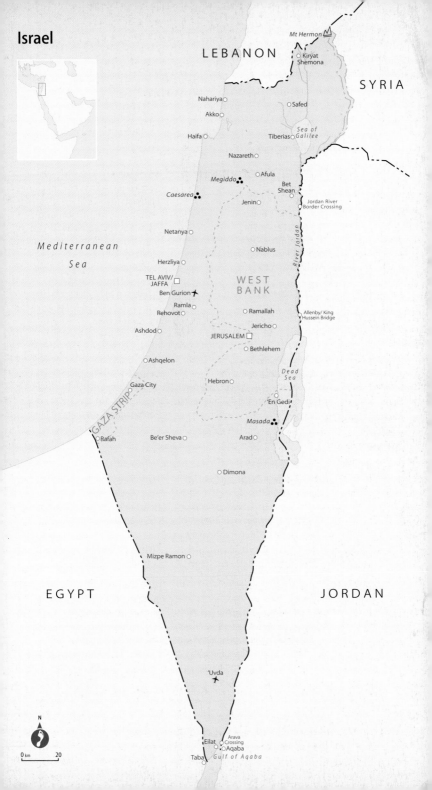

Israel

LEBANON

SYRIA

Mt Hermon

Kiryat
Shemona

Nahariya

Safed

Akko

Sea of
Galilee

Haifa

Tiberias

Nazareth

Afula

Megiddo

Bet
Shean

Caesarea

Jenin

Jordan River
Border Crossing

Netanya

River Jordan

Nablus

Mediterranean

Sea

Herzliya

WEST
BANK

TEL AVIV/
JAFFA

Ben Gurion

Ramla

Ramallah

Rehovot

Allenby/ King
Hussein Bridge

Jericho

Ashdod

JERUSALEM

Bethlehem

Ashqelon

*Dead
Sea*

Hebron

GAZA STRIP

Gaza City

'En Gedi

Masada

Rafah

Be'er Sheva

Arad

Dimona

EGYPT

JORDAN

Mizpe Ramon

N

'Uvda

Eilat

Arava
Crossing

0 km   20

Aqaba

Taba

Gulf of Aqaba

Israel Handbook

Published by Footprint Handbooks
6 Riverside Court
Lower Bristol Road
Bath BA2 3DZ. England
T +44 (0)1225 469141
F +44 (0)1225 469461
Email discover@footprintbooks.com
Web www.footprintbooks.com

ISBN 1 900949 48 2
ISSN 1368-4280
CIP DATA: A catalogue record for this
book is available from the British Library

In USA, published by
Passport Books, a division of
NTC/Contemporary Publishing Group
4255 West Touhy Avenue, Lincolnwood
(Chicago), Illinois 60712-1975, USA
T 847 679 5500 F 847 679 24941
Email NTCPUB2@AOL.COM

ISBN 0-658-00368-2
Library of Congress Catalog Card
Number on file

© Footprint Handbooks Ltd 1999
Second edition

Credits

Series editor
Patrick Dawson
Editorial
Senior editor: Sarah Thorowgood
Editor: Sara Peacock (Bookcraft Ltd)
Maps: Richard Pickvance (Bookcraft Ltd)
and Sarah Sorensen
Production
Pre-press Manager: Jo Morgan
Typesetting and layout: Bookcraft Ltd
Maps: Richard Pickvance (Bookcraft Ltd)
and Kevin Feeney
Proof reading: Lesley Abraham
(Bookcraft Ltd)

Design
Mytton Williams

Photography & drawings
Front cover: Tony Stone Images
Back cover: Pictor International
Inside colour section: Dave Winter;
Tony Stone Images; James Davis Travel
Photography; Eye Ubiquitous; TRIP Photo
Library; IMPACT Photos
Line drawings: Sahra Carter and Gareth
(Tash) Courage

Printed and bound
in Italy by LEGOPRINT

Israel

Footprint

Handbook with the Palestinian Authority Areas

Dave Winter

"Here we are in the holy land of Israel – a Mecca for tourists."

David Vine, *Superstars*, BBC1, (quoted in *Colemanballs*, *Private Eye*, February, 1980).

Contents

Left: view of Jerusalem from the Mount of Olives .In the foreground are the onion-dome spires of the Russian Orthodox church of St Mary Magdalene, whilst the graceful lines of the Dome of the Rock dominate the Old City skyline.

Right: for 2000 years Jews have been coming to the Western (Wailing) Wall to mourn the destruction of the temple in 70CE. Many visitors stuff scraps of paper containing prayers into the cracks between the huge stone blocks.

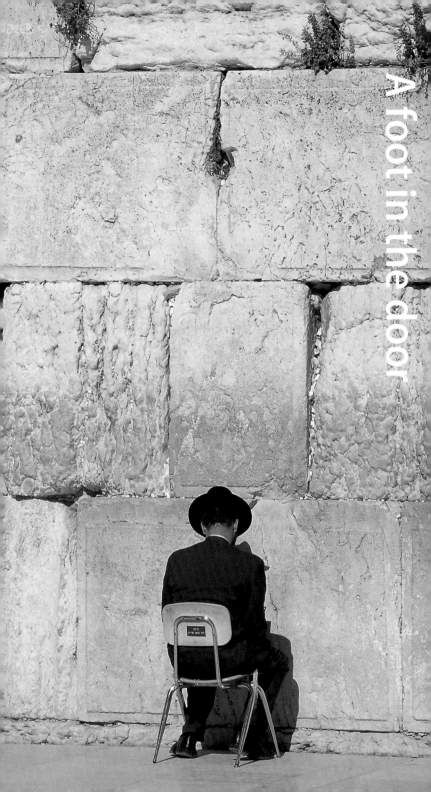

A foot in the door

Highlights

Israel is very nearly the perfect tourist destination. Whether you are there for a two-week sun and sand package holiday; a religious pilgrimage; a journey of personal fulfilment; or simply looking for some casual work to finance the next stage of your travels, you will be hard-pressed to find a country that can match the range and diversity of this small land's attractions. And given Israel's small size, it is very easy to combine a pilgrimage with a bit of sightseeing and some holiday-making: within the space of one day you can pray at the sight of Christ's Crucifixion, then later be seen posing in your thong on the beach in Tel Aviv.

The natural environment Israel is a country of outstanding natural beauty. Its wooded, rolling hills are at their best in Galilee, notably in and around Mount Carmel National Park. The Golan plateau, offers the snowy peak of Mount Hermon at one extreme and unprecedented views down to the Sea of Galilee at the other. And visitors who spend any time exploring the olive-grove covered hills of the West Bank will never doubt that they are in the land of the Bible.

Those seeking more austere and forbidding landscapes will be drawn to the Negev desert and the Dead Sea region. Whilst the latter features the lowest point on Earth and a sea above whose surface you literally float, the former offers a highly eroded landscape of unusual rock formations, deep craters, plus hidden pockets of vegetation and irrigation.

Israel's coastline also offers choices between the white sand beaches of the Mediterranean coast, or the underwater glory of the Red Sea's coral reefs. But marine life is not Israel's only faunal attraction. Standing on the route of the main migratory flight-path between Africa and Europe, Israel is a bird-watcher's paradise, offering the chance to spot nearly 400 species.

All these landscapes are little more than a few hours' drive apart and since Israelis love to hike, the country is criss-crossed by a series of well-marked walking trails that provide perhaps the best way to explore this land. There's even a marked hiking trail from one end of the country to the other.

Living history Over 6,000 years of faith, history and archaeology are packaged and presented at a variety of sites scattered across the country, many of which are so well preserved that you can almost imagine yourself being transported back in time. With a little imagination you could be a Roman legionnaire about to sack Jerusalem; a Jewish zealot defending the hill-top fortress of Masada to the very last; a Crusader knight preparing to face the army of Salah al-Din; or a disciple of Jesus standing on the shores of the Sea of Galilee.

Working and chilling out For several decades now Israel has appealed to young travellers as a place where you can escape from the daily grind. Not just the nine-to-five job, but from the trials of life on the road: you can hang up your backpack for a while without having to go home first. It is also a place to earn a few shekels in order to prolong your travelling.

Such an opportunity is provided by the kibbutz system. In exchange for eight hours' work (albeit usually very hard) a day, all your accommodation and eating requirements are met, plus you earn a little pocket money into the bargain. It won't make you rich, but most former 'kibbutzniks' agree that it is an unforgettable experience. Those prepared to work a little bit harder will find a similar deal on a moshav, where wages are slightly higher. There are also several thousand backpackers in Israel making a living through the 'informal' labour market, staffing the bars and restaurants and helping to construct the hotels that all the other visitors eat, drink and stay in!

Left: the Church of All Nations, at the foot of the Mount of Olives, built in 1924 using subscriptions collected worldwide. To the left is the site of the Garden of Gethsemane, where Jesus was betrayed.

Below: the Dead Sea is rich in supposedly health-giving minerals and has spawned a whole tourism industry based upon the 'health and beauty' potential of the local environment.

Above: the Negev desert is a region of outstanding natural beauty and comprises about half of Israel's land area. The whole desert is criss-crossed by a series of marked trails negotiable on foot, by jeep or on camel back.

Left: though many visitors are attracted by the underwater splendour of the Red Sea coast at Eilat, the Mediterranean coast features kilometre upon kilometre of fine white sand beaches, such as this one at Netanya. **Next page**: St George's monastery clings to the side of the Wadi Qelt ravine. Between the 4th-7th centuries CE, communities of anchorites (religious hermits) established isolated monasteries in the Judean desert.

Right: one of the country's most beautiful religious buildings is the Shrine of the Bab in Haifa, marking the burial place of the martyr-herald who foretold the coming of Baha'ullah, founder of the Baha'i Universalist religion. **Below**: Christian pilgrims visiting Jerusalem recreate Jesus' final walk along Via Dolorosa from the place of his Condemnation to the site of his Crucifixion.

Above: a family celebrating a bar mitzvah at the Western (Wailing) Wall. Jewish males reach adulthood at 13, when they become subject to Jewish Law. On the first Shabbat after his 13th birthday, the boy reads a portion of the Torah in a synagogue for the first time. **Right**: the chalice window above the altar in the church of Dominus Flevit on the Mount of Olives beautifully frames the view of the Dome of the Rock in Jerusalem's old city.

Faith, piety and pilgrimage

For many visitors, a journey to Israel is the journey of a lifetime. This is the centre of the world's three great monotheistic religions: the 'promised land' of 'milk and honey' to Jews; the scene of Christ's Ministry, Crucifixion and Resurrection; and to Muslims, the site of the Prophet Mohammad's night ascent to heaven.

Jews

The whole raison d'être for the creation of the modern State of Israel was the "ingathering of the exiles" (Genesis 15:13-16): to provide a homeland and refuge for the Jewish people in the land that they believe was promised to them by God (Genesis 12:7). The Jewish attachment to this land is undeniable, "next year in Jerusalem" has been a Yom Kippur refrain right round the world for several millenia.

All across Israel you will find sites that bear witness to the major events in Jewish history. Dusty and initially confusing archaeological sites really do become living history when you stand with a Bible or ancient historical document in hand and realize that the text you are reading describes the scene before you. At places associated with the Jewish Revolt of 66-73 CE, such as Masada or Gamla, try reading a contemporary account of the bloodshed, such as Jewish historian Josephus' work *The Jewish War*, to make history come alive.

Christians

By visiting the sites associated with Jesus' birth, his preaching ministry, his crucifixion and resurrection, many Christian pilgrims find that their faith in the teachings of Christ is reaffirmed. There are many who mock pilgrimages to the Holy Land (Monty Python's *Life of Brian* has much to answer for), but it is reassuring to know that archaeological, historical and circumstantial evidence suggests that both the Church of the Nativity in Bethlehem and the Church of the Holy Sepulchre in Jerusalem actually do mark the spots where Jesus was born and crucified.

Of course many sites associated with various events in the life of Jesus are entirely spurious, resulting largely from the desire of Byzantine and medieval period pilgrims to locate precisely each and every event mentioned in the New Testament. However, even those sites that are regarded as 'traditional', as opposed to 'actual', do allow visitors to picture a scene as Jesus may have seen it.

Muslims

The Qur'an states that "Glory be to Him who carried His servant by night from the Holy Mosque to the Farthest Mosque the precincts of which We have blessed" (Sura 17:1), and it is from this line that Jerusalem draws its fundamental importance within the Islamic faith. Though not mentioned by name, the "Farthest Mosque" has come to symbolize the mosque on the Temple Mount in Jerusalem, with Muslims referring to this holy area as the Haram al-Sharif ('Noble Sanctuary'). This is the third holiest site within Islam.

Muslim Arabs account for around three-quarters of Israel's non-Jewish population, and whereas much of Israel leans culturally towards Europe and North America, a visit to the main Arab towns provides a window onto the wider Middle East. Many of the Palestinian population centres now have a degree of autonomy and are administered by the Palestinian Authority, whose President Arafat is pressing hard for an independent Palestinian state.

Other faiths

The 'Holy Land' is in fact a pretty good description. In addition to the three great monotheistic religions, each of which may be subdivided into numerous denominations, sects and sub-sects, Israel is also holy to a number of other faiths. There are a number of Druze communities in Israel, concentrated mainly in the Haifa and Upper Golan regions, whilst the Universalist Baha'i faith have their two holiest sites in the north of the country.

Modern Israel

The old and the new

Never has that old tourist guide cliché about "a land of contrasts" been more applicable than when describing Israel (and we are not just talking about the variety of landscapes). The population is not as simple as a matter of Jews, Muslims or Christians: it's secular and observant; it's Ashkenazi Jews and Sephardi Jews; it's Israeli Arabs and Palestinian Arabs; it's Orthodox Christians and members of the 'Western' Church. Stand on any street corner in Israel and you're likely to observe as many lycra-clad teenage girls teetering past on high heels as you are families of ultra-Orthodox haredim dressed in clothing straight out of the 18th century Eastern European shtetl. For every holy or religious site that Jerusalem has, Tel Aviv boasts a European-style pavement café. And for every testosterone-heavy Israeli soldier that you see with his gun strapped across his back, you'll see a female equivalent in full uniform and make-up with manicured nails. Israel really is a country of the old and the new, past and present living side by side.

From the travel brochure

Israel fits very neatly into the travel agent's brochure. Its benign climate offers long days lying on white Mediterranean sand, with resorts and beaches to suite all tastes. For example, you could join the masses on Shabbat at the metropolitan beaches at Tel Aviv, as the whole city heads seawards for some weekend 'R&R'. Or if you prefer things a little quieter, then check out the almost unlimited stretch of sand at Dor, Tantura and Nahsholim just to the south of Haifa. And if you demand more from your beach than just a strip of fine white sand, then why not visit the beaches at Ashqelon, Caesarea and Akhziv, all of which have an impressive collection of archaeological remains as a back drop.

Israel's premier beach resort is of course Eilat, at the southern tip of the country. Whilst the beaches here do not have the same fine texture as their Mediterranean counterparts, they do offer some of the world's best diving and snorkelling; the coral reefs of the Red Sea coast are one of the world's natural wonders.

Away from the beach, Israel's travel brochure offers you seasonal skiing on the snowy slopes of Mount Hermon; jeep, camel and donkey treks into the Negev and Judean deserts; a surprising range of landscapes and natural features in a country so small; and as much religion, history and archaeology as you could ever want.

Listen and learn

A seemingly intractable dispute takes some of the gloss off Israel's 'brochure' image: this tiny land, smaller than Belgium, or Wales, or the State of New Jersey, is claimed by two peoples: the Israelis and the Palestinians. The struggle between the two co-claimants has been long and bitter, and often violent and deadly, with both sides using terrorism as a means to an end. For the visitor, you are extremely unlikely to be personally touched by outbreaks of violence, though you may be constantly aware of the tension.

However, the election of Ehud Barak as Prime Minister in 1999 has brought fresh hope, with the revival of what had seemed to be a moribund peace process. You will regularly be invited to debate the 'situation' by Israelis, Palestinians and fellow-travellers alike, and this is a great opportunity to learn something about the people whose lives we see discussed so regularly on news broadcasts. In such a situation it is worth bearing in mind the comments of the veteran regional commentator, Thomas Friedman: "When it comes to discussing the Middle East, people go temporarily insane". Make sure that you are well read, and don't pack your prejudices and preconceived notions in your luggage.

Left: recently restored Hassan Beq Mosque in Jaffa's Manshieh Quarter stands in stark contrast to the luxury David Inter-Continental Hotel. **Below**: a church has stood over the reputed home of the Virgin since the 4th or 5th century CE. Nazareth's present Basilica of the Annunciation, dates from 1969, and is expecting a papal visit in March 2000.

Above: orthodoxy and modernity side by side in Jerusalem. **Left**: Mahane Yehuda market stands at the heart of the predominently Sephardi Orthodox neighbourhood in Jerusalem. **Next page**: two elderly residents of the Muslim Quarter of Jerusalem's Old City on their way to the Dome of the Rock.

Essentials

2

Essentials

Planning your trip

Where to go

Israel has so much to offer that it can be hard to know where to begin; it really does have a bit of everything. Statistics from the Ministry of Tourism suggest that around a quarter of visitors to Israel describe themselves as 'pilgrims', a further 25% or so come as 'sightseers', another 25% are 'holiday-makers', whilst the rest come on business or to visit family and friends. This breakdown really does emphasize just how diverse Israel's attractions are.

The vast majority of visitors base themselves in Tel Aviv, Jerusalem, Eilat and Tiberias, then visit the rest of the country in a series of extended day trips. Though many foreign tourists come on pre-arranged package tours, Israel really is very easy to explore independently, and this *Handbook* will provide information for all your accommodation, transport, dining and entertainment needs, whatever your budget. Even relying on public transport it should be possible to see a large percentage of all the key highlights in just 2 weeks, though the more time you have to spend the better; a month dedicated to sightseeing would allow you to see just about everything. Below is a list of Israel's highlights.

Haram al-Sharif/Temple Mount   Sacred to Jews, Muslims and Christians alike, this artificially raised mound in Jerusalem was the site of the Jewish Temples built by Solomon and Herod the Great. Jews still come to the Western (Wailing) Wall here to mourn the destruction of the Temple. The platform is now occupied by one of the world's most beautiful and recognizable monuments: the Dome of the Rock that marks the point of the prophet Mohammad's night ascent to heaven. **Church of the Holy Sepulchre**   The central shrine in Christendom, there is very good evidence to suggest that this church marks the actual site of Jesus' Crucifixion. **Church of the Nativity**   This church in Bethlehem is built over the tradition site of Jesus' birth, and attracts Christian pilgrims from all over the world (particularly at Christmas). **Cave of Machpelah/Haram el-Khalil**   Considered the place where Jewish history effectively began, this is the traditional site of the cave that the patriarch Abraham bought as a family burial tomb. The site is also of profound significance to Muslims. **Tabgha, Capernaum and Mount of the Beatitudes**   Marking traditional sites in Jesus' Galilean Ministry, churches here recall events in the life of Christ, including the 'Sermon on the Mount' and the 'Feeding of the 5,000'. **Shrine of the Bab, Haifa**   This beautiful monument is the tomb of Bab, the Martyr-Herald who foretold the coming of Baha'ullah, the founder of the Baha'i faith.

Holy places

Masada   Undoubtedly one of Israel's key highlights, this mountain-top fortress combines spectacular views and significant archaeological remains from one of the defining events in Jewish history. **Caesarea**   Herod's magnificent port city contains extensive remains from later Roman, Byzantine and Crusader occupation, and is the key archaeological attraction on the Mediterranean coast. **Bet Shean**   Impressive remains from a number of periods, including the best-preserved Roman-Byzantine town in Israel. **Hammat Gader**   A little bit of everything, the site has the best preserved Roman baths in Israel, an active spa, and a terrifying alligator farm. **Avdat (Oboda)**   Substantially restored, this is the best-preserved example of a Nabatean-Roman-Byzantine city, set in a spectacular environment in the Negev desert. **Sepphoris (Zippori)**   Remains from a succession of cities on this site, though noted for the quality of the Roman and Byzantine mosaics and for the dynamic presentation of the attractions. **Nimrod Fortress**   The best-preserved medieval fortress in Israel, with breathtaking views across the Galilee and Golan area.

History & archaeology

Essentials

Natural environment	**Dead Sea** A truly unique experience at the lowest point in the world (400m below sea-level), the high saline content of this lake allows you to experience a sensation akin to floating above the water's surface. The chemical components of the Dead Sea are said to have medicinal and invigorating properties, and a whole health and beauty industry has developed on its shores. **Makhtesh Ramon** This deep erosion crater represents a unique geological feature found only here, in the heart of the Negev desert. Often described as the Israeli equivalent to America's Grand Canyon, it features some spectacular rock formations and vividly coloured rock outcrops. Hiking here, or in the Negev's two smaller erosion craters (Makhtesh HaGadol/Makhtesh HaKatan), is highly recommended. **Banias** This reserve is an area of supreme natural beauty and also of considerable historical and archaeological interest. The site of one of the sources of the Jordan River and the point where several streams collecting snow melt from Mt Hermon converge, the reserve is an area of running water, cascading waterfalls and a dense mix of vegetation types. **Ein Avdat** A short walk along the seasonal Wadi Zin reveals that rarest of desert commodities, water pools, as well as providing some peaceful picnic spots. **Tel Dan** This Nature Reserve compares favourably for beauty with any of Israel's other nature reserves, as the perennial Dan River, the major source of the Jordan River, flows through. Four different marked trails traverse the lush waterscape, taking in the floral and faunal highlights as well as exploring the evidence of mankind's sojourn in the area. **Gamla** The appeal of this viewpoint down onto the Lower Golan and Sea of Galilee region is enhanced by the swooping birds of prey that nest in the cliffs here and the archaeological remains of one of the most dramatic events in the First Jewish Revolt against Rome (66-73 CE). **Underwater Observatory, Eilat** Do not miss this opportunity to descend to the sea bed to observe thousands of brightly coloured fish feeding on the Red Sea's coral reef (and done without getting the slightest bit wet).
'Living museums'	**Old City, Jerusalem** One of the most memorable experiences of a visit to Israel is a wander around the narrow streets of Jerusalem's Old City, exploring sites fundamental to Judaism, Christianity and Islam as you come across them, and taking in the atmosphere of a truly Middle Eastern environment. **Old Akko (Acre)** This last bastion of Crusader rule in the Holy Land features a selection of attractions from the Crusader, Late Arab and Ottoman periods confined within a compact, labyrinthine quarter. **Old Jaffa** Only small sections of the old town remain today, though they have been tastefully restored and provide a pleasant contrast to the modern environs of nearby Tel Aviv. The 'Old Jaffa' area is now a concentration of galleries, antique shops and restaurants, and is a popular destination with evening strollers. **Old Jewish Quarter, Safed** One of the 4 holy cities of the Jews, and the spiritual capital of Jewish mysticism, the town is equally attractive to the secular and gentile alike, who come to admire the views, wander around the narrow streets of the Old City, or browse amongst the galleries and workshops of the Artists' Colony.
Museums	**Israel Museum, Jerusalem** For visitors to Israel who intend exploring the country's major archaeological sites your journey should either begin or end at this museum: Israel's foremost collection of antiquities and art. Highlights displayed include a selection of the 'Dead Sea Scrolls' material. **Diaspora Museum, Tel Aviv** This impressive museum traces the history of the Jewish Diaspora communities throughout the ages and the world.
National Parks and Nature Reserves	Many of Israel's key archaeological and scenic attractions are enclosed within national parks and nature reserves. Previously run by two separate administrations, the two have recently merged to form the **National Parks and Nature Reserves Authority** (4, Rav Aluf Makleff, Tel Aviv, T03 5766888). If you intend visiting more than five National Parks within a 14-day period, it makes

Israel's weather profile

A simplified year-round weather forecast would predict: (i) heavier rainfall in the north and centre of the country than in the south; (ii) humid summers and mild winters on the coast; (iii) dry summers and moderately cold winters in the upland areas; (iv) hot dry summers and pleasant winters in the Jordan Valley; and (v) year-round semi-desert conditions in the Negev.

Essentials

sense to buy the **Green Card**. Costing 60 NIS, in theory you can visit all the National Parks once, as long as you can do so within a 2-week period. Cards are available from the National Parks and Nature Reserves Authority head office, or from the 'main' national parks. **NB** At the time of going to press, it was not clear whether some new 'combined' form of Green Card was going to be produced to reflect the merger of the National Parks Authority and the Nature Reserves Authority.

When to go

There are 2 key factors to bear in mind when timetabling a visit to Israel: climate, and religious holidays/festivals.

Climate

The climatic seasons in Israel are the same as those in Europe (and the northern hemisphere). Thus spring is roughly March-May, summer is June-August, autumn (fall) is September-October and winter is November-February. As a very general guide, **winter** tends to be rather wet and overcast, becoming colder and wetter the further north or the higher up you go. Many visitors are unprepared for just how cold it gets in Jerusalem and Bethlehem in the winter. Nevertheless, the Dead Sea Region and the Negev are particularly appealing at this time of year, with day-time temperatures very comfortable. Since Israel is so small, it does not take much travelling to escape from a cold and wet Jerusalem to a dry and sunny Eilat. Indeed, winter is an ideal time to take a beach holiday in Eilat.

Climatic conditions in **spring** are ideal across most of the country, notably in the Negev and Dead Sea Region, where day-time temperatures have not climbed too high. Temperatures are beginning to pick up on the Mediterranean coast and Jerusalem area, though there will be some rainy days. Galilee (notably Upper Galilee and Golan) may still be cloudy and wet.

Early **summer** is the best time to visit Galilee and the northern areas, with the cooling influence of the sea making the Mediterranean coast an appealing option. At the height of summer, however, the Dead Sea Region and Negev can get far too hot to be comfortable.

As summer turns to **autumn** around September, the entire country becomes an attractive proposition, with comfortable temperatures and little rainfall. As autumn draws to an end, however, the northern areas such as Galilee and Golan become cloudier and wetter.

Holidays

Unless you are coming to Israel to specifically celebrate a religious holiday (whether Jewish or Christian), the main holiday periods are a good time to avoid coming. Flights to and from Israel just before or after religious holidays tend to be heavily booked, and you will almost certainly end up paying more for your ticket. Likewise, accommodation prices rocket (sometimes double), and in some places it can be difficult to find a room without an advance reservation.

The key Christian festivals are of course Easter and Christmas, though the accommodation shortfalls and problems of over-crowding at major sites only really affect visitors to Jerusalem and Bethlehem. Note, however, that different branches of the Church celebrate these events at different times, and hence the Christmas and Easter rush can become quite an extended period. Nevertheless, there is a special atmosphere in Jerusalem and Bethlehem at these times (even if you are non-observant).

Jewish holidays and festivals are numerous, though the key ones are Rosh Hashanah, Yom Kippur, Sukkot and Pesah. Though the holidays are generally brief (usually 1 day), you should bear in mind that the holiday affects all aspects of life in Israel. Not only do accommodation prices sky-rocket, but almost everything else closes down (including places to eat, sights, banks, post offices and transport). When several holidays come along together it can have a major impact on your visit. Dates of Jewish holidays follow the lunar calendar and thus change each year, though the approximate time of year remains the same. Thus, September/October may be a time to avoid since Rosh Hashanah, Yom Kippur and Sukkot all come along together. Likewise, April/May tends to feature Pesah, Independence Day and Holocaust Memorial Day. For full details of holidays and festivals see the section starting on page 59.

What will it cost?

Compared with the rest of the Middle East, South Asia and Southeast Asia, Israel is relatively expensive; costs are more on a par with those in North America, Northern Europe and Australasia. How much you spend per day whilst in Israel largely depends upon how you spend your time, where you stay, and where you eat. The following information is directed mainly at backpackers, to whom the cost of living in a country is usually of primary concern.

Jerusalem's hostels provide the cheapest accommodation in Israel (at $7-8), though generally you should expect to pay around $9-12 for dormitories in the other large cities. In some of the more remote places of interest, IYHA hostels provide the cheapest (and only) accommodation at $18 per night. There is a big jump in price for double rooms, with the cheapest generally $26-$50. For further details on accommodation see page 43.

Dining out in Israel can be an expensive business. The cheapest eating options are provided by the ubiquitous falafel and shwarma stands, though eating at these 3 times a day is neither good for your health nor morale. Expect to spend $15-$20 a day for 1 decent meal plus 2 'street meals'. Hostels with their own kitchens can reduce your food bill. You pay around $5-7 for a beer in a regular bar, though these prices can be halved if you go to one of Israel's many pubs/clubs that are aimed at the backpacker community.

Public transport in Israel is reasonably good value. As a example, the 1-hour bus ride from Tel Aviv to Jerusalem is $5, whilst the country's longest bus journey, the 4½ hrs from Jerusalem to Eilat, is $14. For further details on getting around see page 47.

Your daily budget will be influenced by how much sightseeing you intend doing. Israeli museums, galleries, religious sites, national parks and general sights charge anywhere between nothing and $20 for admission, though the average seems to be around $5. Don't let admission fees deter you from visiting; if you are on a very tight budget, then pick and choose carefully.

Of course, many visitors to Israel finance their stay in Israel by working (whether legally or illegally, see page 64). However, with careful budgeting it should be possible to eat, sleep and see something of the country on $25-$40 per day. You do meet some people surviving on $15 a day or less, though they invariably seem to be miserable and tend to leave Israel having seen next to nothing of the country.

What to take

Most travellers tend to take too much, particularly when you bear in mind that practically everything that you need is available in Israel. However, with few exceptions, most things bought in Israel will be more expensive than back home. There are a few things that you might like to bear in mind before packing your bag for Israel.

Taking appropriate **clothing** is essential. When selecting which clothing to take, you should remember cultural and religious factors as well as climatic considerations. When passing through either Arab or religious Jewish areas, conservative dress is a must. This means no shorts or bare shoulders on either men or women, closed necklines, and loose unrevealing clothes. In Jewish religious areas women are requested to wear long skirts as opposed to trousers. At Jewish religious sites both men and women are requested to cover their heads; yarmulkes and scarfs are often provided, though it is as well to bring some sort of head-covering or hat of your own. **You will be denied entry into churches, mosques and synagogues alike if you are inappropriately dressed.** In summer light loose-fighting cottons are best, though desert and upland areas can get remarkably cold at night. With the exception of day-time in Eilat, the Negev and the Dead Sea Region, winter in Israel can get very cold and wet so bring appropriate warm clothing. Army surplus stores are a cheap source of clothing locally, though it can be inappropriate to wear it in certain areas of Israel and the Palestinian Authority areas.

Toiletries, including tampons, sanitary towels and condoms, are readily available in Israel, though they tend to be more expensive than at home. The same applies to **photographic products**. Those staying in hostels may like to bring their own cotton **sleep-sheet** and **ear-plugs**.

Tours and tour operators

There are any number of tour companies featuring Israel as a destination, and just about any travel agent you walk into will be able to book you on to some sort of package deal. In the UK, the weekly *Jewish Chronicle* frequently has last-minute flight deals as well as competitively priced packages (especially to Eilat, where the advert generally also states which hotel you will be in and whether your room faces a building site or not!). Below is just a small selection of UK-based tour operators offering trips to Israel. For details of flights to Israel see page 31.

Blue Line, 17 Hendon Lane, London, N3 1RT, T0181-3465955. *Broadway Holidays*, 76 The Broadway, Stanmore, Middlesex, HA7 4DU, T0181-4207000. *C-L Bible Tours*, Oakdale, High Ongar Rd, Ongar, Essex, CM5 9LZ, T01277-366137. *Fairlink Christian Travel*, 12-14 Glendower Place, London, SW7 3DP, T0171-2250555. *Israel Travel Service*, 546-550 Royal Exchange, Old Bank St, Manchester, M2 7EN, T0161-8391111. *Jasmin Tours*, 53-55 Balham Hill, London, SW12 9DR, T0181-6758886, F6731204. Escorted tours to the Near and Far East. *McCabe Travel*, 53-55 Balham Hill, London, SW12 9DR, T0181-6756828. Run by the McCabe Educational Trust, who aim to advance religious education through knowledge of the Bible Lands, this is Britain's foremost religious tour operator. We have received many recommendations for this company. *Peltours*, 11 Ballards Lane, London, N3 1UX, T0181-3430590; 14a Cross St, London, EC1N 8XA, T0171-4302230; 240 Station Rd, Edgware, Middlesex, HA8 7AU, T0181-9581144; 27 Church St, Manchester, M4 1QA, T0161-8343721. Long-established firm, specializes in Israel, can arrange discount pre-paid car hire. *Pullman*, 31 Belgrave Rd, London, SW1V 1RB, T0171-9317016. *Rosary Pilgrimage Apostolate*, 12 Farleigh Crescent, The Lawns, Swindon, Wiltshire, SN3 1JY, T01793-422714. Roman Catholic tours. *Saga Holidays*, Saga Building, Middleburg Square, Folkestone, Kent, CT20 1AZ, T0800-318225. Well-reputed firm offering tours for over 50s. *Superstar*, UK House, 180 Oxford St,

Diving code of conduct

Don't touch, kneel on or kick corals *They are delicate animals, which are damaged when touched.*

Don't stir up the sand *Sand settling on coral inhibits its feeding and limits growth; in suspension it reduces the sunlight's penetration with the same effect.*

Don't collect souvenirs *Many dive sites are heavily visited and could become rapidly depleted of their resources.*

Don't feed the marine life *Feeding interferes with the reef's natural food chains. It can produce dependency and in some cases aggression in normally non-aggressive species.*

Don't catch marine life *Fishing and spearfishing is prohibited in National Parks/Protected Areas.*

Do control your buoyancy and body/equipment placement *Much damage is done unknowingly. Proper buoyancy control is crucial; practise away*

from reefs. Be aware of trailing gauges and alternative air sources, which can drag along the reef.

Do respect aquatic life *For the most part, the fish appear indifferent or mildly inquisitive towards divers. However, excessive attention, or activities such as hitching lifts on dolphins or turtles, can cause stress and interfere with mating behaviour.*

Do collect any rubbish you see *Litter is a significant and blatantly unnecessary cause of damage to the reef.*

Do inform divers if they are damaging the reef or acting irresponsibly *Many people act out of ignorance; speaking up helps raise environmental awareness.*

Do report damage to the reef, injured marine life or other disturbances *As a diver, you are in a position to contribute towards the monitoring of reef ecosystems.*

London, W1N 0EL, T0645-125847. Part of El Al. *TravelLink*, 50 Vivian Ave, London, NW4 3XH, T0181-9318000. *WST Holidays*, 65 Wigmore St, London, W1H 9LG, T0171-2240504. Good for students, linked to *issta* in Israel.

Special interest travel

Diving The Gulf of Aqaba is justifiably rated as being home to some of the world's best dive sites, and though most potential divers head to the Sinai (Egypt), there are plenty of diving opportunities in Eilat. All the dive centres in Eilat offer 'introductory dives', which you can do with no previous experience (usually around $40, though a medical may be compulsory). These dives are to a maximum of 6m with a qualified instructor taking full charge.

However, if you really want to appreciate the fascination of diving, the only thing for it is to learn. **Beginners'** (Open Water) courses with PADI, SSI, CMAS or NAUI are available at all the dive centres. They usually last 5 days and include at least 10 dives. Once you have completed the course (and passed) you are free to dive within the limits set by your Open Water qualification. After that there are Advanced courses, usually only 2-3 days, followed by **Rescue** courses and a whole host of speciality courses, including wreck diving, deep diving, night diving, navigation, etc. Finally, there is the **Divemaster** course, which is the minimum qualification needed to work as a dive guide. This takes from 2 to 4 weeks. When enquiring after diving courses check whether the price quoted includes certification and log book. Some dive centres charge for this separately, with the cost being in the region of $30-40 extra.

All dives include tanks and weightbelt. All the other equipment can be rented from the dive centre you go with. If you are going for a full day, or for longer, hire of all the equipment usually costs around $20-35 per day. It is worth checking the state of the equipment you are hiring. Most of it comes under heavy use and begins to wear out quickly; broken fastenings on a buoyancy control jacket or bad-fitting/damaged flippers can be very distracting when what you want to do is give your full attention to the marine life around you. The major dive centres have underwater camera equipment available for hire, and also run underwater photography courses. Eilat also has decompression chambers for dealing with diving accidents. Diving is available along the Mediterranean coast, though most prefer the underwater attractions of the Red Sea.

As an alternative to diving you could try **snuba**, where the air supply remains on a floating raft on the sea's surface and the air is piped down to you. Alternatively, **snorkelling** probably offers an even better means of viewing coral reefs since they tend to grow relatively close to the surface (making diving unnecessary).

A full range of watersports, from water-skiing, sailing, kayaking, wind-surfing, jet-skiing, and being towed along on an inflatable yellow banana, are all available in Eilat and at the Mediterranean coastal resorts. See relevant 'Essentials' sections for details.

Watersports

Israelis love to hike, and Israel is a great country for hiking. Carefully marked colour-coded trails crisscross the country, and in theory it's possible to follow a single trail from the Golan down to Eilat! The best hiking resource is the **SPNI** (Society for the Protection of Nature in Israel), who have offices and field schools across the country. They are generally staffed by dedicated hikers who are keen to share their enthusiasm with you. SPNI also sell detailed 1:50,000 hiking maps (48 NIS), though unfortunately all but the Eilat sheet are only available in Hebrew. However, staff are often keen to translate the relevant details for you. For further information and accommodation booking, contact their head office at 4 Hashfela, 661183 Tel Aviv, T03-6388688, F6877695.

Hiking

See 'Hiking code of conduct' on next page

Serious hikers should buy Joel Roskin's *A Guide to Hiking in Israel with 40 selected one-day hikes* (1994, Jerusalem Post Publications, available at most branches of Steimatsky Bookshops), or his more recent book detailing 'water-hikes' in Israel.

A very subjective list of hikes described in this Handbook would include: Lower Wadi Qelt ('West Bank' chapter); 'En Gedi dry canyon ('Dead Sea Region' chapter); Red Canyon ('Negev' chapter); Mt Ardon-Ein Saharonim ('Negev' chapter); Banias ('Galilee and Golan' chapter); and the Nahal Yehudiya hike, and Upper and Lower Zavitan hikes in Ya'ar Yehudiya Nature Reserve ('Galilee and Golan' chapter).

Israel has 16 graded ski runs and 25km of slopes at the Mount Hermon Ski Centre in Upper Golan. The skiing receives mixed reviews, though at least the option is there (between December and late April).

Skiing

This is available at a number of places, though notably in the Galilee and Golan region. Try *Vered HaGalil*, near the Sea of Galilee, T06-6935785, F6934964; *Texas Ranch*, Eilat, T07-6376663; *Kibbutz Nahsholim*, near Netanya, T06-6399533, F6397614; *HaVatzelet HaSharon*, near Netanya, T09-8663525; *Cactus Ranch*, Netanya, T09-8651239; *Herod's Stables*, Caesarea, T06-8361181; or enquire at the nearest Tourist Office.

Horse-riding

Israel is a superb place for bird-watching because of its location on the main migratory route between Europe and Africa. The International Bird Watching Centre in Eilat (T07-6335339/6374741, F6376922) is a good place to enquire about further information, though there are also noted 'twitching' sites in Upper Galilee and the Golan.

Bird-watching

Peace treaties signed between Israel and Egypt and Israel and Jordan mean that regional travel has never been easier. Many visitors to Israel are now using Eilat as a jumping-off point for making an excursion into southern Jordan. The key attractions here are the 'lost' Nabatean city of **Petra** and the oasis of **Wadi Rum**, the latter made famous by Lawrence of Arabia. Both are just a few hours drive from Eilat, though a 2-day excursion will allow visitors to make more of the major points of interest. Eilat is also the

Onward travel and excursions

Essentials

Hiking code of conduct

Water Few hikes have sources of potable (drinkable) water en route, so you must carry your own supply. The amount you carry will really depend upon the length of the hike and the season, though it should never be less than one litre per person (two litres per person is a better figure). A good way of carrying your water (and keeping it cool) is to buy a thermally insulated jacket that fits around a standard one-litre mineral water bottle. Most have straps attached so they can be carried like a mini rucksack. They are available in camping stores across Israel for around 20 NIS and generally keep water cool for up to six hours.

Clothing Comfortable footwear is essential. This does not necessarily mean walking boots, though the added ankle support is useful. A wide-brimmed hat can also help to prevent sun-stroke. High protection factor sun-block should also be worn.

Season/timing The best time to hike depends upon the location, though in desert regions it is between October and April when the day-time temperatures are more manageable. In winter, however, there is the danger in some areas of flash floods. Hiking is not recommended if it looks like it is about to rain, or has rained in the past few days. If it rains whilst you are walking, avoid entering canyons or seemingly dry river beds. Always take local advice, particularly from park rangers and SPNI officers, before commencing your trek. Hiking in summer is best avoided. High midday temperatures, even in winter, mean that you should aim to make an early start, if necessary resting up during the middle of the day.

Routes The best routes are all marked by colour-coded trail markers. Stick to them. This not only offers you a degree of security, it also provides protection to the environment by controlling the activities of visitors.

Maps The hiking maps provided within the Israel Handbook are for general information, and are not intended to serve as an alternative to the SPNI-prepared 1:50,000 hiking maps. If making an ambitious hike, you are strongly advised to buy the relevant sheet of the SPNI map. These generally cost 48 NIS and are available from most SPNI offices, particularly those in the larger towns. Unfortunately, only the Eilat area sheet has been translated from Hebrew into English, though staff at most SPNI offices and Field Schools are more than happy to translate the relevant data for you.

Expert advice SPNI offices and Field Schools offer expert advice, particularly on local areas, and you are well advised to make use of this free resource. Before attempting any trek, it is worth 'clearing' it with the local SPNI Field School. This is a legal requirement for all hikes in the Golan.

Security This aspect is particularly relevant if you are hiking alone (bad idea). Before commencing your trek, it is strongly advised that you leave details of your planned route and expected return time with somebody, for example the SPNI office or Field School, hostel or hotel manager. You should then 'check-in' with them when you return.

Environmental awareness There is a code of conduct to follow when hiking, some aspects of which are enshrined within Israeli law. Stick to the marked trails. It is generally forbidden to pick, or even touch, plants and flowers. Swimming in most waterholes is usually forbidden. Camping and lighting of fires can only be done in designated areas. Carry out all your waste and be sure not to litter. The old maxim for hiking in Israel is "leave only footprints, take only photos".

point from which you can make an excursion into Egypt's **Sinai peninsula**. In fact, for those not wishing to proceed beyond the Sinai it's possible to get a free 14-day Sinai Permit on the border. Alternatively, those with a full Egyptian visa (available in Israel) can proceed to Cairo and beyond. The key attractions of the Sinai are its diving options, its beach-life, its reputation as a 'traveller hangout', plus Mt Sinai and St Catherine's

Monastery in the interior. For further details on travelling beyond Israel, notably to Egypt and Jordan, see pages 32 and 418. We would also, naturally, recommend Footprint's *Jordan, Syria & Lebanon Handbook* and the *Egypt Handbook*.

Finding out more

Australia: 395 New South Head Rd, Double Bay, Sydney, T02-93261700, F93261676. **Austria**: Rossauer Laende 41/12, A-1090 Vienna, T01-3108174, F3103917. **Canada**: 180 Bloor St West, Suit 700, Toronto, T800-6692369, F416-9642420. **Denmark**: Vesterbrogade 6D, 1620 Copenhagen V, T33-119711, F914801. **France**: 22 Rue des Capucines, 3rd Floor, Paris 75002, T01-42610197, F49270946. **Germany**: Friedrichstr 95, 10117 Berlin, T030-2039970, F2039973; Stollbergstr 6, 80539 Munich, T089-2123860, F21238630; Bettinastr 62, 60325 Frankfurt-am-Maine, T069-7561920, F746249. **Hungary**: Izraeli Nagykovetseg, H-1026 Budapest, Fullank U.8, T02-2000781, F2000794. **Italy**: Corso Europa 12, 20122 Milan, T02-76021051, F76012477. **Japan**: Kojimachi Sanbancho Mansion 406, 9-1, Sanbancho, Chiyoda-Ku, Tokyo 102, T03-32389081, F32389077. **Netherlands**: Stadhouderskade 2, 1054 ES Amsterdam, T020-6128850, F6894288. **South Africa**: 5th floor, Nedbank Gdns, 33 Bath Ave, Rosebank 2196, PO Box 52560, Saxonwold 2132, Johannesburg, T011-7881703, F4473104. **South Korea**: Leema Building, Suite 400, 146-1 Susong-Dong, Chongro-Ku, Seoul 110-140, T02-7380882, F7365193. **Spain**: Gran Via 69, 28013 Madrid, T01-5597903, F5426511. **Sweden**: Sveagagen 28-30, 4 tr., Box 7554, 10393 Stockholm, T08-213386, F217814. **Switzerland**: Lintheschergasse 12, 8021 Zurich, T01-2112344, F2122036. **UK**: 180 Oxford St, London W1N 9DJ, T0171-4343651, F4370527. **USA**: 800 Second Ave, New York, T212-4995650, F4995655; 5 South Wabash Ave, Chicago, T312-7824306, F7821243; 5151 Belt Line Rd, Suite 1280, Dallas, T800-4726364, F214-3923521; 6380 Wiltshire Blvd 1718, Los Angeles, T213-6587462, F6586543.

Tourist offices abroad
For further information on Israel and Palestine on the internet, see page 50.

Essentials

Before you travel

Documents

All visitors require a passport that is valid for 6 months beyond the date of their entry into Israel. You should carry your passport with you (in a secure place) at all times. You may be required to show it when checking in to hotels. You will be asked for your passport at check-posts if travelling around the West Bank and Gaza.

Passport

Almost all nationalities are granted a free **tourist visa** (B2) on arrival. The exceptions to this rule include most African and Central American countries, Arab/Muslim nations, India, Singapore and many of the former Soviet republics. If you arrive by air, the tourist visa is usually valid for a **3-month** stay. If you arrive by land from Egypt or Jordan, or by sea, you are generally given a **1-month** tourist visa. Tourist visas do not permit you to work. They can be extended (see below). Note that upon arrival in Israel, you may be required to show sufficient funds to prove that you can support yourself without having to work illegally. Visas expire on exit from Israel. For further details on arrival protocol see page 35.

Visas
For details of Israeli embassies and consulates overseas see page 29

If you are intending to work on a kibbutz or moshav, it is possible to apply for a 6-12 month **volunteer visa** (B4). This can be arranged once you are already inside Israel. You must take a letter from your kibbutz or moshav (or hospital/institution) confirming your non-salaried post to the Ministry of the Interior (see 'Visa extensions' below). The cost is just 100 NIS, though applicants should be aware that this visa is non-transferable, so if you move kibbutz you need a new visa.

A 12-month **student visa** (A2) is available to those who have been accepted by a university/education institute, though it is non-transferable and does not allow you to work. Take your letter of acceptance to the Ministry of the Interior.

A **work permit** (B1) is very difficult to obtain and your potential employer will be obliged to put up some form of financial bond as a guarantee. You will require proof of medical insurance, the relevant forms from your local Ministry of Labour Employment Office completed by your employer, plus a letter from your employer explaining the need for a foreigner to fill the position. In effect, your employer will have to justify the need to employ a 'foreign expert'. If the Ministry of Labour grant you a work permit, note that it is non-transferable between jobs or employers and you will be liable for tax and national insurance contributions.

Jewish visitors considering returning to Israel permanently may be eligible for **temporary residence**. It is advisable that you contact one of the relevant agencies to guide you through this process: Association of Americans and Canadians in Israel (AACI), 6 Mane St, Talbieh, Jerusalem, T02-661181; 22 Mazeh, Tel Aviv, T03-6299799. British Olim Society (BOS), 13 Ben Maimon, Jerusalem, T02-634822; 76 Ibn Givrol, Tel Aviv, T03-6965244.

Visa extensions In theory, tourist visas can be extended for up to 27 months in total (requiring a visit to the Ministry of the Interior every 3 or 6 months). However, this represents the maximum amount of time that tourist visas can be extended for and is rarely granted. You should remember that granting visa extensions is at the discretion of the Ministry of the Interior and you are in no position to begin demanding your rights. Experience suggests that a 3-month extension is the general rule, though some visitors get 1 month, others 6. However, you will almost certainly be required to produce evidence that you have sufficient funds to support yourself without working illegally. A credit card can come in useful here, though some travellers resort to the old trick of producing now cancelled travellers' cheques that have previously been reported lost or stolen, along with the newly issued travellers' cheques that replaced them. It may work, though the risks are obvious. A tourist visa extension generally costs 100 NIS (plus 1 passport photo) whether you get 1, 3 or 6 months (though it may be free to residents of the Benelux countries).

Dealing with the Ministry of the Interior can be a real bind: Israeli bureaucracy sucks. Most of the Ministry of the Interior offices deal with visa extensions Sunday-Thursday 0800-1200, with later shifts on Wednesday and Sunday (1600-1900). Arrive early since queues outside at 0800 can be very long. It pays to dress smartly and act in a polite manner when visiting the Ministry of the Interior. Having an itinerary of places that you still wish to visit in Israel may assist your application.

The **Ministry of the Interior** can be found at: 1 Shlomzion Hamalka St, New City, Jerusalem, T02-6228211/6290222; 9 Ahad Ha'am St, Tel Aviv, T03-5193333/5193286; Municipality Building, HaTemarim Blvd, Eilat, T07-6376332/6372350.

It has been suggested that the best way to renew your visa is to leave Israel just before your visa expires (eg go to Sinai, Egypt, or Jordan) and get a new visa upon re-entry. This generally seems to work, though it should not be relied upon. Crossing into Egypt for an hour, then returning, tends to raise the suspicions of immigration officials.

Expired visas There can be severe penalties for overstaying your visa, though how rigorously they are enforced appears to be a rather hit-or-miss affair. You may be obliged to pay a monthly charge for each month (or part thereof) that you have overstayed. Telling the immigration clerk at the point of departure that you have no money to pay such a fine may result in a period of sitting in a prison cell waiting for funds to arrive from home (it has been known). You may also be charged for your period of incarceration. If you attempt to leave Israel at a land border with an expired visa you will almost certainly be refused exit and referred back to the Ministry of the Interior. If leaving by air (most notably from Ben-Gurion airport) you will still be due for expired visa fees, though it seems easier to 'do a deal' here on the amount owing. Be polite and repentant. If you overstay your visa, you may be blacklisted and denied re-entry to Israel for 5-10 years (though this normally only applies to those who overstay by 6 months or more).

Australia: 6 Turrana Ave, Yarralumla, Canberra, ACT 2600, T06-2731309; 37 York St, Sydney, NSW 2000, T02-92647933. **Canada**: 50 O'Conner St, Suite 1005, Ottawa, Ontario KIP 6LE, T613-5676450; 115 Blvd René Levesque Ouest, Suite 2620, Montreal, Quebec H3B 4S5, T514-3939372. **France**: 3 Rue Rabelais, 75008 Paris, T01-40765500; 454 Rue Paradis, Marseille 13008, T04-91773990. **Germany**: Simrockallee 2, Bonn 53173, T0228-9346500; Schinkelstrasse 10, Berlin 14193, T30-8932203. **Ireland**: Berkeley Court Hotel, Suite 630, Landsdowne Rd, Ballsbridge, Dublin 4, T01-6680303. **Netherlands**: 47 Buitenhoff, The Hague 2513 AH, T70-3760500. **New Zealand**: BD Tower, The Terrace 111, PO Box 2171, Wellington, T04-4722362. **South Africa**: Dashing Centre, 339 Hilda St, Hatfield, Pretoria, T021-4212222, F3421442; Church Sq House, Plein St, Cape Town, T457205. **UK**: 2 Palace Green, London, W8 4OB, T0171-9579547. **USA**: 3514 International Drive NW, Washington DC 20008, T202-3645500; 800 Second Ave, New York NY 10017, T212-4995300, plus 9 other consulates.

Israeli embassies and consulates around the world

From Israel it is possible to travel on by land to **Egypt** and **Jordan**. For details on visa requirements for Egypt see page 34. For details on visa requirements for Jordan see page 32. Your attention is also drawn to the box on page 37.

Visas for neighbouring countries

Whether you take out travel insurance or not is a personal choice. However, it is strongly recommended that you take out some form of **health insurance**. Health care in Israel is of a very high standard, though the costs are equally high. Receiving the bill from a night's stay in hospital may induce an instant relapse! It is also worth noting that most insurance companies operate an upper age limit and refuse to offer cover above a certain age (or offer cover with a huge premium attached). In the UK, **Age Concern** offer the best-value cover in such circumstances (T01883-346964).

If you do take out travel insurance, make sure that it is a policy that suits your needs. Whilst many policies that cover theft appear to offer comprehensive coverage, they have very low ceiling limits on individual items (often as low as £250). Most policies exclude activities such as diving, skiing, and even hiking. If you intend doing any of these activities, make sure your policy covers them.

Insurance

Anyone in full-time education is entitled to an International Student Identity Card (ISIC). These are issued by student travel offices and travel agencies across the world, and by *issta* in Israel (see under 'Tour companies and travel agents' in major city entries). ISIC cards are particularly useful in Israel, where they entitle you to 10% discount on Egged bus fares over 10 NIS, 20% discount on train fares, and approximately 25% discount on museum and national park entry fees.

ISIC

Money

The unit of currency in Israel is the **New Israeli Shekel**, written as **NIS**. It has in fact been 'new' for over 10 years. The Hebrew plural of shekel is *shekelim*, though the generally used expression is 'shekels' (or 'sheks'). The new shekel is divided into 100 agorot. There are notes of 200, 100, 50, 20 and 10 NIS (though the latter have been largely replaced by coins), plus coins of 10, 5 and 1 NIS. There are also coins of 50 and 10 agorot.

Currency
For a guide to the cost of travelling in Israel see page 22.

....

Exchange rates (October1999)

US$1	=	4.265 NIS	Aus Shilling 10	=	3.3302 NIS
UK£1	=	7.0394 NIS	Swe Krona 1	=	0.5246 NIS
Aus$1	=	2.8057 NIS	Nor Krona 1	=	0.5557 NIS
Can$1	=	2.9103 NIS	Dan Krona 1	=	0.6164 NIS
SA Rand 1	=	0.71 NIS	Fin Mark 1	=	0.7707 NIS
Irish Punt 1	=	5.8186 NIS	Jap Yen 100	=	4.0344 NIS
DM1	=	2.343 NIS	Jord Dinar 1	=	5.9969 NIS
French Fr1	=	0.6986 NIS	Egypt £1	=	1.2484 NIS
Bel Fr10	=	1.136 NIS	Euro 1	=	4.5994 NIS
Dutch Guilder 1	=	2.0795 NIS			
Ita Lira 1,000	=	2.3667 NIS	For very latest rates try the following		
Spa Peseta 100	=	2.7542 NIS	internet web site: http://bankisrael.gov.il		
Swiss Fr 1	=	2.8661 NIS			

....

Which currency? A history of hyper-inflation, now brought somewhat under control, has left a legacy in which many Israelis discuss prices and salaries in **US dollars.** Note that by paying in foreign hard currencies (preferably US dollars) for hotel accommodation, car hire, airline tickets and expensive purchases, you avoid paying the 17% Value Added Tax (VAT). Such transactions can be made using cash, travellers' cheques or credit cards. For details on VAT refunds, see page 37. Though almost all foreign hard currencies are accepted, US Dollars remain the best option. For details of reconverting shekels, see page 36.

Exchanging money **Cash** It is always useful to have some hard currency cash with you, particularly when you are crossing borders. A good mix of high and low denomination US dollars is probably the best bet.

Travellers' cheques These can be cashed at banks and money-changers, or used directly to pay hard currency bills such as hotel accommodation or car hire. They also have the advantage of being replaceable if lost. The disadvantage is that many banks and hotels charge excessive commission charges, or disguise commission charges with criminally poor rates of exchange. Check what the deal is before you sign. Good places to exchange TCs are at offices of companies that issue the cheques (eg American Express offices for Amex cheques), post offices (which all offer commission-free foreign exchange at good rates), or specialized money exchange places that are springing up across the country (in most major cities). Bad places to exchange TCs are most banks (especially at the airports), and hotels. You will need to bring your passport to exchange TCs. Eurocheques are not widely accepted.

Credit cards Many Israelis live on their credit cards, and hence they are widely accepted (and often there is no minimum limit). Visa, American Express, Mastercard and Diners are the most widely accepted cards. Switch cards are not generally accepted, and few places take Eurocard. Many of the banks in the larger cities and towns have 24-hour **ATM** cash dispensers that will give shekel cash advances on most credit cards (Cirrus, +Plus, etc). Exchange rates appear to be competitive, and commission charges not excessive, and hence this can be a good way to carry your travelling funds. If your credit card is lost or stolen call: Amex T03 5242211 (or 24-hr toll-free 177 440 8694); Diners T03 5723572; Visa T03 5723572; Eurocard/Isracard T03 5764444. For further details contact www.visalatam.com, www.mastercard.com, www.americanexpress.com.

Black market There is no real black market to speak of in Israel and there is little to be gained from exchanging money informally. Hostel receptionists will often exchange dollars cash into shekels, though don't expect more than the regular bank rate. Licensed Arab money-changers inside Jerusalem's Damascus Gate (and in most Palestinian towns) may give you marginally better than bank rates for cash and TCs. They are also a good source of Jordanian dinars and Egyptian pounds for those travelling beyond Israel (something worth considering).

Most main post offices act as agents for **Western Union**, through whom you can have money wired to you (call toll-free 177-0222131). Commission charges are high, though. For further details, contact www.westernunion.com.

Transferring money

Essentials

Getting there

Air

The majority of visitors to Israel arrive by air. Most arrivals are at **Ben-Gurion Airport** (at Lod, some 22km southeast of Tel Aviv), though an increasing number of charter flights are landing at **'Uvda Airport** (60km north of Eilat). There are also plans for an 'Israeli terminal' at Jordan's Aqaba Airport that will serve Eilat.

Ben-Gurion Airport (see Tel Aviv) has largely outgrown the volume of traffic now arriving there, and with the tight security checks it can become very crowded. During holidays it can take almost an hour to clear immigration on arrival. For further details on Ben-Gurion Airport, including getting there and away, see the box on page 462.

You are reminded to **reconfirm** your ticket at least 72 hours before departure. **Special needs**, such as vegetarian or kosher food, child's carry-cot, wheelchair assistance, should be arranged in advance with the airline (don't trust your travel agent to do this).

North America It is possible to fly to Israel from Atlanta, Chicago, Los Angeles, Miami and Toronto, though the best deal and widest choice of flights is from New York. There are direct flights from New York to Israel with **El Al** and **Tower Air**, though most airlines have stop-overs somewhere in Europe. Look out for special deals, though don't expect much change from $800. Travel supplements in newspapers such as the *New York Times*, *LA Times*, *Chicago Tribune*, *San Fransisco Examiner*, *Toronto Globe & Mail* and *Vancouver Sun* are good places to look for travel agent deals.

From

UK The London 'bucket-shops' are the best places to pick up a cheap fare to Israel. Look for adverts in *The Jewish Chronicle*, *Time Out* and *TNT Magazine*, the latter being free outside most London tube stations each Tuesday. The broadsheet newspapers all feature weekly travel supplements (usually Saturday). A 1-year open return can cost between £190 and £230 depending upon the season. Shorter stay tickets can be even cheaper. **Air 2000**, **British Caledonian** and **Monarch** all offer cheap charter seats to Israel, though you may have to commit yourself to a return date (or pay a penalty to change it). There are also flights to Israel from Manchester. Try **Israel Travel Service**, T0161-8391111, F8390000, for information.

Europe Discount flights to Israel can be picked up from most major cities in mainland Europe, though they tend to be slightly more expensive than flights from the UK. The cheapest deals tend to be with Eastern European airlines (and thus come with the poor standards of service, time-keeping and safety associated with such operators).

Essentials

Australia/NZ Flying from Australia/NZ will require either stop-overs or plane changes. The cheapest deals are with the national carriers operating via Cairo, Athens or Rome, though expect to pay between A$1,700 and A$2,500 during the low season. A better deal may be to include Israel as part of a round-the-world ticket. Most Aussie/Kiwi backpackers fit Israel in as part of the overland route from Australia to a bar job in London.

Egypt There are weekly flights between Tel Aviv and Sharm el-Sheikh, operated by **Air Sinai**. There are also flights on **El Al** and **Air Sinai** linking Ben-Gurion airport to Cairo (US$160 one way). See 'Airlines' and 'Tour companies and travel agents' in the 'Tel Aviv, Essentials' section on page 465.

Jordan There are now direct flights operating between Tel Aviv and Amman on the Royal Jordanian subsidiary **Royal Wings** (around US$75 single or $100 return). **El Al** offer a similar service. **Royal Jordanian** now also have scheduled flights from Amman to Gaza (US$120 one way).

Peak periods At peak periods not only do air-fares rise dramatically, but it can also be difficult getting a flight in or out of Israel. Such peak periods include the time around Jewish and Christian holidays, plus the peak periods associated with school holidays in the country of the flight's origin. You are advised to book and reconfirm tickets for these periods well in advance.

Airline security For obvious reasons, airline security on planes flying in and out of Israel is probably the tightest in the world, with the national airline **El Al** being like the proverbial duck's arse. Whether you are flying in or out of Israel, you are asked to check-in at least 3 hours prior to departure. **NB** If you are flying with El Al, this pre-flight check-in time can be halved by using the advance baggage check-in service in Jerusalem and Tel Aviv (see relevant 'Essentials' sections for details). At many overseas airports (such as Heathrow and Gatwick in the UK) flights to Israel are checked-in at separate, secure areas of the airport terminal. El Al also use their own airline security staff abroad.

Prior to checking-in at Ben-Gurion or 'Uvda Airport to board a flight out of Israel, you will be questioned thoroughly by the airline security service. How long this cross-examination lasts depends upon a number of factors: your name and ethnic background, the stamps in your passport, your appearance, and where in Israel you admit to having been. Dave Winter's personal record is 1 hour and 55 minutes! However, you can be fairly certain that the plane that you are getting on is unlikely to be bombed or hijacked. As a reminder, keep your luggage in a secure area once it has been packed (by you) and do not offer to carry anything on to the flight for anybody else. If anyone asks you to do this at, or on your way to, the airport, report it to the security personnel.

Overland

Israel has land borders with Lebanon, Syria, Jordan and Egypt, though currently it is only possible to cross overland into the latter two.

To/from Jordan Jordanian visas can be obtained upon entry at most of Jordan's air, sea and land entry/exit points, though visitors arriving at the King Hussein/Allenby Bridge crossing from Israel will not be given visas on arrival. For the sake of convenience, however, get your visa in advance whenever possible. This also applies to Lebanese and Syrian visas (the latter of which are all but impossible to get in Jordan). See 'The entry-exit stamp game' box for further notes on travelling in the region (page 37). Fees vary according to nationality. The following fees were being charged in 1999 for visas issued at point of entry (JD 1=UK£0.91 or US$1.40):

0

Australia Free; Austria JD25; Canada JD31; Denmark JD12; France JD8; Germany JD7; Italy JD8; New Zealand JD4; Spain JD17; UK JD23; USA JD15.

Visas issued at point of entry are valid for a period of 2 weeks, but can be easily extended in Amman. Alternatively, you can apply to the Jordanian Embassy in your own country; for UK nationals this is more expensive (£27 for a single entry). Security procedures for entering Israel from Jordan are very strict and it may take some time to cross the border. Israeli immigration will stamp entry-exit stamps on a separate piece of paper if you so request. For further details see the excellent Footprint *Jordan, Syria and Lebanon Handbook*.

Jordan River Border Crossing/Jisr Sheikh Hussein This is located in the north, 6km to the east of the Lower Galilee town of Bet Shean. Though the least-used of the 3 crossing points, it is actually closer to Jerusalem than the Arava crossing. Leaving Israel you will have to pay 60 NIS departure tax. Jordanian visas are available on the border and a Jordanian entry stamp will appear in your passport. From the Jordanian side, service taxis run to Irbid and then on to Amman. Leaving Jordan, a JD 4 departure tax must be paid and a Jordanian exit stamp will be entered in your passport (even if you previously entered via the King Hussein/Allenby Bridge crossing, where the entry stamp was put on a separate sheet of paper). There are currency exchange facilities on both sides of the border. Buses (11 NIS) and taxis (15 NIS) run to Bet Shean from the border. The crossing is officially open Sunday-Thursday 0630-2000, Friday-Saturday 0800-2000, closed on Yom Kippur and Jordanian holidays (though it's best to try and cross before 1700 on Friday-Saturday). For details on crossing the border from the Israeli side T06-6586442/4.

Allenby/King Hussein Bridge Closest to Jerusalem (16km east of Jericho, see page 284), there are special regulations in force at this crossing point. Leaving Israel, the departure tax is a staggering 120 NIS (since both Israel and the Palestinian Authority collect a share). Jordanian visas are **not** available on the border. The Jordanian entry stamp will not be entered on your passport, but on a separate piece of paper. If you also leave Jordan through this crossing point, the only evidence of your visit to Jordan will be a visa (but no entry/exit stamps). If you leave Jordan through any other exit, you will get a Jordanian exit stamp in your passport. From the crossing point there are buses and taxis to Amman (JD 1). Leaving Jordan, a JD 4 departure tax must be paid. There are currency exchange facilities on both sides of the border. For details of transport between Jerusalem and this crossing point, see 'Transport' in the 'Jerusalem' chapter (page 227). The crossing is open Sunday-Thursday 0800-2400, Friday-Saturday 0800-1500, closed on Yom Kippur and Jordanian holidays, though aim to cross as early in the day as possible. Note that you cannot walk across the bridge (but have to pay an extortionate amount for a 5-minute bus ride). For details of border formalities on the Israeli side T02-9942626.

Arava/Arabah Crossing This is located about 4km north of Eilat on the Israeli side and 10 km northwest of Aqaba on the Jordanian side. From Eilat it can be reached by taxi (20 NIS) or bus 016 (7 NIS); see 'Transport' in the 'Eilat' section on page 404. From Aqaba it can be reached by taxi for an outrageous JD 3. The border is open Sunday-Thursday 0630-2200, Friday-Saturday 0800-2000, closed on Yom Kippur and Jordanian holidays. For details on crossing the border from the Israeli side T07-6336812. If leaving Israel, a departure tax of 60 NIS must be paid. Jordanian visas are available on the border and a Jordanian entry stamp will appear in your passport. If leaving Jordan, a JD 4 departure tax must be paid and a Jordanian exit stamp will be entered in your passport (even if you previously entered via the King Hussein/Allenby Bridge crossing, where the entry stamp was put on a separate sheet of paper). There are currency exchange facilities on both sides of the border.

To/from Egypt There are in fact 3 border crossing points between Israel and Egypt (Eilat/Taba, Rafiah/Rafah and Netafim), though only the first two are of relevance to tourists. Tourists who intend visiting Sinai only need a 14-day **Sinai permit**, though those wishing to travel beyond here will require a **full tourist visa**. Make sure that you get the visa/permit that suits your needs, and remember that tourist visas are **not** issued on the Taba-Eilat border and Sinai permits are not convertible into a full tourist visa. For travelling beyond the Sinai peninsula, see the Footprint *Egypt Handbook*.

Eilat/Taba Travellers wishing to visit Sinai only, or visit Sinai before continuing on to the rest of Egypt, should use this crossing point. In theory it is open 24 hrs, though this can be subject to change at short notice and for those who don't have their own transport it's pointless turning up when there is no onward transport on the other side. For details on reaching the crossing point from the Israeli side, see under 'Transport' in the section on Eilat (and also page 404). Leaving Israel, you will have to pay 60 NIS departure tax, followed by an $8 Egyptian entry tax. You do not have to pay these taxes if you are just visiting the *Taba Hilton* resort facilities at Taba. 14-day Sinai permits are available on the border, but full tourist visas are not. Leaving Egypt there is a $5 departure tax. Security procedures for entering Israel from Egypt are very strict and it may take some time to cross the border. Israeli immigration will stamp entry-exit stamps on a separate piece of paper if you so request. For further details on the Israeli side T07-6362435, F6340539.

Rafiah/Rafah This is the border crossing that you should use if you are heading for Cairo and beyond. Do not come here if you wish to visit Sinai first (there are no transport connections). The majority of travellers using this crossing are generally those booked on a through coach all the way from Tel Aviv or Jerusalem to Cairo (though it's usual to change vehicles at the border). Your best bet for arranging this trip is to go to *Mazada Tours* (141 Ibn Gvirol, Tel Aviv, T03-5444454, F5461928; 9 Koresh St, Jerusalem, T02-6235777, F6255454; 1 Khayat, Haifa, T04-8624446, F8624464). Check the schedule with them, though they usually have daily buses from Tel Aviv at 0900 (arrive 1900), plus night buses at 2030 (arriving 0700) on Tuesday, Thursday and Sunday. From Jerusalem they have daily buses Monday-Friday at 0730, plus night buses at 1900 on Tuesday and Thursday. The fare for all these trips is $35 one-way, $50 return ($5-10 more for night buses), excluding taxes. Egged bus line appear to have finished their regular Bus No 100 to Cairo, though it may be worth enquiring with *Egged Tours* to see if they still run a service (59 Ben Yehuda, Tel Aviv, T03-6371101; 224 Jaffa Rd, Jerusalem, T02-5304883). Leaving Israel there is a 120 NIS departure tax (shared between the Israelis and the Palestinian Authority), and then a $5 Egyptian entry tax. Visas are not available on the border and Sinai permits are invalid. Leaving Egypt there is a $5 departure tax. Security procedures for entering Israel from Egypt are very strict and it may take some time to cross the border. Israeli immigration will stamp entry-exit stamps on a separate piece of paper if you so request. **NB** It is possible to undertake this trip independently, taking a bus from Tel Aviv or Jerusalem to Rafiah, and then taking an Egyptian service taxi from the border to Cairo. It's cheaper, but a lot more hassle. For further details on the Israeli side T07-6734274, F6732974.

Private vehicles For full details on bringing a private vehicle into Israel, check with your nearest Israeli embassy or tourist office. A *Carnet de Passage* is required.

Sea

Ferries A regular ferry service runs between Piraeus (for Athens, Greece), via Rhodes (Greece) and Limassol (Cyprus) and Israel's northern Mediterranean port of Haifa. Two separate

Essentials

shipping lines run these services, handled in **Israel** by the following agents: *J. Caspi* (1 Ben Yehuda, Tel Aviv, T03-5106834/5175749; 76 Ha'Atma'ut, Haifa, T04-8674444/ 8674449, F8674456; 3 Yanai St, Jerusalem, T02-6247315/6252344; 27 Dizengoff, Netanya, T09-8841830); *Mano Passenger Lines* (97 Ben Yehuda, Tel Aviv, T03-5224611; 39/41 HaMeginim St, Haifa, T04-8351631). In **Athens** contact: *Poseidon Lines* (32 Alkyonidon Ave, 16673 Voula POB 70094, 16610 Glyfada, Athens, T01-9658300, F9658310). In **Rhodes** contact: *Kouros Travel Rhodes*, 34 Karpathou St, POB 160 85 100 Rhodes, T0241-22400-76176. In **Limassol** contact: *Poseidon Lines Cyprus* (124 Franklin Roosevelt Ave, POB 6155, 3305 Limassol, T05-745666, F745577).

The fare depends upon the season and the level of comfort that you require. The 'high season' is mid-June to mid-September, and the 'low season' is all other periods (ferries run all year). There are 12 different classes of accommodation, through 'deck space' and 'pullman seat', to 4- and 2-berth cabins with prices varying according to whether you want an attached shower and toilet, and a cabin with a view. As a rough guide, the fares listed below are for 'deck space' (DK), 'aircraft-type seat' (AS) and for sharing '4 berth inside with WC & shower' (AB4) for high season (HS) and low season (LS).

Piraeus: DK $106 HS, $96 LS; AS $116 HS, $106 LS; AB4 $207 HS, $179 LS. **Rhodes:** DK $101 HS, $91 LS; AS $111 HS, $101 LS; AB4 $202 HS, $174 LS. **Limassol:** DK $58 HS, $48 LS; AS $72 HS, $53 LS; AB4 $106 HS, $92 LS. Add $22 port tax to fare.

Though 'deck space' appears to be a bargain, passengers should be prepared for low night-time temperatures, even in summer. Food and drink on board is also fairly expensive. Bicycles are carried free, whilst there are separate fares for cars and motorcycles. If you are under 26 or have a student card, enquire about discounts. At the time of going to press, departures from Haifa were every Sunday and Thursday, though check locally. You should also confirm what time you have to arrive at the port.

Touching down

Customs

Persons over the age of 17 are each allowed to bring in duty free 1 litre of spirits, 2 litres of wine, 250 cigarettes or 250g of tobacco, and personal gifts up to the value of $200. You may have to declare video equipment, personal computers and diving equipment, and pay a deposit, which is refunded when you re-export the goods. Do not lose the receipt.

Duty free allowance

There are no restrictions on the amount of foreign and local currency that you can bring into Israel.

Currency regulations

It is prohibited to bring fruit and vegetables, plants, fresh meat, animals and firearms into Israel.

Prohibited items

Immigration

On arrival (by air, land or sea) you will be requested to fill in a landing card. This effectively will be your tourist visa. If you request (but only if you specifically ask), the immigration official will stamp this card and not your passport. This card must then be surrendered upon departure. **Do not lose this paper**. Note that you may have to provide evidence of means of supporting yourself without working illegally, or a return ticket. See 'Visa' information on page 27.

Passports and visas

Touching down

Time

Israel is 2 hrs ahead of Greenwich Mean Time (GMT+2); 7 hrs ahead of American Eastern Standard Time; 8 hrs behind Australian Eastern Standard Time. Clocks go forward 1 hr for daylight-saving ('summer time') in March, and back again at Rosh Hashana (usually September).

Business hours

*Few first-time visitors to Israel are prepared for the impact of **Shabbat**, or the Jewish Sabbath. Beginning at sun-down on Friday and finishing at sun-down on Saturday, it sees all Israeli offices, banks, post offices, and most shops, restaurants and places of entertainment close down completely. Almost everywhere, both the inter-city and urban transport systems grind to a complete halt. If you don't want to go hungry or get stranded somewhere, plan in advance for Shabbat. Note that in many work environments, the 'weekend' is now adding Friday to the Saturday day of rest. The picture is further confused by the fact that shops and businesses in Muslim*

(Arab) areas observe Friday as their Sabbath, whilst Sunday is the day of rest for Christians. Anyone who claims their religion to be 'monotheism' (as opposed to just Judaism, Christianity or Islam) should in theory be entitled to a very long weekend! The following are a general guide only:
Banks *Sunday, Tuesday, Thursday 0830-1230 1600-1700; Monday, Wednesday, Friday 0830-1200.*
Post offices *Sunday-Thursday 0700-1900; Friday 0700-1200 (though branch offices generally close 1230-1400).*
Government offices *Sunday-Thursday 0800-1300 1400-1730; Friday 0900-1400.*
Shops *Monday-Thursday 0800-1300 1400-1900, Friday 0900-1400.*

Electricity

220 volts, 50 cycle AC. Most plugs are of the round 2-pin variety. Adapters can be bought, though they are probably cheaper in your home country.

Weights and measures

Metric system; speed limits are in km per hour; food is weighed in kg and g; petrol is sold in litres.

Departure

Departure tax There is a 50 NIS departure tax for foreigners flying out of Israel, though this is usually incorporated within the ticket price. Israelis flying out of their country have to pay between $50 and $75! Leaving Israel for Egypt by land, foreigners must pay 60 NIS departure tax at the Eilat/Taba crossing, and 120 NIS at the Rafiah/Rafah crossing. Leaving Israel for Jordan by land, foreigners pay 60 NIS departure tax at the Jordan Valley and Arava crossings, and 120 NIS at the Allenby/King Hussein Bridge. Leaving Israel by sea incurs a $22 port tax, collected when you buy the ferry ticket.

Expired visas See page 28.

Reconverting shekels In theory, it is possible to reconvert up to $500 in shekels upon departure without a foreign currency exchange receipt, though it may be as well to present one. A receipt is definitely needed for transactions above $500. The branch of Bank Leumi in the 'departures' hall of Ben-Gurion Airport charges $3 commission for first $50, $6 commission up to $400 and 1.5% commission over $400 when converting shekels back to hard currency.

The entry-exit stamp game

Anybody intending to travel beyond Israel into Arab and/or Muslim countries may like to avoid having Israeli entry and exit stamps in their passport. Fortunately, Israeli immigration officials are quite happy to assist here and will, on request, stamp a separate sheet of paper rather than your passport. This is fine if you fly in or out of Israel, though if you leave or arrive by land it is difficult to avoid an Egyptian or Jordanian entry-exit stamp. An entry stamp that says that you arrived in Egypt at Taba, for example, means that you can only have come from one place – Israel. In the wider world this is no great hassle, though it will almost certainly prevent you from ever using the same passport to get a Syrian, Lebanese or Sudanese visa (amongst others). Even entering Jordan through the Allenby/King Hussein Bridge, where the Jordanian entry stamp is given on a separate piece of paper, does not appear to help matters. The Syrians will scan your passport for a Jordanian entry stamp, with the lack of one (presuming you've hidden the piece of paper) telling the Syrians where you have come from.

In fact, such is the perseverance with which Syria pursues this matter, some travellers are denied Syrian visas even when they have never visited Israel. Since direct flights began between Israel and Jordan, the Syrians have been reluctant to issue Syrian visas to foreigners who fly into Jordan since the Jordanian entry stamp merely says 'Queen Alia international airport', and gives no clue as to where you boarded the flight – it could have been Israel! Keeping your ticket can help persuade them that you did not board the plane in Israel. Note that if you are planning to fly into Amman from Israel, some flights land at Raghadan Airport (and not Queen Alia International), which is a dead giveaway as to where you boarded the plane!

It helps to get such visas as far in advance as possible, preferably in your home country. Note that it is all but impossible to get a Syrian visa in Jordan, even if you have never been to Israel. If you do have Israeli or Israel-Jordan/Israel-Egypt entry/exit stamps, getting a new passport is one solution, though again, the Syrians, Lebanese and Sudanese are suspicious of new passports issued at embassies in Cairo and Amman. The easiest solution is to plan your trip carefully so that you visit Lebanon and Syria before Israel.

Essentials

Tax refunds

Though there is a 17% Value Added Tax on many goods in Israel, tourists are entitled to a VAT refund on certain products (generally not electrical, photographic or computer equipment). Shops that participate in the scheme generally have a large sign in the window. You should get a 5% discount on the marked price of the goods. Make sure that the VAT paid is marked clearly on the invoice (in shekels and US dollars). The goods should then be placed in one of the special clear-sided bags, with the invoice prominently displayed. You cannot open the bag prior to leaving Israel. At Ben-Gurion Airport and Haifa port, the Bank Leumi in the 'departures' lounge will stamp the invoice and pay the refund, minus a commission (forms up to $30 = $2 comm, up to $100 = $5 comm, over $100 = $8 comm). If you depart Israel elsewhere, customs will stamp the form and the refund will be posted to your home address.

Tourist offices in Israel

Almost all Israeli towns have at least one tourist information office (sometimes a government office and a municipal office), though the standard of service is highly variable. They are generally a good source of free (or cheap) city maps, may be able to assist in booking accommodation, and should stock some sort of free 'What's On' guide to the region that you are in. Beyond this, the help that you get depends upon the dedication of the staff member that you see; to some tourist information office staff, tourists are an inconvenient pain.

Disabled travellers Israel makes more attempt to cater to disabled visitors than most 'Western' countries, though that's not really saying much. Because many visitors to Israel are elderly pilgrims most hotels have access ramps and wheelchair-friendly lifts. Some hotels have rooms specially designed for the disabled, though these tend to be at the top end of the price range. A great deal of effort has been made to make many archaeological sites wheelchair accessible, though the public transport system remains largely off-limits. A useful guide is the *Access in Israel: A Guide for the Disabled and Those with Problems Getting Around*, published by Pauline Hepsaistos Survey Projects (39 Bradley Gardens, London, W13 18HE, UK; Moss Rehabilitation Hospital, 1200 West Tabor Rd, Philadelphia PA 19141, USA, T215-4569603). A selection of useful guides (*Travel for the Disabled* or *Wheelchair Vagabond*) are published by *Twin Peaks Press*, Box 129, Vancouver, WA 98666, Canada, T360-6942462.

Other sources of information include: *ACROD*, PO Box 60, Curtin, Canberra, ACT 2605, Australia, T06-62824333; *Disabled Persons Assembly*, 173-175 Victoria St, Wellington, NZ, T04-8119100; *Irish Wheelchair Association*, Blackheath Drive, Clontarf, Dublin 3, Rep of Ireland, T01-8338241; *JDC-Israel Information Centre*, PO Box 3489, Jerusalem 91043, T02-6787454; *Mobility International*, 25 Rue de Manchester, Bruxelles B-1070, Belgium, T4106297; *RADAR*, 12 City Forum, 250 City Rd, London, EC1V 8AF, UK, T0171-2503222; *Society for the Advancement of Travel for the Handicapped (SATH)*, 347 5th Ave, Suite 610, New York, NY 10016, USA, T212-4477284, http://www.sittravel.com/ *Yad Sarah*, 43 HaNevi'im, PO Box 6992, Jerusalem 91609, T02-6244242.

Companies and organizations running tours to Israel for disabled travellers include: *Across Trust for Disabled*, Bridge House, 70-72 Bridge Rd, East Molesey, Surrey, KT8 9HF, UK, T0181-7831355; *Amir Tours*, 11 Shlomzion HaMalka, Jerusalem 94182, T02-6231261; *Directions Unlimited*, 720 North Bedford Rd, Bedford Hills, NY 10507, USA, T914-2411700; *Flying Wheels Travel Service*, PO Box 382, 143 West Bridge, Owatonna MN 55060, USA, T1-800-5356790.

Gay and lesbian visitors Israel's gay and lesbian scene is not as high profile as that in, say, Sydney, San Francisco or London (largely because male homosexuality only became legal within the last 10 years or so). The best information on gay and lesbian issues in Israel is offered by Aguda, PO Box 37604, Tel Aviv 61375, T03-6293681, email sppr@netvision.net.il. They run a gay and lesbian switchboard (Tue, Thu, Sun, 1930-2330, T03 6292797; Mon, 1930-2330 T04 8525352), and also have a webpage at http://www.geocities.com/WestHollywood/heights/8197.

Rules, customs and etiquette

Bargaining Israel provides almost unlimited shopping potential, particularly in the field of 'souvenirs' for pilgrims/tourists looking for some memento of their visit to the Holy Land. Much of the stuff is garbage, and much is concentrated in Jerusalem's Old City, where nothing has a price tag and you are expected to haggle a deal. Modern economists might feel that bargaining is a way of covering up high-price salesmanship within a commercial system that is designed to exploit the lack of legal protection for the consumer. Even so, haggling over prices is the norm and is run as an art form, with great skills involved. There is great potential for the tourist to be heavily ripped off. Most dealers recognize the gullibility of travellers and start their offers at an exorbitant price. The dealer then appears to drop his price by a fair margin but remains at a final level well above the local price of the goods.

To protect yourself in this situation be relaxed in your approach. Talk at length to the dealer and take as much time as you can afford inspecting the goods and feeling out the last price the seller will accept. Do not belittle or mock the dealer; take the matter seriously but do not show commitment to any particular item you are

The Mossad tie

An amusing incident related to the informality of Israeli dress is recalled by the former Mossad operative Victor Ostrovsky, who went on to spill the beans about the organization in two bestsellers (By Way of Deception, 1990 and The Other Side of Deception, 1994). In Mossad HQ in Tel Aviv there is a photo studio where any operative who needs a photo for something such as a new passport, or accreditation at an Israeli embassy abroad, has his photo taken. Because few Israelis wear a tie to work, and any new 'diplomat' posted abroad has to look smart in his accreditation pictures, two or three ties hang on the rack at the photo studio. When Ostrovsky tipped off the British with a description of the ties hanging on the rack at Mossad HQ, they were able to scan through the accreditation pictures of the staff at the Israeli embassy in London and pick out the Mossad operatives! At a later date Ostrovsky was even able to supply the British secret service with a picture of a new tie that had been donated to the Mossad collection! It rather punches a hole in the popular mythical image of the organization.

Essentials

bargaining for by being prepared to walk away empty handed. Also, it is better to try several shops if you are buying an expensive item such as a carpet or jewellery. This will give a sense of the price range. Walking away from the dealer normally brings the price down rapidly. Do not change money in the same shop where you make your purchases, since this will be expensive.

Clothing

Israelis tend to dress informally. For example, a television shot panning across an Israeli government cabinet meeting will probably show fewer than half of the ministers wearing a tie. A highly visible exception to this rule are the ultra-orthodox Jews, who dress as per the Eastern European Jewish community of the 18th century. As mentioned elsewhere, visitors to Israel (both men and women) should be prepared to dress conservatively when visiting Arab areas, ultra-orthodox Jewish neighbourhoods, and religious and holy sites of any creed. Though light, loose-fitting cottons are excellent for the summer heat, you should bring some sort of jumper whichever season you visit, and cold weather gear if visiting Jerusalem at Christmas.

Conduct

"Back in the 1930s in Tel Aviv's Mughrabi Square there used to be a big clock with no glass covering its face. Legend has it that one day Mayor Meir Dizengoff ordered the clock be removed. When residents in the area asked him why, Mayor Dizengoff explained that it was because every Jew who walked by the clock reset it according to his own watch" *(From Beirut To Jerusalem, Thomas Friedman, 1989)*. Without descending into stereotypes, there are aspects of the Israeli psyche that often take foreign visitors some getting used to. A very rare thing in Israel is a decent standard of service in shops, restaurants, post offices, banks, tourist information offices, and, most notably, Egged bus information booths. Likewise, queuing at bus stops, holding doors open and saying 'please' or 'excuse me' are just not part of the Israeli make-up. There are lots of witticisms floating around that are supposed to sum up the Israeli personality (eg 2 Israelis in a room means 3 different opinions), though the reference that native-born Israelis prefer for themselves is *sabra* – the cactus fruit that is tough and thorny on the outside but remarkably sweet on the inside.

The rules of conduct that most affect foreign visitors to Israel concern visits to holy places, ultra-orthodox Jewish neighbourhoods and Arab areas. The modest dress that you should adopt when visiting such places is discussed elsewhere, though there are a few other rules of etiquette that should be remembered. When visiting mosques, remember to remove shoes before entering. Women are generally permitted entry, though they may have to cover their heads. In synagogues, both men and women are required to cover heads. In churches, it's hats off for men. Public displays of affection at any religious site should be avoided.

Drugs Possession of narcotics in Israel is illegal and those caught in possession risk prison and/or deportation. That said, they are widely available, particularly in the Tel Aviv area where a 'matchbox' of grass sells for around 50 NIS. Police occasionally raid hostels in Eilat and Tel Aviv looking for drugs, whilst visa-violators are also often rounded up in the process. Many visitors now prefer to head down to Dahab in the Sinai (Egypt) for their drugs experience. Given the thoroughness of Israeli security checks, attempting to bring drugs into the country is even more foolish than it would be in normal circumstances.

Photograhpy Ultra-orthodox Jews dislike having their photograph taken. Ask first but be prepared for a refusal. Carrying cameras in certain areas on Shabbat is 'forbidden' (Western Wall, Mea She'arim, Safed). Arab women also dislike being photographed. Again, ask first and be prepared to be disappointed. The old rule applies about whatever you might be inclined to bomb during a war, you can't photograph. Soldiers in uniform are an exception to this rule. If you take any photos of Israeli soldiers in confrontational situations with Palestinians, be wary of getting them developed in Israeli mini-labs: they may be confiscated.

Safety and security Israel and Palestine rarely appears to be out of the news, though this is hardly surprising when you consider that even in the quieter periods Israel plays host to one of the largest press contingents in the world. Many outsiders' perception of Israel come from the nightly news bulletins and newspaper headlines that just depict suicide bombings, political assassinations, stone-throwing Palestinians and rubber-bullet firing Israeli soldiers. It would be dishonest to claim that these reports are entirely sensationalist, and these events completely detached from life in Israel. However, from the foreign visitor's perspective (and to be totally cynical), most of these events take place well away from the main tourist centres, and there has been no deliberate targeting of foreign tourists. Most of the confrontations between Israelis and Palestinians occur on the West Bank, and though there is a chapter on this area in this *Handbook*, the majority of visitors will probably only visit 1 or 2 destinations here.

There is a unique security situation in Israel, and a highly visible one at that, though it should also be remembered that levels of street crime are far lower than in places such as North America and much of Europe. The general advice is to be alert and aware of potentially serious situations, but not to be overly paranoid; relax and enjoy your trip.

Tipping In common with many other countries in the world, bar staff, waiters and waitresses in Israel receive fairly low wages, relying on tips to top up their salaries. Unlike the rest of the world, however, Israeli waiters and waitresses do not go out of their way to provide anything resembling civilized service, and hence it is particularly galling to receive a bill with 'service not included' printed on it. What service? If service is good then add 10%, if not leave nothing. It is not customary to tip taxi drivers. Tipping guides and tour bus drivers is a matter of personal choice.

Women travelling alone Women travelling alone face greater difficulties than men or couples. Despite the fact that levels of conventional crime are considerably lower in Israel than in parts of North America and Europe, women travellers in Israel are likely to face varying degrees of sexual harassment. Instances of physical assault are thankfully rare, though continual verbal abuse can mar your enjoyment of your trip. Most instances of harassment occur in predominantly Arab areas, though the over-hormonal testosterone-heavy Israeli male is a very common species indeed. Young Muslim women rarely travel without the protection of a male or older female, hence a single

Western woman is often regarded by Arab men as strange, and is supposed to be of easy virtue: a view perpetuated by Hollywood. It is not entirely clear what the Israeli male's excuse is for such unacceptable behaviour. It is probably best to steadfastly ignore rude and suggestive comments directed at you but aimed at boosting the caller's ego, though if you feel yourself to be in any immediate danger, don't be afraid to shout and make a scene. Dressing conservatively may minimize the hassle, though this is not guaranteed. Modest dress, however, is required for visiting holy sites so it is perhaps a good habit to get in to. In many parts of Israel you are free to wear whatever you like, as young Israeli women in Tel Aviv and Eilat will so clearly demonstrate. Note, however, that going topless on the beach is still quite rare and can attract unwanted attention.

Certain popular tourist areas that have particularly bad reputations for levels of sexual harassment include: Jerusalem's Old City (notably after dark); the city ramparts walk; the Mount of Olives area; Old Akko, and Nazareth. Sightseeing in pairs is recommended. Specific warnings are given in this *Handbook* where appropriate. Rape crisis hotline: T1202 (24 hours, anywhere in Israel).

Where to stay

Though Israel has a very broad range of hotels, the top end (the **L1**, **L2**, **L3** and **A** price categories used in this *Handbook*) is rather over-represented. As a general rule, the **L1-L3** category hotels live up to their price tag, with facilities and service to match their 'luxury' pricing. Things can be a little more variable in the **A** and **B** categories, with many of the hotels here holding themselves in too high esteem. If you are looking to stay in the 'top end' accommodation, it may be worth noting that the suites in some hotels offer very good value. For a guide to the classifications used, see box on next page or inside the front cover.

Hotels

There are a number of considerations to bear in mind when booking/checking in to a hotel in Israel. Firstly, there is a huge variation in room charges according to the season. 'High' season generally coincides with Jewish and Christian religious festivals and can see prices increase by between 25-50%! Note that the weekend (Friday-Sunday) is usually considered 'high' season. Many Israelis are now voting with their feet and taking their business to Sinai and to Turkey.

Despite this blatant rip-off, in some places (notably Eilat, Tiberias and Jerusalem) it can be hard to find a bed during the 'high' season. Most of the rest of the year is designated 'regular' season, with a couple of weeks of 'low' season when tourist bookings are slack. The classifications in this Handbook are for the **'regular'** season. Note that the prices used here are spot/rack rates: if you book as a group or through a travel agency, you may be getting a significant discount. With all hotel classifications, look out for hidden taxes. An Israeli breakfast is included within the price at many hotels.

Remember that by paying in a foreign hard currency you avoid paying the 17% VAT. Hotel prices are almost always quoted in US dollars, and this is the preferred means of payment (cash, TCs, credit card). Many hotels have specific characteristics that reflect the Jewish nature of Israel, such as in-house synagogues, Shabbat elevators (that stop at every floor and don't require buttons to be pressed) and kosher restaurants.

NB All accommodation in Israel (from 5-star hotels down to backpacker hostels) is required by law to provide a free safe for depositing valuables.

Essentials

 Hotel classifications in the Israel Handbook

Exact prices for hotel rooms are not quoted – price categories are used instead. Note that these are not star ratings and that many hotels in Israel creep into the price category above the one in which they rightly belong. The price categories are based upon the 'regular' season and include taxes. Apart from the hostels, where prices are based upon the cost of one bed in a dormitory, all price categories refer to the price of a double room.

A = $101-150
B = $76-100
C = $51-75
D = $26-50
E = $13-25
F = $8-12
G = $7 and under

Abbreviations *The following abbreviations are used when describing hotel facilities: a/c = air conditioning; T = telephone; F = fax; B&B = bed and breakfast. Attached bath means attached bath and toilet (though 'bath' is used as term to cover bath or shower).*

L1 = $301+
L2 = $201-300
L3 = $151-200

Kibbutz guesthouses Generally classified in this Handbook within the **B-C-D** mid-price categories, Kibbutz guesthouses represent a recent diversification by the beleaguered kibbutz movement. Almost all are located in rural environments, and on the plus side tend to be peaceful and quiet, well run, and with full access to kibbutz facilities such as swimming pools and private beaches, children's entertainment and restaurant/dining hall. The down side is that few are served by regular public transport and that most are probably in the price category above the one in which they belong. It is best to book in advance, preferably through the **Kibbutz Hotels Reservation Centre**, 90 Ben Yehuda, PO Box 3194, Tel Aviv, T03-5246161, F5278088. The various regional *Israel Tourism Guide* brochures have comprehensive listings of kibbutz and moshav guesthouses (free from most tourist offices).

Hospices For those looking to travel in the **D-E** price categories, Christian hospices often provide excellent value. They are run by various denominations of the church and tend to be located close to major Christian pilgrimage sites. Advance reservations are recommended, and essential during major Christian holidays. They tend to be impeccably clean, though most have early curfews, early check-out times, and non-married couples are unlikely to be able to share. Half and full-board deals can be good value.

IYHA hostels There is a need to distinguish between IYHA 'Youth Hostels' and 'backpacker hostels'. You don't need to be a 'youth' to stay at any of Israel's 32 Hostelling International (HI) hostels; in fact most have a number of family rooms. Nor do you have to be a member, though card-holders save 1 or 2 dollars on accommodation and meals. Almost without exception, they are spotlessly clean, offering a choice of spacious a/c dormitories (usually single-sex), generally with attached shower, for $18-21 (**E**); family rooms, sleeping 4-8, a/c with attached shower (adult $26 per person, and $18 for each additional adult); private rooms, with attached shower for $52 (**C**). Check-in is 1600-1900 and you have to be out by 0900. Sheets and blankets are provided. Breakfast is either included or a few dollars extra, and evening meals tend to be generous and reasonable value ($8-13). Bookings are recommended during holidays and weekends, though these hostels can get very noisy with kids then. In some places, such as Masada and 'Ein Gedi, they provide the only budget accommodation. For further details contact the *Israel Youth Hostels Association*, 3 Dorot Rishonim, Jerusalem, T02-6252706, F6250676.

The *Society for the Protection of Nature in Israel (SPNI)* operate 26 Field Schools throughout Israel, many of which have accommodation similar to IYHA hostels (4 Hashfela St, 66183 Tel Aviv, T03-6388688, F6877695).

Backpacker hostels

Israel's cheapest accommodation is provided by the 'backpacker hostels'. Almost all the bed space is in dormitories, though some have generally poor value private rooms in the **D/E** price category (where you share shower and toilet facilities). In Jerusalem's Old City the dorms are usually priced at 25 NIS, and 30-40 NIS elsewhere across the country (**F**). Some allow you to sleep on the roof for less or give discounts for longer stays. Standards are highly variable. Dorm sizes vary between 3 and 46 beds(!), with some being single-sex and others mixed. Other variables include standard of cleanliness, person to bathroom ratio, and chances of getting any sleep. Some hostels pride themselves on their 'party atmosphere', the idea being that they act as a meeting place for backpackers who want to go out and get drunk together. Another problem for the casual visitor is that many of the hostels (notably in Tel Aviv, Jerusalem and Eilat) are full of long-term residents who are in Israel to earn some money; both backpackers and migrant workers. It's not unusual to find someone occupying the same bed in a hostel dorm for 6-12 months. As a result, some tend to be rather 'cliquey' and unless you too are intending to spend the next 6 months in that dorm, you may be looked on as something of an intruder. Another consideration to bear in mind is that most 'workers' either get up very early in the morning to go to work, or work in pubs and nightclubs, and hence come in very late. Sleep is a rare thing in a backpacker hostel. On a positive note, they are great places to meet other travellers, hook up with potential drinking buddies, and to find or ask around about work.

Camping

Though there are a number of fully equipped campsites in Israel, they are only really for those who are dedicated to sleeping under canvas (or whatever); it usually costs as much to pitch your tent as it does to stay in a backpacker hostel. Camping in a hostel grounds is cheaper than sleeping in a dorm and may be a good compromise. You can generally camp for free on beaches (except for the Dead Sea), though theft and security remain major risks. Those determined to camp should contact the *Israeli Camping Organization*, Farm 112, Mishmar Hashiva, T03-9604524, F9604712.

Private homes

Accommodation in private homes is available in a number of towns, notably Netanya, Nahariya, Safed, Eilat and Jerusalem. You can respond to advertisements in the paper, touts at the bus stations, or signs hung outside homes for rent, though it is recommended that you make enquiries through the local tourist office (who should have a list of licensed places). Daily rates vary from $30 to $50 per person, though weekly and monthly deals can be struck. Make sure that you see the place before handing over any money, and be sure that the deal is clear (eg heating, blankets, breakfast, etc). Contact *Israel Bed & Breakfast*, PO Box 24119, Jerusalem, T02-5817001, for further details.

Getting around

Air

Given Israel's compact size very few visitors travel around the country by air, though the domestic airline *Arkia* have flights connecting Tel Aviv, Jerusalem, Rosh Pinna, Kiryat Shemona, Haifa and Eilat. For details on booking flights see the 'Essentials' section of individual towns. The Palestinian Authority's Gaza airport currently only operates a limited number of international flights.

Train

Israel State Railways run a very limited passenger network and an only slightly more expanded freight network. Vulnerability to terrorist attack has always been used as an excuse not to develop the rail network further, though the Ports and Railways Authority have recently announced plans to develop a modern rail transportation system.

The key aim of the plan is to ease road congestion in the Tel Aviv and Haifa areas by constructing a metropolitan rapid transit service, though long-distance rail connections are also under consideration. Where new lines have been developed (eg linking **Tel Aviv** to **Ramla**, **Lod**, **Rehovot**, **Ashdod** and **Be'er Sheva**), the train stations tend to be inconveniently located away from the town centres. Plans are afoot to coordinate train services with local buses that can transport passengers to and from the town centres. There is also talk of extending the line from Tel Aviv to Eilat.

The focus of the present rail network is the coastal line that runs from **Tel Aviv** to **Haifa**, with some trains continuing on to **Akko** and **Nahariya**. Some trains are express, stopping at just Herzliya and Netanya, whilst others stop at all stations *en route*. It is in fact the most pleasant way to make this journey, with fares comparable with the bus service. Those with a student card get 20% discount, making it even more attractive.

The service between **Tel Aviv** and **Jerusalem** which used to run once per day, was very slow, with the station in Jerusalem being inconveniently situated. The service appears currently to be suspended. That's a shame because the scenery *en route* is very attractive and made for a very pleasant journey. For details T03-5774000.

Bus The *Egged Bus Company* provides the back-bone of the Israeli transport system, linking not just the major towns and cities but also all the remote villages, kibbutzim and moshavs. Because of the small size of the country, the longest journey that you are ever likely to undertake is only 4-5 hours (Eilat to Jerusalem or Eilat to Tel Aviv), and costs remain reasonable (under 60 NIS for the two longest journeys). As a very general rule, Egged services operate from around 0530 until about 2230 on Monday-Thursday. **NB** Remember that on Friday and on the eve of Jewish holidays, services stop at around 1500 and don't resume until sunset on Saturday. Plan your journey carefully if travelling at these times. Relying on the bus in the Negev, Golan and Dead Sea Region requires careful planning since services are less regular.

Road distances between towns

	Akko	Ashdod	Ashqelon	Be'er Sheva	Bethlehem	Eilat	Haifa	Hebron	Jericho	Jerusalem	Lod (Ben-Gurion Airport)	Nahariya	Nazareth	Netanya	Rehovot	Tel Aviv	Tiberias	Safed
Ashdod	159																	
Ashqelon	174	33																
Be'er Sheva	231	90	63															
Bethlehem	191	142	145	76														
Eilat	474	333	306	243	319													
Haifa	23	136	151	208	168	451												
Hebron	218	114	117	48	26	291	168											
Jericho	161	102	115	119	43	364	146	67										
Jerusalem	181	72	75	83	10	326	158	37	35									
Lod (Ben-Gurion Airport)	135	40	54	98	61	341	112	88	86	51								
Nahariya	10	169	184	241	193	484	33	217	174	191	145							
Nazareth	65	146	161	218	145	461	38	172	126	135	122	55						
Netanya	86	73	88	145	105	388	63	132	122	95	49	96	73					
Rehovot	140	24	39	85	63	328	117	88	92	50	17	146	127	54				
Tel Aviv	118	41	56	113	73	356	95	100	98	63	18	128	105	32	21			
Tiberias	56	176	191	248	208	491	70	201	181	198	152	66	32	103	157	135		
Safed	51	212	227	284	244	527	74	237	217	234	188	52	57	139	193	171	36	
Zichron Ya'akov	58	105	120	177	128	420	33	153	151	127	85	69	46	32	81	64	78	103

Information General, country-wide bus information can be had by calling T1770-225555 or T03-5375555. You can also call the information office at each bus station (see 'Transport' sections). The information booths at the main bus stations have a very poor reputation for service, justifiably earned. Fortunately, large electronic boards give full details of all departures, including next and last bus and platform number. If travelling to remote areas (notably Negev, Golan and Dead Sea Region), double-check bus times.

Tickets and passes If joining the bus at a bus station you are supposed to buy your ticket from the ticket office, though few Israelis seem to bother with this inconvenience, preferring to pay the driver instead. A student card entitles you to a 10% discount on fares over 10 NIS. During peak periods buses to and from Eilat have to be booked 3 or 4 days in advance. There are a number of passes that provide discount travel on Egged buses, though you need to do a lot of travelling to get your money's worth. **Israbus passes** are available for 7 (270 NIS), 14 (430 NIS) and 21 (540 NIS) days.

Arab buses Travel around the West Bank previously revolved around the Arab bus services operating mainly out of the bus stations opposite Jerusalem's Damascus Gate. However, recent changes in the status of the West Bank road network means that much of the service is currently rather unreliable, and thus Arab service taxis are the most convenient mode of travel here. This situation may change during the life-span of this *Handbook*.

Urban buses Intra-city services around town are operated in most towns by Egged, though the **Dan Bus Company** run the buses in Tel Aviv. At the time of going to press the price of a single journey within a town was 5 NIS, whether you travel 1 stop or all the way across town. (**NB** This fare seems to go up by 50 agorot every 6 months). Be warned: urban bus drivers will shut the doors and pull away as soon as everyone is deemed to be on board. Elderly passengers, the disabled and blind, those carrying children, heavy shopping or backpacks are likely to be sent flying. The driver will then attempt to collect the fares and give change whilst weaving through the traffic. It's all very dangerous and uncivilized.

Those making two or more journeys per day over the period of a single month will save around 25% by buying a **Multifare Discount Pass**. In Tel Aviv, 'sheruts' or service taxis (often a small minibus) operate on the same route as certain buses, displaying the same number. Though costing marginally more than the bus, they can be hailed or stopped anywhere along the fixed route. Many also run on Shabbat (though the fare is 25% more).

Security Cursory searches are sometimes conducted on people entering major bus stations (eg Tel Aviv and Jerusalem), though anyone wearing an IDF uniform (available nationwide in army surplus stores) is likely to be ignored. Bags left unattended, even for a minute, are likely to result in the bus station be evacuated and the offending bag being blown up. Never leave bags unattended and report to security any that appear unclaimed. If you see an unattended bag on a bus, ask around and if nobody claims it inform the driver immediately. Never agree to 'watch' someone's bags for them at a bus station: alert security personnel to their request. Security guards are employed to hop on and off buses at regular intervals to check for suspicious packages. The threat of bombs on buses means that the luggage storage capacity beneath the bus is often kept locked; instead passengers have to negotiate piles of rucksacks in the aisles of the bus.

Taxis that operate around towns are metered, though fares are not particularly cheap. **Taxi** Israeli taxi drivers are like taxi drivers the world over: always keen to rip-off foreign tourists with tales of 'broken meters' and inflated fares. They are obliged to use their

Essentials

meters, though can add a surcharge for a call out, for baggage, and may add 25% for night (2100-0530) and Shabbat services. If you need to make a complaint, call the Controller of Road Transport (Tel Aviv and Central Region, T03-5657272; Jerusalem and the South, T02-6228550; Haifa and the North, T04-8526107).

It is possible to organize a 'special', whether for a tour around a particular town or a visit to a remote site that is poorly served by public transport. Be certain what the exact deal is (eg waiting time, etc), otherwise you are likely to be ripped off. Hotel and hostel receptionists, or the tourist office, may be able to give you some idea of what the fare should be.

Service taxi/sherut An alternative to the intercity bus network is provided by the 'sherut' or service taxi network. Stretch Mercedes seating up to 7, or minibuses, operate on fixed routes between towns for a fare only slightly more than the Egged bus fare. The advantage is that this service is quicker, plus you can get out where you wish. These shared taxis do not run on a fixed schedule but depart when full, though it is surprising how quickly they fill up. In certain areas, service taxis are the only form of transport within or between towns on Shabbat. Service taxis are the best way of exploring the West Bank (where they are referred to as 'servees').

Car hire Hiring a car in Israel makes a lot of sense, particularly for exploring the Negev and Upper Galilee and Golan areas where public transport connections are poor. When divided between 2, 3 or 4 passengers, a hire car can also represent good value. All the major international rental agencies are represented in Israel, along with a number of local firms.

It pays to shop around but you should also be clear as to what exactly it is that you are getting. Adverts that scream at you "hire a car for $20 a day" forget to tell you that insurance will cost at least another $20 per day, and such deals invariably don't include mileage. As a very general rule of thumb, the cheapest category A and B cars (Fiat Uno, Ford Fiesta) cost about $50 per day including insurance. You only generally get unlimited mileage if you hire for 3 days or more. Hiring an A or B category car for a week can reduce daily fees to around $45 per day. Check exactly what the insurance covers. Most policies require you to pay the first $250-350 of any repair bills, and few companies offer collision damage waiver (CDW) where you pay an insurance excess to cover this first $250-350. Availability of CDW even varies between different branches of the same rental firm. Those used to thrashing hire cars and performing wheel-spins should note that insurance excludes all tyre and underbody damage.

Depending upon what time of year you visit, and where you intend going, think very seriously about getting a car with a/c (category B or above). It's often possible to get a free upgrade to an a/c car, though bear in mind that 'free' upgrades mean a higher insurance premium. Most rental agencies require drivers to be over 21, though this rule is sometimes waived. You will require a clean (-ish) licence (international licence not generally necessary) and a credit card. You have to keep your passport, driving licence and rental agreement with you at all times when driving in Israel. Those renting a car for 3 or more days may be able to drive it one-way (eg Tel Aviv to Eilat). Rental cars can not be taken into Sinai (Egypt) or Jordan, whilst yellow- (Israeli-)plated cars may still attract stone-throwers on the West Bank (and some agencies forbid you from taking the car inside the 'Green Line'). Those intending to travel extensively around the West Bank may like to consider hiring a green- or blue-plated car from a Palestinian agency (see entries under various West Bank towns).

Road rules Israeli traffic drives on the right-hand side of the road. It is compulsory for the driver and all passengers (including those in the back seats) to wear seat belts. Children under 14 must be seated in the back seat, and those under 4 must be

Essentials

Driving in Israel

No two ways about it, Israelis are bad drivers. Much pseudo psychological/philosophical rubbish is written to explain Israeli driving habits, generally focusing on the question of the impact of living in a place that is in a perpetual state of war (psychologically at least) with hostile neighbours. The real truth is that many Israeli drivers are impatient, inconsiderate and downright dangerous. Writing in The Jewish Chronicle (London), Simon Round once suggested that Israeli drivers prefer to drive automatic cars so that "they will have at least one hand free to wave to other road users, to eat sandwiches, to adjust the stereo, to turn the pages of the newspaper and to pour the coffee." The Israeli penchant for mobile phones has now added significantly to this list of distractions (though in 1996 a 750 NIS fine was introduced specifically for such an offence).

Those who thought that Athens and Paris drivers were quick on the horn when traffic lights change to green are in for a shock here: "if you are waiting at a traffic light and the car in front of you fails to pull away a nanosecond after the light changes to amber, it is compulsory to give them a prolonged blast on your horn" (Simon Round, ibid). A tourist's guide to driving in Israel, Open Road, gives the following advice/excuse: "Israelis are expressive, passionate people, and this tends to be magnified when behind the wheel. There is more hooting of horns, and unfortunately, more aggressive driving here than in the USA or in northern European countries. We recommend that you do not take this particular style of driving either as a challenge or a personal insult, but remain calm, unintimidated and safe."

strapped in to a suitable car seat. Urban speed limit is 50 kph (31 mph) and 90 kph (56 mph) on inter-city roads. On main arterial roads (eg Routes 1 and 4) 100 kph (62 mph) is permitted. It is compulsory in Israel to drive with headlights on at all times from 1st November to 31st March. Most traffic signs are self-explanatory, or similar to those used in Europe and North America. Other road regulations are similar. When in doubt, give way.

Parking These are general rules with some local variations. Where the kerb is painted red and white, parking and stopping is prohibited at any time. A blue-and-white painted kerb indicates parking permitted with a parking card (available from kiosks, post offices, etc) or by feeding a meter. Parking may be limited to 1 hr during 0700-1700, though a sign should indicate this. Red-and-yellow painted kerbs are for buses and taxis only. Whenever possible, use a designated car park. Do not drive the wrong way in or out of a car-park: the car trap will wreck your tyres.

Israel is an ideal country to explore by bicycle, though some careful planning is required. Freewheeling down into the Jordan Valley basin and the Dead Sea Region is exhilarating; climbing back out on the road up to Jerusalem is not. Likewise, be prepared for some stiff climbs when exploring Upper Galilee and the Golan. The climate is also another major consideration, notably high day-time temperatures in summer, especially in the Negev and Dead Sea Region. Make an early start, rest up during the hottest part of the day, and carry and consume plenty of water. Despite the suicidal tendencies of many Israeli drivers, most roads (particularly the main highways) have wide hard shoulders so you should be able to remain safe. It may also be possible to put your bicycle on a bus for longer/difficult journeys (at 50% of the passenger fare). Those who don't arrive in Israel with their own bicycle can pick up an 18-21 speed form of 'mountain bike' for around 400 NIS (see under 'Shopping' in major cities).

Bicycle

Hitching

Hitch-hiking (*tremping*) remains a popular way of getting around Israel, though as with any other country in the world there are inherent risks attached. A number of measures can be taken to reduce these risks, such as never hitching alone and being selective about whom you get into a car with. It is strongly recommended that women should never hitch without male company. Female soldiers are actively discouraged from hitch-hiking (and forbidden to do so after dark), though half the IDF seems to move around the country by this means. There are special hitching points for soldiers (yellow hand on red background on yellow sign) and potential hitch-hikers should note that Israeli soldiers will always get priority over you. To hitch a ride point down to the road with your index finger (don't use the 'thumb' system used elsewhere).

Keeping in touch

Communications

Language

For list of useful words and phrases, see the back inside cover

If the State of Israel represents the in-gathering of the Jewish people from the Diaspora, then the **Hebrew** language represents one of the main unifying factors. In fact, the very pronunciation of modern Israeli Hebrew (a compromise between Sephardi and Ashkenazi elements) symbolizes its unifying influence. And as Johnson points out, the binding force of Hebrew "prevented Israel from developing a language problem, the curse of so many nations, especially new ones" (*History of the Jews*, 1987).

For several thousand years Hebrew was just used for Jewish liturgy. Indeed, there are some elements in Israeli society (most notably the ultra-orthodox community from Eastern Europe) who believe that it is blasphemous to use Hebrew outside of liturgy, and thus they continue to use native tongues (frequently Yiddish). The modern usage of Hebrew was revived largely through the efforts of Eliezer Ben Yehuda (1858-1922), with the modern Hebrew movement becoming appended to the early Zionist movement. Theodor Herzl is alleged to have wistfully remarked, "Can you imagine buying a train ticket in Hebrew?".

Hebrew is a West Semitic language related to Assyrian and Aramaic. As a general rule, an Israeli could read a Hebrew Bible with relative ease, whilst someone brought up on biblical Hebrew would have some difficulty reading an Israeli newspaper.

The second most widely spoken language in Israel and the Palestinian Authority areas is **Arabic**. It belongs to a branch of the southwestern branch of the Semitic language group, though there are a number of different dialects.

Road signs in Israel are almost always written in Hebrew and English, and in some areas Arabic too. **English** is widely spoken and understood, particularly by those involved in the tourist industry. The Diaspora experience is reflected in the number of other languages spoken in Israel, including French, German, Yiddish, Polish, Romanian, Hungarian, Spanish, and notably Russian.

Postal services

Outgoing mail from Israel is notoriously slow, taking 4-5 days to Europe and 7-10 days to North America and Australia. Incoming mail is rather quicker. Yellow mailboxes are for post within the same city, with red mailboxes for all other destinations. Jerusalem's Central Post Office has a special section for posting parcels (though this is a tedious process involving getting security and customs clearance). Almost all post offices offer poste restante (*doar shamur*), though holders of Amex cards and TCs can use the American Express Clients' Mail service at their offices. Post offices also offer commission-free foreign exchange at good rates for TCs.

Telephone services

The old token- (*asimonim*)-guzzling phone boxes of old have been replaced by a modern phone-card-operated public telephone system. Telecards are available in units of 10 (15 NIS), 20 (25 NIS) and 50 (50 NIS), and can be bought at post offices, shops and kiosks. Telecard-operated public phone boxes can be used for international direct dial (IDD) calls. The standard international access code of 00 has been replaced with the access numbers of three private firms, 012, 013, 014.

Peak rates are Monday-Friday 0800-2200. There is a 25% discount Monday-Friday 2200-0100 and all day Saturday and Sunday. There is a 50% discount Monday-Sunday 0100-0800. Discount calls can be made from offices of Solan Telecommunications in Tel Aviv, Jerusalem, Netanya and Tiberias. For details of dialling codes in Israel, plus operator services, see the inside front cover flap.

Given Israel's contribution to the world of computer technology, there are in fact **Email** remarkably few cyber cafés in the country (perhaps everyone has a computer and modem at home). Most of the major cities have a few, with the going rate being around 30 NIS for 30 mins and 40 NIS for 1 hr (look out for 'happy hours'). They are listed in the 'Communications' sections in the major city entries.

Perhaps as a reflection of their percieved isolation, Palestinians have really taken to the Internet and its potential for access to the outside world. Cyber cafés are springing up in all the major Palestinian towns, and at a very competitive price too (5 NIS for 30 mins, 10 NIS per hour).

Media

Though there are many newspapers in Israel to suit all political leanings, ethnic and **Newspapers** linguistic groupings, and prejudices, there is only one English-language daily, *The Jerusalem Post*. For many years a flag-waving banner-carrying member of the Labour party grouping, a recent take-over has seen the *Post* lurch decidedly to the right. It's hardly a spokesperson for the Likud grouping, though its editorials are now markedly right-wing. On certain days its 'Letters to the Editor' page is full of bigoted, racist rantings (usually originating outside of Israel). It is, however, indispensable for anyone interested in Israeli political life, though it can become a little 'navel-gazing' at times. Its Friday 'what's on' supplement can be very useful. It is not published on Saturday.

The left-wing *Ha'Aretz* daily also has a weekly English edition. Foreign newspapers (generally a day old) and magazines can be bought in larger branches of *Steimatzky* and at 'top end' hotels.

A number of magazines provide good coverage (and often conflicting views) of the **Magazines** contemporary Israeli and Palestinian political, economic and religious scene. The left-leaning *The Jerusalem Report* is like Newsweek or Time in format, though is far better written and much more interesting (22 Rehov Josef Rivlin, PO Box 1805, Jerusalem 91017, T02-6291011, F6291037, email AT&T Mail=!jrep). The Jerusalem Report also has a web site (http://www.jreport.virtual.co.il), with all issues back to 1988 available on CD ROM (about $200 per disc).

News from Within is published monthly by the Alternative Information Centre (6 Koresh St, PO Box 31417, Jerusalem, T02-6241159, F6253151, email aicmail@trendline.co.il); a joint Israeli-Palestinian project that offers an alternative critique of political, economic, social and cultural trends in Israeli and Palestinian society. The Alternative Information Centre provides a valuable resource for visiting journalists. A one-year subscription is $60, plus they have a web-site (http://www.aic.netgate.net).

A pro-Palestinian assessment of contemporary events can be found in *Palestine Report*, published by the Jerusalem Media and Communication Centre (JMCC, PO Box 25047, Nablus Rd, near Mt Scopus Hotel, East Jerusalem, via Israel, T5819777, F5829534, email jmcc@baraka.org). It can usually be picked up at the news-stands around Jerusalem's Damascus Gate.

Essentials

Further information on the internet

Figures released at a 1998 convention at the Israeli Business Management Centre in Tel Aviv suggests that there are some 10,000 Israeli websites, with 170,000 Israeli subscribers. The same convention suggested there were 140 Palestinian websites with some 2,000 Palestinian subscribers. Here are just a small selection of sites that may be of interest to visitors to Israel, and researchers interested in Israeli-Palestinian issues.

Alternative Information Centre
http://www.aic.netgate.net
Publishers of News from Within.

Bir Zeit University
http://www.birzeit.edu/ (university's homepage)
http://www.birzeit.edu/crdps/village.html (looks at the destruction of Palestinian villages)
The West Bank's premier higher education establishment has a number of sites, mainly documenting the work of its Centre for Research and Documentation of Palestinian Society. The university's web master (Nigel Parry nparry@admin.birzeit.edu) runs a very tight ship.

B'Tselem
http://www.btselem.org
Independent Israeli human rights organization.

Complete Guide to Palestine's Websites
http://www.birzeit.edu/links/
Currently lists 117 Palestinian websites with a review of each one.

Complete Guide to the WWW in Israel
http://www.math.technion.ac.il/~nyh/israel/index.html
Over 1,600 links.

Deir Yassin
http://www.deiryassin.org/
Palestinian viewpoint on events of 9th April, 1948. Further information on this subject can be found at
http://www.hanania.com/dybook.htm
(see also under ZOA below).

Government of Israel
http://www.index.gov.il/
Index of government websites, including a list of all the ministries, municipalities and media.

Ha'Aretz
http://www.haaretz.co.il/eng/
Left-wing newspaper.

Hebron Settlers' Website
http://www.virtual.co.il/communities/israel/hebron/

Human Rights Watch Middle East
http://www.hrw.org/about/divisions/mideast.htm
US based, the bane of the Israeli government and the PA!

Israeli Foreign Ministry
http://www.israel.org/ (homepage)
http://www.israel-mfa.gov.il/peace/guide.html (guide to the peace process).

Israel Internet Guide
http://www.neystadt.org/israel/

Israeli Ministry of Tourism
http://www.infotour.co.il
Comprehensive listings.

Jacob Richman's Hotsites

Radio The best frequency for receiving the **BBC World Service** is 1323 kHz (MW), though it is also available on SW bands. **Voice of America** is on 1260 kHz. The FM dial is packed with Israeli stations playing Western music.

Television Israel has two TV stations, imaginatively called Channel 1 and Channel 2. There is persistant talk of privatizing the state-owned Israel Broadcasting Authority (who broadcast Channel 1 and a number of radio stations), though there is doubt as to whether there would be any takers. Commercial Channel 2 has a legal monopoly on all TV advertising, whilst Channel 1 relies largely on an annual licence fee (about $130). Without advertising, it's unlikely that a commercial Channel 1 would be viable, whilst any attempts to allow it to show adverts would be challenged in court by Channel 2! Other critics suggest that Channel 1 is not run by the management but by the unions. Channel 1 shows news in English Sunday-Thursday 1800, Friday 1630, Saturday 1700.

http://www.jr.co.il/hotsites/hotsites.htm
Directory of links to Israel related sites.
Jerusalem Media & Communication Centre
http://www.jmcc.org
Publishers of Palestine Report *and* This Week in Palestine, *good source of info on Palestinian issues.*
Jerusalem Post
http://www.jpost.co.il/
English-language daily newspaper.
Jerusalem Report
http://www.jreport.virtual.co.il
Well-written magazine.
Jewish/Israel Links
http://www.maven.co.il
Huge catalogue of links.
Khalil al-Sakakini Cultural Centre, Ramallah
http://www.sakakini.org/
Palestinian culture and issues. Also has a site dedicated to the Nakba
(http://www.alnakba.org/)
LAW (Palestinian Society for the Protection of Human Rights and the Environment)
http://www.lawsociety.org/
Likud party
http://www.likud.org.il
Ohr Somayach's Top 10 Jewish Humour
http://www.ohr.org.il/judaism/humour/top10/topten.htm
OriNet
http://www.matchroom.com/orient
Leyton Orient homepage.
Palestine National Authority
http://www.pna.org

Homepage of PNA (PA).
Palestine-Net
http://www.palestine-net.com/
Palestinian viewpoint of history, politics, etc.
Peace Now
http://www.peace-now.org
High-profile pressure group.
Ramallah Online Travel Guide
http://www.birzeit.edu/ramallah/
School of Oriental and African Studies' Middle East Water Issues Group
http://www.soas.ac.uk/geography/waterissues/
Excellent database on the subject.
Virtual Jerusalem
http://www.virtualjerusalem.com/
Huge site, with information on just about any subject you care to mention.
Yesha Council
http:www.yesha.virtual.co.il/
Site run by settlers' organization.
Zionist Organization of America (ZOA)
http://www.zoa.org/
The ZOA has a site putting the Israeli spin on events at Deir Yassin
(http://www.zoa.org/archives/pr-980309-99.html).
This list of sights is based largely upon a review of the subject that Nigel Parry presented in a series of articles in the journal Middle East International. Nigel Parry's homepage is
http://www.birzeit.edu/nigelparry/

Essentials

Many homes, hotels and hostels now have 32 cable channels, including BBC World, MTV, Sky and CNN (Cable Netanyahu News, as it used to be known).

Food and drink

Despite a common bond (Judaism) Israelis have a diverse cultural and ethnic background. Not surprisingly, therefore, the dining experience in Israel reflects this diversity. Israel is not quite the gastronomic paradise that the tourist industry would have you believe, and to eat well in this country you have to spend, though by all accounts the present situation is a huge improvement on conditions just 10 or 15 years ago. You can even get good bagels in Israel now!

Food

Kosher

The eating habits of observant Jews are governed by the kashrut *dietary laws laid down by God to Moses (*kosher *being the noun of* kashrut*). Given the standards of hygiene likely to have been practised at this time, many of them make good sense, particularly in the area of prevention of cross-contamination. Many people are familiar with the kosher prohibitions against eating pork and serving meat and dairy products at the same meal, though there is far more to the kashrut laws than just this.*

Beasts that are clovenfooted and chew the cud can be eaten (Leviticus 11:1-47; Deuteronomy 14:6-7). Hence you can eat a cow, which fulfils this criteria, but not a camel (since it chews the cud but is not cleft-hooved). Conversely pigs, despite being clovenfooted, do not chew the cud and so are forbidden. Only birds that do not eat carrion can be considered 'clean', whilst fish must have fins and scales; thus shellfish are forbidden (Deuteronomy 14:8-19). However, to be considered kosher, *animals have to be killed instantly and according to methods supervised by the religious authorities. Animals that*

have died of disease, or in pain, are not considered kosher.

A kosher kitchen, whether in a restaurant or private home, will keep separate plates and dishes for cooking and serving meat and dairy products and will not serve the two together (Exodus 23:19; Deuteronomy 14:14-21). Such have been the culinary habits developed by Israelis over the years, however, you will not simply be given a black coffee to finish off your meal – a milk substitute will be provided. It is permitted for kosher restaurants serving dairy products also to serve fish.

Visitors should note that many restaurants (especially in Jerusalem) are closed on Shabbat, though bar a few extreme cases finding somewhere to eat should not be a problem. Note that a restaurant that offers a kosher menu will probably not be given a kashrut certificate if it prepares or serves food on Shabbat. At some restaurants that are open on Shabbat, food must be ordered and paid for in advance.

Despite the strict regulations regarding kashrut dietary laws, few visitors to Israel will be realistically inconvenienced by them.

Arab food The staple of many Arab restaurants is barbecued meat on skewers (*shashlik*), *shwarma* (known elsewhere as doner kebab) and grilled chicken. Accompaniments include salad, falafel, hummus, bread, and possibly chips (fries), though put together these side dishes can provide a filling meal. One of the most delicious (and cheap) meals served in Israel is *fuul*: a plate of mashed fava beans served in garlic-flavoured oil with hummus and bread. More specialist dishes include *mansaaf*, usually a whole leg of lamb served on a bed of rice with nuts and lemon juice. A diet-busting Arab sweet dish, often served in Jerusalem's Old City for breakfast, is *kanafeh*, a mild cheese mixed with pistachios and baked in a honey syrup shell.

Budget eating It is possible to eat on a budget in Israel, though it is very easy to fall into a predictable diet of nutritionally poor food. The backpacker staple, considered to be Israel's national dish, is the *falafel*. This comprises ground-up chickpeas blended with herbs and spices, rolled into balls and then deep fried. They are usually served stuffed into a pitta bread with *tahini* (a thin paste made from sesame seeds) and salad. Such a sandwich can cost between 3 NIS and 15 NIS depending upon where you buy it. At many such streetside stalls you do the salad-stuffing yourself. A variation of this is the *shwarma*, where the falafel balls are substituted by a form of processed lamb or turkey cut from a revolving spit. Blokes who go down pubs in England know such a dish as a doner kebab. It's funny how a dish that in some cultures would only be eaten after consuming 10 pints of lager can become a staple in others. Many a backpacker in Israel is living on a diet of nothing else.

Many of the bars that have opened to serve Israel's backpacker community provide fairly good-value meals (12-20 NIS), though at some the diet of 'anything and chips' can become a little monotonous. Checking in to a hostel that has cooking facilities may be a means of increasing your intake of fresh vegetables.

Fast food This term used in the Israeli context traditionally meant falafel and shwarma, though today it is more likely to mean Big Mac and fries. Almost all towns of any size have at least one McDonald's, particularly since the chain bought the franchise sites at most of Israel's bus stations. Indigenous versions are also available.

International Diners in Israel can now choose from a global menu, with Argentinian, Mexican, Italian, French, Chinese, Southeast Asian and Indian restaurants found in the main cities. In many cases, the owners/chefs have strong links to the country that their restaurant claims to represent.

Traditional Jewish Some dishes associated with the Ashkenazi, or Eastern European, Jewish immigrants include good old fashioned Hungarian goulash, Viennese schnitzel, chicken livers and gefilte fish. Perhaps more appealing are the Sephardi/Mizrachi, or 'Oriental', restaurants that are becoming more and more popular. Food here reflects the Sephardi roots in the Middle East, with many dishes such as the grilled meats and chicken being very similar to those found in Arab restaurants. Goose livers, baked sinia and stuffed vegetables are all specialities. *Falafel* (see 'budget eating' above) and *hummus* (a thick paste made from ground chickpeas, garlic, seasoning and tahini) are also served as side dishes. It would not be unfair to say that Yemenite restaurants are the current 'flavour of the month' in Israel.

Vegetarian Vegetarians, though not necessarily vegans, are pretty well catered for in Israel, possibly as a by-product of the *kashrut* dietary laws. In addition to the chain of 'dairy' restaurants that can be found across Israel, cities such as Jerusalem, Tel Aviv and Tiberias all have a number of notable restaurants that are preparing imaginative vegetarian dishes. In less cosmopolitan areas vegetarians may have to fall back on the tried and tested falafel and hummus formula, though many hotels prepare good value eat-all-you-want breakfast salads.

Alcohol It used to be said that Israelis were not big drinkers, though the recent massive influx of Eastern Europeans into the country appears to have replaced one stereotype with another. The most popular locally produced beers are Goldstar (4.7%) and Maccabee (4.9%), the latter of which is considered marginally better. Locally brewed-under-licence Carlsberg, Tuborg and Heineken are readily available at similar prices. A half-litre glass in a regular bar will cost 15-20 NIS, or 8-10 NIS if you drink in one of the bars catering to the backpacker crowd. The Ramallah-brewed Taybeh beer wins a lot of friends, though is not widely available.

A number of very good wines are produced in Israel, with notable labels coming from the Golan Heights Winery of Katzrin (see 'Lower Golan' on page 751), the Carmel Oriental Wine Cellars in Zichron Ya'akov (see 'North of Tel Aviv' on page 553) and the Carmel Winery in Rishon LeTzion (see 'South and southeast of Tel Aviv' on page 483). Imported wines tend to be expensive. A variety of spirits and fortified wines are also produced locally, with Israeli vodka renowned for its, er, cheapness.

Non-alcoholic drinks Drinking coffee is a popular Israeli habit. A regular coffee in an Israeli café will probably mean an espresso, though if you want less of a caffeine rush ask for a 'Nescafe'. Coffee served in Arab cafés tends to be of the thick, bitter Turkish-style drink, complete with half a cup of sludge. It is usually served with a palate-cleansing glass of water. The tea served in Arab teahouses is particularly

Essentials

Drink

refreshing; it is served black, in a glass, often with a sprig of mint and plenty of sugar. Carbonated drinks are readily available. Expect to pay 6 NIS for a can of Coke (or 5 NIS for a 1.5 litre unchilled bottle in a supermarket). Bottled water costs 4-5 NIS for a litre.

Entertainment

Bars, cafés & nightclubs

Rather than English-style pubs or American bars, Israel is much more at home with its European style café-bars. In addition to coffee and alcoholic drinks, most also serve light meals. In the more fashionable ones 'being seen' is as important as the quality of the food and drink. Tel Aviv has the greatest concentration of such places, though the rest of the country is catching up.

Of course most towns have good old-fashioned bars, particularly those with large populations of Eastern Europeans. See under 'Food and drink' above for an idea of what to pay for a beer. The larger cities (notably Tel Aviv, Jerusalem, Eilat and, to a lesser extent, Tiberias) have a greater choice of nightlife, with everything from theme-pubs ('English', 'Irish'), through hotel bars, to places aimed primarily at backpackers.

The larger cities all have a selection of nightclubs, though most visitors see little more than the ones aimed at tourists. Hotel nightclubs are rather staid and somewhat dull unless busy. Those aimed at holiday-makers (Israeli and foreign) and backpackers are extremely variable (see 'Essentials' information in each town for the low-down). To really penetrate the 'Israeli scene' you need local contacts. Most of the 'happening' places are in rather remote locations (notably industrial estates on the edges of towns), and you probably won't find out about them unless you ask around locally (try records shops or 'trendy' bars). Entry is typically 50 NIS, drinks are expensive, and most have a selective door policy (dress up; girls wear your shortest skirt).

Cinemas

Almost all towns of any size have at least 1 multi-screen cinema complex, with many US-produced films screened here before they are shown in Europe. Almost all non-Israeli films are shown with their original soundtrack, with Hebrew subtitles added. The diet is standard Hollywood stuff, though there are a few art-house cinemas in Jerusalem and Tel Aviv. Expect to pay around 25 NIS to go to the cinema. Check Friday's *Jerusalem Post* for nationwide listings. At least 1 Jerusalem cinema usually shows Monty Python's *Life of Brian* at Christmas!

Theatres & concerts

Israelis are great theatre and concert goers, with the National Theatre (Habimah) playing to 90% full houses (despite putting on 3 shows a day, 6 days per week). Performances tend to be in Hebrew, with the latest interpretation of Chekov, Beckett or Miller eagerly awaited. See 'Tel Aviv' and 'Jerusalem' sections for main theatre and concert hall listings, and pick up Friday's edition of the *Jerusalem Post*. The Palestinian al-Hakawati theatre group perform regularly in East Jerusalem.

Music

In the first edition of the *Israel Handbook*, it was suggested that the Israelis treated the Eurovision Song Contest with the contempt it deserves, by entering a transsexual singer. Well, Dana International subsequently won the thing (much to the delight of secular Israelis, and the anger of the orthodox who claimed it was shameful), and then stole the show in the following year's event in Jerusalem when she fell off her high heels whilst presenting the trophy.

Sport

Israelis are generally keen on sports, with many of Channel 1's highest viewing figures coming when it screens a major sporting event. However, as a nation Israel is yet to really leave its mark on the sporting world stage (perhaps a reflection of its relatively small population).

Essentials

Palestinian handicrafts

One of the best places to purchase Palestinian handicrafts is in the shop at St Andrew's Church in Jerusalem. The shop is run by Sunbula ('grain of wheat' in Arabic), a non-profit association that acts as an umbrella organization for a number of Palestinian self-help groups (formerly known as 'Craftaid'). Items available include bedouin rugs, embroidery work, olive-wood crafts, etc, with prices ranging from three to several hundred dollars. It is open Monday-Saturday 0900-1800, Sunday 1100-1300, with groups requested to call ahead (T02-6732401, F6731711).

The most popular spectator sports are **basketball and football** ('soccer'). Although Israeli sides have had some success in Europe with the former, they have regularly underachieved with the latter. For many years Israel's most famous soccer export was Ronny Rosenthal, described in the English press as "a rogue rocket, waiting to be aborted by mission control", with a repertoire limited to "running very fast in a straight line – with or without the ball – then falling over"! However, more and more Israeli players are being sought out by European teams, whilst the national team has recently reached its highest-ever FIFA ranking (22nd) and at the time of going to press had just qualified for the Euro 2000 play-offs.

Most towns of any size have a decent **tennis** centre, with the beach version, *matkot*, also being popular. There is currently only one 18-hole **golf course** in Israel, though it's not cheap (see under 'Caesarea' on page 543). For full details of activities such as hiking, skiing, diving, water-sports and horse-riding, see under 'Special interest travel' in 'Planning your trip' at the beginning of the Handbook (page 19). The Israeli **cricket** team is usually viewed as a political creation, forcing nations who play the game but have no diplomatic recognition of Israel (Pakistan, United Arab Emirates and other Gulf States with large South Asian migrant worker populations, Malaysia, etc) into some sort of *de facto* relationship.

Shopping

There is a saying along the lines of "you have to kiss a lot of frogs to find a prince". Something similar could be said with regard to shopping in Israel. Most visitors to Israel seek some sort of **souvenir** of their visit to the Holy Land, though you will have to wade through piles of pilgrim/tourist junk before you find that gem. There's some real *Life of Brian* stuff on offer, including your very own crown of thorns. Another perennial favourite is the 3-D effect picture that is Jesus at one angle, the Virgin Mary at another angle, and the Virgin Mary with a beard if held somewhere in the middle. My personal favourite is the horribly plastic model of Dome of the Rock whose alarm clock wakes you up with a blast of "Allah oh-Akhbar". Jerusalem's Old City remains the main centre for the mass-produced pilgrim trash, though there are some nice pieces there if you look hard enough. Some of the **ceramic** work, **copper** and **brassware**, and **Judaica** is quite interesting. If you can afford them and know what you are dealing with, there are some fabulous **ikons** on sale. Haggling (bargaining) is an integral part of the buying process.

Tel Aviv, Netanya and Tiberias all have showrooms where you can indulge your passion for **diamonds**, whilst Eilat is renowned for its 'gems'. Be careful. As a general rule, anything that Israel exports will be cheaper in your home country, whilst anything that is available in Israel and your own country will be cheaper at home. If buying expensive luxury items, look out for shops participating in the 'VAT refund for tourists' scheme (see page 37).

Essentials

 Months of the Hebrew calendar

Tishrey *(Sep/Oct);* Cheshvan *(Oct/Nov);* Kislev *(Nov/Dec);* Tevet *(Dec/Jan);* Shvat *(Jan/Feb);* Adar.(Feb/Mar, Adar bet *in a* leap year); Nisan *(Mar/Apr);* Iyar *(Apr/May);* Sivan *(May/Jun);* Tamuz *(Jun/Jul);* Av *(Jul/Aug);* Elul *(Aug/Sep).*

The Steimatzky chain is the best source of English-language **books** (including a full range of *Footprint Handbooks*), though prices tend to be more expensive than in the UK and USA at least. Israelis are in fact second on the worldwide list of book readers, despite the prices. There is however a wide range of material on Judaism, Israeli and Palestinian culture, and the Arab-Israeli conflict. *Geographical Tours*, 8 Tverya St, Tel Aviv, T03-5284113 also stock *Footprint Handbooks*.

Film and most camera batteries are readily available in Israel, though it will almost certainly be cheaper if you bring all your photographic equipment needs with you. Outside of larger towns only colour print film may be available. Be wary of buying film from souvenir shops and hawkers; it may be out of date or have been poorly stored.

Holidays and festivals

Holidays and religious festivals in Israel and the Palestinian Authority areas present a very confusing picture. Not only are there 'secular', Jewish, Christian and Islamic holidays, but the dates that they fall on are variously governed by the Hebrew lunar calendar, the solar Gregorian calendar, plus sightings of the new moon at Mecca! It should also be noted that the various branches of the Christian Church celebrate key events on different days.

Jewish holidays

Israel works on the lunar Hebrew calendar (as opposed to the solar Gregorian calendar), and thus all Jewish religious and secular holidays fall on different dates of the Gregorian calendar each year. However, they always remain at roughly the same time of year. Most of the main Jewish holidays fall within the autumn season ('fall'). Unless you are coming to Israel specifically to celebrate one of these holidays, this is a good time to avoid visiting. Transport, banks, offices, shops and restaurants are all affected, whilst accommodation can be difficult to find in spite of the sky-rocketing prices. If you are here for one of the major holidays (Rosh Hashana, Yom Kippur, Sukkot, Pesah) plan ahead. For details of the Jewish Sabbath (*Shabbat*) see under 'Business hours' above. Dates are given here for 1999 (where appropriate), 2000 and 2001. The holidays below are listed in the order in which they occur during the Hebrew calendar year, and not in order of importance.

Rosh Hashana — Rosh Hashana celebrates the beginning of the Hebrew calendar year, though it is also a time of introspection as religious Jews examine their conduct over the previous 12 months. Because it is the only holiday in Israel that lasts for 2 consecutive days, it is considered to be the main vacation period. It is celebrated on the 1st and 2nd of *Tishrey*. In September 1999 the Hebrew year changed from 5759 to 5760. **2000**: September 30-October 1; **2001**: September 18-19.

Yom Kippur — This is the holiest day of the year and the most important date in the Hebrew calendar. It marks the end of 10 days of penitence and moral introspection that began with Rosh Hashana, and finishes with God's judgement and forgiveness: the Day of Atonement. Yom Kippur is characterized by a sunset to sunset fast that is usually observed by even the most 'secular' Israelis. Virtually everything in Israel closes down for Yom Kippur. Since 1973 it has also acted as an unofficial memorial day, commemorating those who died in the surprise war that the Egyptians and Syrians launched on that date. It takes place on the 10th of *Tishrey*. **2000**: 9th October; **2001**: 27th September.

Sukkot

Sukkot commemorates the 40 years spent wandering in the wilderness after the Moses-led Exodus out of bondage in Egypt. Many Jews recreate the *succah*, or moveable shelter, in which the Israelites lived during their wanderings, taking all their meals there for a period of 7 days. Small plywood structures with a roof of loose thatch and branches are built in courtyards, on balconies, in gardens, on roof-tops, and in corners of rooms, all across the country. Many hotels also build a symbolic *succah* in reception. An oft-told story said to derive from a case in the United States tells how a Jew who had built a *succah* on his balcony was taken to court by a bigoted neighbour, who claimed it was an eye-sore. The judge (who was himself Jewish) found in the plaintiff's favour, ordering the Jew to remove the structure within 7 days! Sukkot is often referred to as the Feast of Tabernacles. Zionist tradition associates Sukkot with the celebration of the Harvest Festival. It takes place on the 15th to 21st of *Tishrey*. **2000**: 14th-20th October; **2001**: 2nd-8th October.

Simchat Torah

This is probably the only Jewish religious holiday in Israel that has no accompanying Zionist tradition. It celebrates the giving of the Torah (first five books of the Bible, *Genesis, Exodus, Leviticus, Numbers, Deuteronomy*); literally the Rejoicing of the Law. It falls 1 week after Sukkot, at the end of *Tishrey*. **2000**:21st October;**2001**:9th October.

Hanukkah

Not an official public holiday, since it does not mark an event mentioned in the Torah, Hanukkah celebrates the Maccabean Revolt that began in the 2nd century BCE when the Jews rose up against the pagan reforms of the dominant Hellenistic culture. The revolt culminated in a return to Jewish self-rule under the Hasmonean dynasty (c.152-37 BCE). Hanukkah is celebrated by the nightly ceremonial lighting of the *menorah*, or 7-branched candelabra, and is thus often known as the Feast or Festival of Lights. British readers who used to watch Blue Peter at Christmas will understand. It falls during *Kislev*. **1999**: 4th-11th December; **2000**: 22nd-29th December; **2001**: 9th-17th December.

Tu B'Shevat

This is not a public holiday, though in recent years it has been used as an occasion for tree-planting. Its origins are in the Mishnah, when the 'New Year for Trees' was celebrated by eating fruit and nuts. **2000**: 22nd January; **2001**: 8th February.

Purim

Purim is probably the most bizarre holiday in the Hebrew calendar. It celebrates events in ancient Persia when the Jews were sentenced to death for refusing to bow to the secular authority. Their main persecutor was a man named Haman, though eventually it was Haman whom the authorities executed, whilst the Jews were left unmolested. For some reason Purim, or the Feast of Lots, has been turned into a sort of Jewish Halloween, with children dressing up and adults encouraged to get uncharacteristically drunk. **2000**: 21st March; **2001**: 9th March.

Pesah

Pesah, or Passover, celebrates the Exodus out of Egypt. The festival lasts for a whole week, but even though only the first and last days are official public holidays many shops (including food stores) close for the entire 7 days. Be prepared. During the Israelites' escape from Egypt, the Bible recalls how there wasn't even time for them to wait for their bread to be baked. As a symbolic gesture, no products containing yeast or other leavening agents are eaten. Anyone spending Pesah in Israel will have to content themselves with a special unleavened bread called *matzot*; a rather tasteless

Essentials

substitute in most people's minds. Even McDonald's produces a special bun! The Passover meal also has a symbolic significance in the Christian tradition. Pesah is celebrated from the 15th to 21st of *Nisan*. **2000**: 20th-26th April; **2001**: 8th-14th April.

Mimouna This takes places on the 22nd of *Nisan*, the day after the last day of Pesah. It is only really celebrated by Sephardi Jews, noticeably those from North Africa, and though its exact origin is unclear it is a good excuse for a party! **2000**: 27th April; **2001**: 15th April.

Lag B'Omer Lag B'Omer is really a multiple celebration. Taking place on the 18th of *Iyar*, it marks the end of a 33-day period of mourning and represents a sort of rite of spring when a plague was lifted from the Jewish nation. There's really only one place to celebrate this event, and that's at the Tomb of Rabbi Shimon bar Yochai at Meiron, near Safed (see 'Upper Galilee' section for full details). His teachings in the 2nd century CE were compiled into printed form some 1,100 years after his death, with Lag B'Omer also used as a celebration of the giving of this *Zohar*, or central text of kabbalah. **2000**: 29th May; **2001**: 11th May.

Shavuot in its original form, Shavuot commemorated the 7 weeks that it took the Israelites to reach Mt Sinai, and is thus something of a celebration of the receiving of the Torah. In Hebrew shavuot means 'weeks', though many readers will know this festival as the Jewish Pentecost. Under the Zionist influence of the early kibbutzniks, however, Shavuot has come to represent something of a celebration of the productive capability of the land, and is often referred to as the 'kibbutz holiday'. It takes place on the 6th of *Sivan*. **2000**: 9th June; **2001**: 28th May.

Tisha B'av This is a solemn occasion commemorated mainly at the Western Wall in Jerusalem. It remembers the occasions upon which the First and Second Temples were destroyed. It falls on the 9th of *Av*. **2000**: 10th August; **2001**: 29th July. Some observant Jews also fast on the 17th of *Tamuz*, the date upon which the Romans destroyed Jerusalem's city walls.

Israeli 'secular' holidays

Yom HaSho'ah (Holocaust Memorial) Since 1951, the 27th of *Nisan* has been set aside as a day to remember both the victims of the Holocaust and the heroes of the Jewish resistance. Its official title is in fact Memorial to the Holocaust and the Heroism. At 11 o'clock sharp a siren is heard throughout the country, signalling all traffic (human and vehicular) to stop whilst 2 minutes of silence is observed. It really is a very unusual (and moving) sight, particularly if you are on a normally busy street at the time. Israeli television broadcasts a special service from Yad VaShem. Note that most businesses and places of entertainment close the evening before. **2000**: 2nd May; **2001**: 20th April.

Yom Ha'Atzmaut (Independence Day) David Ben-Gurion declared Israel's independence on 14th May, 1948. Or rather he declared it on the 5th day of the month of *Iyar*. Every 19 years the event can be celebrated on the same day, though otherwise the Hebrew calendar is used. Note that most businesses and places of entertainment close the evening before. **2000**: 10th May; **2001**: 28th April.

May Day May Day reflects the socialist leanings of the early Zionists, though International Labour Day is now only celebrated on some kibbutzim (1st May).

Christian holidays

All the major Christian festivals are celebrated in Israel, though none are official public holidays; Israeli life proceeds as normal. The key festivals are celebrated on different dates by the 'Eastern' Orthodox, 'Oriental' Orthodox and 'Western' Churches ('Latin' ie Roman Catholic, and Protestant).

Christmas Day is celebrated on **25th December** by the 'Western' Church, with the highlight being the midnight mass held at the Church of the Nativity in Bethlehem on the night of Christmas Eve (24th). For full details see the 'Bethlehem' section. The Orthodox ('Eastern') Church celebrates Christmas on **7th January** (except Greek Orthodox which also uses 24-25 December) whilst the Armenian Christmas falls on **19th January**. These dates remain consistent. | **Christmas**

Easter is celebrated on different dates by the 'Western' Church, 'Oriental' and 'Eastern' Orthodox Churches, with the date also changing from year to year. The 'Good Friday' commemorates the Crucifixion, with impressive crowds walking the Via Dolorosa. 'Easter Sunday' (two days later) celebrates the Resurrection. Note that the Orthodox 'Holy Saturday' is the day when the 'Miracle of the Holy Fire' is celebrated (arguably Jerusalem's most intense Christian celebration, see page 142). **2000**: 'Western' Good Friday, 21st April; 'Eastern' Orthodox Good Friday, 28th April; **2001**: 'Western' Good Friday, 13th April; 'Eastern' Orthodox Good Friday, 20th April. | **Easter**

This festival celebrates the revelation by the archangel Gabriel to the Virgin Mary that she was pregnant with Jesus. The most spectacular celebration is held at the Basilica of the Annunciation in Nazareth, and at the time of going to press it was strongly rumoured that the Pope would be in attendance in the year 2000 (25th March). | **Feast of the Annunciation**

For details of various Christian festivals and holidays contact *Christian Information Centre (Catholic)*, PO Box 14308, opposite Citadel, Jaffa Gate, Jerusalem, T6272692, F6286417 and *Franciscan Pilgrim Office*, PO Box 186 (same location), T6272697. | **Other**

Muslim holidays

The Islamic calendar begins on 16th July 622 AD, the date of the *Hijra* ('flight' or 'migration') of the Prophet Mohammad from Mecca to Medina in modern Saudi Arabia, which is denoted 1 AH (Anno Hegirae or year of the Hegira). The Islamic or *Hijri* calendar is lunar rather than solar, each year having 354 or 355 days, meaning that annual festivals do not occur on the same day each year according to the Gregorian calendar. | **The Islamic calendar**

The 12 lunar months of the Islamic calendar, alternating between 29 and 30 days, are; *Muharram, Safar, Rabi-ul-Awwal, Rabi-ul-Sani, Jumada-ul-Awwal, Jumada-ul-Sani, Rajab, Shaban, Ramadan, Shawwal, Ziquad* and *Zilhaj*. To convert a date in the Hijra calendar to the Christian date, express the former in years and decimals of a year, multiply by 0.970225, add 621.54 and the total will correspond exactly with the Christian year!

(Islamic New Year) 1st *Muharram*. The first 10 days of the year are regarded as holy, especially the 10th. **2000**: 5th April; **2001**: 24th March. | **Ras as-Sana/Al-Hijra**

9th and 10th *Muharram*. Anniversary of the killing of Hussain, grandson of the Prophet Mohammad, commemorated by Shi'a Muslims. Ashoura also celebrates the meeting of Adam and Eve after leaving Paradise, and the end of the Flood (Palestinian Muslims are predominantly Sunni Muslim so this event is not widely commemorated here). **2000**: 13th April; **2001**: 1st April. | **Ashoura**

Birth of the Prophet Mohammad: 12th *Rabi-ul-Awwal*. **2000**: 14th June; **2001**: 3rd June. | **Moulid an-Nabi**

Ascension of Mohammad from the Haram al-Sharif in Jerusalem: 27th *Rajab*. **1999**: 4th November; **2000** 23rd October; **2001** 11th October. | **Leilat al-Meiraj**

Essentials

Ramadan The holiest Islamic month, when Muslims observe a complete fast during daylight hours. Businesses and Muslim sites operate on reduced hours during Ramadan. 21st *Ramadan* is the *Shab-e-Qadr* or 'Night of Prayer'. **1999**: 9th December-8th January 2000; **2000**: 27th November-27th December; **2001**: 16th November-16th December.

Eid el-Fitr Literally 'the small feast'. 3 days of celebrations, beginning 1st *Shawwal*, to mark the end of Ramadan. **2000**: 8th January (end of Ramadan 1999); **2000**: 27th December; **2001**: 16th December.

Eid el-Adha Literally 'the great feast' or 'feast of the sacrifice'. 4 days beginning on 10th *Zilhaj*. The principal Islamic festival, commemorating Abraham's sacrifice of his son Ismail, and coinciding with the pilgrimage to Mecca. Marked by the sacrifice of a sheep, by feasting and by donations to the poor. **2000**: 17th March; **2001**: 6th March.

Palestinian 'secular' holidays

There are a number of dates that are celebrated as 'secular' holidays in Palestinian areas, some of which have been designated public holidays by the PA (marked with an asterisk).

Fatah Day   1st January*
Jerusalem Day   22nd February
Palestinian Land Day   30th March
Deir Yassin Day   19th April
Black September Day   18th September
Balfour Day   2nd November
Independence Day   15th November
UN Palestine Day   29th November

Health

Medical insurance Taking out medical insurance prior to visiting Israel is a very good idea. Though healthcare is good and there are few risks not generally encountered at home, treatment costs are sky-high: a weekend in a 5-star hotel is probably cheaper than a night in an Israeli hospital. Check to see whether your policy covers air ambulance and repatriation. Read the policy small print to see if 'high-risk' activities such as diving, riding or hiking are covered. A policy where the insurance company pays the bill direct (rather than you paying, then claiming back the fees later) is probably a better deal, though generally more expensive. Keep all receipts for any treatment that you receive.

Common problems The standard of healthcare in Israel is very high (it leads the world in some fields). There are no special health precautions that visitors should take, except to **avoid dehydration and sun-burn/stroke**. A wide-brimmed hat plus high-factor sun-cream should be worn as protection against the sun, whilst 4 litres of water should be drunk per day to avoid dehydration. Dark-coloured urine, perhaps coupled with a feeling of lethargy, is often a sign of dehydration. Tap water in Israel is safe, though the delivery system in the Old City of Jerusalem may be questionable. Bottled water is widely available. Take a spare pair of glasses (or at least a prescription) if you wear them. Sun-glasses with 100% UV protection are a must. Note that not all clothes offer protection against the sun. As a general rule of thumb, if you can see through it when you hold it up to the light, then you can burn through it.

If you have a **long-standing medical condition** such as diabetes, heart trouble, high blood pressure, etc, get advice from your doctor and carry sufficient medication to last the full duration of your trip. You may want to ask your doctor for a letter explaining your condition. Children should be up to date on basic childhood vaccinations, and adults up to date with vaccinations such as Tetanus.

Travellers continuing on to countries such as Egypt should arrange **malaria prophylaxis** (prevention) before leaving home. Remember that most courses must be started 2 weeks before arriving in the infected area, and continued for 4 weeks after leaving. Consult your doctor or travel clinic.

Travellers should also consider carrying a small **first aid kit** that contains such basic items as headache treatments (eg Paracetamol), preparatory treatments for diarrhoea such as Loperamide (eg *Imodium*, *Arret*), oral rehydration proprietary preparations (ORS), plus sticky plasters and corn plasters (eg *Band Aid*). A good insect repellant may also come in handy, particularly those with around a 40-50% concentration of Diethyl-toluamide (DET). There are also repellants now available that use more natural ingredients. All of these items are available in Israel, though you will probably find that they are cheaper at home.

If **swimming or diving** in an area where there are poisonous fish such as stone or scorpion fish (also called by a variety of local names), sea urchins on rocky coasts, or coral, tread carefully or wear plimsolls. The sting of such fish is intensely painful but can be helped by immersing the stung part in water as hot as you can bear for as long as it remains painful. This is not always very practical and you must take care not to scald yourself. It is highly recommended that you take immediate local medical advice in order to ascertain whether any coral or sting remains in the wound. Such injuries take a long time to heal and can be liable to infection. The main diving resorts in Israel (and across the Egyptian border in Sinai) have medical facilities equipped to deal with **diving accidents**.

In a medical emergency dial T101 (Hebrew) or T911 (English). A special medical help-line for tourists can be reached on T177-0229110. The number of the Magen David Adom (Red Star of David) is given in the 'Essentials' section of all the major towns. The Jerusalem Post carries a daily list of late-night and all-night pharmacies.

Emergency

Working in Israel

What type of work?

Many visitors to Israel, particularly backpackers and students, subsidize their stay in the country (and possibly future travelling) by working. Before committing yourself to anything, it is as well to know what it is exactly that you want from your Israeli work experience. Do you just want to earn some money? Do you want a unique Israeli experience? Do you want to learn something about Israeli life and culture? Or do you want something that will delay your return home, but won't eat into your travelling funds? There are a number of options.

Kibbutz

Several points need to be made about the kibbutz system straight away. It is not a good way to make money, and it is doubtful whether it is a good way to conserve your travelling funds either (with many volunteers drinking away their savings). It is not a good way to get to see Israel since you have to work six days a week, your day off is on the day that the buses don't run, they are usually situated in remote locations and you generally have to stay for more than 3 months to qualify for the kibbutz outings. It is not necessarily a good way to meet Israelis since many kibbutzniks are put off entering into friendship with transitory volunteers, and kibbutzniks only represent a small section of the population anyway (3.8%). It will offer a unique experience, and, according to what your expectations are and what sort of people you share the experience with, it may well be a memorable one. If you are already in Israel, a good way of finding out what to expect on a kibbutz or moshav is by talking to ex-volunteers in the backpacker hostels. Many kibbutzim now prefer to embloy Thai migrant workers since they are invariably more productive than students and backpackers. (**NB** The concept and functioning of the kibbutz and moshav is discussed below).

Work and pay To join a kibbutz as a volunteer you have to be aged 18 to 32, in good mental and physical health, have proof of health insurance (not always asked for) and be willing to submit to a HIV/Aids test (not always enforced). Your work regime will be 6 days per week, 8 hours per day (generally starting very early in the morning), and you will be expected to accept whatever task is assigned to you. There is every reason to believe that volunteers are given the most menial and tedious chores on the kibbutz. Gardening is considered to be a good job. Getting up at 0430 to pick up all the dead chickens that died overnight is not. You have to commit yourself to the kibbutz for a minimum of 2 months.

In return for your labour you will receive free accommodation (usually in a special volunteers' block well away from the regular kibbutzniks), meals, a number of basic requisites such as toiletries, stamps, cigarettes, plus a personal allowance of around US$50 per month. Volunteers generally have access to all the recreational facilities at the kibbutz. You may believe that with all your basic needs provided for it would be possible to save your monthly personal allowance – not necessarily true. An early start to your working day means an early finish, and with so many hours to while away and beer being very cheap in the kibbutz store, many volunteers hit the bottle in a big way. It's very easy to drink away both your monthly allowance and your travelling funds that you're holding in reserve. Poor behaviour resulting from alcohol abuse often leads to considerable tension between kibbutzniks and volunteers. Some nationalities have particularly poor records in this regard, and single men often experience difficulty getting kibbutz placements. On the positive side, like-minded kibbutz volunteers can become lifelong friends (and partners).

Joining a You can organize a kibbutz placement in your home country or wait until you arrive in **kibbutz** Israel. If you go through a kibbutz representative in your own country you will have to pay a $50 registration fee. You then have a choice of flying out to Israel as part of a group, or making your own way there. If you fly with the group you will be met at Ben-Gurion airport on arrival and driven straight to the kibbutz. There may be the opportunity to get together with the other members of your group prior to flying out. The disadvantage with this system is that you have to book your flight through the kibbutz representative in your country, and this can work out more expensive than arranging the flight yourself. If you organize your own flight you have to make your own way to the kibbutz office in Tel Aviv (within 1 month of paying your registration fee at home), and then have to make your own way to your allocated kibbutz. If for any reason you have to wait around for a placement, you are responsible for your own expenses. A list of kibbutz representatives overseas and in Israel is provided below.

To organize a kibbutz placement when already in Israel go to one of the kibbutz representatives in Tel Aviv. Because of the number of students seeking a kibbutz placement, July/August is a bad time to try this approach, whereas harvest period is a good time. Acting like a sober, diligent, hard worker is a good way of getting a placement. It may be possible to apply directly to an individual kibbutz, though this approach is not usually successful. For further details on kibbutz life, including comprehensive details of each individual kibbutz, see John Bedford's ***Kibbutz Volunteer*** (Vacation Work, UK).

Australia: *Kibbutz Program Centre*, 104 Darlinghurst Rd, Darlinghurst, NSW 2010, T02-93606300; *Kibbutz Program Desk*, 306 Hawthorn Rd, South Caulfield, VIC 3162, T03-92725331. **Belgium**: *Bureau de Volontaires*, 68 Ave Ducpetiaux, 1060 Bruxelles, T02-5381050. **Canada**: *Kibbutz Aliyah Desk*, 1000 Finch Ave West, Downsview, Ontario M3J 2E7; *Kibbutz Aliyah Desk*, 5800 Cavendish Blvd, Cote St Luc, Montreal PQ H4W 2TS. **France**: *Objectif Kibbutz*, 15 Rue Beranger, 75003 Paris; *Dror-Habonim*, 9 rue Clement-Roassal, Nice 06000; *Dror-Habonim*, 8 rue Idrac, Toulouse 31000; *Hachomer Hatsair*, 12 Rue Mulet, Lyon 69000; *Dror-Habonim*, 32 rue Estelle, Marseille 13001. **Germany**: *Kibbutz Bewegung*, Savignystrasse 49, 6600 Frankfurt 17, T69-74014. **Netherlands**: *Volunteers Desk*, Jon Veermeerstr 24, Amsterdam 1071. **New Zealand**: *Kibbutz Program Desk*, Jewish Community Centre Building, Kensington St, PO Box 27-156, Wellington, T04-844229. **UK**: *Kibbutz Representatives*, 1A Accommodation Rd, London NW11, T0181-4589235; *Kibbutz Representatives*, 222 Fenwick Rd, Glasgow, T0141-6202194; *Kibbutz Representatives*, Harold House, Dunbabin Rd, Liverpool, T0151-7225671; *Kibbutz Representatives*, 11 Upper Park Rd, Salford, Manchester M7 0HY, T0161-7959447; *Project 67*, 10 Hatton Garden, London EC1N 8AH, T0171-8317626. **USA**: *Israel Aliyah Centre*, Suite 1020, Statler Office Building, 20 Providence St, Boston, Massachusetts 02116; *Israel Aliyah Centre*, 10103 Fondern Rd (354), Houston, Texas 77096; *Israel Aliyah Centre*, 6505 Wiltshire Blvd, Room 807, Los Angeles, California 90048; *Israel Aliyah Centre*, 4200 Biscayne Blvd, Miami, Florida 33137; *Kibbutz Aliyah Desk*, 2320 W Peterson, Suite 503, Chicago, Illinois 60659; *Kibbutz Aliyah Desk*, 110 East 59th St, New York, T212-3186130; *Kibbutz Aliyah Desk*, 870 Market St (1083), San Fransisco, California 94102; *Kibbutz Aliyah Desk*, 6600 West Maple Rd, West Bloomfield, Michigan 48033.

Kibbutz Volunteer Centre, 124 HaYarkon, opposite Sheraton, T03-5221325; *Meira's*, 73 Ben Yehuda, T03-5237369, F5243811; *Project 67*, 94 Ben Yehuda, T03-5230140, F5247474; *Kibbutz HaDati*, 7 Dubnov, T03-5257231, Orthodox observant Jews only.

Kibbutz representatives overseas — (margin)

Kibbutz representatives in Tel Aviv — (margin)

Essentials — (margin)

Moshav

Whilst many kibbutzim are diversifying into light industry and tourism, agriculture remains the backbone of the moshav system. Moshav volunteers are usually assigned to one particular farmer, and the success (or otherwise) of your moshav experience will almost certainly depend upon this relationship. Moshav farmers generally have a reputation for being slave-driving bullies. Moshav work tends to be far harder than that on a kibbutz ('back-breaking' is an often-used term), though the financial rewards are greater. Pay is around US$260 per month for an 8-hour day and 6-day week. Overtime is often compulsory, though getting paid for it can be a problem. The after-hours social scene varies considerably from moshav to moshav; you may be billeted with other volunteers, though don't be surprised if you are on your own. Moshav volunteers generally provide their own food (better get used to tomatoes), though if your farmer supplies your meals expect wages to be halved.

Moshav volunteers have to be aged 18 to 35 and have medical insurance. Don't apply unless you are physically fit and prepared for hard manual labour. To join a moshav go to the representatives office at 19 Leonardo de Vinci St, Tel Aviv, T03-5258473 (bus 70 from central bus station). Good luck!

Working illegally

Estimates of the number of illegal workers in Israel are rather vague, though it is reckoned that almost half of the 110,000 or so foreign workers in Israel are working illegally. In recent years backpackers have to an extent replaced Palestinian labourers since the latter are frequently barred from working in Israel by closures of the West

Bank and Gaza Strip. There are moves to cut the growing dependence on foreign workers in the construction and agriculture sectors, though there are difficulties in attracting Israelis to these menial and low-paid manual labour jobs. Indeed, the official 'Jubilee Bells' event in Jerusalem in 1998 to mark Israel's 50th anniversary would not have been possible without the labouring efforts of backpackers working illegally! Thus, for the foreseeable future, the opportunity for earning money in Israel remains.

If you want to earn money during your stay in Israel (whether to live, or save for further travels), working illegally is a far better option than a kibbutz or moshav placement. It may also be argued that you get to see more of 'real life' too. Unfortunately, the work tends to be poorly paid, often extremely boring, and generally very hard. The main places to seek work are probably Tel Aviv, Eilat and Jerusalem (in that order), though more people are checking out the jobs potential in Tiberias. As a very general rule, men tend to find work in the construction industry (though this term is very broadly defined, with most work likely to be 'destruction' involving stripping out shops and houses). Pay tends to hover around the 15-20 NIS per hour mark, with no insurance or safety equipment provided. It is important not to let wages build up since many employers have reputations for not paying. Daily payment is a good compromise. Remember, working illegally you have no recourse to the law if your employer does not pay up.

Women tend to find work in the service industries, notably bar and restaurant work. In some places there is no salary and wages are made up entirely of tips, though 12-15 NIS per hour is the general rule. Backpacker bars are generally the best place to pick up work. This is Israel, so wear your shortest skirt to the interview. A limited amount of work (receptionist, cleaner, 'runner') is available in the backpacker hostels, though generally this is a pretty good deal. Hostels are a good place to ask around about getting work.

Archaeological digs

If you want to work on an archaeological dig in Israel, contact the *Israeli Antiquities Department* as early in the year as possible and request their list of forthcoming excavations that are open to volunteers (c/o Rockefeller Archaeological Museum, PO Box 586, Jerusalem 91004, T02-6292627, F6292628). Bear in mind that you will have to pay for this experience. The *Institute of Archaeology at the Hebrew University* (Mt Scopus, Jerusalem 91905, T/F02-5825548) provide a similar opportunity (usually costing around $200 per week). One-day digs may be available through *Archaeological Seminars*, PO Box 14002, 34 Habad St, Jerusalem 91140, T02-6273515, F6272660.

Palestinian workcamps

A number of organizations in Palestine and abroad arrange workcamps (usually summer) inside PA areas. Most involve mornings spent working (teaching, renovating schools, planting trees are all popular), followed by an afternoon of 'cultural activites'. A registration fee is normally required ($30-100), as well as proof of medical insurance. You pay your own flight and transport costs, though accommodation and meals are provided. Organizations offering such placements include: *Friends of Bir Zeit University*, 21 Collingham Rd, London, SW5 0NU, T0171-3738414; *International Voluntary Service (IVS)*, 7 Upper Bow, Edinburgh, EH1 2JN, T0131-2266722, F2266723; *Medical Aid for Palestinians*, 33a Islington Park St, London, N1 1QB, T0171-2264114; *Volunteers for Peace*, 43 Tiffany Rd, Belmont, VT 05730, USA, T802-2592759.

Further reading

Where to begin? There is a vast array of literature available that is related to Israel and Palestine, and it has to be said that the following list is highly personal and subjective. Those marked with ** are, in the opinion of the author, essential reading, whilst those marked * are entertaining or informative reads. You may disagree. A list of further reading on **Jerusalem** can be found at the end of the 'Jerusalem, History' section on page 83.

page 83.

Josephus *The Jewish War***, various reprints and translations. See box on page 66. **Paul Johnson** *A History of the Jews***, 1987. A monumental work. Anyone interested in Israel should read this; very accessible. **Walter Laqueur** *A History of Zionism*, Schocken Books, New York, 1989. Probably the definitive general history of the Zionist movement, reasonably accessible. Described as "sympathetic yet critical". **Charles D. Smith** *Palestine and the Arab-Israeli Conflict**, St Martin's Press, New York, 1992. Good, general reader, with no noticeable bias. **Edward W Said** *The Question of Palestine***, 1992; *The Politics of Dispossession: The Struggle for Palestinian Self-Determination 1969-1994**, 1995; *Peace and its Discontents: Gaza-Jericho 1993-1995**, 1995, Vintage, London. All essential reading for those who wish to understand fully the Palestinian-Israeli conflict; they give a rarely aired viewpoint on the current 'peace process'. **Lawrence Joffe** *Keesing's Guide to the Middle-East Peace Process***, Catermill, 1996. Unravels the current 'peace process' in comprehensive yet fathomable detail, with valuable biographies of principal participants. **Benjamin Netanyahu** *A Place Among the Nations: Israel and the World**, Bantam, 1993. Clear presentation of Israeli version of history, though rather patronizing towards its audience. Netanyahu's views and programme clearly laid out. Sample quote: "For international terrorism is the quintessential Middle Eastern export, and its techniques everywhere are those of the Arab regimes and organizations that invented it." **Samuel Katz** *Battleground: Fact & Fantasy in Palestine*, various reprints, 1985. Zionist presentation of Israeli history, but bigoted style leaves a bad taste in the mouth. **Nadav Safran** *Israel: The Embattled Ally*, Yale University Press, 1977. **Shlomo Avineri** *The Making of Modern Zionism: The Intellectual Origins of the Jewish State*, Basic Books, 1981. **Julius Stone** *Israel and Palestine: Assault on the Law of Nations*, John Hopkins University Press, 1981. **Chaim Herzog** *The Arab-Israeli Wars*, Random House, 1984.

A number of seminal texts presenting a pro-Palestinian interpretation of Zionism and its impact can be found in the following: **Ibrahim Abu-Lughod** Transformation of Palestine, Northwestern University Press, 1971. **Walid Khalidi** *From Haven to*

History and politics

Essentials

Essentials

 Josephus' **The Jewish War**

One of the best accompaniments to a visit to Israel is a copy of Josephus' The Jewish War – the key source of information about the First Jewish Revolt against Rome (66-73 CE). Born of a well-connected Jewish family, Joseph ben Matthais famously switched sides during the Revolt, taking the Romanized version of his name (Josephus Flavius) before retiring to an apartment in Imperial Rome to write his memoirs. As a historian Josephus is, in the words of Johnson, "tendentious, contradictory and thoroughly unreliable" (A History of the Jews, 1987), yet his work is never less than absorbing. He is not shy of understanding his own role in the Revolt, so much so that PJ O'Rourke feels moved to suggest that "Josephus must be the most unabashedly contemptible character ever to have left an accurate self-portrait in print" (Give War A Chance, 1992).

One of the key criticisms of Josephus is the number of inconsistencies between The Jewish War and his later work, Antiquities of the Jews. As Johnson points out, however, his motives for producing these works changed between the writing of the two: "he was an example of a Jewish phenomenon which became very common over the centuries: a clever young man who, in his youth, accepted the modernity and sophistication of the day and then, late in middle age, returned to his Jewish roots. He began his writing career as a Roman apologist and ended it close to being a Jewish nationalist" (ibid).

Perhaps the last word on Josephus should be left to PJ O'Rourke, who sees many similarities between the events described in The Jewish War and those in evidence today: "Here, sixty generations ago, is nearly the same cast of characters engaged in exactly the same obsessive, vicious and fatal behaviour for the same terrifying reasons on the same cursed, reeking, ugly chunk of land" (ibid)!

(There are several translations of The Jewish War, though one of the most accessible is G.A. Williamson's translation, revised and annotated by E. Mary Smallwood, published by Penguin Books, London, 1981.)

Conquest: Readings in Zionism and the Palestine Problem until 1948, Institute for Palestine Studies, 1971. **Sami Hadwani** *Bitter Harvest, Palestine 1914-67*, New World Press, 1967. **Maxime Rodinson** *Israel: A Colonial-Settler State?*, Monad Press, 1973. **Elia T Zurayk** *The Palestinians in Israel: A Study in Internal Colonialism*, Routledge, 1979. **Sabri Jiryis** *The Arabs in Israel*, Monthly Review Press, 1976.

Socio-political
travelogues
Robert Fisk Pity the Nation: Lebanon at War**, OUP, 1991. Superb, but immensely depressing, work by one of the Middle East's most respected reporters, the coverage of Israel's 1982 invasion of Lebanon is excellent. Supporters of the Israeli government may not agree. **Thomas Friedman** *From Beirut to Jerusalem***, Harper and Collins, 1993. Very readable, particularly interesting for its examination of the relationship between Israel and the USA and the 'who is a Jew?' question, though Edward Said sees it as a classic example of 'Orientalism'. Friedman is reviled as a 'self-hating Jew' by the Israeli right. **Amos Oz** *In The Land of Israel**, 1985. *The Slopes of Lebanon*, 1989; *Israel, Palestine and Peace*, 1989, various reprints. The doyen of the Israeli left eloquently presents the case for an Israeli-Palestinian compromise, as well as providing an insight into Israeli society. **Stephen Brook** *Winner Takes All: A Season in Israel**, Picador, London, 1990. Interesting political and social journey through Israel. **Amos Elon** *Jerusalem: City of Mirrors***, 1989. Very informative and entertaining read. **PJ O'Rourke** *Holidays in Hell*, Picador, 1988 and *Give War a Chance*, Picador, 1992. Ascerbic wit and no concessions to political correctness, brought briefly to bear on the Holy Land ("God's monkey house"), by 'America's pre-eminent political humorist' who

is said to be able to "irritate both Salman Rushdie and Ayatollah Khomeini"! **Howard Jacobson** *Roots Schmoots*, 1993. Non-observant Jewish intellectual does for Israel what he did for Australia with "In the Land of Oz", ie came along and took the piss. **Saul Bellow** *To Jerusalem and Back*, Secker & Warburg, 1976. **Mark Twain** *The Innocents Abroad*, various reprints, 1871. The PJ O'Rourke of the 19th century.

Robert Slater Rabin of Israel: Warrior for Peace, Robson Books, London, 1996. Interesting biography, though not over-critical. **Andrew Gowers & Tony Walker** *Yasser Arafat and the Palestinian Revolution*, Corgi, London, 1990. Gives an insight into how difficult it is to 'get inside' the man, and you perhaps learn more about the history of the PLO than Arafat himself. **Robert I Friedman** *Zealots for Zion*, Random House, 1992. Rather frightening exposé of the West Bank settler movement. **Michael Bar-Zohar** *Ben-Gurion*, Delacorte, 1978. Regarded as the definitive biography. **Alan Hart** *Arafat*, Sidgwick & Jackson, London, 1994. Incredibly absorbing work, certainly proves the notion that there are 2 sides to every story.

Biography

Ephraim Stern (ed.) The New Encyclopedia of Archaeological Excavations in the Holy Land*, Simon & Schuster, 1993. The ultimate reference work, though at 4 volumes, £265 and 4kg, it's not the book to take into the field!. **Jerome Murphy-O'Connor** *The Holy Land: An Archaeological Guide from Earliest Times to 1700***, OUP, 1998. Excellent, portable guide, concentrates on sites where there is "something significant to see". Father Jerry is extremely entertaining, with almost all TV crews looking him up when producing a piece about the 'Holy Land'. **Kay Prag**, *Blue Guide: Jerusalem**, Black & Norton, London and NY, 1989. Unbeatable reference for anyone exploring Jerusalem in depth. **George Adam Smith** *Historical Geography of the Holy Land*, various reprints, 1894 and 1931. 'Colonial' style, infinite detail and a lovely turn of phrase. The **Bible** isn't a bad guide either!

Archaeology

Larry Collins & Dominique Lapierre O Jerusalem*, 1978. A gushing account of the 1948 Arab-Israeli battle for Jerusalem that reads like a racy novel, though there's a strong pro-Jewish bias. **Victor Ostrovsky** *By Way of Deception*, 1990; *The Other Side of Deception**, 1994, St Martin's Press. Spy enthusiasts will love the revelations about life in the Mossad in the first book, whilst the sequel is a must for all conspiracy-theorists. **Michael Baigent and Richard Leigh** *The Dead Sea Scrolls Deception**, Corgi, 1991. Very entertaining and convincing account of the cover-up that accompanied the discovery of the Dead Sea Scrolls. Other works for the conspiracy-theorists include **Edwin Black** *The Transfer Agreement: The Untold Story of the Secret Pact Between the Third Reich and Jewish Palestine*, MacMillan, 1984; **Edward Tivnan** *The Lobby: Jewish Political Power and American Foreign Policy*, Simon & Schuster, 1987; **John Loftus and Mark Aarons** *The Secret Wars Against the Jews*, St Martin's Press, 1994. When this was reviewed in one journal, the reviewer reminded readers of the authors' own warning, ie only fools take what they are told at face value! It all sounds a bit too Barry Gray. **Norman Wareham and Jill Gill** *Every Pilgrim's Guide to the Holy Land*, Canterbury Press Norwich, 1996. Gentle, pocket-sized guide for Christian visitors. **Joel Roskin** *A Guide to Hiking in Israel*, Jerusalem Post, 1994. Excellent hiking guide featuring 40 1-day walks.

General

A B Yehoshua *The Lover*, Dutton. Israel's best-selling novel. **Amos Oz** *My Michael*; *Black Box*; *To Know A Woman*, various reprints. **Leon Uris** *Exodus*. **James A Michener** *The Source*. **Muriel Spark** *The Mandelbaum Gate*.

Fiction

A well-written monthly journal that is often heavily critical of Israel is *Middle East International* (21 Collingham Rd, London, SW5 0NU, T0171-3735228, F3705956; PO Box 53329, Temple Heights Station, Washington DC 20009; 1-yr subscription £60/$65).

Journals

Essentials

Essentials

Other relevant journals include: *Journal of Israeli History*, Frank Cass and Co Ltd, Newbury Hse, 900 Eastern Ave, London, IG2 7HH, UK (3 per yr, £38); *Israeli Affairs*, same address as above (quarterly, £35); *Middle East Economic Digest (MEED)*, ISS, PO Box 14, Harold Hill, Romford, Essex, RM3 8EQ, UK (weekly, £290); *Middle East Economic Survey*, PO Box 4940, 1355 Nicosia, Cyprus (weekly, $1,525); *Journal of Palestine Studies*, University of California Press, 2120 Berkeley Way, Berkeley, CA 942720, USA (quarterly, $34); *Harvard Middle Eastern and Islamic Review*, 1737 Cambridge St, Cambridge, MA 02138, USA (biannual, $24); *Israel Exploration Journal*, PO Box 7041, Jerusalem 91070, Israel (quarterly, $48); *Journal for the Study of Judaism (in the Persian, Hellenistic and Roman periods)*, EJ Brill, PO Box 9000, 2300 PA Leiden, Netherlands (quarterly, NLG130); *Journal of Jewish Studies*, Oxford Centre for Hebrew and Jewish Studies, 45 St Giles, Oxford, OX1 2LP, UK (half yearly, £23); *British Journal of Middle Eastern Studies*, British Society for ME Studies, c/o Centre for ME and Islamic Studies, South End House, South Rd, Durham, DH1 3TG, UK (half yearly, £20).

Maps Good city maps are usually available free (or cheaply) at most tourist information offices. Reasonable general road maps to Israel include *Hallweg's* 1:500,000 Israel Road Map and *Freytag & Berndt's* 1:400,000 *Israel Sinai*, both of which mark the 'Green Line'. If travelling extensively in the Negev get hold of the Ministry of Tourism's 1:250,000 *Negev Touring Map*. The Israeli company *MAP* produces excellent road atlases in 1:350,000 and 1:150,000, as well as city maps to Jerusalem, Tel Aviv and Haifa. Anyone serious about trekking should get the relevant sheet of the *SPNI* trekking maps (almost all in Hebrew only, though staff may help translate key points). For those travelling beyond Israel we, quite naturally, recommend Footprint's *Jordan, Syria and Lebanon Handbook* and *Egypt Handbook*.

Megiddo

Jerusalem

3

Jerusalem

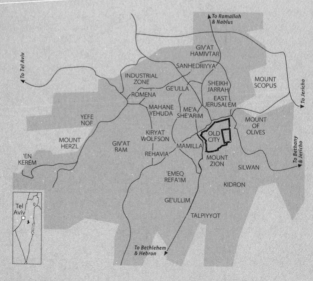

It would not be much of an over-statement to suggest that Jerusalem is the most famous city in the world. In many minds it is also the most important. In one of the best biographies of the city, Amos Elon suggests that "No other historic city evokes such inflammatory argument to this day" (Jerusalem: City of Mirrors, *1989). Here is a city that is of fundamental spiritual importance to one third of humanity, sacred to Jews, Christians and Muslims alike. Three faiths based on a common creed now present mutually exclusive claims to the same city.*

A visit to Jerusalem can be an intense experience, yet it is one that should not be missed. In fact, almost all foreign tourists visiting Israel come to Jerusalem at some stage during their trip, on average spending around half of their time in the city. And there is plenty to justify a prolonged stay, with even the most ardent of non-believers becoming enthralled by its unique atmosphere.

Ins and outs

Getting there   The vast majority of visitors to Jerusalem arrive by bus (whether on the Egged services from just about anywhere in the country, or on a tour bus). Note that the Central Bus Station on the north side of Jaffa Rd (to the west of the New City centre) is currently being rebuilt (it will eventually resemble Tel Aviv's multi-storey terminal and should be completed within the life-span of this *Handbook*). In the meantime, a temporary Central Bus Station is operating some 750m east along Jaffa Rd (on the south side of the street). There are also two minor bus stations in East Jerusalem: Suleiman Street bus station (outside Damascus Gate) serves destinations on the West Bank, though services are irregular and 'service taxis' are a better bet (see page 228); Nablus Road bus station (also near Damascus Gate) serves a number of destinations, but is most useful as the starting/finishing point of Bus 27 around town (see 'Getting around', below).

Service taxis to destinations on the West Bank (Jericho, King Hussein/Allenby Bridge, Bethlehem, Hebron, Ramallah, Nablus, plus Gaza) run from the car-park at the bottom of HaNevi'im (directly outside Damascus Gate), or from Suleiman Street. Sheruts to and from Tel Aviv's Central Bus Station arrive/depart from the corner of HaRav Kook and Jaffa Rd in the New City (just up from Zion Sq and within walking distance of the Old City).

So few people use Jerusalem's once-daily train service to and from Tel Aviv that it appears currently to be suspended. Likewise, given Israel's small size, few visitors use the domestic flights to and from Jerusalem's Atarot Airport, 10km to the north on the road (Route 60) to Ramallah and Nablus.

Getting around   Though many of Jerusalem's sights are within walking distance of each other (notably in and around the Old City), you will almost certainly have to use the city bus service at some stage; few enjoy the walk from the Central Bus Station to the Old City carrying a backpack. Fares are currently 5 NIS whether you go one stop or all the way across town (though this fare increases by about 50 agorot every 6 months). At the time of going to press, local buses from outside the temporary Central Bus Station to the Old City leave from the same side of the road as the bus station; once the original Central Bus Station is renovated, you will need to cross to the south side of Jaffa (Yafo) Rd to catch these services. Below are a selection of the main routes: **1** Central Bus Station – Mea She'arim – Jaffa Gate – Western Wall Plaza; **9** Central Bus Station – Knesset – Israel Museum – Mt Scopus; **13/20/23** Yad VaShem – Central Bus Station – Jaffa Rd – Jaffa Gate; **27** Hadassah Hospital ('En Kerem) – Yad VaShem – Central Bus Station – Nablus Rd bus station (for Damascus Gate); **28** Central Bus Station – National Police HQ – Mt Scopus; **41** Central Bus Station – Atarot airport; **99** Known as the 'Jerusalem Circle Line', this route links many of Jerusalem's main sights on one continuous loop (1½ hrs), with the 1-day (or 2-day) ticket allowing you to get on and off and you please at any designated stop on its route (1-day, 20 NIS). The route is as follows: Ha'Emek St/Jaffa Gate – Daniel Garden – Russian Compound – King David Hotel/YMCA – Jerusalem Theatre – President's House – Laromme Hotel – Liberty Bell Park – Ammon Hanaziv Promenade – Teddy Stadium – Malha Shopping Mall – Holyland Hotel/Second Temple Model – Shalom Hotel – Mt Herzl – Yad VaShem – Sha'arei Zedek Hospital – Israel Museum – Knesset – Hebrew University – Hotels – Central Bus Station – Shmuel Hanavi Junction – Ammunition Hill – Mt Scopus – Meyersdorf Observation – Judean Desert Observation – Mormon University – Tourjeman Post – Damascus Gate – Rockefeller Museum – Church of All Nations – Western Wall – Mt Zion – Railway Station – Radisson Moriah Hotel – Independence Park. This is not a guided tour as such, though the drivers generally announces all the main sites as the buses passes.

Background

Topography

The ancient city extended over a series of hills or ridges intersected by deep valleys, though several thousand years of building, destruction and reconstruction has introduced a man-made topography. The eastern border, the Kidron Valley, remains largely unchanged, dividing the Old City from the low north–south ridge that includes Mt Scopus and the Mount of Olives. The western border of the Old City is the Valley of Hinnom, which then turns southeast, skirting Mount Zion to form the southern border. The ancient city, located on the southeast ridge to the south of the low hill that was to become the Temple Mount, was defined by the Kidron Valley to the east and the Valley of Hinnom to the south. Its western boundary was formed by the Tyropoeon (Cheesemakers') Valley, which runs broadly north to south from the area around the present-day Damascus Gate, along the west side of the Temple Mount, joining with the Kidron Valley and Valley of Hinnom at a point south of the ancient city. The Tyropoeon Valley formerly divided the Temple Mount from the Southwestern Hill (upon which the first-century BCE to first-century CE Upper City was founded, now occupied by the Armenian and Jewish Quarters), though the valley has subsequently being filled in by two millennia of building activity. The northern boundary of the city is less well defined, with the series of hills and ridges upon which Jerusalem is built merging imperceptibly with those further north. For this reason, the north approach has always been the least defensible.

Jerusalem: topography

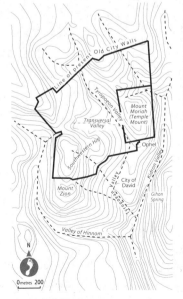

History

The relative lack of archaeological finds and epigraphic evidence make it rather difficult to reconstruct the pre-Israelite settlement here. However, sufficient finds have been discovered that suggest a continuity of settlement from the Chalcolithic period (c. 4500–3300 BCE) up until **David**'s conquest in the 10th century BCE. The location of the walled stronghold that David conquered is in no doubt – the 'Ancient City of the Southeast Ridge' (see page 174) – though who its inhabitants were is less certain. It is generally concluded that the so-called Jebusites (who are described in the biblical account of David's capture of the stronghold) were related to the Hittites, and formed an enclave within Israelite-controlled land.

Pre-Davidic settlement

The City of David   Following David's capture of the stronghold of **Zion** on this southeast ridge late in the 10th century BCE (*II Samuel 5:6-9; I Chronicles 11:4-7*), the true history of Jerusalem may be said to have begun. This relative backwater, so long ignored by the Israelites, suddenly became their new political capital. The choice of location perhaps reflects David's military and political astuteness, selecting a site midway between the northern and southern tribal territories of the Israelites, and on the main north to south axis between the two. Yet it was not just a political capital that David established here. Having brought the **Ark of the Covenant** here (the symbol of the unity of the tribes of Israel and of the covenant between the tribes and God), David effectively made Jerusalem the only legitimate focus of cult for the tribes. The city was now the religious and cultural capital of the Israelites. Following God's command, David bought the threshing floor of Araunah the Jebusite on what was to become the Temple Mount (and much later the Haram al-Sharif), and set up an altar there. It was not unusual for elevated spots close to a city to be used as the local cultic spot, and the Temple Mount was clearly considered sacred prior to David's transaction. In fact the site was linked with the **Mount Moriah** upon which the patriarch **Abraham** offered his son Isaac for sacrifice (*Genesis 22*, though Muslims believe that Ishmael was the offered son), and thus David was considered to be rebuilding the altar of Abraham.

First Temple period   Some suggest that David was considered to have had too much blood on his hands to build the First Temple on Mount Moriah, though it is more likely that he simply wanted to avoid turning Israel into a royal temple-state. Thus, the task of building the Temple fell to his successor **Solomon**.

Jerusalem: 1800 BCE – 1st century CE

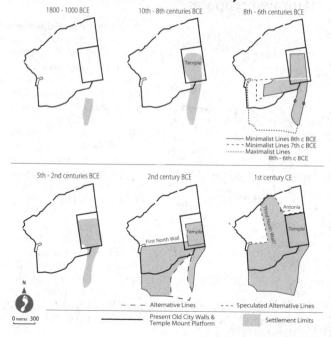

1800 – 1000 BCE   10th – 8th centuries BCE   8th – 6th centuries BCE

Temple

——— Minimalist Lines 8th c BCE
- - - Minimalist Lines 7th c BCE
········· Maximalist Lines
8th – 6th c BCE

5th – 2nd centuries BCE   2nd century BCE   1st century CE

First North Wall   Temple   Third North Wall   Antonia   Temple

N

0 metres 300

- - - Alternative Lines   - - - Speculated Alternative Lines

——— Present Old City Walls & Temple Mount Platform   Settlement Limits

Jerusalem: origins of the name

The earliest written reference to Jerusalem, or more correctly Rushalimum, *appears in the Egyptian Execration texts of the 20th and 19th centuries BCE, whilst the 14th-century BCE el-Amarna letters refer to* Urusalim. *The pre-Israelite city was known as* Jebus, *taking its name from the ethnic group who lived here, and whose last king was Araunah the Jebusite. Araunah's stronghold of Zion (see 'Ancient City of the SE Ridge', page 174) was captured by the Israelites (II Samuel 5:6-7), with David subsequently calling it 'City of David' (II Samuel 5:9; I Chronicles 11:7).*

The earliest Hebrew pronunciation appears to be Yerushalem, *with its meaning presumed to come from the West Semitic elements* yrw *and* slm, *and is generally interpreted as "Foundation of (the God)*

Shalem" (Mazar, *New Encyclopedia of Archaeological Excavations in the Holy Land, 1993). The etymological link between this pagan deity after which the city may have been named, and the Semitic words for peace (Hebrew:* Shalom, *Arabic:* Salaam*), has led many to refer to Jerusalem as the "city of peace", though as can be seen from studying the city's history, this is a most inappropriate name. The Arab name,* al-Quds, *'the Holy', is equally unlikely. Perhaps the best description of the city was given by the 10th century CE Jerusalem-born Arab geographer al-Muqaddasi, who referred to Jerusalem as "a golden basin filled with scorpions".*

During the coregency of David and Solomon the city was centred upon the southeast ridge, though plans were made to expand the city by building the Temple on Mt Moriah and a new palace and royal court complex to the south. It was not until after David's death that construction on the Temple began, though it was to take 20 years for all the building plans to be realized.

Solomon's death c. 928 BCE saw a radical change in Jerusalem's standing. The collapse of the United Monarchy saw the establishment of rival cultic centres in the northern kingdom of **Israel**, (as well as rival political centres), whilst Jerusalem's status was reduced to that of capital of the southern kingdom of **Judah**. It also appears to have been considerably impoverished by the loss of tax revenues from the north.

The key event during the rule of the subsequent **Kings of Judah** was the rise to the east of the **Assyrian empire**. Clashes with the Assyrians during the reign of Uzziah (769-733 BCE) had led to a considerable flow of refugees to Jerusalem, and with the Assyrian destruction of the northern kingdom of Israel c. 722 BCE, Jerusalem now found itself hosting a substantial refugee population. Archaeological evidence points to the incumbent king of Judah, **Hezekiah** (727-698 BCE), making considerable efforts to refortify the expanded city, particularly in the face of the Assyrian king Sennacherib's advance (701 BCE). See for example the 'Broad Wall' in the present Jewish Quarter of the Old City (page 149), or Hezekiah's efforts at defending the city's water supply (page 178). Under Hezekiah's successor, Manasseh (698-642 BCE), further strengthening of the city's defences took place, though under Assyrian supervision.

During Josiah's rule (639-609 BCE) the Assyrian empire fell (613 BCE), though this only served to suck the kingdom of Judah (and Jerusalem) into the power vacuum that the Egyptians and **Babylonians** were trying to fill. Having sided with the Egyptians, Judah saw the victorious Babylonians sack Jerusalem in 597 BCE, and then totally destroy it in 586 BCE. The Babylonians burnt down the Temple, razed the city, and the Israelites were led off in chains: the Exile had begun.

Post-Exilic and Persian periods How many of Jerusalem's population survived the Babylonian sacking and avoided exile is a matter of some debate, though the claim that only the "poorest of the land" (*II Kings 25:8-12*) remained is seemingly supported by the archaeological evidence. The fall of the Babylonian empire in 539 BCE ushered in **Persian** (Achaemenid) rule, and in the following year a proclamation by the Persian ruler Cyrus II (539-529 BCE) allowed Jews to return to Jerusalem and rebuild the Temple (*Ezra 1:2-3*). However, it was not until **Nehemiah** was appointed governor in 445 BCE that the city wall was rebuilt. Even so, Post-Exilic Jerusalem continued to occupy little more than the original southeast ridge and the Temple/Mt Moriah area.

Hellenistic and Hasmonean periods Though Alexander the Great conquered Jerusalem in 332 BCE, his rule was short-lived and impact negligible. By 301 BCE Jerusalem was in the hands of the **Ptolemies of Egypt**, though little is known about their tenure. However, the power struggle between the Ptolemies of Egypt and the **Seleucids of Syria** led to the capture of the city in 200 BCE by the Seleucid ruler Antiochus III (223-187 BCE), who began reorganizing the city along the lines of a Greek polis. **Antiochus III** was fairly subtle in introducing such changes, recruiting the city's wealthy Jews and aristocratic priestly families to his cause, but his successor **Antiochus IV Epiphanes** (175-164 BCE) attempted to bludgeon through fairly radical measures. In particular, the Jews of Jerusalem (and all across the country) objected to the renaming of the city Antiochia, the looting of the Temple treasures, the installation of a graven image in the Temple sanctuary, and its desecration by sacrificing a pig on the sacred altar! The subsequent **Hasmonean (Maccabean) Revolt** reached its climax in 164 BCE when **Judas Maccabaeus** entered Jerusalem and cleansed the Temple (an event celebrated in the Jewish festival of Hannukah). However, the Acra fortress that Antiochus IV had built in the city (and garrisoned with mercenaries) remained in Seleucid hands, and it was not until 141 BCE that **Simeon the Hasmonean** could be said to have firmly established Jewish (Maccabean) control over Jerusalem.

The Hasmonean period saw the expansion of the city, most notably in the move away from settlement on the southeast ridge towards the new Upper City on the Southwestern hill. This new area was protected by the so-called First Wall, sections of which can be seen today within the Citadel and at various places in the Jewish Quarter. The successional dispute among the Hasmoneans brought their period of rule to an end in Jerusalem and saw the first real intervention in the city's affairs of republican Rome. In 63 BCE **Pompey** captured Jerusalem for Rome, subsequently setting up Antipater the Idumean as the head of the Roman client state.

Herodian period and the Second Temple period It was under Antipater the Idumean's second son, **Herod the Great**, that Jerusalem entered into a golden age of prosperity, with building projects on a grandiose scale including the construction of the Antonia fortress (page 123), a new palace defended by three gigantic towers (page 92), an extension of the upper-class Upper City (page 151), and of course the Second Temple (page 100). (**NB** Though the First Temple that was destroyed by the Babylonians in 586 BCE was subsequently rebuilt, the term 'Second Temple' is used to refer to the temple that Herod the Great built.) The result was a beautified city that was also able to provide substantial employment opportunities, particularly within the construction industry. Herod's sons, however, upon inheriting their father's 'kingdom', proved themselves to be generally weak rulers, and Jerusalem found itself ruled by a Roman procurator based in the Roman province's capital at Caesarea. Possibly the most famous of these Roman procurators was **Pontius Pilate**, who ruled 26-36 CE.

The first half of the first century CE saw growing tension between the Jewish population of the Roman province and their Roman rulers, as well as increased resentment between various classes of the population. In particular, Zealot groups emerged, and messianic expectations were heightened. It was into such an atmosphere of uncertainty and expectation that **Jesus** emerged.

By 66 CE minor disturbances had escalated into a full-scale rebellion against Rome, gripping the entire country. Jerusalem's preparations for the inevitable Roman reprisals were not helped by the factional in-fighting that consumed the city's population, with the Zealot leaders conducting a reign of terror not just against those who proposed a peaceful settlement to the dispute with Rome, but against anyone who appeared to challenge their authority. In fact, the internecinal struggle between the three main Zealot leaders, John of Gischala, Simeon bar Giora and Eleazar ben Simeon, led to scenes of brutality against Jerusalem's civilian population that matched the punitive measures that the Romans were to later inflict.

In an action that is described in gripping detail by Josephus (*The Jewish War*) the Vth, Xth, XIIth and XVth Legions of the Roman army, led by the Emperor Vespasian's son **Titus**, eventually succeeded in capturing the city. This culminated in 70 CE in the destruction of most of the city, including the Second Temple. Most of the surviving Jewish population of Jerusalem were exiled, and a decree was issued banning Jews from living in the city.

The First Revolt and the destruction of the Second Temple

Jerusalem

Jerusalem at the end of the Second Temple period

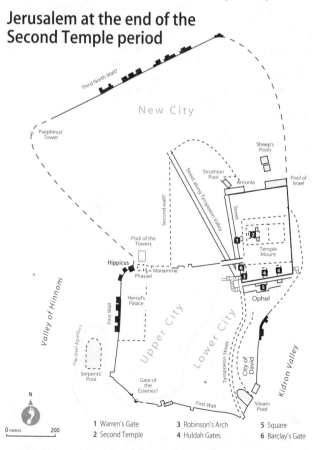

1 Warren's Gate
2 Second Temple
3 Robinson's Arch
4 Huldah Gates
5 Square
6 Barclay's Gate

Early Roman Period and Aelia Capitolina

During a visit to Judea in 130 CE, the Roman emperor **Hadrian** decided to set up a Roman colony on the ruins of Jerusalem. The establishment of Hadrian's **Colonia Aelia Capitolina** led to a second nationwide Jewish protest, this time under the guidance of **Shimon Bar Kokhba**. The brief period of Jewish sovereignty inspired by the Second Jewish Revolt (**Bar Kokhba Revolt**) was short-lived (132-135 CE), and Hadrian's legions soon re-entered Jerusalem. However, it should be noted that during the period of the revolt there is little evidence to suggest that the Jews actually reoccupied Jerusalem. Aelia Capitolina became firmly established, and the decree banning Jewish settlement in the city was more rigorously enforced. The province as a whole was also to become known as Syria Palestine.

The layout of Hadrian's new city is not just preserved in the 'Madaba Map' (page 79), but also largely in the present form of the Old City. The line of the cardo maximus is preserved in Tariq Khan es-Zeit, whilst the secondary (eastern) cardo follows Tariq al-Wad and the Decumanus follows David Street and Bab as-Silsila Street. Meanwhile, the camp of the Tenth Legion Fretensis occupied the large space to the south of the present Citadel (although this traditionally held view has been challenged recently by Doron Bar, who suggests that the camp actually stood to the north of here, in the area now occupied largely by the Christian Quarter).

Byzantine period

By the mid-third century CE Aelia Capitolina had lost much of its standing, and even the Tenth Legion had been posted south to Elath (Eilat). However, Jerusalem's revival was assured in 313 CE by the Imperial Edict of Milan that sanctioned Christianity as a legitimate religion within the Roman Empire. When **Constantine the Great** (306-337 CE) brought Palestine within the Christian Eastern Roman Empire, effectively establishing the **Byzantine Empire**, Jerusalem became a major pilgrimage centre for Byzantine Christians. Inspired by Constantine and his mother, the dowager queen **Helena**, significant efforts were made to identify and locate the major scenes in Christ's

Aelia Capitolina: 2nd century CE

1 'Rock of Antonia'
2 Triumphal Arch
3 Eastern Forum

The Madaba Map

Established as a Christian village by the end of the third to beginning of the 4th century CE at the latest, the small settlement of Madaba (some 30 kilometres south of the Jordanian capital of Amman) gained international fame following the discovery in 1897 of the so-called 'Madaba Map'. The map is in fact part of the mosaic floor of a Byzantine church that is now generally agreed to have been laid in the sixth century CE. The map shows a stylized image of Palestine and may have been intended as a

guide for pilgrims to the Holy Land. Of particular interest is the large (54 centimetres by 93 centimetres) inset showing a bird's-eye view of Jerusalem, confirming how the basic axis of the present Old City largely follows that of the Byzantine city before it, which in turn is based upon Hadrian's Aelia Capitolina. For further details on Madaba see the Jordan, Syria & Lebanon Handbook.

Passion. Numerous churches and religious institutions were established, most notably the Constantine Church of the Holy Sepulchre (page 135).

In the fifth century CE **Eudocia**, wife of the emperor Theodosius II (408-450 CE), was responsible for establishing a number of churches, as the Byzantine passion for identifying the locations of both major and minor gospel scenes reached the point of obsession. It is also clear that by this time Jews were permitted to settle in the city, though the exact date of recolonization is unknown. The zenith of Byzantine Jerusalem was the sixth century CE, during the reign of **Justinian I** (527-565 CE). The Byzantine cardo maximus, (still visible today, page 148), was extended southwards to link the Church of the Holy Sepulchre with Justinian's Nea Church (page 153). The plan of the city at this stage is preserved in the Madaba Map (see above).

Jerusalem: Byzantine period (c 324 - 638 CE)

The decline of the Byzantine empire precipitated the **Persian** invasion of 614 CE, in which the invading Persian forces, aided by the Samaritans and Jews, razed most of the city's churches and religious institutions, massacring some 33,000 Christians in the process. Though the city was returned to the Byzantines by treaty, and attempts were made to restore the city to its former glory (including destroying any remaining Jewish symbols, such as the walls of the Temple Mount), the Byzantines were in no position to resist the advancing **Arabs**, and in 638 CE the city was surrendered to the Muslim army.

Early Arab period

The Arab conquest of Palestine, and in particular their subsequent control over Jerusalem, created reverberations through the region that can still be felt today. Though the caliph **Omar** himself entered the city in 638 CE, famously refusing to pray at the Church of the Holy Sepulchre, little is known about these early years of Arab rule except that the Christian shrines and sanctuaries were left unmolested, and Jews and Arabs were subject to *jizya* (a kind of poll-tax levied on non-Muslims). In fact, early Arab rule was considerably more enlightened than previous and subsequent Christian rule.

The reshaping of Jerusalem along the lines of a Muslim city could be said to have begun under the **Umayyad** dynasty of caliphs (661-750 CE), when the Dome of the Rock and the al-Aqsa Mosque were built on the Temple Mount, and other religious and institutional buildings were constructed. Bahat suggests that these building efforts "expressed the conquerors' desire to demonstrate Islam's superiority over Christianity" (*New Encyclopedia of Archaeological Excavations in the Holy Land*, 1993).

Despite the importance of Jerusalem within Islam, the capital of the province of *Filastin* remained at Ramla on the coastal plain. Even the Umayyad's successors, the **Abbasids** (749-974 CE), ruled Palestine from their capital at Baghdad. A series of earthquakes during the Early Arab period (658 CE, 747 or 749 CE, 756 CE, 808 CE, 1016 CE and 1033 CE) further reduced Jerusalem's status to little more than that of a poor (albeit important) religious pilgrimage centre.

The Abbasid dynasty was soon to be replaced by that of the **Fatimids** (909-1175 CE in Egypt and Syria), based in Cairo. A Shi'ite dynasty, ruling predominantly Sunni Palestine, the Fatimids are perhaps best remembered for the fanatical caliph **al-Hakim** (996-1020 CE), who in 1009 went out of his way to remove all evidence of Christianity from Jerusalem. Muslim rule of the 'Holy Land' was subsequently interrupted by the arrival of the **Crusaders**.

Crusader period

The various periods of Crusader rule in Jerusalem are marked by the construction of grandiose institutions, as well as a large measure of religious intolerance. In fact the first thing that the Crusaders did on capturing Jerusalem on 15 th July, 1099, was to massacre almost the entire Muslim and Jewish population. Many of the earlier Byzantine churches that marked the traditional sites of scenes from the gospels were rebuilt, whilst the defensive capabilities of the city were enhanced by the reconstruction of the Citadel and the remodelling of the city walls. Nevertheless, following the defeat of the Crusaders at the Horns of Hittim in 1187, the city was surrendered to **Salah al-Din** (Saladin).

The subsequent period of **Ayyubid** rule saw many of the Christian institutions turned over to Muslim use, though Christian pilgrims were still permitted to visit the Holy Sepulchre. Salah al-Din refortified the city, with further defensive programmes undertaken by his brother el-Malik el-'Adil and nephew el-Malik el-'Mu'azzem 'Isa. However, in 1219 the latter dismantled much of the city walls in an effort not to provoke another Crusader attack. In fact, the Crusaders did regain Jerusalem in 1229, this time by treaty, though they were subsequently to lose it again in 1244 to the **Khwarizmian Turks**.

Jerusalem soon passed into the hands of the **Mamluks**, the former slave guards of the Ayyubid dynasty who had risen to power in Egypt. Their most notable rulers were the sultan **Baibars** (1260-77) and **al-Nasir Mohammad** (c. 1294-1340), the latter of whom largely rebuilt the Citadel. There are also a number of distinctive tombs and religious institutions dating to the Mamluk period, most notably in the area to the west of the Haram al-Sharif. However, descriptions of Jerusalem in the latter part of the Mamluk period suggest a city decimated by disease, high taxation, internal division and Bedouin incursions.

Late Arab period

The conquest of Syria by Selim the Grim (1512-20) brought Jerusalem under the control of the expansive **Ottoman** empire, though it was **Sulaiman II** ('the Magnificent') who restored Jerusalem to something approaching its former glory; the walls of the Old City that you see today are largely the result of his efforts. However, the Ottoman period in Jerusalem is seen as a metaphor for the rest of Palestine, and widely regarded as a period of corruption, high taxation and neglect. The Ottoman period in Jerusalem was brought to an end on 10th December, 1917, when General Allenby's **British** forces captured the city.

Ottoman period

The British Mandate for Palestine was formalized by the League of Nations in 1922. Though Jerusalem benefitted greatly from the early years of British rule, the Mandate period is generally associated with the growing antagonism between the Arab population of Palestine and the increasing numbers of Jewish immigrants. As calls for the establishment of a Jewish state became louder, confrontations between the Jews and the British, Jews and Arabs, and Arabs and the British became more common. Though this was occuring all across Palestine, major events specific to Jerusalem included the conflict over access to the Western Wall (see page 102) and the bombing of the King David Hotel (see page 208).

British Mandate

With the termination of the British Mandate in May 1948, and the declaration of the State of Israel, Jerusalem became engulfed in war as the neighbouring Arab armies invaded in an attempt to snuff out the infant Jewish state. A dramatic account of the battle for the city of Jerusalem is described in some detail in Collins and Lapierre's distinctly pro-Jewish *O Jerusalem* (1972), whilst a more sober account of the military campaign (from an Israeli perspective) can be found in the late Chaim Herzog's *The Arab-Israeli Wars* (1992).

War of Independence and the Six Day War

The upshot of the war was a divided city, with the Old City and most of East Jerusalem in **Jordanian** hands, and the rest in **Israeli** hands. This tense situation, monitored by the United Nations, continued for almost 20 years until the Israelis captured the whole of the West Bank and Jerusalem in the **Six Day War** of 1967. The Israelis subsequently declared Jerusalem to be "reunified" (though Palestinians would disagree), making it their "eternal, undivided capital".

As the Palestinian Authority and the Israeli government edge towards the 'Final Status Agreement' talks, there can be little doubt that the most explosive issue on the agenda will be the future status of Jerusalem. Even more so than the question of refugees, the right of return, or compensation, the diametrically opposed views of Jerusalem would seem to doom the talks in advance.

Present and future status of Jerusalem

In Israeli eyes the status of Jerusalem in unequivocal: it is the "eternal, undivided capital". Yet most nations have refused to accept Israel's 'annexation' of East Jerusalem, and as a mark of protest retain their diplomatic missions at Tel Aviv (though a bill passed in both houses of the US Congress in October 1996 voted to move the US Embassy to Jerusalem; a piece of legislation seen by many as an attempt to influence Jewish voters in the run-up to the US

The 'centre of life' controversy

In preparation for 'final status' talks, which will determine the status of Jerusalem, each side accuses the other of trying to balance the population in its favour. The Israelis accuse the Palestinians of illegally flooding Jerusalem with thousands of people seeking to gain residence, whilst the Palestinians (supported by a number of Israeli and Palestinian human rights monitoring organizations) are levelling the charge of 'ethnic cleansing' at the Israelis.

The key cause of Palestinian complaint is with regard to the 'centre of life' policy that the Israelis initiated in 1996. Although ID cards of Palestinian Jerusalemites were confiscated prior to 1996 (under the Entry into Israel Law of 1952 and the Entry into Israel Regulations of 1974), incidents of ID

card confiscation have increased by over 600 percent since the implementation of the 'centre of life' policy. Under this policy Palestinians must prove to the Interior Ministry that Jerusalem is the centre of their lives, including proof that all family members were born, reside, work or attend school in the city, and that they have paid all property taxes and utility bills. Palestinians working or living abroad for seven consecutive years are likely to have their residency revoked. This policy was initiated under the government of Benjamin Netanyahu; an irony not lost on opponents of the policy, who point out that if the same law applied to Jews, Netanyahu (who spent many years in the USA) would also find that his residency had lapsed.

Presidential election). Likewise, the Palestinians are seeking to establish 'Arab East Jerusalem' as the capital of a future Palestinian state.

Is there a solution? John V Whitbeck, a London-based international lawyer writing in *Middle East International* (no 538, 22/11/96), draws attention to what he calls the 'condominium' solution. He suggests that "In the context of a two-state solution, Jerusalem could form an undivided part of both states, constitute the capital of both states and be administered by an umbrella municipal council and district councils": effectively, "in the proper terminology of international law, Jerusalem would be a 'condominium' of Israel and Palestine." Whitbeck is at pains to point out how 'sovereignty' is distinct from 'municipal administration', suggesting that joint undivided sovereignty is not some nebulous theory, but a practical, achievable reality. "Jerusalem can be viewed as a cake that could be sliced either vertically or horizontally" continues Whitbeck. "Either way, the Palestinians would get a share of the cake, but, while most Israelis could never voluntarily swallow a vertical slice, they might just be able to swallow a horizontal slice." Whether the two parties could ever agree on such an idea is another matter, and it would have to be some cake to tempt the Israelis. It could be argued that their cherry on the cake would be international recognition of Jerusalem as Israel's capital, though it does not appear that Israel is particularly bothered by this. But as Whitbeck observes, "There will never be a lasting settlement of the Israel-Palestine conflict without a solution to the status of Jerusalem acceptable both to most Israelis and to most Palestinians."

Sights

Jerusalem is a fairly easy city in which to orientate yourself, though it is a little more complex than just an 'Old' and a 'New' city. The places of interest in this chapter of the *Handbook* have been grouped according to location, though most of the attractions are in or close to the walled Old City. In fact, it's not difficult to see all the key attractions in just 2-3 days. The various locations are as follows: the walled Old City, which is itself divided into 4 'quarters' (Muslim, Christian,

Jerusalem: Further reading

Listed here is a selection of books that may greatly increase your understanding and appreciation of Jerusalem. The definitive archaeological guide (with virtually a description of every building in the Old City) is the Blue Guide *by Kay Prag (1989, Norton and Black). Perhaps the best biography of the city is to be found in Amos Elon's hugely entertaining* Jerusalem: City of Mirrors *(1989, Flamingo, London). This book also contains a good bibliography of Jerusalem-related matters. Another personal journey into Jerusalem is made by Colin Thubron in* Jerusalem *(1969, Penguin). A less pompous, but more politically incorrect account can be found in PJ O'Rourke's* Holidays in Hell *(1988, Picador). Events in Jerusalem in the period of the first century BCE to the first century CE are brilliantly told in Josephus'* The Jewish War *(various editions, though GA Williamson's translation with notes by EM Smallwood, published by*

Penguin, 1981, is particularly accessible). Wandering around the Old City with this book is a lot of fun. Literary views of the city have been compiled to form FE Peters' Jerusalem: The Holy City in the Eyes of Chroniclers, Visitors, Pilgrims, and Prophets from the Days of Abraham to Modern Times *(1985, Princetown). For a Zionist view of Jerusalem this century try Martin Gilbert's* Jerusalem in the Twentieth Century *(1996), or for a more balanced view, Karen Armstrong's* A History of Jerusalem: One City, Three Faiths *(1996, HarperCollins). The 1948 battle for Jerusalem is told in gripping, though hardly impartial, style in Collins and Lapierre's* O Jerusalem *(1972, various reprints). Of course a Bible or Torah is not a bad accompaniment to a visit to Jerusalem! Most of these books are available in Jerusalem/Israel bookshops.*

Jewish, Armenian); the Temple Mount/Haram al-Sharif area; Mount Zion; Mount of Olives; Kidron Valley; Ancient City on the Southeast Ridge; Tyropoeon Valley; Valley of Hinnom; East Jerusalem; Northern suburbs; Mt Scopus; New City centre and area north of Jaffa Road; Western suburbs; Western outskirts; Southwestern suburbs; Southern section of the New City.

Mount of Olives

Highlights A wander around the walled Old City, taking in the Citadel, Church of the Holy Sepulchre and the Via Dolorosa; the Temple Mount/Haram al-Sharif area, featuring the Western (Wailing) Wall and Dome of the Rock; the Mount of Olives, for its views and important Christian sites; the Israel Museum and Model of Second Temple period Jerusalem, for putting the city into some sort of historical perspective; and the Yad VaShem Holocaust Memorial.

Jerusalem

Old City

Old City Walls and Gates

Amongst Jerusalem's most striking features are the pale-yellow stone walls that encircle the Old City: for many visitors, the first vision of these walls is a lasting one. They are equally impressive close up, where you can fully appreciate the sheer size of some of the masonry slabs, or from afar, most notably from one of the surrounding hills such as Mt Scopus or the Mt of Olives.

Ins and outs   A complete circuit of the city walls is highly recommended, including sections where you can walk along the top of the walls themselves ('Rampart Walk'). Jerusalem's city walls run for 4.02km and are breached by 8 gates (7 of which are open to passage). Visitors should note that each gate has three names: an Arabic/Muslim version, a Hebrew version, and an Anglicized version that is in common usage (and used here).

History   Relative to Jerusalem's long and ancient history, the city walls and gates that you see today are a recent addition, having been completed by **Sulaiman the Magnificent** (Sulaiman II) between 1537-41. The previous city walls had been dismantled in 1219 by al-Malik al-Mu'azzam in order to discourage the reoccupation of the city by the Crusaders. However, certain stretches of the walls follow the course of far older fortifications, dating back to Crusader and Ayyubid, Byzantine, Herodian/Roman and even Hasmonean times, and in places the earlier defences can still be seen.

Rampart Walk   Not all sections of the ramparts are open, with notable closed sections being the position to the immediate east of the Haram al-Sharif/Temple Mount, and the

Jerusalem: overview

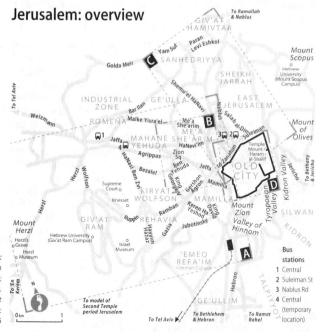

Related maps:
A. New city, western suburbs, page 196;
B. New city, centre, page 195; C. East Jerusalem, page 184;
D. Old City, page 86

Bus stations
1 Central
2 Suleiman St
3 Nablus Rd
4 Central (temporary location)

section that is included within the Citadel. Entrances to the ramparts are at Damascus Gate, Jaffa Gate and the Citadel, with exit-only points at Herod's Gate, New Gate, Zion Gate, Dung Gate and St Stephen's Gate. The various stretches of the ramparts that are open to visitors run for approximately 3.5 kilometres. The following route describes an anti-clockwise circumnavigation, beginning at Damascus Gate, and includes details seen from both inside and outside the walls, and along the Rampart Walk. **Warning** Some instances of sexual assault/harassment and mugging means that it is **not** recommended that women undertake the Rampart Walk unaccompanied. You should also note that the stone path here is particularly slippery when wet. ■ *Saturday-Thursday 0900-1600, Friday 0900-1400, though the section from the Citadel to Zion Gate is closed Friday and Saturday. Adult 10 NIS, valid for four admissions over two days, three at the weekend. **NB** tickets cannot be bought on a Saturday.*

The most impressive gate in the city walls, Damascus Gate is also considered to be one of the best examples of Ottoman architecture in the region. Flanked by two defensive towers, it is solid yet highly decorated with the elaborate *crenellation* (battlements) above often concealing an Israeli soldier keeping an eye on events going on below. In fact, it is not unknown for the *machicolations* above the gate, originally designed for dropping molten lead or boiling oil on to attackers, to have been used for dispensing tear gas canisters! The gateway is set back within a pointed arch of carved wedge-shaped blocks, (known as *voussoirs*) and is reached via a bridge built in 1967 as a temporary structure. The entrance passage to the gate makes a double turn before leading into the heart of the Muslim Quarter. The street inside the gate and the plaza outside are used as informal market-places, whilst a number of money-changers continue to occupy the kiosks inside the gate entrance itself. This is a lively and busy thoroughfare, and arguably the most interesting way to enter the Old City.

Damascus Gate

Sulaiman II's structure is built precisely upon the lines of the former Roman period gate, with excavations in the Damascus Gate area revealing remains from most periods of Jerusalem's history. To view closely the Roman and Crusader remains (and for access to the 'Roman Plaza Museum' and Rampart Walk), take the modern steps down, just to the right of the entrance (as you look at Damascus Gate from the outside). Parts of the revetment walls of the **Crusader city gate** are clearly visible, along with the remains of an ecclesiastical structure from the same period that may be the **Chapel of St Abraham** (its function identifiable by the frescoes of the saints that are still visible). One of the two eighth century CE Umayyad cisterns that flank the gate is located beneath the chapel, though the whole structure appears to have been cleared during al-Malik al-Mu'azzam's 'scorched-earth' policy. Beneath the modern bridge it is possible to observe the **kerbstones of the medieval roadway** that entered the gate on precisely the same line as the modern

Old City overview: gates & quarters

East Jerusalem
Herod Gate
Old City Walls
Damascus Gate
Muslim Quarter
St Stephen's Gate
Haram al-Sharif Temple Mount
Golden Gate
New Gate
Church of the Holy Sepulchre
Dome of the Rock
Christian Quarter
al-Aqsa Mosque
Jewish Quarter
Ophel
Jaffa Gate
Citadel
Armenian Quarter
Dung Gate
N
Ancient City on the southeast ridge
0 metres   200
Zion Gate

Jerusalem

Jerusalem Old City: sights

Jerusalem

Herod Gate

Solomon's Quarries/ Zedekiah's Grotto

Tariq al-M

Suleiman

Nablus

HaNevi'im

Harat al-Su Diyya

Damascus Gate

▲ 58

Tariq al Mawlawiyya

68 ▲

Aqabat er-Rabat

Beit Sharon

Austrian-Arab Clinic

el-Asseileh

Aqabat ash-Sheikh Rihan

MUSLIM

▲ 66

40 ▲ ▲ 26

Via Dolorosa

86 ▲ ▲

III 20

IV

Ghawanima

Toilets

Idzanhanim

Notre Dame de France

New Gate

Custodia di Terra Sancta

CHRISTIAN QUARTER

St Francis

College des Frères

▲ 14

Greek Catholic Patriarchate Bab al-Jadid

Greek Orthodox Patriarchate

Harat al-Wariyya

Latin Seminary & Patriarchate

Casa Nova

▲ 37

▲ 39

Elia Photo

▲ 5

▲ 26

Tariq al-Khanqah

Zalatimo's Sweets

Church of the Holy Sepulchre

IX

▲ 31

▲ 32

VII

Via Dolorosa

VI ▲ 23

(Tariq al-Saray)

V

41 ▲

Aqabat Tekieh

▲ 60

29 ▲

57

Tariq Bab a

▲ 33

Tariq al-Wad

46 ▲

▲ 2

Khan ez-Zeit

Qanatar Khdeir

Aqabat

Christian Quarter

al-Qiama

▲ 63

▲ 73

▲ 55

al-Dabbaghin

Suq al-Lahhamin

Suq al-Attarin

Suq al-Khawajat

King William

56 ▲

Aqabat al-Khalidiyya

Tariq al-Hakkari

▲ 27

52

Suq al-Q

42

54

Tariq Bab al-Silsila

▲ 53

▲ 80

79 ▲ ▲ 2

▲ 78

▲ 71

▲ 36

Christian Quarter St Internet

▲ 64

Pool of the Patriarch's Bath

Suq Aftimos

21 ▲

Fixed Price Shop

Swedish Christian Study Centre

David St

Christian Information Centre

▲ 83

▲ 50

St Mark's

Harat al-Ya'qubiyya

▲ 85

19

Syrian Convent

▲ 77

76 ▲

'Just One Last Day' Museum

47 ▲

Plugat

Shoni Ha-Lakhot

HaKotel

49

Broad Wall

▲ 16

HaKhoma

Misgav Ladakh

▲ 82

JEV QUA

St Mary of the Germans

15

Omar ibn al-Khattab Sq

Jaffa Gate

Citadel

Pol

S

Zion Walking Tours

▲ 22

Arman/ St James

Or HaChaim

Old Yishuv Court Museum

▲ 48

Byzantine

Cardo Maximus

Jewish Quarter

▲ 67

72

Habad

Hurva Sq

Bonei HaKhoma

Tiferet Yisr'el

S

Ha-Karaim

Beit El

Haye Olam

▲ 84

▲ 13

61 ▲

Hechal Convention Yeshivat

▲ 15

▲ 11

Armenian Patriarchate

Armenian Patriarchate

Armenian Garden

Gulbenkian Library

▲ 74

Harat Dair al-Zaituna

Batei Mahase

34

Rothschild Building

65 ▲

Shelter Houses

Mishmerot Hakehuna

Seibenberg House

HaOphel

Jaffa

Latin Patriarchate

Harat

ARMENIAN QUARTER

Hativat Zion

Mardigan Museum

▲ 24

Batei Mahase

Parking

Bus to New City

Zion Gate

Ma'ale Shalom

Hativat Zion

N

0 metres 100

Jerusalem

▲ Sights

1 al-Awhadiyya
2 al-Bistamiyya
3 al-Dawadariyya Khanqah
4 al-Karimiyya
5 al-Khanqah Mosque
6 al-Mujahadin Mosque & Mu'Azzamiyya Madrassa
7 al-Sallamiya Madrassa
8 al-Tankiziyya Madrassa
9 Ariel Visitor Centre
10 Arghuniyya Madrassa
11 Armenian Convent of St James
12 Bethesda Pools
13 Burnt House
14 Casa Nova Monastery
15 Cathedral of St James
16 CE stones 1st CE
17 Chapel of the Condemnation
18 Chapel of the Flagellation
19 Christ Church
20 Church of Our Lady of the Spasm
21 Church of St John the Baptist
22 Church of St Thomas
23 Church of the Holy Face & St Veronica
24 Convent of the Olive Tree
25 Convent of the Sisters of Sion
26 Coptic Orthodox Patriarchate & Coptic Church & Cistern of St Helena
27 Crusader Church of St Julian
28 Dar al Qur'an al-Sallamiya
29 Dar al-Siff Tunshuq
30 Ecce Homo Arch
31 Ethiopian Monastery
32 Ethiopian Patriarchate
33 Fountain
34 Four Sephardi Synagogues
35 Greek Catholic Church of St Anne
36 Greek Catholic Patriarchate
37 Greek Orthodox Museum
38 Greek Orthodox Church of St Anne
39 Greek Orthodox Patriarchate
40 Greek Orthodox Prison of Christ
41 Habash Pharmacy
42 Hammam al-'Ain & Sabil Tariq al-Wad
43 Hamman Sitti Maryam & Sabil Sitti Maryam
44 Hanbaliyya Madrassa
45 Hannam al-Shifa
46 Hasaniyya Mosque & Ribat 'Ala' al-Din Aydughdi al-Basir
47 Hasmonean & Israelite fortifications

48 Hurva Synagogue
49 Israelite Tower & Hasmonean Defenses
50 Jaffa Gate Church of the Nazarene
51 Jawhariyya Madrassa & Ribat
52 Khan al-Qattanim
53 Khan al-Sultan
54 Khan Tankiz
55 Lutheran Church of the Redeemer
56 Madrassa al-Lu'lu'iyya
57 Maktab Bairam Jawish
58 Mamlawiyya
59 Ma'Muniyya Girls' School
60 Mausoleum of Siff Tunshuq
61 Models of the Temple & Vessels
62 Monastery of the Flagellation
63 Mosque of Omar
64 Muristan
65 Nea Church, projected plan
66 Polish Catholic Chapel
67 Ramban Synagogue
68 'Red Minaret'
69 Ribat al-Mansuri
70 Ribat al-Maridini
71 Roman/Byzantine paving stones
72 Sidi 'Umar Mosque
73 St Alexander's Chapel (& Russian Excavations)
74 St George's Convent
75 St Nicodemas
76 Steps to 'roof' of old city
77 Syrian Orthodox Church & Convent of St Mark
78 Tashtamuriyya
79 Tomb of Baraka Khan
80 Tomb of Baybars al-Jaliq
81 Tomb of Turkan Khatun & Tomb of Sa'd al-Din Mas'ud
82 Treasures of the Temple
83 Vicariat Patriarchate Maronite
84 Wohl Archaeological Museum
85 Ya'quibiyya
86 Zawiyat al-Bukharia
87 Zawiyat al- Hunud
88 Zawiya Mahmaziyya

▣ Stations of the Cross I–IX (X–XIV are within the Church of the Holy Sepulchre)

- - Route of the Via Dolorosa

entrance, though at a lower level. The Byzantine and Roman gates also stood at this spot, again at a lower level still, with Roman remains evident in the building bearing the mark of the **Tenth Legion** (**Fretensis**).

Emerging on the east side beneath the modern bridge, the remains of the **East Tower** and **East Gate of the Triple Gate** are clearly distinguishable. This round-arched triple gate flanked by two towers is thought to have been built by the emperor Hadrian in 135 CE at the north end of the cardo maximus of his city of Aelia Capitolina. The fact that no traces of any first century CE walls have been found goes far to support the theory that this triple gate was more a triumphant arch than a defensive structure. However, there is enough archaeological evidence to support the view that **Hadrian** merely rebuilt a gate begun by **Herod Agrippa I** (c. 40-41 CE) as part of the 'Third North wall', possibly reusing some of the drafted stones from the Temple (destroyed in 70 CE). Hadrian's gate opened onto a **monumental paved plaza** at the top of the cardo maximus, at the centre of which stood an honorific column, probably bearing a statue of his likeness. In fact, the Arabic name for Damascus Gate, *Bab al-'Amud*, actually means 'Gate of the Column', though like everything in Jerusalem, the interpretation is not straightforward. Murphy-O'Connor reminds observers (*The Holy Land*, 1992) that Ottoman-period gates invariably take their name from something *outside* them, and consequently the 'column' in question may refer to the huge column drums found within St Stephen's Church, about 200 metres to the north. In the Crusader period the gate was referred to as St Stephen's Gate, with tradition associating the stoning to death of the first Christian martyr just outside. Following the defeat of the Crusader's Latin Kingdom in 1187, Christian pilgrims were forbidden from gathering close to the vulnerable north wall of the city, so the name was conveniently 'moved' to the gate on the east side of the city (see page 91). The Hebrew name for the gate, *Sha'ar Shekhem*, refers to the gate's orientation towards Shechem (Nablus).

Within the Roman Triple Gate is the **Roman Plaza Museum**. The museum contains a small excavated section of the Roman/Byzantine plaza, with some of the polished stone slabs bearing the carved markings of a gaming-board similar to the ones found at the Convent of the Sisters of Sion (page 124). There is also a holographic representation of the honorific column in the plaza, as well as a copy of the sixth century CE 'Madaba Map' (see page 79). ■ *Saturday-Thursday 0900-1700, Friday 0900-1400. Adult 5 NIS*

From the East Tower Chamber of the gate it is possible to climb the steps up to the top of Damascus Gate and the Rampart Walk (see page 84).

Damascus Gate to New Gate	The stretch of wall from Damascus Gate to New Gate is particularly fine Ottoman period work, though excavations suggest that Sulaiman II's architects followed the line of the third or fourth century CE Byzantine walls.
New Gate	As its name suggests, New Gate (*Arabic*: Bab al-Jadid, *Hebrew*: Sha'ar He-Hadash) is a relatively recent access point into the walled city, cut in 1887 by the Ottoman Sultan **'Abd al-Hamid II** in order to facilitate communications with the expanding 'New City' to the northwest. It remained sealed from 1948 until 1967.
New Gate to Jaffa Gate	Just beyond New Gate, inside an angle in the wall, is the small Ottoman-period (16th-century) **al-Qaymari mosque**. At the northwest corner of the Old City walls are the remains of a substantial tower (35 metres by 35 metres) built of re-used Herodian blocks, though almost certainly dating to the Crusader period. The north wall of the tower is best seen in the small 'archaeological garden' outside the Ottoman period walls, whilst parts of the huge internal piers

are preserved within the Christian Brothers' College (viewing is discretionary, and by appointment only). The structure is commonly referred to as **Tancred's Tower**, after the Crusader knight who assisted Godfrey of Bouillon in capturing Jerusalem in July 1099. A medieval legend claims this as the spot where David slew Goliath (*1 Samuel 17*), with the tower referred to in some sources as the *Castle of Goliath* (*Arabic*: Qasr Jalut). A further identification is with Herod Agrippa I's *Psephinus Tower* (described by Josephus in his *Jewish War V: 160*), though not only is the archaeological evidence against such an interpretation, the written evidence is also contrary (Josephus describes an octagonal, as opposed to square, tower). The tower was probably razed in 1219 by al-Malik al-Mu'azzam, nephew of Salah al-Din.

From the site of the former tower, the walls run southeast to Jaffa Gate. Various points along this stretch of the walls are labelled as "Jordanian Post"; a reference to the period between 1948 and 1967 when Jordanian soldiers stationed here looked down upon the no-man's land that divided the Jordanian controlled Old City from Israeli-held Jerusalem. Amos Elon recounts an amusing incident when a nun on the Israeli side of the line managed to 'cough' her dentures into the no man's land: "A brace of blue-helmeted UN truce supervisors, brandishing white flags, combed the debris-covered terrain where few persons had ventured for years and fewer still had come back alive. The false teeth were successfully retrieved" (*Jerusalem: City of Mirrors*, 1989).

Jaffa Gate

Though Sulaiman II's original 1538 gate remains, and is still used for pedestrian access, a section of the curtain wall to the south was demolished in 1898 (and the moat filled in) to allow Sultan 'Abd al-Hamid II's guests, the German **Kaiser Wilhelm II** and his wife, to drive into the city in the splendour of their carriage. **General Allenby** also entered the city with the victorious British Army at this point in December 1917, though he consciously chose humbly to proceed on foot (following the cabled recommendation of the British War Office: "Strongly suggest dismounting at gate. German emperor rode in and the saying went round 'a better man than he walked.' Advantages of contrast will be obvious"). This also contrasts with the entry into Jerusalem of Gustave Flaubert (author of *Madame Bovary*) in 1850, who commented: "We enter through the Jaffa Gate and I let a fart escape as I cross the threshold very involuntarily. I was even annoyed at bottom by this Voltaireanism of my anus" (*Les oeuvres complètes de Gustave Flaubert: Vol.19, Notes de voyage*, edited by L. Conrad, Paris 1910).

Jaffa Gate to southwest corner of Old City walls

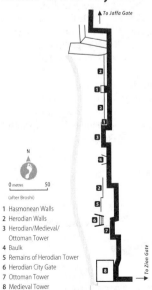

1 Hasmonean Walls
2 Herodian Walls
3 Herodian/Medieval/ Ottoman Tower
4 Baulk
5 Remains of Herodian Tower
6 Herodian City Gate
7 Ottoman Tower
8 Medieval Tower

The gate is referred to by Arabs as *Bab el-Khalil*, or 'Gate of the Friend'; a reference to Abraham, the 'Friend of God', whose tomb lies south of here in Hebron. The Hebrew name, *Sha'ar Yafo*, reflects the gate's orientation towards Jaffa (Yafo). The two graves just inside the gate (behind the railings) are said to belong to two of

Sulaiman II's architects, executed for displeasing him with their penny-pinching (see 'Jaffa Gate to Zion Gate' section below).

Jaffa Gate to Zion Gate To the south of Jaffa Gate is the **Citadel** (see page 92). Those who wish to continue the Rampart Walk must descend at Jaffa Gate, and reascend at the stairs 100 metres south of Jaffa Gate outside the walls (by the Citadel car park). There are a number of points of historical interest along the stretch of wall between the Citadel and the southwest corner (before the wall turns east towards Zion Gate), though most of these features are best seen from outside (as opposed to on top of) the city walls.

This section of the city walls borders the Hinnom Valley to the west, and follows the line of far older defensive fortifications. Sections of the **Hasmonean city walls** (c. 164-63 BCE) are clearly visible in places, as are the slightly later **Herodian tower and walls**. One tower along this stretch is particularly noteworthy, featuring bulging Herodian stones at its base, medieval blocks above, and Ottoman-period work at the top. It was just to the south of here, close to the first century CE city gate, that the Roman army finally broke through into the Upper City in 70 CE, during their suppression of the Jewish Revolt (see Josephus' *Jewish War VI: 374-99*).

At the southwest corner of the Old City walls, just beyond the remains of what must have been an impressive medieval tower, the line of the walls turns sharply east towards Zion Gate. Legend has it that Sulaiman II's walls should have been extended south to encompass the supposed site of the Tomb of David on Mt Zion (see pag 162). However, to save time and money this extension of the walls was not undertaken; a decision taken by the architects that is said to have cost them their lives when a furious Sulaiman II found out.

Zion Gate Completed in 1540, Sulaiman II's *Bab al-Kabi Da'ud* (or 'Gate of the Prophet David') was severely damaged in the 1948 battle for the city: in fact, when the Jewish Palmach forces breached the gate with over 70 kilogrammes of explosives on the night of 18/19th May 1948, they did something that according to Collins and Lapierre "no Jewish soldier had done since the days of Judas Maccabaeus [c. 164 BCE] – they had breached the walls of Jerusalem" (*O Jerusalem*, 1972). Their success was short-lived, however, with the Palmach forces being forced to withdraw almost immediately. Zion Gate still bears the scars of the 1948 fighting, and some of the ornamentation seen here is not original. The small gate chamber houses the country's oldest Holocaust museum.

Zion Gate to Dung Gate Extensive excavations have taken place along the stretch of wall between Zion Gate and Dung Gate, with visible remains from most periods of Jerusalem's history. The area is now designated as a National Park, and most of the points of interest are clearly labelled (see 'Zion Gate to Dung Gate' map). Some of the main points of interest are within the line of the current city walls, though most are outside.

Zion Gate to Dung Gate

1 Ayyubid Tower
2 Fatimid Wall
3 Ayyubid Tower
4 Byzantine Cistern
5 Sulphur Tower
6 Herodian Aqueduct
7 Hospice (?)
8 Nea Church's SE Apse
9 Herodian House
10 Medieval Tower
11 Medieval Tower
12 Cisterns & Ritual Baths

Continuing east from Zion Gate, it is possible to see part of the **Ayyubid tower** built in 1212, but dismantled just seven years later. To the east of the Ayyubid tower, inside the city walls, is a short section of wall dating to the Crusader period, whilst further east still is the **Sulphur Tower** (*Arabic*: Burj al-Kibrit). An inscription on the south side dates it to 1540, though the mixed remains of the tower projecting beneath it date to the medieval period. Close to the Sulphur Tower can be seen a section of the first century BCE **aqueduct** that brought water from Solomon's Pools near Bethlehem to the Temple at Jerusalem. With various repairs, including the insertion of the ceramic pipes in the early Ottoman period, the aqueduct remained in use until early this century!

Just beyond the angle in the wall lie the remains of a sixth century CE building, possibly a hospice, that is thought to be connected with the **Nea Church** just inside the walls, whilst further along the wall itself a small section of the Nea Church's southeast apse protrudes beyond Sulaiman II's walls (see page 153). The massive size of the four revealed courses (the upper of which has been restored) hint at the monumental size of this structure, and serve to confirm its status as the largest basilica in Palestine.

The rest of the section between here and Dung Gate is occupied mainly by rock-cut **cisterns** and **ritual baths** that formed part of first century CE houses. Flanking Dung Gate to the west is a large **medieval tower** that is usually associated with the Crusader *Tanner's Gate*, or *Gate of the Leatherworkers*. Its foundations rest upon a section of **paved Byzantine road** that led down to the Pool of Siloam (see page 180).

Dung Gate

This was probably a small Ottoman postern gate (built 1540-41), but was greatly enlarged between 1948-67 by the Jordanians to allow motor vehicles to enter the Old City (Jaffa and New Gates being sealed during this period). The name in common usage (*Hebrew*: Sha'ar ha-Ashpot) is said to refer to its proximity to a former waste dumping site, though its official name of *Bab al-Maghariba* ('Gate of the Moors') is derived from its position close to the former Moorish (North African) colony.

Dung Gate to St Stephen's Gate

For details of the southeast section of the Old City, where it abuts the south wall of the Haram al-Sharif/Temple Mount, see under the **Ophel Archaeological Park** (page 109). Unfortunately, the sensitive religious and political nature of the Haram al-Sharif/Temple Mount means that it is all but impossible to visit the Golden Gate on the east side of the Old City. Details of this structure are included within the Haram al-Sharif/Temple Mount section (see page 115). The description of the Old City walls and gates continues from St Stephen's Gate.

St Stephen's Gate

Built in 1538 by Sulaiman II, the name that he gave, *Bab al-Ghor* or 'Gate of the Valley (of Jordan)', has never caught on though the Hebrew name, *Sha'ar ha-'Arayot* or Lion's Gate, does refer to the carved lions that adorn either side of the arch. Many Muslim sources still call the gate by its Arabic name, *Bab Sitti Maryam*; an obvious reference to the Church and Tomb of the Virgin Mary just to the east. During the Crusader period the name changed from the 'Gate of Jehoshaphat' to 'St Stephen's Gate' for reasons given above (see under 'Damascus Gate', on page 85). The gate was modified during the British Mandate period to allow access to motor vehicles. It was through St Stephen's Gate that the Jordanian Arab Legion entered the Old City in 1948, but also through here that Colonel 'Motta' Gur led an Israeli parachute brigade in capturing the city on 7th June, 1967. St Stephen's Gate is the starting point of the tour of the **Muslim Quarter** (page 119).

St Stephen's The northeast corner of the Old City has always been considered to be Jerusa-
Gate to Herod lem's weak spot since the terrain is relatively flat and the protective ravines that
Gate defend the other sides are absent. Attempts have been made to improve the
defences on this side by digging a deep ditch from the rock, and building a
large number of insets and off-sets into the walls (thus increasing the field of
fire). The northeast corner is occupied by the **Stork Tower** (or *Burj Laqlaq*). It
was through a breach in the medieval-period walls just to the east of where
Herod Gate is now located that the Crusaders first entered Jerusalem, at noon
on 15th July, 1099.

Herod Gate This small gate in the north wall originally took its name from the rosette panel
above the arch (*Bab al-Zahra*, or 'Gate of Flowers'). Some time in the 16th or
17th century Christian pilgrims mistakenly confused a nearby medieval
house, *Dair Abu 'Adas*, with the palace of the man who condemned Jesus,
Herod Antipas (Abu 'Adas/Antipas?), since when the name Herod Gate has
stuck. Like St Stephen's Gate, this gate has been modified to allow direct
access.

Herod Gate to Between Herod Gate and Damascus Gate the bed-rock is exposed at the sur-
Damascus Gate face. At the mid-point between the two gates, an ancient quarry, '**Solomon's
Quarries/Zedekiah's Grotto**', extends beneath the city walls. The *malaki*
limestone found here was almost certainly exploited by Herod the Great
and/or Herod Agrippa I, and may well be the 'Royal Caverns' that Josephus
mentions (*Jewish War V: 147*). However, it is not unreasonable to speculate
that the tradition associated with Solomon (*I Kings 5:17-18*) is not too far
fetched. The cave complex extends for, well, who knows? It's certain that the
main passageway leads some 200 metres from the cave entrance, though Jewish tradition relates how Zedekiah escaped the besieging Babylonian army in
586 BCE through this hidden network of passages all the way to Jericho! The
Old Testament version is less specific (*II Kings 25:4-5; Jeremiah 52:7-8*),
though the famous 10th century CE Arab geographer al-Muqaddasi seems to
accept this account. ■ *Sunday-Thursday 0900-1700, Friday 0900-1400,
Saturday 0900-1500. Adult 8 NIS. Bring a torch.*

The Citadel ('Tower of David')

*Located on high ground on the west side of the Old City (just south of Jaffa Gate),
the **Citadel of Jerusalem** has been the city's stronghold for around 2,000 years.
Built largely upon the site of Herod the Great's first century BCE palace/fortress
and incorporating the substantial remains of one of the three massive towers that
he built, successive rulers of Jerusalem from the Romans, Arabs, Crusaders,
Mamluks and Ottomans all rebuilt, modified and reused this defensive stronghold. Following the capture of Jerusalem by the Israelis in 1967, the Citadel was
turned into a magnificent museum telling the history of the city through a superb
assembly of scale models, maps, paintings, photographs, holograms and artefacts
found during numerous excavations. Given the superb views from the ramparts,
and the clear and concise museum presentation, the Citadel is an ideal place to
begin a visit to Jerusalem.*

Ins and outs

Getting around There are three marked 'theme-routes' around the Citadel: i) the **Exhibition** tour
(marked in **red**) that reconstructs the chronological history of Jerusalem in a series of

superb exhibits located in various rooms around the Citadel; ii) the **Observation** tour (marked in **blue**) that leads visitors around the towers and upper battlements of the Citadel, providing fantastic views over Jerusalem and beyond; and iii) the **Excavations** tour (marked in **green**) that concentrates mainly on the remains of the 'jumble' of ancient walls and towers that have been excavated in the garden at the centre of the Citadel.

The manner in which you tour the Citadel is a matter of personal choice, though it has to be said that the **Exhibition** tour provides an excellent introduction to the city and gives the greatest rewards when undertaken in chronological order. The tour described here begins with the Exhibition (red) tour, and tries to provide background details on the building within which each exhibit is displayed rather than merely repeating the historical information provided by these museum displays. The **Observation** (blue) tour requires little explanation, with noticeboards posted at the key places detailing what all the major buildings are that you can see from the various vantage points. The tour of the Citadel concludes by descending to the garden in the centre for a closer examination of the **Excavations** (green). Note, however, that in order to gain some perspective on this "jumble of masonry" it is wise to take advantage of the aerial perspective provided from the top of the Northeast (Phasael) tower (**7**). Bold numbers in brackets, for example (**9**), refer to a point marked on the map.

History

Evidence suggests that the site here was used as a stone quarry as early as the seventh century BCE, but was included within the northwest angle of the city walls by the late second century BCE. The dating of this 'First Wall' (which can be seen in the garden on the 'Excavation' tour) remains contentious, though the weight of opinion is behind the argument that it was built by the **Hasmoneans**, probably John Hyrcanus (134-104 BCE).

Early history

What is clear, however, is that **Herod the Great** built three monumental defensive towers here in the first century BCE to protect the magnificent palace that he constructed for himself just to the south. The base of Herod's **Phasael Tower**, named after the king's brother who had fallen in battle, can still be seen today on the northeast side of the Citadel, though there is the possibility that this could be the **Hippicus Tower** named after Herod's great (dead) friend. The latter tower is described by Josephus as being "superior in size, beauty, and strength to any in the whole world" (*Jewish War, V: 162*). The third tower was named after Herod's wife **Mariamme**, whom the king "had himself killed through passionate love" (*ibid*). It could be assumed that the detailed measurements that Josephus provides in describing each of the towers would allow archaeologists to make positive identification relatively straightforward. However, Josephus' penchant for exaggeration must always be borne in mind. As Smallwood points out in her notes to Williamson's translation of *The Jewish War*, Josephus' suggestion that Herod's fortifications included "90 towers 100 yards apart" would create a wall over five miles long, whereas in the text he speaks of a whole circuit of the city walls as $3\frac{3}{4}$ miles!

Josephus provides us with a flowery description of Herod's **palace**, repeatedly referring to its "magnificence", "splendour" and "beauty", concluding that "no words are adequate to portray the Palace" (*V: 176*). Parts of the palace were destroyed at the outbreak of the Jewish Revolt in 66 CE, when the rebels gained access by undermining one of its towers and torched the building (*Jewish War II: 430-440*). The Roman garrison took refuge in the three great towers and sued for terms. Having agreed to surrender, the Romans were then treacherously murdered by the Jews (*Jewish War, II: 431-56*). Josephus suggests that by this act "the city was stained by such guilt that they must expect a visitation from heaven if not the vengeance of Rome" (*ibid*).

Excavation in the 'Armenian Garden' to the south of the Citadel suggest that the palace would have stretched almost to the line of the present south wall of the Old City. Following **Titus'** conquest of Jerusalem in 70 CE, this area became for the next 200 years part of the camp of the Tenth Legion Fretensis (although this traditionally held view has been challenged recently by Doron Bar, who suggests that the camp actually stood to the north of here, in the area now occupied largely by the Christian Quarter).

Of course, much of the interest in Herod's palace lies in its relevance to the Christian tradition of the Crucifixion. Most experts now believe that the Roman Procurator of Palestine, in this case **Pontius Pilate**, would have stayed here in Herod's palace, (as opposed to the Antonia fortress on the opposite side of the city, see page 123) whilst visiting from the Roman capital at Caesarea. Thus, this is would be the site of the **Praetorium** where Pontius Pilate judged Jesus (for example *Mark 15:1-15*). If so, as is probably the case, this completely undermines the authenticity of most of the modern route of the Via Dolorosa (see page 116).

Later history Remains are scant from the Early Arab period of occupation (638-1099 CE), though parts of an **Umayyad** palace have been excavated here (and in the 'Armenian Garden' to the south). When Jerusalem fell to the **Crusaders** in 1099, the **Fatimid** garrison in the Citadel withstood the attack and negotiated their surrender and safe passage from here. The Citadel was subsequently rebuilt into the fortress-palace of the newly established Crusader kings of Jerusalem, but was surrendered to **Salah al-Din** (Saladin) when he took the city in 1187. The fortifications were rebuilt and then dismantled a number of times in the ensuing years, but only when it was clear that the Crusaders were not going to return imminently did the Muslim rulers feel comfortable about extensively refortifying the city. By this time the **Mamluks** had replaced the Ayyubids as the rulers of Palestine, and it was the Mamluk sultan **al-Nasir Mohammad** who gave the Citadel much of its present form (c. 1310-11). Further additions were made in 1531-32 by the Ottoman ruler **Sulaiman II** ('the Magnificent') who was later to build the Old City walls that you see today, and it was from the steps outside the present entrance that the British commander **General Allenby** proclaimed the liberation of the city from Ottoman-Turkish rule in 1917. In recent years the Citadel has been used as barracks by the Jordanian army (1948-67) before being turned over to its present use as a museum following the **Israeli** capture of the city during the Six Day War.

The museum's full title, **The Tower of David Museum of the History of Jerusalem**, perpetuates the use of the popular name for the Citadel that arose in the fourth century CE when Byzantine Christians incorrectly identified the site as the palace of David. The Crusaders revived this erroneous identification, with their reused Herodian tower referred to as the 'Turres David'. In the 19th century the minaret (16th century?) of the 14th-century mosque became known as the **Tower of David**, and the name is now generally applied to the whole Citadel complex.

Sights

The current **entrance** to the Citadel is on the northeast side, opposite Christ Church (a little way inside Jaffa Gate). The **outer steps (1)** here are those from which General Allenby declared the liberation of Jerusalem from Turkish rule in 1917. This ornamental entrance dates to the period of Sulaiman II's rebuilding project (1531-32) and bears his name in a number of inscriptions. A bridge passes over the medieval **moat (2)** and enters the **outer barbican (3)** that the Mamluks, and then Sulaiman II, adapted from the original Crusader gate system. On the left is the **open air mosque (4)** built by Sulaiman II, whilst to the right a series of steps lead down into the moat. The **modern ticket office** is located in this outer barbican.

The main **entrance gate (5)** dates to the 12th century and comprises a guardroom (complete with original stone benches), a portcullis, and the usual L-shaped right-angled turn that was designed to slow down enemy attackers. This Crusader gate complex was also restored by the Mamluk sultan al-Nasir Mohammad. The entrance gate leads into a **hexagonal chamber (6)** built in the 14th century. It is possible to proceed into the courtyard garden from here (for the green **Excavations** tour), though it is recommended that you follow the blue and red arrows up the stairs to the top of the **Northeast (Phasael) tower (7)**. A small room within this tower shows the Italian artist Emannuele Luzzati's 14-minute animated film "Jerusalem" (every half an hour between 1010 and 1640; Hebrew with English translation).

The **Northeast (Phasael) tower (7)** provides one of Jerusalem's best viewpoints. A detailed noticeboard explains the key buildings seen on all sides. The base of this tower is solid all the way through, with the original Herodian construction comprising eight courses above the bedrock rising to just under 19 metres. The base of the tower measures 22.6 metres by 18.3 metres, and 21.4 metres by 17.1 metres at the top. The smaller masonry at the top of the tower dates to al-Nasir Mohammad's building efforts in the early 14th century.

From the Northeast (Phasael) tower it is necessary to decide which colour-coded tour you wish to visit. Since the blue **Observation** tour merely involves a walk around the upper ramparts, from where the key sites in and around Jerusalem are explained on noticeboards, no further explanation of this route is required. The green **Excavations** tour of the mixed remains in the

Citadel (Tower of David)

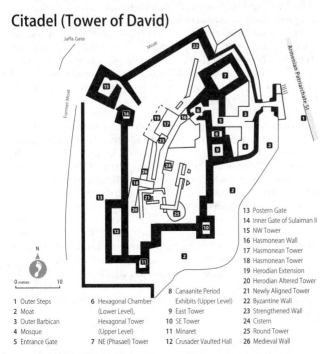

1 Outer Steps
2 Moat
3 Outer Barbican
4 Mosque
5 Entrance Gate
6 Hexagonal Chamber (Lower Level), Hexagonal Tower (Upper Level)
7 NE (Phasael) Tower
8 Canaanite Period Exhibits (Upper Level)
9 East Tower
10 SE Tower
11 Minaret
12 Crusader Vaulted Hall
13 Postern Gate
14 Inner Gate of Sulaiman II
15 NW Tower
16 Hasmonean Wall
17 Hasmonean Tower
18 Hasmonean Tower
19 Herodian Extension
20 Herodian Altered Tower
21 Newly Aligned Tower
22 Byzantine Wall
23 Strengthened Wall
24 Cistern
25 Round Tower
26 Medieval Wall

garden below will be explained at the end. The subsequent commentary explains the red **Exhibition** tour.

Exhibition (red) tour From the top of the **Northeast (Phasael) tower (7)** follow the red arrows down to the adjacent roof of the 14th-century Mamluk **hexagonal tower (6)**. The top of this tower provides a good aerial perspective of the mixed remains in the garden below (described in the green **Excavations** tour). An information board indicates the key points of interest.

To the south of the hexagonal tower, on the same level and still outdoors, there is some information on Jerusalem in the *Canaanite period (c. 3000-1200 BCE)* (**8**). To the south of this exhibit is the **East tower (9)**, probably built during the Mamluk period on Crusader foundations. The chamber that you enter on this level is devoted to the *First Temple period (c. 1000-586 BCE)*, and features among other things a model of the City of David in the 10th century BCE and a hologram of Solomon's Temple. From the roof above this chamber there is another fine view to the east, and of the excavations in the courtyard garden below. The lower level of the east tower (follow the red arrows) is devoted to the *Hellenistic, Hasmonean and Second Temple period (332 BCE-70 CE)*, and features images of Herod's Temple.

Exiting the East tower (**9**) continue south down the ramp to the **Southeast tower (10)**. This too was built in 1310-11 by al-Nasir Mohammad and restored in 1531-32 by Sulaiman II. There are good views from the top, notably of the Armenian Quarter, whilst the chamber inside is devoted to the *Late Roman and Byzantine periods (132-638 CE)*.

Exit the Southeast tower (**10**) and follow the line of the south wall (at either ground or ramparts level) to the southwest corner of the Citadel, passing the 14th-century mosque with its 16th-century (?) **minaret (11)** to your left (south). The southwest corner of the Citadel is occupied by a **Crusader vaulted hall (12)**, orientated on a north to south axis with a now-blocked **postern gate (13)** at its northwest corner. In the 14th century the upper level of the vaulted hall was converted into a mosque by al-Nasir Mohammad. Repairs made to the mosque by Sulaiman II in 1531-32 are noted in an inscription above the *minbar* (pulpit chair). The exhibition in this upper chamber is devoted to the *Early Arab period (638-1099 CE)*, the *Crusader and Ayyubid period (1099-1291)* and the *Late Arab period of the Fatimids and Mamluks (1291-1516)*. The lower level of the Crusader vaulted hall features temporary exhibitions.

Exit the Crusader vaulted hall (**12**) at the lower level and continue north in the shadow of the west wall. In a former deep cistern below the **inner gate of Sulaiman II (14)** is a superb 1:500 scale model of Jerusalem in the mid-19th century CE, built by the Hungarian artist Stefan Illes in 1872 for the following year's World Fair in Vienna. Lost for many years, the model was rediscovered in Geneva in the early 1980s and is now here on an extended loan. The inner gate of Sulaiman II includes an exhibition on the *Ottoman period (1516-1917)* on an upper level, plus a short display titled *Explorers, Scholars and Distinguished Visitors*. The inner gate of Sulaiman II (**14**) links to the **Northwest tower (15)**. From the roof there are excellent views of the New City, and also of the excavations in the courtyard. The middle level of the tower contains information on Jerusalem in the *British Mandate period (1917-1948)* and the establishment of the *State of Israel (1948)*. The cafeteria and toilets are also located here. It is possible to exit the Citadel from the Northwest Tower. The red **Exhibition** tour finishes here.

Though it is possible to wander into the courtyard garden in the centre of the Citadel to examine the excavations up close, it is advisable to view them first from above. Ideally this should be done from the roof of the **hexagonal tower (6)** or from the top of the **Northwest tower (15)**.

Excavations (green) tour

The second century BCE **Hasmonean wall (16)** makes a sweeping curve through what Prag describes as a "jumble of masonry" (*Blue Guide*, 1989). Defended by two **towers (17) (18)** from the same period, this is almost certainly the 'First Wall' described by Josephus (*Jewish War, V: 142-5*). Its continuation can be seen at the start of the tour of the Jewish Quarter (see page 147). The periods of Hasmonean building can be distinguished from later periods by the general use of smaller blocks. Herod the Great's fortification of this northwest corner involved building three great towers, the base of one of which remains today in the **Northeast (Phasael) tower (7)**. The rooms abutting the Hasmonean wall (16) became buried beneath the podium that Herod built to support his palace. He also built an **extension (19)** to one of the Hasmonean towers, whilst reducing the size of the other (20). For some unexplained reason this tower had to be rebuilt early in the first century CE, on a slightly different alignment (21). Evidence of the damage caused to the palace during the Jewish attack of 66 CE was identified just here.

To the north side of the Northeast (Phasael) tower is a section of the **Byzantine wall (22)** added in the fourth century CE; perhaps part of Herod Agrippa's Third North Wall. The original Hasmonean wall (16) was also strengthened (23) and the Herodian tower (21) rebuilt. The **cistern (24)** also dates to this period. Later additions to this "jumble of masonry" include the **round tower (25)**, generally thought to be part of an eighth century CE Umayyad palace, and the stretch of medieval wall (26). ■ *T6265333/6274111, F6283418, 24-hour information service T6294411. April-October Sunday-Thursday 0900-1700, Friday-Saturday 0900-1400; November-March Sunday-Thursday 1000-1600, Friday-Saturday 1000-1400. Adults 30 NIS, student 24 NIS, family of 2 adults and 2 children 60 NIS. Entrance fee includes a free guided tour, Sunday-Friday 1100 English, 1030 Hebrew, Tuesday at 1430 in German. Personal audio guides are available in English and Hebrew at the ticket office. There is a special wheelchair route, though it excludes all the best viewpoints and some of the museum displays. Gift shop, cafeteria, toilets. Buses 1/2/13/19/20/30/38/39/99.*

A **Sound and Light** show is also held here, as well as a '**Murder mystery evening**'. Until July 2000, the Citadel is hosting a spectacular exhibition of glass and polyvitro sculptures from the Seattle workshop of Dale Chihuly (the centrepiece of which is a 15-metre high, 2,000 piece tower). ■ *Sound and Light English: Monday Wednesday 2130, Saturday 2230; French: Monday 2230; German: Wednesday 2230; Hebrew: Monday Wednesday 2030; lasts 45 mins; large groups should book in advance; adult 22 NIS, students 16 NIS, children 12 NIS; bring warm clothes, even in summer. Murder mystery Saturday night 2100 in English; group bookings in Spanish available; bring warm clothing, even in summer.*

Other attractions

Temple Mount/Haram al-Sharif

The Temple Mount/Haram al-Sharif is an artificially raised platform built upon a low hill on the eastern side of the Old City. Whilst representing the architectural and visual focus of Jerusalem, it could also be said to be one of the most contested pieces of real estate in the world. The site of the First and Second Jewish Temples, the latter where Jesus taught, it is now home to a shrine and mosque that make it

Jerusalem

*the third most important place of pilgrimage within the Islamic world. Whilst the status of Jerusalem divides Israelis and Palestinians like no other matter, the custody of the Temple Mount/Haram al-Sharif provides a vivid and terrifying focus to this confrontation. Though there are no standing remains of the Temple, Jews still visit to mourn the Temple's destruction at the **Western (Wailing) Wall**. The central Islamic buildings stand on the Haram al-Sharif/Temple Mount itself and include Jerusalem's main congregational mosque (**al-Aqsa Mosque**), plus one of the world's most beautiful architectural monuments, the **Dome of the Rock**.*

Ins and outs

Getting there There are any number of ways of approaching the Temple Mount/Haram al-Sharif, though most arrive via the Western Wall Plaza (on foot from just about any direction in the Old City, or by Bus 01). The 'sights' information below first describes the **'external features'** (Western 'Wailing' Wall, Western Wall Tunnels, Ophel Archaeological Park, etc), before detailing the **'internal features'** (ie those on the Temple Mount/Haram al-Sharif itself). Though there is (free) 24-hr access to the Western Wall Plaza, entry hours for the Haram al-Sharif are not fixed and revolve around Muslim prayer times. As a general rule, the Haram al-Sharif is open Saturday-Thursday 0800-1500 and closed on Friday. You may be asked to leave the Haram al-Sharif during midday prayers (1230-1330 summer, 1130-1230 winter). During the holy month of Ramadan visiting is restricted to 0730-1000, and the Haram al-Sharif may be closed completely during certain Islamic festivals. Non-Muslims can only enter the Haram al-Sharif through the *Bab al-Maghariba* (Gate of the Moors, via the ramp leading up from the Western Wall Plaza), though you can leave by any of the functioning gates. Entry onto the Haram al-Sharif is free, though there is a 30 NIS (students 18 NIS) charge for a ticket to visit the Dome of the Rock, al-Aqsa Mosque and the Islamic Museum. The ticket office is just inside *Bab al-Maghariba*.

Getting around It is important to dress modestly when visiting both the Muslim and Jewish holy places around the Temple Mount/Haram al-Sharif. This means no shorts (on men or women), with women in particular being reminded to wear loose, non-revealing clothes. Some form of head covering is advisable for both sexes. Decorous behaviour is also essential, with public displays of affection being frowned upon. Non-Muslim visitors are not allowed to conduct prayers on the Haram al-Sharif. Some areas of the Haram al-Sharif are off-limits to visitors, though there are no signs indicating where you can and cannot go. Instead there are officious, self-appointed 'guardians' who will scream and shout and any person who unwittingly wanders where they shouldn't. As a general guide, the whole east side of the Haram al-Sharif to the east of the Dome of the Chain is off limits, as is the south wall (the area to the east of al-Aqsa Mosque, including Solomon's Stables). Most of the self-appointed guides are useless and should be avoided like pork. Shoes must be removed before entering al-Aqsa Mosque and the Dome of the Rock, and cameras and bags left outside. It is not recommended that you leave valuables unattended like this. Photography is not permitted in the Western Wall Plaza on Shabbat or Jewish holidays (and should be treated as a privilege and not a right at other times).

History

Mt Moriah Tradition links the low hill upon which the Temple Mount/Haram al-Sharif stands with the Mt Moriah upon which **Abraham** offered his son Isaac as a sacrifice, as a sign of his obedience to God (*Genesis 22*). There are at least two other versions of this story, with Muslims believing that it was Ishmael, and not Isaac, who was offered by Abraham, whilst Samaritans believe that the biblical

Temple Mount or Haram al-Sharif?

Even for a guidebook that is attempting to be non-partisan, problems arise when it comes to deciding by which name to refer to certain contested sites. In the main, the name commonly used in Western sources has been selected, based largely on the premise that most of the readership is drawn from here and thus the 'common' name used will strike a chord of familiarity. Thus, there is a chapter called 'West Bank' and not 'Judaea and Samaria' or 'Occupied Territories'. With regard to the platform on which the Jewish Temple once stood, but is now occupied by the Dome of the Rock, al-Aqsa Mosque, and a number of Muslim shrines, when referred to in a Jewish context the Handbook will use the term Temple Mount; and when referred to in a Muslim context, it will be referred to as the Haram al-Sharif. In a general context the Handbook will call it the Temple Mount/Haram al-Sharif (though the placing of 'Temple Mount' before 'Haram al-Sharif' signifies nothing). The Hebrew name for the Temple Mount is Har Ha-Bayit, though it is sometimes referred to as Har Ha-Moriyya (Mt Moriah) or Beth Ha-Maqdas (the Holy House). The Arabic name Haram al-Sharif means 'Noble Sanctuary', though Bait al-Maqdis (the Holy House) is occasionally used.

description of the sacrifice site – "Abraham lifted up his eyes, and saw the place afar off" (*Genesis 22:4*) – better fits Mt Gerizim (near Nablus) than the low rise here in Jerusalem. Tradition also places here the "threshing floor of Araunah the Jebusite" that **David** purchased in the 10th century BCE as the site upon which to build an altar to God (*II Samuel 24:18-25*). Other traditions central to Judaism, Christianity and Islam appear to have been placed at this spot retrospectively, with the rock at the spiritual centre of the Temple Mount/Haram al-Sharif also being associated with the place where God took the dust for the creation of Adam, where Adam was buried, where Cain and Abel offered their gift to God and where Noah raised an altar after leaving the ark.

Solomon's Temple

Though it was David who brought the symbol of the Israelites covenant with God (the Ark of the Covenant) to Jerusalem, it is generally claimed that his militaristic past meant that he had too much blood on his hands to build the first Jewish Temple, and thus the task was left to his son **Solomon**. Johnson (*A History of the Jews*, 1987), however, suggests that this argument does not stand up since "war and the Israelite religion were closely associated", citing as an example how the Ark of the Covenant was sometimes carried into battle like a flag or standard. He argues that David chose not to build the Temple since this would have changed the essential nature of the balance between state and religion, and he wished to avoid turning Israel into a royal temple-state.

Work began on Solomon's Temple c. 961/960 BCE, taking seven years to complete, and though no trace remains it is possible to make a tentative reconstruction from the description in the Old Testament of the Bible (*I Kings 5-8*). It was built of stone and timber, with the Phoenician king of Tyre, Hiram, sending both cedars and stonemasons to assist in its construction (*I Kings 5:1-18*). He also sent experts in casting bronze to make the ceremonial vessels. The Temple was tripartite in plan, with an inner **Holy of Holies** housing the Ark of the Covenant. Whether the Ark stood on the 'rock', or the 'rock' served as an altar in the Holy of Holies is unknown. The entrance to the Temple was to the east, flanked by two free-standing columns named for unknown reasons *Jachin* and *Boaz* (*I Kings 7:21*). The Temple was looted of its treasures on a number of occasions before being destroyed in the **Babylonian** sack of Jerusalem in 586 BCE. However, it is important to note that the building style of the

Jerusalem

Temple, similar to Canaanite temples excavated at Lachish and Bet Shean, would have been "put up and equipped in a manner quite alien to the Israelites" (Johnson, *ibid*). In fact, Johnson goes on to argue that "What is clear is that Solomon's Temple, in its size and magnificence, and its location within the fortified walls of a royal upper city or acropolis, had very little to do with the pure religion of Yahweh which Moses brought out of the wilderness" (*ibid*). What Johnson is suggesting is not that Solomon was building a pagan place of worship, but that he was introducing a religious reform that was based upon royal absolutism. This centralization of religious power and cult worship did not survive the death of Solomon, leading to the dissolution of the United Monarchy and the return to the northern (Israel)/southern (Judah) rivalry.

Post-Exilic Temple Following the return from Exile, the Temple was rebuilt by **Zerubbabel** c. 537-515 BCE, probably on the same plan as Solomon's effort but without the ornamentation. The Ark of the Covenant, however, had been lost. **NB** Though the Post-Exilic Temple in reality represents the second Temple built on this site, the term 'Second Temple' is generally used to refer to Herod the Great's creation (see below).

Herod's Temple The decision of **Herod the Great** to construct a grand new temple on the Temple Mount says much about his character. Johnson describes him as being "not merely a notable philanthropist; he was also an inspired propagandist and a great showman" (*ibid*), whose idol was obviously Solomon. The fact that he built the Antonia fortress (page 123) and the three great towers (Phasaeal, Hippicus and Mariamme, see page 92) before commencing work on the Temple further illustrates Herod's standing amongst a suspicious Jewish population. With his Idumean background, his Hellenizing reforms and his dependence for legitimacy on his Roman backers, Herod had to be very careful in how he went about building his Temple since this would require the dismantling of the Post-Exilic Temple then standing on the Temple Mount. He did this by summoning a national council of religious leaders in 22 BCE and laying his plans before them. At every step of the way he was extremely sensitive to charges of desecration, even going so far as to train up to 1,000 priests as builder-craftsmen to work in areas forbidden to the ritually impure. Though

Herod the Great's Temple: the Second Temple

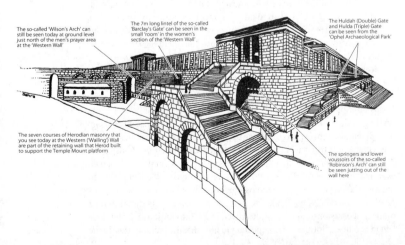

The so-called 'Wilson's Arch' can still be seen today at ground level just north of the men's prayer area at the 'Western Wall'

The 7m long lintel of the so-called 'Barclay's Gate' can be seen in the small 'room' in the women's section of the 'Western Wall'.

The Huldah (Double) Gate and Hulda (Triple) Gate can be seen from the 'Ophel Archaeological Park'

The seven courses of Herodian masonry that you see today at the Western ('Wailing') Wall are part of the retaining wall that Herod built to support the Temple Mount platform

The springers and lower voussoirs of the so-called 'Robinson's Arch' can still be seen jutting out of the wall here

the temple structure itself took less than two years to complete, such was the monumental scale of the entire complex that it was barely finished when the Romans tore it down in 70 CE.

In order to fulfil his ambitions of creating a temple that would not only rival Solomon's effort but also exceed it in splendour, it was necessary to enlarge the Temple Mount platform or enclosure. This was done by bridging the valleys surrounding the Mt Moriah of Solomon's Temple, and filling them in. The Herodian Temple Mount enclosure was shaped like an uneven rectangle, with the following dimensions: west wall 485 metres, east wall 470 metres, north wall 315 metres, south wall 280 metres. Thus, the enclosure covered an area in the region of 144,000 square metres; a remarkable achievement.

The magnificence of Herod's building project can still be appreciated, despite the fact that no trace of the Temple building itself actually remains standing in place. Large sections of the retaining wall can still be seen, rising in various numbers of courses above the bedrock. The most easily visible, and famous, section of Herod's retaining wall is preserved at the so-called Western Wall (see page 102), where seven courses rise above the level of the present plaza with more courses reaching down to bedrock below. See the line drawing on the opposite page to help you visualize the scene. The southeast corner of the mound perhaps best displays the scale of the enclosure, with 35 original courses extending 42 metres above the bedrock. Though most of the courses of stones are a regular size (generally 1 metre high and weighing around 1,800-4,500 kilogrammes), there are some notable exceptions: one stone of the 'mastercourse' in the southeast corner is estimated to weigh 90,000 kilogrammes, whilst another stone to the north of the Western Wall area (and visible on the tour through the Western Wall Tunnel, page 106) is 13.6 metres long, 3.5 metres wide, 3.5 metres high, and estimated to weigh around 570,000 kilogrames!

A fairly accurate picture of the Temple building and the enclose plan has been reconstructed by examining the fragments found on or near the site, the subterranean features remaining *in situ*, and the detailed descriptions found in contemporary accounts (most notably Josephus' *Jewish War V, 1-226* and *Antiquities XV, 380-425*). Standing on a vantage point overlooking the Temple Mount and reading the relevant passage in *The Jewish War* is an enlightening experience. The Temple enclosure probably had nine gates, and was surrounded on three sides by a portico, with a *double (Royal) portico* to the south. It is suggested that this is where the moneychangers and usurers, whose tables Jesus upset, would have been located (*Matthew 21:12-13; Mark 11:15-17; Luke 19:45-48; John 2:13-17*). The outer *Court of the Gentiles* could be entered by non-Jews, though entry to the sacred area was prohibited on pain of death (parts of two tablets, one in Latin and one in Greek, declaring this fact have been found). Within the sacred area itself, the *Beautiful Gate* led from the *Court of the Women* to that of the men (*Court of Israel*), and from thence into the *Court of the Priests*. This is perhaps where the young Jesus was presented (*Luke 2:22-39*). Like the Solomonic Temple, Herod's construction was on a tripartite plan, with the inner chamber veiled by a purple curtain (that tradition says was was rent in two during the Crucifixion: *Matthew 27:51; Mark 15:38; Luke 23:45*). The curtain concealed the inner *Holy of Holies*. Though the exact location of the Holy of Holies is unknown (a factor which prevents religious Jews from visiting the Temple Mount for fear of violating it), it is generally assumed that it stood on the site of the rock that is now enshrined within the Dome of the Rock. The destruction of the Second Temple by the Romans in 70 CE is vividly brought to life by Josephus (*The Jewish War VI, 230-442*).

The 12th century CE rabbi and sage Maimonides ruled that despite the destruction of the Temple, the site still retained its sanctity and hence any Jew wishing to visit had to be ritually pure. Unfortunately, this is not that simple. The ritual purification process is laid out explicitly in *The Fourth Book of Moses, Called Numbers* and features, amongst other things, the "ashes of the burnt heifer of purification for sin" (*Numbers 19:17*). The heifer had to be red and "without spot, wherein is no blemish, and upon which never came yoke", and if only two hairs of the heifer were not red, it couldn't be used. As a further complication, the preparation had to be carried out by Eleazar, the heir apparent of Aaron. Thus, when the Temple was destroyed, no new ashes could be produced, and so purification is not possible until the Messiah arrives to prepare a new supply. As a result, rabbinical consensus is of the opinion that all Jews are now ritually impure.

Haram al-Sharif Following the establishment of Hadrian's Aelia Capitolina c. 132 CE, it is thought that the Roman emperor raised a number of statues on the Temple Mount, though the suggestion that a Temple to Jupiter was built on the site seems unlikely. The platform appears to be largely neglected and ignored by the Byzantines, and it is with the arrival of the Arab armies in 638 CE that the course of the enclosure's history is irreversibly changed. The holiness of the site to Muslims is immediately apparent from the early decision of the caliph Omar to build a mosque on the Temple Mount platform, within a year of the Arab conquest of Jerusalem. The mosque is described as a simple crude affair by the Christian pilgrim Arculf (c. 670 CE), perhaps reusing the columns from Herod's ruined Royal Portico. However, many Israelis suggest that the Arab conquerors of the city 'invented' the religious significance to Muslims of the site as a means of superseding the influence of previous Jewish or Christian claims to Jerusalem (see box on page 103).

By the end of the seventh century CE/start of the eighth century CE, the Muslims had built the **Dome of the Rock** (c. 691-2 CE) and the **al-Aqsa Mosque** (c. 705-15 CE) on the Temple Mount platform, renamed the enclosure the **Haram al-Sharif**, and banned non-Muslims from entering it. Subsequent centuries saw the Crusaders occupy the Temple Mount/Haram al-Sharif, turning the Dome of the Rock into a Christian prayer hall and the al-Aqsa Mosque into a palace for the king, and then the headquarters of the Templars. **Salah al-Din's** conquest of Jerusalem in 1187 saw the main buildings revert to their former use, followed by the continuous additions of Muslim shrines and monuments through the Mamluk and Ottoman periods. Despite the capture of all of Jerusalem by the Israelis in 1967, the Haram al-Sharif has remained in Muslim hands since the 12th century.

Sights

Western Wall The focus of Jewish prayer and pilgrimage, the Western Wall (*Hebrew*: Ha-Kotel Ha-Ma'aravi) is not part of the Temple building itself, but an exposed stretch of the retaining wall that Herod the Great constructed c. 20-17 BCE to support the platform on which the Second Temple was built. Approximately 60 metres of the 485 metre-long western retaining wall is exposed here, allowing Jews and non-Jews alike to appreciate something of the monumental scale of Herod's building project. See the line drawing on page 100 to put the scene before you into historical and archaeological perspective.

Though seven courses of Herodian masonry are visible, there are in fact a further 19 courses below the level of the current pavement. The Herodian blocks are characterized by their carefully drafted edges and are cut with such precision that they are set without mortar. Most of the stones are 1-1.2 metres

The sanctity of the Temple Mount/Haram al-Sharif: competing religious interests

When describing the historical and religious function of the Temple Mount/Haram al-Sharif, Amos Elon suggests that the "main business of this platform, for at least three millenia, has been the traffic in beliefs", adding that by "the curious economy governing sacred sites, the same rock would play a major role in the succession of mutually hostile creeds" (Jerusalem: City of Mirrors, 1989). Whilst the sacredness of the site to Jews is well known (the scene of Abraham's sacrificial offering; David's purchase of the threshing-floor and construction of an altar; site of Solomon's, and then Herod's, Temple) the sanctity within Islam is perhaps less well known to the non-Muslim audience. Abraham, Solomon and Jesus are all revered within Islam, and though the Muslim belief is that Ishmael and not Isaac was offered by Abraham for sacrifice, and that Jesus was a prophet but not son of God, the 'holy' link between Jerusalem and Islam is easily established.

Jerusalem, and more importantly the Haram al-Sharif, was the place where the prophet Mohammad stopped to behold the celestial glories on his isra', or nocturnal flight to heaven. Though the Qur'an does not specify a location by name, the masjid al-aqsa, or 'furthermost sanctuary' has come to be associated with Jerusalem. As a further link between Islam and Jerusalem, the qibla (direction of prayer) in the early days of Islam was not towards Mecca, but to Jerusalem.

A reccuring theme within the right-wing Israeli press has been the premise that Islam merely incorporated Jewish (and to a lesser extent Christian) notions of the 'heavenly' Jerusalem (see Samuel Katz's ranting Battleground: Facts and Fantasy in Palestine, 1973, for example). The fact that Mohammad almost certainly did not visit Jerusalem during his lifetime is irrelevant. As Amos Elon notes, citing such examples as the Immaculate Conception or the parting of the Red Sea, "the lasting power of such legends is in the metaphors they evoke in the religious traditions and in the readiness to believe them" (ibid). He further points out that the "Jewish and Israeli attachment to Jerusalem is equally an amalgam of religious and political sentiments", reflecting Johnson's view that though "The Jews later came to see Solomon's Temple as an essential part of the early faith", it was also a means by which "to push forward his religious reform in the direction of royal absolutism, in which the king controlled the sole shrine where God could be effectively worshipped" (History of the Jews, 1987). Amos Elon also concludes that the fact that the attachment of Islam to Jerusalem is 'late' in no way undermines the significance of that attachment: "the legend of Mohammad's ascent to heaven from the Temple Mount of Jerusalem is by now as central an element in Islam as the Exodus is in Judaism and the cult of Mary is in Christianity" (ibid).

high, and between one and three metres long, though there are some notable exceptions. Visitors to the 'Western Wall Tunnels' will be shown a single stone that measures some 13.6 metres by 3.5 metres by 3.5 metres (see page 106)! Above the seventh Herodian course here the stones are Umayyad (c. seventh century CE), whilst the smaller ones at the top are part of the restoration effort that followed the 1033 earthquake.

It is not entirely clear when Jews first began to gather here to lament the destruction of the Temple, though it is reasonable to assume that it may well have closely followed Hadrian's death in 138 CE. By the third-fourth century CE it was certainly common practice, though following the Arab conquest in 638 CE and the subsequent construction of Islamic monuments on the platform itself it appears that the Western Wall itself became the focus of Jewish pilgrimage. Because of the Jewish lamentations here, it became known as the **Wailing Wall**. Though only a small section of the Wall was available to Jews, as the Jewish population of Jerusalem increased in the 19th century they attempted to change long-standing practices at the Wall (such as bringing chairs for the elderly to rest, and putting up a temporary screen to divide the male worshippers from the women). Though these introductions seem

Haram al-Sharif / Temple Mount overview

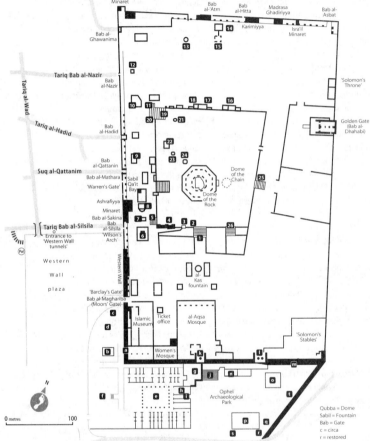

1 South Qanatir (c 10th cent)	r 1429, 1627)	21 Qubbat al-Arwah (c 16th cent)	h Byzantine House
2 Minbar of Burhan al-Din (c 1388, r 1843)	12 Sabil Basiri (c 1456)	22 Masjid al-Nabi (c 1700)	i 'Excavation's Gate'
3 Qubba Yusuf (c 1681)	13 Qubbat Sulaiman (c 1200)	23 Qubbat al-Mi'raj (c 1200)	j Herodian Plaza
4 Qubba Nahwiyya (c 1207)	14 Sabil al-Sultan Sulaiman (c 1537)	24 Qubbat al-Nabi (c 1538, r 1845)	k Double Gate
5 SW Qanatir (c 1472)	15 Pavilion of Sultan Mahmud II (c 1817)	25 E Qanatir (c 10th cent)	l Triple Gate
6 Qubba Musa (Dome of Moses) (c 1249)	16 NE Qanatir (c 1326)	26 SE Qanatir (c 1030, r 1211)	m Single Gate
7 Mastabat al-Tin (c 1760)	17 N Qanatir (c 1321)	a 'Robinson's Arch'	n Mikvehs (Ritual Baths)
8 Sabil Bab al-Mahkama & Birka Ghaghanj (c 1527)	18 Cell of Muhammad Agha (c 1588)	b Pier	o Byzantine Building
9 Mihrab 'Ali Pasha (c 1637)	19 NW Qanatir (c 1376, r 1519,1567)	c Herodian Street	p Umayyad Building
10 Sabil al-Shaikh Budayr (c1740)	20 Qubbat al-Khadir (c 16th cent)	d Umayyad Courtyard	q 7th–6th century BCE remains
11 Sabil Sha'lan (c 1216,		e Umayyad Palace	r Herodian Building
		f Umayyad Hospice?	s Byzantine Homes
		g Medieval Tower	t Byzantine City Wall

God goes on-line

Close inspection of the stone blocks of the Western Wall reveals thousands of slips of paper stuffed into the cracks. This practice of communicating with God through the written form is thought to date to the 18th century CE, though it has taken on a significant new form in the late 20th century. For many years now the Ministry of Religious Affairs has been operating a free prayer-faxing service (T02-5612222), though it is now possible to reach God through cyberspace! An Israeli Internet company will now place your email messages in the wall free of charge. They can be reached via Virtual Jerusalem's home page at http://www.virtualjerusalem.com/

Messages sent via either fax or email are not read prior to being stuffed in the Wall's crevices, and after an appropriate period of time are removed by the custodians and buried on consecrated ground.

innocent enough, the Muslim leaders opposed any change in the status quo for fear that they would lead to further concessions. Attempts by various Jewish groups in the early 20th century to buy the land adjacent to the Wall were seen by the Muslims as part of the Zionist attempt to take over Palestine. Matters were brought to a head on Yom Kippur in 1928 when, following complaints from the Supreme Muslim Council, British policemen forcibly removed a screen from the Wall. Complaints were made to the League of Nations and the British parliament by leading Zionist officials, with Chaim Wizemann writing an open letter to the Yishuv (Jewish community in Palestine) stating that the only solution to this problem of access was to "pour Jews into Palestine". As the Muslims had feared the matter had moved from being a religious one to a political and racial question, and they were quick to link the confrontation at the Wall with the greater question of Jewish designs on Palestine. In mid-August 1929 members of Betar, the youth organization of Jabotinsky's Revisionist party, marched on the wall, raising the Zionist flag and singing the Zionist anthem. The following day at Friday prayers Muslims were exalted to defend the Haram al-Sharif. The following Friday (23rd August, 1929) saw a full-scale riot ensue in which Jewish quarters in Jerusalem, Hebron and Safed were attacked. Zionist groups responded and by the end of the week 133 Jews and 116 Arabs had been killed, with many more injured.

The square, or **Western Wall Plaza**, in front of the Wall took its present form after the Israeli capture of the whole of Jerusalem in the Six Day War of 1967. Until this time the houses and buildings of the Magharibi or 'Moors Quarter' virtually abutted the western retaining wall of the Temple Mount/Haram al-Sharif platform, though these, including the 12th century CE mosque and shrine of Shaikh 'A'id (the Afdaliyya Madrassa), were bull-dozed in June 1967 to allow greater Jewish access. The Western Wall is now divided into two distinct areas for prayer; men have the larger area to the north, whilst women are separated by a screen to a smaller area to the south. Recent years have witnessed a growing number of confrontations between the two sexes as women attempt to assert their rights at the Western Wall. The dispute partly arises from a strict interpretation of *kol ishah*, or the law prohibiting men from hearing a woman's voice in song. The 'Women at the Wall' group, who gather hear to sing for an hour or two per month, maintain that there is no *halackic* ruling stating that the Wall belongs only to men, and thus they have every right to gather here and worship as they please.

In addition to being an excellent places to observe Jews conducting their devotional rituals, there are several points of archaeological interest at the

Western Wall. Just to the north of the men's prayer area (and accessible only to modestly dressed men), a gateway leads to a further prayer area beneath the so-called **Wilson's Arch** (see drawing on page 100). This structure (described in further detail as part of the 'Western Wall Tunnels' tour, below) is generally agreed to be easternmost of the series of arches that supported the causeway spanning the Tyropoeon Valley, linking the Upper City with the Second Temple.

At the southern end of the women's prayer area (and accessible only to modestly dressed women) is the so-called **Barclay's Gate**. Erroneously identified with the *Kiponos Gate* of the *Mishnah*, Barclay's Gate allowed access to the Temple Courts on the Temple Mount platform via a ramp from the street below. All that can be seen today is part of the seven-metre-long lintel of the gate, made from a single stone. It is mainly hidden by the small prayer room for Jewish women that occupies the area beneath the ramp that leads up to the Temple Mount/Haram al-Sharif entrance (Moor's Gate).

Western Wall   The Western Wall Tunnels complex features a number of places of major
Tunnels   archaeological, historical, religious and (arguably) political interest. The key sites date to several important periods in Jerusalem's history, most notably the Hasmonean and Herodian eras, though a number of questions still need to be answered and further excavations are necessary. Unfortunately, fear of desecration (by Jews and Muslims), and the fact that the complex has been turned into a political issue (by Israelis and Palestinians), means that this is unlikely in the very near future. However, some of the more fanciful legends and traditions surrounding the various 'tunnels' round here may be rendered obsolete or mundane if archaeology wins the day, so it is perhaps best that some of the questions remain unanswered.

Tour   The entrance to the Western Wall Tunnels complex is on the northwest side of the Western Wall Plaza (marked by the 'Western Wall Heritage' sign). Turning right you enter a **vaulted passage (A)** (named the 'secret passage' by Warren) that passes a series of arches and vaulted chambers. This is in fact the route of the causeway over the Tyropoeon Valley that connected the Temple with the Upper City on the Southwestern Hill. The original causeway leading to the Temple was destroyed by the Hasmoneans in their defence against Pompey in 63 BCE, rebuilt by Herod the Great when he constructed the Second Temple, and then destroyed again in 70 CE as the Jewish Zealots retreated into the Temple in the face of the Roman advance (see Josephus' *Jewish War II, 344; Antiquities XIV, 58*). The present vaults support Tariq Bab al-Silsila (the Street of the Chain), though their date of construction is uncertain. It is speculated that the vaulted chambers on the south side may date as far back as the first century BCE-first century CE, whilst those to the north are 8th-11th century CE and later. A 15th century CE tradition attributes the construction of the 'secret passage' to David, suggesting that it links the Citadel and the Temple Mount, though this seems rather implausible. According to the tour guides, it took six people 24 years to excavate this section, since they worked with their hands only for fear of alerting the Muslim householders above!

Towards the east end of this passage, to the right (south), a low window-grille reveals a vaulted chamber at a lower level. Warren explored this so called **Masonic Hall (B)** in 1867, suggesting that it was at least as old as the Western Wall (in other words Herodian), though possibly older (Hasmonean). Measuring 14 metres by 25.5 metres, it is well built with a paved floor and a single central column (now broken but still visible) supporting the vaulted roof. Its original function is unknown, though it is said to have been used by Masons who connected it with Solomon's works in the Temple. It has also been identified with the Herodian *Xystos* (Chamber of Hewn Stones), or Council Building to which Josephus refers (*Jewish War V, 144*). A double door in the east wall leads to a series of other rooms. There is all sorts of speculation of further secret passages leading under the Temple Mount/Haram al-Sharif, identified with David and Solomon, that is guarantied to get Jewish archaeologists' pulses racing and Muslim sensibilities bristling.

At the point where the causeway meets the Temple Mount/Haram al-Sharif platform, it is supported by **Wilson's Arch**. Explored and described by Wilson in 1864, it is very similar to 'Robinson's Arch' to the south (see page 109),

Western Wall tunnels

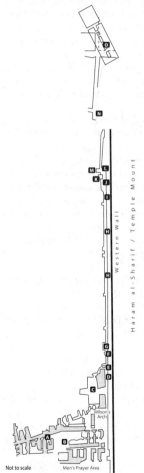

and recent excavations appear to confirm Wilson's assertion that its lower courses and pier at least date to the Second Temple period. The upper courses are probably Umayyad. Modestly dressed men can get a better view of Wilson's Arch via the small entrance to the north of the men's prayer area at the Western Wall.

Turning north on the tour, the narrow passage opens out into a high **cruciform chamber (C)**. The hall is part of four interlocking vaults that were built by the Mamluks (c. 14th century CE) as the substructure supporting the buildings above. The purpose of these vaults was to raise the street level to such an extent that their buildings would be on the same level as those inside the Haram al-Sharif. There is some evidence to suggest that these substructures were used as cisterns. Dominating this hall today is a superb **model of the Second Temple**. Incredibly accurate and detailed, what is even more amazing about this model is the hydraulic action that lowers the whole section along the west wall of the platform (Wilson's Arch etc) and replaces it with the Mamluk and later buildings that occupy this area today. These buildings can also be moved to reveal the Herodian Western Wall of the platform, the bedrock and the Hasmonean cistern along which the tour passes later.

From this hall a series of steps lead down to a **section of the Herodian Western Wall (D)**. The 'mastercourse' can be examined here, including one huge monster stone (c. 13.6 metres by 3.5 metres by 3.5

Jerusalem

Not to scale   Men's Prayer Area

A Vaulted Passage
B Masonic Hall
C Cruciform Chamber
D Section of Herodian wall
E 'Warren's Gate'
F Holy of Holies (?)
G Cistern
H Western Wall Tunnel
I Bedrock
J Hasmonean Cistern
K Guardrail
L Herodian columns & paving stones
M Herodian Period Quarry
N Hasmonean Aqueduct
O Struthion pool

metres) said to weigh 570 metric tons! Though quarried locally it's not sure how it was moved into position.

Continuing north alongside the Western Wall, at a point a little over 40 metres north of Wilson's Arch is **Warren's Gate (E)**. Though little remains of Warren's Gate, it is thought that it was originally similar in size and design to Barclay's Gate (see page 106). The interior of the gate was discovered by Charles Warren in 1867 whilst exploring a cistern on the Temple Mount esplanade. The cistern was in fact originally an underground staircase leading from street level outside the platform, up to the esplanade, and there is reason to suppose that it served the Jewish population as a synagogue during the Early Arab period (638-1099 CE). Its location was chosen due to its presumed proximity to the site of the **Holy of Holies** (which is generally thought to have stood on the west side of the Temple Mount and explains why Jews pray at the west, as opposed to the other walls). In fact, at a point just to the north of Warren's Gate is a section of the wall that is continually wet (**F**). Jewish tradition suggests that the wall is crying over the destruction of the Temple, and many religious Jews stop to kiss the wall and lick the 'holy water'. It may be that the antiquated plumbing of the Arab houses above may provide a more likely, though less uplifting, explanation! A little further to the north of here is another Mamluk period **cistern (G)** that utilizes the space created by the substructure supporting the buildings above.

As the tour continues north, the so-called **Western Wall Tunnel (H)** exposes the entire length of Herod's magnificent Western Wall of the Temple Mount platform. At a point nearing the northwest angle, the retaining wall moves out by some two metres as the **bedrock (I)** is exposed. Part of an open **Hasmonean cistern (J)** can be seen, protected by a large stone serving as a **guard-rail (K)**. Beyond this a number of **Herodian columns and paving stones (L)** that belong to the Herodian street that ran along the outside of the western retaining wall remain *in situ*. It is also possible to see a section of a **quarry (M)** from which stone for the retaining wall was cut.

Until September 1996 the tour stopped here. However, following the excavation of the **Hasmonean aqueduct (N)**, it is now possible to continue further north. Though certainly used by the Hasmoneans to channel water to the Temple from a source in the vicinity of where Damascus Gate now stands, the aqueduct may be older (though links with Solomon are highly unlikely). It was certainly last used by the Hasmoneans since Herod's construction of the Antonia fortress (c. 37-35 BCE) cut off its source of supply. The tunnel now terminates at the **Struthion Pool (O)**; a rock-cut storage pool of the second-first century BCE. The pool appears to have taken its present form in the second century CE during Hadrian's construction of Aelia Capitolina. The pool is split by a dividing wall, the rest of it falling within the property of the Sisters of Sion to the north (see page 124). The Roman blocked steps to the west lead up to a grocery store in the Muslim Quarter, whilst the new exit (to the right) emerges onto the Via Dolorosa in the Muslim Quarter beneath the steps that lead to the Umariyya Boys' School (see page 123). ■ *Advance bookings **must** be made with the Western Wall Heritage Foundation (T6271333, F6264828, though it can take days for someone to answer the phone). Twenty minutes before your tour is due to begin (1400 in English) go to the small police station on the Western Wall Plaza, check that your name is on the manifest (if you're lucky), pay 18 NIS and collect a ticket. It may also be advisable to bring your passport. The entrance to the tunnels is marked by the 'Western Wall Heritage' sign. Yarmulks (provided) or some form of head-covering must be worn. Modest dress is essential. No smoking. The first section is wheelchair accessible, though some prior arrangements should be made. The tour emerges in the*

Muslim Quarter; the tour guide will escort those who feel that they need this ser-
vice back to the Western Wall Plaza. Sunday Tuesday Wednesday 0830-1500,
Monday Thursday 1230-1500, Friday 0830-1200, though these hours appear to
be rather flexible.

Excavations to the south and southwest of the Temple Mount/Haram al-Sharif
enclosure have revealed remains from several key periods in the city's history.
The whole area, variously referred to as the Jerusalem Archaeological Park or
Ophel Archaeological Park, has recently been remodelled, with elevated walkways, explanatory signs, and a marked walking route making it more tourist
friendly.

Ophel
Archaeological
Park

Tour From the entrance to the park head to the southwest angle of the Temple Mount/Haram al-Sharif platform. About 12 metres north of this corner,
look up towards the small section of Herodian masonry jutting out from the
face of the wall. These are the springers and lower *voussoirs* (wedge-shaped
stone blocks that form an arch) of the so-called **Robinson's Arch (a)** (named
after the American who discovered them in 1835). When first excavated it was
presumed to be part of another causeway over the Tyropoeon Valley to the
Upper City, similar in plan and function to 'Wilson's Arch' (see page 107).
However, the discovery of the **base of a pier (b)** to the west, and a careful study
of Josephus (*Antiquities XV, 410-11*), now suggests strongly that the arch supported a series of monumental staircases that actually led south to the Lower
City (see drawing on page 100). In the piers that supported Robinson's Arch
four Herodian shops were discovered, opening on to the Herodian street that
ran beneath the arch. A little further to the north sections of the **Herodian**
street (c) can be seen. Also to be seen here is an Umayyad period **courtyard**
(d) that stands over a former pool from a Byzantine house. Unfortunately, the
build-up of accumulated architectural rubbish over the centuries only serves
to confuse the picture, and mask what are arguably the most interesting features found here (ie those dating to the Herodian period). As some indication
of the quantity of debris that built up here, Robinson's Arch, originally 17.5
metres above the level of the Herodian street, was virtually at ground level in
1968.

   Much of the Ophel Archaeological Park is covered by the remains of an
eighth century CE **Umayyad palace (e)** (85 metres by 95 metres), made more
interesting by the fact that it does not appear to be mentioned in any written
source. The plan of the palace featured a central open court, probably partly
paved and partly planted with trees, whilst covered porticoes ran around the
outside of the court. It is generally agreed that a building with an identical plan,
though smaller, stood directly to the west of the Umayyad palace, possibly
serving as an **Umayyad hospice (f)**. It appears that these buildings were badly
damaged in the Abbasid period, the masonry being reused for construction
elsewhere in the city, though it is not entirely certain whether they were ever
actually completed in the first place.

   In fact, the reuse of masonry and remains from previous eras is a continuous theme in Jerusalem's building history, and this zone is no exception. This
'Ophel' area is presumed to be the site of Solomon's extension of David's city
on the Southeast ridge, though by the first century CE it was a monumental
road and paved plaza that effectively connected the Temple to the Lower City.
Following the Roman destruction of the Temple, the masonry remains were
heavily quarried and used elsewhere in the city, as well as in subsequent
Byzantine constructions here. The whole area was redeveloped by the
Umayyads, partially using Herodian masonry that had found its way into

Jerusalem

Byzantine buildings. Though this area was little used after the Umayyad period, the continued reuse of masonry and architectural fragments has hardly helped archaeologists in recreating the area's past.

To the east of the Umayyad palace, built against the south side of the al-Aqsa Mosque, is what appears to be a **medieval tower (g)**. Possibly built in the 12th century by the Crusaders, it may have been refurbished by Salah al-Din (c. 1191) before finding its present form under the Mamluks (15th century). A flight of modern steps provide a better view, and some perspective, of the excavations in the Ophel Archaeological Park. Further steps descend to the remains of a Byzantine house (**h**), part of whose mosaic floor has been preserved.

Passing through the **'excavation gate' (i)** in the wall, another area of archaeological interest is revealed. Inside the gate to the left (north) is a section of restored pavement and steps belonging to the **Herodian plaza (j)**. The retaining wall of the Temple Mount/Haram al-Sharif platform can be examined in some detail here. A continuous section of the Herodian 'master-course' can be traced all the way to the southeast corner of the platform. Of particular note in this south wall of the Temple Mount/Haram al-Sharif platform are the three gates. About two-thirds of the **Double Gate (k)** is obscured by the medieval tower (**g**), though a section of its eastern part can still be seen. This is certainly the western *Huldah Gate* (*Arabic*: Abwab al-Akhmas) of Herod's Temple, one of the main entrances from the Lower City, though much of the work that you see today is Umayyad. The interior of this gate can be seen within the al-Aqsa Mosque (see page 114). In the third course above the arch's cornice is a reused statue base (upside-down) that mentions the second century CE Roman emperor Hadrian, or possibly his adopted son Antoninus. The **Triple Gate (l)** marks the position of Herod's original eastern *Hulda Gate*, and part of the western door jamb can still be seen, though again this gate largely dates to the Umayyad period. Further east is the **Single Gate (m)**, a postern gate cut by the Crusaders but blocked by Salah al-Din since 1187. It leads to one of the chambers within 'Solomon's Stables' (see page 116). The southeast angle of the Temple Mount/Haram al-Sharif platform, perhaps originally 41 courses of Herodian masonry high (26 above ground, 15 below), is traditionally linked with the *Pinnacle of the Temple* (*Matthew 4:5; Luke 4:9*).

Immediately to the south of the wall between the Double and Triple Gates are a number of Herodian or Roman period **mikvehs (n)**, or Jewish ritual baths. The large building to the southeast of the Triple Gate has proved difficult to identify. Without doubt it is a **Byzantine building (o)**, though the evidence that suggests it was a palace built for Eudocia in the fifth century CE, and later used as the monastery described by Theodosius in 530 CE, remains a source of contention. Whatever its function, a number of vessels that obviously belonged to a Byzantine church, including a bronze cross and door knocker, were discovered here.

Other remains that can be seen in this section of the Ophel Archaeological Park include sections of a large, possibly unfinished, **Umayyad building (p)** built over seventh-sixth century BCE remains; a **tower, gate and storerooms (q)** dating to the seventh-sixth centuries BCE; a **Herodian building (r)** doubtfully linked with Queen Helena of Adiabene (see page 187); further **Byzantine houses (s)** and sections of the **Byzantine city wall (t)**.

■ *T6254403. Sunday-Thursday 0900-1700, Friday 0900-1500. Adult 12 NIS, student 8 NIS, the less scrupulous can climb over the low wall for free at the southeast corner of the Temple Mount. Guided tours in English at 0900, Hebrew at 1200 1500, 25 NIS, T050-512113 or T5602621 for details.*

Dome of the Rock

The Haram al-Sharif, like most views of Jerusalem, is dominated by the graceful lines of the **Dome of the Rock** (*Arabic*: Qubbat al-Sakhra). Though the building's dimensions rest upon a mathematical precision that is related to the piece of rock that it encloses, the overall effect is not one of geometric sterility, but instead what Murphy-O'Connor describes as "mathematical rhythm" (*The Holy Land*, 1992). If it does, as some believe, stand at the centre of the world, then it is a fitting monument. Not only is it the first great building of Islam, it is an architectural masterpiece in its own right.

It was built between 688-692 CE by the fifth Umayyad caliph, **'Abd al-Malik**, following the Arab capture of Jerusalem (638 CE). Though Muslims emphasize that the Dome of the Rock was built to commemorate the prophet Mohammad's night ascent to heaven (*Sura XVII*), there are several less-divinely inspired considerations that must have been in 'Abd al-Malik's mind. In fact during the succeeding (and rival) Abbasid caliphate, attempts were made to discredit the Umayyad caliph 'Abd al-Malik by suggesting that he built the Dome of the Rock in order to lure the lucrative pilgrim trade away from the Ka'ba at Mecca. There is an element of truth in this, though it is generally believed that 'Abd al-Malik was seeking to consolidate a rival political, as opposed to religious, centre in the Jerusalem-Damascus region. However, there are fairly strong grounds to believe that 'Abd al-Malik was seeking to build a striking monument that would reaffirm Islam as the successor to its imperfect predecessors: Judaism and Christianity. As Murphy-O'Connor succinctly puts it, "His building spoke to Jews by its location, to Christians by its interior decoration" (*ibid*).

This point is underlined by the founding inscription around the ambulatories inside the building, quoting a verse from the Qur'an: "O you People of the Book, overstep not bounds in your religion, and of God speak only the truth. The Messiah, Jesus, son of Mary, is only a Messenger of God, and his Word, which he conveyed into Mary, and a Spirit proceeding from him. Believe therefore in God, and his prophets, and say not three. It will be better for you. God is only one God. Far be it from his glory that he should have a son" (*Sura IV, verse 169*). The emphasis on this rejection of the Christian Trinity is aimed at the Byzantine church that had been established for almost four centuries in Jerusalem. The magnificence of the Dome of the Rock was certainly a conscious effort to 'out do' the Christian religious buildings long since established in the city, though it may have been aimed as much at wavering Muslims as towards Christians.

Dome of the Rock

0 metres 10

1 Wooden Screen
2 Reliquary
3 Footprint of the Prophet
4 Steps down to 'Well of Souls'

Tour The architects of the Dome of the Rock are unknown, though the architectural style is a successful synthesis of a number of influences, reflecting the spread of Islam and the consequent use of craftsmen and traditions from these conquered lands. Though numerous repairs have been carried out over the centuries, the basic form remains largely unchanged.

The base is an **octagon** (c. 53.75 metres in diameter) built of local limestone courses. The walls are faced with marble panels, though the original seventh century CE glass mosaic coverings have been replaced this century using polychrome glazed tiles made in Kütahya, Turkey. The predominant colour is a beautiful turquoise-blue, with white, green, black and yellow tiles adding to the overall effect. The stylized floral motifs closely resemble the original patterns, though the colours are far more vivid. Of particular note is the band of blue and white tiles that extends all the way round the octagon, feature verses from the Qur'an (*Sura XXXVI*). Each face of the octagon features five grilled windows, allowing light to penetrate inside.

Above the parapet (at 12.1 metres), the roof of the interior ambulatories slopes up to the **drum** that supports the dome. The drum features sixteen tiled windows, above which a band of blue and white tails features the Qur'anic story of Mohammed's Night Journey (*Sura XVII*). The original dome collapsed in 1016 and was rebuilt in 1022, though many repairs have been made since. The original lead casing proved to be too heavy, leading to instability, and was replaced in 1961 with the brilliant gold-coloured anodized aluminium that you see today. When the Crusaders occupied the Temple Mount/Haram al-Sharif following their capture of Jerusalem in 1099, the Dome of the Rock became the *Templum Domini* (Temple of Our Lord), and a tall cross stood at the pinnacle of the dome. It was replaced with a crescent by Salah al-Din in 1187.

The Dome of the Rock is entered through the west door (remove shoes and leave bags and cameras outside). The interior is divided by eight piers and sixteen columns into an **outer ambulatory** and an inner **octagonal arcade** (inner ambulatory or inner octagon). Such ambulatories are a common feature of Muslim shrines and places of pilgrimage, and emphasize that this is not a congregational mosque (it is sometimes erroneously referred to as the 'Mosque of Omar'). The seventh-century glass mosaic coverings, unlike those on the exterior, are largely preserved on the interior of the octagonal base and bear closer examination. The columns supporting the inner octagon are not regular in size and are thought to have been reused from Roman and Byzantine ruins. A single line of Kufic script, the 'founder's inscription', runs along the top of both sides of the inner octagon (a distance of some 240 metres). It originally featured 'Adb al-Malik's name, the founding date (AH 72, or 691 CE), and Sura IV, verse 169 (see above), though the later Abbasid caliph al-Ma'mun (813-830 CE) inserted his name instead but without altering the founding date. The **ceiling** of the outer ambulatory dates to the 14th century (with later restoration), and is of very fine work. The **ceiling** of the inner ambulatory is comparatively modern (18th century) and is less impressive. The interior of the drum (c. 20.44 metres diameter) is lavishly decorated, with al-Zahir (c. 1027), Salah al-Din (c. 1198) and al-Nasir Mohammad (1318) all leaving their mark. As mentioned earlier, the **dome** is much restored, though the interior decoration remains striking.

At the centre of the inner octagon is the **Holy Rock**. The rock is associated with Abraham's sacrificial offering (*Genesis 22:2-19*), and the place where David built an altar to God (*II Samuel 24:18-25*), and thus is generally believed to be the site of the Holy of Holies in the Solomonic Temple where the Ark of the Covenant stood. Muslims believe that Mohammad began his Night Ascent from this rock, and his supposed footprint in the rock is pointed out to visitors. Tradition relates how the rock attempted to follow Mohammad on his journey, and thus the handprint next to the footprint is where the angel Gabriel held down the rock. During the Crusader period the footprint was venerated as that of Christ, with the result that visiting pilgrims chipped away parts of the rock to keep as souvenirs or sell as relics. By the late 12th century the rock had to be paved with marble, and a beautiful wrought-iron screen built around it to keep the souvenir-hunters away. The 12th-century French-made screen can be seen in the Islamic Museum here. The present intricately carved **wooden screen** was presented by the Ayyubid sultan al-'Aziz 'Imad al-Din in 1199. At the southwest corner of the rock is a tall gilded **reliquary** that houses a number of relics, including a hair from the prophet Mohammad's head. Nearby is the place where the **footprint** is located.

At the southeast angle of the rock a Crusader period marble entrance gives way to a **cave** beneath the rock. Muslim tradition holds that the rock overlies the centre of the world, lying above a bottomless pit whilst the waters of Paradise flow beneath the cave. The spirits of the dead can supposedly be heard here awaiting Judgement Day, and hence the popular name of the **Well of Souls** (*Arabic*: Bir al-Arwah). Similar themes can be found within the Jewish Talmud.

Immediately to the east of the Dome of the Rock is a small dome supported by 17 columns (all of which can be seen from any point). Referred to as the **Dome of the Chain** (*Arabic*: Qubbat al-Silsila), the function of this structure is still a matter of scholarly debate. Built in 691-692 CE by 'Adb al-Malik, it has been suggested that this was the architect's model for the Dome of the Rock, though this is unlikely. Much has been made of the fact that it, and not the Dome of the Rock, stands at the centre of the Temple Mount/Haram al-Sharif platform, and it has been speculated that it stood above the Solomonic (and then Herodian) sacrificial altar. Its position on the platform has also been used to suggest that it marks the *omphalos*, or navel of the world. In all likelihood it was built to house the treasury of the Haram al-Sharif, though the traditions surrounding it may have created a sense of sacredness that may have acted as a deterrence to would-be thieves. The popular name derives from the tradition that a chain once stretched across the entrance, hung there by either David, Solomon, or God. Those who swore falsely whilst holding the chain were either struck by lightening, or a link would fall, thus giving judgement on them as a liar. Such a supernatural tradition may also have been invented in order to act as a further security measure.

Dome of the Chain

The Dome of the Rock stands on a **platform** that is raised between 2.5 and 6 metres above the level of the rest of the esplanade. Eight **staircases** ascend the platform from the esplanade; two to the north, one to the east, two to the south, and three to the west. At the top of each staircase is a *qanatir*, a series of arches or arcade. They are popularly referred to by Muslims by the Arabic word *mawazin*, meaning 'scales'; a reference that derives from the tradition that on the Day of Judgement, scales will be hung from them to weigh the souls of the dead. The oldest is the west qanatir, dating to 951-52 CE, with the rest dating to the 10th, 14th and 15th centuries (with later refurbishments). Also of interest on the dome platform itself is the **Qubbat al-Mi'raj**, or Dome of the Ascension of the Prophet. Murphy-O'Connor proposes that the "mere existence of this structure shows that the original purpose of the Dome of the Rock was not to commemorate the Ascension of Mohammad" (*ibid*), though this argument can be challenged on two counts. Firstly, as Prag points out (*Blue Guide, 1989*), this commemorates not the spot from which Mohammad ascended, but rather where he prayed prior to his Ascension. Secondly, the identification of the Temple Mount/Haram al-Sharif with *al-Masjid al-Aqsa al-Mubarak*, "the furthermost Blessed Mosque" where Mohammad made his Night Ascent is very old, with the pilgrim Arculf describing a rudimentary mosque here by 680 CE, and the Dome of the Rock being constructed a little over 10 years later. The Qubbat al-Mi'raj, by contrast, dates to 1200-01, and thus any tradition

Platform of the Dome of the Rock

Jerusalem

Plots against the Haram al-Sharif

The Temple Mount/Haram al-Sharif is more than just a symbol of nationalism between the Israelis and the Palestinians, whilst those playing a part in trying to alter the present status quo are not necessarily Jewish or Muslim. In August 1969, a 29-year-old Australian by the name of Denis Michael Rohan set fire to al-Aqsa Mosque, and then proceeded to take photos of his handiwork. By the time Rohan was apprehended the mosque had been badly damaged and the 12th century CE minbar presented by Salah al-Din completely destroyed. He was to claim later that the "abominations" on the Temple Mount were delaying the rebuilding of the Temple, and thus putting the Second Coming on ice. Rohan's aim was to see the Jewish Temple rebuilt "for sweet Jesus to return and pray in". In an oft-quoted aside, then Prime Minister Golda Meir's comment to her cabinet colleagues that "we must condemn this outrage" was met by Menachem Begin's "yes of course, but not too much".

Yet the Rohan incident is not an isolated case. A series of attempts were made through the 1980s and 90s by radical Jewish groups to penetrate the Haram al-Sharif, and destroy the Muslim monuments there. However, more and more of these extremist groups are actually being bankrolled by Christian fundamentalists: "Fundamentalist Evangelicals, who interpret the Bible literally, believe the Jews' return to Israel and the restoration of the Temple will precede the Second Coming of Christ – at which point the Jews will be forcibly converted. Zionist fundamentalists … accept the Christians' patronage because they are convinced the Messiah will be a Jew. The alliance between Jewish and Christian fundamentalists is perhaps the ultimate marriage of convenience, with the two groups united to bring on the Messiah, and each side convinced the Messiah will be its own" (Friedman, Zealots for Zion, 1992).

Of course the danger of such groups is that they do not fear the consequences. They know full well that the success of any attack on the Muslim holy places on the Haram al-Sharif would trigger a bloodbath – perhaps the Armageddon for which they are waiting.

---

surrounding it is far later. Also of note on the dome platform is the **Minbar of Burhan al-Din**, next to the south qanatir; a 14th-century pulpit (restored in 1843) which is associated with praying for rain.

Al-Aqsa Mosque   Whilst the Dome of the Rock is a shrine and place of pilgrimage, **al-Aqsa Mosque** serves as Jerusalem's Jama'i Masjid, or main Friday congregational mosque. Though not an unattractive building, it loses out in inevitable comparison with the Dome of the Rock, (this is by no means something to be ashamed of), though the two do rather complement one another. However, its architectural history is far more complex than that of its near neighbour, and as a result of its numerous restorations it original form is far more difficult to discern.

The Aqsa Mosque has rather been a victim of its position at the southern end of the Temple Mount/Haram al-Sharif platform. Whilst the northern and central areas of the platform (including the spot where the Dome of the Rock stands) are presumed to stand largely on solid bedrock, the topography of the site upon which the Jewish Temple was located meant that the southern area had to be raised by the construction of a series of vaults. These vulnerable hollow spaces have largely contributed to the mosque's destruction during the numerous earthquakes that have struck Jerusalem.

The date of the first mosque built on the former Temple Mount platform is uncertain. It is not entirely clear whether the caliph **Omar** built a mosque here following the Arab capture of the city in 638 CE, though the Christian pilgrim Arculf describes a rudimentary mosque standing in the ruins of Herod's Royal Stoa (portico) in 680 CE. A mosque certainly was standing here by 715 CE, presumably built by the Umayyad caliph **al-Walid I**, though possibly by one of his predecessors. This mosque may well have formed the basis of the plan of the mosque seen today. By c. 775 CE the mosque had been enlarged to a fifteen-aisled basilica-like structure, though whether the work was carried out by the Umayyads or the Abbasid caliph **al-Mahdi** (775-785 CE) is also uncertain (though the general consensus is that the work was Umayyad). The main entrance to the mosque was via the Double Gate and the passage beneath the mosque (see Ophel Archaeological Park, page 109). The steps down can be seen outside the main entrance to the mosque, though they are not open to the public. Two major earthquakes in 747/48 CE and 774 CE caused extensive damage, though every set-back saw repairs swiftly made. By the ninth century the mosque probably had seven aisles on either side of a central nave, a central door in the north wall, with a marble portico along the north façade, and a large lead-sheathed dome.

The earthquake of 1033 devastated the mosque, with the relative impoverishment of the city at this time meaning that al-Aqsa was restored as a more modest five-aisled building. Crusader rule in Jerusalem saw the mosque used first as a palace of the king, then as a headquarters of the **Order of the Knights Templar**. They made a number of structural alterations, including the construction of the Templar Hall to the west (now occupied by the Women's Mosque and Islamic Museum). In 1187 **Salah al-Din** restored the building to its original purpose, making a number of changes including endowing the mosque with a beautiful **minbar** (pulpit) of carved, inlaid and gilded cedar wood. In 1969, a mad Australian (what other type is there?) started a fire in the al-Aqsa and the pulpit was destroyed (see box on page 114).

Numerous restorations have taken place since Salah al-Din's time, and many of the features that you see inside the mosque today date to the 20th century. However, there do appear to be small fragments from almost every phase of the mosque's troubled history.

The Islamic Museum in the southwest angle of the Haram al-Sharif was established in 1927 within a number of Crusader- and Ayyubid-period buildings. It features items found on the Haram al-Sharif, including important architectural fragments removed from the various structures here during restoration work. Though some of the items are remarkable, the presentation is less than dynamic and labelling and explanation is inadequate. In recent years the museum has become highly politicized, with visitors greeted on arrival by the blood-soaked garments of victims who have been 'martyred' in the Palestinian struggle against the Israelis. The most notable architectural exhibits include the copper-plated **great doors of the Dome of the Rock**, presented by Sultan Qa'it Bay in 1467-68, and the superbly carved cypress **roof beams** that were used in the eighth-century Umayyad al-Aqsa Mosque.

Islamic Museum

There are a number of other points of interest on the Haram al-Sharif, though not all are accessible to tourists. One of the more interesting features that cannot be examined close up, though can be observed from either the Haram al-Sharif or the Mount of Olives to the east, is the **Golden Gate** (*Arabic*: Bab al-Dhahabi). There is a Jewish tradition linking it with the purification ritual of the red heifer (*Numbers 19:1-10*), though the date of this gate is unknown. There are links with Eudocia (mid-fifth century CE) and the triumphant entry into Jerusalem by the Emperor Heraclius (631 CE), though there are

Other features on the Haram al-Sharif

architectural features that are distinctly Umayyad. It is very similar in style to the Double Gate in the south wall, which is generally believed to be Herodian with Umayyad (amongst others) modifications. Its north entrance is often referred to as the **Gate of Mercy** (*Arabic*: Bab al-Rahma), and the south entrance the **Gate of Repentance** (*Arabic*: Bab al-Tawba). The gate, blocked in the eighth century CE, is the source of a number of traditions. It is variously believed that the just will enter through this gate on the Day of Judgement – hence its popularity as a burial site. A Muslim tradition seems to suggest that a Christian conqueror will enter through this gate; perhaps a byproduct of the tradition that Jesus entered this gate on Palm Sunday, and will appear here at the Second Coming. The theory has also been proposed that the purpose of the Muslim cemetery is to deter any Jewish or Christian messiah!

Just to the north of the Golden Gate is **'Solomon's Throne'** (*Arabic*: Kursi Sulaiman), a small rectangular structure with twin shallow domes. A Muslim tradition holds that when Solomon died, his body was propped up here so as to conceal his death from the demons, and thus avoid fulfilling the prophesy that said that the Temple would be destroyed following his death. The structure probably dates to the 16th century CE, with the fact that it may have been built by Sulaiman II ('the Magnificent') perpetuating the tradition.

Another feature that is also off-limits to non-Muslims is the so-called **Solomon's Stables** complex in the southeast angle of the Haram al-Sharif. These are in fact part of the subterranean vaulting system that Herod the Great built to support his Temple Mount, and have no connection whatsoever with Solomon. Much of the upper parts and arches were actually built by the Crusaders (who introduced the Solomonic link) when they used the vaulted chambers as a stables for their war-horses. In late 1996 the halls were opened as a prayer chamber capable of accommodating 10,000 people, with the 'Solomon's Stables' name being dropped in favour of the **Marwani Mosque** title.

Over 200 architectural units have been recorded on the Haram al-Sharif. Amongst the minor features that can be inspected close, the most interesting include the following three. The **Sabil Qa'it Bay**, to the west of the Dome of the Rock, is an attractive structure built in the late 15th century CE, but largely restored in 1883. Though it is built in the style of a funerary monument, it is in fact a public fountain drawing water from what may well be a Herodian cistern below. This is possibly the same cistern that is described in relation to the 'cave' synagogue close to Warren's Gate (see 'Western Wall Tunnels' tour, page 106). The isolated structure to the north of the Dome of the Rock is the **Qubbat Sulaiman**, possibly an Ayyubid-modified Crusader building (c. 1200 CE) that tradition links with the spot at which Solomon prayed after completing the Temple. Also of note between al-Aqsa Mosque and the Dome of the Rock is **al-Kas**, the main fountain at which Muslims perform their ritual ablutions before praying at al-Aqsa.

Via Dolorosa and the Stations of the Cross

The Via Dolorosa, or 'Way of Sorrows', is the traditional route along which Jesus carried his cross on his way from his Condemnation to his Crucifixion. It remains a major draw for Christian pilgrims, many of whom carry crosses and prostrate themselves at the various 'Stations'. Because of the confused, sometimes amusing, process by which the modern route came into being, it is easy to mock the hordes of pilgrims who continue to walk the route. Even those who haven't seen Monty

Python's Life of Brian will raise a smile on seeing the numerous souvenir shops along the route where you can buy your very own crown of thorns (haggling essential). Yet the Via Dolorosa remains a triumph of faith over fact, and if you go with the philosophy that "these are probably not the places where the actual incidents happened, but that is not important: what is important is that the incidents did happen, and that is what we are here to commemorate", then the experience can be a means of renewing a relationship with God.

The first seven Stations of the Cross fall within the Muslim Quarter of the Old City, and **Ins and outs** full details of the various sites are described within the description of this quarter beginning on page 119 below (and see the map on page 86). The VIIIth and IXth Stations are on the 'border' between the Christian Quarter and the Muslim Quarter, with full details of these stations found in the description of the latter beginning on page 119. The final five Stations are all found within the Church of the Holy Sepulchre (see page 135). You can walk the entire route in as little as 30 minutes, though most prefer to spend more time (human traffic jams can also make this walk considerably longer).

The origins of recreating Jesus' steps as part of an act of pious remembrance **History** are very old indeed, with Egeria describing such a procession (from the Eleona Church on the top of the Mount of Olives, via the place of Jesus' arrest at Gethsemane on the evening of Maundy Thursday, arriving at Calvary on the morning of Good Friday) as far back as 384 CE. Though the latter section of the route was largely the one followed today, there were no devotional stops at various 'Stations' marking specific incidents on Christ's journey. Within a couple of centuries such devotional stops had been introduced, though the route itself had substantially changed. From Gethsemane the route passed around the outside of the city walls to the south, to the reputed House of the High Priest Caiaphas on Mount Zion, and then on to the site where eighth-century pilgrims placed the Praetorium of Pilate (marked by the Church of St Sophia somewhere near the Temple Mount, though this site has yet to be positively identified). Pilgrims then continued to the Holy Sepulchre.

However, it was the medieval pilgrims who took up this devotional walk with relish. The various sects into which the Christian church had long since split each provided their own version of the Via Dolorosa, the route of which generally reflected where in Jerusalem their churches were located. Yet it was not just in Jerusalem, or indeed the Holy Land, that the Via Dolorosa was created; by the 15th century cities all across Europe had their own symbolic Via Dolorosas! This was later to become a source of some confusion for visiting pilgrims; they were used to 14 'Stations' or devotional stops and were surprised to find that the Jerusalem Via Dolorosa had just eight. The solution was simple: they added six more! The modern route was established in the 17th century, though some 'Stations' were not fixed at their present point until the 19th.

Whilst the authenticity of the site of the Crucifixion and Tomb of Christ at the Church of the Holy Sepulchre is strongly supported, retracing Jesus' route to Calvary depends entirely upon locating the Praetorium where he was condemned. The modern route is based upon the assumption that Pilate would have stayed at the Antonia fortress (page 123) when visiting the city from the Roman capital at Caesarea. However, most scholars now agree that Pilate would almost certainly have resided at the palace that Herod built just to the south of the present Citadel, on the opposite side of the city (see page 92). Gospel descriptions of the trial setting (*Matthew 27:19; Luke 23:4; John 18:28*) match other descriptions of the Herodian palace, such as those found in Josephus (*Jewish War II, 301*). Thus, a more likely route would involve Jesus heading east along what is now David Street, perhaps turning north towards

Jerusalem

Jerusalem

Calvary at the three parallel suqs at the current junction of David Street, the Cardo and Tariq Khan es-Zeit. In fact, it is a miracle that the trinket salesmen on David Street have not campaigned more rigorously to have this route introduced!

Tour The following is just a brief summary of the Via Dolorosa; fuller details can be found within the sections on the 'Muslim Quarter' and the 'Church of the Holy Sepulchre'. The route is marked by the dotted lines on the 'Old City: Sights' map on page 86.

Ist Station This commemorates the spot where Jesus was condemned to death by Pilate. The present tradition suggests that this took place at the Antonia fortress, a site now occupied by the 'Umariyya Boys School (page 123). Because access to this site is restricted, the **Chapel of the Condemnation** opposite serves as the first Station on most processions (page 123). The 'Eastern Orthodox' begin their procession at the **Greek Orthodox Prison of Christ** just to the west.

IInd Station The site where Jesus traditionally took up the cross, this event was previously commemorated in the street outside, though is now more commonly associated with the courtyard of the **Monastery of the Flagellation/Chapel of Condemnation** (page 123). The route then passes beneath what is known as the Ecce Homo Arch (page 125).

IIIrd Station Where Jesus fell for the first time, marked by a small carving outside the **Polish Catholic Chapel** at the junction of the Via Dolorosa and Tariq al-Wad (page 126).

IVth Station Where Jesus met his mother, commemorated by a carving of the event outside the **Armenian Catholic Patriarchate and Church of Our Lady of the Spasm** on Tariq al-Wad (page 126).

Vth Station Jesus falls again and Simon of Cyrene is compelled to carry the cross, the station is marked by a small 'V' at the junction of Tariq al-Wad and Tariq al-Saray (also known as the Via Dolorosa, see page 126).

VIth Station A Roman numeral VI on the door of the **Church of the Holy Face and St Veronica** commemorates the spot where Veronica wiped the face of Jesus with her handkerchief, the imprint of the face remaining on the cloth (p126). The present location is part of the 13th-century tradition.

VIIth Station At the top of the street, at the junction with Tariq Khan es-Zeit, a small VII above a doorway opposite marks the VIIth Station (page 127). This is sometimes commemorated as the spot where Jesus fell for a second time, though it also marks the **Porta Judicaria** where legend relates that the death decree was posted. This Station was seemingly introduced in the 13th century to prove to confused medieval pilgrims that the Holy Sepulchre site was indeed outside the city walls at the time of the Crucifixion. The door here is sometimes open, revealing an altar set next to a pillar from the Constantine Church of the Holy Sepulchre, as well as a small chapel.

VIIIth Station Located a little way up Aqabat al-Khanqah Street (see page 127) , this Station marks the traditional site where Jesus addressed the women of Jerusalem: "Daughters of Jerusalem, weep not for me", and is is marked by a VIII on the wall of the **Monastery of St Caralambos**. Now return to Tariq Khan es-Zeit and continue along it, ascending the steps to the right just beyond *Zalitimo's Sweets*. Follow the narrow street to the end.

Where Jesus fell for a third time, marked by a IX on the pillar at the entrance to the **Ethiopian Monastery** on the 'roof' of the Church of the Holy Sepulchre (page 135). From here there are a number of options. If open, you can descend via the Chapel of the Ethiopians to the 'Parvis' (courtyard outside the present entrance to the Church of the Holy Sepulchre). Alternatively, retrace your steps to Tariq Khan es-Zeit, take the first right onto Harat al-Dabbaghin, and this also leads to the Parvis. **IXth Station**

Located in the **Latin Chapel of the Nailing to the Cross** on Calvary (inside the Church of the Holy Sepulchre, page 141), the Xth and XIth Stations commemorate where Jesus was stripped of his robes and nailed to the cross. **Xth and XIth Stations**

The **Greek Chapel of the Exaltation or Raising of the Cross** marks where the cross was raised and Jesus died (inside the Church of the Holy Sepulchre, page 142). **XIIth Station**

The **Stabat Mater altar** between the two chapels is where Jesus' body was taken down from the cross and handed over to Mary (inside the Church of the Holy Sepulchre, page 142). **XIIIth Station**

The **Tomb of Christ** at the centre of the Rotunda is the final Station of the Cross (inside the Church of the Holy Sepulchre, p143). **XIVth Station**

Muslim Quarter of the Old City

The Muslim Quarter is both the largest quarter in the Old City (c. 28 hectares) and the most densely populated part of Israel (with population estimates varying between 14,000 and 20,000 residents). For many visitors it is also their first experience of a truly Middle Eastern city. Although there are a number of fine Islamic institutions (notably those dating to the Mamluk period), the majority of visitors are primarily interested in the Christian sites associated with the route of the Via Dolorosa.

Ins and outs

There are a number of ways to approach the Muslim Quarter, though most visitors arrive via the Christian Quarter (along David St from Jaffa Gate), or from Damascus Gate. Although many begin their tour of this quarter at the Chapel of the Condemnation on Via Dolorosa/Tariq Bab Sitti Maryam (because it's the Ist Station of the Cross), there are a number of points of interest towards St Stephen's Gate to the east. With most visitors following the route of the Via Dolorosa, the main dilemma comes when you reach the Vth Station of the Cross. The description below follows the most popular choice: it details the rest of the sites along the Via Dolorosa as far as the Church of the Holy Sepulchre (subsequently described in the 'Christian Quarter' on page 135), and then gives details of the various points of interest on Tariq al-Wad, Aqabat Tekieh, Tariq al-Khalidiyya and Tariq Bab al-Silsila (roughly the area to the west of the Temple Mount/Haram al-Sharif, see map on page 86). **Getting in and getting around**

Warning The Muslim Quarter is a conservative area and you should dress accordingly; you will probably be denied access to both Muslim and Christian sites if your dress is not deemed to be modest enough (no shorts/bare

Jerusalem

shoulders/revealing clothes on either sex). **NB** 'bab' = gate; 'tariq' = street; 'madrasa' = Islamic religious school; 'sabil' = fountain; 'ribat' = hospice; 'turba' = tomb; 'hamman' = bathhouse.

History

During the Umayyad period (seventh to eighth centuries CE), the division of the Old City into well defined 'quarters' was far less regimented (or political) than today, and there is considerable evidence to suggest that the main Muslim residential and commercial districts lay west and southwest of the Haram al-Sharif (the current Jewish Quarter!). Though there is evidence of continued Muslim activity in this northeast corner of the Old City, by the Fatimid period (10th to 12th centuries CE) this was in fact the Jewish Quarter. Following the arrival of the Crusaders through a breach in the medieval walls near Herod Gate in 1099, the present Muslim Quarter was occupied largely by Christian Crusaders, with several major churches constructed.

This northeast quarter of the Old City can be said to have become firmly Muslim in the 12th century CE, when the Ayyubid Caliphs (12th to 13th centuries CE), and then the Mamluks (13th to early 16th century CE) established large numbers of schools, mosques and foundations in the quarter. The Mamluks in particular developed the areas adjacent to the Haram al-Sharif, building many fine madrasses, tombs, and town houses, the exteriors of which can still be viewed today (since most are in private use, it is not generally possible to view the interiors).

The period of Ottoman rule in Jerusalem (1512-1917) saw the establishment of the Ottoman administration in the Muslim Quarter (including the governor's palace), as well as commercial interests (most notably in the caravanserais to the west of the Haram al-Sharif). It also saw the return of many of the Crusader-period buildings (particularly along the Via Dolorosa) to Christian use. The fact that this northeast quarter of the Old City has been the key 'Muslim Quarter' for the last 800 years or so explains why Palestinian Muslims find it so provocative when Jewish groups buy or lease property in the area, then move in to establish a 'Jewish presence'. However, the latter group argue that Jews continued to live in the 'Muslim Quarter' throughout this period, until being driven out by Arab mobs in 1936.

Sights

Around St Stephen's Gate — Immediately inside St Stephen's Gate, to the north, is the **Hamman Sitti Maryam**: a bathhouse named for the Virgin Mary and still in use until quite recently. The adjacent **Sabil Sitti Maryam** ('fountain of the Virgin Mary') was built by Sulaiman II in 1537. The doorway just beyond the fountain belongs to the **Greek Orthodox Church of St Anna** and displays a sign claiming it as the "birthplace of the Virgin Mary". For a small donation you will be led down a few steps inside the doorway to the right, and shown a small room with a mosaic floor that is claimed to be the spot in question.

Bethesda Pools — Entering this Greek Catholic complex (labelled 'Basilique Sainte Anne et Bassins de Bethesda'), you emerge into a rather attractive square court containing a number of fragments of masonry excavated in the immediate vicinity, set amongst flower beds that are carefully tended by the French White Fathers who occupy the seminary. The bust at the centre of the court is of Cardinal Lavigerie, founder of the order. Beyond this medieval cloister is the Greek Catholic Church of St Anne (details on page 121) and the Bethesda Pools.

The healing of the paralytic

"Now there is at Jerusalem by the sheep market a pool, which is called in the Hebrew tongue Bethesda, having five porches. In these lay a great multitude of sick folk, blind, lame, paralysed, waiting for the moving of the water. For an angel went down at a certain season into the pool, and troubled the water: whosoever then first after the troubling of the water stepped in was made whole of whatever disease he had.

"And a certain man there was, who had been crippled for 38 years. When Jesus saw him lie, and knew that he had been now a long time in that condition, he saith to him, 'Wilt thou be made whole?' The crippled man answered him, 'Sir, I have no man, when the water is troubled, to put me into the pool: while I am coming, another steppeth down before me.'*

"Jesus saith unto him, 'Rise, take up thy bed, and walk.' And immediately the man was made whole, and took up his bed, and walked." (John 5:2-9)

A pool here is thought to have been first cut around the eighth century BCE to channel rainwater to the First Temple, and may well be the **'upper pool'** referred to in the Bible (*II Kings 18:17*). The high priest Simon the Just is thought to have added the second pool c. 200 BCE. By the Early Roman period healing properties had been attributed to the pools, with additional baths and pools having been dug from the bedrock just to the east. The sick, blind, lame and paralysed gathered here awaiting the 'disturbing of the water', as recounted in John's gospel, and this was the scene of Jesus' miracle that so infuriated the Jewish elders since it was performed on the Sabbath (*John 5:1-12*, see box above).

Hadrian's paganizing of Jerusalem (into Aelia Capitolina) in 132-135 CE saw the construction of a small temple/shrine to Serapis (Aesculapius) featuring five colonnades, which Origen described following his visit c. 231 CE (though he mistakenly believed that he was describing the five 'porches' mentioned in the gospel account). By the mid-fifth century CE a small church on the site commemorated the miracle, whilst shortly afterwards the tradition developed linking this spot with the birthplace of the Virgin Mary (with a subsequent church taking her name). The early church was probably destroyed during the Persian invasion of 614 CE, though ninth century CE records record some form of church on the site.

The church seems to have survived the anti-Christian edicts of the Fatimid sultan al-Hakim in the early 11th century CE, and there appears to have been a church standing on the site when the Crusaders arrived in 1099 (though it may not have been serving a Christian purpose). A small chapel was erected on the site of the Byzantine church and a convent church for Benedictine nuns was also built. In fact, the Crusader king Baldwin I placed his repudiated Armenian wife Arda into the care of the Benedictine nuns here. The Crusader period saw the revival of the tradition concerning the birthplace of the Virgin Mary, and the house of her parents Anne and Joachim. In the early 12th century CE the Church of St Anne that you see today was constructed. Next to the niche, opposite the Church of St Anne, a number of steps lead down to the southeast corner of the rather deep southern pool.

Many commentators consider the Greek Catholic Church of St Anne to be the finest example of Crusader ecclesiastic architecture in the Old City, and despite the rather plain and austere interior it is easy to see why. In spite of an extension to the church that saw the façade shifted west by seven metres (you can clearly see the 'join'), the church retains the clean lines of classic

Greek Catholic Church of St Anne

Romanesque architecture. It is also renowned for its superb acoustics. There is a fine entrance portal, above which remains the inscription of Salah al-Din that records the conversion of the church into the Salahiyya Madrassa in 1192. Franciscans were granted permission to continue to hold Mass in the madrasa on the annual Feasts of the Immaculate Conception and the Nativity.

The present church was probably built sometime around 1140, though it is clear that the area around the Bethesda Pools has been venerated by Christians since the mid-fifth century at least. St Anne's is a basilica with three naves. From the south aisle a number of steps lead down into the crypt of the earlier Byzantine chapel that tradition holds was built over part of Joachim and Anne's home (the parents of the Virgin Mary). One of the small chambers holds an altar above which stands a statue of the Virgin Mary, whilst a second chamber contains an icon depicting the 'Nativity of the Virgin'.

By the mid-19th century, the property was all but abandoned, with some sources saying the Muslims believed it to be haunted. In 1856 the Ottoman Sultan 'Abd-al-Majid I offered the site to Napoleon III in recognition of French support for the empire during the Crimean war. The building had previously been offered to Queen Victoria for similar services rendered, though she chose to take Cyprus as a gift instead: much to the continued regret of the Anglican Church! ■ T6281992, F6280764. *Monday-Saturday 0800-1145 1400-1700, 1800 in summer, closed Sunday. Adult 5 NIS. Small souvenir shop and toilets.*

Mamluk-period buildings around Tariq Bab Sitti Maryam At the top of Tariq Bab Hitta (at its junction with Tariq Bab Sitti Maryam) is the **Ribat al-Maridini**, a mid-14th-century hospice built to house pilgrims from Mardin (now in southeast Turkey). Further down Tariq Bab Hitta on the same side of the street is the **al-Awhadiyya**, the supposed tomb of Salah al-Din's great-great-nephew al-Malik al-Awhad (d. 1298). The recessed arch entrance is guarded by two recessed re-used Crusader columns. The decorative cloister vault uses a design similar to the fleur-de-lis, but is often obscured by a painting of the Dome of the Rock. Opposite is the **al-Karimiyya**, a madrasa built in 1319 by a former Inspector of the Privy Purse in the Mamluk administration. A Copt converted to Islam, Karim was responsible for a number of religious endowments in Cairo and Damascus, though he was later disgraced and forced to leave office (supposedly for protecting Christians). The road finishes at the *Bab Hitta* (Muslims only).

Continuing west along Tariq Bab Sitti Maryam, the vault spanning the road belongs to the former **al-Mujahidin mosque**, built in 1274. As recently as the 1860s a square Syrian-style minaret was still standing, as depicted by C.W. Wilson in his *Picturesque Palestine* (1880). Only its base can now be seen. Attached to the north side of the mosque is the **Mu'azzamiyya madrasa**, established in 1217.

Just beyond the vaulted arch across the road, a vaulted street (Tariq Bab al-'Atm, sign-posted as 'King Faisal Street') leads left (south) towards the al-'Atm Gate to the Haram al-Sharif (*Bab al-'Atm*). At the top of the street on the left is the **al-Sallamiyya madrasa**, built by an Iraqi merchant c. 1338. It is noted for its attractive recessed entrance doorway with typically Mamluk style red and cream door jambs, and for the three grilled windows of the assembly hall (another architectural feature typical of the period). Further down the street on the same side is the **al-Dawadariyya Khanqah**. Built in 1295 by a Mamluk amir who served under six different sultans, this is amongst the finest Mamluk buildings in the quarter. Unfortunately, it is not open to visitors though the entrance can still be admired. The road finishes at the *Bab al-'Atm* (Muslims only).

Continuing west along Tariq Bab Sitti Maryam, it is possible to take a short diversion north along Aqabat Darwish Street (follow the signs for the *Black Horse Hostel*), though in reality there is very little to see at the three main sites on this diversion: **Church of St Mary Magdalene (Ma'muniyya School)**, **St Agnes Church (Mawlawiyya Mosque)** and **Greek Orthodox Church of St Nicodemus** (but the street itself is very attractive and is blissfully free of traffic).

The site upon which the Antonia fortress used to stand, (now occupied by the 'Umariyya Boys' School), has been of military significance since the time of Nehemiah at least (c. 445 BCE), and may have been the location of his 'tower of Hananeel' (*Nehemiah 3:1*). It is also likely that a stronghold existed on this site during the overlapping periods of Ptolemic (304-30 BCE), Hasmonean (152-37 BCE) and Seleucid (311-65 BCE) rule. In fact, great effort has been exerted by archaeologists attempting to locate the Seleucid fortress of Acra since this would greatly assist in reconstructing the plan of Hellenistic (pre-Hasmonean) Jerusalem. Though the debate is not settled, there is a considerable weight of opinion that supports the theory that Acra was a forerunner of the Antonia.

Antonia fortress

The Antonia fortress was built some time between 37 and 35 BCE by **Herod the Great** in order to protect, but perhaps also control, the Temple. It was named on behalf of his patron Mark Anthony and is described in some detail by Josephus: "[it] was built on a rock 75 feet high and precipitous on every side ... the interior was like a palace in spaciousness and completeness ... it was virtually a town, in its splendour a palace ... in general design it was a tower with four other towers attached, one at each corner; of these three were 75 feet high, and the one at the SE corner 105 feet ... the city was dominated by the Temple and the Temple by Antonia ... " (*Jewish War V: 237-245*). Captured by the rebels in 66 CE, the conquest of Antonia became a priority for Titus and was one of the principal foci of attack for the Roman Fifth and Twelve Legions. Josephus graphically describes the bitter two-month campaign that finally led to its capture on 24th July, 70 CE (*Jewish War V: 466; 523; VI: 5*). Titus ordered his soldiers to "lay Antonia flat" (*VI: 93*) to allow his troops easy access to the Temple, and now all that remains is a section of the four-metre-thick south wall.

Christian tradition identifies Antonia with the **Praetorium** (seat of Roman procurators in Jerusalem) where Pilate judged and sentenced Jesus (*Mark 15:1-15*), though archaeologists generally dispute this claim. However, the former site of the Antonia fortress marks the traditional **First Station of the Cross**.

NB The 'Umariyya Boys' School is not generally open to visitors, though you may be admitted if you speak to the caretaker outside of school hours. There is little to see that relates to its ancient history, though it does command a superb view of the Haram al-Sharif. The iron door in the alcove under the flight of steps leading up to the entrance is the controversial new exit to the 'Western Wall Tunnel' (see page 106).

Within this complex stands the Chapel of the Flagellation (to the right, east), the Chapel of the Condemnation (to the left, west) and the Monastery of the Flagellation (straight ahead, north). The latter is an eminent Franciscan school of biblical and archaeological studies and houses a small museum with a number of interesting finds.

Chapels of the Flagellation and Condemnation

It remains unclear as to when Christian tradition first placed events in Christ's Passion at this site, though Crusader churches commemorating the Flagellation and Condemnation certainly once stood here. During the Ottoman period it is reported that the buildings were being used as stables, and later as a private house, until the whole complex was given to the Franciscans by Ibrahim Pasha in the early 19th century.

The current **Chapel of the Flagellation** was built in 1927-29 to a design by

Jerusalem

the Italian architect Antonio Barluzzi. A simple single-aisled chapel, the gold dome above the altar features a representation of the crown of thorns (*Matthew 27:29; Mark 15:17*), plus images of Jesus being scourged at the pillar (*Mark 15:15; John 19:1*), Pilate washing his hands (*Matthew 27:24*), and the release and triumph of Barabbas (*Matthew 27:26; Mark 15:15; Luke 23:24-25*).

The **Chapel of the Condemnation** is an early 20th-century structure built upon the site of a medieval three-aisled chapel. The most interesting feature of the chapel is the section of pavement that continues under the wall into the property of the Sisters of Sion next door. This is part of the ***lithostrotos*** (Greek for 'pavement', *Gabbatha* in Aramaic, see *John 19:13*) upon which Pilate is said to have set up his judgement seat. For full details of the *lithostrotos*, see the 'Convent of the Sisters of Sion', below.

The Chapel of the Condemnation is the **First Station of the Cross** in the Franciscan's procession, whilst the **Second Station of the Cross** where Jesus took up the Cross is the courtyard outside. Every Friday at 1500 the Franciscans lead a procession carrying a heavy wooden cross from here along the route of the Via Dolorosa (see page 116). ■ *T6280271/6282936. April-September 0800-1145 1400-1800 daily, October-March 0800-1145 1300-1700 daily. Free.*

Convent of the Sisters of Sion The Convent of the Sisters of Sion (Ecce Homo Convent) contains several very interesting items connected to the tradition of this area as the site of the Passion of Christ. These include the Struthion pool, sections of the pavement (*lithostrotos*) laid over the pool that have an earlier connection with Christ's condemnation, and a lateral section of the 'Ecce Homo Arch' that passes over the Via Dolorosa outside.

Struthion pool The Struthion ('sparrow') pool is a rock-cut cistern that dates to the end of the second/beginning of the first century BCE. Originally an open pool measuring around 52 metres by 14 metres, it was fed by a channel from the region of what is now Damascus Gate, itself supplying the Temple via a Hasmonean aqueduct from its southwest corner. The construction of the

Convent of the Sisters of Sion

1 Sign reading 'Lithostrotos'
2 Entrance
3 Ticket Desk
4 Lecture areas
5 Steps
6 Struthion Pool (lower level)
7 Museum
8 Northern Gallery
9 Audio-Visual Presentation
10 'Lithostrotos' (upper level)
11 Eastern gallery
12 Prayer Chapel
13 Exit Staircase
14 Ecce Homo Arch
15 Viewpoint for Ecce Homo Arch
16 Basilica

N
Not to scale

Antonia fortress in 37-35 BCE cut the aqueduct to the Temple and led to a change in the plan of the pool. Mentions in Josephus suggest that the pool formed part of a reservoir cut into the moat to the north of the Antonia fortress, though this point is still debated. If so, it would suggest that the present position of the Convent of the Sisters of Sion (and the Chapel of the Condemnation) lie outside the former limits of the Antonia fortress, calling into question the authenticity of the Christian tradition of the modern Via Dolorosa route.

The pool was roofed over in the second century CE, with the outstanding barrel vaults that supported Hadrian's pavement above still clearly visible. It was discovered during the construction of the convent in the early 1860s, though until 1996 it was only possible to view a small section of the pool. The controversial decision to extend the 'Western Wall Tunnel' by excavating the former Hasmonean aqueduct means that it is now possible to view the whole pool: though you have to visit two different sites to do so! The northwest section of the Struthion pool is visible from here, whilst the southeast section (obscured behind a thick dividing wall) can be viewed by visiting the Western Wall Tunnel (page 106). When the Israeli authorities first decided to extend the Western Wall Tunnel, the original plan was for the new exit from the Hasmonean aqueduct to be into the Struthion pool. However, the Convent of the Sisters of Sion rejected this plan, and hence the new exit pops out beneath the steps of the 'Umariyya Boys' School (see page 123).

Lithostrotos   This impressive pavement of large smooth slabs is associated with the Christian tradition of Pilate's condemnation of Jesus: "When Pilate therefore heard that saying, he brought Jesus forth, and sat down in the judgement seat in a place that is called the Pavement, but in the Hebrew, Gabbatha" (*John 19:13*). The fact that incised gaming-boards of a dice game called 'King's Game' are carved into the *lithostrotos* recalls to Christians the scene of the Roman guards mockery of Jesus (*John 19:2-3*) and the casting of lots for his garments after his crucifixion (*John 19:23-24*). The flaw in this argument is the fact that this pavement was laid by the emperor Hadrian in 135 CE as part of the eastern forum for his city of Aelia Capitolina. However, some sources suggest that Hadrian's pavement may have used re-cut and re-laid Herodian flagstones, and thus there is still hope that Jesus may have walked on these stones. ▦ *T6277292, F6282224. Daily 0830-1230 1400-1700, closed Sunday. Adult 5 NIS. Enter through small door on Aqabat er-Rahbat sign-posted "lithostrotos".* **NB** *this place is an absolute nightmare when packed with several tour groups.*

The arch spanning the Via Dolorosa outside the Convent of the Sisters of Sion is popularly known as the 'Ecce Homo Arch'. Christian tradition has it that this is the spot at which Pilate presented Jesus in his crown of thorns and purple robe to the baying crowd, and declared "Behold the man!" (in Latin, *Ecce Homo*, see *John 19:5*). However, it is not claimed that this is the actual arch from which Pilate made his declaration. The arch that you see spanning the Via Dolorosa today is part of the central arch of a triple-arched gate that has generally been attributed to Hadrian's eastern forum, built for Aelia Capitolina in 135 CE. However, recent analysis of the building style and construction technique has led to a reappraisal and it is now attributed to Herod Agrippa I (41-44 CE). The northern lateral arch of what was probably Herod Agrippa I's east gate to the city can be seen within the Basilica of the Ecce Homo (property of the Convent of the Sisters of Sion). To see this section, pass under the Ecce Homo Arch on the Via Dolorosa and climb the steps on your right to the Basilica. A glass screen allows sightseers to view the northern lateral arch without disturbing proceedings within the Basilica.

Ecce Homo Arch

Jerusalem

Greek Orthodox Prison of Christ

Just to the west of the Ecce Homo Arch is the Greek Orthodox Prison of Christ, which serves as the **Ist Station of the Cross** in the Orthodox Church's Easter procession. Visitors are shown three 'cells' (one for Jesus, the other two for the criminals he was crucified with). ■ *Summer 0800-1200 1500-1800, closes one hour earlier in winter.*

Beit Sharon

Standing at the junction of the Via Dolorosa and Tariq al-Wad (one of the Muslim Quarter's main thoroughfares), if you look north (right) towards Damascus Gate you will see a two-metre-high menorah on the top of the house that bridges the street (with a huge Israeli flag hanging down). This is the Old City 'home' of veteran right-wing politician **Ariel Sharon**. It is generally assumed that the ownership of this apartment has more to do with a display of Israeli power than providing a place of residence; outrageous figures for the annual cost of 'protecting' this apartment are frequently banded about. From this junction Tariq al-Wad leads south to the Western Wall Plaza.

Polish Catholic Chapel (IIIrd Station of the Cross)

Just to the south of the junction of the Via Dolorosa and Tariq al-Wad is the **Polish Catholic Chapel** (so named because it was restored in 1948 with donations from Polish soldiers who had served in the Palestine campaigns of the Second World War). The tiny chapel outside, marked by two fallen pillars, commemorates the **IIIrd Station of the Cross** where Jesus fell for the first time. The scene is depicted in a small carving above the chapel.

IVth Station of the Cross

About 25 m south of the Polish Catholic Chapel is the **Armenian Catholic Patriarchate and Church of Our Lady of the Spasm**, marking the **IVth Station of the Cross** where Jesus met his mother. A small bas-relief of Mary touching Jesus' face recalls the scene.

Vth Station of the Cross

At the junction of Tariq al-Wad and the street variously known as Tariq al-Alam or Tariq al-Saray (though invariably referred to and sign-posted as the Via Dolorosa), a Roman numeral 'V' marks the modern site of the **Vth Station of the Cross** where Simon of Cyrene took up the cross. Before turning along here, if you look ahead down Tariq al-Wad, the house built over the road was referred to as the 'House of the Rich Man' in the 14th century. Next door, the 'House of the Poor Man' was the site of the 14th-century Vth station. **NB** The rest of this description of the Muslim Quarter first details the sites along the rest of the Via Dolorosa as far as the Church of the Holy Sepulchre, and then returns to the various points of interest on Tariq al-Wad, Aqabat Tekieh, Tariq al-Khalidiyya and Tariq Bab al-Silsila (roughly the area to the west of the Temple Mount/Haram al-Sharif; see map on page 86).

VIth Station of the Cross

Continuing up the slight incline on the Via Dolorosa, at the point where a vault stretches over the street the Roman numeral 'VI' on the left indicates the **VIth Station of the Cross**. Tradition claims this as the site of the home of St Veronica, who used her veil or handkerchief to wipe the face of Christ. A medieval tradition claims that an imprint of his face was left on the cloth, which has subsequently been involved in a number of miracles and is now the property of St Peter's in Rome (though the Greek Orthodox Patriarchate in the Christian Quarter also have one!). The identification of this site as the VIth Station is medieval. Bullfighting fans will know that a 'Veronica' is a pass made with the cape, so called because the cape is grasped in two hands in the manner in which St Veronica is shown in religious paintings as holding the veil/handkerchief with which she wiped the face of Christ. The **Church of the Holy Face and St Veronica**, just beyond the 'VI', is not generally open to visitors, which is a great pity since it is another example of Antonio Barluzzi's work (restoring the 19th-century chapel).

The point where the Via Dolorosa meets Tariq Khan es-Zeit is one of the most congested spots in the Old City, with a crush of Palestinian shoppers meeting hoards of bewildered and disorientated camera-wielding tourists walking the Via Dolorosa. Pedestrian chaos at this busy crossroads is further exacerbated by the fact that the junction marks the **VIIth Station of the Cross** (marked by a small 'VII' above a doorway on the west side of Tariq Khan es-Zeit). There are varying views as to which event this station commemorates. Some hold that this is where Jesus fell for a second time, whilst others refer to it as the **Porta Judicaria** (or 'Gate of Judgement') where the death sentence notice would have been posted. The latter argument was seemingly introduced in the 13th century to remind pilgrims that this was the former city limit in the first century, thus confirming that the place of crucifixion ('Golgotha') was outside the city walls.

Porta Judicaria (VIIth Station of the Cross)

Tariq Khan es-Zeit effectively marks the western limits of the Muslim Quarter, with points to the west of here effectively being in the Christian Quarter. However, for ease of use the various places of interest on this 'boundary' are detailed here.

The **VIIIth Station of the Cross** is located a little way up Aqabat al-Khanqah on the left (the road leading west from Tariq Khan es-Zeit next to the VIIth Station). It is marked by a small 'VIII' on the wall of the **Monastery of St Caralambos** and commemorates Jesus addressing the women of Jerusalem: "Daughters of Jerusalem, weep not for me".

VIIIth Station of the Cross

Returning to Tariq Khan es-Zeit, you come to a wide stone staircase on the right. In the angle beneath the stairs is a private shop selling traditional Arab sweets: **Zalatimo's Sweets**. Within the storeroom here lies the superb remains of Constantine's massive doorway between the propylaea and east atrium of his fourth century CE Church of the Holy Sepulchre (see page 135). **NB** It is customary to make a purchase if seeking permission to view the doorway.

Zalatimo's Sweets

Ascending the staircase, follow the winding street (Aqabat Dair al-Sultan) to its dead end. The column on the left marks the **IXth Station of the Cross** where Jesus is said to have fallen for the third time. Passing through the gate on to the 'roof' of the Holy Sepulchre, you encounter the **Ethiopian Monastery**, occupying the ruins of the 12th-century Canons' Cloister (itself built upon the ruins of the Constantine basilica). Unable to fulfil their tax obligations to the Ottoman sultan in the 16th-17th century, they lost their ownership to various parts of the Holy Sepulchre to the Copts, and were forced up to these small cells on the 'roof'. The dome that you see at floor level is the same one that you see from the Chapel of St Helena below.

IXth Station of the Cross

A doorway in the southwest corner of this 'roof' leads into the narrow **Chapel of the Ethiopians**, from where steps descend via the Coptic Chapel of St Michael to the courtyard (Parvis) outside the Church of the Holy Sepulchre (see page 135). The last five Stations of the Cross are all within the Church of the Holy Sepulchre. If the door to the Chapel of the Ethiopians is locked (as it frequently is), retrace your steps to Tariq Khan es-Zeit, continue south to the next right turn (Harat al-Dabbaghin), and follow this street to the Parvis.

Jerusalem

Jerusalem

The Ethiopians in Jerusalem

The Ethiopians have a long association with Jerusalem dating back to King Solomon; in fact, the Ethiopian emperors claimed a line of descent from Solomon as a result of his union with the Queen of Sheba. The Ethiopians have fared badly in the sectarian squabbles for control of the Holy Sepulchre, with rising debts forcing them to relinquish control of most of their sites within the church itself in favour of their bitter rivals the Copts. Their rivalry with the Copts is all the more ironic because both groups belong to the Monophysites who believe in the single composite nature of Christ (as opposed to the dual composite nature). "Divided by a common faith" is how Amos Elon describes it. The Ethiopians now largely occupy the 'roof' of the Holy Sepulchre, where their simple annual Searching for the Body of Christ ceremony forms one of the gentlest and most interesting annual religious festivals. More details on the Ethiopian church can be learned at the Ethiopian Compound on Ethiopia Street, between the Russian Compound and Me'a She'arim in the New City.

Coptic Orthodox Patriarchate and Coptic Church and Cistern of St Helena Next to the pillar marking the IXth Station of the Cross is the Coptic Orthodox Patriarchate, whilst opposite is the Coptic Church of St Helena. At the far end of this small church, about 70 steps descend to the large (and generally full) 'Cistern of St Helena'. The cistern has not yet been dated. Make sure the priest turns on the light at the top of the stairs otherwise you will see nothing (a small donation is expected).

St Alexander's Chapel and Russian Excavations Located at the junction of Tariq Khan es-Zeit, Harat al-Dabbaghin, and the main Muslim-Quarter suqs (see 'Old City: Sights' map on page 86), is the so-called **St Alexander's Chapel and Russian Excavations** (also known as the Russian Mission in Exile). Beneath this 19th-century building lay a number of remains from Constantine's fourth-century CE church, as well as Hadrian's second-century CE building (though unless you are keen on archaeology, you may not be particularly excited by these exhibits). The site was acquired by Russia in 1859 (for the very fact that it contained elements of the original Holy Sepulchre), with the present structure built to protect them following the visit of the Grand Duke Sergei Alexandrovitch in 1881. The building subsequently became known as the Alexandrovsky Hospice (of the Russian Palestine Society).

Tour The column (1) at the bottom of the stairs (2) is part of a poorly built triumphant arch built by the (poor) Christian community of Jerusalem to show their gratitude to Constantine Monomachos for his 11th-century rebuilding efforts. It was probably modelled on the far more impressive

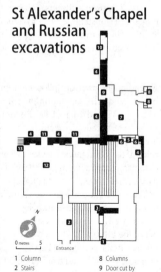

St Alexander's Chapel and Russian excavations

1 Column
2 Stairs
3 Pier of 2nd century Arch
4 Walls of Hadrian's Platform
5 Gate
6 Blocks
7 Pavement of Cardo Maximus
8 Columns
9 Door cut by Constantine
10 Main Entrance (Zalatimo's Sweets)
11 Doors
12 Modern Chapel
13 Medieval Arch

Hadrianic arch that previously marked this spot, part of which can still be seen (**3**). Pass through the arch and turn left. Some of the walls of Hadrian's monumental structure can still be seen (**4**). These utilized some Herodian blocks, and were in turn reused in Constantine's basilica. According to legend, the gate (**5**) ahead was the gate through which Jesus was led out of the city on his way to Golgotha (hence the protective glass over the sill), though it is in fact a Constantinian entrance to the south cloister (that may previously have been a Hadrianic arch). At a later date this gate was modified, possibly being enlarged by cutting back the walls on either side and inserting the two blocks (**6**). Beyond this gate was the pavement of Hadrian's cardo maximus (**7**), flanked by a row of columns of which part of two remains (**8**). To the left (west) is a door (**9**) that Constantine cut through the Hadrianic wall (**4**) as a minor entrance into the basilica. The main entrance lies (**10**) just to the north and can be seen within a private shop (see 'Zalatimo's Sweets', page 127).

The two doors to the south (**11**) are thought to be entrances from the south cloister to the atrium of Constantine's basilica. Beyond the modern chapel (**12**) a doorway leads to a small museum. The medieval arch (**13**) next to the museum entrance led to the Canons' Cloister, now occupied by the Ethiopian Monastery (see page 127). ■ *Monday-Saturday 0900-1300 1500-1700, ring the bell. Adult 5 NIS. St Alexander's Chapel is only open at 0700 on Thursday, when prayers are said for Tsar Alexander III.*

Muslim Quarter suqs

Jerusalem's most atmospheric **bazaar** stands at the junction of the Muslim, Christian and Jewish Quarters, at the point where Tariq Khan es-Zeit, David Street, Tariq Bab al-Silsila and the Cardo converge (see map on page 86). Three parallel streets are linked by narrow lanes along the route of the Roman-Byzantine town's cardo maximus, though much of the structure that you see here is Crusader. For much of the 12th century, the central street of the covered market was property of St Anne's Church (see page 121), and the monogram 'SA' appears in the masonry above some of the arched entrances to the shops. When St Anne's Church was converted into the Salahiyya Madrassa by Salah al-Din in 1192, he also transferred the title deed. The other two streets on either side were *waqf* of al-Aqsa Mosque. The street on the west was the vegetable market in Crusader Jerusalem, but it is now the **Suq al-Lahhamin** (or 'Street of the Meat Sellers'). Visiting tourists tend to find this street particularly nauseous. The central street is the **Suq al-'Attarin** ('Street of the Spice Sellers'), though it previously fulfilled all the Crusaders' drapery needs. The east street is **Suq al-Khawajat** ('Street of the Merchants'). If you continue south on the most westerly of these suqs (Habad, see 'Old City: Sights' map on page 86), a flight of iron steps to the left leads up to the **rooftops** above these suqs. There are excellent views from here (as well as some peace and quiet).

Muslim Quarter: area to the west of the Haram al-Sharif

Dar al-Sitt Tunshuq ('Palace of the Lady Tunshuq')

Considered by some to be one of the finest Mamluk monuments in the city, it is in some need of restoration though it is still possible to admire some typical features of Mamluk building style. The entrance portals are of particularly good work, notably the now-blocked east door, whilst some of the inlaid work is well executed. Little is known about 'Lady Tunshuq', except that she died in 1398 ten years after the palace was built. It is suggested that she fled to Jerusalem to escape the campaigns of Timur (Tamerlane), though to be able to build such a palace, she was no ordinary refugee. In later years (c. 1552) the building was incorporated within a charitable foundation ('Imaret of Khassaki Sultan') established by a wife of Sulaiman II, and was then used in the 19th century as the residence of the Ottoman governor. Part of the palace was subsequently used as an orphanage. Opposite the palace is the **Mausoleum of Sitt Tunshuq**, which also features some nice detail, though it too is in a poor state of repair. The palace and mausoleum are located on Aqabat Tekieh, at the midpoint between Tariq Khan es-Zeit and Tariq al-Wad.

Maktab Bairam Jawish

Though an early Ottoman structure, built in 1540 by the Amir Bairam Jawish as either a school or pilgrim hospice, the inference is that the architects and craftsmen were Mamluk trained since it incorporates so many features from this earlier period. Its most notable points are the lead plates that bond the courses (the source of the madrassa's name 'Rasasiyya'), and the decorative arch. This building is at the east end of Aqabat Tekiek, at its junction with Tariq al-Wad.

Sights along Tariq Bab al-Nazir

From the Aqabat Tekieh/Tariq al-Wad junction, proceed straight ahead (east) into the narrow street opposite that leads to the Haram al-Sharif. The top of this street is marked by a **fountain** built by Sulaiman II in 1537 (called 'Sabil Tariq Bab al-Nazir' or 'Sabil al-Haram'). The street, Tariq Bab al-Nazir, leads to the *Bab al-Nazir* ('Gate of the Inspector': hence the street name), though confusingly this gate is sometimes referred to as the *Bab al-Habs* ('Gate of the Prison') and hence the street has a second name (Tariq Bab al-Habs).

Fifty metres down Tariq Bab al-Nazir, on the left, is the **Hasaniyya madrasa**, built by Husam al-Din al-Hasan in 1434. Next door is the **Ribat 'Ala' al-Din Aydughdi al-Basir**, built as a pilgrim hospice around 1267, and probably the oldest Mamluk building in the city. An official in the Mamluk administration, such was the reputation of 'Ala' al-Din Aydughdi that despite his blindness in later years he was referred to as 'al-Basir' ('the clear sighted'). Following the loss of his vision he was made Superintendant of the Jerusalem and Hebron Harams ('sanctuaries'). The building was later used as quarters for the Sudanese Muslims who guarded the Haram al-Sharif, and then during the Ottoman period as a prison (hence the gate/street name).

Opposite, occupying much of the south side of Tariq Bab al-Nazir, is the **Ribat al-Mansuri**. This was also built as a pilgrim hospice (c. 1282) but later used as barracks for the Haram guards and then as a prison. Many North African Muslim families still live here, and though an invitation into their home is a rarely extended privilege, it is a fascinating experience. The road continues to the *Bab al-Nazir* (Muslims only).

Sights along Tariq al-Hadid

About 50 metres along Tariq al-Hadid, at the point where the path divides, located on the right is the **Hanbaliyya madrasa**, founded in 1380 by the Mamluk official Baidamur al-Khwarizmi. Taking the left fork, the lane runs all the way to the *Bab al-Hadid* (Muslims only). Just before the gate is the **Jawhariyya madrasa and ribat** that is now occupied by the offices of the Administration of Waqfs and Islamic Affairs, Department of Archaeology. It was built in 1440 by an Abyssinian eunuch by the name of Jawhar al-Qunuqbayi who later became Steward of the Royal Harem. The entrance portal has the now familiar red and cream masonry, whilst the upper windows are well worked. The upper storey extends above the adjacent **Ribat Kurt al-Mansuri** (hospice built in 1293 by the renowned soldier Sayf ed-Din Kurt who died fighting the Tartars in 1299), linking it to the Haram al-Sharif complex itself. Other buildings from the period close to the *Bab al-Hadid* include the **Arghuniyya madrasa** (c. 1358), **Khatuniyya madrasa** (c. 1354) and the **Muzhiriyya madrasa** (c. 1480).

This superb 95-metre-long Mamluk covered bazaar has been substantially restored, and is an impressive sight featuring 50 or so shops, two bathhouses and a caravanserai. Unfortunately, few of the shops are open for trade (most are used for storage), and hence it has a somewhat abandoned feel. Burgoyne, who extensively surveyed the Mamluk buildings in the Muslim Quarter between 1968-75, believes that the arcade represents two distinct construction periods, going as far as to suggest that the east section was built merely to fill the space between the market and the walls of the Haram al-Sharif. Even to the untrained eye it is easy to see that this is the case, though the block to the east is in no way inferior. It is now generally assumed that the west block was originally a Crusader market (the lower four courses of masonry are certainly Crusader) that was repaired at the same time that the east section was built. The 'join' in the middle is particularly well executed. The market is generally attributed to **Tankiz al-Nasiri**, with a number of inscriptions in the structure mentioning his gift (including on the doors of the *Bab al-Qattanin* at the east end, on the lintel above these doors, and on the keystone of the relieving arch to the Khan Tankiz to the north of bays eight and nine). Two of these inscriptions indicate 1336 as the date of construction.

Suq al-Qattanin (Market of the Cotton Merchants)

To the north side of bays six to ten is the vaulted hall of the **Khan al-Qattanin** (a caravanserai) founded c. 1453-61. Further along the north side the stairs at bay 16 provide access to the living accommodation above the shops. At the east end the steps in bay 29 lead up to the elaborate *Bab al-Qattanin* (Muslims only).

On the south side of the bazaar there is an entrance (closed) that leads to a 12th-century Ablutions Place that serves the Haram al-Sharif. Adjacent to bays 17-20 is the entrance to the **Hamman al-Shifa** (closed), a bathhouse built in 1330 in the Roman-Byzantine style. A 26-metre-deep well-shaft draws water from a source below, though it is renowned for its poor quality. Also on the south side of the bazaar, between bays eight and nine, is the entrance to the **Khan Tankiz** (closed). Restoration of this caravanserai appears to be in progress.

At the entrance to the Suq al-Qattanin (with its north wall adjoining bays one to three) is the **Hamman al-'Ain**. This typical Mamluk bath, built c. 1330, is supposedly being restored, though there appears to be little activity inside. Just to the south of the bathhouse entrance on Tariq al-Wad is the **Sabil Tariq al-Wad**, a fountain constructed by Sulaiman II in 1536.

Diagonally opposite Suq al-Qattanin is a street heading west called Aqabat al-Khalidiyya. Just 15 metres along the street on the right is a small workshop/furniture maker's showroom. Examination of this structure in 1978 by Bahat and Solar tentatively identified it as the **Crusader Church of St Julian** (though some other sources claim that it may have been dedicated to St John the Evangelist). Despite a number of structural changes throughout the years, this is still identifiable as a three-aisled basilica with three apses. The owner does not welcome visitors (unless you're buying furniture!).

Crusader Church of St Julian (?)

This historic street has remained the main east to west artery of the Old City throughout history. The eastern part follows the course of the Hasmonean causeway that crossed the deep Tyropoeon valley (the ravine that ran along the side of the Temple Mount/Haram al-Sharif but has now been filled by centuries of construction). Herod the Great enlarged the vaulted causeway (sections of the Hasmonean/Herodian causeway can be seen in the 'Western Wall Tunnels', page 106), and the Mamluks built over it further. In between time, the current Tariq Bab al-Silsila formed one of the main east to west routes in

Tariq Bab al-Silsila

Jerusalem

Hadrian's Aelia Capitolina, and the Street of the Temple during Crusader rule. It now leads to one of the main gates to the Haram al-Sharif, *Bab al-Silsila* (usually Muslims only). There are several noteworthy buildings located just outside the gate, including the ornate **Tomb of Turkan Khatun** (c. 1352), the **Tomb of Sa'd al-Din Mas'ud** ('al-Sa'diyya', c. 1311) and the splendid **al-Tankiziyya madrasa** (c. 1328).

The **Tashtamuriyya** is an interesting complex on Tariq Bab al-Silsila that was built c. 1382 by Sayf al-Din Tashtamur, a former First Secretary of State to the Mamluk sultan. Not only a residence, the Tashtamuriyya was also built as a tomb, religious school and charitable institution. It's now divided into a number of private residences (some Jewish), and though not open, it is still possible to admire the impressive façade.

Further along the street on the same side is the **Tomb of Baraka Khan**. A chief of one of the Tartar Khwarizmian tribes that swept through Syria and Palestine in the early 13th century, he ended his days with his severed head impaled on the citadel gate at Aleppo (c. 1246). His memory was rehabilitated when one of his daughters married the Mamluk sultan Baibars. One of his sons is thought to have built this tomb some time between 1265 and 1280. A number of structural alterations have been made to the building, including its conversion into the Khalidi Library in 1900, and little remains of its original splendour bar the façade. Almost next door you can see the arched entrances to the **Dar al-Qur'an al-Sallamiyya**, a Koranic school built in 1360. Given the building's history and function, the Israeli flag flying from the much later upper storey is particularly provocative. The building opposite, at the junction with Tariq al-Wad, is the **Tomb of Baybars al-Jaliq**, a Mamluk official who died c. 1281. You can just about see into the tomb chamber through the green metal grille over the window (though there's not much to see).

Other minor sights

The **Khan al-Sultan** (just off Tariq Bab al-Silsila) is a former Crusader caravanserai that was restored in 1386 by the Mamluk sultan al-Zahir Sayf-al-Din Barquq, and continued to be used in this role during the Ottoman period (with some structural modifications). It still pretty much retains this function, with the lower floors used for storage (though no longer as stables), and the upper floors providing living accommodation.

The **Madrassa al-Lu'lu'iyya** (on Aqabat al-Khalidiyya) was built c. 1373. The street that it stands on is noted for some fine views back to the Dome of the Rock.

Christian Quarter of the Old City

The Christian Quarter is the second largest of the four divisions of the Old City (c. 18 hectares), with a permanent resident population estimated at around 4,500 (3,800 Christian, 700 Muslim). Spiritually (though certainly not physically or aesthetically) it is dominated by the central shrine of Christendom, the Church of the Holy Sepulchre – revered as the scene of Christ's Crucifixion and Resurrection. The quarter contains numerous other Christian institutions (churches, hospices, convents, patriarchates, seminaries, etc) built to serve the various Christian sects. Today, in excess of 20 different major Christian denominations compete for influence within the quarter, often displaying a distinct lack of Christian brotherly love in the process. Meanwhile, the predominantly Muslim traders along two of the Old City's main shopping streets, David Street and Christian Quarter Road, compete for the tourist dollar.

Ins and outs

There are a number of possible entry points into the Christian Quarter. Most visitors arrive through Jaffa Gate, though many enter from the Muslim Quarter whilst following the route of the Stations of the Cross on the Via Dolorosa ('Old City: Sights' map, page 86). **Warning** Given the high tourist flow through this area (notably Omar ibn al-Khattab Square inside Jaffa gate), it is popular with hustlers offering their services as guides, or trying to tempt you to various shops where you will get a 'special discount' (and they will get a commission). Some of the offers are genuine, and many of the guides are very knowledgeable and speak a number of foreign languages fluently. However, there is no way of sorting the 'wheat from the chaff', and it may be wise to err on the side of caution: licensed guided tours can be arranged at the Tourist Information Office just inside Jaffa Gate whilst shopping discounts can be negotiated yourself. **NB** David Street's gently sloping incline, with graded steps and ramps, can be treacherous when wet.

Getting there and getting around

Jerusalem

History

Though the line of Herod Agrippa I's 'Third North Wall' around the first century CE city is still a matter of speculation, the lack of archaeological evidence for pre-second century CE construction on the spot now occupied by the Christian Quarter seems to confirm that this whole area was undeveloped until the construction of Hadrian's city of Aelia Capitolina in 135 CE (though this view has recently been challenged by Doron Bar, who argues that the camp of the Roman Tenth Legion Fretensis was here, and not to the south of the Citadel).

Much of this area was subsequently levelled for Hadrian's forum (though most archaeologists still believe that the city was largely unwalled at this point). The Christian Quarter really owes its historical foundation to the rapid expansion of the Christian community in Jerusalem during the Byzantine period, who clustered their institutions around the Holy Sepulchre. This is also true of the Crusaders, who built in this quarter on a monumental scale.

For the best view of this sight you will need to ask permission (and sometimes pay a small fee) to climb up to the roof of the *Petra Hostel*. Surrounded on all sides by later period buildings, the Pool of the Patriarch's Bath takes its current name from its medieval function as a source of water for the baths located close to the palace of the Crusader patriarch. However, despite a lack of systematic archaeological investigation, it is clear that the origins of the pool are far older. The area was extensively quarried in the seventh century BCE and a small rain-fed pool could well have existed at that time: hence the alternative name, **Pool of Hezekiah**. It is equally likely that the pool has its origins in the Hasmonean (152-37 BCE) or Herodian (37-4 BCE) quarries that were dug in this vicinity, and it may well be the 'Amygdalon' or 'Tower Pool' mentioned by Josephus in his account of the Roman suppression of the Jewish Revolt in 70 CE (*Jewish War V: 468*). The Crusader period saw the water from the pool used by the patriarch, and later by the nearby bathhouse. Measuring 72 metres by 44 metres, this large pool is probably only worth seeing if it has recently rained (unless of course you like looking down upon several generations' worth of accumulated trash).

Pool of the Patriarch's Bath

This small church has a complex history, which is not surprising given the fact that it is one of the oldest churches in Jerusalem. Its crypt and foundations date to the fifth century CE, and it is quite possible that it was built to mark the

Church of St John the Baptist

presence in Jerusalem of relics related to John the Baptist. Largely destroyed in the Persian invasion of 614 CE (when the relics were looted and large numbers of Christians massacred), it was restored shortly after pretty much on the same plan by the Patriarch of Alexandria, St John Almoner. It has what is known as a trefoil shape, with three apses to the north, east and south. The upper storey (ie bar the crypt and foundations, most of what you see today) belongs to the 11th century CE reconstruction that was undertaken by the merchant community of Amalfi, Italy. The façade and two small bell-towers are a later addition still. Visitors to the church are welcome, though it may be necessary to ring the bell in the little courtyard to summon the priest.

The Crusader period saw much confusion arise as to the tradition of the site upon which the church is built. The tradition that the church stood on the site of the house of Zechariah, father of John the Baptist, was challenged by the Latins in the 14th century, who claimed that it in fact stood above the former residence of Zebedee, father of St John the Evangelist. The Greek Orthodox, who are now the custodians of the church, have been rejecting this claim since the 17th century.

Whilst the crypt was being cleared of accumulated debris in the 19th century, a magnificent reliquary (object used to hold religious relics) was located hidden amongst the masonry. Inlaid with precious stones and bound with gilded copper bands, it was made from a piece of rock crystal formed into the shape of a mitre. Amongst the relics it held were 'fragments of the True Cross' and items associated with St Peter, John the Baptist and most of the apostles. It is now held in the Greek Orthodox Treasury of the Church of the Holy Sepulchre.

Christian Quarter Street This thoroughfare features numerous shops selling religious icons and Christian-related souvenirs. Some of the large, smooth **paving stones** along this street date to the Roman/Byzantine city of the third to fourth century CE, and were discovered some metres below the present surface during work on the sewers in 1977.

'Mosque of Omar' The present mosque was built in 1193 by **Afdal 'Ali** following the defeat of the Crusaders six years earlier by his father Salah al-Din. It takes its popular name from the seventh century CE story relating to the Caliph Omar's refusal to pray inside the Church of the Holy Sepulchre (see 'Church of the Holy Sepulchre' on page 135), though it was originally referred to as the Mosque of Afdal 'Ali. The original mosque reuses much Crusader masonry from the Muristan (page 146), perhaps from the Hospital of the Knights itself, though much of the work was completed later.

The outer entrance gate dates to the mid-19th century, whilst the minaret had to be rebuilt after the 1458 earthquake (possibly in 1465). The top of the minaret has much in common with its counterpart on the al-Khanqah Mosque (page 147), 100 metres to the north; in fact, they are at exactly the same height and a line drawn between them is absolutely parallel to the ground. Further, a line drawn between the two minarets has its mid-point at the entrance to the tomb of Christ in the Holy Sepulchre. Murphy-O'Connor (*The Holy Land, 1992*) believes that there is no doubt that this was intentional, and may have been a crude effort to 'nullify' the resurrection of Jesus, which Muslims reject. **NB** This is not considered a 'tourist site' by the Muslim community, and non-Muslims are not allowed entry. Do not confuse this mosque with the title 'Mosque of Omar' erroneously applied to the Dome of the Rock on the Haram al-Sharif.

Church of the Holy Sepulchre

The Church of the Holy Sepulchre is built upon the traditional site of the Crucifixion and Resurrection of Jesus, and is thus the most important site within Christendom. The church that you see today dates to a number of periods, having been partially destroyed and rebuilt on a number of occasions, reflecting the Christian experience in the Holy Land. It is admittedly a rather confusing place and getting to grips with the complexity of not only the setting and history (not least of all the events that it was built to celebrate), as well as the confusing architectural elements, is not easy in the crush of bodies milling around here. If you can, make a series of visits at different times of the day, and it may be an idea to read the account below before entering the church.

Ins and outs There are several approaches to the Church of the Holy Sepulchre, though the only entrance is via the Parvis (courtyard) on the south side (1). Those walking the Via Dolorosa route will, on reaching the Ninth Station of the Cross, have two options. If the door is open, it is possible to descend to the Parvis via the Ethiopian Monastery on the 'roof' (through the Chapel of the Ethiopians at the upper level, and the Coptic Chapel of St Michael (7) at the lower level). Note that this route is not suitable for large processions (or those carrying crosses). The second option for those walking the Via Dolorosa is for them to retrace their steps to Tariq Khan es-Zeit, turn right onto Harat al-Dabbaghin, and follow this street through the low doorway into the Parvis. The final approach is from Christian Quarter Rd, via Qantarat al-Qiama (sometimes referred to as St Helena St), and into the Parvis from the west side. **NB** Modest dress is essential to enter the church.

Church of Constantine Work begun on the Church of Constantine in 326 CE, and it was dedicated on 17th September, 335 CE. This truly was a monumental edifice, dwarfing all later efforts including what you see today. It comprised four main elements (atrium, basilica, court and rotunda), and at its longest and widest points it measured around 180 metres by 100 metres (see plan). The main entrance was from the cardo maximus to the east, into the slightly irregularly shaped **atrium**. This led via either three or five doorways into the basilica itself, often referred to as the **Basilica of Constantine** or **Martyrium** ('place of witness'). This comprised five aisles, the central one of which was widest at around 13.5 metres, whilst the lateral aisles had upper and lower galleries. The roof was lead, and the ceiling was lined with gold that according to Eusebius "like some

Church of the Holy Sepulchre: 4th century CE

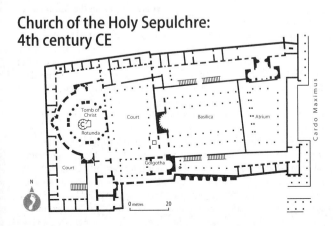

Jerusalem

The Tomb of Christ: is this the place it claims to be?

The first question that many visitors ask concerns the authenticity of the site. Amos Elon records the alleged remark of one young visitor, no doubt repeated by numerous other visitors since: "I didn't know that our Lord was crucified indoors!" (Jerusalem: City of Mirrors, 1989).

The information that the gospel accounts give us is useful but limited. They refer to "a place called Golgotha, that is to say, a place of a skull" (Matthew 27:33; Mark 15:22; John 19:16), whilst John further adds that "there was a garden; and in this garden a new sepulchre" (19:41). Looking at the church today, such a scene is hard to imagine (and compare with the 'Garden Tomb', page 183).

Of course, a first century CE Jewish graveyard would have been outside the city walls, though proving that this site once fitted this criteria is not difficult. Evidence for the alignment of the city walls in the early first century CE has admittedly been rather elusive (ie the location of the 'Second North Wall', and its immediate successor the 'Third North Wall'), but extensive archaeological examination of this northwest corner of the Old City has revealed no significant construction that **predates** the early second century CE. Therefore it is more than reasonable to assume that the site of the present Church of the Holy Sepulchre did indeed stand outside the limits of the first century CE walls.

Thus, when Bishop Makarios of Jerusalem (with the permission of the emperor Constantine) began his search for the burial place of Christ in 325/6 CE, he concentrated his excavations on this site here, within the city walls. Why he chose this particular spot is still not certain, though there is the very real possibility that this place was still being pointed out as the site of the Crucifixion. Tradition records that the early Christian population of Jerusalem continued to venerate the site of the Crucifixion and Resurrection right through the early years of persecution, including the destruction of Jerusalem by the Romans in 70 CE. It is also important to note that although the actual Tomb of Christ may have been 'lost', the rock of Golgotha was still being pointed out to visitors.

Much has also been made of the fact that Hadrian chose to redevelop this site around 135 CE, the inference being that he deliberately built a large pagan temple here in order to snuff out reminders of the nascent Christian faith. But as Biddle points out, such assumptions reflect more "fourth-century assumptions about pagan attitudes to Christianity than second-century reality" (The Tomb of

great ocean, covered the whole basilica with its endless swell". To the west of the basilica was a porticoed court, with the block of stone venerated as Golgotha in the southeast corner. The court gave on to the **Rotunda** (or **Anastasis**, meaning 'Resurrection') around the Tomb of Christ. Construction of this great circular edifice required substantial quarrying and levelling of the rock around the tomb itself, and there is evidence to suggest that it was not completed when the church was dedicated (though certainly by 384 CE, and possibly by 340 CE). A dome (probably wood with a lead covering) capped the rotunda, supported by 12 columns 10.5 metres high and 8 piers. The exact form of the structure over the tomb (**The Edicule**) is not entirely clear, though attempts have been made to reconstruct it from representations on souvenirs brought back from the Holy Land by early pilgrims.

The **Persian** invasion of 614 CE saw the church burnt, the wooden roof destroyed, the relics looted and the monks murdered. Repairs were undertaken by **Modestus**, Abbot of St Theodosius, though the description of the church given by the pilgrim Arculf in 680 CE varies little from the descriptions of the original Constantine church. The **Arab** conquest of Palestine in 638 CE placed Jerusalem under Muslim control, and led to an amusing, though

Christ, 1999); it is doubtful if the nature of Hadrian's monumental public building will ever be determined, and claiming that a statue of either Venus, Aphrodite or Tyche was placed above the Tomb of Christ is mere speculation. The fact that Bishop Makarios was prepared to go to the expense of demolishing Hadrian's building, excavating the former quarry, and then shifting all the debris when it would have been far easier (and cheaper) to use the large open space just to the south as the site for his church (and have it 'near' to the site of the Passion, as opposed to being actually 'on' it) is cited as evidence that the precise location of Golgotha was known.

However, when Bishop Makarios did find a typical Jewish burial cave of the first century CE during his excavations in 325/6 CE, it is still not clear why it was immediately accepted as the Tomb of Christ. In fact, another rock-cut tomb typical of the first century BCE/first century CE can be seen in the west exedra of the Rotunda in the present church (see *(27)* on map). Amos Elon notes how in Eusebius' account of the discovery of the holy tomb at this spot, he describes it as being "contrary to all expectation" (Life of Constantine, 3:28). Elon asks: "Why contrary? Could it be that, in ordering the

basilica to be built on the site of the greatest pagan shrine in Jerusalem, Constantine, with the zeal of a new convert, was catering as much to politics as to theology?" (ibid). There could be a far simpler explanation for this discovery being "contrary to all expectation"; as Biddle notes, the tomb hadn't been seen in 200 years and "Makarios dug more in hope than expectation and was, to Eusebius's surprise, proved 'right'" (ibid). Biddle also speculates that Makarios was able to proclaim his find as the Tomb of Christ because it "could have been marked in some way, possibly with cut or painted graffiti which were legible in 325/6", noting how the tomb of St Peter in the Vatican was also identified in this way.

Thus, in conclusion, the authenticity of the claim that this is the site of the Tomb of Christ is best summed up by Dan Bahat, former City Archaeologist of Jerusalem: "We may not be absolutely certain that the site of the Holy Sepulchre Church is the site of Jesus' burial, but we certainly have no other site that can lay a claim nearly as weighty, and we really have no reason to reject the authenticity of the site" (Biblical Archaeology Review, May/June 1986).

subsequently fateful, incident in the building's history. Following a tour of the church conducted by the Christian patriarch Sophronis, the Muslim Caliph **Omar** was invited to pray in the church. Omar considerately declined, stating "if I had prayed in the church it would have been lost to you, for the believers would have taken it saying 'Omar prayed here'". Ironically, had it been converted into a mosque it is unlikely that it would have fallen victim to the subsequent desecration at the hands of the Fatimid **Caliph al-Hakim**.

There is evidence that various desecrations of the church took place in the 10th century CE, often at the

Church of the Holy Sepulchre

hands of combined Muslim and Jewish mobs, but the vandalism of 1009 was the most systematic and complete. Al-Hakim ordered Yaruk, governor of Ramla, to "demolish the church of the Resurrection … and to get rid of all traces and remembrance of it". Thus, Constantine's grand church was all but destroyed, though much of the Rotunda remained intact and the lower levels of the Edicule and much of the rock-cut tomb itself may have been protected from the hammer-wielding vandals by the sheer volume of accumulated debris.

The church rebuilt Until very recently it has always been assumed that the church was rebuilt between 1042 and 1048 by the Byzantine emperor **Constantine Monomachos** (subsequently becoming known as the **Church of Constantine Monomachos**). However, it is now clear that the Christian community of Jerusalem began rebuilding the church in 1012, just three years after the al-Hakim inspired attack. Indeed, as early as 1020 al-Hakim himself had permitted the resumption of Christian liturgies at the site. The most likely scenario is that provided by Biddle (*ibid*), who suggests that the period 1012-23 saw locally inspired reconstruction, followed by a second phase of imperial (Byzantine) reconstruction around 1037 to 1040. However, the individual nature of the work completed within these two phases is not entirely clear; just the result. The subsequent church was a much more modest affair, occupying just the court, Rotunda and some minor chapels and courts of the former building. The original basilica and atrium disappeared (though fragments of these sections of Constantine's church can be seen at the 'St Alexander's Chapel and Russian Excavations', page 128, and 'Zalatimo's Sweets', page 127). The columns of the rotunda were cut in half and re-erected (giving the visitor today some sense of the scale of the original Constantine church), and several other modifications made, including the construction of a new apse on the east side. The entrance was as it is today: from the courtyard to the south. This is more or less how the **Crusaders** found the church when they captured Jerusalem in 1099.

Crusader Church of the Holy Sepulchre There are further misconceptions with regard to dating the Crusader modifications to the church. It has largely been assumed that the 50th anniversary of Crusader rule in Jerusalem was celebrated on 15th July, 1149 by the dedication of the modified and restored **Crusader Church of the Holy Sepulchre**. This assumption has been drawn from the wording of a (now disappeared) Latin inscription above or around the western arch that led to the Chapel of Golgotha (now the Chapel of Adam (**17**)). However, it is now clear that this date of dedication refers solely to the Chapel of Golgotha and not the whole **Church of the Holy Sepulchre**. In fact, it is more likely that the Crusader Church of the Holy Sepulchre was not completed until around 1163-69.

The work undertaken by the Crusader masons was substantial. In addition to rebuilding the chapels around Calvary, they extended the church to the east across Constantine's previously open court by building a choir with an ambulatory and three radiating chapels in the finest late Romanesque style. This was linked to the Rotunda by a crossing covered by a dome and flanked to the north and south by transepts. The principal entrance was (as today) through the portal in the south transept. To the east of the choir, upon the site of Constantine's basilica and atrium, was built the complex needed to house those tending the church.

Although Jerusalem was surrendered to Salah al-Din in 1187, the Church was left unmolested. Pilgrims were permitted to return under the truce signed between Richard Coeur de Lion and Salah al-Din in 1192, and Latin priests were able to join the Syrian priests who had remained since 1187. However, much of the Church was badly damaged in 1244 when the **Khwarismian Turks** rode into the city, and the Edicule itself is said to have been in a particularly parlous state by the time **Boniface of Ragusa** began his restoration programme in 1555.

A major fire in 1808 had a catastrophic effect on the Church, destroying 7 out of 10 of the remaining original 4th/11th-century columns in the Rotunda, with the collapsing roof badly damaging the exterior of the Edicule. In 1809 the Greek Orthodox community obtained permission from the Ottoman sultan to restore the Church, with the subsequent work being completed in a little over 18 months under the supervision of the Greek architect **Nikolaos Komnenos**. In Biddle's words, "Komnenos' work has not commended itself to non-Orthodox critics" (*ibid*), with the rebuilt Edicule having been described as a "gaudy newspaper kiosk" (Amos Elon). There is even evidence to suggest that the Greeks systematically removed the tombs of the various Crusader kings simply to remove as much trace as possible of the church's Latin past (though it is not really known what state these tombs were in following their looting by the **Khwarismian Turks** in 1244). It should also be noted that Komnenos' restoration was not a structural success either, with the dome of the Rotunda having to be rebuilt in 1868. The whole Church was further weakened by a major earthquake in 1927, and it took until 1959 for a mutually acceptable restoration plan to be agreed by all sides. In the meantime, the Public Works Department of the British Mandatory Government in Palestine (in 1947) had to strap the whole place (including the Edicule) together with iron girders to prevent it collapsing.

Much has been made of the sectarian squabbles within the Holy Sepulchre in recent years. The split between the 'Eastern' and 'Western' churches dates to the fifth or sixth centuries, though the theological split subsequently became influenced by political and geopolitical manoeuvres, notably during the Crusades. As a result, the Church of the Holy Sepulchre now finds itself not united by a common belief in Christ's Resurrection, but divided in a territorial battle between Latins, Greeks, Copts, Armenians, Ethiopians and Syrian Jacobites for control of a piece of real estate. Physical fights have broken out over such trivial matters as the positioning of a Greek Orthodox rug a few centimetres into Armenian 'space', or "the sweeping of Greek dust with brooms held by Franciscan hands" (Amos Elon, *ibid*); the wooden ladder seen resting against the outer façade of the main entrance is perhaps the best illustration of such territorial wars (see (**14**) below). However, it is suggested that the three 'Great Communities' (Greek Orthodox, Latins, Armenians) are now working closely together through the Common Technical Bureau; perhaps best exemplified by the dedication in 1997 of the brilliantly restored columns, walls and dome of the Rotunda. There are plans to resurface the floor of the Rotunda in time for the Millennium, before discussions begin on the desperately needed restoration of the decaying Edicule.

Recent history

Jerusalem

Tour

The tour of the Church of the Holy Sepulchre begins in the **Parvis (courtyard)** (**1**) on the south side. Standing in the **Parvis (1)** looking towards the entrance doorway of the Holy Sepulchre (north), one can see three Greek Orthodox chapels to your left (west) that were built on the former site of the Constantine baptistery in the 11th century CE. The first (south) is the **Chapel of St James the Less (2)**, the brother of Christ. In the centre is the **Chapel of the Forty Martyrs (3)**, formerly referred to as the Chapel of the Trinity. The north

The exterior

chapel, adjoining the Holy Sepulchre, is dedicated to **St John the Baptist (4)**. The bell-tower was added in 1170, though it had become so unstable by the early 18th century that almost half of it had to be removed. These three chapels are generally closed.

To your right (east) are entrances to three other buildings. The first, furthest away from the Holy Sepulchre, is the **Greek Monastery of Abraham (5)**, from where there is (restricted) access to the upper storey of the Holy Sepulchre (including the 'Church of Abraham'). In the centre is the **Armenian Chapel of St James (6)** (sometimes open), whilst in the northeast (top right) corner of the courtyard is the **Coptic Chapel of St Michael (7)**. A staircase inside this chapel leads up to the **Chapel of the Ethiopians**, the **Ethiopian Monastery** up on the roof, and the nearby Ninth Station of the Cross (see page 127).

The structure with the small dome in the northeast corner of the courtyard, against the wall of the Holy Sepulchre, is known as the **Chapel of the Franks (8)**. This was originally designed as a 12th-century Crusader ceremonial entrance to Calvary/Golgotha, which is on an upper level inside the Holy Sepulchre. It was closed up following the fall of Jerusalem in 1187, though the stairs up **(9)** can still be seen. The lower storey is referred to as the **Greek Chapel of St Mary of Egypt**, whilst the upper storey is the **Latin Chapel of the Agony of the Virgin**. You can see into the latter from a window in the Latin chapel on Calvary inside **(15)**.

Church of the Holy Sepulchre: 12th century to present day

1 Courtyard (Parvis)
2 Chapel of St James the Less
3 Chapel of the Forty Martyrs
4 Chapel of St John the Baptist
5 Greek Monastery of Abraham
6 Armenian Chapel of St James
7 Coptic Chapel of St Michael (and stairs to Ethiopian Monastery)
8 Chapel of the Franks
9 Stairs
10 Tomb of Philip d'Aubigny
11 Redundant wall
12 Steps up to Golgotha
13 Blocked doorway
14 Entrance
15 Latin Chapel of the Nailing to the Cross (upper level)

16 Greek Chapel of the Exaltation or Raising of the Cross (upper level)
17 Chapel of Adam (lower level)
18 Stone of Unction
19 Three Mary's Place
20 Rotunda

21 11th century columns
22 Tomb Monument
23 Chapel of the Angels
24 Chapel of the Holy Sepulchre
25 Coptic Chapel
26 Syrian Chapel
27 Rock-cut Tomb

28 Greek Orthodox Catholicon
29 Arch of the Emperor Monomachos
30 Crusader period side aisles
31 Mary Magdalene Altar
32 Chapel of the Apparition
33 North Aisle
34 'Seven Arches of the Virgin'
35 Prison of Christ
36 Ambulatory
37 Chapel of St Longinus
38 Chapel of the Parting of the Raiment
39 Chapel of the Derision
40 Doorway to Canon's Monastery
41 Step
42 Chapel of St Helena
43 Chapel of the Invention or Finding of the Cross

Before entering the Holy Sepulchre, it's worth taking a few minutes to admire some of the finer points of the **Crusader façade**, particularly the delicately carved stonework on the upper storeys. The entrance doors are flanked by marble triple columns, topped by carved capitals. You may see Greek Orthodox worshippers kissing the central of the three columns on the left side of the main doorway (**14**). This tradition relates to the miracle of 'The Descent of the Holy Fire' (see page 142). Seemingly, members of the Armenian community locked the Greek Orthodox Patriarch outside the Church so that only their group would be able to receive the Holy Fire inside the Tomb of Christ. But according to Greek Orthodox tradition, the Holy Fire suddenly burst forth from the central of the three columns outside, lighting the torch of the Patriarch. If you closely examine the column in question you will find that it is blackened by fire!

The right (east) door (**13**) was sealed shut by the Muslim rulers following the fall of Jerusalem in 1187. The original 12th-century carved lintels above the doorway are now in the Rockefeller Museum (see page 183). If you look above the sealed east door (**13**), you may notice a small wooden ladder. This is probably the most potent symbol of the tension between the different sects that control the Holy Sepulchre. Under the 'status quo' agreement of 1757 (implemented by the Ottomans and reapplied during the British Mandate), existing arrangements within the church cannot be changed. Thus, this ladder which belongs to one sect cannot be removed since it stands on property 'owned' by another sect. In fact, the ladder even appears in the watercolours painted by David Roberts during his tour of the Holy Land in 1839!

The wooden boards just outside the entrance cover the **tomb of Philip d'Aubigny (10)** (d. 1236), discovered by accident in 1867 when a bench concealing it was removed! It thus escaped the fate of the other tombs of the Crusader knights that the Greeks removed during their reconstruction work after the 1808 fire. He was an English knight and councillor to King John at the time of the signing of the Magna Carta, and also Tutor to Henry III.

The interior

The entrance (**14**) to the Holy Sepulchre leads into the south transept of the Crusader church. Notice how the clear view across the church is blocked by the wall in front of you (**11**). This wall was first constructed shortly after the catastrophic fire of 1808 and was designed to support the badly damaged arch. The Greek Orthodox subsequently used it to hang their icons (and it now features an unimaginative mosaic of Christ's Passion). However, recent restoration of the arch above has made this wall superfluous and it now serves no structural purpose whatsoever. The logical thing to do would be to remove it, allowing the clear view across the church that was originally intended, but then the Greeks would have nowhere to hang their icons! Hence the wall stays. When you visit there may well be a metal step ladder in front of this wall; this appears to be a modern re-run of the wooden ladder noted outside (see above). The south transept is dominated by the Stone of Unction (**18**), though we shall come to this shortly.

Having entered the Holy Sepulchre, the logical route is to take the steps (**12**) up to **Calvary/Golgotha** immediately to the right. The steps were built subsequent to the blocking of the doorway (**13**) in the 12th century. They lead to an upper floor that reveals the top of the rock outcrop upon which tradition claims Jesus and the two thieves were crucified – Calvary or Golgotha. The first chapel (south) is the **Latin Chapel of the Nailing to the Cross (15)**, and forms the **Xth and XIth Stations of the Cross** where Jesus was disrobed and nailed to the Cross. Most of the mosaic decoration here is relatively modern, though the ceiling medallion depicting the Ascension is 12th century. It is possible

Jerusalem

☞ *Miracle of the Descent of the Holy Fire'*

Every year the Church of the Holy Sepulchre is the scene of what Amos Elon describes as "a barbaric ceremony that is part Greek-Dionysiac, part Christian and part Zoroastrian fire worship" (Jerusalem: City of Mirrors, 1989). The origins of the 'Miracle of the Descent of the Holy Fire' are obscure, though it may be derived from the story of Solomon's consecration of the First Temple. On 'Holy Saturday' (the day after the Orthodox Good Friday) the Greek Orthodox Patriarch and an Armenian prelate are locked inside the Tomb of Christ. Then, by miracle, fire descends from heaven, the Patriarch receives it, and proceeds to light a great torch with it before passing it out to the crowd. What this has to do with Christianity is questionable, though it is usually justified by some line about a supernatural event marking the spot of the Resurrection (and is often seen by the Orthodox Church as a symbol of God favouring them). Whether anybody actually believes in this 'miracle' is another matter, with Amos Elon suggesting that "the ceremony is reminiscent of a professional wrestling match where everyone but the most ignorant knows that the blows are not real, but everyone is nevertheless thrilled by the spectacle" (ibid). Sorry to shatter your illusions (not about the miracle, but about professional wrestling).

'Holy Saturday' is arguably the most exciting time to be in Jerusalem. Up to 15,000 people cram into the Church of the Holy Sepulchre on this day, with thousands more locked outside (all streets to the Church are closed off by the Israeli police from about 0700 onwards). If you can't get inside the Church, then Christian Quarter Street is not a bad place to spend your day (particularly when the Catholic Scouts and sword swirling Armenians march past). When you eventually manage to get into the Church (often not before 1500), the resulting scene is reminiscent of the aftermath of an outdoor rock festival; clothing, drinks containers and food remains strewn everywhere!

The ceremony can be a considerable source of tension between the various Orthodox communities: in 1834 over 300 worshippers were said to have died in the mêlée. The whole event, like everything else in the Church, is governed by the 'status quo' agreement of 1757. For example, the spaces between columns 18 and 15 and 11 and 8 of the Rotunda are reserved for Armenians, whilst 14 to 12 and 8 to 5 are for the Greek Orthodox. A knife fight broke out in the Church in 1998 when members of the Syrian Church "displayed religious exuberance" at the Miracle, and were subsequently attacked by Armenians; under the 'status quo' only the Greek Orthodox are allowed to display religious zeal when the Miracle is performed!

from here to see through the window grille into the Latin Chapel of the Agony of the Virgin (see page 140). The second chapel (north) on Calvary is the **Greek Chapel of the Exaltation or Raising of the Cross (16)**, and represents the **XIIth Station of the Cross**. The slots cut in the rock for the three crosses can be seen in the east apse here, whilst it is also possible to touch the rock itself beneath the Greek altar (leading to some very unholy scenes involving video cameras). The Latin **'Stabat Mater altar'** (Our Lady of Sorrows) between the two chapels is said to mark the spot where Mary received the body from the cross, and is the **XIIIth Station of the Cross**.

Descending the stairs from the Greek chapel, it is possible to see further sections of the rock of Golgotha (behind perspex) in the recently restored **Chapel of Adam (17)** (directly below the Greek chapel, (16)). Early tradition claims that Christ died where Adam was buried, so hence the name. The concept of the blood of Christ on the Cross dripping on to the first guilty head is particularly strong within the Greek Orthodox, and may explain why many Greek depictions of the Crucifixion feature a skull at the foot of the Cross. You can chose the explanation for the large fissure seen in the rock here according to your personal spiritual leaning. It is either a natural fault in the rock that led the workmen to abandon this section of the quarry prior to its use as a place of execution/burial, or it is the direct result of the earthquake that occured at the time of the Crucifixion. The tombs of the first two Crusader 'kings' of Jerusalem, Godfrey of Bouillon and Baldwin I, previously lay just inside this chapel, though they were removed by the Greeks during the restoration programme that followed the 1808 fire.

Beyond this chapel, dominating the entrance to the Holy Sepulchre, is the **Stone of Unction (18)**, commemorating the anointing of Jesus' body by Nicodemus prior to its burial (*John 19:38-40*). The previous 12th-century stone was lost in the fire of 1808 and the present limestone slab dates only to 1810. The lamps hanging above it belong to the Armenians, Copts, Greeks and Latins. It is not uncommon to find worshippers prostrating themselves on this 19th-century stone, or scooping up the now 'holy' water that they have poured on to it.

Ahead, to the left, the small canopy supported by four pillars marks the traditional site where the three Marys are said to have watched the Crucifixion (**19**). The steps lead up to the Armenian Chapel (closed).

From here you enter the **Rotunda** or **Anastasis (20)** that was originally part of Constantine's fourth century CE church, and later restored in the 11th, 12th and 20th centuries. The columns and piers are thought to closely follow the line of the fourth century CE supports, whilst two of the columns to the northeast (**21**) are originals from the 11th-century reconstruction. This was originally a single column used in Constantine's church (and possibly reused from Hadrian's structure), and thus gives some idea of the scale of second and fourth century CE monumental building projects in Jerusalem. It was cut in half for the 11th-century rebuilding programme. The walls and columns have recently been restored, as has the magnificent new dome (dedicated in 1997). The 'starburst' on the interior of the dome represents the Twelve Apostles and the spreading out of the Church in the World. It is hoped that the floor of the Rotunda will be relaid in time for the Millennium.

At the centre of the Rotunda is the **Tomb of Christ**, covered by the Edicule (**22**) (or tomb monument, see box on page 144). The entrance to the marble tomb monument is to the east, and the approach is lined by tall candles belonging to the Armenians, Greek and Latins. The interior is divided into two tiny chapels. The first, the **Chapel of the Angels (23)** (3.4 metres by 3 metres), is said to contain a part of the rolling stone used to seal Christ's tomb, (and subsequently rolled away by the angels). The steps lead to the roof, and the scene of the 'Miracle of the Descent of the Holy Fire' (see page 142). A low doorway leads from the Chapel of the Angels into the tiny **Chapel of the Holy Sepulchre (24)** (2 metres by 1.8 metres), the **XIVth Station of the Cross**. There's just about room inside for three people to pray, plus the priest who accepts a monetary offering to light a candle. The streaked honey-coloured marble slab covering the burial couch is actually one stone, and dates to at least 1345. Legend suggests that the cut in the slab was deliberately made in order to deter looters from removing it. Marble shelves run around the west, north and east sides of the burial slab. The central part of the shelf is 'owned' by the Greek Orthodox, the left-hand part and left angle by the Latins, and the right-hand part and right angle by the Armenians. The marble icon in the centre (north) belongs to the Greek Orthodox, and is part of the 1809-10 restoration. The silver-coated picture to the left belongs to the Latins, and the painting to the right to the Armenians. The positioning of the candlesticks, vases and pictures is

Jerusalem

 The Edicule over the Tomb of Christ

Probably the greatest authority on the Edicule is Professor Martin Biddle, whose recent publication The Tomb of Christ *(Sutton, 1999) breaks new ground in the study of the Holy Sepulchre. Having been granted unprecedented access to the Tomb, and using all resources at his disposal (such as photogrammetry), Biddle's insight is largely as a result of applying one of the basic rules of systematical archaeological enquiry: starting with what is there at the present and working your way backwards! Remarkably, this fundamental approach has never before been used here, largely because it was always assumed that nothing could be learnt from the relatively modern Edicule. However, Biddle believes that the anomalies in the form of the present Edicule reveal clues to the form of previous monuments: "Inside the skin of 1809-10 as in an onion lie the remains of earlier Edicules" (ibid).*

The exterior of the present Edicule (22) dates to the 1809-10 restoration, and is thought to be perilously close to collapse (partly as a result of the 1927 earthquake).

In fact, it is largely held together by the timber and steel cradle put there in 1947 by the British Mandate government. It appears that the east and west walls are largely unsupported, and Biddle estimates that "elements in the east front [have] moved as much as 3cm in the years 1990-3" (ibid). Because the spike on the top of the cupola has moved no more than two millimetres between 1989 and 1992, it is believed that the outer cladding is moving independently of the vault and cupola over the Tomb Chamber.

Since the state of the Edicule is so 'parlous', it is hoped that a restoration plan that is acceptable to all the interested parties can be worked out. This will require dismantling stone by stone the present Edicule, though such a programme will reveal what is actually left of the original Tomb Chamber.

If you are looking for some souvenir of your visit to the Holy Land, you may be better off saving your money until you get home and buying Martin Biddle's The Tomb of Christ.

strictly governed by the 'status quo' agreement. On the west wall is a hinged painted icon of the Virgin that opens to reveal a rough masonry wall (possibly part of the 11th-century Byzantine reconstruction).

Leaving the tomb monument, walk round to the far (west) side. It is thought that the small **Coptic Chapel (25)** was built against the west wall between 1809/10 and 1818. The cupboard under the altar here reveals what is generally believed to be the west face of the west wall of the rock cut Tomb Chamber.

Opposite the Coptic Chapel, in the west exedra of the fourth century CE Rotunda, is the **Syrian Chapel (26)**. Peering into the candlelit hole in the wall on the left (south) side it is possible to see part of the first century BCE to first century CE rock-cut tomb (**27**) that was a deciding factor in the argument aimed at establishing the authenticity of the site. The north, west, and south exedras of the fourth century CE Rotunda have all survived, and much of the west rear wall (not visible from the interior) is original up to a height of 11 metres. The gallery and tower above this west end of the church are not accessible from the Church, though may be from the Greek Orthodox Patriarchate (see page 147).

Return to the entrance to the tomb monument. Facing east you are confronted by the central aisle of the 12th-century Romanesque Crusader Church, now functioning as the **Greek Orthodox Katholikon (28)**. It is entered through the incorrectly attributed **Arch of the Emperor Monomachos (29)** that was originally built to support the east apse of the 11th-century restoration programme. The 'eastern' influence in the Crusader

Church is not necessarily solely the result of the Greek Orthodox ownership (and subsequent decorative style). Much of the Crusader sculpture, as well as the cupola, displays the conscious decision of the Crusader craftsmen to merge their work with the existing 'eastern' stylistic elements that were already in place in the church. The partition walls (**11**) that divide the Katholikon from the Crusader side aisles (**30**) are now redundant following recent renovations, though they are yet to be removed. The 'omphalos' (navel) on the floor relates to the tradition of the site of the Crucifixion and Resurrection as being at the centre of the world.

Return to the tomb monument and turn right (north). Passing the two original 4th/11th century pillars (**21**), and continuing straight ahead, to the right stands an **altar** dedicated to **St Mary Magdalene (31)**, and commemorating Christ's appearance to her on the morning of the Resurrection. The double-doors ahead lead to the **Chapel of the Apparition (32)**, sometimes referred to as the **Chapel of St Mary**. The principal Franciscan chapel in the Holy Sepulchre, it honours the ancient tradition of Jesus' appearance to his mother after the Resurrection (though the gospels do not record the event). A small fragment of the **Column of the Scourging** is displayed just inside the door, to the right. To the east of the chapel is the **Latin Sacristy**.

Leave the chapel and turn left (east) after the altar dedicated to St Mary Magdalene. In this **north aisle (33)**, the 12th-century architect went to considerable lengths to preserve the portico of the 11th-century courtyard (built using Byzantine pillars), though what resulted is described as a "remarkable jumble" of decorative pillars and weight-bearing piers that is referred to as the **Seven Arches of the Virgin (34)**. At the east end of this aisle is the so-called **Prison of Christ (35)**, a small chapel that honours the 8th-century tradition that Christ was held in a small room with the two thieves whilst their crosses were being prepared. By the 12th century, this spot was claimed as the site of the tradition.

Continuing around the ambulatory (**36**) of the Crusader church, there are three small chapels set in the three apses. The first (northeast) is the Greek **Chapel of St Longinus (37)**, and dedicated to the Roman soldier who pierced Jesus' side with a spear whilst on the Cross (*John 19:34*). A fifth century CE tradition relates how Longinus (later made famous by John Wayne with his interpretation of the "surely this man is the Son of God" line) was cured of his blindness in one eye by the blood that spurted out. He subsequently repented and became an early Christian convert. The Armenian chapel in the centre (east) apse is the **Chapel of the Parting of the Raiment (38)**, whilst the third (southeast) apse is occupied by the Greek **Chapel of the Derision** or the **Crowning with Thorns (39)**.

The 12th-century doorway (**40**) between the first northeast and east apses led to the Canon's Monastery, built on the ruins of the Constantine basilica. The flight of steps (**41**) between the east and southeast apses leads down into the **Chapel of St Helena (42)** (known to its Armenian custodians as the Chapel of St Krikor, or Gregory). Note the crosses carved into the walls by early pilgrims. The chapel is generally thought to date to the Crusaders' 12th-century building programme (the vaulted ceiling certainly does) though the north and south walls are almost certainly part of the foundations of Constantine's basilica. There is some speculation that this chapel was formerly the crypt of the Constantine basilica, though this view is largely discounted. The dome above is the one that you meet at floor level when visiting the Ethiopian Monastery (see page 127).

A further 22 steps in the southeast corner of the Chapel of St Helena lead down to the **Chapel of the Invention or Finding of the Cross (43)**. Remarkably, in his account of the discovery of the tomb of Christ (*Life of Constantine,* written c. 337-40) Eusebius neglects to mention how Constantine's mother, the Empress Dowager Helena, discovered the True Cross in a cistern close to the rock of Golgotha. Perhaps it slipped his mind! In fact, the tradition did not appear until 351 CE, 16 years after the completion of Constantine's church. Nevertheless, this spot is revered as the place where Helena found the True Cross. Custody of the chapel is divided between the Greeks and Latins.

Returning up the steps to the ambulatory of the Crusader Church (**36**), continue west along the south aisle, passing the Chapel of Adam (**17**), and ending the tour of the Church of the Holy Sepulchre back at the entrance. ■ *T6273314. Daily 0400-2000, 1900 in winter. Free. For details of service times, contact the Christian Information Centre opposite the Citadel – midnight mass is highly recommended here, with an atmosphere totally different to the camera-clicking disturbances of the daytime.*

Muristan   The whole block to the south of the Church of the Holy Sepulchre was formerly occupied by the **Muristan**, which became the headquarters of the Crusader Knights of St John – the Hospitallers. Between the 11th and early 16th century this block was occupied by the great hospital, the knights' hospice, the residence of the Grand Master, plus a number of churches. Today there is nothing to see, with much of the Crusader structures being plundered for masonry to be used in Sulaiman the Magnificent's 16thcentury Old City walls.

The Muristan was developed in the early 11th century by wealthy, but pious, traders from **Amalfi** in Italy. They constructed, or reconstructed, a number of churches and hospices including the Church of St John the Baptist (page 133), the Church of St Mary of the Latins (the site now being occupied by the Lutheran Church of the Redeemer, see page 147), and the now-disappeared Church of St Mary Minor (which subsequently became known as St Mary Major). All trace of the latter was obliterated by the market built here by the Greeks in 1901, though the attendant hospice would probably have been located where you see the fountain today.

The turning point in the development of the area came with the conquest of the city in 1099 by the **Crusaders**. Many of the knights wounded in the assault were admitted to the small hospital for sick pilgrims that was attached to the Church of St John the Baptist. Some of these knights were to go on to serve the hospital, primarily protecting the sick pilgrims, and with generous endowments from the first two Crusader kings of Jerusalem (Godfrey of Bouillon and Baldwin I) within a short space of time an order known as the **Knights of St John of the Hospital** had been established. This later became the military order known as the **Hospitallers**; subsequently one of the most powerful and wealthy medieval orders whose military role "almost overshadowed its primary charitable purpose". A huge hospice housing 400 knights was built during the mid-12th century, whilst according to one contemporary source, over 2,000 patients of both sexes were being treated in the enlarged hospital in the 1170s.

The fall of Jerusalem in 1187 saw the Hospitallers involved in negotiating the terms of surrender with Salah al-Din, and though the Order lost their property the hospital continued to function. The present name, Muristan, is taken from the Persian word for 'hospital' or 'hospice'. Reports from the 15th century suggest an area in terminal decline, with most of the buildings in a state of dilapidation and decay, and by c. 1524 the whole area appears to have been abandoned. As Prag notes (*Blue Guide*, 1989), "It requires considerable imagination to visualize the area as the well-built and busy 12th century headquarters of a great hospital and military order". There are now several rather pleasant cafés and restaurants in the Muristan area.

Built in 1898 on the lines of the Church of St Mary of the Latins, the 178-step tower of the Lutheran Church of the Redeemer can proudly boast one of Jerusalem's best views. ■ *T6276111/6282543. Monday-Saturday 0900-1300 1500-1700. Use modern entrance on Frederick William Street. Adult 3 NIS. Prior arrangement is needed to view the medieval excavations below. English service Sunday 0900.* **Lutheran Church of the Redeemer**

Presents an insight into the history of one of Jerusalem's largest Christian groups, and displays some items of archaeological interest. There is also access via the Patriarchate to the roof of the Holy Sepulchre, with spectacular views into the recently restored dome above the Rotunda. ■ *T6284006. Tuesday-Friday 0900-1300 1500-1700, Saturday 0900-1300. Adult 5 NIS. From Jaffa Gate head up Greek Catholic Patriarchate Street, then turn right into Greek Orthodox Patriarchate Street.* **Greek Orthodox Patriarchate and Museum**

Formerly the palace of the Latin Patriarch in Jerusalem, it became a *khanqah* (convent for Sufi mystics) following the Crusader surrender of the city to Salah al-Din in 1187. The minaret was built c. 1417 (see also 'Mosque of Omar', page 112). **Al-Khanqah Mosque**

Jewish Quarter of the Old City

The Jewish Quarter is the smallest of the four divisions of the Old City (c. nine hectares), and the population is exclusively Jewish. The Israeli High Court ruled in 1981 that non-Jews could not buy property there (to preserve the quarter's homogeneity), though similar legislation does not apply to the Old City's other three quarters. The quarter was badly neglected during the period of Jordanian occupation (1948-67), even systematically looted, and was devastated during its capture by the Israelis in the Six Day War of 1967. However, one positive consequence of this devastation was the opportunity afforded to archaeologists to excavate here thoroughly before the bulldozers of the rebuilding contractors moved in. The time and effort invested by the archaeologists has been amply rewarded, and there are now a number of important and interesting sites to be seen in the quarter.

Ins and outs

There are several key access points into the Jewish Quarter: from the 'Western Wall Plaza', having arrived there via either Dung Gate to the south or from the Muslim Quarter to the north; from Zion Gate, at the southern tip of the Armenian Quarter; or along the Byzantine cardo maximus, from its north end, at the junction with the Muslim and Christian Quarters. The tour of the Jewish Quarter entails a fair amount of back-tracking, not least because most of the sites are now covered by a single entrance ticket (only available from the Wohl Archaeological Museum). Photography and smoking are frowned upon here on Shabbat, and the bank ATM machine closes. See 'Old City Sights' map on page 86. **Getting there and around**

History

The ancient city that David established on the southeast ridge (see page 174), and Solomon expanded northwards with the construction of the Temple, gradually developed to occupy the land now comprising the Jewish Quarter during the period of Hezekiah's rule (727-698 BCE). In fact, remains of Hezekiah's fortification of the area are key sites on the Jewish Quarter tour. The

Babylonian sacking of the city in 586 BCE led to the virtual abandonment of this land for the next three centuries or so. Hasmonean and then Herodian rule in Jerusalem saw the rapid expansion of the city, and by the end of the first century BCE the main focus of the Upper City was shifted here. The evidence of this is superbly presented at the Wohl Archaeological Museum in the quarter.

The devastation wreaked upon the Upper City by the Romans in 70 CE is also evidenced by the archaeological remains, and following the second rebellion by the Jews (Bar Kokhba Revolt 132-135 CE), much of what is now the Jewish Quarter was occupied by the Roman Tenth Legion (Fretensis). There is little evidence of occupation of this area by Jews in the Byzantine, Early Arab or even Crusader periods (though it should be remembered that the Crusaders massacred most of the Muslim and Jewish population upon their capture of the city in 1099). However, there is considerable weight of evidence to suggest that Jerusalem's only medieval synagogue was built here (see Ramban Synagogue, page 154). It was during the Ottoman period that this south central area of the Old City became known as the Jewish Quarter. The Sephardi community became established here at the beginning of the 16th century, with the Ashkenazi Jews firmly planting roots around 1700. The Karaites sect had been long established by then. All were driven out by the war in 1948.

The reconstruction of the Jewish Quarter following its capture by the Israelis in 1967 has been carefully planned. Although most of the new buildings are modern in design and function, an old byelaw dating to the early years of the British Mandate was invoked, requiring all new buildings to be faced with dressed, natural Jerusalem stone.

Byzantine cardo maximus

Whilst the three parallel streets of the covered bazaar just to the north overlie the Roman-Byzantine cardo maximus of Hadrian's city of Aelia Capitolina, the section of the cardo maximus exposed here is a later southern extension of the main north to south thoroughfare. At the time of the construction of Aelia Capitolina (135 CE), the area in which you are now standing (and indeed most of the present Jewish and Armenian Quarters) was occupied by the camp of the Tenth Legion (Fretensis), and would not have been considered part of Aelia Capitolina itself. Thus, Aelia Capitolina's cardo maximus ran roughly from the present site of Damascus Gate to the junction of Tariq Khan es-Zeit, David Street and Tariq Bab al-Silsila.

The section of restored cardo maximus presented for viewing here represents the **Byzantine** extension of the city, and is usually attributed to **Justinian** (527-565 CE). It is generally believed that the cardo was extended in order to link the two principal churches of the city: the Church of the Holy Sepulchre and Justinian's own Nea Church (page 153). A "magnificent street" some 22.5 metres wide, it comprised a broad uncovered roadway (12 metres wide) flanked by two rows of five-metre-high columns forming a *stoa* (covered passageway) on either side. The road was paved with large well-dressed stones laid in parallel rows at right angles to the street, with a raised ridge along the centre assisting with drainage. About 180 metres of the cardo maximus has been exposed here.

The northern section was laid upon earth fills that covered sections of the **Hasmonean wall** (second to first century BCE) and earlier seventh century BCE **Israelite wall** (see 'Israelite Tower and Hasmonean defences', page 149). In fact, glass-covered shafts allow visitors to look down upon excavated remains that the Byzantine cardo maximus overlies, thus giving some idea of how the successive levels of construction and destruction of Jerusalem have changed the city's landscape. The southern section of the Byzantine cardo maximus was laid upon the quarried bedrock; a process that left a six-metre-high scarp to the west of the street. A number of shops were created here by quarrying into the rock scarp, and some remains can still be seen (including one high-vaulted shop preserved almost intact). For a full understanding of how the Byzantine cardo maximus operated (and looked), read the informative noticeboards that mark all the key points of interest.

The **'Just One Last Day' Museum** on the cardo maximus has a collection of 27 not particularly good photographs taken by John Philips of *Life* magazine during the Jordanian capture of the Jewish Quarter in 1948. The pictures are poorly presented and slightly yellowing, whilst the captions are equally jaundiced. The cardo also features a number of restaurants and galleries selling Judaica. ■ *T6288141. Sunday-Thursday 0900-1700, Friday 0900-1300. Adult 8 NIS, or 26 NIS on 'combined' ticket from Wohl Archaeological Museum*

'Broad Wall'

The section of wall exposed here is part of Hezekiah's expansion of the fortified city (c. 727-698 BCE). The original wall is thought to have run west from the Temple Mount to the present location of the Citadel, though only a 65-metre section is exposed here. It takes its popular name from the fact that it is seven metres wide, though what you see here is merely the foundations of partly hewn stones that have been laid without mortar. A line drawn on the adjacent modern building indicates how high the original wall may have been. The function of the wall was to protect the area of the city that had grown up outside the original Solomonic city walls, quite possibly as a result of the Assyrian invasion of Samaria in 722 BCE and the subsequent flow of refugees. The wall was hastily built in advance of Sennacherib's march on Jerusalem in 701 BCE (see *II Kings 18:13*), and required the demolition of a number of eighth century CE private houses that stood in its way. The archaeological evidence fits perfectly with the written record: "And ye have numbered the houses of Jerusalem, and the houses have ye broken down to fortify the wall" (*Isaiah 22:10*). A map here shows the plan of Jerusalem in the First Temple period. Further information on Jerusalem during the First Temple period be found in the **Ariel Visitor Centre**, a little further north along Plugat HaKotel. ■ *T6286288. Sunday-Thursday 0900-1600, Friday 0900-1300. Adult 11 NIS.*

Probable relationship between Israelite & Hasmonean Fortifications

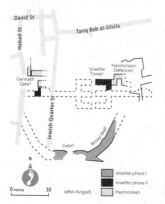

Israelite Tower and Hasmonean defences

At the junction of Plugat HaKotel and Shonei HaLakhot is a section of an Israelite Tower and Hasmonean defences preserved beneath a modern building (the sign on the door says 'Israelite Tower').

Beneath the modern building are the remains of the corner of a massive tower, preserved to a height of eight metres and with walls up to four metres deep. Abutting and incorporating the tower are the remains of a further tower and city wall that clearly belongs to a different period.

The relationship between the fortifications here, the 'Broad Wall', and the sections of Israelite and Hasmonean fortifications that can be seen in the area of the Byzantine cardo maximus excavations (see page 148) is not entirely certain, and indeed the modern buildings of the Jewish Quarter were constructed before the archaeologists had the chance fully to exhaust all possible theories on their relationship. However, the most likely scenario is as follows: The **Israelite Tower** seen here is part of a gate dating to the seventh century BCE, and possibly built by Manasseh (698-642 BCE). If so, this may be the "middle gate" where the Babylonian generals met after breaching the city walls in 586 BCE (*Jeremiah 39:3*). In fact, a number of arrowheads dating to the Babylonian sack of Jerusalem in 586 BCE were found in the vicinity, scattered amidst signs of the burning that followed the conquest. The other Israelite wall near here, the earlier 'Broad Wall', is on a totally different alignment and is not part of the same system of fortifications.

The later tower and city walls that abut the 'Israelite Tower/Middle Gate' here are now thought to be part of the second century BCE **Hasmonean defences**. Probably begun by Jonathon Maccabaeus (see *I Maccabees 10:10-11*) around 160 BCE and completed by his brother Simon (see *I Maccabees 13:10*) in 134 BCE, the fact that the Hasmonean defences are so closely aligned with the earlier Israelite fortifications may be the reason why Josephus attributes this 'First Wall' to David, Solomon and the subsequent kings of Judah (*The Jewish War V: 142-4*). The extension of this 'First Wall' can be seen beneath the Byzantine cardo maximus to the west (see page 148). ■ *T6288141. Sunday-Thursday 0900-1700, Friday 0900-1300. You have to buy your ticket at the Wohl Archaeological Museum (see page 151), 4 NIS or 26 NIS on 'combined' ticket.*

Burnt House The archaeological evidence to support Josephus' graphic description of the Roman sacking of Jerusalem following the destruction of the Temple in 70 CE can be seen here at the 'Burnt House'. Josephus relates how the Romans "poured into the streets sword in hand, cut down without mercy all who came within reach, and burnt the houses of any who took refuge indoors, occupants and all" (*Jewish War VI: 403*). Such was the scale of slaughter that the city was deluged with gore "so that many of the fires were quenched by the blood of the slain" (*ibid*). Though the latter is a typical Josephus exaggeration, the debris-filled rooms of this house contained charred wooden beams and fallen stones scorched by fire, thus confirming part of Josephus' account. The date of the fire was further confirmed by the discovery of a coin dated 69 CE amongst the debris, as well as an iron spear leaning against a wall and the bones of a young woman's hand and arm.

The plan of the house is that of a large complex belonging to a fairly wealthy family, though you should bear in mind that what you see today is merely the remains of the basement: the rest of the building could not be excavated. The identity of the owner was established following the discovery of a stone weight inscribed "[belonging] to the son of Katros". The Babylonian Talmud refers to such a priestly family who served in the Temple, though the line in question (*Pes. 57a*; Tosefta, *Men 13:21*) suggests that they were not the most popular people in town. The museum includes a rich display of household items discovered *in situ*, the labelled plan of the 'Burnt House', and a short multi-lingual audio-visual presentation. ■ *T6287211. Sunday-Thursday 0900-1700, Friday 0900-1300. You have to buy your ticket at the Wohl Archaeological Museum (see below), 9 NIS or 26 NIS with 'combined' ticket. Wheelchair access.*

St Mary of the Germans During the medieval period, this area of the present Jewish Quarter was regarded as the German quarter of Crusader Jerusalem (and Misgav Ladakh was the 'Street of the Germans'). A complex containing a church (St Mary of the Germans), a hospice and hospital was built here around 1128 by the **German Knights of the Hospitallers Order** (from which developed the Order of the Teutonic Knights in the next century) to serve the needs of German-speaking pilgrims. The church was built on a simple basilical plan with two rows of piers dividing the central nave from the two aisles, and was adjoined on the north side by a large hostel. To the south was a two-storeyed structure; above, more or less at the same level as the church, was a ceremonial hall, whilst below stood the hospital. Modifications were made to the building during the Mamluk period, and there is even evidence to suggest that the church was used as a residence for dervishes. The complex was excavated and restored following the Israeli capture of the Old City in 1967.

The steps descending from St Mary of the Germans lead via one of Jerusalem's best **viewpoints** down to the Western Wall Plaza (see page 102). The nearby **Hechal Wohl Convocation Hall of Yeshivat HaKotel** contains a number of exhibits related to the First Temple ("Treasures of the Temple"), including models and vessels. ■ *Sunday-Thursday 1000-1700, Friday 0900-1300. Adult 10 NIS.*

Also close by is the exit (no entry here) to the Wohl Archaeological Museum (see below).

This museum contains the superbly presented remains of a residential area dating to the first century BCE/first century CE, generally referred to as the **Herodian Quarter** (it appears as such in some guidebooks, or by the name of its principal attraction, the 'Palatial Mansion'). A visit to this museum is highly recommended.

Wohl Archaeological Museum

The area referred to by its excavators as the 'Herodian Quarter' covers some 2,700 square metres of the Upper City of Jerusalem. During the Herodian period (37 BCE-70 CE) Jerusalem experienced great prosperity and rapid growth, with the Upper City becoming the most exclusive residential address. The value of the excavated section of the Upper City that is presented in this museum is that it "provides evidence of an urban plan for a residential neighbourhood, house plans, domestic architecture and art, the living conditions of the city's inhabitants, and various aspects of everyday life in the city in the Second Temple period" (Avigad, *New Encyclopedia of Archaeological Excavations in the Holy Land*, 1993).

Tour Now located some three to seven metres below the present street level, the site here presents the remains of a series of six or seven houses from the Herodian period. Descending the steps from the entrance you arrive at an elevated walkway around the **Western Building**. The plan before you here is only the basement of the house, though it superbly illustrates the layout of the water installations and service rooms of a wealthy household. It comprises a

Wohl Archaeological Museum

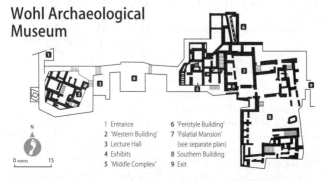

N
0 metres 15

1 Entrance
2 'Western Building'
3 Lecture Hall
4 Exhibits
5 'Middle Complex'
6 'Peristyle Building'
7 'Palatial Mansion'
   (see separate plan)
8 Southern Building
9 Exit

number of cisterns, a vestibule, a bathroom, and two *mikvehs* (ritual baths), of which one is preserved intact. Parts of the mosaic floor from the bathroom remains. The site is enhanced by a hologram depicting "scenes from bathrooms and ritual baths".

The tour continues east along the corridor, passing the gift shop, lecture hall and a pictorial history of the excavations. A number of finds from the Second Temple period (retrieved from the debris) are also displayed.

The '**Middle Complex**' comprises the remains of two separate houses, apparently divided by a common wall. There is a fine mosaic preserved in the large living room, though when first discovered it was covered by a layer of debris directly related to the fire of 70 CE (see 'Burnt House' on page 150). Amongst the artefacts recovered from the house were a number of stone tables: the first pieces of furniture from the Second Temple period ever found. Restored examples are displayed here.

The walkway descends into "the largest and most magnificent of the buildings discovered in the Jewish Quarter" (Avigad, *ibid*) – the '**Palatial Mansion**'. The topography of this residential quarter of the Upper City dictated that the floor level here is some distance lower than that of the houses in the Middle Complex (and seven metres below the present street level). This large mansion, covering 600 square metres, comprises two storeys, though experts speculate that there may originally have been a third. The ground floor contains a series of rooms around a central court, some of which have survived remarkably intact, though most of what you see on the plan before you belongs to the basement. The number of *mikvehs* found in the complex, including one where the vaulting, double entrance and mosaic-paved corridor were found in a superb state of preservation, has led to speculation that this large villa may have been the residence of members of the family of a high priest at the Temple. Other experts have challenged this assumption, looking to the stylistic Hellenistic influences to dismiss this argument. The 1:25 scale model of the reconstructed mansion allows the visitor to picture the building in its prime, with presentation here further enhanced by the information boards and pictorial reconstructions. Further restoration of the mansion's stucco panels remains in progress.

Abutting the Palatial Mansion to the south is the '**Southern Building**', again comprising a series of rooms around a central courtyard. To the north of the Palatial Mansion is an intriguing '**Peristyle Building**'. Sometimes referred to as the 'House of Columns', this is the only such building discovered in the Herodian Quarter, though its exact plan is uncertain. Comparisons have been drawn with luxurious contemporary Roman villas (Avigad), as well as with Herod's palaces at Masada and Jericho.

Further remains from this period (and earlier) can be seen in a private home – **Seibenberg House** (viewing by prior appointment only) – just to the south of here. ■ *T6283448/ 6288141 Sunday-Thursday 0900-1700, Friday 0900-1300. This is the main ticket office for most of the sites in the Jewish Quarter, and there is a 'combined' ticket available for 26 NIS. The entrance is on Hurva Square and the*

'Palatial Mansion'

1 Ritual Bath (Mikveh)	7 Bathroom	12 Reception Hall
2 Ritual Bath	8 Cisterns	13 Living Quarters
3 Pool	9 Storerooms	14 Wall Paintings (Frescoes)
4 Ritual Bath	10 Ritual Baths under Courtyard	15 Vault
5 Cistern	11 Courtyard	16 Alley
6 Courtyard		

exit close to the Hechal Wohl Convocation Hall of Yeshivat HaKotel. No
photography.

This large square, often filled with playing Jewish schoolchildren, has a number of fragments of columns, capitals and Attic bases scattered about. None
was found *in situ* and their exact origins are unclear, though it is certain that
they formed part of some monumental structure(s) built nearby during the
Hasmonean or Herodian period. The building along the west side of Batei
Mahasseh Square, the **Rothschild Building**, dates to 1871, whilst the complex
of buildings along the south side, the **Shelter Houses**, were built nine years
earlier to house poor immigrant Jews from Holland and Germany. Their base-
ments provided shelter for the quarter's residents during the last weeks of the
battle for the Old City in 1948. This area was also badly damaged in the fighting
for the city in 1967, though the subsequent archaeological excavations that
ensued led to the discovery of remains of the Nea Church beneath the square.

Batei Mahasseh Square

Next to nothing remains of Justinian's Nea Church, dedicated to 'St Mary,
Mother of God', though when dedicated in 543 CE it was (and remains) the
largest basilica built in Palestine. Because so little remains it has been difficult
to reconstruct the Nea Church's plan, though Avigad, one of the site's (and
Jewish Quarter's) principal excavators suggests that it is a basilica with a
narthex to the west, with three inscribed apses in the east wall. Its external measurements are something in the region of 116 metres by 57 metres, which is not
so difficult to imagine when you see that the seemingly meagre remains (part
of the northeast apse, vaults to the south, external southeast corner) have walls
up to four metres thick.

Nea or New Church of Justinian

   Though the approximate location of the church just to the east of the south
end of the Byzantine cardo maximus was known from the sixth-century
Madaba Map (see page 79), and sections of it had been exposed during the
construction of the Batei Mahasseh complex in 1862, it wasn't until Avigad's
excavations (1970-82) that the true identity of the structure was firmly established. It was probably badly damaged in either the Persian invasion of 614 CE
or the Arab conquest of 638 CE, and finally destroyed in the ninth century CE.

   To view the preserved section of the **northeast apse**, walk down the steps

Nea Church

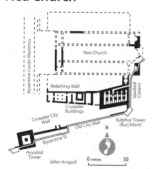

(after Avigad)

away from the Rothschild Building to
the southeast corner of Batei
Mahasseh Square. Descend the steps
to the right and turn left under the
arch on Nachamu Street. Descend a
further seven steps, then take the
double flight of stairs down. Behind
the green metal grille is the entrance
to the northeast apse (not always
accessible). Sections of the vaulted
cistern and external structures can be
seen in the archaeological garden to
the south (just inside the present Old
City walls).

Construction of synagogues to serve the Sephardi community on this site date
to 1610, with the completion of the **ben Zakkai Synagogue** (named after the
first century CE rabbi and noted sage). A study hall was added on the northwest side in 1625, and converted into the **Prophet Elijiah Synagogue** some 70
years later. Further modification to the complex saw the **Middle Synagogue**

Four Sephardi Synagogues

added some point later, and the **Stambouli Synagogue** completed by 1857. The entire complex became badly neglected during the period of Jordanian occupation of the Jewish Quarter (1948-67), though subsequent restoration work has been completed using items recovered from Italian synagogues destroyed during the Second World War. ■ *Sunday-Thursday 0930-1600, Friday 0930-1230. Adult 3 NIS.*

Hurva Square To the north of the Four Sephardi Synagogues complex is Hurva Square. The large **undressed stones** in the northwest corner of the square may be the foundations of a street laid in 62-64 CE as part of a public works programme implemented by Herod Agrippa II to provide relief to the workmen (perhaps up to 20,000) who were made redundant following the completion of the major structural work on the Temple.

Ramban and Hurva Synagogues The west side of the square is occupied by the Hurva and Ramban Synagogues, and the Sidi 'Umar Mosque. Visiting Jerusalem in 1267, the noted Jewish scholar **Rabbi Moses ben Nachman** (known as **Ramban** or **Nachmanides**) discovered that there were only enough Jews in Jerusalem for a game of chess (out of a total population of around 2,000). He settled in the city (meaning that the Jewish population were now just one short for a hand of Bridge) and founded a synagogue on Mount Zion. Some time in the 14th century CE the **Ramban Synagogue** was moved to the present site, occupying the ruins of a Crusader church (possibly 'St Peter in Chains' or 'Church of St Martin'). The building collapsed in 1474 but was rebuilt in 1523 (possibly as the only synagogue in Jerusalem). Ottoman edicts subsequently banned its use as a Jewish place of worship.

In 1700 a group of Ashkenazi Jews (from Eastern Europe) arrived in Jerusalem and established themselves on a site just to the north of the Ramban Synagogue. Their attempts to build their own synagogue were complicated by internal squabbling following the death of their leader, and the half-built structure was confiscated by the Ottomans to settle the group's debts. Hence the synagogue's name: **Hurva**, or 'the Ruin'. The Hurva was returned to the Ashkenazi community by Ibrahim Pasha in 1836, finally completed in 1856 but destroyed in the fighting of 1948. One of the slender arches (13 metres high) that formerly supported the synagogue's dome was restored in 1977, and remains one of the Jewish Quarter's noted landmarks.

The small **minaret** nearby belongs to the **Sidi 'Umar Mosque** (also known as **Jabi Kabir**), which may well have occupied a former Crusader structure (Church of St Martin?) some time in the 14th century. The minaret shows a number of 15th-century characteristics and is built in the square Syrian style.

Armenian Quarter of the Old City

Marginally bigger than the Jewish Quarter (c. 10.5 hectares), the Armenian Quarter occupies the southwest corner of the Old City. Visitors should note that many of the quarter's would-be attractions are behind high walls and closed doors, and are not open to the casual visitor. Indeed, Amos Elon suggests that the Armenian Quarter "bristles with defensive measures. It is an enclave, a closed compound, a miniature city within a larger one, entirely surrounded by a high, fortress-like wall. The heavy gates are guarded and locked at night as during the Middle Ages" (Jerusalem: City of Mirrors, 1989). Perhaps this explains why this is the only ethnic/religious quarter of the Old City that occupies the same site as it did in the fifth century CE.

Ins and outs

The two main approaches to the Armenian Quarter are from Jaffa Gate or from Zion Gate. Visitors should beware of sometimes heavy traffic on Armenian Patriarchate Street. Perhaps the most interesting time to visit the quarter is at the end of April, when the community commemorates the genocide of the Armenian people at the hands of the Turks during World War One. Following a moving service at the atmospheric Cathedral of St James, the Partiarch leads a silent procession along Armenian Patriarchate Street to the Armenian Church of the Holy Saviour on Mount Zion. See 'Old City: sights' map on page 86.

Getting there and around

History

Much of this quarter was formerly occupied by Herod the Great's palace, though next to no traces remain. The Armenians were quick to establish a presence in Jerusalem following the adoption of Christianity as the state religion in 301 CE (the first nation to do so), and the period of exile that followed the collapse of the Armenian state in the fourth century CE seemed to strengthen the Armenian community in the Holy Land. Indeed, by the seventh century CE an Armenian visitor to Jerusalem noted 70 Armenian convents/monasteries in the city. Many of these were established by St Gregory (Krikor) the Illuminator, though most were destroyed during the Persian (614 CE) and Arab (638 CE) invasions, and their remains are now scant.

The re-established Armenian kingdom in Cilica (c. 1098-1375) had close links with the Latin kingdom in Jerusalem (with Baldwin I, Jerusalem's second Crusader ruler, also being the Count of Armenian Edessa), and the Armenian revival in the Holy Land was further cemented by the purchase of the Church of St James from the Georgians (some time in the 12th century prior to 1151). Armenian fortunes in Jerusalem fluctuated in subsequent centuries, though not necessarily reflecting fortunes in the home land. However, the genocide committed by the Turks early in the 20th century has galvanized the Armenian community in Jerusalem, who now see themselves not only as the custodians of the religious centre of the Armenian diaspora, but also as the guardians of the Armenian cultural identity.

Sights

Consecrated in 1849, the Anglican Christ Church is the oldest Protestant church in Jerusalem (though the meaning of its claim to be the "first major 'modern' building in Jerusalem" is less clear). Though the initial impression of the church is one of simplicity, closer inspection reveals a number of details that are a clue to the church's unusual history and function. Note, for example, the Hebrew writing and Jewish symbols on the reredos at the front of the church, on the stained-glass windows, and the Star of David on the altar.

Christ Church

The church was built by an Anglican missionary society called the **London Society for Promoting Christianity amongst the Jews** (later the **Church's Ministry among the Jews**, or **CMJ**). The society, founded in 1809, drew its inspiration from a line in the opening chapter of *The Epistle of Paul the Apostle to the Romans*, which declared: "For I am not ashamed of the gospel of Christ: for it is the power of God unto salvation to every one who believeth; *to the Jew first*, and also to the Greek" (*Romans 1:16*, emphasis added). Like other evangelical groups of the period (and indeed today), the CMJ's founders believed that before the Messiah returned, the Jewish people would be restored to the promised land and that a good many of them would acknowledge Jesus Christ

Jerusalem

 The Armenian genocide: a rehearsal for Hitler?

On 24th April each year a day of mourning is held in the Armenian Quarter to commemorate what many Armenians refer to as the first European Holocaust. In the period 1915-18, over 1,000,000 Armenian civilians were murdered by the Turks, not, as Fisk points out, using the "sophisticated machinery that the Nazis were to employ against another minority community less than 30 years later," but "shot or knifed to death, the women often raped before being murdered" (Pity the Nation: Lebanon at War, 1990). A further 75,000 Armenians were murdered during Turkey's 1918 invasion of the Caucasus, whilst Walker estimates that 250,000 more may have died between 1919 and 1922 (Armenia: The Survival of a Nation, 1980).

The fact that the genocide was largely ignored by the rest of the world was tragic not just for the people of Armenia, but also for European Jewry. As Fisk observes whilst studying a photograph of Armenian villagers being led away by Turkish troops,

"Double take. Is this Lake Van or Lvov, western Armenia or eastern Poland? Are the soldiers Ottoman or Wehrmacht?" (ibid). Describing the Armenian genocide as "a rehearsal for Auschwitz", Amos Elon quotes an Armenian spokesman as saying "The Armenian holocaust was forgotten or ignored. If it had not been ignored, perhaps Auschwitz would not have happened" (Jerusalem: City of Mirrors, 1989). This may not necessarily be true, yet Hitler is said to have told those generals who questioned the possible international reaction to his Final Solution, "Who remembers today the fate of the Armenians?" As Turkey continues to deny its culpability in the Armenian genocide (unlike the Germans), perhaps it is only the Armenian people themselves who remember the fate of their ancestors. Amos Elon again: "The ghastly memory of the past nourishes a central collective trauma among Armenians, as it does among Jews."

as the Messiah. The CMJ's presence was established in Jerusalem in 1833 both in anticipation, and to precipitate, such events. Thus, the founders of Christ Church incorporated Jewish symbols into the church design so that Jews would feel comfortable about entering, and could see how the Christian church acknowledged its Jewish origins. ■ *T6277727, F6277730. Daily 0800-2000. Services at 0930 1030 1830. The church runs a very attractive guest-house to the rear.*

Ya'qubiyya   This small mosque (not always accessible to visitors) occupies a former 12th century CE Crusader church dedicated to St James (the Less). The site may originally have been the site of a monastery founded c. 430 CE by Peter the Iberian to house the relics of **St James Intercisus** (or St James the Cut-up), a Persian Christian martyred in 422 CE. Muslim documents of the 14th century CE refer to the building as the Zawiya (tomb) of Shaikh Ya'aqub al-'Ajami (James the Foreigner), and this medieval dedication has been preserved in the name of the mosque today. Parts of 12th century CE Crusader masonry can be seen in the arch and choir.

Syrian Orthodox   A remarkable number of traditions are related to this site, occupied intermit-
Church and   tently since the 12th century by the Syrian Orthodox (or **Jacobite**) commu-
Convent of St   nity. A Byzantine tradition links the site to Mary of Jerusalem, mother of
Mark   (John) Mark (St Mark), and suggests that i) the Last Supper was eaten here (*Matthew 26:17-30; Mark 14:12-36; Luke 22:7-38; John 13-17*); ii) the Descent of the Holy Spirit at Pentecost took place here (*Acts 2:1-47*); iii) the Virgin Mary was baptized in the stone font against the present south wall; and iv) that St Peter came here after his miraculous release from prison by the Angel (*Acts*

12:12)! Little wonder that the site was chosen for a church during the Byzantine period.

The present church was built in the 12th century, with numerous later modifications, though its constructors have not been positively identified. The confusion arises from the fact that the Jacobites fled Jerusalem prior to its capture by the Crusaders in 1099, with much of their property being passed to a Frankish knight. His apparent death in Egypt in 1103 saw the property returned to the Jacobites, though his subsequent reappearance in 1137 (alive and well) further confused the rights to the title deeds. A settlement in favour of the Jacobites was eventually reached.

The entrance portal of the convent is 12th century, and leads to a much more recent courtyard. The key feature of the 12th-century church is the stone font in which the Virgin Mary is said to have been baptized. The portrait of the Virgin and Child above the font is attributed to St Luke, though it is generally agreed that it dates only to the Byzantine period. Other points of interest include the inscription on the west pillar inside the entrance (said to be 6th century CE), and the beautiful 18th-century blue and white tiles that also decorate the Armenian Convent of St James (see below). ■ *Monday-Saturday 0700-1200 1400-1700, closed Sunday. Free, donations accepted.*

Armenian Convent of St James

This large complex, containing the Cathedral of St James, the residence of the Patriarchate, a pilgrim hospice, accommodation for nuns and monks, a seminary, library, museum, printing press, and various other related buildings, is the centre of the Armenian Christian community.

Cathedral of St James

Those who make the effort to visit or worship in the Cathedral of St James are rarely disappointed; not only is it the finest church in town, the atmosphere inside during services and festivals, in the words of Murphy-O'Connor, "mirrors the life and vigour of a colourful and unified people" (*The Holy Land*, 1992). Laden with incense, the interior of the cathedral is at its best on fine days, when "sunlight from the high windows and the lights of all the lamps create a dazzling and memorable reflection on the rich vestments, ornaments, tiles and other treasures" (Prag, 1989).

The central part of the present cathedral dates to the 11th century, though it is believed that a friend of the Byzantine empress Eudocia may have endowed some form of Christian establishment near here as early as 444 CE, and installed an Armenian as abbot. It was almost certainly destroyed during the Persian invasion of 614 CE. Between 1072 and 1088 the **Georgian** Christian community established a church and monastery here dedicated to St James the Great. An early Christian martyr, St James (son of Zebedee) was one of the first of the apostles, and was executed c. 44 CE on the orders of Herod Agrippa I. The fortunes of the Georgians took a turn for the worse in the 12th century and they were forced to sell the church to the **Armenians**. A number of alterations were made to the church, including the rededication of a number of side chapels and some minor structural changes, though the Armenians retained the link with St James (in fact the principal relic was said to be his severed head).

During the Ottoman period the Armenian church fell into heavy debt through both mismanagement of its finances and its financial commitments to the Church of the Holy Sepulchre. The arrival of **Gregory the Chainbearer** in 1721 (so called because he wore a chain around his neck for three years whilst begging for restoration donations in the doorway of the Church of the Holy Mother of God in Constantinople) saw the debts repaid and the cathedral lavishly restored. Most of the precious stone and metal ornamentation dates to this period. The appearance of the cathedral was further enhanced by the

Jerusalem

addition of the decorative blue and white tile work (in the Kütahya style) between 1727 and 1737. **NB** Only the monastic compound and main church (excluding the chapels to the north) are open to visitors. ■ *T6284549. Open during afternoon service only, Monday-Friday 1500-1530, Saturday-Sunday 1430-1500. Free, donations accepted. It may occasionally be possible to visit during the morning service (0630-0700), or by seeking written permission from the Patriarchate.*

Armenian Garden

The walled compound to the west of Armenian Patriarchate Rd – the **Armenian Garden** – contains a number of institutions related to the Armenian community, though the area is not open to the public. This area to the south of the Citadel was previously occupied by Herod's palace, though precious little survived the 70 CE sacking. Despite the extensive excavations, it is not possible to view the meagre remains here.

Mardigan Museum

Housed in a very attractive former seminary (built 1843), this small museum explains the history and culture of Armenia (including a number of gruesome photos documenting the genocide of 1915-18), and also houses some of the gifts that pilgrims have given to the cathedral. More detailed information on Armenian history and culture can be researched at the nearby **Gulbenkian Library**. ■ *T6282331. Monday-Saturday 1000-1700, closed Sunday. Adults 5 NIS. Cameras must be left outside. Gulbenkian Library: Monday-Friday 1530-1800.*

Church and Convent of the Holy Archangels (Convent of the Olive Tree)

It is sometimes also possible to visit the **Church and Convent of the Holy Archangels** (also known as the **Convent of the Olive Tree**) within the grounds of the Armenian Convent, to the southeast of the Cathedral of St James. A 14th century CE tradition places the 'House of Annas' here, to whom Jesus was taken after his arrest prior to being sent to the House of the High Priest Caiaphas. The olive tree is said to mark the site of the scourging. The

Cathedral of St James

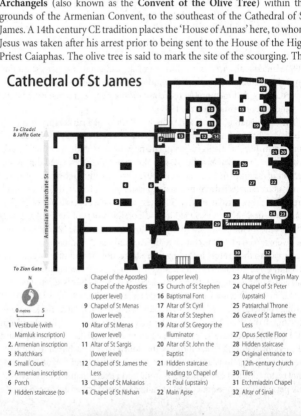

To Citadel & Jaffa Gate

Armenian Patriarchate St

To Zion Gate

N

0 metres   5

1 Vestibule (with Mamluk inscription)
2. Armenian inscription
3 Khatchkars
4 Small Court
5 Armenian inscription
6 Porch
7 Hidden staircase (to

Chapel of the Apostles)
8 Chapel of the Apostles (upper level)
9 Chapel of St Menas (lower level)
10 Altar of St Menas (lower level)
11 Altar of St Sargis (lower level)
12 Chapel of St James the Less
13 Chapel of St Makarios
14 Chapel of St Nishan

(upper level)
15 Church of St Stephen
16 Baptismal Font
17 Altar of St Cyril
18 Altar of St Stephen
19 Altar of St Gregory the Illuminator
20 Altar of St John the Baptist
21 Hidden staircase leading to Chapel of St Paul (upstairs)
22 Main Apse

23 Altar of the Virgin Mary
24 Chapel of St Peter (upstairs)
25 Patriarchal Throne
26 Grave of St James the Less
27 Opus Sectile Floor
28 Hidden staircase
29 Original entrance to 12th-century church
30 Tiles
31 Etchmiadzin Chapel
32 Altar of Sinai

outer wall of the church is also said to contain one of the stones that would have cried out aloud had the disciples not praised God (*Luke 19:40*). This may seem risible to some, though as Murphy-O'Connor has pointed out, this is a tradition that "no one can ever prove false"!

Mount Zion

The area now referred to as Mount Zion is a low hill just below the southwest corner of the Old City, outside the current walls. Tradition links it with a number of important Christian events, including the Last Supper, the imprisonment of Jesus in the House of the High Priest Caiaphas, Peter's denial of Jesus (thrice), the Descent of the Holy Spirit at Pentecost, the falling asleep (death) of the Virgin Mary, and the location of the earliest Christian church. Also sited here is the 'Tomb of David', though it is 99.9 percent certain that he is not buried on this hill, but rather on the 'Ancient City of the Southeast Ridge' – the real Mount Zion (see box on page 160, and page 174).

Ins and outs

For those arriving on foot, the principal point of access to Mount Zion is from Zion **Getting there** Gate (a natural continuation of the tour of the Armenian Quarter). There is also extensive parking available at the main entrance to the hill's attractions.

History

Evidence strongly suggests that the hill now referred to as Mt Zion was enclosed within the city walls as early as the second century BCE, with the walls remaining in place until the Roman sack of Jerusalem in 70 CE, and thus this area was part of the walled city at the time of the crucifixion of Jesus. The hill probably marked the southern limit of the Tenth Legion (Fretensis) camp after the establishment of Aelia Capitolina (135 CE), and remained unwalled until the Byzantine empress **Eudocia** rebuilt the ruined walls around the hill between 444 and 460 CE.

By this time many (though not all) of the Christian traditions associated with this site had been firmly established, and several churches had been built and rebuilt. Though the New Testament does not specify the exact location of many of the key events in the final days of Jesus' life, identifying and locating the sites became a fixation amongst **Byzantine Christians**, who sought to localize every detail of the gospels.

Thus, by the fifth century CE Mount Zion had become associated with the Descent of the Holy Spirit at Pentecost, Jesus' imprisonment in the House of the High Priest Caiaphas on the night before the Crucifixion, Peter's three denials of Jesus before the crowing of the cock (and his subsequent weeping on the rock), and as the site of the seat of the patriarchal throne of James the Less (brother of Jesus) and hence the location of the first church. By the end of the sixth century the tradition surrounding the Upper Room (where the Descent of the Holy Spirit at Pentecost had taken place) had been extended to include the Last Supper in this same room. The tradition surrounding the location of the House of John, where the Virgin Mary fell asleep (and died), was also added to the list. All of these sites were marked by Byzantine churches, and a detailed picture is provided by the sixth century CE Madaba Map (see page 79). By the end of the 10th-beginning of the 11th scentury CE, this hill now referred to as Mt Zion had also become associated (incorrectly as it happens) with the burial place of King David.

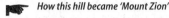

How this hill became 'Mount Zion'

The first biblical reference to 'Mount Zion' describes how "David took the stronghold of Zion" and "dwelt in the castle; therefore they called it the city of David" (II Samuel 5:7-9; I Chronicles 11:5-7). Though the word 'Zion' later came to have a deeply symbolic meaning generally associated with the Temple (but also of great spiritual importance to Christians), the 'Mount Zion' of David's fortified city clearly refers to the ridge to the southeast of Jerusalem, now referred to as the 'Ancient City of the Southeast Ridge' (see page 174).

The transfer of the name 'Mount Zion' to this southwest ridge can be dated to the fourth century CE, and is generally attributed to either a misreading or a new interpretation of religious texts by Christians. Murphy-O'Connor (The Holy Land, 1992), for example, draws

attention to the Bordeaux pilgrim's (c. 333 CE) interpretation of a line in Book of Micah that suggests that "Zion shall be ploughed as a field, Jerusalem shall become a heap of ruins, and the Mountain of the Lord [Temple Mount] a wooded hill" (Micah 3:12). Rather than reading this as a warning of how the city would be ploughed as a field and would become a heap of ruins and the Temple Mount a wooded hill, the Bordeaux pilgrim saw this as a physical description of Jerusalem: if the hill to the east was the Temple Mount, then the one to the west must be Mount Zion! As David's ruined city on the southeast ridge became 'lost', the Christian reference to the hill here as 'Mount Zion' stuck, and the name has remained for the past 1,600 years.

Having been sacked by the Persians in 614 CE, the various churches on Mount Zion were rebuilt, but stood outside the city walls in a state of ruin when the Crusaders took Jerusalem in 1099. The Crusaders restored and refurbished the venerated New Testament sites, and built the **Monastery and Church of St Mary on Mount Zion**. The upper level commemorated the room of the Last Supper (the Cenacle, or Coenaculum), whilst below the Tomb of David was located. Salah al-Din's capture of Jerusalem in 1192 saw Mt Zion once again enclosed within the city walls, though al-Malik al-Mu'azzam's subsequent dismantling of the city's fortifications in 1219 may have also included many of the defensive features that the Crusaders had incorporated into the church.

The **Franciscans** acquired permission to establish a presence on Mt Zion in 1335, and within 10 years had obtained control of most of the venerated places including the Cenacle. Within 50 years they had built a number of hospices on the hill and a cloister along the south side of the Cenacle. The **Tomb of David**, which had only created minor interest amongst the Crusaders, suddenly became a contested site in the late 14th century CE, with both Muslims and Jews laying claim to it. The reason for this sudden interest, according to Murphy-O'Connor, was the "legend of treasures buried with the king" (*ibid*), and by 1450 the Muslims had gained control of the site and built a mosque into the lower storey of the church. Franciscan (and other Christian, as well as Jewish) rights of access were gradually eroded over the following years, culminating in the 1523-24 decree of **Sulaiman II** ('the Magnificent') that forbade all Jewish and Christian access. In fact, access to the site for non-Muslims remained difficult right up until 1948 when the **Israelis** captured the hill. Between 1948-67, when Jewish access to the Western Wall was impossible, the 'Tomb of David' became the *de facto* main Jewish pilgrimage site in Jerusalem.

Armenian Church of the Holy Saviour The property of the Armenian church has been thoroughly excavated and has revealed a number of interesting finds. In addition to remains of first century BCE homes and Byzantine-period streets and houses, part of a fifth century CE apse was also excavated: tentatively linked with the 'Zion, Mother of all the Churches', though most experts believe that this was located slightly further south (see line superimposed on map of Mt Zion). Far more likely is a church associated with the site of the **House of the High Priest Caiaphas**, where Jesus was tried before the High Priest on the night before his Crucifixion, and where Peter thrice denied Jesus before the crowing on the cock, as prophesied (*Matthew 26:57-75; Mark 14:53-72; Luke 22:54-71; John 18:13-27*). Note that there is an alternative proposed site on Mt Zion for these same scenes (page 163, and another in the Armenian Quarter, page 156).

The 12th-century Crusader church that commemorates these events stands in the southeast corner of the compound. It was acquired by the Armenians in the 14th century CE, repaired and rebuilt in the next century, and is now referred to as the **Armenian Church of the Holy Saviour**. Its key points of interest are the 'Chapel of the Second Prison of Christ' in the southeast corner, and the piece of the 'Stone of Angels' taken from the Church of the Holy Sepulchre in the 13th century CE and placed in the altar here. The church was badly damaged during the 1948 war (and was used by the Israelis as a gun emplacement between 1948-67), and a new **Church of St Saviour** is nearing completion in the northeast corner of the compound.

Built in Romanesque style, with a tall circular tower capped with a grey conical roof and four turrets, the Church of the Dormition is one of Jerusalem's most prominent landmarks. Built between 1901 and 1910 on land presented to the **Church of the Dormition**

Mount Zion

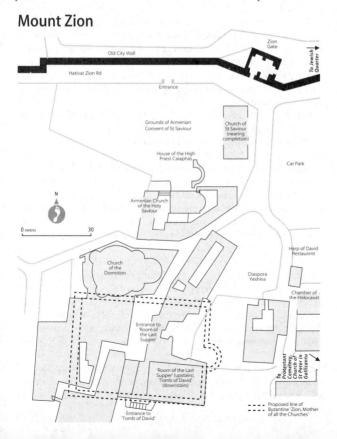

Jerusalem

Church of the Domition

German Catholic Society of the Holy Land by William II of Prussia, the church commemorates the fifth century CE tradition of the site of the House of John on Mt Zion where the Virgin Mary fell asleep (ie died). The Latin name of the church is *Dormitio Sanctae Mariae*: the falling asleep of St Mary. Though the church is elaborately decorated and some careful examination of the detail is highly rewarding, the main draw of the church is the **Chapel of the Dormition** in the crypt. A life-sized statue shows a sleeping Mary, with the mosaic in the dome above showing Christ receiving her soul, surrounded by six women of the Old Testament (Eve, Miriam, Jael, Judith, Ruth, Esther). ■ *T6719927. Daily 0800-1200 1400-1800. Free, donations accepted. Toilets, souvenir shop, cafeteria. No photography.*

Room of the Last Supper (Cenacle/Coena culum)

The whole block of medieval buildings to the south of the Church of the Dormition is part of the 'Monastery and Church of St Mary' on Mt Zion that the Crusaders built in the 12th century, though it has undergone significant modification since then. Much of this complex overlies the site of the fifth century CE **Zion, Mother of all the Churches** (see the superimposed plan on the map of Mount Zion), though the fact that so few remains have been discovered means that it is difficult to talk of its exact plan with any degree of certainty.

The pointed-arched entrance to the left (east, no sign) leads to a small courtyard that continues on to the Diaspora Yeshiva. Ascend the steps in the corner of the courtyard, pass through the first room and along the open passage, then enter the groin-vaulted hall. Tradition relates that this is the **Room of the Last Supper** (also known as the **Cenacle** or **Coenaculum**).

Mt Zion has been associated with the site of the Last Supper (*Matthew 26:17-30; Mark 14:12-36; Luke 22:7-38; John 13-17*) since the sixth century CE, though this belief may well have developed from the site's association with the tradition of the Upper Room of the Descent of the Holy Spirit at Pentecost (*Acts 2:1-47*) that developed a century or so earlier. Note that the Syrian Orthodox Church of St Mark in the Armenian Quarter also claims this honour (see page 156). The hall here was probably built in the 12th century, but significantly restored in the 14th century when the Franciscans gained control of the Cenacle. The altar and choir to the east were removed during the later construction of the dome over the 'Tomb of David' in the level below, and a sculptured mihrab (indicating Muslim direction of prayer) was added to the south wall during the early Ottoman period. The coloured glass windows also date to this period. The pelicans adorning the canopy over the steps in the corner are a medieval Christian symbol of charity. The steps descend to an antechamber of the tomb below, though access is not permitted. ■ *Daily 0800-1200 1400-1600, sometimes closed Friday afternoon. Free.*

'Tomb of David'

Retracing your steps to the lane outside, turn left and pass beneath a second pointed arch. The cloister that you enter is the one built by the Franciscans c. 1377 after gaining rights to the Cenacle. To the left is the so-called **'Tomb of David'**.

As explained in the introduction, King David is not buried here, but somewhere in the 'Ancient City on the Southeast Ridge/City of David' (*I Kings 2:10*; see page 174). However, the late 10th-early 11th century CE tradition has survived, following the revival of interest in the legend in the 14th century CE. A second revival of interest in the site as the Tomb of David stemmed from the Jordanian occupation of the Old City between 1948 and 1967, when Jews denied access to the Western Wall chose this Israeli-held position at which to pray.

The controversy surrounding the site does not end there, though. The relationship between the lines of the 12th century CE Crusader 'Church of St Mary on Mt Zion' that you see today and the fourth century CE 'Zion, Mother of all the Churches' has not been definitively established, and thus it is also claimed that the ancient foundations of the present Crusader church are in fact part of a first or fourth century CE **synagogue**. A synagogue on Mt Zion is mentioned by both the Bordeaux pilgrim (c. 333 CE) and Epiphanius of Salamis (c. 374-94 CE), though its position in relation to the early Christian buildings on the hill is not made clear. A particular point of contention is the **niche** in the wall behind the cloth-draped **cenotaph** itself. It has been suggested that the niche, orientated 'correctly' towards the Temple Mount, would have held the Torah Scrolls of the synagogue. The another view is that the niche is an inscribed arch of the fourth century CE church. And finally, in order perhaps to allow all competing interests to find an answer that suits their prejudices, it may also be part of an earlier Roman pagan building whose remains were incorporated within the fourth century CE 'Zion, Mother of all the Churches'. ■ *T6719767. Saturday-Thursday 0800-1800, Friday 0800-1400. Free. Men must cover heads, cardboard yarmulkes provided for use free.*

The cloisters outside the Tomb of David features the **Museum of King David**, which contains an eclectic collection of exhibits centred around a display of modern art. ■ *T6716141: no fixed hours; admission by donation.*

Exiting the cloister, across the path is the Chamber of the Holocaust: a memorial to the six million Jews murdered by the Nazis. ■ *T6715105: Sunday-Thursday 0830-1800, Friday 0800-1500. Adult 10 NIS).*

A number of prominent Christians are buried here, including three important Middle East/Holy Land archaeologists, **Sir WM Flinders Petrie**, **Leslie Starkey**, **CS. Fisher**, and the German industrialist **Oskar Schindler**. The cemetery is on the lower southwest slope of Mt Zion. To find Schindler's Grave (immortalized in the Speilberg film), enter the cemetery gate, then drop down to the second (lower) level. The grave is fairly central (it has no headstone so can be hard to find, though it is usually adorned by small piles of stones). **Protestant cemetery**

Although now venerated as the site of the **House of the High Priest Caiaphas** (again!), and thus the place where St Peter thrice denied Jesus before the crowing of the cock (whence the church derives its name, *Matthew 26:57-75; Mark 14:53-72; Luke 22:54-71; John 18:13-27*), it is still not certain when tradition first placed this event at this particular spot. Excavations at the site have revealed a rock-cut crypt (now referred to as the 'First Prison of Christ') above which was built a monastic church some time in the Byzantine period (probably sixth century CE). However, the earliest mention of this as the place where Peter "went outside, and wept bitterly" (*Luke 22:62*) is recorded several centuries later. By the 11th-12th centuries CE the site was firmly on the pilgrim trail, billed (as today) as the 'Church of St Peter in Gallicantu', though this structure had been destroyed by the mid-15th century CE. The present church was built in 1928-32 and has a fine view over the 'Ancient City on the Southeast Ridge' (the 'real' Mt Zion! See page 174). **Church of St Peter in Gallicantu**

Jerusalem

As a further challenge to the identification of this site as the location of the House of the High Priest Caiaphas, the question has been raised as to the positioning of the home of such an important figure on the *lower* slopes of Mount Zion. Though one can be fairly sure that the city walls enclosed Mount Zion at the time of Jesus' crucifixion, it is less sure that they extended this far down to the edge of the Tyropoeon Valley. Thus, would such an important figure as the High Priest have his house *outside* the city walls? Further, such a wealthy and influential man as Caiaphas would surely have had his property on the very top of the hill, thus making the case of the alternative site to the north of the Church of the Dormition (within the Armenian St Saviour compound) a more compelling one. Either way, the exact position remains pure conjecture. ■ *T6731739. 0830-1200, 1400-1700, closed Sunday. Souvenir shop, refreshments, toilets.*

Mount of Olives

The Mount of Olives stands to the east of Jerusalem, separated from the Old City by the Kidron Valley (see page 172). It is part of a ridge of soft sandstone that has Mt Scopus at its northern end, the Mount of Olives at the centre, and the low rise above the Arab village of Silwan to the south. Much of its west and south slopes are covered by a vast ancient Jewish cemetery, whilst several major events in the life of Jesus in the days leading up to the Crucifixion are commemorated in a number of churches located here. The various viewpoints high up on the Mount of Olives also offer arguably the best panorama of the whole city.

Ins and outs

Getting there and around The logical place to begin a tour of the Mount of Olives is at the top, thus avoiding a steep upward climb. Bus 37 from the junction of HaNevi'im and Shivtei Yisra'el in the New City comes here, or you could spend 15 NIS on a taxi. If you are part of a guided tour you will probably be dropped at the summit, though the majority of independent sightseers will reach the Mount of Olives at the bottom: from St Stephen's Gate in the Old City walls; from the junction of Jericho Rd and Sulaiman St at the northeast corner of the Old City; or by making their way up from the tombs in the Kidron Valley below. Hence, the description below is from the bottom up.

Warning This route can become particularly congested when several tour buses arrive simultaneously (as is usually the case). In addition to making both sightseeing and prayer/contemplation difficult, the sheer numbers of visitors here attracts both hawkers and salesmen, as well as crooks. In the crush of bodies and confusion, be careful not to get your pocket picked, and be cautious of having a bag full of valuables slung unattended over your shoulder. There are also reports of cases of sexual harassment (and even assault) of lone female visitors wandering around here. Be particularly careful in the high-walled cemeteries; it may be wise **not** to come here unaccompanied. Lone females should definitely not continue down the east side of the hill from Bethphage to Bethany. **NB** Suitably modest clothing must be worn when visiting these sites.

History

The earliest history of the Mount of Olives relates to a function still undertaken here today: that of a **burial place**. Burial shafts dating to the late third millennium have been found on the east and south slopes of the ridge, whilst by the Late Bronze Age (c. 1550-1200 BCE) the west slope of the Mount of Olives formed part of the main cemetery of Jerusalem. This tradition of burial here on the southwest slopes of the Mount of Olives, and on the other side of the Kidron Valley beneath the east side of the Temple Mount/Haram al-Sharif, stems from the belief that the Kidron is in fact the **Valley of Jehoshaphat** where the whole of humanity will assemble to be judged by God: "I will also gather all nations, and will bring them down into the valley of Jehoshaphat" (*Joel 3:2*), and "Then shall the Lord go forth, and fight against those nations, as when he fought in the day of battle. And his feet shall stand in that day upon the mount of Olives, which is before Jerusalem on the east, and the mount of Olives shall cleave in the midst thereof toward the east and toward the west, and there shall be a very great valley" (*Zechariah 14:3-4*). As well as the Jewish cemeteries here, there are also Muslim and Christian graveyards. Many of the Jewish tombs here were systematically desecrated during the Jordanian occupation of part of Jerusalem (1948-67), when the graves were allegedly broken up for use as paving stones in the latrines. One notable recent burial in the large Jewish cemetery here is fat crook Robert Maxwell (whose grave would make an excellent latrine).

There is some evidence to suggest that the Mount of Olives was the site of an Iron Age Jewish sanctuary, possibly David's 'Nob' (*II Samuel 15:30-32*) or Solomon's temples to foreign gods on the Mount of Corruption (*II Kings 23:13*): the low rise above Silwan. After the construction of the Temple by Solomon, the Mount of Olives became associated with the Ceremony of the Red Heifer (*Numbers 19:1-10*).

The importance of the Mount of Olives to Christians stems from the episodes in the life of **Jesus** that were enacted here, most notably in the days leading up to his arrest and Crucifixion. It is highly probable that on his visits to Jerusalem, particularly during festivals when the costs of accommodation in the city would sky-rocket (as today), Jesus stayed with friends at Bethany (for example, see *Mark 11:11-12; Luke 10:38*). Thus the road between Bethany and the Temple (pretty much following the route of the tour outlined below) would have been well known to him. It was from Bethphage on the top of the Mount of Olives that Jesus begun his triumphal entry into Jerusalem before the Passover (*Matthew 21:1-11; Mark 11:1-11; Luke 19:28-40; John 12:12-15*); where Jesus foretold the future of the city (*Matthew 24-25; Mark 13:1-4*) and

Jerusalem

Mount of Olives

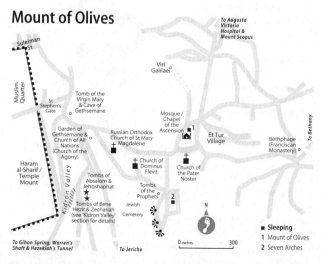

wept over it (*Luke 19:37, 41-44*); and in the garden at the foot of the slope, Gethsemane, that he was betrayed and arrested (*Matthew 26:36-56; Mark 14:32-50; Luke 22:39-54; John 18:1-12*). Luke's gospel also places the Ascension on the Mount of Olives (*Luke 24:50-52*).

The early **Byzantine** period saw numerous churches established on the Mount of Olives to commemorate these events, and by the sixth century CE a Christian visitor (Theodosius, c. 518) noted 24 churches on the hill. Many were destroyed during the Persian invasion of 614 CE, though some were rebuilt immediately afterwards and others later by the Crusaders. However, subsequent years of neglect left the area in a state of ruination and many of the churches that you see today are primarily the result of late 19th-and early 20th-century restoration efforts.

Tomb of the Virgin Mary The bend in the road outside the Tomb of the Virgin Mary is marked by the reputed **Tomb of Mujir al-Din** (1456-1522), a noted Arab scholar who has provided a valuable commentary on 15th-century Jerusalem and Hebron. A 20th-century dome, supported by four pillars, stands above a simple white stone shrine within a walled enclosure.

The entrance to the **Tomb of the Virgin Mary** (sometimes referred to as the **Church of the Assumption**) is located off an open square courtyard below, and to the left of, the Jericho Road. Descending into the sunken courtyard (**1**), before you stands the Crusader built entrance portal (**2**). The church was built by the Benedictines c. 1130 on the ruins of previous Christian shrines. After one has passed through the Crusader entrance, 44 steps descend to the remains of the Byzantine church. Much of the masonry at the upper end of this staircase, including the steps themselves, dates to the 12th century CE. At the 20th step, to the right, is the **tomb of the Crusader Queen Melisande** (died 1161) (**3**). Her body was moved to a new tomb at the foot of the stairs in the 14th century, though this has subsequently become lost. In later years Queen Melisande's tomb became associated with the burial place of the Virgin Mary's parents, **Joachim** and **Anne**. Almost opposite, several steps further down, is another **burial niche** (**4**) related to the family of the Crusader king Baldwin II. This was later identified with the tomb of the Virgin's husband, **Joseph**.

As you continue to the bottom of the stairs, the pointed Crusader arches give way to the round vaults of the Byzantine period church. It is not entirely certain when the Valley of Jehoshaphat first became associated as the place of the Virgin Mary's death (it's not mentioned in the gospels), though it is identified as the place of her burial in the anonymous second-third century CE *Transitus Mariae* (Assumption of Mary). A church may have been built above a rock-cut tomb on this site as early as 455 CE, with a bench *arcosolium*

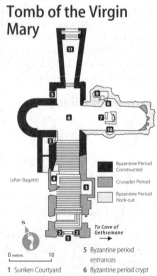

Tomb of the Virgin Mary

(after Bagatti)

■ Byzantine Period Constructed
■ Crusader Period
□ Byzantine Period Rock-cut

To Cave of Gethsemane →

N

0 metres 10

1 Sunken Courtyard
2 Crusader entrance portal
3 Tomb of the Crusader Queen Melisande
4 Burial niche of family of Baldwin II
5 Byzantine period entrances
6 Byzantine period crypt
7 Tomb of the Virgin
8 Niche
9 1st century CE style tomb
10 Mihrab
11 Original entrance to Cemetery

being venerated as the burial place of Mary. This **Church of St Mary in the Valley of Jehoshaphat** may have been destroyed during the Persian invasion of 614 CE, though it must have been rebuilt since it is described by Arculf c. 680 CE. It comprised an upper and lower church, both on a round plan. Though the seventh century CE saw Mt Zion identified as the site of the Dormition (see page 161), the church here was certainly still functioning in the ninth century CE. It was probably destroyed by the caliph al-Hakim in 1009 before the Benedictines rebuilt the church and added a large monastery. This was largely effaced by Salah al-Din in 1187, with many of the stones from the monastery finding their way into the sultan's new city wall.

The Byzantine **crypt (6)** at the bottom of the steps is 10.6 metres below the level of the entrance. The built apse to the left belongs to the Ethiopians, whilst the rock-cut apse to the right (east) is under the custodianship of the Armenians, Greeks, Copts and Syrians. The Eastern Orthodox influence is manifested in the darkness of the church and the incense-thickened atmosphere. At the centre of east apse (right) is a small square chapel marking the supposed site of the **tomb of the Virgin (7)**. As with the tomb of Christ in the Church of the Holy Sepulchre, this tomb has been cut away from the surrounding rock. To its north, a niche **(8)** stands at the entrance to another tomb of the first century CE style **(9)**. To the south of the Virgin's tomb a *mihrab* **(10)** marks the direction of Mecca: Muslims revere Mary as the mother of the prophet Jesus. ■ *0600-1145, 1430-1700 daily. Free though donation is expected.*

Returning to the sunken courtyard, a passageway to the east leads to the **Cave of Gethsemane** (or 'Cave of the Oil Press'). Quite possibly a natural cave, it contains a pre-Christian water cistern that appears to have been used later as a Byzantine and then Crusader burial place. At the time of Jesus it appears that an oil press (*Hebrew*: Gat Shemen) was operating here, whilst the cave may have been used as a shelter at other times. During the Byzantine period the cave became associated with a number of traditions surrounding Jesus, including the site where the Disciples rested whilst he prayed "a stone's throw away" (*Luke 22:41*), and where he was betrayed and arrested. ■ *T6283264. 0800-1200 1430-1800. Free.*

Before entering the Garden of Gethsemane, it is worth continuing a short distance south along the Jericho Road in order to admire the superb west façade of the church. Above the colonnaded portico of Corinthian columns is a glittering gold mosaic depicting Christ as mediator between God and man, and assuming the suffering of the world (hence the alternative name, Church of the Agony). The quote is from the *Epistle of Paul the Apostle to the Hebrews* (*Hebrews 5:7*). **NB** Beware of the heavy speeding traffic on this road.

Enter the **Garden of Gethsemane** by the small gate in the north wall. Due to heavy pilgrim/tourist congestion you are supposed to walk around the garden in an anti-clockwise direction. This garden was identified as early as the fourth century CE as the place where Jesus prayed, was betrayed by Judas and arrested (*Matthew 26:36-56; Mark 14:32-50; Luke 22:39-54; John 18:1-12*), though the tradition may be earlier. The dating of the olive trees in the garden varies between 300 and 2300 years old, though this upper limit seems unlikely since the Romans are widely believed to have stripped the entire region around Jerusalem bare during their siege of 70 CE (see for example Josephus, *Jewish War*, V, 264).

The present **Church of All Nations (Church of the Agony)** was built in 1924 from subscriptions collected worldwide (hence the popular name). It was designed by the Italian architect **Antonio Barluzzi** as a triple-aisled

Cave of Gethsemane

Garden of Gethsemane and Church of All Nations

Jerusalem

basilica, with the twelve low domes in the ceiling being decorated with the coats of arms of the countries that donated towards the church's construction. The purple glass in the windows dims the light entering the church, perhaps representing the "hour when darkness reigns" (*Luke 22:53*) of Jesus' arrest. The focal point of the church is the section of bedrock upon which Jesus is said to have prayed prior to his arrest.

The present church largely follows the line of the Byzantine basilica built here between 379 and 384 CE by Theodosius I; in fact the two internal lateral apses include some courses of the Byzantine church, plus sections of the original mosaic floor, can also be seen. It is generally believed that the church was destroyed in the earthquake of 747/8 CE. The Crusaders rebuilt the church c. 1170, though this time on a slightly different orientation. The church appears to have been abandoned by 1345. ■ *T6283264. 0800-1145, 1430-1800. Free.*

Russian Orthodox Church of St Mary Magdalene	This attractive church was built by Czar Alexander III in 1888 and is most noted for its seven Kremlin-style gold onion-shaped domes. Only limited access to the church is possible. Buried within the convent grounds is Princess Alice of Greece, mother of Prince Philip, Duke of Edinburgh. ■ *T6284371. Tuesday and Thursday 1000-1130.*

Church of Dominus Flevit

This attractive 20th-century church is built on a site that was associated by medieval pilgrims with the tradition of Jesus weeping over the city as he rode towards it (on Palm Sunday). However, the land upon which the church was built shows signs of far earlier usage, the evidence of which can be seen just inside the gate of the grounds, to the right. Excavations in the early 1950s revealed the remains of a **cemetery** first used in the Late Bronze Age (c. 1550-1200 BCE) that later became the **largest necropolis** of the Roman period thus far discovered in Jerusalem. Covering 0.6 hectares, the necropolis contained at least 20 *arcosolium* burial caves (arched recesses) and 38 pit tombs, most dating to the third-fourth centuries CE, though the site continued in use during the Byzantine period. Seven hard limestone sarcophagi were found, some of which were elaborately decorated. In addition, over 120 *ossuaries* (secondary burial receptacles into which bones are put after the flesh has decayed) were discovered, about a third of which bear inscriptions (in Aramaic, Hebrew and Greek). The first two tombs on display just inside the gate are thought to date to the period 100 BCE-135 CE, and were generally used for secondary burial in ossuaries. The tomb fell out of use in 135 CE when Hadrian created his city of Aelia Capitolina on the ruins of Jerusalem, and forbade Jews access to the city. The third tomb is of an arcosolium type, with the bodies places in the arched recesses, and is thought to date to the third-fourth century CE. The fourth tomb is somewhat older. The Late Bronze Age tombs could not be preserved, though they provided a very rich assemblage of pottery, plus some alabaster and faience vessels and Egyptian scarabs.

Continuing along the path brings you to the **Church of Dominus Flevit** ('the Lord wept'), built in 1955 to a tear-shaped design by Antonio Barluzzi. Its most notable feature is the 'Chalice' window, which beautifully frames the view of the Old City to the west. The present church stands on the site of a Byzantine-style chapel, though experts are quick to point out that it almost certainly dates to the Early Arab period, c. 675 CE. From at least the seventh century CE onwards a liturgical procession began at the top of the Mount of Olives on Maundy Thursday, arriving in Jerusalem on the morning of Good Friday. This may be when the tradition of this site as the place where Jesus wept began. However, the fourth century CE pilgrim Egeria also mentions such a procession, and excavations have also revealed the remains of a fourth century

Jesus weeps over the city

"When Jesus came in sight of the city, he wept over it and said, 'If only you had known this day the way that leads to peace! But now it is hidden from your sight. For a time will come upon you, when your enemy shall cast a trench about you, and encircle you and hem you in on all sides. And they will bring you to the ground, you and your children within your walls, and not leave you one stone standing on another, because you did not recognize the time of God's visitation'." (Luke 19:41-44)

CE monastery here. Its dedication has not been established. The small terrace in front of the Church of Dominus Flevit provides an excellent viewpoint for secular visitors, and a quiet place for prayer and meditation for pilgrims. ■ *T6274931. Daily 0800-1145 1430-1700. Free. Toilets, small souvenir shop.*

Tombs of the Prophets Despite the claim that these are the tombs of the prophets **Haggai**, **Zechariah** and **Malachi**, who lived c. sixth-fifth centuries BCE, this tomb complex is in fact part of the first century BCE-135 CE necropolis that you may already have seen within the grounds of the Church of Dominus Flevit. In fact, these style tombs (*kokhim*) did not come into use for Jewish burials until the first century BCE. Its radiating fan-shape is unusual, however. Some of the inscriptions discovered here suggest that the complex was reused for the burial of foreign Christians in the fourth and fifth centuries CE. ■ *Sunday-Friday 0900-1500, closed Saturday. Admission is free in theory, though you may be expected to pay a tip if you don't have your own torch and have to be shown round. Cold drinks are available here.*

Old City viewpoint Climbing the steps and turning right brings you to the Old City viewpoint; one of Jerusalem's best panoramas. The sun is best placed for photography early in the morning. The IDF soldiers normally stationed here will pose for photos for free, though the old Arab men with the camels make their income this way, so you will be expected to pay. Those who like to pose sitting on a camel in front of a spectacular backdrop will not be disappointed here.

Church of the Pater Noster Early Christian visitors such as Eusebius (c. 260-340 CE) and the Bordeaux Pilgrim (c. 333 CE) record that the Emperor Constantine ordered a church built on the Mount of Olives above a cave that was venerated as a place at which Jesus taught the disciples. The site also became identified with the Ascension (*Luke 24:50-52*). Constantine's church, possibly built under the supervision of his mother Queen Helena, was formerly dedicated as the Church of the Disciples and the Ascension, though most early sources refer to it by its popular name, **Eleona** ('Church of the Olive Groves': an Aramaic 'a' added to the Greek 'elaion' creates 'of olives'). Visiting the church in c. 384, the pilgrim Egeria noted that the site was identified with Jesus' teaching on the ultimate conflict between good and evil (*Matthew 24, 25*), and no mention is made of the Ascension, the site of which had supposedly been moved further up the hill.

Following the destruction of the church in 614 CE by the Persians, the fate of the site is not entirely clear. Though visiting pilgrims mention the Church of the Ascension, there are few references to Eleona, yet a "Church where Christ Taught his Disciples" is mentioned in a ninth century CE list. It is now widely believed that the site here lay in ruins until the arrival of the Crusaders, when the cave became associated specifically with Jesus' teaching to the Disciples of the **Lord's Prayer**. Early in the 12th century CE a modest oratory was built, followed by a succession of churches destroyed and rebuilt as the fortunes of the Crusaders and Muslims ebbed and flowed.

The property was bought in 1857 by the Princesse de la Tour d'Auvergne, who spent the rest of her life searching for the cave. She is responsible for the cloister here (1868) and the adjacent Carmelite convent (1872). In 1910 the White Fathers discovered the remains of the Byzantine Church of Eleona, and further excavations were made by the Dominicans in 1918. Subsequent appeals were made to raise a basilica above the ancient foundations, though work stopped when funds ran out. The unfinished structure remains as it was left and is now referred to as the **Church of the Pater Noster** ('Our Father').

The site is perhaps most famous today for the 60 plus renditions of the Lord's Prayer inscribed onto ceramic tiles, each in a different language. The collection originally occupied the cloister, though recent additions have expanded into the church, vestibule, and all available walls. More recent translations include Gujarati, Hausa and Igbo. The small gift shop sells postcards of each panel, though certain languages tend to sell out quicker than others (not necessarily English, Spanish, French, etc, but more obscure ones such as Rwandan). It is also possible to view the cave at the centre of the reconstructed (but unfinished) basilica. The 20th-century basilica was supposed to recreate the fourth century CE building, though the fact that it was never finished perhaps avoided the controversy over what form the original building actually took: there is still lively debate as to whether the fourth-century basilica's internal apse was polygonal or rectangular! The crypt of the basilica was built around the cave, and it is still possible to descend inside today. It is not thought that the cave itself was originally part of a tomb, though it certainly cuts part of a first century CE *kokhim* tomb. ■ *T5894904. 0830-1145, 1500-1645. Free. Souvenir shop.*

Mosque/Chapel of the Ascension
Of the four gospels, only Luke mentions the Ascension of Jesus into heaven (*Luke 24:50-52* and *Acts 1:9*). Murphy-O'Connor (*The Holy Land*, 1992) suggests that the discrepancy in the two accounts (written by the same hand) lies in the fact that Luke "was aware that he was not recording an historical event; from his point of view the Ascension was much more a literary way of drawing a line between the terrestrial mission of Jesus and that of the apostles". Of course the actual site of the Ascension is not specified, though the Byzantine pilgrims in their zeal to localize every detail of the gospels came to venerate a cave on the Mount of Olives as the scene. The choice of a cave as the place to venerate the Ascension arises probably not from some unusual interpretation of the gospels, but rather from the realities of life in Jerusalem for early Christians: the fear of persecution meant that it was probably safer to congregate in a cave than in the open. As mentioned in the background to the Church of Eleona/Church of the Pater Noster (see page 169), the cave was rapidly forgotten as the place of the Ascension and the venerated site 'moved up the hill'. In c. 384 CE the pilgrim Egeria records that the Ascension was celebrated at the site now occupied by the Mosque/Chapel of the Ascension.

The first church on this site appears to have been built some time before 392 CE by Poimenia, a wealthy and pious Roman woman. It was almost certainly destroyed by the Persians in 614 CE and then restored by Modestus. The round building, open to the sky, is described c. 680 CE by Arculf, including the footprints of Jesus in the dust. Arculf's description is largely confirmed by excavations undertaken in 1960 by the Franciscan Fathers. The present octagonal form dates to the Crusader restoration of 1102, when several other alterations were made. At the end of the 12th century Salah al-Din granted the site

The Ascension

"Jesus led the disciples out as far as to Bethany, and he lifted up his hands, and blessed them. And it came to pass, while he blessed them, he was parted from them, and carried up into heaven." (Luke 24:50-52)

to two of his pious followers (Wali al-Din and Abu'l Hasan), and the custodians have been Muslim ever since.

The small mosque and minaret at the entrance to the site date to 1620. If the Crusader-built chapel is closed it may be necessary to find the custodian of the mosque (ask around and someone is bound to assist you). The original Crusader shrine featured an outer colonnaded cloister within which stood an octagon of columns and arches, open to the sky. A stone dome on an octagonal drum now covers the octagonal Crusader chapel, and some of the arches have been blocked. The octagon has also been truncated to the east. Of particular note are the 12th century CE Crusader capitals on the columns surrounding the octagon, especially the two featuring bird-headed winged quadrupeds. A sectioned-off area of the floor bears the supposed imprint of Jesus' right foot; the imprint of his left foot was removed to the al-Aqsa Mosque some time around 1200 CE. ■ *No fixed opening hours. Admission 3 NIS. Modest dress essential, shoes must be removed.*

Russian Orthodox Convent of the Ascension and Viri Galilaei A little to the north of the Mosque/Chapel of the Ascension is the **Russian Orthodox Convent of the Ascension**, whose tower provides one of the best views from the top of the Mount of Olives, but is unfortunately rarely open to visitors. Also to the north is the site of **Viri Galilaei** (see Mount of Olives map), where tradition relates that the disciples were referred to as 'Men of Galilee' immediately after the Ascension (*Acts 1:11*). The site is marked by a Greek Orthodox Church, though a Byzantine chapel may well have stood here originally.

Bethphage Bethphage is mentioned in the gospels as the place where Jesus mounted the donkey to make his triumphal entry into Jerusalem; an event that Christians now celebrate as 'Palm Sunday' (*Matthew 21:1-11; Mark 11:1-11; Luke 19:28-40; John 12:12-15*). Though the gospels do not reveal the specific place where the procession begun, the **Franciscan monastery** that now commemorates the event is in all likelihood pretty much 'in the vicinity' of Bethphage.

Within the courtyard of the monastery (ring the bell for admission) is a late 19th-century church (1883) built upon the remains of a medieval chapel. Enshrined within the Crusader chapel is a stone block that is venerated as the mounting-stone that Jesus used to mount the donkey. As Murphy-O'Connor dryly observes (*The Holy Land*, 1993), a mounting-stone may have been necessary to mount a huge battle-charging Crusader steed, but would it really have been necessary for your average Palestinian donkey? Nevertheless, the Franciscans Palm Sunday procession begins from this chapel. ■ *T6284352. 0700-1145 1400-1730, closes one hour earlier in winter, ring the bell for admission. Free, though gatekeeper may expect a small tip.*

Routes From Bethphage it is logical to follow the path along the wall behind the monastery and continue down to **Bethany** (see page 264). **NB** This route is not recommended for unaccompanied females or those making an ostentatious display of wealth.

Jerusalem

Kidron Valley

*The Kidron Valley (Arabic: Wadi Jauz) forms Jerusalem's eastern border, divid-
ing the Old City and East Jerusalem area from Mt Scopus, the Mount of Olives
and the Arab village of Silwan. The valley is at its deepest between the Temple
Mount/Haram al-Sharif and the Mount of Olives, where it is often referred to by
its biblical name, the **Valley of Jehoshaphat** ('Yahweh judges'). The Kidron
owes its importance to this identification as the place where the **Last Judgement**
is due to take place (see for example Jeremiah 31:40; Joel 3:2; Zechariah 14:3-4),
and this is why so many cemeteries and burial grounds are located on the valley's
slopes. There are a number of tombs and monuments of particular note in the
Kidron Valley, though a succession of legends, traditions and popular stories
have served to obscure many of their original functions.*

Ins and outs

**Getting there
and getting
around**
There are several points of access to the main sites of the Kidron Valley. A path leads
down from opposite the Garden of Gethsemane and Church of All Nations at the
beginning of the Mount of Olives tour described above; they can be reached by walking up the valley from Warren's Shaft and the Gihon Spring on the tour of the 'Ancient
City on the Southeast Ridge' (page 177); or they can be reached by the modern flight
of steps (labelled 'Abshalom's Pillar Observation Point') at the southeast corner of the
Old City. **NB** Unaccompanied women should not venture down here alone. In recent
visits the author has encountered a variety of suspicious characters 'concealed' within
the tombs, ranging from argumentative monks, through groups of Arab youths, to
gangs of drunken Russians. For a map showing the position of these tombs, see the
'Mount of Olives' map on page 165.

**Tombs of
Absalom and
Jehoshaphat**
The most imposing monument here is the so-called **Tomb of Absalom**.
Resembling a bottle-shape at the top, the upper section is masonry whilst the
base below the cornice is cut directly from the rock. It stands 20 metres high
and is described by Geva as "probably the most complete tomb monument in
Israel" (*New Encyclopedia of Archaeological Excavations in the Holy Land*,
1993). The square, rock-hewn base features an unusual combination of styles,
including Ionic columns at each corner, a Doric frieze above, and an Egyp-
tian-influenced cavetto cornice. The upper masonry section features a concave conical roof resting on a stone pedestal (*tholos*). The entrance to the tomb
within is on the south side, above the level of the cornice, whilst the other holes
hacked in the side were made by
grave-robbers. It is generally believed
to have been built in the second half
of the first century BCE.

The dating of the tomb has negated
the popular association with **Absalom**, son of David, who lived almost
1,000 years before this tomb was cut.
In fact, this association with Absalom
was probably first made by Benjamin
of Tudela c. 1170 from the reading of
a line in the *Second Book of Samuel*:
"Now Absalom in his lifetime had
taken and reared up for himself a pillar, which is in the king's valley" (*II*

'Tombs of Absalom
& Jehoshaphat'

Entrance

'Tomb of
Jehoshaphat'
complex

Nephesh
('Tomb of Absalom')

N

0 metres 5

Samuel 18:18). In fact, an 18th century CE commentator relates how passers-by used to throw stones at the tomb because of Absalom's treachery towards his father.

Though the Tomb of Absalom is a tomb in its own right, it also forms part of the **Tomb of Jehoshaphat** that is located behind (to the northeast, cut into the rock). In fact, the Tomb of Absalom may well have acted as a *nephesh*, or memorial ceno-

Tombs of Absalom and Jehoshaphat

taph, for the burial complex cut in the cliff behind. For whom the eight-chambered catacomb-like burial complex was built for is not certain, and it is now popularly known as the Tomb of Jehoshaphat. Its entrance is in the northeast corner of the court, behind the Tomb of Absalom, and features a finely carved pediment. Without a torch it is difficult to locate the intricate carvings inside, though their style suggests a Herodian period dating (c. 37 BCE-70 CE). The Byzantine period saw these catacombs occupied by hermits.

Just to the south is a further burial complex, also featuring a *nephesh* (funerary monument) and a catacomb burial complex. The **Tomb of the Bene Hezir** is the rock-cut catacomb that you come to first. It has a Doric façade comprising two free-standing and two engaged columns with Doric capitals supporting a Doric frieze. A Hebrew inscription on the *architrave* (beam resting on the capitals) above the Doric columns identifies individual members of the priestly family of the **Bene Hezir** (see *I Chronicles 24:15*). The burial complex comprises a porch, several burial chambers, a flight of steps that leads to ground level, and a passageway that connects with the *nephesh*. It almost certainly dates to the late second-early first century BCE, though a 12th century CE tradition linked it with **St James the Less**, and you still sometimes see it referred to as his tomb.

Tombs of the Bene Hezir and Zechariah

'Tombs of the Bene Hezir & Zechariah'

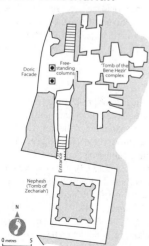

Just to the south is the *nephesh* belonging to the Tomb of the Bene Hezir. This freestanding monument was carved directly out of the rock and comprises a five-metre by five-metre cube base supporting a pyramid. All four sides of the cube are decorated with Ionic columns and an Egyptian cavetto cornice. The decorative style strongly suggests that it is contemporary with the Bene Hezir complex, though it is still referred to as the **Tomb of Zechariah**.

From these tombs it is possible to continue down the Kidron Valley to Warren's Shaft and the Gihon Spring (see page 177), or take the upper path leading up to the Arab village of **Silwan**.

The village of Silwan (from 'Siloam') occupies the east side of the Kidron

Silwan

(Map labels: Doric Facade, Free-standing columns, 'Tomb of the Bene Hezir' complex, Entrance, Nephesh ('Tomb of Zechariah'), N, 0 metres 5)

Jerusalem

Valley, and looks down upon the 'Ancient City on the Southeast Ridge' (page 174). Though this village has been an Arab village for centuries, the fact that it was the location of the City of David 3,000 years ago has now made it the target of the Jewish settler movement.

Sometimes referred to as the 'Tomb of the Pharaoh's Wife/Daughter', the **Monolith of Silwan** is located on the edge of an escarpment as you enter the village. It comprises a free-standing cube (5.5 metres by 4.8 metres) cut from the rock, and previously capped by a pyramid (presumably similar to the 'Tomb of Zechariah' described above). The pyramid was removed in the Roman period (for an unknown reason) and the Monolith now blends in with the rest of the houses making it difficult to locate without local help. It is a funerary monument probably dating to the ninth-seventh centuries BCE, with a distinct Phoenician-Egyptian influence. The hole cut through the Hebrew inscription was made by the Byzantine hermit who made his home inside.

Ancient City on the Southeast Ridge ('City of David')

The low ridge to the south of the Temple Mount/Haram al-Sharif (sandwiched between the Tyropoeon Valley to the west and the Kidron Valley to the east) is the site where David built his capital early in his reign, effectively founding the new city of Jerusalem. Referred to variously as the 'City of David', 'Ancient City on the Southeast Ridge', or the 'Ophel Ridge', the site today presents an insight into 4,000 years of continuous occupation, of which David's building efforts were just a small part. Remains from most periods of occupation can be seen in the City of David Archaeological Garden, though the name is somewhat misleading since not all are from David's city. Further down the ridge are a number of interesting sites related to the sophisticated water-supply system that served the city, most notably Warren's Shaft and Hezekiah's Tunnel.

Ins and outs

Getting there and around The best place to begin a tour of the 'Ancient City on the Southeast Ridge' is at Dung Gate. Exit the gate and turn left (east) along HaOphel Rd. Almost immediately on your right, just after the car-park, a road leads south down into the Tyropoeon Valley (see page 180). Take this road downhill, looking out for the entrance to the City of David Archaeological Garden (just before the 'Shuiki Grosserie' shop). The path just beyond this shop leads down to Warren's Shaft.

History

Archaeological, epigraphic and biblical evidence of pre-Davidic Jerusalem does not allow a detailed reconstruction of the city's development and history prior to the Israelite conquest, though the exact location of the early city has been irrefutably established – here on the southeast ridge. The background of the city's inhabitants is not entirely clear either, though biblical sources appear to suggest a mixture of Amorites and Hittites (*Ezekial 16:3*). The exact year of **David's** conquest is unknown, though it is generally believed to have been fairly early in his reign (997 BCE is often mentioned). The capture of the city is graphically described in biblical sources (*II Samuel 5:6-9*), though some of the key action events are also ascribed to Joab (*I Chronicles 11:4-7*). What is clear, however, is that the resident population, known as the **Jebusites**, were not murdered or expelled but continued to live amongst their Israelite conquerors (*Judges 1:21*).

David subsequently shifted his capital here, and as the city developed to the north and west during the reigns of David's successors (Solomon, then the kings of Judah), the seat of power shifted also. However, this southeast ridge remained settled and within the city walls until the first century CE at least. The subsequent centuries saw the settlement on this ridge alternately enclosed, then excluded from the confines of the city walls, and since about the 11th century CE it has been located outside. It remained an important part of Jerusalem, however, not least because of the complex water-supply system built here

Ancient City on the southeast ridge, Kidron Valley & Tyropoean Valley

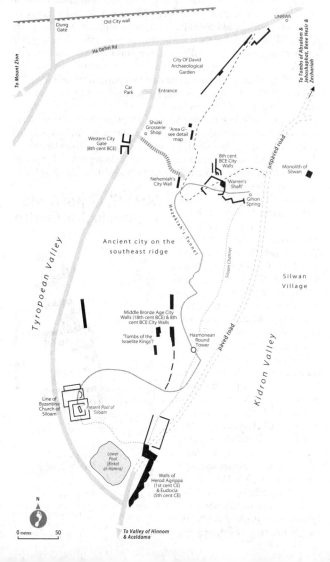

Jerusalem

that drew water from the Gihon Spring in the Kidron Valley and supplied it to the city. Extensive excavations were begun by Warren in 1867, and have continued intermittently until the present day. Some questions remain unresolved, such as the precise location of **'Millo'** upon which David's city was centred (*I Chronicles 11:8; II Samuel 5:9*).

City of David Archaeological Garden

The City of David Archaeological Garden represents a century's worth of archaeological excavation of some 14 centuries of settlement. The site is well presented and clearly labelled. Though there are fragments scattered throughout the 'garden', the key point of interest is **Area G** excavated primarily by Yigal Shiloh between 1978-85, and often referred to as the 'Acropolis' (see map below).

Archaeologists believe that the houses built on the ridge c. 1800 BCE were constructed on the natural slopes and terraces. Some time in the 14th-13th centuries BCE a stone podium was built to flatten the ridge and to make construction easier. This was done by building stone compartments, filling them with rubble, then building above them. Some of these 14th-13th century BCE **compartment walls (1)** can still be seen, though no trace of the citadel that the Jebusites built on the podium (that was captured by David) has ever been found. The podium was extensively modified and repaired by David, then Solomon (10th-9th centuries BCE), and strengthened by means of a massive **stone ramp** or **glacis (2)**.

During the seventh century BCE terraces were cut into this ramp and a number of houses were constructed. One such house, notable for its thick walls and ashlar blocks set into its corners, can still be seen today. This four-roomed **'House of Ahiel' (3)** has been partially preserved, including its west side **(4)** and **two monoliths (5)** that supported the roof, the base of the retaining wall to the east **(6)**, an **outer stairway (7)**, and a small room over a cesspit to the north that is presumably a **toilet (8)**. Part of a separate house to the north has also been identified, taking is name, the **'Burnt Room' (9)**, from the destruction debris found here that resulted from the Babylonian sacking of the city in 586 BCE (*II Kings 25:9*). A good description of the destruction inflicted here by the Babylonians is provided by Nehemiah (*Nehemiah 2:13-16*).

The origin of the high defensive **wall (10)** along the crest of the ridge is still a matter of debate. Some sources believe that this is the fifth century BCE wall built by Nehemiah, that was later rebuilt in the second century BCE by the Hasmoneans. Others believe that it is entirely the work of the Hasmoneans; the two **towers (11)** are certainly Hasmonean work. This is a section of the 'First Wall' that Josephus describes (*The Jewish War, V, 4*). ■ *Sunday-Thursday 0900-1700, Friday 0900-1300. Adult 8 NIS.* **NB** *It may be necessary to buy your entry*

'Area G', City of David Archaeological Garden

N
0 metres 5

1 14th–13th century BCE compartment walls
2 Stone ramp (Glacis)
3 'House of Ahiel'
4 W section of 'House of Ahiel'
5 Monoliths
6 Retaining wall of 'House of Ahiel'
7 Outer stairway
8 Toilet
9 'Burnt Room'
10 Nehemiah's wall rebuilt by Hasmoneans (?)
11 Hasmonean towers

Jerusalem's early water-supply system

The primary source of water for the 'Ancient City on the Southeast Ridge/City of David' was the Gihon Spring. This rises to the surface in the Kidron Valley beneath the east slope of the ridge upon which the ancient city stood. Though perennially full, the **Gihon Spring** is an intermittent spring, gushing forth into the Kidron several times a day and thus requiring the construction of a series of reservoir pools to store the water. The main drainage channel linking these pools was the **'Siloam Channel'** (part channel, part tunnel) that ran for some 400 metres along the floor of the west side of the Kidron Valley, filling the reservoirs and irrigating the crops grown on the floor of the valley. A 120-metre section of this channel has been cleared.

The overwhelming disadvantage of this system is that the majority of it lay outside the city walls, and so was vulnerable when the city was under siege. Thus, two further tunnels were cut or enlarged as part of Jerusalem's early defensive water system. The dating of the first, **'Warren's Shaft'**, remains a matter of conjecture. Early opinion suggested that this shaft was cut by the Jebusites prior to David's capture of the city on the ridge, and may even have been the zinnor (gutter) up which the young king, or his general Joab, gained entrance to the city (II Samuel 5:8; I Chronicles 11:6). However, Yigal Shiloh, who was responsible for the most complete excavation of Warren's Shaft, rejects this view suggesting that the identification of the shaft as a Canaanite (Jebusite) water system "is unsubstantiated by any concrete archaeological evidence" and has been "rejected for various reasons – textual, architectural, and archaeological – by most scholars" (New Encyclopedia of Archaeological Excavations in the Holy Land, 1993). Shiloh suggests that the shaft is

Section through Warren's Shaft, Gihon Spring & Hezekiah's Tunnel

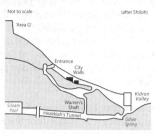

Not to scale   (after Shiloh)

characteristic of the Israelites, and dates it to the 10th or 9th century BCE.

The purpose of Warren's Shaft, (a natural fissure in the rock enlarged to form a vertical shaft), was to allow buckets to be lowered to the spring below without the water-drawers having to leave the city walls. This explanation took a long time to become accepted, and it wasn't until Kenyon's excavations of 1961-67 that it could be proved that the entrance to the shaft was indeed within the Canaanite and Israelite city walls.

The second tunnel of the defensive water system, **'Hezekiah's Tunnel'**, is far less controversial. It was, according to Shiloh, "planned and executed as part of a comprehensive design by Hezekiah's town planners" (ibid) in the eighth century BCE, with the archaeological evidence matching the biblical record (II Kings 20:20; II Chronicles 32:3-4, 32:20). It replaced the lower section of the Siloam Channel, and brought the water-supply system within the city walls.

ticket from the Wohl Archaeological Museum in the Jewish Quarter of the Old City ('combined' ticket costs 26 NIS).

'Warren's Shaft' is part of a defensive system designed to protect Jerusalem's early water source. It takes its name from one of the men who 'discovered' it in 1867, Sir Charles Warren (who later went on to become Commissioner of the Metropolitan Police in London at the time of the 'Jack the Ripper' murders). It

Warren's Shaft

Jerusalem

is entered today through an Ottoman-period building that houses a small museum explaining the excavation of the shaft and how the water-supply system functioned. Passing through a short tunnel you enter a rather steep section. The barrel-vaulted roof here is almost certainly Roman, suggesting an earlier collapse of the original roof. Descending the modern iron steps you reach the Israelite tunnel, which gradually widens to a platform before dropping down to a large natural cave. A natural vertical fissure, enlarged into 'Warren's Shaft' descends about 13 metres to a horizontal tunnel that delivered water from the Gihon Spring to the base of the shaft (this horizontal shaft later evolved into 'Hezekiah's Tunnel', see below). The water below cannot be seen from the top of the shaft, and drawing the water in buckets would have been particularly hard work. ■ *T6288141. Sunday-Thursday 0900-1700, Friday 0900-1300. Adult 8 NIS. Bring a torch and do not visit this site if you are any way claustrophobic – it also features a steep descent of over 80 steps.*

Ancient walls If you continue down to the floor of the Kidron Valley, on your way down you pass sections of the **Middle Bronze Age city wall** (18th century BCE) that may have been part of towers built to protect the city's water gate. The ancient wall, distinguishable by the massive blocks of roughly cut masonry, is overlain by sections of the **eighth century BCE city walls**, preserved in places to a height of three metres.

Gihon Spring and Hezekiah's Tunnel The first written reference to the **Gihon Spring** is the biblical account of Solomon's anointment as king by Zadok the priest and Nathan the prophet (*I Kings 1:33, 38, 45*). It takes its name from the Hebrew 'to gush forth', which describes the way in which this siphon works. As discussed earlier, the ancient city's water source was vulnerable to attack during sieges, so with the prospect of the Assyrian king Sennacherib's advance on the city, **Hezekiah** (727-698 BCE) began work on constructing defensive measures. After all, "why should the kings of Assyria come and find so much water?" (*II Chronicles 32:4*). The Siloam Channel that led from the Gihon Spring to the Lower Pool (now the 'Birkat al-Hamra') was blocked, and the source disguised. Hezekiah's water engineers then embarked upon an ambition construction project to divert the waters from the Gihon Spring to the Lower Pool via a new channel cut in the rock, but within the city walls: **Hezekiah's Tunnel**.

The gradient between the spring and the end of the tunnel is very slight, around 35 centimetres, and thus the tunnel required considerable planning. Running for approximately 533 metres, it follows a particularly winding course, which is attributed to three major factors: i) the necessity of avoiding bands of hard rock whilst exploiting natural fissures; ii) the inadequacies of surveying techniques; and iii) the need to avoid the burial places on the south end of the ridge (see 'Tombs of the Israelite kings' on page 187). Hezekiah's engineers worked towards each other from either end; a process described in the so-called **Siloam Inscription** found mounted on the wall at the south end of the tunnel. This contemporary account, written in Hebrew, is now in the Istanbul Museum, though the Israel Museum in Jerusalem has a copy. Murphy-O'Connor (*The Holy Land*, 1992) suggests that the inscription must be the work of a "proud engineer" since the king would have placed any such declaration in a far more prominent position!

Tour It's possible to walk along the entire length of the tunnel, emerging at the 'Pool of Siloam' after about half an hour (this will mean skipping the 'Tombs of the Israelite kings' and the 'Hasmonean round tower' at the southern end of the Kidron Valley, though this is no great loss). For the most part the

The 'Siloam Inscription'

"Behold the tunnel. This is the story of its cutting. While the miners swung their picks, one towards the other, and when there remained only three cubits to cut, the voice of one calling his fellow was heard – for there was a resonance in the rock coming from both north and south. So the day they broke through the miners struck, one against the other, pick against pick, and the water flowed from the spring towards the pool, 1,200 cubits. The height of the rock above the head of the miners was 100 cubits."

water is about one metre deep, though it is sometimes a little deeper at the beginning and end. You will be walking in this water so some form of footwear is recommended. If you are lucky enough to experience the siphon effect of the spring there is no need for concern: the water only rises 15-20 centimetres. Bringing a torch is essential, unless you want to pay a tip to a 'guide' holding a useless candle. It is impossible to get lost, though women should probably not attempt this walk unaccompanied.

The tunnel is entered via two flights of steps, the dates of which are uncertain (though probably medieval). About 20 metres into the tunnel it takes a sharp turn to the left. The chest-high wall here blocks a channel that leads to Warren's Shaft (see page 177). The point where the two groups of miners met is clearly visible, though the group working from the south had to lower the level of the floor because they had started too high. The tunnel eventually emerges into the Pool of Siloam. Details of the Pool of Siloam can be found in the section dealing with the brief Tyropoeon Valley tour (see page 180).
■ *Sunday-Thursday 0900-1700, Friday 0900-1500. Adult 8 NIS, though you will have to pay for any guides, however inadequate, and any candles used.*

Tombs of the Israelite kings

On the lower slopes of the Southeast Ridge is a large area that has been substantially, but inconclusively, excavated. The area has undoubtedly been worked as a quarry, probably some time between the second century BCE and second century CE (though experts can't agree), but there are also some far older shafts cut into the bedrock that are suggested as the **Tombs of the Israelite kings**.

As discussed in the description of the so-called Tomb of David on the Mt Zion tour (page 160), all the written evidence suggests that David and his sons and successors were buried within the walls of his city (*I Kings 2:10*); in other words, the 'Ancient City on the Southeast Ridge'. Weill, who excavated this area in 1913-14, proposed that the two 'tombs' located here belonged to David and his family members. The most impressive one is entered by a deep shaft leading to a vaulted tunnel 16.5 metres long and 4 metres high. A stone bench with a niche may have been intended for a coffin. In addition to the area being used as a quarry, the 'tombs' had been looted in antiquity, which fits in neatly with Josephus' observation that Hyrcanus took 3,000 talents from the Tomb of David to finance his mercenary army and pay off Antiochus VII Sidetes in the early second century BCE (*The Jewish War, I, 61*). The jury is still out on this one.

Round tower

Below the Tombs of the Israelite kings are the remains of a **round tower** generally attributed to the Hasmoneans. Could this be the "tower in Siloam" that fell and killed 18 people, as described by Jesus (*Luke 13:4*)? Below here, further to the south, are the remains of city walls built by Herod Agrippa (first century CE) and Eudocia (fifth century CE). At the apex of the 'triangle' formed by the ridge, the Kidron Valley meets the **Tyropoeon Valley** (below). From this point it is best to head north along the Tyropoeon Valley, back towards the Old City.

Tyropoeon Valley

The Tyropoeon Valley defines the western limits of the ridge upon which the 'Ancient City on the Southeast Ridge/City of David' stood. In antiquity it was a considerably deeper ravine, extending as far north as the present location of Damascus Gate, though centuries of building, destruction and rebuilding have filled it in somewhat. The name translates as Cheesemakers' Valley, though the origins are unclear. It may have been the inspiration for the "Blessed are the Cheesemakers" line in Monty Python's Life of Brian, *though as the Samaritan observes, "it's not supposed to be taken literally, and obviously refers to any manufacturer of dairy products".*

Ins and outs

Getting there and getting around   Though the tour of the limited sights in the Tyropoeon Valley can begin at the carpark just to the southeast of Dung Gate, the logical thing to do is to make the Tyropoeon Valley an extension of the 'Ancient City on the Southeast Ridge' tour (see above and colour map 2 for orientation).

Lower Pool (Birkat al-Hamra)   This pool was part of the reservoir system through which the Gihon Spring was exploited, and probably acted as an overflow from the Pool of Siloam as well as collecting the winter flood waters that gushed down the Tyropoeon Valley. The garden here is owned by the village of Silwan and is not generally open to visitors. It is possible to see the overflow channel between the Pool of Siloam and the Lower Pool, though. If you continue south from here you would eventually come to the **Monastery of St Onuphrius (Aceldama)** in the **Valley of Hinnom** (see page 182).

Pool of Siloam   Though it was fed by the Gihon Spring via Hezekiah's Tunnel, nobody is quite sure of the original form of the pool that Hezekiah cut. It seems highly likely that knowledge of the existence of Hezekiah's Tunnel became lost, and Siloam was thought to be a natural spring (Josephus refers to it as such). In fact, the pool was used by Jews for ritual purification ceremonies, particularly around the Feast of Tabernacles when water from the pool was carried up to the Temple in a gold ewer, possibly in the mistaken belief that this was the actual spring of the City of David. The pool may have been part of Herod's extensive building programme, possibly forming part of the huge bathhouse that is thought to have existed at the bottom of the Tyropoeon Valley. It is unlikely to have survived the Roman sack of Jerusalem in 70 CE.

It seems almost certain that this was the site of the Shrine of the Four Nymphs that Hadrian built for his new city of Aelia Capitolina in 135 CE, and this may well be the building that the Bordeaux pilgrim describes c. 333 CE. By the mid-fifth century CE the pool had become firmly linked with Jesus' miracle of giving sight to the man born blind (*John 9:1-12*), and the Empress Eudocia had the pool rebuilt with the **Church of Siloam** constructed above it. The **Byzantine pool** appears to have been almost square (22.8 metres by 21.6 metres), with an arcade on all four sides and a paved court to the south that was approached by a stepped street to the west. The church stood to the north, though topographical constraints meant that it had an odd plan. It was entered through the atrium to the north, which led into a stepped narthex, with the main body of the church (28 metres by 16 metres) divided into a nave and two aisles by four square piers. The south aisle overhung the north end of the pool, with the Piacenza pilgrim (c. 570 CE) describing the church as a "hanging basilica".

All that remains to be seen today is a narrow stone-lined pit (c. 18 metres by 5 metres) occupying a fraction of the Byzantine pool, with Hezekiah's Tunnel entering from the north. The church was destroyed by the Persians in 614 CE, the whole area being left in a state of desolation and villagers from Silwan occasionally shifting the accumulated debris so that they could draw water. The mosque was built in the late 19th century CE. ■ *Open when the representative of the custodians, the Islamic Waqf, is in attendance. Admission is officially free, though a tip may be expected for opening the gate. Children will lead you a short distance into Hezekiah's Tunnel for a small fee, though you are supposed to enter from the other end.*

Valley of Hinnom

The Valley of Hinnom begins to the northwest of the Old City, in the vicinity of the Mamilla Pool in Independence Park. It sweeps down in a gently curving northwest to southeast arc, defining the western boundary of the Old City, before turning east to join up with the Tyropoean and Kidron Valleys at a point to the south of the Old City (see topographical map of Jerusalem, page 84).

Much of the west side of the Valley of Hinnom is now occupied by the **New City***, so the various places there are included within the description of the 'New City, Southwestern suburbs'* *(see page 196).* *Described below are the points of interest on the east side of the valley, notably the* **Sultan's Pool** *and the* **Monastery of St Onuphrius (Aceldama)***.*

Ins and outs

To reach the sights described here on the east side of the Valley of Hinnom, exit Jaffa Gate and head south along the busy Hativat Yerushalayim. Just before the junction where Hativat Yerushalayim swings east (left) in a loop around Mount Zion, and the Hebron Road heads southwest (right), to the right of the road is the **Sultan's Pool**. Rather than following either Hativat Yerushalayim (left) or Hebron Rd (right), take the smaller road straight ahead (southeast) to reach the Greek monastery on the site of **Aceldama** (600m).

Getting there and around

History

The Valley of Hinnom has traditionally marked the boundary between the tribes of Benjamin and Judah (*Joshua 15:8, 18:16*), and was often the site of cultic places for the worship of non-Israelite gods (*II Kings 23:10; Jeremiah 32:35*). This is probably the reason why the valley became associated with the 'Valley of Slaughter' on the 'Day of Vengeance' that Jeremiah describes so vividly: "And the carcases of this people shall be meat for the fowls of the heaven, and for the beasts of the earth; and none shall fray them away" (*Jeremiah 7:32-33*). This tradition evolved into the Jewish concept of the 'hell of fire', or *Gehenna* (the latter word being the Greek and Latin form of 'Hinnom Valley'). The valley was used as a burial place in Roman and Byzantine times, notably at the southern end, and from this developed the tradition of Aceldama (see below). The 20th century CE has seen the construction of much of the 'New City' of Jerusalem on the west side of the valley.

The 'Sultan's Pool' (*Arabic*: Birkat al-Sultan) takes its name from Sulaiman II ('the Magnificent') who restored much of Jerusalem in the 16th century CE, including the present city walls and this pool. However, the origins of the pool

Sultan's Pool

here are much older, perhaps being part of the Herodian low-level aqueduct system that brought water to the city from 'Solomon's Pools' close to Bethlehem. The pool here was known to the Crusaders as the 'Germain's Pool', and was also restored by al-Nasir Mohammad in the 13th century CE. Despite Sulaiman II's restoration work, it soon fell into disrepair and by the 19th century it was generally referred to as just a muddy pool. It has now been filled in, and contains the Merrill Hasenfield Amphitheatre as the centrepiece to a large public park. This is one of Jerusalem's most atmospheric venues for live music, and tends to be the place where major international acts perform. Check listings in the *Jerusalem Post* and *What's On In Jerusalem*.

Monastery of St Onuphrius (Aceldama) St Onuphrius was a Byzantine-period Egyptian hermit whose claim to fame was the length of his beard, worn long to hide his nakedness! He may have been the inspiration for the character played by Terry Jones in Monty Python's *Life of Brian*, whose 18-year vow of silence was broken when Brian jumped on his toes! This site became associated with a number of traditions in the Byzantine period (and revived by the Crusaders), most notably as the Aceldama or 'Field of Blood' that the high priests bought as a burial place for foreigners with the 30 pieces of silver with which Judas betrayed Jesus. 'Field of Sleeping' is a more accurate translation of the Aramaic, and thus the site is also claimed as the traditional place where Judas hung himself. The monastery features a small cave (now used as a chapel) that a 16th century CE tradition claimed as the place where eight of the apostles hid during the Crucifixion. The cave is part of a series of first century BCE to first century CE rock-cut Jewish tombs that are to be found in the vicinity. Two distinct burial complexes close to the monastery are associated with Aceldama; one belonging to the Western Church and one belonging to the Eastern Church. Also nearby is the medieval charnel house built by the Order of the Knights of the Hospital of St John for the burial of pilgrims. ■ *Flexible hours. Free, though donations expected.*

East Jerusalem

To Palestinians, the term 'East Jerusalem' refers to the whole of the walled Old City, the districts just to the north such as Sheikh Jarrah, and those to the east and southeast including the Mount of Olives, Kidron Valley, Silwan, Tyropoeon Valley and Mt Zion. If some form of Palestinian state ever evolved, these various districts would be the desired capital. For most tourists and visitors to Jerusalem (and for the purposes of this Israel Handbook), 'East Jerusalem' is considered to be the area of the city just to the north of Damascus Gate.

Ins and outs

Getting there and getting around Bus 27 from the Central Bus Station terminates at the Nablus Rd Bus Station at the heart of East Jerusalem, whilst service taxis from most West Bank towns (Ramallah, Nablus, Jericho, Allenby/King Hussein Bridge) and Gaza run to or from the street just outside Damascus Gate. Most visitors to the various sites in East Jerusalem arrive via Damascus Gate.

Sights

Notre Dame de France Founded as a pilgrim hospice by the Augustinian Fathers of the Assumption in 1887, this imposing building is very much a statement about 19th-century Catholic France. It was built with subscriptions raised in every parish in France so that the French presence in the Holy City "would no longer be a nomad camped under a tent … but ensconced in her own palace, equal to her rivals" (quoted in Collins and Lapierre, *O Jerusalem*, 1972).

The building's solid granite walls and defensive capabilities meant that it was immediately pressed into service during the battle for Jerusalem in 1948; in fact it was to play a pivotal role. As former President of Israel Chaim Herzog observes, "a few hundred yards from the centre of the Jewish city in Jerusalem, the Arab Legion was halted. The Jewish city had been saved by the stubborn struggle of the defenders of Notre Dame" (*The Arab-Israeli Wars*, 1982).

The considerable damage inflicted in 1948 has subsequently been restored and the Notre Dame now functions again as a very pleasant pilgrim hostel. The five-metre-high statue of the Virgin Mary presenting her child to Jerusalem remains the building's crowning glory. ■ *T6279111, F6271995.*

Schmidt's College

This large building opposite Damascus Gate (on the corner of Nablus Road) was built as the German Catholic Hospice and College in 1886, though it later served as the temporary headquarters of the British administration following General Allenby's capture of the city in 1917, and later as the HQ of the Royal Air Force.

Rockefeller Archaeological Museum

This magnificent building (constructed in 1927-29) was built using funds from J.D. Rockefeller to house the antiquities of Palestine that had been gathered together by the Department of Antiquities of the Mandate Government. Built in neo-Gothic style, the architect incorporated aspects of local Byzantine and Islamic design, most notably the peaceful garden courtyard at the heart of the building. The exhibits are superb, though the presentation has changed little since the museum opened, and there is no sense of the dynamism that is a feature of most museums in Israel; a visit to the Israel Museum in Jerusalem illustrates how archaeology should be presented. The exhibits are presented in chronological order, starting in the south octagon and following a clockwise route. Notable features include the eighth century CE wooden panels from al-Aqsa Mosque (South Room); stucco work and other decorative fragments from Hisham's Palace in Jericho (West Hall); and the 12th century CE marble lintels from the Church of the Holy Sepulchre (North Room). ■ *T6282251. Sunday-Thursday 1000-1700, Friday-Saturday 1000-1400. Adult 22 NIS, student 14 NIS, though keep ticket since this allows admission into Israel Museum within one week for just 10 NIS. Toilets, small book/souvenir shop.*

Garden Tomb

The Garden Tomb is proposed as an alternative site for the Crucifixion and Resurrection of Jesus Christ, and for those who have already visited the Church of the Holy Sepulchre and come away confused and disappointed, then this is the place for you. There is indeed a very pleasant garden (*John 19:41*), and a tomb cut in the rock-face (*Matthew 27:60; Mark 14:46; Luke 23:53; John 19:41*) complete with what appears to be a groove for a rolling stone (*Matthew 27:60; Mark 15:46; Luke 24:2*), and from the vantage point overlooking the Sulaiman Street Arab bus station, the cliff-face does appear to resemble a skull (*Matthew 27:33; Mark 15:22; John 19:16*). Yet this is where imagination must be tempered with the hard facts of reality. Notwithstanding the convincing evidence that suggests that the Church of the Holy Sepulchre does in fact stand upon the site of Christ's Crucifixion (see page 135), the archaeological evidence supporting the claim of the Garden Tomb is conspicuous by its absence. The tomb chamber features none of the characteristics of a first century CE burial place, such as *arcosolia* (rock-cut troughs or burial benches beneath an arched opening), with the configuration of the tombs that you see today characteristic of the ninth-sixth centuries BCE. Thus, it can not

East Jerusalem & northern suburbs

Jerusalem

Tombs of the Sanhedrin

Grapes Tomb

Yam Suf

Mishmar Ha-Gvul

GIV'AT Ha-MIVTAR

Paran

Six Days War

Tomb of Simon the Temple Builder

Family Tomb

16

To Mount Scopus & Ramallah

SANHEDRIYYA

Levi Eshkol

AMMUNITION HILL

Sinai

To Mount Scopus

Universita Ha-Ivrit

Shemu'el Ha Nevi (Samuel the Prophet)

HaShalam

SHEIKH JARRAH

Nablus

St Joseph

Danish Consulate

St John's

Palestinian Needle Workshop

Swedish Consulate

French Consulate

Belgium Consulate

JMCC

12

1

2

18

Tomb of Simon the Just

HaZeitim

Ibn Jubair

Abu Bakr e-Sadik

Othman ibn Afan

Khalid ibn el-Walid

Wadi Jauz Rd

Zawiyya Jarrahiyya

Louis Vincent

Abou Obiedah el-Jarah

Orient House

St George St

Al-Kasaba Theatre

British Council

Palestinian National Theatre

Seventh Day Adventist Centre

Ali Ibn

Abitaleb

3

1

8

14

St Georges School

Nazarene Church

Mandelbaum Gate

Tourjeman Post

St George's Anglican Cathedral

Tombs of the Kings (Queen Helena of Adiabene)

Ibn Khalid

Ibn Batura

27

7

US Consulate

W F Albright Institute of Archaeological Research

Petrol Stations

Palestinian Pottery

Mosque

Amar Ben Ela'as

French Cultural Centre

Bible Society

5

29

6

15

19

Az-Zahra

3

4

Syrian Catholic Patriarchate

Ecole Biblioteque et Archéologique Francaise

13

21

30

Al-Masudi

Ibn Sina

Rashid

Antara Ben-Shadad

Armenian Mosaic

Dominican Convent & Church of St Stephen

Garden Tomb

Al-Asfahani

11

Ha Nevi'im St

26

1

25

23

20

17

24

9

Schmidt's College

Service Taxis to Ramallah

2

10

28

Suleiman St

Rockefeller Archaeological Museum

Service Taxis to Hebron, Bethlehem, Jericho, Allenby/King Hussein Bridge, Gazza

Notre Dame de France

Id Zanhanim

22

Damascus Gate

Herod Gate

OLD CITY

New Gate

St Stephen's Gate

Mount of Olives

N

0 metres 200

have been the "new" or "unfinished" tomb that the gospels describe. There is also evidence to suggest that the body benches here were cut back significantly in the Byzantine period, and this would have been highly unlikely if the early Christians had considered this to be the tomb of Jesus. Further modifications were also made by the Crusaders, when the site was used as a stable!

Though the rock-face above the Sulaiman Street Arab bus station had already been identified as a possible Golgotha (Thenius 1842; Fisher Howe 1871; Conder 1878), it was the "feverish mind" of **General Charles George Gordon** ('of Khartoum') who popularized the Garden Tomb as Christ's sepulchre. As Amos Elon points out, it was not the form of the cliff face (now above the bus station) that so convinced Gordon that this was the 'place of the skull', but rather the 1864 British Military Ordnance Map of Jerusalem! Apparently, the contour line marking 2,549 feet makes a perfect "death's-head, complete with eye-sockets, crushed nose and gaping mouth" (Amos Elon, *Jerusalem: City of Mirrors*, 1989)!

Cynics would argue that the speed with which the Anglican Church rushed to endorse Gordon's identification had more to do with the absence of any Protestant-owned 'holy sites' within the city than with actual belief in Gordon's claims. Though their support has subsequently been withdrawn, as Murphy-O'Connor so eloquently puts it, "in Jerusalem the prudence of reason has little chance against the certitude of piety" (*The Holy Land*, 1992). The Garden Tomb is now administered by the (British) Garden Tomb Association, and to their credit their very pleasant guides are the first to point out that the archaeological evidence is deficient in supporting Gordon's claim. However, the Garden Tomb not only provides a quiet and pleasant place for prayer or contemplation, it also acts as a valuable visual aid in recreating an image of the Crucifixion. ■ *T6272745. Monday-Saturday 0830-1200 1400-1730, closed Sunday except for an interdenominational service in English at 0900. Admission and guided tour free. Toilets, good souvenir shop.*

Dominican Convent and Church of St Stephen

The present Church of St Stephen (1900) is part of a complex founded some 10 years earlier as the first graduate school in the Holy Land dedicated to the study of the Bible and biblical archaeology: **Ecole Biblique et Archéologique Français de St Etienne**. The school, run by Dominican monks and financed in part by the French government, has been instrumental in deciphering the Dead Sea Scrolls.

The first church on this site was built c. 455-60 by the Empress Eudocia to house the shrine for the bones of St Stephen, the first Christian martyr (*Acts 6:5 to 8:1*), whilst the empress herself was later buried here. The relics had been brought here in 438/9 by Cyril of Alexandria, though less than a century later the resting place of the bones had become confused with the site of the stoning itself.

The sixth century CE monastery built here was destroyed by the Persians in 614 CE, and though a small chapel was built here soon after, it was the Crusaders who substantially redeveloped the site. By this time the site of St Stephen's bones and the site of his stoning had become firmly confused. The Knights Hospitallers restored the chapel in the 12th century CE, though the whole complex, including large stables, was pulled down in 1187 so as not to provide the advancing Salah al-Din with a strategically placed stronghold. The stables were redeveloped in 1192 as a hospice to house pilgrims since the Ayyubids forbade Christians from lodging within the city walls. It was at this time that the name 'St Stephen's Gate' was shifted from its original position (the present 'Damascus Gate') to its present one at the northeast gate in the walls. Excavations within the walls of the Dominicans property have revealed the plan of the **Byzantine church** (upon which the present church is built, and incorporating some of the original mosaics), some of the **Hospitallers' stables**, the **Byzantine and medieval chapel**, and a **Byzantine tomb complex**. Murphy-O'Connor (*The Holy Land*, 1992) is amongst those who suggest that the presence of the many reused columns found here is the reason why Sulaiman II chose the title *Bab al-'Amud* ('Gate of the Column') for the entrance to the Old City that is now referred to as Damascus Gate. He notes that Ottoman-period gates invariably took their name from something *outside* them, and thus the association with the column of Hadrian's Roman paved square *inside* Damascus Gate may be erroneous. ■ *T6264468, F6282567. The Ecole has an excellent research library (Monday-Saturday 0900-1145, $40 per year), and offers a programme of lectures. The Church offers Mass at 0730 and 1130 on Sunday, 0630 and 1200 weekdays, plus Vespers at 1925.*

Dominican Convent & Church of St Stephen

1 Hospitallers' Stables
2 Byzantine & Medieval Chapel
3 Byzantine Church
4 Byzantine Tomb Complex

(after Vincent)

0 metres 20

Armenian Mosaic Of outstanding workmanship, the mosaic (measuring 6.3 metres by 3.9 metres) was discovered in 1894 during the digging of the foundations of a new house. Its decorative style has led to a sixth century CE dating, though the exact year that it was laid is not certain. An Armenian inscription reading "To the memory and for the salvation of all the Armenians the names of whom the Lord knoweth", together with the discovery of several burial caves in the vicinity, have led to the assumption that this was a Byzantine mortuary chapel (though it has been identified by some as the Church of St Polyeucht). The multi-coloured tesserae feature a number of birds, including peacocks (drinking the elixir of life, and thus symbolizing life after death), ducks, storks, pigeons, fowl, an eagle (symbolizing evil), and a caged bird (parrot?) representing an interpretation of the relationship between the body and the soul. ■ *The mosaic is not easy to find, and the building is rarely open (officially 0700-1700 daily, but don't rely on this). On HaNevi'im Street, just south of the Ramsis Hostel, is a small cul-de-sac behind rusted iron gates that resembles Steptoe & Son's yard (full of old fridges). The entrance is behind the grill on the left.*

Mandelbaum Gate and Tourjeman Post The huge swathe of 'empty' land on either side of Shivtei Isra'el Street and Shemu'el HaNevi Street was the no man's land between the Israelis and Jordanians in the years that control of the city was divided (1948-67). The only crossing point between the two spheres of influence was the UN-supervised spot that became known as the **Mandelbaum Gate**; the crossroads were marked not by a gate, but by a house belonging to a wealthy businessman – Mandelbaum. The house (marked by a plaque) is located at the meeting point of the following roads: Shivtei Israel, Samuel the Prophet (Shmuel HaNevi), Hel Hahandasa (Engineer Corps) and St George.

Just across the road is the **Tourjeman Post**. Formerly a small museum offering a Zionist perspective on the years 1948-67, it is now known as the **Museum of the Seam** and seeks to "promote dialogue, understanding and coexistence". ■ *4 Hel Hahandasa, T6281278. Sunday-Thursday 0900-1700, Friday 0900-1300. Adult 5 NIS*

St George's Anglican Cathedral

Built in 1898, this church now acts as the cathedral of the Anglican Episcopal Diocese of Jerusalem and the Middle East. The church has an interesting history. There are many British links to the past, including a font donated by Queen Victoria and a tower dedicated to the memory of Edward VII, though the years 1910-17 saw the complex occupied by the Ottoman army's High Command. Following General Allenby's capture of the city on 9th December, 1917, the instrument of Turkish surrender was signed in the bishop's study here. ■ *T6283302, F6282253. No set opening hours. Free. Within the complex is a highly recommended guesthouse.*

'Tombs of the Kings' (Queen Helena of Adiabene)

Described by the prominent archaeologist Nahman Avigad as the "largest and most magnificent [Roman period] tomb in Jerusalem" (*New Encyclopedia of Archaeological Excavations in the Holy Land*, 1993), the so-called **'Tombs of the Kings'** has been labouring under a misnomer for over a century now. Although mentioned in several ancient sources including Josephus (*Jewish War V, 147; Antiquities XX: 17-96*), and well known to travellers from the 16th century CE onwards, the tomb was excavated in 1863 by de Saulcy, who was so struck by the magnificence of the monument that he identified it as the Tombs of the Kings of Judah (and hence the popular name). A wealthy family of French Jews bought the tomb for this reason shortly afterwards, donating it to the French Republic in 1886. The French government still remains the custodian.

The tomb was in fact cut c. 50 CE and belongs to **Queen Helena of Adiabene** (died c. 65 CE). Much is known about this woman, thanks largely to Josephus. Helena was the dowager queen of Adiabene in northern Mesopotamia (now in northeast Iraq), a town with a sizeable Jewish merchant community who had converted the royal family to Judaism. Some time between 44 and 48 CE the dowager came on a pilgrimage to Jerusalem, her visit coinciding with the great famine that struck the city. Helena immediately threw herself into a one-woman famine relief programme, procuring food from such far-away

'Tomb of the Kings' (Queen Helena of Adiabene)

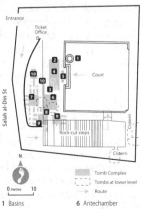

- 1 Basins
- 2 Architectural Fragments
- 3 Tomb Entrance
- 4 Vestibule
- 5 Free-standing Columns
- 6 Antechamber
- 7 Burial Chamber
- 8 Secret Stairway
- 9 Other Burial Chambers
- 10 Unfinished Burial Chambers

places as Egypt and Cyprus. Helena subsequently settled here and built herself a palace in the Lower City (Josephus, *Jewish War, V, 253*), remaining in Jerusalem until the death of her son, King Izates, c. 65 CE. She died in Adiabene shortly after her return there, and upon the succession of another son (Monobazes), her body (along with that of Izates) was sent to Jerusalem for burial.

Tour Entering the gate of the property on Salah al-Din Street, turn right past the ticket kiosk to the top of the stairs. As you descend the 24 rock-cut steps, note the channels that fed the rain into the two cisterns at the bottom. Passing through a rock-cut arch to the left, you enter into a vast square court (approx 26 metres by 27 metres) that was almost certainly a former quarry of the famous Jerusalem *malaki* limestone. The 24 steps down would probably have been a ramp for dragging up the blocks. On the west side of the court is the entrance to the tomb complex, with its elaborate (though badly damaged) façade. The architrave, decorated with a band of carved leaves, supports a Doric frieze, above which three pyramids once stood (Josephus, *Antiquities, XX, 95*). The two free-standing (**5**) and two engaged end-columns are missing, replaced by the metal scaffolding supports that you see today. Inside the vestibule (**4**) to the right (north) are fragments of columns and capitals that were found *in situ* (**2**). Outside the vestibule are two rock-hewn basins that were used in the ritual purification of the dead (**1**).

Inside the vestibule to the left (south) is the entrance to the tomb chambers (**3**). The tiny entrance was closed using a rolling stone, with further measures taken to disguise the entrance. Nevertheless, the tomb was heavily looted in antiquity, and some of the sarcophagi found here can now be found in a new role as flower troughs on in the Old City and on the Haram al-Sharif. Squeezing through the low doorway you enter an antechamber (**6**), from which four doors lead to a complex of burial chambers (some unfinished). The first chamber on the right (west) (**7**) furnished a superb sarcophagus, now housed in the Louvre. At a lower level, entered by a secret stairway (**8**) hidden below the floor of a grave, was discovered a superb sarcophagus bearing the name 'Queen Saddan'. The corners had been knocked off its lid so that it could fit through the entrance. It is now generally agreed that 'Queen Saddan' is the Aramaic version of the Greek name of Queen Helena of Adiabene. There are compelling reasons for this deception, and for the fact that the queen's sarcophagus was hidden away from the main burial chamber. Helena's death and burial coincided with the upheaval and uncertainty of events leading up to the First Jewish Revolt (66-73 CE), and the risks of looting or desecration would have been very real. As it happens, the sarcophagus escaped the tomb-robbers, though the fact that it is now displayed in the Louvre may suggest to some that the deception was ultimately pointless. ■ *Monday-Saturday 0800-1200 1400-1700. Adult 5 NIS. Bring a torch/flashlight.*

American Colony Hotel The 'American Colony' was one of several new suburbs of Jerusalem established outside the old walled city at the end of the 19th century. Its founding members were the American lawyer and church leader Horatio Spafford and his Norwegian wife Anna, whose religious consciousness had been raised in a tragic shipwreck in 1874 in which their four young children were drowned. In 1881, with a group of friends, the Spaffords settled in the Holy Land, occupying a large house in the Old City between Damascus Gate and Herod Gate and devoting their lives to charitable work amongst Jerusalem's poor.

Fifteen years later they were joined by a large group from the Swedish Evangelical Church, the story of their journey being fictionalized and told in Selma Lagerlof's Nobel-prize-winning *"Jerusalem"*. The large influx of new settlers required more space, and so the group rented (and later bought) a large mansion built outside the walled city by a rich Arab landowner, Rabbah Daoud Amin Effendi el Husseini. The community soon expanded further, requiring adjacent properties to also be rented, and in a very short space of time the whole area was being referred to as the American Colony.

In the opening years of the 20th century, the foundations of the subsequent American Colony Hotel were laid when Baron Ustinov (grandfather of Peter Ustinov) made an arrangement to lodge visiting pilgrims there. The main function of the building, however, continued to be charitable, with hospital and clinic facilities being run through the Turkish occupation, the First and Second World Wars, the Israeli-Arab war of 1948 and subsequent Jordanian occupation, and the Six Day War of 1967. It was not until the Colony became a *de facto* part of Israel that the hospital facilities were deemed no longer necessary, and the building became upgraded to form the *American Colony Hotel*. This remains one of Jerusalem's most prestigious addresses, having played host over the years to (in alphabetical order): General Allenby, Lauren Bacall, Joan Baez, Gertrude Bell, Saul Bellow, Carl Bernstein, John Betjeman, John Le Carré, Marc Chagall, Graham Greene, Alec Guinness, Gail Hunnycut, T.E. Lawrence, Malcolm Muggeridge, Peter O'Toole, Dominique LaPierre, Donald Pleasance, John Simpson, Leon Uris, Peter Ustinov and Richard Widmark. The hotel is a favourite haunt of journalists and Palestinian officials (hence the Israeli nickname the 'PLO Hotel'!).

Further along the same street (Abu Obiedah ibn el-Jarrah) is **Orient House** (T6273330), the *de facto* headquarters in Jerusalem of the Palestinian Authority. Just to the north of the American Colony Hotel, on Nablus Road, is the **Zawiyya Jarrahiyya**, or tomb of Amir Husam al-Din al-Jarrahi (died c. 1201; an early 13th century CE holy man). The shrine is meant to bring good fortune to those who pray here, (with special good luck available to those involved in raising chickens and egg production!). The mosque was added in 1895.

Jewish tradition relates that this is the tomb of Simon the Just (*Hebrew:* **Tomb of Simon** Shimon ha-Zaddiq), a High Priest at the Temple in the fourth century BCE **the Just** who was renowned for his piety. The rock-cut tomb undoubtedly dates to the Middle to Late Roman period, with a Roman inscription mentioning a Roman woman by the name of Julia Sabina, and is certainly not that of Simon. Nevertheless, the tomb remains a place of Jewish pilgrimage, particularly popular amongst Sephardi (Oriental) Jews. ■ *To reach the tomb head north along the Nablus Road past the American Colony Hotel. Where the road dips before the hill up to Sheikh Jarrah, take the road to the right (east). Take the left fork and then the next left fork, and the tomb is on the left. Head coverings must be worn. There is little to see here, however.*

Northern suburbs

There are several points of interest in the Northern suburbs of Jerusalem, to the immediate north of the area covered in the 'East Jerusalem' section. The location of the various places of interest here can be found on the 'East Jerusalem and northern suburbs' map (see page 184).

To the north of the American Colony Hotel is the suburb of Sheikh Jarrah. **Ammunition** Taking its name from the small Arab village established here at the end of the **Hill** 19th century CE, the district is now home to a number of administrative buildings and foreign embassies. The low hill to the north, between Sheikh Jarrah and the newer Jewish suburbs of Sanhedriyya and Giv'at Ha-Mivtar, is **Ammunition Hill**.

During the period 1948-67, when most of East Jerusalem (including the Old City) was controlled by Jordan, this low hill not only controlled the road leading to the Israeli enclave on Mt Scopus, but also the road between Ramallah and the Old City. The Jordanians, recognizing the strategic importance of the hill as well as remembering the fierce battles that had taken place here in 1948, had heavily fortified what had come to be known as 'Ammunition Hill'. The night of 5/6th June, 1967, saw Israeli paratroopers take the hill in a particularly bloody and hard-fought battle. The hill is now a war memorial to the 183 Israeli dead, and features an underground museum (basically the Jordanian command bunker), an auditorium (screening a number of film and multimedia presentations that explain the Israeli version of history), an outdoor museum (tanks, pillboxes, trenches) that explains the battle for Ammunition Hill, plus picnic gardens. ■ *T5828442, F5829132. Sunday-Thursday 0830-1700, Friday 0900-1300, occasionally open evenings. Adults 8 NIS, students 5 NIS. Buses 4/9/25/28 to bottom of hill. Wheelchair access.*

Giv'at Ha-Mivtar To the north of Ammunition Hill is the new Jewish suburb of Giv'at Ha-Mivtar. A couple of minor tombs – **Tomb of Simon the Temple Builder** and **The Family Tomb** – are hidden within this residential district. This suburb has also revealed the world's only archaeological evidence of crucifixion. Despite the fact that thousands were crucified by the Romans, archaeological evidence for this form of execution was completely lacking until **Yehohanan ben Hagkol** ('The Crucified Man from Giv'at Ha-Mivtar') was excavated here in 1968. Nothing is known about him except his name and the fact that he died some time between 7 and 70 CE, with the iron nail driven through his heel bone confirming how he died. A replica is displayed in the Israel Museum (the real bones having been given a Jewish burial).

Gibeah of Saul Located on the Nablus Road a little to the north of the suburb of Giv'at **(Tell el-Fûl)** Ha-Mivtar (and five kilometres north of Damascus Gate) is a low mound that forms an isolated part of the Mt Scopus to Mount of Olives ridge. A series of excavations at the site suggests that it is the **Gibeah of Saul** (*Arabic*: Tell el-Fûl, or 'Mound of Horse Beans'): the home and capital of the Israelite king, **Saul**.

On the route of the main north to south road (as today, Nablus Road), this was the site of the capital of the **Benjamites**, though it appears to have been destroyed when the other tribes of Israel took their revenge against the Benjamites (see *Judges 19-20*). It appears that Saul lived here as a young man (*I Samuel 10:26, 11:4*), and later it became his royal residence (*I Samuel 15:34*), the name changing from Gibeah of Benjamin to Gibeah of Saul.

The principal remains at the site are what's left of the fortress built during the time of Saul, that remained for some years after his death (c. 1025-950 BCE). In fact, all that remains are the base of the southwest corner tower and parts of the adjacent casement walls, though the excavators have projected the plan of the fortress as being rectangular (52 metres by 35 metres) with towers at all four corners.

The fortress appears to have been destroyed, (though the settlement not necessarily abandoned), and rebuilt a number of times, notably following the Assyrian expedition of 701 BCE and the Babylonian invasion led by Nebuchadnezzar in 588-586 BCE. Later occupants of the mound include the Roman army, whom Josephus describes as camping close to "Gabath Saul" on the night before they reached Jerusalem in 70 CE (*Jewish War V, 51*). There is not a great deal to see, and only those with a keen interest in the period are likely to be rewarded by a visit here. There is no public transport directly to the mound, though a Ramallah- or Nablus-bound service taxi may be persuaded to drop you off as it passes.

A small park in Jerusalem's northern suburb of Sanhedriyya contains a number of tombs characteristic in style and workmanship of Jewish tombs from the first century CE. Because the number of burials is approximate to the 70 judges of the Sanhedrin who met in the Temple and monitored and maintained Jewish religious law, the site became known as the **Tombs of the Sanhedrin**. There are in fact 55 *kokhim* (roughly oven-shaped rock-cut burial places), 4 *arcosolia* (rock-cut bench burial beneath arched opening) and 2 cave/ossuaries (secondary burial containers), though there is nothing to suggest that the tombs have any connection with the Sanhedrin; in fact, they appear to be standard family burial places.

> **Tombs of the Sanhedrin (The Judges)**

The most notable of the tombs in this quiet fir-strewn park are **tomb 14** towards the northwest corner and **tomb 8** to the east. The former has an intricately carved pediment, though both now look fairly forlorn, with the entrances barred and the courtyards full of rubbish. An interest in first century CE Jewish tombs would have to be your reason for coming here (Bus 039 from the city centre stops outside).

The so-called 'Grapes Tomb' is part of the same tombs complex, though located outside the park some 200 metres to the east. At a point along Red Sea (Yam Suf) Road, opposite Mishmar Ha-Guvl Street, take the steps down between apartment blocks 8 and 10 (sign-posted 'Doris Weiler Garden'). At the bottom of the steps is another first century CE Jewish burial cave, comprising a porch, central chamber, three rooms with *loculi* and one chamber with *arcosolia*. The pediment above the entrance is decorated with vine tendrils and bunches of grapes (hence the name). Bus 039 also passes this site.

> **Grapes Tomb**

Mount Scopus

Mount Scopus is a low hill (903 metres) to the northeast of the Old City; part of the soft sandstone ridge of which the Mount of Olives is also a part. It is a strategic highpoint overlooking the city (the name deriving from the Greek skopus, meaning 'look out'), and the list of generals and armies that have camped out on this high ground is long and impressive. The Roman general Cestius camped here in 66 CE during the early stages of the Jewish Revolt (Josephus, Jewish War II, 528), though he was subsequently forced to beat a hasty and costly retreat. Titus was more successful four years later, launching his attack on the city from this vantage point (Jewish War, V, 67). The Crusaders also camped here in 1099, whilst more recent conquerors have included the British in 1917 and Moshe Dayan's Israeli forces in 1967. The 20th century has seen a number of institutions established on Mount Scopus.

Ins and outs

Egged Buses **4/4a/9/9a/23/28** run to Mt Scopus, plus Bus 82 from the Nablus Road Bus Station.

> **Getting there**

Though proposals for a modern Jewish university in Jerusalem had existed since the end of the 19th century, and land for this purpose had been bought on Mt Scopus in 1913, it was not until 1925 that the university was formerly opened.

> **Hebrew University**

Though the **Hebrew University** set itself the task of resurrecting Hebrew culture, it was also charged with, in the words of its first president, Dr Judah Magnes, "reconciling Arab and Jew, East and West". It success as a centre of learning is unquestioned, though whether it has fulfilled the latter requirement is a point of contention. By the late 1980s just six percent of its students were Arab, with almost all of these being 'Israeli Arabs' drawn from Galilee. Jerusalemite Palestinians shunned, or were shunned by, the university.

To its early institutes of Chemistry, Microbiology and Jewish Studies were added faculties of Humanities and Medicine, plus other minor sections. However, come 1948, the university spent the next 20 years isolated from the rest of Jerusalem; a pocket under Israeli control at the centre of the Jordanian-held West Bank. The new campus was subsequently established in the suburb of Giv'at Ram, on Jerusalem's western side. Following the Israeli victory in the Six Day War of 1967, the campus on Mt Scopus not only reopened, but also expanded significantly, with many new faculties being added. Free guided tours of the university campus are available. ■ *T6585111. One-hour guided tours in English are conducted each day at 1100 from the Broniman Family Reception Centre.*

Tombs on Mt Scopus
Excavations on Mt Scopus have revealed a number of tomb complexes. Several can be found within the Botanical Gardens of the Hebrew University, and are generally included within the tour.

The **Five Tombs complex** dates to the first century CE, and forms part of the vast Jewish necropolis that spread across this hill. The tombs are in fact separate entities, though overcrowding on the necropolis meant that they were so close together, the *kokhim* actually interconnected.

Dating to the same period is the **Tomb of Nicanor**, located approximately 50 metres to the southeast. A Greek inscription on one of several decorated ossuaries that were found when the cave was excavated in 1902 mentions "the sons of Nicanor of Alexandria", (who is said to have donated one of the gates of the Temple). His two sons, Nicanor and Alexa, are mentioned by name in Greek and Hebrew inscriptions below. The burial cave is one of the largest of the period in Jerusalem, and features a 17-metre-long façade entered through a pillared porch. The burial catacomb is complex, featuring four burial chambers containing *loculi* on several levels.

The **Tomb of a Nazirite Family** was discovered in 1967 during the extension of the university, and was subsequently dismantled and moved to its present position on the southeast side of the Botanical Gardens. The tomb comprises a central chamber roofed with a barrel vault, with three side chambers branching off. No burial installations are cut in the tomb, though two sarcophagi and fourteen ossuaries were found. An inscription in Hebrew on one names "Hananiah son of Jehonathan the Nazirite", whilst another mentions "Salome wife of Hanahiah son of the Nazirite". Both are thought to date to the second half of the first century CE. Comparisons are often made between this tomb and the Tomb of Herod's Family near the King David Hotel in the New City (see page 209).

Brigham Young University
Tours of the 'Jerusalem Centre' at the Brigham Young University (Mormon University) (whose establishment religious Jews opposed) are also available. ■ *T6273195. Free tours Tuesday-Friday 1000 1030 1100 1130 1430 1500 1530. Buses 9/9a.*

Hadassah Hospital
Designed and built in a fortress-like style by Mendelson, the Jewish Rothschild-Hadassah University Hospital opened in 1938. This

world-renowned medical centre was closed during the Jordanian occupation of East Jerusalem and the West Bank (1948-67), and the new Hadassah Hospital was established to the west of the city, near 'En Kerem (see page 207). After 1967 the hospital reopened, and continues to serve the city. Tours are available. ■ *T5818111. Tours Sunday-Friday, hourly from 0900-1200.*

On the northwest slope of Mt Scopus is the British World War One cemetery, superbly maintained by the Commonwealth War Graves Commission.

British WW1 cemetery

On the south side of Mt Scopus, on the road to the Mount of Olives, is the Augusta Victoria Hospital (T6279911). Built in 1898 by Emperor Wilhelm II of Germany, and dedicated to his wife, the Empress Augusta Victoria, the most striking feature of the hospital and hospice complex is the 60-metre-high tower. When open (1200-1600 daily), it provides excellent views of the city and surrounding area.

Augusta Victoria Hospital

New City

*The area to the northwest, west and southwest of the walled Old City is variously described as the **New City**, or **West Jerusalem**. There are numerous places of interest within the New City; some very ancient and others post-dating the establishment of the State of Israel. The various sites are fairly spread out, and there is no fixed route for conveniently viewing all the main attractions. However, the information given below attempts to broadly group the various places of interest by location. These include the **City centre and area north of Jaffa Road**; **Western suburbs**; **Western outskirts**; **Southwestern suburbs**; and the **Southern section of the New City**. For orientation refer to the following maps: 'New City (including Western suburbs, Western outskirts and Southwestern suburbs)', page 196; and 'City centre and area north of Jaffa Road', page 195.*

City centre and area north of the Jaffa Road

Though now containing the City Hall, police district headquarters, and law courts, the large area to the northwest of the Old City was previously owned by Imperial Russia, and is still referred to as the **Russian Compound**. The four-hectare plot was bought with a grant from the Imperial Treasury following a visit to the Holy Land by the Grand Duke Constantine Nicholaevitch in 1859. Growing numbers of visiting Russian pilgrims through the course of the 19th century meant that the traditional hospices and monasteries within the Old City could no longer cope with the demand, and the Grand Duke's assessment was that new facilities needed to be provided. Of course, the construction of grand edifices such as the Cathedral of the Holy Trinity (consecrated in 1864) would also reflect Russia's sense of its standing in the world, and thus the building here was on a grand scale. Within 20 years the high-walled enclosure of the Russian Compound housed a cathedral, consulate, monastery, hospital and hospice capable of accommodating 2,000 Russian pilgrims annually.

Russian Compound

The mass flow of Russian pilgrims, generally poor peasants, continued, and in 1881 additional accommodation was provided by the 'Alexandrovsky Hospice' (see page 128). By the beginning of the 20th century, each Easter saw the arrival of up to 9,000 Russian pilgrims, though events soon took a dramatic turn. The Russian Revolution saw the number of pilgrims slow to a trickle, and the buildings of the Russian Compound were taken over by the British Mandate administration who used them as a police headquarters and prison. This is the complex that became known to Jews fighting for an independent state as 'Bevingrad', after the British Foreign Secretary Ernest Bevin. The Israeli government purchased the estate in 1955, though its British function remains largely unchanged. Recent renovation has produced a pleasing, 'open-plaza' feel to the public space (Safra Square). To the north of the Russian Compound (on the north side of HaMalka Street and east side of Monbaz Street) are some of Jerusalem's trendiest bars (see 'Bars' on page 223).

The **Cathedral of the Holy Trinity** still stands at the heart of the Russian Compound, though it is not open to visitors. The grand Kremlin-style onion-shaped domes are executed far better on the Russian Orthodox Church of St Mary Magdalene (on the Mount of Olives tour).

An interesting feature near the church (by the police station) is the large **monolithic column** still laying in its quarry bed. Its size (12.15 metres long, approximately 1.75 metres diameter) is comparable with the description of the columns in the Royal Portico of Herod the Great's Temple, and it is suggested that this is what it was intended for until the fault at one end was discovered.

The former British prison nearby now houses the **Hall of Heroism**; a museum dedicated to the memory of Jewish freedom-fighters (or terrorists, according to your viewpoint) from the British Mandate period. ■ *T6233166. Sunday-Thursday 0800-1600, Friday 1000-1300. Adult 8 NIS students 5 NIS.*

Me'a She'arim
Quarter

To the north of the Russian Compound is the **Me'a She'arim Quarter**: Jerusalem's principal ultra-Orthodox Jewish neighbourhood. The name literally means 'hundred gates'; a reference to the defensive architectural style of the quarter that sees the outer walls of the houses providing a continuous protective façade, with the '100 gates' leading to the main, and then private courts. These design practices provide not only privacy, but also defensive measures; considered essential when the quarter was built away from the walled Old City in 1874. The name is also a pun; an invocation of fruitfulness and plenty drawn from a line in the First Book of Moses, *Genesis*: "Then Isaac sowed in that land, and received in the same year an hundredfold: and the Lord blessed him" (*Genesis 26:12*).

Yet it is not just the architectural features that conjure to mind the *shtetl* (Jewish ghettoes) of pre-Holocaust Eastern Europe; it is the quarter's residents. The most visible attachment to the past is the appearance of the ultra-Orthodox men, (in their black frock-coats, wide fur-brimmed hats, stockinged feet, and speaking Yiddish), who would appear to be more at home in a ghetto of 18th-century Poland or Lithuania than a 20th-century Mediterranean/Middle Eastern nation. Amos Elon describes Me'a She'arim as a "medieval world of poverty and unbroken faith – and of fanatical intolerance of other worlds of thought or ways of life" (*Jerusalem: City of Mirrors*, 1988), though there is a concession to the Israeli novelist Amos Oz's point that "because of Hitler you have no right to oppose this kind of Judaism" (*Here and There in the Land of Israel*, 1982; *In the Land of Israel* in English translation). Many of the more confrontational ultra-Orthodox groups who oppose the modern State of Israel, such as the radical Neturei Karta ('Guardians of the City'), have a popular base in Me'a She'arim and conduct their campaigns through the inflammatory posters that are present throughout the quarter. In fact, more than one observer has suggested were it not for the posters that hold the old stone blocks of the houses together, the whole quarter would have fallen down years ago!

Most visitors now know Ticho House (Beit Ticho) for its superb vegetarian **Ticho House**
restaurant (see 'Eating', page 220), though this former home of prominent
ophthalmologist Dr Abraham Ticho, and his artist wife Anna, features a small
museum detailing the couple's lives and work. It is an excellent place for sitting
and 'chilling out'. ■ *7 Harav Kook Sreet, T6245068. Sunday Monday*
Wednesday Thursday 1000-1700, Tuesday 1000-2200, Friday 1000-1400. Free.

The focus of the New City is Zion Square and the pedestianized streets that **Zion Square**
radiate from it. Ben Yehuda, Yoel Salomon, Josef Rivlin, Dorot Rishonim and
Mordechai Ben Hillel Streets are all lined with shops, cafés, restaurants, bars
and nightclubs where young Jerusalemites and foreign backpackers gather to

Jerusalem

New City: centre & area north of Jaffa Road

shop, eat, drink and be seen. On Friday and Saturday afternoons, when the weather is fine, there's barely enough elbow space to hold your knife and fork, though early Friday and Saturday evenings see the whole area eerily deserted. Come the early hours of the morning, any night of the week, you're almost guaranteed to see some drunken backpacker throwing up following a long session at the *Underground* nightclub.

Time Elevator Jerusalem A new "multi-sensory experience" (three giant screens, moving seats and stage) takes you through 3,000 years of Jerusalem's history (six languages,

New City: western suburbs, western outskirts, southwestern suburbs

To Kastel, Abu Ghosh
Latrun & Tel Aviv

Central Bus Station

Yirmiyahu

Weizmann

Herzl

Weizmann

Jaffa

Shazar

Binyanei Ha'ooma 6

Wolfson

■19
■18
22

Ze'ev Vilna'i

KIRYAT BEN GURIO

Wolfson

Bank of Israel

Kaplan

Prime Minister's Office

HaMuze'onim

Mordechai Ish Shalom

Herzl

YEFE NOF

Bloomfield Science Museum

Ruppin

Yefe Nof

Rubin Academy of Music

Balfour

Hebrew University

Brodetski

Wise

Bible Lands Museum

Military Cemetery

Herzl

Road no. 4 (under construction)

GIV'AT RAM

Magnes

Shrine of the Book

Yehuda Burla

Isr Mu

To Yad VaShem

Mount Herzl

Herzl Museum

Uziel

Shmu'el Bait

Eli'oshar

To 'En Kerem

Uziel

Rokakh

Rokakh

Zalman Sh

Betsal'el Bazak

Betsal'el Bazak

N

MALKHA

Shakal

Uziel

Herzog

0 metres 200

To model of Second Temple period Jerusalem, Holyland Hotel (west) & Jerusalem Mall (Malkha)

To Jerusalem Mall (Malkha), Teddy Stadium & Tennis Centre

■ Sleeping	6 Holiday Inn Crowne Plaza	13 King Solomon	19 Park Plaza
1 Ariel	7 Hilton Jerusalem	14 Laromme Jerusalem	20 Prima Kings
2 Caesar	8 IYHA Beit Bernstein	15 Lev Yerushalam	21 Radisson Moriah Plaz
3 Dan Pearl	9 IYHA Beit Shmuel	Apartment	22 Renaissance Jerusale
4 David's Royal Residence,	10 IYHA HaDavidka	16 Mount Zion	23 Sheraton Jerusalem F
David's Village	11 Jerusalem Tower	17 Notre Dame de France	24 St Andrew's Hospice
5 Eldan	12 King David	18 Paradise	25 Tirat Bat-Shava

Related maps:
A. *Old City, page 86;*
B. *East Jerusalem,*
page 184; C. New city,
centre, page 195

Jerusalem

shows every 40 mins). ■ *Beit Agron, 37 Hillel, T6252227, F6252228. Sunday-Thursday 0900-2200, Friday 0900-1530, Saturday 0940-2200. Not recommended for pregnant women or children under five!*

In the heart of the predominantly Sephardi Orthodox neighbourhood of Mahane Yehuda (about a kilometre northwest of Zion Square) is a market that provides a fitting contrast to the 'civilized' shopping experience of Ben Yehuda Street; this is a true Middle Eastern market. It is particularly exhilarating/crowded in the pre-Shabbat rush.

Mahane Yehuda Market

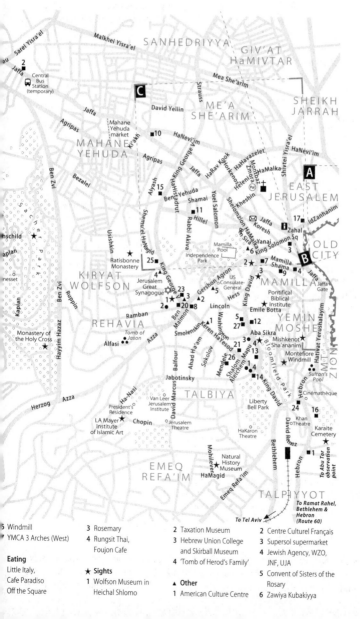

5 Windmill
YMCA 3 Arches (West)

Eating
Little Italy,
Cafe Paradiso
Off the Square

3 Rosemary
4 Rungsit Thai,
Foujon Cafe

★ **Sights**
1 Wolfson Museum in
Heichal Shlomo

2 Taxation Museum
3 Hebrew Union College
and Skirball Museum
4 'Tomb of Herod's Family'

▲ **Other**
1 American Culture Centre

2 Centre Culturel Français
3 Supersol supermarket
4 Jewish Agency, WZO,
JNF, UJA
5 Convent of Sisters of the
Rosary
6 Zawiya Kubakiyya

Visiting Me'a She'arim

There are a number of important things to bear in mind if you decide to visit Me'a She'arim. Quite naturally, the people who live in this quarter do not consider themselves to be a 'tourist attraction', and find nothing unusual in the way that they dress and conduct themselves; in fact, they consider themselves to be the norm. As Thomas Friedman succinctly puts it: "Forty years ago, when secular Israeli fathers were taking their sons down to Me'a She'arim to show them the Haredim before they supposedly disappeared, what they didn't know was that the Haredim were taking their sons over to the secular neighbourhoods of Jerusalem and telling them: 'Behold these empty secular Jews! In another generation they will realize that the Jews' return to their land is not a political act but a spiritual one – and one which demands a spiritual response. Forty years from now, they will all be like us.'" (From Beirut to Jerusalem, 1989).

Thus, visitors to Me'a She'arim should conduct themselves, and dress, in a modest manner. Men should wear long trousers, and preferably a long-sleeved shirt. Women must wear a long, loose-fitting skirt (even long trousers are unacceptable), a long-sleeved, loose-fitting shirt, and it may also be wise to cover hair (though shaving it off and wearing a wig is not necessary). Public shows of affection should be avoided. Both male and female residents of the quarter dislike being photographed, so discretion, or better still abstinence, is recommended. Photography should be avoided on Shabbat (Sabbath) at all costs (and it's probably best not to visit on Shabbat either).

The reaction to those who do not act or dress in an appropriate manner is unpredictable. Immodestly dressed women may find men crossing the road to avoid them, or being hissed at and called a 'whore', though spitting and stone-throwing are not unknown. Those who sneak photographs with long lenses risk expensive repair bills.

Nahom Museum of Italian Jewish Art The Nahom Museum of Italian Jewish Art is a collection of religious art and artefacts from Italy housed in the former 18th-century synagogue from Conegliano Veneto near Venice. At the end of the Second World War Conegliano Veneto no longer had a Jewish population, so in 1952 the interior of the town's synagogue was carefully dismantled and shipped to Israel. A Shabbat service in Italian is still held here. ■ *27 Hillel, T6241610. Sunday-Thursday 1000-1300, Wednesday 1600-1900. Adult 5 NIS.*

Western suburbs

The western suburbs of the New City, particularly Giv'at Ram, are home to most of Israel's public institutions, most notably the Parliament building (Knesset), Supreme Court, Prime Minister's Office and the new campus of the Hebrew University. This large, green, open space to the south of the Central Bus Station also contains a number of places of interest (such as the Israel Museum, Bible Lands Museum, Monastery of the Holy Cross), and some of the city's more upmarket hotels. Allow a full day to explore all these sites (though the Israel Museum alone could probably justify a day in itself).

Ins and outs

Getting there and getting around There are buses direct to most of the buildings and museums, though many visitors with spare time on their hands choose to take a bus to the Central Bus Station, cross the road, then work their way north to south through the landscaped park. For orientation, refer to the 'New City (including Western suburbs, Western outskirts and Southwestern suburbs)' map on page 195.

The attractive **Israeli Supreme Court**, opened in 1992, stands at the north end of Sacher Park, to the south of the Central Bus Station. Guided tours are available. Between the Supreme Court building and the Knesset to the south is the pleasant **Wohl Rose Park**, featuring many species of roses. ■ *Qiryat Ben-Gurion Street, T6759612. Free guided tours in English Sunday-Thursday 1200,* **NB** *you must bring your* **passport***.*

Supreme Court

The Israeli Parliament, or **Knesset**, stands at the centre of Sacher Park, to the south of the Israeli Supreme Court building. A modern, futuristic building (inaugurated in 1966), the rather unattractive exterior belies the lavishly decorated interior. Of particular interest are the tapestries and mosaics designed by Marc Chagall. The public gallery is open to visitors when the Knesset is in session, and though the debate is in Hebrew, the body language and decibel level translates into any tongue. Guided tours of the building are also available. The large bronze menorah opposite the entrance (to the north) was a gift from the British Parliament. ■ *Off Rehov Ruppin, T6753333. Guided tours in variety of languages Sunday and Thursday 0830-1430. Public gallery Monday-Tuesday 1600-2100, Wednesday 1100-1300. Enter from north side.* **NB** *you must bring your* **passport** *and be prepared for a thorough body/bag search. Buses 31 and 32a from Central Bus Station, Buses 9/24/28 from Jaffa Road.*

Knesset (Israel Parliament)

Jerusalem

Israel Museum

The Israel Museum in Jerusalem has the country's foremost collection of antiquities and art, housed within a complex of low-rise, interconnected pavilions, each with a different theme. The galleries are light and airy, the presentation dynamic yet concise, with the historical, archaeological and monetary value of many of the exhibits too vast to contemplate. For visitors to Israel who intend exploring the country's major archaeological sites, your journey should either begin or end here. To get the most out of the museum either a series of visits or a guided tour of the sections that interest you is highly recommended. The museum complex features a full programme of lectures, films, concerts and temporary exhibits (a monthly listings guide is available from the museum shop or from the tourist office). ■ *Rehov Ruppin, PO Box 71117, T6708811, F5631833. Sunday Monday Wednesday Thursday 1000-1700, Tuesday 1600-2200, though the Shrine of the Book stays open 1000-2200, Friday 1000-1400, Saturday 1000-1600. Adult 30 NIS, student 25 NIS, repeat visit within two weeks 15 NIS, family ticket of two adults two children 90 NIS, keep ticket for free entry to Rockefeller Museum within one week.* **NB** *If you visit the Rockefeller Museum first, then come here within one week, you can see both for 32 NIS. Tickets for Saturday must be bought in advance. With the exception of the Shrine of the Book, where access is possible but difficult, wheelchair access is generally excellent. Buses 9/17/24/99 run from the city centre to the museum. The museum has its own website: http:// www.imj.org.il*

One of the highlights of the Israel Museum complex, the Shrine of the Book houses part of the collection of manuscripts known as the **Dead Sea Scrolls**. The distinctive white-tiled roof of the building is designed to resemble the lid of one of the jars in which the scrolls were stored. For further details of the scrolls, see page 308.

Shrine of the Book

The Shrine of the Book building is divided into three section: the corridor; the main hall; and the lower exhibition area. Displayed in the corridor are manuscripts from the 'Cave of Letters' in Nahal Hever, plus associated documents and fragments of manuscripts. The centrepiece of the main hall is the **Isaiah scroll**, whilst in the wall cases are fragments from the **Habbakuk Commentary**, **War of the Sons of the Light against the Sons of Darkness**, and the **Manual of Discipline**, amongst others. Some are originals whilst others are accurate copies. The lower exhibition hall contains a number of remarkably well preserved artefacts dating to the time of the Bar Kokhba Revolt (132-135 CE) that were retrieved from a cave in the Nahal Hever near Qumran. ■ *Free tours of the Shrine of the Book in English take place on Sunday 1330, Monday 1330, Tuesday 1500, Wednesday 1330, Thursday 1330, Friday 1245. No photography allowed inside.*

Israel Museum

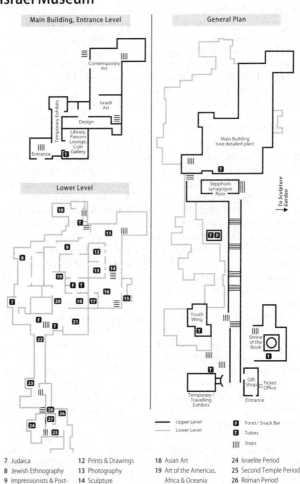

7 Judaica
8 Jewish Ethnography
9 Impressionists & Post-impressionists
10 Old Masters & Period Rooms
11 Modern Art
12 Prints & Drawings
13 Photography
14 Sculpture
15 Temporary Exhibitions
16 Israeli Art
17 Information Centre for Israeli Art
18 Asian Art
19 Art of the Americas, Africa & Oceania
20 Islamic Art
21 Springer Auditorium
22 Prehistoric Period
23 Canaanite Period
24 Israelite Period
25 Second Temple Period
26 Roman Period
27 Hebrew Script Pavilion
28 Glass Gallery

Israel Museum: Guided Tours

The following free English-language guided tours are for individuals only. Meet at the Main Building Information desk (for group guided tours call T6708884). **Museum highlights**: *Sun Mon Wed Thu Fri 1100, Tue 1630;* **Jewish heritage**: *Sun Wed 1500;*

Archaeological treasures: Mon Thu 1500; **Shrine of the Book**: *Sun Mon Wed Thu 1330, Tue 1500, Fri 1245. Tours in French (Sun 1100) and German (Sun 1400) begin from the Entrance Pavilion Information Desk.*

The Bible Lands Museum ("your passport to the ancient world"!) features one of the largest (and most valuable) private collections of antiquities from the Middle East. Presentation is excellent, and enlivened by the use of interactive computer programs and hands-on displays. The museum also hosts a wide range of events, from cheese and wine evenings to lectures, workshops and recitals. Pick up a copy of the monthly *Museum Events* listings from the tourist office. ■ *25 Granot, opppsite Israel Museum, T5611066. Sunday Monday Tuesday Thursday 0930-1230, Wednesday 0930-2130, Friday 0930-1430, Saturday 1100-1500. Adult 22 NIS, student 15 NIS. Guided tours in English every day at 1015, except Wednesday at 1730 and none on Saturday. Buses 9/17/24/99.* **Bible Lands Museum**

To the west of the Israel Museum is the Giv'at Ram campus of the Hebrew University. When studies were suspended at the original Hebrew University on Mt Scopus (see page 191) between 1948 and 1967, this new campus was established here. After 1967 some of the faculties returned to Mt Scopus, though the campus here still houses the Faculty of Science, the Science Library, the Institute for Life Sciences, the Institute for Advanced Studies, as well as the Jewish National Library (*T6585027*) and halls for 3,000 students. Of particular interest in the National Library is the superb **Ardon Window**; a huge stained-glass window featuring Kabbalistic symbols. ■ *Free guided tours of the campus are available on weekdays at 0900 and 1100 (T5632548).* **Hebrew University**

Also part of the Hebrew University is the new **Bloomfield Science Museum**, featuring interactive "science is fun" displays that are particularly appealing to children. ■ *Ruppin Street, T5618128. Monday Wednesday Thursday 1000-1800, Tuesday 1000-2000, Friday 1000-1300, Saturday 1000-1500. Adult 15 NIS, students 12 NIS, children 6 NIS. Buses 9/17/24/28.*

The best view of the Monastery of the Holy Cross is from the square outside the Main Building of the Israel Museum (see page 199). Though the monastery complex is incongruously set next to a major road on the edge of one of Jerusalem's more upmarket suburbs (Rehavia), it is still sufficiently isolated to give some impression of how it may have appeared some 950 years ago. When the monastery was founded in 1039-56 it was quite isolated from the defensive walls of the Old City, and hence its thick buttressed walls and fortress-like appearance. Though dating from the 11th century, the monastery that was founded here by King Bagrat of Georgia actually stands upon the site of a fifth century CE Byzantine church (also founded by a Georgian, the confusingly named Peter the Iberian). The original church marked the traditional Byzantine site of the tree from which the cross used in Jesus' crucifixion was made. The Byzantine church was destroyed by the Persians in 614 CE, though a section of the original mosaic floor to the right of the altar can still be seen. **Monastery of the Holy Cross**

Much of the church that you see today dates to the 11th century, though alterations have been made throughout the years. The Georgians fell upon hard

Jerusalem

times during the 16th century and the church was subsequently sold to the Greek Orthodox in the latter half of the century. The unusual frescoes were added in the 17th century ('unusual' since they feature the heady mix of Christian saints, pagan gods and Greek philosophers!), whilst the clock-tower dates to the 19th century. ■ *Sederot Hayyim Hazaz. Monday-Friday 0900-1500. Adult 5 NIS.*

Tomb of Jason About 500 metres northeast of the Monastery of the Holy Cross, in the Rehavia suburb of Jerusalem, is the Tomb of Jason. Excavated in 1956, the tomb takes its name from one of several Aramaic and Greek inscriptions, one of the former of which is a three-line lament to Jason. Though robbed in antiquity, it is suggested that the tomb was actually used by several generations (about 25 burials in all), with the mixture of Hasmonean and Herodian pottery suggesting that it was in use from the early first century BCE to the early first century CE. Beyond the forecourt and the outer and inner courts is one of the tomb's more interesting features. The entrance porch is marked by a single Doric column (made of stone drums) between two pilasters; a unique feature on any tomb of this period thus far excavated in Israel. The plastered walls within the porch feature a charcoal drawing of three ships, plus the reference to Jason. Several further charcoal drawings of ships were found in the irregularly shaped burial chamber. ■ *Alfasi Street, between Ramban and Azza Streets, Rehavia. Monday-Thursday 1000-1300. Nearest buses 9/17/22.*

Western outskirts of the New City

*There are a number of notable places of interests in the western outskirts of the New City that visitors to Jerusalem should make every effort to see. In particular, the Holocaust Memorial at **Yad VaShem** should be on everybody's 'must visit' list, whilst the **Model of Second Temple period Jerusalem** is invaluable visual tool for getting to grips with the Old City.*

Ins and outs

Getting there and around Public transport access to the various sights in the western outskirts is extremely straightforward: with the exception of the **Model of Second Temple period Jerusalem** (Buses 21 and 21a), all the other places are on the route of Bus 27. For orientation, refer to the 'New City (including Western suburbs, Western outskirts and Southwestern suburbs)' map on page 196.

Model of Second Temple period Jerusalem An interesting attraction in the grounds of the *Holyland Hotel (West)* is a 1:50 scale model of Jerusalem as it may have appeared at the end of the Second Temple period, as the First Jewish Revolt was beginning (66 CE). It is extremely useful in allowing visitors to visualize how the city would have appeared at this time. ■ *Holyland Hotel West, Bayit Vagan, T6437777. Sunday-Thursday 0800-2200, Friday-Saturday 0800-1700, tickets for Saturday must be bought in advance. Adult 15 NIS, student 12 NIS, 30 NIS for use of video camera. The hotel is located about 1.5 kilometres southwest of the Hebrew University Giv'at Ram campus, between Herzog Street and Herzl Avenue. It is accessed via Uziel Street, which is signposted at both ends. Buses 21 and 21a go directly there.*

Biblical Zoo Recently opened zoo features rare animals common to Israel and mentioned in the Bible. ■ *T6430111. Sunday-Thursday 0900-1930, Friday 0900-1630, Saturday 1000-1800. The zoo is located just to the southwest of Jerusalem (Malkha) Mall. Buses 26/33/99.*

Theodore Herzl (1860-1904)

Herzl is described by Johnson as "one of the most complex characters in Jewish history" (A History of the Jews, 1989). He was born to wealthy parents in Budapest in 1860 (his father subsequently loosing everything in the crash of 1873), and studied for the bar, though writing was to remain his first great love. To his dying day he was to lament his lack of appreciation as a playwright.

The turning point in Herzl's life came in the last decade of the 19th century, when the Dreyfus trial in Paris served to convince him that Jews would never fully be accepted into European society because anti-Semitism was so deeply engrained.

Herzl's publication of Judenstaat in 1896, in which he called for the establishment as a Jewish state on the grounds that Jews were a distinct race as opposed to just being a religious grouping, effectively marked the birth of what is known today as political Zionism. It was not a concept that Herzl invented; instead he was the catalyst that began a chain of events that eventually led to the foundation of the State of Israel some 44 years after his death. But as Johnson remarks, "he gave Zionism a lead of nearly twenty years over its Arab nationalist equivalent, and that was to prove absolutely decisive in the event" (ibid).

The hill on the western outskirts of Jerusalem, **Mt Herzl** (Har Herzl), is home to a number of institutions fundamental to the state of Israel. In addition to the **Military Cemetery**, Mt Herzl also features the tombs of Israel's past prime ministers and presidents, including Levi Eshkol, Golda Meir, Menachem Begin, and, more recently, Yitzhak Rabin. Other 'Great Leaders of the Nation' buried on Mt Herzl include Vladimir (Ze'ev) Jabotinsky (1880-1940), with the centrepiece of the cemetery being the **Tomb of Theodore Herzl**. The life and works of Herzl, including a reconstruction of his Vienna study, are presented in the **Herzl Museum**, just inside the gates of Mt Herzl. The western slopes of Mt Herzl are occupied by the extensive **Jerusalem Forest** and the memorial to the Holocaust, **Yad VaShem** (see below). ■ *Cemetery Sunday-Thursday 0800-1615, Friday 0800-1300. Free. Buses 13/17/18/20/23/27 stop outside. Herzl Museum T6511108. Sunday-Thursday 0900-1615, Friday 0800-1300. Adult 5 NIS, student 3 NIS.*

Mt Herzl

Yad VaShem

See next page for description of Yad VaShem

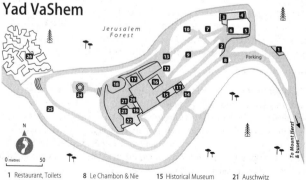

1 Restaurant, Toilets	8 Le Chambon & Nie Lande Monuments	15 Historical Museum	21 Auschwitz
2 Information Booth	9 Pillar of Heroism	16 Hall of Remembrance	22 Art Gallery
3 World Holocaust Teaching Centre	10 Children's Memorial	17 In Memory of the Victims of the Death	23 Auditorium
4 Offices & Archives	11 The Boat	Camps	24 Monument to Soldiers & Partisans
5 In Memory of Chemy	12 Silent Cry	18 Warsaw Ghetto Uprising	25 Boxcar Monument
6 Hativka	13 Cossack & Children	19 Hall of Names	26 Valley of the Destroyed Communities
7 Menorah	14 Avenue of Righteous Gentiles	20 Synagogue	

Jerusalem

 Controversial views of Yad VaShem

Controversy surrounding Yad VaShem arises from the fact that many commentators view it as far more than a shrine or memorial to the six million plus Jews who died in the Holocaust: it clearly has a political statement to make. Whether Yad VaShem "bears witness to the fact that Israel is founded on new ashes as much as on its biblical past" as Amos Elon suggests (Jerusalem: City of Mirrors, 1989), or that its theme is that "the Holocaust produced the state of Israel and anyone who opposed the creation of that state is on the level of the Nazis" as Robert Fisk concludes (Pity the Nation: Lebanon at War, 1990) is a starting point for further debate.

Fisk, one of the most experienced and respected journalists commenting on the Middle East, pulls no punches in his assessment of Yad VaShem's role: "in the same building as the photographs of SS officers selecting the Jews on the ramps at Birkenau are news pictures of British paratroopers ordering the concentration camp survivors away from post-war Palestine. The British, it says in effect, were like the Nazis; they too were criminals. When I first visited Yad VaShem in 1978, I found it a place of unanswerable accusation. When I went there in 1987, after my journey to Auschwitz, it seemed somehow facile, an instrument of propaganda that used the horror of what happened in Auschwitz and Treblinka and all the other camps to justify not just the existence of Israel but all that Israel has

done since."

So is it possible to strike the balance between honouring the victims of the Holocaust, explaining the forces that created it, and pointing the finger of accusation? Undoubtedly so, but what reviles Fisk within Yad VaShem is the very deliberate way in which the finger is pointed not just at the Nazis (and the British), but also at the Palestinians: "It is also a place of accusation against the Arabs of Palestine. For there are pictures at Yad VaShem of the Grand Mufti of Jerusalem being greeted in Nazi Germany by Heinrich Hitler. The photographs are perfectly clear. Here we can see Sheikh Haj Amin al-Husseini shaking hands with the leader of the SS, there he proudly inspects a volunteer Muslim contingent of the Wehrmacht. On the wall are his words – an accurate translation – exhorting the German government to prevent the Jews of Europe going to Palestine. The inference is clear: the Muslim religious leader of the Palestinian Arabs is also a war criminal. So why should not his political successors be war criminals? If the Arab Palestinians who saw in the Nazis some hope of preventing Jewish immigration into Palestine were on the same level as the SS, were not those Palestinians who oppose Israel today equally guilty?"

It is common to see Fisk dismissed as 'anti-Israel', 'pro-Arab' or 'pro-Palestinian', though such labels miss the point (in fact, a theme underlying Fisk's writing, notably in Pity the Nation, is how political leaders,

Yad VaShem (Holocaust Memorial) The most moving experience for many visitors to Israel, Yad VaShem ("a memorial and a name", from *Isaiah 56:5*) pays homage to the six million Jews who died in the Holocaust. Entering from the east, you pass along the **Avenue of Righteous Gentiles** – a memorial garden to non-Jews who risked their lives protecting Jews – to the **Historical Museum**. This museum features harrowing photographs and testimony documenting the Holocaust in Europe, and the factors that created it, though some of the presentation is controversial (see box). To the west of the museum is the **Hall of Names**, where 'Pages of Testimony' by Holocaust survivors and their families fill over three million pages. ■ *Sunday-Tuesday and Thursday 1000-1400, Wednesday 1000-1700, Friday 1000-1230*

The same building also features an **art museum** of work produced in the concentration camps and Jewish ghettoes. To the west of here is a **railway**

whether Arab, Palestinian or Israeli, have invariably let their people down, and Fisk's sympathy and loyalty lies with the ordinary people who have become the victims). Yet the Israeli right, most notably former Prime Minister Menachem Begin, but also Ariel Sharon (Defence Minister at the time of the Israeli invasion of Lebanon in 1982), continue to draw unsubtle parallels between the Palestinian leadership and the Nazis. During the 1982 invasion of Lebanon, Begin (then Prime Minister) repeatedly drew parallels between Arafat's position in Beirut and Hitler trapped in his Berlin bunker. Israeli writer Amos Oz was moved to pen a piece titled Hitler's Dead, Mr Prime Minister, berating Begin for his "weird urge to resurrect Hitler from the dead just so that you may kill him over and over again each day" (The Slopes of Lebanon, 1989). In 1989, in an interview with the Wall Street Journal (10th-11th Feb 1989), Sharon declared that Arafat was "like Hitler who wanted so much to negotiate with the Allies in the second half of the Second World War ... and the allies said no. They said there are enemies with whom you don't talk. They pushed him to the bunker in Berlin where he found his death, and Arafat is the same kind of enemy, that with whom you don't talk. [He's] got too much blood on his hands."

Yet it is not just Yad VaShem's role as accuser that is criticized; it is the way in which the Holocaust is used to promote the concept of 'the Jew as victim' within the Israeli consciousness. This is perhaps an even more controversial view. Thomas Friedman, Pulitzer-Prize-winning Middle East reporter, reviled by the Israeli right as a "self-hating Jew", and author of a popular book about his time based in the region (From Beirut to Jerusalem, 1989) that Palestinian intellectual Edward Said describes as "purest Orientalism", has strong views on the subject. He reviles the "'Holocausting' of the Israeli psyche ... turning the Palestinians into the new Nazis and Israel into a modern-day Warsaw Ghetto aligned against the world." He sees Yad VaShem as the means of delivering "the subliminal message" that the various concentration camps "are what the state of Israel is all about" and deplores the "Yad Vasheming" of Israel.

There is no doubt that the Holocaust is a defining feature of Israeli society – how could it not be? – yet it is far from being the defining feature (if such a feature could exist). And it is true that Yad VaShem is more than just a memorial to the victims of the Holocaust, with its political or propaganda purposes in many ways devaluing the memory of the victims that it sets out to honour. Yet a visit to Yad VaShem is still a very moving experience, with its true value as a lesson and a warning encapsulated in Egyptian president Anwar Sadat's comments in the visitors' book, made during his visit in 1977: "May God guide our steps toward peace. Let us end all suffering for mankind."

boxcar that was used to transport Jews to the camps, and now serves as a memorial monument. Below is the **Valley of the Destroyed Communities** that commemorates the Jewish communities in Europe that were eliminated during World War Two. North of the Historical Museum is the **Hall of Remembrance**, where an eternal flame (*ner tamid*) is a memorial to the six million Jewish victims of the Holocaust, with the names of the 21 major concentration and death camps engraved on the floor. ■ T6751611. *Sunday-Thursday 0900-1645, Friday 0900-1300. Free. Take buses 13/17/18/20/27 to Mount Herzl and get off there. Then take the 'En Kerem road where is branches to the right at the large red metal sculpture. Instead of following the hill down to the left towards 'En Kerem, take the downhill path to the right, to Yad VaShem. **NB** Respectful dress should be worn. There are free guided tours in English at 1000 on Sunday and Wednesday. Toilets and cafeteria are available.*

Jerusalem

'En Kerem

Though Jerusalem continues its relentless expansion westwards, the former Arab village of 'En Kerem still retains something of its former rural feel. The village is traditionally associated with the home of Zechariah and Elizabeth, the parents of John the Baptist, and consequently as the birthplace and early home of John. The Virgin Mary's visit to her cousin Elizabeth is also commemorated here.

Ins and outs Buses 27 and 184 both run through the village from Jerusalem. Alternatively, it is possible to follow the road down from Mt Herzl (see page 203). Look out for a restaurant called *Le Château* in the centre of the village, close to the police station. Just beyond *Le Château*, an alley leads right (north) to the **Franciscan Church of John the Baptist**. The road to the left (Ha-Ma'yan St, with sign indicating "to the Virgin's Spring") leads to the **Virgin's Spring** and then up the hill to the right to the **Church of the Visitation**. There are a number of attractive mid-range restaurants in the village.

Franciscan Church of John the Baptist Most of the present church dates to the late 17th century, though it stands on far older foundations. Its somewhat fortress-like appearance reflects its remote location away from Jerusalem and its eventful past. Parts of a fifth to sixth century CE church underlie the present structure, hinting at the Byzantine tradition linking the village with John the Baptist, though the remains of a Roman marble statue of Venus/Aphrodite found here suggest that an earlier pagan temple may well have once stood on this spot. The original Byzantine church was damaged and rebuilt a number of times until the Crusader Knights Hospitallers, and then the Templars, took it over. Following the Crusader defeat in 1187 it was occupied by the Muslims, not returning to Christian hands until the Franciscans acquired it in 1621. However, they were unable to establish a presence and restore the church until 1674: the year to which much of the present structure belongs. It was expanded in 1860, the main doorway to the west added in 1885, and a new bell-tower (resplendent with a cross and TV aerial) constructed in 1895. The main feature of the church is the Grotto of St John, reputedly built over the house of Zechariah and Elizabeth, and thus the Baptist's birthplace (*Luke 1:5-25, 57-66*).

Two fifth to sixth century CE chapels are also visible from the courtyard outside, built against the southwest wall of the present church. The most interesting of these is the **Chapel of the Martyrs**, to the north. Discovered in 1885 during the construction of the west doorway, the chapel contains a mosaic with a Greek inscription offering "Greetings, Martyrs of God". It is still unclear as to whom this dedication refers. ■ *T6413636. Monday-Friday 0800-1200 1430-1800, Sunday 0800-1200 1430-1700, closed Saturday and closes one hour earlier in winter. Free. Souvenir shop.*

Virgin's Spring About 400 metres to the south of the Church of John the Baptist (follow the sign) is a small abandoned mosque built over a spring. A 14th century CE tradition notes this as the place where the Virgin Mary drew water during her three-month stay with her cousin Elizabeth (*Luke 1:39-56*).

Church of the Visitation Climbing the hill to the right past the Russian Convent (1871) and Rosary Sisters Orphanage, you eventually come to the Church of the Visitatio Mariae, or **Church of the Visitation**. The present 'upper' church is described as "probably one of the most beautiful of all the Gospel sites in the Holy Land" (Wareham and Gill, 1996), and was built in 1955 over 'lower' Crusader and

Byzantine remains. The west façade of the church features a mosaic depicting the Virgin Mary mounted on a donkey meeting with her cousin Elizabeth (the 'Visitation', *Luke 1:39-56*). Though the modern 'upper' church features a number of paintings depicting events in the life of Mary, plus the glorification of the Virgin throughout the centuries, it is the older 'lower' church that is of the greatest interest. The Crusader church is built above the Byzantine remains around a cave that tradition links with the story of Elizabeth hiding the baby John from Herod's soldiers. ■ *T6417291. Sunday-Friday 0800-1145 1430-1800, closed Saturday, closes one hour earlier in winter. Free. Souvenir shop. Toilets.*

The Hadassah Medical Centre was built here in 1963 when the original hospital of the same name on Mt Scopus was inaccessible (1948-67). It is one of the world's foremost teaching hospitals, with a reputation for also providing treatment to Israel's Arab neighbours. Those without medical insurance who intend using the facilities should bear in mind that a night here can cost more than a night at the *Sheraton Jerusalem Plaza Hotel*!

Hadassah Medical Centre

The hospital is worth visiting just to see the magnificent **stained-glass windows** by **Marc Chagall** in the synagogue. Depicting the 12 tribes of Israel (based on *Genesis 49* and *Deuteronomy 33*), four of the windows were badly damaged in the 1967 war, requiring delicate repair work by the artist himself. Chagall decided to remember the war by leaving some of the bullet holes in place. ■ *Hospital T6427427, Chagall Windows T6776271. Free English-language tours are held every hour on the half-hour Sunday-Thursday 0830-1230, Friday 0930-1130. The synagogue is open Sunday-Thursday 0800-1315 1400-1545, Friday 0800-1245. Adults 10 NIS, students 5 NIS. Buses 19/27.*

Southwestern suburbs

The Southwestern section of the New City largely comprises the suburbs of Mamilla, Yemin Moshe, Talbiyeh, 'Emeq Refa'im and Rehavia. These suburbs are divided from the walled Old City by the Valley of Hinnom. The background to the Valley of Hinnom, and the sites on the east and southeast side of the valley, are included in the section that begins on page 181. The places described below are largely associated with the expansion of Jerusalem beyond the confines of the Old City at the end of the 19th century CE.

Ins and outs

Most of the sites detailed below can be reached by heading to the east end of Independence Park, then heading south-southeast down **King David Street** (all pretty much within walking distance of the Old City and New City centre). For orientation, refer to the 'New City (including Western suburbs, Western outskirts and Southwestern suburbs)' map on page 196.

Getting there

At the centre of Independence Park is the **Mamilla Pool** (89 metres by 59 metres by 5.8 metres deep); probably once part of the Herodian aqueduct system that brought water to the head of the Valley of Hinnom from Solomon's Pools near Bethlehem. A number of traditions surround this location, invariably involving massacres of innocents by various groups. The nearby Lion's Cave commemorates, in Jewish tradition, the massacre of Jews by the Greeks. The same cave, meantime, serves as a reminder of the massacre of Christians

Independence Park

by Jews in 614 CE (or by Jews and Persians in other sources). What is certain about this site is that the Mamilla Pool became part of the Mamluk water system sometime in the 15th century CE, with a channel linking it to the Pool of the Patriarch's Bath in the Christian Quarter.

In the 13th century CE the main Muslim graveyard was established here, continuing in use until the 20th century. In a grove to the east of the park, about 100 metres from the Mamilla Pool, is the **Zawiya Kubakiyya** – the burial place of Amir Aidughidi al-Kubaki (d. 1289). A former slave in Syria, al-Kubaki rose to become Governor of Safed under the Mamluk sultan Baibars, though in later years he fell from grace and was banished to Jerusalem. The cube-shaped tomb, supporting a low dome on a drum, uses much secondary Crusader material, and it has been suggested that it was originally the mortuary chapel used to bury the Canons of the Church of the Holy Sepulchre. In fact, in the centre of the mausoleum stands a Romanesque Crusader sarcophagus. **NB** Independence Park has something of a reputation as a "meeting place" after dark for gay men.

Dominating the southwest corner of the park is the prestigious *Sheraton Jerusalem Plaza Hotel*. Opposite is the **Jerusalem Great Synagogue**, seat of the Chief Rabbinate. Next door is the **Wolfson Museum in Heichal Shlomo**, which features Jewish liturgical art and folklore, plus a Torah library. Slightly further up the road is the **Jewish Agency**, the headquarters of the **World Zionist Organization** (and its archives), the **Jewish National Fund** (JNF) and **United Jewish Agencies**. ■ *Synagogue: 58 King George/HaMelekh George Street. Tours Sunday-Thursday 0900-1300, Friday 0900-1200. Museum: T6247112. Sunday-Thursday 0900-1300. Buses 4/7/9/14/31. Jewish Agency: 48 HaMelekh George, T6202222*

Taxation Museum As dull as it sounds, the Taxation Museum at the top of King David Street presents the history of the taxation of Jews in Palestine and the Diaspora. ■ *32 Agron, T6258978. Monday Wednesday Friday 1000-1400, Sunday Tuesday Thursday 1300-1600. Free.*

Hebrew Union College The **Skirball Museum** at the Hebrew Union College (at the north end of King David Street) has a small collection of items excavated by the Biblical Archaeology School here. ■ *14 King David Street, T6203333. Sunday-Thursday 1000-1600, Saturday 1000-1400. Free. Buses 15/18/21/30.*

Jerusalem International YMCA Three Arches Not your run-of-the-mill YMCA, this Jerusalem landmark was built in 1933 to a design produced by the firm of architects responsible for the Empire State Building, and with funds provided by the New Jersey millionaire James Jarvie. Considering the synthesis of styles, the building is remarkably attractive, as well as being a very nice place to stay (see 'Sleeping' on page 213). The tower, at 90 metres high, provides good views of the city. ■ *Monday-Saturday 0900-1400. 3 NIS.*

King David Hotel The *King David Hotel* is still considered the most prestigious residence in Jerusalem. In a head-to-head contest, its celebrity guest list of former residents easily matches the American Colony Hotel in East Jerusalem (see page 188).

However, the King David Hotel is less famous for its celebrity roll-call (such as the scene in the film version of Leon Uris' *Exodus* in which Paul Newman and Eva-Marie Saint share a drink on the terrace), than for the events of 22nd July, 1946. Around lunchtime on that day over 300 kilogrammes of explosives placed in a milk-crate detonated, demolishing one wing of the hotel. The bomb had been placed by the Irgun- the Jewish resistance (or 'terrorist', according to your viewpoint) movement headed by the future Prime Minister of Israel, Menachem Begin. Its target was the British Mandate administration, whose offices occupied most of the building. The victims included 28 British, 41 Arabs, 17 Jews and 5 'others' dead, with hundreds injured: most were civilians. The controversy over the bombing, including details of the sequence of events, continues to this day. Begin publicly mourned the Jewish victims alone, blaming the British for failing to act on the telephone warning in time (which was phoned through by a 16-year-old girl). Other sources suggest that the bomb detonated six minutes early, but, even so, insufficient time had been given to evacuate the building. The Jewish establishment condemned the outrage, and the British called it the "ninth worst terrorist act this century", yet it achieved its objective: the cost of a continued British presence in Palestine was too much to bear, and the decision on the future of Palestine was handed over to the United Nations.

Just to the south of the *King David Hotel*, a short road (Aba Sikra Street) leads east to the north end of Bloomfield Park. Just inside the park here is the so-called **'Tomb of Herod's Family'**. Though Herod himself was buried at the Herodium (see page 250), Josephus mentions a family tomb belonging to Herod to the west of the city (*Jewish War I, 228; I, 581; V, 108; V, 507*). However, the evidence that this is indeed the burial place of Herod's family is purely circumstantial, based on Josephus' vague description and the fact that the tomb lies directly across the Valley of Hinnom from Herod's former palace (to the south of the Citadel, see above). The tomb was robbed in antiquity, which has not helped in its identification.

'Tomb of Herod's Family'

However, the tomb itself is fairly well constructed, suggesting that it was indeed the burial place of someone rich or important. It is entered through a modern structure at the surface, leading down to a rock-cut forecourt (10 metres by 6.5 metres). The foundation courses to the northwest may have belonged to the tomb's *nephesh* (funerary monument). The entrance to the catacomb was sealed by a very large rolling stone, and leads to a small antechamber from which four chambers branch off. A noticeable feature of the complex is the fine workmanship of the ashlar masonry that was used to face the tombs. There is some uncertainty concerning the dating of the tomb. Some of the features could be of the second half of the first century BCE, thus making it reasonable that Herod's father Antipater (d. 43 BCE) was buried here, as suggested by Josephus (*Jewish War, I, 228*). However, some of the features are certainly later, though this could simply mean that the tomb was intended for later descendants. ■ *Daily 1000-1600. Adult 3 NIS.*

On the east side of **Bloomfield Park**, facing across the Valley of Hinnom towards Mount Zion, is the **Yemin Moshe Quarter**; a small neighbourhood of some 130 houses established outside the walled Old City in 1891. The quarter was abandoned during the period of Jordanian occupation (1948-67), but has subsequently been redeveloped. Running to the south of the Yemin Moshe Quarter, at the bottom of the hill, are two rows of terraced houses known as **Mishkenot Sha'ananim** ('tranquil settlement'). These were amongst the first houses to be built outside the city walls (c. 1860), and formed part of an attempt to provide affordable, comfortable accommodation for poor Jewish immigrants in the 19th century. Their benefactor was the Anglo-Jewish philantropist, **Sir Moses Montefiore**.

Mishkenot Sha'ananim and the Montefiore Windmill

The **Montefiore Windmill** was built to enable the community to produce their own flour, though the scheme never really came to fruition. It is now a museum detailing the campaigns and achievements of Montefiore. The houses have been restored as part of a music centre complex, designed to accommodate musicians, scholars and performers, and the whole area (including Yemin Moshe) has something of the 'artists' colony' about it. ■ *Sunday-Thursday 0900-1600, Friday 0900-1300. Free*

Sunset from this point (or anywhere in Bloomfield Park overlooking the Old City) is particularly scenic, as the walls of the Old City gradually shift colour as the sun goes down.

Liberty Bell Park and the 'German Colony' Popular with strollers and picnicking families, this park was laid out to commemorate the bicentennial of Israel's patron and ally, the United States of America. It contains a replica of the Liberty Bell in Philadelphia.

The suburb to the southwest of Liberty Bell Park, **'Emeq Refa'im**, was the main German Colony' of 19th-century Jerusalem, with many of the houses displaying a northern European influence. The colony was founded by the same 'Templars' German Protestant Christian group who established the German Colony in Haifa some three years earlier. Most of the community were expelled during the Second World War.

There are several notable museums located in this district, including the highly recommended **L A Mayer Institute of Islamic Art** and the **Natural History Museum**. ■ *Institute of Art: 2 HaPalmach, T5661291. Sunday Monday Wednesday Thursday 1000-1700, Tuesday 1600-2000, Friday-Saturday 1000-1400. Adult 8 NIS, student 6 NIS, tickets for Saturday must be bought in advance, or at the King David Hotel, Bus 15. Natural History Museum: 6 Mohilever, T5631116. Sunday-Thursday 0830-1300, may be closed in August. Adult 6 NIS. Buses 4/14/18.*

St Andrew's Church St Andrew's Church of Scotland, to the south of Bloomfield Park, was built in 1927 to commemorate the Allied victory in the First World War, and the capture of the Holy Land. The church was designed by Clifford Holliday and his said to reflect his interest in the Armenian style of monastic architecture. The church operates a highly recommended pilgrim guesthouse (see 'Sleeping' on page 213) and a handicraft shop from which profits go to a number of Palestinian self-help groups.

Khan Theatre The road that heads south, passing on the west side of St Andrew's Church, leads to the **Jerusalem Railway Station** (opened in 1892 when the line to Jaffa was completed). Just before the station, housed in a former Ottoman period caravanserai, is the **Khan Theatre** (■ *2 David Remez Square, T6718281. For details of programme see 'Jerusalem Post', 'What's On in Jerusalem', or enquire at the tourist office. Buses 4/6/8/10/14/18/21*).

Cinémathèque Just below the Hebron Road running southeast from Bloomfield Park (passing on the east side of St Andrew's Church) is the **Jerusalem Film Centre and Cinémathèque**, which features nightly screenings, film festivals, theme nights, and 'movie marathons'. The cafés here, notably the *Cacao*, are particularly popular. ■ *T6724131. Call for listings, or consult 'Jerusalem Post'. Buses 4/4a/7/8/14/18/21/48.*

Abu Tor Observation Point Further southeast along Hebron Road is the **cable car monument**; a site that was previously occupied by the St John's Ophthalmic Hospital (built 1882), part of which now forms the old wing of the *Mount Zion Hotel*. There are also several cafés here, with fine views across the Valley of Hinnom to Mount Zion and the Old City.

Continuing south along Hebron Road, just before the *Ariel Hotel*, a road

Security and safety in Jerusalem

There are a number of security and safety considerations that should be borne in mind when visiting Jerusalem. Though acts of terrorism are rare, they do occasionally happen. Most likely 'targets' seem to be buses and bus stations, so be wary of unattended bags and report their presence to security personnel/bus staff.

Attacks on Jews in East Jerusalem and the Old City are rare, though they have occurred, so the choice of wearing a kippa or making other outward displays of Jewishness is something that ought to be considered (though of course there is the argument that you shouldn't be intimidated by racist attacks). Likewise, tourists who wander around in 'amusing' IDF t-shirts should not be surprised if they are greeted with hostility (or worse) when wandering around the Muslim Quarter.

Note that not all terrorist attacks in Jerusalem are committed against Jews/Israelis by Palestinians; you need to be equally vigilant in the vicinity of institutions (bus stations, government offices, places of worship) where the likely targets of any attacks are Palestinians. Likewise, when Israeli police go wading into crowds at Damascus Gate with clubs and tear gas, they don't discriminate.

Women may experience varying levels of harassment in the East Jerusalem/Old City area, ranging from disparaging remarks to actual physical touching. Beware of pressing crowds when the human traffic jams on Tariq Khan es-Zeit reach their peak. The Old City should be considered **unsafe** for lone females at night (as should the 'Rampart Walk' around the city walls , and the Mount of Olives area during the day). A particularly sinister development in recent years has been the groups of Arab youths hanging around outside the Tabasco Tearooms late at night, harassing women as they leave. If possible, take a (male) escort, and if cornered make a scene and as much noise as you can. Conversely, wandering around the Old City (particularly the Muslim Quarter) at any time whilst dressed in skimpy clothes remains a bad idea; it may seem like a good idea to wear your shorts when you get on the bus at Eilat or Tel Aviv etc, but by the time you have reached the Old City and are wandering around looking for a hostel, you will soon realize your mistake. Recent years have also seen the phenomenon of large groups of drunken Eastern European men hanging around the booze shops inside New Gate.

As with any city that attracts huge numbers of tourists, Jerusalem (and the Old City in particular) has its share of pickpockets, bag-snatchers and confidence tricksters. On the whole, however, despite the religious and political tensions, Jerusalem is considerably safer than most cities in the 'West' (and has a considerable 'security presence'). Being sensible and vigilant, though not over-paranoid, is the best way to approach the issue of safety in Jerusalem.

leads left (east) to the **Abu Tor Observation Point**. In Crusader times this hill was known as the 'Hill of Evil Counsel', from the tradition that this was the site of the House of the High Priest Caiaphas (yes, another one!) where Jesus was taken the night before his crucifixion. The present name is taken form the tradition that one of Salah al-Din's warriors, to whom the hill was given, used to ride into battle on the back of a bull. His tomb on the hill became a place of Muslim pilgrimage, though most visitors nowadays come to admire the view across to the Old City.

Southern section of the New City

There is a scenic viewpoint and an archaeological site in this southern section of the New City (directly south of the Abu Tor Observation Point, see above). The Talpiyyot industrial estate here is home to some of Jerusalem's trendiest nightclubs.

Haas Promenade Another fine view of the Old City, Valley of Hinnom and Mount Zion can be had from the south of the city, on the **Haas Promenade**. This is a particularly popular spot in the early evening or night-time. It is reached by heading south towards the suburb of Talpiyyot on the Hebron Road, turning left (east) just beyond the 'Peace Forest'.

Ramat Rahel Running parallel to the Hebron Road as it runs south through the suburb of Talpiyyot is the Betar Road. This road leads to **Kibbutz Ramat Rahel**, an independent collective within the municipal borders of Jerusalem. In addition to its agricultural activities, the kibbutz also has a luxury Guesthouse (T6702555, F6733155) and leisure/recreation centre, plus some interesting archaeological remains. The kibbutz was also the scene of heavy fighting in the 1948 war, with control of the hill fluctuating between the Jews and the Arabs. The kibbutz has a museum related to the war, and guided tours are available (call ahead). Bus 7 from the Central Bus Station goes to the kibbutz.

   Remains at Ramat Rahel: The modern kibbutz of Ramat Rahel occupies a prominent hill (818 metres above sea level) at a point roughly equidistant from the Old City and Bethlehem. Not a great deal is known about the ancient site, and even its name has not been preserved, though many scholars now support an identification with the biblical **Beth-Haccherem** (*Jeremiah 6:1, 22:13-19; Nehemiah 3:14*). The earliest settlement suggests a stronghold dating to the ninth or eighth century BCE, though the most prominent ancient remains are from a magnificent **citadel-palace** built by one of the later kings of Judah, probably **Jehoiakim** (608-597 BCE). Aharoni, who excavated the site between 1954-62, believes that this new construction "must have required a large measure of technical skill and enterprise", involving razing existing buildings and levelling the site (*New Encyclopedia of Archaeological Excavations in the Holy Land*, 1993). The walls of the outer citadel probably enclosed an area in excess of two hectares. The inner citadel, or palace (its function identifiable by the level of workmanship), measured around 75 metres by 50 metres. Sections can still be seen here, though the best preserved decorative remains, (three complete proto-Aeolic capitals and several incomplete fragments), have been removed to the Israel Museum. The citadel-palace complex was almost certainly destroyed during the Babylonian invasion of 586 BCE.

   Though remains have been found from the Babylonian-Hellenistic periods (586-37 BCE), and the Herodian period (37 BCE-70 CE), the next significant finds date to the third century CE. These comprise a **Roman bathhouse** and **villa** built by the Tenth Roman Legion c. 250 CE. Both were renovated and used during the Byzantine period. Also in the Byzantine period, c. 455 CE, a large **church** and **monastery** were built on the hill by Lady Ikelia, possibly to mark the traditional site where Mary rested on her way to Bethlehem. This large basilica, to the northeast of the site, is referred to in a number of contemporary sources as the **Church of Kathisma**. The plan of the church is readily identifiable, though only a small section of the mosaic floor was preserved. The site appears to have been abandoned since the seventh to eighth century CE.

Essentials

Sleeping

The hotels, hospices and hostels below are listed by area (Old City; East Jerusalem; Northern Suburbs, Mt Scopus and Mount of Olives; New City). The majority of the upmarket accommodation is found in the New City, whereas budget hotels, hospices and budget hostels tend to be in the Old City and East Jerusalem. The Old City/East Jerusalem area is more atmospheric, but has little nightlife and can be more risky at night (Israelis/Jews rarely stay here). The New City is blander but has better shopping, dining out and nightlife options. You pays your money and takes your choice (though in reality the two areas are little more than a half-hour walk apart). Advance booking is highly recommended during holidays (all denominations, all price categories), and essential at hospices and places orientated to pilgrimage-tours. Note that tour groups get significant discounts on the 'spot rates' used here. The Old City backpacker hostels offer the cheapest accommodation in Israel (under 25 NIS per night).

■ *on maps; price codes see inside front cover*

Jerusalem

(See the 'Old City: sleeping and eating' map on the next page).

Old City

B *Gloria*, 33 Latin Patriarchate, Jaffa Gate, T6282431, F6282401. Good location and fine views from restaurant and rooftop, fairly large rooms with heating, a/c, phone, décor a bit 70s, reasonable value, especially at off-season rates.

C *Austrian Hospice*, 37 Via Dolorosa, T6274636, F6271472. Busy, well-maintained pilgrim hospice, dorms (**E**), single and double rooms, check-out 1000, curfew 2200 (but key available), reservations recommended. **C** *Casa Nova Pilgrims' Hospice*, 10 Casa Nova, New Gate, T6282791. Franciscan-run hospice, reasonable rooms, imposing dining hall, reservations recommended. **C** *Christ Church Guesthouse*, Omar ibn al-Khattab Sq, Jaffa Gate, T6277727, F6282999. Spartan but clean rooms, some triple and family rooms, meals available, 2300 curfew, non-married couples cannot share, reservations recommended. **C** *Lark*, 4 Latin Patriarchate, T6283620. Basic rooms, attached bath, good Armenian restaurant downstairs. **C** *Lutheran Hospice and Hostel*, 7 St Mark's, T6282120, F6285107. Very well-run guesthouse, clean doubles (**C**) set around a peaceful courtyard, plus large, staid single-sex dorms (**E**), 2230 curfew, 0900-1200 lock-out, no smoking. **C** *New Imperial*, Omar ibn al-Khattab Sq, Jaffa Gate, T6282261, F6271530. Historic building (previous guests include Kaiser Wilhelm II in 1898), remarkably good value, cheap dbles with shared bath and no views (**D**), dbles with att bath and views (**C**), very friendly, bookings essential. Recommended. **C** *Notre Dame de Sion Ecce Homo Convent*, 41 Via Dolorosa, T6277293, F6276797. Rather austere, women-only dorms (**E**), some private rooms, 1000-1200 lock-out, 2200 curfew, reservations recommended.

D *Greek Catholic Patriarchate Hospice*, St Dimitri, off Greek Catholic Patriarchate St, T6282023. Aimed at Greek Catholics, reservations recommended. **D** *Jaffa Gate Hostel*, Armenian Patriarchate, next to Christian Information Centre, T6276402. Recently refurbished, no longer has dorms, doubles with attached bath (**D**) or shared bath (**E**).

E *IYHA Old City Youth Hostel*, 2 Ararat, T6288611. Well maintained and clean, though rather staid atmosphere, stone building can be cold in winter (but nice in summer), 2300 curfew, 0900-1700 lock-out, advance reservations essential.

G *Al-Ahram*, 64 Tariq al-Wad, T6280926. Quiet 4-8 bed dorms (**G**) and private rooms (**E**), though not so quiet when neighbouring mosque is in full cry, midnight curfew.

Jerusalem Old City: sleeping & eating

Jerusalem

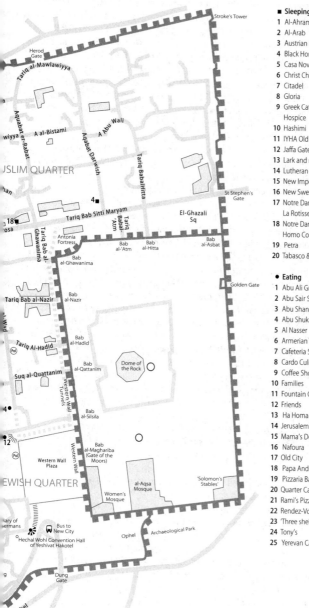

G *Al-Arab*, Tariq Khan es-Zeit, near Damascus Gate, T6283537. Long-established backpacker favourite and cheapest in town, recently refurbished but still rather run down, grubby toilets and showers (irregular hot water and peep-holes), variously sized dorms (including one with 46 beds on the roof!), private rooms (**D-E**) though couples should beware of peepholes, new kitchen but still unhygienic, no curfew, Masada Tours, popular despite many shortcomings. **G** *Black Horse*, 28 Aqabat Darwish, off Via Dolorosa, T6276011. Dorms plus some private rooms (**E**), kitchen, TV room, lots of long-term guests but other Old City hostel managers all have 'low opinions' of the owners of this place. **G** *Citadel*, 20 St Mark's, T6274375. Good for those after peace and quiet, large cavern-like dorms, small TV lounge, kitchen, good views from the roof. **G** *Hashimi*, 73 Tariq Khan es-Zeit, near Damascus Gate, T6284410, F6284667. Excellent choice for those after some peace and quiet, cheap dorms, private rooms with or without a/c (**D**), kitchen, free tea and coffee. Recommended. **G** *Heritage House*, Head Office at 90 Habad, T6271916, F6288302, men's hostel at 2 Or Hayim, T6272224, women's hostel at 7 Hamalah, T6281820. Jewish Quarter hostels welcome religious and non-observant Jews, though there is some pressure to attend 'Jewish education classes', dorm accommodation is often free (except Shabbat), check-in Sunday-Thursday 0700-0900, 1700-2300, or before 1600 on Shabbat. **G** *New Swedish*, 29 David, T6277855. Dorms rather crowded with old cast-iron bunks (mixed plus women-only), some cheap doubles (**E**), clean showers, cosy kitchen, free tea/coffee, friendly and more peaceful than competitors. **G** *Petra*, 1 David St, T6286618, F6262434. Excellent location just inside Jaffa Gate with fabulous views from the roof (plans for rooftop bar/barbeque), rambling historic building is slowly being refurbished, regular dorms (6-8 beds), cheap private rooms (**E**) plus nicer rooms with balcony views (**D**), clean linen, free use of three kitchens, fridges on each floor, internet access, cheap bar (beer 7 NIS), 24-hr reception, no curfew, 1000 check-out, baggage storage, 'interesting' clientele (lots of 'Jerusalem Syndrome' types), well run, takes credit cards. Recommended. **G** *Tabasco*, 8 Aqabat Tekieh, off Tariq Khan es-Zeit, T6281101. Remains Jerusalem's most popular backpacker hostel, spacious dorms have 10-26 beds (but not crowded), some women-only dorms, cheaper dorm on the roof, some private rooms (**E**), cleaned daily, very clean hot showers and toilets, cheap meals (12-20 NIS) and drinks (beer 6-10 NIS) in *Tearooms* downstairs, can be a little noisy until bar closes at midnight, friendly staff, 'Masada Sunrise' tours, cheap air tickets (see Yassin), overpriced laundry service, no curfew. Recommended. To reach the hostel enter Old City through Damascus Gate, take the right fork on to Tariq Khan es-Zeit, pass *Al-Arab Hostel* (200m), and it's just down the second small street on the left (there's a sign).

East Jerusalem (See the 'East Jerusalem and Northern Suburbs' map on page 184).

L2 *American Colony*, 1 Louis Vincent, off Nablus, T6279777, F6279779. Historical building (see page 188) now houses East Jerusalem's classiest hotel, there's a certain simplicity to the interior décor though the antiques and wall-hangings dotted about the public places add style. Attractive pool area and quiet courtyard garden. To appreciate your stay fully, go for the more luxurious rooms or Pasha's Suite (**L1**), excellent restaurant (see 'Eating' on page 220). Recommended.

L3 *Addar*, 53 Nablus, T6263111, F6260791. Luxury new suite hotel, beautifully furnished rooms with balcony or terrace, kitchenette, bathrooms with Jacuzzis, all rooms feature fax and email facilities, a/c, cable TV, lobby coffee shop, friendly staff. Recommended. **L3** *St George International*, Amar Ben Ela'as, off Salah al-Din, T6277232. 150 rooms with a/c, heating, some with small balconies (but not all with views), large atmospheric dining hall, small pool, though rather old fashioned and difficult to see how they can justify these prices.

A *Ambassador*, Nabus, Sheikh Jarrah, T5828515, F5828202. Favoured by tour groups (though overpriced without their discounts), rooms a/c, cable TV, Italian and 'Oriental' restaurants. **A** *Golden Walls (Tulip Inn)*, Suleiman, T6272135, F6264658. Formerly the *Pilgrim's Palace*, excellent though noisy location between Damascus and Herod Gates, refurbished a/c rooms, good group discounts, busy lobby lounge. **A** *Holy Land (East)*, 6 Rashid, T6284841, F6280265. Large comfortable hotel, popular with groups, revel in the 70s décor, reasonable rates (particularly at group rates). **A** *Ritz*, corner of Ibn Khaldun/Ibn Batura, T6273233, F6286768. 103 a/c rms, though no sense of 'luxury' that you should expect with this price tag.

B *Az-Zahra*, 13 Az-Zahra, T6282447, F6282415. Very pleasant a/c rooms in quiet old building, tranquil courtyard/restaurant, would be much better value if you can bargain price down. **B** *Capitolina (YMCA EAST)*, 29 Nablus, T6286888, F6276301. Pool, squash and tennis, though hotel itself is lacking in atmosphere, large rooms some with small balconies. **B** *Christmas*, 1 Ali Ibn Abitaleb, T6282588, F5894417. Modest hotel catering for pilgrims, recent refurbishment has seen a significant price hike. **B** *Jerusalem*, 4 Antara Ben-Shadad, off Nablus, T6271356, F6283282. Attractively refurbished old building, well-furnished rooms (some with excellent balcony views), cable TV, phone, appealing patio restaurant or Bedouin 'diwan' indoors, friendly management. Recommended. **B** *Mt Scopus*, Nablus, Sheikh Jarrah, T5828891, F5828825. Fair-sized rooms with small balconies, though rather old fashioned and overpriced. **B** *National Palace*, 4 Az-Zahra, T6273273, F6282139. Probably the best value in this category, all rms a/c, TV available, well situated rooftop Middle Eastern restaurant. **B** *New Regent*, 20 Az-Zahra, T6284540, F5894023. Rooms are a reasonable size, plus there's a nice rooftop restaurant, though it's a little run-down to justify this price tag. **B** *Victoria*, 8 al-Masudi, T6223870, F6274171. A/c, heating, quiet location, restaurant, though a little overpriced.

C *Capitol*, 17 Salah al-Din, T6282561, F5894352. Small but smart a/c rooms, TV available, better value at group rates. **C** *Jerusalem Meridian*, 5 Ali Ibn Abitaleb, T6285212, F6285214. All rooms recently upgraded, standard rooms reasonable value, 'club' rooms (**B**) and suites (**A**) have central a/c, cable TV, some with small balconies, restaurant, discounts for long stays, good value if you can get the 'corporate' discount. **C** *Lawrence*, 18 Salah al-Din, T6264208, F6271285. Rather old fashioned and run down, but friendly and good value if you haggle. **C** *Metropole*, 6 Salah al-Din, T6282507, F6285134. Rather old fashioned, if business is slack can negotiate a good deal. **C** *New Metropole*, 8 Salah al-Din, T6283846, F6277485. Actually looks older and more run down that its namesake next door, though pricier. **C** *Notre Dame de France Guesthouse*, IdZanhanim, T6279111, F6271995. Historic building opposite New Gate, aimed primarily at Roman Catholic pilgrims (though others welcome), lovely building, fine views, well-kept rooms, recommended restaurant (*La Rotisserie*), reservations recommended. **C** *Pilgrim's Inn*, Rashid, T6272420, F5894658. Small and well furnished, but currently rather run down. **C** *Rivoli*, 3 Salah al-Din, T6284871, F6274879. 31 rooms, some a/c, though hard to justify this price. **C** *St George's Anglican Cathedral Pilgrim Guesthouse*, 20 Nablus, T6283302, F6282253. Delightfully tranquil setting around cloistered garden, sensibly run, reservations recommended. Reasonable value by Jerusalem standards.

G *Cairo Youth Hostel*, 21 Nablus, T6277216. Dorms plus a couple of private rooms (**D-E**), recently received a long overdue lick of paint, popular with gap-year volunteers. **G** *Faisal*, 4 HaNevi'im, T6272492. Crowded single-sex dorms, kitchen, TV, laundry, flexible curfew, rooftop views of Damascus Gate. **G** *Palm*, 6 HaNevi'im, T6273189. Formerly a real 'travellers' hang-out, change of management has made the hostel more frigid, though certainly cleaner and more orderly. Crowded dorms (6-10 beds), some with attached bath, various private rooms (**D**), flexible midnight curfew. **G** *Raghadan*, 10 HaNevi'im, T6283348. Some dorms but mainly private rooms (**D**), flexible curfew. **G** *Ramsis*, 20 Hanevi'im, T6271651. Mainly private rooms, but currently looks closed up.

Northern Suburbs (See the following maps: 'East Jerusalem and Northern Suburbs', page 195. 'Mount of Olives', page 165).

L2 *Hyatt Regency*, 32 Lehi, Mt Scopus, T5331234, F5815947. Bold, modern design featuring hanging gardens and waterfalls in the lobby, palm-fringed pool area, plus true 5-star facilities (including Jerusalem Spa complex). Recommended.

A *7 Arches*, Mount of Olives, T6277555, F6271319. Fabulous views (though unless you have your own transport you may feel rather isolated), good facilities for the price (with a competitive pricing policy). Not a bad deal.

B *Commodore*, Shmuel Ben 'Adava, T6284845, F6284701. Reasonable, though rather remote location on north side of the Mount of Olives.

C *Mount of Olives*, 53 Mount of Olives Rd, Mount of Olives, T6284877, F5894427. Very popular with evangelical Christians (and 'Jerusalem Syndrome' types) since Jesus made a 'visitation' in the reception area last year!

Apartment rental and B&Bs C-D *Le sixteen*, 16 Midbar Sinai, Giv'at Ha-Mivtar, T5328008, F5819159. Five comfortable rooms (sleeping 2-5) with attached bath, kitchenette, cable TV, a/c, breakfast, parking, private entrance, internet access (and site, http://www.Le16-BnB.co.il), very welcoming, Buses 4/22/28/48.

New City (See the following maps: 'New City (including Western suburbs, Western suburbs, Western outskirts and Southwestern suburbs)', page 196; 'New City: centre and area north of Jaffa Road', page 195).

L1 *Hilton Jerusalem*, King David, T6212121, F6211000. Recently opened, full services and facilities that you would expect, if you can afford the extra $25-50 for executive floors and Old City views then go for it. Recommended. **L1** *Holiday Inn Crowne Plaza*, Ha-Aliya, (just north of Knesset), T6588888, F6514555. Rooms in former *Hilton* are rather small, though facilities good, nice pool area, health club, tennis, good choice of restaurants. **L1** *King David*, 23 King David, T6208888, F6208882. Flagship of the *Dan* chain with a famous history (see page 208), this places oozes class, though to appreciate the experience fully you really need to stay in one of the 'deluxe' or 'executive' rooms facing the Old City ($500+). Recommended if you can afford it. **L1** *Laromme Jerusalem*, 3 Jabotinsky, T6756666, F5610158. This is where Bill Clinton and Madeleine Albright stay when they're in town (it sort of acts as the temporary US Embassy), full facilities that you would expect (including $1,300-a-night suites), though off-season standard rooms are remarkably good value for Jerusalem. Recommended. **L1** *Sheraton Jerusalem Plaza*, 47 King George, T6298666, F6231667. Excellent service and facilities that you would expect, regular rooms are surprisingly good value out of season, expect to pay extra $25 for an Old City view or extra $60 for balcony or 'smart room'. Excellent restaurant choice (see 'Eating' on page 220). Recommended.

L2 *Dan Pearl*, Zahal Sq, T6226666, F6226600. At the junction of the 'Old' and 'New' City, 110 rooms including 22 luxury suites ($600+!), standard rooms nice but expect to pay more for an Old City view, indoor pool, health club, choice of restaurants.

L2 *Prima Kings*, 60 King George, T6201201, F6201211. Recently had a face-lift though prices have shot up, neat flower-filled balconies, fair sized rooms, attractive restaurant and lobby coffee shop, only good value if you get tour group rates. **L2** *Radisson Moriah Plaza*, 39 Keren Ha-Yesod, T5695695, F6232411. Popular with tour groups though rooms rather small, few with balconies, disabled and non-smoking rooms, rooftop pool, choice of dining options.

L3 *King Solomon*, 32 King David, T5695555, F6241774. Standard rooms rather small, bigger 'deluxe' rooms and suites, full facilities, choice of restaurants, dramatic view from the pool though not quite the sense of luxury. **L3** *Paradise*, 4 Wolfson, T6558888, F6512266. A/c rooms with small balconies, cable TV, indoor and kid's pool, health club. Reasonable. **L3** *Park Plaza*, 2 Wolfson, T6528221, F6528423. Rooms rather small and no pool (though free use of Jerusalem Recreation Centre some distance away), though light and airy patio restaurant area. **L3** *Renaissance Jerusalem*, 6 Wolfson, T6528111, F6511824. West of the city centre (but free shuttle to main sites), large pool set in extensive gardens, indoor pool, health centre, rooms a good size (especially 'Royal Wing'), good deals for long-stay and out of season guests.

A *Ariel*, 31 Hebron, T6719222, F6734066. Some distance to south of city centre, larger rooms are more like mini-suites and ideal for families. **A** *Caesar*, 208 Jaffa, T5382156, F5382802. Uninspiring location with lack of views and character. **A** *Eldan*, 24 King David, T5679777, F6249525. Formerly the *Menorah* and now owned by the car-hire firm (offices next door), fully refurbished, rooms large with picture windows, a/c, cable TV, minibar, safe, new furniture, even a phone in the bathroom, restaurant, coffee shop, keen staff. Not a bad deal. **A** *Jerusalem Tower*, 23 Hillel, T6209209, F6252167. Central location, though little else to justify price tag (though groups get a discount), rooms rather small. **A** *Kikar Zion*, 25 Shamai, T6244644, F6244136. Overlooking Zion Sq, restaurant, pool, fitness centre, not really luxurious. **A** *Lev Yerushalam Apartment*, 18 King George, T5300333, F6232432. Excellent value apartment hotel with 1-2 bedroom suites, kitchenette, lounge, dining area, (20% discount for 7 nights, though prices raise during high season), health club, central location. Recommended. **A** *Mount Zion*, 17 Hebron, T6724222, F6731425. Excellent views (especially at sunset), best deals are the 'superior' rooms in the 19th-century Ottoman-period old wing, modern pool and health club, 4 restaurants. Recommended. **A** *Tirat Bat-Sheva*, 42 King George, T6232121, F6240697. Nothing exceptional for the price, offers 'specials' when business is slack, go for the rooms with the larger balconies. **A** *Windmill*, 3 Mendele, T5663111, F5610964. Not as luxurious as the price tag suggests, a/c, cable TV, Shabbat elevator, kosher restaurant. **A** *YMCA 3 Arches*, 26 King David, T5692692, F6235192. Famous Jerusalem landmark (see page 208), very appealing building and public areas though rooms rather plain, indoor pool, fitness room, squash and tennis.

B *Golden Jerusalem*, 40 Jaffa, T6233074, F6233513. Rooms small but have a/c, central location. **B** *Palatin*, 4 Agripas (entrance on Even Israel), T6231141, F6259323. Rather box-like rooms, hard to see why it's so expensive. **B** *Ron*, Zion Sq, 44 Jaffa, T6253471, F6250707. Hard to find a more central location (though can be noisy), rooms don't really justify the price, considered a historical site by fans of Menachem Begin. **B** *Zion*, 10 Dorot Rishonim, T6232367, F6257585. Central location, a/c, TV, not bad value.

C *Arcadia*, 57 Jaffa, T6221998, F6221858. Reasonable value for central location, breakfast included, friendly. **C** *Jerusalem Inn Guesthouse*, 7 Eliashar, T6252757, F6251297. Small guesthouse close to city centre, though we've received a number of serious complaints about 'overcharging'. **C** *Kaplan*, 1 HaHavazelet, off Zion Sq, T6254591, F6249623. Small rooms, central location. **C** *St Andrew's Hospice*, near Bloomfield Park,

T6732401, F6731711. Hospice rund by the Church of Scotland offers good views, quiet rooms in grand early 20th-century building, good value meals, a little remote but tranquil.

C-D *Noga*, 4 Bezalel, T6254590, F5661888. More apartment than hotel, self-contained rooms (sleep 2-4) with kitchenette, heating, minimum 2-night stay, advance booking essential. Not a bad deal.

E *IYHA Beit Bernstein Youth Hostel*, junction of Keren Ha-Yesod/Gershon Agron, T6258286. Spacious single-sex dorms (4-8 beds), a/c, heating, TV lounge, check-in after 1500, check-out 0900, advance reservations recommended, Buses 7/8/9/31/32. **E** *IYHA Beit Shmuel Guesthouse*, 6 Shamma, behind Hebrew Union College, T6203473. Part of Beit Shmuel Centre for Progressive Judaism, a/c dorms and private rooms (**D**), check-out 0900, no curfew. **E** *IYHA 'En Kerem Youth Hostel*, off Ma'ayan, 'En Kerem, T6416282. Clean IYHA-style facilities in wonderful rural setting, reservations recommended, Bus 027. **E** *IYHA HaDavidka Youth Hostel*, 67 HaNevi'im, junction with Jaffa, T6252706, F6250676. Standard IYHA place, popular with Israeli groups, reservations recommended. **E** *IYHA Louise Waterman Wise Youth Hostel*, 8 Pisgah, near Mt Herzl, T6423366, F6423362. Jerusalem's biggest IYHA hostel, usual facilities plus kitchen, Buses 018/020/027 then walk. **E** *Jerusalem Inn Hostel*, 6 HaHistadrut, T6251294, F6251297. Rather crowded 4-6 bed dorms, popular (though there's much better value places in the Old City). **E** *My Home*, 15 King George, T6232235, F6232236. Run-down hostel with grotty showers and toilets (why do other guidebooks recommend this place?). Poor value. **E** *The House in the Centre*, 23 Ben Yehuda, T6248021. Formerly the *Jasmine Ben Yehuda*, uncrowded 6-8 bed dorms, some private rooms (**D**), no curfew, popular with Israelis.

F *Jasmine Ben Yehuda*, 1 Yoel Salomon, T6248021, F6253032. Formerly the *Capitol Hostel*, right above a noisy nightclub, suitable for dedicated clubbers only.

Apartment rental and B&Bs *Good Morning Jerusalem*, Binyenei Ha'ooma, Jerusalem Convention Centre, Jaffa Rd, T6511270, F6511272. Specializes in finding B&B accommodation to fit your needs. *Jerusalem Inns*, PO Box 4233, T5611745, F5618541. Offers a similar service. The Municipal Tourist Office in Safra Sq may also be able to help.

Eating

Those who are serious about their food should pick up a free copy of *Jerusalem's Menus*, *Jerusalem's Best Menus* and the *Jerusalem Restaurant Guide* from the Tourist Office (though bear in mind that the places mentioned have paid to appear in these brochures). As a general rule, restaurants in the New City and Jewish Quarter of the Old City are kosher and close on Shabbat (whilst those in East Jerusalem and the rest of the Old City aren't and don't!). Most places in the New City take credit cards, whilst those in the Old City tend not to.

Old City and East Jerusalem **Budget** The cheapest places to eat are probably the three 'hummus and fuul' places on HaNevi'im, just outside Damascus Gate (6 NIS). There are plenty of 'falafel and shwarma' places in East Jerusalem and in the Muslim Quarter. Many swear by the 'three falafel man' at the junction of Tariq al-Wad and Tariq Khan es-Zeit just inside Damascus Gate, whilst others claim that he must be on commission from the shops selling toilet paper nearby! *Tabasco Tearooms*, 8 Aqabat Tekieh, off Tariq Khan es-Zeit, T6281101. Serves generous, cheap and greasy meals all day ('anything and chips') for 12-20 NIS, crowded in the evening with beer drinkers (see 'Bars' on page 223).

Café/bars *Cafeteria St Michael*, Omar ibn al-Khattab Sq, Jaffa Gate. Good for break-fasts. *Coffee Shop*, Omar ibn al-Khattab Sq, opposite Citadel, T6286812. Very 'English tea-room' atmosphere, good soups and salads. *Fountain Grill*, Muristan. Nice spot for tea or a cold drink, excellent toasted sandwiches, one of the owners has the most spectacular 'comb-over' hairstyle you'll ever see! *Quarter Café*, Tiferet Yisra'el, Jewish Quarter, T6287770. Light meals, though most come for coffee and cake and views of the Temple Mount/Haram al-Sharif, closed Shabbat. *Rendez-Vous*, Latin Patriarchate, Jaffa Gate. Pleasant little café/bar, pasta 25 NIS, salad 18 NIS, beer 10-15 NIS, internet access. *Tony's (between the arches)*, 174 Tariq al-Wad (Hagai), T6277761. Located 'between the arches' in the alleyway that leads to Tariq al-Wad (or 'Hagai' to Israelis) from the northwest corner of the Western Wall Plaza. Breakfasts, salads, toasted sand-wiches, unique atmosphere.

French *La Rotisserie, Notre Dame de France Guesthouse*, IdZanhanim, T6279111. Well reviewed and nicely located, main dishes 40-50 NIS.

Hotel restaurants *American Colony Hotel*, 1 Louis Vincent, off Nablus, T6279778. Good food, very pleasant environment, Saturday lunchtime buffet is good value (around 100 NIS). *National Palace*, 4 Az-Zahra, East Jerusalem, T6273273. Good Arabic food complements the excellent views.

Middle Eastern *Abu Sair Sweets* and *Jaffar Sweets* on Tariq Khan es-Zeit, are two good places to get your daily sugar fix. Try the *kanafeh*, a mild cheese mixed with pis-tachios and baked in a honey syrup shell. *Abu Shukri*, 63 Tariq al-Wad, Muslim Quar-ter, T6271538. Jerusalem's best-known hummus place, eat well for under 15 NIS. *Al-Nasser* and *Families*, Tariq Khan es-Zeit, just down from *Al-Arab Hostel*. Both serve half-chicken, chips and salad for 25 NIS, falafel, hummus, etc. *Armenian Tavern*, 79 Armenian Patriarchate, Armenian Quarter, T6273854. Atmospheric setting in part of Crusader-period church, excellent food, try the *khaghoghi derev* (stuffed vine leaves), starters from 12 NIS, main dishes 40 NIS, pasta 28 NIS, recommended. *Lark*, 4 Latin Patriarchate, Jaffa Gate. Recommended Armenian dishes, main courses 25 NIS. *Phila-delphia*, 9 Az-Zahra, East Jerusalem, T6289770. Well reputed restaurant serving Arabic food with long and famous clientele list, main dishes around 25-55 NIS, or go for the *mezze*. *Select*, Armenian Patriarchate, Armenian Quarter, T6283325. Mixed menu, main dishes 40-60 NIS. We have received several recommendation for this restaurant.

Miscellaneous *Abu Ali Green Door Bakery*, Aqabat esh-Sheikh Rihan, near Damas-cus Gate, T6276171. Jerusalem's cheapest filling dinner is the 'Arabic pizza' baked here. Essentially it's a bread base smeared with cheese, tomato purée, with added onions, capsicum, meat (best avoided), with a couple of eggs cracked on top (5 NIS). It's tastier than it sounds. Bring a book to read whilst you're waiting. *Abu Shanab*, 35 Latin Patriarchate, near Jaffa Gate, T6260752. Good value, choice of 3 sizes of tasty pizza (10/20/35 NIS), pasta dishes, cheap bar with 2-for-10 NIS beer (1800-1900, 2100-2200), open 1000-2200 daily, closed Sunday. *Cardo Culinaria*, The Cardo, Jew-ish Quarter, T5894155. Billed as an "authentic 1st-century dining experience", diners are encouraged to dress up in Roman Legionnaire helmets, etc, whilst young female backpackers dressed in togas (earning 12 NIS per hour plus tips) feed them grapes. The whole concept would be rather tacky if it were not for the fact that the food is rather good. Lunch (1200-1400) $15 per head, dinner (reservations essential) $25 per head, kosher, closed Shabbat. *Papa Andreas*, 64 Suq Aftimos, Muristan, T6284433. Pleasant rooftop restaurant, nice atmosphere, St Peter's Fish 30 NIS, spinach pie and salad 24 NIS, shashlik 36-50 NIS, *mezze* with salad and hot pitta 60 NIS, good lunch-time specials, or just smoke a nargila. *Pizzaria Basti*, 70 Tariq al-Wad. Excellent place for 'people-watching' (opposite IIIrd Station of the Cross), cheap meals (under 25 NIS), or just stop for a mint tea.

New City **Budget** The New City's shwarma and falafel places are located on and around Ben Yehuda, though they're pricier than those found in the Old City. Cheapest fruit and veg is found in Mahane Yehuda Market.

Café/bars *Biankini*, Angelo Levi Bianchini. Very snug bar/restaurant. *Café Chagall*, Luntz/Ben Yehuda. Very popular, especially on Friday afternoon. *Café Paradiso*, Keren Ha-Yesod. Pleasant ambiance. *Casa Italiana*, Yoel Salomon. *Little Italy*, Keren Ha-Yesod. Swish location. *King David Hotel*, 23 King David, T6251111. If you can't afford to stay, check out the lobby coffee shop (though the price of coffee and cake here will feed a hostel full of backpackers for a week). *Rose*, Rabbi Akiva. Nice terrace café/restaurant. *Rosemary*, corner of King David/Mapu. Pleasant dairy café/restaurant. *Second Cup Coffee Shop*, Ezra M Mizrachi (alley next to *McDonald's* on Shamai), T6234533. Open 24 hrs, part of North American *Coffee Plantation & Gloria Jean's* chain. *Trio*, Luntz. Nice spot for a coffee.

Central/North/South American *Amigo's*, 19 Yoel Salomon, T6234177. Pleasant Mexican restaurant, have a full blow-out for 50 NIS. *Blues Brothers Steakhouse*, 3 Luntz, T6258621. Well-reviewed Argentinian steakhouse, it's not cheap (60-80 NIS) but the meat is good.

Chinese/Southeast Asian *Crazy Chicken*, Jaffa Rd. Excellent Thai stir-frys stuffed into a baguette (14-25 NIS). Filling, tasty and good value. *Korea House*, 7 Makhalat Shiv'a, T6254756. Fashionable Korean restaurant, main dishes 40-60 NIS, business lunch 36 NIS. *Mandarin*, 2 Shlomzion HaMalka, T6252890. One of Israel's oldest, Hong Kong/Chinese chefs, main dishes 30-50 NIS. *Master Wok*, 15 King George. Cheap chicken/beef stir-fry (18 NIS). *Rungsit*, 2 Jabotinsky, T5611757. Upmarket Thai-Japanese cuisine, classy but pricey. *Sakura*, Feingold Courtyard, off 31 Jaffa, T6235464. Israel's best Tokyo-style sushi bar, main dishes around 60 NIS. Recommended.

Fast food/chain *Bonkers Bagels*, 41 Jaffa, near Zion Sq, T6244115. Best in Israel, open late, also home catering (T1-800-bagels). *Burger Ranch*, 18 King George; 3 Luntz; 43 Emeq Refa'im; *Dunkin Donuts*, Jaffa, near Zion Sq. *McDonald's*, 4 Shamai.

French *Chez Simon*, 15 Shamai, T6255602. 3-course set menu around 120 NIS, excellent quality. *Stanley's*, 3 Horkenos, T6259459. Seeks to combine French cuisine with South African cuts of meat, main courses 56-70 NIS.

Hotel restaurants *Cow on the Roof*, Sheraton Jerusalem Plaza, 47 King George, T6259111. Advance reservations and a healthy bank balance are required to dine at this popular meeting place for parents of prospective brides and grooms from the affluent classes. The food's good too.

Italian *Alla Gondola*, 2nd floor, 14 King George, T6255944. Long-established favourite with wide selection of non-kosher dishes, 130 NIS for 3-course meal. *Angelo*, 9 Horkenos, T6236095. Possibly the best homemade pasta in town, main dishes around 40 NIS. *Cacao*, Cinémathèque, Hebron, T6710632. Italian veggie menu in appealing setting, 25-40 NIS main courses. *Etnachta*, 12 Yoel Salomon, T6256584. Pleasant Italian dairy and fish restaurant, main dishes 28-45 NIS. *Pepperoni's*, Rabbi Akiva, T6257829. Daily specials 55-65 NIS, good value business lunches, nice setting. *Spaghettim*, 8 Rabbi Akiva, T6235547. Pasta with a choice of 50 different sauces, generous portions and high quality (main dishes 20-40 NIS), good wine list, pleasant setting. Recommended.

Indian *The 7th Place*, Beit Agron, 37 Hillel, T6254495. Located in the same building as the Ministry of Information's press office, excellent *veg thalis* 38 NIS, *dosas* 25 NIS, *gulab jamun* 13 NIS, also has a dairy and fish menu. Recommended.

Middle Eastern *Eucalyptus*, 4 Safra Sq, T6244331. New location but continued rave reviews, Moshe Basson is one of Israel's most renowned chefs yet the innovative Middle Eastern menu remains moderately priced (40-70 NIS). Recommended. *Fantasia*, 3 Horkanos, T6245406. Upmarket Moroccan cuisine, pricey but good. *Misadonet*, 12 Yoel Salomon, T6248396. Nice setting, traditional 'home-style' Kurdish cuisine, soups 20 NIS, main dishes 40-60 NIS, plus some veggie specials. *Yemenite Step*, 10 Yoel Salomon, T6240477. Many imitators, but few can match the original. Excellent Yemenite food, main dishes 25-45 NIS, nice setting.

Miscellaneous *Askadinya*, Shimon Hatzadik, T5324590. Jerusalem's current 'flavour of the month', upmarket French-Italian cuisine, main dishes 40-80 NIS, endearing setting. *Fink's*, 2 HaHistadrut, T6234523. Seemingly modest bar-cum-restaurant is a long-established haunt of journos and politicians, main dishes 50 NIS-infinity, good food, interesting atmosphere. *Gizmongolia*, 9 Heleni HaMalka, T6240490. 'Eat-all-you-can' for 75 NIS Mongolian grill. *Rimon Café*, Luntz. Good Israeli breakfasts and light meals (40 NIS). *Shemesh*, Ben Yehuda. Main dishes 35-60 NIS, fish 59 NIS.

Seafood *Hadagia*, 72 Agrippas, T6222867. Kosher fish dishes, main courses 50-75 NIS. *Ocean*, 7 Josef Rivlin, T6247501. Innovative menu featuring creatively presented seafood (main dishes 100 NIS).

Supermarkets *Supersol*, Gershon Agron. Sunday-Tuesday 0700-2400, Wednesday 0700-0100, Thursday 24 hrs, Saturday end of Shabbat-2400. *2000 Drugstore*, Shamai. Booze, fags, groceries, but controversially open 24 hrs, 7 days per week.

Vegetarian *Little Italy*, 38 Keren Ha-Yesod, T5617638. Excellent Italian vegetarian food, main dishes 35 NIS+. *New Age Café*, Dorot Rishonim. Nice organic vegetarian restaurant and juice bar. *Off The Square*, The Mill, 8 Ramban, T5665956. Mouth-watering pot pies, stuffed crêpes/potatoes, or veggie pasta, 35 NIS, huge salads 27 NIS. Recommended. *Sahara Tulip*, Jaffa, T6254239. Excellent veggie food, main dishes 35 NIS (eg curried egg plant and chick peas), soup 15 NIS, salads 33 NIS. *The 7th Place*, 37 Hillel, T6254495. See under 'Indian' on page 223. *Ticho House*, Abraham Ticho, off HaRav Kook, T6244186. Light meals (15-25 NIS) or coffee and cake in a delightfully tranquil setting. *Village Green*, 1 Bezalel, T6251464, and 33 Jaffa, T6253065. Excellent choice of wholesome veggie dishes, self-service canteen style, pay by weight so don't pile your plate too high, about 25 NIS for a huge feed.

Bars and nightclubs

Jerusalem's night-life used to be a standing joke, particularly amongst Tel Avivians, though this is certainly no longer the case. There is now a selection of bars and nightclubs to suit most tastes and pockets, with many staying open until the early hours. With very few exceptions, most bars are located in the New City, most notably around Zion Sq. The fashionable nightclubs tend to be out in the suburbs, notably Talpiyyot to the south.

Cellar Bar, *American Colony Hotel*, 1 Louis Vincent, off Nablus. For those on expense **Bars** accounts, notably journalists, aid workers and Palestinian officials. *Champ's Bar*, 19 Jaffa. A Jerusalem institution popular with backpackers and Eastern Europeans alike, very seedy atmosphere, strippers every Tuesday and Saturday, giant screen for sports,

(Guinness 20 NIS per pint), 50% discount during 'happy hour' (1600-1900), open Sunday-Friday 1300-0300, Saturday 2000-0300. Recommended if you like this sort of thing. *Fink's Bar Restaurant*, 2 HaHistadrut, T6234523. Long-established favourite with politicians and journalists, expensive, good food, closes at midnight. *La Bulta Rece*, Jaffa. Popular with Eastern Europeans, also offers discount international phone calls. *Mike's Place*, 14 Horkenos. Tiny place specializing in live (usually blues) music, cheapish beer plus happy hours. *Strudel*, 11 Monbaz, Russian Compound, T6232101, F6221445. Not just an internet café/bar, but also a very pleasant place for a night out (serves good snacks and bar food too). Open Sunday-Friday 1000-'late', Saturday 1500-'late', 'happy hours' 1900-2100 and 2400-0030 (for net and for bar). *Tabasco Tearooms*, 8 Aqabat Tekieh, off Tariq Khan es-Zeit, Old City, T6281101. Backpacker haven serving cheap beer (6-10 NIS) and food (12-20 NIS), fills up for happy hour (1800-1900, 2100-2200, 2 beers for 8 NIS). The friday night 'punch party' is legendary, with half the country's kibbutz volunteers turning up for the 1-hr 'drink-all-the-punch-you-can-for 10 NIS'. The party really kicks off when the hour is up (loud music and dancing), closes at midnight. There are a number of bars and pubs on Yoel Salomon and Josef Rivlin, many of which have some sort of 'happy hour', including: *Admiral Pub*, *Blue Hole*, *Godfather Bar*, *The Tavern*, *Zolli's Pub*. There are also a whole host of 'trendy' bars in the Russian Compound, including *Al-cool*, *Cannabis*, *Casso*, *Gizmo*, *Glasnost* and *Sergey*, though beer is fairly expensive (15-20 NIS) and some have a dress code and cover charge if a band is playing.

Nightclubs Club A1-11, Talpiyott suburb. Trendy club full of sexy Israeli girls and guys, 50 NIS entry (bouncers have to like the look of you so dress up), beer 16 NIS, 25 NIS taxi ride from city centre, 2300-late. *Underground*, 1 Yoel Salomon, off Zion Sq. This Jerusalem institution seems to have been around for ever. It used to be a real travellers' place, though in recent years Israelis have outnumbered tourists and we have received many complaints about shabby treatment afforded to backpackers by bar and security staff. In April 1998 the place was closed up for a while whilst a judge investigated an allegation of a gang-rape by staff members. The case eventually collapsed, with conspiracy theorists suggesting that the whole thing was part of an elaborate charade to claim insurance for loss of business! The main room features chart/classic music (and lots of dancing on tables), whilst downstairs is more dance/house orientated. Bar prices are reasonable, and there are some 'happy hour' promotions. Sometimes it's free and other times there is an entry fee (usually offset by a free drink).

Entertainment

For full details of cultural, cinematical and theatrical performances, check the 'entertainment' section of Friday's *Jerusalem Post*, *This Week in Jerusalem*, *This Week in Palestine*, and other such freebies that can be picked up at tourist offices and hotel receptions.

Cinemas *Cinémathèque*, Israel Film Archive, Hebron, T6724131. Jerusalem's main 'art-house' cinema. *GG Gil*, Jerusalem (Malha) Mall, T6788448; *Mevaseret Tzion*, T5700868. *Rav Chen*, 19 Ha'oman, Talpiyyot, T6792799.

Concert halls The world-renowned **Israel Philharmonic Orchestra** perform at the *Binyanei Ha'ooma*, opposite Central Bus Station, T6558558, whilst the **Jerusalem Symphony Orchestra** and **Israel Chamber Ensemble** often play the *Jerusalem Theatre/Jerusalem Centre for the Performing Arts*, 20 David Marcus, T5617167. Classical music concerts and recitals are also held at: *Beit Ticho*, off Harav Kook, T6245068. *Gerard Behar Centre*, 11 Bezalel, T6251139; *Van Leer Jerusalem Institute*, Einstein Sq, 43 Jabotinsky,

T5617141; *YMCA (West)*, 26 King David, T6257111; *Zionist Confederation House*, Emil Botta, T6245206; also *Israel Museum*, see 'Sights' on page 199, every Tuesday at 1800. Live outdoor concerts (classical/folk/rock) are occasionally held at *The Sultan's Pool*, just to the southwest of Jaffa Gate. For details, see the 'Entertainment' section of the *Jerusalem Post*, its Friday *In Jerusalem* section, or pick up a free copy of *This Week in Jerusalem* and *Events in Jerusalem* from your hotel or the Tourist Office.

Tzabarim Arab and Jewish folklore show every Monday, Thursday, Saturday at 2100 at *YMCA Auditorium* (T050-233210). **Cultural shows**

Balkan Dancing, Moadon Hasport, 30 Hatsfira, German Colony, T5662682. *Folk Dancing*, Philip Leon Community Centre, 8 Chile, Kiryat Yovel, T5643111; Gerard Behar Center, Leo Model Hall, 11 Bezalel, T6251139. *'Modern Dancing'*, Merkaz Hamagshimim, 7a Dor V'dorshav, T5619233. *Sixties Dancing*, Cosell Centre, Hebrew University, Givat Ram, T050-408579. Lessons, tennis shoes compulsory. *ICCY*, 12 Emeq Refaim. **Dancing**

Al-Hakawati Theatre, Nunza (near *American Colony Hotel*), T5854513/6280957. Critically acclaimed (and highly politicized) theatre, usually in Arabic but sometimes with English translation; *Al-Kasaba*, Abou Obiedah Ibn el-Jarah, East Jerusalem, T6264052, F6276310. Palestinian theatre, cultural shows, etc (usually in Arabic). *The Khan*, 2 David Remez (near train station), T6718281. Theatre, music, stand-up comedy, restaurant, art gallery, most performances in Hebrew. **Theatres**

Shopping

It's difficult to exhaust Jerusalem's potential for shopping, though if you're looking for a trinket or souvenir you will have to wade through a sea of rubbish before you find anything tasteful. As a general rule, shops in the New City tend to be 'fixed-price', with prices prominently displayed. In the Old City it's a free-for-all, with protracted bargaining required to make the most of your spending power. For those who prefer the easy option, there are a few 'fixed-price' shops in the Old City, also allowing *Life of Brian* fans the perfect opportunity to quote another line ("'ere, this bloke won't haggle"). There is a fixed-price souvenir shop just north of the *New Swedish Hostel* in the Christian Quarter of the Old City. At all costs avoid the aggressive and foul-mouthed scumbags in *Jim's Shop* and the un-named place just to the west on the Via Dolorosa opposite the Greek Orthodox Prison of Christ. In the Old City, David St/St of the Chain and the Via Dolorosa are crammed with small shops staffed by multi-lingual merchants with a keen eye for the tourist dollar. Initially stunned by the bright colours, unusual objects and accumulated junk, closer inspection usually reveals that all the stalls are pretty much selling the same stuff. There's some choice rubbish aimed at the pilgrim market, most notably the 3-D picture of Jesus with the winking eyes, or your own personal crown of thorns. Another favourite is the inflatable Yasir Arafat face! More upmarket wares, including some nice Judaica pieces, are found in the shops along the Cardo, in the Jewish Quarter. Shops listed below are just a tiny selection of what's on offer.

Gallery Anadiel, 27 Salah al-Din, T6288750, contemporary Palestinian art. *Gift Box*, American Colony Hotel, T6734046. Open 1000-1200 1730-2000, closed Saturday morning. Nice range of classy gifts, including some appealing watercolours. *Jerusalem Artists' House Gallery*, 12 Shmuel HaNagid, T6252636. New and established Israeli artists. *Alix de Rothschild Craft Centre*, 4 Or Hayim, Jewish Quarter, Old City, T6286076, *Arieh Klein*, 3 Ziv, off Bar Ilan, T5820992. Offers more expensive, up-market olive-wood products. *Palestinian Needle Workshop*, 79 Nablus. Open **Arts and crafts**

Monday-Saturday 0800-1800. *Sunbula*, St Andrew's Hospice, junction of King David and David Remez, T6732401. Quality embroidered work, with profits again going to good causes.

Books *Dani Books*, Jaffa/Even Israel. Good selection, will buy and swop second hand. *Gur Arieh*, 8 Yoel Salomon, T6257486. Offers an eclectic collection of overpriced second-hand stuff. *Libraire Française*, Jaffa, sells French-language books, newspapers and magazines. *Sefer va-Sefel*, 2 Ya'Avetz/49 Jaffa, T6248237. New and second-hand odds and ends. *Steimatsky*, 7 Ben Yehuda, 9 King George, and at 39 Jaffa (next to *Arizona Bar*). The latter is the main branch, and stocks the full range of *Footprint Handbooks*. *Stein Books*, 52 King George, T6247877. Mainly 'Judaism', some second-hand books;

Camping gear Camping Jerusalem, Ben Hillel. Army surplus, etc; *Mr T*, 13 Ben Yehuda, T6251644. Enough ex-IDF gear to kit out several Soldier of Fortune conventions. *Steve's Packs*, Ben Hillel. Outdoor and camping gear, also has a branch in Jerusalem Mall, Malkha.

Ceramics *Eight Ceramists*, 6 Yoel Salomon, T6255155. Handmade ceramics from pottery cooperative, much in demand. *House of Quality*, 12 Hebron, near Mt Zion Hotel, T6717430. *Jerusalem Pottery*, 15 Via Dolorosa. Specializes in Persian-style hand-painted tiles and plates, generally in turquoise. *Palestinian Pottery*, 14 Nablus, opposite US Consulate, T6282826. Hand-painted designs.

Glass *Nekker Glass Co*, 6 Beit Israel, T6286683. Superb hand-blown glass items, imaginative designs.

Jewellery *National Diamond Centre*, 143 Bethlehem, T6733770. Offers tours and sales. *Ophir*, 38 Jaffa, T6249078. Hand-made, quality items.

Judaica *Engel Gallery*, 13 Shlomzion Hamalka, T6253523. *Frank Meisler Galleries*, Annex of King David Hotel, 21 King David, T6242759. *Chaim Peretz*, 1 Rabbi Ariye, T6250859. Full range of Judaica made to order. *Shlomo Mishaly Metal Work*, 8 Yoel Salomon, T6257856. New City's original Judaica store. *Danny Azoulay*, 5 Yoel Salomon, T6233918. Specializes in fine porcelain items. *Oded Davidson*, Nahalat Shiva Artists' Gallery, 6 Yoel Salomon, T6245728. Very collectable silver-work.

Photography *Elia Photo Service*, Tariq al-Khanqah, Christian Quarter. Sells superb black and white photos of Jerusalem taken in the 1930s, 40s and 50s, or a compilation book of the late Kerouk Kahredjian's pictures in *Jerusalem Through My Father's Eyes*. *Photo Prisma*, 44 Jaffa Rd (near *Hotel Ron*). Israel's best outlet for all your film needs (pro and amateur). *Takel*, Ben Hillel. Cameras, films, developing and printing.

Sports

Bowling (ten-pin) *Jerusalem Bowling Centre*, Achim Yisrael Mall, Kenyon Talpiot, 18 Yad Harutzim, Talpiyyot, T6732195. 10 lanes, 20 NIS per game. **Bowls** *Jerusalem Lawn Bowls Club*, Jerusalem Forest, T5865206 (Alec). **Bridge** Each Monday at 1900 at *AACI*, 6 Mane St, T5617151. **Cycling** *Jerusalem Bicycling Club*, 16 Ha'Arazim, T6438386. **Health & fitness** *Bodyline*, 18 King George, T6232763. Gym, aerobics, weights, 25 NIS single visit, 175 NIS monthly. *Great Shape*, YMCA West, 26 King David, T6257111. Aerobic classes, etc. *Jerusalem Spa*, Hyatt Regency Hotel, French Hill, T5322906. Full facilities, fabulous setting. *Renaissance Jerusalem Hotel*, 6 Wolfson, T6528111. Indoor and outdoor pools, aerobic classes, saunas and Jacuzzis, massage, tennis. *Woman's Club*, 9 HaUman, Talpiot, T6795318. Exercise classes, fitness room, beauty centre. **Hiking** Those intending to hike in the Jerusalem area (and elsewhere in Israel) are advised first to consult with the *SPNI* (see under 'Tour companies and travel agents' below). **Pool (8-ball)** *Galliano's Pool Bar*, Horkenos, off Zion Sq. **Scrabble** Each Monday at 1900 at *AACI*, 6 Mane St, T5617151. **Swimming** *Djanogly*, Bet Avraham Community Centre, Ramot Allon, T5868055. *Jerusalem Pool*, 43 Emek Refaim, T5632092. City's only Olympic-sized pool, sauna, fitness room, lawns, 30 NIS, Buses 04/018, open daily 0700-1900, Shabbat tickets must be bought in advance. *Mitzpeh Ramat Rahel Pool*, Kibbutz Ramat Rahel, T6702920. Balloon-covered heated pool, weight and fitness room, coffee shop, tennis, year and half-year membership. **Squash** *YMCA (West)*, 26 King David, T6257111. 3 courts, 30 NIS per 40 mins, book ahead. **Tennis** *Hebrew University*, Mt Scopus, T5817579. 10 courts, 25 NIS per hr, advance reservations essential. *Israel Tennis Centre*, 5 Almaliach, Katamon Tet, T6791866/6792726. 18 courts, 30 NIS per hr, advance reservations essential. *YMCA (West)*, 26 King David, T6257111. 4 courts, 30 NIS per hr, call ahead for booking.

Transport

Car hire Most of the car hire firms have their offices on King David, near the Hilton **Local** Jerusalem. Note that most will not cover damage or theft that occurs on the West Bank (including East Jerusalem). *Avis*, 22 King David, T6249001. *Budget*, 8 King David, T6248991, F6259456. *Eldan*, *Eldan Hotel*, 24 King David, T6252151. *Hertz*, 18 King David, T6231351. *Perry*, 36 Keren Hayesod, T5619690. *Sa-Gal*, 14 King David, T6248003. *Sun Tours*, 5 Pines, T5383943, F5383903. *Thrifty*, 8 King David, T6250833. *Traffic*, T6241410.

Taxis *Atarot Transportation*, T5830691. Run a luxury transport sevice to Jerusalem's Atarot airport. *Aviv*, T6257366. *Damascus Gate Taxis*, T6288880. *Hapisga*, T6421111. *Nesher Taxis*, 21 King George, T6231231, F6241114. The best way to get to **Ben-Gurion Airport** (40 NIS per person, 45 mins), book ahead and they will pick you up. Allow plenty of time since the taxi may drive all over Jerusalem picking up other pre-booked passengers. In the Old City they will usually only arrange to pick you up from outside the tourist office at Jaffa Gate. *Yisrael*, HaHistadrut, T6252333.

Air **Atarot (Jerusalem) Airport** (T5833980) is located 10km north of Jerusalem along **Long distance** the road (Route 60) to Ramallah and Nablus. **Arkia**, Room 121, Klal Building, 97 Jaffa, T6255888, offer limited services from the tiny airstrip to **Eilat** (1 hr), **Haifa** (30 mins) and **Rosh Pinna** (30 mins). Bus 041 runs to Jerusalem's Atarot airport from the Central Bus Station (or see under 'Taxis' on page 227). For details of air tours around Jerusalem, see under 'Tour companies and travel agencies', on page 232. There are buses from Jerusalem's Central Bus Station to Ben-Gurion Airport (see page 227), as well as taxis (see page 227).

Long-distance buses Jerusalem's **Central Bus Station** (T5304555) is located on Jaffa Rd, to the west of the New City centre. **NB** See note in 'Getting there' at the beginning of the 'Jerusalem' chapter on page 72. The information booth here is very busy (and not particularly helpful), though there is a large electronic board. The bus station has shops, toilets and places to eat. Although the exact timetable may change during the lifespan of this *Handbook*, frequencies rarely do. Central Egged bus information, T03-6948888.

Akko: go to Haifa and charge. **Ashdod**: 448 via Latrun, every 2 hrs, 1½ hrs, 20 NIS. **Ashqelon**: 437, Sunday-Thursday half-hourly 0630-2000, Friday last at 1545, Saturday

Jerusalem

first at 1800, 1 hr 20 mins, 22 NIS. **Bat Yam**: 404, Sunday-Thursday hourly 0610-1940, Friday last at 1545, Saturday first at 1820. **Be'er Sheva** direct: 470, Sunday-Thursday every 1-2 hrs 0620-1815, Friday last at 1500, 1½ hrs, 22 NIS. **Be'er Sheva** via Kiryat Gat: 446, Sunday-Thursday 2 per hr, Friday last at 1545, Saturday first at 1745. **Ben-Gurion Airport**: 945/947, every 30 mins, Sunday-Thursday 0600-2200, Friday last at 1540, Saturday first at 1815, 1 hr, 20 NIS. **Bet El**: 170, (outside bus station, south side of road to right), 1 per hr. **Bet Shean**: 961/963/964, see 'Tiberias' below, 1½ hrs, 25 NIS. **Bet Shemesh**: 415, Sunday-Thursday 2 per hr 0550-2400, Friday last at 1550, Saturday first at 1810. **Bnei Brak**: 400, Sunday-Thursday every 15 mins 0630-2330, Friday last at 1500, Saturday first at 1815. **Cairo**: due to lack of demand, the daily Egged Bus No 100 to Cairo via Tel Aviv ($35) has been suspended. For buses to Cairo see under 'Tour companies and travel agents' on page 232. **Eilat**: 444, Sunday-Thursday 0700 1000 1400 1700, Friday 0700 1000 1400, Saturday 0030, 4½ hrs, 56 NIS, book 2-3 days in advance. **'En Gedi**: 486, 0845 1100 1200 1300; or Bus 487, 1600 1945 2140; or Bus 444 (see 'Eilat, above') 1½ hrs, 24 NIS. **Hadera**: 945, see 'Haifa via Hadera' below. **Haifa** direct: 940, Sunday-Thursday every 15 mins 0550-2000, Friday last at 1520, Saturday first at 1745, 3 hrs, 30 NIS. **Haifa** via **Ben-Gurion Airport** and **Hadera**: 945, 8 per day, Sunday-Thursday last at 1930, Friday last at 1510, Saturday first at 1915. **Haifa** via **Ben-Gurion Airport** and **Netanya**: 947, 2 per hour, Sunday-Thursday 0600-2200, Friday last at 1540, Saturday first at 1815. **Kfar Etzion**: 161 (outside bus station, south side of road), Sunday-Thursday hourly 0830-2330, Friday hourly 0830-1500, Saturday 2230 2400. **Kiryat Arba**: 160 (outside bus station, south side of road), Sunday-Thursday every 30 mins 0530-2200, Friday last at 1430, Saturday first at 1830. **Kiryat Shemona**: 963, see 'Tiberias' below; **Latrun**: 404, see 'Bat Yam' above, or 435, every 2 hrs. **Masada**: see 'En Gedi' and 'Eilat' buses above; **Nahariya**: go to Haifa and change. **Netanya**: 947, see 'Haifa via Netanya' above. **Ramla**: 433, Sunday-Thursday every 20 mins 0630-2050, Friday last at 1515, Saturday first at 1800, 1½ hrs, 26 NIS. **Rehovot**: 433, see 'Ramla', above. **Safed**: 964, Sunday-Thursday 1430, Friday 1445, 3½ hrs, 50 NIS. **Tekoa**: 166 (outside bus station, south side of road), Sunday-Thursday every 2 hrs 1200-2300, Friday 1200 1430, Saturday 2030. **Tel Aviv** direct: 405, Sunday-Thursday every 15-20 mins 0550-2340, Friday last at 1600, Saturday first at 1745, 1 hr, 20 NIS, plus numerous other slower services. **Tiberias** via **Bet Shean**: 961/963/964, Sunday-Thursday hourly 0645-1830, Friday last at 1445, Saturday first at 2000, 2½ hrs, 40 NIS.

Sherut/service taxi Sheruts to and from **Tel Aviv** arrive and depart from the junction of HaRav Kook and Jaffa, close to Zion Sq (50 mins, 20 NIS). There are occasionally service taxis to Tel Aviv from the car-park at the bottom of HaNevi'im, outside Damascus Gate.

West Bank and Gaza Service taxis are the main transport link to the various West Bank towns from Jerusalem. Shared taxi/minibus to **Ramallah** (30 mins, 3 NIS) depart from Suleiman, just outside Damascus Gate (exit Damascus Gate, turn right, and they're lined up on the opposite side of the road). For **Nablus**, go to Ramallah and change. Service taxis to **Bethlehem** (15 mins, 3 NIS, to checkpoint then change), **Jericho** (35 mins, 8 NIS), **Hebron** (30 mins, 9 NIS) depart from the car-park opposite Damascus Gate, at the bottom of HaNevi'im. It's also possible to get a shared taxi to **Gaza**, though this can be difficult. In the morning, most of the traffic is in the opposite direction (ie from Gaza to Jerusalem), with most vehicles taking migrant workers back to Gaza at night. It may be possible to round up enough people for a shared taxi, though you may end up paying for a 'special' (1½ hrs, 200 NIS). It's probably cheaper to take an Egged bus to Ashqelon, and take a taxi/hitch from there.

For the **King Hussein/Allenby Bridge** [XR:96 031] crossing into **Jordan**, it's quicker and just as cheap to take a shared taxi from the car-park opposite Damascus Gate all the way to the border (45 mins, 26 NIS). Taking a shared taxi to Jericho, and a taxi from there, saves you no money, and costs a lot of time.

Train Jerusalem's train station is inconveniently located on Remez Sq (Kikar Remez), to the southwest of the Old City (T6733764). Take Bus 05/06/08/014/021/048, though it's probably quicker to walk. There's a daily service to **Tel Aviv** (1455, 2 hrs, 25 NIS), and though it's slower than the bus, it's a very pleasant journey. **NB** The service appears to currently be suspended due to lack of demand. Central train information, T03-5774000.

Working

Employment options are probably more limited than in Tel Aviv and Eilat, with most positions in the 'construction' industry being filled by Palestinians. Israeli contractors pick up casual labourers from 'the wall' (by the shared-taxi stand, opposite Damascus Gate) early each morning, though it would be unfair to deprive a Palestinian of one of the few opportunities of work that he has.

Pubs, clubs and restaurants are another source of possible work, generally paying 12-15 NIS per hour plus tips, though most employers prefer attractive girls. The Cardo Culinaria Restaurant on the Cardo in the Jewish Quarter employs a procession of backpacker girls who are not adverse to wearing a toga over their shorts and t-shirt. *Abu Shanab Restaurant*, Jaffa Gate, also employs backpackers, though nobody who works the washing-up shift ever seems to go back for a second night.

Hostel work, though not making you rich, will give you a roof over your head in exchange for 4 hours or so work, generally manning reception or cleaning. 'Running' (meeting would-be guests at the bus station and persuading them to go to a certain hostel) reaps similar rewards, plus a 'per head' commission. Finally, asking around amongst fellow long-stay hostellers can also bring employment leads.

Directory

El-Al, 12 Hillel. Sun-Thu 0830-1830, Fri 0830-1300. Advance baggage check-in available at 7 Kanfei Nesharih, Giv'at Sha'ul, Sun-Thu 1300-2000, Fri 1100-1500, Sat Sabbath end-2300 or 49 Yermiyahu, T6246725 (same hours, call first). *Air France*, 1 Shlomzion Hamalka, T6252495. *Alitalia*, 23 Hillel, T6258653. *Arkia*, 97 Jaffa, T6255888. *British Airways*, 33 Jaffa, T6256111. *Delta*, 15 Shammai, T6248199; *Iberian*, 8 Shammai, T6232919. *KLM*, 33 Jaffa, T6284896. *Lufthansa*, 16a King George, T6244941. *Olympic*, 33 Jaffa, T6234538. *Sabena*, 2 Emil Bota, T6234971. *SAS*, 14 Az-Zahara, T6283235. *Swissair*, 31 HaNevi'im, T6231373. *TWA*, 34 Ben Yehuda, T6241576. **Airline offices**

Banking hours Sun Tue Thu 0830-1230 1600-1700, Mon Wed Fri 0830-1200. Shop around for best exchange rates/commission charges. Most of the banks listed below have 24-hr ATM machines ('cashpoints') offering shekel advances on most cards. Hotels are bad places to change money. Note that **post offices** offer commission-free foreign exchange for travellers' cheques. There are also a number of legal **money changers** inside Damascus Gate who offer good deals on travellers' cheques and cash. Those travelling on to Egypt or Jordan are recommended to buy a supply of Jordanian Dinars/Egyptian Pounds in advance. *American Express*, junction of Hillel/Ezra M Mizrachi (alley next to *McDonald's*). Newish location, Sun-Thu 0900-1700, 0900-1300, member services including clients' mail. *Bank Leumi*, 21 Jaffa, T6291611. *Change +*, 25 Jaffa, T6244226. *ChangePoint*, 33 Jaffa, T6255572 and 2 Ben Yehuda, T6240011. *First International*, 64 Agrippas, T6254311. *HaPoalim*, 1 Zion Sq, T6207118 or 16 King George, T6207676. *Israel Discount*, 62 King George, T5637902. *MoneyNet*, Ben Hillel. **Banks**

Area code T02. **NB** Telephone numbers in Jerusalem are now 7-digit. Some of the old 6-digit numbers still work, though if you encounter problems, use the following formula: for numbers starting with the digit 3, 6, or 8, add 5 before the number. For those starting with the digit 2, 4, or 7, **Communications**

Jerusalem

add 6 before the number. **Internet/email** *No 74*, 74 Christian Quarter St. Internet access in the Old City. *Rendez-Vous*, Latin Patriarchate, Jaffa Gate. Currently experimenting with 1 computer, nice setting. *Strudel*, 11 Monbaz, Russian Compound, T6232101, F6221445. Jerusalem's original and only true internet bar, full internet/email service, good place for a drink, snacks and bar food, Sun-Fri 1000-'late', Sat 1500-'late', 'happy hours' 1900-2100 and 2400-0030(for net and for bar). **Post offices** *General Post Office*, 23 Jaffa, T6244745. Open Sun-Thu 0700-1900, Fri 0700-1200. Offers poste restante, parcel mail, fax, telegram (dial 171), and international phone calls. There are branch offices in the New City on Ezra M Mizrachi (alley next to *McDonald's*), in East Jerusalem on Salah al-Din, in the Old City on Armenian Patriarchate (opposite Citadel). **Telephones** *Solan*, Dorot Rishonim. Discount international calls, cellular phone hire, open 0800-2400 daily. See also *La Bulta Rece* "international phone pub" under 'Bars' on page 223.

Cultural centres *American Cultural Centre*, 19 Keren Ha-Yesod, T6255755. *British Council*, 2 Abou Obiedah Ibn el-Jarah, East Jerusalem, T6282545. Mon-Thu 1100-1600, Fri 0930-1330; or 3 Shimshon, New City, T6736733. Mon-Thu 1000-1300 1600-1900, Fri 1000-1300. *Centre Culturel Français*, 21 Salah al-Din, East Jerusalem. Mon-Fri 1000-1300 1400-1800, Sat 1400-1800.

Embassies and consulates Many nations still refuse to recognize Jerusalem as Israel's "eternal undivided capital", and so retain their embassies in Tel Aviv. Some, however, maintain consulates in Jerusalem though you may be referred to Tel Aviv for certain matters. Note that a bill was passed in both houses of the US Congress in October 1996 to move the US Embassy to Jerusalem by May 1999. To some, this was seen as a cynical attempt to 'buy' crucial Jewish votes (and money) during the last presidential election campaign. In June 1999 President Clinton signed an order delaying the implementation of this law.

   Austria, 8 Hovevei Zion, T5630765; **Belgium**, 5 Biber, Sheikh Jarrah, East Jerusalem, T5828263; **Denmark**, 5 Bnei Brith, T6258083; **France**, 5 Emil Botta, T6259481 and Sheikh Jarrah, East Jerusalem, T6282387; **Greece**, 31 Rachel Imenu Katam, T5619583; **Italy**, 16 November, T5618966; **Spain**, 53 Rambam, T5633473; **Sweden**, 58 Nablus, East Jerusalem, T5828117; **Turkey**, Sheikh Jarrah, T5828238; **UK**, 19 Nashashibi, Sheikh Jarrah, East Jerusalem, T5828281; **US**, 27 Nablus, East Jerusalem, T6282231 (come here for most services), or 16 Agron, T6253288.

Hospitals and medical services **Chemists** There are several chemists in the Zion Sq area, including the following. *Super-Pharm*, HaHistadrut, T6412516. Sun-Thu 0830-2300, Fri 0830-1500. *Alba*, 7 Ben Yehuda, T6257785, Sun-Thu 0830-1900, Fri 0830-1500, Sat sunset-2300. For details of rotating night/Shabbat service consult hotel reception, Tourist Office, *Jerusalem Post*, or signs on pharmacy doors (usually in Hebrew).

   Hospitals The world-famous *Hadassah Hospital* in 'En Kerem (T6427427), or its sister on Mt Scopus (T5818111), are capable of dealing with all emergencies, though you should make sure that your medical insurance is up to it: a night here can cost more than a weekend at the *King David Hotel*. Holders of Blue Cross-Blue Shield are eligible for pre-paid hospitalization (T6776040 for details). *Bikur Holim Hospital*, 74 HaNevi'im, T6701111, may be a better bet for the budget-minded. *Terem Immediate Medical Care*, Magen David Adom Building, 7 HaMemGimel, T6521748, offers what its name suggests.

Laundries Laundry Place, 12 Shamai, T6257714. Sun-Thu 0830-2400, Fri 0830-1530, Sat 1830-2330. *Michali*, 36 Azza, Rehavia. Sun-Thu 0700-2200, Fri until Shabbat. *Natali*, 1 Etzel, French Hill. Sun-Thu 24 hrs, Fri until Shabbat, Sat from end of Shabbat. *Shimoni*, 24 Shimoni, Rasko. Sun-Thu 0700-2200, Fri until Shabbat. *Suzana*, 46 Emeq Refa'im. Sun-Thu 24 hrs, Fri until Shabbat, Sat from end of Shabbat.

Places of worship **Christian** *Christian Information Centre (Latin/Catholic)*, PO Box 14308, opposite Citadel, Jaffa Gate, T6272692, F6286417. Open weekdays 0830-1300, offers 'Christian tourist information', some free maps, details of Christian sites in Jerusalem, and is the place to 'blag' a ticket for midnight Christmas mass in Bethlehem by pretending to be Catholic. *Franciscan Pilgrim Office*, PO Box 186, same location as above, T6272697. Can arrange mass at any Franciscan church in Israel, and buy a 'pilgrimage certificate'. **Anglican**: St George's Cathedral, 20 Nablus Rd, T6283302. Holy Communion Sun 0800, weekdays 0700; Eucharist Sun 1100; Mattins weekdays 0830; Evensong daily 1800. **Baptist**: 4 Narkis, T6255942, Sat 1700 Hebrew, Sun 1100 English. **Bible Society**: 1 Ibn Khaldun, East Jerusalem. **Chaldean**: 7 Chaldean, off Nablus, T6284519. **Coptic**: St Francis, Old City, T6282868.

'Masada Sunrise Tour'

Few backpackers to Jerusalem escape the 'Masada Sunrise Tour' soft-sell; in fact, as you check-in to certain hostels the sales-pitch begins (reception staff get 2NIS for every tour they sell). There never seems to be any shortage of participants, so is it such a good deal?

For those visitors to Israel with limited time and limited funds, the 'Masada Sunrise Tour' offers a cheap and convenient way of seeing some of Israel's most spectacular (but remote) sights. Packed into a non-stop 12 hours you will get to "climb Masada and watch the sunrise over the Dead Sea", "float in the Dead Sea", "hike through 'En Gedi Nature Reserve", "pass by Qumran", "visit Jericho", "see St George's Monastery in the Wadi Qelt Gorge" before finally "enjoying the panoramic view of Jerusalem from the Mount of Olives". And all this for just 80NIS (excluding entrance fees, though the tour goes up by about 10NIS every year). Too good to be true?

Of course there are both advantages and disadvantages to seeing Israel in this way. For a start, the tour is extremely rushed. Mount of Olives, St George's Monastery, Jericho and Qumran are little more than 'photo stops' (with most people too knackered to even bother getting out the minibus at the latter), whilst the short time spent at 'En Gedi Nature Reserve does not allow you to get away from the hordes of visitors who just pop in for an hour or so. Further, the 0300 departure time is a real killer (and very cold if the minibus is late as usual), whilst the "sunrise over the Dead Sea" is not all it's cracked up to be!

That said, there are enough advantages to make this tour worthwhile, particularly to those on a tight budget. For example, the cheapest accommodation at Masada and 'En Gedi is some $18 per night, so you've virtually saved the tour price already. Also, you need not worry about the Dead Sea Region's irregular transport connections; to do the same tour by public transport would probably take 3-4 days. And finally, by travelling as a group you gain the advantage of reduced admission prices.

If you do take the tour, make sure that you bring some warm clothes for the Masada climb (and wait for the bus), drinking water and food (most the places you pass are expensive), swimming costume and towel for the Dead Sea, and money for admission fees. And please, organise all these things the night before so you don't wake up the rest of the dorm with the rustling of those bloody bags!

Christ Church: Omar ibn al-Khattab Sq, Jaffa Gate. Sat 1430 Messianic Hebrew, Sat 1800 Romanian, Sun 0930 English communion, Sun 1530 Filipino communion, Sun 1830 English communion, Mon 1900 Hebrew prayer meeting. **Christian Science Society**: YMCA (East), 29 Nablus, T6286888. **Greek Catholic (Melkite)**: Greek Catholic Patriarchate, Old City, T6282023. **International Evangelical Church**: 55 HaNevi'im, T5356954. **Lutheran**: Church of the Redeemer, Muristan, Old City, T6276111. Danish Israel Mission, 91 Bar Kokhba, T5825149. Finnish Evangelical Lutheran Mission, 25 Shivtei Israel, T6288631. Norwegian Home, 26 Hatzfira, T5638923. **Maronite**, 25 Maronite Rd, T6282158. **Orthodox Churches**: Armenian, Armenian Orthodox Patriarchate St, T6282331. Coptic, IXth Station of the Cross, T6272645. Ethiopian, VIIIth Station of the Cross, T6282848. Romanian, 46 Shivtei Israel, T6271676. Russian Ecclesial Mission, St Mary Magdalene, Gethsemane, T6282897. Syrian, St Marks Rd, Old City, T6283304. **Pentecostal**, St Paul's Church, 32 Shivtei Israel, T6717988, Sun 1830 English. **Presbyterian**, St Andrew's Church, near Bloomfield Park, T6732401, Sun 1000 English. **Seventh Day Adventist Centre**, Ali Ibn Abitaleb, East Jerusalem. **St John's Chapel**, Lutheran Church of the Redeemer, T6276111. English service Sun 0900 (female clergy). See also the various churches in the 'Sights' section beginning on page 82.

Jewish *Beit Knesset Moreshet Yisrael, Yerushalayim* (Conservative), T6253539; *Beit Knesset Yeshuran*, 44 King George, T6243942; *Central Synagogue*, 17 Beit Haram, Beit Hakerem, T6513043; *Centre for Conservative Judaism*, 2 Agron, T6256386; *Chabad House of the Old City*, Tzemach Tzedek Synagogue, 31 Chabad, T6273118; *Great Synagogue*, 56 King George,

T6247112; *Harel Community* (Reform), Shmuel Hanagid, T6253841; *Hebrew Union College*, Jewish Institute of Religion (Reform), 13 King David, T6203333; *Italian Synagogue*, 27 Hillel, T6241610.

Muslim *Al-Aqsa Mosque*, Haram al-Sharif, T6283313; *Mosque of Umar*, al-Qiama, near Church of the Holy Sepulchre; plus other mosques in the Old City.

Tour companies and travel agents *Alternative Tours*, c/o *Jerusalem Hotel*, 4 Antara Ben-Shadad, off Nablus, T6277216. Experienced and reliable Abu Hassan (T052-864205) runs a variety of Palestinian-orientated tours including Bethlehem (3-4 hrs, 35 NIS), Gaza Strip (1 day, 130 NIS), Hebron (1 day, 60 NIS), Jericho (half-day, 50 NIS), Ramallah and Nablus (1 day, 90 NIS), plus refugee camp visits (half-day, 35 NIS). *Archaeological Seminars*, Jaffa Gate, T6273515, F6272660. A variety of walking tours (all depart from 34 Habad in the Jewish Quarter), including the Western Wall Tunnels (advance booking necessary), $16, plus digs at archaeological sites such as Bet Guvrin ($60, full day). *Ateret Cohanim*, T5895101/6284101. This organization is involved with 'settling' Jews in the Christian and Muslim Quarters of the Old City. They arrange tours and will explain their viewpoint. *Egged Tours*, Shlomzion Hamalkah. Run a variety of city- and country-wide tours, and can give information on '99-Jerusalem Circle Line' bus. *issta*, Yoel Salomon, T6257257. Good for student-priced flights, etc. *Kanfei Jerusalem*, T5831444, F5831880. 30-minute flights over Jerusalem ($50), or 1-hr flight over Jerusalem and Masada ($85). *Mazada Tours*, 9 Koresh, T6235777, F6255454. Runs 2 buses daily to Cairo ('day' bus $35 single, $50 return, departs 0730; 'night' bus $40 single, $60 return, departs 1900; prices exclude border taxes; buses also depart from Tel Aviv). Their Cairo office is at the *Cairo Sheraton* (T3488600). Also run day tours from Eilat to Petra ($139), plus choice of other tours. *Society for the Protection of Nature in Israel (SPNI)*, 13 Heleni HaMalkha, T6244605, F6254953. SPNI organize a series of excellent guided tours in Israel, including 3-day Galilee and Golan hiking and kayaking ($298, Tue), 4-day Negev and Eilat ($396, Fri), 2-day Masada, 'En Gedi and Dead Sea ($185, Fri), 1-day Wadi Qelt ($59, Mon), and Jerusalem Old City ($59, Thu). For 2000 they are organizing a 'jubillennium march in the footsteps of Jesus'. *United Tours*, *King David Hotel*, 23 King David, T6252187, F6255013. *Zion Tours*, Ezra M Mizrachi (alley next to *McDonald's*), off 19 Hillel, T6254326. Cheap airfares to the US. *Zion Walking Tours*, Armenian Patriarchate, near Jaffa Gate, T/F6287866. Long-established tour company, Old City $10, Mount of Olives $18, 'Underground' and Western Wall Tunnels $14, Judean Desert and Jericho $45, Mt Zion and Ancient City on the Southeast Ridge $17, Old City walls $16.

Tourist offices *Municipal Tourist Offices*, Safra Sq, T6258844. Sun-Thu 0900-1600, Fri 0900-1230; Jaffa Gate, T6280382. Sun-Thu 0800-1700, Fri 0800-1300. The Municipality run free guided tours (English) of various Jerusalem sites each Sat at 1000 (leaving from Russian Compound, 32 Jaffa, call ahead T6298065). There is a 1-2 hr (Eng) tour of the Municipality complex on Safra Sq at 0930 each Mon (meet near the palm trees, 6 NIS). *Christian Information Centre*, Jaffa Gate, T6272692. Mon-Sat 0830-1300. *Jewish Student Info Centre*, 5 Beit-El, Jewish Quarter. Free tours, hostel accommodation, etc.

Useful addresses and phone numbers **Ambulance** T101 (or T6522607). **Fire** T102. **Police** T100 (tourist police: T5391254). **Rape Crisis Centre Hotline** T1202 (24 hrs, anywhere in Israel), or T6255558. **Other** *AACI*, 6 Mane St, T5617151. *Alcoholics Anonymous*, 24 Hapalmach, T5630524. English Mon 2045, Tue noon, Wed 2000, Thu 2045, Fri 1230, Sat 1930, Bus 015. *Beit New York-Jerusalem*, Safra Sq, T6244681. Affiliated to UJA New York, organizes volunteer work, cultural exchanges, etc. *B'nei Brith*, 3-5 Keren HaYesod, T5661989. *Bizzart Studios*, 16 Hillel. For all your body piercing needs. *Hebrew lessons*, c/o YMCA, 26 King David, T5692673/05-2674770. *HIV/Aids Tests*, Strauss Health Center, 24 Strauss, T6231921. *Israel Center*, 10 Strauss, T5384206. *Jerusalem Media & Communications Centre*, PO Box 25047, Nablus Rd, near *Mt Scopus Hotel*, East Jerusalem, T5819777, F5829534. Publishers of *Palestine Report*, prepares daily briefings on events in Palestine. *Ministry of Foreign Affairs*, Press Office, T5303343. *Ministry of Information*, Beit Agron, 37 Hillel. The place to come for your Israeli press card. *Nishmat*, 27 Michlin, Bayit Vegan, T6421051. Jerusalem Center for Advanced Jewish Study for Women, *Orient House*, Abou Obiedah Ibn el-Jarah, East Jerusalem, T6273330. Controversial *de facto* Jerusalem HQ of the Palestinian Authority.

Consult the *In Jerusalem* section in Friday's *Jerusalem Post* for a full list of support groups ranging from 'Mainstream Overeaters Anonymous', through 'Women Who Love Too Much' to 'Religiously Observant Women Considering Single Motherhood'.

The West Bank

The West Bank

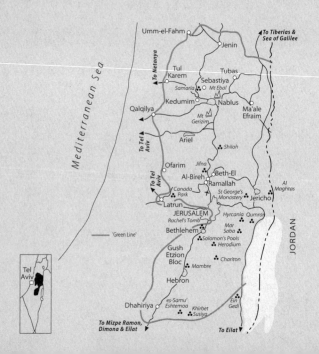

The area known to most of the world as the 'West Bank' (of the Jordan River) is the heart of the biblical regions of Judaea and Samaria, and as such, contains a number of important historical-archaeological sites. However, the majority of the population is overwhelming Arab Palestinian (Muslim and Christian); a population that rejects the Israeli rule that has been imposed upon it since the Six Day War of 1967.

The Declaration of Principles signed between Israel and the PLO in 1993, and the subsequent Israeli-Palestinian Interim Agreement on the West Bank and Gaza Strip ('Oslo II Accords' signed in 1995), plus the 'Wye Plantation Agreement' of 1999, has seen parts of the West Bank granted a degree of limited autonomy under the auspices of the Palestinian Authority (PA).

Most of the international community regard the West Bank as territory 'occupied' by Israel, thus making any Israeli (Jewish) settlement there illegal, whilst many Palestinians view the West Bank as the heart of some future Palestinian state. To the visitor, this means that there are still some problems involved in visiting the various West Bank sights. However, with some caution it should still be possible to visit all the sites that are included within the 'West Bank' chapter of this Israel Handbook. A subjective list of the highlights of the West Bank could include: the Church of the Nativity in Bethlehem, the birthplace of Jesus; the Herodium, Herod's palace-fortress to the southeast of Bethlehem; Mar Saba Monastery, standing in splendid isolation in the Judean Desert; the Haram el-Khalil/Cave of Machpelah in Hebron, where some suggest that Jewish history began; the beauty of the Wadi Qelt ravine, and the lonely St George's Monastery; Jericho, the world's oldest walled city; and finally the view of the country from Mount Ebal and Mount Gerizim, near Nablus.

Ins and outs

This chapter refers to this area as the 'West Bank' simply because this is the term most familiar to an English-speaking audience. Used in the context of the *Israel Handbook* it has no political connotations. If this *Handbook* was written in Hebrew it would use the expression 'Judaea and Samaria', and in French 'Cisjordanie'. For a brief summary of the politicization of the geographical nomenclature, see 'Historical overview' below.

With the exception of Bethlehem and possibly Jericho, the majority of hotels in the various West Bank towns were forced to close during the *intifada* due to lack of business. Though new hotels are beginning to open all across the West Bank (notably in Ramallah), the uncertain nature of the current 'peace process' means that conditions in the various towns under PA control can change rapidly. Thus, the general recommendation is that tourists use Jerusalem as a base to visit the various West Bank sites in a series of extended day-trips. Hopefully this situation will soon change, allowing the Palestinian economy to benefit from the much needed tourist dollar.

Transport arrangements have been complicated somewhat by the division of the West Bank into areas 'A', 'B' and 'C' (see below), and the rules governing which coloured number-plates can go where. Most of the Jewish settlements are served by Egged buses from the Central Bus Station in Jerusalem (or from the street outside). The Palestinian towns and villages are best served by service-taxis which can be picked up from outside Jerusalem's Damascus Gate. Some of the sites described in this 'West Bank' chapter are fairly remote, and are not served by public transport. Those with access to rental vehicles should note that yellow (Israeli) licence-plated vehicles still attract stone-throwers (or worse) on the West Bank, and thus are best avoided. Some car rental agencies actually place bans on you taking their vehicles beyond the 'Green Line', or cancel the insurance (this can also apply to East Jerusalem). Thus, the best way to reach these outlying sites is to hire a car and local driver at the nearest town.

This 'West Bank' chapter is divided into three sections: 'South of Jerusalem', 'East of Jerusalem' and 'North of Jerusalem'.

Background

Geography

Covering a total land area of 5,860 square kilometres, the West Bank has a surprising diversity of geographical features. Topographically it is dominated by the Central Range that is made up of the rolling hills of Judaea and Samaria, described as presenting "a mosaic of rocky hilltops and fertile valleys, dotted with age-old silver-green olive groves" (Israel Information Centre *Facts about Israel*, 1995). And though the West Bank is today demarcated by a political boundary, the 'Green Line', there are very clear physical boundaries. To the north the Jezreel Valley (Plain of Esdraelon, see page 633) divides the Central Range between Samaria and Judaea to the south, and Galilee to the north; to the west the West Bank is defined in topographical terms by the Maritime Coastal Plain (see page 482), and to the southwest by the Shephelah (see page 585); to the south the hills of the Central Range around Hebron meet the Negev arid area (see page 334); to the southeast is the stark yet beautiful Judean Desert, whilst the eastern limits of the West Bank are defined by the Jordan River itself. Much of the Jordan Valley and the northern section of the Dead Sea are included within the political boundary of the West Bank's 'Green Line'.

Warning: travelling around the West Bank

There are a number of security and safety considerations that must be borne in mind when visiting the various sites on the West Bank. Situations can change very quickly here, and thus you are advised to seek up-to-date advice on recent events in the places that you are intending to visit. Though your embassy or consulate is a good place to start, you should realize that they tend to provide the most pessimistic view of safety levels in various West Bank towns, and may attempt to discourage you from going. In theory, tourist offices should be a good place to seek further information, though those in Jerusalem at least are more likely to question why you want to go to one of those 'horrible towns full of Arabs anyway'. A better bet is to ask around other travellers who have visited these places, though you should of course be aware of the travellers' tales gossip machine, which thrives on rumours and half-truths. A reliable source of information on the prevailing situation in various West Bank towns is the local and international media (see 'Useful media addresses' section in 'Jerusalem – Local information' on page 232), of which the Jerusalem Media & Communications Centre is particularly useful. As a very general rule (at the time of going to press), in towns such as Bethlehem that are very much part of the tourist trail, there are no special security precautions. In towns such as Nablus, Ramallah and Jericho, despite fearsome reputations during the intifada, you are likely to be greeted cordially, perhaps looked on as something of an oddity. Hebron remains the most volatile town and you should seek further authoritative advice before visiting.

Transport arrangements have been complicated somewhat by the division of the West Bank into areas A, B and C (see page 239), and the rules governing which coloured number-plates can go where. Most of the Jewish settlements are served by Egged buses from the Central Bus Station in Jerusalem (or from the street outside). The Palestinian towns and villages are best served by service-taxis, which can be picked up from outside Jerusalem's Damascus Gate. Some of the sites described in this West Bank chapter are fairly remote, and are not served by public transport. Those with access to rental vehicles should note that yellow (Israeli) licence-plated vehicles still attract stone-throwers (or worse) on the West Bank, and thus are best avoided. Some car rental agencies actually place bans on you taking their vehicles beyond the Green Line. Thus, the best way to reach these outlying sites is to hire a car and local driver at the nearest town.

When visiting Palestinian towns and villages, it is worth making your 'foreign tourist' status very clear, though this does not necessarily mean flashing expensive cameras around or wearing a Hawaiian shirt. Appearing non-Israeli/Jewish is the key, unless of course you are visiting Jewish settlements. Fraternizing with IDF patrols or Jewish settlers in predominantly Palestinian areas remains a bad idea, as does voicing pro-Israeli opinions. In effect, caution and common-sense should be your watchwords. **NB** There are ID paper checks on many West Bank roads, particularly at the entry/exit points to Jerusalem: you must **carry your passport at all times**. Backpackers who have overstayed their visa may have to forego visiting the West Bank since a random ID check may ultimately result in deportation.

Visitors to the West Bank should remember to dress conservatively, with upper arms and legs covered. Women should also consider bringing some form of headscarf.

West Bank

Climate Most of the West Bank falls within a Mediterranean climatic zone, featuring dry hot summers and mild humid winters. Aspect and altitude have an important influence, with winter snows not uncommon on the higher ground, and rainfall higher on west-facing slopes than on the relatively arid east-facing slopes. The further east you move, the greater the fluctuations in temperature, with an extreme climate in evidence in the Jordan rift valley and Judean Desert regions.

Historical overview

The idea of 'the West Bank' as a single political or geographical unit is a comparatively recent phenomenon. Prior to the founding of the State of Israel in 1948, Palestinians living on the West Bank tended to refer to themselves as citizens of a particular city, town or village. The UN Partition Plan of 1947 (Resolution 181), however, envisaged the bulk of what is now known as the 'West Bank' as forming the heart of a future Arab state, though most Palestinians rejected this as a 'division of the homeland'. Following Israel's independence war, the term 'West Bank' was used to describe the area to the west of the Jordan River that King Abdullah incorporated into Transjordan (subsequently the Hashemite Kingdom of Jordan). It is important to note that Abdullah deliberately avoided using the term 'Palestine' in an attempt to stifle nascent Palestinian identity, thus hoping to legitimize his rule over the 'West Bank'. Right-wing Israelis, such as the former prime minister Benjamin Netanyahu, suggest that Abdullah "invented" the term "West Bank" "in order to obliterate the historic and on-going Jewish connection to the land" (*A Place Among the Nations: Israel and the World*, 1993). There is a degree of truth in this argument (though it is not as simple as Netanyahu makes out), but it seems likely that Abdullah was seeking as much to "obliterate" Palestinian connections as Jewish ones. Only Britain and Pakistan recognized Abdullah's claim to the West Bank.

However, there are far older names for the West Bank. As much as Palestinians and left-wing Israeli 'doves' would like to dispute the point, this is the land of *Eretz Yisrael*; the centre of the biblical Israelite kingdoms of **Judaea** and **Samaria**. Those looking for the heart of the Jewish connection to the land need not look to Galilee, the Mediterranean coast, or the Negev: it is here, on the West Bank. Naturally, the Israeli religious-right who want the right to settle anywhere in the land of *Eretz Yisrael* don't want to live in Tel Aviv or Eilat; they want to settle in Shechem, Samaria, Shiloh and Hebron. The more secular settlers have tended to develop towns in the commuter belt, closer to the Green Line, and within easy access of the Israeli towns where they work. Israel's settlement of the West Bank/Judaea and Samaria was facilitated by its capture in the Six Day War of 1967. The revival by Israel of the terms Judaea and Samaria to describe the West Bank is often described as a politicization of the geographic nomenclature, though in reality the name West Bank is equally loaded.

The Israeli claim to this land is of course complicated by the fact that, for the past millennium, the population of West Bank has been predominantly (Muslim) Arab. The current population estimates for the West Bank suggest fewer than 150,000 Jewish settlers (plus a similar number in East Jerusalem) and 1,300,000 Palestinians. Few nations recognize the Israeli claim to the land (though Israel has not attempted to annex it, unlike East Jerusalem), with most states regarding the West Bank as being 'occupied territories', thus making any settlement activity there illegal under international law. To the international community, biblical arguments are irrelevant.

There are also, inevitably, two contradictory views of the Israeli occupation. One is of benign rule bringing economic and social benefits to an underprivileged Arab population, as espoused by Netanyahu: "[the Israeli administration has] built five universities for the Palestinian Arab population, places severe restraints on its soldiers and court-martials offenders, and enables the Arabs to appeal to the Israeli Supreme Court to reverse the decision of the army" (*A Place Among the Nations: Israel and the World*, 1993). As Joffe observes, however, the "prevailing Palestinian view ... painted a picture of an alien and oppressive regime which stifled political independence, and used the threat of armed force to ensure that settlers had access to water, land and security, at the locals' expense" (*ibid*). Independent human rights reports are most enlightening on this subject. Yes, as Netanyahu suggests, Israeli soldiers are answerable to the courts, but is justice dispensed? According to the US State Department's "The Occupied Territories Report on Human Rights Practices for 1996", released by the Bureau of Democracy, Human Rights, and Labour, January 30, 1997: "A fine of less than $0.01 (one agora) fine [*sic*] was passed down by a military court in November on four soldiers who confessed to having killed a Palestinian in 1993", whilst Amnesty International's 1996 Report details how "An Israeli colonel who shot dead a 14-year-old girl, Ra'eda al-Qarra, in March 1993 was found guilty by a military court in March 1995 of causing her death through failure to exercise proper caution. He received a six-month suspended prison sentence." Both reports detail systematic torture and human rights abuses by the Israeli security forces. Separate reports prepared by the US State Department and Amnesty International suggest that systematic torture, extra-judicial killing, arbitrary arrest and unfair trials are widespread amongst the security services controlled by the Palestinian Authority (see page 822).

Israeli-Palestinian Interim Agreement (Oslo II)

At the time of this *Israel Handbook* going to press, the present situation on the West Bank is determined by the Israeli-Palestinian Interim Agreement on the West Bank and the Gaza Strip, Washington DC, 28th September 1995 (usually referred to as Oslo II Accords). According to the Declaration of Principles that Israel and the PLO signed in Washington in September 1993, final status negotiations should have begun by December 1995, been concluded by April 1996, with the permanent status agreement to be implemented by April 1999. Thus in theory, during the life-span of this *Israel Handbook*, the status of the West Bank should have changed significantly. In reality this is highly unlikely since at the time of going to press (autumn 1999) final status negotiations had not yet begun.

The Oslo II Accords divide the West Bank into three categories. In **Area A**, consisting of the main urban areas (and four percent of the land), the PA has powers and responsibilities for internal security and public order. In **Area B**, consisting of 440 West Bank villages, the PA has responsibility for public order for Palestinians while Israel maintains overriding responsibility for security with the purpose of protecting Israeli nationals and confronting the threat of 'terrorism'. Areas A and B cover about 23 percent of the land area in the West Bank and 68 percent of the population. **Area C** covers Jewish settlements and areas of 'strategic importance', with Israel responsible for civil affairs and all security, though certain areas and civil powers are due to be transferred to Palestinian jurisdiction up until the permanent status negotiations. Arguing the case for the Oslo II Accords before his cabinet, then prime minister Shimon Peres said that this agreement allowed Israel to keep "73 percent of the lands, 97 percent of the security and 80 percent of the water". The percentage of the West Bank's population that are Jewish settlers (excluding East Jerusalem) is around 11.5 percent. For further details of the Israeli-Palestinian negotiations, see Lawrence Joffe's comprehensive *Keesing's Guide to the Middle-East Peace Process* (Cartermill, 1996).

South of Jerusalem

There are a number of major places of interest on the West Bank to the south of Jerusalem. The major sights such as **Bethlehem** *and* **Hebron** *are located on the main Route 60 (Hebron Road), whereas some of the more remote spots such as* **Herodium** *and* **Mar Saba Monastery** *will require you to have (or to hire) your own transport.*

Bethlehem

Phone code: 02
Colour map 2, grid C4

In appearance Bethlehem is a typical Palestinian Arab town; but one whose economic base is distorted out of all proportion by its dependence on the pilgrim and tourist trade arising from the fact that this is the site of the birth of Jesus. The town's key attraction is Christendom's oldest complete and working church, built over the traditional site of the Nativity. A number of other sites in and around the Bethlehem area are also based upon (less well founded) biblical traditions.

Ins and outs

Getting there Bethlehem is easily visited as a short excursion from Jerusalem. Take a service taxi from outside Damascus Gate to the Israeli check-post on the northern outskirts of Bethlehem (near Rachel's Tomb). To avoid hassles here, make sure that you have your passport. Sometimes you have to change to another service taxi that will take you to Manger Square, or your original vehicle may continue southwest along Route 60 to the junction with Paul VI Rd (see map). Alternatively, you can walk from the checkpost.

Those on an organized tour from Jerusalem may be taken on the 'scenic route' (Route 398) to Bethlehem (20 km). This heads southeast from the Mount of Olives, approaching Bethlehem in a wide loop to the east that includes the **St Theodosius' Monastery** (see page 254) and the **Shepherd's Fields** (see page 249), before arriving in Bethlehem via the neighbouring village of Beit Sahur.

Getting around Bethlehem is compact enough to get around on foot. Those planning trips to places in the vicinity of Bethlehem should go to the local bus stand just below Manger Square, or negotiate a deal with the numerous taxi drivers and 'guides' hanging around the square itself (see 'Transport' on page 248). The main places of interest in Bethlehem are centred around **Manger Square**, the heart of the town (and recently the centrepiece of the town's ambitious 'Bethlehem 2000' refurbishment programme). The Church of the Nativity stands at the east end of the square, with Milk Grotto Street leading off to the southeast to Milk Grotto Chapel. An interesting market lies to the west of Manger Square, in addition to the Bethlehem Museum and St Mary's Syrian Orthodox Church.

History

Jewish Bethlehem Though usually associated with Christianity, the biblical town of Bethlehem features prominently in Jewish history. It is first mentioned in the Bible in defining Ephrath, on the road to which Rachel died and was buried, though it is through **David** that Bethlehem rises to prominence. A son of the city, he was anointed here as king (*I Samuel 16:1-23*), though Bethlehem was to remain a small town in the shadow of Jerusalem. David's grandfather, Obed, was the son of Ruth and Boaz, who met and married in the town (*Ruth 4:17*). The supposed field belonging to Boaz in which he first encountered Ruth is a popular attraction in the nearby village of Beit Sahur (see page 249).

Bethlehem was included within Rehoboam's (929-911 BCE) line of fortifications defending Jerusalem, and some nine centuries later it again became strategically important guarding the road to Herod the Great's palace-fortresses at the Herodium and Masada.

There can be little doubt that the Christian tradition of Bethlehem as the birthplace of Jesus determined the destiny of the town. There are strong

Christian Bethlehem

West Bank

Bethlehem

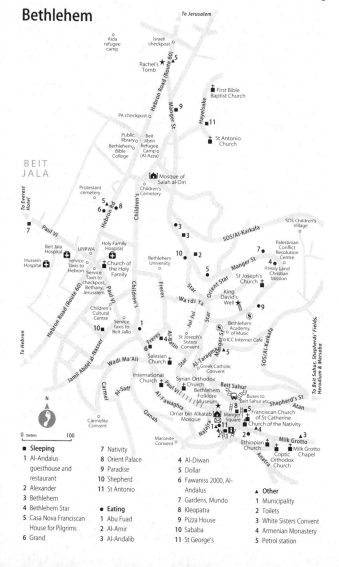

Sleeping
1 Al-Andalus guesthouse and restaurant
2 Alexander
3 Bethlehem
4 Bethlehem Star
5 Casa Nova Franciscan House for Pilgrims
6 Grand
7 Nativity
8 Orient Palace
9 Paradise
10 Shepherd
11 St Antonio

Eating
1 Abu Fuad
2 Al-Amir
3 Al-Andalib
4 Al-Diwan
5 Dollar
6 Fawaniss 2000, Al-Andalus
7 Gardens, Mundo
8 Kleopatra
9 Pizza House
10 Sababa
11 St George's

Other
1 Municipality
2 Toilets
3 White Sisters Convent
4 Armenian Monastery
5 Petrol station

☞ *Luke's gospel and the birth of Jesus*

Luke's assumption that Mary and Joseph lived in Nazareth prior to Jesus' birth (Luke 2:4) is largely based on the premise that since Jesus was brought up there as a child (Matthew 13:54; Luke 4:16), and had relatives there (Matthew 13:55-56), his parents must have lived there before his birth. A reading of Matthew's gospel, however, suggests that Mary and Joseph were in fact natives of Bethlehem (Matthew 2), only later moving to Nazareth in order to avoid the murderous designs of the Herodian dynasty, or perhaps seeking work at the grand building project at Sepphoris (Zippori). This presented Luke with a dilemma since he needed to place the couple at Bethlehem for the birth of Jesus. He did this by invoking the census of Quirinius (Cyrenius, governor of Syria), suggesting that Joseph had to come to Bethlehem since he was "of the house and lineage of David" (Luke 2:4). However, this census did not actually take place until 6 CE.

Luke's gospel is largely responsible for the image of the Nativity that most adults from some form of Western Christian background grow up with; the Christmas carol picture of "no room at the inn" and

Jesus' subsequent birth in a stable. However, this whole image could largely be based upon a flawed translation of the gospel, with the Greek underlying the line "she laid him in a manger because there was no room for them at the inn" (Luke 2:7) also capable of being translated as "she laid him in a manger because they had no space in the room" (see Murphy-O'Connor, 1992). Though there is no specific mention of a cave in the gospel account of the Nativity, it may be possible that in order to avoid the overcrowding within the house that Joseph shared with his parents, the couple moved to the cave area at the back of the house that was a feature of most of the homes in the Bethlehem area at the time. The manger element of the story is probably derived from the fact that such a cave would have been used as a shelter for the domestic animals during periods of bad weather. Interestingly, second century CE Christian references to the Nativity all speak of Jesus' birth in a cave, whilst the area beneath the Church of the Nativity that is today venerated as the birthplace of Christ is part of a cave complex.

archaeological and circumstantial grounds for accepting that the Church of the Nativity in Bethlehem marks the place of Jesus' birth. In fact, the Roman emperor Hadrian's decision in 135 CE to plant a grove dedicated to the pagan god Adonis at the traditional cave site of Jesus' birth did not so much divert Christian attention away from the spot as mark the site out for the next two centuries. However, it is fairly safe to assume that Luke's gospel account of the events leading up to the birth of Jesus is fundamentally flawed (see box, above).

The first church built to commemorate the site of the Nativity was constructed by the emperor **Constantine**, and dedicated by his mother **Queen Helena** in 339 CE. Just under 50 years later, **St Jerome** settled in Bethlehem with a group of Roman matrons (including St Paula and St Eustochium), thus founding an important monastic tradition in the town. During his period of residence in Bethlehem, St Jerome translated the Bible from Greek and Hebrew into Latin, creating *The Vulgate*, or authoritative version of the Bible that the Roman Catholic Church used right up until this century. The 'study' that he used whilst working on the translation is said to be one of the caves in the complex beneath the Church of the Nativity.

The subsequent history of Bethlehem is effectively the history of the Church of the Nativity. Like the rest of the town it was largely damaged in the Samaritan revolt of 529 CE, before being rebuilt on a much grander scale by the emperor **Justinian I** (527-565 CE). Remarkably, the church survived the Persian invasion of 614 CE that brought destruction to most churches in the country (Jerusalem in particular). Legend suggests that the invaders recognized the dress of the Magi ('three wise men') in the mosaic on the west façade, and spared the church out of respect for their ancestors. It even survived al-Hakim's destructive edict of 1009, probably because Muslims had been allowed to perform devotions here for several centuries (Jesus is a prophet within Islam, though not the son of God).

The Church of the Nativity was held particularly dear to the **Crusaders**, with Baldwin I crowning himself king there on Christmas Day 1100. When the Latin Kingdom collapsed following defeat at the Horns of Hittim in 1187, the Ayyubid dynasty respected the sanctity of the church, though subsequent dynasties such as the Mamluks and Ottomans systematically looted the place. The **British** captured the town from the Turks without a shot being fired three days before General Allenby entered Jerusalem in 1917. The town was occupied by the **Jordanians** following the termination of the British Mandate in 1948, finally coming under **Israeli** control during the Six Day War of 1967.

Bethlehem remains a very vulnerable town, with its economic well-being relying almost entirely on the pilgrim and tourist trade. This sector of the economy was very badly hit by the lack of visitors during the *intifada*, and remains hostage to the state of the current Israeli-Palestinian 'peace process'; unemployment in the town currently runs at about 40 percent. There have been a number of clashes between Bethlehem and the neighbouring Jewish settlement of Efrat over matters such as water rights, access roads and land confiscations. The permanent population of Bethlehem (c. 30,000) was previously evenly split between Christian Arabs and Muslim Arabs, though the recent exodus of Christian families has now put the Muslims in the majority. In December 1995 the town became autonomous of Israel under the remit of the Palestinian Authority; an event marked at the traditional Christmas Eve celebrations in the Church of the Nativity by the presence of a beaming Yasir Arafat.	**Recent history**

Sights

Most visitors using public transport take Route 60 (Hebron Road) to reach Bethlehem (eight kilometres), passing the **Greek Orthodox Monastery of Mar Elias** after five kilometres to the left. This marks the traditional site where the prophet Elijah rested, although there are some later traditions associated with this spot. ■ *Monday-Saturday 0800-1100 1300-1700. Modest dress essential.*	**Greek Orthodox Monastery of Mar Elias**
From the outside, the Church of the Nativity bears a greater resemblance to a medieval citadel than a place of worship, neatly encapsulating the history of competing faiths in the Holy Land. Looking at the west façade from Manger Square, the comparatively modern church adjoining it to the north (left) is Franciscan Church of St Catherine (see page 245), whilst immediately to the south (right) is the Armenian Convent. The higher tower to the right belongs to the Greek Orthodox Convent.	**Church of the Nativity**

The entrance to the church through the **western façade** has been considerably altered down the years, though evidence of the three sixth century CE entrances can still be seen. The tips of the **lintels (1) (2)** of two lateral doors can be seen projecting beyond the 19th-century **buttress (3)**. It is easy to see how the **main entrance doorway (4)** has been reduced in size, firstly by the Crusaders and then in the Mamluk or Ottoman period. The entrance is often referred to as

☞ *Christmas in Bethlehem*

Bethlehem hosts three Christmases. The (Latin) Roman Catholic and Protestant celebrations are held on 24th-25th December, and the Greek Orthodox church also uses this date. Those wishing to attend the midnight mass will require a special ticket, available from the Franciscan Pilgrim's Office (T6272697) at the Christian Information Office opposite the Citadel, inside Jerusalem's Jaffa Gate (T6272692, F6286417). It's free, though you may have to pretend that you are Catholic (and you should have your passport with you when you go to the

service). The Orthodox churches (except for the Greek) celebrate Christmas on 6th January, whilst the Oriental Orthodox (Armenian, Coptic, Ethiopian, Syrian, etcetera) church holds its services on 17th and 18th January. Though extra transport is laid on from Jerusalem during these holiday periods, visitors should note that accommodation rates in Bethlehem sky-rocket and those without confirmed reservations may find 'no room at the inn'. NB Christmas in Bethlehem can be very cold, and heavy snow is not unknown.

the **Door of Humility (4)**, though this probably has far less to do with the idea of all visitors having to bow their heads to enter than with the very practical measure of defence; not only did it prevent horsemen from riding directly into the church, it also stopped looters wheeling their carts all the way in!

The Door of Humility leads into the rather dark Justinian **narthex (5)**, though the partitions are of a later date. Only one doorway (**6**) now leads into the central **nave (7)**. A few carved panels are all that remain of the heavy wooden entrance door made by an Armenian carpenter in 1227. The main body of the church remains largely unchanged since Justinian had it built in the sixth century CE, though in the tradition of the Eastern Orthodox church the nave is devoid of furniture. The graceful red limestone **pillars** were probably part of the original fourth century CE Constantine church, with the stone having been quarried locally. Many of the pillars were decorated with paintings of saints during the Crusader era, with the most notable images being those of Canute of Denmark and England (**8**), Olaf of Norway (**9**) and Cathal of Ireland (**10**). One of the columns bears an image of Christ, with reports in December 1996 suggesting that it was "weeping for the sins of the world". The original **octagonal baptismal font (11)** from the Justinian church occupies a new position in the south aisle (**12**). It was probably moved here during the Crusader restoration of the church, having previously stood above a cistern close to the present high altar (**13**).

Church of the Nativity

0 metres 20

Caves beneath Church
(see 'Grotto of Nativity' map)

1 Lintel, 6th century
2 Lintel, 6th century
3 19th-century Buttress
4 Main Entrance / Door of Humility
5 Narthex
6 Doorway
7 Nave
8 St Canute
9 St Olaf
10 St Cathal
11 Baptismal Font
12 South Aisle
13 Greek Orthodox High Altar
14 North Aisle
15 South Wall
16 North Wall
17 4th-century Mosaic below trapdoors
18 South Transept
19 Altar commemorating Circumcision
20 Steps to Grotto of the Nativity
21 Steps up from Grotto of the Nativity
22 North Transept
23 Door in North Aisle
24 Entrance to Cave Complex
25 Toilets

The interior walls of the north (**14**) and south (**12**) aisles of the nave were decorated with mosaics during the Crusader period, very small sections of which remain intact. The **south wall** (**15**) featured depictions of the seven ecumenical councils, below which were images of the genealogy of Jesus according to the Gospel of Matthew (*Matthew 1:1-17*). The **north wall** (**16**) bore themes representing six of the provincial councils (Antioch, Ancyra, Sardica, Gangra, Laodicea and Carthage) above figures illustrating the genealogy of Jesus according to the Gospel of Luke (*Luke 3:23-38*). A series of **trapdoors** (**17**) in the floor of the nave reveal parts of the mosaic floor of the original fourth century CE Constantine church.

The **high altar** (**13**) is hidden by the *iconostasis*, or ornately carved screen hung with icons. The **altar** (**19**) in the **south transept** (**18**) belongs to the Greek Orthodox Church and commemorates the Circumcision. Two flights of steps lead down to the **Grotto of the Nativity** (those to the south (**20**) for going down, those to the north (**21**) for coming up).

The **Grotto of the Nativity** is part of a complex of caves that marks the traditional site of the birth of Jesus. At the bottom of the steps (**20**) a large silver star (**a**) in the floor marks the scene of the Nativity. The present star belongs to the (Latin) Catholic church and dates to 1717, though it was removed by the Orthodox church in 1847 following a dispute. Though the Ottoman authorities ordered the star returned some six years later, this trivial quarrel was one of the factors that led to the Crimean War between Russia and the alliance of Britain, France and Turkey (1853-56). Like the Church of the Holy Sepulchre in Jerusalem, different sects of the Christian church battle it out for guardianship of this holy place. Fortunately here there are only three players (Greek Orthodox, Roman Catholics, Armenians), though this has not prevented some bitter and bloody battles over such trivial matters as cleaning rotas, prayer times, and the acceptance of daylight saving hours! Close to the star marking the Nativity is a representation of the Manger (**b**). A narrow passage reputedly cut by St Jerome leads to other points of interest within the cave complex, though this passage is usually blocked by a locked gate (**c**). They are accessible however through the entrance (**24**) in the Franciscan Church of St Catherine (see page 245). Return to the main church above via the steps (**21**).

Grotto of the Nativity

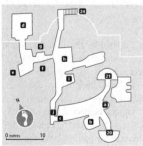

0 metres 10

20 Entrance from Church of the Nativity	**c** (Locked) Gate
21 Exit from Church of the Nativity	**d** Cave of St Jerome
	e Tomb of St Jerome
24 Entrance from Franciscan Church of St Catherine	**f** Tombs of St Paula & St Eustochia
	g Tomb of Eusebius
a Silver Star marking Birth Place	**h** Chapel of the Holy Innocents
b Representation of the Manger	**i** Altar to Joseph's Dream
	j St Jerome's Passage

Exit the Church of the Nativity via the door in the north transept (**22**) into the Franciscan Church of St Catherine, or via the door in the north aisle (**23**) into the attractive Franciscan cloister. ■ *Summer 0600-1800, winter 0800-1700. Free, donations accepted. Modest dress essential.*

Franciscan Church of St Catherine

Based on an original Crusader construction, this Roman Catholic church was rebuilt in 1882 and then modified again in 1949. The midnight mass held here on Christmas Eve is broadcast around the world. The medieval cloister to the west of the church is particularly attractive, and features a large statue of St Jerome.

West Bank

A number of steps in the south aisle lead down to the cave complex connected to the Grotto of the Nativity (see page 245). Amongst these are: the **Cave of St Jerome (d)**, where he reputedly completed the translation of the Hebrew and Greek Bibles into the Vulgate; the **tomb of St Jerome** (d. 420 CE) (**e**); the **tombs of St Paula** (d. 404 CE) and **St Eustochia** (d. 419 CE) (**f**); the **tomb of Eusebius (g)**; the **Chapel of the Holy Innocents (h)**, dedicated to those massacred by Herod (*Matthew 2:16*), and an altar commemorating Joseph's dream that he should flee to Egypt (**i**); and finally the passageway (**j**) to the Grotto of the Nativity reputedly cut by St Jerome. These identifications have no archaeological value. ■ *T2742425. Open daily 0500-1200 1400-1800. Free, donations accepted. Modest dress essential.*

Armenian Monastery It is sometimes possible to visit the Armenian Monastery, adjacent to the Church of the Nativity. It is particularly noted for its use of blue tile work on the chapel, as well as the splendid view from the roof. ■ *Daily 0530-1800, closes one hour earlier in winter. Free, donations accepted.*

Milk Grotto Chapel The truly gullible and desperate may like to visit the Milk Grotto Chapel, five minutes walk along Milk Grotto Street to the southeast of the Church of the Nativity. The Franciscan chapel is built above the cave where the Holy Family reputedly hid prior to their flight into Egypt. It takes its name from the white-coloured rock on the floor that supposedly turned that colour when a drop of Mary's milk fell on it whilst she was nursing Jesus. The chapel is popular with women praying for fertility, and presumably good lactation. The present chapel dates to 1871, though the tradition dates to the sixth century CE. ■ *Daily 0800-1130 1400-1700. Free, donations accepted. Junk souvenirs on sale.*

Bethlehem Folklore Museum This small museum attempts to recreate 19th-century Bethlehem using exhibits of costumes, furniture, handicrafts, documents and the mock-up of a Palestinian home. ■ *Off Paul VI Street, T2742589. Monday-Saturday 1000-1200 1430-1700. 5 NIS.*

King David's Well The *Second Book of Samuel* tells how David declared "O that someone would give me water to drink from the well of Bethlehem which is by the gate!" (*II Samuel 23:15*), but then refused to drink because of the risks taken by three of his followers when they broke through the Philistine lines to fetch the water. Instead he offered it to God. During the Crusader period the cistern in the Church of the Nativity above which the octagonal baptismal font originally stood (see page 243) became associated with this tradition, though now the revered site is a series of three restored cisterns in the parking lot of the King David Cinema (see map). The cinema features a truly awful film of Jesus' life based on Luke's gospel. ■ *Off Manger Street, known here as King David Street, T2742477. 0700-1200 1400-1900.*

Rachel's Tomb The traditional site of the tomb of Rachel, Jacob's fourth (and favourite?) wife, is located on the northern outskirts of Bethlehem; the town to which she was travelling when she died giving birth to Benjamin (*Genesis 35:16-19*). Rachel is venerated by Jews, Christians and Muslims alike, though within Jewish tradition she is regarded as something of a 'mother of the nation', and the shrine here is particularly busy with Jewish women praying for fertility and safe birth. The tomb itself is probably medieval, though substantial repairs were carried out in the 19th century. The velvet-draped cenotaph inside the tomb is certainly not the one described in the Bible (*Genesis 35:20*). In recent years the shrine has been the scene of disputes between the Israelis and the Palestinian

Authority, and is now largely obscured from the road by a high 'protective' wall. ■ *T2742020. Sunday-Thursday 0800-1600, Friday 0800-1300. Free. Sexes are segregated by a screen; modest dress must be worn, and men must wear a head covering or one of the cardboard yarmulkes provided. Service taxis from Jerusalem's Damascus Gate stop at the check-post just to the north of the tomb.*

Essentials

Bethlehem's hoteliers have suffered from the closure of areas under PA rule by the Israelis, and the close proximity of a wide range of accommodation at Jerusalem, just 15 mins away. However, the need to drum up business means that prices can be very competitive, with determined haggling producing good deals. Further, Bethlehem's hotels tend not to be as overpriced as those in Jerusalem. Unfortunately there is nothing in the budget price range. Advance booking is essential over the Christmas period. Since Bethlehem came under the control of the PA, most hotels prefer letters to them to be addressed as "Bethlehem, Palestine" or "Bethlehem via Israel".

A *Shepherd*, Jamil Abdel al-Nasser, T2740656, F2744888. Recently refurbished and 'stone-clad' in true Vera Duckworth style, spacious and nicely furnished rooms, central a/c and heating, very large bathrooms, cable TV, phone, minibar, dining hall, bar, garden restaurant. Not a bad deal especially at group rates. **A** *Orient Palace*, Manger Sq, T2777766/2742798, F2741562. Superb setting right on Manger Sq, very successful recent refurbishment has left the hotel looking very plush. Nicely furnished a/c rooms, orthopaedic mattresses, cable TV, phone, minibar, pleasant *Al-Madafah* coffee shop, *As-Sabil* French/Italian restaurant and attractive *Al-Bustan* terrace restaurant. Very nice, especially with group discounts, advance booking essential.

B *Bethlehem*, Manger St, T2770702, F2770706. Large 160-room hotel with spacious a/c rooms, central heating, TV, phone, nice terrace restaurant, coffee shop, bar, generous group rates, keen staff.

C *Al Andalus Guest House*, Manger Sq, T2741348, F2742280. Only 10 rooms, all with tiny shower, clean but sparsely furnished, TV lounge, dining hall. Good value if you can negotiate a big enough discount. **C** *Alexander*, Manger St, T2770780, F2770782. Double rooms (**C**) plus excellent value 2-room apartments (**B**) with lounge, fitted kitchen, TV, panoramic views, sleeping up to 4, very friendly staff. Recommended. **C** *Bethlehem Star*, Freres, T2743249, F2741494. Modern, light and spacious rooms, central a/c, cable TV, attractive roof restaurant, 'American' bar, coffee shop, not a bad choice. **C** *Everest*, Paul VI, Beit Jala, T2742604, F2741278. Small, modest hotel in Beit Jala, restaurant. **C** *Grand*, Freres, T2741603, F2741604. Long established 'luxury' hotel, 50 rooms, a/c, cable TV, phone, plus 18 apartments (slightly bigger rooms, some with connecting doors), dining hall for breakfast plus recently opened *Mariachi* Mexican restaurant/bar, keen staff, good discounts for groups. **C** *Nativity*, Paul VI, T2770650, F2744083. Large 89-room hotel on outskirts of town (Beit Jala), a/c, restaurant. **C** *Paradise*, Manger St, T2743760, F2744544. Large, modern a/c rooms. phone, radio, TV lounge, restaurant, bar, though not particularly friendly.

D *Casa Nova Franciscan House for Pilgrims*, Manger Sq, T2743981, F2743540. Attractive, well-run pilgrim hostel, good value at $20 per person B&B, $25 per person half-board, $30 per person full-board, group dorms available, heated in winter, 2300 curfew, advance reservation essential. **D** *St Antonio*, Hayelsake, T2744308. Friendly, unpretentious hotel catering mainly to (Catholic) pilgrims, simple rooms with attached bath or shower, dining hall, small bar, group rates available, advanced booking advised. Recommended.

Sleeping
■ *on map;*
price codes see inside
front cover

West Bank

Eating In addition to the hotel restaurants, there are a number of places around Manger Sq that you may care to consider (though they are very much aimed at the tourist market). ***Al Andalus***, T2743519, serves basic Middle Eastern fayre, plus 'Western' meals such as burgers and chips or hot-dogs; ***St George***, T2743780, receives good reviews for its Middle Eastern cuisine. There are also a number of restaurants on Manger St and Hebron Rd.

Bars & nightclubs **Bars** Bethlehem is not a place to head for if you're after nightlife, although most of the hotels have a bar. **Entertainment** Concert halls: ***Bethlehem Academy of Music/Bethlehem Music Society***, Manger St, T2777141, F2777142; ***National Conservatory of Music***, T2745989, F2770048.

Shopping Most of the tacky tourist junk is found on Manger Sq, Milk Grotto St, al-Nizhma (Star) St and Paul VI St.

Transport **Local** Car hire: ***Murad***, T2747092; ***Orabi***, T050-372687. Most hotels can arrange car (and driver) hire. **Taxis**: the taxi stand just below (north of) Manger Sq is the place to enquire about hiring a taxi to visit places such as Shepherds' Fields (Beit Sahur), Herodium, Chariton, Mar Saba, St Theodosius' Monastery and Hyrcania. Haggle like mad and make sure the conditions are clear (price, waiting time, etc). If you want to book a taxi try ***Asha'b***, T2742309, or ***Beit Jala***, T2742629.

Long distance **Buses**: minibuses and ancient buses run from the bus stands on Beit Sahur/Shepherd's St, the road just below (north of) Manger Sq. No 47 runs to **Beit Sahur** (1 NIS, 5 mins), whilst there are also services to **Beit Jala** (10 mins) and **Solomon's Pools/Artas** (30 mins). Lumbering buses to **East Jerusalem**'s Suleiman St bus station can also be picked up at the junction of Hebron/Paul VI St, and sometimes there are services continuing on to **Ramallah**. **Service taxi**: the best way to get to/from Bethlehem is by service taxi. A service taxi from Jerusalem's Damascus Gate to the check-post at the north end of town costs 3 NIS (15 mins). To return to **Jerusalem** either walk up to the check-post and take a service taxi from there, or walk to the junction of Hebron Rd/Paul VI St and flag one down. Service taxis to **Beit Jallo** run from a yard at the junction of Paul VI/Children's Rd (see map), and there are service taxis to **Bethany** from the junction of Hebron Rd/Paul VI St.

Directory **Banks** There are plenty of money-changers at the Manger Sq end of Paul VI St. **Communications** **Area code**: T02. **NB**: Bethlehem numbers have recently changed to 7 digits. If you have a 6-digit number try prefacing it with a 2. **Post offices**: *Main Post Office*, Manger Sq, T2742668 (Mon-Fri 0800-1700, Sat 0800-1430). **Internet/email**: *ICC Internet Café*, Manger St (see map). **Cultural centres** *Al-Liqa' Centre for Religious & Heritage Studies in the Holy Land*, T/F2741639; *International Centre of Bethlehem*, T6470047, F6470048, http://www.annadwa.org *Palestinian Group for the Revival of Popular Heritage*, T/F2747945. **Hospitals and medical services** Chemists: *Al-Razi*, T2741647; *Al-Sha'ab*, T2742472. Hospitals: *Holy Family*, Paul VI, T2741151. There are several other hospitals in Bethlehem, though your best bet is to get to Jerusalem. **Tour companies and travel agents** Most of the tour companies covering Bethlehem are actually based in Jerusalem. If you want a tour led by a Palestinian (as opposed to an Israeli) try ***Palestinian Association for Cultural Exchange (PACE)***, Ramallah, T02-2986854; ***Amani Tours***, Ramallah, T02-2987013 or ***Alternative Tours***, Jerusalem, T052-864205. **Tourist offices** Ministry of Tourism & Antiquities, 2nd floor, Manger Sq, T2741581. May be able to provide you with a map, plus the useful ***This Week in Palestine*** brochure. **Useful addresses and phone numbers** Police: Manger Sq, T2748231. **Ambulance**: T101 (T2743225). **Fire**: T2741123. **Municipality**: T2741323.

Around Bethlehem

Field of Ruth and Shepherds' Fields

The small Arab village of **Beit Sahur** lies 1.5 kilometres east of Bethlehem and is the scene of a number of biblical traditions. It is supposedly the setting for much of the *Book of Ruth*, including the scene in which Boaz (David's great-grandfather) first observed **Ruth** in his field gleaning the ears of corn (*Ruth 2:2-3*). A particular site in the village is referred to as the **Field of Ruth**, whilst the Hebrew translation of Beit Sahur means 'Village of the Watching'.

Beit Sahur is also home to the Christian tradition of the **Shepherds' Fields** where according to Luke's gospel and the popular Christmas carol, the shepherds "watched their flocks by night" and were then greeted by the angel with the news of Jesus' birth (*Luke 2:8-20*). The site was first noted in the fourth century CE by Christian pilgrims anxious to see the spot where the angel appeared to the shepherds and there are now competing Greek Orthodox and Roman Catholic sites marking the traditional spot.

Ins and outs Bus 47 runs to Beit Sahur from the bus stand behind and below the Manger Sq police station in Bethlehem (5 mins, 1 NIS). The square where Bus 47 terminates (before returning to Bethlehem) is where you may be able to get a service taxi (and definitely able to get a 'special' taxi) to the **Herodium**. From here the sites are marked, with the left fork leading to the Roman Catholic site, and the right fork leading 250m further on to the Greek Catholic site.

Greek Orthodox site The Greek Orthodox site is marked by an attractive red-domed church completed in 1989. The earliest remains here date to the fourth century CE, and comprise one of the earliest Christian mosaic floors excavated in the country. The floor is believed to belong to the "splendid cave with an altar" first described by the pilgrim Egeria in 384 CE, and later enlarged in the fifth century CE with the construction of a simple church above it. Vigils were held in this 'Church of the Shepherds' (known locally as **Kaniset er-Ru'at**) on the eve of Epiphany in the early fifth century CE. In the following century a new basilica was built above the existing church. Its northern aisle became a burial place for nuns and monks serving the church, with over a hundred skeletons having been excavated. A much more elaborate basilica was built in the sixth century CE, emphasizing the importance of the site to the early Christian church. The basilica was destroyed in the Persian invasion of 614 CE, rebuilt in the seventh century CE, before finally being destroyed in the 10th century CE. In addition to the ancient remains, the modern church is also worth visiting, though the whole complex is often closed. ■ *Daily 0800-1130 1400-1700. 10 NIS.*

Roman Catholic site The Roman Catholic site is administered by the Franciscans, and is known locally as **Siyar el-Ghanam**. The compound includes the remains of a church built in the late fourth or early fifth centuries CE, later converted into a monastery in the sixth to eighth centuries CE. Most observers now believe that this complex was simply another Byzantine monastery in the Judean Desert, and not specifically connected with the tradition of the Shepherds' Fields. The modern **Chapel of the Angels**, completed in 1954, is another attractive ecclesiastical design by the Italian architect Antonio Barluzzi. ■ *T6472413. Daily 0800-1130 1400-1730.*

West Bank

Herodium

*Located some 10 kilometres southeast of Bethlehem is a low hill, on the summit of which is the **Herodium** (Herodion, or in Arabic Jebel Fureidis). This palace-fortress complex represents one of **Herod the Great's** most ambitious building projects. At the base of the hill is a series of palace annexes and entertainment facilities known as **Lower Herodium**. The site is well preserved, extremely well presented, and highly recommended not just for its historical/archaeological value, but for the fine view that it affords across the surrounding Judean Desert area.*

Ins and outs

Getting there It is surprisingly difficult to reach the Herodium by public transport. You can take Bus 47 from Bethlehem to Beit Sahur, and then wait around in the parking lot that serves as a bus stop until there are enough people to fill a service taxi heading in that direction (though you could be in for a very long wait). Alternatively you can hire a taxi privately ('special'). Bargain hard, though expect to pay around 30 NIS for the vehicle to take you there, wait, and return. Make sure you specify how long you wish to stay at the site; at least one hour is needed to explore the upper and lower sites. Of course it is possible to walk there, though the road is a real killer since it is a series of long up and down hills. From Jerusalem, Egged Bus 166 to Tekoa passes reasonably close to the site (Sunday-Thursday every two hours 1200-2300, Friday and Saturday very resticted service). Make sure the driver knows where you want to get off. It's a couple of kilometres walk from the nearest stop.

History

Much of our knowledge of the Herodium's history is derived from the writings of Josephus (*The Jewish War; Antiquities*), with a series of excavations at the site confirming many of the details he gives. It is worth standing facing the site and reading Josephus' description (*Antiquities XV, 324-325*).

Dating construction here can be narrowed down to a period of nine years between Herod's wedding to Mariamne (24 BCE) and the visit to Judea (including the Herodium) of Marcus Agrippa, son-in-law of Herod's patron the emperor Augustus (15 BCE). It was built at the site of one of Herod's key victories over the Hasmoneans during his flight from Jerusalem to Masada in 40 BCE. The site appears to have been particularly dear to Herod for not only did he give it his name, he also requested that he be buried there. Though Josephus gives great detail of Herod's funeral cortège (*Jewish War I, 670-673; Antiquities XVII, 196-199*), the two sources contain contrary information so it is not sure whether Herod was actually buried here; certainly no tomb has been found despite extensive excavations.

The fortress was in Jewish hands at the beginning of the First Jewish Revolt (66 CE) but fell to the Romans after the capture of Jerusalem (70 CE). It was also a command post for the Jewish rebels during the Second (Bar Kokhba) Revolt of 132-135 CE. In the fifth to seventh centuries CE Byzantine monks established a monastery in the palace-fortress and built at least three churches in the Lower Herodium area.

Herodium Palace-Fortress

0 metres 10

1 Herodium Monumental Staircase
2 Outer Wall
3 Inner Wall
4 N, W, S Semi-circular Towers
5 Monumental Tower or Keep
6 Courtyard or Garden
7 N Exedra
8 S Exedra
9 Underground Entrance
10 Apodyterium
11 Tepidarium
12 Frigidarium
13 Caldarium
14 Byzantine Chapel
15 Triclinium
16 Mikveh
17 Furnace

Sights

Herod's palace-fortress complex is reached by a winding staircase around the outside of the mound. The original **monumental staircase (1)** was a far grander affair, comprising 200 white marble steps descending in a straight line from the summit's northeast corner. The palace-fortress comprises **two parallel circular walls (2) (3)**, the outer one having a diameter of 62 metres. The wall is defended by **three semi-circular towers (4)** at the north, west and south compass points. To the east stood a monumental tower or **keep (5)**, the base (18 metres in diameter) of which is extremely well preserved. It is believed that five storeys of living space were built above it. Both the circular walls and defensive towers are built on a series of vaults that were built to produce an artificially flat top to this natural hill.

The palace appears to have been divided into two distinct areas. The eastern section beneath the keep was occupied by a large **garden** or **courtyard (6)**, and enclosed to the north, south and west by columns, and by a wall with pilasters to the east. Two symmetrical exedrae lie to the north and south **(7) (8)**. In the northeast corner is an **underground entrance (9)** that probably dates to the First Jewish Revolt (66-73 CE), though it is usually locked. The tunnel leads to the Herodian cisterns outside **(a)**.

The western section of the palace comprised dwellings and service rooms.

Herodium: overview

To Chariton

To Bethlehem

610m

650m

670m

N

Ticket Office

Herodium Palace-Fortress

Parking

730m

710m

690m

0 metres 100

a Cisterns
b Pool
c Circular Pavilion
d Ornamental Garden
e Bath House
f Artificial Course (funerary path)
g Monumental building
h Palace
i,j,k Byzantine Churches

Of particular note here is the bathhouse, featuring an *apodyterium* **(10)** with an attractive mosaic floor, a circular *tepidarium* **(11)** topped with a hemispherical dome, a small *frigidarium* **(12)** and a large rectangular *caldarium* **(13)**. During the Byzantine period the monks mainly occupied the still-roofed bathhouse, setting up their oven in the *caldarium*. They also built a small chapel to the south of the bathhouse **(14)**. In the southern part of the western section stood a rectangular **triclinium (15)** with four columns supporting the roof (the base of one remains). This dining hall appears to have been converted into a synagogue during the Bar Kokhba Revolt, with a **mikveh (16)** also being added. The Jewish rebels were also responsible for the **furnace (17)** that they used to make arrow and spear heads.

Lower Herodium   The Herodian structures at the foot of the hill were undoubtedly built at the same time as the palace-fortress. Standing at the top of the hill provides a good perspective. In the centre of Lower Herodium is the **pool complex**, featuring a large uncovered **pool (b)** that was fed by aqueduct from the Artas spring near 'Solomon's Pools' (see page 254). The presence of the **circular pavilion (c)** at the centre of the pool suggests that the pool's primary function was not as a reservoir, but as an artificial lake for swimming and sailing small boats that acted as the architectural focal point of the complex. The pool was contained within a large rectangular **ornamental garden (d)**. At the southwest corner stood a large **bathhouse (e)**, built in the Roman-style with mosaic floors and frescoes similar to those found at Masada, Jericho and Cypros.

Extending west–east from the southeast corner of the ornamental garden is a large **artificial course (f)**, some 350 metres long and 30 metres wide. It was originally suggested that this was a hippodrome or race course, though most commentators now believe that it is far too narrow to have served such a purpose. It is certainly connected with the **monumental building (g)** at its western end. The thickness of the monumental building's walls (three metres) suggests that they supported a vaulted ceiling, and quite conceivably a pyramidal roof. This, along with the discovery nearby of architectural fragments such as decorative Doric friezes, has led to speculation that the monumental building may in fact be Herod's funerary monument. If this is the case, the artificial course may well be a special funerary path. Along part of its south side stands the remains of a large **palace (h)**. Three **Byzantine churches (i) (j) (k)** have also been excavated in Lower Herodium. ■ *Saturday-Thursday 0800-1700, Friday 0800-1600, closes one hour earlier in winter. Palace-fortress 17 NIS, student 14 NIS, entrance to Lower Herodium free. Toilets at car park.*

Chariton   This little visited monastery was founded in the mid-fourth century CE by the monk **Chariton** and, despite considerable hardship and persistent attacks, monks continued to occupy the monastery until the Crusader period, possibly finally abandoning it in the Mamluk period. About 1.5 kilometres to the south of the monastery, beyond the 'Ein en-Natuf spring, is a small opening in the cliff face some 15 metres above ground level known as the **Hanging Cave of Chariton**. Decorations on the cave's walls suggest that it could indeed be Chariton's cave, occupied in later years by another monk, Cyriac of Corinth (449-557 CE). Precious little remains of the monastery itself.

Ins and outs There's no public transport to here. To reach the site, continue along the road past the Herodium for 2km until it crosses the deep ravine of the Wadi Khureitun (Nahal Tekoa). A walking path along the west side of the wadi heads south, passing a number of prehistoric caves before arriving at the ruins of the Chariton Monastery (3km).

Mar Saba Monastery   Few of the Byzantine desert monasteries can match **Mar Saba** as a spot for solitude and quiet contemplation in a stark and austere landscape. Located some 15 kilometres east of Bethlehem, the monastic complex here clings to the cliff-face of the Kidron Valley, sprawling down from top to bottom and stretching along either side of the ravine for some two kilometres.

The monastery is named after **Saint Sabas** (439-532 CE), who settled in a cave on the opposite side of the valley from the present main complex (look for the cave with the cross and letters 'A' and 'C') around 478 CE. Such was his

Monasteries, laurae, coenobium, anchorites and archimandrites

From the fourth century CE onwards, monasticism spread throughout Palestine, with monasteries being established close to holy places generally connected with the life of Jesus. However, the monasteries that developed in more isolated environs, most notably in the Judean Desert, were rather different in character. These desert monasteries can be divided into two types, the laura and the coenobium, according to a number of factors such as the type of life practised there and the plan and architecture of the complex. Most, however, began with the decision of a single hermit to withdraw from the world (usually to a cave with water close by), with other monks perhaps joining at a later stage and thus forming a community. Whether the community became a laura or a coenobium was generally a decision of the founding hermit (**archimandrite**).

The laura was a monastery for an **anchorite** community (a term used to describe religious hermits), with monks living in solitude in individual cells but meeting for communal meals and prayers perhaps once per week. The laura comprised a series of dispersed cells connected to each other or a central building by a path. In a **coenobium** the monks tended to meet on a daily basis for prayers and meals, whilst the various monastic buildings (often including a hostel for visitors, a sick-bay, church, storerooms and workshops) were enclosed within a wall.

Mar Saba is a particularly fine example of a Byzantine period Judean Desert monastic complex since it appears that it gradually evolved from a laura into a coenobium, though the original individual cell of its founder can still be seen.

West Bank

fame that his period of seclusion lasted just five years, and by 483 CE so many other anchorites had sought to settle close to him that a *de facto* monastic community had come into being. By 486 CE as many as 70 monks were living here. Within the next 20 years the community doubled in size and two churches were built and dedicated. From 494 CE he was recognized as the archimandrite of Palestine's anchorite community (see box).

The monks here suffered greatly during the Persian invasion of 614 CE, yet despite repeated attacks throughout the Early Arab period (638-1099 CE) the laura reached its golden age during the eighth and ninth centuries CE. Mar Saba had a reputation during this period as a centre of scholarly and literary activity.

The core of the laura is still inhabited, though Mar Saba is now a coenobium covering an area some 60 metres by 100 metres. Many of the buildings are relatively recent, following the destructive earthquake of 1834. The **body of Saint Sabas** can be seen in the principal church, whilst his tomb is in the paved courtyard outside. The **chapel of St Nicholas** marks the site of the first church founded here by St Sabas. If it is open, it is possible to enter the 18-metre-high **Tower of St Simeon** (built c. 1612). The tower is sometimes referred to as Justinian's Tower, though the inscription dating it to 529 CE in the reign of the emperor Justinian is a forgery. Women are allowed to enter this tower, plus the **Women's Tower** (c. 1605) built outside the monastery walls, but not the rest of the complex. Be sure to drop down into the Kidron Valley and climb the other side for a memorable view of Mar Saba Monastery. ■ *Daily 0700-1100 1330-1700, though Sundays and meal times are a bad time to call. Free, but donations expected. Modest dress is essential.*

Ins and outs The easiest way to get here is to hire a taxi from Bethlehem (around 90 NIS for the return trip and waiting time, after serious bargaining). Make sure it is clear how long waiting time will be; you will need a couple of hours here if you wish to cross the ravine to get the best view. Public transport is difficult. Bus 60 from Bethlehem goes as far as the Arab village of Ubeidiya. From here it is a 7-8km walk (1½-2 hr walk). Take the left fork after 1km or so. The last bus back to Bethlehem from Ubeidiya is around 1600, though you should allow longer for the return trip because of the uphill climb from the monastery.

St Theodosius' Monastery The road from Bethlehem to Ubeidiya (for Mar Saba Monastery) passes St Theodosius' Monastery. Founded by St Theodosius in the late fifth to early sixth century, it stands above the reputed site where the Magi (three wise men) rested on their way back from visiting the infant Jesus at Bethlehem. By the time of the founder's death in 529 CE there were said to be some 400 monks living at the monastery, though many of the residents here were massacred during the Persian invasion of 614 CE. The monastery (also known by the Arabic name of Deir Dosi) was largely restored in 1893, but visitors are rarely admitted. ■ *Monday-Saturday 0800-1100.*

Hyrcania (Khirbet el-Mird) A remote Hasmonean period fortress in the Judean Desert hills, **Hyrcania** is not the best preserved archaeological site in the area, nor the easiest to get to. Yet the setting is extraordinary and makes the considerable effort attached to getting here all the more worthwhile.

It was probably first built by John Hyrcanus (134-104 BCE), and was used as a treasure house by his daughter-in-law Alexandra Salome (76-67 BCE). Having been rebuilt by Herod in 31 BCE, it became infamous as a place of imprisonment, internal exile and execution. One of Herod's last victims to be buried here was his own son Antipater, just days before his own death, and it is speculated that Antipater's grave may be amongst those in the plain below the fortress (identifiable by the stone circles in the square enclosure). It was abandoned after Herod's death (its isolation making it of little strategic value), with the ruins being reoccupied by monks in the Byzantine period. St Sabas built a coenobium here in 492 CE, calling it Castellion, with the site not being abandoned until the 14th century (though an ultimately futile attempt was made to reoccupy the monastery between 1923-39).

Remains on the hill are from the Herodian, Byzantine and early 20th century CE periods of occupation, though a detailed site description is not really necessary; better to admire the view and feeling of solitude.

Ins and outs There is no public transport to the site. Continue along the road from Mar Saba as far as you can. It is then a matter of parking in the lot on the south shoulder of the 524-metre-high Jebel Muntar, before following the path to the cistern known as Bir el-Amarah. From there, black trail markings lead you along the course of a wadi, until you begin to follow the course of an ancient aqueduct. Eventually you see the ruins on the summit of the hill to the north (1½ hrs walk from the parking spot). Entrance is via the path to the northwest. In theory it is also possible to reach Hyrcania on the track that leads south from Nebi Musa, though how safe or practical that is cannot be ascertained.

Bethlehem to Hebron

Solomon's Pools and Artas The erroneously named **Solomon's Pools** are the closest perennial springs to Jerusalem at an altitude above that of the city, and have provided one of the oldest and most reliable supplies of water. A low-level aqueduct taking water from here to Jerusalem dates at least to the time of Herod the Great (first century BCE), sections of which can be seen here and around the 'Sultan's Pool' in Jerusalem (see page 181). A second, higher aqueduct was built in the late second century CE by the Romans to bring water to Jerusalem; parts of the great stone pipe of which can be seen some 400 metres south of Rachel's Tomb. The entire aqueduct system is a remarkable technical achievement, dropping as it does only one metre every kilometre. In later years this water-supply system was repaired by the Mamluks, then refurbished by the Ottomans, who built the fort here to defend the pools. The British also exploited the water from Solomon's Pools, and they continued to supply Jerusalem until well into the 20th century.

The **Ein Salah** spring in the nearby village of **Artas** (two kilometres away) fed the aqueduct that Herod built to supply the Herodium, though a Crusader period tradition has associated this village with the "enclosed garden of Solomon" from the *Song of Songs*. Such biblical traditions associated with Artas saw several Europeans, including a son of Queen Victoria, buy land in and around the village. In 1894 the Italian Order of the Sisters of Mary of the Garden built the **Hortus Conclusus Convent** in Artas.

Ins and outs The pools are about 5km southwest of Bethlehem, just east of Route 60. To get there, take Minibus 1 from Bethlehem to the nearby Arab village of Dashit. There is a small café (*King Solomon's Gardens*) at the pools, and an amphitheatre has recently been completed. One of the best ways to appreciate the Artas area is on a tour organized by the *Bethlehem Artas Folklore Centre*, T02-2744046. They can also fill you in on the annual Artas Lettuce Festival (April).

West Bank

Located almost at the mid-point between Bethlehem and Hebron are the Jewish settlements of Kfar Etzion and the Gush Etzion bloc (including Efrat and Alon Shevut). The kibbutz at Kfar Etzion was established in 1942, and some six years later formed the "southernmost anchor" (Collins and Lapierre, 1972) of Jerusalem's defences during Israel's independence war. After repeated attacks the kibbutz and its satellite settlements fell to the Arab forces, and there is considerable evidence to suggest that many of the Jews here were murdered by the Arab irregular forces after having surrendered (supposedly in revenge for a similar massacre at Deir Yassin, see page 781).

Kfar Etzion and Gush Etzion bloc

Following the Six Day War of 1967, the kibbutz at Kfar Etzion was resurrected, with many of those settling there being the descendants of those who had died defending it in 1948. A small museum at Kfar Etzion tells the story of the 1948 battles for the kibbutz, plus the history of Jewish settlement in the area. There is also a *Youth Hostel* here (T9935133). ■ *T02-9935160. Sunday-Thursday 0830-1230, Friday 0830-1100. 5 NIS. Prior appointment should be made. Kfar Etzion is best reached from Jerusalem on Egged Bus 160.*

The small attractive Arab village of Halhoul is the traditional site of the tombs of **Nathan the prophet** and **Gad the seer** (*I Chronicles 29:29*). They are located off to the left (east) of the ancient well at the north entrance to the village.

Halhoul

The site of **Mamre** (Arabic:*Ramat el-Khalil*) lies approximately half-way between Halhoul and Hebron, just off the present main Jerusalem–Hebron road (and on the ancient Jerusalem–Hebron road). The Bible describes Elonei (oaks of) Mamre as the place where **Abraham** dwelt in his tent and built an altar to God (*Genesis 13:18*), and where he received three men, and pleaded with God for the salvation of Sodom (*Genesis 18:1-33*). The site was traditionally marked by an oak tree, though in some sources a terebinth is mentioned. **NB** There is an alternative site in Hebron (see page 262).

Mamre (Ramat el-Khalil)

There is little to see here within the enclosure wall (probably Herodian, though doubts remain), other than a **pagan altar** (dating to the period after the destruction of the Second Temple when the site became a pagan cultic centre and the scene of an annual fair closely associated with idolatry), plus the **narthex, nave, aisles, prothesis and diakonikon** of a Christian basilica that Constantine founded here c. 325 CE in a (futile) attempt to supplant the pagan practices (though it is suggested that much of what you see is a later Crusader adaptation of the original Byzantine church). Tradition suggests that the **well** in the southwest corner was hand-dug by Abraham, though it almost certainly dates to the same period as the enclosure wall.

Hebron (al-Khalil)

Phone code: 02
Colour map 2, grid C4

The City of the Patriarchs, Hebron is the burial-place of Abraham, Isaac and Jacob, and consequently sacred to Jews, Muslims and Christians alike. Built on a series of hills and wadi beds in the Judean Hills, the modern city of Hebron is also home to a Jewish community of some 45 families (350 people) and 150 yeshiva students living amongst a Palestinian population of 120,000 mainly Muslim Arabs. Around 1,000 Israeli soldiers and 400 Palestinian policemen attempt, with limited success, to keep the two communities apart. In many ways Hebron can be seen as a microcosm of the Israeli-Palestinian conflict, and after Jerusalem, is perhaps the biggest potential flashpoint between the two sides.

Ins and outs

Getting there Hebron is best reached by a service taxi from Jerusalem's Damascus Gate (9 NIS, 30 mins), which drops passengers close to the centre of town (see map). Alternatively, take Egged Bus 160 from outside Jerusalem's Central Bus Station to the nearby Jewish settlement of Kiryat Arba, from where it's a 20-min walk to central Hebron. From Hebron there are service taxis to Ramallah (2 hrs, change here for destinations further north), Bethlehem, and sometimes south to es-Samu' (see page 263).

Getting around Central Hebron is extremely compact, and easily tackled on foot. Note that certain roads are sometimes closed off. You should carry your passport with you at all times (you may well be asked to show it at various roadblocks).

Getting out It goes without saying that Hebron is one of the most fascinating cities in the Holy Land and a visit is highly recommended. However, there are several factors that should be borne in mind. Acts of seemingly random violence are perpetrated by both Arabs and Jews, often in the crowded market area. It may be as well to take advice from embassies, tourist offices, journalists and other travellers before visiting Hebron. Expressing pro-Israeli views in the Arab areas is not recommended. Though it is not necessary to dress in a Hawaiian shirt and check trousers, it is useful to look like a tourist and not an Israeli when wandering around town. Likewise, fraternizing with Israeli soldiers and Jewish settlers may not be a good idea for the casual visitor. Any problems that you encounter should be reported to the (generally Norwegian) Temporary International Presence in Hebron (TIPH) representatives (wandering around town with TIPH armbands). As with all other West Bank towns, men and women should dress conservatively.

History

According to the Bible, it was at Hebron that **Abraham**, the progenitor of the Jewish people, first bought land in *Eretz Yisrael* (*Genesis 23*). Johnson, in his acclaimed study *A History of the Jews* (1987), suggests that this "is where the

4,000-year history of the Jews, in so far as it can be anchored in time and place, began". Indeed, the purchase by Abraham of the **Cave of Machpelah** as a burial place for his wife Sarah and ultimately himself is probably the first actual, witnessed event in the Bible.

Abraham was buried in the Cave of Machpelah alongside Sarah, as were Isaac and his wife Rebecca, and Jacob and Leah (*Genesis 49:30-31; 50:13*). With so many important events in Jewish history having taken place here (*II Samuel 2:1-4; II Samuel 5:1-3; Samuel 15:7-12*), it is little wonder that Jews have such a spiritual and physical attachment to Hebron. Ironically, some of the antagonism between Muslims and Jews in Hebron is derived from the common origins of their faith: Hebron is holy to Muslims because Abraham (Ibrahim) is regarded in the Qur'an as "the first Muslim". Indeed in Arabic, Hebron is referred to as 'Al-Khalil' (the friend) in honour of Ibrahim's closeness to God.

The original City of the Patriarchs largely occupied the low spur of the hill referred to now as Jebel Rumeida (or **Tel Hebron**, sometimes erroneously referred to as Tell Rumeida). Excavations have revealed evidence of occupation from around 3300 BCE, through the period of Abraham's land purchase (c. 1650 BCE), through to around 586 BCE (though there is little to see today). The focus of the city subsequently shifted to a new site on the valley floor at the foot of Jebel Rumeida, largely on the site of the present city.

Following the destruction of the Temple in 70 CE, Jews were banned from living in Hebron. The date of the Jewish return to Hebron is unclear, though Eusebius' *Onomasticon* (written before 340 CE) describes Hebron as a "large Jewish village". It is also clear that both Christian and Jewish pilgrims were visiting Hebron in the Byzantine period, whilst the superb Herodian enclosure built around the Cave of Machpelah now incorporated a Christian basilica.

The bishop Arculf (who visited c. 680 CE) describes a half-ruined town, though the Tomb of the Patriarchs/Cave of Machpelah complex remained undamaged; it subsequently became the Ibrahimi Mosque, and is now referred to in all Muslim sources as the Haram el-Khalil. Jews continued to settle in Hebron and pray at the Cave of Machpelah, but were then banned from the town by the Crusaders before being permitted to return under the Mamluks (though in 1266 they were banned by ordinance from entering the cave to pray). In 1588 the Jewish population suffered a massacre at the hands of the Ottoman Turks.

Recent events

Twentieth-century Hebron has seen a depressing cycle of violence resulting from competing Jewish and Muslim, Israeli and Palestinian, claims to the holy city. A word that visitors to Hebron will repeatedly hear is *tarpat*. It is not a word as such, but the Hebrew name for the Jewish year 5689. In the Gregorian calendar this is the year **1929**; the year of the Arab riots all across British Mandate Palestine, and the year in which 67 members of the Jewish community of Hebron were massacred by their Muslim neighbours. What made this attack all the more despicable was that the majority of the victims were the old and defenceless, women and children. The Arab revolt of 1936 saw the British authorities evacuate the remaining Jewish population of Hebron.

The importance of the 1929 massacre in the minds of the present Jewish community in Hebron is summed up by a recent article by Herb Keinon in the *Jerusalem Post*: "More often than not, Hebron's Jews say they moved there fuelled by a desire not to give Hebron's Arabs a prize for the massacre of 1929. For the Jews living in Hebron today, 1929 is as real as yesterday, and to move back into Hebron is to redeem those who were massacred. To now pull out is in their minds equivalent to saying the victims of 1929 died for nothing".

West Bank

Indeed, a large sign on a Jewish property next to Hebron's central casbah reads "This market was built on Jewish property, stolen by Arabs, after the 1929 massacre" (see Casbah in 'Sights' on page 261).

Following Israel's victory in the Six Day War of 1967, Hebron, by now a wholly Arab town, came under Israeli control. Out of sensitivity to Muslim wishes, however, the Israeli military were under strict instructions not to allow Jewish settlement in Hebron. On 12th April 1968, **Rabbi Moshe Levinger** led 32 Jewish families into the Park Hotel in downtown Hebron and rented all 40 rooms from its owner. The original rental period was for 10 days, ostensibly to celebrate Passover, though there was an agreement between Levinger and the owner that the lease could be extended indefinitely: "Until the Messiah comes", Levinger is said to have muttered under his breath in Hebrew, according to the journalist Robert I. Friedman (*Zealots for Zion*, 1992). The incident is said to have deeply embarrassed the Israeli government, though the truth of the matter is that Levinger's plan was perhaps the worst kept secret in Israel. A month later the cabinet voted to allow the community to remain in Hebron, subsequently moving them into a military compound. After some bitter negotiations the Israeli government eventually established (in 1970) the new Jewish settlement of **Kiryat Arba** (see page 262) on the slopes overlooking Hebron.

In March 1979 Levinger's wife Miriam led a group of 40 women and children down from Kiryat Arba and occupied the old derelict Jewish health clinic in Hebron (Beit Hadassah, see page 261), thus reestablishing a Jewish presence in the city proper. They have remained ever since.

As Lawrence Joffe observes, "Small though their numbers may be, the Jews of Hebron tend to be amongst the most radical of the Israeli religious right-wing. Likewise, Hebron is the main West Bank centre for the Islamic fundamentalist *Hamas* movement. Not surprisingly, many Israelis and Palestinians fear that Hebron is a powder keg which could explode and destroy the fragile peace process" (*Keesing's Guide to the Middle-East Peace Process*, 1996).

Hebron

To Jerusalem & Bethlehem

To Jerusalem

✝ Russian Church

KIRYAT ARBA

∴ Masqobiya

University Graduates Union

PA Headquarters

Hebron Hotel

Malik Abdallah

Hebron Municipality

Fire Station

∴ Abraham's Oak

Es-Salam

Malik Hussein

Fruit & Veg Market

Palestine Red Crescent

al-Saba

Wadi el-Jadid

Service Taxis to Jerusalem

Ali Baka Mosque

Nasr ed-Din

Service Taxis to Ramallah

Omar ben Alkhattab

CASBAH

Beit Hadassah

Avraham Avinu Complex

Haram el-Khalil/ Cave of Machpelah

Cemetery

Shavei Hebron Yeshiva

al-Shahada

Gutnick Centre

Al-Khalil er-Rahman

RUMEIDA (TEL HEBRON)

★ Birket el-Sultan

N

0 metres   500

To es-Samu (Eshtemoa)

One such attempt to derail the peace process was the attack by a Kiryat Arba resident, Dr Baruch Goldstein, on Muslim worshippers at the Ibrahim Mosque in February 1994. Twenty-nine were murdered and scores injured when Goldstein, wearing his IDF uniform and carrying his IDF-issued gun, opened fire on Muslim worshippers as they prayed. A further 30 Palestinians were killed by Israeli soldiers following the demonstrations across the country that Goldstein's act triggered. To the Israeli religious right Goldstein is a hero (his grave in Kiryat Arba mentions a "martyr" who died "sanctifying God's name") whilst Hebron's Jews dismiss comparisons between the massacres of 1929 and 1994, stating that the massacre of Jews was perpetrated by the Arab masses rather than one individual.

The long delayed Israeli redeployment in Hebron that was a condition of the Oslo Accords eventually took place in 1997 after a long and tense period of uncertainty. Hebron is now divided into **H1**, under Palestinian Authority control, and the Israeli controlled **H2** enclave at the centre of the town.

Sights

The central focus of Hebron is the complex built around the traditional burial place of Abraham, Sarah, Isaac, Rebecca, Jacob, Leah and Joseph (the latter to Muslims only, with Jews believing that he is buried in Shechem, see 'Nablus' on page 290). There is also a tradition that Adam and Eve are buried here. In Jewish sources it referred to as the **Cave of Machpelah** or **Tomb of the Patriarchs**, whilst Muslims refer to it as **Haram el-Khalil** or **Ibrahimi Mosque**. Both faiths rank the site second only to the Western Wall and Dome of the Rock respectively as a sacred site in the Holy Land.

(margin note: Cave of Machpelah/ Haram el-Khalil)

(margin note: West Bank)

The architectural highlight is the superb enclosure wall that Herod the Great built around the Cave of Machpelah in the first century BCE. The workmanship is excellent, with the surface of the exterior wall neatly broken up by the pilasters. The two minarets were added in the 12th century CE by Salah al-Din, though there were originally four. The top section of the exterior wall is later still, though as Murphy-O'Connor observes, "Oblivion is too kind a fate for the unknown responsible for the crenellated monstrosity that still disfigures the summit of the Herodian wall" (*The Holy Land*, 1993). It is difficult not to think of a medieval citadel when you first see the Haram el-Khalil/Cave of Machpelah.

From the 13th century CE onwards Muslims forbade Jews from worshipping at the Cave of Machpelah; they were limited to praying on the steps outside. The Israeli victory of 1967 saw a compromise worked out that meant the complex would remain within Muslim hands, but would allow Jews free and easy access. This all changed following Goldstein's shooting spree in 1994, and now the shrine is divided into Jewish and Muslim sections with two separate entrances. Security is obviously very tight, and you may well be searched two or three times before you are allowed inside. Make sure that you are carrying your passport. **Modest dress is essential**.

Muslim section The Muslim entrance is via the **Mamluk period staircase (1)** on the west side of the Haram el-Khalil. ■ *Sunday-Thursday 0700-1900, Saturday 1130-1900, no non-Muslims on Friday*. Your attention is drawn to the fine Herodian blocks adjacent to the staircase, some of which still have the projecting knobs that protected them on their journey from the quarry to the wall. At the top of the staircase, on the north side of the Herodian enclosure, is the **Djaouliyeh mosque**, built c. 1318-20 (**NB** women can remain in the corridor but not enter the body of the Djaouliyeh mosque itself). The Muslim section is entered through a break in the Herodian wall (2). This passage is of uncertain date, though it was cut before 918 CE. Within the enclosure to the right (west) partitions (**3**) (and armed soldiers) divide the Muslim and Jewish sections. A small window grille straight ahead allows you to peer into the **tomb of Sarah (4)**.

Entering the Muslim main prayer hall (**5**) it is easy to see the Mamluk influence in the use of coloured inlaid marble. The hall has changed hands and hence form through the centuries, revealing Byzantine, Crusader and Mamluk influence. The cenotaphs marking the **tomb of Rebecca (6)** and the **tomb of Isaac (7)** date to the the visit in 1332 of Tankiz, Mamluk viceroy of Syria, though like all the other cenotaphs here they are merely symbolic, with the true burial place being somewhere in the caves below. Tankiz was also responsible for much of the decorative marble work on the walls. To the right of the **mihrab (8)** is the beautifully carved **minbar (9)**, or pulpit. It was originally carved c. 1091 for a mosque in Ashqelon though it was brought here in 1191 by Salah al-Din. Following the destruction in 1969 of a similar minbar in Jerusalem's al-Aqsa mosque, this is the finest period piece in the country. Close to the minbar is the **medieval entrance (10)** to the cave complex beneath the Haram el-Khalil. The first recorded exploration of the original Cave of Machpelah was made by the Augustinian Canons in 1119. They were lowered down via a rope from this spot, though a staircase was later built. They described a Herodian passage leading to a circular chamber, from which a door opened out into a large cavern. A further doorway gave access to a square rock-cut tomb chamber. A more recent clandestine Israeli investigation described a straight corridor linking the stairs with the tomb chamber. The medieval entrance (**10**) sealed in 1394. A small **cupola (11)** covers an entrance to the rock-cut tomb below.

Haram el-Khalil / Cave of Machpelah

Djaouliyeh Mosque

Jewish Section

Muslim Section

Herodian Enclosure Later Periods

Entrance to Muslim Section

Entrance to Jewish Section

0 metres 10

Staircase

N

1 Mamluk Period Staircase
2 Break in Herodian Wall (Modern Entrance)
3 Partitions
4 Tomb of Sarah

5 Main Muslim Prayer hall
6 Tomb of Rebecca
7 Tomb of Isaac
8 Mihrab
9 Minbar
10 Medieval Entrance to Caves below
11 Cupola

12 Herodian Gutter
13 Women's Mosque
14 Tomb of Abraham
15 Footprint of Adam Shrine
16 Tomb of Joseph
17 Tomb of Leah
18 Tomb of Jacob
19 Synagogue

Though now obscured by carpets, the paved floor is also Herodian. There is a slight slope from east–west terminating in a gutter (**12**), suggesting that the enclosure built by Herod was unroofed. A small chamber of the main hall is now referred to as the Women's Mosque (**13**). A window grille allows you to peer inside the tomb of Abraham (**14**). Like the other tombs it is draped with a richly embroidered cloth, though again the cenotaph is merely symbolic. It almost certainly dates to the ninth century CE. Muslim tradition attributes the footprint (**15**) in the stone to Adam; a result of his persistent praying here. It is marked by a small shrine.

Jewish section   The designated entrance to the Jewish section of the Cave of Machpelah is via the Crusader buttresses adjacent to the original entrance *Sunday-Thursday 0800-1600, closed to non-Jews on Friday, Saturday and Muslim and Jewish holidays*. In the 10th century CE this entrance was blocked by the construction of the tomb of Joseph (**16**), with the cut in the Herodian wall (**2**) providing the new access point. The Crusader adaptations to the building retain the façade of the Byzantine church (built after 570 CE), though nothing else of this structure remains. Perhaps the architectural highlight of the Jewish section is the unimpeded view of the Herodian wall and paved floor, with the former attracting scenes similar to those seen at the Western Wall in Jerusalem. The tomb of Leah (**17**) and tomb of Jacob (**18**) both date to the Mamluk period (14th century CE), whilst the cenotaphs marking the symbolic tomb of Abraham (**14**) and tomb of Sarah (**4**) are both ninth century CE. Between the two latter tombs is a small synagogue (**19**) built after 1967.

Jewish Community of Hebron   According to the Israeli Government Press Office, the Jewish population of Hebron is 500 persons, comprising some 45 families and a relay of 150 yeshiva students (many from North America). They are concentrated in a number of buildings and housing complexes in the centre of the city. Nineteen families live in buildings adjacent to the **Avraham Avinu** courtyard, which also includes a synagogue, two kindergartens, the municipal committee offices and a guest house. The synagogue was rededicated in 1981, having been rebuilt and restored according to plans drawn in the 1940s; the Jordanians had razed the building in 1948 and turned it into an open market. Seven families live in mobile homes at Tel Rumeida, whilst twelve families live in Beit Hadassah, the former Jewish clinic. There is supposedly a museum to the 1929 massacre inside the **Beit Hadassah** complex, though a prior appointment is probably necessary (see 'Visit Hebron' below). Six families live in **Beit Schneersohn**, one in **Beit Kastel** and six in **Beit Chason**. **Beit Romano** is home to the Shavei Hebron yeshiva, and is currently being refurbished.

Visit Hebron   Guided tours of the Jewish Community of Hebron (in English) can be booked by calling Moria on T02-9962323 or T050-279002; they leave from the lobby of the *Sheraton Plaza Hotel* in Jerusalem every Monday and Wednesday at 0900 (returning 1600). Alternatively, visit the Hebron Settlers' Website (http://www.virtual.co.il/communities/israel/hebron/). For the Jewish Community of Hebron's viewpoint you can buy their *'Hebron: Past, Present and Forever'* booklet from the Gutnick Centre near to the Cave of Machpelah.

Casbah   The town's main casbah or souq is a typically fascinating Arab bazaar, featuring amongst other things, a number of butcher shops selling camel meat. There is ample opportunity to engage in discussion with local residents about life in Hebron/West Bank, though pro-Israeli views should not be aired and you are recommended to make it clear that you are a tourist and not Jewish or Israeli.

West Bank

Masqobiya and Abraham's Oak	A very dead-looking oak tree on Shariah al-Masqobiya (to the west of the town centre) competes with Mamre (see page 255) for the title of 'Abraham's Oak'. The Russian Orthodox church have a 19th-century monastery here.
Birket el-Sultan	The Birket el-Sultan (Sultan's Pool) is the traditional site where David had the murderers of Saul's last son, Ish-bosheth, executed (*II Samuel 4:7-12*), though there is little to see.

Essentials

Sleeping & eating	Most people visit Hebron as a day trip from Jerusalem, although there is a recently opened hotel: **C–D** *Hebron*, Shahrah Malik al-Faisal (opposite the Municipality), T9926760. Comfortable, recently opened place, friendly but not particularly busy. The stalls around the Casbah sell some of the cheapest falafel in the country, whilst good value grilled chicken, hummus, salad, etc is available at a number of places in the Casbah.
Transport	Car hire: *Holy Land*, T2220811. Taxis: *Al-Isdiqa*, T2229436; *Al-Badawi*, T2228545; *Al-Itihad*, T2228750; *Al-Tahhan*, T2222525.
Directory	**Communications Post office**: on Shahrah Malik al-Faisal. **Cultural centres** *Association* D'Echanges Culturels Hebron-France, T2224811; *Beit Ula Cultural Centre*, T6264089, F6288448; *British Council*, T2224813; *Palestinian Child Arts Centre*, T2220272. **Hospitals & medical services** Chemists: *Al-Hikmah*, T2228254; *Ibn Sina*, T2229649. Hospitals: *Al-Ahli*, T2220212; *Amria Alia*, T2228126; *Mohammad Ali Muhtaseb*, T2220246; Red Crescent Society, T2227450. **Useful addresses & phone numbers** Police: T100. Ambulance: T101 (T2228598). Fire: T222844.

Kiryat Arba

The Jewish settlement of Kiryat Arba, built on a low rise to the north of the Cave of the Machpelah, preserves a biblical name for Hebron: Kiriath-Arba. Meaning literally 'town of the four', it alternatively stands for the four couples who tradition says are buried here (Adam and Eve, Abraham and Sarah, Isaac and Rebecca, Jacob and Leah), or as evidence that the ancient town was divided into four quarters or clans.

The population of Kiryat Arba is around 6,000, with many of its residents followers of the right-wing messianic *Gush Emunim* movement, and the settlement is considered the most militant on the West Bank. Kiryat Arba's most notorious former resident is Baruch Goldstein, the Jewish settler who murdered 29 Muslims at the Haram el-Khalil in 1994. His grave stands at the entrance to the settlement, in a park named after the assassinated founder of the now illegal fascist party *Kach*, Meir Kahane (for an enlightening biography of Kahane see Robert I. Friedman's *The False Prophet: Rabbi Meir Kahane – From FBI Informant to Knesset Member*). Since the massacre, Goldstein's family have laid a tile floor around the grave, put in bookshelves, a wash-basin and lights, whilst the wording on the tomb refers to a "martyr" who died "sanctifying God's name". There have been moves to have the grave shifted to a less prominent spot, though the IDF have already once refused permission for him to be buried in the Jewish cemetery in Hebron.

Ins and outs	Egged Bus 160 runs from the stop outside Jerusalem's Central Bus Station to Kiryat Arba (Sun-Thu every 30 mins 0530-2200, Fri last at 1430, Sat first at 1830).

South of Hebron

From Hebron, Route 60 continues southwest all the way to Be'er Sheva (50 kilometres). At 17 kilometres along this route a road turns southeast to es-Samu' (seven kilometres, take a service taxi from Hebron). This is believed to be the site of the biblical city of **Eshtemoa**; a town in the territory of Judah (*Joshua 15:50*) that was granted to the Levites (*Joshua 21:14; I Chronicles 6:42*). The Bible recalls how David sent part of the spoils of his campaign against the Amalekites to the elders of Eshtemoa (*I Samuel 30:26-28*), whilst excavations at the site in 1968 revealed a hoard containing 26 kilogrammes of silver. Unfortunately, the dates do not quite match. A large synagogue, complete with mosaic floor and walls preserved in places to seven metres, has been excavated, with tentative dating suggesting that it was in use around the fourth to fifth centuries CE. The present Palestinian village is famed for its carpets.

Es-Samu'/Eshtemoa

Located approximately five kilometres east of es-Samu' is a site known by the Arabic name of **Khirbet Susiya**. Identification is not certain, though this may be the biblical town of **Carmel** in the territory of Judah (*Joshua 15:55*) that was the birthplace of one of David's mighty men (*II Samuel 23:24*). There are a number of remains at the site, the best preserved of which is the **synagogue** founded in the third or fourth century CE that continued in use until the eighth or ninth century CE when it was replaced by a mosque.

Kirbet Susiya

West Bank

East of Jerusalem

*Travelling east from Jerusalem the drive along Route 1 to **Jericho** is only 40 kilometres long, yet it is a spectacular one. The landscape becomes increasingly barren and austere as the road rapidly drops down to the Jordan Valley via the Judean Desert. Amos Elon suggests that a "traveller with a historical bent might be forgiven if he or she insisted on approaching Jerusalem from the desert in the east. The early Hebrews came in this way – from the desert to the sown – after their crossing of the Jordan; and the Romans and Arabs after them. It is the most*

East of Jerusalem

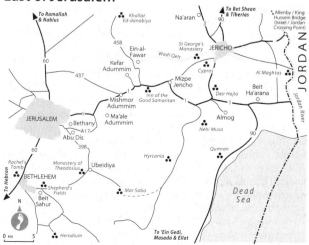

spectacular route. The stage is set. The colour is switched on. The hills suddenly part like curtains. The drama of the scene, like a trumpet blast in Fidelio, is enhanced by its suddenness" (Jerusalem: City of Mirrors, 1989).

There are a number of notable sights along this route, including a rewarding hike, though some spots are only accessible if you have your own transport.

Bethany (al-Azariyya)

Phone code: 02
Colour map 2, grid B4

Bethany is generally associated with the village in which Jesus' friends Martha, Mary and Lazarus lived (Mark 10:38-42), with whom Jesus and the Disciples usually stayed when visiting Jerusalem. It was to this village that Jesus returned after his triumphant entry into Jerusalem (Mark 11:11-12), and also the home of Simon the Leper, where Jesus was anointed by Mary (Matthew 26:6-13; Mark 14:3-9; John 12:1-9). But perhaps the best known gospel scene associated with Bethany is Jesus' raising of Lazarus from the dead (John 11:1-44). A number of religious buildings in the village commemorate these events.

Ins and outs

Getting there The village of Bethany lies on the lower east flanks of the Mount of Olives. Most visitors come to Bethany as part of a brief stop on a longer tour (such as to Jericho or the Dead Sea). However, it is very easy to visit independently. Bethany can be reached by walking down from Bethphage on the Mount of Olives. **NB** This walk is not recommended for unaccompanied females. Buses to Bethany (ask for the Arabic name, 'al-Azariyya') run from the Suleiman St Arab bus station opposite Damascus Gate. However, Jericho-bound service-taxis can drop you here, and can easily be flagged down for the return trip.

History

Bethany was known to early Christians (for example, Eusebius, c. 330 CE) by its Greek name *Lazarion*, 'place of Lazarus'; a name that was also used by Byzantine and medieval pilgrims. This name is also preserved in the Arabic name in common usage today, '**al-Azariyya**'.

Christians appear to have venerated this site from an early stage, with Egeria (384 CE) describing a service held at the 'Lazarium' (tomb of Lazarus and guest room of Mary and Martha) commencing the Easter service. Egeria's mention of the large numbers gathered here, who "fill not only the Lazarium itself, but all the fields around", may have inspired the construction of the first church here.

The church/Lazarium appears to have been destroyed in an earthquake, and was subsequently replaced by a new church in the fifth century CE. The Byzantine church was refurbished by the Crusaders, and a completely new church built over the tomb of Lazarus. This almost certainly served as the chapel for the vast new Benedictine convent that the Crusader Queen Melisande built adjacent to the tomb in 1138-43. Though this was to become one of the richest convents in the Crusader kingdom, it was abandoned following the Crusader surrender of Jerusalem in 1187, and by all accounts the whole complex was lying in ruins by the 14th century. The tradition of the raising of Lazarus appears to have been revived in the 15th century, and in the 16th century the Muslims built the Mosque of al-'Uzair above the forecourt of the Byzantine church, adjoining the tomb (since Islam also venerates the raising of Lazarus). Between 1566-75 the Franciscans cut the present stepped entrance to the tomb so that Christians could also have access. The

West Bank

Bethany

To Bethphage

Coach Parking

To Jericho

B E T H A N Y   *To Abu Dis, Jerusalem*

N

0 m   50

1 Franciscan Church
2 12th-century Benedictine Convent
3 Mosque of al-'Uzair
4 Tomb of Lazarus
5 Greek Orthodox Church & Convent
6 Crusader Tower
7 'Oldest House in Bethany'

present Franciscan Church was completed in 1954 whilst the Greek Orthodox Church is a little over 10 years younger.

Sights

Franciscan Church

The **Franciscan Church (1)** is one of a number of churches in the Holy Land designed by the Italian architect Antonio Barluzzi. It is cruciform in shape, and features a mosaic depicting Martha, Mary and Lazarus on the façade. The apse of the **fourth-century church (2)** can be seen beneath trapdoors immediately inside the modern entrance. Further grilles and trapdoors reveal mosaics from the fourth-century church, whilst clearly defined in white marble close to the modern east altar is the apse of the **fifth-century church (3)**. Masonry from the fourth-century church can be seen in the courtyard outside the **modern church (4)**, plus piers from the fifth-century church **(5)** and masonry from the **fifth-century façade (6)**. To the south are some Crusader remains relating to the **Benedictine convent (7) (8)**. Return to the street by the stairs **(9)**. ■ *T6749291. 0800-1125 1400-1700, closes one hour earlier in winter.*

Mosque of al-'Uzair

The 16th-century **mosque (12)** is not generally open to non-Muslims. The **courtyard** of the mosque **(11)** occupies what previously had been the atrium of the fourth- and fifth-century churches. An earlier (though not necessarily the original) entrance to the tomb of Lazarus can be seen in the **west wall** of the mosque **(13)**. Opposite the mosque is what is billed as the "oldest house in Bethany" (visitors welcome for a 'donation').

Tomb of Lazarus

The current entrance to the **tomb of Lazarus (14)**, via 26 steep, rock-hewn **steps (15)** cut by the Franciscans in the 16th century, is through a small doorway a little further up the street. The owners of the shop opposite hold the key, and generally ask for 2 NIS to unlock the tomb. At the bottom of the shaft, further

West Bank

Church, Mosque & Tomb of Lazarus, Bethany

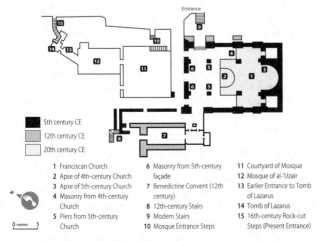

Entrance

5th century CE
12th century CE
20th century CE

0 metres   5

1 Franciscan Church
2 Apse of 4th-century Church
3 Apse of 5th-century Church
4 Masonry from 4th-century Church
5 Piers from 5th-century Church
6 Masonry from 5th-century façade
7 Benedictine Convent (12th century)
8 12th-century Stairs
9 Modern Stairs
10 Mosque Entrance Steps
11 Courtyard of Mosque
12 Mosque of al-'Uzair
13 Earlier Entrance to Tomb of Lazarus
14 Tomb of Lazarus
15 16th-century Rock-cut Steps (Present Entrance)

steps lead under a low slab into a small antechamber. You have to be something of a contortionist to get in here, and visitors should also note that getting stuck in here with a tour group is a real nightmare. Visitors should note that next to none of the original rock-cut walls of the tomb are visible (they are obscured by Crusader masonry) and the floor level of the tomb has probably been raised substantially. Thus, what you are really seeing is a Crusader-built chamber.

Greek Orthodox Church and Convent   The Greek Orthodox complex incorporates part of the Crusader chapel built over the tomb of Lazarus. Behind the church are the remains of a **Crusader tower** (14.6 metres by 14.8 metres) that was part of the 12th-century convent.

Ma'ale Adummim

Phone code: 02
Colour map 2, grid B5

This new Jewish settlement is named after the biblical Ma'ale Adummim, or 'ascent of the red rocks', that provided a pass leading up to Jerusalem from Jericho on the border of the tribes of Benjamin and Judah (Joshua 15:7). The settlement is a rather striking sight, modern white apartments perched on a high, reddish hill above the Judean wilderness, though not necessarily an attractive one. It is planned to extend Ma'ale Adummim to house around 35,000 people, acting as a Jewish overspill from Jerusalem.

*Incongruously located in the heart of Ma'ale Adummim's residential centre is the large Byzantine **Martyrius Monastery**, described by Murphy-O'Connor as "an elevated island of rock in the midst of graceless urban development" (The Holy Land, 1992).*

Ins and outs

Getting there and around   This settlement is about eight kilometres east of Jerusalem along Route 1. Bus 174 goes to Ma'ale Adummim from Jerusalem. Note that in addition to the Jerusalem–Jericho road, there is an 'Israeli' road linking the town to the Jewish northern suburbs of Jerusalem. For those arriving along the Jerusalem–Jericho road (Route 1) there is a street plan of Ma'ale Adummim at the entrance to the town. The monastery is referred to as 'Archaeological Site' on the map, and is reached by following such signs along Hagai Road.

Sights

Martyrius Monastery   The Martyrius Monastery (Arabic: *Khirbet Murasas*) was established by **Martyrius the Cappadocian** in the fifth century CE, though founding such an extensive monastic complex does not appear to have been the monk's original intention when he settled here. He arrived in the Holy Land from Egypt in 457 CE, settling at the laura of St Euthymius some four kilometres to the east. However, it appears that he found that laura too overcrowded, and thus retreated to a cave that has been identified here. He subsequently founded the monastery that bears his name, though during this early phase it was not particularly large and was certainly not walled. Martyrius was later appointed priest of the Church of Anastasis (The Holy Sepulchre) in Jerusalem, and later patriarch of Jerusalem (478-486 CE); a position that he used to develop the monastery here. The complex was subsequently enlarged to become one of the central monasteries in the Judean Desert.

Martyrius' Monastery reached its peak in the late sixth century CE, under the archimandrite Genesius. A new pilgrim hostel was built outside the monastery walls, the refectory was constructed, alterations were made to the church and a new chapel was added. The monastery was abandoned after the Arab conquest of 636 CE.

Monastery of St Euthymius

A couple of kilometres east of Ma'ale Adummim, Route 1 passes the industrial suburb of **Mishmor Adummim**. Taking the turn-off that leads all the way through the industrial zone, after 1.5 kilometres on the left are the ruins of a monastery (Arabic: *Khan el-Ahmar*).

Born in Lesser Armenia in 377 CE, **Euthymius** became an important figure in Byzantine desert monasticism. Arriving in the Holy Land in 406 CE, he was an early disciple of Chariton before establishing a new laura with Theoctistus in 411 CE. Like many of the charismatic desert anchorites he was something of a victim of his own personality, forced constantly to wander the Judean Desert in search of quiet spots away from the disciples who chose to follow him. He eventually established a new laura here in 428 CE. Such was the success of Euthymius' laura in attracting followers that he left orders that it be transformed into a coenobium upon his death. In 482 CE, nine years after his death, the coenobium was dedicated.

The monastery was severely damaged in the major earthquake of 659 CE, with most of the remains visible today being eighth- or ninth-century CE repairs. The monastery continued to function well into the 12th century CE, when further extensive repairs were carried out. The site was abandoned in the early 13th century CE, though it appears to have been used as a caravanserai by Muslim pilgrims travelling from Jerusalem to Nebi Musa.

The complex is surrounded by a well preserved ashlar wall. The most prominent building is the **church**, built after the earthquake of 659 CE (though largely restored in the 12th century CE). The attractive mosaic floor in the south aisle is dated to the seventh century CE, though the paving work in the nave is 12th century CE. To the north of the church is the **crypt of St Euthymius**. Thirteen steps lead down into the crypt, which featured the main burial chamber of St Euthymius, plus a secondary chamber to the west that revealed the burial troughs of a hundred or so monks.

West Bank

Martyrius Monastery

1 Modern Steps	8 Niche for Rolling Stone	15 Cave
2 Pilgrim Hostel	9 Gate Keeper's Chamber	16 Refectory
3 Chapel	10 Groom's Restroom	17 Kitchen
4 High Wall	11 Stables	18 8th-century CE Farmhouse
5 Northern Gate in E Wall	12 Church	19 Bath House
6 Southern Gate in E Wall	13 Chapel	20 Storeroom
7 Paved Courtyard	14 Burial Hall	21 Chapel

N

0 metres 20

Khallat ed-Danabiya This little visited site is located along Route 458, a turning north off Route 1 (see 'East of Jerusalem' map). Very little is known about the laura complex here, and even an identification with any of the 41 Byzantine desert monasteries known from contemporary literary sources is not possible. However, the series of small cells linked by a network of stairways on the narrow ridge above the deep ravine of the Wadi Makkuk is quite an impressive sight, leading to comparisons with Peru's Machu Picchu! The focus of the laura, presumably founded in the fourth century CE, is a small cave with a natural apse known as the 'cave-church'.

Inn of the Good Samaritan The desire of Christian pilgrims from the Byzantine and Crusader periods to localize every event mentioned in the gospels leads to the often spurious adoption of many places as the traditional site of events in the life of Jesus. It is not entirely certain when this spot first became associated with the story of the Good Samaritan (*Luke 10:30-37*), though the connection has been milked to death ever since, and this remains a popular coach party stop on the Jerusalem–Jericho road. What makes this all the more ridiculous is that Jesus was not recounting an actual event or describing a specific inn, but rather using the inn as a setting for a parable in response to the question "Who is my neighbour?" The building here dates to the Ottoman period and variously served as a caravanserai, police-post, and now tourist trap.

Far more authentic is the old Bedouin bloke just down the road (beyond the Wadi Qelt turning) who poses his camel next to the **sea-level** sign by the road. (**NB** Remember, this is how he makes his living so photos of the camel should be paid for).

On the hill above the Inn of the Good Samaritan (on the north side of the road) lie the unspectacular remains of the Crusader-built **Tour Rouge** fortress, constructed by the Templars to protect pilgrims on the Jerusalem–Jericho road. It stands on the site of the **Maledomni** fortress, built in the early Byzantine period for the same purpose.

Wadi Qelt

Colour map 2, grid B5 *Wadi Qelt is a seasonal stream (Hebrew: Nahal Perat) that drains an area of 180 square kilometres on its course from close to Jerusalem, all the way to the Jordan River to the east of Jericho. Twenty-eight kilometres long, the ravine of the Wadi Qelt forms three distinct stages, each providing a challenging hike. The most popular hike is along the **Lower Wadi Qelt**, taking in **St George's Monastery**, and terminating at the Tulul Abu el-'Alayiq site to the southwest of Jericho. There is also a driving route along the Roman road above the ravine, which provides great views down to the monastery and the opportunity to visit the Herodian fortress of **Cypros**.*

Ins and outs

Getting there The turning for Lower Wadi Qelt is at the major bend in the road just before Route 1 drops down to sea-level after the Inn of the Good Samaritan (look for an orange sign indicating "Nahal Perat", a white sign saying "Mizpe Jericho" and a big brown sign announcing "Al-Wadi Qelt"). To reach this point take a Jericho-bound service taxi from outside Damascus Gate. Make sure that the driver knows that you want to get off at Wadi Qelt (ask for Mizpe Jericho) a little before Jericho (though you may have to pay the full Jericho fare of 8 NIS). Head left towards the cluster of small white buildings until you get to the T-junction. There are two options here. Hikers attempting the

Lower Wadi Qelt hike should turn left (see below for details). The (Roman) road to the right runs parallel to Wadi Qelt, and has a coach park/viewpoint from where there are excellent views down to St George's Monastery (there is also a steep walking path down). This road passes Cypros, continues on to Jericho, and is the route generally taken by tour coaches.

There are several important points that must be remembered before tackling this hike. Do not enter the canyon if rain is forecast since there is very real danger of flash-floods. Take plenty of drinking water since there is none *en route*. There are also a number of security concerns that should be considered before making this hike. Take advice from the tourist office and SPNI in Jerusalem before making the trip. It is almost certainly safe, though it does not hurt to ask around beforehand. Women should certainly not hike here without male companions, and nobody should hike alone. SPNI in Jerusalem offer guided hikes (US$44). This hike takes six to eight hours (about 12 kilometres), depending upon how long your stops are at the various points of interest.

Lower Wadi Qelt hike

Head left (**1**) along the road parallel to the main Jerusalem-Jericho road for about one kilometre towards the group of white buildings. At the T-junction (**2**) turn left (the turning right follows the old Roman road to Jericho).

After a very short distance, opposite a group of ruined buildings (**3**), an unpaved road heads north. As it curves down to the left, a viewpoint (**4**) on the right provides an excellent view across the northern Judean Desert before you. Begin to follow the unpaved road as it drops down, though to make the hike more interesting follow the trail indicated by the small green sign to the left. This leads down via a twisting and turning wadi, and is more scenic than the unpaved road. After some walking you pass through what appears to be a natural rock arch supporting a former aqueduct that was built to supply Cypros (see page 270). Ahead of you is the British built pumping station (**5**) that used to pump water to Jerusalem, but now supplies Jericho. A path and then steps to your left (green-and-white arrows) lead to a bridge across the wadi. Though signs here say no wading or diving, few hikers can resist taking off their shoes and socks and wading up the Ein Qelt canyon. Water flows here via an aqueduct from En Fawar, and though the waterfall (**6**) is man-made this is still a very attractive spot.

Return to the pumping station, then follow the course of the aqueduct eastwards. The red-and-white route climbs upwards, linking with the Central Wadi Qelt hike; ignore these trail-markers and follow the signs along the aqueduct marked "picnic site – circular trail". Beyond the buildings attached to the pumping station are a number of picnic tables set amongst some shady trees. Follow the aqueduct until it crosses a small tributary on a bridge (**7**). There are

Lower Wadi Qelt hike

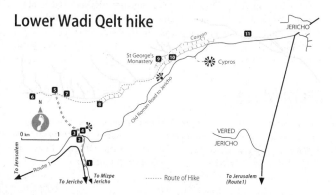

two options here: you can either follow the course of the aqueduct, or better still, drop down into the Wadi Qelt canyon itself. Continuing along the course of Wadi Qelt (red trail markers again), it shortly becomes more and more canyon-like (**8**). Note that there is one reasonably tricky descent shortly after entering the canyon. After about two kilometres scrambling along the canyon, the floor of the wadi becomes increasingly thick with vegetation, and the aqueduct crosses above you to the southern bank. As you round a corner **St George's Monastery** (**9**) comes spectacularly into view (see box on next page).

Beyond the monastery there are a number of options. The least interesting is to return the way you came. The next option is to cross the bridge across the canyon, and climb the path up the cliff to the south side of Wadi Qelt. This path leads to the parking lot and viewpoint (**10**) from which most tour groups view the monastery. From here you can continue east along the Roman road towards Jericho (passing the site of Cypros), or return along the road to the hike's starting point (**2**). Note that it may be difficult to flag down service taxis that are not full from here (whilst it is not recommended that you leave your car unattended here whilst you complete the loop trip).

The most interesting option, however, is to continue along Wadi Qelt to Jericho. Follow the red markers up the steps beyond the monastery, following the path along the north side of the canyon. Eventually the path begins to drop down again, passing the ruins of Tulul Abu el-'Alayiq (**11**) on either side of you. From here it is a fairly unrewarding two-kilometre walk into Jericho.

Cypros   Often described as a 'mini-Masada', most of the building remains here are attributed to Herod the Great, and form one of the Judean Desert **palace-fortresses** that he was so keen on building. Despite having a magnificent palace at Tulul Abu el-'Alayiq just below, it was relatively exposed, and thus it is believed that Cypros (Arabic: *Tell el-'Aqaba*) was built as the nearest citadel in which Herod could take refuge during periods of revolt. It appears that Herod's fear of revolt was only matched by his fear of having to suffer any hardship, and hence the construction of two very fine Roman-style **bathhouses**, one on the summit and one on the lower level. Further finds confirm Josephus' account of a luxurious palace-fortress. The complex takes its name from Herod's mother.

Excavations at the site suggest that the hill was a fortified stronghold in Hasmonean times, and may very well be either one of the two fortresses (**Threx** or **Taurus**) that the Syrian general Baccides built during the Maccabean wars. Strabo recounts their destruction by Pompey in 63 BCE during the Roman invasion. Certainly the round tower on the lower level is pre-Herodian. To build his palace-fortress Herod enlarged the summit by means of packed earth fills supported by retaining walls, whilst the lower level was also built up. Archaeological evidence supports Josephus' account of the palace-fortress' destruction at the beginning of the First Jewish Revolt (66-73 CE), though the picture is confused slightly by the buildings of a group of monks in the Byzantine period (324-638 CE). The square building on the lower level is believed to be a Byzantine period chapel.

Nebi Musa

Colour map 2, grid B5   *This important Muslim shrine has an interesting and colourful history. Situated on one of the old roads up to Jerusalem from the Jordan Valley, tradition has it that Muslim pilgrims on their way to/from Mecca used to stop here to look across the Jordan Valley to **Mt Nebo**, site of Moses' death (Deuteronomy 34:1-7).*

St George's Monastery

Clinging to the side of the Wadi Qelt ravine, this monastery takes its name from St George of Koziba; a monk born in Cyprus c. 550, but who spent much of his life at various lauras in the Judean Desert. The caves in the Wadi Qelt cliffs were originally occupied by anchorites in the early fifth century CE, though it was John of Thebes who transformed the small oratory here into a monastery complex (c. 480 CE). Though the height of the monastery's fame coincided with George of Koziba's period of residence in the late sixth century CE, it is almost certain that St George's Monastery was one of the victims of the Persian invasion of 614 CE. It was restored by the Crusaders in the 12th century, with several new traditions being introduced as well. The story of Elijah hiding in a cave and being fed by ravens during his flight to Sinai is now credited to the Church of the Cave at the upper level, whilst the legend of Joachim weeping over the sterility of his wife Anne, and the angel subsequently announcing to her the impending conception of the Virgin Mary, are both commemorated at churches on the middle level. All these buildings are relatively recent, however. A pilgrim passing in 1483 recalls seeing the entire complex in ruins, and it was not until the Greek Orthodox church's reconstruction programme of 1878-1901 that St George's Monastery took its present form. The large bell-tower was added by Timothy the First in 1952.   Flexible opening hours, officially Monday-Saturday 0800-1300 1500-1700, closes one hour earlier in winter. Donation expected. Modest dress required; women admitted.

Ins and outs

Getting there

Shortly after the turn off for Wadi Qelt along Route 1 (and eight kilometres short of Jericho), a new road branches off to Nebi Musa (look for the orange sign). A bus or service taxi between Jerusalem and Jericho can drop you here, though there is no public transport for the two kilometres to the site. Perhaps the best way to reach Nebi Musa is to hire a Palestinian service taxi ('special') from Jericho. The path heading west from Nebi Musa leads all the way to the Monastery of St Euthymius, though it may not necessarily be safe to follow this route. To the south of Nebi Musa lies Hyrcania (Khirbet el-Mird), though this is included within the 'South of Jerusalem' section.

The shrine

In 1269 CE the Mamluk sultan Baibars built a small shrine to Moses here (Arabic: *Musa*), and in time the shrine came to be venerated as the tomb of Moses himself. The legend was helped by several factors, one of which was the fact that the line in *Deuteronomy* describing Moses' death on Mt Nebo does not claim that he is buried there, instead stating that "no man knows the place of his burial to this day". This site was also convenient in that it was exactly one day's march from Jerusalem on the pilgrimage to Mecca.

Early in the 19th century CE the Ottoman Turks initiated a complete restoration of the shrine, hospice and auxiliary pilgrim-related buildings here, and Nebi Musa then became the venue for a 7-day pilgrimage that coincided with the Christian Holy Week (*mawsim*). The timing of this event was no coincidence, it even being set annually not by the Islamic lunar calendar but by the Christian calendar; to all intents and purposes, it was in competition with the Christian Easter. In later years the week-long festival, which began with a procession from al-Aqsa Mosque in Jerusalem to Nebi Musa, became a focus for political agitation, with tight controls on the event being imposed by the British Mandate authority. The festival was cancelled altogether in the period of Jordanian occupation of the West Bank (1948-67), and following the Yom

Kippur war of 1973 the shrine was used as a military base by the Israelis. The *mawsim* was briefly revived in 1987 but was quickly stopped by the Israelis. It is yet to be seen whether the Palestinian Authority will attempt seriously to revive it. ■ *Daily 0800-sunset. Free, but donations accepted.*

Jericho

Phone code: 02
Colour map 2, grid B5

Located on the wide plain of the Jordan Valley some 40 kilometres east of Jerusalem, Jericho's position at 250 metres below sea-level makes it the lowest town in the world. Jericho's benign winter climate and productive soils made this spot an obvious choice for human settlement, and by general consensus the defensive walls built around this settlement c. 8000 BCE make Jericho the oldest walled city on earth.

Not surprisingly, the area in and around Jericho is rich in archaeological-historical sites from just about every period you care to mention. The modern town of Jericho sprawls somewhat throughout the oasis, though the fact that it is almost entirely low-rise, and there remains plenty of splashes of green, makes it rather attractive in a ramshackle kind of way.

Ins and outs

Getting there Many visitors come to Jericho as part of an organized tour, though it is easy to reach independently. Service taxis from Jerusalem's Damascus Gate will drop you in the main square (Palestine Square), though the return to Jerusalem is a little more complicated (see 'Transport' on page 279).

Getting around With an early start it is possible to see all of Jericho's main attractions in one day, though a second day is needed if you wish to explore the other sites in the Jericho area (see page 280 onwards). The sites in Jericho itself are fairly spread out, involving a 6 or 7km walk to see them all, though they do neatly fit into a loop that begins and ends at the main square. Taxis can be hired for a tour around Jericho's attractions for around 60 NIS, though you'll need to bargain hard and establish exactly what the deal is. A guided return trip to the Mount of Temptation will cost around 25 NIS. You may also be able to negotiate a deal to take you to Nebi Musa. An excellent way to explore the Jericho area is on a bike hired from *Zaki Bike Rental* on the main square (3 NIS per hour, 15 NIS all day, open 0900-1700, cash deposit preferable to leaving passport).

History

The beginnings The evidence of early human settlement at this oasis is most spectacularly seen at the 8000 BCE walls and tower at Tel Jericho/Tell es-Sultan. Early settlers were no doubt attracted by the plentiful water supply, productive soils and benign winter climate, with a succession of cultures establishing themselves here in the Mesolithic, Pre-Pottery Neolithic, Pottery Neolithic, Early and Middle Bronze Age periods. It seems that the wandering hunter-gatherers made the shift to sedentary agriculture some 11,000 years ago.

The Israelites The most famous incident in Jericho's history comes with the return of the Israelites from the Exodus, c. 1250 BCE. The prophet-general Joshua commanded the priests to carry the Ark around the walled city for six consecutive days. On the seventh day the priests blew their trumpets and "Joshua said unto the people 'Shout; for the Lord hath given you the city.' ... So the people shouted when the priests blew the trumpets; and it came to pass, when the people heard the sound of the trumpet, and the people shouted with a great shout, that the wall fell down flat" (*Joshua 6:16-20*). Ancient Jericho never recovered its former importance (a fact confirmed by archaeological evidence from Tel Jericho), with the ancient city being abandoned from the time of the Babylonian Exile (586 BCE). Subsequent centres of Jericho established themselves elsewhere in the oasis.

Jericho's fortunes were revived in the first century BCE by the Hasmonean dynasty, who began to establish a number of winter palaces here (Tulul Abu el-'Alayiq, see page 281). The Jericho plain was soon to feature prominently in the struggle between the Hasmoneans and the upstart Herod. It is possible that at this time Jericho was considered to be Roman property, so much so that Mark Anthony saw fit to make a present of the estate to his paramour Cleopatra. In turn she leased part of the estate to Herod, allowing him to build the first of his three palaces here. With the death of Cleopatra c. 31 BCE, the Roman emperor Octavian (Augustus Caesar) granted Jericho to Herod. In a dramatic 25-year period Herod built two further palaces, had the surviving male heir to the Hasmonean dynasty drowned here, and planned his final tyrannical act (see Tell es-Samrat, page 276), before finally dying in Jericho in 4 BCE. Jericho subsequently reverted to Roman rule, though was largely destroyed in the recriminations that followed the First Jewish Revolt (66-73 CE).

Hasmoneans & Herod

In the Byzantine period it appears that the oasis of Jericho was heavily populated, with the new town established largely on the area of the present settlement. Jericho had a large Christian population at this juncture, though the presence of the 'Peace Upon Israel' synagogue (see page 276) suggests that a Jewish community continued to exist here.

Byzantines, Arabs & British

Jericho was one of the first cities taken in the Arab conquest of Palestine, and judging by the opulence of the palace of Khirbet el-Mafjar (Hisham's Palace) it enjoyed the same reputation as a winter playground of the wealthy as it had eight centuries before.

The town was captured by the Crusaders in 1099 and still carries several reminders of this European heritage (Mount of Temptation, amongst others). Though Jericho returned to Muslim rule following Salah al-Din's victories in 1187, the town's lack of defences (it was unwalled) and its apparent wealth (based on agriculture) made it a persistent target for Bedouin raids to such an extent that Murphy-O'Connor suggests that "a thriving town degenerated into a miserable village" (*The Holy Land*, 1992). The decline continued throughout Ottoman rule and it was not until the British repaired the aqueducts and irrigation facilities that Jericho once again became a centre of agricultural production specializing in dates and fruit.

Jericho fell to Transjordan in the war of 1948, with the town's population being boosted by Arab refugees from areas now controlled by Israel. Jericho's reputation as a winter resort continued, with many of the wealthy classes from Amman taking their holidays here.

Modern history

The 1993 Declaration of Principles signed by Israel and the PLO envisaged a degree of autonomy in areas that Israel had occupied since the Six Day War of 1967. Since the Gaza Strip alone did not appear to be a sufficient inducement to entice the Palestinians, Jericho was included within a package that became known as 'Gaza-Jericho first', and in May 1994 the Jericho area came under the control of the newly established Palestinian Authority (PA).

West Bank

Sights

Tel Jericho (Tell es-Sultan) It is now generally accepted that this site is the location of the oldest city at Jericho, though early excavations here were not promising. Charles Warren's dig in 1868 had no success, with Warren himself concluding that there was nothing of significance to be found here. It later transpired that one of the shafts that he sunk missed the stunning Pre-Pottery Neolithic stone tower by just one metre! Subsequent excavations, culminating in the major dig at the site by Kathleen Kenyon between 1952-58, have revealed up to 23 levels of occupation.

Jericho

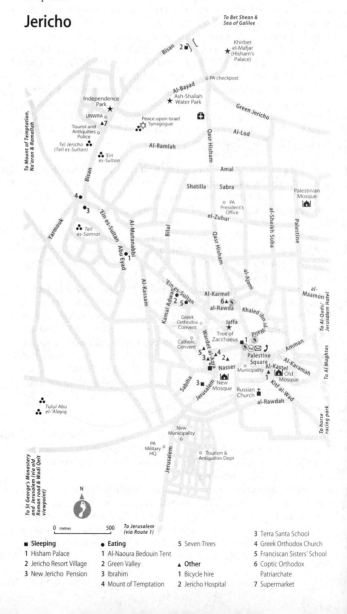

■ Sleeping	● Eating	5 Seven Trees	3 Terra Santa School
1 Hisham Palace	1 Al-Naoura Bedouin Tent		4 Greek Orthodox Church
2 Jericho Resort Village	2 Green Valley	▲ Other	5 Franciscan Sisters' School
3 New Jericho Pension	3 Ibrahim	1 Bicycle hire	6 Coptic Orthodox
	4 Mount of Temptation	2 Jericho Hospital	Patriarchate
			7 Supermarket

West Bank

In truth, those without a deep interest in archaeology may fail to be impressed by the significance of the finds here since, with few exceptions, Tel Jericho is not the most visually exciting historical site. Thus, the details below concentrate on the major finds and sights only.

The earliest remains date to around 9600-7700 BCE, though a major change took place here in the late ninth millennium BCE with the construction of a town wall. Such a step suggests a move in human society from food-gatherer to food-producer, with this Pre-Pottery Neolithic date suggesting that Jericho was one of the first places on earth to experience this shift (and thus justifying to a certain extent the mantle of 'world's oldest city'). The focus of this wall is the **great stone tower** built against the inner side. Built of solid stone, except for the centre where an entirely preserved staircase winds its way to the very top, the tower is preserved to a height of 7.75 metres and has a diameter of 8.5 metres. Murphy-O'Connor suggests that "this supreme achievement of a Stone Age people is without parallel elsewhere in the world" (*The Holy Land*, 1992). The sedentary population at this stage must have been in the region of 2,000, largely dependent upon agriculture.

This phase of occupation came to an end around 6800 BCE, to be replaced by a far more sophisticated culture from outside the region (possibly originating in Anatolia). After a period of about 2,000 years this culture disappeared as quickly as it had arrived, being succeeded (after a gap) by a distinctly inferior culture.

A completely new group settled here in the Early Bronze Age (3300-2200 BCE), and though interpreting the remains from this period has proved difficult, parts of the **mud-brick wall** can still be seen. The Middle Bronze Age (2200-1550 BCE) saw yet another building style in evidence at Jericho, with the lack of a true urban centre suggesting that they were nomads and pastoralists. Towards the end of the Middle Bronze Age Jericho had developed significantly, including the construction of a new-style **defensive wall** that featured a 17-metre-high curtain wall standing on top of an artificial glacis that served to steepen the slope to an angle of 35 degrees. This glacis is one of the best preserved sights on view today.

Tel Jericho (Tell es-Sultan)

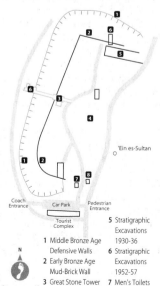

'Ein es-Sultan

Coach Entrance
Car Park
Pedestrian Entrance

Tourist Complex

N

0 metres 40

1 Middle Bronze Age Defensive Walls
2 Early Bronze Age Mud-Brick Wall
3 Great Stone Tower
4 Iron Age structures
5 Stratigraphic Excavations 1930-36
6 Stratigraphic Excavations 1952-57
7 Men's Toilets
8 Women's Toilets

West Bank

The remains from the Late Bronze Age (1550-1200 BCE) are fairly inconclusive. Jericho's destruction in the Late Bronze Age II ties in with the Israelite entry into the country after the Exodus. Whether the walls of Jericho were sent tumbling by the blasts from the Israelites' trumpets is another matter (*Joshua 6*). The site here remained largely abandoned until the seventh century BCE, though subsequent occupation appears to have only lasted until the Babylonian Exile (586 BCE). Thereafter Tel Jericho (Tell es-Sultan) was abandoned. ■ *T2322909. Open daily 0800-1700, one hour later in summer. 10 NIS adult, 7 NIS student. Toilets, souvenir shops, expensive café, Mount of Temptation restaurant.*

West Bank

'Ein es-Sultan
The perennial spring opposite Tel Jericho is the reason why this site was first occupied around 9000 BCE, and some 11,000 years later it is still a vital source of water to the oasis of Jericho. The spring is also identified with the story of Elisha purifying Jericho's water supply by adding salt (*II Kings 2:19-22*), and is sometimes referred to as Elisha's Spring. There is nothing of interest to see at the pumping station today.

Tell es-Samrat
Located 600 metres southwest of Tel Jericho is a small artificial mound known as Tell es-Samrat. Excavations here have revealed remains of a large **racetrack** adjoined to the north by a theatre. Behind the theatre is a large **square structure** that appears to have been some sort of residence or reception room connected with the racecourse, or perhaps a gymnasium. All have been positively identified with the Herodian period and general consensus suggests that this site is associated with the last days of Herod (d. 4 BCE) that Josephus recounts in such detail (*Antiquities XVII, 161, 173-179, 193-195; Jewish War 1, 647-73*). Josephus describes Herod as being "melancholy-mad, and in a virtual challenge to death itself he proceeded to devise a monstrous outrage." Having locked up the head men of every village in Judaea at the racetrack here he summoned his sister Salome, telling her "I know Jews will greet my death with wild rejoicing; but I can be mourned on other people's account ... These men under guard – as soon as I die, kill them all ... then all Judaea and every family will weep for me – they can't help it." Fortunately for the head men Salome ignored his dying wishes, instead choosing to release them.

'Peace Upon Israel Synagogue'
This synagogue was constructed in the late sixth or early seventh century CE, and remained in common use until the eighth century CE. It is noted for its fine **mosaic floor**. The nave mosaic is divided into two sections, with the northern one (closest to the door) featuring a six-line Aramaic inscription set below a pattern of alternating interwoven squares and circles. The southern section (furthest from the entrance) features a pattern of lozenges featuring heart-shaped ivy leaves alternating with rhomboid-shaped plain lozenges. The centrepiece is an image of the Ark of the Law supported on four legs, with a stylized conch above. Below is a panel containing a seven-branched menorah flanked by a lulab and shofar. The Hebrew inscription, 'Peace upon Israel', gives the synagogue its common name. ■ *0800-1600 daily. 10 NIS.*

Khirbet el-Mafjar (Hisham's Palace)
Visitors disappointed by Tel Jericho are far more likely to be impressed by Khirbet el-Mafjar, popularly known as **Hisham's Palace**. It was built as a hunting-lodge or spring/winter resort in the Umayyad period, though surprisingly little is known about its history, whilst its ancient name is unknown and it has not been identified in ancient literature.

The popular name comes from an association with the Umayyad caliph **el-Hisham ibn Abd el-Malik** (724-43 CE), though the palace's "sumptuous architecture" that provides a "congenial setting for the life of esthetic hedonism" (Hamilton, 1993) better suits the known character of el-Hisham's nephew and successor **el-Walid ibn el-Yazid II** (743-744 CE). It is generally agreed that though the bath area was constructed during el-Hisham's reign, the palace was still being built when el-Yazid assumed the caliphate. When the latter's career was cut short by assassination in 744 CE, it appears that the palace was abandoned unfinished. It was probably badly damaged in the major earthquake of 749 CE and subsequently became a source of cut stones for the local population.

Tour Khirbet el-Mafjar comprises three main elements: the palace, the mosque and the bath, though only the latter was completed. The **modern entrance (1)** leads into a **forecourt (2)** where a number of architectural fragments brought down by the earthquake of 749 CE have been rearranged. The palace was originally a two-storied square building planned around a central courtyard and enclosed by four arcaded galleries. A **vaulted porch (3)** set in the base of a projecting tower to the east formed the main entrance, with the architectural style exhibiting an Iraqi influence. At the centre of the unroofed **courtyard (4)** is a **stone sculpture (5)** that was erected by the excavators from fragments found *in situ*. The **rooms (6)** around the courtyard appear to have been used to accommodate guests and servants, and not for domestic use. Hamilton suggests that the preponderance of non-domestic rooms in the palace suggests "a numerous retinue and hospitality lavishly dispensed" (*ibid*). A **small mosque (7)** complete with *mihrab* stands to the south of the courtyard. A flight of **steps (8)** in the western gallery leads to an underground vaulted room with an attractive mosaic floor. The water spout, wall benches and brick-lined waterproofed space confirms that it was a **bathing hall (9)**. The large hall in the northern gallery may have served as a **banqueting hall (10)**.

West Bank

Khirbet el-Mafjar (Hisham's Palace)

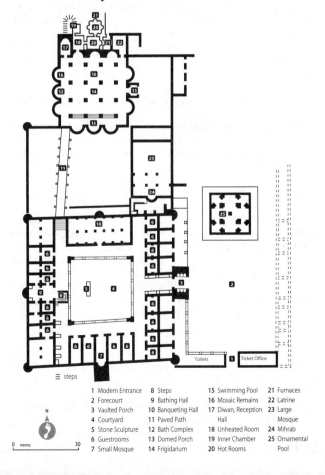

≡ steps

N

0 — 30 metres

1	Modern Entrance	8	Steps	15	Swimming Pool
2	Forecourt	9	Bathing Hall	16	Mosaic Remains
3	Vaulted Porch	10	Banqueting Hall	17	Diwan, Reception
4	Courtyard	11	Paved Path		Hall
5	Stone Sculpture	12	Bath Complex	18	Unheated Room
6	Guestrooms	13	Domed Porch	19	Inner Chamber
7	Small Mosque	14	Frigidarium	20	Hot Rooms

21	Furnaces
22	Latrine
23	Large
	Mosque
24	Mihrab
25	Ornamental
	Pool

The bath is connected to the palace by a **paved path (11)** that may have been for the exclusive use of the caliph. The **bath complex (12)** is in fact the architectural highlight of Khirbet el-Mafjar. It comprised a **domed porch (13)** on the east side, a large **frigidarium (14)**, a **swimming pool (15)** (that el-Yazid reputedly filled with rosewater mixed with musk and turmeric), plus a complex of rooms to the north. The frigidarium (**14**) was paved with a spectacular coloured stone mosaic divided into separate circular panels or carpets that were designed to give the optical effect of a series of large rugs. Though largely preserved intact, only sections now remain *in situ* (**16**). The complex of rooms to the north of the frigidarium includes a **diwan** or **reception hall (17)**, an unheated room (**18**) that led into a small inner chamber (**19**) that contained two hip-baths, two caldaria or hot rooms (**20**) heated by a hypocaust connected to two furnaces (**21**), plus a latrine (**22**). Of particular note is the **diwan (17)**, decorated with one of the best preserved mosaics in the country, whilst the benches, vaults and dome feature extensive use of carved plaster. Also of note is the room with the **hip-baths (19)**: according to legend el-Yazid used to fill these with wine, immerse himself fully, then drink until the level of the bath was 'distinctly lowered'!

To the south of the bath complex is the **large mosque (23)** (23.6 metres by 17.1 metres). The southern section closest to the mihrab (**24**) appears to have been sheltered by a roof, though there is evidence to suggest that the mosque and roof were never completed. The tour finishes at the **ornamental pool (25)** in the forecourt. A shallow basin, the pool featured an octagonal pavilion set on a series of piers as the centre-piece. ■ *T2322522. Saturday-Thursday 0800-1700, Friday 0800-1600, closes one hour earlier in winter. 10 NIS adult, 7 NIS student. Toilets, snack-bar.*

Tree of Zacchaeus Jericho is the scene of several events in the life of Jesus. It is here that he healed the two blind beggars (*Matthew 20:29-34*), healed blind Bartimaeus (*Mark 10:46-52*), and where he dined with the rich tax collector Zacchaeus, who had climbed a sycamore tree to see Jesus better (*Luke 19:1-10*). There is a sycamore tree on 'Ein es-Sultan St that is called the 'Tree of Zacchaeus', but it's not really 2,000 years old.

Essentials

Sleeping
■ *on map;*
price codes see inside
front cover

A *Jericho Resort Village*, Qasr Hisham, T2321255, F2322189. Recently completed, this splendid new hotel is excellent value (with facilities that you would pay double the price for in Jerusalem). Standard rooms are large, modern, nicely furnished with cable TV, phone, balconies. Pool-view rooms are $20 more, though the views are probably more dramatic from the other side. The main block also features some suites and connecting rooms (**L3**). Poolside bungalows accommodate up to 4 on a 1-4 week basis (**L3**). Large pool, pool bar, kid's pool, jacuzzi, Dead Sea pool, tennis, kid's playground, *Fountain* outdoor grill, *Andalous* buffet restaurant, friendly service. Highly recommended.

C *Al-Quds/Jerusalem*, Amman, T2321329/2322444, F2323109. Recently completed hotel, 'deluxe' rooms with a/c and balconies (**C**), plus some cheaper standard rooms downstairs (**D, E**), restaurant.

D *Deir Hajla Monastery*, Jericho by-pass road, T9943038 or T050-348892. The monastery on the edge of town (see 'Around Jericho' section, page 280) offers accommodation for pilgrims: private rooms or large dorms for groups. **D** *New Jericho Pension*, Jerusalem, T2322215. Set in an attractive rose garden, most rooms with attached bath (make sure you inspect room before taking it), though in late 1999 this place looked closed up.

E, F *Hisham Palace*, 'Ein es-Sultan, T2322414, F2323645. You could be forgiven for thinking that this British Mandate period hotel closed down (during the British Mandate!), but it remains open. It's extremely shabby, though renovations are proceeding at a snail's pace. Inspect the rooms first and make sure it's clear what the deal is (ie paying for the whole room or just 1 bed). Haggle like mad.

Most visitors stay just long enough to have an overpriced meal or snack at the tourist complex at the Tel Jericho site (eg *Mount of Temptation*, T2322614). This is a shame since there are some pleasant restaurants in Jericho. Many of the outdoor restaurants are spread along 'Ein es-Sultan St, including *Al-Naora Bedouin Tent*, T2322585, *Green Valley*, T2322349, *Ibrahim*, T2323252 and *Seven Trees*, T2322781, amongst others. Most offer a spread of grilled meats, hummus, salad etc for around 25-30 NIS per head (group rates available). Cheap falafel and shwarma can be found around Palestine Sq. **Eating**

Bars The *Jericho Resort Village* has a bar, although it is aimed primarily at residents. **Casinos** The huge new *Oasis Casino* has recently opened to the south of the town centre, on Jerusalem Rd (the road south to the junction with Route 1). **Bars & nightclubs**

Theatres *Municipality Theatre*, T2322417, F2322604 (see map). **Festivals** For details of the annual **Jericho Winter Festival** T2323836, F2322604. **Entertainment**

Football Following recognition by FIFA, the Palestinian national team played their first sanctioned international at the recently built, 7,000-capacity *Jericho International Stadium* (a boring 0-0 draw with Jordan). The stadium hosts regular fixtures as well as having **basketball** and **tennis** courts. **Horse-racing** There is a horse-racing track to the southeast of Palestine Sq (along the road to Al Maghtas). **Swimming** *Ash-Shallal*, T050-570094/520932. Large water park, restaurants, etc. **Sports**

Car hire *Orabi*, T050-405095 or T2323230. **Taxis** *Al Petra*, T2322525; *Hisham Palace*, T2321958. **Service taxi** With the continued uncertainty over the fate of the West Bank bus services, the best way to get around is by service taxi. Jericho is best reached by service taxi from outside Jerusalem's Damascus Gate (8 NIS, 30 minutes). To return to **Jerusalem**, green/blue plated service taxis from Palestine Sq run as far as **Abu Dis** (6 NIS), where you change to a yellow-plated service taxi that runs over the Mount of Olives to Damascus Gate (2 NIS). Service taxis from Palestine Sq also run to the Israel/Jordan border at **Allenby/King Hussein Bridge** . Note that if you are travelling direct between Jerusalem and the border crossing it is quicker and cheaper to miss out Jericho altogether. There are also service taxis from Palestine Sq to **Ramallah**. **Transport**

Banks Most of the banks and money-changers are in and around Palestine Sq, and at the southern end of Qasr Hisham (including *Cairo Amman*, T2323628; *Arab Bank*, T2321310). Jordanian dinars are available. **Communications** Area code: T02. NB Phone numbers in Jericho have recently changed. As a general rule, if you have an 'old' number beginning '99' substitute this with '23'. **Post offices**: main post office is on Al-Karamah, T2323574. This is a good place to buy PA stamps. **Telephones**: *Palestine Telecom*, Al-Karamah, T2322499/2322514. **Cultural centres** *Jericho Culture & Art Centre*, Wardet al-Azra, T2321047. **Embassies and Representative Offices to the PA** Denmark: T2323193, F2322300; Switzerland, T5828805, F5823757. **Hospitals and medical services** Chemists: *Al Arabi*, T2322325; *Hijazi*, T2322630/2322694. Hospitals: *Jericho Government Hospital*, near Palestine Sq, T2321966/7. A **Directory**

West Bank

new hospital is planned for Jerusalem St to the south of town. **Tourist offices** Tourism and Antiquities Department, T2322935/2321229. **Useful addresses and phone numbers** Police: Palestine Sq, T100 (T2322521). **Ambulance:** T101 (T2957574). **Fire:** T102 (T2322658). **Municipality:** T2322418. Allenby/King Hussein Bridge border crossing: T2323661. **President's Office:** T2321301. **UNRWA:** T2322411.

Around Jericho

Mount of Temptation (Jebel Quruntul)

The association of this cliff to the northwest of Jericho with the first and third temptation of Christ (*Matthew 4:1-11*) dates only to the 12th century CE. The Crusaders built two churches at the site; one in a cave halfway up the cliff face and one on the summit. The present monastery halfway up the cliff dates to 1874-1904 and contains the **medieval cave church** within its grounds. Visitors are shown the traditional site of the conversation between Christ and the devil, including the stone upon which the former sat!

Permission should be sought (and a small fee paid) to continue up the path to the summit (30 minutes). The Crusader church here had been destroyed by the 14th century, whilst a 19th-century attempt to rebuild it did not come to much. This is the site of the second century BCE **Fortress of Doq**, built by the Syrian general Baccides and scene of the murder of Simon Maccabaeus in 134 BCE by his son-in-law Ptolemy. Little remains of the fortress bar parts of a ditch, retaining wall and tower. The view down to the Plain of Jericho and across to the Dead Sea certainly makes the climb up here worthwhile. The present name of the hill, **Quruntul**, is an Arabic translation of the Crusader

Around Jericho

To Ramallah
To Bet Shean, Sea of Galilee & Khirbet el-Beiyudat
Na'aran
Jericho Tourist Village
Khirbet el-Mafjar (Hisham's Palace)
Mount of Temptation (Jebel Quruntul)
Mount of Temptation Tourist Complex
Tel Jericho
Peace upon Israel Synagogue
'Ein es-Sultan
Tell es-Samrat
Ibrahim Restaurant
Palestinian Mosque
JERICHO TOWN CENTRE
To Al Maghtas
Ancient Graveyard
Tulul Abu el-'Alayiq
Wadi Qelt
Wadi Qelt
St George's Monastery
Cypros
To Jerusalem via Route 1
N
To Jerusalem via 'Old Road'
0 km 1

name Mont Quarantana, meaning 'Mount of Forty': a reference to the 40 days and 40 nights that Jesus spent in the wilderness. ■ *Monday-Saturday 0700-1400 1500-1700, closes one hour earlier in winter, early visit recommended. Modest dress essential. Free, donation expected. There's no public transport to the site and it's a long walk, though the path up the cliff is not as steep as it first appears. Plans are in hand to build a 'tourist cable car' to the summit (T2321591).*

Tulul Abu el-'Alayiq

Located to the west of the modern city of Jericho, at the eastern end of the Wadi Qelt gorge, is the site known by the Arabic name of Tulul Abu el-'Alayiq. Initially confusing and spread over a considerable area, this site represents the winter playground of the first century BCE Jewish aristocracy. Attracted by Jericho's benign winter environment, when Jerusalem was shivering, the Hasmonean (and later Herodian) court decamped to their palaces here.

West Bank

Ins and outs

It should be noted that the site is poorly maintained and rather confusing. The description below concentrates on the main sights that can still be discerned; without the site plans printed here you will almost certainly be lost. There is no public transport to the site, though there's a snack bar with cold drinks nearby. Entrance is officially 10 NIS, though there's rarely anyone here to collect it.

Getting there and around

History

The site was first extensively developed by the Hasmonean king Alexander Jannaeus (103-76 BCE), though two building phases from his reign are discernible. A third Hasmonean construction phase is attributed to his widow and successor, Salome Alexandra (76-67 BCE). The Hasmoneans built a large winter palace complex on the north side of the Wadi Qelt though the plan is somewhat confused by later modifications. Alexander Jannaeus' palace may also have been severely damaged by the earthquake of 31 BCE.

During the period 35-30 BCE Herod the Great built the first of three palaces here. **Herod's first palace** is located on the south side of Wadi Qelt and was presumably built whilst Alexander Jannaeus' palace was still standing and in the possession of the Hasmonean family. Following the earthquake of 31 BCE and the death of Cleopatra following the battle of Actium, it appears that Herod took control of the Hasmonean palace complex and built his own **second palace** over the top of it (30-25 BCE). Some time between 15-10 BCE, **Herod's third palace** was built; a magnificent complex straddling Wadi Qelt. However, as Netzer notes, "Herod's three palaces at Jericho should be viewed as a single unit that developed in stages; all three palaces probably coexisted in the last years of his reign" (*New Encyclopedia of Archaeological Excavations in the Holy Land*, 1993).

Sights

Herod's third palace (**D**) may have been built to commemorate Marcus Agrippa's visit to Palestine in 15 BCE. As a mark of appreciation it seems likely that a Roman construction team was sent to assist in the building work since it is certain that local and Roman builders worked on the palace simultaneously.

Herod's third palace

Any differences in styles were disguised by covering all the walls with a fine lime plaster. The third palace was built on both sides of Wadi Qelt rather in the Roman style of building homes and palaces alongside lakes and seas; here the residents were able to enjoy the seasonal flow at least.

The key feature on the south side of the wadi is the **sunken garden (12)**. It features rows of **double colonnades (13)** flanking the east and west ends, set two metres above the level of the garden with a portico in front of the colonnades acting as a viewing area. To the east is a large **pool (14)**, whose waters cooled the atmosphere. The bridge across Wadi Qelt has not survived. The plan of the northern wing of the third palace is clearly discernible. The **main reception hall (18)** would have been capable of accommodating several hundred guests and served as the palace's central triclinium (used for banquets, ceremonies and receptions). Three rows of columns ran parallel to the west, north and east walls, with an opening to the south providing a view of the sunken garden. Though the large paving stones from the floor are missing, their impressions remain. The walls of the hall would have been decorated with frescoes and stucco mouldings.

To the east of the main reception hall is a **peristyle courtyard (19)** with a semi-circular exedra (20) on its north side. Several guest rooms open on to the courtyard, with the one to the north perhaps being the **throne room (21)**. A garden stood at the centre of the courtyard, and a number of embedded flowerpots have been found here. A second, smaller **peristyle courtyard (22)** is located to the east. The Roman-style **bathhouse (23)**, built mainly of Roman 'concrete', features a circular room with four semicircular niches that may have served as a **laconicum (24)**. Similar examples have been excavated at Pompeii. The rectangular room at the east end of the bathhouse served as a **caldarium (25)** and was

Tulul Abu el-'Alayiq

A **Hasmonean Palace**
1 Central Building
2 Pools
3 Swimming Pools
4 Tower
5 Pavilion
6 Artificial Mound
7 Twin-Palaces
8 Garden & Swimming Pool
9 Pool

B **Herod's 'First Palace'**

C **Herod's 'Second Palace'**
10 East Wing

D **Herod's 'Third Palace'** (see detail map)
11 North Wing
12 Sunken Garden
13 Double Colonnades
14 Pool
15 Southern Mound
16 Dwellings / Service Wing
17 Industrial Installations

after Netzer

N

0 metres 100

Wadi Qelt

Wadi Qelt

see North Wing of Herod's Third Palace' plan

heated by the same hypocaust as the adjacent **tepidarium** (26). The frigidarium was probably part of another Herodian building that predated the third palace. The adjacent wing (27) was built on a lower level and may in fact be part of an earlier villa incorporated into the third palace.

Herod's first palace (**B**) is located to the south of the site, and comprises a rectangular building facing inwards around a peristyle court. There's not a great deal left to see.

Herod's first palace

The plan of the Hasmonean palace complex (**A**) is rather confusing. This is due to the fact that significant alterations were made during the Hasmonean period, and then again under Herod. The **central building** (1) of the original palace has only been partially excavated, mainly because it was later filled in to form an artificial mound for another structure. An interesting structure to the southwest is a **tower** (4) that predates the Hasmonean palace. It was initially speculated that this was one of the towers known as Threx or Taurus, though this view has now been discounted (see 'Cypros' on page 270). The two **pools** (2) to the west of the central building may also predate it, having probably been

Hasmonean palace complex (and Herod's second palace)

West Bank

Northern wing of Herod's 'Third Palace'

after Netzer

18	Main Reception Hall	23	Bath House
19	Peristyle Courtyard	24	Laconicum
20	Exedra	25	Caldarium
21	Throne Room	26	Tepidarium
22	Smaller Peristyle Courtyard	27	Adjacent Wing

0 metres 10

built by John Hyrcanus I (134-104 BCE).

Early in the reign of Alexander Jannaeus (103-76 BCE) a new complex was built to the east of the central building. The focus of this complex was the two large **swimming pools** (3), with a colonnaded **pavilion** (5) built in the Doric style to the south. Later, in the period of Herod's rule (c. 35 BCE), these pools were to be the scene of a typically Herodian act. On a hot evening Herod encouraged the seventeen-year-old high priest Aristobulus III, the last in the Hasmonean line, to take a cooling dip in the pool here. He didn't get out of the pool alive (see Josephus, *Antiquities XV, 50-61; Jewish War I, 435-437*).

During the middle part of Alexander Jannaeus' reign (c. 92-83 BCE), the increasingly turbulent situation saw the need to fortify the palace complex here. This was done by filling in the central building (1) area to create an **artificial mound** (6), and cutting a fosse to defend it. Nothing of substance remains of the fortified structure built on the artificial mound. Alexander Jannaeus' successor, his wife Salome Alexandra (76-67 BCE), extended the palace complex, building a new wing to the east. The key features here are the **twin-palaces** (7), so called because they were built next to each other as mirror images. A decorative **garden and swimming pool** (**8**) stood to the west, with a larger **pool** (**9**) built later in the east court. This latter pool was incorporated into Herod's second palace.

Though the main Hasmonean palace complex was badly damaged in the earthquake of 31 BCE, it is still not entirely clear whether it was repaired, rebuilt, or just left to crumble. Some time in the period 30-25 BCE Herod took over the site and begun construction of his second palace (**C**). Amongst the alterations he made was to turn the two large swimming pools (**3**) into a single pool, with the second palace featuring an ample provision of gardens. According to Netzer the second palace did "not follow high architectural standards" (*ibid*), which may explain Herod's decision to build the third palace.

Na'aran A couple of kilometres northwest of Jericho is the site of the ancient Jewish village of **Na'aran**. The sixth century CE **synagogue** here contains one of the most interesting synagogue mosaic floors in the Holy Land. It was first exposed in 1918 by a stray artillery shell that the Turks fired at the British fort at Wadi en-Nu'eima. Most of the figurative drawings in the mosaic floor were defaced by ultra-religious Jews, though they went to great lengths to preserve the Hebrew lettering. The floor has been removed to the Israel Museum in Jerusalem. ■ *Daily 0800-1700, one hour later in summer. Adult 10 NIS.*

Khirbet el-Beiyudat Twelve kilometres to the north of Jericho is the site of Khirbet el-Beiyudat, identified as the **village of Archelais** that Herod's son Archelaus established as a date plantation (Josephus, *Antiquities XVII, 340*). Amongst the remains excavated here is a **Byzantine basilica** that features an attractive mosaic in red, black, white and mustard. Construction of the church belongs to a number of periods, though it was certainly in use during the fifth and sixth centuries CE.

Al Maghtas Some 10 kilometres southeast of Jericho is **Al Maghtas**, one of five traditional sites on the Jordan River where John is said to have baptized Jesus (*Matthew 3:13-17; Mark 1:9-11; Luke 3:21-22*). This particular one is marked by an attractive 19th-century Greek Orthodox monastery, though excavations continue at the site with the hope of discovering first century CE remains in time for the tourist beano in 2000! However, Al Maghtas is within a closed military area and hence public visits are restricted to the Greek Orthodox and Roman Catholic Epiphanies (in January and October respectively). ■ *Contact the Christian Information Centre (Catholic), PO Box 14308, opposite the Citadel, Jaffa Gate, Jerusalem, T6272692, F6286417 for further information.*

Deir Hajla To the east of Route 90, just off the Jericho by-pass road, is the **Greek Orthodox Monastery** known as Deir Hajla. With its large silver dome and isolated position it is a regular landmark for travellers on Route 90. The present name is said to preserve the biblical Beth-hogla (*Joshua 15:6; 18:19, 21*). The current monastery dates to the end of the 19th century, though it stands on foundations laid by the patriarch of Jerusalem in the 12th century CE. Within 500 metres of the monastery is the site of the laura founded by the eminent monastic figure of the Judean wilderness, **St Gerasimus** (c. 455 CE). Accommodation is available at the monastery (see under 'Jericho' on page 272).

Allenby/King Hussein Bridge A mere 16 kilometres east of Jericho is the Allenby/King Hussein Bridge, one of the main crossing points between Israel and Jordan. For full details see page 33 in 'Getting there: overland'.

North of Jerusalem

The area to the north of Jerusalem is probably the part of the West Bank least visited by foreign tourists, yet in a historical, cultural or political context it is as important as any other part. This is the heartland of the Jewish region of Samaria, with numerous biblical sites deserving some attention. It is also the main Arab population centre and would form the core of any proposed Palestinian state. In addition, it is a region of natural, rugged beauty.

The **prophet Samuel** was supposedly buried in Rama (*I Samuel 25:1*), but since the sixth century CE at least his tomb has been marked at this spot. A Crusader church was built on top of the existing Byzantine crypt (the Crusaders called this spot 'Mountjoy'), but since the 15th century the tomb has been housed within a mosque. The views from the minaret are particularly rewarding. The village of Nabi Samwil is located a couple of kilometres north of Jerusalem, off the main Nablus Road. Take Egged bus 36 from Jaffa Road to the suburb of Ramot and walk from there.

Nabi Samwil

The Palestinian village of al-Jib recalls the biblical Gibeon (*Joshua 9:3-21; 10:12*), noteworthy for its superbly preserved 12th to 11th century BCE water system (see *II Samuel 2:13*). In addition to the rock-cut pool and 10th-century BCE tunnels, you can also see the eighth to seventh century BCE wine cellars. Al-Jib is several kilometres (walking distance) north of Nabi Samwil. To reach the excavations from al-Jib, take the Biddu road and continue up the hill to the parking lot. Follow the path from there.

Gibeon (al-Jib)

Located on the Nablus Road a little to the north of the Jerusalem suburb of Giv'at Ha-Mivtar (and five kilometres north of Damascus Gate) is a low mound that forms an isolated part of the Mt Scopus–Mount of Olives ridge. A series of excavations at the site suggest that it is the Gibeah of Saul (Arabic: *Tell el-Fûl*, or 'Mound of Horse Beans'): the home and capital of the Israelite king Saul (*I Samuel 10:26; 11:4; 15:34*).

Gibeah of Saul (Tell el-Fül)

All that remains are the base of the south corner tower and parts of the adjacent casement walls of the fortress built during the time of Saul, though the excavators have projected the plan of the fortress as being rectangular (52 metres by 35 metres) with towers at all four corners. It appears to have been destroyed and rebuilt a number of times, notably following the Assyrian expedition of 701 BCE and the Babylonian invasion of 588-586 BCE. Later occupants of the mound include the Roman army, who camped close to 'Gabath Saul' on the night before they reached Jerusalem in 70 CE (Josephus, *Jewish War V, 51*). There is not a great deal to see and only those with a keen interest in the period are likely to be rewarded by a visit here. There is no public transport directly to the mound, though a Ramallah- or Nablus-bound service taxi may be persuaded to drop you off as it passes.

Ramallah

Situated on the crest of a hill just 16 kilometres north of Jerusalem, Ramallah's cooling breezes formerly made it a popular resort during the Jordanian occupation (1948-67). The Arabic name Ramallah means 'Heights of God'. Blessed with good olive plantations and viticulture, plus an expanding industrial base, it

Phone code: 02
Colour map 1, grid B4

West Bank

is probably the West Bank's most affluent town. It was previously a predominantly Christian town, though its population of some 25,000 Arabs is now roughly divided equally between Christianity and Islam. Ramallah is considered by young Palestinians to be the West Bank's 'hippiest' town.

Ins and outs

Getting there Ramallah is best reached by a service taxi from outside Damascus Gate in Jerusalem (30 minutes). It also acts as a place to change service taxis on the way to Nablus. Shout out where you want to go and someone will quickly propel you in the right direction (see also under 'Transport' on page 288). The town is compact enough to get around on foot, with most services in and around the main square, Midan Manara. Most of the government offices (and more upmarket residences) are in the Al-Bireh suburb to the north/northeast.

Sights

A piece in *Palestine Report* titled "So hip it hurts" reports how "when *Newsweek* went on a search for the hippest hangouts on earth, it obviously overlooked Ramallah. Coming soon to the City of Returness: an Internet Café. A cinema/café/artspace. A Kentucky Fried Chicken. And, the ultimate symbol of arrival, a McDonalds" (*Vol 2 No 26, 6/12/96*). An earlier edition of the same

Ramallah

■ Sleeping	5 Golden Fried Chicken	▲ Other	8 Internet International
1 Al-Hajal	6 Karamesh Coffee Shop	1 Athens Supermarket	Centre
2 Al-Wehdeh	7 Kit Kat Koffee, Black	2 Carma Cyber Club	9 Police
3 Merryland	Horse Bar, Al-Bayat	3 Service taxis to/from	10 Friends' Boys School
4 Miami Pension	al-Filistini	Jerusalem	11 Football pitch
	8 Nazareth	4 Service taxis to/from	12 Ali 'Tmad supermarket
● Eating	9 Nevertiti	Nablus	13 Cinema
1 Al-Bardauni, Plaza	10 Rumours	5 Service taxis to/from	14 Mukhmas Shopping
2 Antika, Jaffar Sweets,	11 Taboun	Jericho	Centre (and Zoom
Al-Bahri Seafood	12 Tony's Pizza, NT	6 Service taxis to/from	Internet Cafe)
3 Damascus Sweets	Internet Cafe	Bir Zeit	
4 Flamingo's		7 Taxis around town	

journal also claimed that "Robert DeNiro was spotted sipping a cappuccino in the European Bakery a few months back, after a tough day scouting locations for a new film insiders say will be set partially in ... Ramallah" (*Vol 2 No 23, 15/11/96*). Despite these favourable reviews there's not a great deal to see in Ramallah itself, though its population extends a warm welcome to visiting foreigners. The Khalil al-Sakakini Cultural Centre is one place to start (http://www.sakakini.org/). For more information on the town see the Ramallah Online Travel Guide (http://www.birzeit.edu/ramallah/).

Essentials

There's not really much choice in Ramallah, with most people taking advantage of the proximity of Jerusalem's far greater selection of hotels.

Sleeping
■ *on map;
price codes see inside
front cover*

A *Best Eastern*, El-Ersal, Al-Bireh, T2958451, F2958452. Located near the Ministry of Information in the upmarket Al-Bireh suburb, this new 91-room hotel features large standard rooms, slightly bigger deluxe rooms ($20 extra), plus some suites (**L3**) and business rooms (**L3**). All have a/c, cable TV, minibar, phone. Hotel has *Olive Garden* restaurant, Italian *Al Massa* plus *Popeye's* "chicken & biscuits", pool, taxi service, helpful and friendly staff. **A** *Grand Park*, T2986194, F2956950. Large, luxurious hotel on the edge of town, very grand public areas, some of the more deluxe rooms and suites in the **L3** category, very nice *Fountain Terrace* restaurant.

B–C *City Inn*, T2959191, F2959189. Located on the Nablus Rd to the north of town, 33 rooms, restaurant, conference facilities.

C, **D** *Al-Bireh Tourist Hotel*, Al-Quds/Jerusalem, T2986803, F2986802. Newish 50-room comfortable hotel on road south of Ramallah. **D** *Al-Hajal*, Faisal, T2986759. Rooms a little box-like, though with a/c and attached bath. **D** *Al-Wehdeh*, 26 Al-Nahda, T2980412. Clean, functional rooms, attached basic bath, TV/video, discounts for longer stays. **D** *Merryland*, Al-Ma'ahed, T2987176. Fairly basic place above a very noisy shopping complex. **D** *Miami Pension*, Jaffa, T2956808. Reasonable rooms with attached bath and neat little balconies, terrace restaurant, breakfast included, though on a noisy road.

Ramallah has a particularly good selection of restaurants, notably the *muntazaat* (outdoor restaurants) where both local dignitaries and Palestinian families come to eat and relax. Most of these outdoor restaurants are to be found along Jaffa Road, close to the Municipal Park. Perhaps the most famous is *Al-Bardauni*, Jaffa, T2951410, where all the 'big nobs' on expense accounts come to dine and entertain (expensive, takes Visa, best to book in advance). There are also several upmarket café/bars on Al-Rasheed, near its junction with Jaffa, including the trendy *Kit Kat Koffee* bar/restaurant and *Al Bayat al-Filistini*, T2987188.

Eating

A selection of slightly cheaper (and mostly good value) restaurants can be found on Rokab, as it runs west from the central square (Midan Manara), and also along Ahliyyah College St. These include *Rumours*; *Angelo's*, T2956408; *Karamesh Coffee Shop*; *Nazareth*; *Flamingo's*, T2985813; *Taboun*, T2980505; and *Nevertiti*.

Those on a tight budget will find very cheap falafel and shwarma in the places close to Midan Manara.

Unlike most of the other towns on the West Bank, you will find that many of Ramallah's restaurants also serve alcohol (beer and usually locally produced arak). Alcohol is also sold in shops and supermarkets. Ramallah's most happening spot is, apparently, the Black Horse Bar, located above the *Kit Kat Koffee* restaurant on

**Bars &
nightclubs**

West Bank

Al-Rasheed. It bills itself as the only nightclub in the PA territories, with a DJ playing 'Western' dance music on Friday nights.

Entertainment **Art galleries** *Al-Mattal Gallery*, T2958218; *Ziryab Gallery*, T2959093. **Cinemas** *Al-Walid*, Nadha, T2952295. Specializes in 'shoot-'em-up' style blockbusters. The *Popular Art Centre*, see 'Cultural centres' below, also shows Hollywood films. **Concert halls** *National Conservatory of Music*, T2959070, F2959071. **Theatres** *Ashtar Theatre*, T2980037.

Transport **Local** Car hire: *Abu Laban*, T2954010. *Good Luck*, T2950160. *Orabi*, near *Al-Bireh Tourist Hotel*, T2953521: probably the most reputable of the Palestinian car hire companies (good for Palestinian-plated cars for touring the West Bank, though yellow Israeli plates also available). *Universal*, T2986080. *You Save*, T2955954. **Buses**: buses to Bir Zeit run from the stand on Al-Adha'a, opposite Mukhmas Shopping Centre. **Taxis**: *Al-Bireh*, T2952956. *Al-Salam*, T2955805. *Al-Wafa*, T2955544. *Al-Itihad*, T2955887. *Omaya*, T2956120. The taxi rank for journeys around town is on Al-Adha'a.

Long distance Air: *Atarot Airport* is located just off Route 60 about halfway between Ramallah and Jerusalem (see page 227 for details). **Long distance buses**: the main bus station (currently undergoing redevelopment) is on Nadha, just to the east of Midan Manara. There are services to most places on the West Bank (plus East Jerusalem's Suleiman St bus station), though service taxis provide a much quicker and more convenient option. **Service taxi**: service taxis arrive/depart from a variety of places close to Midan Manara, depending largely upon where you have come from/are going to. The easiest option is to call out where you want to go and then allow yourself to be propelled in the right direction. Jerusalem (3 NIS, 30 mins) service taxis arrive/depart from Al-Quds (sometimes called Palestine St) just southeast of Midan Manara (see map). For **Nablus** go to Nadha, near the *Al-Walid Cinema* (10 NIS, 1 hr). *Darwish* run service taxis to **Jericho (Allenby/King Hussein Bridge)** from their office at the bottom of Ein Misbah (10 NIS, 1 hr). Service taxis to **Bir Zeit** run from the stand further up Ein Misbah.

Directory **Airline offices** *Cyprus*, T2984894; *Egyptair*, T2986950; *Qatar*, T2984894; *Royal Jordanian*, T2987060; *Sabena*, T2952180. **Banks** *British Bank*, junction of Jaffa/Rasheed, has an ATM machine. There are numerous banks and money-changers in and around Midan Manara. **Communications** Area code: T02. NB If you have one of the old 7-digit phone numbers beginning with '99' and it doesn't work, try replacing the first '9' with a '2'. **Post offices**: the main post office is on Al-Mutaza. **Internet/email**: there are a number of cybercafés around town offering very cheap internet access (usually 5 NIS for 30 mins, 10 NIS for 1 hr). *Carma Cyber Club*, 8th floor, Rokab; *Internet International Centre*, Rokab; *NT Internet Café*, 6th floor of building above *Tony's Pizza*, Midan Mughtabireen; *Zoom Internet Café*, 4th floor, Mukhmas Shopping Centre, Al-Adha'a. See map for locations. **Cultural centres** Ramallah is the base for a number of organizations that are geared towards raising awareness of Palestinian culture and heritage. Call ahead for details of their programmes. *As-Siraj for Culture, Arts & Theatre*, T2957037, F2957073; *Baladna Cultural Centre*, Nadha, T2958435, F2958434; *British Institute*, T2958763; *Carmel Cultural Foundation*, T2987375, F2987374; *First Ramallah Group*, T2952706, F2980583; *French Cultural Centre*, T2987727, F2987728; *Goethe Institute*, T2980546, F2981923; *In'ash Al-Usra Society (Centre for Heritage & Folklore Studies*, T2956876, F2956544 (http://www.inash.org); *Khalil al-Sakakini Cultural Centre*, T2987374, F2987375; *Manar Cultural Centre*, T2957937; *Popular Art Centre*, T2953891, F2952851. Most noted for screening Hollywood films. **Embassies and Representative Office to the PA** *Austria*, T2958477, F2958479; *Canada*, T2958604, F2958606; *Germany*, T2984788, F2984786; *Netherlands*, T2987639, F2987638; *South Africa*, T2987355, F2987356. **Hospitals and medical services** Chemists: there are numerous pharmacies around the town centre, and on the Nablus Rd in Al-Bireh. Hospitals: *Arabcare Hospital*, Al-Adha'a, T2986420; *Ramallah Government Hospital*, T2982222; *Red Crescent*

Hospital, T2956260. **Tour companies and travel agents** There are a number of companies/associations based in Ramallah that organize guided bus tours all over Palestine: *Palestinian Association for Cultural Exchange (PACE)*, T2986854; *Amani Tours*, T2987013. **Useful addresses and phone numbers** Police: T2956571. Ambulance: T101 (T2957574). **Fire:** T2956102. **Ministry of Information:** 23 Akka, T2954042, F2954043, www.pna.org/mininfo This is the place to come for your Palestinian Authority press card.

Located about five kilometres northeast of Ramallah is the small Arab village of **Beitin** Beitin, almost certainly the site of the biblical **Bethel** or 'House of God' (formerly Luz, see *Judges 1:23*). It is best known as the scene of Jacob's dream (*Genesis 28:12*), and a low hill here is referred to as '**Jacob's Ladder**' though it is indistinguishable from the other low hills in the area. Bethel was captured by Joshua c. 1240-1235 BCE, but subsequently conquered by the Canaanites. Ephraim recaptured it for the Israelites (*Judges 1:22-26*), though it was soon overshadowed by the rise of nearby Jerusalem. It continued to be occupied during the rule of the kings of Judah, and was also settled in the Hellenistic, Roman and Byzantine periods. The minimal Bronze and Iron Age remains are hardly worth a visit. The controversial Jewish West Bank settlement of **Beth-El** is located nearby.

This Palestinian town some 20 kilometres north of Ramallah is best known as **Bir Zeit** the home of **Bir Zeit University**, the premier further education centre on the West Bank. The university has a noted Centre for Research and Documentation of Palestinian Society, and full details of the university can be found on its web site (http://www.birzeit.edu). Its webmaster is Nigel Parry (http://www.birzeit.edu/nigelparry/). Regular buses and service taxis run to the university from Ramallah.

The PA have recently restored a Crusader period **Manor House** at Jifna (just **Jifna** off Route 60 about five kilometres north of Ramallah on the road to Bir Zeit). For further details see Pringle's *Gazeteer of Secular Crusader Buildings in the Holy Land*.

The site of Shiloh is located about one kilometre off Route 60 at a point some **Shiloh** 30 kilometres north of Jerusalem (look for the orange sign). It is the scene of a number of biblical traditions (*Joshua 18:1; 18:8-10; 21:2; Judges 21:19; I Samuel 1-3; 4:1-22; Jeremiah 7:12-14; Psalms 78:60*). Archaeological excavations have confirmed a number of the biblical descriptions.
    Remains from the **Middle Bronze Age IIB** (1750-1550 BCE) have been found, plus a few finds from the **Late Bronze Age** (1550-1200 BCE), though it appears that the site was used more as a cultic place than a permanent residential settlement. **Iron Age IA** (1200-1150 BCE) structures have also been identified, though few visitors to Shiloh will be impressed by the sight before them. The later remains are more substantial, particularly the mosaic floors in the Byzantine **Pilgrim's Church** and **basilica**. There are also several structures from the Early Arab period (638-1099 CE), including the **Jama' es-Sittin** (Mosque of the Sixty) which re-uses fragments from earlier churches, and may well originally have been a synagogue.

Ins and outs For those determined to visit, a Nablus-bound service taxi from Ramallah can be persuaded to stop (though you may have to pay the full Nablus fare). To return, flag down any passing traffic. The nearest settlement is the Arab village of Sailun.

Nablus (Shechem)

Phone code: 09
Colour map 2, grid A4

Nablus is the largest city on the West Bank (barring East Jerusalem), and is now run by the Palestinian Authority. Biblical references to the various sites here abound, with the ancient town of Shechem filling a significant spot within Jewish history (Israeli sources, including road signs, still refer to the town by this name). Nablus has been an important Arab settlement since the seventh century CE and one of the main centres of Palestinian resistance to Israeli rule. There are plenty of points of interest in and around the town to visit, or you can come here just to discuss the 'Arab-Israeli Question'.

Ins and outs

Getting there The easiest way to reach Nablus is by service taxi from Ramallah (occasionally all the way from Jerusalem). Service taxis and buses to most destinations on the West Bank leave/depart from the stand to the west of the town centre (see map, and 'Transport' on page 296).

Getting around The town centre is compact enough to get around on foot, and most of the sights around Nablus (including Tell Balâtah, Jacob's Well and Joseph's Tomb) are probably easier to reach by walking rather than by service taxi. A walk up to the top of Mount Gerizim or Mount Ebal will take about two hours each, or a 50 NIS taxi ride (wait and return). The main focus of the new town is Palestine Square (Midan Filistin), though this square is sometimes known as Midan al-Hussein.

Warning It should be noted that the ancient sites of Nablus probably hold most appeal to Jews yet, ironically, making a display of your Jewishness in Nablus remains a bad idea. Visitors should note that Nablus is a conservative city, so modest dress and behaviour is essential. Nablus was considered very much a 'no-go' area during the *intifada*, and though the city remains tense it is considered safe for foreign tourists to visit.

History

Ancient Shechem The long history of settlement at this spot is a function of its location on a major north–south route through the central hill country, and at the mouth of the region's only east–west pass. It was at this spot c. 1850 BCE that the patriarch **Abraham** entered the land of Canaan, and where "the Lord appeared unto Abraham, and said, 'Unto thy seed will I give this land'" (*Genesis 12:7*). It was also at Shechem that Jacob bought land for himself and his family (*Genesis 33:18-20*), whilst his son Joseph, following his death in Egypt, was buried here (*Joshua 24:32*). Edward Campbell suggests that, to the Israelite kings, Shechem "was the place to go to establish one's right to rule the region", and hence the desire of modern Israel's political and religious right wing to hang on to the West Bank (in other words, Judaea and Samaria): this is the land of the patriarchs, not Tel Aviv or Eilat.

At the end of the United Monarchy (928 BCE) the city became the capital of the northern kingdom ('Israel' as opposed to 'Judah'), but its political significance was soon eroded when the capital was switched to Samaria (see page 297).

Shechem suffered greatly from the Assyrian invasion of 724-722 BCE but experienced something of a revival in the Early Hellenistic period (332-167 BCE), and most notably in the wake of the construction of the **Samaritan** temple on nearby Mt Gerizim in the fifth to fourth century BCE (see page 292). The temple was razed during the Hasmonean ruler John Hyrcanus' sack of Shechem in 108/107 BCE, when the town was largely destroyed. Insubstantial remains of ancient Shechem, most notably from the Hellenistic period, can be seen at **Tell Balâtah** about two kilometres southeast of the modern town of Nablus.

Neapolis

Following the suppression of the First Jewish Revolt by the Roman army (66-73 BCE), a new Roman colony was established just to the west of the site of ancient Shechem: **Neapolis**. The fertile lands around Neapolis were divided amongst veterans of Titus' army, whilst a temple to Zeus was built on Mt Gerizim (see Tell er-Ras, page 295). Later centuries saw the construction of a hippodrome, amphitheatre and theatre, though the remains are not well presented today.

Arab arrival

Christianity became established here quite early, perhaps as a result of the gospel story of Jesus stopping to drink at Jacob's Well (*John 4:5-42*). In 484 CE the Church of Mary Mother of God was built on the site of the Samaritan temple on Mount Gerizim, resulting in several periods of conflict between the Samaritans and the Byzantine rulers.

Since the capture of the city by the **Arabs** in 636 CE Nablus has been a thriving Muslim population centre (apart from a brief interregnum from 1099-1187 when the Crusaders established a presence here). It became the capital of a governorate during the Ottoman period (1516-1917) when Jerusalem was a relative backwater, and later became the administrative centre during the period of the British Mandate. It has always been a focus of Arab opposition to Zionism, and subsequently to Israeli control, and was a centre of resistance during the *intifada*.

Reality of life under the Palestinian Authority has come as something of a shock to many of Nablus' citizens, with the experience of human rights abuses that were commonplace under Israeli military rule now being perpetuated by the Palestinian Authority's own security forces. Nablus' economy today is largely based on agriculture and the manufacture of soap and olive oil, plus the recent expansion of the city's industrial base.

Sights

Old City

Nablus' most attractive neighbourhood is the Old City, just to the south of Palestine Square. In many ways this is a welcome change from Jerusalem's Old City; the same narrow streets and alleyways are here but without the rampant commercialism. Strolling through these back streets is a fine way to spend some time. Amongst the more interesting buildings are the **Touqan Castle** and the **al-Shifa Turkish baths**. The former is a mansion dating to the Ottoman period. It remains occupied (by a number of families) though you can still appreciate the building from the courtyard. Nearby on Nasir Street (also known as Khalid ben el-Walid Street) are the 15th-century Turkish baths, recently restored and now the oldest working hammam in the country. ■ *T2381176. Daily 0800-2200. Women only on Wednesday 0800-1600. Baths 10 NIS, massage 10 NIS.* The **Hamman al-Hana** in the Old City offers similar services, with women only on Tuesday.

Of the city's many mosques perhaps the **al-Kabir mosque** is the most impressive, featuring a columned vaulted hall that was originally part of a Crusader church (built c. 1168). The mosque is easily identified by the tall minaret with silver cupola and crescent moon. Nearby is the blue-domed **al-Nasir**

West Bank

mosque. Neither is open to non-Muslims. It may be possible, however, to visit one of Nablus' traditional **soap factories** (try *al-Bader* at 20 Nasir Street, who are keen to show you around but speak little English).

Samaritan Quarter A community of Samaritans live in a small quarter of the old city of Nablus, just to the west of the town centre and in the shadow of their sacred mountain, Mt Gerizim (see page 294). There is a small synagogue here housing what is claimed to be the world's oldest Torah scroll. Nablus has one of just two Samaritan communities in the world (the other being at Holon).

Roman theatre The second century CE Roman theatre is located on the northern slope of Mt Gerizim, just above the old city (see map). With a projected diameter of around 110 metres it would have been one of the largest in the country, with three *cavea* (spectator seating areas). Unfortunately it was plundered by the Mamluks during the building of Nablus, and all that remains is a section of the lower *cavea* and some architectural fragments. The guy in the neighbouring metalwork shop has the key to the gate and will happily let you in.

Roman amphitheatre & hippodrome Insubstantial remains of the second century CE hippodrome lie on the south-west slope of Mount Ebal, formerly at the western approach to the Roman city. Superimposed on the circular end of the hippodrome are the remains of the third century CE amphitheatre, though both are difficult to find and not well presented.

Former British prison The former British prison, once used to house Arab and Jewish opponents of the British Mandate authority, is now the Palestinian Authority's Ministry of the Interior. Ironically, if reports from Amnesty International and the US Department of State are to be believed, the building remains a centre of repression. It is located to the east of the town centre, on the way to Tell Balâtah (you can't mistake its fortress-like appearance, with its huge portraits of Arafat beaming down).

Nablus

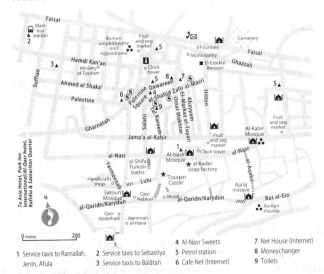

1 Service taxis to Ramallah, Jenin, Afula
2 Service taxis to Sebastiya
3 Service taxis to Balâtah
4 Al-Nasr Sweets
5 Petrol station
6 Cafe Net (Internet)
7 Net House (Internet)
8 Moneychanger
9 Toilets

Around Nablus

The first church built on this site dates to the end of the fourth century CE, and was **Jacob's Well**
built to commemorate the story of Jesus' meeting with the Samaritan woman where
he spoke about the "living water" (*John 4:4-30*). The incident is said to have taken
place at the site of the well dug by Jacob when he purchased land in the area (*Genesis
33:18-20*), with the 35-metre-deep well forming the centrepiece of the crypt beneath
the high altar. The church is mentioned by St Jerome in 404 CE though it was largely
destroyed in the Samaritan revolt against the Byzantine rulers in 529 CE. Despite
being repaired by the Emperor Justinian it was again levelled during the Persian
invasion of 614 CE. The Crusaders constructed a new church on the Byzantine
foundations in the 12th century CE though this church too stood in ruins until the
Russian Orthodox church acquired it in 1860. Unfortunately, their reconstructions
efforts were interrupted by the Russian Revolution and though the garden in which
it stands is currently subject to refurbishment work, the church itself remains a
roof-less shell. It is now owned by the Greek Orthodox church. The church is some
six metres below the present ground level, and is entered via the arched gate to the
west. Two flights of steps lead down from the main aisle of the basilica to the crypt,
where the well is located. If enough people are present the Greek Orthodox priest will
draw water from the well; it is remarkably cool and sweet. ■ *T2375123. 0800-1200
1400-1700 daily. Free. Souvenir shop in the crypt, toilets and café at entrance. Work
continues slowly but surely to complete the building of the church. To reach the site head
southeast from Nablus, take the left fork down the hill and look out for the white-walled
compound with the Greek and Palestinian flags above the gate.*

Today, ancient Shechem is little more than a series of unimpressive remains **Ancient**
occupying three dips in an area of open ground usually populated by lounging **Shechem (Tell**
Palestinian policemen and kids playing football. Excavations at the site have **Balâtah)**
revealed 24 distinct strata of occupation dating from the Chalcolithic period
(c. 4000 BCE at the earliest) until the Late Hellenistic period (the sacking by
John Hyrcanus c. 107 BCE). The only gaps within this period of occupation are
c.3300-1900 BCE, 1540-1450 BCE, 1150/1125-975 BCE and 475-331 BCE.
The most impressive (or is that the least unimpressive?) remains are on the
north side of the tel, and feature the defensive **Cyclopean wall** (c. 1650 BCE),
the **northwest gate complex**, and the *migdal* or **fortress temple**. The **east
gate** is also reasonably well preserved.

Service taxis pass the modern village of Balâtah that surrounds the site,
though it is in fact probably easier to walk (see 'Around Nablus' map). Balâtah
is a refugee overspill from Nablus.

Though comparisons are frequently made between the similar architectural **Joseph's Tomb**
styles of Joseph's Tomb in Nablus and Rachel's Tomb near Bethlehem, this
small domed structure bears a closer resemblance to an Israeli military position. Along with the Temple Mount in Jerusalem and the Cave of Machpelah
(Tomb of the Patriarchs) in Hebron, this is one of the three places that Jews
claim as theirs by right of historically documented purchase. The *Book of
Joshua* recalls how, following his death, "the bones of Joseph, which the children of Israel brought up out of Egypt, buried they in Shechem, in a parcel of
ground which Jacob bought of the sons of Hamor the father of Shechem for an
hundred pieces of silver: and it became the inheritance of the children of
Joseph" (*Joshua 24:32*). After centuries of Muslim control the last decade has
seen the tomb in the hands of the Israelis, or more accurately the Israeli army.
In the protests that followed the controversial opening of the Hasmonean tunnel in Jerusalem in September 1996, the Israelis and Palestinians turned their

West Bank

guns on each other at Joseph's Tomb, leaving five Israeli soldiers dead, and the yeshiva here ransacked (and its books burned). Not surprisingly the site remains tense and visitors may not be allowed access. Morning seems to be the best time to try, though officially it's open 0800-1800. Modest dress must be worn (including head coverings for both sexes).

Mt Gerizim The Samaritan sacred mountain of Mount Gerizim stands 868 metres above sea-level, and 500 metres above Nablus below. Those who make the two-hour hike to the summit (or 50 NIS taxi ride) will not be disappointed by the view across Samaria; on a clear day the Mediterranean coast to the west is clearly visible. Samaritan religious celebrations reach their peak at Passover, when the community who have spent the 40-day period living on the summit of Mt Gerizim (in the modern houses on the plateau below the summit) ritually slaughter a sheep in the manner laid down by Moses (*Exodus 12:1-51*).

The Samaritan community believe that it was on Mt Gerizim and not Mt Moriah (Temple Mount) in Jerusalem that Abraham offered his son Isaac for sacrifice. In part, this belief derives from the view that the biblical description of the sacrifice site – "Abraham lifted up his eyes, and saw the place afar off" (*Genesis 22:4*) – better fits Mt Gerizim than the insignificant hill that is Mt Moriah.

Josephus (*Jewish War; Antiquities*) provides much of the early history of settlement on Mount Gerizim, documenting the various disputes between the Samaritan and Jewish communities. A walled city of about 40 hectares was built on the upper ridge during the Hellenistic period, with the thick layer of ash on the floor of all the buildings confirming the city's destruction by John Hyrcanus c. 108/107 BCE. Of the buildings from this period still discernible, the most impressive are remains of the **residential quarters**, the **sacred precinct** (modelled on the Temple Mount in Jerusalem), and the so-called **Twelve Stones** (part of a second century BCE building).

Related map:
A. Nablus, page 267.

Around Nablus

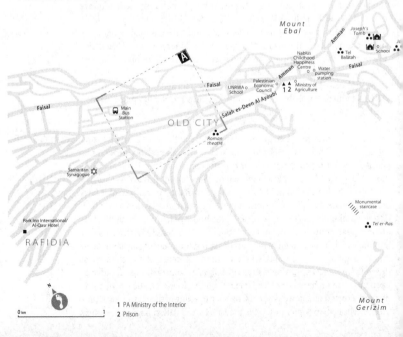

1 PA Ministry of the Interior
2 Prison

West Bank

The Samaritans

Best known to the Christian world through Jesus' parable of the "Good Samaritan" (Luke 10:30-37), the Samaritans are a dissident sect of Judaism numbering probably less than 600 adherents worldwide. Almost the entire community live in Nablus or Holon (near Tel Aviv). Recognizing only the first five Books of Moses as their Torah, plus its immediate sequel, the Book of Joshua, the Samaritans consider themselves as true Jews. Their origins lie within the demise of the United Monarchy following the death of Solomon (928 BCE), and the subsequent split between the northern kingdom of Israel and the southern kingdom of Judah. The settlement of large numbers of foreigners in Samaria following the Assyrian invasion of 722-721 BCE led many Jews in the southern kingdom of Judah to suspect the purity of the Judaism in the northern kingdom (Israel), yet when the Jews of Judah returned from the exile imposed upon them in 586 BCE by the Babylonians, they were rather perturbed to find the Samaritans claiming to be the true guardians of the pure faith of Moses. The

final break between the Samaritans and the Jews came in the second century BCE.

Samaritan power was concentrated around the site of their sacred mountain, Mt Gerizim, though the rise to prominence of Christianity in the area brought them into open conflict with the Byzantine empire. The first shot in this war was fired by the Byzantine emperor Zeno (474-491 CE), who in 484 CE built the Church of Mary, Mother of God on the Samaritan sacred area on Mt Gerizim. Skirmishes between the two communities continued, reaching a bloody climax in the Samaritan revolt of 529 CE. The emperor Justinian's response to the Samaritans' nationwide church-burning and Christian-massacring spree was swift and equally brutal, effectively reducing the Samaritan community to the relatively insignificant relic that it remains today.

Following the destruction of the settlement on Mt Gerizim, Samaritans continued to ascend the mountain to pray. According to the writings of Procopius (*Buildings 1-17, v, vii*) this was because they worshipped the summit itself, and not because they had ever built a temple there. During the struggle between the Samaritans and the (Christian) Byzantine empire, the Emperor Zenon built a large octagonal church on the summit. It is clear that the siting of the **Church of Mary, Mother of God** on an area sacred to Samaritans was deliberate, possibly as an attempt to convert them but definitely as a demonstration of superiority. The church was partially destroyed on a number of occasions in the ensuing conflict between the Byzantines and Samaritans, with many of the later additions to the church comprising defensive fortifications. Looking at the plan of the remains today the lines of the octagonal church within a wall fortified by defensive towers are immediately apparent. It was largely destroyed by the Arabs in the eighth century CE, and the fortress walls dismantled. The modern tomb at the northeast corner belongs to Abu Ghanen, a Muslim holy man.

Mt Gerizim actually comprises two perpendicular ridges; the lower one running east–west and the upper one running north–south. Facing Nablus on the north face of the lower ridge are the remains of a **temple** dedicated to **Zeus Hyposistos** (the supreme). The remains stand upon an artificial mound that is now referred to as Tell er-Ras. Nearly all the coins minted at Neapolis between the mid-second century CE and the mid-third century CE depict the temple, reached by a long monumental staircase. Later writers (such as the Bordeaux Pilgrim c. 333 CE and Epiphanius c. 315-403 CE) mention the 1,300-1,500 step staircase ascending Mount Gerizim. Excavations have revealed two main

Tell er-Ras (Roman temple)

phases of construction at the temple (mid-second century CE then early third century CE), though only 65 or so of the stairs remain intact.

Mt Ebal   Whilst Mt Gerizim stands to the south of Nablus, the town is defined to the north by Mt Ebal. The former is blessed, whilst the latter is considered cursed (*Deuteronomy, 11:29*). Though a site dating from the Iron Age I (1200-1150 BCE) has been found on the northeast slope (and variously interpreted as an Israelite cultic site or a fortified tower), most visitors to Mount Ebal come for the view. As the great biblical geographer George Adam Smith observed, "No geography of Palestine can afford to dispense with the view from the top of Ebal".

Essentials

Sleeping   **A** *Asia*, PO Box 88, Rafidia, T2392321, F2386220. New hotel in Rafidia district on the western outskirts, furnished a/c rooms with small balconies, modern bath, dish TV, phone, minibar, lobby coffee shop, *Layali Zaman* restaurant. **A** *Park Inn International/Al-Qasr*, Omar Ibn al-Khattab, Rafidia, T2385444, F2385944. Located on the western outskirts of town, 40 recently renovated and furnished a/c rooms, dish TV, phone, minibar, 2 restaurants plus roof terrace, lobby bar. **G** *El-Esteklal Bension (Al-Estiqlal Pension)*, 11 Hitten, T2383618. Light and airy (but not very private) basic 4-bed dorms, shared bath, plus some basic private rooms with shared bath (**E**). Friendly; women allowed but may feel uncomfortable.

Eating   Sticky sweets, most notably *kanafe* (soft cheese in an orange wheat flake jacket and covered in honey), are Nablus' speciality and can be tried at numerous stalls and shops in the Old City area. One of the best is *Al-Nasr Sweets* (see map), which serves excellent *kanafe* for 3 NIS per plate. There are any number of restaurants in the town centre (mainly around Palestine Sq) offering good value kebabs, grills, falafel and shwarma.

Transport   **Local**   Car hire: *Orabi*, T2383383. Taxis: *Al-Ittimad*, T2371439; *Al-Madina*, T2373501.

Long distance   Buses: Nablus' main bus station is a parking lot to the west of the town centre (see map). Most of the buses run to surrounding Palestinian villages, although there is a slow, lumbering service to **Ramallah** that stops at all points in between (8 NIS, 1 hour 20 minutes). Service taxis are a better bet. **Service taxi**: the easiest way to reach Nablus is by service taxi. Coming from **Jerusalem** you will have to take one from outside Damascus Gate and change at Ramallah (3 NIS, 30 minutes). From **Ramallah** it takes 1 hour (10 NIS). From Nablus, service taxis to **Ramallah**, **Jenin** and **Afula** run from outside the main bus station to the west of the town centre (see map). Service taxis to **Sebastiya** (for the site of **Samaria (Sebaste)**, 5 NIS, 20 minutes) run from a spot on Suffian, near its junction with Hamdi Kan'an (see map). Service taxis along Faisal St to Tell Balatah, Joseph's Tomb and Jacob's Well (1 NIS) run from just north of Palestine Sq (ask for 'Balatah').

Directory   **Airline offices** *Gulf*, T2386312; *Lufthansa*, T2382065; *Royal Jordanian* have an office near the post office. **Banks** There are branches of most of the Arab banks (plus a few money-changers) in and around Palestine Sq, though it's probably best to change money before coming to Nablus. **Communications** Area code: T09. **NB** Nablus numbers are now 7 digit and begin with a '2'. **Post offices**: *Central Post Office* on Faisal (Sat-Wed 0800-1300 1500-1700, Thu 0800-1300, Fri closed) sells PA stamps. **Internet/email**: *Café Net*, 2nd floor, Palestine St (see map), T2392843. 10 NIS per 1 hr. *Net House*, Na'em Abdul Hadi Building, Omar Mokhtar (though entrance is on Omar Khayyam), T/F2392086, email jawad@net-house.net 10 NIS per 1 hr. **Telephones**: the telephone exchange is next to the Central Post Office. **Cultural centres** *Al-Yasmin-Assalah Centre*, T2386723, F2384568; *British Council*, T2385951, F2375953; *French Cultural Centre*, T/F2385914; *Palestinian Scientific Society (Palestinian Cultural Project Network)*, T/F2942111. **Hospitals and**

West Bank

medical services **Chemists**: most of the chemists are located close to the hospitals, and around Palestine Sq. **Hospitals**: *Al-Amal Centre*, T2383778; *Al-Ittihad*, T2371491; *Al-Watani*, T2380039; *Arab Medical Centre*, T2371515; *St Luke's*, T2383818; *Rafidia*, T2390390; *Red Crescent Society*, T2382153. **Tour companies and travel agents** *Palestinian Association for Cultural Exchange (PACE)*, Ramallah, T02-2986854, and *Amani Tours*, Ramallah, T02-2987013, offer tours to Nablus (from Ramallah). *Unlimited*, T2385949, based in Nablus, can also arrange tours. **Tourist offices** The Tourist Information Kiosk is located on the traffic island to the north of Palestine Sq (see map). They have a few maps and brochures and are keen to help. The **Ministry of Tourism** is housed on the eighth floor of a building on Hamdi Kan'an (see map), though they are genuinely surprised to receive visitors. **Useful addresses and phone numbers** Police: T2383518. Ambulance: T101 (T2385077). Fire: T2383444.

Samaria (Sebaste)

Located on the low hill above the Arab village of Sebastiya, 12 kilometres north-west of Nablus, is the site of the city of Samaria: the former capital of the northern kingdom of Israel and centre of the region of Samaria. The site has been extensively excavated and contains remains from a number of periods of occupation.

Phone code: 02
Colour map 2, grid A4

West Bank

Ins and outs

The easiest way to reach the site is to take a Jenin-bound service taxi from Nablus to the Arab village of Sebastiya, and then climb the hill. Make sure the driver knows where you want to get off (5 NIS, 20 minutes). There are also service taxis direct to the village of Sebastiya from Nablus (see page 296). To return, flag down any passing traffic.

Getting there

History

A city was founded here by **Omri** c. 876 BCE (*I Kings 16:23-24*), and subsequently added to by his son and successor **Ahab** (871-852 BCE). The masonry used for the Israelite construction at Samaria is renowned for its high quality of

Samaria (Sebaste)

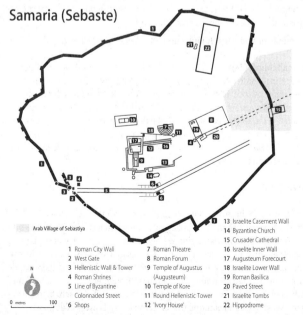

Arab Village of Sebastiya

1 Roman City Wall	7 Roman Theatre	13 Israelite Casement Wall
2 West Gate	8 Roman Forum	14 Byzantine Church
3 Hellenistic Wall & Tower	9 Temple of Augustus	15 Crusader Cathedral
4 Roman Shrines	(Augusteum)	16 Israelite Inner Wall
5 Line of Byzantine	10 Temple of Kore	17 Augusteum Forecourt
Colonnaded Street	11 Round Hellenistic Tower	18 Israelite Lower Wall
6 Shops	12 'Ivory House'	19 Roman Basilica
		20 Paved Street
		21 Israelite Tombs
		22 Hippodrome

0 metres 100
N

workmanship, largely learnt from the Phoenicians.

It was during the reign of **Jeroboam II** (784-748 BCE) that Samaria reached its peak of prosperity, though the evolution of a privileged ruling class was to raise the ire of the prophet Amos (*Amos 3:9-15*). Jeroboam's death saw a decline in fortune of the Israelites at Samaria, with increasing **Assyrian** influence being felt in the region, most notably in the large numbers of foreigners that they settled here (*II Kings 17:24*). This was one factor in the rise to prominence of the **Samaritan** community, and their subsequent split from the Jews.

Samaria remained the administrative capital of the province of the same name, with successive Assyrian, Babylonian and Persian governors, until **Alexander the Great** conquered the city (332 BCE). Large numbers of Macedonians were settled in Samaria, giving it a largely Greek ethnic, cultural and political feel, whilst the Samaritan community were expelled to Shechem. Hellenistic influence was terminated by the arrival of the Hasmonean ruler **John Hyrcanus**, who razed the city and sold its inhabitants into slavery (c. 108/107 BCE).

The city was subsequently granted to **Herod the Great** in 30 BCE by the Romans. He completely rebuilt the city, naming it **Sebaste** after his sponsor (Sebaste being Greek for Augustus), and it soon developed into a great and splendid city. The rise of neighbouring Neapolis (Nablus) saw Samaria enter into a terminal decline, despite some modest building projects at the site by the **Byzantines** and **Crusaders** (related to the tradition that John the Baptist, or his head at least, lay buried here).

Sights

Remains from almost all building periods can still be found at Samaria. The most striking remains from the various periods are as follows:

Israelite   The **casement wall (13)** around the acropolis; the artefacts from the **Ivory House (12)**, with the group of ivory objects found here comprising the most important collection of Iron Age miniature art found in Israel (see *I Kings 22:39* and *Amos 6:4*).

Hellenistic   The **round tower (11)**, described by the site's excavators as one of the most impressive remnants of the Hellenistic period found in Israel.

Roman   The **Temple of Augustus (Augusteum) (9)**, theatre (7) and forum (8).

Byzantine and Crusader   The **small church (14)** on the south side of the hill began life as a three-aisled monastic chapel in the sixth century (celebrating the finding of John the Baptist's head), but underwent substantial alterations in the Crusader period; the **Crusader cathedral (15)** in the village of Sebastiya itself was built on the site of a Byzantine church commemorating the reputed burial place of John the Baptist, though in later years it was converted into a mosque by Salah al-Din. ■ *T09-2342235. Saturday-Thursday 0800-1700, Friday 0800-1600, closes one hour earlier in winter. Adult 10 NIS, student 6 NIS. Toilets, refreshments.*

Moving on

From Samaria/Sebastiya, Route 60 continues north through 'Emeq Dothan, or the **Valley of Dothan**. The biblical city of Dothan has been identified with the mound of **Tel Dothan** rising 60 metres above the valley at a point 22 kilometres north of Nablus. The city is associated with the story of Joseph being sold into slavery by his brothers (*Genesis 37:15-36*), though there is little to see at the site today. Route 60 continues through the small Arab town of **Jenin** (44 kilometres from Nablus), passing the site of **Ta'anach**, before leaving the West Bank and entering the Jezreel Valley of Lower Galilee.

Dead Sea Region

5

Dead Sea Region

In describing the Dead Sea Region, the great biblical geographer George Adam Smith was moved to say: "Surely there is no region of earth where Nature and History have more cruelly conspired, where so tragic a drama has obtained so awful a theatre." (Historical Geography of the Holy Land, 1894).

Visitors to the Dead Sea Region today are attracted by this combination of the "natural" and the "historical". A region of stunning, almost shocking, beauty, this section of the Great Syrian/African Rift Valley combines the lowest point on earth (some 400 metres below sea-level) with one of the world's most singular features – the Dead Sea. This large lake, with its high salt content, enables bathers actually to float above the water's surface. A whole tourist industry has grown up from the desire to experience this peculiar sensation, whilst 'health resorts' have sprouted at points along the coast to take advantage of the supposed therapeutic and cosmetic benefits of the Dead Sea muds and minerals. The region's natural beauty can also be appreciated in a number of hikes through protected areas such as the Nahal David ('En Gedi) Nature Reserve.

The Dead Sea Region also contains two of Israel's most important historical-archaeological sites. Though Qumran can hardly be called the most spectacular of attractions, its importance derives from the fact that this is where the famous and controversial Dead Sea Scrolls were discovered. Masada, on the other hand, is one of those rare species where its importance as a historical-archaeological site is actually matched by its visual impact. Scene of the famous last stand of the Zealots in the First Jewish Revolt against the Romans (66-73 CE), Masada combines panoramic views from its mountain-top location with archaeological remains that bring its past alive. This is a site in Israel that should not be missed.

Ins and outs

The Dead Sea Region is linked via Route 90 (then Route 1) to Jerusalem to the north-west, and by Route 90 to Eilat to the south. Although the main sites have good bus connections to Jerusalem (1½ hours) or Eilat (3 hours), travelling around the Dead Sea region itself by public transport requires some advanced planning. Bus schedules to most destinations are posted outside the 'En Gedi Youth Hostel and the Masada Youth Hostel. Of course, a hired car is the ideal way to explore the region. Those on a tighter budget may like to try one of the day package tours organized from Jerusalem, although these provide only very limited time at each spot.

It should be noted that most of the accommodation in the region is in the **L2**, **L3**, and **A** price categories, with the cheapest options being the **E** category Youth Hostels at 'En Gedi and Masada.

Background

Geography

The Dead Sea, in reality a lake, is a substantial body of water some 80 kilometres in length, up to 18 kilometres wide, and situated at 395 metres below sea level. Its surface area is contracting but is generally put at 1,049 square kilometres. The deepest point in the lake is estimated at 400 metres. The Dead Sea is divided into two unequal sectors; a larger northern area of very salty receding lake, and a shallow, smaller southern basin. Between the two is a dried out, gradually expanding, isthmus or interlaken. The land surrounding the Sea is arid and bleak, with the heavily saline soils being useless for agriculture without special treatment and expensive irrigation.

The Dead Sea is fed primarily by the Jordan River, and the effect of upstream exploitation (such as the Israeli National Water Carrier and the Jordanian pumping of the Yarmuk) has led to a significant fall in its water levels; in fact less than 100 years ago the Sea was 12 metres higher (and possibly 10 metres higher as recently as 1960), whilst 50,000 years ago it was some 225 metres higher. With no outlet, water from the Dead Sea is lost via evaporation; as much as 25 millimetres per 24 hours during the summer peak. A number of interesting proposals are being investigated that imagine water from the Mediterranean replenishing the Dead Sea, with further exploitation of the power generation potential of the water falling into the Jordan Valley.

The northern basin is the focus of most tourist activity, particularly on the west (Israeli) side, with special designated 'beaches' providing changing rooms and fresh-water showers, plus health and beauty treatment centres. The southern basin is comparatively shallow and has suffered severely from the combined effects of falling water level and the exploitation of the area for potash extraction. Both the Jordanian and Israeli sides feature large evaporation pans.

The Dead Sea has special chemical characteristics given its low altitude and the lack of external drainage. Evaporation has helped to increase the salt content of the sea, while the wadis that run into it include heavily sulphurous spring waters. The waters of the Dead Sea are saline and increase in salt content with depth. In the surface layer of water to a depth of 40 metres the salt content of the water is approximately 300 parts per 1,000 and temperatures are some 20°C-37°C. Few people can submerge themselves in densities of this kind so the effects of the lower layers are academic! The surface layer is very rich in bicarbonates and sulphates (and heavy in health-giving iodine, bromine and magnesium if Dead Sea resort literature is to be believed) and the Sea is underlain by natural salts and a mud layer of silts brought down by the Jordan River. Certainly, the high salinity of the Dead Sea means that there are few bacteria in the water, which is therefore safe for bathing and other forms of immersion.

History

Despite the seemingly inhospitable nature of the Dead Sea region, there is in fact a long record of human activity in the surrounding area. The history of the Dead Sea region is very closely intertwined with the history of the Judean Desert that lays to the northwest and west; in fact, the Judean Desert has acted more as a point of contact than a physical barrier between the Dead Sea and the population centres to the northwest and west. Human occupation along the shores of the Dead Sea did not end with God's destruction of Sodom and Gomorrah (*Genesis 18, 19*).

The region has primarily been seen as both a place of refuge and as a centre for commercial exploitation. The Dead Sea Works that was established here by the British in 1930 is merely a continuation of a process of commercial exploitation that may have begun almost 2,500 years ago with the Nabateans, who sold the surface bitumen to the Egyptians for use in the embalming business; an industry that continued well into Roman times. Whilst the Dead Sea Works continue to produce significant quantities of potash, bromine, magnesium, chloride and salts (as well as being an important employer of residents of towns such as Dimona), the Dead Sea region is increasingly looking towards tourism as its major source of revenue and employment. But once again, like the industrial exploitation of the Dead Sea's resources, this is not a new phenomenon. A great deal of the Dead Sea's tourism industry is geared towards the apparent 'health and beauty' potential of the local environment. Much is made of the increased oxygen in the air (a function of the Dead Sea's position vis-à-vis sea level), the pollution-free environment, and the medicinal properties of the various bromine, magnesium, iodine and mud treatments. Yet, as stressed before, this idea of the Dead Sea region as a 'refuge' from the rigours of the modern world is not new. Communities of hermits and ascetics (possibly including groups such as Essenes or individuals like John the Baptist) appear to have sought refuge in the region over 2,000 years ago, in addition to political refugees who include amongst their number King David, Herod the Great and the Jewish Zealots (at Masada and possibly Qumran). Thus the fat old men and women who jostle you for position in the 'En Gedi Spa may be the latest link in a chain that began three millennia ago with King David.

Qumran

Though this site is rather unprepossessing, its significance derives from the fact that this is where most of the Dead Sea Scrolls were discovered (see box on page 308). There are few sites in Israel/Palestine that create more controversy and ill-feeling between theologians, archaeologists and historians than Qumran, yet few issues surrounding the site and the treasures found here have been satisfactorily resolved. For example, there is still ferocious debate with regard to the date of the founding of the community, the nature of the community settled here, their period of occupation, their reason for abandoning the site, and the date that the occupation finished. In fact, every single aspect of life at Qumran!

Phone code: 07
Colour map 2, grid C5

Ins and outs

Getting there — All buses between Jerusalem and 'En Gedi, Masada, Eilat etc on Route 90 stop opposite the turning to the site (5-minute walk uphill), though you should take care to remind the driver to stop. Qumran is also accessible by bus from Arad, but not from Jericho (service taxis only). For bus timings, see entries under the destinations mentioned on page 302. Most visitors to Qumran just visit the National Park and then continue on their way, though there is some pleasant accommodation just up the road at the **B-C** *Kalia/Qalya Holiday Village*, Kibbutz Kalia, T02-9942833, F9942710. This quiet guesthouse features 16 a/c doubles with fridge, TV, phone, or 6 a/c family apartments, bar, kosher dining hall, restaurant, mini-market, solarium, pool, children's entertainment.

Getting around — The compact nature of the site, and the fact that it is clearly labelled, means that a detailed tour description is not necessary. It is worth seeing the short film about the site in the new 'cinema' at the entrance. Note that it is not possible to explore many of the caves in which the Dead Sea Scrolls were found. Cave 6 to the northwest is the most readily accessible, whilst Cave 4 is clearly visible in the cliff face across the ravine from the observation point.

The site

Who lived at Qumran? — The 'consensus' view is that Qumran was occupied by a Jewish break-away group referred to as the **Essenes**. This sect, or sub-sect, of Judaism is generally characterized as celibate, ascetic, reclusive, pacifist, and divorced from the mainstream of religious, political and social thought; hence Qumran would appear to be a perfect location for such a group. Such an image of the Essenes is derived from their depiction in the works of Josephus (*Jewish War II, VIII; Antiquities XVIII, I*), Philo (*Every Good Man is Free, XII-XIII; Hypothetica, 11*) and Pliny (*Natural History, V, XV*), with the inference being that they closely resemble the modern idea of a monastic order.

This image is challenged by a number of commentators, most spectacularly Baigent and Leigh (see *Dead Sea Scrolls Deception* box, page 306), who claim that evidence from both the Qumran site itself and found within the Dead Sea Scrolls not only fails to support the idea of a pacifist, celibate and isolated community, but in fact suggests the complete opposite. They base their claims on a number of points: i) If the community here were celibate, why are there graves of women and children in Qumran's main burial ground? ii) If the group were pacifist, why does Qumran contain such a prominent defensive tower, and what is the purpose of the forge nearby? Linking this point to the Dead Sea Scrolls themselves, Baigent and Leigh highlight how the so-called War Scroll is hardly pacifist. iii) Why is there no reference to the term 'Essene' in the Dead Sea Scrolls? iv) If, as Philo suggests, the Essenes have no cult of animal sacrifice, what is the purpose of the animal bones carefully placed in pots that were discovered at the site? v) If, as Josephus asserts, the Essenes were on such good terms with Herod the Great, why does the site appear to be have been destroyed shortly after the start of his reign, and only reoccupied immediately following his death? Further, why does the corpus of Dead Sea Scrolls material make several criticisms of uncle–niece marriages; criticism for which Herod (a practitioner) had John the Baptist executed?

Of course, there are equally compelling, but equally difficult to prove, counter-arguments. For example, with regard to the burial ground, the fact that the sheer number of burials (possibly 1,200, of which only 50 have been excavated) vastly exceeds the accommodation capacity of Qumran has been suggested as an indication that many of the burials (notably the women and

Dead Sea Region

children) may have been brought from some distance away, perhaps been linked to the Qumran community by kinship or ideology. Further, the idea that Qumran was in fact a military fortress is countered by the suggestion that Qumran "is of inferior strategic value and the flimsy walls of the complex could not have had military value" (Broshi, 1993).

Indulging Baigent and Leigh for a moment, if Qumran was not occupied by Essenes, then who occupied the site? Pointing to similarities in the text and nomenclature between the Dead Sea Scrolls and the Gospels, Baigent and Leigh suggest that the Dead Sea Scrolls (particularly the "Habakkuk Commentary") are actually referring to the same events depicted in Acts of the Apostles (*Acts*), Josephus, and the works of early Christian historians. Yet they are far from suggesting that Qumran was occupied by the 'early Christians' as we know them; far from it. Baigent and Leigh suggest that Qumran was occupied by the "**zealots for the Law**" who were led by Jesus' brother James, and strictly followed Jesus' teachings of the supremacy of the Law. As such, they were more of a Jewish revivalist movement, rather than seeking to create a new religion (subsequently Christianity). It is further suggested that the group at Qumran had more in common with the image of the **Zealots** at Masada (see page 318) than with the traditional image of the Essenes (pointing out that Qumran-style Dead Sea Scrolls were also excavated at Masada).

Naturally, to proponents of the counter-arguments as to who actually occupied Qumran, the dating of the period of occupation is essential. Believers in the 'conspiracy-theory' argument would claim that those presenting the 'consensus' view have sought to establish an early date for the settlement of Qumran so as to give credence to the theory that the Dead Sea Scrolls were written in the Hasmonean period (mid-second to mid-first-centuries BCE), and thus are safely pre-Christian. Likewise, those challenging the 'consensus'

When did they live here?

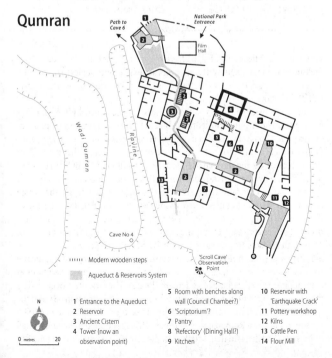

☞ **"The Dead Sea Scrolls Deception"**

Amongst the huge body of literature on the subject of the Dead Sea Scrolls probably the most accessible and entertaining read is provided by Michael Baigent and Richard Leigh's "The Dead Sea Scrolls Deception" (1991, plus later reprints). It is difficult to dismiss easily many of the conclusions drawn by Baigent and Leigh, and in many regards the points that they make appear far more credible than the framework of assumptions and interpretations that has been presented as undisputed fact (the so-called données, or 'givens' of history) by many of the disseminaters of the Dead Sea Scrolls material.

There are three main themes running through "The Dead Sea Scrolls Deception". Firstly, Baigent and Leigh explore what has been widely referred to as the "academic scandal par excellence of the twentieth century", whereby "a small enclave of scholars with vested interests and a biased orientation" (who may not even be best qualified to examine the body of scroll material) have unfairly monopolized all research on the original Dead Sea Scrolls.

Access has invariably been denied to academics not associated with the "international team" of scholars who hold the original material in their possession, whilst only a negligible percentage of the Qumran material was actually finding its way into print.

Secondly, the question of why so much of the Qumran material is being withheld is examined in some detail, with Baigent and Leigh concluding that the prime reason is some form of conspiracy surrounding the Catholic Church. In a progressive and logical argument, the authors suggest that the scroll material reveals some unpalatable truths about the origins of Christianity, which the Catholic Church (through the Ecole Biblique et Archéologique Française, which is heavily represented in the "international team" charged with deciphering the scrolls) is seeking to suppress. Baigent and Leigh contend that this is why the "international team" have sought to distance the scrolls (by dating and chronology) from the early Christian church. The authors draw attention in

---

view (such as Baigent and Leigh) have sought to establish a later date, thus making settlement at Qumran contemporary with events depicted in the New Testament (*Acts of the Apostles*), Josephus (*Jewish War*) and the works of early Christian historians.

The 'consensus' view is that the site was first occupied by the Israelites between the eighth and sixth centuries BCE. The first really important phase of occupation (Phase Ib) is dated to the Hasmonean ruler John Hyrcanus (134-104 BCE). A number of coins found at the site suggest that the peak of Phase Ib came during the rule of Alexander Janaeus (103-76 BCE). The site's principle excavator Roland de Vaux (head of the Ecole Biblique et Archéologique Française, and according to Baigent and Leigh the prime mover in the Catholic conspiracy over the Dead Sea Scrolls), dates the end of this phase of occupation to 31 BCE. For his evidence, he points to a long crack in one of the cisterns, suggesting that this was caused by the great earthquake of 31 BCE that Josephus describes (*Jewish War I, 19, 3-370; Antiquities XV, 5, 2-122*). De Vaux then suggests that the earthquake caused the catastrophic fire (of which deep ash remains have been found) that consumed the Qumran community. The next phase of settlement (Phase II) saw the site reoccupied by the same group c. 4 BCE, before being destroyed by the Romans in 68 CE at the height of the Jewish Revolt. It is then claimed that the settlement was occupied for some years by a Roman garrison (Phase III), abandoned following the fall of Masada (73 CE), and then briefly occupied by Jewish rebels during the Bar

particular to the way in which a "consensus" has been reached regarding the dating of the community, the nature of the group who lived at Qumran, and the date and reasons for the community's demise. For example, even the free brochure that you get when you visit the National Park today follows the "consensus" view on the date of the foundation of the site (second century BCE), the nature of the community (Essenes) and the date the settlement was abandoned by them (68 CE). Robert Eisenman (Chairman of the Department of Religious Studies and Professor of Middle East Religions at California State University in Long Beach, and leading opponent of the "consensus" view) suggests that a "small group of specialists, largely working together, developed a consensus ... in lieu of clear historical insight ... [and that] preconceptions and reconstructions, such as they were, were stated as facts, and these results, which were used to corroborate each other, in turn became new assumptions, that were used to draw away a whole generation of students

unwilling (or simply unable) to question the work of their mentors" (Maccabees, Zadokites, Christians and Qumran, 1983).

Finally, Baigent and Leigh examine what it is within the Dead Sea Scrolls that can be so unpalatable to the Catholic Church, and reach dramatic conclusions. They suggest that, contrary to the "consensus" view, the community at Qumran were not the pacifist Essenes, but in fact the "zealots for the Law" that characterized the dramatic last stand against the Romans at Masada (see page 318). They further suggest that at the centre of the scrolls material is the story of the community's leader, none other than Jesus' brother St James, "whose dispute with Paul precipitated the formulation of the new religion subsequently known as Christianity"! They further suggest that Paul (who was perhaps a Roman agent or informer) effectively moved in the completely opposite direction to Jesus' teachings of the supremacy the Law (Matthew 5:17-19), instead propagating the Pauline philosophy of supremacy of faith (Romans 1:17; Galatians 3:11) – now a basic tenet of Christianity.

Dead Sea Region

Kokhba (Second Jewish) Revolt (132-135 CE). Much of de Vaux's evidence is based on coins found at the site, and on an interpretation of historical-literary sources.

This 'consensus' view is dissected and challenged point by point by Baigent and Leigh, notably de Vaux's emphasis on the one coin dating to 135-104 BCE, when in reality the number of coins from 103-76 BCE (143) suggests that this was nearer the date that the community was founded (the two earlier coins presumably being older ones remaining in circulation). Baigent and Leigh next challenge de Vaux's earthquake-fire theory, suggesting that "instead of trying to identify the cause of the crack ... de Vaux went rummaging for an earthquake that might have been responsible." Conveniently he found one in Josephus. Baigent and Leigh point to the relationship between the approximate date of the fire (c. 31 BCE) and the date of the site's reoccupation (c. 4 BCE), stressing how closely these dates match the period of rule and then death of Herod the Great (37-4 BCE). The implication is that the community was deliberately destroyed on Herod's orders, possibly because he saw the movement as a challenge to his rule (note the criticism of uncle–niece marriages mentioned on page 304). Of course, once again this challenges the idea of a community "divorced from the mainstream of religious, political and social thought", and contradicts Josephus' image of the Essenes as being supported by Herod. Baigent and Leigh once again assert that the Qumran community were not Essenes as traditionally depicted.

☞ **The Dead Sea Scrolls**

A chance discovery in 1947 by a young Bedouin shepherd boy, Mohammad adh-Dhib of the Ta'amireh tribe, has now passed from being one of the greatest archaeological finds of this century to what some describe as the "religious scandal of the century" and "academic scandal par excellence" (see Dead Sea Scrolls Deception box, page 306). Whilst searching for a stray goat in caves on the northwest shore of the Dead Sea, the shepherd boy came across a number of earthenware jars containing leather scrolls wrapped in linen. Once it became apparent that something of value had been found here, a series of excavations and bounty-hunting expeditions began (though it's difficult to distinguish between the archaeologists and the Bedouins as to who were the bigger trophy-hunters). A veritable corpus of material has now been gathered from caves in the region, much of it in fragments, but other sections, such as the "Isaiah Scroll" being several metres long. Most of the material has been divided into two broad categories, 'religious' and 'secular', though most scholars now consider the latter category as more interesting (and controversial)

since it seems to indicate much about the community at Qumran and elsewhere. Briefly summarized below are what some commentators who oppose the 'consensus' interpretation of the Dead Sea Scrolls consider to be the most interesting finds.

The Copper Scroll: Discovered in Cave 3, and so named because the scroll is actually a roll of copper with the writing punched in to the metal, this is an inventory of buried treasure concealed at 64 sites (none of which has been identified). If the figures listed are to be believed, the treasure comprises almost 25,000 kilogrammes of gold and over 59,000 kilogrammes of silver. The treasure is generally thought to derive from the Temple, though some commentators (notably the 'international team', see Dead Sea Scrolls Deception box, page 306) deem the treasure to be fictitious. If the inventory was compiled in anticipation of the Roman invasion following the outbreak of the Jewish Revolt (66 CE), it gives a CE date to the Dead Sea Scrolls, with major implications for dating the Qumran community.

The Community Rule: Found in Cave 1, this scroll documents the rules and

De Vaux's conclusions about Phase II of Qumran's occupation are also challenged, in particular his dating of the termination of the community in 68 CE (based primarily on findings of coins). By setting such a date, Baigent and Leigh claim, de Vaux is able to state that "none of the manuscripts belonging to the community is later than the ruin of Khirbet Qumran in AD 68" (*Archaeology and the Dead Sea Scrolls*, 1977), and thus the events that they discuss cannot be contemporary with events depicted in Acts of the Apostles (*Acts*), Josephus, and the works of early Christian historians. However, Baigent and Leigh believe that the distribution of coins from after 68 CE actually proves nothing, countering that de Vaux's emphasis on the fact that most of the coins are not Judaic is spurious since "in the years following the revolt, Roman coins were the *only* currency in Judaea. This being the case, they need hardly have been dropped solely by Romans." Thus, the latest date for the scrolls being deposited at Qumran is not 68 CE, but Bar Kokhba's time (ie 136 CE). It is also possible to challenge de Vaux's assumptions about Phase III (the brief Roman occupation between 68 CE and 73 CE), with Driver in particular noting that de Vaux's "greatly simplified" canal system that the Roman garrison is claimed to have built is in fact too crude to be considered Roman (Driver GR, *The Judaean Scrolls*, 1965). Thus, many of the buildings at Qumran may have been destroyed in 68 CE, but the site was not necessarily abandoned, and may have been occupied right up until 136

rituals governing the community at Qumran. Of particular interest to scholars who see links between the Qumran community and what is known as the 'early Christian church' (eg Baigent and Leigh) are the numerous similarities between both the various laws and rituals described, and the nomenclature by which they are called.

The War Scroll: Found in Caves 1 and 4, this scroll operates on two levels. On the one hand it is clearly a manual for conducting war, whilst on the other hand it is an order of battle for an apocryphal war between the "Children of Light" and the "Children of Darkness". As such, it challenges the 'consensus' view of a pacifist group settled at Qumran. Baigent and Leigh also argue that it clearly refers to the soldiers of imperial as opposed to republican Rome (ie post-27 BCE), and thus must refer to the Roman invasion of 66 CE and not 63 BCE.

The Temple Scroll: Possibly found in Cave 11, though this is not certain, this scroll deals with both rituals and rites of observance at the Temple in Jerusalem, plus details of design, furnishings, fixtures and fittings. As such, it suggests that

contrary to the 'consensus' view, the community at Qumran were not divorced from mainstream Jewish life or contemporary religious affairs. The Temple Scroll is also the source of one of the references to the condemnation of uncle–niece marriages that Baigent and Leigh suggest as an indication of the animosity between the Qumran community and Herod the Great.

The Habakkuk Commentary: Found in Cave 1, this document appears to be a chronicle of the life and times of the Qumran community, and hence dating this text would go a long way towards proving who exactly they were, and when they occupied this site. Its reference to the victorious Roman troops sacrificing to their standards (as opposed to gods) again suggests the imperial Roman invasion, as opposed to the republican Roman invasion, and thus a CE and not BCE date. Interestingly, Josephus describes such a practice following the fall of the Temple in 70 CE (Jewish War, VI, vi). Baigent and Leigh also see parallels between events described in the Habakkuk Commentary and those outlined in the Acts of the Apostles.

CE. Of course, it should also be pointed out that if the community at Qumran were indeed Zealots, or closely linked with the group holding out at Masada, they would hardly be left unmolested at Qumran whilst the Roman army was besieging Masada (until 73 CE). However, if it proves nothing else, the argument over Qumran shows how open to interpretation the field of archaeology is. ■ T02-9942235. Winter 0800-1700 daily, summer 0800-1700 daily. Adult 16 NIS, adult in group 14 NIS. Cafeteria, huge souvenir shop, toilets.

This large reserve features a series of winding streams and freshwater pools amongst the reeds and grass, and is unique in having such natural freshwater bathing spots so close to the Dead Sea itself. In theory it is possible to view a selection of animals in the reserve, though on busy days they seem to be driven away by the sheer numbers of visitors. There are a number of ruins within the reserve that appear to be contemporary with those at Qumran, though they are less well presented. **NB** It may be necessary to dress a bit more modestly if bathing in the pools or Dead Sea here (women in particular). This spot is popular with Palestinian families. ■ T02-942355/9942355. April-October 0800-1700, November-March 0800-1600. Adult 25 NIS, child 15 NIS. Cafeteria, freshwater showers, toilets.

'En Feshka (Einot Zvquim Nature Reserve)

Dead Sea Region

Qalya/Kalia Beach Water Park This (fresh) water park, featuring slides, wave-machines, beach with fresh-water showers, and go-kart track is located on the shores of the Dead Sea, five kilometres north of Qumran. ■ *T02-9942391. March-December 0900-1700 daily. 64 NIS, or 40 NIS after 1400. Follow sign for "Water Park, Qalya Beach and Karting 2000". Buses 486/487 stop at the junction for the water park.*

Metzoke Dragot

Phone code: 07
Colour map 2, grid C5

The Metzoke Dragot area (including the Mazoq HaHe'teqim Nature Reserve) is the centre of 'adventure tourism' in the area, offering rock climbing, rappelling, mountain biking, jeep tours, plus several treks of varying degrees of difficulty. This area is also the home of the Wadi Murabba'at Caves, where a number of important artefacts have been found.

Ins and outs About 17km south of 'En Feshka along Route 90, a road winds steeply up to the west (signposted "Metzoke Dragot International Centre for Desert Tourism"). Any bus between Jerusalem and 'En Gedi (on to Eilat) will drop you at the turning (give the driver plenty of warning), although it is at least a 1-hour walk from Route 90 up to the Centre.

Metzoke Dragot International Centre for Desert Tourism The Centre offers rock climbing courses (450 NIS), rappelling courses (275 NIS), as well as taking one-day rock climbing (750 NIS) and rappelling (600 NIS) expeditions to designated sites in the cliffs of the Judean Desert. Most of the hikes in this area require a guide; note that the **Lower Wadi Darga (Deragot)** hike is for experienced hikers only, and requires climbing with ropes and swimming across deep pools. Enquire at the Centre about desert treks, jeep tours, mountain biking and motorcycling tours. **Accommodation** in the **C** price category is provided by nearby *Kibbutz Mizpe-Shalem*, T02-9944222, F9944333.

Nahal Tekoa hike This hike can be attempted without a guide, and is highly recommended, featuring some of the area's best views, and taking in interesting archaeological sites such as the Wadi Murabba'at Caves. **Warning**: a long section of this hike passes through an IDF live firing range, so **can only be attempted on Saturdays and holidays**. Check with the Metzoke Dragot Centre before attempting it.

Metzoke Dragot area (including Nahal Tekoa hike)

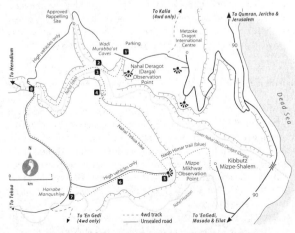

The Wadi Murabba'at (Bar Kokhba) Caves

A number of caves are dotted along this section of the Wadi Murabba'at, four of which have been found to contain important remains from the Chalcolithic period (4500-3300 BCE) onwards. Of particular note were the documents found here relating to the Bar Kokhba Revolt (Second Jewish Revolt) of 132-136 CE. The majority of finds date to the Roman period, and include pottery, coins, weapons, tools, keys, sandals, bone dice, and an interesting wooden stamp. Many documents were also found, including seventh-century BCE papyrus fragments, plus an ancient Torah scroll containing portions of Genesis, Exodus and Numbers. There are also fragments from Deuteronomy, Isaiah, and a number of minor prophets. Of special interest are the Hebrew and Aramaic documents from the time of the Bar Kokhba Revolt, most notably a letter sent to Joshua son of Galgula, and believed to be signed by Shimon ben Kosiba. Most of these finds are now displayed in the Shrine of the Book at Jerusalem's Israel Museum.

The complete loop is 14 kilometres and takes eight to nine hours to complete. The starting point (**1**) is at the parking lot some two kilometres west of the Metzoke Dragot Centre. Follow the black trail-markers down to the southwest, towards the **Nahal Deragot** (known here as **Wadi Murabba'at**). The black trail heads sharply west, parallel and above Nahal Deragot, eventually ascending to the **Wadi Murabba'at Caves** (**2**).

Just beyond the caves the black trail is joined by a red trail, at the point where the Nahal Deragot meets **Nahal Tekoa** (**3**). The Nahal Tekoa valley traverses the Judean Desert in a broadly northwest-to-southeast direction, rising at the settlement of Tekoa close to the Herodian, before joining the Nahal Deragot here and draining into the Dead Sea. The word 'deragot' roughly translates as 'descent' in Hebrew, and describes the way in which the two seasonal streams drop down to the Dead Sea.

Having crossed the Nahal Tekoa/Deragot junction (**3**), follow the red trail in a southeasterly direction along the south bank of the wadi. After a short distance it begins a steep ascent up the cliff-face, via a series of switchbacks (**4**). From the top there is a good view of the Wadi Murabba'at Caves. The red trail continues in a southeasterly direction, gradually moving away from the cliff-face. Continue towards the communications antenna at the **Mizpe Mikhwar Observation Point** (**5**). The view from here fully justifies all the exertion thus far. To the west can be seen the Hebron Hills, with the Judean Desert to the west, northwest and north. However, it is probably to the east, across the Dead Sea, that the view is most spectacular. Almost directly east across the Dead Sea, where the hills seem to form a natural amphitheatre, lie the hot springs of **Callirrhoe**, made famous by Herod the Great (see *Jordan, Syria and Lebanon Handbook* for further details). The whitish cone in the hills just to the south is believed to be the site of **Machaerus**, where Herod had John the Baptist beheaded (*Matthew 14:9-12*, see *Jordan, Syria and Lebanon Handbook* for further details).

From the observation point a very steep blue trail descends to the southeast. If you are not hiking on a Saturday, it is impossible to continue the Nahal Tekoa hike west from Mizpe Mikhwar Observation Point since you will be entering an IDF live firing zone. The options are to return the way that you came, or head down the blue trail towards Kibbutz Mizpe-Shalem and Route 90. Note that this trail, **Naqb Himar** ('trail of the donkey'), is very steep and great care must be taken. It is thought to be part of the original supply trail cut by the Romans between Tekoa and Masada.

For those hiking on a Saturday (and who have ascertained that it is safe to pass through the IDF firing range), head west along the rough road that runs along the cliffs above Nahal Hazezon (**6**). After about two kilometres you reach **Harrabe Manqushiye** (**7**), a rock-cut reservoir that also served as a rest-stop on the Tekoa–Naqb Himar–Masada road. Having crossed the wadi here, take the dirt road heading northwest, eventually reaching the Nahal Tekoa after three kilometres or so (**8**). Follow the black trail-markers southeast (right) into the gradually narrowing Nahal Tekoa canyon, and follow it as far as the Wadi Murabba'at Caves (**2**). From here you climb back up to the starting point.

'En Gedi Region

Phone code: 07
Colour map 2, grid C5

*'En Gedi is a large oasis on the western shore of the Dead Sea, taking its name from a perennial spring that rises some 200 metres above and one kilometre west of the Dead Sea. It was held as a biblical symbol of beauty (Song of Solomon 1:14), retaining that image today as a vibrant splash of greenery, rich vegetation, pools and waterscapes amongst the austere hills of the Judean Desert and the sterile depths of the Dead Sea. The 'En Gedi Region includes two Nature Reserves (the Nahal David and the Nahal 'Arugot; sometimes known collectively as **'En Gedi Nature Reserve**), one of the Dead Sea's best established bathing beaches (**'En Gedi Beach**) and a health and beauty resort providing therapeutic bathing (**'En Gedi Spa**). There are also a number of accommodation options, which make 'En Gedi a good spot from which to explore the Dead Sea Region.*

Ins and outs

Getting there   The 'En Gedi region is easily accessible by bus from Jerusalem, Eilat, Arad and Be'er Sheva (see page 316 for timings), although many visitors come on a day trip that does not really do justice to the region.

Getting around   There is a shuttle bus that runs between Kibbutz 'En Gedi Guesthouse and 'En Gedi Spa (details on page 316), although you really have to walk between the various sites (unless you have your own transport).

History

The most celebrated story concerning 'En Gedi recalls David's flight from Saul, when he sought sanctuary in the "wilderness of En-gedi" (*I Samuel 24:1*). David passed up the opportunity to kill Saul when the latter went into a cave to "cover his feet" (*I Samuel 24:3*), ie take a dump. David chose instead to prostate himself at Saul's feet (after he'd finished his business), leading to the reconciliation of the two. There is significant evidence of settlement throughout the region in the Chalcolithic period (4500-3300 BCE), most notably at the Chalcolithic temple inside the

'En Gedi region

To Qumran

Nahal David

To Nahal 'Arugot National Park

Nahal 'Arugot

'En Gedi Beach, Pundak Restaurant

Dead Sea

Kibbutz 'En Gedi & Guesthouse / Holiday Resort

N

0   metres   500

To 'En Gedi Spa, Masada

1 'En Gedi Youth Hostel
2 SPNI Field School
3 Main entrance to Nahal David Nature Reserve

Nahal David Nature Reserve, whilst 'En-Gedi is then listed amongst the wilderness cities of Judah (*Joshua 15:62*) prior to reaching its fame during Saul's reign (c.1020-1004 BCE).

In later years it is mentioned by Josephus in the context of raids by the Sicarii during the First Jewish Revolt (66-73 CE, see *Jewish War IV, 402*), with documents found in the Cave of Letters in Nahal Hever to the south suggesting that it was also a centre of Jewish activity during the Bar Kokhba Revolt (132-136 CE). 'En Gedi remained a large Jewish village cultivating dates and balsam-producing plants throughout the Byzantine period, though subsequent occupation has been far more intermittent.

Sights

Many people spend insufficient time here and end up following the hordes of visitors who pop in, head up to **David Falls** (15 minutes), continue to **Dodim Cave** (40 minutes), head up to the Chalcolithic temple (10 minutes), on to **'En Gedi Spring** (5 minutes), and then leave again after little more than an hour. If you come on one of the 'see the Dead Sea in one day' type tours, this is what you will end up doing, though for those with children or unable to walk long distances this will probably be enough. If you can spare the time, base yourself locally and spend four to six hours on the **Dry canyon hike** that takes in all the main sites and gets you away from the crowds. **NB** This hike is not suitable for all, and involves some steep ascents and descents. Do not forget to bring plenty of drinking water.

Nahal David Nature Reserve

This hike begins at the SPNI Field School (**2**) above the 'En Gedi Youth Hostel (**1**). From the parking lot outside the Field School, follow the road up to the

Dry canyon hike

Dead Sea Region

Nahal David Nature Reserve (including the 'dry canyon hike')

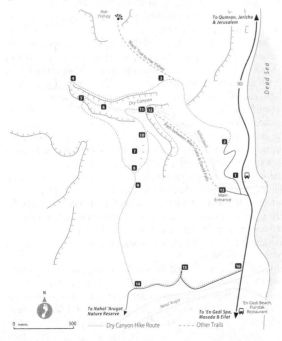

Har Yishay

To Qumran, Jericho & Jerusalem

Black Trail to Har Yishay

Dry Canyon

Dead Sea

90

Path between Main Gate & David Falls

Nahal David

2

1

13
Main Entrance

4

5

6

11 **12**

10

7

8

9

15

16

14

N

To Nahal 'Arugot Nature Reserve

Nahal 'Arugot

To 'En Gedi Spa, Masada & Eilat

'En Gedi Beach, Pundak Restaurant

0 metres 500

······ Dry Canyon Hike Route   – – – Other Trails

Chalcolithic temple at 'En Gedi

The Chalcolithic temple at 'En Gedi dates to the Ghassulian phase of the Chalcolithic period (nearer to 3300 BCE than 4500 BCE), with all the remains found at the site suggesting that it was used solely as a cult place with no indication of domestic use. It comprises a broadhouse to the north, opening on to an enclosed courtyard, with a smaller broadhouse to the east. The circular structure built of small stones at the centre of the courtyard served some cultic purpose. A gateway in the northeast corner leads to Nahal David, whilst a more elaborate gate in the south wall leads to 'En Gedi Spring. It appears that the main altar stood in the north wall of the larger broadhouse: a conclusion drawn from the remains found there (including a clay statuette of a laden bull, animal bones, ashes, etc). The sunken pits at the east and west ends of the larger broadhouse also contained burned bones, horns and pottery amongst the ashes.

small amphitheatre and exit through the gate in the fence. There is nobody here to collect your admission fee. Follow the black trail in a steep upwards direction (it is sign-posted "Ma'ale Har Yishay"). After a short distance the trail divides, with the black trail continuing up to Har Yishay to the right (at least one hour), and the red trail continuing straight ahead. Follow the red trail towards the four-metre-high cliff (**3**), and continue up it. **NB** It is very easy to lose the trail here since one of the red trail markers appears to be missing, and if you're not careful you'll climb too high and re-meet the black trail. Thus, after ascending the low cliff, take the lower path to your left towards the edge of the cliff above the Nahal David canyon, and you'll soon see the next red marker. Continue along the path above Nahal David and David Falls (which you can hear below) until you reach a small gully (**4**). Drop down into the gully and follow it round to the left where it enters the **dry canyon** above the Nahal David. **NB** Do not enter this canyon if there is the slightest possibility of rain, since it is subject to flash-floods. Also note that the rocks in this canyon have been worn treacherously slippery by water action.

Not far into the dry canyon, shortly after it has become steeper and narrower, a number of metal stakes have been hammered into the rock to your right (**5**) to show you the route out of the canyon, and to assist your ascent. However, before exiting the dry canyon, it is possible to follow it to the Window Fall at its end. **NB** If you continue past this point (**5**) towards Window Fall (**6**), you should note that not only are there are some difficult descents (usually involving sliding down on your backside), but that you must also return this same way: ascending these almost sheer faces, where the rock is smooth and very slippery, is not easy. If you do feel confident enough to take on this challenge, the view is certainly worthwhile. Several water-hollows that fill up in winter and spring need to be negotiated, though their level will depend upon the season and recent rainfall. The canyon ends at **Window Fall** (**6**), where the view down upon Nahal David and the Dead Sea is beautifully framed by the canyon sides. There is a large pool here, though it often appears too murky for bathing (though it is much better after a recent flashflood when it has been washed out and its level is higher). From the beginning of the hike to this point should take about one hour.

Return to the metal stakes (**5**) and climb back out of the canyon to the south. You soon hit a green trail running parallel to the dry canyon. Follow it to the left (southeast), and then continue to the top of the small hill in front of you. The hill looks down upon the whole 'En Gedi area, with the **Chalcolithic temple** (**7**) below you.

Tel Goren

Five levels of occupation have been identified at Tel Goren: (v) End of Iron Age (c. 630-582 BCE); (iv) Persian period (fifth to fourth centuries BCE); (iii) Hellenistic period (mainly Hasmonean period from Alexander Janaeus to Herod, 103-37 BCE); (ii) Early Roman *period (mainly Herodian dynasty, 4 BCE-68 CE); (i) Late Roman and Byzantine periods (second to sixth centuries CE). Unfortunately, there is little to see here today.*

Follow the path down from the Chalcolithic temple, taking the right (south) at the trail intersection (**8**) to **'En Gedi Spring** (**9**). The spring provides welcome relief on a hot day, though it has to be noted that it is only mid-shin deep, and is impossibly crowded if more than five people are gathered here. There are several options from here: i) Continue south along the trail, taking in Tel Goren (**14**) and the Ancient Synagogue (**15**), before returning to Route 90 (**16**) at a point 500 metres south of the Youth Hostel (**1**); ii) Follow the loop trail to the north, visiting Dodim Cave (**11**), then David Falls (**12**), before exiting the Nature Reserve at the main gate (**13**); iii) Visiting Dodim Cave (**11**) and David Falls (**12**) as described in option ii), then returning to 'En Gedi Spring (**9**) to pursue option i). The route described here follows option iii).

Head north from 'En Gedi Spring, taking the right fork at the intersection (**8**), and passing beneath the ledge upon which the Chalcolithic temple stands (**7**). After several minutes walking, you reach another trail intersection (**10**). To visit the Dodim Cave take the signposted trail down to your left. Leopards are said to inhabit this area occasionally, though it is extremely unlikely that you will meet any. If you do, however, pick up a few stones and retreat slowly, occasionally throwing a few stones to discourage the leopard from following you. It should be noted that the leopards do all they can to avoid contact with humans. You are likely to come across ibex here, though, whose rustling in the reeds may scare the life out of you. The trail soon reaches the banks of Nahal David, though it is forbidden to follow it up to its source for fear of disturbing the flora and fauna. Note above you the 'mouth' of Window Falls. Descend to Nahal David using a series of ladders-cum-steps cut from the rock, before crossing the stream. Follow the path along the north bank to a large boulder. On the path below you it is possible to see swarms of visitors making their way up to David Falls. To reach Dodim Cave (**11**) (sometimes called Shulamit Cave), climb down the series of metal steps and grab rails. Unless you climb down (there are two separate ladders), the cave is largely hidden, though a full descent really means getting wet in the lovely pool here.

From here, retrace your steps to the intersection (**10**), then follow the path in a loop round to **David Falls** (**12**). Though the streams and falls here are very pleasant, unless you're very lucky this section of the Nature Reserve tends to be very busy. From David Falls you can either follow the path back to the main entrance (**13**), or climb back up to the intersection (**10**) to return to 'En Gedi Spring (**9**) and continue the tour.

From 'En Gedi Spring, follow the sign for 'Tel Goren' heading south. Crossing a modern water pipe, and passing a **Crusader flour mill**, descend the hill following the green-and-white arrows. Cross the first dirt road that you meet on your descent, then turn right when you meet the second. As you pass through a gate, a small yard with a stone circle marked out within it serves as a monument to eight members of the early Jewish settlers' self-defence organization, the 'Hashomer' or 'watchmen', who were killed here. The low mound just above this monument, surrounded by a wire fence that appears to have given up long ago, is the site of **Tel Goren** (**14**) (see box).

Beyond Tel Goren is the exit to the Nahal David Nature Reserve, where you hit the surfaced road. A right turn (west) here leads to Nahal 'Arugot Nature Reserve (see page 316), whilst by following the road to the left (east) you soon come to the **Ancient Synagogue (15)** (easily identifiable by the tent-like roof built over it for protection).

From the Ancient Synagogue, follow the paved road until it hits the main road, Route 90 (**16**). From here it is approximately 500 metres back to the Youth Hostel (**1**). ■ *Summer 0800-1700, winter 0800-1600. Adult 20 NIS, adult in a group 17 NIS, ticket allows access to Nahal 'Arugot Nature Reserve on the same day. Snack-bar, drinking water and toilets at the entrance. There are some rules that must be observed: you must leave Dodim Cave by 1430, 'En Gedi Spring by 1500 and Shulamit waterfall by 1530; it is forbidden to smoke or eat within the reserve; it is preferred that you walk in groups of three or more to deter possible leopard attack, though there is no recorded instance of any ever having taken place here.*

Nahal 'Arugot Nature Reserve Less famous than its neighbour, the Nahal 'Arugot Nature Reserve receives far fewer visitors than the Nahal David Nature Reserve, and it is easier to get away from the crowds. The most popular walk is up to the Hidden Waterfall, about one and a half hours from the entrance (follow the marked trail along the stream), though you can continue up to the Upper Pools. The entrance to Nahal 'Arugot Nature Reserve is about two kilometres along the turn-off from Route 90, a kilometre south of the 'En Gedi Youth Hostel. ■ *0800-1500 daily. Adult 12 NIS, or free if you have same day ticket from Nahal David NR.*

Essentials

Sleeping & eating E *IYHA Beit Sarah 'En Gedi Youth Hostel*, T6584165, F6584445. Massive new extension now complete though still necessary to book during weekends and Jewish holidays. Single-sex 5-8 bed a/c dorms with attached bath, some private doubles (**C**) or $18 per additional adult, breakfast $6, dinner $10, check-in 1600, check-out 0900, usual standards of cleanliness. E *SPNI Field School*, T6584288. Some 5-6 bed a/c dorms, plus private rooms (**C**), kitchen, advance booking recommended.

Transport Although the bus times given here may change during the life-span of this book, they give some idea as to the frequency of services. The timetables are usually posted at the *Youth Hostel* reception. All the buses heading south stop at 'En Gedi Spa, Masada Junction (2.6km from Masada, with some continuing to the site itself) and 'En Boqeq. The number in brackets is the bus number.

Arad: Bus 385, Sunday-Friday 1115. **Be'er Sheva**: Bus 384, Sunday-Thursday 0800 1230 1530 1800, Friday same but last at 1530. **Eilat** (via **Masada**, **'En Boqeq** and **Arava Road**): Bus 444, Sunday-Thursday 0750 1050 1450 1750, Friday same but last at 1450. **Jerusalem**: Sunday-Thursday 0545 (487) 0855 (486) 1005 (444) 1215 (486) 1300 (444) 1445 (421) 1545 (486) 1640 (486) 1700 (444) 1800 (487) 2000 (444), Friday same but last bus at 1445, Saturday 1800 (487). Add or substract about 5 minutes if catching the bus at 'En Gedi Beach, Kibbutz 'En Gedi or 'En Gedi Spa.

'En Gedi Beach

The main (though not necessarily the best) bathing spot in the northern Dead Sea Region is the 'En Gedi Beach, a little over one kilometre south of the 'En Gedi Youth Hostel and Nahal David Nature Reserve. The beach is rather stony and unattractive, but has changing rooms (5 NIS), toilets (1 NIS), left luggage (5 NIS), some shade and freshwater showers. A lifeguard is on duty 0800-1600. **NB** Keep an eye on your possessions whilst bathing here. The *'En*

'Swimming' in the Dead Sea

With a salt concentration of over 20 percent, the Dead Sea actually supports one's body on the surface, and prevents 'swimming' as such: 'floating' in the Dead Sea is a far more accurate description. There are several points to bear in mind before taking the almost obligatory dip in the Dead Sea. Firstly, it is best to use one of the recognized 'beaches' since these have fresh-water showers that allow you thoroughly to wash off the residue that is left on your skin after bathing. Secondly, it is important to avoid getting the water in your eyes since it will sting like hell and may cause inflammation. If you do get the water in your eyes, rinse immediately and continuously with fresh water. For this reason, noticeboards at the beaches outlaw splashing. The water of the Dead Sea also tastes extremely unpleasant, and may make you feel sick if swallowed. Because of the high salt content, the water causes agony in every minute scratch and cut (including some that you may not know that you had); thus the Dead Sea region is a haven for designer stubble and George Michael look-a-likes since shaving prior to a dip in the sea is not to be recommended.

Because floating in the Dead Sea is such an unusual experience, it is not recommended that you attempt to lie on your front in the water; flicking yourself over onto your back is not as easy as it sounds, and might be a cue to splash water in your eyes/mouth. In fact most of the beaches have noticeboards giving information on how to get into the water (walk backwards and then assume a sitting position). Children should be supervised, with the 'ground-rules' carefully explained to them.

Gedi Pundak Beach Restaurant offers kosher bland cafeteria-style food (eg shnitzel and chips 30 NIS, portion of chips 7 NIS, credit cards over 30 NIS) from 0730-1730, including Saturdays and holidays. The overpriced *'En Gedi Camping Village* is currently (permanently?) closed. There is **Tourist Information** at the *Paz* gas station (T6584444, 0900-1300 1330-1600). For onward travel see page 316 (though you will have to add/subtract five minutes or so, and bear in mind that some services stop at 'En Gedi Beach for a break).

Kibbutz 'En Gedi

Kibbutz 'En Gedi is located about one and a half kilometres off Route 90, about one and a half kilometres south of 'En Gedi Beach. Though agriculture plays a large part in the economy of the kibbutz, it is sustained through tourism (most notably through the hotel it runs).

A-B *'En Gedi Guesthouse/Resort Hotel*, Kibbutz 'En Gedi, T6594222, F6584328. Offers **Sleeping** half or full-board in "rustic-style units" in rural setting, a/c, phone, cable TV, dining hall, bar, tennis, gym, indoor and outdoor pools, restaurant, discount at spa.

A free (for guests) shuttle bus runs 8 times per day between the kibbutz and the spa. **Transport** For onward travel see page 316 (though you will have to add/subtract 5 minutes or so, and bear in mind that some services stop at 'En Gedi Beach for a break).

'En Gedi Spa

Four kilometres south of the turning for Kibbutz 'En Gedi is the 'En Gedi Spa. The spa offers "the famous Dead Sea black mud and natural minerals" treatment, as well as therapeutic bathing in sulphurous pools. *Facilities may be free to Guesthouse/Resort Hotel guests, but check. Otherwise, admission 54 NIS with*

Ancient Synagogue at 'En Gedi

It is believed that several synagogues have stood on this site, the first possibly dating to the end of the second or beginning of the third century CE, and prominently featuring the swastika as either a decorative element or as a symbol of good luck. Substantial changes were made to the building some time between the mid-third and the beginning of the fourth century CE, at a time when 'En Gedi was described as "a very large Jewish village" (Eusebius, Onomasticon). Again, the synagogue was rebuilt in the late fifth century CE,

and a colourful new mosaic pavement laid. An interesting feature of the mosaic pavement from this period is the fact that although it includes the names of the signs of the zodiac in inscriptions, unlike contemporary synagogues at Hammath-Tiberias and Beit Alpha, it does not bear their images. This has led some to suggest that the community here was rather conservative. Dating the synagogue's demise is not conclusive, though it could date to the persecutions of the early years of Justinian I's reign (527-565 CE).

discounts for weekly/monthly tickets, deposits required for lockers, towels and bathrobes, massage from 130 NIS, spa open 0700-1800, beach open 0700-1730. For onward travel see page 316 (though you will have to add or subtract five minutes or so, bear in mind some services stop at 'En Gedi Beach for a break).

'En Gedi to Masada Approximately seven kilometres south of 'En Gedi the **Nahal Hever**, one of the deepest canyons in the Judean Desert, drains into the Dead Sea. During the Bar Kokhba Revolt (132-136 CE), Jewish fighters sought refuge from the Romans in the deep caves on both sides of Nahal Hever's valley. Two caves in particular have revealed remains, artefacts and documents that, in the words of the Israeli archaeologist Yigael Yadin, "have enriched the body of knowledge about the material culture of this period" (*New Encyclopedia of Archaeological Excavations in the Holy Land*, 1993). The **Cave of Horrors** revealed the skeletons of 40 men women and children who had been starved to death by the Roman siege of the cave. In the nearby **Cave of Letters** archaeologists discovered "the largest group of complete documents yet uncovered in the Judean Desert" (Yadin, *ibid*), with the 'archive of Babata' and the 'Bar Kokhba Letters' being considered of such importance that they are now displayed in the Shrine of the Book in Jerusalem's Israel Museum. Neither cave is accessible to visitors.

Two kilometres south on Route 90, the **Nahal Mishmar** drops sharply over a steep cliff into the Dead Sea Valley (from 270 metres above sea level to 30 metres below). About 50 metres below the top of the cliff it is just possible to discern the **Cave of Treasure**, where valuable objects from the Chalcolithic (4500-3300 BCE) and Bar Kokhba (132-136 CE) periods were found.

A further four kilometres south on Route 90, one of the longest canyons in the Judean Desert, **Nahal Ze'elim**, flows into the Dead Sea. A number of caves in this valley revealed items from the Chalcolithic (4500-3300 BCE), Iron Age II (1000-586 BCE) and Bar Kokhba (132-136 CE) periods.

Masada

Phone code: 07
Colour map 3, grid A6

The high fortress at Masada must be one of the greatest and most exciting viewpoints in the Middle East, overlooking vast areas of the Dead Sea/Rift Valley and the Jordanian Heights. Yet Masada is more than just a spectacular viewpoint. The extensive excavations carried out here have confirmed as fact much of the

Jewish historian Josephus' account of the extraordinary events here in the first century CE. As the last outpost of resistance in the Jewish Revolt of 66-73 CE, it was here that 967 Jewish 'Zealots' preferred mass suicide to submission to Rome. Today, Masada is one of Israel's most popular (and most visited) archaeological sites, though within the Israeli psyche Masada represents far more than just an ancient place of archaeological interest.

Ins and outs

Masada is located just off Route 90, around 18km south of 'En Gedi (and 15km north of 'En Boqeq). Some of the buses between Jerusalem and Eilat (via 'En Gedi) will take you all the way to the site, whilst others will only drop you at the turn-off (from where it's 2.6km to the site). Make sure that the driver knows you want to get off at Masada. **Getting there**

Many visitors to Masada take advantage of the early opening hours of the site (0430) to climb to the top so that they can watch the sun rise over the Dead Sea and the Jordanian Heights. It is advisable to bring warm clothes since it can be rather cold waiting for the sun, even in summer. Cold drinking water is available at the *Youth Hostel* at the bottom of the Snake Path, and at the summit. Site entrance fee is paid at the bottom. **Getting around**

The site

Viewed from the north, Masada is an enormous rock pinnacle standing out from the main ridges and peaks of the hills of the Western Dead Sea coast. The site is separated from its surroundings on all sides by precipitous slopes: 120 metres on the west where it connects to the hill range behind, 400 metres on its northern and southern sides and more than 434 metres on the coastal cliff. The cliff top is rhomboid in shape, measuring approximately 600 metres north–south and 300 metres east–west at the centre. The fortress has immense natural barriers and land access is possible only by two steep paths. In addition, the approach to the site as a whole from the west is through the bleak and poorly watered hills of Judaea or from the east through the wilderness of the Wadi Arava. Both were difficult to penetrate and gave the Masada site a unique strength, exploited in the Jewish revolts against Roman rule.

History

The main written historical sources on Masada are the works of Josephus (*Antiquities*; *The Jewish War*), though like everything else from this source, a healthy degree of scepticism is required when examining details. There still remains some doubt as to the nature of the site here during the Hasmonean period, and things only become clearer during the Herodian era.

   Most of the remains seen today at Masada date to the reign of **Herod the Great** (37 BCE-4 BCE), though some structures were certainly built later by the Zealots. Most archaeologists now conclude that building at Masada under Herod falls into three main phases: i) early phase **c. 35 BCE**; ii) main phase **c. 25 BCE**; iii) late phase **c. 15 BCE**. Herod's association with Masada began in 40 BCE, when he was fleeing with his family from the pretender Antigonus and the Parthian army. Herod's brother Joseph, with 800 men, resisted Antigonus' siege, though they are only said to have survived dying of thirst by a fortuitous cloud-burst that filled the rock-cut cisterns on the summit. When Herod returned from Rome in 39 BCE, he rescued his family and then set about adding to Masada's considerable natural defences. It should be noted that Herod viewed Masada as less of a strategic stronghold protecting his kingdom, but more as a place of refuge for himself. Though Josephus suggests that the greatest threat to Herod's newly legitimated kingdom came from "Cleopatra, queen of Egypt", the threat of "peril … from the Jewish people, lest they should depose him and restore their former dynasty to power" should not be dismissed too lightly (*Jewish War, VII, 300*).

Masada's history subsequent to Herod's death in 4 BCE is unclear, though it was certainly occupied by a Roman garrison at the outbreak of the Jewish Revolt in 66 CE. Though Josephus does not give details, Masada was captured "by stealth" by the Jews, and its Roman garrison exterminated (*Jewish War, II, 408*). It subsequently became a refuge for the duration of the Revolt, ruled by the "tyrant" or "autocrat" **Eleazar, son of Jair, son of Judah** (Eleazar ben Yair/Jair). The origin of Masada's fame, other than its astonishingly fine site, comes from the events here which led to the self-inflicted massacre of the Hebrew **Zealots**. The story of the Masada siege arose following the Jewish flight from Jerusalem in 70 CE after the destruction of the Temple, and forms one of the most riveting passages in Josephus' *The Jewish War* (*VII, 275-407*). The Zealots increased the level of fortification at Masada (72-73 BC) and held out against a 15,000-man Roman army for two years before a ramp and iron tower were constructed up the mountain slope by the Romans to gain entry by force. At the first sign that the defences would be overwhelmed as the outer Herodian stone wall was breached and then the inner wooden retaining walls were set on fire, the Zealots took their own lives, leaving only two women and five children alive out of the garrison estimated at nearly 1,000 persons. A section of Eleazar ben Jair's speech that incited the mass suicide, as reported by Josephus, is included in the free brochure and site plan that you are given upon entry to the National Park. It is generally believed that Josephus used considerable artistic licence in his account of Eleazar ben Jair's stirring words (some suggest that he made the entire thing up), though archaeology has largely confirmed the events that he outlined. Evidence has been discovered to suggest that the storerooms of the defenders remained well stocked (to show the Romans that the mass suicide had not been dictated by hunger), whilst eleven small ostraca discovered close to the Water Gate may even contain the original 'lots' that were cast to decide who should kill whom (*Jewish War, VII, 396*).

The site was occupied by a Roman garrison for some years after the siege and mass suicide of 73 CE, perhaps as late as 111 CE if the evidence of coinage found here is taken into consideration. Pottery finds have also suggested that Nabatean soldiers were included amongst the Roman siege troops and subsequent garrison. Christian monks appear to have occupied Masada during the fifth and sixth centuries CE, constructing a church to the northeast of the Western Palace. Following their demise, Masada appears to have been largely forgotten until being correctly identified by Robinson and Smith in 1838 (from 'En Gedi, via a telescope!). It is interesting to note that the name 'Masada' appears only in Greek and Latin transcriptions. Yadin speculates that it may be an Aramaic form of *ha-mesad*, or 'the fortress' (*New Encyclopedia of Archaeological Excavations in the Holy Land*, 1993).

Masada – overview

Sights

The site is well labelled in Hebrew and English so a detailed tour description in this *Handbook* is not really necessary. However, some further details of the key places of interest are included below. **NB** The black line indicates the height of the walls found *in situ*, whilst construction above this line represents reconstruction made by archaeologists using masonry found scattered nearby.

The great walls of Masada comprise the outer walls of the site built by the Romans during the siege of 72-73 AD, which straggle round the foot of the escarpments with garrison camps at intervals (see 'Masada, overview' map). On the heights is the main fortress wall with its towers and bastions running for some 1,400 metres. It is constructed of two encasing limestone block walls infilled with rubble, giving an overall width of some four metres. It is generally assumed that the 70 or so rooms in the casement wall were used as living quarters by the Zealots and their families, and have revealed a large number of artefacts. Thirty towers are built into the walls at irregular intervals, according to the terrain and defensive considerations. There are four gates from the time of Herod, all built on the same general plan: the **Western Gate**, **Eastern Snake Path Gate**, the **Southern Gate** and the **Northern (Water) Gate**. It was in a building (**1**) close to the Water Gate that the 'lots' associated with the mass suicide were found (see page 320).

The walls & gates

Masada is dominated by the palaces built by Herod the Great. They comprise distinct areas within the fortress: the **Northern Palace-Villa**, the **Western Palace**, the **royal apartments** (building XI(**2**), building XII(**3**) and building XIII(**4**)), plus the **administrative buildings** (in the northwest corner of the Western Palace).

The palaces

Northern Palace-Villa The most spectacular building on the site, and described in some detail by Josephus, it is built in three tiers on the northern edge of the cliff and belongs to the 'main phase' (c. 25 BCE) of Herod's building programme. The **upper terrace (5)** comprised a semi-circular balcony with the living quarters to the south, whilst the **middle terrace (6)** some 20 metres below almost certainly featured some form of entertainment complex. A further 15 metres below is the **lower terrace (7)**, where a central hall surrounded by porticoes also served some form of entertainment purpose. Remains of the sandstone columns, with fluted drums and Corinthian capitals, along with decorative frescoes, can still be seen. A small bathhouse stands to the east. During the period of the Revolt, the living quarters on the upper terrace retained their original function, whilst the lower levels were used as part of the strategic defence of the water source. A thick layer of ash suggests that the middle and lower terraces were consumed by fire, with remains from the Revolt including numerous arrowheads, plus the skeletons of a man, woman and child. The woman's scalp was complete with braids.

Western Palace The largest residential structure on Masada covering almost 4,000 square metres, the Western Palace served as the ceremonial and administrative centre and belongs to the 'early phase' of Herod's construction (c. 35 BCE) with a substantial enlargement in the 'main phase' (c. 25 BCE). It comprises four blocks of buildings: i) the royal apartments in the southeast; ii) the service wing and workshops in the northeast; iii) the storerooms in the southwest; iv) the administrative wing and residence of palace officials in the northwest. Recent research suggests that the so-called

Dead Sea Region

 'Masada complex'

The suicide of the Jewish Zealots at Masada has given rise to a phrase, 'Masada complex', that is considered by some to have become the symbol of the modern State of Israel: a state of psychology under siege where death by one's own hand is better than defeat. However, if anything, the sentiment of modern Israel is not so much reflected in a 'you'll never take us alive' attitude, but more in the 'no more Masadas' sentiment. The importance of Masada within the Israeli consciousness is manifested in the swearing-in ceremonies that some units of the IDF hold here, whilst the site is a compulsory stop for all Israeli children in what is less of an educational visit, and more an exercise in nation building. In this regard, there are parallels between Masada and the Holocaust memorial at Yad VaShem; a link explored by Johnson in his comprehensive A History of the Jews (1987). Johnson points out how "One of the most important developments in the history of the Jews, one of the ways in which Judaism differed most strongly from primitive Israelite religion, was the growing stress on peace ... Jewish valour and heroism was pushed into the background as a sustaining theme; Jewish irenicism came to the foreground. To countless generations of Jews, what happened at Jabneh, where the scholar finally took over from the warrior, was far more significant than what happened at Masada. The lost fortress, indeed, was virtually forgotten until, in the lurid flames of the twentieth-century Holocaust, it became a national myth, displacing the myth of Jabneh."

Herodian **'swimming pool' (8)** to the southeast of the Western Palace, and close to building XI (**2**), is in fact a *mikveh* (ritual bath) dating to the period of the Zealot community.

The storehouses Yadin identifies two types of storehouses for food and weapons at Masada: public storehouses, and storehouses attached to specific buildings such as palaces and administrative centres. The largest **public storeroom complex** is located just to the south of the Northern Palace-Villa's upper terrace. It is believed that oil, wine, flour and other foodstuffs were each stored in separate rooms in special jars. Most of the storehouses containing foodstuffs were burnt at the climax of the siege, though some were left undamaged in order to prove to the Romans that the mass suicide was not a result of starvation.

The bathhouse The bathhouses attached to the palaces are supplemented by a magnificent **bathhouse** built during the 'main phase' (c. 25 BCE) by Herod. It is located in the complex just to the south of the upper terrace of the Northern Palace-Villa. It comprises a large open court and four rooms: the *apodyterium* (entrance room), *tepidarium* (warm room), *frigidarium* (cold room) and the *caldarium* (hot room). The remains of the *hypocaust* (under-floor heating system) and *praefurnium* (furnace) are well preserved. Immersion pools and *mikvehs* were added to many buildings during the period of the Revolt (66-73 CE), and the large bathhouse underwent significant alterations.

Religious buildings All of the buildings attributed to the period of the Revolt are religious in nature. These include the synagogue in the northwest wall, to the west of building VII, whilst an alteration to **building XIII (9)** suggests that its northern hall was perhaps converted for use as a **Beth Midrash** (study hall). A number of *mikvehs*, or ritual baths, were built across the site.

The key element at Masada, at an elevation of over 400 metres in the middle of **The water** a harsh desert, was the provision of water. The Israeli excavations have shown **system** that the water system was made up of three parts, including setting up a water catchment to bring water to the vicinity of the fortress from the Ben Jair and Masada wadis. Water was carried in places in the Wadi Masada on aqueducts to storage pools. Lower down, water was delivered also by aqueduct to rock cisterns from the wadi Ben Jair. Water was stored in square cisterns, 4,000 cubic metres in volume, cut into the rock: eight above and four below. Water was also carried to the site by animal and led to the cisterns by channels running from the Water Gate in the north of the fortress. Small scattered cisterns for storing rain water falling in the summit area were also in use and were important if minor supplies.

Masada – site plan

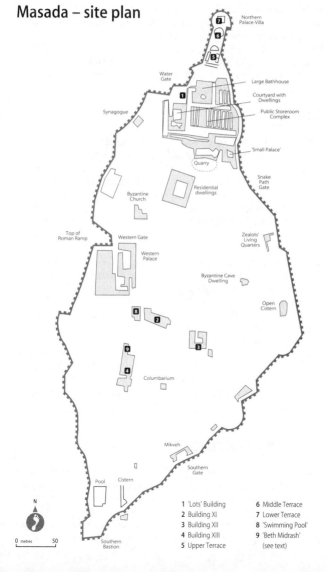

1 'Lots' Building
2 Building XI
3 Building XII
4 Building XIII
5 Upper Terrace
6 Middle Terrace
7 Lower Terrace
8 'Swimming Pool'
9 'Beth Midrash'
(see text)

0 metres 50

The Roman Outside the fortress are the structural remains of the Roman siege, led by
siege remains Flavius Silva (see 'Masada, overview' map). In addition to the siege wall built
to contain the site, there are clear signs of the Roman camps, the ramp built by
the Roman general on the west close to the Western Gate that enabled siege
weapons to destroy the entrance to the citadel. In all they are a memorial to the
dedication of Flavius Silva to his task and the effectiveness of Roman military
engineering.■ *T6584207/8 or T6584464. Sunrise to 1700 daily, closed Yom
Kippur. Adult 20 NIS, student 15 NIS. Cable car operates 0800-1600; one-way
ticket adult 20 NIS, student 14 NIS return ticket adult 36 NIS, student 22 NIS;
price excludes admission fee. Cafeteria (fairly pricey, closes early), souvenirs, toilets at the bottom, (free) cold drinking water at the top. It is forbidden to camp out
on top of Masada at night.*

Sound & light Each Tuesday and Thursday a 50-minute *Son et Lumière* (sound and light)
show show takes place at the amphitheatre on the Roman ramp side of Masada.
Though commentary is in Hebrew, headphones provide simultaneous translation into English, French, German, Spanish or Russian. ■ *Bookings should be
made at the Arad Tourist Information Centre (T9958144 or T05-7959333,
F05-7955052), where you can enquire about transport. Performances take place
at 2100 April-August, 1900 September-October, and cost 30 NIS.*

Essentials

Sleeping & **E** *IYHA Masada Youth Hostel/Isaac H Taylor Hostel*, T6584349, F6584650.
eating Well-maintained hostel, single-sex a/c dorms (8 beds) with attached bath, or doubles
and family rooms (**D**). Breakfast $5 (0730-0800, or delivered at 2000 the night before),
hot meal $7 (or $9 at weekends), check-in 1600-1900, check-out 0830, camping area,
BBQ/sitting area, free cold drinking water, lockers (6 NIS), safe. Advance reservations
recommended (essential at weekends and holidays). On request, reception staff may
separate those who are rising early to climb Masada from those after an undisturbed
lie-in.

Transport Exact times may change during the life-span of this book. Check at reception for latest
timetable, or call Tel Aviv (T03-6948888). Note that all Jerusalem-bound services also
stop at 'En Gedi and Qumran, whilst southbound services stop at 'En Boqeq. Number
in brackets is bus number. **Be'er Sheva**: Sunday-Thursday 0815 (384) 1245 (384)
1545 (384, **Arad** only) 1815 (385), Friday 0815 (384) 1245 (384), Saturday 1545 (384,
Arad only), 2 hours. **Eilat**: Sunday-Thursday 0800 (444) 1100 (444) 1500 (444) 1800
(444), Friday same, last at 1500, 3¾ hours. **'En Gedi**: Sunday-Thursday 1055 (384)
1340 (384) 1625 (384), Fri 0955 (384) 1325 (384) 1430 (385), 30 minutes. **Jerusalem**:
Sunday-Thursday 0830 (486) 0920 (444) 1150 (486) 1220 (444) 1520 (486) 1620 (486
and 444), 1920 (444), Friday 0830 (486) 0920 (444) 1150 (486)1220 (444) 1520 (444),
Saturday 1850 (444) 2120 (444), 2¼ hours. **Tel Aviv**: Sunday-Friday 1425 (421). There
are also thrice-weekly *Arkia* flights between Tel Aviv's Sde Dov airport and Masada.

'En Boqeq Region

Phone code: 07 'En Boqeq (Ein Bokek or Umm Bagheq) is another oasis on the western shore of
Colour map 3, grid A6 the Dead Sea, similar to 'En Gedi though somewhat smaller. It was probably first
settled in the Hasmonean period (152-37 BCE), though its fame dates from the
Herodian period (37 BCE-70 CE) when it became a centre for the manufacture of
cosmetics and pharmaceuticals. The settlement was probably destroyed during
the First Jewish Revolt (66-73 CE), though it appears to have been resettled by the

*time of the (Second Jewish) Bar Kokhba Revolt (132-136 CE). A Roman fort was built here in the early fourth century CE, though it was almost certainly destroyed by earthquake in the fourth or fifth century CE. Settlement continued following the Arab conquest of 636 CE, though ancient remains at 'En Boqeq are few and far between today. 'En Boqeq is now the Dead Sea's major **tourist resort**, with upmarket hotels accommodating guests seeking to use the **spa and health facilities**. Several kilometres further south of 'En Boqeq, there are further hotel and hot spa facilities at **Hamme Zohar** (see page 326). The only remains of 'En Boqeq's historical past are the **Mezad Boqeq** (Roman fort) and **officina** (Herodian workshop) located in the canyon of the Nahal Boqeq just to the northwest of the main hotel/tourist area. The area's main administrative centre is **Neve Zohar**.*

Sights

This small Roman **fort** on the north side of the Nahal Boqeq valley was probably built as part of the *Limes Palaestinae* eastern frontier defences. A short section (two metres out of one kilometre) of the **aqueduct** that served 'En Boqeq is visible to the northwest of the fort, as are two of the **cisterns** that stored water at the oasis. Less easy to find, to the east of the fort (nearer to the main Route 90), are the remains of the Herodian workshop, or **officina**. This building contained ovens, basins and vessels used in the perfume, cosmetic and pharmaceutical production process. It is speculated that raw materials such as, buds, blossoms, seeds, fruits, resins, twigs, bark and leaves of aromatic plants were perhaps provided from the Far East and Arabia by the Nabatean trade caravans.

Mezad Boqeq & Officina

'En Boqeq's modern *raison d'être* is the tourism industry associated with its **spa and health resort** facilities. Most of the hotels listed below have their own 'health and beauty' centres. The **beaches** here at 'En Boqeq are amongst the most attractive on the Dead Sea, though they can be prone to overcrowding.

'En Boqeq Tourist Complex

Essentials

Note that most of the hotels in 'En Boqeq offer significant discounts to long-stay guests; just as well since their room rates are grossly overpriced.

Sleeping & eating
■ *on map; price codes see inside front cover*

L2 *Caesar Premier*, T6689666, F6520301. Fairly modern, landscaped pool area, spa, restaurants, balconies with sea views. **L2** *Carlton Galei Zohar*, T6584311, F6584503. New block features balconies and larger rooms ($30 extra), all rooms a/c, cable TV, sea-view, indoor and outdoor pools, full spa facilities, *Max's Beer Garden*, restaurant, pub. **L2** *Crowne Plaza*[D], T6591919, F6591911. Lots of glass and great views, so why couldn't they have added balconies? Very grand and airy entrance, rooms a good size, deluxe rooms and suites, very attractive pool area, restaurant. Reasonable choice. **L2** *Golden Tulip Privilège* T6689999, F6689900. Wow! Opened mid-1999, grand public areas with sweeping staircases and glass lifts, large rooms and impressive suites, very appealing pool area, choice of restaurants, bowling hall, very attractive spa. Given the prices other places charge you may as well spend your money here (there are some good special offers available): recommended. **L2** *Hod*, T6584644, F6584606. Exterior looking rather old fashioned, but despite very small balconies rooms are quite pleasant and a fair size. Appealing sun-deck around pool, health and fitness centre, restaurant, nightclub. Very expensive, however (I thought the price quoted was shekels but it was dollars!). **L2** *Hyatt Regency Dead Sea*, T6591234, F6591235. Huge, 600-room hotel, all rooms a/c with balconies and sea-views, plus suites, disabled rooms, choice of 4 restaurants, children's activities and pool, tennis, squash, plus

Dead Sea Region

arguably the region's most luxurious spa (guest entry 30 NIS, visitor entrance 100 NIS, mud wraps 160-480 NIS, massages 120-350 NIS, hydro-baths 85 NIS, facials 150-350 NIS, plus various other weird and wonderful treatments). High-quality hotel, but very expensive. **L2** *Radisson Moriah Gardens*, T6584351, F6584383. This place looks so old it's hard to see how they justify the price (though you do get breakfast included!). 196 a/c rooms, cable TV, some connecting and disabled rooms, outdoor pool, kid's pool, heated indoor Dead Sea pool, spa facilities, nightclub, restaurants. But that price!

L3 *Lot*, T6584321, F6689200. Attractive poolside area though not all rooms have sea-views or balconies, spa and health club (massages 100-199 NIS, mud bath 100 NIS, sulphur pool 38 NIS), restaurant, bar. Rather overpriced. **L3** *Tsell Harim*, T6584121, F6584666. Nicer inside than the exterior suggests, rooms rather plain though their saving grace is the individual solarium for private sunbathing. Pool, tennis, bar, restaurant.

A *Park Inn*, T6591666, F6584162. Smallish a/c rooms with small balconies, cable TV, breakfast included, pool, dining hall, solarium.

Transport For onward public transport see page 316 (though you will have to add or subtract 20 minutes or so, and bear in mind that some services stop at 'En Gedi Beach for a break). Note also that some services use the new by-pass between 'En Boqeq and Hamme Zohar, and no longer run along the beach road.

Hamme Zohar

Phone code: 07
Colour map 3, grid A6

In addition to some of the Dead Sea's most attractive (though private) beaches, Hamme Zohar's (Hamei Zohar, Zohar, Zohar Springs) major attractions are the health spas. The most luxurious (with prices to match the opulence) are at the Radisson Moriah Plaza Dead Sea Hotel and the Nirvana on the Dead Sea Hotel. Some facilities are offered free, or at a reduced price, to hotel residents, though most are an additional expense.

Sleeping &
eating

L1 *Nirvana on the Dead Sea*, T6584614, F6584620. Fabulous, luxury hotel, rooms have a/c, TV, video, radio (all controlled

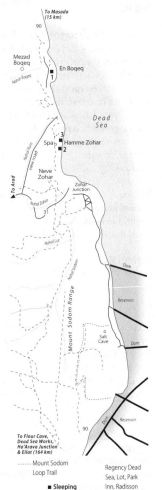

'En Boqeq & Sodom regions

To Masada (15 km)

Mezad Boqeq

En Boqeq

Dead Sea

Spa — Hamme Zohar

Neve Zohar

To Arad

Zohar Junction

Mount Sodom Range

Salt Cave

Reservoir

Dam

Dam

Reservoir

To Flour Cave, Dead Sea Works, Ha'Arava Junction & Eilat (164 km)

...... Mount Sodom Loop Trail

■ **Sleeping**
1 Caesar Premier, Carlton Galei Zohar, Crowne Plaza, Golden Tulip Privilège, Hod, Hyatt

Regency Dead Sea, Lot, Park Inn, Radisson Moriah Gardens, Tsell Harim
2 Nirvana on the Dead Sea
3 Radisson Moriah Plaza

0 km 1

N

from bedside panel), suites, apartments and family rooms, private beach, choice of pools, plus full spa facilities. Recommended. **L1** *Radisson Moriah Plaza*, T6591591, F6584238. 220 sea-facing rooms, small balconies, a/c, cable TV, guests have free use of indoor heated pool, Dead Sea pool, outdoor pool, jacuzzi, sauna, fitness room, plus access to other spa facilities (extra).

For onward public transport see page316 (though you will have to add or subtract 20 minutes or so, and bear in mind that some services stop at 'En Gedi Beach for a break). Note also that some services use the new by-pass between 'En Boqeq and Hamme Zohar, and no longer run along the beach road. **Transport**

Sodom (Sedom) Region

*Tradition holds that this is the cursed land of **Sodom and Gomorrah**, Smith's region where "History and Nature have ... cruelly conspired", though many Israelis will tell you that the night-spots of Tel Aviv or Eilat are the modern Sodom and Gomorrah. The region is one of austere, terrifying beauty; a fitting scene for where "the Lord rained upon Sodom and upon Gomorrah brimstone and fire ... and he overthrew those cities, and all the plain, and all the inhabitants of the cities, and that which grew upon the ground" (Genesis 19:24-25).*

Phone code: 07
Colour map 3, grid B6

Dead Sea Region

*The dominant geographical features are the salt flats of the Dead Sea to the east, with their bizarre sculptured forms, and the **Mt Sodom (Sedom) Range** to the west. This range, 11 kilometres long but just 2 kilometres wide, began to form some 2,000,000 years BP, with sedimentary rocks being laid down upon the layers of salt deposits. Over time, the sedimentary layers began to crack, with plastic salt layers rising to form Mt Sedom, and some of the harder sedimentary layers being pushed to the summit. The highest point of the range is 240 metres above the Dead Sea, but still beneath sea-level. The range is underlain by a salt rock layer 2750 metres deep. Though annual rainfall is less than 50 millimetres, water leaking into the fissures between the harder rock and the salt rock has formed vertical chimneys and lateral caves and tunnels. Other formations formed by the erosive action of water resemble pillars and statues, including the famous **Lot's wife** (see Genesis 19:26).*

The cliff face lining this section of Route 90 is riddled with cave complexes, including the spectacular **Salt (or Sedom) Cave**. With a properly equipped and fully trained guide (contact SPNI) these caves are fascinating to explore, **though it is essential that you do not attempt this on your own**. The caves are prone to rockfalls and it is very easy to get lost. **Salt (Sedom) Cave**

A further three and a half kilometres south along Route 90, a sign to the west indicates the **Flour Cave** and the **Mt Sodom Observation Point**.

The road to the Flour Cave is semi-paved, and passable in a normal car. Unfortunately the cave is not accessible by public transport, whilst on foot it is almost eight kilometres from Route 90. If you have your own transport this trip is highly recommended. After just over two kilometres of spectacular scenery the track forks. To the right, a steep (and less hire-car suitable) path leads almost four and a half kilometres up to **Mt Sodom Observation Point**. The track to the left forks again after two kilometres; take the right fork and follow it three and a half kilometres to the Flour Cave. So named because of the flour-like residue that lines the canyons, the soft limestone cliffs have been carved by water action into spectacular, swirling shapes. It's very hot down in the canyon, though a number of caves provide some deliciously cool shade. Bring a torch and plenty of drinking water. **Flour Cave**

👉 **The Arava**

The Arava Road (Route 90), from the Dead Sea to the Gulf of Aqaba at Eilat, follows the course of the great Syrian-African Rift Valley; an extension of the East African Rift Valley. The valley was formed in antiquity when this whole region lay under the ocean, with only the granite peaks of Sinai protruding above sea-level, and great deposits of limestone were laid upon the ocean-bed. Early in the Miocene epoch, pressure on the earth's surface from both east and west caused the limestone to rise above the water in two long, north–south running folds. The violent rupture of the strata between the two folds, and the subsequent slumping of the land between the two north–south linear faults, created the Syrian-African Rift Valley. The Rift Valley in its southern reaches is one of the "most singular features of the earth's surface" according to the great Middle Eastern writer, Hitti (1951). The Jordan River and the Wadi Arava form Israel's eastern border with Jordan.

The northern section of the Rift Valley (north of the Dead Sea) is dominated by the Jordan River. The southern section (south of the Dead Sea to the Gulf of Aqaba) is occupied by the Wadi Arava (Arabic 'Arabah); a highly braided stream that only occasionally has water. The two sections are separated by a diagonal ridge of limestone that contrived to shut in a section of the old ocean-bed complete with a large quantity of salt water; hence the Dead Sea.

The Wadi Arava is a wide wadi in the north, with several broad lateral valleys. The western, Israeli, side of the wadi is defined by the ranges of the Tih, and the east by the west-facing scarp of the Jordanian Heights. At the head of the Gulf of Aqaba, the generally flatter western side is in Israeli territory. As the wadi approaches the Gulf of Aqaba, hills encroach on the west. Throughout the northern Wadi Arava the vegetation is sparse according with the highly saline and alkaline nature of the soils, especially in the area of the plains around Sodom. Further south, beginning some 50 kilometres north of Eilat (near the mines of Timna) the valley bottom looks like a poor savannah area with a scattering of acacia and tamarisk and some indigenous salt bushes and grasses surviving throughout the year.

The Wadi Arava defined by the Rift Valley is fairly flat. The maximum altitude is at a slightly elevated line of rocks and low hillocks in the land lying about 60 kilometres north of Eilat between Yahel and Be'er Menuha at an elevation of approximately 192 metres above sea level. The Rift Valley between the Dead Sea and Eilat has two distinct areas, the northern area draining into the Dead Sea and the southern to the Gulf of Aqaba. Above the valley itself the land rises steeply to the west, with elevations immediately adjacent standing at 476 metres at Yahel and elsewhere at 200-400 metres, rising inland west of Yotvata to 710 metres.

Dead Sea Works   This is an unattractive industrial complex (located just south of the turn-off to the Flour Cave) that is vital to the economic needs of Israel. The original Dead Sea Works were founded on the northern shore in 1930, with those here being built four years later. The truly desperate may be able to arrange a tour through the tourist office in Arad (T05-7958144, or by calling direct, T07-6665111).

Moving on   From the southern end of the Dead Sea (Ha'Arava/Sodom Junction), Route 90 continues 164 kilometres south to Eilat. This stretch of highway is known as the Arava Road. This is a pleasant enough journey, although there are no real major sights *en route* until you get closer to Eilat. These sights are included in the 'Around Eilat' section of 'The Negev' chapter (see page 407).

The Negev

6

The Negev

There is far more to the Negev than just the hedonistic beach resort of Eilat stuck on the bottom of a large stretch of desert. In fact, the Negev hardly fits most people's preconceptions of what a desert is anyway; this is more the austere, wind-eroded stone-strewn landscape than the sweeping sand dunes of 'Lawrence of Arabia' cinematography. This is an area to explore in depth, rather than viewed through the window of a bus heading from Tel Aviv to the beach at Eilat. Although public transport does serve all the key sites, careful planning must be made to ensure connections. If the option is available to you, this is the place to hire a car (or camel).

The first lesson that you will learn about the Negev is how adaptable people are. And a visit to the superbly preserved remains of the Nabatean-Roman-Byzantine cities at Avdat, Mamshit and Shivta will soon show you that, contrary to the oft-presented image, the Israelis were not the first to 'make the desert bloom'. The Negev is also a physically beautiful environment, no more so than at Ein Avdat National Park, where the contrast between icy blue pools of water and dry, brown barren hills is brought sharply into focus. Meanwhile, at the very heart of the Negev is a natural geological phenomenon that is as spectacular as Israel's more famous natural wonders, the Dead Sea and the Red Sea coral reefs: the Makhtesh Ramon erosion crater is the place to get your hiking boots on and your 'Every Boy's Guide to Rocks and Minerals' out of your luggage. And finally there is Eilat, Israel's premier resort.

Background

Geography

The Negev, Hebrew for 'arid land', comprises approximately half of the State of Israel's land area, but is home to just seven percent of the population. The Negev is shaped like an isosceles triangle, with the long sides being the Egyptian border to the west, and the Jordanian border to the east, with the short side comprising a line drawn roughly between the Dead Sea to the east, and the Mediterranean Sea at Gaza to the west. The apex of the triangle is marked by the city of Eilat, on the Gulf of Aqaba.

History

Early history Despite the Negev's seemingly difficult and inhospitable nature, the region has been settled continuously since prehistoric times. Systematic study has provided irrefutable evidence of widespread occupation of the Negev throughout much of prehistory. The information on this early prehistory is still being considered and digested, though early statements suggest that the link between human occupation dates and environmental change needs to be examined thoroughly.

During the Late Bronze Age-Iron Age I-II, the 19th and 20th dynasties of the **Egyptian** New Kingdom were involved in extensive copper mining and smelting activities in the southern Negev and Sinai regions, with the **Midianites** continuing this activity after the 12th century BCE.

Biblical references to Negev settlements abound, with excavations having revealed a rich assemblage of sites from the **Bronze Age** (c. 3300-1200 BCE) and the **Iron Age** (1200-586 BCE). The first five books of the Old Testament of the Bible, (*Genesis, Exodus, Leviticus, Numbers* and *Deuteronomy*), which also form the Jewish *Torah*, are filled with references to settlements in the Negev that have since been identified, such as Be'er Sheva (*Genesis 21:31-33; 26:23-33; 46:1-5*), Arad (*Numbers 21:1; 33:40*), Kadesh Barnea (*Genesis 14:7; Numbers 13:26; 20:14; Deuteronomy 1:46*), amongst others. This, after all, is the land of the route into Exodus, the return, and the wanderings of the children of Israel.

By the beginning of the second millennium BCE, three main groups occupied the Negev: the **Canaanites** to the north, particularly around Arad; the **Amalekites** to the south, who were defeated by the United Monarchy's expansion into the Negev; and the **Edomites** to the east, who later moved north and northwest into the Shephelah, and subsequently became known as the Idumaeans.

The expansion of the **United Monarchy** (c. 1020-928 BCE) into the Negev Hills is reflected in a number of Iron Age IIA sites (1000-900 BCE), though the area was probably abandoned by the succeeding kings of Judah until the beginning of the Persian period (586 BCE). The reasons are not altogether clear, though the devastating invasion of Pharaoh Shishak in 924 BCE may have been a factor. Be'er Sheva (Beersheba), for example, is repeatedly mentioned in the Bible as defining the southern limits of Israel, the United Monarchy, or Judah (*Joshua 15:28; I Samuel 3:20; II Samuel 3:10, 17:11, 24:15; I Chronicles 21:2*). Other areas of the Negev remained occupied: Arad, for example, has remains of a series of Israelite citadels dating from the ninth to the sixth centuries BCE.

Perhaps one of the key defining moments in the history of the Negev was the **The Nabateans**
arrival of the Nabateans, some time in the fourth or third century BCE. Their origins are unclear, though their impact is undisputed. As controllers of the trade route, the Spice Road, between their Edom capital at Petra and the Mediterranean Sea at Gaza, the Nabateans constructed a string of road stations across the Negev, many of which can still be seen today. Their mastery of advanced irrigation techniques, in particular their control of surface water run-off, led to the establishment of urban centres of considerable size, such as Oboda (Avdat), Mamphis (Mamshit), Sobata (Shivta), and to a lesser extent, Elusa (Haluza) and Nessana (Nizzana). Spectacular remains can still be seen today.

The independent Nabatean empire probably reached its peak in the first cen-   **Roman &**
tury CE, though the towns and routes that they established seem to have been   **Byzantine**
little affected by the annexation of their kingdom into the Roman *Provincia*   **periods**
Arabia in 106 CE. In fact, the majority of the population of these towns were
ethnically Nabatean, and as such, the Early Roman period (37 BCE-132 CE)
may accurately be referred to here as the Middle Nabatean period.

A major administrative reorganization of the Eastern Roman Empire under
Diocletian (284-305 CE) incorporated many of the Nabatean towns within
the empire's southern defence system. New trade routes also led to the rise or
demise of certain Nabatean towns.

The major development in the Negev region during the fourth century CE
was the conversion of much of the population to Christianity. Thus ushered in
the era of the Christian Roman Empire, or the **Byzantine period** (324-638
CE). Many of the former Nabatean towns flourished during this era, with the
monumental churches that can be seen today at a number of sites bearing testimony to this prosperity. The decline of Byzantine power allowed the Arabs to
conquer the Negev in 636 CE, and for the next 1,000 years or so, the region was
inhabited solely by the **Bedouin**.

The Negev region remained a relative backwater of the Ottoman Empire right   **Modern history**
up until the **First World War**, when its strategic value was recognized. The
British Army's Palestine campaign featured largely in the northern and western areas of the Negev, with Be'er Sheva being the first town in Palestine to fall
into British hands (1917). In addition to General Allenby's campaign, this was
also the stomping ground of T.E. Lawrence ('of Arabia'). Before his wartime
efforts at disrupting Turkish communications and supply lines, Lawrence had
spent much of 1914 surveying the archaeological sites of the area for the Palestine Exploration Fund. After the war, the Negev fell within the mandated area
of the British, though there were few attempts to develop it. Population levels
still remained extremely low, comprising mainly Bedouin tribesmen. In fact,
the **Peel Commission Partition Plan** of 1937 granted the Negev region to the
Arabs since they represented the only people living there.

Partially in response to this situation, and partially out of a desire to settle
the region that Moses wandered through with the children of Israel, Jewish
pioneers began to establish isolated communities within the Negev. This
programme was to prove significant in its foresight in later years. By the time
the **United Nations Partition Recommendation** was published in 1947,
the presence of these isolated Jewish communities was enough for the UN to
allocate the entire Negev region (bar a narrow strip to the south of Gaza) to
the Jewish State. With the Arab rejection of the plan, and the subsequent war,
these Jewish settlements played an invaluable, and often heroic, role in
holding up the Egyptian army's advance. In one of the final acts of the war, the
Golani Brigade managed to establish control of a stretch of the Gulf of Aqaba

(subsequently Eilat), that allowed Israel an outlet to the Red Sea.

There remains much controversy over Israel's claims that it has 'turned the desert green', but there can be little doubt that Israel leads the world in developing semi-arid and arid irrigation techniques. Thus, large areas of the Negev have been brought under cultivation. The results of establishing 'development towns' in the Negev are more contentious; for every 'success' (see Arad), the example of at least one 'failure' (see Dimona) is held up. **Tourism** is now providing a major source of income in the Negev region.

Northern Negev

*The Northern Negev has a number of points of interest to the visitor, particularly those who have their own transport. The commercial capital of the Negev, **Be'er Sheva**, is an easy-going place, with several interesting attractions in the immediate vicinity. The bulk of the sights, however, lie to the east and southeast of Be'er Sheva, notably the archaeological sites at **Tel Arad** and **Mamshit**. For those with their own vehicles, the **Makhtesh HaGadol** and **Makhtesh HaKatan** (craters) provide a wonderfully scenic backdrop to a number of hikes.*

Be'er Sheva (Beersheba)

Phone code: 07
Colour map 3, grid A3

The ancient biblical city of the Patriarchs, Be'er Sheva is now redefining itself as the modern administrative and commercial capital of the Negev. Attractions in the town itself are limited, and though there are good transport connections its potential as a base from which to explore the surrounding area is constrained by the limited choice of hotels. However, the Old City down-town area has a relaxed, laid-back atmosphere that belies Be'er Sheva's headlong rush for expansion.

Ins and outs

Getting there Most visitors arrive at the large Egged Central Bus Station located just off Derekh Eilat (T6294311/2 or T6294333). Be'er Sheva has good bus connections, with major destinations such as Eilat, 'En Gedi, Jerusalem and Tel Aviv being served by express, regular and local buses. There is a trial train service between Be'er Sheva and Tel Aviv (and beyond), with plans to improve transport between the rather remote train station and the town centre.

Getting around The town centre is fairly small, so you can easily get around on foot. The main routes around town (5 NIS) leave from the Egged Central Bus Station, with most running regularly from 0520-2300. For details of city buses, T6277381.

History

Ancient history & biblical references There are numerous biblical references to the early settlement of Be'er Sheva (Beersheba), with the etymology of the name being discussed in *Genesis*. The meaning of the name may refer to either the 'Well of Seven' (see 'Abraham's Well', page 338) from the Hebrew *shiv'a*, or 'Well of (the) Oath' from the Hebrew *shevu'a*, with the origin of Beersheba attributed to both Abraham (*Genesis 21:29-33*) and Isaac (*Genesis 26:15-33*). Jacob received the vision here that told him to take his family into Egypt (*Genesis 46:1-2*); the city was a place of importance under Samuel, with his sons Joel and Abiah judging here (*I*

Samuel 8:1-2); and Elijah fled here from Jezreel on his journey to Mount Horeb (*I Kings 19:3*).

Many of the biblical references mention Beersheba as the limits of the kingdom of Judah (*Joshua 15:28*), the lands of Israel (*I Samuel 3:20*) and the United Monarchy (*II Samuel 3:10, 17:11, 24:15; I Chronicles 21:2*), with the most common incantations being 'from Dan to Beersheba' and 'from Beersheba to Dan'.

Excavations at a site known as **Tel Be'er Sheva** five kilometres northeast of the modern city (see page 341) have revealed levels of occupation dating back to the Iron Age. However, identification of the tel with biblical Beersheba has been problematic due to the lack of remains dating to the Late Bronze and Late Iron Age periods that would coincide with the Beersheba of the Patriarchs. Academic opinion is divided, though there is strong circumstantial evidence.

Much of Be'er Sheva's history during the **Persian period** and the **Roman-Byzantine period** is told at the site of Tel Be'er Sheva (see page 341).

The Crusaders never made it as far south as here, mistaking the site of Bet Jibrin (Bet Guvrin) for biblical Beersheba. It was the Turks who revived Be'er Sheva's fortunes at the turn of the 20th century, establishing a new town to act as an administrative centre for the Bedouin tribes of the Negev, thus strengthening the declining Ottoman empire. Jewish settlement also began during this period. The British forces of General Allenby captured the town in 1917 as part of the World War One Palestine campaign. It subsequently expanded rapidly, with the population rising to around 7,000.

Ottoman Empire & British Mandate

The British government's White Paper of 1943 forbade the Jewish purchase of land in the Negev, though the reality of isolated Jewish settlements in the Negev convinced the architects of the 1947 United Nations Partition Plan to include most of the Negev within the proposed Jewish state. Be'er Sheva, however, was just within the boundaries of the proposed Arab state. When war broke out following the declaration of the State of Israel, Be'er Sheva was occupied by the Egyptians, who established their command centre here. The city was subsequently captured by the Negev Brigade of the Israeli army in October 1948.

The Negev

Be'er Sheva

Sleeping
1 Desert Inn/ Ne'ot Midbar Hotel
2 Hilton Be'er Sheva

Eating
1 New York, New York Cafe

0 metres 500

Related map:
A. Be'er Sheva Centre & Old City, page 337.

Modern city The initiative for transforming the city into the administrative and commercial capital of the Negev was taken by the city's first mayor, David Tuvyahu. The population of Be'er Sheva is now approaching 150,000, helped in no small part by the massive influx of immigrants that followed the city's designation as an 'immigration absorption city'. In addition to Moroccan and Ethiopian Jews, the city is now home to a sizeable and highly visible Eastern European community.

Sights

Walking tour of the Old City Many of Be'er Sheva's places of interest are located in the attractive Old City area, the grid pattern of streets built by the Turks as their regional headquarters around the turn of the twentieth century. A walking tour of the Old City has now been marked, taking in mainly Ottoman and British Mandate period buildings (under one hour). The route is in a figure-of-eight, divided into a North Ring and a South Ring. The usual starting place is the Negev Museum. You may feel that some of the 'attractions' on the walking tour are not worth the effort.

Negev Museum This is housed in the former Turkish **Governor's Residence (5)**, a small mansion built in 1906 that later served as Be'er Sheva's first City Hall. It features an art collection, plus temporary exhibits. Just to the north of the Governor's House is a former Ottoman period **mosque (6)**, also built in 1906, that now houses the 'archaeology' department of the museum. Displays focus on finds from the Be'er Sheva region, and Tel Be'er Sheva in particular. However, both are currently closed for refurbishment. **NB** Due to the proximity of the military base, photography is not permitted in this area. ■ *Remez Gardens, Ha'Atzma'ut, T6282056. Sunday-Thursday 1000-1700, Friday 1000-1300, Saturday 1000-1300. Currently free.*

Former Bedouin School (12) This building was erected by the Turks in 1913 for use as a boarding school for Bedouin boys. During the First World War it was used as a military hospital. Today, the building, and the palm trees lining the front path, all look a bit the worse for wear, though there are plans to refurbish the building as part of the Negev Museum.

World War One cemetery (11) During the autumn of 1917, the Allied forces broke through the Turkish lines and captured Be'er Sheva. The battle was not without cost, and today 1,239 Allied soldiers are buried here, the biggest World War One cemetery in Israel. Many of the graves belong to members of Commonwealth regiments, with Australians and New Zealanders buried next to Welsh and English soldiers. A lot of graves are simply marked 'A Soldier of the Great War'. As with all cemeteries administered by the Commonwealth War Graves Commission, it is superbly maintained.

Turkish railway remains The northernmost section of the walking tour features a series of buildings connected with the old Turkish railway. This is the line that features so prominently in the writing and exploits of Lawrence of Arabia. The track was dismantled by General Allenby in 1917, but it is possible here to see the former **Turkish Station Master's House (10)** (now the offices of the *Society for the Protection of Nature, Israel*). A little further to the south along David Tuvyahu is the former **Turkish Railway Station (9)**, now under renovation, but previously used as a gallery and visual arts centre. The original station platform remains. Further south still, but now hidden amongst a residential area, is the **water-tower (8)** used to fill the trains' boilers.

This school was built by the British in the 1940s and is still in use today. This completes the North Ring of the tour, bringing you back to the Negev Museum on Ha'Atzma'ut.

Be'eri School (7)

Opposite the former Turkish Governor's Residence, at the junction of Herzl and Ha'Atzma'ut, is the **former home of the Arab historian Araf al-Araf (4)** (1892-1973). He also served as a district ruler under the Ottomans, and now has the indignity of his splendid former home being turned into a mini-market cum bakery. A similar fate has befallen the **former home of Sheikh Brich Abu-Medin (3)**, Bedouin sheikh, British appointed Mayor of Be'er Sheva, and Bedouin representative to the British government. His former house on the junction of Ha'Atzmaut and Ha-Histadrut is now a falafel café and a chemists. Continuing south on the pedestrianized Keren Kayemet Le-Israel, you pass a number of restored buildings from the Ottoman period; the most notable being the building at no 94 that now serves as the HaNegev Pharmacy. At the junction with Trumpeldor is the site of the **first grain mill (2)** in the Negev, established by two Jewish families in 1901.

Ottoman period buildings

Be'er Sheva Centre & Old City

★ Sights
1 Abraham's Well
2 Jewish Grain Mill
3 House of Sheikh Brich Abu-Medin
4 Home of Araf al-Araf
5 Governor's Residence
6 Ha-Negev Museum (Former Mosque)
7 Be'eri School
8 Water Tower
9 Turkish Railway Station
10 Turkish Station Master's House
11 World War 1 Cemetery
12 Bedouin School
13 Allenby Garden
14 Bet Haseraya
15 Bet Hanegbi
16 First High School
17 Bet Hamision
18 Artists' Quarter (Shuq Hilman)

▲ Other
1 Herzl car rental
2 Traffic car rental
3 Taxi rank
4 Restaurants/cafes
5 Arkia
6 Petrol stations
7 Supermarkets
8 Electrical substation
9 Bedouin market

■ Sleeping
1 Arava
2 Aviv
3 Beit Sadot Yalev IYHA Youth Hostel
4 Ha-Negev

0 — metres — 250

...... Route of walking tour of old city

Abraham's Well (1) "And Abimelech said unto Abraham, What mean these seven ewe lambs which thou hast set by themselves? And he said, For these seven ewe lambs shalt thou take of my hand, that they may be a witness unto me, that I have digged this well. Wherefore he called that place Beersheba; because there they sware both of them. Thus they made a covenant at Beersheba: then Abimelech rose up, and Phichol the chief captain of his host, and they returned into the land of the Philistines. And Abraham planted a grove in Beersheba, and called there on the name of the Lord, the everlasting God." (*Genesis 21:29-33*). And so it came to pass that a tacky attraction would be built around a well in Be'er Sheba, and lo, tourists would come and taketh their photo at this spot, wherein they shalt purchase a Coca-Cola and a souvenir t-shirt. The well itself is thought to be 12th century CE, with current water-drawing constructions dating to the Ottoman period. The owner is a good source of information on Be'er Sheva's history, and will enthusiastically show you a book containing a number of old photos that show the ancient Bedouin watering hole here, as well as providing an insight into how the modern town has expanded. ■ *1 Hebron Road, T6234613, F6282073. Sunday-Thursday 0800-1600, Friday 0830-1300. Free. This is as close to a 'tourist information' centre as you'll find in town.*

Artists' Quarter (18) This area is fairly quiet during the day, but becomes lively at night, with a concentration of cafés and pubs doing business until the small hours.

Bet Hamision (17) This is one of the first houses in the city (built 1903). The house is pretty much obscured by a high wall, and admittedly the 'walking tour of the Old City' is getting a bit desperate now. The tour passes the city's first **high-school (16)**; the home of the first military ruler of Be'er Sheva after the 1948 war, **Bet Hanegbi (15)**, (now home of the Institute for Industrial Mathematics, and covered by beautiful purple and yellow flowering trees); before arriving at the former Turkish government building, **Bet Haseraya (14)**, now used by the Israeli military (no photography) and the memorial **Allenby Garden (13)**. The walking tour finishes here.

Bedouin Market There has been a formal weekly Bedouin market in Be'er Sheva since 1905, though the exact location has changed on several occasions. The market now takes place each **Thursday** at the grounds on the north bank of the Nahal Be'er Sheva, just off the Eilat Rd, south of the Central Bus Station (see maps). **NB** During holiday weeks, the market takes place on the Monday of the same week. Although there are Bedouin wares on sale (jewellery, ceramics, rugs, clothes, fabrics and copperware), to many this market is no more exotic than the average car-boot sale. To the south of the market grounds you can see the **Turkish Bridge**.

Ben-Gurion University & the Institute for Applied Research The Negev Institute of Higher Education, founded in 1965, has since evolved into the Ben-Gurion University. An important postgraduate faculty now attached to the university is the Institute for Applied Research, initially founded by David Ben-Gurion in 1957. The institute specializes in researching living conditions in desert and semi-arid zones, attracting many top scientists from this field. Tours of both establishments are available by prior arrangement. ■ *Ben-Gurion Boulevard, T6461111. Institute for Applied Research, HaShalom, T6461901.*

Bet Yad-Labanim This hall is a memorial centre for 'Be'er Sheva's soldiers who fell in Israel's wars', and features displays detailing Israel's wars, with particular reference to the battle for control of the Negev. ■ *HaNessi'im, T6237744. Admission free.*

Designed by the innovative Israeli artist Dani Karavan (also responsible for the Holocaust Memorial at Rehovot's Weizmann Institute of Science), this unusual work serves as a memorial to the Negev Brigade of the Palmach that distinguished itself in the 1948 War of Independence. Various parts of the sculpture symbolize different aspects of the campaign, with Hebrew inscriptions giving blow-by-blow accounts of the battles. The memorial is on the Be'er Sheva plateau, overlooking the Be'er Sheva Valley, though it can be difficult to reach by public transport. ■ *Off Be'er Sheva-Omer Road, several kilometres out of town to the northeast. Bus 055 passes within two kilometres.* **Negev-Palmach Brigade Memorial (Andarta Memorial)**

Details of this ancient site are found in the 'Around Be'er Sheva' section, page 341. **Tel Be'er Sheva**

Essentials

L3 *Hilton Be'er Sheva*, Henrietta Szold, T6405444, F6405445. 257-room tower-block opened in 1997, 'regular' rooms rather bare, 'business' rooms (**L2**) have fridge, cable TV, desk, minibar, plus 'mini-suites' with sitting room and 2 rather overpriced 'Presidential' suites (**L1**) with kitchenette and jacuzzi. Large lobby dining area, poolside patio BBQ (entertainment on Thu), Chinese restaurant, fully equipped gym (30 NIS per visit, non-guests 65 NIS, or 12,000 NIS per year), large heated pool. Good facilities but without the real feel of luxury. **Sleeping**
■ *on maps; Price codes: see inside front cover*

B *Desert Inn/Ne'ot Midbar*, David Tuvyahu, T6424922, F6412772. Set in large grounds in remote residential neighbourhood, recently renovated and modernized, restaurants, 2 pools, sauna and jacuzzi, children's activities.

D *Aviv*, 48 Mordey HaGeta'ot, T6278059, F6281961. Simple and old fashioned but clean enough, some rooms with balconies, at lower end of **D** price category. **D** *HaNegev*, 26 Ha'Atzma'ut, T6277026, F6278744. Rooms at different prices. Those in annex are rather squalid with shared bath (**E**), extra $5 gets you a poor room with attached bath (**D-E**), plus nicer rooms in new block with a/c, attached bath, TV (**D**).

E *Arava*, 37 Ha-Histadrut, T6278792. Not much English spoken but friendly, full of ancient Eastern Europeans, modest but spotlessly clean rooms, attached bath, best value in town for couples (upper end of **E** category). **E** *Beit Sadot Yalev* IYHA Youth Hostel, 79 Ha'Atzma'ut, T6277444/6271490, F6275735. Very well maintained a/c 3 or 4 bed dorms (no bunks!) but quite expensive ($21-23 per person). *'Old Guesthouse'* has dbles (**C-D**), with larger dbles in the *'New Guesthouse'* (**B-C**). Check-in 1500-1900, check-out 0900, no curfew, lunch/dinner $11, pool. Nice but not great value.

There are no truly outstanding restaurants in Be'er Sheva, though the main square at the north end of the pedestrianized Keren Kayemet Le-Israel is a nice place to sit with your falafel or shwarma. Note that the *Café Maurice* here uses extremely small pitta – try next door. If you're doing it yourself there are several supermarkets in the Old City, with fresh fruit and vegetables available at the Municipal Shuq. **Eating**

The Kanyon HaNegev Centre has branches of *Burger Ranch*, *Kapulsky* and *Pizza Hut*, whilst there's a *McDonald's* at the bus station. *Bulgarit*, 112 Keren Kayemet Le-Israel, T6238504, is a long established modest Bulgarian place serving hearty meals for 30-45 NIS. *Ilie's*, 21 Herzl, T6278685, is considered the best place in town for a steak (35-55 NIS). *Beit Ha-Ful*, 15 Ha-Histadrut, T6234253, is excellent value, with Be'er Sheva's best fowl, hummus, falafel and shwarma. *Beer-Teva*, next to *Hilton Be'er Sheva*, T1-800-225577, is a bio-organic health food store.

The Negev

Bars & When it comes to night-time entertainment, Be'er Sheva is rather deceptive. What
nightclubs appears to be a sleepy, quiet town has quite a number of lively bars and cafés. The
whole area around Keren Kayemet Le-Israel has a number of pleasant evening-time
watering holes, whilst those seeking later entertainment (2100-0300) should head for
the bars around Trumpeldor, Ha-Avot and Silansky. Eastern Europeans are particularly
in evidence. Consistently recommended in this area are *Trombone*, *HaSimta* (*The
Alley*) and *The Wall*.

Entertainment **Cinemas** *GG Ori*, T6103111; *Rav-Negev*, Kanyon HaNegev Centre, T6235278.
Concert halls *Be'er Sheva Chamber Orchestra*, HaMeshahrerim, T6231616/6276019;
Rubin Music Conservatory, Ha-Nessi'im, T6231616. **Folk-dancing** Sat evening at
Ben Gurion University, Thu evening at *Makiv Gimel High School*, Mivza Yo'av,
Shekhuna Bet neighbourhood, bus 3. **Theatres** *Be'er Sheva Theatre Co*, Be'er Sheva
Theatre, Gan Moshe, T6278111.

Sports **Gym** Non-guests can use the gym, saunas and jacuzzis at the *Hilton Be'er Sheva*
(Sun-Thu 0700-2200, Fri 0700-1800, Sat 0700-1800, 30 NIS). **Swimming** Non-guests
can pay to use the pools at the *Desert Inn* and *Beit Sadot Yalev IYHA Youth Hostel*.
There is a *Municipal Pool* out to the northwest of the city and the *Galei HaNegev Pool*
on Yehuda HaLevi, nr Sheni Eliyahu Park to the north. **Tennis** *Samson Tennis Centre*,
Yehuda HaLevi, Shekhuna Bet neighbourhood.

Transport **Local Bus**: The town centre is fairly small, so you can easily get around on foot. The
main routes around town (5 NIS) leave from the Egged Central Bus Station, with most
running regularly from 0520-2300: **2** Egged–Shuq–Old City; **3** Egged–Shuq–Old
City–Kanyon HaNegev Centre (Mall)–Main Post Office–Magen David Adom–Techno-
logical College; **4** Old City–Shuq–Egged–Shekem Courthouse–Central Clinic–Ben
Gurion University; **6** Egged–Shuq–Old City–Kanyon HaNegev Centre–Central Post
Office–Courthouse–Conservatory–Technological College–Psychiatric Hospital; **7**
Egged–Shuq–Old City–HaNegev Mall–Main Post Office–Courthouse–Municipal-
ity–Soroka Hospital; **10** Egged-Be'er Sheva Country Club; **16** Soroka Hospital–Ben
Gurion University. For details of city buses, T6277381. **Car hire**: *Avis*, 11 Ha-Nessi'im,
T6271777; *Budget*, Shazar Blvd, 8 Poaley Binyan, T6280755; *Eldan*, Desert Inn Hotel,
T6430344; *Europcar*, 1/9 Hebron, T6231013; *Hertz*, 5a Ben-Zvi, T6273878; *Reliable*, 1
Ha'Atzmaut, T6237123. **Taxis**: *Hazui*, Nordau, T6239333; *Mezada*, 45 Ha'Atzma'ut,
T6275555; *Sinai*, 48 Ha-Histadrut, T6277525.

Long distance Buses: The large **Central Bus Station** is located off Derekh Eilat,
T6294311/2 or 6294333 or 177 0225555. The bus information office is particularly
unhelpful. Tickets should be bought in advance from the ticket office, though few
seem to bother. Main destinations such as Eilat, Jerusalem and Tel Aviv are served by
express, regular and local buses. Actual departure times may change during the lifetime of this book, but they still serve as a guide to the frequency of the services.

Arad: Bus 388 direct, 2-3 per hour, Sunday-Thursday 0645-2230, Friday until 1730,
Saturday 1700-2300, pl 9, 45 minutes, 19 NIS; **Ashqelon**: Bus 363/364,
Sunday-Thursday 0615-2045, Friday last 1615, Saturday 2015, pl 2; **Avdat/Ein Avdat**:
Bus 060, every 1-2 hours, Friday last at 1430; Dimona: Bus 048/056, 2 per hour,
Sunday-Thursday 0600-2300, Friday until 1700, Sat 1730-2330, pl 7; **Eilat** (via Mizpe
Ramon): Bus 392/393/394, Sunday-Thursday 0745 0915 1100 1200 1545, Friday 0745
0800 0915 1200, Saturday 1730 2120, pl 4, 3 hours, 45 NIS; **Eilat** (via Arava road): Bus
397, Sunday-Thursday 0730 1030 1230 1530 1830, Friday last at 1530, Saturday 1830,
pl 3, 45 NIS; **Ein Bokek** (via Arad): Bus 384/385, Sunday-Thursday 0800 1230 1530
1800, Friday 0230, pl 9; **Ein Gedi**: as per Ein Bokek; **Jerusalem**: Bus 470 direct,

Sunday-Thursday 0700 0750 0820 0910 1500 1600 1700, Friday 0720 1100 1200 1300, Saturday 2015, pl 13, 2 hours, 29 NIS; **Jerusalem** via **Hebron**: Bus 440, Sunday-Thursday 0720 1035, Friday 0715 1035, pl 13; **Jerusalem** via **Kiryat Gat**: Bus 446, 2 per hour, Sunday-Thursday 0600-2000, Friday last 1530, Sat 2020-2300, pl 13; **Lahav**: Bus 042/047, Sunday-Thursday 9 per day, Friday 4 per day, Sat 1 per day, pl 1; **Mizpe Ramon**: Bus 392/393 (to Eilat), Sunday-Thursday 0745 0915 1100 1200 1545, Friday 0745 0800 0915 1200, Sat 1730 2120, pl 4, 1½ hours; **Retaim** via **Revivim** and **Mash'abbe Sade**: Bus 045, Sunday-Thursday 0600 1020 1220 1415 1615 1805 2000, Friday 0600 1230 1600, Sat 2100, pl 4; **Sde Boker**: Bus 060, every 1-2 hours; **Tel Aviv**: Bus 370/375/380/383/391/394, every 15 minutes, Sunday-Thursday 0530-2145, Friday 0545-1700, Saturday 2015-2200, pl 15-16, 1½ hours, 22 NIS.

Sherut/service taxi: Shared taxis (*Moniot Ayal*, T6233033) run to **Eilat**, **Jerusalem** and **Tel Aviv** from outside the Central Bus Station (same fare as bus), but they only depart when full. **Train**:The train station is on Ben Gurion, to the east of town, T6237245. Formerly just used for freight services, there are now trial passenger services to Tel Aviv (and beyond), though the train station is rather inconveniently located.

Directory

Airline offices *Arkia*, corner of Ha'Atzma'ut/Keren Kayemet Le-Israel, T6287444; *El Al*, 123 He-Haluz, T6270660 or 136 He-Haluz, T6231855. **Banks & money changers** There are numerous banks in and around the town centre, most of which offer foreign exchange (though check rates and commission charges first). Banks marked on the map are those with ATM machines. The post office also offers commission-free foreign exchange. **Communications** **Area code**: T07. **Post office:** Main branch at corner of Ha-Nessi'im and Ben Zvi offers poste restante, international phone calls and foreign exchange. There are 6 other post offices, including a branch at the junction of Hadassah and Ha-Histradrut in the Old City. **Hospitals and medical services** Chemists: *PharmLin*, 34 Herzl, T6277034; *Super Pharm*, Kanyon HaNegev Centre, T6281371; plus several on Herzl and Keren Kayemet Le-Israel. Hospitals: *Soroka Medical Centre*, Ha-Nessi'im, nr Ben Gurion University, T6660111. **Tour companies and travel agencies** *Egged Tours*, Central Bus Station, T6232532; *issta*, New Campus, Ben Gurion University, T6237255. **Tourist offices** The nearest you will find to a tourist office is the Visitors' Centre at Abraham's Well, 1 Hebron Rd, T6234613, F6282073 (Sunday-Thursday 0800-1600, Friday 0830-1230). **Useful addresses and phone numbers** Police: T100 (emergency); 30 Herzl, T6462744. **Ambulance:** Magen David Adom T101 (emergency); corner of Weizmann and Sokolov, T6278333. **Fire:** T102. **Municipality:** T6463666; T6463777 ('hotline').

Around Be'er Sheva

There are a number of places of interest in the area immediately surrounding Be'er Sheva, though public transport connections are not particularly convenient.

Tel Be'er Sheva

The most impressive remains on view at Tel Be'er Sheva today are from the Iron Age city, of which some two-thirds have been excavated. In order for the remains to have been left uncovered, they have had to have been sealed by new, fired bricks. A number of levels of occupation have been identified, labelled strata IX-II. At the lower levels, stratum VIII may date to the biblical reference to Samuel, and his sons Joel and Abiah serving as judges (*1 Samuel 8:1-2*).

Stratum V was probably destroyed during the campaign of the Pharaoh Shishak c. 925 BCE, though it is suggested that the town could not have been of any great importance since it is not mentioned amongst the list of captured cities on the Karnak temple relief. There is a view, however, that Be'er Sheva may be the 'Hagar of Abra(ha)m' that is mentioned.

Tour of the site Much of what you see today is from stratum III, and its continuation, stratum II, the latter being destroyed in a violent conflagration probably dating to the Assyrian king Sennacherib's campaign in 701 BCE. The main (and only) **city gate** (**1**) probably dates to the 10th century BCE. Two guard rooms stand on either side, and it was protected by an **outer gate** (**2**). This, however, was not reconstructed following Sennacherib's sacking of the city, though the **outer piers** (**3**) were enlarged as additional protection. An **irrigation channel** (**4**) runs through the city gate, to a deep **well** (**5**) outside. This well is thought to date to the 12th century BCE, though it is curious why it was not enclosed within the latter city walls.

The city gate emerges on to the city square (**6**). To the left (west) side of the square is what is thought to have been the **Governor's Residence** (**7**). Note how the entrance is built using ashlars, rectangular hewn stones laid in horizontal courses, whereas the rest of the site is built from field stones. The building contains two dwelling units, a kitchen and storerooms. The cellar below may have previously formed part of a temple site.

To the right (east) of the city gate is the largest building; three pillared structures that probably formed part of the city storehouse (**8**). Broken pottery vessels attest to their usage, with commentators suggesting that these storage facilities were part of a taxation system established by Solomon. Stones from a **horned altar** were found incorporated into one of the storeroom walls. The original reconstructed horned altar (1.6 metres by 1.6 metres) now stands in the Israel Museum in Jerusalem, though you can see a copy in the HaNegev Museum in Be'er Sheva. The interesting aspect of this altar is the fact that the stones were cut (ie it was 'horned'). Biblical law is quite strict in saying that the altar should be made from uncut stone: "And there thou shalt build an altar unto the Lord thy God, an altar of stones: thou shalt not lift up any iron tool upon them" (*Deuteronomy 27:5*); and again, "an altar of whole stones, over which no man hath lift up any iron" (*Joshua 8:31*). The altar may well have been broken up during the religious reforms of Hezekiah, King of Judah (727-698 BCE).

Also to be seen on the tel are a number of later ruins, the most noticeable of which is the rhomboid shaped Roman fortress (**11**), opposite the storehouse.

Around Be'er Sheva

■ *T6469981, F6469979. 0900-1700 daily. Admission free. Small visitors' centre, information booth and cafeteria at the site. The site is located on the Be'er Sheva to Omer-Hebron road (Route 60) five kilometres northeast of the modern city. Bus 055 from the Central Bus Station runs irregularly (thrice a day, Sunday-Thursday) past the Tel Be'er Sheva access road, from where it is a two-kilometre walk to the site. Last bus returns at 1800.*

This open-air museum features almost one hundred assorted planes parked on a huge concrete airfield. The museum tells the story of the Israeli Air Force (IAF) since its inception, and has a diverse collection of planes. The 2 hour tour of the museum features a short film screened inside the belly of a Boeing 707 that played a minor role in the 1977 rescue at Entebbe. ■ *T6906855. Sunday-Thursday 0800-1700, Friday 0800-1200. Adult 15 NIS. The museum is located some seven kilometres west of Be'er Sheva on Route 2357, though there is unfortunately no regular public transport to the site. An infrequent service goes to Hazerim from the Central Bus Station (check there for further details).*

Israeli Air Force Museum, Hazerim

Within the Centre is the '**Museum of Bedouin Culture**'; an attempt to explain aspects of the traditional Bedouin way of life. Activities such as cooking, bread-baking, the coffee ceremony and carpet weaving are demonstrated, whilst displays present artefacts such as jewellery, clothing, agricultural

Joe Alon Centre: Museum of Bedouin Culture

The Negev

Tel Be'er Sheva (Iron Age city)

Approximate position of Roman fortress

1 City Gate	5 Well
2 Outer Gate	6 City Square
3 Outer Piers	7 Governor's Residence
4 Main Irrigation Channel	8 City Storehouse
9 Dwellings	
10 Cellar House	
11 Roman Fortress	
12 Water Supply System	

0 metres 20

Main Drainage Channel

implements and household utensils. Many of the items have been donated by the various Bedouin tribes of the Negev and the Sinai, with some of the things on display having now gone out of general usage. ■ *Kibbutz Lahav, T9918597/9913322, F9919889. Saturday-Thursday 0900-1600, Friday 0900-1400. Adult 10 NIS. To reach the museum, head north from Be'er Sheva for 21 kilometres on Route 40. Turn right (east) at Dvira Junction on to Route 3255 and follow orange signs to the museum (eight kilometres). By public transport, buses 042/047 run from Be'er Sheva to Kibbutz Lahav nearby nine times per day (Sunday-Thursday). The more regular bus 369 (to Kiryat Gat and onto Tel Aviv) regularly passes Dvira Junction, from where it's an eight-kilometre walk.*

Bedouin Heritage Centre, Rahat The small development town of Rahat is an attempt to settle the Bedouin. The housing is modern, with schools and medical facilities, but it is hard to see the sustainable economic basis of the settlement. A recent report on child poverty in Israel claims that 34 percent of youngsters in Rahat live below the poverty line, and unemployment is way above the national average (*Jerusalem Report*, 29/3/99). The proprietors of the **Bedouin Heritage Centre** have struck upon a means of making ends meet by offering a sanitized version of Bedouin life to tourists. Drink freshly roasted coffee, or suck on a hubbly-bubbly, whilst sitting on a rug in a Bedouin tent listening to traditional music, before taking a ride on a camel. Locally produced handicrafts are on sale. ■ *T05-7918263. Sunday-Friday 0830-2000, Saturday 1130-1700. Adult 12 NIS. From Be'er Sheva, head north on Route 40 for 25 kilometres to the Beit Kama (Qama) Junction. Turn left (west) on to Route 293, then left (south) again immediately, opposite the petrol station. Head south along Route 264 for four kilometres, turning left again at the sign for Rahat. The centre is two kilometres along this road, just before the main centre of Rahat. There is no convenient public transport to the site from Be'er Sheva.*

West of Be'er Sheva

The area to the west of Be'er Sheva, towards the Gaza Strip, is little visited by tourists though there are a couple of places of interest that are accessible if you have your own transport.

This is one of Israel's most neglected regions economically, with few employment opportunities to sustain the so-called 'development towns'. One resident describes Ofakim, one of the largest towns in the area, thus: "This town is Death Valley. There's nothing here. Not even anger. Just mass depression. The children are doomed" (Jerusalem Report, 29/3/99).

Eshkol National Park

Eshkol National Park was developed to provide recreational facilities for towns in the surrounding area following Israel's final withdrawal from Sinai in 1982. The key attraction of the park is the **swimming pool**, at 3,500 square metres not surprisingly the largest in Israel. An observation tower gives a good all-round view of the park, with wide expanses of lawn and several lakes providing unlimited potential for picnics. Shade is provided by palm, pistacia, olive, California pepper and acacia trees.

The western boundary of the park is formed by the Nahal HaBesor (The Besor River), the largest wadi in the country. The Besor is mentioned in the Bible, as David pursued those who had kidnapped his two wives (*I Samuel 30:9-10*). A number of unspectacular remains from the Chalcolithic to the

Eshkol National Park

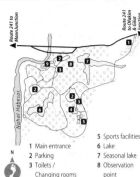

5 Sports facilities
1 Main entrance   6 Lake
2 Parking   7 Seasonal lake
3 Toilets /   8 Observation
  Changing rooms   point
4 Swimming Pool   9 Springs

Byzantine period dot the park. ■ 0800-1700, pool 1100-1700. Adult 18 NIS. You need your own transport to reach Eshkol National Park. From Be'er Sheva head northwest on Route 25, turning left (west) at the Gilat Junction (21 kilometres) on to Route 241. Eshkol National Park is a further 16 kilometres west (via Ofakim).

Nahal HaBesor Scenic Route

A driving route has been prepared through the centre of the **HaBesor Reserve**; a 1,300 hectare section of the middle Besor wadi. Though the road is not sealed, it should be suitable for most vehicles. The sites en route are not particularly stunning, though the drive is pleasant enough. The route described below is north to south. Total length: 21 kilometres.

1 Old railway bridge

A number of actions were fought in this area between the Allied forces and the Turks during World War One, with the Australian and New Zealand (ANZAC) regiments playing a major role. During this period, a vital communications and supply link ran through here in the form of the thrice weekly Rafiah–Be'er Sheva train. The train continued to run along this route until 1927. Parts of the stone foundations of the wooden railway bridge built in 1917 can still be seen.

2 Chalcolithic site, ancient quarry

200 metres from the road, on the left, is a site dating to the Chalcolithic period (fourth century BCE). The remains of pits dug as living quarters and storage rooms are still discernible. A path leads a further 250 metres down to an ancient quarry dug on the banks of the wadi.

3 Badlands border

A ridge 150 metres to the left of the road marks the boundary of the sand and sandstone based subsoil on the west of the Nahal HaBesor with the distinct badlands soil and vegetation classification area to the north. The sandstone ridge, reddish sand and beachrocks on the opposite bank of the wadi suggest the existence of an ancient beach.

4 Tel Sharuhen (Tel el-Far'ah, South)

Marked by the observation tower to the left of the road, this ancient mound or tel is identified by most scholars as the site of the biblical city of Sharuhen. Excavations have revealed an almost continuous occupation from the Middle Bronze Age IIB (1750-1550 BCE) until the first century CE Roman period. The surface of the site is scarred by the criss-cross lines of trenches dug during the First World War.

Several ancient written sources refer to Sharuhen, including the Bible (Joshua 19:6), and at least three different Egyptian sources. In the account of Hyksos' expulsion during the second millennium BCE, Ahmose describes a siege of Sharuhen that lasts for three years.

Not that much remains to be seen, though the Late Bronze Age residency to the north of the mound is impressive. The building was still in use until the 11th century BCE. The plan of the Roman fortress and city can be barely discerned.

The Negev

5 Sharuhen well The settlement's well (not marked) is to the northeast.

6 Sharuhen pool This natural, perennial pool provided the main supply of water to the town of Sharuhen. To the south of the pool are traces of the ancient Roman road, *Limes Palaestina*, that once connected Rafiah to the Dead Sea.

7 Site B There is little to see at this fourth millennium BCE Chalcolithic site, though it is thought that it was once a centre of flint tool production.

8 Tel Sawauin An Iron Age IA (1200-1150 BCE) settlement previously occupied this site, with the Arab name that the site has come to be known by, 'Sawauin', being derived from the Arabic word for 'flint'; an obvious reference to the nearby Chalcolithic site (above). A late Lower Palaeolithic (c. 120,000 BP) site has been identified nearby. It is also possible to see parts of the railway rampart laid by the Egyptian Expeditionary Force of the British Army in 1917.

9 Revuva well (Bir Ruweiba) An early 20th century Ottoman built well, drawing water using the 'Antilliya' method of a water wheel and a system of jugs, operated by draft animals, can be seen 250 metres to the right of the road. Restored during the British Mandate period, the well falls within the boundaries of the Bedouin village of Ruweiba.

10 Drain cliff A man-made drain cliff stands to the left of the road, though you will have to climb down to see it in detail. A sunken drain collects water for irrigation from beneath the pebble layer, with water collecting in the basins during the winter. The spot is popular with a number of birds, and it is not unusual to come across a large number of cranes browsing.

11 Conglomerate pool Further south is the conglomerate pool, where water from the springs collects in the reservoir. This has been a rich area for archaeologists, with finds from the Chalcolithic, Israelite (Iron Age), Hellenistic, Roman and Byzantine periods being found. Just to the south of here is a 3-way fork. The right fork leads to the main road (Route 222), whilst the second left continues the tour.

12 Remains of ancient farm Across a very dubious-looking suspension bridge is a cluster of settlements comprising a few huts, grain pits, millstones, ovens and some bits of pottery. All bar one date to the Iron Age IIA (1000-900 BCE), the other dating to the Iron Age IIC (700-586 BCE), with the suggestion being that they are biblical *hazerim* (farms) attached to Sharuhen. Little remains to be seen today, however, and it is not thought that these ancient farms were occupied for long.

Nahal HaBesor scenic route

The water of the cliff pool is apparently contaminated, and not fit for drinking or even bathing in. A display board gives a brief description of the geological phenomenon that the cliff in front of you presents: 'a geological story of the area during the past 3 million years'. **13 Cliff pool**

The tour finishes at a high observation tower that gives a good general view of the surrounding area.

From here, the option is to **i)** head north on Route 234 and return to Be'er Sheva, Gaza, or in the direction of Tel Aviv;or **ii)** head southeast on Route 222 in the direction of **Mash'abbe Sade Junction**, passing **Elusa** (Haluza) and the turning for **Rehovot-in-the-Negev** (see 'Southern Negev' page 363). **Moving on**

East and southeast of Be'er Sheva

From Be'er Sheva, it is possible to take one of two routes towards the Dead Sea Region. The east route takes in the Canaanite/Israelite city at Tel Arad and its modern neighbour Arad, before dropping below sea-level down to the Dead Sea at Neve Zohar.

The southeast route to the Dead Sea, with a number of diversions, passes the modern town of Dimona, the ancient Nabatean city of Mamshit, and the two smaller of the Negev's three main craters, Makhtesh HaGadol and Makhtesh HaKatan. If travelling with your own transport, with an early start it is possible to take in the best of both routes in one grand loop that can return you to Be'er Sheva the same day. If relying on public transport, it would take several days to cover the key sites (with some remoter areas not accessible at all).

Tel Arad

*At one time the site of the most important city in the Negev, Tel Arad has substantial remains from both the **Canaanite** and the later **Israelite** settlements. The site has been considerably restored, particularly the Israelite (and later) citadel at the top of the hill, which has been largely rebuilt using original material. The lower Canaanite city is the largest, most complete Early Bronze Age city yet excavated in Israel. A walking tour is marked down through the Canaanite city, with the key points of interest all labelled.*

Ins and outs

Regular buses between Be'er Sheva and Arad (along Route 31) will drop you at the turning for the site, known as Tel Arad Junction (24 kilometres east of Be'er Sheva). From here it is a two and a half kilometre walk to the site. An irregular bus service from Arad (052) goes all the way to the site entrance. **Getting there**

History

The Canaanite city probably reached its peak towards the beginning of the Early Bronze Age II (3000-2700 BCE). The economy of the city was based primarily on agriculture, including production and processing of barley, wheat, peas, lentils, flax and olives, plus the rearing of livestock. Another important sector of the economy involved extensive trade with southern Sinai, Egypt, plus other Canaanite cities. Many of the jars, cooking pots and other artefacts **The Canaanite city**

The Negev

found at Tel Arad are now in the Israel Museum in Jerusalem, with others in the Arad Visitors Centre, in the modern town of Arad (see below). Evidence from Stratum III (c. 2950-2800 BCE) suggests that much of the town was destroyed in some major conflagration, almost certainly the result of an enemy attack. The town appears to have been rebuilt almost immediately, though occupation was not to last long with the city being abandoned by 2650 BCE. The reasons for this are not entirely clear, though climatic change, Egyptian encroachment or political unrest throughout Canaan have all been suggested. The fact that the Canaanite city site itself was never reoccupied explains why the remains are so extensive and well preserved.

The Israelite citadels site After a gap of around 1,600 years, parts of the site were reoccupied by the Israelites. The early settlement was clustered around a *bamah*, or cultic high place. The *bamah* became a royal Israelite sanctuary during the reign of Solomon (965-928 BCE), and was protected by a citadel. Five further Israelite citadels were built on the site between the ninth century BCE and the early sixth century BCE.

After the destruction of the last of the Israelite citadels at the end of the First Temple period (587-586 BCE), the site was abandoned for a while. A brief occupation during the fifth century BCE led to some Persian building activity, though most of this was destroyed in the third to second century BCE when a large Hellenistic tower was built. The tower stood until the second century BCE.

The Romans built a fortress on the mound (c. 70-100 CE), possibly as part of the network of fortifications guarding the *Limes Palaestinae* (Dead Sea–Rafiah road). No remains were found on the tel from the Byzantine village mentioned in Eusebius' *Onomasticon*, though evidence suggests that the Roman fort was repaired and reoccupied during the Early Arab period (638-1099 CE). The mound was later used as a Muslim graveyard from the 10th to 16th centuries CE. The citadel has been rebuilt by archaeologists, with distinct sections from the tenth, ninth to eighth, and sixth centuries BCE, and the Hellenistic tower, clearly identifiable.

Tour of the site

Before commencing your tour of the site, it is worth supplementing the free map (that you are given upon entry) with the 2 NIS plan that shows an isometric reconstruction of the early Canaanite city; it is a good aid in visualizing the form of the city. Be sure to also pick up an English translation. The tour does not proceed in chronological order, but begins at the Israelite citadel, from where there is an all-encompassing view of the site.

Israelite citadel The mound upon which the **Israelite citadel (1)** stands rises above the lower (Canaanite) city to the southwest. The citadel that you see today has been largely rebuilt by the archaeologists who excavated the site, though they used the original materials. Six successive Israelite citadels stood on this site, plus later Persian, Hellenistic, Roman and Arab

Tel Arad

National Park entrance & car park

0 metres 40

1 Israelite Citadel (see separate plan)	6 Projected line of city walls
2 Sanctuary/Temple	7 Western Gate
3 Sacred Precinct (see separate plan)	8 Southwestern Gate
4 Palace	9 Residential Quarters & restored 'Arad House'
5 City Walls	10 Water Reservoir Area

The Negev

structures, though the plan today is relatively clear, with distinct phases from Stratum XI (10th century BCE), Strata VII-X (ninth to eighth centuries BCE), Stratum VI (sixth century BCE), plus the later Hellenistic tower (third to second century BCE) all labelled. Climbing to the observation point in the southwest corner gives the best view of the citadel's plan, the Canaanite city below, and the surrounding countryside.

Though finds in the citadel area have revealed a hoard of silver ingots and jewellery, as well as evidence of a perfume industry, the most significant building within the citadel is the **sanctuary (2)**, or **temple**, located in the northwest corner. Its construction began in the Solomonic period (late 10th century BCE, Stratum XI), though the *bamah* and altar predate it to the late 12th to early 11th centuries BCE (Stratum XII). The temple is orientated east–west, like the Solomonic Temple in Jerusalem, and comprises three rooms; a hall, the sanctuary, and the **holy of holies**. A *masseba*, or ritual standing stone, was found in the holy of holies. The temple remained in use until the seventh century BCE, though the use of the sacrificial altar may have gone out of use during the religious reforms of Hezekiah (727-698 BCE). Other structures within the citadel that remain (and are labelled) include the artisans' quarter and the water system.

The Sacred Precinct (3) comprises a large twin temple, a small twin temple, and a large ceremonial structure, all within a self-contained complex separated from the other city buildings by a wall. The **large twin temple** to the west consists of two large halls identical in size, both opening on to courtyards. The northern hall is divided into three cells, and a large altar and a cult basin were found in its courtyard. The southern hall proved to be rich in finds, most notable of which is what is thought to be a *masseba*. The **small twin temple** in the centre of the Sacred Precinct is similar in plan. A number of finds were unearthed here, including a stone altar in the courtyard of the northern hall. The **ceremonial building** to the southeast comprises a large hall opening on to a wide courtyard. All the buildings in the Sacred Precinct open to the east, with the twin temples closely resembling the twin temples at Megiddo.

Sacred Precinct

The Negev

Sacred Precinct, Tel Arad

N

0 metres 10

1 Large Twin Temple
2 Small Twin Temple
3 Ceremonial Building

Courtyard

The Palace complex (4) was sealed off from the rest of the city buildings, with no doors or windows to the west, a main entrance to the north, and small doorways to the east and south. A large room is at the core of the palace complex, featuring what is thought to be a large ritual ablutions basin as well as a *stela* (similar to a *masseba*). The location of the complex near to the Sacred Precinct was significant in determining its function.

The Palace complex

The market area comprises two large, thin-walled buildings set either side of an open area. Large numbers of *pithoi* (large storage jars) were found in the buildings.

Market

City walls & gates Though not all of the **Canaanite city walls (5)** have been excavated, they probably extend for some 1,200 metres, enclosing an area of 10 hectares. The wall is almost 2.5 metres thick in most parts and is built of large, semi-dressed stones with a fill of smaller stones. The walls are reinforced by posterns, towers and gates, of which a number have been excavated. The **western gate (7)** was possibly the main gate, suggested by its wide entrance (2.3 metres). It is protected by a semi-circular tower to its north. The other gate that has been excavated, the **southwestern gate (8)**, is protected by a rectangular gate.

Residential quarter The area between the western gate and the southwestern gate and the area to the very south of the city are the city's **main residential quarter (9)**. The Canaanite city plan is well ordered, with a functional separation of districts. Most of the residential quarters are located inside the curve of the southern part of the city wall, and between the western and southwestern gates. Typical dwelling units comprise a main room with benches running along the walls, a stone base for a wooden pillar to support the roof in the centre of the room, a smaller subsidiary room, plus a courtyard. Such is the regularity of this building within the Canaanite city, such a broadhouse is now referred to as **Arad House**. A restored Arad House, complete with vessels and utensils, is located to the south of the Canaanite city.

Water reservoir area It should be noted that the Canaanite city lacks a natural spring or well and is thus dependent upon collection and storage of rainwater. The Eocenic rock that the mound stands upon is different in character to the Senonian rock that surrounds it and, being impervious to water, it allows the storage of water in large cisterns.

The water reservoir area (**10**) of the Canaanite city is a distinct complex of buildings surrounding the main reservoir on three sides. A dam probably stood to the east. The largest building in the complex has been dubbed the **water citadel**, and may well have been associated with the control and distribution of this most valuable of commodities. It comprises five long, narrow chambers, with its very thick outer walls (over 1.5 metres) leading to the references to its fortified character. A large building resembling a residential unit, but with a unique stone-paved courtyard, is located close to the water citadel and has been dubbed the **water commissioner's house**.

The plan of the original Canaanite city reservoir is not clear due to the later digging of an Israelite period well. The deep well, tapping the upper aquifer, supplied water that was carried in vessels to the cistern inside the Israelite citadel. The well was restored during the Herodian period, some time between 37 BCE and 70 CE. ■ *0800-1700 daily. Adult 10 NIS, student 7 NIS. There is a free map, though it is also worth buying the additional sheet for 2 NIS that features an isometric reconstruction of the Canaanite city.*

Arad

Phone code: 07
Colour map 3, grid A5

Though there are few attractions in Arad itself, the town provides a base from which to explore the surrounding area. Arad is also worth visiting since it is one of the few development towns in the Negev that has been deemed to have worked. Arad lies close to the ancient Canaanite city at Tel Arad (see page 347), though its main claim to fame nowadays is as home to the renowned Israeli writer Amos Oz, and as the venue for the annual Hebrew Music Festival.

Ins and outs

Getting there

The easiest way to reach Arad is by bus from Be'er Sheva (you'll have to change at Be'er Sheva if coming by bus from Eilat, and all Arad-bound buses from Tel Aviv also pass through Be'er Sheva). Arriving from the direction of the Dead Sea, there are several buses per day from 'En Boqeq, 'En Gedi and Masada to Arad.

Getting around

The town centre is very compact, though if you're heading out towards the hotels on the eastern edge of town it is easier to hop on bus 1 (which makes a long circuit all the way around the town).

History

Earmarked as a Negev development town by the government in the early 1960s, the site for the new town was selected by a group of founding fathers. The lay-out of the town was developed by an interdisciplinary team who took into consideration physical, social, economic and demographic factors. Thus, there is a distinct separation of industrial, commercial and residential zones, with sufficient room for the town to expand in stages. Compared with other Negev development towns, Arad has been a success. As one long-time resident pointed out, "Those who planned towns such as Dimona never lived in them. The opposite is true of Arad" (Brook, *Winner Takes All*).

Arad is situated 600 metres above sea-level, at the point where the Judean Hills meet the Negev desert. With a dry desert climate, pollen-free air, and pollution-free environment, Arad has gained a reputation as a centre for the treatment of asthma and other respiratory problems. Several of the hotels have private clinics treating asthma sufferers and there is also a national centre for the rehabilitation of asthmatic children.

The Negev

Arad

■ **Sleeping**	4 Margoa Arad	▲ **Other**	4 Muza pub
1 Arad	5 Masada (not finished)	1 Municipality	5 School
2 Blau Weiss	6 Nof Arad	2 Stadium	6 Supermarket
3 Inbar		3 TV towers	7 Cinema

Not to scale

The Negev

Sights

Arad Visitors' Centre   The Arad Visitors' Centre features a small museum that concentrates primarily on the nearby site of Tel Arad, as well as a number of audio-visual presentations explaining aspects of the Negev and Dead Sea environment. The Visitors' Centre also doubles as the tourist information office. ■ *Eliezar Ben Yair, between Commercial Centre and Arad Mall, T9954409. Sunday-Thursday 0900-1700, Friday 0900-1430. Adult 15 NIS.*

Essentials

Sleeping
■ *on map;*
price codes see inside
front cover

Arad has a very narrow choice of hotels, with all of them being hugely overpriced for the facilities on offer. You may get a better deal for a long term stay.

A *Inbar*, 38 Yehuda, T9973303, F9973322. Large, new 103 room hotel in centre of town, though rooms fairly simple for the price. Spa has heated indoor pool, sauna, jacuzzi, mud treatments, plus a skin clinic. **A** *Margoa Arad*, Moav, T9951222, F9957778. Rooms quite large though still a little old fashioned, gardens, pool, TV room, nightclub, restaurant, asthma treatment clinic. But where do they get these prices from? **A** *Nof Arad*, Moav, T9957056, F9954053. Rather cramped rooms in main block plus slightly cheaper chalets in garden, breakfast included, pool, *Aviv* clinic for respiratory diseases (T9972262), kosher restaurant.

C-D *Arad*, 6 Palmach, T9957040, F9957272. This place is a bit of a joke, resembling more a prison or barrack block than a hotel. It features very basic chalets with ancient TVs and very tatty bathrooms. The dining hall is a throwback to the 1960s. Very poor value.

E *Blau Weiss Youth Hostel & Guesthouse*, Atad, T9957150. Clean 4-6 bed dorms with a/c, plus some private doubles (**D**), breakfast included, check-in 1600-2000, check-out 1000, no curfew. The only real budget option.

Rooms for rent   The Arad Visitors' Centre can supply a complete list of registered rooms for rent, and may be able to help in making reservations. *David's House*, 38 Narkis, T9953173; *Lav's House*, 13 Irit, T9954791; *Oasis (Ronen's House)*, 7 Moav, T9950308; *Paz'z House*, 37 HaGilad, T9957177; *Raber's House*, 35 Shoham, T9952961; *Ron's House*, 54 Odem, T9950697; *Rontal's House*, 21 HaGilad, T9952207; *Schachter's House*, 5 Shoham, T9954423.

Eating   There are no really outstanding restaurants in Arad. There are plenty of cafés, pizza parlours and kebab places in the Commercial Centre, plus several supermarkets nearby. *Mister Shay*, 32 Palmach, behind the Municipality, T9971956, serves reasonable Chinese food. Otherwise you could try *Apropo* in the Kanyon Arad Mall, T9950766, for Thai and Italian light meals, or *Steiner's*, behind the petrol station on Route 31 at the entrance to town, which serves large, filling meals. The liveliest pub is probably *Muza* on Artist Square, T9958764.

Entertainment   **Cinemas** *Star*, T9950904. **Sports** Sports Centre: *Arad Sports Centre*, HaSport/Ayanot, T9957702, features indoor and outdoor swimming pools, tennis, gym, football and roller skating. **Tennis**: *Tennis Centre*, Achva, T9956877. **Festivals** Once a year, for 4 days in mid-July, the population of Arad doubles (some say trebles), as the town plays host to the Hebrew Music Festival (*Festival Arad*). Many of the concerts are free, with tickets for shows by better known Israeli rock and pop stars costing around 50 NIS. Whatever your musical tastes, Arad is worth visiting during the festival just to

Access to the 'Roman Ramp' entrance to Masada

The western entrance to the fortress at Masada, (the 'Roman Ramp'), is accessible by vehicle only from Arad (though there is no public transport to the site). The west side of Masada is also the venue for the Son et Lumière (Sound & Light) show. The Roman Ramp entrance is 20 km northeast of Arad, along Route 3199. To reach Route 3199, head along Moav to the eastern limits of Arad, before turning left onto Tzur just before the Margoa Arad Hotel. Masada is then sign-posted along the road to the right (northeast).

sample something of the atmosphere; it's the nearest Israel comes to Woodstock/Reading/Glastonbury. Accommodation is not a problem if you don't mind dossing down in the giant (free) marquees erected by the Municipality (otherwise, book your accommodation well in advance). Tickets for individual shows go on sale nationwide about a month before the event.

Shopping The main shopping area is the Kanyon Arad (Arad Mall) between Eliezar Ben Yair and Ha'Kanaim, or the Commercial Centre between Eliezar Ben Yair and Yehuda. Arad Market takes place each Monday (see map).

Transport **Local** Taxi: T9950888, T9969565. **Car hire**: the main car rental agencies (or their representatives) are in the Commercial Centre, between Eliezar Ben Yair and Yehuda.

Long distance buses Arad's 'Bus Station' is a shed and a dirt parking lot on Yehuda, T9957393/9957377. **Tel Aviv** 1-2 buses per hour, 389 direct, 2 hours, 35 NIS; 384/385/388 via **Be'er Sheva** (45 minutes, 19 NIS), last bus Fri 1330. **Jerusalem** 441, Sunday only. **'En Boqeq** (30 minutes, 17 NIS), **Masada** (45 minutes, 20 NIS) and **'En Gedi** (1 hour, 22 NIS) 384/385 several services per day. The best option for **Eilat** is to change at Be'er Sheva. For **Tel Arad**, take one of the buses bound for Be'er Sheva and ask to be dropped at the **Tel Arad Junction** (2.5 km walk to the site).

Directory **Banks** There are several banks in the Mall/Commercial Centre area, though the best option for foreign exchange is probably the Post Office. **Communications** Area code: T07. **Post office**: the main post office is on the corner of Eliezar Ben Yair and Hebron, opposite the Arad Visitors' Centre, and offers poste restante, international phone calls and commission-free foreign exchange. **Cultural centres** *Samuel Rubin Cultural Centre*, Eliezar Ben Yair, T9957747, features a small museum, a library and a theatre. **Hospitals and medical services** Chemists: *Super-Pharm*, Kanyon Arad/Arad Mall, Ha'Kanaim, T9971621, only chemist in the area open on Sat and Jewish holidays, (Sun-Thu 0900-2200, Fri 0900-1500, Sat 1100-2200); *Pharmacy*, Commercial Centre, T9957439. Hospitals: *Soroka Hospital*, T9400111; *Bet Mazor*, Yehuda, T9953339, regional rehabilitation centre for asthmatic children. Several of the hotels also have asthma treatment facilities. **Libraries** *Public Library*, Yerushalaym, nr Arad Mall, T9958517. **Tour companies and travel agents** *Kfar Hanokdim*, T9957326, offers camel tours or a 'Bedouin experience'. From Arad, you can also organize various jeep tours (T9952388, F9954116) and desert tours (*Yoel Tours*, T9954791). The Arad Visitors' Centre (see below, page 353) is a good source of information on various tours and excursions. **Tourist offices** The nearest you'll find to a tourist office is the *Arad Visitors' Centre* on Eliezar Ben Yair (between the Commercial Centre and Arad Mall, T9954409, Sun-Thu 0900-1700, Fri 0900-1420). **Useful addresses and phone numbers** Police: T100 (emergency); Yehuda, next to Bus Station, T9957044. Ambulance: T101 (emergency); Magen David Adom, Yehuda, next to Bus Station, T9957222. Fire: T102 (emergency); Hata'asiya, Industrial Zone, T9950222.

Nevatim To the southeast of Be'er Sheva, just off Route 25, is the moshav of Nevatim. Settled by Jews in 1946, Nevatim was abandoned following the 1948 War of Independence, with attempts to resettle it with recently demobbed soldiers

The Negev

The 'Black Hebrews'

Arriving in Israel in 1969 and settling largely in Dimona (and to some extent in Arad and Mizpe Ramon), this sect has caused considerable controversy within Israel. The group are largely English-speakers from the United States, led by Ben-Ami Ben Israel (formerly Ben-Ami Carter), and claim to be descendants of the 'real Jews'. Amongst their beliefs is that the 'original Jews' were expelled from Israel by the Romans following the destruction of the Second Temple in 70 CE. Many settled in West Africa but were subsequently forcibly transferred to the United States as part of the slave trade. The Black Hebrews are descended from these former slaves and

have now returned to Israel to reclaim the Holy Land for the 'real Jews'. Their initial claim to be Ethiopian Jews was exposed to be fraudulent by an Arad bus driver, himself an Ethiopian Jew, though nowadays they make no attempt to conceal what they consider to be their origins.

Not surprisingly, their claims brought them into conflict with the Israeli government. The group are now tolerated (if largely ignored) by central government, but hope to soon achieve full citizenship rights. Their profile was raised recently when two members of the community formed part of the group that represented Israel in the 1999 Eurovision Song Contest!

and immigrants not proving successful. In 1955 a community of Jews from the province of Cochin in western India (Kochi, in Kerala State) established themselves at Nevatim, constructing a distinct new synagogue and furnishing it with the ritual objects from the original Cochin synagogue. It is possible to visit the synagogue, as well as the Cochin Jewry Heritage Centre; a small museum detailing the history of the community (visitors should call ahead, T07-6277277).

Dimona

Phone code: 07
Colour map 3, grid B4

Whilst Arad is often held up as a model for the Negev development towns, Dimona is frequently selected by commentators as the example of the one that didn't work. From modest beginnings in 1955, the population has increased to around 35,000, a sizeable proportion of whom are Jews of North African origin. The economy of the town has traditionally been sustained by four major industries, despite the fact that the remoteness of the location increases transport costs considerably. Severe staff cut-backs at the textile factories, the chemical factory, and to a certain extent at the Dead Sea Works, have led to high levels of unemployment in the town. By the early 1990s almost 20% of the population were unemployed, with the town finding it difficult to attract new industries despite generous tax concessions.

Dimona's other major 'business', sometimes euphemistically referred to as the 'chocolate factory', is the country's leading **nuclear research station**. The facility is located off the road 13 kilometres east of the town, though sightseers are not encouraged and it's not recommended that you stop to take a look. When a former employee at the site, **Mordechai Vanunu**, spilled the beans about Israel's nuclear capacity to the London *Sunday Times*, he was lured to Rome by a female Mossad agent, kidnapped, and brought back to Israel to stand trial. He's currently serving a long term of imprisonment.

Dimona's other main talking point is the presence of the 2,000-strong community of African Hebrew Israelites, popularly referred to as the **Black Hebrews** (see box). The group have established their own 'village' within Dimona, and the community of a thousand or so welcome visitors who take an interest in their beliefs and the way that they live. ■ *Prior appointment is advisable, T6555400; their compound is on Herzl, close to the bus station.*

D *Drachim Guest House & Youth Hostel*, 1 HaNassi, T6556811. Choice of 6-bed dorms or private rooms, a/c, attached bath, pool, sauna, jacuzzi, kosher dining hall, check-out 1000, lock-out 1200-1400. Clean but expensive. **D-E** *Black Hebrews' Guesthouse*, T6555400. Advance booking essential. Easily the best (and cheapest) place in town to eat is at the Black Hebrews' vegan restaurant (Sunday-Thursday 0730-1530, 1700-2300, Friday 0730-1600). **Sleeping & eating**

Central Bus Station, T05-7552421. Be'er Sheva, buses 048/056, 2 per hour, 45 minutes, 16 NIS; **Eilat**, buses 395/397, 1-2 per 2 hours, 3 hours, 44 NIS; **Tel Aviv**, buses 375/393/394, hourly, 2 hours 45 minutes, 33 NIS. *Dimona Taxis*, Ha'Mahpilim, T6555008. **Transport**

Mamshit

During the reign of their King Obodas III (c. 28 BCE-9 CE), the **Nabateans** *established a number of large settlements in the Negev, ostensibly as way-stations on the network of roads that comprised the Spice Road between their Edom capital at Petra and the Mediterranean Sea at Gaza. The extensive and impressive remains commonly referred to by the Hebrew name* **Mamshit** *are generally accepted as being the site of one such Nabatean city,* **Memphis** *(also known in Arabic as Kurnub). Mamshit is particularly well preserved, with the remains of the city now part of a National Park.*

Phone code: 07
Colour map 3, grid B4

The Negev

Ins and outs

Mamshit is located six kilometres southeast of Dimona (**NB** the signpost to the site is not particularly prominent, and so the turning comes upon you rather quickly). The Dimona–Eilat bus (395/397) passes the turning for the site. Turning off Route 25, the site is approximately one and a half kilometres due south. After 200 metres, a track leads left to the Mamshit Camel Ranch, T05-7551054, from where you can take a camel safari into the desert. **Getting there**

Organized tours visiting the site may encounter the old city full of actors, employed by the Ministry of Tourism to play the role of Nabateans (call ahead for details). The site is well presented, with many of the more important buildings labelled. **Getting around**

History

A town was probably established here during the reign of the Nabatean king Obodas III, in the Early Roman period (also known as the Middle Nabatean period, 37 BCE-132 CE). Roads almost certainly connected Memphis to other Nabatean towns, most notably Gaza via Oboda (Hebrew: Avdat), though it should be noted that Memphis was on a secondary and not the main trade route. Its status and prosperity may well have increased in the Late Nabatean period when Roman engineers cut steps forming the Ma'ale Aqrabim (or Scorpions' Ascent, see page 362) to the southeast, on the road to Petra. **Early Roman/Middle Nabatean period**

Much of the Nabatean kingdom was annexed by the Roman Empire in 106 CE, though this is not considered to have lessened the general prosperity of the Negev. The Nabateans had begun to establish a sophisticated system of agriculture in the central Negev, cultivating the desert by collecting rainwater in carefully constructed terraces in the narrow valleys. Potential arable land at Mamphis was scarce, however, and thus much of the town's economy was based upon the rearing of race-horses. This lack of arable land may also explain why Mamphis, with a population of around 1,500, is considerably smaller than Nessana (Nizzana, population 4,000) and Oboda (Avdat, population 3,000).

Middle and Late Roman/Late Nabatean period

One of the key features of Nabatean towns is the quality of the architecture, and Mamphis is no exception. Initially, the towns featured the characteristic Nabatean large public buildings, with only the army living in permanent quarters and most of the population living in tents. The Late Nabatean period saw a new town plan laid out, initiated largely by the construction of upper-class housing, and with the main north–south axis now dividing public buildings from the residential areas. The Nabateans used their knowledge and mastery of constructing grand building designs, and adapted it to their domestic architecture. The Middle and Late Roman periods (Late Nabatean period) saw the construction of large, spacious houses around a central courtyard, sometimes up to three storeys high. The homes were designed to be cool in summer and warm in winter. Many of the sizeable Nabatean buildings seen at the site today date to the Late Nabatean period.

During the Late Roman period, Mamphis was integrated within the southern defence system of the Roman Empire, probably guarding the Jerusalem–Aila (Eilat) road, and a fortified wall was built around the settlement. It appears that the Romans made few additions to the built environment, instead taking advantage of the high-quality building techniques of the Nabateans. It is interesting to note that much of the town's economy became based upon the payment of salaries from the imperial treasury to resident soldiers. When the Eternal Peace agreement was concluded by the Emperor Justinian in 561 CE and the military payments ceased, the economy of Mamphis went into severe decline. Some commentators believe that Roman units were replaced by a locally recruited militia in the fourth century CE.

Byzantine period

The major change at Mamphis during the Byzantine period (324-638 CE) was that most of the population became Christian. Two of Mamphis' most prominent buildings, the Eastern Church and the Western Church, date to this period. A number of buildings were destroyed by a strong earthquake in 363 CE.

As mentioned earlier, Mamphis went into serious decline following the suspension of the military payments system in 561 CE, and was probably destroyed by local Arab tribesmen prior to the full-scale occupation of the Negev by the Arabs in 636 CE.

Tour of the site

The following tour of the site proceeds in a roughly clockwise direction from the entrance, though the buildings are not viewed in chronological order.

Nabatean caravanserai

Though this large building (23 metres by 42 metres) stands outside the later city walls, remains from a Middle Nabatean wall run south to the main body of the city's buildings, suggesting that previously the **caravanserai (1)** was not so isolated. It did remain buried by deep sand dunes for a long period of time, however, and is missing from the plan of the site that T.E. Lawrence (Lawrence of Arabia) helped prepare in 1914.

The caravanserai comprises a central court, with large halls along its west and south sides, and a row of rooms to the north and east. The southernmost of the rooms on the east side may possibly have been a bathhouse. The building has been largely restored, during which process a large number of coins were found, dating between c. 9 BCE and 408 CE.

Opposite the modern café, and behind the National Park ticket office, is the city's **main gate (2)**. It was defended by two unequally sized towers, later expanded, and closed by sturdy wooden doors. Remains of the burnt doors were found in the debris of the gate. It is interesting to note that the main gate is not aligned with the main street of the Late Nabatean town.

Main city gate

Most Nabatean settlements were unwalled, relying instead for their defence on a series of strategically placed towers within the town itself. When the Romans absorbed the central Negev area within the southern defence system of their empire, Mamphis' compact size meant that it could be encircled by a defensive wall. Built in the Late Roman period, Mamphis' **city walls (3)** were initially a little under a metre wide, though they were subsequently doubled in size. The walls run for just under one kilometre, taking advantage of the contours of the land and taking into account existing buildings. They are reinforced by a number of towers.

Late Roman city walls

On the east side of the town are the remains of a bathhouse and public pool, though both are currently sealed off due to their fragility. Dating of the **bathhouse (4)** is uncertain; it was certainly in use during the Byzantine period,

Bathhouse & public pool

The Negev

Mamshit (Mamphis)

1 Nabatean Caravanserai
2 Main City Gate
3 Late Roman City Walls
4 Bathhouse
5 Public Pool
6 Building XII (House of Frescoes)
7 Hoard of silver coins found here
8 British Mandate Period Police Station
9 Eastern Church
10 Market Area
11 Quarters for Militia or Pilgrims/Hermits?
12 Nabatean Tower
13 Western Church
14 Late Nabatean Tower (Building II)
15 Mill
16 Palace of City Governor
17 Early Nabatean Dwellings
18 Water Gate

N

0 metres 10

though it may actually have been built during the Late Nabatean period. The entrance is to the west, leading to a central courtyard lined with stone benches. This probably served as the changing room. The cold room (*frigidarium*) is in the northeast corner of the bathhouse and has two sitting baths. A connecting door leads to the *tepidarium*, or lukewarm room, with the hot baths comprising three rooms (*caldarium*) sunk into the ground. Remains of the plumbing system that brought water and took away the waste can also be seen.

To the east of the bathhouse, adjacent to the city walls, is a large complex featuring a **public pool (5)**. This was used as a reservoir and was supplied by water carried by man and beast from the wadi to the west of the town.

Building XII To the south of the bathhouse and public pool is a large complex of buildings sometimes referred to as the **House of Frescoes (6)**, (though the site's excavators have labelled it **Building XII**). One of the finest examples of the ability of Late Nabatean architects, the complex features a central courtyard lined with columns topped by well-formed capitals, standing on a *stylobate*. Stables lead off from the courtyard, along with "a most elaborately planned lavatory" (Avraham Negev, 1993). The residential wing of the complex is to the northeast, with the well-executed mosaics on the upper floor providing the building with its popular name. The treasure room stood to the south of the courtyard, and is identifiable by the paintings and frescoes on the arches and upper walls of its vestibule. A **hoard (7)** of 10,500 silver dinars and tetradrachms was found in a bronze jar concealed beneath the ruins of a staircase. The oldest of the coins date to the reign of the Nabatean King Rabbel II (70-106 CE), with the latest dating to the rule of the Roman Emperor Elagabalus (218-222 CE). It is speculated that the Building XII complex, and hence the hoard of coins, belonged to a wealthy horse-breeder.

British police station The relatively modern building at the southeast point of the town is the former headquarters of the Negev police during the British Mandate period. Along with the construction of the Eastern Church (see page 358) during the Byzantine period (324-638 CE), the construction of the **police station (8)** destroyed much of what may have been the Middle Nabatean fortress building.

Water-supply system Accomplished engineers as well as architects and masons, the Nabateans thrived in their desert environment through their ability to construct complex, but reliable, water-supply systems. Mamphis' water was controlled by three well-built dams on Nahal Mamshit, a water-conservation system built above the high waterfall of a tributary of the Nahal Mamshit, plus several water retaining pools engineered to the south and west (none shown on map).

Eastern Church The **Eastern Church (9)** is notable for its high standard of workmanship, and, unusually for a Byzantine period building, the construction methods are Roman. Dating the church precisely has not been possible, though a number of clues have enabled experts to make an educated guess. The geometric mosaic pavement in the nave has two crosses incorporated into the design. Since the practice of depicting the cross on a church floor was banned in 427 CE, it is concluded that the Eastern Church must predate this decree. Further, coins dating to the reigns of the Eastern Roman Emperors Diocletian (284-305 CE, in the pre-church era) and Theodosius I (379-395 CE) were discovered in the foundations, suggesting the church was built some time during the latter's reign. The Eastern Church complex also features a chapel, a baptistry, a small bathhouse, a bell tower, and an annexe that may have served as a monastery.

Small reliquaries sunk into the floor next to the altar, and a simple grave in a side room, contain the bones of supposed saints or martyrs.

The main **market area (10)** is to the north of the Eastern Church, and comprises three rows of shops lining two streets. The market was in use from the Late Nabatean to the Byzantine period. The building in the southern part of the market area (**11**), and also joined to the Eastern Church, is thought not to be related to the market; its function may have been as quarters for either militia members or for hermits/pilgrims.

Market area

The plan of the Byzantine **Western Church (13)** is almost identical to that of the Eastern Church and, though a little smaller, it may have been more elaborate in its execution. The nave mosaic (currently under repair) depicts birds, fruit, swastikas and flowers on a geometric pattern, with an inscription within a medallion reading: "Lord, Help your servant Nilus, the builder of this place, Amen." Several other inscriptions also mention Nilus, plus two church wardens, and the church is sometimes referred to as the **Church of the Nile**. The Western Church was destroyed in a violent conflagration. Once again, dating the church has been problematic, with the mosaic inscriptions providing no clues. A coin found in the upper levels of the church foundations belongs to the reign of the Roman Emperor Probus (276-282 CE), whilst another coin found amongst the fill of the foundation pit dates to the late fourth century CE.

Western Church

A good view of the entire city can be had from the top of the **Late Nabatean tower (14)** ('Building II'), which is five metres high. The square tower (10 metres by 10 metres) adjoins a courtyard containing a reservoir, around which are a number of storerooms and a suite of guestrooms. The tower may have served as a combined observation tower/administrative centre during the Middle and Late Nabatean periods. Just to the south of the tower are the remains of a **mill (15)**.

Late Nabatean tower (Building II)

The large (35 metres by 20 metres) building to the northeast of the tower may have been the **palace of the city's governor (16)** during the Late Nabatean period. The complex features a guardroom, guest quarters and offices, with the main residential area on the upper balconied storey. The poorly preserved remains to the west of the palace may well be **Early Nabatean dwellings (17)** from the first century CE.

Late Nabatean palace (Building I)

The small **Water Gate (18)** was added to the western wall in the Late Roman period to allow water to be brought into the town from the three dams on the Nahal Mamshit (see page 358).

Water Gate

Though not enclosed within the Mamshit National Park area (nor shown on the map), three main cemeteries associated with the site have been excavated; the main Nabatean necropolis one kilometre to the north of the city, a Roman cemetery 200 metres to the northeast, and a Byzantine cemetery 500 metres to the west of the city. ■ *T6556478. 0800-1700 daily. Adult 12 NIS, student 8 NIS.*

Cemeteries

The Negev

Makhtesh HaGadol and Makhtesh HaKatan (craters)

Lying to the southeast of Be'er Sheva are two impressive erosion craters, formed by the same geological process as the Negev's more famous erosion crater, Makhtesh Ramon (see page 382). There are several interesting hikes that can be made in the Makhtesh HaGadol (Great Makhtesh) and Makhtesh HaKatan (Little Makhtesh) area, as well as a number of archaeological remains, though many visitors just drive through and admire the views.

Ins and outs

Getting there Unfortunately, the sites and hiking trail heads described below are not accessible by public transport, and as none of the hikes is circular, you will need transport waiting at the finishing points. However, the area is highly recommended if you have your own transport.

There are several points of access to the two craters (see east and southeast of Be'er Sheva on colour map 3 for orientation). They can be approached from the northwest via Yeroham (a Negev development town 13 kilometres southwest of Dimona, and 32 kilometres south of Be'er Sheva); from the north, via Hatrurim Junction at the junction of Routes 31 and 258; and from the southeast, from Hazeva Junction at the meeting point of Route 90 (The Arava Road) and Route 227.

Sights

Mezad Zafir This was a square fort used to defend the Ma'ale 'Aqrabim ascent (see page 362). Little remains bar the very lower courses, though evidence suggests that this was a two-storey building dating to the second or third century CE. The fort was surrounded by an unroofed courtyard that housed a number of animal pens.

The Makhtesh HaGadol & Makhtesh HaKatan

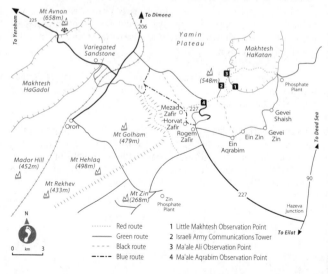

.... Red route	1 Little Makhtesh Observation Point
—— Green route	2 Israeli Army Communications Tower
– – – Black route	3 Ma'ale Ali Observation Point
–·–·– Blue route	4 Ma'ale Aqrabim Observation Point

The Negev

This was another square, two-storey Roman fortress used to guard this route. **Horvat Zafir**
The walls here are preserved to a height of about two and a half metres. The
building just to the west was probably a Nabatean road station, though much
of it was destroyed in order to use the building materials in the fort's
construction.

Rogem Zafir The larger of the two structures here is a fort, measuring 9.35 **Ma'ale 'Aqrabim**
metres by 9.1 metres, and formerly two storeys high. A number of coins were **(Scorpion's**
found here, mostly depicting the images of Roman emperors and dating from **Ascent).**
the third and fourth centuries CE. The smaller structure comprises five rooms
and an anteroom, and probably served as a hostel. The two structures served as
a staging post on the Petra–Gaza Spice Road. Rogem Zafir is the starting or finishing point for a number of hikes, most of which are marked on the
sign-board and map.

Mezad Hazeva The remains of the fortress here were first discovered in 1902,
though subsequent damage to the structure 28 years later rendered the original
conjectured site plan indiscernible. The structure was initially thought to have
been a Nabatean road station on the Petra–Gaza Spice Road, with signs of continued usage well into the Late Roman period. Further excavation, however,
has revealed that what remains here is actually a second–fourth century CE
Roman fortress built upon the ruins of several Iron Age fortresses. The later
Iron Age fortress is associated with the reign of Josiah (639-609 BCE) and may
well have been destroyed at the time of the destruction of the first Temple in
Jerusalem (586 BCE). The earlier fortress may well date to the reign of Uzziah
(769-733 BCE). If this is true, the site may well mark the southeast border of
the kingdom of Judah, and as such may be the possible location of the biblical
Tamar.

The Negev

Makhtesh HaKatan & Ma'ale Aqrabim (Scorpion's Ascent)

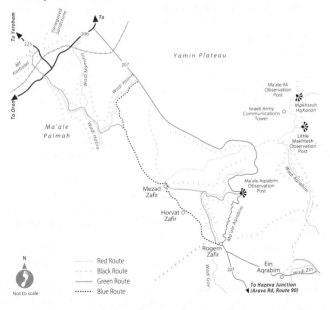

The Negev

Roman Ma'ale 'Aqrabim hike

The starting point for this strenuous six- to seven-hour hike is the **Rogem Zafir** (see page 361), with the route being described here running in a southeast to northwest direction. The route follows blue trail markers for most of its journey, with a number of diversions and extensions marked in green and black.

The route incorporates the Ma'ale 'Aqrabim, or **Scorpions' Ascent**, part of an ancient route linking the northern Arava area with the northern Negev Hills. The Scorpions' Ascent leads up from the Wadi Zin and the area known as the Wilderness of Zin. This area featured heavily in the wanderings of Moses and the children of Israel, though his followers were not impressed: "And why have ye brought up the congregation of the Lord into this wilderness, that we and our cattle should die there?" (*Numbers 20:4*). This area was later described to Moses by God as the southern border of the land that the Jews should settle: "And your border shall turn from the south to the ascent of Akrabbim, and pass on to Zin ..." (*Numbers 34:4*, with further mentions in *Joshua 15:3* and *Judges 1:36*).

The turning point in the fortunes of this route was when the Roman engineers cut a cliff road into the steep escarpment during the Late Roman period (132-324 CE). Whereas the average slope of the natural escarpment was 34°, and thus unsuitable for pack animals, the sharp curves and terraced steps that the Romans constructed reduced this gradient to a manageable 16°. As you climb up, you may wish that the Romans had reduced the gradient by a bit more. The staircase was largely rebuilt during the British Mandate period.

There is a shorter, but steeper path off to the right, leading to the Ma'ale 'Aqrabim Observation Point, though the route described here continues in a northwest direction, between two wadis, before you encounter the first staircase. Five flights of stairs later, you arrive at the top of the Roman **Ma'ale 'Aqrabim**. The building remains here are Horvat Zafir (see page 361). About 500 metres to the south are the remains of an ancient dam.

The blue trail continues north, in the direction of the remains of the fort on the top of the hill about one and a half kilometres in front of you. This is Mezad Zafir (see page 360). From Mezad Zafir, there are several options. The red trail leads east, towards the **Ma'ale Ali Observation Point** and the **Little Makhtesh Observation Point**, intersecting the main road, Route 227, on the way (see map). The black trail heads northwest, rejoining Route 227 after about four and a half kilometres. The blue trail continues west-north-west, after four and a half kilometres either following the Ma'ale Yamin (Yamin ascent) back to Route 227, or allowing a diversion for a further six kilometres along the green route of the Big Fin trail back to the **Variegated Sandstone** (some beautiful sandstone formations featuring a bold display of yellows, ochres, reds and purples).

Wadi Zin, Wadi 'Aqrabim, Ein Zin, Wadi Hazeva hikes

This is another long, strenuous eight-hour hike, with some steep climbs and descents, though there are several options for shortening the hike. As described here the hike begins at Rogem Zafir, though this requires a steep ascent at the end of the hike.

The unpaved road heading east from Rogem Zafir is passable to cars for the first two kilometres or so. This hike begins by following the course of the bed of the **Wadi Zin**. About one kilometre beyond the car parking area you reach **Ein Aqrabim** (Aqrabim Spring). Levels of water found in the springs and cisterns on this route vary according to the season, though more often than not they're virtually dry. The trail to here is marked with black. From Ein Aqrabim there are two options. The black route heads north along the Wadi Aqrabim, making a steep ascent to the parking lot near the **Little Makhtesh Observation Point** . The better, though far longer, hike is to follow the green trail markers in an easterly direction along the Wadi Zin, passing **Ein Zin** (Zin Spring) and **Gevei Zin** (Zin Cisterns), where the wadi and the green trail turns north. Head past the **Gevei Shaish** (Shaish Cisterns), and head for the unattractive **Phosphate Plant**. This point is actually accessible by road from Route 25 to the north. The trail is now indicated by red markers, and drops down into the **Makhtesh HaKatan** (Little Makhtesh) along the course of the **Wadi Hazera**. Looking very much like the result of a massive meteorite impacting on the earth's surface, the Makhtesh HaKatan (like Makhtesh HaGadol) was actually created by the same process that formed the Negev's larger crater, the Makhtesh Ramon (see page 382). The red route continues across the floor of the crater, before climaxing in the steep and tiring **Ma'ale Ali** (Ali Ascent) up to the **Ma'ale Ali Observation Point**. There's then a magnificent view of where you've just walked.

NB The usual rules about hiking in the desert apply. The maps here are for information only, and should be complemented with the relevant sheets of the SPNI 1:50,000 map. These are available from SPNI offices in main towns. The words 'wadi' and 'nahal' (river) are used interchangeably above.

Southern Negev

*This Southern Negev section principally follows the 220-kilometre journey south from **Be'er Sheva** via **Mizpe Ramon** to **Eilat**. Most of the journey follows the main Route 40, before joining up with the Arava Road for the run-in to Eilat (Route 90). Notable sights en route include the **Ein Avdat Nature Reserve**, the Nabatean city of **Avdat** (Oboda), the Negev's most significant natural feature, the **Makhtesh Ramon**, as well as the resort city of **Eilat** itself. In addition to the sights on the main Route 40 (all accessible by public transport), there are a number of excursions to sights off this road, most of which require you to have your own transport.*

Haluza (Elusa)

Haluza is the Nabatean settlement of Elusa, established as part of the Petra–Oboda–Gaza Spice Road (see page 385) some time in the third century BCE. Because of its remote location, Elusa receives few visitors and hence the presentation is not up to much. Most of the site is covered by wind-blown sand and dust; pretty much as it was when Robinson discovered and identified it in 1838, and Woolley and Lawrence (of Arabia) described it in 1914. The most substantial remains are the theatre and the east church, located close together on the southeast side of the site.

Phone code: 07
Colour map 3, grid B3

Haluza is located southwest of Be'er Sheva, although you need to head south of Be'er Sheva along Route 40 for 30 kilometres to Mash'abbe Sade Junction, then head north-west along Route 222 for 20 kilometres to reach the site. See 'Be'er Sheva to Mizpe Ramon' map for orientation. You really need your own transport to reach Haluza, although there are a few irregular buses (045, six per day) from Be'er Sheva to Kibbutz Revivim (continuing northwest along Route 222). The nearest accommodation to Haluza is the 48-room hostel (**D-E**) at Kibbutz Tlalim, 6563615, 6563614.

Ins and outs

The principal Nabatean finds from the site date to the reigns of the Nabatean kings Aretas I (c. 168 BCE) and Aretas IV (c. 9 BCE-40 CE). However, it was

History

during the Late Nabatean and Late Roman periods that Elusa reached its peak, eventually becoming the major Byzantine city in the Negev.

There are numerous written references to Elusa, providing some insight into the city's history. Ptolemy refers to Elusa, as does the writer Libanius in two mid-fourth century CE letters. Elusa is also listed on the Roman cartographer Castorius' 'road atlas' of the Roman Empire, *Tabula Peutingeriana* (c. 365 CE). Christian references to Elusa, however, are more problematic. The assertion by both Jerome and Nilus that Christians and idolaters lived side by side in Elusa during the early fifth century cannot be proven since the earliest Christian epitaph thus found at the site dates to 519 CE. There are also important references to Elusa in the Nessana papyri (see page 367).

The site   The **theatre** was first constructed in the Middle Nabatean period, in the first half of the first century CE. Later additions were made, and it seems to have remained in use until the middle of the Byzantine period at least. The *cavea*, or spectators' seating area, is about 35 metres in diameter, though it is not well preserved. The 'VIP' box in the centre is still discernible, however. The *orchestra* area in front of the stage is quite well preserved, though inscriptions suggest that a new floor was laid as recently as 455 CE. The Nabatean theatre at Elusa had cultic uses, with the site's excavators believing that a Nabatean temple stood nearby.

Part of the reason that the east church was excavated so thoroughly was because it was thought that it may stand on the site of the Nabatean temple connected with the theatre. Because of this attention paid to the east church, it is probably the most impressive attraction at Elusa today. The church is particularly large (27 metres by 77 metres), with many well-preserved limestone columns and Proconessian marble Corinthian capitals still *in situ*. The base of a bishop's throne has been identified within the central apse, suggesting that the church was in fact the region's cathedral. It has not been possible to date the church conclusively, though the building style is comparable with other churches built in the Negev between 350 CE and 450 CE.

Rehovot-in-the-Negev

The Hebrew translation of the name for this site, 'Rehovot-in-the-Negev', is somewhat misleading. Though it refers to the *Rehoboth* where Isaac dug a well (*Genesis 26:22*), there is absolutely no evidence that this is the right spot. The Arabic name, *Khirbet Ruheibeh* (ruins of Ruheibeh), refers to the Wadi Ruheibeh (Hebrew: Nahal Shunra) that seasonally flows along the river bed below the city. There is a well in the river bed 50 metres deep, however, though it was quite probably dug by the Nabateans. The Nessana (Nizzana) papyri (see page 367) lists a number of settlements in the area, of which Beth Malchu is the most likely identity of Rehovot-in-the-Negev.

With no positive identification of the site it is hard to piece together its history, though the general consensus is that it was founded as a way-station between Elusa and Nessana on the Petra–Gaza Spice Road (see page 385).

Though the site contains an important **cemetery** (the only Byzantine cemetery thus far excavated in the Negev), a number of **Nabatean dwellings**, and the most impressive **North Church** (dating to the late fifth century CE at least), there is not a lot to justify the effort of getting here.

Ins and outs   The site is located 12 kilometres southwest of Haluza, and accessible only by four-wheel drive vehicle. The journey between the Haluza Dunes and the **Shunera Dunes** to reach the site, however, is exhilarating, bringing to mind the old maxim that 'getting there is half the fun'.

Shivta (Sobata)

Though not part of the main Petra–Oboda–Gaza Spice Road (see page 385), the Nabatean town of Sobata (Arabic: Subeita) was still linked to Oboda (Avdat) and Nessana (Nizzana) by road. Because of its remoteness, Shivta receives few visitors. Consequently, though the National Park has free admission, labelling and sign-posting at the site is almost nonexistent. The principal points of interest are the churches, though parts of the Nabatean and Byzantine towns remain. *Colour map 3, grid B2*

Shivta is not accessible by public transport. From Tlalim Junction on Route 40, head southwest for 20 kilometres, then turn south for 8 kilometres to the site (passing a number of burnt-out Egyptian tanks from the 1948 war). **Ins and outs**

Sobata was probably founded during the time of the Nabatean king Aretas IV (c. 9 BCE-40 CE), or perhaps during the reign of his predecessor Obodas III (c. 28-9 BCE). The peak of the city's prosperity during Nabatean rule was probably towards the end of the dynasty, just prior to the Roman annexation of the Nabatean empire in 106 CE. The Romans seem to have had little impact upon Sobata, probably not even stationing a garrison or fortifying the town. Sobata increased in importance during the Byzantine period (324-638 CE), possibly becoming a centre of Christian scholarship and pilgrimage. The Nessana Papyri (see page 367) again suggest no permanent military garrison during this period, though there are plenty of references to the agricultural economy of Sobata. **History**

There is evidence to suggest that following the Arab conquest of the region (636 CE), Christians and Muslims lived in peace together here. As one of the site's chief excavators, Avraham Negev, points out, the builders of the mosque were at pains not to damage the adjoining baptistry of the South Church.

Shivta (Sobata)

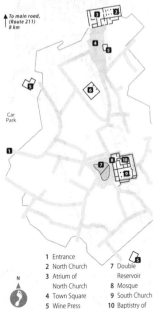

To main road,
(Route 211)
8 km

Car
Park

1 Entrance
2 North Church
3 Atrium of
   North Church
4 Town Square
5 Wine Press
6 Middle Church

7 Double
   Reservoir
8 Mosque
9 South Church
10 Baptistry of
   South Church

N

0 metres 50

The **North Church** was probably built in two separate phases, beginning life as a single apsidal basilica some time in the middle of the fourth century CE. Considerable additions were made in the first half of the sixth century CE to make the church triapsidal. The church is attended by a monastery, a chapel, a baptistry and a mortuary chapel. **Sights**

The **South Church** is smaller, constrained in its construction by the positioning of the double reservoir on its west side. For this reason there is no *atrium* (entrance forecourt); an unusual feature considering that the contemporary churches at Elusa, Rehovot-in-the-Negev, and the North Church here all have particularly large atriums. The apses were previously plastered and painted, with one such scene depicting the Transfiguration of Jesus, though it is hard to make out the subject of the paintings today. The

The Negev

well-preserved baptistry to the north of the church is adjoined by a small **mosque**. ■ *Open all hours. Admission free.*

Nizzana (Nessana)

Colour map 3, grid B2 Nizzana is the site of the important Nabatean Spice Road town of Nessana, and is famed as the place where the so-called Nessana Papyri were found (see page 367). The mound that Nessana stands upon looks quite impressive from a distance, though upon closer inspection it is clear that many significant archaeological remains have been lost. The construction of the North Church in the Byzantine period obscured many of the Nabatean buildings, perhaps including the main Nabatean temple. Further, the use of the site by the Turkish administration early in the 20th century, including the 'recycling' of building material for construction of buildings throughout the area, destroyed many of the older remains.

Ins and outs Nizzana is not accessible by public transport. It lies around 20 kilometres further west along Route 211 from the turning for Shivta (see 'Be'er Sheva to Mizpe Ramon' map for orientation).

History Dating the first Nabatean settlement at **Nessana** remains controversial, although the site has few remains from the Middle Nabatean, Late Nabatean and Roman periods. The Byzantine period (324-638 CE) was the period of Nessana's greatest prosperity, with the settlement expanding significantly and the major buildings at the site today dating from this period. The significant Nessana Papyri also date to this period, between the sixth and late seventh centuries CE (see page 367). Though there was a smooth transition to Arab rule in the seventh century CE, there are no remains at Nessana (Arabic: 'Auja el-Hafir) suggesting occupation later than the eighth century CE. With no evidence of a conflagration or a violent end, it is suggested that the agricultural land that supported the settlement fell into disuse, thus accelerating the city's decline.

Nizzana (Nessana)

Sights The Roman fortress, probably built in the first half of the fourth century CE (though this date is disputed), occupies much of the mound to the south of the North Church. There are a series of rooms along the long (85-metre) west and east walls, though the rooms on the east side are thought to have been added later. The fortress is defended by a number of towers, with the main gate in the south tower and a secondary entrance in the east tower. The long monumental staircase up to the mound is now thought to date to the second

To South Church

1 Roman Fortress	6 Baptistry
2 Later Period Rooms	7 North Court
3 MonumentalStaircase	8 Covered Gallery
4 Southern Court	9 Courtyard
5 Mono-Apsidal Basilica	10 Covered Gallery
(Church of Sergius &	11 Chapel
Bacchus)	12 Sacristy

The Negev

The Nessana Papyri

During excavations at Nessana undertaken by the British School of Archaeology in Jerusalem, a significant discovery was made in a small room in the southern part of the North Church: the Nessana Papyri. Written in Greek and bilingual Greek-Arabic, the papyri cover a number of subjects from the literary and theological to military, administrative and petty legal matters, and all date from the period of the sixth to late seventh century CE.

Though the literary and theological documents are important, and include several chapters of the Gospel of St John, details of the exploits and martyrdom of Saint George, plus a Greek dictionary accompanying Virgil's Aeneas, the nonliterary documents are particularly significant for the information that they provide on the economic, social and military life of the central Negev region during the period 512 CE to 689 CE.

Amongst the subjects discussed are marriage, divorce, inheritance, plus various bills of sale and financial contracts. There are also important references to wheat and grain yields, taxes, and payments of annona militaris, or monthly salaries paid to the militias stationed at places such as Oboda and Mamphis, thus allowing a partial reconstruction of the socio-political administration of the region. Extracts from the cache of papyri can be seen at the Israel Museum in Jerusalem.

half of the first century BCE, and not the Byzantine period as initially thought, and thus is assumed to have led to a Nabatean temple and not the fortress.

Dating the North Church is not precise, though two burials within the church have epigraphic references mentioning the dates 464 CE and 474 CE. Remains of three saints were found in a marble reliquary in one of the small rooms within the church, with inscriptions within the church dedicating it to the saints Sergius and Bacchus (with a mention of St Stephen). The Southern Court opens into the mono-apsidal basilica. To the west of the basilica is a baptistry, though at some stage parts of the east end were removed in order to make the basilica longer. Other later additions, including the North Court and the covered gallery date to the reign of the (East) Byzantine Emperor Justinian (527-565 CE).

On a separate mound some 60 metres southwest of the fortress is the South Church. An inscription dates the church to 601-602 CE, and dedicates it to the Virgin Mary. The three-apse style was a feature of churches in this region.

Horvat Haluqim

During the United Monarchy (1004-928 BCE), a network of citadels was built in the central Negev region, each protecting state-initiated agricultural settlements. (Similarities between this process and that of the Zionist pioneers of the early 20th century are hard to ignore). Horvat Haluqim is thought to be one such 10th century BCE fortified settlement (the original desert kibbutz?).

Today, it is still possible to see the remains of the oval-shaped fortress, with its central courtyard and seven casement rooms, plus the remains of twenty-five or so private dwellings that formed the agricultural settlement. The initial settlement was probably destroyed during the Pharaoh Shishak's invasion in 923 BCE, though evidence suggests that the site was reoccupied in the second-third centuries CE. The site is labelled in English, though is only of limited interest.

Ins and outs This site is to the north of Route 204, just northeast of Halukim Junction (see colour map 3 for orientation). You can walk here from Kibbutz Sde Boker (see page 368).

Kibbutz Sde Boker

The kibbutz is best known today for its association with Israel's first Prime Minister and statesman, David Ben-Gurion. In 1953 Ben-Gurion unexpectedly retired from politics, choosing instead to settle on the fledgling Kibbutz Sde Boker. It is possible to visit Ben-Gurion's 'Desert Home', the Memorial National Park where he is buried next to his wife, as well as the Ben-Gurion University of the Negev. The kibbutz is also a base for tours into the 'Wilderness of Zin' as well as the access point for the beautiful Nahal Zin Nature Trail through the Ein Avdat National Park.

Ins and outs   Sde Boker is on the main Route 40, though you should note that the express buses between Be'er Sheva and Eilat are not scheduled to stop here. Bus 060 between Be'er Sheva and Mizpe Ramon stops here (once every 1-2 hours). For orientation see colour map 3.

History   Kibbutz Sde Boker was founded on the fourth anniversary of the Declaration of the State of Israel, 15th May 1952. Situated at the head of the Nahal Zin, (a seasonal wadi), the settlement stood above the inhospitable 'Wilderness of Zin'. The original intention of the settlers, predominantly ex-soldiers, was to ranch cattle; hence the name Sde Boker, roughly translated from the Hebrew as 'Rancher's/Cowboy's/Farmer's Field'. Livestock rearing now plays a less important role in the agricultural economy of the kibbutz, with sophisticated irrigation techniques now producing out of season olives and fruits for export, as well as some cereals.

Sights   **Ben-Gurion's Desert Home**   Ben-Gurion's initial stay at Sde Boker was limited to just 14 months, after which time he was drawn back into politics. He finally retired to Sde Boker with his wife Paula in 1963, living here until his death (in Tel Aviv) 10 years later. Ben-Gurion's low, green prefab home, with its red roof and narrow verandah, has been left fairly much as it was when David and Paula lived here. The museum is extremely well presented, with almost every article on display labelled, from the photograph of Gandhi on the bedroom wall, to the biblical quotes copied in his own handwriting on his desk. ■ *T6560320/6558444, F6560119. Sunday-Thursday 0830-1530, Friday 0830-1400, Saturday 0900-1430. Admission free. Guided tours by prior appointment.*

Ben-Gurion University of the Negev   Sign-posted three kilometres south of Ben-Gurion's Desert Home is the Sde Boker University, variously referred to as Ben-Gurion College of the Negev, Sde Boker Institute of Arid Zone Research, etc. Whatever title you use to refer to it, the academic speciality of this establishment is clear: the study of land and life in arid and semi-arid environments. The various institutes affiliated here attract specialists from around the world, in addition to producing much home-grown talent in this field. However, social sciences are also taught at this campus, with the Ben-Gurion Research Institute housing priceless archival material relating to the foundation of the State of Israel, and the history of the Jews in this century. ■ *T6535333. Call ahead for tours.*

Ben-Gurion Memorial National Park (Ben-Gurion's grave)   The road towards the main university campus also leads to the site of David and Paula Ben-Gurion's graves. And what a place to be buried! Two simple white slabs stand amidst a landscaped garden, featuring both rock and flora indigenous to

··

David Ben-Gurion (1886-1973)

Born in Plonsk in Russian Poland, Ben-Gurion (born David Gruen) was one of the crucial links in the chain that brought Theodor Herzl's dream of Jewish homeland to fruition. He also had a very clear idea of what sort of entity the Jewish state should be, believing that the so-called Jewish Question could not be resolved within a capitalist framework (Johnson, A History of the Jews, 1987). His 3 principles remained consistent throughout his long political career: Jews must return to the land; the new state must be built within a socialist framework; the Hebrew language must act as the binding cultural element of

the Zionist society.

Described by Johnson as a "notorious creator and divider of parties" (ibid), Ben-Gurion's post-independence political career was marked by a number of major feuds with cabinet and party colleagues. In 1953 he quit politics and joined the kibbutz here, though he was lured back to government just 14 months later. He eventually resigned from the Knesset in 1970, dividing his last years between his home in Tel Aviv and the modest prefab here.

··

the area, on the edge of a sheer rockface that provides a magnificent vista down into the canyon of the 'Wilderness of Zin'.

A winding path leads down from near the grave-site to the 'Lower Parking Lot' of the Ein Avdat National Park and Nahal Zin Nature Trail (see below for details). ■ *T6565717, F6565721. Call ahead for tours.*

Sleeping C-D *Sherman Guest House*, T6565933/6565079. Well-equipped rooms, good views from common lounge, reservations reccommended. E *SPNI Field School & Hamburg Guest House*, T6532016/6565902, F6565721. Attractive 6-bed dorms (**E**) plus double rooms (**D**), all a/c with private bath, very clean, great views, pool, kitchen, reservations essential. Good value.

Eating Next door to Ben-Gurion's Desert Home is the *Sde Boker Inn*, where you can get good value meals and snacks (and fill your water bottle with cold drinking water for free). In the kibbutz's main plaza there is also a supermarket (Sunday-Thursday 0800-1900, Friday 0800-1400) and a cafeteria, the *Zin Inn* (Sunday-Thursday 0800-2300, Friday 0800-1400).

Directory **Communications** Area code: T07. **Post office**: in the kibbutz's main plaza (Sun-Thu 0900-1100 and 1300-1400, Fri 0900-1100). **Tourist information** Anyone attempting to hike in the region (excepting the simple Nahal Zin Nature Trail in Ein Avdat National Park) should first contact the *SPNI Field School*, T6565828/6565016, F6565721, for advice. They sell (and can translate the Hebrew) detailed 1:50,000 maps of the area, which you are advised to carry along with other necessities for hiking in the desert. If you book in advance, they can also organize guided treks (or you could try *Petra Jeep*, T6557156, who organize jeep tours of the Wilderness of Zin).

Ein Avdat National Park

The **Nahal Zin Nature Trail** *provides a delightful walk along the bed of the Nahal (River) Zin, with the option of a gentle jaunt for the less intrepid (short, circuitous route taking one to two hours), or the more strenuous long, one-way route (two to three hours), featuring a stiff climb up the rock-cut steps in the cliff face. There are some excellent picnic sites, as well as some peaceful spots beside that rarest of desert commodities, water pools.* *Colour map 4, grid C2*

The Negev

Ins and outs

Getting there For details of public transport to Ein Avdat National Park, see 'Ins and outs' under Kibbutz Sde Boker, page 368. For orientation see colour map 3.

Getting around Some advanced thought is required before commencing either the **long, one-way route** (two to three hours) or the **short, circuitous route** (one to two hours). Both begin at the **Lower Parking Lot** (actually to the north, near to Sde Boker), with the long route finishing at the **Upper Parking Lot** (actually to the south) and the short route finishing where it began. It is important to note, however, that the rock-cut steps from the valley bottom to the Upper Parking Lot are one-way only, and **cannot be descended**. What this means in reality is that if you park your car at the Lower Parking Lot (or are staying at Sde Boker), if you take the long, one-way route, you finish your walk at the Upper Parking Lot. Since it is forbidden to descend the rock-cut steps back to the valley bottom and retrace your route, you'll have to arrange for somebody to drive down Route 40 to the Upper Parking Lot to pick you up, or you'll have to walk back to Sde Boker along Route 40 (an unrewarding seven and a half kilometre slog). If lucky, you may be able to flag down a passing bus (060), though you may be in for a long wait.

If you don't have someone to drive your car down to the Upper Parking Lot, one option is to complete the short, circuitous route, returning to your car at the Lower Parking Lot. Then you can drive down Route 40 to the Upper Parking Lot, from where you can still visit the Ein Avdat Observation Point, and its spectacular views. All that you will have really missed is the steep climb up the rock-cut steps (though some claim this to be the highlight of the trail!). Make sure that you keep your entrance ticket because this must be presented when entering either the Lower or Upper Parking Lots. The National Park can become crowded on weekends and public holidays. **NB** Do not confuse the Ein Avdat National Park with the Nabatean-Roman-Byzantine city within Avdat National Park, some 11 kilometres further south along Route 40 (see page 372).

Nahal Zin Nature Trail Both the long, one-way route and the short, circuitous walk begin at the **Lower Parking Lot (1)**. Just to the west (right) of the Lower Parking Lot, marked by the profusion of vegetation, is the **Ein Mor spring (2)**. This spring feeds the main wadi from the surrounding clayey water-bearing strata. The trail passes a fine specimen of **Atlantic Terebinth (3)**

Ein Avdat National Park & 'Nahal Zin nature trail'

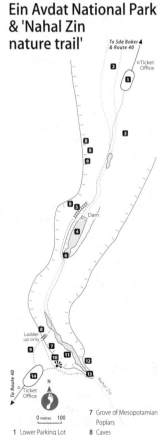

7 Grove of Mesopotamian Poplars
1 Lower Parking Lot
2 Ein Mor Spring
3 Atlantic Terebinth
4 Ein Avdat Lower Pool
5 Rock-hewn Steps
6 Ein Avdat Waterfall
8 Caves
9 Tower
10 Observation Point
11 Upper Pools
12 Ein Ma'arif Spring
13 Dry Waterfall
14 Upper Parking Lot

(*Pistacia atlantica*) to the left (east), looking exactly as it is represented as the symbol of the Israel National Parks Authority. Thought to be in the region of 250 years old, this deciduous native of the Irano-Turanian steppe is testament to environmental change in the region, suggesting a previously wetter climate. Cross the bed of the wadi to the right (west) side, and continue following the trail. Large caves are cut into the cliffs to your right, and those with sharp eyes may be able to spot ibexes on the cliffs above you. Initially ignore the rock-cut steps to your right, and cross the artificial dam that creates the **Ein Avdat lower pool (4)**. Either side of you are the tight canyon walls of white limestone, with thin seams of black-brown flint, whilst at your feet is an inviting looking pool of dark greeny-blue water (**NB** Drinking and swimming is forbidden). The approach path passes along the left (east) bank of the pool to the base of the **Ein Avdat waterfall (6)**. This must be one of the Negev's most popular photo-opportunities, though, being a dead-end, this point can become quite congested. Having other people in your picture, however, does give a sense of appreciation of the scale. The intensity of the waterfall (or lack of) will depend upon the season.

From the waterfall retrace your route and climb the rock-hewn steps (**5**) around the pool (take care with children). The path leads to the head of the **Ein Avdat waterfall (6)**, about 15 metres above the pool below. There is another terrific view from here back down the canyon. The trail continues along the left (east) side of the wadi, entering into an area of relatively lush vegetation. Some relaxing shade is provided by the **grove of Mesopotamian Poplars (7)** (*Populus euphratica*) on the opposite bank. This is probably the finest grove of such specimens in the whole of the Negev, since these deep-rooted trees are considered something of a rarity in such environments.

Cut into the cliffs above you are a number of caves (**8**), thought to have been occupied by monks during the Byzantine period (324-638 CE) (**NB** If you are taking the short, circuitous route, this is the point where you must turn round and retrace your steps back to the Lower Parking Lot). Those following the long, one-way route should begin to follow the main path up the escarpment. In places, progress is made by suitably positioned metal stairs and ladders. On a hot day (or on any day for that matter), this is a tiring climb. **NB** The ladders and stairs are one-way: **up only**. Don't forget to stop and admire the view on the way up.

At the top of the climb is a small, square **tower (9)**, probably dating to the Byzantine period and connected with the monk's habitation in the caves below. The trail continues along the top of the escarpment to the **observation point (10)**. With the ravine bottom some 50-60 metres below you and great views across the Wilderness of Zin, this is a spectacle not to be missed. Those who still have some energy left can follow the trail south along the top of the ravine for a further 150 metres to the site of the **huge dry waterfall (13)**, 60 metres above the bed of the Nahal Zin. Here you can see Ein Avdat's **upper pools (11)** and the **Ein Ma'arif spring (12)** that also feeds the wadi below. From here you retrace your steps to the observation point, finishing the tour at the **Upper Parking Lot (14)**. ■ *T6555684. Open daily 0800-1600; one hour later in summer. Adults 16 NIS, students 12 NIS. Admission to both the Upper and Lower entrances is permitted on one ticket, on the same day only.*

The Negev

Avdat (Oboda)

Phone code: 07
Colour map 3, grid C3

Of all the Nabatean-Roman-Byzantine towns in the Negev region, Avdat, (referred to by the Nabateans as Oboda) is probably the best preserved. As one of the major way-stations on the Petra–Gaza Spice Road (see 385), Oboda also evolved as the centre of a major agricultural region. The town flourished during the Late Roman period, with the prosperity continuing into the Byzantine period. There are impressive buildings from all three periods of the town's history. The remains of the town have been substantially restored, with a marked walking route taking in the key structures. A black line marks reconstructed areas; anything below the line indicates original remains, whilst anything above the line was reconstructed from ruins found at the site. ('Avdat' is the Hebrew version of the Arabic name for Oboda, 'Abdah').

Ins and outs

Getting there and around Avdat National Park is located on the main Be'er Sheva–Eilat road (Route 40). Drivers on the express Be'er Sheva–Eilat buses 392/393 may be persuaded to set you down at the park entrance. A more definite option is to take the slower bus 060 that runs every one or two hours between Be'er Sheva and Mizpe Ramon. For orientation see colour map 3.

History

Early & Middle Nabatean period Oboda was founded as a caravan stop on the Petra–Gaza Spice Road at the end of the fourth century/beginning of the third century BCE, though the original settlement may have comprised temporary structures only, possibly tents.

The oldest Nabatean structures date to the Middle Nabatean period, in particular the reign of the Nabatean kings Obodas III (c. 28-9 BCE) and **Aretas IV** (c. 9 BCE-40 CE). In addition to becoming a centre of pottery manufacture during this period, agriculture developed significantly. The mainstay of the local economy was still the caravan route, though the rearing of goats, sheep and camels was important. The Nabatean camel corps, used to police the Spice Road, were stationed locally. The Middle Nabatean period town came to an end during the reign of the Nabatean king **Malichus II** (40-70 CE), when Oboda was destroyed by non-Nabatean Arabian tribesmen.

Late Nabatean/Late Roman period Oboda was revived in the Late Nabatean period by Rabbel II (70-106 CE), who initiated renewed agricultural activity in the region. Even the annexation of the Nabatean's empire by Rome in 106 CE failed to interrupt Oboda's expansion; indeed, it may have given it renewed impetus. Despite being part of the Roman's *Provincia Arabia*, Oboda in the second and third centuries CE can be considered as much a Late Nabatean as a Late Roman period town, since the majority of the population were still ethnically Nabatean. The temple was re-dedicated to the local Zeus (Zeus Oboda), and construction began on a new Roman town to the southeast of the mound. The Emperor **Diocletian** (284-305 CE) incorporated Oboda within the defensive system of the Eastern Roman Empire, building the fortress on the east side of the mound, and recruiting local people to serve in the militia. Much building took place during this period of prosperity, though much of the Roman quarter was destroyed by an earthquake early in the fourth century CE.

Many of the buildings seen at Oboda today date to the Byzantine period, with the continuing prosperity being based largely upon sophisticated irrigation techniques extending the cultivated area. Grape cultivation and wine production were important to the local economic and social scene. Most of the Byzantine town, dating approximately from the mid-fourth century CE to 636 CE, occupied the west slope of the mound, comprising 350–400 homes in both houses and caves. The Christian nature of the town is evident in the substantial remains of several fine churches. **Byzantine period**

With the gradual decline of the Byzantine empire, Oboda was subject to increasingly regular incursions by Arab tribesmen, with the decline in security gravely affecting the town's economic base. Oboda was finally abandoned after the Arab conquest of 636 CE.

Tour of the Park

The recommended tour of the site begins at the National Park entrance, just off the main Be'er Sheva–Eilat road (Route 40). This route may require some doubling back, since, having driven up to the upper parking lot, the tour actually finishes at the lower parking lot. One alternative is to return to the upper parking lot having reached the observation point and Nabatean temple, drive to the lower parking lot, then ascend the steps back up to the observation point/temple, taking in the sites *en route*. There are drinking water fountains in the upper and lower parking lots, and a snack-bar and toilets near the main entrance. Note that you have to go to the ticket office (**24**) to get a token for the car-park barrier.

Numbers (marked in bold) refer to points marked on the 'Avdat National Park' map. Additional detail of the mound/acropolis area is shown on the plan of 'Oboda (Avdat) Acropolis', with points of detail marked by letters in **bold.**

From the **National Park entrance (1)**, the paved road leads up a steep climb to the **upper parking lot (6)**. Two points of interest, the **Burial Cave (en-Nusrah) (21)** and a **Roman villa (8)**, are passed on the way up.

The Negev

Avdat National Park

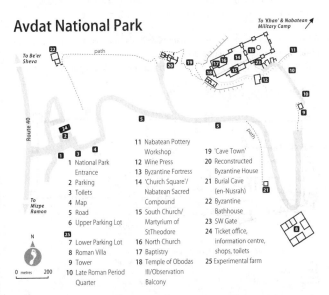

To 'Khan' & Nabatean
Military Camp

To Be'er
Sheva

path

Route 40

To
Mizpe
Ramon

N

0 metres 200

1 National Park Entrance
2 Parking
3 Toilets
4 Map
5 Road
6 Upper Parking Lot
7 Lower Parking Lot
8 Roman Villa
9 Tower
10 Late Roman Period Quarter

11 Nabatean Pottery Workshop
12 Wine Press
13 Byzantine Fortress
14 'Church Square'/ Nabatean Sacred Compound
15 South Church/ Martyrium of St Theodore
16 North Church
17 Baptistry
18 Temple of Obodas III/Observation Balcony

19 'Cave Town'
20 Reconstructed Byzantine House
21 Burial Cave (en-Nusrah)
22 Byzantine Bathhouse
23 SW Gate
24 Ticket office, information centre, shops, toilets
25 Experimental farm

Burial Cave (en-Nusrah) (21) The 1904 excavations at Obodas identified this tomb as the burial place of the Nabatean king Obodas III (c. 28-9 BCE). Subsequent investigations throw doubt on this claim, suggesting that the cave (located on a spur to the southwest of the acropolis mound) was probably cut in the first half of the first century CE. Other evidence that refutes the claim is the fact that it is not a solitary grave, with the 22 double *loculi* coves making this a multi-burial site, including the graves of some women. Greek inscriptions in the vaulted entrance hall (that mention, amongst other things, the women buried here) are dated to the third century CE, suggesting that the original Middle Nabatean period burial cave was later reused.

Roman villa (8) To the south of the main acropolis mound, just off the new access road, lie the remains of a Roman period villa. The plan of the building is typical of the period, with the rooms located around a central courtyard. A water cistern has been cut in the centre of the courtyard. An observation point provides an excellent view of Oboda's setting and the reconstructed Nabatean farm (see page 377).

Tower (9) This well preserved tower stands at the southwest corner of the Late Roman period quarter (see page 374). An inscription above the lintel on the tower's north wall suggests that it was built in 293-294 CE. Standing three storeys high, the tower probably served as an observation point; a function that it still retains today. Though often labelled on site plans as the 'Roman tower', it may in fact be Nabatean. The skilful architect has even contrived to make the tower earthquake proof.

Late Roman period quarter (10) The Late Roman period quarter is probably best seen from the top of the tower (see above). The quarter was constructed as a suburb of the early town some time in the third century CE, with building work continuing until 296 CE at least. The main street ran on a north–south axis, with most of the dwellings comprising houses built around courtyards, and constructed from well-dressed stone. The fact that there is no evidence of Christian occupation of the site suggests that the quarter had been abandoned by the Byzantine period (324-638 CE). There is a strong consensus that the quarter was destroyed by the devastating earthquake of 363 CE.

Nabatean pottery workshop (11) A brief excursion away from the main path leads right (east) to the Nabatean pottery workshop. Oboda became an important centre of pottery manufacture in the Early and Middle Nabatean periods, with a reputation for high

Oboda (Avdat) Acropolis

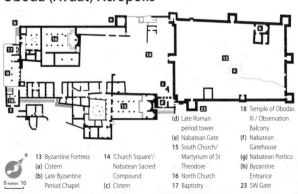

0 metres 10

13 Byzantine Fortress
(a) Cistern
(b) Late Byzantine Period Chapel
14 'Church Square'/ Nabatean Sacred Compound
(c) Cistern
(d) Late Roman period tower
(e) Nabatean Gate
15 South Church/ Martyrium of St Theodore
16 North Church
17 Baptistry
18 Temple of Obodas III / Observation Balcony
(f) Nabatean Gatehouse
(g) Nabatean Portico
(h) Byzantine Entrance
23 SW Gate

quality and delicate workmanship. This particular workshop appears to have been in use from around 30 CE until the middle of the first century CE. There are three distinct rooms: for clay preparation, the potter's wheel and the kiln.

There are a couple of buildings to the north and northeast of the acropolis mound that were important during the Middle and Late Nabatean periods. Neither is formally included on the walking tour of the site, nor marked on the map.

A **khan** (caravanserai), probably dating to the Late Nabatean period and in use until the mid-fourth century CE, stands to the north of the Nabatean pottery workshop. The large building (23 metres by 31 metres) stands around a central courtyard, and probably stood two storeys high. The large halls were used for storing goods traded along the Spice Road.

About 400 metres northeast of the acropolis mound is the site of the original **Nabatean military camp**. The compound measures 100 square metres, with a well-built stone wall reinforced by two corner towers and two central towers on each side. The camp was the home of the camel corps during the Middle Nabatean period, with barracks and camel sheds still discernible. As with other Nabatean towns in the Negev, it appears that only the garrisons were housed in permanent structures, with the rest of the population almost certainly living in tents. A large encampment probably stood to the east of the Nabatean military camp. The camp was probably abandoned when the Roman-Byzantine fortress was built on the acropolis.

Four wine-presses were discovered at Oboda, though this one, dating to the Byzantine period, is the best example. A notice-board provides an explanation of the production process. From the wine-press, the tour enters the Byzantine fortress through the southwest gate. **Wine-press (12)**

The Byzantine fortress was probably built at the beginning of the fourth century CE, though much of its two-metre-thick walls was built by stone 'recycled' from the Nabatean military camp (see above) and dismantled Late Nabatean period houses. The fortress is approximately 61 metres long (east–west) and 40 metres wide (north–south), with twelve towers defending the walls. The main entrance to the fortress is the **Southwest gate (23)**, though there is a smaller entrance to the northwest. A deep **cistern (a)**, with a capacity of 200 cubic metres, has been dug in the centre of the courtyard, supplied by two rainwater channels. In the northeast corner of the fortress is a **Late Byzantine period chapel (b)**, built of locally quarried limestone previously used at the Nabatean military camp. Excavations beneath the chapel revealed the presence of a Middle Nabatean period oven. **Byzantine fortress (13)**

To the west of the fortress is what was previously the Nabatean sacred compound during the Middle and Late Nabatean period. The construction of the adjacent churches during the Byzantine period has given the compound the moniker 'Church Square'. The sacred compound (51 metres by 40 metres) was probably built during the reign of Obodas III, to serve what is thought to be the Temple of Obodas III (see page 376), on the southwest side of the acropolis. One of the main entrances to the acropolis is the **Nabatean gate (e)** in the north wall, though the portals of the gate's tower were both altered during the Byzantine period. The **cistern (c)** in the southeast corner provided water to the Temple of Obodas III. The cistern stands near to a **Late Roman period tower (d)**. **Church Square/ Nabatean sacred compound (14)**

The Negev

South Church/ Martyrium of St Theodore (15) An epitaph on a tomb within the South Church, and the name of the same saint found engraved on fragments of a marble chancel screen, suggests that the church was dedicated to St Theodore. It was almost certainly built in the middle of the fifth century CE, but was destroyed by fire during the Arab invasion of 636 CE. The church is mono-basilical, with a central nave and two aisles divided by two rows of seven columns respectively. A three-dimensional model illustrates typical Byzantine church architecture. The Nabatean style of some of the capitals suggest that they were 'recycled' from the Nabatean temple.

North Church (16) The North Church is older, probably dating from some time in the mid to late fourth century. Again, it is thought that blocks from the former Nabatean temple were used in its construction. It is a basilica, with a single apse containing a pedestal for the bishop's seat. To the west of the atrium a flight of steps leads to the **baptistry (17)**. The church was largely destroyed during the Arab invasion, and latter used briefly as a sheep pen.

Temple of Obodas III/observation balcony (18) The present observation balcony is thought to stand largely upon the site of a former Nabatean temple. Excavations have revealed the plan of a structure similar in detail to the plan of other Nabatean temples in Moab, with dedications to the deities of Dushara and Allat. Inscriptions mention various members of the Nabatean royal family, suggesting the tentative link with Obodas III, though this connection is not assured. Later Byzantine construction has confused the mental reconstruction of the temple and sacred compound. Parts of the modern observation platform's previous functions have been identified as a **Nabatean gatehouse (f)**, a **Nabatean portico (g)**, and a **Byzantine entrance (h)**.

From the observation balcony, stairs descend towards the lower parking lot, taking in the last few items on the tour. Alternatively, return to the upper parking lot, drive to the lower parking lot, and ascend the stairs to see the last few points of interest.

Cave Town (19) From the observation balcony, stairs and a path descend through the main Byzantine town area, along Oboda's western slope. The town comprised around 350 to 400 residencies, and, given the nature of the typical Byzantine house here, the area has been dubbed Cave Town: many of the dwellings feature a cave cut into the hillside. The **reconstructed Byzantine house (20)** provides a good example of the typical dwelling unit here at Oboda. The complex comprises an enclosed court, with a hall to the north leading into two rock-cut chambers of the house-cave unit. The cave area almost certainly served as a wine-cellar cum pantry, in summer remaining beautifully cool, oblivious to the temperature outside. In the example here, the entrance to the cave features some red ochre drawings of St George and St Theodore, with some Greek inscriptions.

Below the Cave Town area is the lower parking lot (7), though it is possible to follow the footpath as far as the Byzantine bathhouse (22), down near the petrol station. From the bathhouse, a path leads back to the National Park entrance.

Byzantine bathhouse (22) The Byzantine bathhouse here at Oboda is certainly worth the short extra walk since it is considered to be amongst the best preserved structures from this period found anywhere in Israel. The courtyard is not particularly fine, since it was probably only a temporary structure, but the quality of the rest of the building is evident once you pass through one of the two entrances in the north wall. The right doorway leads into the *frigidarium*, or cold room, where there is a plaster-coated plunge pool one and a half metres deep. The left doorway from the courtyard leads into the *apodyterium*, or changing room. Beyond this

Byzantine bathhouse, Oboda (Avdat)

1 Entrance Courtyard
2 Frigidarium
  (Cold Room)
3 Apodyterium
  (Changing Room)
4 Tepidarium
  (Lukewarm Room)
5 Hypocaust system
6 Caldarium
  (Hot Bath Room)
7 Furnace

room is the *tepidarium*, or lukewarm room.

Water was supplied to the bathhouse from a 64-metre-deep well nearby, with the waste water removed via a channel, parts of which can be seen to the north of the building. Though the ceiling of the *hypocaust* (the hollow space beneath the *tepidarium* and *caldarium* through which the hot air was circulated) has not survived, it is still possible to see the brick pillar bases that supported it. The furnace was to the south of the building, with the brick flues and clay pipes through which the hot air was circulated still in fine condition.

The hot bath room, or *caldarium*, is on the west side of the building, and is built in the shape of a cross. The bathtubs were heated by channels fed from the *hypocaust*, whilst hot air was provided by a furnace to the west. Parts of the domed roof remain.

The reconstructed Nabatean farm is an experimental station first established here in 1959 in order to investigate, and attempt to recreate, the irrigation techniques of the Nabateans (see box on next page). Groups can arrange tours of the farm by booking in advance, T07-6565741/6558462. ■ *T6586391, F6550954. Open daily 0800-1700; closes one hour earlier in winter. Adults 18 NIS, students 14 NIS. There is a restaurant and toilets at the site entrance.*

Reconstructed Nabatean farm

Mizpe Ramon (Mitzpe Ramon)

Mizpe Ramon stands on the lip of arguably the Negev's greatest natural wonder, the Makhtesh Ramon (Ramon crater, see page 382). For the tourist, the town provides an excellent base from which to explore the stunning surrounding area.

*Phone code: 07
Colour map 3, grid C3*

Ins and outs

Mizpe Ramon is located on the northern edge of the Makhtesh Ramon (Ramon crater), some 24 kilometres south of Avdat National Park along Route 40. For orientation see colour map 3. For details on getting down into the crater, see under 'Makhtesh Ramon' on page 382. The town centre is very compact, though it is a fair walk out to the sights on the edge of town.

Getting there and around

Sights

The town was only founded in 1956, primarily as a seventeen-man co-operative providing road services. Today the population stands at around 6,000, swelled recently by the resettlement of Russian and Eastern European Jews. Without tourism, it's difficult to see any concrete economic base that could support the town, and unemployment in the town is said to be running at 20 percent.

The Negev

Turning the desert green: how the Nabateans beat the Israelis by 2,000 years

The idea that the Israelis "turned the desert green" has its origins not in the astounding contribution towards the world's knowledge of arid and semi-arid eco-system management that Israeli scientists have made, but in a political sentiment. The implication is that prior to the return of the early Zionists, the land was 'abandoned', 'uncared for', and 'empty': thus the idea that the Palestinians had any deep attachment to the land can be negated.

However, political arguments aside, Israeli researchers have been amongst the quickest to provide the evidence that they were not the first to "make the desert bloom". The Nabateans, a race probably of Arab origin, established sustainable desert agriculture in the Negev 2,000 years

before the foundation of the State of Israel. Their success was down to the development of sophisticated irrigation techniques.

In areas where rainfall is limited, the key factor in desert agriculture is the control of surface run-off. The loess soil of the Negev quickly develops an impermeable crust when exposed to water, thus preventing penetration into the soil of the surplus rain. The water that cannot be absorbed into the soil is the surface run-off. By managing efficiently the control of the surface run-off, the Nabateans were able to create a system whereby each field received the water equivalent of twenty times the actual level of rainfall that falls.

Low walls (approx 15 cm high) (**1**) dividing the water catchment area into manageable sizes also acted as conduits for directing the water. Small heaps of stones (**2**) also served a similar purpose, and were particularly successful in increasing the rate of water collection from light rains. Underground cisterns in adjacent farm dwellings (**3**) were connected to the conduits, and allowed the prolonged storage of water. The cultivated area at the centre of the shallow wadi was terraced and walled (**4**), with the different levels of stepped terracing allowing the passage of surplus water to the field below (**5**). Along with trade on the Spice Road, the management of the water environment allowed the Nabateans to establish relatively high density settlements in this harsh desert environment.

Nabatean irrigation technique

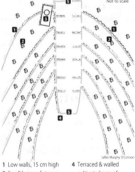

Not to scale

(after Murphy O'Connor)

1 Low walls, 15 cm high
2 Small heaps of stones
3 Cistern in farm dwelling
4 Terraced & walled cultivated area of shallow wadi
5 Surplus overflow channel

Mizpe Ramon Visitors' Centre Mizpe Ramon's best starting point is the excellent Visitors' Centre, built on the crater's edge. Not only are there superb views from the observation platform, there is a good audio-visual show (if a little OTT on the hyperbole) explaining all aspects of the crater, informative display boards instructing on the crater's formation, geological composition, and floral and faunal occupation, plus staff who can give advice to potential hikers. Recommended. ■ T6587392/6588691, F6588390. *Sunday-Thursday 0900-1700, Friday 0900-1600, Saturday 0900-1700. Adult 20 NIS, or combined ticket with Bio-Ramon Centre 23 NIS.*

The garden outside the Visitors' Centre is designed to comprise six different desert habitats, and is often occupied by a family of grazing ibex. The Bio-Ramon Centre features a small zoo, comprising animal, vegetable and mineral life indigenous to the crater. The collection of animal life may dissuade you from hiking in the crater: it features scorpions, spiders, snakes, other reptiles, rodents and insects. ■ *T6588755. Sunday-Thursday 0800-1500, Friday 0800-1300, Saturday 0900-1600. Adult on combined ticket 23 NIS. Guided tours by prior appointment.*

Bio-Ramon Centre

Staring into Makhtesh Ramon from the crater's rim is a pleasant way to pass the time, and is particularly rewarding at sundown as the rocks seemingly change colour. One of the best viewpoints is from the HaGamal Observation Point, to the southwest of the Visitors' Centre. It's so named because it is shaped like a camel.

HaGamal Observation Point

To the north of the Visitors' Centre is the Desert Sculpture Park; an unusual collection of stone 'sculptures' inspired by the surrounding environment, and gathered here under the direction of the Israeli artist Ezra Orion.

Desert Sculpture Park

This unique collection of llamas and alpacas, said to be the largest herd outside South America, was gathered here some years ago by an Israeli couple with a

Alpaca Farm

The Negev

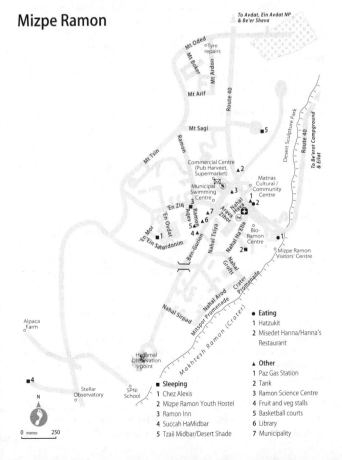

Mizpe Ramon

To Avdat, Ein Avdat NP
& Be'er Sheva

Mt Oded
Tyre repairs
Mt Boker
Mt Ardon
Mt Arif
Route 40
Mt Sagi
■ 5
Mt Tsin
Ramon
Desert Sculpture Park
Route 40
To Be'erot Campground & Eilat
Commercial Centre (Pub Harveet, Supermarket)
▲ 2
Municipal Swimming Centre
▲ 3
Matnas Cultural / Community Centre
1 ▲ 2
'En Ziq
Ramon
3 ■ 7
▲ 7
Arava Zihor
Nahal Hava
'En Ovdat
5 ▲ 6
'En Mor
4 ▲ 4
Nahal Tsiya
Ben-Gurion
Nahal Ha Ella
Bio-Ramon Centre
■ 1.
'En Ein Sahardonim
Nahal Gvit
2 ■
Mizpe Ramon Visitors' Centre
Nahal Sirpad
Nahal Arod
Mitspor Promenade
Crater Promenade
● Eating
1 Hatzukit
2 Misedet Hanna/Hanna's Restaurant
Makhtesh Ramon (Crater)
Alpaca Farm
HaGamal Observation point
Stellar Observatory
SPNI School
■ 4
▲ Other
1 Paz Gas Station
2 Tank
3 Ramon Science Centre
4 Fruit and veg stalls
5 Basketball courts
6 Library
7 Municipality
N
0 metres 250
■ **Sleeping**
1 Chez Alexis
2 Mizpe Ramon Youth Hostel
3 Ramon Inn
4 Succah HaMidbar
5 Tzail Midbar/Desert Shade

love of all things South American. The herd has grown from around 180 specimens to over 300, and provides a supply of high-quality wool. It's possible to
feed the animals, ride the llamas, plus observe the other animals here such as
peacocks, camels, angora goats, and reputedly, a kangaroo. Children will love
it, whilst adults can enjoy some fine South American coffee. ■ *On road southwest of town, T6588047, F6586104. Open daily 0900-1800. Adult 15 NIS. Call
ahead for details of feeding and shearing times. Guided tours in English available
if requested in advance.*

Essentials

Sleeping

■ *on maps*
*price codes see inside
front cover*

A *Ramon Inn*, 1 Aqev, T6588822, F6588151. I've always thought this place is rather
overpriced, especially given the lack of facilities (no pool) and the weekend price hike,
though several readers have suggested it is 'warm, intimate, unpretentious and welcoming' with 'home cooking at its ethnic best'. The improvement may be due to its
incorporation into the *Isrotel* chain. Features studio apartments sleeping 2-6 adults
(larger apartments are the best value) with kitchenette, lounge, cable TV, tours and
activities booked at the front desk. The best in town.

B *Succah HaMidbar/Succah in the Desert*, 7 km southwest of Mizpe Ramon on
Alpaca Farm Rd, T6586280. People are not sure what to make of this place. Basically,
you pay in the region of $100 for 3 nights recreating the desert living experience of
the wandering Children of Israel during their desert Exodus. Accommodation is in one
of 6 *succots*; a portable dwelling made of stone walls and a palm-frond roof, carpeted,
with mattresses and blankets. Lighting and showers are solar-powered, whilst other
bodily functions are performed *au naturel*. A central *succot* is used for meals, as a
meeting place, meditation centre, etc. If this is your thing, it really is superb. If not, at
the price, you may think someone's 'aving a larf.

C *Tzail Midbar/Desert Shade*, Mizpe Ramon, see map, T6586229, F6586208. This tour
company that organizes treks and tours into the crater (see 'Tour companies', page
381) also offers campsite and small cabins.

D *Chez Alexis*, 7 Ein Sahardonim, T6588258. A good alternative to the *Youth Hostel*,
this converted villa offers doubles and beds at cheaper prices. Free use of kitchen and
TV lounge. It's wise to call in advance.

E *Mizpe Ramon Youth Hostel*, opposite Visitors' Centre, T6588443, F6588074. Single-sex 6-bed dorms plus family rooms (**C**), all a/c with attached bath, very clean, TV
lounge, conference rooms, kiosk, breakfast included, dinner expensive at $10 but a
big feed, check-in 1600-2100, check-out 0900, advance reservations highly recommended. Can get noisy at weekends. **E** *SPNI Field School Hostel*, west of town beyond
HaGamal Observation Point, T6588615. Dorms for students only, a/c doubles (**D**) with
attached bath, breakfast available and sometimes other meals, essential to book in
advance, check-in 1400-1900, check-out 0830. Good info for hikers.

F *Be'erot Campground*, Makhtesh Ramon, T6588691. Pitch your own tent or stay in
one of their Bedouin tents at this official campsite some 18 kilometres inside the
crater. Toilets (no showers), limited snack-bar, bookings and payment to be made at
the Visitors' Centre. Day visitors can use the facilities for 10 NIS.

Eating The restaurant at the Ramon Inn has been well reviewed (book ahead if not staying
there), and for those on a budget the *Youth Hostel* offers a good feed for $10.
Hatzukit next to the Visitors' Centre offers canteen-style meals for 32-35 NIS (fight for

a window seat). *Misedet Hannal/Hanna's Restaurant* at the Paz Gas Station is a home-style roadhouse restaurant serving filling breakfasts, lunches and snacks. There is a supermarket in the Commercial Centre on Ben-Gurion.

Bars There are a couple of pubs in the Commercial Centre, including *Pub Harveet* (often open until 0200-0300). There's sometimes a teenyboppers' disco at the *Youth Hostel*. **Sports** Cycling: for mountain bike hire see under 'Tour companies', page 381. **Desert archery**: located on the road to the west of town, T6587274 or T05-0344598. Same principle as golf, but using a bow and arrow. **Hiking**: for organized hikes in the crater, see under 'Tour companies', page 381. Also see under 'Tourist offices', page.381. **Swimming**: *Municipal Pool*, corner of Ben-Gurion and 'En Ziq (1000-1800 most days, 22 NIS).

Entertainment

Buses stop at the Paz Gas Station on Route 40, at the Commercial Centre on Ben Gurion, or on the road outside the Youth Hostel. Bus 060 runs every one to two hours (0600-2100) between Mizpe Ramon and **Be'er Sheva** (1½ hours), passing **Avdat National Park, Ein Avdat National Park,** and **Sde Boker**. Bus 392 between **Be'er Sheva** and **Eilat** (1½ hours) passes through in both directions 5 times per day Sunday-Thursday and once on Friday, though there is no guarantee that there will be empty seats. Buses are at about 0800 1000 1200 1600 1900, though you should check exact timetable locally.

Transport

Banks *Bank HaPoalim* in the Commercial Centre does foreign exchange and has an ATM machine. You could also try the post office. **Communications** Post office: in the Commercial Centre on Ben-Gurion, T6588416 (Sunday-Tuesday and Thursday 0800-1230, 1600-1830, Wednesday 0800-1300, Friday 0800-1230), offers international phone calls, foreign exchange. **Hospitals & medical services** Chemists: there's a pharmacy in the Commercial Centre on Ben Gurion, T6586112. **Hospitals**: the nearest hospital is in Be'er Sheva, though there is a fully equipped *Magen David Adom* first aid station open 24 hrs on Nahal Have, T6588333 or T101. **Tour companies and travel agents** Shop around. *Avi Chaklai*, T6588205, organized tours, camping in Bedouin tents, etc. *Desert Shade/ Tzail Midbar*, T6586229, F6586208, one of the most reputable of the tour companies, offering camping and cabin accommodation, jeep tours ($30 for 3-4 hrs), camel treks ($15 per hr), guided hikes ($100-$150 depending on duration), or combined jeep and walking tours along the Spice Road. They also rent mountain bikes. *Midreshet Ramon*, T6587042, part of the College for Judaic/Land of Israel studies, offer special Shabbat observant weekends. *Ramon Desert Adventures*, T6595106, offer jeep tours, night drives and mountain biking. *Ramon Tours*, T6588623, organized tours, etc. *Shu'alei Shimshom/Samson's Foxes*, T6588868, offers jeep tours, 'Bedouin hospitality' etc. *SPNI Field School*, T6588615 organize walking tours. **Tourist offices** The staff at the *Mizpe Ramon Visitors' Centre* can offer advice on hikes and driving tours in the region. It's certainly worth calling in here for advice before heading off into the crater. The only problem is, by the time the centre opens at 0900, it's probably too hot to start a hike. If possible, try to call in before it closes (1700) the day before you plan to go. It is important that you buy the SPNI 1:50,000 map of the crater (50 NIS) before attempting anything too adventurous. It's available (in Hebrew only) from the gift-shop opposite, though the staff are willing to translate all important details. *Society for the Protection of Nature in Israel* (SPNI): T6588615/6586101 (open Sun-Thu 0800-1730, Fri 0800-1200). The Field School is to the west of town, beyond the HaGamal Observation Point. It is highly recommended that you call in here before attempting a hike into the crater. It is also a good idea to leave a copy of your planned itinerary, as the SPNI (with their communication links to the army) are your only hope of rescue if you get into difficulty. **Useful addresses & phone numbers** Police: T6588444. Magen David Adom (ambulance): T101 (or T6588333). **Other**: there's a tyre repair workshop along the first right turn as you arrive from Be'er Sheva (see map), T6588885, and 2 petrol stations.

Directory

Makhtesh Ramon

The Makhtesh Ramon can justifiably compete with the coral reefs of the Red Sea, and the unique environment of the Dead Sea, for the title of Israel's most stunning natural site. Forty kilometres long, nine kilometres wide, and in places four hundred metres deep, the Makhtesh Ramon is the largest erosion crater in the world. Though comparisons with the landscapes of both the Grand Canyon and the Moon are somewhat clichéd, they do serve to suggest something of the grandeur and splendour of the scenery here. Though the crater's beauty can still be appreciated from the window of a coach, this is a good place to get your walking boots on. The crater is now administered by the Nature Reserves Authority, with a number of marked walking and driving routes.

Ins and outs

Getting there and getting around The main problem with hiking in the Ramon crater is that the trail-heads are so far from Mizpe Ramon. Unless you have your own transport, or take a very early bus down into the crater, you will expend a lot of energy just getting to the trail-head. One possibility is to stay overnight at the *Be'erot Campground* (see 'Sleeping', page 380). It is very important to make a preliminary visit to the Visitors' Centre or SPNI Field School in Mizpe Ramon before commencing any hikes. The SPNI 1:50,000 map is invaluable.

Geology

The Hebrew word *makhtesh*, meaning mortar (as in mortar and pestle), has now entered the glossary of geological terminology since it describes a geological process that has been identified only here, in the Negev. During the Miocene geological epoch, (70 million years BP), pressure on the Earth's surface created a range of low mountains running broadly northeast-southwest through the Central Negev region. At some point the 'dome' cracked, allowing water to penetrate. Over a prolonged period the penetrating water eroded the lower, softer sandstone beneath the higher, harder limestone and dolomite, eventually creating three major erosion craters: Ramon, HaGadol and HaKatan. The term *makhtesh* is now used to describe an erosion valley surrounded by steep cliff walls and drained by a single wadi (water-course).

Because of its geological age, the Makhtesh Ramon presents a three-dimensional model of the geological history of the Earth. The layered rock beds of the cliff walls, and the bed of the makhtesh floor, display magma solidified into igneous intrusions, basalt, essexite, trachyte, clay, sandstone, mudstone, quartzite, thin layered limestone, bituminous limestone, limestone, chalk, conglomerate, flint, chert, dolomite, gypsum, ferriferous sandstone, sandstone and siltstone. What this list means to the non-geologically minded (99 percent of the population?), is that the crater is full of colourful and bizarre rock formations that should not be missed.

Flora and fauna

The Makhtesh Ramon is also the junction of four climatic-vegetation zones (Mediterranean, Irano-Turanian, Sahoro-Arabian and Sudand-Oceanic), thus accounting for the range of landscapes and vegetation types. It is estimated that there are 1,200 different kinds of desert vegetation in the Makhtesh Ramon, including such flowers as sun roses, hairy storkbills, Negev tulips and

Eco-friendly tourism in Makhtesh Ramon

The Ramon Park is Israel's largest nature reserve, and is administered by the Nature Reserves Authority (NRA), in association with the Society for the Protection of Nature in Israel (SPNI). It is estimated that the park receives between three-quarters and one million visitors per year, promoting serious concerns about the environmental impact of such large numbers.

There are several ways in which the NRA are attempting to deal with this threat, particularly when you bear in mind that the lack of an broad economic base in Mizpe Ramon means that tourism is seen as the future mainstay of the town's economy. A web of marked paths (and driving routes, where appropriate) is being introduced across the makhtesh floor, linking various places of geomorphological, geochemical, botanical, faunal or human interest, with

explanation boards and specified observation points. The idea is to channel visitors along certain routes, confining them to manageable areas where any negative impact can be monitored. For visitors to the crater, the usual rules apply. Stick to the marked paths, do not pick any flowers or plants, and carry out all your rubbish with you.

The Ramon Research Centre in Mizpe Ramon will continue its programme of research in the crater, as well as expanding its educational programme. The crater is widely used for training purposes by the Israeli Defense Forces, though all recruits are now given lectures and taken on guided tours to 'increase their awareness of the nature and history' of the region.

asphodelines. Some floral features, such as the Atlantic Terebinth (*Pistacia atlantica*), are remnants of a wetter period and provide symbols of environmental change.

The range of fauna at home in the crater is equally remarkable. You are most likely to see the crater's ibex and gazelle population, as well as raptors and other birds of prey such as Egyptian vultures, short-toed eagle, griffin vulture, kestrel and a variety of owls. Less conspicuous residents are wolves, foxes, porcupines, hyaenas, a lovely selection of snakes, spiders, scorpions and rodents, and reputedly, a number of leopards. You may also come across evidence of man's occupation, dating back to Byzantine, Roman, Nabatean, Israelite and Canaanite times.

Sights and hikes

The **Haminsara** or **Carpenter's Workshop** (or 'saw-mill') can be reached by driving or walking six kilometres down into the Makhtesh Ramon (crater) on Route 40 from Mizpe Ramon. Alternatively, a steep walking path leads down from the cliff-top promenade to the west of the Mizpe Ramon Visitors' Centre. The name is taken from the resemblance of the rock here to pieces of sawn timber. The unusual prism shapes were created by cross-fissuring under pressure in the quartzite rock. The direction of the fissures determines the number of facets (eg triagonal to hexagonal). A walkway has been built to protect the various exhibits, and you should not stray from it, though you are free to handle the samples of rock in the box placed at the start. Different rock formations are labelled. This poor man's Giant's Causeway takes no more than 10 minutes to view.

You can continue from here on to the **Ammonite Wall** about five kilometres away. The rock face here contains hundreds of ammonite fossils, named after the ram-headed Egyptian god Ammon, whom they resemble. From here, it a long walk back up to Mizpe Ramon, though it may be possible to hitchhike or flag down a passing bus.

Carpenter's Workshop and Ammonite Wall

The Negev

Short driving tour For those with their own transport, and not wishing to travel too far on foot, it is possible to make a short driving tour of some of the crater's attractions. Leaving Mizpe Ramon to the south on Route 40, the road descends the twisting 'Atzmaut Ascent' into the Ramon crater. After six kilometres, a sign indicates right for the **Haminsara**, or **Carpenter's Workshop** (see page 383 for full details).

Continuing on Route 40, take the next left at the orange sign for Saharonim Plateau, Ein Saharonim and the Be'erot Campground. The road is unpaved for the five and a half kilometres to the **Be'erot Campground**, though it is suitable for all vehicles. Immediately past the campsite, the road divides. The path straight ahead leads to **Mt Ardon** (see page 385) at four kilometres, or the Ma'ale Noah ascent out of the crater at ten and a half kilometres. Both routes are only suitable for walkers or four-wheel drive vehicles. This route also leads to the **Ma'ale Mahmal**, or 'Camel Driver's Ascent'. This is a difficult ascent, though it is also one of the most dramatic sections of the Petra–Gaza Spice Road. In order to climb the face of the cliffs out of the Makhtesh Ramon, 300 metres high, the Nabateans widened a natural fissure in the rock and constructed supporting terrace walls. At the top of the cliff is **Mezad Ma'ale Mahmal**, a small fort dating to the first century CE.

The right turn beyond the campsite leads to Ein Saharonim and the Saharonim Plateau. Taking the right fork, after one and a half kilometres the road divides again. At this junction, the left fork leads one kilometre to the top of the Saharonim Plateau, whilst the right fork leads two and a half kilometres to Ein Saharonim. Marked at this junction is a section of the Nabatean's Petra–Gaza Spice Road (see page 385). You have to walk a little way to see anything, with the nearest preserved 'milestone' about two kilometres north.

Taking the left fork first, the road leads across the **Saharonim Plateau** to the foot of **Harut Hill**. It's possible to walk to the top of this hill, 492 metres high, and back in about two hours; well worth it for the excellent views around the crater. Other options from here include following the blue markers north to **Mt Ardon** (included in the 'Mt Ardon–Ein Saharonim' hike described on page 385), or following the black or blue markers southeast along the Wadi Ardon towards Ein Saharonim (also included in the 'Mt Ardon–Ein Saharonim' hike described on page 385). This latter route is also passable by four-wheel drive vehicles.

Returning to the road junction, the left fork leads a winding two and a half kilometres to **Ein Saharonim**. This is the site of a small spring (Ein

Makhtesh Ramon, showing route of the 'Spice Road'

The Petra–Oboda–Gaza Highway: The Nabatean Spice Road

Penetrating the Negev as early as the 4th century BCE, the Nabateans came to dominate the trade and transport of spices, incense, salt and bitumen between the Arabian Peninsula, through the Levant, to the Mediterranean Sea. The main route, the Spice Road, led from the Nabatean's Edom capital at Petra, via Oboda (Avdat) to Gaza.

The route taken by the Spice Road is fairly easy to determine today, not just through the identification of the various fortresses and way-stations at intervals along its path, but also through the discovery of large sections of paved road. Detecting a Roman influence, scholars believe that the Nabateans imitated these road-building techniques, including the placing of milestones; this practice became prevalent in the Roman Empire during the reign of Augustus (27 BCE-14 CE). This period is contemporary with the zenith

of the Spice Road's fortunes, during the reign of the Nabatean kings Obodas III (c. 28-9 BCE) and his successor Aretas IV (c. 9 BCE-40 CE).

The Romans forced the Nabateans to relinquish their hold on the Arabian spice trade in the mid-1st century CE, severely weakening their power, and allowing non-Nabatean tribes from the Arabian Peninsula to plunder the way-stations. Despite a brief renaissance under their last king, Rabbel II (70/71-106 CE), the Spice Road fell into disuse, with new commercial routes being redirected. Some of the former Nabatean way-stations became fortified outposts of the Roman Empire following the Emperor Trajan's annexation of the Negev in 106 CE.

The Negev

Saharonim) and oasis, though in summer it may be little more than a brown puddle. Also located here are the remains of a Nabatean fortress, **Mezad Sha'ar Ramon**, that served as part of the chain of stations along the Spice Road.

There are a number of hiking options from here. You can head east via the **Ma'ale Dekalim** (ascent) to Wadi Neqarot, from where you can continue southeast on the Spice Road hike (see page 387), or you can head north-northwest from Wadi Neqarot to Harut Hill (described in reverse in 'Mt Ardon–Ein Saharonim' hike on page 385). Most of this route is also accessible by four-wheel drive. Alternatively, you can head southwest on the green trail to **Mt Saharonim** (see 'Mt Saharonim hike', on page 387). If you don't have a four-wheel drive vehicle, or do not intend walking, you return the way you came. Once you have returned to Route 40, you can turn left (south), continuing for a further two and a half kilometres, until you see a sign on the right that indicates the **Ammonite Wall**, several kilometres west from the main road (see page 383 for details).

This is a long hike to complete in one day, seven to nine hours, and may best be split into two separate trips. The hike begins at the **Be'erot Campground**. Those on foot should note that the Be'erot Campground is 17 kilometres from Mizpe Ramon (for route description see 'Short driving tour', page 384). Bus 392 from Mizpe Ramon (heading to Eilat) will drop you at the junction on Route 40, but it's still a five and a half kilometre walk from here to Be'erot Campground. It may be possible to hitch here but, bearing in mind the fact that you will need to make an early start, it may be best to spend the night before the trek at the Be'erot Campsite (see under Mizpe Ramon 'Essentials' for details, page 380).

Mt Ardon–Ein Saharonim hike

Turn left out of the **Be'erot Campground** and head north, ignoring the turning on your right for Ein Saharonim and Saharonim Plateau. After about three kilometres, a blue marked trail leads off to the right (east), where the path begins a gradual, and then a steep ascent to the top of Mt Ardon (702 metres). There are tremendous views from here, making the effort more than worthwhile. The descent of the south side of **Mt Ardon** should be undertaken with care, though once back near to the valley floor you will begin to appreciate the extraordinary coloured rock formations. This upper section of the Ardon Valley is sometimes referred to as Red Valley, due to the profusion of dark red sandstone. Dark volcanic intrusions provide some fascinating rock formations. There are also remains of fossilized tress *en route*. The blue trail eventually leads to **Harut Hill** (492 metres). There are several options here: i) you can return along the unpaved road back to the Be'erot Campground (just over three kilometres away). This whole trip should have taken four to five hours in total; ii) you can climb to the top of Harut Hill, and then return to the Be'erot Campground (total trip six to seven hours); iii) you can continue on to Ein Saharonim, adding a further four to five hours to what you have already completed.

Turning left (southeast) at Harut Hill, the trail towards Ein Saharonim is marked in blue or black (according to which map you use). The trail here follows the bed of the Wadi Ardon, passing a number of spectacular volcanic

Makhtesh Ramon, showing Mt Ardon-Ein Saharonim & Mt Saharonim hikes

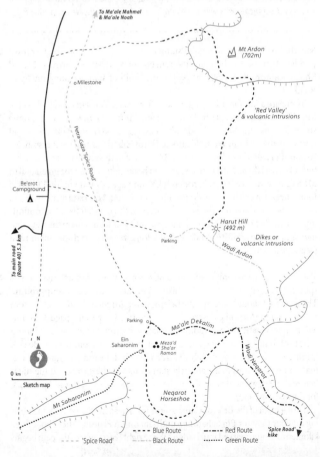

rock intrusions known as **dikes**. After two kilometres or so of walking, you arrive at a three-way fork. The first left red route leads southeast, into the Wadi Neqarot, and forms part of the Spice Road hike (see page 387). The second path is the blue route, and involves walking in the lee of some steep cliffs (with shady caves) along the **Neqarot Horseshoe** (Parsat Neqarot), and on to **Ein Saharonim**. The third route, the red trail to the right, leads west to Ein Saharonim via the **Ma'ale Dekalim** ascent. The spring at Ein Saharonim, even after a day's hard walking, is not the sort that you would wish to dive into for some relief; it's often little more than a muddy puddle. Also sited at Ein Saharonim is the Nabatean fortress of **Mezad Sha'ar Ramon**. From Ein Saharonim, it is about three kilometres back to the Be'erot Campground.

This four to five hour hour hike also begins at the Be'erot Campground (see 'Mt Ardon-Ein Saharonim' hike on page 385 for starting details). Turn right out of the campground, and head south along the four-wheel drive 'Oil Road'. After almost four kilometres, a green marked trail leads left (east), ascending Mt Saharonim, on the southern edge of the Makhtesh Ramon (crater). The walk proceeds along the top of the cliffs, along the crater's edge, before descending to **Ein Saharonim** (see hikes on page 385 for details). On the descent to Ein Saharonim, the green trail passes **Sha'ar Ramon** (Roman Gate), where the main wadi that flows through the crater makes its exit.

Mt Saharonim hike

This is a very long trek, covering over 40 kilometres, and best undertaken by experienced desert hikers, preferably with a local guide, and with suitable equipment for camping out. There is no reliable drinking water supply on this route. You should consult with the SPNI in Mizpe Ramon before attempting this journey, seeking the permission of their rangers, and possibly the army. The map here is for information only, and not comprehensive enough for this hike. You will need the SPNI 1:50,000 map. The hike emerges onto the Arava Road (see the end of the Dead Sea Region chapter).

Spice Road hike

The Negev

Borot Lotz (The Loz Cisterns)

Borot Lotz (or Loz Cisterns) refers to a series of seventeen waterholes that were thought to have been first dug around the 10th century BCE, with later modifications undertaken by the Nabateans from the fourth century until the end of the Byzantine period (seventh century CE). A four kilometre walking trail has been marked by the Nature Reserves Authority, encompassing the best preserved cisterns, a number of ancient remains, and passing through lush terraces of recently planted indigenous trees. The whole tour takes one to two hours.

There is no public transport to the site. To reach Borot Lotz, head north from Mizpe Ramon on Route 40, turning left (southwest) five kilometres out of town at Haruhot Junction. Continue southwest on Route 171 for approximately 34 kilometres, before turning right (northwest) on to the track at the sign for Borot Lotz. The parking lot and the beginning of the tour is one kilometre along the track (taking the right fork). There are toilets, camping facilities and drinking water near the parking lot. The tour around the principal sites is marked by red-and-white trail signs. **NB** It is forbidden to bathe in the cisterns or drink the water. Lighting fires, picking plants and flowers, and littering are all forbidden.

Ins and outs

During the reign of King Solomon (965-928 BCE), efforts were made to populate the Negev in order to provide a buffer zone between the settled kingdom and the desert nomads. Borot Lotz was part of this settlement programme

History

along the northern ridge of the Makhtesh Ramon. A series of cisterns were dug, primarily to store water from the winter rains, with evidence suggesting that most of the waterholes at Borot Lotz were dug during this period.

When those advanced water engineers, the Nabateans, settled in the Negev around the fourth or third century BCE, they refined the cisterns at Borot Lotz and incorporated them within their high-tech surface run-off irrigation system. Remnants of ancient farms and terraces suggest that agriculture continued at Borot Lotz until the end of the Byzantine period (seventh century CE). The recently planted orchard, fed by a Nabatean system of surface run-off irrigation, gives some idea as to how Borot Lotz may have appeared 1,500 to 2,000 years ago.

Tour Leaving the parking lot and camping area heading north, after 50 metres you come to what is popularly known as the **'good water cistern' (1)**, so named because of the quality of water it once supplied. The bullrush that now occupies the cistern would have been cut out in ancient times, since it would have impaired the quality of the water and possibly have caused physical damage to the structure. The 'good water cistern' is an open cistern, cut into the soft impermeable rock and lined with a series of layers of uncut stone. Two diversion channels funnel the surface run-off water via sedimentation pools into the cistern. These pools serve to filter out silt deposits from the water (see the cross-section diagram).

The trail leads downhill, crossing the jeep track, and following an ancient drainage channel to a large cistern, 30 metres in diameter, that over the years has become filled by sediment (the 'clogged cistern'). Just beyond here are the

Borot Lotz (Loz Cisterns)

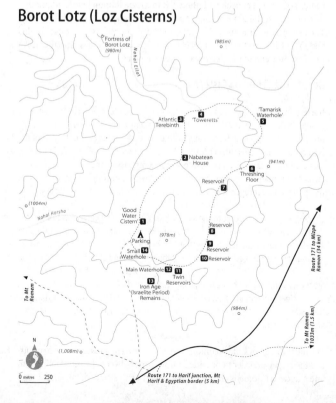

Cross-section of a Nabatean cistern

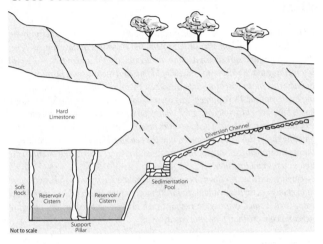

Hard
Limestone

Diversion Channel

Soft
Rock

Reservoir /
Cistern

Reservoir /
Cistern

Sedimentation
Pool

Not to scale

Support
Pillar

remains of a **Nabatean house (2)**, **probably dating to the first century CE.**

Continuing downhill, in a northerly direction, lies a grove of **Atlantic Terebinth (3)** (*Pistacia atlantica*). As with other specimens of this tree elsewhere in the Negev, the presence of pistachio trees here suggests that this region was once wetter than it is now. These particular trees are thought to be several hundred years old. A diversion may be made northwest of here to climb to the viewpoint at the top of the 980-metre peak known locally as the 'Fortress of Borot Lotz'.

The trail climbs slightly to the east, following the course of a seasonal wadi. Lavender cotton, cat thyme, white wormwood and wild pyretrum grow here, and were all previously used for medicinal purposes. Also present in the river-bed are fossil remains of snails, **toweretts (4)**, that previously lived here 70 million years ago. (**NB** Do not touch.)

Climbing the ridge above you, to the east-southeast, the marked trail leads to a second cistern. This one is semi-enclosed, dug into a layer of hard, impermeable rock. The tamarisk tree growing here gives it the name, the **'tamarisk waterhole' (5)**. There are remains nearby of a low stone wall; almost certainly part of the Nabatean system of surface run-off agriculture.

Ascending the next ridge, the trail leads to a **threshing floor (6)** that also probably dates to the Nabatean, or possibly Byzantine, period. It was also used in later years by Bedouins. The threshing floor stands amongst a number of ancient agricultural buildings, including livestock pens and grain storage rooms.

Crossing another dry wadi bed, the trail passes another **reservoir (7)**, though this one is in a poor state of repair and seemingly over-run by saltbushes (*Atriplex halimus*). A number of **reservoirs (8) (9) (10)** further on are in far better condition. They are reached by ascending the ridge from the wadi bed, passing a number of remains of Middle Bronze Age I (2200-2000 BCE) settlements. Of the **twin reservoirs (11)** ahead, the northernmost is in the best condition, having been refurbished earlier this century.

The main **waterhole (12)** to the west is the largest at Borot Lotz, being fed by four different conduits. To the southwest of the main waterhole, off the red-and-white marked trail, lie the remains of settlements from the Iron Age, or Israelite period (1200-586 BCE) **(13)**. The tour returns to its starting point, passing a **small waterhole (14)** on the way.

Eilat

Phone code: 07
Colour map 4, grid C2

Eilat is Israel's premier resort town, frequently billed as a hedonistic alternative to the 'cultural tourism' on offer at Jerusalem and elsewhere in the country. True, the all-year-round sunshine is a major attraction, and the under-sea coral world is something that no visitor to Israel should miss, but there is some justification in the view that the tourist brochures are somewhat over-enthusiastic when describing Eilat's appeal. Development has been rapid, and though many of the larger hotels have been tastefully designed, many have not. And with the desire to provide more and more tourist beds, you can be sure that you will never be far from a building site. It should also be noted that the beaches do not have the fine sand of the Mediterranean coastal resorts, but rather sand more akin to that found on the ubiquitous building sites.

Having said that, the town does have a very relaxed, easy-going feel, with more than enough activities available to satisfy most holiday-makers. And with Israel being such a small country, attractions such as the Dead Sea or Jerusalem are never much more than four hours away.

Ins and outs

Getting there

Related maps:
A. Eilat Centre,
page 399.
B. Eilat North Beach
Area, page 396.
C. South of Eilat,
page 393.

If arriving on a package tour or charter flight, you will arrive at 'Uvda (Ovda) Airport, the military airport some 60 kilometres to the north. Charter airlines usually arrange transport to and from Eilat and the airport: otherwise it's a 150 NIS taxi fare or an irregular bus service (392 between Eilat and Be'er Sheva, six per day, one hour). Domestic *Arkia* flights use Eilat Airport, literally in the centre of town (see map). Note that there are plans to build an 'Israeli terminal' at Jordan's Aqaba airport, 14 kilometres north of Aqaba.

Eilat

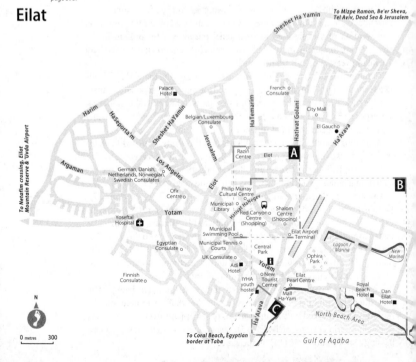

The Central Bus Station is located on HaTemarim, and is within easy walking distance of the hostels (though a little further from the main hotels area). Connections are good to the rest of the country, though on popular routes (Dead Sea, Jerusalem) it is as well to book seats two to four days in advance. See page 418 for details of buses to/from Jordan and Egypt (Sinai).

Eilat centre is fairly compact, although there are two important bus services that most visitors will use at some point. Bus 015 runs twice hourly from the Central Bus Station via Glass Boat, Dolphin Reef, Coral Beach, Underwater Observatory to the Egyptian border at Taba (first bus 0700, last at 2030, restricted service on Friday and Saturday). Bus 016 runs from the Arava boder crossing with Jordan, via the Central Bus Station, then follows the same route as bus 015 to Taba (twice hourly, 0900-1930, restricted service on Friday and Saturday). **Getting around**

History

Though the modern town of Eilat was established less than fifty years ago, the advantages of this location – with its fresh water supply, natural anchorage, and commanding position on the trade crossroads between Egypt, Arabia and on to the Mediterranean – have been recognized since antiquity. When Moses led the wandering children of Israel out of Sinai, into the wilderness of Moab, he passed through here (*Deuteronomy 2:8*), and the port here (Ezion-Geber?) was established some 3,000 years ago to serve the copper mines at Timna (see page 407). During Solomon's reign (965-928 BCE), the port of Ezion-Geber had a firmly established ship-building industry (*I Kings 9:26*), and it is often speculated that the Queen of Sheba landed here on her way to visit Solomon in Jerusalem (*I Kings 10:1-2*). The Ptolemies, Nabateans, Romans, Crusaders and Mamluks all ruled Eilat down through the centuries, though few left any permanent mark. **Ancient history**

The problem for archaeologists has been the positive identification of the sites of biblical Elath and Ezion-Geber. A number of sites have been proposed (including Tell el-Kheleifeh, near to the Jordanian town of Aqaba, and 'Coral Island', see page 394), but it is far more likely that any remains that could have led to a positive identification have long since been built over during the construction of the modern towns of Eilat and Aqaba. It is also possible that any remains may have been completely washed away by the flash-floods that periodically inundated the site prior to the construction of water control measures. What this means for the visitor to Eilat is that there are no ancient sites in the town itself to divert you away from the beach.

The modern history of Eilat begins as recently as 1949, when the settlement was little more than a hostelry for camel caravans and a British Mandate police station. Recognising the strategic and economic importance of access to the Red Sea, the Israeli army occupied a strip of land adjacent to the Gulf of Eilat during the closing stages of the 1948-49 War of Independence. This territorial gain was confirmed in the Armistice Accords of 1949, a kibbutz was founded (Eilot, later moved a couple of kilometres inland), and in 1951 a port was opened. It was not until 1956 that the Israelis were able to establish the right of innocent passage through the Straits of Tiran into the Gulf of Aqaba, though Israeli ships were constantly harassed by her Arab neighbours, contrary to international law. Attempts by the Egyptians in 1967 to block the Straits to Israeli shipping was one of the factors that led to the Six Day War. **Modern history**

The Negev

Eilat has developed considerably since then (permanent population around 30,000), and though the port remains Israel's major link to the Far East and the southern hemisphere, it is tourism that represents the town's major earner.

Sights

Beaches
Though Eilat's beaches are considered its main attraction, unless you intend exploring the underwater splendour, or partaking in the various watersports on offer, you may think that the hype is a little overdone. The sand is of the building-site variety, and some beaches can become unpleasantly crowded. Most beaches are free, charging just for sun-lounge chairs (10 NIS per day), though some do charge an admission fee. Women rarely go topless in Eilat.

The nearest beach to the town centre (and the most crowded) is North Beach, which is subdivided into a number of smaller beaches generally named after a nearby landmark such as a hotel (Neptune Beach, Royal Beach, etc). They have freshwater showers, bed-chairs for hire, and are generally supervised by lifeguards. A stroll along the promenade and around the lagoon/marina is a popular early evening entertainment.

Quieter beaches are to be found by heading out along the Eilat–Taba road towards the Egyptian border (bus 015). Beaches here include HaNesiha, Ofir, HaMigdalor and HaDekel, though they are sometimes referred to collectively as South Beach. Eilat's underwater attractions are probably best explored at the Coral Beach Reserve (see below). Dolphin Reef is becoming an increasingly popular attraction (see below).

Coral Beach
Nature Reserve
By far the most spectacular attraction in Eilat is the underwater world of the coral reef, populated by a diverse collection of garishly coloured fish, sharks, octopuses, crustaceans and sea-urchins. The best place to view the coral reef first hand is at the Coral Beach Nature Reserve, on the Eilat–Taba road towards the Egyptian border (bus 015). The one kilometre coral reef here is protected by the Nature Reserves Authority, with part of the 20 NIS entrance fee going towards the management and preservation of this resource. Potential snorkellers can hire equipment here (35 NIS) and follow the marked trails through the highlights of the coral bed. It is also possible to hire scuba diving equipment, or take tuition (see under 'Sports' on page 402). Note that 'Aqua-Sport' Beach (at the northern end) is free.

Warning There are a number of rules to bear in mind. **Don't touch anything**. Not only is it illegal to damage or remove anything, you may also be putting yourself at considerable risk of injury. Some of the creatures, whether plant or animal (or perhaps simply appearing to be a rock) are venomous, and an encounter with one of these may be an experience that you remember long after the glorious underwater colours have faded from your memory. It is recommended that you always wear some form of footwear in the water (also available for hire). If you do have an accident, even if it is just a scratch, seek the immediate medical advice at the dive-shops and equipment hire places, and then consult a doctor. ■ *Winter 0900-1700 daily, summer 0900-1800 daily. Adult 20 NIS. Private beach, hot showers, sunbeds (10 NIS), snack-bar.*

Dolphin Reef
Also located along the Eilat-Taba road is **Dolphin Reef**. In addition to a very pleasant private beach with a popular pub and restaurant, beach chairs, sun-shades and freshwater showers, Dolphin Reef also offers the opportunity to observe and swim with the dolphins. The centre was seemingly founded for 'scientific purposes', though it is sometimes argued that this is little more than the commercial exploitation that can be found in dolphinariums the world

over. However, the centre here does conduct valuable research into behavioural patterns of the species, in particular human–dolphin interactions. The 'swim with the dolphins' scheme is also used as a form of therapy for emotionally disturbed or physically handicapped humans. The intentions of the centre's staff are certainly sincere and honourable.

The admission fee entitles you to use the beach, see a natural history film

South of Eilat: the Eilat–Taba road

■ Sleeping
1 Ambassador, Red Sea Sports Club
2 Club
3 Club In
4 Club Mediterranee Coral Beach
5 Dortel Sol
6 Edomit
7 Eilat Princess
8 IYHA Youth Hostel
9 Le Meridien
10 Orchid
11 Prima Carlton
12 Red Rock
13 Reef

● Eating
1 Bedouin Tent
2 Casa Italia, Mandy's Chinese, Goldstar Village Beach Pub
3 Fisherman's House, Piggy's Pub, Baruch Fish, Supermarket
4 Greek Fisherman
5 The Last Refuge

▲ Other
1 World Class Diving Centre, Aqua-Line Dive Centre
2 Marina Divers, Parasailing, Glass-bottom boats
3 Texas Ranch
4 Camel Ranch, Solomon's Chariots
5 New Tourist Centre

about dolphins, whales and sea-lions, plus observe the dolphins from the observation piers. Feeding/training takes place daily at 1000 1200 1400 1600. For an additional 115 NIS, you can spend half an hour or so swimming with the dolphins (minimum age for children 10 years), or you can pay to join in the feeding/training session. **NB** You should not wear sun-cream or sun-block when swimming with the dolphins since this can damage their skin. ■ *T6375935. Open 0900-1700 daily all year (pub open until late). Beach admission adult 35 NIS, child 28 NIS; swimming with dolphins 150 NIS adult, 135 NIS child (book in advance). Diving and snorkelling equipment is also available (243 NIS adult, 235 NIS child).*

If you don't want to get wet, this is the best way to see Eilat's coral world and the creatures that live within it. This is an attraction that should not be missed. The Underwater Observatory comprises two large, glass-windowed rooms submerged five metres below the sea's surface. Spectacular coral grows all around the observatory, with thousands of brightly coloured fish flitting in and out of the reef. There's a very attractive circular restaurant within the Underwater Observatory, as well as an observation deck at the top of the tower. At over 20 metres high, not only does the deck give a great view down through the clear blue sea to the coral bed below, there is also a 360° vista that takes in four countries (Israel, Egypt, Jordan, Saudi Arabia).

Moored against the pier that extends out to the Underwater Observatory is the **Yellow Submarine** (T6373193). A 45 minute trip in the submarine allows you to do what scuba divers can't: descend to a

Underwater Observatory/ Oceanarium/ Yellow Submarine

The Negev

depth of 60 metres. The submarine then rises to 30 metres below the surface, where marine life is rich.

Back on dry land is the **Oceanarium**, with excellent shark, turtle and sting-ray pools, as well as a darkened room where you can view a collection of phos-phorescent fish. Make sure you pick up the free fish identification chart and hand-held electronic guide (English, French, German, Hebrew). ■ *T6376666. Saturday-Thursday 0830-1700, Friday 0830-1500. Adult 80 NIS, child 66 NIS. Yellow Submarine trip costs 280 NIS adult, 170 NIS child for 45 minute trip, including admission to the Underwater Observatory. Entrance to Oceanarium only 65 NIS adult, 45 NIS child. Take bus 015 from the Central Bus Station; buses return at half past every hour. If you wish to take photographs, load your camera with a fast film (flash photography and thick glass are not compatible).*

Glass-bottom boat tours Another great way to explore the undersea world, without getting your feet wet, is to take a cruise in one of the glass-bottom boats (see 'Tour companies and travel agents', page 406, and 'Sports and activities', page 402).

Coral Island A popular cruise destination from Eilat is Coral Island (also known as 'Pha-raoh's Island'), about 13 kilometres to the south in the Gulf of Aqaba. It has been suggested that this is Solomon's port of Ezion-Geber. The lagoon on the west side of the island is not natural, and the island was used as an anchorage in later years, with fortified remains from the Hellenistic (332-37 BCE) and Byzantine periods (324-638 CE) as well as the remnants of a Crusader castle (built in 1116). The Crusader fortress was subsequently lost to Salah al-Din in 1170, recovered by Reynald of Châtillon, and lost again to the Mamluks in the 13th century (see 'Tour companies and travel agents' on page 406 for details of how to get here).

International Bird-watching Centre Eilat is on the main migration route between Africa and Europe, via the Great Syrian-African Rift Valley, with over 400 species of migratory birds having been observed in the region. Forty different species of raptors alone have been noted here. The main bird-watching park is to the east of the 'North beach area'. Observation points have been marked, and arc linked by hiking trails. Guided tours are available. ■ *Those who are interested should contact the International Bird-watching Centre on HaTemarim, opposite the bus sta-tion, T6335339, F6376922, where you can get advice and book tours (Sunday, Tuesday, Thursday 0900-1600, Monday, Wednesday 0900-1300 1600-1900). You can also call the information centre (T6374741). There is also a 'Birdwatching Club' at the SPNI Field Study Centre at Coral Beach (T6371127).*

Ostrich Farm Similar fare on offer nearby at the Ostrich Farm (T6372405, F6373213), where you can take a ride in 'Solomon's Chariots'; a glorified donkey cart. There's also 30 or so birds, plus sundry other animals. The Ya'eni Pub is a popular attraction at night.

Eilat Stone Mines Though there is a tour of the mine 70 metres below the surface, emphasis here is on the opportunity to purchase at 'manufacturer's prices'. They'll even send a limousine to pick you up, or refund your taxi fare, and get you in the mood with free cocktails. ■ *Industrial Area, T6336363. Sunday-Thursday 0800-2200, Friday 0800-1500, Saturday 0900-2200.*

Camel Riders is a desert tours company based at Shacharut, about 40 kilo- **Camel Riders,**
metres due north of Eilat. They organize camel tours of the Negev, from two **Shacharut**
days up to two weeks, allowing you to reach places otherwise inaccessible.
Food and tent accommodation is provided, as well as English-speaking
guides. Tours cost from $120 to $1200 depending upon the length. T6373218
for details.

Eilat is a good base from which to make tours into the Negev, to Jordan, and **Tours**
into the Sinai. See 'Tour companies & travel agents' on page 406 and the 'Excursions to Sinai and Jordan' at the end of this chapter (page 418).

Essentials

There are at least 50 hotels in Eilat offering more than 8,000 beds, with plans for 55 **Sleeping**
hotels offering 12,000 beds by the year 2000. This can mean that your room is facing ■ *on maps;*
on to a building site (check this when making your reservation; some hotels adver- *price codes see inside*
tise cheaper rates for such rooms). With so many hotels available there should be *front cover*
some scope for bargaining over the price (in all price categories), though at certain
times of the year (Jewish and Christian holidays, weekends, etc) rooms must be
booked well in advance (and prices sky-rocket to double or treble). The price categories quoted here are for the regular season. Note that there are significant discounts to be had by booking through a travel agent. Most of the hotels in the more
expensive categories are very fine indeed, whilst those in the mid-price range tend
to be rather overpriced.

L1 *Dan Eilat*, North Beach, T6362222, F6362333. One of Israel's most luxurious hotels
but still manages to retain an informal atmosphere. 7 categories of room from standard to 'mega-suites' ($700-1,400) all facing the sea. Lebanese, French, Italian, Orien-
tal, South American restaurants, piano bar, nightclub, 3 pools set in landscaped
gardens, off season prices remarkably good value. Recommended. **L1** *Eilat Princess*,
Eilat–Taba Rd near border with Egypt, T6365555, F6376333. One of Eilat's best hotels,
real sense of luxury, all rooms with extra large beds, some beautiful suites and themed
'club' rooms (Indian, Thai, Chinese, Moroccan, Russian, etc), 7 restaurants, bar, nightclub, series of swimming pools connected by waterfalls and slides, fully equipped
gym and health centre, tennis, private beach. Good choice if you can afford it; recommended. **L1** *Herod's Palace/Herod's Vitalis/Herod's Forum*, North Beach, T6380000,
F6380010. Wow! This place almost makes it into the 'sights' section! *Herod's Palace*
features 300 luxurious rooms, plus 30 or so suites ($510-635), opulent *Salome Lobby*
built in the style of a Nabatean Temple (bar, shows), *Four Winds* 'quiet lobby' (including romantic candlelit terrace), *Officer's Club* bar (over 18s only), *Tamarind* restaurant,
Punchline pub, *Giraffe* noodle bar, *Saparine* terrace restaurant, *scardo* shopping
arcade running down to the beach, several pools, kid's pool, swim-up bar. *Herod's
Vitalis* is a 64-room self-contained health spa hotel with separate check-in: over 18s
only, no smoking, no mobile phones, plus full spa facilities (not open to non-*Vitalis*
guests). *Herod's Forum* is a self-contained 104-room conference hotel with banqueting halls catering for up to 1,200 guests. A lot of thought and money has gone into
this hotel (rumoured to be over $200 million!), and there's a real feeling of quality.
There are even plans to import proper sand for the public beach opposite the hotel! If
you can afford it, stay here. If you can't, at least come and have a look. Recommended.
L1 *Hilton Queen of Sheba*, Lagoon, North Beach. Still under construction, but this
place is going to be impressive. **L1** *Le Meridien*, HaPalmah, North Shore, T6383333,
F6383300. Recently opened right on the airport flight-path (must have tyre marks
on the roof!), 2-3 room suites, extra for deluxe sea-view and pool-view (around
$500). Very luxurious. **L1** *Royal Beach*, North Beach, T6368888, F6368811. Flagship

The Negev

of the *Isrotel* chain, luxurious and well laid out, beautifully furnished, $125 supplements for better rooms, plus suites in the $600-1,000 price range, hefty high and peak season price hike (cheapest rooms $630 during Pesach), all the facilities that you would expect. Recommended (if you can afford it). **L1** *Taba Hilton*, Taba Beach, across Egyptian border, T6379222, F6379660. One of the best hotels in region, has superb facilities in quiet setting, 5 restaurants, 3 bars, nightclub, pool, private beach, watersports, tennis, free transport to/from hotel. Recommended.

L2 *Ambassador*, Coral Beach, T6382222, F6382200. Busier and more luxurious hotel associated with the *Red Sea Sports Club Hotel* and *Manta Diving Centre*, 4 pools, kiddie club, nightclub, restaurants. **L2** *Crowne Plaza*, Lagoon, T6367777, F6330821. Tastefully decorated rooms, all facilities but exterior rather shabby, formerly the *Holiday Inn*. **L2** *Lagoona*, King Solomon's Wharf, T6366666, F6366699. *Isrotel*-run 'all inclusive' hotel (all food and drink), $20-30 supplement for pool views, family rooms available. Good for families, not a bad deal. **L2** *Orchid*, Coral Beach, Eilat–Taba Rd,

Eilat: North Beach area

Beaches
A HaDayagim (no swimming)
B HaSela HaAdom
C Um Rashrash
D Hapenina
E Neptune
F Moriah
G Tarshish
H Nevi'ot
I Royal
J Hazahav
K Kokhav Ha Yam
L Edum
M Ha Shehafim

To Mizpe Ramon, Be'er Sheva, Tel Aviv, Dead Sea & Jerusalem

Gulf of Aqaba

North Beach Area

Not to scale

To Coral Beach and Egyptian border at Taba

To Jordanian border 650m

Related maps
A. Eilat Centre, page 399; **B**. South of Eilat, page 393

Sleeping
1 Americana Inn
2 Caesar Resort
3 Club
4 Crowne Plaza
5 Dalia
6 Dan Eilat
7 Dortel Sun
8 Edomit
9 Four Points
10 Four Points Red Sea
11 Galei Eilat
12 Grand Plaza
13 Herod's Forum
14 Herod's Palace/ Herod's Vitalis
15 Hilton Queen of Sheba
16 IYHA Youth Hostel
17 King Solomon's Palace
18 La Coquille
19 Lagoona
20 Le Meridien
21 Marina Club
22 Moon Valley
23 Neptune Eilat
24 Palmira
25 Radisson Moriah Plaza
26 Red Rock
27 Riviera Club
28 Royal Beach
29 Royal Gardens Suites
30 Sharbat (under construction)
31 Sport
32 Vista

● Eating
1 Burger King
2 Burger Ranch, Spiral Club Cafe, Milky Way
3 Cafe Royal Brasserie
4 Grill House
5 Hemingway's Pub
6 La Trattoria
7 Lemon Beach Pub
8 Lotus Chinese
9 Maman
10 McDonald's, Domino's Pizza
11 New York, New York
12 Pago Pago
13 Pizza Hut
14 Pubs and Restaurants
15 Regatta, Satchmo Jazz Bar
16 Rotunda Pub
17 Tandoori, Ben and Jerry's
18 Teddy's Resto-Pub
19 Three Monkeys Pub
20 Wang's Grill, Ranch House
21 Yacht Pub

▲ Other
1 Supermarkets
2 Um Rashrash (flag)
3 Nautical and Sports Association of Eilat
4 Kids' playground

T6360360, F6375323. Beautiful Thai-style resort village featuring 136 charming chalets with sea-facing balconies, well furnished, picturesque pool area, supervised kids' entertainment. Recommended. *Chao-Phya* Thai restaurant, a very good choice (**L1** in high season). Recommended. **L2** *Palmira*, Kamen, North Beach, T6366000, F6337279. Friendly place popular with tour groups, lots of activities (pool aerobics, cocktail games, disco, bingo, kids' activities), set around nice pool area. Good value at tour group rates. **L2** *Royal Gardens Suites*, HaYam, North Beach. Huge 3-sided apartment hotel around attractive pool/garden area, due to open in 2000.

L3 *Caesar Resort*, Lagoon, T6305555, F6332624. Rack rate is vastly overpriced though most guests come as part of a group (and hence get a much better deal). Very busy, pool area rather crowded and noisy, shabby exterior belies rather nicer interior. **L3** *Club*, Hel HaHandassa, T6361666, F6326113. Nautical theme (from décor to staff uniforms), pool- or sea-facing balcony rooms, mainly suites, tropical garden with pools, waterfalls etc. Busy and service rather off-hand, very much for the family. **L3** *Club In*, Coral Beach, T6334555, F6334519. Self-contained villas with kitchenette, living room, TV, pool, kid's pool, restaurant, quiet location. **L3** *Four Points*, Kamen, North Beach, T6304444, F6363640. Formerly *Paradise*, run by *Sheraton* but service rather off-hand. Balconies but no real sea views, large pool and sun deck, kid's pool, health club (extra). **L3** *Four Points Red Sea*, Kamen, North Beach, T6363636, F6363630. Rooms set around pool and garden area, balcony, a/c, TV, restaurant, solarium, tennis, run by *Sheraton*. **L3** *Galei Eilat*, North Beach, T6367444, F6334184. Eilat's original hotel but looking very old now despite being refurbished by the *Howard Johnson* chain. There are much better value places than this. **L3** *Grand Plaza*, Lagoon, T6389999, F6389990. Built on site of old *Shulamit Gardens*, fairly large rooms with sea or marina views, balconies, cable TV, plus some suites with jacuzzi on balcony, considerable price hike at weekends and holidays. **L3** *King Solomon's Palace*, King Solomon's Wharf, T6368818, F6368886. Huge 373 room hotel, 25 family rooms (**L2**) plus 'King's Rooms' on upper floors (**L1**), huge pool area, choice of restaurants, health club, lots of children's activities. Reasonable value for Eilat. **L3** *Neptune Eilat*, North Beach, T6369369, F6334389. Now part of *Howard Johnson* chain, all rooms with balcony and sea-views, choice of restaurants, sports facilities. New block nicer. **L3** *Radisson Moriah Plaza*, North Beach, T6361111, F6334158. One of Eilat's best. All the usual facilities including a/c, TV/video, fridge, some deluxe rooms and suites (**L2**), 3 pools, health club, several restaurants and coffee bars. Recommended. **L3** *Red Sea Sports Club*, Coral Beach, T6333666. Hotel catering for divers using the *Manta Diving Centre* (T6370688, F6370655), close to beach. Fairly simple functional rooms (greater luxury at the *Ambassador Hotel*, see page 396). **L3** *Sharbat*, Lagoon. Under construction.

A *Club Mediterranee Coral Beach*, Coral Beach, T6384444, F6370559. Usually booked through travel agencies (and cheaper too), lots of entertainment such as nightclub, billiards, tennis, volleyball, minigolf, health club, daily programme of activities. Now looking a little old fashioned, though. **A** *Dortel Sol*, Hel HaHandassa, T6376222, F6375888. Formerly *Sonesta/Sun Suites*, all-suite hotel, most with balcony, pool, kid's club. Half-board deals quite good, family orientated. **A** *Edomit*, New Tourist Centre, Yotam, T6379512, F6379738. Ugly tower-block away from beach, spacious rooms, pool. Good restaurant, but overpriced. **A** *Holiday Inn Eilat-Patio*, 3 Shfifon, T6364364, F6340118. Smaller, more intimate branch of the chain. Rooms small but comfortable though some readers suggest that the kid's entertainment, disco and variety show make it 'very noisy'. **A** *Marina Club*, Antibes, North Beach, T6334191, F6334206. Mini suites sleeping 4-6 set around central pool area, most with small but not very private balconies. Pretty good value. Recommended. **A** *Mercure*, 3 Hativat HaNegev, T6382333, F6382301. Central location, all rooms with balcony though a little cramped, small pool. Somewhat overpriced. **A** *Nova*, Hativat HaNegev, T6382444,

F6382455. Large, package-tour orientated hotel set around large pool, lots of activities. Good for children though not for those after peace and quiet. **A** *Prima Carlton*, Eilat–Taba Rd, T6334088, F6333555. Rather 'block-like' and looking a little old fashioned, pool, restaurant. **A** *Riviera Club*, Antibes, North Beach, T6333944, F6333939. Spacious apartments with kitchenette, lounge, some with private garden and patio, pool, kid's entertainment. **A** *Shalom Plaza*, 2 Hatmarim, T6366777, F6376865. Modern hotel built above the shopping plaza (a little noisy), large rooms, pool, Swiss restaurant. **A** *Vista*, Kamen, North Beach, T6303030. New hotel, small pool. Rather overpriced.

B *Americana Inn*, Kamen, North Beach, T6333777, F6334174. Rooms and small chalets set around large pool area, but no real views (a little like a 70s motel), service 'Israeli' and not 'American', larger rooms in new wing with kitchenette, bar, nightclub, classic brochure. **B** *Briza*, Hatmarim, T6388888, F6388889. Central location. Rather overpriced for facilities on offer. **B** *Etzion*, HaTemarim, T6370003, F6370002. Functional rooms, a/c, TV, heated pool, health club, restaurant, nightclub. **B** *Moon Valley*, Kamen North Beach, T6366888, F6334110. Attractive low-rise motel with pleasant sun deck and pool area. Candidate for rudest staff in Eilat. **B** *Red Rock*, HaPalmah, T6373171, F6371530. Spacious rooms but now looking a bit old and overpriced. **B** *Reef*, Eilat–Taba Rd, T6364444, F6364488. Quiet location, pool. Rather old fashioned and not particularly good value. **B** *Sport*, North Beach, T6303333, F6332765. Noted for its sports facilities in the neighbouring *Country Club*, 2 outdoor pools (1 heated), kid's pool, tennis, squash, raquetball, handball, baseball, gym, jacuzzi, sauna, health centre, plus nightly entertainment. Remarkably good value for the standard of rooms.

C *Dalia*, Tarshish, North Beach, T6334004, F6334072. Old fashioned exterior but completely refurbished inside, restaurant, nice lobby area, small pool. Not bad value (especially out of season). **C** *La Coquille Suites*, Tarshish, North Beach, T6370031, F6370032. Friendly family run apartment hotel, family rooms with kitchen, dining area, some with balconies and jacuzzi. Pretty good value. **C** *Pierre*, 123 Ofarim, T6326601, F6326602. Brand new hotel looking rather out of place in this 'hostel area', pretty good value a/c rooms, bar, restaurant. **C** *Red Mountain*, 137 Hativat HaNegev, T6363222, F6363200. Reasonable value, central location, a/c, cable TV, pool, restaurants. **C** *Red Sea*, HaTemarim, T6372171, F6374605. Small, away from beach, noisy location, small pool, discounts for longer stays. **C** *SPNI Field School*, Coral Beach, Eilat–Taba Rd, T6372021, F6371771. Private a/c rooms, breakfast included, dorms currently not open, camping possible (**G**) in shady picnic area with clean shower blocks, convenient for beach. **C** *Topaz*, Hatmarim, T6362111, F6362121. 30 suites and 50 studios with kitchenette and diner, all fairly large, heated pool, kid's pool, restaurants, not a bad deal.

D *Aqua-Sport Divers Lodge*, Ofarim, T6376289. Formerly *Ofarim Street Rooms*, now used to accommodate divers on packages with *Aqua-Sport*. **D** *Sunset*, 130/1 Retamim, T6373817. No longer has dorms, rooms and mini-suites with fridge, kitchenette, TV, attached bath, though rates negotiable, rather noisy bar area.

Budget hotels and hostels Eilat's budget accommodation is almost entirely confined to a small area one block north of the Central Bus Station (see 'Eilat centre' map). **NB** This area can be rather raucous at night: the eastern end of Al Mogim should be considered to be extremely dangerous, populated mainly by Eastern European drunks, prostitutes and druggies.

Most of the dorm beds are in the 25-30 NIS price range, with private doubles costing 80-140 NIS (depending upon your negotiating skills). Many of the hostels in Eilat are populated by long-stay 'travellers' who are working here (hostels are good places to ask around about picking up jobs), and for short term visitors they may appear a little cliquey. Other hostels pride themselves on their party atmosphere, and hence getting some sleep can be difficult. Few have curfews. Sleeping on the beach away from the city centre is legal, but is not recommended.

E *IYHA Youth Hostel*, Hel HaHandassa, T6372358, F6375835. 370 beds in 4 or 6 bed a/c dorms, some private doubles (**C**), reservations recommended, hefty price hike in high season. Clean and well run.

F *Shalom*, Hativat HaNegev, T6376544, F6376544. Choice of dorms or doubles (**E**), but rather run down. **F** *Spring*, 126/1 Ofarim/Agmonim, T6374660. Popular with young Israelis (and rather noisy), clean but extremely crowded dorms, 24 hour bar with pool table.

Eilat centre

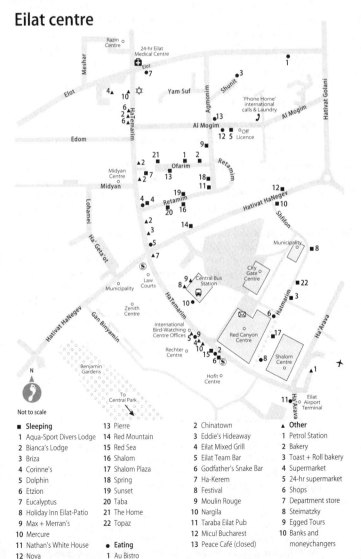

The Negev

■ Sleeping
1 Aqua-Sport Divers Lodge
2 Bianca's Lodge
3 Briza
4 Corinne's
5 Dolphin
6 Etzion
7 Eucalyptus
8 Holiday Inn Eilat-Patio
9 Max + Merran's
10 Mercure
11 Nathan's White House
12 Nova
13 Pierre
14 Red Mountain
15 Red Sea
16 Shalom
17 Shalom Plaza
18 Spring
19 Sunset
20 Taba
21 The Home
22 Topaz

● Eating
1 Au Bistro
2 Chinatown
3 Eddie's Hideaway
4 Eilat Mixed Grill
5 Eilat Team Bar
6 Godfather's Snake Bar
7 Ha-Kerem
8 Festival
9 Moulin Rouge
10 Nargila
11 Taraba Eilat Pub
12 Micul Bucharest
13 Peace Café (closed)

▲ Other
1 Petrol Station
2 Bakery
3 Toast + Roll bakery
4 Supermarket
5 24-hr supermarket
6 Shops
7 Department store
8 Steimatzky
9 Egged Tours
10 Banks and moneychangers

G *Bianca's Lodge*, 117/2 Ofarim, T6372371. Formerly *Fawlty Towers*, rather cramped dorms. **G** *Corinne's*, 127/1 Retamim, T6371472. Reasonable a/c dorms with attached bath (though a little dark), some cosy a/c wooden cabins (**E**), and probably the area's cheapest double rooms (**E**), a/c, attached bath, clean and quiet. Not a bad deal if you bargain hard. **G** *Dolphin*, Al Mogin. Caters for Eastern European skinheads and migrant workers, run down crowded dorms, kitchen, bar, located in very dodgy area. **G** *Eucalyptus*, 121 HaTemarim, T6370592. Cheap dorm, some private a/c rooms with attached bath (**D-E**), owner also has some very nice apartments for rent. **G** *Max and Merran's*, 111/1 Agmonim, T6371333. New ownership but trading on the reputation of previous owners, cheap dorms, 1 cheap private room, only 1 shower. Not really 'traveller' orientated. **G** *Nathan's White House*, 131/1 Retamim, T6376572. Friendly and clean, good for long stay guests, smallish rooms with attached bath, sociable kitchen area. **G** *Red Sea Hostel*, New Tourist Centre. On the 3rd floor above *Underground Pub*, very noisy. Good location for pub goers. **G** *Taba*, Retamim, T6375982, F6371435. Cheap dorms plus a variety of private rooms (price depending on size, a/c, attached or shared bath, **D-E**), kitchen, garden, BBQ area, rates negotiable. Not a bad deal; **G** *The Home*, Ofarim, T6372403, F6373513. One of those 'love it or hate it' hostels, full of long term workers and rather cliquey for those just passing through. Crowded dorms, fully equipped kitchen, breakfast included, TV lounge, no curfew. Good place to pick up work, good choice for a long stay.

Apartment rental and B&Bs   The Tourist Information should be able to provide you with a copy of *Essentially Eilat*, which features a list of 'holiday units' for rent.

Camping   Fairly shady camping is available at the (**G**) *SPNI Field School* at Coral Beach, with some 'permanent' tents available at (**G**) *Coral Beach Campground*, T6375063, though there is precious little shade here. Camping on the beach is legal away from the town centre, though is not recommended and is **unsafe for women**.

Eating   **Budget**   Most of the falafel/shwarma stalls and bakeries are located along HaTemarim. Most of the 'backpacker bars' offer cheap meals ('anything and chips' for under 20 NIS), particularly those in the New Tourist Centre. There is also a reasonably good value food court in Mall Ha'Yam. The nearest supermarket to the hostels area is at the junction of Hatemarim and Elot (see 'Eilat centre' map). *Taverna*, New Tourist Centre, T6373406. Bar serving cheap meals, open 24 hours, happy hours, takes credit cards. *Underground*, New Tourist Centre. Pub serving cheap meals, spaghetti 15 NIS, beans on toast 10 NIS, chips 7 NIS, plus popular all-day breakfast 20 NIS; *Unplugged*, New Tourist Centre. Internet bar/café serving good meals, pizza 20-30 NIS, salad 20 NIS, schnitzel 20 NIS.

Café/bars   There are numerous cafés (also offering light meals) in the Shalom Centre, Red Canyon Centre, Mall Ha'Yam and Eilat Pearl Centre.

Central/North/South American   *Eddie's Hideaway*, 68 Almogim (off Eilot), T6371137. Perennial favourite in Eilat, best known for its steaks, reservations recommended. *El Gaucho*, Ha'Arava, T6331549. Slabs of Argentinian style beef from 40 NIS. *New York New York*, next to *Moon Valley Hotel*, T6336380. 'Genuine American style restaurant'. *Salsa*, Dan Eilat Promenade, T6362295. Californian kitchen with a Latin American flavour, nice setting. *The Last Cigaro*, Holiday Inn Promenade, T6367777. See under 'Bars', page 401.

Chinese/Southeast Asian   *China Town*, Etzion Hotel Centre, HaTemarim, T6370004. Chinese-Thai menu, 'Oriental' chef. *Mai Thai*, New Tourist Centre, T6372517. One of the best in town, authentic Thai food, main courses 35-70 NIS.

Mandy's Chinese, Coral Beach, T6372238. Cantonese and Szechuan styles, receives good reviews, main dishes 30-60 NIS.

Fast food/chain *Burger Ranch*, Mall Ha'Yam. *McDonald's*, Mall Ha'Yam. *Crowne Plaza Hotel*, Tourist Information Centre. *Pizza Hut*, King Solomon's Wharf, T6378197, also Eilat Pearl Centre.

French *Au Bistro*, Eilot, T6374333. Very well reviewed classical French cuisine. *Chez Simon*, New Tourist Centre, T6371965. French-Italian place specializing in grilled meats and fish.

Hotel restaurants *Bedouin Tent*, *Lagoona Hotel*, T6333666. Middle Eastern food and belly dancing, (not Fri), expensive. *Café Royal Brasserie*, *King Solomon's Palace Hotel*, T6363439. Excellent chateaubriand, main courses 80-175 NIS. *Hemingway's*, *Royal Beach Hotel*, T6368989. Good seafood in nice setting, though rather expensive. *Off the Wharf*, *King Solomon's Palace Hotel*, T6363439. Good, though pricey. *Ranch House*, *Royal Beach Hotel* Promenade, T6368989. American steak house using beef imported from the US, expensive. *Wang's Grill*, *Royal Beach Hotel* Promenade, T6368989. Interesting Californian menu with 'Far East' touch, expensive. I have never dined at the various restaurants in *Herod's Palace Hotel*, but the setting is certainly impressive. Any one of the restaurants at the *Dan Eilat* or *Eilat Princess* can be recommended for a treat.

Italian *Regata*, Dan Eilat Promenade, T6362293. Nice location, wide choice though fairly expensive.

Indian *Maharaja*, New Tourist Centre. Reasonably priced, main dishes 30-50 NIS. *Tandoori Kohinoor*, King Solomon's Wharf, T6333879. Subtle tandoori dishes, meat main dishes 40-50 NIS, veg dishes 21-35 NIS, rice 15 NIS, good value fixed lunch menu 43 NIS, sometimes live music.

Middle Eastern *El Morocco*, New Tourist Centre, T6371296. Best known for its tagines and couscous, 53 NIS. *Ha-Kerem*, Eilot, T6374577. Long established unpretentious family-run restaurant serving filling Yemenite dishes for 25-40 NIS.

Miscellaneous *Country Chicken*, New Tourist Centre, T6371312. A variety of dishes (including chicken), often hand out flyers with special discount deals. *Lido*, New Tourist Centre. Main dishes 39-54 NIS, take-away pizza 45 NIS. *Malibu*, Coral Beach opposite *Ambassador Hotel*, T6341990. Very nice setting on beachfront.

Seafood *Barracuda*, next to *Dortel Sol*. Main dishes 55-75 NIS. Described by one reader as 'overpriced, understaffed and totally lacking in good service'. *Fisherman's House*, Coral Beach, T6379830. Good value eat-all-you-want fish buffet 32 NIS. *Greek Fisherman*, Coral Beach. Main fish courses 60 NIS. *Pago Pago*, Lagoon, T6376660. Floating restaurant and bar, seafood main dishes 55 NIS, beer 12 NIS. *Red Lobster*, North Beach (next to Mall Ha'Yam), T6371760. Israeli seafood, good value brunch menu (90 NIS for 2). *The Last Refuge*, Coral Beach, T6372437. Considered by locals to be the best seafood restaurant in town, main dishes 40-80 NIS.

Bars Most of the top hotels have fairly unatmospheric pubs and nightclubs. Better options are those around the New Tourist Centre (backpacker/budget orientated) or those along the Eilat–Taba Road (particularly Coral Beach area, 15 NIS taxi ride). Few get going much before 2300. Sadly the (in)famous *Peace Café* has now closed down. *Eilat Team*, junction HaTemarim/Hativat HaNegev. Unpretentious travellers' place,

Bars & nightclubs

The Negev

cheap food. *Flying Pig*, Coral Beach. Bills itself as offering English country pub grub, well reviewed. *Hemingway's*, Marina/Lagoon. Rather upmarket but it has its moments. *Lemon Beach Pub*, North Beach. Nice during 'beach hours' for drinking beer in the sun. *The Last Cigaro*, Holiday Inn Promenade, T6367777. Bills itself as an 'authentic South American pub', live music, food, cigar menu. *Punchkok Pub*, Philip Morley House, T6344111. With its singing waiters this place is just so tacky you have to try it. *Taverna*, New Tourist Centre. Backpackers bar open 24 hours, beer 7-11 NIS per ⅓ litre, cheap meals, rather raucous, 'the first and oldest pub in Eilat'. *Teddy's Resto-Pub*, Ophira Park, North Beach, T6373949. Bar-restaurant, good value fixed menu (99-119 NIS for 2). *The Three Monkeys*, Royal Beach Promenade. 'Plastic' English pub (makes a change from 'plastic' Irish pubs), live entertainment. *Underground*, New Tourist Centre. Very popular with backpackers, cheap beer and cheap food, loud music and hard drinking, sports shown on giant screen, open 24 hours. *Unplugged*, New Tourist Centre. Internet bar, cosy sofas, very busy in the evening, beer 10-15 NIS, good value meals 18-30 NIS, shows movies or plays loud music. Quite nice. *Yacht Pub*, King Solomon's Wharf. Rather 'plastic' English-style pub, not very atmospheric unless full (doesn't get going until late). *Ya'eni*, Ostrich Farm, near Coral Beach. Spectacular lightshow to accompany 'outback' feel.   **Casinos** *Victoria*, T6341356, F6341357. Floating casino operating out of the marina.   **Nightclubs** The top hotels have fairly unatmospheric nightclubs. A more enjoyable time is likely at the various beach parties that are usually held near Coral Beach (ask around in the 'backpacker' pubs). Nothing gets going in Eilat much before midnight. 'Club nights' come and go at places in the Industrial Area; ask young locals what's 'in'. *Disco Sheba*, *King Solomon's Palace Hotel*. Nightly from 2300 (except Sunday), claims to be 'most spectacular laser light show in Israel', but more 'Saturday Night Fever' than Ibiza rave club. *Pat-Pong Club*, New Tourist Centre, T6330999. Claims to be 'the bast in the country' (sic), offers 'striptease and lesbian show...rhythmic music and nice atmosphere', open daily 2200 until late, lots of Eastern European girls; *Ronnie's*, *Americana Inn*, T6336908. Popular with young Israelis.

Entertainment   **Cinemas** *Red Canyon*, Red Canyon Centre, HaTemarim. *Gil*, Mall Ha'Yam, T1-700-505050. *Sega City*, Sega World, Mall Ha'Yam, T6340491. '6-D sky ride'. A giant *IMAX* screen is due to be constructed soon in Central Park.   **Festivals** For further details and precise dates contact the Tourist Information Office (T6372111). **Red Sea Classical Music Festival**: an international festival held every December or January. **Red Sea Rock Festival**: 3-day festival held every April (finding budget accommodation can be a problem). **Jazz on the Red Sea**: extremely popular 4-day jazz festival, Monday-Thursday during the last week in August. **Teymaniyada**: 3-day celebration of the Middle East (music, singing, dancing, food) held every August. **Triathlon**: usually held in December.

Sports   **Airodium** Near to *Sport Hotel*, North Beach, T6372745, F6331676. Put on a special baggy suit, lay on a large mattress and then get shot into the air by a blast of air allowing you to simulate the sky-diving experience ($40). They also organize tandem sky-diving ($250). **Bird-watching** *Birders Club*, SPNI Field School, T6372021. *International Bird-watching Centre*, HaTemarim, opposite the bus station, T6335339, F6376922. (Sunday, Tuesday, Thursday 0900-1600, Monday, Wednesday 0900-1300, 1600-1900). **Bridge** *Philip Murray Cultural Centre* every Monday night (see 'Cultural centres', page 405). **Cycling** *Red Sea Sports Club* (see 'Tour companies', page 406) offer mountain bike hire ($8 per hr, $20 per day). **Desert safaris** *Red Sea Sports Club* (see 'Tour companies', page 406) offer self-drive jeep safaris ($35 half-day; $48 full day) or full day guided tours $55. **Diving** There are numerous companies offering diving and dive equipment rental. Note that you'll have to pay for a medical examination ($10-25) and insurance ($15). Yoseftal Hospital has a decompression chamber. Most of the dive companies also hire out snorkelling gear for around 35 NIS per day. The prices below are from the Red Sea Sports Club and are about the going rate: Full equipment rental (including unlimited air refill) $50; introductory dive $45; check out dive $42; refresh dive $42; private guided dive $50; guided night dive $35; boat dive to Japanese Gardens $40; boat trip to Coral Island (including 2 dives, full equipment, lunch, visa) $130; 1 dive (including full gear, transfer to dive site) $30; 2 dives (including full gear, transfer to dive site) $54; introductory dive with dolphins $61; guided swim with dolphins $51; 6 day package (12 dives, tanks, weights) $120-200; 1 week package with dive with dolphins, dive at Coral Island, 2 dives in Sinai, 2 dives in Jordan, trip to Petra, 1 dive in Eilat (including transfers, accommodation, tanks, weights, but not visas, border taxes, entry fees) $632; Sinai diving safaris, 1-5 days, $99-495 (excluding visas, border taxes); Jordan diving safari including 4 dives, accommodation, trip to Petra $260; PADI Open Water 5 day course $275 (logbook $15); PADI Advanced 2 day course $220. *Aqua-Line Diving*, Almog (Coral Beach), T6326628. *Aqua-Sport*, Almog (Coral Beach), T6334404, F6333771. Variety of dive packages, night dives, wreck dives, PADI courses etc. *Coral Sea Divers*, *Carlton Hotel*, Coral Beach, T6370337, F6370486. *Diver's Village*, South Beach, T6372268. *Eilat Divers Supply*, Amtal Export Park, off Ha'Arava, T6315552, F6315554. Diving supplies discount warehouse, all you need. *Leonardo*, *Holiday Inn*, T6317772; *Lucky Divers*, *Galei Eilat Hotel*, T6335990; *Marina Divers*, near *Reef Hotel*, Eilat–Taba Rd, T6376787, F6373130. Full equipment rental $42 per day, refresher dive $44, check-out dive $44, guided dive (full equipment and transfers) $28 1 dive or $44 2 dives, plus all sorts of excursions and dive packages. *PADI 5-Star Dive Centre*, *Crowne Plaza Hotel*, Lagoon. *Siam Diving Centre*, Almog (Coral Beach), T6370581. Guided dives, PADI courses, diving safaris to Sinai and Jordan. *Snuba*, Coral Beach, T6372722, F6376767. 'Snuba' is similar to diving except that the tank remains on a small raft on the surface (ages 8 and above, max depth 6 metres, approx 1¼ hours). **Fishing** Red Sea Sports Club rent out boats and gear for a 6 hour deep sea trip (around $400 for 6 people). **Glass bottom boat tours** *Coral 2000*, Underwater Observatory, T6373214, F6376337. Tours at 1000 1130 1300 1430. *Galaxy*, Spiral House, near *Moriah Hotel*, T6316360, F6316354. Tours at 1000 1200 1330 1530 1700. *Israel-Yam*, T6375528. Tours at 1030 1300 1530. *Jules Verne Explorer*, T6377702. Departs 1000 1230 1500 daily. **Gym** Try the *Country Club* at the *Sport Hotel*, T6333333. **Hiking** *Nature's Way*, HaTemarim, T6370648. Ecology hikes to Eilat Mountain Reserve. *SPNI Field School*, Coral Beach, Eilat–Taba Rd, T6372021, F6371771. This is an indispensable source for information on hiking in the region (and the Negev in general). They also sell the 1:50,000 map of the Eilat Mountain Reserve (the only sheet that has been translated into English). **Horse and camel riding** *Red Sea Sports Club* (see 'Tour companies', page 406) offer 2½ hour camel trips $30, 4 hour camel trip $40, horse-riding $35 per hour, $45 for 2 hours. *Texas Ranch*, near to Dolphin Reef, T6376663. Horse and camel riding as well as full and half-day treks further afield (2½ hours $30 adult, $22 child). *Camel Ranch*, Wadi Shlomo, T6370022. (Summer 0900-1300 1700-2100, winter 0900-1300 1500-1900). *Solomon's Chariots*, Nahal Shlomo, T6340990. Donkey-cart chariot rides. **Quad bikes** Red Sea Sports Club (see 'Tour companies', page 406) lead 1 hour guided tours $35. **Sailing** *Nautical & Sport Association*, Northern Marina, T6334272, F6378114. Hires out 420s, Lasers, Toppers by the hour. *Nirvana*, T05-0349190. Sailing cruises plus some water-sports. *Yacht Eilat*, T6376768, F6337787. **Shooting** *Red Sea Sports Club* , T6382243, (see 'Tour companies', page 406) offer lessons ($30), live firing, and computer-generated shooting at their range at the *Ambassador Hotel*. **Skydiving** Tandem skydiving from 12,000 feet (40-45 seconds free fall), T6372745 or T05-2629004. **Squash** *Country Club*, *Sport Hotel*, T6303338. **Swimming** *Municipal Swimming Pool*, Yotam, near the Tourist Information Centre, T6367236. May-October daily 0900-1745. Most hotels have at least one pool. **Tennis** *Isrotel Tennis Centre* , *Sport Hotel* , T6303338. **Water-sports** There are numerous

The Negev

companies in Eilat offering a variety of watersports. The following prices are from the Red Sea Sports Club and are about the going rates (see 'Tour companies', page 406). **Boating**: paddle boat $14 per hour; canoe $8 per hour; motor boat $35 per hour; speed boat $65 for half an hour, $120 per hour; bob-ski $8 per half-hour; jet ski $25 per half-hour; banana $8 per 10 minutes. **Parasailing**: $35 per 10 minutes. **Water-skiing**: $30 per 15 minutes; $60 per half-hour lesson. **Windsurfing**: lessons $25 per hour ($100 per 5 hours, $175 per 10 hours); board rental $17 per hour, $68 per 5 hours, $120 per 10 hours, $205 per week, $375 per 2 weeks.

Shopping   **Books**   B.J.'s Books, New Tourist Centre, T6340905. Buys and sells used books, 50% credit when returning used books, also internet and email facilities. **Steimatzky** have branches at the Central Bus Station and in Mall Ha'Yam. **Camping/outdoor gear** There's a good place in Mall Ha'Yam. **Clothes** *Gianni Versace* have a boutique at the *Royal Beach Hotel*, T6368876. **Duty free** *Sakal Bros.* have branches at both airports, T6372274. **Jewellery** *Caprice*, 3 Hatushiya Lane, T1-800-202929. *H Stern*, at Mall Ha'Yam plus *Dan Eilat*, *King Solomon Palace*, *Moriah Plaza*, *Neptune*, *Princess*, *Royal Beach* hotels. *Malkit*, 457 Hadekel, T6373372. see also *Eilat Stone Mines* in 'Sights' on page 394. **Market**   There's a craft market every Thursday on Hatmarim, opposite the bus station. **Photography** *Marina Photo*, Royal Beach Promenade, T6334103. Film, 1 hour developing and printing. **Shopping centres** *Mall Ha'Yam*, North Shore, T6340006. Sunday-Thursdaay 0930-2300, Friday 0900-1530, Saturday sunset-2400. Now eclipses Eilat's older malls: food court, cinema, Sega World, fast food restaurant, just about any type of shop you could want.

Transport   **Local buses**   The most important local bus services are routes 015 and 016 (see 'Getting around' on page 391).

Long distance buses   The **Central Bus Station** is on HaTemarim (information T6365111). Tickets should be reserved at least 2 days in advance (4 days during the high season). The information office is surprisingly helpful (timetable in English). There are toilets and snack places. The exact times may change during the lifespan of this handbook, though frequencies rarely alter.

   Be'er Sheva via **Eilat Mountain Reserve** and **'Uvda airport** (Route 12): Bus 392, Sunday-Thursday 0630 0900 1300 1500 1700, Friday 0630 1230, 3 hours, 45 NIS. **Haifa** (via **Be'er Sheva**, **Hadera** and **Netanya**: Bus 991, Sunday-Thursday 0830 1430, 2330, Friday 0830, Saturday 1530 2330. **Jerusalem** via **'En Boqeq**, **Masada** (2 hours 20 minutes), **'En Gedi** (3 hours): Bus 444, Sunday-Thursday 0700 1000 1400 1700, Friday 0700 1000 1300, Saturday 1630 1900(peak season), 4 $\frac{1}{2}$ hours, 56 NIS. **Tel Aviv** via **Mizpe Ramon** and **Be'er Sheva** (3 hours, 45 NIS): Bus 394, Sunday-Thursday 0100 0400 0500 0630 0800 0930 1100 1200 1300 1400 1500 1600 1700 1800, Fri 0100 0500 0630 0800 0930 1100 1230 1400, Sat 1130 1300 1400 1500 1600 1700 1800, 4 $\frac{1}{2}$ hours, 56 NIS. **Tel Aviv**: Bus 393, Sunday-Thursday 1900 2000, Friday 1500, Saturday 1900 2000.

   For details on getting to Jordan and **Sinai (Egypt)**, see box on page 418, and the relevant 'Getting there – overland' section on pages 32-34.

Car hire *Avis*, Tourist Information Centre, T6373164. *Budget*, Shalom Centre, T6374124. *Eldan*, Shalom Centre, T6374027. *Eurodollar*, T6371813. *Europcar*, Shalom Centre, T6374014. *Hertz*, Red Canyon Centre, T6376682. *Reliable*, *Etzion Hotel*, HaTemarim, T6374126. *Thrifty*, Shalom Centre, T6373511.

Taxis   Drivers must always use their meters. Fares are the same whatever the number of passengers (maximum 4). There's an extra charge 2100-0500. They can charge 2 NIS per piece of luggage (and are entitled to charge 2 NIS extra for telephone

Working in Eilat

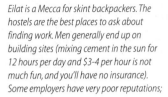

Eilat is a Mecca for skint backpackers. The hostels are the best places to ask about finding work. Men generally end up on building sites (mixing cement in the sun for 12 hours per day and $3-4 per hour is not much fun, and you'll have no insurance). Some employers have very poor reputations; do not allow wages to build up (insist on daily payment). Women tend to find work in bars and restaurants (wages may be minimal or even non-existent and you'll be dependent on tips). Sexism rules in Eilat: wear your shortest skirt to the interview.

call-outs). *Adom*, T6333365. *King Solomon's*, T6332424. *Sivan*, T6330444. *Taba*, T6333339.

Air 'Uvda (Ovda) Airport (T6375884/6375880) is located some 60 km north of Eilat, (1 hour along Route 12, see 'Around Eilat' map), and handles most international flights. Since it is primarily a military airport it is not shown on most maps. Bus 392 (between Eilat and Be'er Sheva) passes the airport 5 times per day (only twice on Friday), or a taxi between the airport and Eilat will cost around 150 NIS. If arriving on a package tour, transfers are usually arranged for you. The airport is rather basic, although there is a tourist information counter, cafeteria and a bank (T6375696). Note that there are plans to build an 'Israeli terminal' at Jordan's Aqaba airport (14 km north of Aqaba). **Eilat Airport** (T6373553) is slap bang in the city centre (the travel brochures don't mention the noise when they describe Eilat), and handles mainly domestic flights run by *Arkia, IsrAir, El Al* and *Laufer*. You can probably walk there from most hotels (otherwise it's a short taxi ride or bus 015 stops outside).

Sherut/service taxi *Yael Daroma*, T6336001, offers inter-city taxi service.

Sea/boat Those arriving in Eilat by private boat should contact *Eilat Marina* in advance (T6376761, F6315454).

Airline offices *Arkia*, 12 Bridge House Tourist Service Centre, T6384888/6338001 (flight information T6371711; 'Uvda T6376344; Eilat airport T6376102). *IsrAir*, T6340666 (Eilat airport T6325966). *El Al*, Khan Amiel Centre, Ophira Park, North Beach, T6331515 ('Uvda T6372580; Eilat airport T6371515). *Laufer*, T6376890 ('Uvda T6372377; Eilat airport T6376890).

Banks There are numerous banks on HaTemarim, Hativat HaNegev and in the New Tourist Centre (beware of poor rates or high commission), with most having ATMs. There are a number of money changers including *Change*, Reichter Centre, T6371646, Spiral Centre Marina (opposite Bridge House), T6316440. *ChangeSpot*, Mall Ha'Yam, T6340049, King's Wharf, T6318450, Etzion Hotel Shopping Centre, T6325151. The post office offers commission-free foreign exchange. Hotels are bad places to change money.

Communications Area code: T07. **Post offices**: main branch for poste restante, international phone calls and foreign exchange is in Red Canyon Centre, HaTemarim, T6372302 (Sun Mon Thu 0745-1230 1600-1830, Wed 0745-1400, Fri 0745-1300). There is a branch post office in Mall Ha'Yam. **Internet/email**: *B.J.'s Books*, New Tourist Centre, T6340905. Internet, email, scanning, word processing (Sun-Thu 1000-2200, Fri 1000-1800). *Internet One Alls*, Bridge House Tourist Service Centre. 12 NIS per 15 mins, 22 NIS per 30 mins, 35 NIS per 1 hr, Eilat (and Israel's) most expensive internet café? *Unplugged*, New Tourist Centre. Internet use 7 NIS per 15 mins, 25 NIS per hour, see also under 'Bars', page 401, and 'Budget eating', page 400. **Telephones**: HaTemarim is the best bet for discount phone call offices. *Phone Home* on Al Mogim is in a very dodgy area.

Cultural centres *Philip Murray Cultural Centre*, Hativat HaNegev/HaTemarim, T6372131. Classical music concerts, theatre, plus other events.

Directory

The Negev

Embassies and consulates See 'Eilat' map for locations. **Belgium, Luxembourg**, T6375556; **Denmark, Germany, Norway, Sweden**, T6334277; **Egypt**, 68 Ha'Efroni, T6376882 (visa services Sun-Thu 0900-1100, morning deposit, afternoon collection, see page 418; **Finland**, T6373761; **France**, T6332826; **Italy**, T6340505; **Switzerland**, T6372749; **UK**, T6372344 (may be able to assist other English-speaking countries).

Hospitals and medical services Chemists: at least a dozen, including *Pharmacy Eilat*, Eliot, 25/4 Beit Evrona, T6375002. Specializes in homoeopathy (0815-1315 1615-2000); *Super Pharm*, City Gate Centre, T6376870. Sun-Thu 0900-2200, Fri 0900-1500, Sat 0900-2200, or Mall Ha'Yam, T6340880, Sun-Thu 0900-2400, Fri 0900-2300, Sat 1100-2400. **Hospitals**: *Yoseftal Hospital*, Yotam, T6358011. The hospital has a decompression chamber.

Laundries *Kviskal*, Razin Centre, HaTemarim, T6374838. Open 0800-2200, laundry and dry cleaners, will collect and deliver. *Micky Mouse Laundromat*, 99/1 Al Mogim. **Libraries** *Municipal Library*, Hativat HaNegev.

Tour companies and travel agents *Arkia*, 12 Bridge House Tourist Service Centre, T6338001. *Camel Riders*, Shacharut, 40 km north of Eilat, T6373218, F6371944. 2-day Negev camel safari $165, 4 days $320, 6 days $480. *Egged Tlalim*, near Central Bus Station, T6365122. Offers a variety of 'around Israel' tours (1-day Masada, Dead Sea, 'En Gedi $80; 1-day Jerusalem, Bethlehem $66; 2-day Masada, Jerusalem, Bethlehem $190). *Johnny Tours*, Bridge House, T6316215, F6316217. Sinai, Cairo, Jordan, in English, French, German, 33 years experience. *Kisuki Water Sports*, near Mall Ha'Yam, T6372088. Parasailing, jet-ski, tubes, banana boat, speed boat, pedal boats, kayak rentals. *Manta Diving Centre*, Coral Beach, T6370688, F6370655. *Neot Hakikar*, Tourism Information Centre, 1 Yotam, T6326281, F6326297. Reputed agency offering Sinai tours (various lengths, tailor-made), Petra trips (1-day $139, 2-days $210), St Catherine's (1-day $60, 2 days $165). *Peltours*, **Neptune Hotel**, North Beach. *Red Sea Sports Club*, King Solomon's Wharf, T6333666, F6333307. Full range of diving and water-sport options (see 'Sports', page 402), plus yachting, jeep safaris, tours etc. Their 1-day cruise to Coral Island is $49 (including lunch and all taxes). *Sea World*, Coral Beach Marina, T6371659. Parasailing, dolphin cruise, glass bottom boat, yacht cruise, water-skiing, motor boat, banana boat. *Thru Us Travel*, Bridge House Tourist Service Centre, T6316886. 1-day tours to Petra ($139 excluding visa fees and border taxes, service described as 'impeccable' by one reader), 2-day tours to Cairo ($165). *Travelis Eilat*, Khan Centre, Ophira Park, T6331329, F6331087. 1-day tours to Petra ($139), 2-day tours to Cairo ($150), 1-day tours to St Catherine's ($60), 1-day to Dead Sea ($29), 5 hrs to Timna Park and Hai-Bar ($39), discounts often on offer. *United Tours*, New Tourist Centre, T6371726, F6371752. Daily tours all over Israel. *Y.L. Johny VIP*, Shalom Centre, 2nd floor, T6340368, F6340389. Half-day Timna $42, 1-day Masada and Dead Sea $78, 1-day Masada and 'En Gedi $96, 1-day St Catherine's (Sinai, not including border taxes) $58, 2-day Sinai and St Catherine's $140 (not including border taxes), 1-day Petra (Jordan, not including border taxes/visas) $139, 2-day Petra and Wadi Rhum (not including border taxes/visas) $250, Cairo 2-days $180, Cairo 3-days $265 (not including border taxes/visas).

Tourist offices Tourist Information Office: junction of Yotam/Ha'Arava, T6372111. Sun-Thu 0800-1800, Fri 0800-1400, Sat 0800-1200, lots of brochures, free maps, discount vouchers etc. There is a *Commercial Information Office* nr Mall Ha'Yam, which will assist in booking accommodation.

Useful addresses and phone numbers Police: T100 (T6362444). Ambulance: *Magen David Adom* T101 (T6372333). Fire: T102 (T6372022). Other: *Eco Peace Friends of the Earth*, T6336575. *Municipality*, T106. *Tourist Patrol*, T6367296.

Around Eilat

There are a number of attractions in the area around Eilat, most of which are located along Route 90 to the north. Descriptions of the various hikes in the Eilat Mountain Nature Reserve begin on page 412 below.

Hai-Bar Yotvata Wildlife Reserve

This reserve is located off Route 90 (Arava Road) about 35 kilometres north of Eilat. It has its origins in the Hai-Bar Society, an organization founded in the 1960s with the twin aims of reintroducing populations of wild animals indigenous to Israel that had disappeared, and the increased protection of existing endangered species. Now under the administration of the Nature Reserves Authority, the reserve has developed significantly, with a programme that has reintroduced many of the animals mentioned in the Bible, such as the Arabian oryx, African wild ass and onagers. Some species not indigenous to Israel, such as addax and Scimitar-horned oryx, are now being bred here for reintroduction into their original habitats abroad. A successful predators breeding centre, featuring canines, felines, hyenas, raptors and reptiles, was established in 1986.

There are three sections to the reserve. The first section is the **open area**, where the various species are left to wander in a quasi-natural space. The **Predators Centre** features a number of endangered species, plus an 'unpleasant' collection of rodents and scorpions. There is also a large enclosure housing a variety of vultures. The reserve also features a **Desert Night Life Exhibition Hall**, where it is possible to observe nocturnal and semi-nocturnal wildlife. A minibus tours the 10 kilometres of tracks within the reserve every hour on the hour (summer 0900-1300, winter 0900-1400), with a guided tour of the Predators Centre and the nocturnal room. It is also possible to watch the evening feeding sessions. ■ *Route 90/Arava Road, T07 63673057. 0830-1530 daily. Admission including tour , adults 20 NIS, children 12 NIS. Call ahead to book tours. Public transport options from Eilat are the same as for Timna Park, see below.*

Timna Park

Timna Park covers 60 square kilometres and is an expanse of unusual rock formations, stunning views, archaeological sites, and the oldest known copper mines in the world. A variety of hiking and driving trails are marked through the park, taking in the most spectacular and unusual sights, and requiring different levels of physical exertion from seven hours walking to no more than 30 minutes away from the car.

Phone code: 07
Colour map 4, grid C3

Ins and outs

Getting there

Timna Park is located 27 kilometres north of Eilat on Route 90 (Arava Road), so virtually any bus leaving Eilat can drop you at the turning to the site (from where it's three kilometres to the entrance). **NB** Get off at the sign for Timna Park, and not for Timna Mines. Returning to Eilat requires standing by the main road and flagging down any passing vehicles. Most Eilat travel agents run tours to Timna Park (half-day for $40).

Getting around

The driving tour can also be undertaken on foot, though hikers should be aware that most of the attractions are three to four kilometres apart. If you intend undertaking one of the longer walking routes, you should be suitably equipped with a plentiful

The Negev

water supply, sun-block and a wide-brimmed hat. It is also advisable that you inform the park staff at the entrance where you intend going, how long you plan to take, and to check in with them when you complete your trip. Keep to the marked paths, and beware of unmarked (and very deep) mine shafts. Before commencing any tour, it is worth viewing the short video about the park that is shown at the park entrance. You can also hire an Easy Guide for 15 NIS.

The Park

Geology   The park is encircled on three sides by the high Timna Cliffs, formed of light-coloured geologically continental sandstone, overlaid with marine sedimentary rock stacked in distinct layers of dolomite, limestone and marl. Copper carbonate ore nodules, mixed with azurite, cuprite and paratacamite, as well as copper silicate deposits, are located at the base of the cliffs and provided the basis of the substantial copper mining and smelting industry that developed here. The Timna Cliffs are open on the east side, where the four wadis that drain the valley (Wadi Timna, Nehustan, Mangan and Nimra) drain into the Arava depression. At the centre of the park stands the Mt Timna plateau, a darker igneous intrusion of granite and syenite.

History   The copper mines at Timna were previously popularly known as 'King Solomon's Mines', with the Bible relating how Solomon (965-928 BCE) derived great wealth from the export of this valuable commodity. However, copper mining and production at Timna predates Solomon by a considerable period and, further, there is absolutely no archaeological evidence that suggests that the people of Israel or Judah were engaged in any form of mining in this area. In fact, the Bible makes no actual reference to King Solomon's Mines, and it is probably true that throughout almost the entire period of the United Monarchy and the subsequent Kingdoms of Judah and Israel, the mines at Timna lay abandoned.

Excavations suggest that quarrying for copper ore and primitive copper-smelting began at Timna around 6,000 years ago. The most intense period of activity at the site was during the 19th and 20th dynasties of the Egyptian New Kingdom (c. 1320-1085 BCE), with mining continuing through the Iron Age IA-IIB (c. 1200-700 BCE), and periodically through to the second century CE of the Roman period. Production in the region has subsequently continued from the beginning of the Early Arab period (638 CE) until present day.

Sights

Driving/short walking route   This is the main marked route, and it begins at the main park entrance. Total tour time is about three and a half hours (on foot). Head west along the bed of the Wadi Timna, passing the Mt Timna plateau to your left. After three and a half kilometres, turn right at the sign for the Mushroom, Chariots and Arches. After one and a half kilometres you pass the parking area for the Mushroom (stop here on the way back), before reaching the junction for the Chariots and the Arches 500 metres further on. Turn left here for the Arches (three and a half kilometres further).

The arches & ancient mines (1)   From the car-park, follow the blue-and-white signs. These lead to a series of attractive rock formations in the white sandstone at the foot of the cliffs, most notably a series of eroded arches created by wind and water action. The right fork leads to a cave entrance to the Late Bronze Age–Iron Age I (c. 1550-1000 BCE) mining system, and a number of ancient shafts. This area was one of the major mining centres, with approximately 10,000 shafts found in the immediate vicinity. Investigation has revealed two different systems of mining here. One technique involved the sinking of shafts, some as deep as 37 metres, into the conglomerate rock in search of rich veins of copper ore. Alternatively, narrow galleries (1 metre high and 70 centimetres wide) were driven horizontally into the white sandstone, sometimes being widened if the copper strike was rich enough. The galleries were reached via vertical shafts. The Late Chalcolithic shaft-and-gallery system mines found here (c. 3300 BCE) are the earliest known examples of such copper mining techniques. Many of the highly advanced Egyptian New Kingdom shaft-and-gallery mines (Late Bronze Age–Iron Age I, c. 1550-1000 BCE) display a level of sophistication only known previously in Roman and later period mine engineering. According to Rothenberg, the discoveries made here "called for the revision of the history of mining".

Returning to the marked trail, you descend some steps (on your bum) into a ravine, climbing out via a series of rock cut steps. At the top of the low hill is a mine shaft 37 metres deep, plus an all-round panoramic view of the area. The saucer-shaped round areas that are visible all around are actually silt-filled mining shafts that were dug through the rock cover into the sandstone below. The route passes a number of mining dugouts and Chalcolithic shaft sites. This walk takes about one hour. Just before returning to the parking lot, the route passes the start of the 'Arches ancient mines and canyons trail' (see page 411).

Return to the first junction, and turn left at the sign for the Chariots (two and a half kilometres).

The Chariots (2)

From the parking lot, a steep, marked path leads to a cliff-face that contains a number of drawings thought to date from the Egyptian/Midianite era. The Midianites, along with the Kenites, were a northern Arabian people who operated many of the Egyptian mines in the region. The drawings on the sandstone cliffs feature deer and ostriches, plus a chariot drawn by ibexes. A walkway leads into a canyon where it is possible to see the better preserved chariot drawings. On the right are oxen-drawn chariots containing Egyptian soldiers armed with shields and axes. In the centre a group of hunters handle dagger, bows and arrows. This short walk takes around 20 minutes.

Return to the junction, and the Mushroom is indicated on your right.

The Negev

Timna Park

Sketch Map

1	Arches & ancient mines
2	Chariots
3	Mushroom & smelting camps
4	Slave's Hill
5	Solomon's Pillars
6	Hathor Temple
7	Timna Lake
8	Geological Trail
9	Ancient Mines
10	Ma'ale Milhan

Timna Mushroom

The Negev

The Mushroom & the smelting camps (3) Although the Mushroom, an excellent example of desert erosion, is the main photo opportunity here, the importance of this site lies in the New Kingdom smelting camp located here (c. 13th-12th centuries BCE). Within a fenced-off area lie the remains of a number of buildings that were formerly accommodation units and storerooms around the main courtyard of the smelting camp. Four furnaces were discovered here, and it's possible to see a reconstruction, complete with a description of the smelting process (the original furnaces being in the Eretz Israel Museum in Tel Aviv). Amongst the many finds at this site was a corbeled vault containing the remains of two Proto-Boskopoid skeletons of African origin. 70 metres to the west of the smelting camp, at the top of the low hill, is some form of sacred area, perhaps a *bamah* or cultic high place.

Returning to the junction on the main road that leads from the park entrance, turn right (west). Take the first left, leading to Slave's Hill, Solomon's Pillars and the Hathor Temple.

Slave's Hill (4) Approximately 500 metres along this road, to your right, is a low, flat hill labelled Slave's Hill (though there is no explanation as to why this name has been given). This is the site of a large smelting camp dating to the 14th-12th centuries BCE, with some evidence of a brief period of reoccupation in the 10th century BCE. The camp was surrounded by a strong defensive wall, parts of which remain, with two towers guarding the entrance gateway. Large quantities of slag, as well as remains of furnaces and workshops, attest to the function of the site.

Solomon's Pillars (5) Further along the road (one kilometre), you come to Timna Park's most outstanding natural phenomenon; huge eroded columns of Nubian sandstone known as Solomon's Pillars. It is thought that the 'pillars' here were created over time by water seeping into deep cracks that formed in the sandstone cliffs of Mt Timna during the creation of the Great Syrian-African Rift Valley. The pillars are particularly attractive in the late afternoon light (if they're not obscured by tour coaches that is). A path to the right leads to some Egyptian rock carvings, though it's very difficult to see anything at all (look high above you, at the bottom of the flat bit of rock). The path descends via some steps to the Hathor Temple/Sanctuary.

Hathor Temple/ Sanctuary (6) The discovery of the Hathor Temple by Rothenberg in 1966 proved conclusively that the copper mining activities in the southern Negev region were controlled by the Egyptian pharaohs, in collaboration with the Midianites (though local people were employed as workers). An open shrine was built here on the site of Chalcolithic remains during the reign of the Egyptian pharaoh Seti I (1318-1304 BCE). Two well dressed pillars survive, although the image of the head of Hathor, the Egyptian goddess with the cow-like ears, appears to have been deliberately defaced by the Midianites. The temple appears to have been rebuilt numerous times, having been severely damaged by earthquake on at least one occasion. Votive offerings, both Egyptian and Midianite, were found within the site.

Retracing your steps to the main road, a left turn leads three and a half kilometres to Timna Lake. This attractive man-made lake provides a welcome splash of blue in the parched, semi-arid environment. Though the signs say 'no swimming', this doesn't seem to stop anyone. In addition to a kiosk, and shaded picnic tables, there is the very pleasant *Timna Oasis Restaurant* that serves very good meals and snacks plus a 'Bedouin tent' snack bar. It is also possible to camp at the lake. From the lake, return to the park entrance. **Timna Lake (7)**

The Geological Trail begins at the park entrance, and climbs up the east side (8) of Mt Timna for breathtaking views of the surrounding valley from the granite plateau. The trail follows red trail markers, descending at Solomon's Pillars after around three hours. It's still an hour's walk to the park entrance from here (and three kilometres back to Route 90). **Geological Trail**

This three to four hour hike begins at the Arches and Ancient Mines (1), (though these are actually seven kilometres from the park entrance). Follow the blue signs until you come to the sign-post marked 'Roman Cave, White and Pink Canyons, Solomon's Pillars'. The trail then follows black-and-white trail markers along the course of the Wadi Timna bed, via the sites known as Roman Cave, White Canyon and Pink Canyon, before arriving at Slave's Hill and Solomon's Pillars. **Arches, Ancient Mines & Canyons Trail**

This is the most demanding of all the hikes, taking around seven hours but providing some excellent views. The hike begins at the park entrance, heading north, skirting the bases of Sasgon Hill and Mt Mikhrot. There is then a steep ascent, Ma'ale Milhan (10) to Mt Milhan. The route passes along the top of Timna Cliffs, providing great views into the valley below, before making a descent between Mt Berekh and Mt Etek. The trail then joins up with the latter stages of the Arches, Ancient Mines and Canyons trail. The route is marked in brown and white. ■ *T07-6372542. 0730-1700 daily. Adults 25 NIS. For guided tours call Kibbutz Elifaz, T07-6356215. For restaurant bookings at Timna Oasis T07-6374937, open 0900-1800 daily.* **Ma'ale Milhan, Timna Cliffs & Mt Berekh hike**

Yotvata

Most people visiting Yotvata see little more than the roadhouse, made famous by its fabulous selection of dairy products, produced locally at Kibbutz Yotvata and sold throughout the country. Other visitors come to stay or use the facilities at **Ye'elim Holiday Village**. However, the oasis at Yotvata has been an important settlement since antiquity, with some scholars suggesting that it may be the "Jotbathah, a land of rivers of water" that is mentioned in the Bible (Deuteronomy 10:7). *Phone code: 07*
Colour map 4, grid B3

Located on Route 90 (Arava Road) some 51 kilometres north of Eilat (and 113 kilometres south of Ha'Arava/Sodom Junction), just about any bus to/from Eilat can drop you here. **Ins and outs**

Sights   The **Early Iron Age Fortress** (c. 1200-1000 BCE) on the small hill to the south of the kibbutz, was built to protect the Yotvata oasis since this was a major source of water and supplies for the people producing copper at nearby Timna. The **Roman fortress**, to the west of Route 90 near to Yotvata's main spring, was also built to protect the water supply, probably during the reign of the emperor Diocletian (284-305 CE). It was partially destroyed, then rebuilt, in the mid-fourth century CE, before finally being destroyed in the late fourth century CE. Parts of the ruins were converted into a police station during the British Mandate period and the remains of this building can still be seen on the east rampart.

Also in Yotvata, opposite the fuel station, is the **Red Sea Desert Visitors Centre** (T6326555), which can offer advice on exploring the region.

Sleeping and eating   C *Ye'elim Holiday Village*, Yotvata, T07-6371870. Guests can stay in pleasant a/c, 2-bed chalets around the garden, or pay to use swimming pool and water-slide facilities as day-visitors. Very popular on Shabbat. There is a restaurant at the *Holiday Village*, and a more informal cafeteria at the roadhouse/petrol station. Both serve the dairy products for which Kibbutz Yotvata is famous.

Hikes around Eilat

*The area above Eilat has been declared the **Eilat Mountain Nature Reserve**, and provides some excellent hiking ground. The reserve extends as far north as Timna Park, bounded on the west by the Egypt/Israel border, and on the east by the Edom Mountains in Jordan. With the three major rock types found here being dark hard igneous, red stained sandstone, and lighter yellow sandstone, the area is marked by some stunning rock formations in bright, vivid colours.*

Ins and outs   The only drawback to hiking here is that few of the trail-heads can be reached by regular public transport. The usual rules about hiking in the desert apply. None of the routes described below has drinking water *en route*, so you must bring your own (minimum one to two litres per person). It is not recommended that you walk during the middle of the day, so an early start is recommended, and summer is certainly not the best time to undertake these hikes. Sun-block and a sun-hat are essential. Walking boots, with some ankle support, are recommended, though by no means compulsory. It is a good idea to tell someone exactly where you are going, and what time you are due back. **NB** The hiking maps below are for **general information only**, and should not be seen as a substitute for the SPNI 1:50,000 hiking map of the area around Eilat. This is currently the only sheet of the series that has been translated into English, and it is strongly recommended that you buy it if you intend making any of these hikes (see 'Eilat – Essentials', page 403, for SPNI address).

Mt Tz'Fahot hike

Ins and outs   This hike offers good views of the Gulf of Aqaba, with the advantage that it is accessible by public transport. The trail is fairly easy, taking 2-3 hours. To reach the trail-head, take bus 015 from Eilat to the turn off for Texas Ranch (see map 'South of Eilat: the Eilat-Taba road').

The trail begins at the estuary of the Shlomo River, at the turning for Texas Ranch and the Ostrich farm. The path leads upstream for some two kilometres or so, where it meets the Wadi Tz'Fahot (**1**). The buildings here were originally scheduled to be used as a quarantine centre for animals being placed in Israeli zoos, though the project never came to fruition. Continue along the path of the Wadi Tz'Fahot, with its numerous Acacia trees in its bed, in a southerly direction. The valley becomes narrower, and is joined by a small waterfall to the right (west) (**2**). About 250 metres beyond here the path forks (**3**). A black-marked path leads right (west) towards the Gishron River, though we take the left, green trail. The path starts to climb up the ravine quite steeply (**4**), before a narrow valley joins from the right (south) (**5**). It's quite a slog up this last stretch, until you eventually reach the top of 278-metre Mt Tz'Fahot (**6**). The views down to the Gulf of Aqaba are particularly attractive in the late afternoon light, though the temptation to wait around for the sunset must be avoided, since this will require a difficult descent in the dark. The trail is marked down the east side of the mountain, joining the Garinit River, and reaching the beach area at the Coral Beach Nature Reserve. Bus 015 runs back to Eilat from here.

Mt Tz'Fahot hike

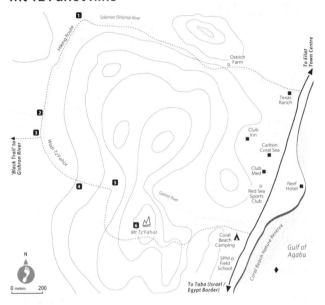

Mt Shlomo hike

This is quite a long hike, five to six hours, beginning from Route 12 to the northwest of **Ins and outs** Eilat, and finishing on Route 90 (Arava Road) to the north of Eilat. Unless you want an uninspiring walk back into town, you'll have to arrange for someone to pick you up from where the hike finishes. The hike features an excellent view from the top of Mt Shlomo, as well as passing numerous waterfalls of varying size. The trail-head is reached by leaving Eilat to the west, on the road next to the Tourist Information Centre (Yotam, then Route 12). After seven kilometres, a sign indicates right for Mt Shlomo (Solomon's Mountain). Irregular bus 392 from Eilat runs along Route 12 (see 'Eilat – transport' on page 404).

Leaving the parking lot (**1**), head north along the course of the Solomon River. The cleave through which the river runs was formed as a result of the process that created the Great Syrian-African Rift Valley. Continue north along the river bed until you come to a point where two stream beds join the Solomon River (**2**). Follow the course of the stream to the east (right) until you reach the mountain's saddle (**3**). A path leads up to the observation point at the top of Mt Shlomo (**4**), from where there are terrific views of the surrounding area. Particular impressive is the view into Moon Valley, in the Sinai to the west.

Descend Mt Shlomo on the path to the east, dropping down to the bed of the Mapalim River (**5**). The walk north along the river bed is most attractive, passing a number of waterfalls. The height and power of the water will depend upon the season (they may be dry in summer), though it's usually possible to walk through them all. You eventually reach a point where there are two falls together (**6**). Turn right (east) here, and follow the trail until you reach the Netafim River (**7**). After walking for a half-hour or so, you reach a point that is accessible by vehicle from Route 90 (**8**). If you are not being picked up here, it is a four kilometre walk down to Eilat.

Mt Shlomo Hike

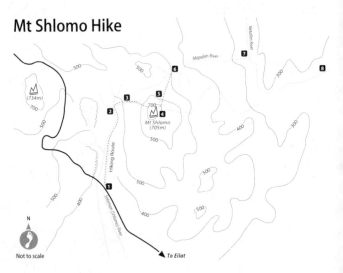

Ein Netafim and Mt Yoash hike

Ins and outs This short hike is in two parts. The first section visits Ein Netafim; a perennial spring above Eilat, where there is a good chance of seeing some bird and animal life. The second section of the hike visits the Mt Yoash Observation Point, from where there are excellent views of the surrounding area, with the option of continuing down to the Gishron River. Total walking time is around two and a half hours for the two early sections, five to six hours if you continue on to the Gishron River hike. The trail-head is reached by leaving Eilat to the west on the road next to the Tourist Information Centre (Yotam, then Route 12). After ten and a half kilometres, a sign on the left indicates Mt Yoash whilst a sign on the right points towards Ein Netafim. Irregular bus 392 from Eilat runs along Route 12 (see 'Eilat – transport' on page 404).

Turning right off Route 12, there is a sort of parking lot (**1**). It is possible to drive further down towards Ein Netafim and park there, but the road is only really suitable for four-wheel drive vehicles (and you will almost certainly be reluctant to take a hire car down here). It's a 20 minute walk down the twisting dirt path and across a dry wadi, to the lower parking lot (**2**). Having arrived at the head of the waterfall (dry), it is a treacherous descent to the spring below. You often see mountain goats here, who apparently assemble to have a good laugh at the humans attempting the narrow paths.

Having reached the bottom of the waterfall, hopefully in one piece, take the path marked in black along the right bank of the Netafim River (**3**). The path is marked by green powdered shards that, when wet, form a clayey substance from which pottery is made. After several minutes walking, a series of rock-cut steps lead down to a section of superbly coloured sandstone, with a collection of hues from pale yellow, through deep reds, to purple. Crossing the river bed, you turn left, after several minutes reaching the head of the spring (**4**). It is not uncommon to see wildlife assembled around the spring. In addition to the goats, rabbits and rodents, quite a lot of bird-life congregates here, including the Desert Swallow and the Onychognathus Tristami, with its orange-tipped wings. Though Ein Netafim is a perennial spring, this does not mean that the flow of water will be much more than a trickle flowing into a muddy puddle during the hotter months of the year. The pool here is not natural, having been built by the British in 1942, and then later refurbished.

From here, you can either retrace your steps, or follow the green trail signs back up to the lower parking lot (**2**).

To do the second section of the hike, return to the upper parking lot (**1**), and

Ein Netafim &
Mt Yoash hike

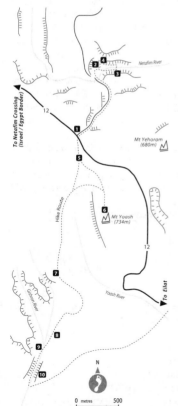

drive diagonally across Route 12 to the turning marked 'Mt Yoash'. About 100 metres along this trail is a parking lot (**5**), from where it is a 20 minute walk along the path on the left to the top of the 734-metre Mt Yoash (**6**). (You can take a four-wheel drive vehicle all the way up here). The observation point here has great views over the whole Gulf of Aqaba, with Jordan and Saudi Arabia clearly visible across the water. The Sinai Desert, in Egypt, is to the west, whilst the dark mountain to the north is Mt Shlomo (Solomon). On the return to the parking lot, it is possible to make a left turn and walk down to the Gishron River Observation Point (**7**).

From here, if you wish, you can follow the blue trail markings down to the Upper Gishron River, or return to your car. If you descend to the river, about a kilometre further along the river course is a 20-metre high waterfall (**8**). You can climb around the falls on a path to the right just before it. The path continues along the right bank of the river, passing a number of rock drawings illustrating ships, camels, goats and a mounted rider (**9**). Follow the green trail into the narrow crevice to the left (**10**). This pass is reputedly named after a larger than average girl, Tsafra, who was unable to squeeze through! The narrow canyon reaches the Yehoshafat River, then passes through the saddle between the Yehoshafat and Solomon Rivers, before reaching Route 12 several kilometres south of the turning for Mt Yoash.

Mt Hizqiyyahu Observation Point and Moon Valley

This is not really a hike, though the observation point here is worth visiting for the fine views it offers, particularly of Moon Valley. The observation point is 300 metres east of Route 12, at a point 18 kilometres from Eilat (and six kilometres from the Netafim crossing point into Egypt). Irregular bus 392 from Eilat runs along Route 12 (see 'Eilat – transport' on page 404). Information boards at the two viewpoints here explain the topography of the land. The view into the moonscape of Moon Valley, across the border in Sinai, is very attractive. It is also possible to see the Egyptian military guard post across the border, as well as the UN base that was used to monitor the international border.

Red Canyon hike

Ins and outs This is one of the best short hikes in the Eilat Mountain Nature Reserve and is suitable for all ages, though there are a couple of steep descents using ladders, and one steep ascent. Total walking time is about two and a half hours. The trail-head is reached by leaving Eilat to the west, on the road next to the Tourist Information Centre (Yotam, then Route 12). Route 12 passes the starting point for a number of other hikes, before reaching the junction for the Netafim border crossing point into Egypt after eleven and a half kilometres. Irregular bus 392 from Eilat runs along Route 12 (see 'Eilat – transport' on page 404). The road bears right (northeast) here, and after a further ten kilometres a sign indicates right for Red Canyon. Take this unpaved road (but reasonably good, even for a hire car), taking the right fork after one kilometre (the left fork, indicated as Old Petra Road emerges back on to Route 12 about 11 kilometres further on). After one and a half kilometres, you reach the parking spot (**1**).

Follow the path leading from the parking lot. After five minutes walking, there is the option of dropping down into the ravine on your left, or continuing along the path above it. The upper path eventually drops down into the ravine (**2**). There are some stunningly coloured rocks here, including some very vivid purples. Turning right, after several minutes walking, the ravine is joined from the left by the course of the Shani River (**3**). This is a seasonal wadi, dry for most of the year, though its bed is the habitat of a number of plants adapted to the seasonal drought and extreme temperatures. These include the Raetam bush, identifiable by its stork-like branches, which are bare for most of the year but sprout small green leaves and then flower after the rains. Other small shrubs found here include the Atriplex, Spinosa, Baccatus and Anabasis, some of which are edible or

Red Canyon hike

have medicinal purposes. (It is forbidden to touch or pick any plants).

As you continue along the ravine, another small wadi joins from the right. The ravine begins to narrow significantly, until you reach the Red Canyon (**4**). The Red Canyon was created by the cutting action of the Shani River. The flowing water gradually wore down the dark igneous rock into fine layers of sand. Ferrous (iron) acids gradually turned these sand layers into a harder substance: sandstone. The ferrous acids also gave the rock its deep red colour, with higher concentrations of acid producing the darker reds. The subsequent water and wind action created the beautiful shapes in the canyon. Where the canyon narrows, there are a series of metal hand rails to help you down. Unfortunately, after a couple of hours in the sun, the metal rails can become red-hot to touch. The canyon subsequently becomes even narrower, with some metal steps placed to help your descent. Further metal steps drop down another level, where the canyon walls provide some deliciously cool and welcome shade.

The narrow canyon emerges into a wider one, where a sign (**5**) offers you the option of climbing back above the Red Canyon and returning to the parking lot (about one hour), or continuing on the green route along the Shani River. The latter is recommended. The Shani River takes a sharp southeast turn (**6**), marked by a green clay wall to the left. The river bed is dotted with numerous Tamarisk trees that not only sink deep roots into the ground, but have also evolved a system whereby salt is excreted onto their leaves, collecting the night dew and then feeding off the dew as it drops to the ground. The salt left on the ground around the tree deters competitors for the water nearby.

After a further 500 metres, the Shani River is joined by another ravine from the right (west) (**7**). Turn right into this narrow ravine, and follow its gently uphill sloping course (marked by black trail signs). Numerous rock rabbits (*Procavia capanis*) can be seen scuttling about here. After several hundred metres, the black trail markers indicate an ascent to the left, above the dry waterfall (**8**). The path here is very steep and care must be taken. Follow the black trail markers past the large Acacia tree (**9**) until a junction is reached (**10**). The black route bears left, following the course of the Shani River South towards the dark bulk of the Neshef Mountains, before reaching the main road (Route 12) near to the turn-off for Red Canyon. The better route, however, is to turn right at the junction (**10**) and follow the red trail markers back to the parking area. This last section is quite up and down, and frustrating in that you keep thinking that the parking lot will be just over the next rise. It's easy to feel disorientated, but keep to the main path and it will lead to the parking lot.

Amran's Pillars and Black Canyon hike

Ins and outs This hike begins from Route 90, about 12 kilometres to the north of Eilat, where an orange sign with blue-and-white and green-and-white trail markers indicates the hiking routes. The track leads five and a half kilometres to Amran's Pillars (though it is sign-posted as '6.5 km').

The track is unpaved, though with care you should be able to get a car along here. After two and a half kilometres the path forks, with the route to the left following the green-and-white trail along the Nahal Shehoret for the Black Canyon hike. (This hike follows Nahal Shehoret on the green-and-white trail, the sandstone plain on the red-and-white trail, before arriving at Amran's Pillars on the black-and-white and then blue-and-white trails).

The right fork follows the blue-and-white trail to Amran's Pillars. After two and a half kilometres or so, the rock formations become stunning, with the

The Negev

> ### Excursions into Sinai (Egypt) and Jordan from Eilat
>
> *Many visitors to Eilat (particularly those on package tours) like to book short trips across Israel's borders into Jordan and Sinai (Egypt) respectively. A 1-day trip to Petra in Jordan (allowing you around 4 hours at Petra) will cost around $140 excluding visas (available on the border, free-$50 depending upon nationality) and border taxes (about $30 total). Four hours is nowhere near enough time at Petra (1-2 full days is really the minimum to fully appreciate it), but if this is your only chance to visit then you must go for it. A 2-day tour to Petra and Wadi Rhum will cost around $250 including accommodation and food but excluding visas/border taxes. Consult Footprint's*
>
> *Jordan, Syria & Lebanon Handbook for extensive information about these sites. A 1-day trip to St Catherine's Monastery at the foot of Mount Sinai costs around $60 excluding visa (a `Sinai permit' is available on the border) and border taxes (around $30 total). A 2-day Sinai tour (beach and St Catherine's) will cost around $140. See `Tour companies and travel agents' in the Eilat section, page 406, for a list of places offering these tours. For those wanting to book a tour to Egypt (and not just Sinai), they will require a full tourist visa (not available on the border).*
>
> *For further information see the Footprint Handbooks to Jordan and Egypt.*

lines of faulted and folded strata displayed at the surface in beautiful blacks, reds, browns and greens. Less than 500 metres further on you reach Amran's Pillars. Yellow buttressed cliffs top the huge eroded red columns of sandstone that form the pillars. They may not be as large or domineering as Solomon's Pillars in Timna National Park, but the colouration of the rock here is certainly more strident.

A popular overnight campground for trekkers (on foot and on horse or camel back) is 500 metres beyond Amran's Pillars, though the track beyond here is suitable for foot or four-wheel drive travel only. If you wish to continue on foot beyond here, you should be well equipped, and be carrying the SPNI 1:50,000 map of the area (the only sheet of the series published in English).

Hidden Valley

About 17 kilometres north of Eilat on Route 90 (and 10 kilometres south of Timna Park), an unmarked track heads west towards what is popularly known as Hidden Valley. There is a hiking route marked through this valley (black-and-white markers), though the sealed road is abruptly fenced off four kilometres west of Route 90, just as the valley sides begin to close in and the route becomes interesting. The Tourist Office or Nature Reserves Authority in Eilat may be able to offer advice on this hiking route.

Hieroglyphs at Timna

Gaza

7

Gaza

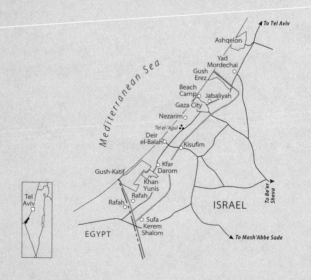

The Gaza Strip rivals Hong Kong as the most densely populated place on earth. Population density would seem to be the only point that could possibly link these two very different places, though both in fact have recently seen an end to a period of what may be regarded as colonial rule. The Declaration of Principles signed by Israel and the PLO in 1993 has seen a form of limited autonomy granted to the Palestinian Authority in some 60 percent of the Gaza Strip, though, like the Hong Kong comparison, the end of colonial rule does not appear to have ushered in an era of democracy and freedom. The published results of a recent investigation by Amnesty International provide a damning catalogue of human rights abuses committed by the Palestinian Authority against its own people, particularly in Gaza. Coupled with the 'de-development' of the Gazan economy that was a feature of the Israeli occupation and the continued ability of Israel to seal the border with Gaza at will (thus preventing migrant workers from reaching their jobs and exports from getting to market), the immediate prospects for the Palestinians of Gaza do not seem good. Promised investment from the international community has either not materialized, or has been delivered in an uncoordinated, ad hoc manner, with substantial sums possibly having been squandered or embezzled.

So why visit Gaza? Like many of the world's 'trouble-spots' it has a perverse attraction, where the depth of human kindness and personal generosity of a people who have so little to give, but are so prepared to share, is a deeply humbling experience.

Background

Geography

Geographically, the Gaza Strip is the part of the Mediterranean coastal strip of Israel known in antiquity as the Plain of Philistia (after its Philistine population). Like the coastal plain to the north, the land is agriculturally productive though soils tend to be somewhat sandier. Despite its population of 963,000 Palestinians and 3,500 Jews, the Gaza Strip is just 40 kilometres long, 10 kilometres wide, with a total land area of around 360 square kilometres.

Climate   Gaza is located in a climatic transition zone between a typical Mediterranean climate of dry, hot summers and mild, humid winters, and a steppe climate where diurnal and seasonal fluctuations in temperature are much greater. Generally, however, the Mediterranean exerts a moderating effect on temperature extremes.

History

The area known today as the 'Gaza Strip' is actually an artificial creation of Israel's independence war of 1947-48, though the main urban conurbation of Gaza City and its rural hinterland represent an ancient trading centre marking the nexus between the continents of Africa and Asia. The earliest literary reference to Gaza City (the list of Pharaoh Thutmose III's conquests from the 15th century BCE), gives a clue as to the esteem within which the city was held: 'Gazat' is described as being "a prize city of the governor". Its position as the last major town through which travellers and traders must pass before entering the Sinai desert *en route* to Egypt has ensured a long and eventful history (see 'Gaza City', page 425).

Given the reputation that Gaza has been saddled with in the last 50 years, it is difficult to imagine its former status as a "prize city". Palestinian intellectual Edward W Said describes Gaza as "the essential core of the Palestinian problem, an overcrowded hell on earth largely made up of destitute refugees, abused, oppressed, and difficult, always a center of resistance and struggle" (*Peace and Its Discontents*, 1995). Though Gaza's degeneration into this "hell on earth" is usually attributed to events surrounding the birth of the State of Israel, noted social scientist Sara Roy (who has probably written the best informed assessments of the impact of Israeli occupation of the Gaza Strip), observes that the British Mandate government was largely responsible for sowing the seeds of the territory's underdevelopment. The systematic 'de-development' of the Gazan economy, according to Roy, has been a result of successive Israeli governments' policy ever since (see box, page 425).

The 1947-48   The first major turning point in Gaza's recent history was the war of 1947-48
war   that accompanied the establishment of Israel. In a three-month period between November 1948 and January 1949, the influx of Palestinian refugees who had fled in the wake of Israel's military successes in the northern Negev and Mediterranean coastal plain saw the Gaza district's population rise from 60,000 to some 230,000. Most were accommodated in the eight large camps that developed (Jabaliyah, Beach, Nuseirat, Bureij, Maghazi, Deir al-Balah, Khan Yunis and Rafah), with a disproportionate number of Gazans still living in these camps today. Though the tents and temporary shelters have been replaced by concrete structures, the image of these camps today still remains

one of a transitory nature. Pro-Israeli commentators note how an equal number of Jewish refugees expelled from Arab countries after the 1947-48 war have been absorbed into Israeli society, whilst the Palestinians remain in camps. In the words of Benjamin Netanyahu, "Israel's attempts to dismantle the remaining camps and rehabilitate their residents have been continually obstructed by the PLO and the Arab world" (*A Place Among the Nations*, 1993). Whilst the refugees have been used as a tool in the hands of regional Arab power players, the point that Netanyahu chooses to ignore is that the refugees in the camps represent to the Palestinians a physical reminder of Palestinian dispossession, and thus constitute a powerful symbol.

Israel's offer to take Gaza Strip (including its refugees) under her suzerainty following the armistice with her Arab neighbours was rejected by Egypt. Thus, the present territorial division known as the Gaza Strip is largely the area of which Egypt assumed control throughout the period 1948-67. The strip was never formally annexed by Egypt "as it was believed that one day Gaza would be re-absorbed into a renascent Arab Palestine on the ruins of the State of Israel" (Joffe, *Keesing's Guide to the Middle-East Peace Process*, 1996).

The Gaza Strip was briefly occupied by Israel during the Suez Crisis of 1956, though it was returned to Egypt later that same year. The second major turning point in Gaza's recent history came with the Six Day War of 1967, and the subsequent Israeli military occupation. Israeli statistics indicate that in the Gaza Strip significant steps were taken in reducing infant mortality and adult morbidity during the period 1970-90, whilst both living conditions and agricultural production were improved. NGOs and human rights organizations, however, recall a régime of systematic abuse and torture of Palestinians by the Israeli military, whilst the Gazan economy was made subservient to, but not integrated with, the Israeli economy. In effect, Gaza became a source of cheap labour and a market for Israeli produced goods. Sara Roy suggests that this 'de-development' of the Gazan economy (see box, page 425) led to a situation where the GNP per capita in 1992 was in the region of $600 (compared with $13,760 in Israel in 1994), and recalls a situation in 1992 when the United Nations Relief and Works Agency (UNWRA) advertised eight garbage collectors' jobs and received 11,655 applications (see Said's *Peace and Its Discontents*, 1995).

Six Day War and Israeli occupation

The *intifada*, which effectively began in the Jabaliyah refugee camp on 9th December 1987, forced Israeli society to examine its role and objectives in Gaza more closely. As Joffe observes, "Popular unease grew over the hardship imposed on young Israeli conscripts who had to guard the area. Similarly, as the heartland for *Hamas* (see box, page 426), some Israeli analysts felt that bequeathing Gaza to PLO jurisdiction was a clever way of handing them a poisoned chalice" (*ibid*). Gaza was also seen as easier to relinquish than the West Bank for two key reasons. Firstly, unlike the West Bank, it was never really part of biblical *Eretz Yisrael*, and though Jewish settlements have existed in Gaza since antiquity they have always been seen as removed from the mainstream of the Jewish Commonwealth. "The biblical phrase 'eyeless in Gaza' refers to the plight of Samson, blinded and forced into exile in Gaza. But it also implies a region considered by Jews as unfriendly and hostile, populated as it was then by their Philistine enemies" (Joffe, *ibid*). Secondly, the signing of the peace treaty with Egypt in 1979 largely negated the argument that the Gaza Strip was required as a buffer zone.

Limited autonomy

Thus, in 1993, Israel and the PLO signed the Declaration of Principles (known as Oslo I) that provided for an immediate transfer to Palestinian

Gaza

self-rule in Gaza (and Jericho). One of the key features of all the agreements signed between the Israelis and the Palestinians is that Israel remains responsible for all movements in and out of Gaza (and the West Bank). Therefore, at any time it chooses, Israel can close the border between the Palestinian Authority (PA) areas and Israel. This has happened for prolonged periods on numerous occasions following terrorist attacks inside Israel (including, in some instances, acts of Jewish terrorism against Palestinians). As Amnesty International observe, "While the Israeli Government states that this is done in an attempt to avoid such attacks, *it is widely perceived as a form of collective punishment*" (AI Index: MDE 15/68/96). With many Gazans unable to go to work inside Israel, considerable hardship has been experienced, with recently published economic indicators underlying the gravity of the situation. The Israeli-imposed closure of Feb 1996 (that lasted until Nov 1996) saw unemployment rates in Gaza rise from 29.4 percent in September/October 1995 to 39.2 percent in April/May 1996 (source: Palestinian Central Bureau of Statistics). The problem of unemployment is compounded by the high dependency ratio in Gaza, with 53.2 percent of the population under the age of 15 and over the age of 65. Further, the low participation rate of females in the labour force has led to a process of feminization of poverty.

The rapid level of population growth (4.55 percent pa in 1994) has led to severe levels of overcrowding, with the average number of individuals per room at a staggering 2.57 (as opposed to 1.02 among Jewish families in Israel). Over 11 percent of households in Gaza that have piped water suffer from weekly water shortages, whilst it is claimed that the 3,500 or so Jewish settlers in Gaza consume 15 million cubic metres of water annually, even though the 963,000 Palestinians consume just 110 million cubic metres. The average per capita annual income in the Gaza Strip is below $800, with an estimated one-third of all households subject to absolute poverty. These figures are made all the more depressing when you bear in mind the rampant corruption and incompetence that has been a feature of PA rule (some $340 million of the PA's declared 1996-97 budget, about half, was either squandered or embezzled). It does indeed seem that the PA have accepted a poisoned chalice, and then proceeded to increase the deadliness of the poison. Critics of the 'peace process' suggest that the PA has merely become Israel's enforcer in Gaza.

Ins and outs

Getting there and getting around The Israeli-Palestinian Interim Agreement of 1995 (Oslo II) provides passage between the Gaza Strip and Israel at the following crossing points: Erez, Nahal Oz, Sufa, Karni (mainly commercial), Kisufim, Kerem Shalom and Elei Sinai. In reality, however, foreigners who wish to visit Gaza (whether as tourists or part of delegations) should use the Erez crossing point in the north (T07-6741672). On the Israeli side of the check-post foreigners should go to the hut marked 'VIP/International Organizations Office' where their passports will be examined. You will be issued with a pass that you give up as you leave Israeli territory. Once on the PA side, you will be asked to enter your passport details in the log-book. Note that the security checks are far stricter when you return to Israel, where there is the possibility of a body-search and bag X-ray. Travellers who have overstayed their Israeli visas are not recommended to attempt this trip.

The biggest problem in reaching Gaza is that, in all probability, most of the transport will be travelling in the opposite direction to which you wish to go. Presuming the border is open, early morning (pre-dawn) sees all the transport carrying migrant workers **from** Gaza **into** Israel proper. The evening sees the transport returning

The 'de-development' of the Gaza Strip

Sara Roy is amongst the most authoritative writers on the political economy of the Gaza Strip and the effects of Israeli occupation there. Roy's conclusions in papers for the West Bank Data Project, and more recently in The Gaza Strip: the political economy of de-development (Institute for Palestine Studies, Washington, 1996) bring Israel's political ideology and economic rationale into critical focus. She suggests that Israel has "sought primarily to dispossess the Arabs of their economic and political resources with the ultimate aim of removing them from the land, making possible the realisation of the ideological goal of building a strong exclusively Jewish state." Reviewing Roy's book for Middle East International (No 543, 7/2/97), Wendy Kristianasen Levitt summarizes the effect of this policy on Gaza: "So, Israel's exploitation of Gaza was not deliberate, rather part and parcel of the greater design, although it was, on the yardstick of settler states, unusually severe, depriving the population of its key resources – land, water and labour – and also of its means of developing those resources." Roy chooses to define the results of Israel's role as a process of 'de-development', or the "deliberate, systematic deconstruction of an indigenous economy by a dominant power."

Whilst the leanings of Middle East International are undeniably pro-Arab, it might be of interest to know that Sara Roy is in fact Jewish, the daughter of two Holocaust survivors whose mother was in the Lodz ghetto and Auschwitz death camp, whilst her father was only one of two Jewish survivors from the Polish town of Chelmnow. It is unlikely that her family history has influenced her writings; this information is given here since it now appears customary to delve into the background of anyone who writes anything that criticizes the State of Israel.

workers **to** Gaza. From **Jerusalem**, service taxis (or minibuses) leave from the car park opposite Damascus Gate. The one-way trip costs 25 NIS and takes about one and a half hours. Unfortunately, there can be a very long wait for the vehicle to fill up. A privately hired taxi ('special') will cost between 150-200 NIS one-way (depending upon whether it's a taxi or minibus). Bear in mind that if you return from Gaza in the evening you will have the same problem of all the traffic going in the opposite direction, and you may be forced to hire a 'special'.

An alternative way of reaching Gaza (and the best way if coming from **Tel Aviv**) is to go to **Ashqelon** on the southern Mediterranean coast. From there, take a south-bound bus towards Be'er Sheva (036/037/364/365/366) and ask to be let off at **Yad Mordechai junction**. From this junction it is just a five-kilometre walk to the Erez crossing, though there are normally service taxis waiting. The last bus back from Yad Mordechai junction to Ashqelon is at 1815 (366). If you get stuck at the Erez crossing it is often possible to hitch a lift as far as Ashqelon. The last bus from Ashqelon to Jerusalem is at 1915 (22 NIS, one hour and 20 mins) and from Ashqelon to Tel Aviv at 2240 (25 NIS, one hour).

To reach **Gaza City** from the Erez check-point pay no more than 20 NIS to hire a taxi, though it is much cheaper if you can persuade a service taxi to take you.

Gaza City

It has to be said that there is not really a great deal to see in Gaza City, with precious few reminders of its long and eventful past. In fact, most visitors are struck by the unattractiveness of the place, typified by the recent proliferation of ugly concrete block buildings. However, it is very interesting to see at first hand the

Phone code: 07
Colour map 2, grid C1

Hamas

Hamas is an acronym for 'Islamic Resistance Movement', though it roughly corresponds with the Arabic word for 'zeal'. The organization was founded in Gaza in February 1988 as an offshoot of Sheikh Ahmed Ismail Yassin's Islamic Congress, itself an organization in the mould of the Ikhwan al-Muslimun, or Muslim Brotherhood. Lawrence Joffe describes Hamas as "the pre-eminent Islamic fundamentalist movement in the occupied territories, and the biggest single rival to the PLO for support amongst Palestinians." (Keesing's Guide to the Middle-East Peace Process, 1996). The irony is that although Israel banned Hamas in September 1989 and imprisoned Yassin in 1990, Israel was partially responsible for nurturing such a movement in the first place by encouraging the growth of fundamentalists in the 1980s as a counter-weight to the secular nationalist PLO.

The organization is largely opposed to the Israeli-PLO joint accords and still calls for a jihad to liberate Palestine, though there have been recent calls by Yassin for his followers to participate in the Palestinian Authority (PA). There are persistent rumours of splits in the organization, with the mainstream political movement seeking to disassociate itself from the armed wing that has been responsible for a number of deadly suicide bombings inside Israel. The PA has arrested thousands of Hamas supporters, ostensibly to prove to Israel that it is committed to countering terrorism, though privately it is suggested that it is in Arafat's interest to silence his political rivals.

contrast between Gaza City and an average Israeli town, and this is perhaps above all a place where the people are the prime 'attraction'; a place to talk and listen to Palestinians explaining their lives.

Ins and outs

Getting there Gaza City is usually reached in a private/service taxi from the Erez crossing (see 'Ins and outs' on page 424 for full details). Most service taxis arrive/depart from Palestine Square (Midan Filastin) in Gaza City, including those to/from other Palestinian towns in the Gaza Strip (see 'Transport', page 430). Gaza's airport (located near to the Rafiah border post) is now up and running, though services remain limited (see 'Transport, air', page 430).

Getting around There are two foci of interest in Gaza: the 'Old City' area around Palestine Sq, and the beach area that is developing rapidly as Gaza's most desirable residential address. The two districts are linked by Omar al-Mokhtar St, Gaza City's main thoroughfare. You can easily walk between these two districts, or take one of the service taxis that run up and down Omar al-Mokhtar (1 NIS).

History

The importance of Gaza in antiquity as a strategically placed trading centre is best emphasized by the fact that, following its capture in the 15th century BCE by Pharaoh Thutmose III, more than fifty military campaigns were conducted in this area by the Egyptians.

Gaza is mentioned in biblical sources as being allotted to the tribe of Judah (*Joshua* 15:47; *Judges* 1:18), though in reality Israelite influence here was minimal. In fact, from the beginning of the 12th century BCE Gaza was the southernmost city of the Philistine Pentapolis that also included Askalon (Ashqelon), Ashdod, Ekron and Gath (*Joshua* 13:3; *I Samuel* 6:17; *Jeremiah* 25:20). It was here that Samson met the 'harlot' Delilah, got the haircut, was imprisoned by the

Philistines, then pulled down their temple of Dagon (*Judges 16:1-31*).

Though Gaza was conquered by the Assyrian king Tiglath-pileser III in 734 BCE, and by the Judaean king Hezekiah shortly afterwards (*II Kings 18:8*), Gaza undoubtedly remained a Philistine city. The city was subsequently occupied by the Persians, who turned it into an important royal fortress. Alexander the Great's arrival in 332 BCE saw Gaza as the only city in the region to resist the introduction of Hellenistic rule, though this resistance was short lived and Gaza was swiftly conquered and its inhabitants sold into slavery. Gaza became a northern outpost of the Ptolemies until 198 BCE, when it fell to the Seleucid king Antiochus III. Early Hasmonean attempts to take the city were unsuccessful and it wasn't until 96 BCE that Alexander Jannaeus conquered it for the Jews. However, rather than occupying the city Alexander Jannaeus chose largely to destroy it, hence the reference to "desert Gaza" in the New Testament (*Acts 8:26*).

The city's fortunes were revived under Roman rule, with a number of splendid temples built here. In fact pagan practices continued long after Byzantine Christian rule was established, only ceasing in the fifth century CE. The famous school of rhetoric that was established in the Roman period flourished under the Byzantines, whilst Palestine's reputedly largest church (the Eudoxiana) was built here. No trace of it has ever been found. Though predominantly a Christian city, it is believed that Jews began to settle in Gaza during the Roman and Byzantine periods. Remains of the mosaic floor of an early sixth-century CE synagogue have been excavated at a spot 300 metres south of the present harbour.

Gaza fell to the Arabs in 635 CE, shortly after they had defeated the Byzantine army in battle nearby. The small Jewish and Samaritan communities in Gaza both flourished under Arab rule. The Crusaders captured the city in 1149, turning it into a Templar stronghold. The 12th-century CE Crusader cathedral dedicated to St John the Baptist is preserved in the Djami el-Kebir, or Great Mosque (see below). Salah al-Din captured Gaza in 1170 and under later Mamluk rule it became the administrative capital of the Mediterranean coastal plain as far as 'Atlit. Gaza retained its administrative duties under the Ottomans, continuing in its role as a trading station on the route between Syria and

Egypt. Napoleon passed through briefly in 1799 before embarking on his Egypt campaign, before Ottoman rule was brought to an end during the First World War by the British Palestine campaign of 1917-18. Gaza's subsequent history is dealt with in the general introduction to the Gaza Strip above.

Sights

Great Mosque (Djami el-Kebir) Located to the southeast of Palestine Square, the Great Mosque (also referred to as Djami el-Kebir or Great Umari Mosque) preserves the 12th-century CE Crusader cathedral of St John the Baptist. Its façade, complete with grand arched entrance, is a typical piece of Crusader ecclesiastical architecture. The original church was a basilical building with rows of double columns

Gaza City

■ **Hotels**
1 Adam
2 Al-Amal
3 Al-Quds International
4 Cliff

5 Marna House
6 Palestine

● **Eating**
1 Al-Mankal Chicken

2 Gaza
3 Love Boat/
  Al-Andalus/
  La Mirage
4 Palm Beach

0 metres 400

separating the nave from the aisles, though the south and southeast sides were enlarged when it was converted into a mosque. The octagonal minaret was probably built on the site of the Crusader belfry. Though not certain, it is thought that the Crusader church was probably built on the site of the Byzantine Eudoxiana. ■ *Modestly dressed non-Muslims may be escorted round outside of prayer times.*

Old City

The label 'Old City' is slightly misleading since the bazaar area around Palestine Square can hardly compete with Jerusalem for character. Some of the older buildings around the Great Mosque use the *ablaq* style of decoration prevalent in the Mamluk period that features bands of red and white masonry. The short, vaulted gold market is rather similar to the medieval souq found in Jerusalem's Old City (though on a far smaller scale).

Napoleon's Citadel

The truly desperate may care to take a look at the Mamluk period villa that Napoleon used as his headquarters during his brief sojourn in Gaza in 1799. It is now a girl's school and can be found on al-Wehda Street to the east of the Great Mosque.

Al-Jundi (Square of the Unknown Soldier)

Heading down al-Mokhtar Street towards the sea you reach al-Jundi, or the Square of the Unknown Soldier. A small park has been developed here, sometimes known as Norwegian Gardens in deference to the Scandinavians' role in the Israeli-Palestinian peace negotiations. It's popular with unemployed Gazans during the day and promenading families in the evenings. The offices of UNRWA and the Islamic University lie just to the southwest of here (see map).

Gaza

Beach area

The focus of Gaza's hotels and upmarket restaurants is along the strip of coast next to Gaza's incomplete port development and rather forlorn UN Beach Club (which still has signs declaring it as the 'UN reporting and evacuation point'). The hotels and restaurants here are the places to come if you want to be in with the movers and the shakers of the PA (though you may wonder who's picking up the tab for all this entertainment). The beach here is rather dirty and miserable and will probably not appeal to visiting tourists.

'Old City' centre, Gaza City

Note that women in Gaza go to the beach and bathe fully clothed. The fishing market here is quite interesting. A road block on Ahmad Orabi/al-Rasheed Street prevents those without an appointment visiting Arafat's palace and offices.

British War Cemetery

In the Altofah East district of Gaza City (about two kilometres east of Palestine Square) is the British War Cemetery, maintained by the the Commonwealth War Graves Commission, containing the graves of Commonwealth soldiers killed in the 1917 Palestine campaign. There are also the graves of some soldiers who were brought to Gaza hospital for treatment during the Second World War North Africa campaign.

Essentials

Sleeping
■ *on maps;*
price codes see inside
front cover

There's not a wide range of accommodation in Gaza, with nothing at the cheaper end of the market, though demand for rooms is not great anyway. However, most of the hotels in Gaza are used to dealing with journalists, foreign delegations and NGO workers, all on expense accounts, and thus are all priced well above the market rate.

B *Al-Quds International*, Omar al-Mokhtar, Almena's Roundabout, T2825181, F2823240. New skyscraper at beach end of the main street, sea-view rooms with balcony, TV, phone, fridge, carpet (**A**), land-facing rooms with same facilities (**B**), plus cheaper rooms with no balcony, fridge or TV (**C**), breakfast and short orders available on room service, restaurant. **B** *Cliff*, al-Rashid, Gaza Beach, T2861353, F2820742. Comprises 4 blocks of 3 storeys, all rooms with a/c, cable TV, phone, fridge, attached bath, *Love Boat* restaurant adjacent, at cheaper end of B price category. **C** *Adam*, al-Rasheed, Gaza Beach, T2823521, F2823519. Rooms a/c with cable TV, attached bath, restaurant features reasonable meals at $10-12 a head, or $16 for fish, breakfast included. **C** *Marna House*, al-Ozyez, 1 block east of Omar al-Mokhtar, T2822624, F2823322. Attractive private villa, pleasant garden and terrace, breakfast included. **C** *Palestine*, al-Rasheed, Gaza Beach, T2823355, F2860056. Little run-down tower-block, all rooms with cable TV, a/c, fridge, some suites in **B** price category, has restaurant and large function hall popular for wedding receptions. **D** *Al-Amal*, Omar al-Mokhtar, T/F2861832. Good value 28-room hotel, most rooms with a/c, TV, attached bath, some cheaper with shared bath, intimate restaurant plus outdoor dining area, very friendly. Recommended.

Eating

In addition to the hotel restaurants, there are a number of 'upmarket' (by Gaza standard) places to eat down by the beach-front on al-Rasheed St. These include the *Love Boat*, *Al-Andalus* and *La Mirage*, and tend to specialize in fish dishes for around $15-20 per head. A form of **Indian** food can be found at *Al-Mankal Chicken Tikka* on al-Mokhtar St, next to *Al-Amal Hotel*. Very cheap falafel, shwarma and grilled meat and chicken places can be found around Palestine Sq.

Shopping

Fras Market, selling **fruit and vegetables**, is just northwest of the Municipality building. Al-Shajaia **clothes** market is southeast of Palestine Sq. Traditional Palestinian garments and decorative pieces can be bought at the **UNRWA Embroidery Shop** located close to the UNWRA HQ and the Islamic University (see map). All profits go to refugee welfare programmes. Palestinian and PLO-related souvenirs can be found at a small store to the east of al-Jundi Sq (see map).

Transport

Local Car hire *Al-Ahli*, 84 Omar al-Mokhtar, T2864007; *Imad*, T2864000; *Palestine Rent-a-Car*, 49 Omar al-Mokhtar, T2823841; *Yafa*, T2865907. Or enquire at your hotel about hiring a vehicle (usually with driver). **Taxi** *Al-Nasser*, T2861844; *Azhar*, T2868858; *Central*, T2861744; *Imad*, T2865390; *Midan Filastin*, T2865242.

Air Gaza International Airport is located close to the Rafah border post. Currently there are flights with *Egyptair* to/from **El Arish**, plus flights with *Royal Jordanian* between Gaza and **Amman** ($120 one-way). At the time of going to press a number of airlines (including *Palestine Airways* (T2822800) were planning flights to/from **Cairo**, **Larnaca** plus all the main Arab capitals. Call T2135696 for further details. **Buses** *Gaza Bus Company* run buses to **Khan Yunis** (40 minutes) and **Rafah town** (1 hour) from Palestine Sq. Service taxis are much quicker. **Service taxis**: Palestine Sq is the place to pick up a service taxi to most places on the Gaza Strip, including **Khan Yunis** (4 NIS, 25 minutes), **Rafah town** (5 NIS, 45 minutes, to get to the **Rafah border crossing** you have to change at Rafah town), **Bureji** (2 NIS),

Nuseirat (2 NIS), **Maghazi** (2 NIS) and **Deir el-Balah** (2 NIS).

Service taxis to the **Erez border crossing** tend to leave from al-Shajaia Sq, south of Palestine Sq. A service taxi should cost 4 NIS and a 'special' no more than 20 NIS. Service taxis for **Jabaliyah** (1 NIS) also leave from here. For details of getting to the Gaza Strip from points in Israel see 'Ins and outs' on page 424.

Airline offices *Egyptair*, 170 al-Wehda, T2825180; *Palestine Airway*, T2822800 (also handles most other airlines); *Royal Jordanian*, 171 Omar al-Mokhtar, T2825413. **Banks** There are money-changers around the gold market in the Old City plus various banks on Palestine Sq, though it's probably best to bring sufficient funds with you. Most banks will cash US$ TCs and some will give advances on Visa cards (with a hefty commission). **Communications NB** Gaza phone numbers have recently changed to 7 digits; if you have a 6-digit number try prefacing it with a 2. **Post offices**: *Main Post Office* is at the Ministry of Post and Telecommunications, 'Ministries Complex', al-Mokhtar, opposite Municipal Park. **Internet**: *Cyber Internet Café*, T2844704. **Telephones**: International calls can be made from *El-Baz*, 173 Omar al-Mokhtar, T2821910, F2864120, or from most hotels. **Cultural centres** The British Council have offices on Alnasrah St, just off Omar al-Mokhtar, T2825574, F2820512 (see map, Sun-Wed 1100-1530, Thu 1100-1400). See map for location of *Goethe Institute*, T/F2825584, and *French Cultural Centre*, T2867883, F2828811. *Culture & Light Centre*, T/F 2865896; *Gaza Theatre*, T2824870, F2824860; *Rashad Shawwa Cultural Centre*, T2864599, F2868965; *Science & Culture Centre*, T2830101, F2832085. **Embassies and Representative Offices to the PA** The *European Commission* have offices just off Omar al-Mokhtar (see map). **Egypt**, T2824290, F2820718; **India**, T2825423, F2825433; **Jordan**, T2825134, F2825124; **Morocco**, T2824264, F2824104; **Norway**, T2824615, F2821902; **Qatar**, T2825922, F2825932; **Russian Federation**, T2821819, F2821819; **Tunisia**, T2825018, F2825028. **Hospitals and medical services** Chemists: there are a number of chemists on Omar al-Mokhtar, al-Wehda and Ez el-Deer el-Qassam, including *Al-Fayrouz*, T2865502 and *Al-Rimal*, T2822522. Hospitals: *Al-Shifa*, off Ez el-Deer el-Qassam (see map), T2865520; *Al-Ahli Al-Arabi Hospital*, Palestine Sq, T2820325. **Places of worship** There are Baptist, Greek Orthodox and Roman Catholic churches close to Palestine Sq (see map). **Tourist offices** The *Ministry of Tourism* is on Yarmouk St, to the east of al-Saraya Sq. It may be easier to get information (and a large map of Gaza City) at the Municipality Building (see below). **Useful addresses and phone numbers** Police: T2863400. Ambulance: T101 (T2868400). Fire: T2863633. *Municipality of Gaza*, al-Mokhtar, just north of Palestine Sq; *Palestine Centre for Human Rights*, 29/21-54, next to *Al-Amal Hotel*, Omar al-Mokhtar, T2825893. There are police stations on al-Mokhtar south of Palestine Sq and on al-Mokhtar north of al-Jundi Sq.

Rest of the Gaza Strip

Beyond Gaza City there is not a great deal to attract tourists to the Gaza Strip. The site of **Tell el-'Ajjul** some six kilometres southwest of Gaza City features remains from ancient Egyptian settlements dating from c. 1670 BCE to 1450 BCE, though they are hardly inspiring. Excavations at **Deir el-Balah**, 13 kilometres southwest of Gaza City, have revealed remains from the Late Bronze Age (c. 1550 BCE) to the Byzantine period (324-638 CE), including the largest group of anthropoid coffins thus far discovered in Palestine. The site is now largely abandoned and anthropoid coffins are best seen in the Israel Museum in Jerusalem. Likewise, the site of **Ruqeish** on the coast near to Deir al-Balah (18 kilometres southwest of Gaza City) does not really warrant a special visit, despite the fact that it was the scene of a flourishing Phoenician settlement in the Late Iron Age and Persian period.

The two other major Palestinian towns in the Gaza Strip are Khan Yunis (population 200,704) and **Rafah** (population 122,865). Though neither has a great deal to see, both have lively weekly markets (Khan Yunis on Wednesday and Thursday; Rafah on Saturday and Sunday). Both can be reached by service taxi from Palestine Sqare in Gaza City. Details of the international border

UNRWA

The United Nations Relief and Works Agency (UNRWA) was created in December 1949 by UN General Assembly resolution 302 [IV], having evolved through a series of improvised organizations that sought to take active responsibility for Palestinian refugees displaced during the war that marked the creation of the State of Israel. The temporary nature of UNRWA's mandate is an affirmation that the 'refugee problem' was still perceived as being a transitory one. It was initially given a three-year life-span, but for the past 50 years the UN General Assembly has dutifully gone through the process of extending its mandate on a yearly basis. Despite this, UNRWA has grown to become by far the UN's largest organization, its 18,000 employees constituting more than the entire work force of all the other UN agencies combined.

The W in the acronym provides an insight into the duties that UNRWA was expected to perform, the term 'Works' relating to the implementation of economic development schemes centred on labour provision and economic infrastructure.

The reluctance of refugees to accept long-term infrastructural projects has led UNRWA to reassess its targets and it has now chosen to focus its resources on the provision of education and health care. About two-thirds of its employees are teachers, with UNRWA's schooling system being amongst the most admired education system in the Arab world. Almost 20 percent of its budget is spent on health care.

As large areas of the West Bank and Gaza Strip come under Palestinian Authority control, it becomes difficult to predict UNRWA's future. Some suggest that this bureaucratic dinosaur, with its anachronistic mandate, may soon die out, though as Michael Crichton and Steven Spielberg have recently proved, there's plenty of life left in the dinosaurs.

crossing between Israel and Egypt at Rafah (T07-6734205) can be found on page 34.

There are a number of Jewish settlements in the Gaza Strip and they are home to around 3,500 settlers (despite the fact that they occupy some 25 percent of the land and have hugely disproportionate access to resources such as water). The largest settlements are **Nezarim**, **Kfar Darom** and the **Gush-Katif** bloc in the south, connected to the outside world by the infamous 'lateral roads'. The latter has a number of reasonable beaches, though coming all this way just to swim and sunbathe is rather perverse. There are a couple of hotels and a youth hostel in Gush-Katif.

Refugee camp visits

Contrary to popular belief, UNRWA does not 'run' the eight major refugee camps in the Gaza Strip, but instead takes responsibility for them. With advance notice it may be possible to arrange a guided visit to one of the camps: contact UNRWA at its offices on al-Azhar St (opposite the Islamic University) in Gaza City, T07-6867044. Alternatively it is possible to visit the camps on your own (though it is courteous to inform UNRWA first). The largest camp, Jabaliyah, is conveniently located between the Erez crossing point and Gaza City. To some visitors it merely resembles a regular Indian or Pakistani town, though the contrast with neighbouring towns in Israel puts this image into perspective. Beach camp (Alshati) is located a 15-minute walk along the beach from the sea end of al-Mokhtar Street in Gaza City. The other camps are Nuseirat, Bureij, Maghazi, Deir al-Balah, Khan Yunis and Rafah.

Tel Aviv/Jaffa

8

Tel Aviv/Jaffa

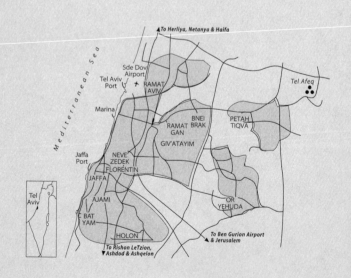

Tel Aviv is a large, dynamic metropolis on the Mediterranean coast, incorporating the ancient port town of Jaffa and blending almost imperceptibly into the surrounding settlements on the maritime coastal plain. Few foreign visitors to Tel Aviv would describe it as a beautiful city, with its sky-scrapers and urban sprawl, traffic congestion and muggy atmosphere, and apparent absence of a history in a land that is steeped in the events of the past. But Tel Aviv has attitude, and bags of it. The city's residents, and indeed visitors from the rest of Israel, love its pavement cafés, its bars and nightclubs, its shopping districts and beaches, and revel in the very fact that it is not a city dominated by ancient history. Tel Aviv is seen as a city to make money, and to spend it; if you want religion or history, the sentiment goes, then Jerusalem is just 45 minutes away. Tel Aviv is considered to be the 'most Israeli' of all the towns in the country.

Those who do spend some time in Tel Aviv will find that there is more to do than just lie on the beach, or relax in cafés and bars. There is a rich cultural life, with numerous museums, galleries, theatres and concert halls, and if you look carefully enough you will find some attractive older neighbourhoods in the process of being tastefully restored. Many visitors just pass through Tel Aviv on their way to or from Israel's main international airport nearby, which is a shame since the city has much to offer.

Ins and outs

Getting there   Most visitors arrive in Israel through Ben-Gurion Airport, some 22km southeast of Tel Aviv at Lod (see box on page 462 for details on getting to/from the airport). The Central Bus Station is located southeast of the city centre (see 'South central Tel Aviv' map), and is well connected with just about anywhere in Israel you could wish to go. Tel Aviv also forms part of the country's limited train network.

Getting around   Although most of Tel Aviv's hotels and hostels are a 5-10 mins walk from the beaches, and most of the key sights are clustered in one or two areas, it is still something of a sprawling city; it is certainly too far to walk to either the Central Bus Station or Central Railway Station. At some stage it will almost certainly be necessary to take a bus. The main routes of use to tourists are on buses 4 and 5 (see 'Transport' on page 461 for full details). Sheruts also run along routes 4 and 5, and metered taxis are also available (flag down or book in advance).

Buses running within Tel Aviv are operated by the **Dan Bus Company**. A single ride (one stop, or all the way across Tel Aviv) costs 5 NIS. A monthly pass can save you money during a prolonged stay if you use the bus more than twice per day. It is also worth buying the Ministry of Transport's *Map of Tel Aviv and Suburbs* that includes all the Dan bus routes. It is available (5 NIS) from the **Dan Information Office**, 2nd Floor, Central Bus Station. For information on Dan bus routes call T6394444 or T5614444. Most services run Sunday-Thursday 0500-2415, Friday 0500-1745, Saturday 2015-2415 and **do not run on Shabbat**.

The four bus terminals in Tel Aviv are: Reading Terminal (north of city, of little relevance to tourists); **Central Railway Station Terminal,**(sometimes referred to as Arlozorov); **Carmelit Terminal** (nr Carmel Market); and the main terminal at the **Central Bus Station** (also the departure and arrival point of most inter-city buses).

History

The origins of the modern city   Tel Aviv's modern history is probably best appreciated whilst admiring the panoramic view from the top of the Shalom Tower. It is only then, as the skyscrapers and suburbs stretch before you, that you realize how rapid the development has been; at the turn of this century, you would still have seen the predominantly Arab city of Jaffa to the south, but the area that Tel Aviv stood upon was little more than sand dunes and isolated Palestinian villages.

In 1909, a group of 66 Jewish families selected this spot to build a new Jewish settlement, having decided to leave the overcrowded confines of Jaffa. Thus, work on the construction of Tel Aviv began, financed by the Jewish National Fund, but ironically using predominantly Arab labour. Early Jewish neighbourhoods such as Newe Tzedek and Newe Shalom had been established just outside Jaffa since the end of the 19th century, but it was the gathering of the 66 families on the sand dunes of Jibalis Vineyard that heralded the foundation of modern Tel Aviv.

The early growth of Tel Aviv   By the 1920s the population of Tel Aviv stood at some 35,000, thanks largely to the third *Aliya* (1919-23) and the arrival of Jews attempting to avoid the increasingly violent Jewish-Arab conflict in nearby Jaffa. Some of these bloody confrontations had their origins in events seemingly unrelated to the Jewish-Arab conflict (the battles of 1st May, 1921, for example, actually had their origins in clashes between Jewish communists parading on May Day in support of a Soviet Palestine, and Jewish socialists who opposed them), though as

Footprint Handbooks

Travel guides to discover

Affix
Stamp
Here

Footprint Handbooks
6 Riverside Court
Lower Bristol Road
Bath
BA2 3DZ
England

Ancient city – modern name

Though the history of the city of Tel Aviv dates only to this century, there is considerable evidence of previous periods of occupation on this site. The history of nearby Jaffa can be traced back to the 15th century BCE, whilst a variety of sites now largely buried under Tel Aviv date from the fifth millennium BCE onwards. Few remains can be seen today, with the best example easily being Tell Qasileh, now within the grounds of the Eretz Israel Museum in Northern Tel Aviv (see page 449).

Tel Aviv derives its name from the title of the Utopian novel by the 'father of political Zionism', Theodor Herzl (1860-1904). The novel, published in 1902 but set in 1923, describes the visit of the two narrators to an imaginary modern Jewish state in Palestine. The title, Altneuland, means 'Old-New Land', with Nahum Sokolov's translation into Hebrew bearing the title 'Tel Aviv'. This was also the name of a Babylonian town mentioned in the Bible (Ezekiel 3:15).

the decade progressed they became more bitter and more violent. The British Mandate authorities were slow to respond, being reluctant to commit their own troops.

With continued Jewish immigration into Palestine, Tel Aviv's population (including Jaffa) stood at around 46,000 in 1931, increasing to 135,000 by 1935. The Arab Revolt of 1936, comprising increased Arab-Jewish fighting as well as strikes and civil disobedience, led to the closing of Jaffa's port and the construction of a new harbour facility at Tel Aviv.

The town continued to grow rapidly, by now far beyond the expectation of the early urban planners. Many fine buildings from this period remain, most notably those in the International Style of Bauhaus, Mies van der Rohe, Le Corbusier and Mendelsohn, though this generally unplanned expansion has today made Tel Aviv a city associated with urban sprawl. By 1947 Tel Aviv's population stood at around 200,000, with a further 30,000 Jews in Jaffa comprising about one-third of the population there. The UN vote on the partition of Palestine in 1947 led to more bitter Arab-Jewish fighting, and just prior to the expiry of the British Mandate Jaffa fell to the Jewish forces. Almost the entire Arab population of the town fled.

Independence and the 1948/49 war

On 14th May 1948, David Ben-Gurion announced the foundation of the State of Israel from the former home of one of Tel Aviv's founding fathers, Meir Dizengoff. At the conclusion of the subsequent War of Independence, Jaffa was incorporated within the municipality of Tel Aviv. The city was the country's first capital, with the original parliament building standing on what is now the site of the Opera Tower. The subsequent decision to declare Jerusalem as the undisputed and eternal capital of Israel is a move that has not been recognized by most nations, with the majority of foreign embassies still located in Tel Aviv.

Modern town

As the city expanded outwards, it all but swallowed up its former outer suburbs. Though the population of Tel Aviv is now given as around 350,000, it should be noted that their are some sizeable satellite towns all but joined to the outer municipal limits. These include Bat Yam (population 143,000), Holon (population 163,000), Ramat Gan (population 123,000), Petah Tiqva (population 151,000) and Bnei Brak (population 125,000) to name just five. Tel Aviv is happy to allow Jerusalem the title of spiritual, cultural and political capital of Israel, though Tel Aviv remains the business and entertainment centre, as well as the major international gateway.

Tel Aviv: overview

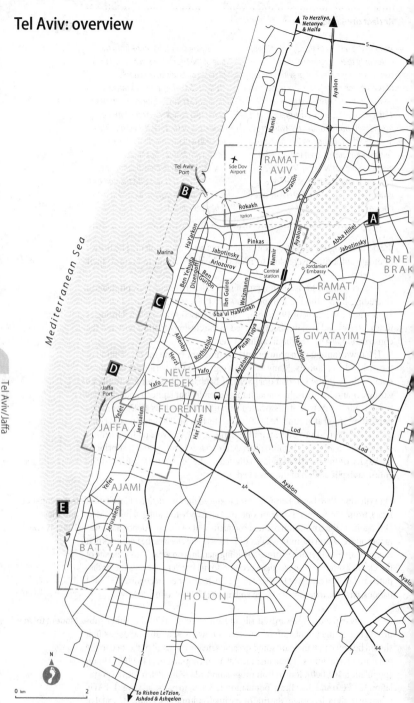

Related maps: **A.** *South central Tel Aviv, page 442;* **B.** *North central Tel Aviv, page 446;*
C. *Northern Tel Aviv, page 446;* **D.** *Jaffa, page 468;* **E.** *Old Jaffa, page 470*

Tel Aviv attitude

No guidebook to Israel would be complete without that old cliché, "Haifa works, Jerusalem prays, Tel Aviv plays". Comparisons with New York, including references to the 'Big Orange', are stretching reality a little, but visitors and residents alike are well catered for in terms of entertainment and action. In addition to the pavement cafés and bars, restaurants, cinemas, pubs and nightclubs, plus the beaches, Tel Aviv is also home to the 'higher' cultures of theatre, art and orchestra. But it is not just the presence of such entertainment facilities that appeals to many who live here: it's also 'Tel Aviv attitude'. Tel Aviv is seen as the symbol of the new Jewish state, and though many of the early Zionist pioneers spoke of a return to Zion and Jerusalem, there was also the desire to begin anew. Too much history was attached to Jerusalem; too much tragedy in the memory of the Jewish people. Places such as Tel Aviv offered the opportunity of a fresh start. Founders of the modern state such as David Ben-Gurion saw Israel as "a new socialist society of free men and women" and was less interested in the "national icons and religious relics" that Jerusalem represented

(Amos Elon, Jerusalem: City of Mirrors, 1989). Tel Aviv offered this new vision. Israel's national poet Chaim Nachman Bialik (1873-1934), who revived the literary use of Hebrew, prefered Tel Aviv to Jerusalem because "our hands have built it from its foundations to the roof. This after all is the purpose of our national renaissance: to cease being indebted to others, to be our own masters, in body and spirit". He also adapted the biblical image of Jerusalem – "joy of many generations" (Isaiah 60:15) – and applied it to Tel Aviv (Amos Elon, Jerusalem: City of Mirrors, 1989).

So whilst Tel Avivians enthuse about the city's nightlife, its beaches where you can wear and do what you like, and talk of this 'secular city' that is so different from 'boring' and 'constraining' Jerusalem, you should look beyond these symbols of a materialistic culture. They are not symbols of moral decline or frivolity; they represent confidence, and above all, normality.

Sights

Beaches

Tel Aviv's five-kilometre strip of fine white sand is less than five minutes walk from most hotels and hostels, and under 10 minutes walk from the city centre. For metropolitan beaches they are remarkably clean, though they can become very crowded and on Shabbat or holidays it's almost standing room only.

Phone code: 03

Most beaches have freshwater showers, changing rooms and toilets. The main beaches are served by lifeguards (look for the wooden huts raised on stilts), though they are not always on duty. **Black** flags mean **no swimming**, **red** flags mean **swim with caution**, and **white** flags indicate **safe swimming**. **NB** There are some deadly undertows along Israel's Mediterranean coastline, including here at Tel Aviv, and **drownings** are common. Take care. During the life-guards' strike of 1999, 20 people drowned in two months along the Mediterranean coast. **Theft** is also rife; do not leave valuables unattended. Sleeping on the beach at night is **not** recommended. Topless bathing by women is extremely rare and may attract unwanted attention. ■ *Lifeguards on duty April, May, September 0700-1700, June 0700-1800, July-August 0700-1900, T6916450.*

Each beach is named after a local landmark, generally a large hotel or a street. The northernmost beaches (north of the marina) and around the Hilton's private beach tend to be quieter, whilst the stretch from Gordon to the

Tel Aviv/Jaffa

☞ **'Orange' Walking Routes**

The Municipal Tourist Office have produced a number of walking routes (and one driving route) through Tel Aviv that take in most of the city's places of interest. Known as **Orange Routes**, ('Tapouz' in Hebrew), they are marked on the free map from the Tourist Office, and are well signposted throughout the city. Orange Routes 1 and 2 are certainly worth following if you wish to see most of Tel Aviv's sights.

Orange Route 1 takes approximately 3½ hours (including viewing museums), and takes in the following places of interest: **Museum of the History of Tel Aviv/Jaffa**, **Bialik House**, **Rubin House**, **Yemenite Quarter**, **Nahalat Binyamin**, **Shalom Tower**, **Independence Hall**,

Haganah Museum, **Newe Zedek neighbourhood**, **Suzanne Delal Centre**. Orange Route 1 begins at the junction of Ben Yehuda and Idelson.

Orange Route 2 walk takes approximately 2½ hours (excluding time spent in the art museums), and includes the following attractions: Kikar Dizengoff, **Museum of the Irgun Zvai Leumi**, **Habimah Theatre**, **Helena Rubinstein Pavilion of the Tel Aviv Museum of Art**, **Frederic Mann Auditorium**, **Tel Aviv Performing Arts Centre**, **Tel Aviv Museum of Art**, **City Hall**. Orange Route 2 begins on Shalom Aleichem (though it only begins here because this is where the Tourist Office **used** to be located).

Opera Tower is popular with tourists, young Tel Avivians, and over-hormonal Israeli males on the make. Yes, some Israeli males do still try to impress girls by dropping to the sand and doing press-ups in front of them!

The West Beach and **Charles Clore Park** are popular with families and features some of the most elaborate barbeques you are ever likely to see. Arab families tend to occupy the beach/park areas further to the south towards Jaffa, where the women bathe fully clothed. Surfers and wind-surfers tend to use the beaches around the marina, Hilton beach to the north, or the furthest beaches to the south near Jaffa.

South Central Tel Aviv

Museum of the History of Tel Aviv/Jaffa Designed by the architect Czerner and originally constructed as a hotel in 1925, this building housed the offices of the Municipality of Tel Aviv until 1965. It now has a number of displays related to the history of the city. The unusual sculpture outside is by Nahum Gutman. ■ T5255052. Sunday-Thursday 0900-1400. Free.

Bialik House This beautifully designed and furnished house, built in 1925, was for eight years the home of Israel's national poet, **Chaim Nachman Bialik** (1873-1934). Bialik was not just a great Hebrew poet, he was also an essayist, a noted story teller, a writer of children's stories, a translator into Hebrew of noted works such as *Don Quixote* and *Wilhelm Tell*, a researcher into the field of Jewish folklore, as well as being a religious scholar who worked on an important compilation of rabbinic law.

Following his death in 1934, his wife bequeathed the house and its contents to the City, since when it has been renovated and opened as a museum. ■ 22 Bialik, T5254530. Sunday-Thursday 0900-1700, Friday closed, Saturday 1100-1400. Free.

Rubin House Former home of **Reuven Rubin** (1893-1974), one of Israel's most renowned artists, the building is now home to a permanent collection of his works, as well

··

Tel Aviv: strutting your stuff

The promenade that runs the length of the sandy strip is a poseur's delight, with many young Israeli girls wearing less off the beach than they do on it. Current fashion is based around crop-tops, mini-skirts, and the type of boots Gary Glitter made popular in the 1970s, whilst for young Israeli males, wrap-around sun-glasses, a mobile phone, and an unusual breed of dog are de rigeur *fashion accessories. With the mix of Israel's youth, Eastern European immigrants, ultra-orthodox Jews, foreign tourists and backpackers, it's a great place for people-watching. Look out for the dancing outside the Ramada Hotel beachfront on Shabbat: it's extraordinary.*

··

as housing temporary exhibits. 14 Bialik, T5255961. Sunday, Monday, Wednesday, Thursday 1000-1400, Tuesday 1000-1300, 1600-2000, Friday closed, Saturday 1100-1400. 10 NIS.

This is one of Tel Aviv's oldest districts – and it shows. Yet to be gentrified like, say, the Newe Zedek neighbourhood, the Yemenite Quarter has some fine old buildings, housing some excellent traditional restaurants. To the west, the district borders the Carmel Market (see 'Shopping' on page 459).

Kerem HaTemanim (Yemenite Quarter)

On the northeast margin of the Yemenite Quarter is Kikar Magen David, so called because the road junction of six converging streets resembles the Star ('magen') of David. The road leading broadly southeast from here, **Nahalat Binyamin**, is a lively area, home to pavement cafés, street entertainers, craft-stalls and general sightseers. It is particularly appealing on Tuesdays and Fridays. About a third of the way down the street, at No 8, is a beautiful old building that serves as a reminder of Kerem HaTemanim at its peak. It's a good idea to allow some extra time to explore this area and maybe have lunch. The road leading east off Kikar Magen David, **Rehov Shenkin**, is the hunting ground of Tel Aviv's 'beautiful people', and is lined with fashionable shops and cafés.

Nahalat Binyamin and around

Just off Nahalat Binyamin to the southeast is the imposing domed structure of the **Great Synagogue**, built in 1926, though it has a bit too much concrete to be really attractive.

This museum traces the development of the Jewish Defence Force, Haganah, that later evolved into the Israeli army (IDF). The first floor of the museum opens with reconstructions of the establishment of Bar Giora and Hashomer: the early settlers' defence movements. A section of the floor is devoted to the contribution of Jewish Brigades, and their role in the British Army during World War I. The 'riots' of 1920/21 and of the 1930s are lingered over at some length.

Haganah Museum

The second floor deals with the procurement and manufacture of arms during the 1930s and 1940s, with a large collection of weaponry on display. The floor also deals with the role of the Jewish Brigade in the Second World War, and the resumption of the struggle against the British at the war's conclusion. The third floor houses more military paraphernalia, and details the establishment of the Palmach: the striking arm of the Haganah.

The new museum building adjoins the former home of **Eliahu Golomb** (1893-1945), the unofficial defence minister of the yet-to-be born State of Israel. His house served as the Central Headquarters of the Haganah, and some of his private rooms and the Haganah archive can be viewed on the

Tel Aviv/Jaffa

South central Tel Aviv

Tel Aviv/Jaffa

Related maps:
A. North-Central Tel
Aviv, page 446.
B. Jaffa, page 468.
C. Old Jaffa, page 470.

■ **Sleeping**

1 Bell
2 Beit Immanuel
3 Dan Panorama
4 David Inter-
  Continental
5 Galim
6 HaYarkon
7 Miami, Tayelet,
  Ambassador
8 Mugraby
9 Nes Ziona, Moss
10 Sea Side
11 The Office

● **Eating**

1 Arcaffe Expresso
  Gourmet, Birnbaum
  & Mendelbaum
2 Barracuda Bar,
  Dream Bar
3 Buzz Stop
4 Cafe Tamer
5 Cafe Up
6 Crazy Bagel
7 Dita Bar
8 Dr Lek, Camembert
9 Euro Bar
10 Esther's Deli,
  Zanzibar
11 Expresso Bar
12 Expresso Bar
13 Il Pastaio
14 Java Bar
15 Joey's Bar, Vog
  Dance Bar
16 Leon Cafe
17 Minzar Bar, Sandy Bar
18 Pastalina
19 Pet Cafe
20 Pimenta
21 Pitz Bar
22 Planet Hollywood
23 Rebecca Cafe
24 Seafood House
25 Spaghettim
26 Tampadulu
27 Tarkari
28 Tel Aviv Brew House,
  Session Kitchen Bar
29 The Chicago, Soweto
  Club
30 Y-Ale Bar
31 Yin Yang
32 Yotvala
33 Yuppies Bar
34 'Z' Cafe
35 Zion

ground floor. The house and museum are now run by the Ministry of Defence. ■ *25 Rothschild, T5608624. Sunday, Tuesday, Wednesday, Thursday 0800-1600, Friday/Saturday closed. 8 NIS.*

Independence Hall

On 29th November, 1947 the General Assembly of the United Nations voted by a margin of 33 in favour, 13 against, and 10 abstentions, to partition Palestine. On the day that the British Mandate was due to expire, 14th May 1948, members of the Civil Administration, People's Council, and invited guests, met here at 16 Rothschild Boulevard to hear **David Ben-Gurion** announce to the world:

'Accordingly we, the members of the National Council, representing the Jewish people in the Land of Israel and the Zionist Movement, have assembled on the day of the termination of the British Mandate for Palestine, and by virtue of our natural and historic right and of the resolution of the General Assembly of the United Nations, do hereby proclaim the establishment of a Jewish State in the Land of Israel – the State of Israel'.

The 'Independence Hall' where this historic announcement took place has been preserved as it was on that day. The rest of the building serves as a small museum detailing a pro-Zionist view of history.

The shell of the building that houses the Independence Hall is one of Tel Aviv's original structures, formerly occupied by **Meir Dizengoff**, the city's first mayor. ■ *16 Rothschild, T5173942. Sunday-Thursday 0900-1400, Friday and Saturday closed. Adult 10 NIS, student 6 NIS.*

Sotherby's

Hosting auctions, exhibitions and functions, this is one of Tel Aviv's most appealing buildings (especially the way it is lit at night). ■ *46 Rothschild, T5601666.*

Shalom Tower

Standing at the north end of one of Tel Aviv's first roads, Herzl Street, the Shalom Tower occupies the former site of Israel's first secular Hebrew language grammar school, Gymnasia Herzlia. Built in 1959, the Shalom Tower at one time claimed to be the tallest building in the Middle East. Today it functions mainly as an office block, with a few shops at the base. On the 34th floor, however, is an **Observatory** that offers a tremendous panoramic view of Tel Aviv and beyond. A small museum displays a selection of old maps that plot Tel Aviv's relentless growth, and an interactive audio-visual unit illustrates the history of Tel Aviv/Jaffa. A trip to the observatory is highly recommended for those new to Tel Aviv. ■ *9 Ahad Ha'am, T5177304. Sunday-Thursday 1000-1830, Friday 1000-1400, Saturday 1100-1600. Adults 15 NIS, students 12 NIS, tickets from first floor, elevator 9.*

Newe Zedek

Perhaps Tel Aviv's oldest residential district, Newe Zedek was established in 1887 by Jewish families moving out of the congested Jaffa neighbourhood. Many fine old building remain (eg 11 Lilienbaum), and following substantial renovation work Newe Zedek has become a much sought after address for Tel Aviv's upwardly mobile classes. It's difficult not to be charmed by the relaxed 'Mediterranean' ambience.

In the southern part of the quarter is the **Suzanne Dellal Centre**. The restored hall is now a centre for dance and drama and the plaza is used for open air performances (check *Jerusalem Post* or *What's On In Tel Aviv* for programme). With its dwarf trees, shady garden, benches and coffee shop, the centre is very well appointed. The coffee shop is popular with 'theatrical' types. ■ *6 Yehielli, T5105656.*

Formerly the centrepiece to Jaffa's long since disappeared Manshieh Quarter, the mosque found fame during the 1948 war when its tall, slender minaret was used as a vantage point by snipers. Neglected for so long, the mosque has now been elegantly restored and is once again a working place of worship, though it appears rather incongruous set against the 5-star tower-block hotels nearby.

Hassan Bek Mosque

North Central Tel Aviv

Kikar Dizengoff (Dizengoff Square) is the centrepiece of the street that's described by Stephen Brook in his book *Winner Takes All: A Season in Israel* as "the street in Israel the *haredim* would disapprove of most". To many Tel Avivians, the square symbolizes both the secular and fun-loving nature of their city, though unless you visit on a Friday evening as Shabbat gets underway you may be wondering what all the hype is about. From the onset of Shabbat until the early hours of the morning, the square's numerous cafés, bars and pizza parlours are crowded with young and old alike, many of them escaping the Shabbat restrictions of Jerusalem. At any other time the square has more in common with Birmingham's Bullring; a traffic island that happens to have a few shops, restaurants and cafés.

Kikar Dizengoff

At the centre of the square is the 'unusual' **Agam Fountain Sculpture of Fire and Water**. Created in 1958 by Israeli sculptor Yaacov Agam, the fountain periodically (1100 1300 1900 2100) shoots a flame aloft whilst the coloured panels revolve to the sound of music (from classical to The Beatles). The sculpture is a good example of the willingness of Israelis to place daring works of art in public places.

Housed in the buildings of the **Jabotinsky Institute** (an Israeli right-wing historical research body) is a museum presenting the history of the **Irgun Zvai Leumi** (National Military Organization). Some see this organization as a freedom movement struggling to end the British Mandate rule, whilst to others it was a vicious terrorist organization that failed to distinguish between the military and civilian non-combatants.

Museum of the Irgun Zvai Leumi (Etzel Museum)

The museum presents the history of the Irgun and its key 'actions'. Perhaps the most notorious of these 'actions' was the attack on the King David Hotel in Jerusalem on 22nd July 1946, then headquarters of the British administration in Palestine. Ninety-one Jews, Arabs and Britons, the majority civilians, died in this 'action', with many hundreds more injured.

NB There is a second museum devoted to the role of the Irgun, known as the **Etzel Museum in War of Independence 1947-1948**, located in the attractively reconstructed building at the southern end of Charles Clore Park. Sometimes referred to as Gidi House, the building is named after the Irgun's former operations officer, Amihai Paglin: 'Gidi'. The exhibits here deal primarily with the 1948 battle for control of Jaffa. If you visit both museums on the same day you can use the same admission ticket. ■ *Museum of the Irgun Zvai Leumi/Etzel Museum, 38 Hamelekh George, T5284001. Sunday-Thursday 0830-1600, Friday 0830-1200, Saturday closed. 8 NIS. Etzel Museum in War of Independence 1947-1948, Charles Clore Park, T5172044. Sunday-Thursday 0830-1600. 8 NIS.*

The Habimah Theatre is home to Israel's National Theatre; a company that has its origins in revolutionary Russia. Following early Hebrew performances in Moscow around 1917/18, several company members settled in Palestine and established the Habimah. The name is taken from the Hebrew word for 'The Stage'. The current theatre building dates to the mid-1930s, with substantial additions in the 1970s, and features three auditoriums seating a total of

Habimah Theatre

Tel Aviv/Jaffa

North central Tel Aviv

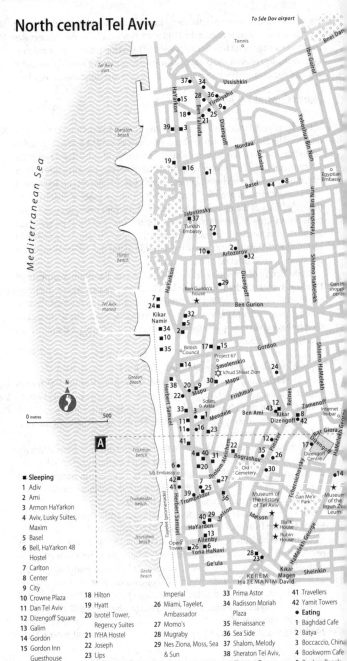

To Sde Dov airport

Tennis

Mediterranean Sea

Tel Aviv port

Sheraton beach

Hilton beach

Tel Aviv marina

Gordon beach

Frishman beach

Trumpeldor beach

Jerusalem beach

Geula beach

A

Ussishkin

Yirmiyahu

Dizengoff

Nordau

Sokolov

Basel

Jabotinsky
Turkish Embassy

Arlozorov

Ben Gurion's house

Ben Gurion

Kikar Namir

British Council

Project 67
Smolenskin
Ichud Shivat Zion

Gordon

Mapu

Frishman

Herbert Samuel

Solan, Arkia
Mendele
Ben Ami
Kikar Dizengoff

Shlomo HaMelekh

Plonit

Bograshov
Old Cemetery

US Embassy

Tchernichovsky

Gan Me'ir Park

Museum of the History of Tel Aviv

Museum of the Irgun Zva Leumi

HaMelekh George

Opera Tower

Allenby

Yona HaNavi

Ge'ula

KEREM HaTEMANIM

Kikar Magen David

Sheinkin

Ibn Gvirol

Bnei Dan

Yehoshua Bin Nun

Egyptian Embassy

Gan H shoppi centre

Shlomo HaMelekh

Shlomo HaMelekh

Reines

Zamenoff

Internet In-bar

Bar Giora

Dizengoff Centre

Idelson
Bialik House
Rubin House

HaYarkon

Ben Yehuda

Ben Yehuda

HaYarkon

Sholom Aleichem

Herbert Samuel (promenade)

Allenby (promenade)

N

0 metres   500

Related maps:
A. South-Central
Tel Aviv, page 442.

■ Sleeping
1 Adiv
2 Ami
3 Armon HaYarkon
4 Aviv, Lusky Suites, Maxim
5 Basel
6 Bell, HaYarkon 48 Hostel
7 Carlton
8 Center
9 City
10 Crowne Plaza
11 Dan Tel Aviv
12 Dizengoff Square
13 Galim
14 Gordon
15 Gordon Inn Guesthouse
16 Grand Beach
17 Grand Hotel Deborah
18 Hilton
19 Hyatt
20 Isrotel Tower, Regency Suites
21 IYHA Hostel
22 Joseph
23 Lips
24 Mercure Marina Tel Aviv
25 Metropolitan, Imperial
26 Miami, Tayelet, Ambassador
27 Momo's
28 Mugraby
29 Nes Ziona, Moss, Sea & Sun
30 No 1 Hostel
31 Noah
32 Olympia
33 Prima Astor
34 Radisson Moriah Plaza
35 Renaissance
36 Sea Side
37 Shalom, Melody
38 Sheraton Tel Aviv, Sheraton Towers
39 Tal
40 Top
41 Travellers
42 Yamit Towers

● Eating
1 Baghdad Cafe
2 Batya
3 Boccaccio, China
4 Bookworm Cafe
5 Bonkers Bagels, New York Bagel McDonalds

Tel Aviv/Jaffa

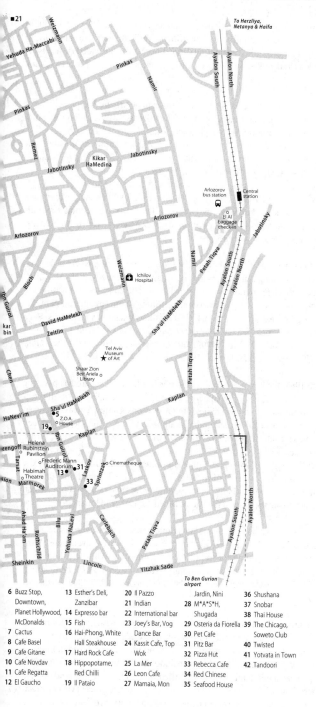

■21

To Herzliya,
Netanya & Haifa

Ayalon South

Ayalon North

Weizmann

Yehuda Ha-Maccabi

Pinkas

Pinkas

Remez

Namir

Jabotinsky

Kikar
HaMedina

Jabotinsky

Jabotinsky

Arlozorov
bus station

Central
station

El Al
baggage
check-in

Arlozorov

Arlozorov

Namir

Petah Tiqva

Ayalon South

Ayalon North

Jabotinsky

Bloch

Ibn Guirol

Weizmann

Ichilov
Hospital

David HaMelekh

kar
bin

Zeitlin

Sha'ul HaMelekh

Chen

Tel Aviv
Museum
of Art

Shaar Zion
Beit Ariela
Library

Kaplan

Petah Tiqva

HaNevi'm

Sha'ul HaMelekh

5
Z.O.A.
House

19

Kaplan

zengoff

Helena
Rubinstein
Pavilion

Frederic Mann
Auditorium

Laskov

Sprintzak

Cinematheque

Ayalon North

Tarsat

Habimah
Theatre

13

31

33

Marmorek

sion

Ibn Guirol

Bilu

Yehuda HaLevi

Carlebach

Petah Tiqva

Ahad Ha'am

Rothschild

Lincoln

Yitzhak Sade

Sheinkin

Ayalon South

Ayalon North

To Ben Gurion
airport

6 Buzz Stop, Downtown, Planet Hollywood, McDonalds	**13** Esther's Deli, Zanzibar	**20** Il Pazzo	Jardin, Nini
7 Cactus	**14** Expresso bar	**21** Indian	**28** M*A*S*H, Shugada
8 Cafe Basel	**15** Fish	**22** International bar	**29** Osteria da Fiorella
9 Cafe Gitane	**16** Hai-Phong, White Hall Steakhouse	**23** Joey's Bar, Vog Dance Bar	**30** Pet Cafe
10 Cafe Novdav	**17** Hard Rock Cafe	**24** Kassit Cafe, Top Wok	**31** Pitz Bar
11 Cafe Regatta	**18** Hippopotame, Red Chilli	**25** La Mer	**32** Pizza Hut
12 El Gaucho	**19** Il Pataio	**26** Leon Cafe	**33** Rebecca Cafe
		27 Mamaia, Mon	**34** Red Chinese
			35 Seafood House

36 Shushana
37 Snobar
38 Thai House
39 The Chicago, Soweto Club
40 Twisted
41 Yotvata in Town
42 Tandoori

Tel Aviv/Jaffa

1,520 people. Average attendance rates are said to be around 90 percent, due in part to the large number of subscribers. Performances are generally in Hebrew, though simultaneous translation is sometimes provided via headsets. Check *Jerusalem Post* or *What's On In Tel Aviv* for listings. ■ *Kikar Habimah, T5209888. Buses 5, 26.*

Helena Rubinstein Pavilion Run under the auspices of the Tel Aviv Museum of Art, this hall plays home to temporary exhibits of contemporary art. The cost of admission includes entrance to the main Museum of Art, though tickets do not have to be used on the same day. Check listings magazines for programmme. ■ *6 Tarsat, T5287196. Sunday, Monday, Wednesday, Thursday 1000-1800, Tuesday 1000-2200, Friday, Saturday 1000-1400. Adult 24 NIS, student 16 NIS. Buses 5, 26.*

Frederic Mann Auditorium Adjacent to the Helena Rubinstein Pavilion is this 3,000-seater concert hall, home to the Israeli Philharmonic Orchestra. In order to pay the bills, the auditorium also hosts rock and pop concerts. Check listings magazines for details. ■ *Tarsat, T5289163. Buses 5, 26.*

Tel Aviv Museum of Art The finest art collection in the country, the museum features works by leading Israeli and foreign artists, including: Chagall, Degas, Kokoschka, Monet, Picasso, Pissarro, Renoir and Reuven Rubin. The complex also feature the Helena Rubinstein Art Library, a Graphics Study Room (by appointment, Tel Ex 230), and temporary exhibits. Check listings magazines for details. ■ *27 Sha'ul Hamelekh, T6961297 F6958099. Sunday, Monday, Wednesday, Thursday 1000-1800, Tuesday 1000-2200, Friday, Saturday 1000-1400. Adult 24 NIS, student 16 NIS. Buses 9, 18, 28, 32, 70, 111.*

Kikar Rabin/Malkhe Y'Isra'el Plaza. Since 1965, the large City Hall on the north side of the square has been the home to the Tel Aviv Municipality (T5218438), whilst the square itself is frequently the site of political rallies, demonstrations, cultural events, and even street parties when the local football team wins the cup. The square has been renamed recently in honour of **Yitzhak Rabin**, who was murdered here on 4th November, 1995.

At the centre of the plaza is the **Monument to the Holocaust and the Rebirth of the Jewish Nation**. At the base of Yigael Tumarkin's unusual sculpture is a yellow triangle surmounted by an inverted pyramid, which together create the form of the Star of David: "A dungeon burst open".

Ben-Gurion's House This simple town house is maintained more or less as it was when Israel's first Prime Minister David Ben-Gurion, and his wife Paula, lived here. Most impressive is the library of some 20,000 volumes, as well as a collection of Ben-Gurion's letters to contemporary world leaders. ■ *17 Ben-Gurion, T5221010. Sunday-Thursday 0830-1400, Friday 0830-1300, Saturday 1100-1300 (call ahead). Free.*

Old Cemetery Sometimes referred to as the 'First Cemetery', this Jewish burial ground was established in 1903, and is the final resting place of a number of leading Zionists and Tel Aviv residents as well as a large number of Jews killed in the 1921 and 1929 riots. Those buried here include Chaim Arlosorov, Max Nordau, Meir Dizengoff, and the poets Chaim Nahman Bialik and Sha'ul Tchernikowsky. Stones scattered across a tomb indicate a recent visit by a relative; a longer-lasting equivalent to the Christian traditions of leaving flowers at a grave. ■ *Trumpeldor, T5164595. Sunday-Thursday 0930-1430, Friday 0930-1200.*

Northern Tel Aviv

The suburbs of Northern Tel Aviv are divided from the rest of the city by the River Yarqon. In ancient times the river formed a natural division boundary between the tribes of Ephraim to the north, from those of the Dan to the south. The river also marks a topographical boundary between the Sharon Plain, which runs north of Tel Aviv, and the Shefela Plain, which runs south. The northern suburbs are home to some of Tel Aviv's (and Israel's) leading museums, as well as one of Israel's premier educational establishments, Tel Aviv University (T6408111).

Comprising a number of pavilions and smaller museums constructed around an ancient archaeological site, the theme of the Eretz Israel Museum is, as the name suggests, "in the land of Israel". The three-hour guided tour (advance booking) is recommended, as is the more 'hands-on' Family Tour. Hand-woven rugs, ceramics, jewellery, glass and silver *objets d'art*, Judaica, and other souvenirs are available at the Museum Shop.

Eretz Israel Museum

Tell Qasileh Central to the Eretz Israel Museum site are the excavations of Tell Qasileh. At least 12 levels of occupation have been identified here, the oldest dating back to the 12th century BCE. These comprise a brick building at Level XII, and a wall and two copper-smelting furnaces that are a century younger at level XI. Both are attributed to the Philistines. The Philistines also constructed three large temples, each at a different level of occupancy. These finds are significant in that they provide an insight into Philistine temple architecture through different ages.

Evidence from Level X dates to the 10th century BCE and suggests that following David's conquest of the region, a port was constructed on this site. In fact, some scholars go as far as to suggest that the Lebanese cedars that were used by Soloman to construct the Temple arrived through the port here, and not further down the coast at Jaffa. Four centuries later the process was repeated for the construction of the Second Temple (see *II Chronicles 2:16; Ezra 3:7*).

Other stratum levels indicate occupation in Hellenistic, Roman, Byzantine, Crusader and Islamic times, though it was during the latter occupation that the development of Jaffa led to the decline, and eventual abandonment, of the port at Tell Qasileh. Findings from the tel are displayed in the adjacent pavilion.

Glass Museum Tracing the history of glass manufacturing techniques, this museum houses a superb collection of glassware, said to be amongst the most valuable in the world. Demonstrations of glass-blowing are sometimes given.

Kadman Numismatic Museum a large collection of ancient coinage, tracing the history and development of currencies of the whole region, is housed in this hall. **Ceramics Museum**: amongst the highlights of exhibits in this museum are the excellent examples of the Gaza and Akko style of ceramic pottery. The **Alphabet Museum** traces the development and use of alphabets, writing and language in the region.

Pavilions The **Nechushtan Pavilion** concentrates mainly on finds at the Timna copper mines, while the **Man and his Works Pavilion** contains predominantly Arab folk crafts and agricultural tools and techniques, and the

Tel Aviv/Jaffa

Folklore Pavilion comprises mainly Jewish religious art, ceremonial objects and clothing. The **Postal and Philatelic Pavilion** is currently under construction.

Lasky Planetarium Using a 360-degree screen, surround sound and computerized special effects, the Planetarium takes you on a "Journey Through the Universe" (Hebrew only). The promotional brochure reminds viewers that "people suffering from heart conditions or vertigo, and women who are pregnant, attend the show at their own risk". However, it's no more frightening than a drive along an Israeli highway. ■ *2 Haim Levanon Ramat Aviv, T6415244. Sunday, Monday, Tuesday, Thursday 0900-1400, Wednesday 0900-1800, Saturday 1000-1400. 20 NIS including Planetarium, no concessions. Buses 24, 27, 45, 74, 86.*

Diaspora Museum This impressive museum traces the history of the Jewish Diaspora communities throughout the ages and the world. Rather than presenting the story of the Diaspora in chronological order, the museum is divided into a number of themes, including: the family, community, faith, culture, among the nations, and return.

The museum makes use of many audio-visual displays (most in Hebrew and English), has study and educational areas, and is extremely well presented and labelled. The museum guides suggest that you need five or six hours to appreciate fully the full range of exhibits, though non-Jewish visitors should be able to appreciate most aspects of the museum in one or two hours. ■ *University of Tel Aviv Campus, Klausner, T6462151. Sunday, Monday, Tuesday, Thursday 1000-1600, Wednesday 1000-1800, Friday 0900-1300, Saturday closed. Adult 25 NIS, student 18 NIS. Buses 25, 74.*

Northern Tel Aviv

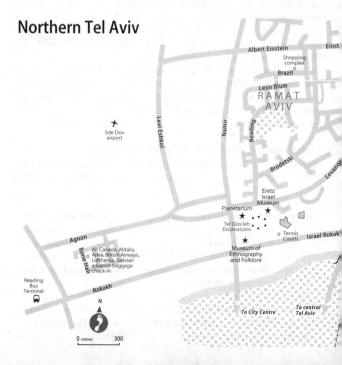

On the banks of the Yarqon River lies Tel Aviv's largest and most attractive **Yehoshua' Park**
open, green space area. Yehoshua' Park (Ganei Yehoshua') features a boating
lake (T6420541), children's zoo, adventure playground, puppet theatre, bird
park, mini-train ride, pedaloes, Wohl Amphitheatre for open-air concerts,
and a tropical garden. It is very popular with picnicking families, particularly
from the ultra-Orthodox community.

To the northeast of the park is the Maymadian Water Park (T6422777), and
to the north of the park lie the Exhibition Grounds (T6462422), the Israel
Trade Fairs & Convention Centre (T6957361), and the Luna Park
(T6423070).

To the southwest of the park is **Tel Gerisa**, an ancient archaeological site on
a small mound dating to the 18th century BCE. In reality, there's nothing
much to see besides an overgrown, fenced-off trench in the ground, though
the views of Tel Aviv's suburbs aren't bad. The mound is sometimes referred
to as **Napoleon's Hill**, after the legend that Napoleon threatened to shell Jaffa
in 1799 with a mighty cannon placed on top of this elevated position.

Ramat Gan

A number of attractions lie in Tel Aviv's eastern suburb of **Ramat Gan**. This
suburb is also home to Bar Ilan University (T531811); established in 1955, and
named after the leader of Orthodox Jewry, the university specializes in all
aspects of Jewish religious studies.

This small museum is located just behind the Diamond Exchange, the world's **Harry**
largest trading house for this valuable commodity. The value of Israel's dia- **Oppenheimer**
mond industry exports in 1993 exceeded $3.3 billion. Israel is responsible for **Diamond**
around 80 percent of the world's output of small polished stones, and 40 **Museum**

Tel Aviv/Jaffa

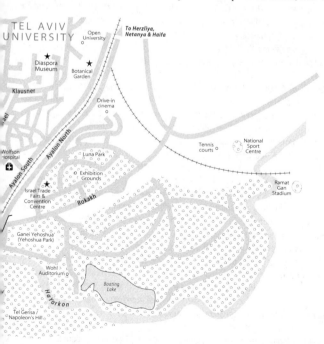

percent of the polishing of diamonds of all other sizes, making Israel the world's leading diamond polishing centre in terms of production and marketing. What is most remarkable about these statistics is that no diamonds are actually mined in Israel! The museum explains the process of mining, polishing, cutting, setting and selling the stones, with a number of extremely valuable visiting exhibitions on display. ■ *1 Jabotinsky, T5576029. Sunday-Thursday 1000-1600, Tuesday 1000-1700, Friday, Saturday closed. Adult 14 NIS, student 9 NIS. Buses 23, 40, 42, 50, 68, 70.*

Ramat Gan Safari Park A selection of African and other wildlife can be seen in this 100-hectare safari park. Closed vehicles only are permitted to drive through, though tours are organized for pedestrians. ■ *T6312181. Sunday-Thursday 0900-1600, Friday 0900-1300, Saturday closed. Adult 30 NIS, student 22 NIS. Buses 30, 35, 40, 43.*

Essentials

Sleeping

Expensive
■ *on maps; price codes see inside front cover*

Tel Aviv has a large number of hotels, with new ones opening all the time. Whilst most in the **L1**, **L2** and **L3** categories are very fine indeed, there is a distinct lack of good value places in the mid-price range.

L1 *Dan Tel Aviv*, 99 HaYarkon, T5202525, F5249755. Long established classy hotel with reputation for good service, 84 of the 286 rooms are sea-facing (more expensive), plus some luxury suites (much more expensive). Choice of restaurants, indoor freshwater pool, outdoor seawater pool, health club. Recommended. **L1** *Hilton*, Independence Park, T5202222, F5272711. One of Israel's priciest hotels, though standard of service and facilities is high, popular with business travellers, full facilities as you would expect, plus excellent restaurant choice. Recommended. **L1** *Sheraton Tel Aviv & Sheraton Towers*, 115 HaYarkon, T5211111, F5233322. Good reputation for service and intimacy, full facilities, choice of restaurants. Recommended.

L2 *Crowne Plaza*, 145 HaYarkon, T5201111, F5201122. Variety of rooms and suites, including disabled and non-smoking rms, fully equipped rooms, choice of restaurants, full leisure facilities. **L2** *Hyatt*, under construction. **L2** *Dan Panorama*, 10 Kaufman, T5190190, F5171777. 500 rooms, 6 suites and 133 deluxe rooms on upper floors ('Carmel floors' have separate check-in), with small balconies overlooking either Jaffa or Tel Aviv, full facilities and slightly cheaper than other hotels in this category. **L2** *Isrotel Tower*, 78 HaYarkon, T5113636, F5113666. Attractive suites sleeping 2 adults and 2 children, or 2-person 'executive' suites, all with sitting rooms, kitchenettes, 2 cable TVs, phones, a/c. Small supplement for sea views, costly price hike in high season though discounts for long stays. Bars, business lounges, conference facilities, attractive rooftop pool. Not a bad choice if you can afford it. **L2** *Radisson Moriah Plaza*, 155 HaYarkon, T5216666, F5271065. Nicely refurbished, rooms have balconies and sea views plus full facilities, choice of dining options, business facilities, seawater pool, choice location. **L2** *Renaissance*, 121 HaYarkon, T5215555, F5215588. Formerly the *Ramada*, pleasant rooms with balconies and sea views, full range of facilities including heated indoor pool. **L2** *Yamit Towers*, 79 HaYarkon, T5191111, F5174719. Strange-looking tower in heart of sea-front area features mini suites and 2-bed apartments with kitchen, lounge, standard rooms cheaper.

L3 *David Inter-Continental*, 12 Kaufman, T7951111, F7951112. Opened in 1999, features reasonably priced standard rooms (though no balconies), plus a variety of superior 'deluxe', 'club' and 'executive' rooms and suites that reach up into the **L2** and **L1** price categories. Full facilities that you would expect, including choice of restaurants, pools, health club, business and conference rooms. Certainly worth considering if you can afford it. **L3** *Mercure Marina Tel Aviv*, 167 HaYarkon, T5211777, F5211770. Recently refurbished, features large attractive rooms, a/c, cable TV, business facilities, pool and health club. Not a bad choice. **L3** *Metropolitan*, 11-15 Trumpeldor, T5192727, F5172626. Modern block close to beach, fully equipped rooms but no balconies, terrace pool, choice of restaurants. **L3** *Regency Suites*, 80 HaYarkon, T5173939, F5163610. All suite hotel, though 'second' beds are mainly sofa-beds, kitchenette, cable TV, a/c.

A *Adiv*, 5 Mendele, T5229141, F5229144. Impressive reception, pleasant rooms and nicer inside than exterior suggests, but lack of sea views should really make it cheaper. **A** *Basel*, 156 HaYarkon, T5244161, F5270005. Probably the best value of the *Atlas* chain, has a large number of returning guests who wouldn't stay anywhere else. Most rooms with sea views. **A** *Carlton*, 10 Eliezer Peri, T5201818, F5271043. Though not as luxurious as surrounding hotels, has pleasant attentive service, rooftop pool, rooms without sea views cheaper. **A** *Center*, 2 Zamenhoff, T6296181, F6296751. Central location, but for these prices why not go for a seafront location? 56 a/c rooms, some with balconies, cable TV, phone. Overpriced. **A** *City*, 9 Mapu, T5246253, F5246250. Another *Atlas* hotel that in terms of facilities should struggle to get into this category. **A** *Grand Beach*, 250 HaYarkon, T5433333, F5466589. Though the hotel has no real sense of luxury and rather lacks the personal touch, it's competitively priced and probably the best value in this category. Choice of restaurants, rooftop pool. Tentatively recommended. **A** *Grand Hotel Deborah*, 87 Ben Yehuda, T5278282, F5278304. Part of *Atlas* chain, 60 a/c rooms, cable TV, phone, but no sense of luxury and no pool. **A** *Maxim*, 86 HaYarkon, T5173721, F5173726. 60 a/c rooms, cable TV, recently refurbished, prime location. **A** *Metropolitan*, 11-15 Trumpeldor, T5192727, F5172626. Better value if you're getting the tour group price, otherwise overpriced. **A** *Olympia*, 164 HaYarkon, T5242184, F5247278. New hotel, a/c, cable TV, restaurant, most rooms sea facing. **A** *Prima Astor*, HaYarkon. Under construction. **A** *Shalom*, 216 HaYarkon, T5343277, F5235895. Long established place, though recently refurbished after joining *Howard Johnson* chain, *Stagecoach* bar/restaurant downstairs. **A** *Tal*, 287 HaYarkon, T5468126, F5467687. Part of *Atlas* chain though somewhat overpriced.

B *Ami*, 4 Am Yisrael Hai/152 HaYarkon, T5249141, F5231151. Small, simple, homely **Mid-range** hotel with quiet atmosphere, some rooms with balcony. **B** *Armon HaYarkon*, 268 HaYarkon, T6055271, F6058485. Rooms have a/c, cable TV, but a little box-like and on noisy road. **B** *Aviv*, 88 HaYarkon, T5102784, F5223060. Simple hotel with few facilities though rooms have a/c. **B** *Bell*, 12 Allenby, T5174291, F5174352. Exterior rather shabby but newly refurbished inside, friendly. Can be good value if you bargain hard. **B** *Imperial*, 66 HaYarkon, T5177002, F5178314. Rooms a little box-like with no picture windows or real views. A little old-fashioned but reasonable value by Tel Aviv standards. **B** *The Home*, 106 HaYarkon, corner of 6 Frishman, 5222695, F5240815. A good option for long-term residents, *The Home* offers simple studio apartments complete with kitchenette, at weekly rates. Small studio $250 pw, studio 'A' $300 pw, studio 'B' $325 pw, 2-room apartment $350 pw (add $50 pw in high season). Discount monthly rates. Reception 0900-1500. **B** *Top*, 35 Ben Yehuda, T5170941. Another overpriced *Atlas* hotel. The *Miami* and *Tatelet* hotels on Allenby look as if you could hire their rooms by the hour. **B/C** *Moss*, 6 Nes Ziona, T/F5171655. Rather box-like rooms, very old fashioned but that's the type of guests it attracts.

Tel Aviv/Jaffa

C *Eilat*, 58 HaYarkon, T5160594, F5102453. Homely atmosphere, room price depends upon view, above noisy bar. **C** *Gordon Inn Guesthouse*, 17 Gordon, T5238239, F5237419. Some reasonable value private rooms ($10-15 cheaper with shared bathroom), doubles, triples, quads and group rooms, coffee shop, clean and quiet. **C/D** *Nes Ziona*, 10 Nes Ziona, T5106084. Simple, quiet, old fashioned place, a/c, cable TV.

D *Galim*, 9 Allenby, T5175703, F5271885. Very friendly small place, attached bath, some rooms with nice views, reasonably priced. **D** *Sea & Sun*, 62 HaYarkon, T5173313, F5173562. Could do with a lick of paint, but some reasonably priced double rooms with attached bath.

Cheap   Most of Tel Aviv's budget accommodation is found around the south end of Ben Yehuda and HaYarkon, and can be reached by Buses 4 and 5 from the Central Bus Station, or 222 from the airport. Because of the large number of long-stay visitors working in Tel Aviv, some hostels can appear a little cliquey to short-stay visitors. Others are 'party places' where a good night's sleep can be hard to find. Most charge between 35-40 NIS per night for a dorm bed, with discounts for longer stays and private rooms in the **D/E** categories. **NB** Sleeping on the beach is not advised.

E *IYHA Hostel and Guest House*, 36 Bnei Dan, T5441748, F5441030. Usual clean and orderly dorms, plus private rooms (**D**), though a little remote (Buses 5, 24, 25 and 222).

F *Dizengoff Square*, 13 Ben Ami, Kikar Dizengoff, T5225184, F5225181. Large hostel in central location, dorms of varying size (some with balconies) and varying degrees of airiness, pretty clean but showers rather cramped, price includes a poor value breakfast, cable TV lounge, kitchen, good place to pick up work, annoying paging system that announces 'phone call for...' all night, no curfew. Tentative recommendation. **F** *Gordon*, 2 Gordon, T5229870. Excellent location close to the beach, spacious dorms are light and airy with lots of balconies, bar/sitting area, party atmosphere, no curfew. Recommended. **F** *Jambo*, 56 HaYarkon, T5106698. Rather crowded dorms, some private rooms with showers (**E**), food/snacks available. **F** *Lips*, 54 Ben Yehuda. Closed. **F** *Momo's*, 28 Ben Yehuda, T5297421. You'll either love or hate this place: most visitors either flee after one night or stay forever. Loud music and loud traffic all night, 24-hr bar (Dave Winter was once refused service for being too smart!) and cheap food (burger and chips 12 NIS), single-sex and mixed graffiti-covered dorms, dirty showers/toilets, no curfew and no sleep. **F** *Mugraby*, 30 Allenby, T5102443. Friendly, dorms a little crowded, private rooms with attached bath (**D**) and cheaper private rooms with shared bath (**D/E**), small café with internet access. **F** *No 1 Hostel*, 84 Ben Yehuda, T5237807. Recently redecorated, dorms (4-6 beds) a little cramped but OK, some with not very private showers in the room, some private rooms with shared bath (**D/E**), no curfew but lockout 1100-1400, kitchen, lockers, breezy bar on the roof. **F** *Noah*, 34 Ben Yehuda, T6200044. Popular with Israelis, noisy location, some private rooms (**D/E**), no curfew, lockers, TV lounge. **F** *Sea Side*, 20a Trumpeldor, T6200513, F5256965. Rooms near reception rather noisy (avoid), those upstairs more spacious (4-8 beds), cheaper rooftop bungalows (**G**) plus private rooms with attached bath (**E**), bar (beer 7 NIS), kitchenette, rooftop sitting area, recently refurbished, close to beach, no curfew. Recommended. **F** *The Hostel (Hayarkon 48)*, 48 HaYarkon, T5168989, F5103113. Probably the best hostel in Tel Aviv with everything well thought out. Large, clean, uncrowded dorms, discounts for stays of 3 days, plenty of clean, modern and roomy showers (actually space to hang clothes!) with constant hot water. Some dorms with 4-6 beds and attached shower (**E/F**) with balconies, plus a selection of breezy, light and airy private rooms (**D**) also with semi-private balconies. Large kitchen (free tea/coffee), TV room/bar with pool table, large roof area with great views and bar/BBQ, laundry, no curfew. Friendly and highly recommended. **F** *The Office*, 57 Allenby, T5289984. Still a popular hostel, although not necessarily the cleanest (especially the showers), mixed and single-sex dorms, some private rooms (**D/E**), kitchen, lockers, no curfew, popular and lively bar. **F** *Travellers*, 47 Ben Yehuda, T5232451, F5237281. A little run down but one of the cheapest hostels, special weekly/monthly rates, dorms (including some women-only) plus private rooms with shared bath (**D/E**), fridges in rooms, kitchen, storeroom, no bar so fairly quiet, welcoming atmosphere, cheap backpacker tours (ask for Duncan).

Holiday 2000, T5271438, F5274556. Short- and long-term lets. *Joseph*, 15 Bograshov, T051 623089. Former *Josef* hostel now given over to long-term room lets. *Kikar Dizengoff Apartments*, Kikar Dizengoff, T6200107, F6200108. *Nativex*, 27 Mapu, T5273088. Luxury apartment lets. **Apartment rental and B&Bs**

Eating

Tel Aviv has arguably Israel's best and most diverse selection of restaurants, and a number of distinct 'dining areas'. Little Tel Aviv at the north end of Dizengoff has a number of long-established places and is generally seen as being rather upmarket. Two 'up and coming' areas are Florentin, and to a lesser extent Neve Zedek, whilst Jaffa has a number of recommended (and not so recommended) restaurants (see 'Jaffa' section on page 475). Unsuprisingly, the Yemenite Quarter (Keren Hataymanim) is home to a number of Yemeni Jewish places, whilst the sea-front promenade is the venue of places aimed primarily at tourists (foreign and Israeli alike). Note that most Tel Aviv restaurants are not kosher.

Many of the hostels have kitchens that guests can use for free. Carmel Market is the cheapest place for fruit and veg; see 'Shopping' on page 459 for details of supermarkets. There are numerous falafel and shwarma places towards the south end of Ben Yehuda, and also around Kikar Dizengoff and Kikar Magen David. *Buzz Stop*, 86 Herbert Samuel, T5100869. Long-established backpacker favourite, though move to more salubrious location now brings in a much more mixed clientele (look at the photos on the wall to see what it used to be like!). Bar open 24 hrs, kitchen 0900-0300, full English breakfast 20 NIS, most meals (anything and chips) under 20 NIS, cheap drinks (beer 10/12 NIS), waitresses survive on 8 NIS per hour plus tips! Recommended. *Momo's Hostel*, 28 Ben Yehuda. The 24-hr bar has cheap meals (burger and chips 12 NIS, chips 7 NIS), though there's a strict dress code ('New Age Traveller'). **Budget**

Tel Aviv is famous (in Israel anyway) for its 'café society'. There are a number of streets that are distinctly 'chic', though what is and isn't 'in' changes remarkably quickly. Below are just a small selection. Currently the 'trendiest' street is Shenkin, which features amongst others *Camembert*, très Parisien; *Tamar* at 57; *Up* at 56, small diner area plus larger restaurant section, meals 30 NIS; *Yuppies* at 42, with meals from 40 NIS. There are plenty of attractive café/bars on Dizengoff, including *Baghdad Café*, at 226; *Café Gitane* at 302; *Green Bar Café* at 286; *Kassit* at 117; *Snobar*, at the north end, with meals for 30 NIS, salads 20 NIS. Basel, which runs east from the north end of Dizengoff, has a number of 'trendy' cafés, notably *Bookworm*, 30 Basel, T5462714, and *Café Basel*. Ben Yehuda also features some attractive café/bars, including *Café Nordau* at 145, a popular gay meeting place; and *Ernesto* at 90. **Café/bars**

Other attractive café/bars include *Arcaffe Expresso Gourmet*, Rothschild, very continental; *Expresso Bar*, 46 HaMelekh George, or junction of Rothschild/Herzl; *Hippopotame*, 12 Yirmiyahu; *Java Bar*, 12 Marmorek; *Leon Café*, 42 Pinsker; *Pet Café*, 34 Pinsker, T6202586, open 7 days (0800-0200), bring your dog and he gets fed too!; *Pimenta*, corner of Nahalat Binyamina and Yehuda HaLevi, T5661661, very nice with light meals 40-60 NIS, good atmosphere; *Pitz Bar*, Ibn Gvirol; *Rebecca Café*, corner Laskov/Carlebach; *Red Chili*, 12 Yirmiyahu; *Rose Café*, corner Marmorek/Ha-Levi; *Twisted*, 9 HaYarden; *Zanzibar*, Ibn Gvirol, particularly 'trendy'.

Central/North/South American *Cactus*, 66 HaYarkon. Tex-Mex menu, burritos, enchilladas, fajitas 50 NIS, salad 45 NIS, burgers 40 NIS. *El Gaucho*, 57 Pinsker, T5283788. Argentine steakhouse chain, steaks 60-80 NIS. *Papagaio*, 14 HaArba'a, T5626888. Brazilian grill-churesccaria (eat all you can), moderately expensive but good, reservations essential, live show most nights. *Pimenta*, see 'café/bars' above. *The Chicago*, 63 HaYarkon, T5177505. Deep pan pizzas for 2 55-75 NIS, salad 40 NIS, diet-busting cakes and pies. *White Hall Steakhouse*, 6 Mendele, T5249282, or 44 Rothschild, T5663747. American-style steaks 60-80 NIS.

Chinese/Southeast Asian *China Lee*, 102 HaYarkon. Main dishes 60-80 NIS. *Hai-Phong*, 100 HaYarkon. Main dishes 40-50 NIS. *Mika*, 27 Montefiore, T5283255. Cheaper bar meals and business lunch at chic Japanese restaurant, otherwise pricey. *Mongolian Grill Bar*, 62 HaYarkon, T5174010. All you can eat menu 90 NIS, or à la carte, good value business lunch, reservations recommended. *Red Chinese*, 326 Dizengoff, T5466347. Good quality Thai and Chinese, 40-75 NIS main courses. *Sushi Bar*, 20 Ashtori Haparhi, T5460575. Japanese, moderately expensive. *Takamaru*, 10 HaArba'a, T5621628 and 118 HaYarkon, T5273950. Japanese dishes. *Tampadulu*, 1 Florentin, T5180012. Pricy, upmarket place specializing in satays and other Indonesian dishes, high standard, main courses 50-75 NIS. *Thai House*, 8 Bograshov, junction Ben Yehuda, T5178568. Rather nice and relaxed feel, stir-fry 40 NIS, 'specials' 50 NIS, veg dishes 26 NIS. *Top Wok*, corner of Frishman and Dizengoff. Tasty stir-frys, 22-35 NIS. *Yin Yang*, 64 Rothschild, T5604121/5606833. Considered to be Tel Aviv's best, around 100 NIS per head, reservations recommended.

Fast food/chain restaurants *Ben and Jerry's*, 286 Dizengoff and on sea-front outside *Radisson Moriah Hotel*. *Bonkers Bagels*, corner of Ibn Gvirol and Sha'ul HaMelekh. *Burger King*, Dizengoff Centre. *Dr Lek*, Ben Yehuda. Ice-cream parlour. *McDonald's*, Kikar Dizengoff. Dizengoff Centre, corner of Ibn Gvirol and Sha'ul HaMelekh. *New York Bagel*, Ben Yehuda, and corner of Ibn Gvirol and Sha'ul HaMelekh. *Pizza Hut*, junction of Dizengoff and Arlozorov, T5275656. Pizzas 19-25 NIS. *Planet Hollywood*, 86-88 Herbert Samuel. Usual fayre, burgers 40 NIS, nightclub. *Subway*, Kikar Dizengoff. 12-inch sandwich 25 NIS, 6-inch 17 NIS.

Hotel restaurants *King Solomon's Grill*, *Hilton*, Independence Park, T5202222. Chinese, continental, Middle Eastern, Japanese, one of the best in town. *Twelve Tribes*, *Sheraton Tel Aviv*, 115 HaYarkon, T5211111. Highly recommended with a diverse selection of 'Israeli' dishes (100 NIS+), reservations recommended.

Italian *Boccaccio*, 106 HaYarkon, T5246837. Italian/seafood, main dishes 60 NIS, business lunch 40-70 NIS. *Café Regata*, *King David Tower*, 87 HaYarkon. Italian Venetian restaurant, very chic. *Il Pataio*, Ibn Gvirol, T5251166. Nice setting, good pasta 40 NIS, meat dishes 75 NIS, run by an Italian 'wonderful host' who has lived here for 30 years, highly recommended. *Il Pazzo*, 114 HaYarkon, T5241875. 30-50 NIS main courses. *Mama*, 12 Rabbi Akiva, T5175096. Excellent pizza, more 'Italian' than 'American', 40 NIS, lunchtime only. *Osteria da Fiorella*, 148 Ben Yehuda, T5248818. Attractive setting, pleasant family-run place. *Pastalina*, 16 Elifelet, T6836401. New style upmarket pasta bar. *Prego*, 9 Rothschild, T5179545. Well appointed restaurant, pleasant atmosphere, good food (75-100 NIS for 3 courses). *Spaghettim*, 18 Yavne, T5664479, and 7 Rival, T6876097. Over 50 different spaghetti dishes (25-45 NIS), plus traditional Italian country cooking, reservations recommended.

Indian, junction of Ben Yehuda and Yirimyahu. Main dishes 20-30 NIS. *Tandoori*, 2 **Indian**
Zamenhof, Kikar Dizengoff, T6296185. One of Israel's best, lunch buffet 60 NIS
(1200-1330, Saturday 1300-1600), main dishes 40-50 NIS. See also 'vegetarian', page
457.

Batya, junction of 197 Dizengoff and Arlozorov. Family run place, open for Shabbat **Jewish**
lunch also. *Elimelekh*, 35 Wolfson. The epitomy of good old-fashioned traditional **(traditional)**
Jewish home cooking. *Esther's Deli*, Ibn Gvirol. Home-style cooking.. *Gamliel*, 38
HaKovshim, Keren Hataymanim, T5178779. Yemenite style grilled meats 20 NIS, fried
goose liver 45 NIS, baked sinia 25 NIS. *Judith's Csarda*, Gan Ha'Ir Shopping Centre, 71
Ibn Gvirol, T5279214. Noted Hungarian restaurant, try the stuffed cabbage. *Nini*, 182
Ben Yehuda, T5290597. Highly recommended Glatt Kosher Tunisian menu, guillades
70 NIS, couscous 60 NIS. *Pletz'l*, 70 Frishman, T5238761. Traditional Jewish with
old-time Yiddish atmosphere, schitzel, goulash, chicken livers, main courses
25-30 NIS. *Shushana*, 33-35 Yirimyahu. Noted Hungarian dishes, pancakes 26 NIS,
blintzes 35-40 NIS, soups 16 NIS, closed Shabbat. *Tiv*, 130 Allenby, junction with
Yehuda HaLevi. Cheap lunchtime self-service canteen. *Zion*, 28 Peduyim, Keren
Hataymanim. Busy Yemenite restaurant.

Birnbaum & Mendelbaum, 35 Rothschild. Very, very swish bar and grill, main courses **Miscellaneous**
90 NIS. Recommended. *Catch 21*, corner HaYarkon and Bograshov. Breakfast 25 NIS,
salad 40 NIS, main courses 40-60 NIS. *Hippopotame*, 12 Yirimyahu, T5466348. Main
dishes 45-50 NIS, fish 50-75 NIS, house speciality is chateaubriand (140 NIS for 2).
L'entrecôte, 195 Ben Yehuda, T5466726. Intimate atmosphere with choice of
3-course meals 50-75 NIS. *Mamaia*, 192 Ben Yehuda, T5239621. Appealing and
highly praised Romanian restaurant, steak 75 NIS, chateaubriand 80 NIS. *Mon Jardin*,
184 Ben Yehuda, T5231792. Well reviewed, main courses 50-60 NIS, stuffed vegetables highly recommended. *Picasso*, 88 HaYarkon/Mendele, T5102784. Sunny, nice
views, fish 70 NIS, pasta 50 NIS, 3-course business lunch 60 NIS. *Tel Aviv Brew House*,
see 'Bars' on page 457. *Yotvata In Town*, 83 Herbert Samuel, T5107985. Billed as offering "the best dairy food of the kibbutz", its prime location makes it impossibly
crowded on Shabbat.

Fish Restaurant, 256 Ben Yehuda. Very popular with locals. *La Mer*, 265 Dizengoff, **Seafood**
T5467077. Very attractive setting, fish 50-70 NIS, good value business lunches
60-80 NIS (3 courses, 1200-1800). *Manta Ray*, Alma Beach, T5174773. Pricey but
highly recommended, upmarket beachfront location, reservations recommended.
Pundag, 8 Frishman, T5222948. Kosher fish restaurant, main dishes 60 NIS. *Seafood
House*, 45 Pinsker. Pleasant setting, fish main course 60-70 NIS. *Shugada*, 267
Dizengoff, T5467484. Main dishes 55-65 NIS, plus eat-all-you-want, long established.

There aren't many places aimed primarily at vegetarians, though *LeHayyim/A Taste* **Vegetarian**
of Life, 60 Ben Yehuda (no English sign but often referred to as the *Eternity Restau-*
rant), is highly recommended for its vegan veg burgers, vegetarian steaks, tofu dishes
and salads (Sunday-Thursday 0900-2300, Friday 0900-1500, Saturday sun-
down-2400). *Ha'Ikar Habriyut*, 18 Ashtori Haparhi, T5444432. Organic vegetarian
dishes. *Tarkari*, 68 HaKishon. Undoubtedly influenced by all those Israelis spending
their post-army days hanging out in India, offers excellent (if pricey) South Indian
thalis.

Bars and clubs

Bars *Buzz Stop*, see under 'Budget eating' on page 455. *Dita Bar*, 61 Rothschild. Very
pleasant bar inside, or sit on the candlelit terrace outside, snacks available. *Down*

South Pub, *Hotel Eilat*, 58 HaYarkon. Bar with pool tables (and competitions). *Embassy*, 22 Ben Yehuda. Aimed at backpackers, cheapish booze and food. *Hard Rock Café*, Dizengoff Centre. As per any other around the world. *International Bar*, 109 HaYarkon. Loud, cheap hard-drinking backpacker place. *Joey's Bar and Vog Dance Bar*, 42 Allenby. Slice of Americana, popular with tourists and ex-pats. *M*A*S*H*, 275 Dizengoff, T6051007. Long established (1982) bar, open 1000-0300, happy hour 1700-2000, giant screen shows sport and films, food available (all-day breakfast 28 NIS). *Momo's*, see under 'Sleeping' on page 454 and 'Budget eating' on page 455. *Session Kitchen Bar*, 11 Rothschild. Pleasant spot, especially the terrace. *Tel Aviv Brew House*, 11 Rothschild, T5168666. Currently one of the 'in' places (reservations recommended), featues working brewery at its centre, excellent food (good value business lunch til 1830, 42 NIS), happy hour 1600-1900, open til 0300, live jazz, Dixie, swing and blues Friday 1430-1730, Sunday 2100-2400. *The Office*, 57 Allenby. Part of the hostel, backpacker-friendly prices, pool, darts, occasional live music. See also 'Café/bars' on page 455. The Eastern European bars on Allenby, and in the area just to the north of the Central Bus Station, tend to be a bit 'rougher' (with the latter area in particular being the main brothel area of Tel Aviv).

Nightclubs *Clab 38* (sic), 38 Allenby. Sex club, 170 NIS per half-hour (apparently!). *Coliseum*, Kikar Namir, T5271177. Women free (men 30 NIS), bit of a pick-up joint for tourists, loud, lots of dancing, Monday-Saturday 2330-0500. *Collimbarium*, 49 Kibbutz Giluiot. Cover charge 25-30 NIS, you may not get in if you don't look 'cool' enough, though once inside there is a choice of 2 halls, one offering house/dance, the other playing latest hits. *Deca Dance*, 16 Allenby. Formerly site of *Beers* bar, open Thursday-Friday 2300-late, strict dress code so dress up. *58 Allenby*, 58 Allenby, T5176019, Wednesday-Saturday midnight onwards (dress up to get in), Friday night gay night, voted by British *Ministry* magazine as "fifth best club in the world outside the UK", and as "the place to go in Israel" by *The Face*, although currently there is talk of the Tel Aviv Municipality closing it down for operating without a licence! *Golem*, 7 Hillel Hazaken. Thursday and Friday 2400-late, cover charge 30-40 NIS, popular with the trendy Israeli crowd, mixed music. *Lemon*, 17 Hangarim, Florentin, T6813313. Best known for its Monday night gay night, and Shabbat parties on Jaffa beach. *Playboy Club*, Allenby. Entry 50 NIS, beer 20 NIS, 'shows' at 2200 onwards, it's a brothel really. *Shanbo*, 25 Lillenblum, T5106739. Monday for 20 yrs +, Thursday and Friday 24 yrs +, Saturday open to all, 2200-late, cover charge 25-35 NIS. On 3 floors, first room (*Shanbo*) features 80s, 90s and MTV, second floor features *Josefine Trance Club*, whilst upper floor is for those who manage to score on either of the 2 previous floors. *Soweto Club*, 61 HaYarkon, T5160222. Roots reggae, dance, ragga muffin, rap, hip-hop, Caribbean, and other theme nights, 20-50 NIS entry.

Entertainment

Cinemas *Cinematheque*, 2 Sprintzak, T6917181. *Dizengoff*, Dizengoff Centre, T6200485. *Gan Ha'Ir*, 71 Ibn Gvirol, T5279215. *Gordon*, 87 Ben Yehuda, T5244373. *Hod*, 101 Dizengoff, T5226226. *Khen*, Kikar Dizengoff, T5282288. *Lev*, Dizengoff Centre, T5288288. *Or*, Opera Tower, 1 Allenby, T5102674. *Tel Aviv*, 65 Pinsker, T5281181, amongst numerous others, check *Jerusalem Post* for programme.

Theatres and concert halls *Bat Dor Dance Troupe*, 30 Ibn Gvirol, T6963175. *Batsheva Dance Company*, T5171471. Innovative and controversial. *Cameri*, 101 Dizengoff, T5233335/5279888. Simultaneous translation into English on Tuesdays. *Habimah*, Habima Sq, T6296071/5266666. See page 445. *Hasimta*, 8 Simtat Mazal Dagim, Old Jaffa, T6812126. 'café-theatre' style presentations. *Inbal Dance Theatre*, 6 Yehieli, Neve Zedek, T5173711. *Israel Conservatory of Music* , 19 Shtrieker, T5466228. *Mann*

Auditorium, 1 Huberman, T5289163. See page 448. *National Yiddish Theatre*, c/o ZOA House, 1 Daniel Friesch, T1-800-444660. *Noga*, Noga Sq, 7 Jerusalem, Jaffa, T6816427. *Ohel Shem Auditorium*, 30 Balfour, T5252266. *Suzanne Dellal Centre*, 6 Yehielli, Neve Zedek, T5105656. See page 444. *Tel Aviv Performing Arts Centre*, 19 Shaul HaMelekh, T6927707. Home of the new Israeli opera. *Tsavta*, 30 Ibn Gvirol, T6950156. *Wohl Amphitheatre*, Ganei Yehoshua, T5218210/6420487. Check *Jerusalem Post* for listings.

Castel, 153 Ibn Gvirol, T6044725. *Hadran*, 90 Ibn Gvirol, T5279797. *Le'an*, 101 Dizengoff, T5247373. *Rococo*, 93 Dizengoff, T5223663/5276677. **Ticket outlets**

Call T5160259 for details of festivals and special events. February: **Jazz, Movies and Videoclips**, Tel Aviv Cinematheque, 2 Sprintzak, T6917181. March: **Theatroneto** (week-long festival of one-actor performances), Suzanne Dellal Centre, 5 Yekhi'eli, T5105656. **Tel Aviv Marathon**, T5613322. April (Passover): **Tel Aviv Music Festival**, Old Jaffa, T5160259. June: **International Street Theatre Festival**, T5160259. **A Week of Israeli Theatre Productions**, Hasimta Theatre, 8 Mazal Dagim St, Old Jaffa, T5160259. July: **Jaffa Nights** (concerts and drama), Old Jaffa, T5160259. July-August: **Beach Festivals**, various activities and parties on Tel Aviv's beaches, T5160259. August: **A Week of Storytelling**, Suzanne Dellal Centre, 5 Yekhi'eli, T5105656. **Festivals**

Shopping

Dizengoff has traditionally been Tel Aviv's most upmarket shopping street, and at its northern end this is probably still true. However, most now agree that it's no longer 'what it was', with a distinct shift down market. In fact, comparisons with London's Oxford Street are fairly accurate in this regard. The **Dizengoff Center** at Kikar Dizengoff remains proof that 'hanging out' at the mall is as popular with the youth of Israel as it is in the States. The *Hamashbir* department store here is the outlet for *Marks & Spencer*.

Upmarket shoppers head for the designer shops on Kikar HaMedina, where an Israeli designed and manufactured Gottex swimsuit costs more than it does in the States. The 'in' place to shop and to be 'seen' whilst shopping is Sheinkin, between Allenby and Rothschild. It compares itself with the Village in New York and London's Hampstead High Street, claiming to have 'banned the banal'. It's really trying a bit too hard, but if it's over-priced art, over-priced clothes or an over-priced coffee that you're after, this is the place for you. Far more fun is the **Shuk Hasishpeshim**, or Jaffa's 'flea market' (see page 472).

Also more authentic is **Carmel Market**, located on the edge of Keren Hat.aymanim. Though a wide selection of goods are on sale, the markets main produce comprises fruit and vegetables. It is loud, raucous, and a lot of fun.

Home-made jewellery, amongst other things, can be found on the pedestrianized **Nahalat Binyamin**: a popular location for street entertainers, people-watchers, or those wanting an alfresco lunch or coffee.

Shuk Hasishpeshim (Jaffa's 'flea market') is the best bet; see page 472. **Bicycles** New, 18-speed mountain bikes cost around 400 NIS from a couple of shops at 78 and 80 Levinsky (near Central Bus Station). **Books** *Book Boutique*, 190 Dizengoff, T5274527. Used English books. *Steimatsky* have a number of branches across town, including 101 and 109 Dizengoff, inside the Dizengoff Centre, Central Bus Station, and at the airport. There are some small second-hand bookstalls on Allenby, which also sell the world's least desirable product (secondhand porno mags!). **Camping/outdoor gear** *Maslol*, 47 Bograshov, T6203508/5280141. Well-run shop with all the outdoor **Antiques/Junk** gear you could need, guidebooks, free tourist information readily dispensed, travel agency, on-line travel information, free/cheap bikes for city tours. Recommended. **Jewellery** *H Stern*, Israel's prestigious jewellery and diamond merchants have outlets at the airport and in all the top hotels. *Israel Diamond Exchange Centre*, 1 Jabotinsky, Ramat Gan, T5757979. Try also the outdoor market on Nahalat Binyamin. **Shopping malls** *Dizengoff Centre*, junction of Dizengoff and HaMelekh George (Buses 5, 13, 24, 25, 61, 99). *Gan Ha'ir*, 71 Ibn Gvirol (near City Hall, Buses 8, 10, 13, 24, 32, 66). *Opera Tower*, 1 Allenby (Buses 4, 8, 10, 90). **Supermarkets** *Supersol*, Ben Yehuda (Sunday-Tuesday 0700-2400, Wednesday-Thursday 24 hrs, closed Shabbat).

Sports

Diving *Dugit*, 250 Ben Yehuda, T6045034. Fishing and diving centre, sells and rents gear, will put you in touch with their diving club (Mr Atzmon Maiky, T5441712). *Israeli Diving Association*, 94 HaYarkon, T5236436. *Leonardo*, Dive Centre, Dolphinarium, T5105871, F5108439. PADI open-water courses (around $350), intro dives ($50), equipment hire etc. *Lucky Divers*, 44 HaYarkon, T5178361. *Octopus*, Tel Aviv Marina, T5440730.

Flying *Aero Club of Israel*, 67 HaYarkon, T5175038. A number of companies organize plane and helicopter flights over Tel Aviv/Israel. Try: *Chim-Nir Aviation*, T09-9520520; *FN Aviation*, T09-9548525; *Moon Air Aviation*, T09-9587280; *Nesher Aviation*, T6993197. Most are based at Herzliya Airport.

Football International fixtures are played at the **Ramat Gan Stadium**, whilst domestic fixtures take place at the **Bloomfield Stadium** in Jaffa (eg Maccabi Tel Aviv) or at the **Maccabi Yafo Stadium** in Jaffa. Check local press for fixtures (usually Saturday afternoon).

Hiking *Society for the Protection of Nature (SPNI)*, 4 Hashfela, T6388666 (info office T6388642, Sunday-Thursday 0900-1400, Friday 0800-1300). Invaluable resource centre for potential hikers anywhere in Israel, also arranges guided trips (T6388675).

Jet-ski hire *Dolphinarium*, T6822131.

Running Tel Aviv Marathon is held in March; T5613322 for details.

Shooting *Bul Shooting Ranges*, T5373046; *Lahav*, T5376423; *Ramat Gan Shooting Range*, T5793320.

Skiing *Rosen & Meents*, 40 HaYarkon, T5162031; *Snow Ski Center*, 2 Ben Zakai, T5660645.

Swimming Many of Tel Aviv's swimming pools are in private clubs, so it's best to call ahead. *Galit Pool*, 3 Wingate, T5375031; *Kiryat Shalom Sports Center*, 7 Amikam, T6812158; *Tel Aviv Swimming Pool Gordon*, Kikar Atarim, T5271555.

Tennis *Israel Tennis Centre*, PO Box 51, Ramat HaSharon, T6456666.

Ten-pin bowling *American Bowling Center*, 299 Abba Hillel, Ramat Gan, T5700834; *Petah Tikva Bowling*, 7 Basel, Petah Tikva, T9242615.

Transport

Buses For tourists, the routes listed below are the most useful: **4** Central Bus Station **Local**
– HaGalil – Saloman – HaShomron – Petah Tiqva – Allenby – Ben Yehuda – Dizengoff
– HaTa'arukha – Reading Terminal (every 3-10 mins, 0500-2415). **5** Central Bus Sta-
tion – HaSharon – HaShomron – Petah Tiqva – Kikkar HaMoshavot – Allenby –
Rothschild – Tarsat – Dizengoff – Nordau – Ibn Gvirol – Pinkas – Meizmann – Yehuda
HaMakkabi – Namir – Pinkas – Beyt HaHayal (every 3-8 mins, 0450-2415). **10** Central
Railway Station – Al Parashat – Arlozorov – Bloch – Ben-Gurion – Adam HaCohen –
Manger – Arlozorov – Ben Yehuda – Allenby – Herbert Samuel – Daniel –
HaKoveshim – HaSokhnut – Kikar HaSharon – Yefet (for Jaffa) – on to Bat Yam (every
10-25 mins, 0525-2420). **25** Bat Yam – Jerusalem (for Jaffa) – Allenby – Tel Aviv Uni-
versity (every 5-10 mins, 0515-2410). **46** Central Bus Station – HaGalil – HaSharon –
HaShomron – Petah Tiqva – Yafo – Elat – Raziel – Yefet (for Jaffa) – on to Bat Yam
(every 5-15 mins, 0515-2425).

Car hire There are numerous car hire companies in Tel Aviv; those listed below are
just a selection. Most have offices at Ben-Gurion Airport, which are open 24 hrs. *Avis*,
113 HaYarkon, T5271752 (airport T9773200); *Budget*, 99 HaYarkon, T5245233 (airport
T9711504); *Eldan*, 112 HaYarkon, T5271168 (airport T9773400); *Eurodollar*, 2 Mapu,
T5271122 (airport T9731271); *Europcar*, 126 HaYarkon, T5248181 (airport T9721097);
Hertz, 144 HaYarkon, T5223332 (airport T9711165); *Perry*, 112 HaYarkon, T5233311;
Reliable, 96 HaYarkon, T5249764 (airport T9772511); *Sa-Gal*, 84 HaYarkon, T5106103;
Thrifty, 122 HaYarkon, T5612050 (airport T9711750); *TIP*, 94 HaYarkon, T5240281;
Traffic, 130 HaYarkon, T5249187.

Sheruts/shared taxis Minibuses operating as shared taxis (sheruts) run along local
bus routes 4 and 5, and are more flexible since you can flag them down and get on or
off anywhere along the route. They also run later at night, and on Shabbat. Fares are
the same as the buses (though 25% more on Shabbat).

Taxis *Balfour*, T5604545; *Castel*, T6993322; *Gordon*, T5272999; *Habima*, T5283132;
New York, T5226660; *Nordau*, T5466222, amongst many others, all 24 hrs. For complaints about taxis in the Tel Aviv and Central Region, T5657272, F5657216.

Air Most visitors to Israel arrive at **Ben-Gurion Airport**, close to Tel Aviv. See box on **Long distance**
next page for full details. Also see 'Flying' in the 'Sports' section on page and 'Getting
there, Air' on page 31.
  Domestic flights tend to use Sede Dov Airport (see 'Tel Aviv: overview' map), with
Arkia (T1-800-444888, or at Sede Dov T6902222) offering hourly flights to **Eilat** (1 hr),
several daily to **Rosh Pinna** (30 mins) and **Kiryat Shemona** (40 mins) respectively,
and a number weekly to **Neve Zohar** (30 mins).

Buses Tel Aviv's **Central Bus Station** is on Levinsky, to the southeast of the city centre (see 'South Central Tel Aviv' map). Buses 4 and 5 run from the Central Bus Station
past most of the hotels and hostels (see 'Local buses' on page 461). The Central Bus
Station is on 6 floors and features, in addition to the McDonald's and numerous
fast-food places, a bank, post office, children's adventure playground, army surplus
shop where you can buy an electronic stun gun or a new case for your M16, and even
a peep show!
  Initially confusing, it is actually quite well signposted: 1st floor: Dan departure platforms 101-118 (for journeys within Tel Aviv); 2nd floor: Dan alighting platforms and
Dan information counter (for Dan Tel Aviv bus routes map); 3rd floor: Parking
entrance; 4th floor: Taxi/Sherut platform 414, 'special transport' Egged and Dan

☞ *Ben-Gurion Airport*

General: Ben-Gurion Airport is located at Lod, some 22 km southeast of Tel Aviv. For general airport information, T9710000; for computerized recorded information T9723344 (English) or T9723333 (Hebrew).

To/from the airport: United Tours *Bus 222 (T1-800-876787) runs hourly between the airport arrivals hall and Tel Aviv (via the railway station and along the sea-front, terminating at the* Dan Panorama Hotel *and passing many of the hotels and hostels), 20 NIS, Sunday-Thursday 0400-2400, Friday 0400-2000, Saturday 1300-2400.* Egged Bus 475 runs every 30 mins between Tel Aviv's Central Bus Station and the airport (12 NIS, 25 mins, Sunday-Thursday 0530-2300, Friday last at 1545, Saturday first at 1815). From the Central Bus Station, Buses 4 and 5 pass most of the hostels. Buses 945/947 connect the airport to Jerusalem (20 NIS, 55 mins, Sunday-Thursday 0600-2200, Friday last at 1540, Saturday first at 1815). There are 1-2 services per hour between the airport and Haifa (Buses 945/947, 42 NIS, 1 hr), and to a number of other destinations. Sheruts are available 24 hrs from outside the arrivals hall to Jerusalem (Nesher taxis, T9721818 40 NIS, 1 hr), Tel Aviv (26 NIS, 20 mins) and Haifa/Akko/Nahariya (Amal, T04-8676444, 70 NIS, 1 ½ hrs). Taxis are also available 24 hrs (T9711103, about 50 NIS to central Tel Aviv).

Arrival formalities: You have to fill out a landing card on arrival (this is effectively your visa), retaining it until you depart Israel (don't lose it). Immigration will stamp this card and not your passport, **but only if you ask in advance**. The volume of traffic using the airport has largely outgrown the terminal, and it's not unusual to have to queue for an hour to clear Immigration.

Departure formalities: Ensure that you arrive no less than 3 hrs before your flight departs. Be prepared for thorough questioning by the security staff before you check in (my own personal record is 1 hr 55 mins). See page 32 for further details on airport security. Bear in mind that this is done for your own safety. You must return your landing card to Immigration upon departure (and if you avoided an Israeli stamp when you arrived you can avoid getting one now, but only if you ask).

Airport facilities: There is limited **duty-free** available upon arrival, plus more extensive duty-free shopping upon departure (but not the world's best value). All the major **car-hire** firms have offices at the airport, most of which are open 24 hrs. A number of companies offer **cellular phone** hire, plus regular telecommunications facilities. **Banks** here do not offer the best deals; change just enough to tide you over until you can go to more competitive places in Tel Aviv or Jerusalem. VAT refunds are processed at the Bank Leumi in the Departures lounge (forms up to \$30=\$2 commission, up to \$100=\$5 commission, over \$100=\$8 commission). There's a post office, shops (including branches of Steimatzky bookshop) and café/restaurants. There are no left luggage facilities.

Advance baggage check-in: El Al have advance baggage check-in at Arlozorov Bus Terminal (in front of the train station), T6917198. Air Canada, Alitalia, Arkia, British Airways, Lufthansa and Swissair have advance baggage check-in at 2 Bonei Halr, T6903306 (near Reading Bus Terminal; see 'Northern Tel Aviv' map). Advance baggage check-in allows you to arrive at the airport 1 ½ hrs (and not 3 hrs) before your flight. For pre-recorded advance check-in info T9723388 (English) or T9723377 (Hebrew).

Tel Aviv/Jaffa

platforms 410-413, Dan departure platforms 415-418 (including routes 4, 5, 50, 51), post office, bank, shops, McDonald's; 6th floor: Tourist Information (near platform 630), left luggage (Sunday-Thursday 0700-1900, Friday 0700-1500, 10 NIS per item per day), Egged bus information, Egged ticket office, Egged departure platforms 601-636, Egged alighting area.

Almost all inter-city services are operated by the Egged Bus Company. The Egged information counter on the 6th floor has the usual level of Israeli service (ie none), and the timetables are available in Hebrew only. However, there are large electronic time-tables in English that list nearly all destinations, next departure time, final departure time, platform number and bus number. Tickets are supposed to be bought before boarding the bus (essential if using a student card), but few Israelis do. **Egged bus information** T5375555.

NB Security is tight here; you may be stopped and searched on arrival. Do not leave bags unattended, do not look after bags for anyone else, and report to security any unattended luggage. Listed below are a small selection of services (generally those offering the quickest, most direct route): **Destination**: bus no; platform no; regularity; timetable; fare; journey time.

Arad: 389; pl 604; 3 per day; Sunday-Thursday 1000 1300 1830, Friday same Saturday 2100. **Ashdod**: 312/314/320; 2-3 per hr; 15 NIS; 35 mins. **Ashqelon**: 362 exp, 300 exp, 311 via Yavne; 2-3 per hr; 25 NIS; 1 hr. **Be'er Sheva**: 370; pl 605; every 20 mins; Sunday-Thursday 0540-2100, Friday 0600-1640, Saturday 1950-2300; 22 NIS; 1¾ hrs. **Eilat**: 394; pl 628; 8 per day; Sunday-Thursday 0800-1700 plus 0100, Friday 0800-1400, Saturday 1700 and 0030; 56 NIS; 4½ hrs; book in advance. **Hadera** for **Caesarea**: 921; pl 602/3; 1-2 per hour; Sunday-Thursday 0630-2030, Friday 0730-1600, Saturday 1830-2200; 19 NIS; 1 hr 20 mins. **Haifa**: 900; pl 602/3; every 20 mins; Sunday-Thursday 0630-2030, Friday 0730-1600, Saturday 1830-2200; 25 NIS; 1¼ hrs. **Jerusalem**: 405; pl 609; every 15 mins; Sunday-Thursday 0550-2340, Friday 0550-1720, Saturday 2000-2400; 20 NIS; 50 mins. **Nazareth**: 823; pl 622; 9 per day; Sunday-Thursday 0525-2100, Friday 0525-1630, Saturday 1730-2210; 34 NIS; 1½ hrs. **Netanya**: 600; pl 619; every 20 mins; Sunday-Thursday 0530-2300, Friday 0530-1715, Saturday 2000-2300; 15 NIS; up to 1 hr. **Ramla**: 455 direct; 2-3 per hr; 11 NIS; 30 mins. **Rishon LeTzion**: numerous services; 8 NIS; 25 mins. **Safed**: 846; pl 625; Sunday-Friday 0535 0815, Saturday 0815; 40 NIS; 3½ hrs. **Tiberias**: 830; pl 623; every hr; Sunday-Thursday 0550-1830, Friday 0600-1530, Saturday 1730-2030; 40 NIS; 2 hrs. The regular Egged service to **Cairo** appears to have been suspended due to lack of interest. Tour companies still organize a bus on this route (see page 465).

Sherut/service taxi Inter-city sheruts leave from platform 414 (4th floor) of the Central Bus Station to a number of towns (usually providing a cheaper, quicker and more convenient service than the buses). Key destinations include: **Ashdod**; **Ashqelon**; **Be'er Sheva**; **Haifa**; **Jerusalem** (particularly convenient, arrives near Zion Sq); **Lod**; **Nazareth**; **Netanya** and **Ramla**.

Train Tel Aviv's **Central Railway Station** (formerly known as 'Arlozorov') is to the north of the city centre (see 'Central North Tel Aviv' map), T6937515/5774000, or T7652200 for recorded message. Bus 222 from the airport stops outside (Arlozorov Bus Terminal), as do buses 10, 20 and 64 amongst others. Although the network is limited it is a very pleasant way to travel, and cheaper than the bus network (especially with a student card). Services run every hour or so north via **Herzliya**, **Bet Yehoshua**, **Netanya**, **Kfar Vitkin**, **Hadera**, **Binyamina**, **Zikhron Ya'aqov**, **'Atlit** to **Haifa**, (with additional trains per hour calling at the main towns), plus certain services continuing to **Akko** and **Nahariya**. A line also runs southeast and east to **Lod**, **Ramla** and **Rehovot**, though at the time of writing there was talk of suspending the charming line up to **Jerusalem** (slow, but very picturesque). New services are being developed for **Ashdod** and **Be'er Sheva**, though massive rapid transit transportation plans remain on the drawing board.

Tel Aviv/Jaffa

Sea/boat Tickets for the Cyprus/Greece ferry to/from Haifa can be bought at *Caspi Travel*, 1 Ben Yehuda, T5175749. To land your own craft at Tel Aviv's Atarim Marina, T52722596.

Directory

Airline offices *El Al*, 32 Ben Yehuda, T5261222. Sun-Thu 0830-1645, Fri-Sat closed, late hours at *Hilton* office and 24 hrs at airport. A number of airlines have their offices at 1 Ben Yehuda, including *Aeroflot*, T5107050; *Air France*, T5161144/5110000; *Air Sinai*, T5102481; *American Airlines*, T5104322; *British Airways*, T5101581/5; *Canadian*, T5172163; *Cyprus*, T5278065; *Lufthansa*, T5142350; *Olympic*, T5112121; *Qantas*, T5172163; *SAA*, T5102828; *SAS*, T5101177; *Swissair*, T5116666. Other airlines include: *Adria*, 66 Ben Yehuda, T5223161; *Aerolineas Argentinas*, Shalom Alechem; *Air Canada*, 59 Ben Yehuda, T5273781/5107893; *Air India*, 32 Ben Yehuda, T5259222; *Air Kazakhstan*, 14 Trumpeldor; *Air UK*, 27 Ben Yehuda, T5173812; *Alitalia*, 98 Dizengoff, T5200000; *Arkia*, 11 Frishman, T1-800-444888, (or at Dov airport T6902222); *Austrian*, 17 Ben Yehuda, T5173535/5172244; *Bolivian*, 44 HaYarkon, T5174072; *British Midland*, 32 Ben Yehuda, T6290972; *Cathay Pacific*, 43 Ben Yehuda, T5228444; *Cubana*, 44 HaYarkon, T5174072; *Cyprus*, 32 Ben Yehuda, T5258171; *Delta*, 29 Allenby, T6201101; *Georgia*, 71a Ben Yehuda, T5277863; *Iberia*, 14 Ben Yehuda, T2900976/5163239; *KLM*, 128 Ibn Gvirol, T5219999; *Malev*, 94 Ben Yehuda, T5246171; *Olympic*, 13 Idelson, T6294381; *Royal Jordanian*, 5 Shalom Alechem, T5165566, F5106615. One-way tickets to Amman $80; *Sabena*, 74 HaYarkon, T5174471; *Tarom*, 46 Herbert Samuel, T5162030; *Thai*, 1 Trumpeldor, T5160908; *Tower Air*, 78 HaYarkon, T5179421; *Turkish*, 78 HaYarkon, T5172333; *TWA*, 74 HaYarkon, T5171212. Charter flights to the UK on *Air 2000*, *British Caledonian* and *Monarch* are usually handled by *Flying Carpet*, 44 Ben Yehuda (entrance on Bograshov), T5256655.

Banks There are numerous banks offering foreign exchange in Tel Aviv (though check rates and commission charges before committing yourself). Those marked with the '$' bank symbol on the maps are those with ATM machines. Note that **post offices** offer commission-free foreign exchange. **Lost credit cards: American Express, Eurocard, Mastercard**, T5764666; **Diners Club**, T5723666; **Thomas Cook**, T177-4408424; **Visa**, T177-440-666. **Money changers: American Express**, 53 Ben Yehuda; 52 HaMelekh George; **Change Spot** 140 Dizengoff, T5243393, 13 Ben Yehuda, T5100573; 26 Rambam, T5166699, Opera Tower, 1 Allenby, T5106035; **Change**, 52 HaMelekh George, T5256908 and 37 Ben Yehuda, T5106252; **Change Bar**, 94 HaYarkon, T5245505; **Change Point**, 106 HaYarkon, T5245505, 70 Ben Yehuda, T5279035, amongst many others.

Communications Phone code: 03. **Post offices:** *Central Post Office*, 132 Allenby, T5643760, plus numerous branch offices marked on map. **Post Restante:** 7 Mikve Yisra'el, (counter 1, Sun-Thu 0800-1800, Fri 0800-1400). **Internet/email:** *EBC Executive Business Centre*, 99 HaYarkon, T5226999. *Internet In-bar*, 2 Shlomo HaMelekh (corner of 87 HaMelekh George), T5282228, F5282225. Sun-Thu 0900-0100, Fri 0900-1700, Sat 1600-0100, 30 NIS for 30 mins, 40 NIS for 1 hr, 'happy hour' 1200-1800 (30% discount). **Telephones:** *Central Telegraph Office*, 7 Mikve Yisra'el, T5643654 (open 24 hrs including Shabbat). *RSM*, 80 HaYarkon, T5168366. Daily cellular phone rental, free incoming calls. *Solan Communications*, 13 Frishman, T5229424, open 7 days 0800-2300, UK and USA 2 NIS per min, Aus 3 NIS per min, cellular phone rental (first 2 weeks free, 39 cents incoming calls, 69 cents per min outgoing, plus 19 cents for overseas calls). **Overseas operator:** T188.

Cultural centres American Cultural Center, 5th floor, 1 Ben Yehuda, T5106935, Mon-Thu 1000-1600, Fri 1000-1400. **British Council**, see under 'Libraries' below. **Hungarian Cultural and Business Centre**, 38 Allenby. Sells gifts, junk, and a good selection of porno mags!

Embassies and consulates Most countries have failed to recognize Israel's decision to choose Jerusalem as their capital, and hence most embassies and consulates remain in Tel Aviv. **Argentina**, 3a Jabotinsky, T5759173. **Australia**, 37 Sha'ul Ha-Melekh, Europe House, 4th floor, T6950451. **Austria**, 11 Herman Cohen, T5246168. **Belarus**, 2 Kaufman, T5102236. **Belgium**, 266 HaYarkon, T6054164. **Brazil**, 2 Kaplan, T6919292. **Canada**, 3 Nirim, T6363300. **Cyprus**, 50 Dizengoff, Top Tower, T5250212. **Czech Republic**, 23 Zeitlin, T6918282. **Denmark**, 23 Bnei Moshe, T5442144. **Egypt**, 54 Basel, (off Ibn Gvirol), T5464151. Open Sun-Thu 0900-1100 for visa services (arrive early). In theory visa can be collected the same afternoon, but don't count on it. Visa fee depends upon nationality; bring 3 photos. Tourist visas are not available on the border, but non-extendable 14-day 'Sinai permits' are. **France**, 112 Herbert Samuel, T5245371. **Germany**, 3 Daniel Frisch, T6931313. **Greece**, 47 Bodenheimer, T6055461. **Hungary**, 18 Pinkas, T5466860. **India**, 4 Kaufman, T5101431. **Ireland**, 266 HaYarkon, T9509055. **Italy**, 4 Weizmann, T6964223. **Japan**, 4 Weizmann, T6957292. **Jordan**, 14 Aba Hillel, Ramat Gan, T7517722. Open Sun-Thu 0900-1600 for visas (arrive early). Visas can take up to 14 days to be processed. Most nationalities (not Israelis) can get a visa on the border, but not at the Allenby/King Hussein Bridge. **Netherlands**, 4 Weizmann, T6957377. **New Zealand**, see under UK. **Norway**, 40 Namal, T5442030. **Philippines**, 2 Kaufman, T5175263. **Poland**, 16 Soutine, T5240188. **Portugal**, 4 Weizmann, T6956373. **Romania**, 24 Adam HaCohen, T5244644. **Russia**, 120 HaYarkon, T5226733. **Slovenia**, 12th Floor, Textile Centre, 2 Kaufman, T5163530. **South Africa**, Top Tower, 16th Floor, 50 Dizengoff, T5252566. **Spain**, 3 Daniel Frish, T5965218. **Sweden**, 4 Weizmann, T6958111. **Switzerland**, 228 HaYarkon, T5464455. **Thailand**, 21 Sha'ul HaMelekh, T6958980. **Turkey**, 34 Amos, T6054155. **UK**, 192, HaYarkon, T5249171. **Ukraine**, 12 Striker, T6040311. **USA**, 71 HaYarkon, T5197575, after-hours T5174347. **Uzbekistan**, 1 Ben Yehuda, T5104684.

Hospitals and medical services

Ambulance: *Magen David Adom*, 2 Alkalai, T101 (T5460111 for intensive care ambulance). **Chemists**: *Dizengoff Pharmacy*, 133 Dizengoff; *HaGalil*, 80 Ben Yehuda, corner of Mapu, T5240861. Homeopathic pharmacy, open 0830-1900; *Pharma Plus*, 185 Dizengoff; *SuperPharm*, junction of Dizengoff and Gordon; plus numerous others. Although the night/Shabbat rota is displayed outside most pharmacies, it's in Hebrew only. **Dentists**: *Adent*, 93 Yehuda HaMaccabi, T5466328; *Dental Clinic*, 4 Zeitin, T6969542; *Israel Dental Association*, 49 Bar Kokhba, T5280507; *Levdent*, 1 Zeitlin, T6914414; *Tai Dental Clinic*, Dizengoff Centre, T5254186. **Doctors**: *SOS Doctors*, T177-022-5006 (24-hr house calls). **Mental Health Hotline**, T1201 (children T5467799). **Hospitals**: *Basel Heights Medical Centre*, 35 Basel, T5462330; *Beit Harophim Medical Centre*, 3 Sprintzak, T6968840; *Ichilov Medical Centre*, 6 Weizman, T6974444/6974226, Tel Aviv's main hospital; *Wolfson*, 62 Halohamim, Tel Giborim, Holon, T5028211.

Laundries

Kikar Dizengoff Laundry, Kikar Dizengoff, open 24 hrs, 12 NIS for 7 kg, dryer 5 NIS for 15 mins; *Nikita*, 98 and 191 Ben Yehuda; *Uni Wash*, 64 Ben Yehuda; *Zikit*, 117 Ibn Gvirol; *Zukush*, 245 Dizengoff.

Libraries

British Council, 140 HaYarkon, T5222194, F5221229. Library (with BBC TV) Mon-Thu 1000-1300 1600-1900, Fri 1000-1300; *Shaar Zion Beit Ariela Public Library*, next to Tel Aviv Performing Arts Centre, Sha'ul HaMelekh. See also under 'Cultural centres', page 464.

Places of worship

Christian: *Anglican*, 12 Bar Hofman (Jaffa), T6821459; *Emmanuel (Lutheran)*, 9 Bar Hofman (Jaffa), T6820654; *Russian*, Herzl (Jaffa); *St Anthony (Catholic)*, 51 Yefet (Jaffa), T6822667; *St Michael (Greek Orthodox)*, Netiv Ha-Mazalot (Jaffa), T6823451; *St Peter's (Catholic)*, Kikar Kedumim (Jaffa), T6822871; *Baptist*, Baptist Village (northeast of Tel Aviv), T9311965. **Jewish**: *Beit Daniel (Reform)*, 62 Bnei Dan, T5442740; *Great Synagogue (Ashkenazi)*, 110 Allenby, T5604905; *Ichud Shivat Zion (German)*, 86 Ben Yehuda, T5224047; *Kehilat Sinai (Conservative)*, 88 Bograshov, T5174701; *Ohel Moed (Sephardi)*, 5 Shadal, T5609764. **Muslim**: *El Ajami*, HaSfina (Jaffa); *Hanamal*, Jaffa Port; *Great Mosque*, Russian St (Jaffa).

Tour companies and travel agents

There are numerous tour companies based in Tel Aviv, mainly found at the hotels and along Ben Yehuda. Most offer Israel tours, trips to Jordan (especially Petra), plus Egypt trips. *Egged Tlalim*, 59 Ben Yehuda, T5271212, F5272020. Variety of tours, daily bus to Cairo. *issta*, 128 Ben Yehuda, T5230006/7. Sun, Mon, Tue, Thu 0900-1800, Wed, Fri 0830-1300, good for student/under-26 discounts. *Mazada Tours*, 141 Ibn Gvirol, T5444454, F5461928, or 24 hrs T7653696. Long established, specializing in trips to Egypt and Jordan, daily bus to Cairo (day $35 plus departure tax), night $40 plus departure tax), see entry under Jerusalem on page 237 for full details. *Mona Tours*, 25 Bograshov, T6211433, F5251079. Claims to be able to beat anyone else's price, good for standby flights to Europe and Australia. *Late Night Ltd*, 53 Gordon, T5276346, F5276350. Offers the 'Nightline', a night tour of Tel Aviv (Mon-Thu 2100-0030). *Peltours*, 33 Ben Yehuda. Experienced operator. *Pullman Tours*, 98 HaYarkon, T5270474, F5270477. Bus to Cairo every Sun, Mon, Wed, Thu, $40 one-way, $60 return (excludes visa and border taxes). *United Tours*, 88 HaYarkon, T5179606.

Tel Aviv/Jaffa

Tourist offices   The IGTO **Tourist Information Office** is at Room 6108, 6th floor (near platform 630), Central Bus Station, T6395660, F6395659. It has free maps of Tel Aviv/Jaffa, all the brochures/flyers you could ever need, plus *Hello Israel* and *This Week in Tel Aviv*. The staff can also help in booking accommodation.

Useful addresses and phone numbers   Police: T100 or T6284444 (Police Lost and Found T6818107). **Magen David Adom (ambulance)**: 2 Alkalai, T101. **Fire**: T102 or T6994111. **Alcoholics Anonymous**, T5225255. **Association of Americans and Canadians in Israel (AACI)**, 22 Mazeh, T6299799. **British Olim Society (BOS)**, 76 Ibn Gvirol, T6965244. **Gay and Lesbian Hotline**, T6292797, or try T6293681. **Jewish National Fund**, 96 HaYarkon, T5234367. 'Plant a young tree in Israel'. **Narcotics Anonymous**, T5758869. **Rape Crisis Centre**, T5234819. **VIP International Escort Service**, T5607510, 'medically certified'! **Visa extension office**, Shalom Tower, East Wing, 14th floor. Open Sun-Thu 0700-1200, arrive as early as possible and look smart. Bring passport, photos, air ticket (if you have one) and proof of funds.

Working   **Kibbutz Moshav Volunteers Office**, 169 HaYarkon, T5271386. **Kibbutz Program Centre**, 3rd floor, 18 Frishman, T5278874, F5239966. **Meira's Volunteers for Moshav and Kibbutz**, 1st floor, 73 Ben Yehuda, T5237369, F5241604. **Project 67**, 94 Ben Yehuda, T5230140. See page 62 for further information. **Other**   Tel Aviv is probably the best place in Israel (with Eilat) to pick up (illegal) casual work. Many potential employers call the hostels in search of day labourers, so make friends with the receptionist. Men tend to get work in the 'construction' industry (14-20 NIS per hour), or as dish-washers in restaurants (10-12 NIS per hour). Women tend to find work as hostel receptionists or as waitresses and barmaids (nothing-10 NIS per hour, plus tips), though you're more likely to find work if you're attractive and own a short skirt! You could also try **Au-Pair Intermediary**, T9659937 or **Au-Pair International**, T6190423. See page 63 for further information.

Jaffa

Phone code: 03
Colour map 2, grid B2

Jaffa has a long and incident-packed history, with repeated periods of capture and destruction followed by bouts of reconstruction and prosperity. Only small sections of the old town remain today, though they have been tastefully restored and provide a pleasant contrast to the modern environs of nearby Tel Aviv. The 'Old Jaffa' area is now a concentration of galleries, antique shops and restaurants, and is a popular destination with evening strollers. The Shuq Hapishpeshim, or Jaffa's famous 'Flea Market', is another experience that should not be missed.

Ins and outs

Getting there   Most visitors to Jaffa arrive along Yefet St, via the clock-tower square area, although those on coach tours may be driven straight into the heart of the restored Old Jaffa area. The seafront promenade walk has now been extended all the way from Tel Aviv to Old Jaffa, and is just awaiting the final beautification touches. Bus 46 runs from the Central Bus Station to the Jaffa clock-tower (every 5-15 mins, 0515-0025). Bus **10** runs from downtown Tel Aviv to the clock-tower (every 10-25 mins, 0525-0020). Several buses run from the Central Bus Station along Sederot Jerusalem, just inland of Old Jaffa, including **7** (every 30 mins, 0515-2000), **40** (every 10-20 mins, 0450-2120) and **44** (every 7-20 mins, 0515-1940).

Getting around   There is no single walking route that takes in all the sights of Jaffa in a set order, but given the compact size of the district, it is easy to just wander around and still see all the attractions.

History

Legend, and Jewish tradition, suggests that Jaffa (**Yafo** in Hebrew and **Joppa** in most biblical references) was founded after the Flood by Japheth, son of Noah. Jaffa also became the setting for the legend of Andromeda, and the supporting cast of the rock, the sea-monster, Perseus and Pegasus (see 'Jaffa legends', page 470).

There are numerous early written references to Jaffa, most notably in the Bible; the port here is mentioned as the landing place for the Cedars of Lebanon that were brought by sea for use in the construction of the First and Second Temples at Jerusalem (*II Chronicles 2:16; Ezra 3:7*).

There is evidence that by 1200 BCE Jaffa was established as a Philistine city, although about 200 years later **David** conquered the city. As with much of the kingdom of Judah, Jaffa was captured by the Assyrian king **Sennacherib** during his successful campaign of 701 BCE. In subsequent years Jaffa became a largely Phoenician town, with a fifth century BCE inscription of **Eshmunazar of Sidon** describing how the king of Persia presented him with Dor and Jaffa.

Jaffa became a largely Greek city during the Early Hellenistic period (332-167). In fact, according to Greek legend, Joppa is daughter of the wind god Aeolus. Jaffa came under control of the Ptolemies until the capture of Palestine by **Antiochus III** of Syria in 223 BCE. The ethnically Greek population of Syrian-controlled Jaffa came into conflict with the **Maccabees** during the Hasmonean period, with much of the town being burned by Judas Maccabaeus (*II Maccabees 12:3-7*). This was in response to the deliberate drowning of 200 Jaffa Jews. The port town was subsequently conquered by his brother Jonathan, and annexed to Judaea by the older brother Simon (*I Maccabees 12:34*).

Pompey declared the town independent in 63 BCE, though **Julius Caesar** returned it to Jewish control 16 years later. It was reputedly given to **Cleopatra** by a love-struck Mark Anthony, though nominal control was passed to **Herod the Great** following her death in 30 BCE. The port went into serious decline in the first century BCE with Herod's establishment of the port of Sebastos at Caesarea, and was largely destroyed by **Vespasian** in 67 CE. The Roman emperor later rebuilt the town, giving it an independent charter. A biblical reference to Jaffa describes how Peter "tarried many days in Joppa with one Simon a tanner", having raised Tabitha (known as Dorcas) from the dead (*Acts 9:36-43*), and also received a vision here that revealed that pagans should be admitted into the church (*Acts 10:10-48*).

In latter centuries Jaffa was conquered by the **Arabs** (636 CE) and then by the **Crusaders**, with the port becoming a major landing place for pilgrims visiting the Holy Land. After the Mamluk sultan Baibars finally dispatched the Crusaders in 1267, the town was largely abandoned for the next three centuries.

Jaffa's modern history begins with **Ottoman** rule in Palestine around 1520. **Napoleon** besieged Jaffa in 1799, with the town falling under the control of **Ibrahim Pasha** some years later. Many of the buildings to be seen in Old Jaffa today were built during this period. The mid- to late 19th century saw the establishment of new settlements outside Jaffa, populated mainly by Christian and Jewish Zionists. Numerous Christian hostelries, churches and monasteries were established in and around Jaffa during this period. The early 20th century saw the tentative beginnings of the new Jewish town of Tel Aviv.

The decade of the 1920s saw increased tension between the Jewish and Arab communities leading to violent clashes. Vast swathes of the town's narrow labyrinthine streets were cleared by the British in order to facilitate military control, though parts have now been restored in the Old Jaffa area. The town's port suffered a terminal blow following its closure during the 1936 Arab Revolt, and the establishment of a new port at Tel Aviv. The UN vote on the partition of Palestine in November 1947 led to prolonged clashes all across Palestine, with Jewish forces capturing Jaffa in April 1948 after a short but bloody battle. The flight of almost the entire Arab population has remained a point of contention ever since.

Following the 1948/49 War of Independence, Jaffa was amalgamated within the municipality of Tel Aviv. In recent years, parts of Old Jaffa have been substantially restored.

Jaffa

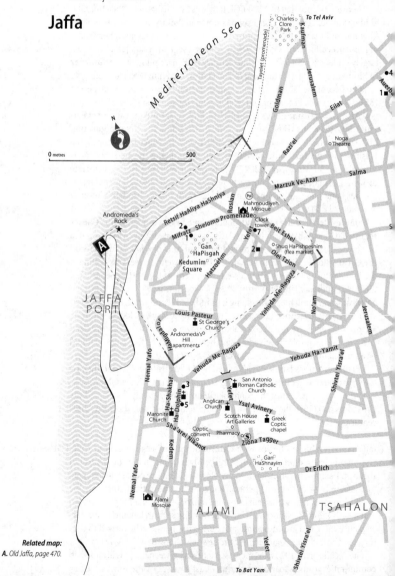

Related map:
A. Old Jaffa, page 470.

Sights

Built in 1906 to mark the anniversary of the accession to the throne of the Otto- **Ottoman**
man Sultan Abdul Hamid II, the occasionally working clock-tower serves as one **Clock-tower**
of several prominent Jaffa landmarks. There is some dispute as to whether the
clock-tower was built to mark the 25th or the 30th anniversary of the Sultan's
reign, though this confusion probably derives from the fact that construction
actually began in 1901 and took five years to complete. Similar clock-towers
were built in Jerusalem and Akko to mark the same event. More recent renovations added the plaque commemorating the Israelis killed in the 1948 battle for
the town, and the stained glass windows which date to the mid-1960s.

Tel Aviv/Jaffa

■ Sleeping	● Eating	5 Le Relais Jaffa
1 Beit Immanuel	1 Abouelafiya	6 Pastalina
Christian Hostel	2 Aladin	7 Said Abou Elafia & Sons
2 Old Jaffa Hotel	3 Eli's Caravan	8 Tampadulu
	4 Keren	9 Tarkari

Jaffa Legends

There are many legends attached to Jaffa, spanning almost every age in history. Perhaps the most famous biblical reference to Jaffa concerns the story of Jonah, and his experience with the "great fish" (Jonah 1:17), or whale. It was from Jaffa that **Jonah** embarked on his ill-fated expedition, ignoring God's commandment to go to the "wicked" city of Nineveh, and instead attempting to sail to Tarshish (Jonah 1:1-3).

There is also the story of the **Pharaoh Thutmose III**'s capture of the city in the 15th century BCE, when he sent the governor of Jaffa a number of baskets said to contain bounty. Having accepted the gift, the governor discovered too late that the baskets actually contained soldiers, who went on to capture the city from within.

Then there is the legend of **Andromeda**. It seems that Queen Cassiopeia, wife of King Copeus of Ethiopia, boasted that her daughter Andromeda was more beautiful than any mermaid. This seriously pissed off Nireus (father of mermaids), who begged Poseidon (god of the sea) to take revenge for this sleight. Duly obliging, Poseidon sent a sea-monster to terrorize the coast. In an attempt to assuage the fury of Poseidon, King Copeus tied his daughter Andromeda to the rock as a sacrifice to the monster. Fortunately for Andromeda she had a daring suitor in Perseus, who swooped down from the skies on his winged steed Pegasus, slew the monster, and carried her off to safety. Legend doesn't recount what Andromeda later said to her father about the incident.

Also on the clock-tower square stands the '**Kishleh**', a building that dates to the Ottoman period, but was later used as a detention centre by the British. Today, the building serves as Jaffa Police Station, though the seal of Sultan Abdul Hamid II can still be seen above the door.

Mahmoudiyeh Mosque Located at the southwest corner of the square is the Great, or **Mahmoudiyeh Mosque**. Though dating to 1809, the mosque was extensively renovated just three years later by the Turkish Sultan's representative in Jaffa, Governor Mohammad 'Abu Nabut' Aja, during whose rule Jaffa experienced a period of rejuvenation and expansion. Amongst building materials used on the renovation were columns taken from Ashqelon and Caesarea, and popular legend has it that the masons set them upside down, so that today their capitals stand at the base.

The main entrance to the mosque is in the south wall, though a separate entrance was built in the

Old Jaffa

Tel Aviv/Jaffa

east wall during the late 19th century for exclusive use of the governor and other notables. Also in the south wall is the **Suleiman Fountain**, though it retains little of its former splendour. The mosque has a tall, slender minaret, two white domes and a pleasant interior courtyard, though it is not generally open to non-Muslims.

Before one wanders up the hill into the restored area of Old Jaffa itself, there are a few places of interest in the vicinity of **Yefet Street**. Diagonally opposite the mosque, just off Yefet Street, is the old Jerusalem road (now Beit Eshel Street), the former business district. At No 11 stands the 19th-century **Manouli Khan**, a caravanserai formerly run by an Armenian family. Today, it is a furniture/antique store, though you can still see something of its previous form as a hostel and stables.

Other buildings of note on Yefet Street include the **Anglo-Palestine House** (site of the first Zionist Bank), **Emigrant House** (a 19th-century hostel for Jewish immigrants), and the **'St Louis' French Hospital**. The two former buildings, bar the shops downstairs, are now pretty much derelict, though the latter is still used as a community health centre. Named after the leader of the Seventh Crusade, Louis IX who landed at Jaffa in 1251, this attractive neo-Renaissance building was established as a hospital in the 19th century.

Further south on Yefet Street, and still very much in use, is the **Tabitha School for Girls**, established and run by the Presbyterian Church of Scotland since 1863. The small graveyard to the rear of the building contains the grave

Other sights along Yefet Street

Tel Aviv/Jaffa

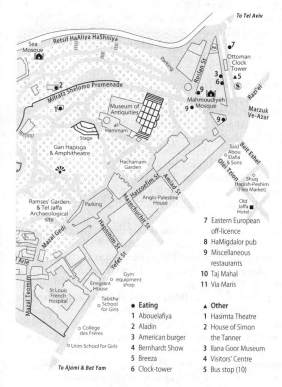

To Tel Aviv

Sea Mosque

Retsif HaAliya HaShniya

Parking

Roslan St

Ottoman Clock Tower

Mifratz Shelomo Promenade

Museum of Antiquities

al-Hammam

Stage

Gan Hapisga & Amphitheatre

Hachamam Garden

Mahmoudiyeh Mosque

Razi'el

Marzuk Ve-Azar

Said Abou Elafia & Sons

Beit Eshel

Olei Tzion

Shuq Hapish-Peshim (Flea Market)

Ramses' Garden & Tel Jaffa Archaeological site

Parking

Hatzoefim St

Amiad St

Hechuchu St

Anglo-Palestine House

Old Jaffa Hotel

Mazal Gedi

HaNinim St

Yefet St

7 Eastern European off-licence
8 HaMigdalor pub
9 Miscellaneous restaurants
10 Taj Mahal
11 Via Maris

Mazal Teomim

'Arie

St Louis French Hospital

Emigrant House

Gym equipment shop

Tabitha School for Girls

● **Eating**
1 Abouelafiya
2 Aladin
3 American burger
4 Bernhardt Show
5 Breeza
6 Clock-tower

Collège des Frères

Urim School for Girls

To Ajami & Bat Yam

▲ **Other**
1 Hasimta Theatre
2 House of Simon the Tanner
3 Ilana Goor Museum
4 Visitors' Centre
5 Bus stop (10)

of, amongst other notables, Dr Thomas Hodgkin, the man who diagnosed Hodgkin's Disease, and who himself died in Jaffa in 1866. Next door stands the **College des Frères**, a former late 19th-century French catholic school for boys, and further along the **Urim School for Girls**, founded by Catholic nuns in 1882 and still used as a school to this day.

Shuq Hapishpeshim (Flea Market)   Also located just off Yefet Street, at the clock-tower end, is Jaffa's brilliant flea market. Opinions are divided as to whether you are likely to pick up a bargain or not, but it's certainly worth a visit. In addition to some genuine antiques, there are even more not-so-genuine antiques, plus some real rubbish, particularly amongst those traders whose pitch is just a few square metres of pavement on Olei Zion Street. Odd shoes, electrical equipment that has no hope of ever working, seedy videos with extremely pornographic covers that turn out to be blank tapes (so I'm told!), piles of rags that are actually second-hand clothes: the street vendors have them all. The traders with permanent shops have more upmarket wares, particularly furniture, carpets, jewellery, plus clothing of a style that sells well in both London's Camden Market, and the bazaars of Rajasthan. Whoever you are dealing with, bargaining is an essential part of the purchasing process. Closed Saturday.

Museum of Antiquities/ Jaffa Museum   Formerly the A-Saraya al-Atiqa (old Turkish Government House) the building now houses an interesting collection of finds from the Jaffa/Tel Aviv area dating from the Neolithic (7500-4500 BCE) period to the 19th century CE. The museum works particularly hard to emphasize the historical Jewish presence in Jaffa. ■ *10 Mifratz Shelomo, Old Jaffa, T6825375. Sunday, Monday, Thursday 0900-1400, Tuesday, Wednesday 0900-1900, Friday closed, Saturday 1000-1400. Adult 12 NIS, student 8 NIS.*

Directly behind the museum is **al-Hammam**, the former Turkish bath-house, and now part of the theatre/restaurant building.

St Peter's Monastery   Old Jaffa's most prominent landmark is the ochre and pale yellow **St Peter's Monastery**. Franciscans built a monastery on this site in 1654 upon the ruins of a 13th-century Crusader castle, though the present building dates to the late 19th century. It is still possible to see the remarkably intact vaulted chambers of the Crusader halls by descending the stairs in the monastery's courtyard.

The apostle Peter is said to have visited Jaffa, where he performed the Miracle of the Resurrected Tabitha, also known as Dorcas (*Acts 9:36-37, 38-39, 40*). A later guest at the old monastery built in Peter's honour was Napoleon, who is alleged to have stayed there during his 1799 campaign. ■ *1 Mifratz Shlomo, Old Jaffa, T8222871. 0800-1145, 1500-1800. Free.*

Kedumim Square Visitor's Centre   The large open plaza at the centre of the restored area of Old Jaffa, Kedumim Square, is at its most lively during the evening, when it fills up with promenading families, young couples, tourists and restaurant-goers. On the west side of the square is a **viewpoint**, offering exceptional views of the Jaffa port area, and **Andromeda's Rock** (see box, page 470).

At the centre of the square is a below-ground **Visitor's Centre**, housing a number of excavations and an exhibition detailing the history of Jaffa. The excavations include a 3-room subterranean complex dating from the end of the third century BCE, the walls of a Jewish dwelling abandoned in 67 CE, and a number of walls containing inscribed references to Yehuda ben Tozomenos, Jaffa's *agoranomos* (official in charge of weights and measures) during the reign of Emperor Trajan (98-117 CE). A short video lasting nine minutes (shown every six minutes, with subtitles in all languages) tells the story of

Jaffa's history. ■ *Sunday-Thursday 0900-2300, Friday 0900-1400, Saturday 1000-2300. Free; disabled access.*

On the landward (south-southeast) side of Kedumim Square are the archaeological excavations known as 'Tel Jaffa, Area A'. Excavated between 1955 and 1974, the site now forms part of a landscaped lawn, referred to as Ramses' Garden. Though not spectacular, the finds have proved important in piecing together Jaffa's long history. Remains on display include: "stone foundations of a citadel dating to the Hellenistic period (332-140 BCE); a lower wall dating to the Persian period (539-332 BCE); gateway foundations destroyed in a conflagration towards the end of the late Canaanite period (end of 13th, beginning of 12th century BCE); lower section of city's gateway dating to the reign of the Pharaoh Ramses II (1304-1237 BCE), including four jamb-stones of the gateway with incised hieroglyphic inscriptions featuring named titles of Ramses II; beneath the gateway, remains of brick walls dating to the late Canaanite era (16th-14th century BCE); structural remains dating to the Middle Ages, and finally, a soap production building from the British Mandate period". **Ramses' Garden and Tel Jaffa**

To the north of Ramses' Garden lies the **Gan Hapisga**, or Summit Garden. The large lawn is popular with picnicking families, and also provides the seating area for productions on the outdoor stage. The observation point at the summit, featuring an uninspiring sculpture titled 'Statue of Faith', is a favourite spot with newly weds for a photographic opportunity.

To the south of Kedumim Square is the Artists' Quarter, a superbly restored labyrinth of narrow alleyways, arched streets and cul-de-sacs. Most buildings are now studios, galleries and upmarket souvenir shops, though the blatantly commercial nature of the quarter does not really detract from its architectural charm. Also in this area is the **Hasimta Theatre and Bar**, and the **Ilana Goor Museum**. The latter building dates to the mid-18th century and was originally used as a hostel for Jewish pilgrims arriving in the Holy Land at Jaffa Port. After 1949 it served as a synagogue for Libyan Jews, and since 1955 it was first the home of the "internationally renowned artist, designer and sculptress" Ilana Goor, and then a museum displaying her life's work. It is a nice building, with some interesting pieces on display, but whether "your senses awaken to the diversity of shapes and images, the subtle play of texture and light" in this experiment of "living with art" as the brochure claims, may depend on whether you think 15 NIS admission fee is a bit steep. ■ *4 Mazal Dagim, Old Jaffa, T6837676. Sunday, Monday, Wednesday, Saturday 1000-2200, Tuesday, Thursday 1000-1400, Friday 1000-1600. Adult 15 NIS.* **Artists' Quarter**

Returning to Kedumim Square, a number of narrow alleys and staircases descend towards the Jaffa Port area. One such path, Shimon Habursekai, passes the House of **Simon the Tanner**, where Peter is said to have stayed following the Miracle of the Resurrection of Tabitha. It is a private house, and the owner may show you around, though there is little of historic interest to see. **Jaffa Port**

Jaffa Port is one of the oldest known harbours in the Middle East, perhaps the world (see above for history), and finds many references in the Bible (*Chronicles II 2:16; Zechariah 14:10; 2 Maccabees 12:3-6; Jonah 1:1-3, 4, 15, 17, 2:1, 10*). Today, it is primarily a marina for fishing boats and pleasure craft, with a number of quayside restaurants specializing in sea-food. A fine view of Jaffa can be had by walking out along the breakwater, or by taking a short trip around Andromeda's Rock on one of the pleasure cruisers (T6825753, 15 NIS for ½-hour trip).

There are a number of religious institutions along the quayside, including **St**

Jaffa Harbour

Michael's Greek Orthodox Church, The Armenian Church and St Nicholas' Monastery, and the Jama'a el-Bah'r, or Sea Mosque, where fishermen traditionally came to pray.

Andromeda's Rock   Just beyond the breakwater lies an unspectacular cluster of small rocks (you could hardly call them islands), known collectively as Andromeda's Rock (see box, page 470).

South of Old Jaffa   To the south of Old Jaffa stands the **San Antonio Roman Catholic Church**. This modern church, with its red-tile roof and tall steeple was built in 1932, and dedicated to St Antonius of Padua, a contemporary of St Francis of Assisi. Further along Ysal Avinery Street, behind San Antonio's, is a Greek Coptic chapel and convent with a small red dome, arched cloisters and squat, square tower. Further along the same street is a rather attractive basilica.

Opposite San Antonio's is the **Church of St Peter**, though it rather appears now as if somebody is living in this building. The small road beside St Peter's leads to a **Greek Catholic Church and Convent**, built in 1924. Nearby, on HaDolphin, is a **Maronite Church**.

Further to the east, approximately 2½ km from Old Jaffa, and distinguishable by its tall, slender tower, is the **Russian Monastery of St Peter**. Dedicated in 1860 by the Russian government, the chamber beneath the monastery is said to be the site of St Peter's resurrection of Tabitha.

Essentials

Sleeping   **C-E** *Beit Immanuel Christian Hostel*, 8 Auerbach, corner of 17 Eilat, T6821459, F6829817. Beautiful building (apparently constructed by Peter Ustinov's grandfather) now run as hostel by Anglican Church. Light and airy private rooms with attached bath sleep 2-4 (**C**), 'deluxe' dorms with attached bath or cheaper 'regular' 10-bed dorms (**E**), extremely clean and well run, dinner available ($10) including Shabbat dinner ($15), shady garden, reception 0700-1100, curfew 2300. Recommended.

F *Old Jaffa Hostel*, 8 Olei Tzion, T6822370. Very popular hostel in excellent location (overlooking the flea market) housed in fine old building. Single-sex and mixed dorms (discounts for paying in advance), private rooms with shared bath (**E**), private rooms with balconies and shared bath (**D**) and private rooms with balcony, kitchenette, bath, TV (**D**), no curfew, lovely roof garden, kitchen, cable TV lounge. This place receives rave reviews in most other guidebooks, though it has rested on its laurels somewhat and is no less crowded nor cleaner than most Tel Aviv hostels. Still worth considering though. Tentatively recommended.

Jaffa has a number of appealing restaurants, though those in prime locations charge more than similar-quality places in Tel Aviv. **Eating**

French *Le Relais Jaffa*, 13 HaDolphin, Jaffa, T6810637. One of Jaffa's (and Tel Aviv's) most highly recommended restaurants, serves traditional French cuisine in a beautiful 19th-century building, entrees 30-35 NIS, les viandes 60-85 NIS, specials 70-95 NIS, les desserts 16-25 NIS, reservations recommended. Recommended.

Miscellaneous *Abouelafiya*, Mifratz Shlemo Promenade. Attractive historic building with large dining hall serving traditional North African/Middle Eastern fayre, fish 60 NIS, meat 60 NIS, tajeen 66 NIS. *Aladin*, Mifratz Shlemo Promenade. Pay for the setting and views, fish 70 NIS, meat 60 NIS. *Eli's Caravan*, 1 HaDolphin, Jaffa. Sign in Hebrew only, renowned locally for its hummus. *Keren*, 12 Eilat, junction Auerbach, Jaffa, T6816565. Located in the American Colony area of Jaffa, has pleasant bar downstairs and highly recommended restaurant upstairs, renowned for its stuffed zucchini, reservations recommended. Recommended. *Little Spain*, 5 Mazal Arie Lane, Old Jaffa, T5180932. Israel's only Spanish restaurant, with live flamenco on Friday and Saturday, tapas 25 NIS, seafood 50-65 NIS, paella 55-85 NIS. *PastaLine*, 16 Elifelet, Jaffa, T6836401. Also located near the American Colony, offers pasta-based fixed menu for around 60 NIS, reservations recommended. Recommended. *Said Abou Elafia & Sons*, Yefet. This bakery is famous throughout Israel (so much so that people queue 15 deep on the pavement outside). In addition to fresh bread, baguettes, bagels, croissants, etc, they serve an excellent indigenous form of pizza, plus sambusas (baked pitta stuffed with egg, cheese and vegetables). The bakery is take-away only, open 24 hrs including Shabbat (very busy). *Taj Mahal*, Kedumim Sq. Indian dishes, eat-all-you-want buffet (60 NIS) is the best deal, à la carte is a little expensive (60 NIS main dishes) though there is a 20% discount 1200-1500.

Seafood There are several restaurants down on the quayside at the Old Jaffa Port including: *Blue Sea Devil*, Quayside, Old Jaffa Port, T5181069. Specializes in 'catch of the day', particularly monkfish, bass, trout, red mullet, St Peter's fish, 55-75 NIS main course, a/c. *Breeza*, Old Jaffa Port. Air-conditioned, grill 50 NIS, fish 70-100 NIS main courses. *Fisherman's*, Old Jaffa Port, T6813870. Main fish courses 60-100 NIS. *Pirate*, Old Jaffa Port. Variety of fish, 60 NIS main course. *Taboon*, Main Gate, Jaffa, T6811176. Good atmosphere and good food, reservations recommended.

Tel Aviv's suburbs

There are a number places of interest in the satellite towns around Tel Aviv that are now effectively suburbs of the metropolis. Even using public transport it is possible to visit more than one town in a day.

Bat Yam

Claims by the Bat Yam Tourist Office that the town is "one of Israel's most beautiful holiday resorts" is stretching the truth somewhat. Though Bat Yam was initially a separate town established in 1925, Tel Aviv's relentless expansion has virtually incorporated it as one of its larger suburbs (population 143,000). Its one saving grace is an attractive 3.5-kilometre stretch of white

Phone code: 03
Colour map 2, grid B2

Tel Aviv/Jaffa

Tel Aviv/Jaffa

sandy beach (Bat Yam is Hebrew for 'Daughter of the Sea'). A promenade has recently been built along the seafront, complete with a number of restaurants and snack-bars, plus a small water-park. The stretch of beach between Jabotinsky and HaAtzma'ut, known as the model beach, has a breakwater so is fairly calm for swimming. There are also wading pools for children, showers, changing rooms and beach chairs. Just south of here is a popular area for surfers. A yacht club on the seafront offers boat and board hire, plus the chance to go hang-gliding.

Essentials

Sleeping   **A** *Sun*, 136 Ben-Gurion, T5532553, F5527796. Recently taken over by *Howard Johnson* chain, Bat Yam's premier hotel with 300 rooms and suites, full features including pool, kid's pool, sauna, variety of sports, good facilities for families at a competitive price.   **B** *Colony Beach*, 138 Ben-Gurion, T5551555, F5523783. Apartment hotel with 1- and 2-bedroom suites, sea views but no balconies, price hike in season (**A**). Not quite as plush as when new.   **C** *Armon Yam*, 95 Ben-Gurion, T5522424, F5522430. 66 fairly modern rooms, a/c, cable TV and fridges available (extra), rooms a little small but cheaper than equivalent in Tel Aviv. **C** *Bat Yam*, 53 Ben-Gurion, T5064373. 20 modest a/c rooms, has had a recent modernizing face-lift. **C** *Shenhav*, 2 Jerusalem, T5075231. Rather old fashioned and very little English spoken, some rooms with private 'internal' balcony.   **D** *Via Maris*, 43 Ben-Gurion, T5060171. Another modest pension, though very little English spoken. *Sarita Hotel* remains closed.

Eating   There are a number of restaurants along Ben-Gurion, including *Blue Lagoon*, *Casablanca*, *Champagne*, *Dolphin*, *Domino Pizza*, *Dr Fish*, *El-Moroco*, *Fanan Yamani*, *Little Turkey*, *Marrakech* and *Mozart Café*, though none is particularly outstanding. *Il Forno*, 83 Ben-Gurion, is not a bad choice, with a wide choice of pasta dishes (most 30-40 NIS).

Bars & nightclubs   There's quite a choice of bars and nightclubs along Ben-Gurion, many reflecting the towns's sizeable Turkish and North African populations. They include: Big Bos Bar, *Marrakech Nite Club*, *127 Bar*, *Pub Deep Purple*, *Pub Exstaza*, *Pub Hatagelet* and the charming *Puzzy Bar*.

Transport   Bat Yam is located 5.5 km south of Tel Aviv. To reach Bat Yam, continue south through Jaffa along either Yefet or Jerusalem, before turning right (west) on to Rothschild. This leads down to the seafront, with all the hotels located here on Ben-Gurion. Dan buses 10, **18**, **25**, **26** and **46** run to/from Tel Aviv, and Egged bus **83** (Central Bus Station) to Rishon LeTzion) pass the *Colony Beach Hotel*. There is a 24-hr taxi office outside the *Sun Hotel* (T5523131).

Bat Yam

Sleeping
1 Armon Yam
2 Bat Yam
3 Colony Beach
4 Sarita
5 Shenhav
6 Sun
7 Via Maris

Eating
1 Blue Lagoon, Pub Hatagelet
2 Casablanca
3 Champagne, Dolphin, Dr Fish
4 Domino Pizza,

Big Bos Bar
5 El-Moroco
6 Fanan Yamani, Puzzy Bar
7 Il Forno
8 Little Turkey, Marrakech Nite Club
9 Mozart Cafe
10 '127' Bar
11 Pub Deep Purple, Pub Exstaza, Ha-Janta Pub

0 metres 400

Though this is just another industrialized suburb of Tel Aviv (population **Holon**
163,000), Holon is noted for its community of 300 or so **Samaritans**; one of
only two communities in the world (the other being in Nablus, see page 292).
Best known to Christians through the biblical "Story of the Good Samaritan",
the community use Arabic to converse in their daily life and an archaic form of
Hebrew in their liturgy.

The suburb of B'nei B'rak to the northeast of Tel Aviv is home to a community **B'nei B'rak**
of some 125,000 Orthodox Jews, and comparisons are often drawn with Jerusalem's Mea She'arim district. Thomas Friedman notes in his book *From Beirut To Jerusalem* that "Jewish life in B'nei B'rak today has much more in
common with Jewish life in 18th century Lithuania than anything happening
in north Tel Aviv. If they wanted to film the movie 'Hester Street' here, they
would not have needed to bring in many props or costumes".

The town was founded in the 1920s by Warsaw Hasidim, though the name
B'nei B'rak is mentioned as a city of the Dan tribe in *Joshua 19:45*, later to
become a centre of religious study during the Roman occupation. B'nei B'rak
continues this tradition. **NB** If you do decide to visit B'nei B'rak, it is important
to dress modestly (men: long trousers, long sleeves; women: long skirt, closed
neckline), and not to act as if in a zoo: it's really a residential neighbourhood
and not a tourist site.

Transport Many of the buses that run from the Central Bus Station to Petah Tiqva
(eg **68, 69**) pass through B'nei B'rak. There are numerous sherut services from B'nei
B'rak to Jerusalem.

The large satellite town of Petah Tiqva to the northeast of Tel Aviv (population **Petah Tiqva**
151,000) has grown significantly from modest beginnings as the first Jewish
agricultural settlement in Palestine. Founded as little more than a collective
farming village in 1878, the Hebrew name Petah Tiqva, meaning 'Gate of
Hope', (from *Hoshea 2:17*), is perhaps an indication of the mind-set of those
early settlers as they struggled to succeed in an area not easily farmed. Without
the financial support of Baron Edmond de Rothschild they may not have progressed beyond those difficult early stages, and he is duly honoured in a stone
arch erected at the western end of the town. A Founders' Garden (Gan
Hameyasdim) in the centre of Petah Tiqva commemorates the early settlers,
with the original synagogue located nearby.

Artiefacts from nearby Tel Afeq (see page 477) are displayed in the **Yad
Lebanim Museum**, 30 Arlosorov, Petah Tiqva. ■ *Monday-Friday 1630-1930,
Saturday 1000-1300.*

Transport Petah Tiqva can be reached by numerous bus services from the Central
Bus Station.

Though not strictly a suburb of Tel Aviv, the town of **Rosh Ha'ayin** lies just **Tel Afeq**
four kilometres east of Petah Tiqva. Located near the source of the Yarqon **(Antipatris) and**
(Rosh Ha'ayin means 'Head of the Spring'), the town is most noted for the **Migdal Afeq**
nearby sites of **Tel Afeq (Antipatris)** and **Migdal Afeq (Migdal Zedeq)**.

Ins and outs Rosh Ha'ayin can be reached from Tel Aviv's Central Bus Station on
buses **77** (every 10-20 mins, 0520-2330) and **151** (every 15 mins between 0530-0630
and 1330-1630). From Rosh Ha'ayin there is no regular public transport directly to
either site.

Tel Aviv/Jaffa

History   Excavations at **Tel Afeq** have revealed a continuous occupation of the site from the Early Bronze Age (3300-2200 BCE) until the early part of the current century. Afeq probably reached its peak in the Middle Bronze Age IIA (2000-1750 BCE) when it covered an area of over 10 hectares, and is listed in the Bible as one of the conquered Canaanite cities (*Joshua 12:18*). It was at Afeq (Aphek), around 1080 BCE, that the Philistines' army gathered before capturing the Ark of the Covenant from the Israelites at Eben-ezer (*I Samuel 4:1-11*).

A town (called Pegae) developed at the Afeq mound during the Early Hellenistic period (332-167 BCE), and was later expanded by **Herod**. He built a fort on the site in 35 BCE, naming the city after his father **Antipatris**. Josephus (*The Jewish War II, 513*) refers to the tower at "Aphek" as a refuge for Jews during the First Jewish Revolt (66-73 CE). **Paul** spent a night here on his journey from Jerusalem to Caesarea (*Acts 23:31*). Much of Antipatris was destroyed in a major earthquake in 363 CE.

The Crusaders also occupied Afeq, as did the Mamluks and Ottoman Turks. To the Crusaders, the nearby hill of **Migdal Afeq** (three kilometres southeast of Tel Afeq) was of far greater strategic value. Though there is evidence to suggest that Byzantine fortifications had previously been built here, almost certainly to protect the source of the perennial River Yarqon, the site is now occupied by the ruins of the Crusader castle of **Mirabel**. Though somewhat overgrown and neglected, the site is still worth a visit, though it is certainly not the best preserved Crusader castle in Israel.

Sights   The dominant structure on the ancient Tel Afeq mound is the **Ottoman fortress** (Binar Bashi) that was used to administer and garrison the coastal road from Haifa to Gaza. The large square fortress is strengthened by towers at each corner, of which the one to the southwest is octagonal, whilst the others are square. The main entrance to the west opens indirectly on to a large courtyard, around which barracks and stables were built. A mosque stands at the centre of the courtyard. To the north of the fortress can be seen the **Bronze Age fortified city walls**.

Tel Afeq / Tel Aphek

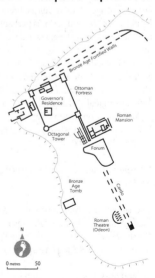

The main Roman remains date to the Herodian period (37 BCE-70 CE), and comprise a series of buildings built on either side of the **cardo** (main street of Roman city). The cardo extends down to a small **Roman theatre**, or **odeon**. The stage, supported by ten arches, remains intact, along with a small section of the spectator seating area. However, the odeon was still unfinished when the earthquake of 363 CE struck.

Mediterranean Coastal Strip

9

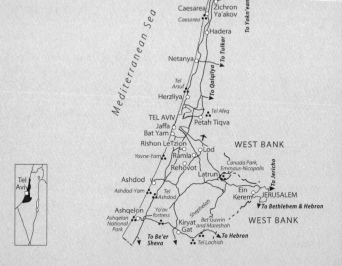

Visitors seeking a sun, sea and sand holiday tend to head to Eilat, at the southern tip of the Negev. This is a great pity since the beaches along the Mediterranean coast, despite lacking the underwater splendour of the Red Sea's coral reefs, are infinitely superior. Yet there is more to Israel's Mediterranean coast than kilometre after kilometre of golden sand. After all, this coast has been a major zone of transition between Europe and Asia, and the coastal plain is replete with archaeological remains from several millennia of contact and interaction. Indeed, in typical Israeli style, there is often no separation between history and everyday life; in many places, to make your way down to the beach you have to pick your way through the archaeological remains.

Four of the key highlights on the coast contain that combination of beach and archaeology that makes Israel so appealing: Caesarea, Ashqelon, 'Atlit and Dor. Information is also included on two very different coastal resorts, Herzliya and Netanya, plus the wine producing region centred around Zichron Ya'akov.

To the south of Tel Aviv, a little inland from the coastal plain, lie a cluster of important archaeological sites in the area known as The Shephelah, including Bet Guvrin-Mareshah and Lachish. Also nearby is the natural wonder of the Soreq Stalactite Cave. There are also a number of points of interest along the Ajalon Valley, an ancient trading route that the modern Tel Aviv to Jerusalem highway now follows.

Mediterranean Coastal Strip

Ins and outs

This chapter of the *Israel Handbook* has been divided into two sections. The first describes the key attractions to the "South and southeast of Tel Aviv". This section is divided into two further sub-sections: one describing "The Shephelah" region (the area broadly inland of the towns of Ashdod and Ashqelon), and the other describing the main attractions on and around the main "Tel Aviv to Jerusalem road". The second section of this chapter concentrates on "North of Tel Aviv". The main Mediterranean coastal city of Tel Aviv/Jaffa is described in the previous chapter.

Background

Geography

The **Mediterranean coast** of Israel is a more or less straight line running north to south, with a slight inclination westward. It has neither a sheltered gulf, nor deep estuary for its entire length, and no large islands off-shore. Though harbours were eventually established in places along this coast, none is natural, and it should be noted that no invader from the west ever landed an army on this coast south of Mt Carmel (Haifa) without first having established a presence inland. This holds true for the Philistines, Alexander, Pompey, the Romans, the Crusaders and Napoleon. It could also be said that this section of the Mediterranean coast never produced a maritime people, with even the Phoenicians who settled south of Mt Carmel being predominantly agriculturalists.

The Mediterranean coastal strip, or **Maritime Plain**, is at the very heart of the history of the region. Described by Smith as "one of the most famous war-paths of the world" (*Historical Geography of the Holy Land*, 1894), the Maritime Plain has seen the march of the armies of Thothmes, Ramses, Sennacherib, Alexander, Pompey, Vespasian, Titus, Salah al-Din and Napoleon, to name but a few. It has also been part of a great trading route: the southern extension, or Great South Road, of the famous *Via Maris* or *Way of the Sea*. For millennia, this was the main trading route between Damascus and Egypt.

The Maritime Plain can be broadly divided into two distinct regions. To the north of Tel Aviv, running for 55 kilometres almost all the way to Mt Carmel (Haifa), is the **Plain of Sharon**. In antiquity, much of this area was forested, possibly for almost its entire length, with numerous written references (from the Bible to Josephus, Crusader sources, and even Napoleon) referring to the woodlands here. In subsequent centuries, following years of exploitation and then neglect, much of this land became the malaria-infested swamps that became such a challenge to the early Zionist pioneers. The draining and management of the swamps has turned the Plain of Sharon into a rich agricultural region, with improved communications allowing the development of large urban industrial centres.

The other section of the Maritime Plain stretches south from Tel Aviv, down to Gaza. Older sources refer to this region as the **Plain of Philistia**, after its early inhabitants, the Philistines. You may also see this region referred to as the **Shephelah** (or Shefela), though strictly speaking this is the region of low hills between the Maritime Plain and the Central Range. The Plain of Philistia is also rich agricultural land, though soils tend to be sandier.

A number of significant cities developed along the Maritime Plain, not least of which were the five chief Philistine cities: Gaza, Askalon (Ashqelon), Ashdod, Ekron and Gath. Further north lie Yavne, Ramla and Lod (Lydda), Jaffa (Joppa), and, most significantly on the Plain of Sharon, Caesarea and

Dor. Few of these cities have Jewish origins, though the modern Jewish towns established at the end of the 19th or early 20th centuries have come to dominate the Mediterranean coastal strip. These include Tel Aviv and its 'satellites', plus Herzliya, Netanya and Hadera.

South and Southeast of Tel Aviv

Rishon LeTzion

Rishon LeTzion was one of the first of the Jewish agricultural settlements established by the early Zionist pioneers, but is now one of Israel's fastest-growing cities. The town's history and development is documented in an interesting museum, with significant buildings from the early years marked on a short walking route.

Phone code: 03
Colour map 2, grid B2

Ins and outs

Getting there and around Rishon LeTzion is a 25-min bus ride (8 NIS, numerous frequent services) from Tel Aviv's Central Bus Station, and can be visited as a day trip that also includes Rehovot, Ramla and Lod. Rishon LeTzion's bus station (T9535555/6948888) is on the junction of Herzl and Eyn HaKore, and has frequent connections to Tel Aviv and other parts of the country (Ashqelon, 301; Be'er Sheva, 351; Be'er Sheva via Kiryat Gat, 371; Jerusalem, 433; Petah Tiqva, 164; Ramla, 247, 50 mins, 10 NIS; Rehovot via Nes Tziona, 200/274/164/201/166/317, 15 mins, 7 NIS). There are also sheruts available (T9672754, see map) to Tel Aviv and Jerusalem. All the sights are within walking distance of one another.

History

The town was founded in 1882 by 17 families of Russian and Romanian immigrants, who were escaping from the pogroms in Eastern Europe. As they were inexperienced in agricultural techniques, beset by disease incubated in the malarial swamps that they were attempting to settle, and occasionally harassed by Arab bandits, the settlement very nearly didn't survive. Without the determination and stubborness of the founding fathers, and a large measure of financial support from **Baron Edmond de Rothschild**, the baby settlement may well have been stillborn.

Rishon LeTzion claims the distinction of being 'first' in a number of fields of Jewish life. Not only was it the forerunner of other Jewish agricultural settlements ('Rishon LeTzion' meaning 'First to Zion'), it claims to be the site of the first singing of the *Hatikva* (the Jewish national anthem, though this is claimed elsewhere), the place where the current Israeli flag was first flown, the location where Hebrew was taught in the first Hebrew school, and the place where the first 'Hebrew' plough was built. It is also home of the Israeli wine producing industry, following the introduction of Burgundy and Bordeaux vines in 1887.

Rishon LeTzion Museum The town's history is well presented in the compact museum overlooking Founders' Square. A guided tour is usually offered (Hebrew, English, plus several European languages, no extra charge), though it is very intense. The

Mediterranean Coastal Strip

museum features a number of mock-ups of homes and shops from the early settlement, a short audio-visual presentation tracing the story of 'The Pioneers', and a concise history of the town's development. ■ *Founders' Square, Rothschild, T9644292/9682435. Sunday, Tuesday, Wednesday, Thursday 0900-1400, Monday 0900-1300 1600-2000. Adult 12 NIS, free on first Saturday of the month.*

Rishon Le Tzion Museum

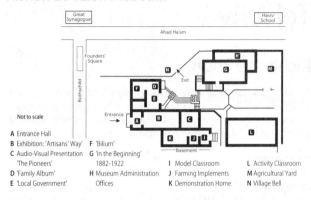

Not to scale

A Entrance Hall
B Exhibition: 'Artisans' Way'
C Audio-Visual Presentation 'The Pioneers'
D 'Family Album'
E 'Local Government'

F 'Bilium'
G 'In the Beginning' 1882-1922
H Museum Administration Offices

I Model Classroom
J Farming Implements
K Demonstration Home

L Activity Classroom
M Agricultural Yard
N Village Bell

Pioneer's Way	A short walking route around the town centre (marked by a fading yellow painted trail) takes the visitor past many of Rishon LeTzion's earliest buildings and most interesting sites. **NB** Some of the attractions are incorrectly numbered on the free map available at the museum.
The Great Synagogue (1)	The foundations of the synagogue were laid on the hill at the centre of the village in 1885. An Ottoman ordinance in effect at the time banned the construction of new synagogues in Palestine, so the early settlers obtained a building permit for the construction of an agricultural warehouse. The two windows at the top of the synagogues façade are said to symbolize the tablet stones of the Ten Commandments, whilst the twelve windows represent the 'Twelve Tribes'.
Founders' Square (2)	This site at the top of the hill is where the first 17 families set up their tents on 15th August, 1882.
Farmer's House (3)	One of the first permanent buildings in the village of Rishon LeTzion, this sandstone house is built in Eastern European style, with a shingled roof, square windows, and a large cellar. It is not in a particularly good state of repair.
House of Aharon Mordechai and Miriam Freiman (17)	Aharon Mordechai Freiman was one of the founding fathers of the town, and he lived in this house after its construction in 1883. It is claimed that the National Hebrew song *Hushu Ahim Hushu* was composed by Yehiel Michel Piress for the house-warming. A Hasidic synagogue and Talmud Torah School was built behind the house on land donated by Freiman, and the house itself was also used as a courthouse. Today it is a kitchen utensils store.
Ya'akov Kanner's House (4)	Built in 1900 by Ya'akov Kanner, one of the more prosperous farmers of the community, this elegant townhouse later housed the Magen David Adom (equivalent of the Red Cross) from 1940-85, and was used as the headquarters of the Haganah during the 1948 war.

....

'Hatikva': The Israeli National Anthem

*The **Hatikva**, later Israel's National Anthem, was said to have been written by Naftali Herz Imber during his stay in Rishon LeTzion (1883-84). The work was later edited by Israel Belkind, Mordchai Lubman and David Yudilovits, with the melody adapted by Samuel Cohen in 1888 from a popular Romanian folk song. Meaning "The Hope", the Hatikva does not specifically mention the land of Israel, but rather the hope to be "a free people in the land of Zion and Jerusalem".*

....

One of the major crises facing the community of settlers in the early days of Rishon LeTzion's existence was the provision of water. Yosef Feinberg was sent to Europe to solicit funds from the Jewish community to ensure the survival of Rishon LeTzion. With the aid of an 'anonymous' loan from Edmond de Rothschild, who was to become the town's benefactor, the founding fathers were able to construct this village well. Water was eventually found at a depth of 48 metres. The image of the well's water tower is now included in the town crest of Rishon LeTzion since it played such a large part in deciding the fate of the settlement. There is an interesting 'Sound and Light' performance at the well (included in the price of the museum admission) ■ *Monday-Thursday 0900-1400 1600-2000, Friday 0900-1300).*

Joseph Feinberg Village Well (7) and Water Tower (8)

The building was originally erected in 1888 to provide accommodation for Rothschild administrators, agronomists, doctor, and as a wine cellar. The building now houses the town's Municipal Offices.

City Hall (18)

Major redevelopment of the park area (Zadal Project) continues, and the former **Community Hall (9)** is no longer accessible.

City Park (10)

Rishon LeTzion including 'Pioneer's Way'

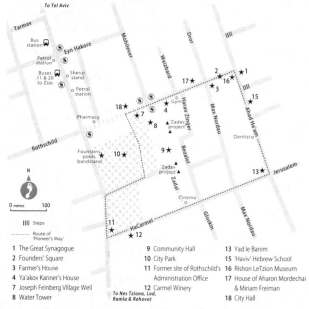

1 The Great Synagogue	9 Community Hall	13 Yad le Banim
2 Founders' Square	10 City Park	15 'Haviv' Hebrew School
3 Farmer's House	11 Former site of Rothschild's	16 Rishon LeTzion Museum
4 Ya'akov Kanner's House	Administration Office	17 House of Aharon Mordechai
7 Joseph Feinberg Village Well	12 Carmel Winery	& Miriam Freiman
8 Water Tower		18 City Hall

Mediterranean Coastal Strip

Administrative Offices (11)	Baron de Rothschild's administrative offices are now actually gone, and the site is marked by a memorial to "the Fallen of Rishon LeTzion".

Carmel Winery (12)	This is Rishon LeTzion's most famous landmark. The wine cellars were completed in 1897, though the building served as more than just a wine producer. Whole workshops were included on the premises for use in auxiliary trades, such as the manufacture of barrels and pumps. From 1929 onwards, the winery was also used by the Haganah for arms practice, including live firing and the manufacture of guns. It is claimed that the Arabs were so scared of the building's reputation that no attempts were made to attack Rishon LeTzion. Guided tours and tasting sessions are available. ■ *T9643248, F9673914. Tours 0900 1100 1300 1500. Adult 15 NIS.*

Yad le Banim (13)	For years this was the grandest building in early Rishon LeTzion, serving as the centre of Baron de Rothschild's activities in Palestine.

Haviv Hebrew School (15)	Founded in 1886, this is said to be not only the first Hebrew school in Eretz Israel, but also in the whole world. It was named after Haviv Lubman, a noted public figure of the time, and it taught Jewish studies, literature, and science – in Hebrew. It is now a mixed school and a second storey has been added. The walking tour finishes back at the **Rishon LeTzion Museum**.

Chai Kef Zoo	Rishon LeTzion has a modest zoo, including children's interaction section. ■ *T9613360. Summer Sunday-Saturday 0900-1800, Friday 0900-1700; winter Sunday-Saturday 0900-1700, Friday 0900-1600. To reach by public transport, turn south out of Rishon LeTzion bus station, walk on the right-hand side of the road for 50 metres to the bus stop, take bus 11 or 20, every 10 mins.*

Rehovot

Phone code: 08
Colour map 2, grid B2

Though situated in the heart of an agricultural region particularly famed for citrus production, Rehovot is best known as the home of the **Weizmann Institute**: Israel's greatest centre of fundamental and applied research.

Ins and outs

Getting there and around	Rehovot can be reached on regular buses (200/201) from Tel Aviv's Central Bus Station (11 NIS, 30 mins). These buses arrive via Rishon LeTzion and stop right outside the Weizmann Institute's main gate. Rehovot's Central Bus Station (T9446060) is a longish walk to the southwest. The Weizmann Institute is also conveniently located near to Rehovot's **train** station, from where there are regular services to and from Tel Aviv (about 1 per hr). For **Sherut** inter-city taxis, try *Gordon Taxis* T9451818 or *Rehovot Taxis* T9474478.

History

The town was initially established in 1890 by early Zionists from a community of Polish Jews. The name is taken from Rehoboth, a well dug in the Negev by Isaac (*Genesis 26:22*), though the settlement did not expand much beyond a collection of farming villages until it was connected to the Lod to Gaza railway line towards the end of World War I. This outlet to greater markets facilitated by the rail link led to an expansion in citrus production, plus the development of an industrial base. During the 'Second Aliya', Rehovot

Chaim Weizmann (1874-1952)

Born in 1874 near to the border between White Russia, Lithuania and Poland, Weizmann's greatest legacy to the Zionist movement (and the subsequent State of Israel) was the way in which he paved the way for the Balfour Declaration. A great admirer of the British, believing them to be as fair-minded and just as they claimed to be, he used his not inconsiderable charm (which Laquer suggests he could "turn on and off abruptly", A History of Zionism, 1989) to win over support amongst the ruling British élite

for the establishment of a Jewish homeland. Johnson suggests that, despite teaching biochemistry at Manchester University, Weizmann's life-task was in fact "to exploit the existence of the British Empire, and the goodwill of its ruling classes, to bring the Jewish national home into existence" (A History of the Jews, 1989). By 1948 all his lobbying efforts had paid off, and the following year he became Israel's first President.

became an important social and cultural centre in the history of Jewish resettlement, and the first Hebrew language instruction to the Sephardic community was given here.

It was around this time that **Chaim Weizmann** (see box, page 487) settled in Rehovot, establishing an agricultural research station. In 1944, on the occasion of Weizmann's 70th birthday, The Weizmann Institute of Science was inaugurated. The town of Rehovot now has a population of around 83,000.

Sights

The Weizmann Institute is one of the world's leading research bodies in the fields of physics, chemistry, biology, microbiology and plant genetics. Set in a wonderful park area, comprising over 80 hectares of manicured lawns, gardens and shady paths, the Institute provides the workplace for almost 2,000 staff, researchers and students. One of the Institute's most recent innovations is the 'smart-card' used by Rupert Murdoch's 'pay-per-view' satellite TV stations. **Weizmann Institute**

Besides the lovely parkland, the main attractions for the non-scienti- fically minded are **Weizmann House** (Weizmann's family home between 1949-52, designed by the renowned architect Erich Mendelsohn), the **Weizmann Archives** (open to the public) and the simple **Weizmann Graves** of Weizmann (1874-1952) and his wife (1881-1966). Nearby is a memorial plaza containing a **Holocaust Memorial** by sculptor Dani Karavan. ■ *Just inside the main gate is a plan of the grounds; just as well, since there are over 60 buildings. (**NB** Weizmann House is No 56, Weizmann Graves No 57 and Archives No 55). Excellent guided tours are available by prior appointment (T9343852), which include a short audio-visual presentation in the **Wix Auditorium** that details the work of the Institute (1100 and 1445 daily, 1100 only on Friday). Weizmann House is open Sunday-Thursday 1000-1500, closed Friday Saturday, admission free.*

Mediterranean Coastal Strip

Rehovot

Yavne The modern town of Yavne is probably best known in Israel today as the site of the country's first nuclear reactor, though the town has ancient origins. Very little remains of the ancient city of Yavne, known in antiquity as Jabneh or **Jabneel** (*Joshua 15:11*), though in the 12th century BCE it ranked comparably with the five great Philistine cities (Gaza, 'Ashkalon, 'Ashdod, 'Ekron and Gath). Jabneel, with 'Ashkalon, had the distinction of being a harbour city, and excavations at **Yavneh-Yam** (eight kilometres northwest), have revealed remains of a large square defensive coastal enclosure occupied between the Middle Bronze IIA and Late Bronze I.

The town subsequently passed through Phoenician, Greek and Maccabean hands, before Vespasian captured it for Rome in 68 CE. Yavne already had a large Jewish population at this stage, and it was here that **Rabbi Yohanan ben Zakkai** established the centre of learning that laid the foundations of the *Mishnah*. Following the destruction of the Temple in Jerusalem (70 CE), Yavne became the seat of the Sanhedrin, with prominent rabbis such as **Yohanan ben Zakkai** and **Ben Akiba** teaching at the school of rabbinic theology. The school, and much of Yavne, was destroyed during the Roman suppression of the Bar Kokhba Rebellion (Second Jewish Revolt, 135 CE). At one point Yavne was occupied by the Crusaders, though the remains of the 12th-century church are insubstantial.

Ramla (Ramleh)

Phone code: 09
Colour map 2, grid B3

*The name Ramla almost certainly derives from the Arabic word 'raml', meaning 'sand', and is probably a reference to the dunes upon which the town was built. The city became the capital of **Filistin** and is the only city in Palestine that was founded by the **Arabs** (early in the eighth century CE by the Umayyad caliph **Suleiman ibn 'Abd el-Malik**). Ramla owes its strategic importance to its location at the junction of three ancient communication routes. Thus, the town has been fought over and occupied by the Arabs, Crusaders, Mamluks, Napoleon's army, the Ottomans, the British army, Palestinian Arabs, and finally the Israelis. Ramla has a number of interesting remains, and a very laid-back feel.*

Ins and outs

Getting there and getting around Ramla can be easily visited in a day excursion from Tel Aviv that also takes in Lod, Rishon LeTzion and Rehovot. Buses run direct to Ramla's new Bus Station (information T9220222) from Tel Aviv's Central Bus Station. There are plenty of buses from Ramla to Lod and hourly services to Jerusalem. All the main sights are within easy walking distance of each other, and the souk is a pleasant place to stroll (and eat).

History

Until the conquest of Ramla by the Crusaders in 1099, the town had a long history of religious tolerance, both between faiths, and between different sects of the main faiths. A large number of *Sufis*, (from the mystical aspect of Islam, emphasizing the importance of personal spiritual development that is found only through the Qu'ran), came to settle in Ramla during the Abbasid Caliphate (c 750 CE). It is documented that Ramla was already home to members of both the *Sunni* and *Shia* (Shi'ite) branches of Islam, as well as indigenous Jews. Ramla was (and continues to be) centre of one of the main communities of *Karaites*, a Jewish sect dating back to the eighth century. Their settlement is at **Matsliah**, two kilometres to the south of Ramla.

Much of Ramla's early splendour was destroyed in the 11th century by a series of earthquakes, and in the 12th century by the arrival of the **Crusaders**. Thrice the Crusaders fought the Fatimids for control of Ramla, and in the 90 years or so that they controlled the town it became an important staging post on the pilgrimage route to Jerusalem. Christian tradition relates that Ramla was the site of **Arimathea**, the domicile of **Joseph**, who arranged for Jesus to be brought down from the cross and buried in his family's tomb. The Crusaders were eventually evicted in 1187 by the forces of **Salah al-Din**, who were in turn succeeded by **Baibars** in 1267. Substantial rebuilding took place during this period of Mamluk rule, including the construction of the White Tower.

Later visitors to Ramla have included **Napoleon**, who is alleged to have spent a night at the Church and Hospice of St Nicodemus and St Joseph of Arimathea during his ill-fated 1799 campaign, and General Allenby, who arrived at the head of the British forces during the First World War.

During the Arab uprising and riots of 1936, many of the town's Jewish residents left, only to return after the Arab exodus in the wake of the Israeli capture of the town in 1948. Indeed, much has been made recently of David Ben-Gurion's role in this 'population transfer'. The population of Ramla today is around 60,000, 20 percent of whom are Arabs.

Sights

Originally the 12th-century Crusader Church of St John, the Great (Omari) Mosque was converted to its present function during the Mamluk period. A tall, white minaret was built on the foundations of the church's bell-tower, though evidence of the Crusader's aisled basilica can still be seen inside. The mosque is not generally open to casual visitors, though you may be lucky.

Great (Omari) Mosque

There are considerable reminders of Ramla's ancient past, and a stroll around the old residential quarter has much to recommend it. Just north of the Great (Omari) Mosque, and beyond the commercial bazaar, is the main neighbourhood place of worship: the **Zeitouni Mosque**. The mosque contains the tomb of Sheikh Zeitouni. Also to be seen close by are the Ottoman period **Radwan Baths**, still in use until around 1948. Just to the north of the baths is the **Greek**

Old City

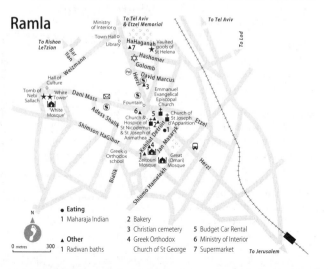

Ramla

To Tel Aviv & Etzel Memorial

To Tel Aviv

To Rishon LeTzion

Ministry of Interior

Town Hall
Library

HaHaganah
Vaulted pools of St Helena

Hashomer

Golomb

Hall of Culture

David Marcus

Tomb of Nebi Sallach

'White Tower'

Dani Mass

Emmanuel Evangelical Episcopal Church

To Lod

Fountain

'White Mosque'

Adess Shalik

Church & Hospice of St Nicodemus & St Joseph of Arimathea

Church of St Joseph d'Apparition

Etzel

Shimson HaGibor

Bialik

Greek Orthodox school

Zeitouni Mosque

Great (Omari) Mosque

Kehilat Detroit

Jlan Masryk

Herzl

Shlomo Hamelekh

To Jerusalem

Eating
1 Maharaja Indian

Other
1 Radwan baths

2 Bakery
3 Christian cemetery
4 Greek Orthodox Church of St George

5 Budget Car Rental
6 Ministry of Interior
7 Supermarket

N

0 metres 300

Orthodox Church of St George, identifiable by its blue dome on its bell-tower and image of George and the Dragon above the entrance. The traditional houses in this part of town, built as they are around courtyards and clustered together along narrow streets, are rather appealing, though you will find yourself continually coming up against dead-ends.

Church and Hospice of St Nicodemus and St Joseph Arimathea The compound is entered through a gate on Bialik, which leads to an enclosed courtyard containing a statue of a praying St Nicodemus holding a child. Originally built by the Franciscans in the 16th century, most of the building actually dates to early this century (1902), thus making something of a mockery of the tour that includes Napoleon's alleged bed chamber. The interior of the church is remarkably simple. ■ *0900-1130, excluding Saturday or Sunday. Admission free. Modest dress required.*

'White Tower' and 'White Mosque' Known as the 'Tower of the Forty Companions of the Prophet' to Muslims and 'Tower of the Forty Martyrs' to Christians (or simply 'White Tower'), this is a later addition to a mosque (**al-Jama'a al-Abyad**) commonly attributed to the Umayyad period. Although an Arabic inscription over the entrace to the tower claims that it was built in 1318 CE by Sultan Mohammad ibn Qala'un, it is known that repairs to the mosque had been carried out earlier, during the reign of the Mamluk sultan Baibars. The 27-metre-high square tower is built in Gothic style, and is said to offer a fine view from its upper platform (both Napoleon and General Allenby used it as a reconnaissance tower). It remains closed for repairs.

To the south of the tower/minaret are the remains of a substantial mosque compound (93 metres by 84 metres). The compound includes the mosque itself along the southern side of the quadrangle, two porticoes to the east and west, the north wall and 'White Tower' to the north, plus what is thought to be an ablutions fountain in the centre. Beneath the compound are a series of subterranean cisterns. In the northwest corner of the compound is the **Tomb of Nebi Sallach**, a Muslim holy man who is reputed to have turned a rock into a camel in the name of Allah.

It is now assumed that the mosque complex was constructed in three main periods. The first stage saw the laying out of the complex in its present form during the Umayyad period. All that remains from this period are parts of the mosque walls, the east wall and portico, the north wall, and the underground cisterns. The cisterns were built using arched pillars, thus supporting the barrel-shaped vaults. They may well have been fed by a spring originating in Gezer, as well as collecting rainwater run-off. The second period of construction, attributed to Saladin, was responsible for the west wall and the ablutions fountain. During the final period of construction, the minaret (tower) was added. ■ *Sunday-Thursday 0800-1500, Friday 0800-1200, Saturday 0800-1600. 5 NIS.*

White Tower and White Mosque

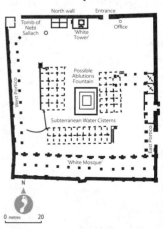

Stealing the White Tower

A popular legend exists in Ramla concerning an attempt by the neighbouring town of Lod to steal the White Tower. A long history of emnity apparently existed between Ramla and Lod, with much of the building material used to construct Ramla being taken from the ruins of Lod. A large section of Lod's population was seemingly forcibly removed to Ramla in order to promote the latter's growth.

Envying Ramla's square tower, the residents of Lod resolved to steal it, and remove it to their town. Borrowing some ropes from an 'old sheikh', the boys from Lod, in the dead of night, tied the ropes to the tower and began to heave it back to Lod. Unbeknown to them, the old sheikh, who was a bit of a wag, had given them rubber cords rather than rope. As the boys arrived in Lod pulling their 'ropes', they cried out "Ramla's tower arrives", at which point the town turned out to greet them. Unfortunately for them, the tower remained in Ramla.

Vaulted Pools of St Helena

These vaulted pools, located in the basement of a small building in a garden between HaHaganah and Hashomer, are named after the fourth century CE Roman empress dowager St Helena. She is credited with, three centuries after the event, 'rediscovering' the tomb of Christ, Golgotha, the true cross, the instruments of the passion, the cave of the nativity and the site of the Ascension of Christ! As such, Amos Elon refers to her ironically as "the most successful archaeologist in all history"! True to form, the pools have no connection whatsoever with St Helena (except the name), since they were built in 789 CE during the reign of the fifth Abbasid Caliph, Haroun al-Rashid. The reference to the name 'St Helena's Pools' appears for the first time in the books of Christian pilgrims in the early 19th century. 'Haroun al-Rashid's Pools' would be a far more evocative name, since he is best known for his association with the tale of *A Thousand and One Nights*. The Arab name for the pools is **Birket al-Anzia**.

The pool measures 21.17 metres by 19.82 metres, and is covered by a series of 24 groined vaults. The 24 square openings in the roof allowed a large number of people to draw water from the pool at one time. The cistern is beautifully cool, and the light reflecting on the rippling pool creates a very pleasing effect. Rowing boats are available to take you on a rumbustious ride around the pool. ■ *Sunday-Thursday 0800-1500, Friday 0800-1200, Saturday 0800-1600. Adult 8 NIS, boat-hire negotiable.*

British War Cemetery

To the east of Ramla, 2 kilometres beyond the town, is the large First World War cemetery where the troops of General Allenby's forces, who died fighting the Turks, are buried. The cemetery is cared for by the Commonwealth War Graves Commission.

Essentials

Eating

There are plenty of falafel and shwarma places along Herzl, and in the Old City area, though for a treat try the *Maharaja Indian Restaurant* on Herzl, T9223534. Run by one of Ramla's 800-strong Indian community, it offers excellent veg thali (28 NIS), dhal and rice (18 NIS), curry and rice (18 NIS), masala dosa (14 NIS), as well as samosas, snacks and sweets.

Mediterranean Coastal Strip

Transport From Ramla's new bus station (T9220222) there are regular buses to Jerusalem via **Latrun** (404/433/435/439, 26 NIS, 1½ hrs) or **Bet Shemesh** (401); **Lod** (011, 6 NIS, 15 mins); **Rehovot** (248/249/432/435); **Rishon LeTzion** (247/432/433, 10 NIS, 50 mins); **Tel Aviv** (455 direct, 10 NIS, 30 mins), plus less regular services to other destinations. For Sheruts to Tel Aviv or Lod try **Shimshon Taxis** T9220888 on Herzl.

Lod (Lydda)

Phone code: 08
Colour map 2, grid B3

*Most visitors to Israel come to Lod (Lydda) without knowing it: Tel Aviv's Ben-Gurion Airport is located on the outskirts. Although the modern town is rather unattractive, it is Lod's association with the Christian matyr **St George** that draws most visitors.*

Ins and outs

Getting there and getting around There are numerous buses from Tel Aviv's Central Bus Station to Lod, including the bus via Ben-Gurion Airport (475), or a direct bus (460, every 15 mins, 12 NIS, 40 mins). Lod's bus station (T9773555) is a small yard in the heart of the Old City, from where the key attractions are within easy walking distance. There are regular buses to and from Ramla (011, 6 NIS, 15 mins), Rehovot (248/249 via Ramla) and Rishon LeTzion (247, 11 NIS, 50 mins), though to get to Jerusalem you must change at Ramla. Sheruts to Tel Aviv leave when full from outside Dahamash Mosque. There are trains from Tel Aviv (hourly), though Lod's station is not conveniently located.

History

The town has its origins in the arrival of the Israelites in the Promised Land (*Chronicles 8:12*), with the first written mention of Lod being in the 15th century BCE 'City Lists of Thutmose III'. The town was later occupied by the Greeks in the fourth century BCE ('Lydda'), the Hasmoneans in the second century BCE (*I Maccabees 11:34*), and the Romans in 67 CE ('Diospolis', City of Zeus).

Lod has a lengthy Christian association, dating back to the visit of Paul when he cured Aeneas (*Acts 9: 32-35*), and continued through the town's association with **St George**. Legend suggests that he was born in Lydda, and it was to here that his remains were brought following his martyrdom in 303. St George's Church, with the saint's sarcophagus, is Lod's main attraction.

Lod was razed by the Omayyad Caliph Abd el-Malik, rebuilt by the Crusaders, though its subsequent history is not particularly noteworthy. In fact, it was not until the termination of the British Mandate in 1948 and the creation of the State of Israel that Lod once again came to prominence, when the decision was made to expand the nearby former British airstrip.

Sights

St George's Church/ el-Chodr Mosque In addition to being canonized by the Christian c hurch, St George is also revered by Muslims as the 'bright spirit', **el-Chodr**, who will vanquish the demon Dajal on the Day of

Lod (old city)

To Tel Aviv

Katzenson
Pharmacy
Herzl
Dahamash Mosque
Uziel
Egged bus office
Ha'Haluts
El-Chodr Mosque
St George's Church
To Kikar Ha'Atzma'ut & new city
Priman Derekh

N

0 metres 100

1 Ruined caravanserai
2 Greek Orthodox monastery
3 Shops & restaurants
4 Weekly markets
5 Sheruts
6 Taxis
7 Parking lot

St George's Church / el-Chodr Mosque, Lod

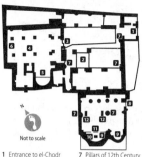

Not to scale

1 Entrance to el-Chodr Mosque
2 Ablutions Fountain
3 Entrance to Prayer Chamber
4 Byzantine Column with Greek inscription (high up)
5 Apse of Byzantine Basilica
6 Mihrab
7 Pillars of 12th Century Crusader Church
8 Entrance to St George's Church
9 Apses of Crusader Church
10 Greek Orthodox Altar
11 Greek Orthodox Altar Screen
12 Staircases to Crypt & Tomb of St George

Judgement. Thus, the complex that houses his remains is shared by the two faiths.

The complex has its origins in a sixth-century Byzantine basilica, remains of which are best seen in the **el-Chodr Mosque** in the southern part of the complex. One of the main columns supporting the prayer hall belongs to the Byzantine church, and can be identified by the Greek inscription. To the north of this column is an apse from the Byzantine structure. Modestly dressed non-Muslims are permitted entry into the mosque (on removal of shoes, and excluding prayer times), though it may be necessary to emphasize that you are non-Israeli. Enter through the green-domed gate to the west.

The original **St George's Church** was built by the Crusaders, though much of the present structure was built in 1870 by the Greek Orthodox church. Two apses and two central columns from the Crusader church still form a central component of the present St George's Church. The interior of the church is ornately decorated in the style typical of Greek Orthodox places of worship in the Holy Land. The altar screen is particularly intricate. Two staircases lead down to the crypt, and the simple tomb of St George. The sarcophagus, restored in 1871, is of white marble, with an image of the saint holding a spear and a cross. Above is a painting of the dragon being slain.

The church/mosque is at its busiest (and most interesting) on St George's Day (23rd April) and on the saint's burial date (15th November).

Dahamash Mosque This recently refurbished mosque has a contentious history. During fighting between Jordanian and Israeli forces in Lod in 1948, a number of civilians took refuge in the mosque. Local Palestinians tell visitors that Israeli troops deliberately targeted the mosque with mortar fire, killing a hundred or so civilians sheltering inside.

Museum of Jewish Heritage This small museum mainly details the life of Sephardi and Mizrachi Jews. ■ *20 David HaMelekh, T2949569. Sunday-Thursday 0900-1600. 10 NIS.*

Gezer

Ins and outs Gezer is located seven kilometres southeast of Ramla, from where buses (16/18) run to Kibbutz Gezer. From here, it is a short walk to the tel. Alternatively, Buses 404/433/435/439 from Jerusalem pass the turn-off to the site.

History Though pottery remains indicate habitation of ancient **Tel Gezer** in the Chalcolithic period (fourth millennium BCE), the site only really developed when its strategic situation on the road from Jerusalem to the coast was fully realized by, in turn, Canaanites, Egyptians, Israelites and Philistines. Solomon fortified the town as one of his 'chariot cities' (*I Kings 9:16-17*), and it was only after this time that the city could be considered to be Israelite. Even after

Mediterranean Coastal Strip

Gezer

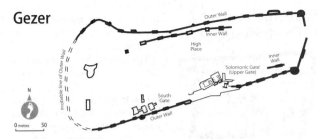

Joshua's earlier conquest, it appears that the Canaanites remained in the city. Further, Gezer acted more as a buffer zone between the Philistines and Israelites, perhaps more under Philistine influence (*II Samuel 5:25; II Chronicles 14:16; 20: 4*).

Periods of great calamity, followed by reconstruction, have been the fate of Gezer during the ensuing centuries. In 142 BCE, **Simon the Hasmonean** took the town for the Maccabees and built a large palace and fortress (*I Maccabees 13:43-48*), whilst his son **John Hyrcanus** used Gezer as his headquarters (*I Maccabees 13:53*). However, during the Jewish insurrections of the Roman era Gezer was all but destroyed. In the 12th century CE the region was the scene of many great battles between the **Crusaders** and the **Arabs**, and it has been suggested that Gezer served as Saladin's command post.

Near to the site is the Kibbutz Gezer, founded in 1945 on land provided by the British for Jewish settlers. The kibbutz was captured by the Jordanian Arab Legion during the 1948 war, though was recaptured hours later.

Visiting the site You can only fully appreciate Gezer's strategic value by climbing to the top of the mound and surveying the 360-degree view. The sweep of the coastal plain is particularly impressive. When first excavated at the beginning of this century, the dig was the most ambitious yet undertaken by the Palestine Exploration Fund. Excavations have revealed evidence from all levels of occupation, though easily the most significant find is the Gezer Calendar; a limestone plaque from Solomon's era (965-928 BCE) describing the agricultural cycle in an early form of Hebrew. Other important finds were the bilingual (Hebrew and Greek) boundary stones inscribed with "the boundary of Gezer" that helped identify the site.

Unfortunately, the site is not well marked and at certain times of year is substantially overgrown. The most notable remains are as follows: the **South Gate**, defended by a 15-metre stone tower, built in the 17th century BCE; the **Solomonic Gate (Upper Gate)**, an impressive four-entry gateway built in the 10th century BCE (and later rebuilt as a three-entry gateway in the ninth century BCE); and the **High Place**, a row of 10 monoliths dating to the Middle Bronze Age II (1300-1200 BCE), some exceeding 3 metres high, erected on a north-south axis and probably used in some form of cult worship.

Modi'im

Ins and outs Modi'im can be difficult to reach by public transport since the main road from Tel Aviv by-passes Modi'im and runs through Latrun to the south (it may be possible to get off Route 1 at Ben Shemen, and continue the 5km to Modi'im on foot). Private transport poses no such problem.

History The ancient site of Modi'im features significantly in the history of the Jews as the scene of the beginning of the **Maccabee rebellion** in 167 BCE. The catalyst in the revolt was the decision of the Syrian ruler Antiochus IV Epiphanes to attempt to make the Jewish community perform sacrifices to pagan gods. Mattathias (Mathityahu), a priest in Modi'im, defied Antiochus' envoys and refused to participate. Another Jew was prepared to appease Antiochus, so Mattathias and his five sons killed the man and chased the Syrian envoys away (*1 Maccabees 2:15-28*). This small incident precipitated the rebellion that ultimately led to the establishment of the 130-year Maccabean (or Hasmonean) state.

The rock-cut tombs of Mattathias and four of his sons remain, though the monument built over the tombs by the fifth son, Simeon, has been destroyed (see *1 Maccabees 13:27*). Each year, during the *Hanukkah* commemoration of the Maccabee victory over the Assyrians, the Modi'im Torchlighting ceremony takes place here, with the torch being carried by a relay of runners to the President's house in Jerusalem.

Ashdod

Although 'Ancient Ashdod' is very ancient indeed, there are few remains dating to its long and eventful past. However, the modern town has a pleasing enough ambience, with the provision of green space and leisure facilities having been a priority of the urban planners: Ashdod is probably quite a nice place to live. For visiting tourists, the main attraction is eight kilometres of Mediterranean beaches.

Phone code: 07
Colour map 2, grid B2

Ins and outs

Ashdod is best reached by the numerous bus services connecting it to Tel Aviv (45 mins), Ashqelon (15 mins), Be'er Sheva and Jerusalem. The new bus station is to the southeast of the town centre, at the junction of Herzl and Begin. The beaches are a 20- to 25-min walk away. Buses to local destinations (with some continuing on to Tel Aviv), as well as sheruts, can be picked up from the stands on Shavei Tzion.

Getting there and around

Mediterranean Coastal Strip

History

During the 12th and 11th centuries BCE Ashdod was one of the five great **Philistine** cities (*Joshua 13:3*); following the capture of the Ark of the Covenant from the Israelites it was for a time kept by the Philistines in the Temple of Dagon here (*I Samuel 5:1-5*). The town was subsequently captured in turn by the Israelites (*II Chronicles, 26:6*), Assyrians (*Isaiah 20:1*) and Babylonians (foretold in *Jeremiah 25:20; Zephaniah 2:4; Zechariah 9:6*).

It was during the period of **Persian** occupation that Ashdod developed significantly as a port (sixth to fourth century BCE), and this process continued following the arrival of the Greeks in the third century BCE, when the town became known as **Azotus** (Ashdod-Yam).

The old town has strong Christian links as the site where **Philip the Evangelist** (Philipe the Deacon) preached the gospel, and near to where he converted and baptised a eunuch in the employ of the Queen of Ethiopia (*Acts 8:26-40*). Along with Ashqelon (see page 498), Ashdod was extensively used by the Crusaders. The port was further developed by Arab seafarers, who called it Minat el-Qila (Fortress Port).

Ashdod's modern history really begins in 1965, when the construction of a deep-water harbour facility provided the catalyst for the town's rapid expansion. The town's population has been boosted by an influx of North African

Jews, and more recently by the arrival of immigrants from Eastern Europe. It is very noticeable just how many bars and restaurants have their sign-boards written not in Hebrew, or even English, but in Cyrillic.

Sights

Ancient Ashdod It's hardly worthwhile visiting the scant remains of **Tel Ashdod**, some six kilometres south of the modern town. Excavations have revealed remains from the Middle Bronze Age II, the Iron Age I (including evidence from the Philistine city), plus all later periods up to the Early Arab period. Most of the site has been destroyed by later cultivation and construction. Likewise, the remains of the coastal settlement of **Ashdod-Yam** (two kilometres south of the city centre) are few and far between, though it is possible to see parts of a large defensive rampart probably built around 713 BCE. There are also sections of the 13th-century Crusader fortress (Bus 6a or 10 from the local bus station goes nearest to the site).

Beaches Attempts have been made in recent years to provide more facilities at the beaches. This includes not just showers, changing rooms and toilets, but promenades, public seating, street furniture and sculptures, picnic areas, children's playgrounds, plus complexes that house restaurants, cafés, nightclubs

Ashdod

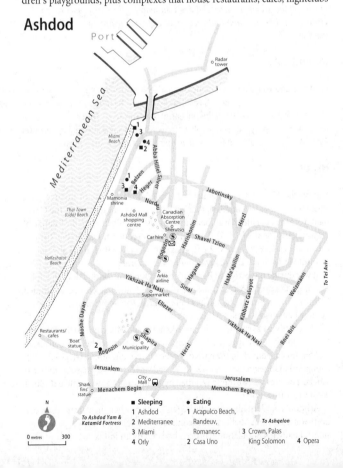

■ Sleeping
1 Ashdod
2 Mediterranee
3 Miami
4 Orly

● Eating
1 Acapulco Beach, Randeuv, Romanesc
2 Casa Uno
3 Crown, Palas King Solomon
4 Opera

To Ashdod Yam & Katamid Fortress

To Ashqelon

0 metres 300

and beach bars. It has worked, to some extent, though in order to attract more tourists, greater improvements must be made in tackling the problem of pollution from the port nearby.

Miami Beach has newish facilities, and is near to a number of (Russian) restaurants and nightclubs, and the town's two operational hotels (plus a third, under construction). The harbour directly to the north does not provide a very attractive backdrop. South of here is **Thai-Town Beach** (or **Lido Beach** as it's better known). Significant work has been done to spruce up the beachfront, with many of the facilities mentioned above found here. On Wednesday, a large 'flea market' is held in the car-park here. The southernmost urban beach is Hakeshatot Beach, where a large complex housing cafés, restaurants and bars has been built. It also appears that there are plans to develop the beach hinterland further to the south, possibly as a marina.

Essentials

The 2,000 new rooms planned by the Ashdod Tourism Development Company have yet to materialize, and the Mediterranee Hotel remains half-built. Thus, sleeping options remain extremely limited.

Sleeping
■ *on map;*
Price codes:
see inside front cover

C *Orly*, 22 Nordau, T8565380, F8565382. Rather old fashioned and a little overpriced, but rooms have a/c, cable TV, phone, some with small balconies, friendly and 'sunny', close to the beach, restaurants. **D** *Ashdod*, Miami Beach, T8560477. New place opened in 1999 very close to the beach, a/c, cable TV (extra), modern tiled bathrooms, everything brand new. Pretty good value; best deal in town. **D** *Miami*, 18 Nordau, T8522085. Looks closed up but it isn't! Run-down rooms, some a/c, not much English spoken, poor value. **Rooms to let** *Aliza*, T8542102; *Ashdod Beach*, T8555741; *Maison Harrel*, Nahal Zehelim, T8540885; *Michael Ben Shitrit*, T8554837.

Cafés *Blues Café*, 9 Rogozin, T8522901. *Graffiti*, 7 Rogozin, T8566291. *La Lyonnaise*, T8569878. *Nus Café*, 9 Rogozin, T8566922. *Shagal*, Hakshatot Beach, T8662339. *Shakespeare*, 15 Rogozin, T8566758. **Fast food** *Burger Ranch*, City Mall, T8664411. *Burger King*, Lev Ashdod Mall, T8561010. *Domino's Pizza*, City Mall, T8663388. *McDonald's*, City Mall, T8651008. *Pizza Don Pedro*, 5 Kineret, T8550042. *Santos Pizza*, Lev Ashdod Mall, T8652233. **Miscellaneous** *Apropo*, City Mall, T8663311. Dairy and light meals. *Ashdod Ha'ktana*, 19 Jabotinsky, T8523568. Middle Eastern grilled meats, fish, salad, nice setting. *Bombay*, Ashdod Mall, T8564687. *Casa Uno*, 74 Rogozin, T8553179. Italian food recommended by one reader. *Chan Lee*, Ha'Bonim, T8565299. Moderately priced Chinese dishes. *El Gaucho*, Hakshatot Beach, T8649981. Part of Argentinian steakhouse chain, steaks 75-100 NIS. *Golden Phoenix*, 20 Nordau, T8562688. Chinese restaurant at *Orly Hotel*. *Kapulsky*, Lev Ashdod Mall, T8643923. Diet-busting cakes, light meals. *Opera*, next to *Mediterranee Hotel*. Recently opened Eastern European place. *Pina Argentina*, Hakshatot Beach, T8655485. Huge steaks. There are also a couple of extremely attractive restaurants in the Mamonia Shrine.

Eating

Brilliant, Hakshatot Beach, T8651610 (daily 1000-0200). *Buffalo*, 19 Haorgim, T8528887 (daily 0800-2400). *Dux*, Lido Beach, T8528288. *Happy Days*, Hakshatot Beach, T8550835. *Lachish Gardens*, Ha'Oman, T8566955 (daily 2130-0130). *Maze Bar*, 4 HaBonim, T050-733700. *Patshanga Beach*, Lido Beach, T050-355323 (Sunday-Thursday 0900-0300, Friday-Saturday until 0430). *Pigal*, HaBonim, T8561524 (daily 2100-0400). *Q*, HaBonim, T052-885234. *X-O-Bar*, 19 Haorgim, T8528120 (daily 2000 until late). *Tembel*, Hakshatat Beach, T8649779.

Bars & nightclubs

Mediterranean Coastal Strip

Entertainment   **Cinemas** *Gil*, Lev Ashdod Mall, T8647202; *Ori*, Ashdod Mall, T8568073; *Rav-Hen*, City Hall, Maerkaz Ha-ir, T8661120.

Sports   **Diving and sailing** Ashdod Yam, 2 Yona Hanavi, T8522339 (Sunday-Thursday 0830-1400 1600-1900, Friday 0830-1600). **Ten-pin bowling** *Alon Bowling*, 2 Ha'Orgim, T8529311 (daily 1000-0200).

Shopping   Ashdod has three large shopping centres: *Ashdod Mall*, Nordau, T8567031; *Lev Ashdod Mall*, Yehuda HaLevi, T8544051; and *City Mall-Merkez Ha-ir*, Herzl, T8662020 (this is where the bus station is).

Transport   **Buses** Ashdod's new bus station (City Mall – Merkaz Ha-ir, T8547213/8507213) is to the southeast of the town centre, at the junction of Herzl and Begin. It has a McDonald's, shops, clean toilets, etc. **Ashqelon**: 015, every 20 mins, last at 2000, 13 NIS, 25 mins; **Be'er Sheva**: 360 direct, 368 via Kiryat Gat, 4 per day, 17 NIS, 1 hr 40 mins; **Jerusalem**: 448 via Latrun, every 2 hrs, 20 NIS, 1½ hrs; **Rehovot**: 212/323; **Tel Aviv**: 312/314/320, every 15 mins, last at 2230, 15 NIS, 40 mins; plus a number of other services. Some of the buses bound for Tel Aviv (312/314) pick up passengers from the stops on Shavei Tzion. There are also sheruts to Tel Aviv from here (T8563533), and a taxi office (*Port Taxi*, T8532497). **Car hire** Most of the car hire offices are at the junction of Rogozin and Shavei Tzion (Avis, T8564162; *Eldan*, T8534177; *Europcar*, T8527779; *Uricar*, T8562415). **Train** Ashdod is envisaged as being part of the revamped Israeli train network (T8522567), though currently the station is rather remote, and poorly connected to the town itself (irregular Bus 6). There are 2 trains per day via Rehovot and **Lod** to **Tel Aviv**, with one continuing north to **Netanya**, **Haifa**, **Akko** and **Nahariya**.

Directory   **Airlines offices** *Arkia*, Rogozin, T8521212, F8568838 (Sun-Thu 0800-1900, Fri 0800-1300). **Banks** *Bank Leumi* and *Bank HaPoalim* have branches on Shapira and Rogozin. The post offices offer commission-free foreign exchange. **Communications** Post offices: the General Post Office is on Shapira (Sun, Mon, Tue, Thu 0800-1230 1600-1830, Wed 0800-1300, Fri 0800-1230). The branch office is on Rogozin (both offer foreign exchange). **Telephones**: *Videomit*, Ashdod Mall, T8528005 and *Pele-Call*, Lev Ashdod Mall, T8660366. Both offer cellular phone rental. **Tourist offices** This is handled by the *Hofit-Ashdod Tourism Development Company*, Ashdod City Hall, 12 Ha'Banim, T8545481, F8545472. **Useful phone numbers** Police: T100. Ambulance: *Magen David Adom*, T101. Fire: T102.

Ashqelon (Ashkelon)

Phone code: 07
Colour map 2, grid C1

With a natural port site, and a rich hinterland of fertile agricultural land and abundant water, there should be little surprise that Ashqelon developed as an important city, with a history spanning 6,000 years. Much of the town's history is presented in an excellent National Park, where substantial remains are set amongst picnic lawns. The town is also attempting to appeal more to holiday-makers, with a refurbishing of the beach area.

Ins and outs

Getting there   Ashqelon has good bus connections with the rest of the country, notably Tel Aviv and Jerusalem. It can also be used as the 'jumping off' point for Yad Mordechai Junction, for onward travel to Gaza. The Central Bus Station is on Ben-Gurion (T6750221), with sheruts leaving from the opposite side of the road.

Buses 1, 6 and 10 run infrequently from the Central Bus Station to Ashqelon National Park (or it's a 20-min walk). Bus 5 runs to Kikar Zefanya (for Antiquities' Courtyard) from the Central Bus Station (or an uphill 20-min walk), continuing on to Barnea. Buses 1, 2, 4, 4a and 10 run between Migdal and the Central Bus Station, with buses 2 and 3 calling at Barnea.

Getting around

History

Despite an earlier settlement having been established here, it was the movement of the **Sea Peoples** into this area that saw Ashqelon become a **Philistine** city around the 12th century BCE, and there are numerous references in the Bible to 'Ashkelon' as one of the five leading cities of the Philistines (*Joshua 13:3, 3*; *I Samuel 6:17*). Of the five cities (Gaza, Ashqelon, Ashdod, Ekron and Gath), Ashqelon was perhaps the most important due to its status as a port.

Early rulers

Subsequent centuries saw Ashqelon conquered by a series of rulers, including Assyrians and Egyptians, with the last Philistine ruler of Ashqelon being forced into exile in Babylon around 604 BCE by **Nebuchadnezzar**. The city later came under the rule of the Persians, during whose tenure the maritime **Phoenicians** expanded Ashqelon's commercial wealth. A succession of dynasties followed, though whoever the nominal rulers were Ashqelon retained a fair degree of autonomy, and by the first century BCE was minting its own silver coins. In subsequent years, most notably during the period of the *Mishnah* and *Talmud* (second to fifth centuries CE), Ashqelon was considered to be outside the limits of Eretz Israel ('land of Israel'), and had resisted Jewish forces during the First Jewish Revolt (66 CE).

Ashqelon flourished in the Late Roman period (132-324 CE), adding to the splendour that **Herod** had endowed the city with during his earlier period of rule. Josephus (*The Jewish War I: 21, 42*) details a number of Herod's ambitious building projects, and it is suggested in a number of sources that Ashqelon was Herod's birthplace. Trade continued to develop in Byzantine times (324-638 CE), with Ashqelon becoming the major outlet for wine produced in the Levant. The city also became a focus of Christian pilgrimage.

Roman and Byzantine rule

Muslim rule began in 636 CE and continued until the Crusaders defeated the Fatimids in 1153. The city then changed hands five times between the Christians and the Muslims within the next century. **Salah al-Din** took the city in 1187, only for **Richard Coeur de Lion** to recapture it four years later. In the meantime, Salah al-Din had razed most of the fortifications and attempted to destroy the harbour. Richard subsequently rebuilt some of the fortifications, only to return the city to Salah al-Din by treaty. Once again Salah al-Din dismantled the fortified walls, only for them to be partially rebuilt in 1240 by the Duke of Cornwall. The fortress was finally destroyed in 1265 by the Mamluk sultan **Baibars**. The Ottoman ruler Ahmed el-Jazzer subsequently used stone from the site to help build his sea wall at Akko.

Arab and Crusader periods

For most of this century Ashqelon merely comprised the small Arab village of Migdal, where parts of an old caravanserai and mosque remain. In 1952, following the controversial forced removal of the Arab population, South African Jews founded the settlement of Afridar from which Ashqelon has grown to a city of some 75,000 people.

Recent history

Mediterranean Coastal Strip

Ashqelon: what's in a name?

There are a number of spellings of the city name, including Ashqelon, Ashkelon, Ashkalon, and Ascalon. Classical sources (including Josephus, Strabo and Pliny) refer to Ascalon, with the city subsequently giving its name to a variety of onion (caepa Ascalonia) that was grown nearby in Roman times. The name of the scallion variety of onion still derives its name from this source.

The origin of the name probably lies in the Northwest Semitic language, possibly used in Canaanite times. The root of the word is also closely related to the Canaanite verb 'to weigh', from where the word 'shekel' is derived.

Sights

Ashqelon National Park
Set adjacent to the beach, within 80 hectares of sculptured lawns, the Ashqelon National Park contains a number of antiquities that hint at the city's long and distant past. Though there are remains from most levels of occupation, including Canaanite, Philistine and Hellenistic, it is those from the Roman, Byzantine, Arab and Crusader periods that dominate.

The park is enclosed within well-preserved **fortified walls** that are best seen to the east and south. These ruined walls are usually mistakenly attributed to the Crusaders. They were in fact built in the Fatimid period (10th-12th centuries CE) by the Arabs, though they were partially rebuilt and reinforced in 1192 by Richard Coeur de Lion. There were originally gates at each of the cardinal points; Jaffa Gate to the north, Jerusalem Gate to the east, Gaza Gate to the south, and Sea Gate to the west. Today, just the eastern gate remains standing.

The most dramatic view of the surrounding wall can be seen by dropping

Ashqelon

Sleeping		Eating		2 Antiquities Courtyard
1 Hachof		● 1 El Poncho		3 Bus stops (2 & 3)
2 Holiday Inn				4 Luxury apartment
3 King Saul	5 Shulamit Gardens	▲ Other		blocks
4 Samson's Gardens	6 Village	1 Roman Painted Tomb		5 Private health club

Mediterranean Coastal Strip

down on to the beach, and viewing the fortifications from there. Parts of the western wall have succumbed to the years and have been reclaimed by the sea; other parts lay broken on the beach. Much of the debris, including Roman columns, was dumped here by Salah al-Din in an attempt to render the harbour unusable by the Crusaders. In the southwest corner, at the site of the old quay, the ancient **Byzantine wall** remains, buttressed by **Roman columns** that have been likened to the barrels of coastal cannons.

In the centre of the park is the **Bouleuterion**, a colonnade and assembly hall, according to an inscription, "built for the council of the free city of Ascalon under the seven emperors". This quadrangle, containing Corinthian capitals and column bases, probably dates to the third century CE when Ashqelon was ruled as a semi-autonomous state by Severius. The building was 110 metres long and 35 metres wide, with an open central courtyard surrounded by a portico (colonnade) of 24 columns on each side, and 6 at either end. The columns stood eight metres high. At the southern end is an apse, set at its original level several metres below the current ground level. The entrance to the apse is flanked by a couple of remarkable marble pillars. One depicts the **goddess of victory**, Victoria-Nike, stood holding a wreath and palm on a globe supported by Atlas. The other is a representation of the Egyptian **goddess Isis**, with the **child-god Horus**. This evidence, along with other statues, busts, inscriptions and reliefs found nearby, point to construction of the complex in the Severan era (possibly early third century CE), rather than by Herod the Great, as suggested by some sources.

The park also contains a 10,000 seat **amphitheatre** that is used for concerts and drama presentations, plus two **Turkish wells** dating to the Ottoman period, one of which has been significantly restored. With ample parking places and large expanses of lawn, the National Park is very popular at weekends with picnicking families. There is a designated **bathing beach** here,

Ashqelon National Park

though it is rather polluted. It is possible to tour the park on foot, though it is quite a long walk if you wish to take in a complete circuit of the Arab/Crusader walls. There is a café and two restaurants within the park. ■ *T6736444. Summer 0800-1830 daily, winter 0800-1600 daily. Admission free for pedestrians, 10 NIS for 'citizens', 50 NIS bus, 20 NIS minibus. Bus 6 runs here hourly from the Central Bus Station.*

Roman painted tomb To the north of the National Park, near to the *Shulamit Gardens Hotel*, is a **Roman painted tomb** from the third or fourth century CE. The barrel-vaulted tomb is decorated with frescoes depicting, amongst other images from classic Greek mythology, water-nymphs seated by a stream, and Pan with his flute. The tomb has places for four bodies, and the quality of work suggests that it was built for a wealthy family, whose figures are perhaps represented on the north wall. ■ *Sunday-Friday 0900-1300, Saturday 1000-1400. Admission free.* **NB** *The tomb is currently closed whilst the beachfront area is being redeveloped.*

Sheikh Awad Tomb This 13th-century Mamluk tomb stand above the beach, its dome providing an interesting counterpoint to the nearby 'golf-ball' *Holiday Inn*. The central chamber holds the local saint's tomb, with two later rooms on either side.

Antiquities Courtyard Located in the heart of the Afridar district is the compact **Antiquities Courtyard**. An interesting collection of archaeological finds from the Ashqelon area, the key attractions are two third-century CE **Roman sarcophagi**. The first is complete with a cover depicting reclining figures, symbolizing the deceased. You may notice that the faces on these figures are yet to be completed: this suggests that the sarcophagus had not yet been purchased and was still waiting to be completed with a likeness of the deceased. The superb carvings on the side depict the abduction of Persephone, whilst the two shorter ends have two griffins, and a pitcher between two lions, respectively. The other sarcophagus probably had a similar cover, though this was not found when the two items were excavated in 1972. On three sides are carved scenes from a battle between the Romans and the Gauls (or Trojans), whilst on the fourth side there is a depiction of bulls being attacked by lions.

Other items in the Antiquities Courtyard include: a broken column containing a Greek inscription acclaiming Emperor Julian, (361-363 CE); a Roman copy of a Hellenistic statue of a man wearing a toga; a Byzantine sarcophagus from Barnea; and a number of eighth- to ninth-century sculptures in a neo-Hittite style. ■ *Kikar Zefanya, Afridar. Sunday-Thursday 0930-1530, Friday 0830-1330. Free. Buses 4, 4a, 5.*

Byzantine basilica and mosaic pavement During the construction of the suburb of Barnea, the remains of a Byzantine basilica church were discovered. The nave is flanked by two side aisles (with a *prothesis* and *diaconicon*), with a small prayer room to the south. Coloured glass *tesserae* found on the floor suggest that the walls and floor were decorated with mosaic. Work continues on restoring the site.

A second, smaller basilica was found 200 metres to the northwest. An inscription in Greek in the *diaconicon* (storehouse in Byzantine churches) dates construction to 499 CE, with a second inscription in the antechamber pavement quoting Psalm 93:5 ("holiness becometh thine house, O Lord ... "), and a date of 493-494 CE. A third Greek inscription quotes Psalm 23:1 ("The Lord is My Shepherd ... "). The **mosaic pavement** in the main aisle is very well executed. ■ *Buses 2 and 3 stop nearby.*

Mediterranean Coastal Strip

There are a number of interesting things to see in Ashqelon's older district of **Migdal district**
Migdal, to the east of the town centre. The **Ashqelon Museum** traces the history of the town from Roman times through to the establishment of the State of
Israel, with an audio-visual presentation in Hebrew, English and French. The
museum is located on **Kikar Ha'Atzmaut**, site of an old caravanserai on an
ancient trading route. ■ *Kikar Ha'Atzmaut, T6727002. Sunday-Thursday
0900-1300, 1600-1800, Friday 0900-1300, Saturday 1000-1300. Admission free*

The **Khan Mosque** on the square is currently closed to visitors. Migdal is
the town's main market area and is best seen on a Thursday. Local Buses 4, 5, 6
and 7 run to Migdal.

There are a number of distinct beaches along Ashqelon's Mediterranean coast. **Beaches**
From north to south they are: **North Beach**, fairly quiet, popular for nude
bathing; **Barnea Beach** becomes quite busy at weekends with residents of this
fairly affluent suburb; **Bar Kochba** is the town's religious beach, which has
separate bathing hours for men and women; **Delilah Beach** has a number of
wading pools and three small island within swimming distance, and is the
town's busiest beach, particularly for families at weekends; **Yamia Club** is a
non-bathing beach (water-sports only); finally, on the coastal side of the
National Park, is the **Park Beach**. **NB** There are very strong undercurrents
along this stretch of coastline, and it is advised that you only swim at sanctioned beaches where life-guards are present.

Ashqelon has a large water park featuring five water slides, three pools, and **'Ashkeluna'**
water slides for young children. Out of season it looks pretty forlorn, and
would seem to be in need of substantial repairs and refurbishing before it could
re-open. Best to call ahead ■ *T6739970/050-540831. Bus 6 from Central Bus
Station.*

Excursions from Ashqelon

This kibbutz was founded in 1943 and named after **Mordechai Anilewicz**, **Kibbutz Yad**
heroic leader of the Jewish Uprising against the Nazis in the Warsaw Ghetto. **Mordechai**
During Israel's War of Independence, the 165 members of the kibbutz played a
significant role in holding up the advancing Egyptian army (despite being outnumbered fifteen to one). Though the Egyptians captured the kibbutz after
five days of fighting, this gave sufficient breathing spaces for the Israeli forces
to regroup around Tel Aviv, and thus saved the fledgling Israeli capital. A
museum in the kibbutz tells the story of the Jewish resistance in the Warsaw
Ghetto, whilst outdoors a mock **battlefield**, complete with model tanks, soldiers and a full recorded explanation, tells the story of the 1948 battle.
■ *T07-6720529. 0800-1600 daily. 8 NIS. The kibbutz is 10km south of Ashqelon
on Route 4. For details of buses here, see 'Transport' on page 505. Buses return to
Ashqelon Sunday-Thursday 0710 (035) 1224 (019) and 1620 (037), Friday
0710 (037) 1420 (037).*

A complex has been built around the natural hot sulphur spa (12km east of **Hamei Yoav Hot**
Ashqelon), featuring a hot sulphur pool, "thermo-mineral water massage and **Springs**
jacuzzi", some cooler plunge pools and a cafeteria. ■ *Hamei Yoav Spa Vacation, T07-6722184, F6723305. Accommodation is available nearby at the Kibbutz Negba Guesthouse and the Kibbutz Ein Tzurim (see 'Sleeping', next page).*

Mediterranean Coastal Strip

Essentials

Sleeping
■ *on map;*
Price codes:
see inside front cover

Despite its 'resort' reputation there isn't much accommodation choice in Ashqelon (nothing in the budget category), and most of what there is remains rather over-priced. The *Paradise* and *Park Plaza* hotels are still not completed.

L2 *Holiday Inn*, 9 Yekutiel Adam, T6748888, F6718822. Opened November 1998, this luxury hotel resembles a giant golf ball from certain angles. All rooms face the sea, with some 'business', 'deluxe' and 'chalet' rooms. Full facilities include pleasant pool area, tennis, basketball, petanque and health club. Restaurants include *Giraffe Noo-dle Bar*, *Veranda* Viennese coffee house, *Rosemarin* Romanian plus lobby lounge. Overall quite plush, though surrounding area is still a little tatty.

A *Shulamit Gardens*, 11 Hatayassim, T6711261, F6710066. 270-room hotel with full leisure facilities (large pool, gym, sauna, tennis, nightclub, choice of restaurants), though rooms are a little box-like and few have balconies. Full and half-board also available.

B *Hachof (Holiday Beach)*, Delilah Beach, T6735111. Rather run down (looks aban-doned from some angles) and somewhat disorganized, rooms have a/c, cable TV, but are bare and old fashioned. Staff are friendly but it's hard to see how they can justify these prices. **B** *King Saul*, 28 Harakefet, T6734124, F6734129. Recently renovated but still has rather 70s feel, some more expensive chalets, pool, tennis, restaurant, Shabbat restrictions apply, very overpriced for what it is. **B-C** *Kibbutz Ein Tzurim*, Sde Gat 79510, T08-6580263. Religious kibbutz near the Hamei Yoav Hot Springs (see above), 2-bedroom a/c holiday chalets, kosher meals in the kibbutz dining hall. **B-C** *Kibbutz Negba Guesthouse*, Kibbutz Negba, T07-6774799, F6774899. Bed and breakfast accommodation also near the Hamei Yoav Hot Springs (see above).

C *Samson's Gardens*, 38 Hatamar, T6734666. Old-fashioned chalets set around gar-den in quiet residential neighbourhood, though rooms have a/c, cable TV, are large and have modern bathrooms, (religious) family orientated. **C** *Village*, 2 Moshe Dorot, corner of Hatayassim, T6736111, F6730666. 52 chalets with a/c, TV, phone set Butlins-style in private grounds around a pool. Bar, restaurant, horse-riding facilities. Not much English spoken. Reasonable value.

Eating All the hotels have their own restaurants though none stand out (bar perhaps the *Holiday Inn*). There are some reasonable cafés on Kikar Zefanya/'Sundial Square', plus a collection of cafés, pizzerias and seafood joints on Delilah Square (facing the beach). Falafel and shwarma is at its cheapest in Migdal. The shopping malls all have fast-food outlets and a couple of café/restaurants.

Bars & nightclubs There are several pubs on Kikar Zefanya/'Sundial Square' (eg *Signon*), and down by the beach on Delilah Square.

Entertainment **Cinemas** *Gil*, Huzot Mall, Ben-Gurion (just off map); *Rav Chen 5*, Giron Mall, 21 Ben-Gurion, near Central Bus Station.

Shopping The two main shopping malls are *Huzot Mall* on Ben-Gurion, and *Giron Mall*, just west of the Central Bus Station. *Le Ha-Ir Mall* is at the southern end of HaHistadrut.

Sports **Diving** *Southern Divers*, Delilah Beach, T6711375. **Horse riding** *Municipal Ranch*, Eli Cohen, T6726608. **Snooker** There's a snooker club (T6731925) on Kikar Zefanya/'Sundial Square'. **Swimming** see 'Ashkeluna' and 'beaches' on page 503.

Municipal Pool, Stretch Henry, off Ofer. **Tennis** *Israel Tennis Centre*, Ofer, T6722286.
17 courts. **Ten-pin bowling** Huzot Mall, T6753153.

Local Buses See 'Getting around' at the beginning of the Ashqelon section on page **Transport**
498. **Car hire** *Amado*, 97 Ha'Nassi, T6735777; *Eldan*, junction of Herzl/Ben-Gurion,
T6722724; *Mal Mor*, T6750622. **Taxis** *Ashkelon Tours* taxi stand on 'Sundial Square',
T6751361; *HaMerkez*, T6733077; *Shimshon*, T6751333.

Long distance Buses The Central Bus Station is located on Ben-Gurion
(T6750221). The bus station has a McDonald's, toilets (1 NIS), etc. **Ashdod**: 015,
every 20 mins, last at 2015, 13 NIS, 25 mins. **Be'er Sheva**: 364/366, hourly, last at
2000, 1½ hrs. **Erez** (for Gaza): 019, Sunday-Thursday 1200, Friday 1615 (see also
Netiv Ha'asara), 30 mins. **Haifa**: 992, every 2 hrs, 2¾ hrs. **Jerusalem**: 436/437, hourly,
last at 1915, 22 NIS, 1 hr 20 mins. **Kiryat Gat**: 025, hourly, last at 2130. **Netiv
Ha'asara/Nisanit** (near Erez): 037, Sunday-Thursday 0915 1415 1810, Fri 1245, 30
mins. **Rafiah Terminal** (for Egypt): 362, 0900 Sunday-Friday, 1 hr. **Rehovot** and
Rishon LeTzion: 301 (continues to Tel Aviv), every 15 mins. **Tel Aviv**: 300 express
(also 301 express, 311 via Yavne), every 15 mins, last at 2245, 25 NIS, 1 hr. **Yad
Mordechai**: 019, Sunday-Thursday 1200, Friday 1615 (see also Netiv Ha'asara). Note
also that Bus 364 for Be'er Sheva passes through **Yad Mordechai Junction** (3 km
from the kibbutz, and within hitching range of the Erez crossing into Gaza).
Sherut/service taxi *Muniyot HaMerkazit*, opposite the Central Bus Station,
T6739977, offer 24-hr services to **Tel Aviv** via **Ashdod**.

Banks Several banks with ATM machines are found on Kikar Zefanya/'Sundial Square'. Banks **Directory**
are also found on Herzl in Migdal. Post offices offer commission-free foreign exchange.
Communications Phone code: T07. **Post offices**: GPO, 18 Herzl, Migdal (post restante).
Branch offices behind Central Bus Station and on Orit, near to Kikar Zefanya/'Sundial Square'.
Hospitals and medical services Ambulance: *Magen David Adom*, Ben-Gurion, T101
(T6723333). Chemists: *Super-Pharm*, Giron Mall, T6711431, amongst others. **Hospitals**:
Barzilai Medical Centre, 3 HaHistadrut, T6745555; *Central Clinic*, Ben-Gurion, just west of
Central Bus Station. **Tour companies and travel agents**: *Ashkelon Tours*, Municipal Centre,
T6751055; *Mona Tours*, 31 Herzl, T6724932; *Nir Ashkelon*, 63 Herzl, T6750930. **Tourist offices**:
Tourist Information Office, Ha'Nassi, T6710312. Sun-Thu 0800-1900, Fri 0830-1200, helpful
small kiosk opposite the 'Sundial Square', has large-scale map of Ashqelon. **Useful addresses
and phone numbers** Ambulance: T101. Fire: T102. Police: junction of Ha'Nassi and Eli
Cohen, T100 (emergency), T6771444.

The Shephelah

The Shephelah (Shefela) correctly refers to the region of low hills between the Colour map 2,
Plains of Philistia and the higher Central Range (see chapter introduction on grid C2-3
*page 481). This is the area broadly inland of Ashdod and Ashqelon. This distinct
region has played a significant role in the history of Palestine/Israel, and as such
warrants its own sub-section within this chapter. There are a number of places of
interest here, though access by public transport is not always straightforward.*

History

The name Shephelah translates as 'low' or 'lowland', describing a region of
low, broken hills scattered amongst areas of plain. This line of hills runs in a
gently curving arc, enclosing the Maritime Plain from Jaffa to Gaza. The
Shephelah is cut by several wide valleys that run broadly east to west from the
foot of the Judean Hills to the Mediterranean. These are the **Ajalon Valley** (see

Mediterranean Coastal Strip

'The Tel Aviv to Jerusalem road' on page 516), the **Vale of Soreq**, the **Vale of Elah** and the **Wadi el-'Afranj**.

Because of these valleys, the Shephelah has not functioned as a physical barrier between the people dwelling on the plains and those living further east. If anything, the Shephelah has provided a point of contact between the different groups. Smith thus describes it as "a famous theatre of the history of Palestine – the debatable ground between Israel and the Philistines, between the Maccabees and the Syrians, between Salah al-Din and the Crusaders" (*Historical Geography of the Holy Land*, 1894). Many of the great battles between groups contesting this ground either took place in the four valleys that run east to west and cut through the hills, or were facilitated by these valleys acting as lines of communication into the heart of the protagonist's territories.

The **Vale of Soreq**, the modern route of the Tel Aviv to Jerusalem rail link, is the traditional site of the towns of Zorah and Eshtaol, and the Camp of Dan, where a "woman bare as son, and called him Samson: and the child grew, and the Lord blessed him" (*Judges 13:24*). Over the low hills from the Vale of Soreq is Timnah, where Samson took a Philistine wife (*Judges 14:1*) and killed the young lion (*Judges 14:6*). The head of the Vale of Soreq has been suggested as the site where the Philistines captured the **Ark of the Covenant** from the Israelites (*I Samuel 4:1-11*), though neither the exact site of battle nor the "Stone of Help" where they rested the Ark has been definitively identified. It seems more logical, however, to suggest that the battle is more likely to have taken place at the head of the Ajalon Valley. The route of the Ark's return, however, is more certain, following the "highway" along the Vale of Soreq from Ashdod up to Beth-Shemesh (*I Samuel 6:1-21*).

The entrance to the Philistine Plain of the **Vale of Elah** is guarded by **Tel Zafit**, site of the Crusader castle of 'Blanche Garde' ('White Citadel'). Though unconfirmed, this site is tentatively described by some scholars as being the location of the great Philistine city of Gath (though there is precious little to see here). As the Vale of Elah winds up into the Shephelah, at the junction of two further wadis, one leading south towards Hebron and the other striking out towards Bethlehem, there is a broad flat plain (along Route 38, just north of Ha'Ela Junction). This is suggested as the scene of the contest between **David and Goliath** (*I Samuel 17:1-52*), and though there is nothing specific to see, the description in the biblical passage does rather match the setting here.

The fourth valley running through the Shephelah is cut by the **Wadi el-'Afranj**, running broadly northwest from Hebron to the coast at Ashdod. This route is particularly important since it takes in the sites of **Lachish**, **Mareshah** and **Bet Guvrin** (see below). For orientation, see colour map 2 at the end of the book.

Kiryat Gat This modern industrial town is located 22 kilometres east of Ashqelon, and is the administrative centre of the surrounding Lachish region. There is little of interest in the town itself, though there are some major attractions nearby (see below). Most visitors will only use Kiryat Gat as a transport stop on the way to either of these sites, though even then the transport connections are not particularly good. Those with their own transport can by-pass Kiryat Gat altogether.

Transport To/from **Tel Aviv** 333/369, every 20 mins, 22 NIS; **Jerusalem** 446, every 30 mins, 22 NIS; **Ashqelon** 025, every 30 mins, 12 NIS. For details on getting to **Bet Guvrin National Park** and **Tel Lakhish** by bus, see below.

Bet Guvrin and Mareshah

*The interesting remains of the two ancient cities of **Bet Guvrin** and **Mareshah***   *Colour map 2, grid C3*
*are well presented within **Bet Guvrin National Park**. Of particular note are the*
underground cave complexes, the 'Sidonian burial caves', and the ancient 'tel' of
Mareshah. Several other attractions are located on the grounds of Kibbutz Bet
Guvrin, and between the kibbutz entrance and the petrol station, though these
are less well presented.

Ins and outs

To reach Bet Guvrin National Park from Kiryat Gat, you must take bus 011 to Kibbutz   **Getting there**
Bet Guvrin (Sunday-Thursday 0805 and 1730 only, Friday 0805 and 1415 only, 10 NIS;   **and around**
return Sunday-Thursday 0825 and 1730 only, Friday 0825 1430 only). As you can see,
these times are not very convenient, and require a very early start if making a day-trip
from Tel Aviv, or even Ashqelon. Some of the Kiryat Gat-Hebron buses pass along this
road (route 35), so it may be possible to flag one down.

If travelling in your own transport, take Route 35 (by-passing the town of Kiryat
Gat) towards Hebron. The park is signposted (orange sign) 17 km southeast of Kiryat
Gat.

Mareshah (Marisa)

Following the end of the United Monarchy (c. 928), Mareshah was one of the   **History**
cities given to Judah (*Joshua 15:44*), and during the reign of Asa (908-867
BCE) a major battle was fought just to the north of Mareshah (described in
some detail in the Bible, *II Chronicles 14:9; 15:12*).

In the Early Hellenistic period (332-167 BCE) Mareshah replaced Lachish
(see page 511) as the capital of western Idumaea (Edom), and a sizeable
Sidonian community came to settle here.

During the Hasmonean wars Mareshah was repeatedly attacked by the
Maccabees (*I Maccabees 5:66, 2 Maccabees 12:35*), and upon its capture by
Hyrcanus I the population was forcibly Judaized by the imposition of circumcision (Josephus, *The Jewish War I, 63*). Mareshah remained under
Hasmonean rule until its recapture by Pompey (*Jewish War I, 156*) and was
then later rebuilt by Gabinius, governor of Syria, around 56 BCE. The city was
incorporated as part of the domain granted to Herod (c. 40 BCE), though it
was almost immediately destroyed by the Parthians. Once stability returned,
Bet Guvrin replaced Mareshah as the district capital and Mareshah ceased to
exist.

Bet Guvrin

Bet Guvrin became the capital of the district following the destruction of   **History**
nearby Mareshah in 40 BCE (see page 507), though it was not until the Late
Roman era that the village developed into a flourishing city. It became a
Roman polis in 200 CE under the emperor Septimus Severus, and was granted
one of the largest tracts of land in Palestine stretching from 'En Gedi to the sea.
He gave the city the name Eleutheropolis, 'City of Freedom'. The
Roman-Byzantine city probably extended for a little under 50 hectares and
later became the seat of a bishop.

During the Early Arab period (638-1099) the city became known as Bet
Jibrin, and in the 12th century the Crusaders built a small city here. The

Crusader king Fulk of Anjou built a castle here in 1136 as part of the plan to encircle Ashqelon, though once that city fell in 1153, Bet Guvrin's strategic significance was lessened. The Knights Hospitaller continued to occupy the fortress, perhaps mindful of its location on the Jerusalem road.

Bet Guvrin National Park

Colour map 2, grid C3

The main attractions are well marked on a walking trail. The complete walking tour takes four to five hours, though if you have your own transport it is possible to drive between sites and park in the spaces provided. This will, however, involve some degree of doubling back on foot. Cold drinks, snacks and toilets are available outside the Bell Caves (13). The numbers below correspond to the numbers on the map.

Mareshah's Northern Burial Site (1)

Two caves dating back to the third to second centuries BCE are open for viewing, though there are far more impressive caves within the park. There is a parking lot and picnic site nearby, though most visitors drive on to parking lots I and II and begin the tour there.

'Polish Cave' (2)

Forty or so steps lead down into this water cistern, cut from the rock in the 4th or 3rd century BCE. The 'artefact' (Latin for 'an installation for the raising of pigeons') niches were added in the late Byzantine/early Arab period. Like other cisterns on this site, the cave has a vaulted ceiling and rock-cut steps with handrail. The 'Polish' reference is to the soldiers of General Anders' army who visited the caves in 1943, carving the words 'Warsaw', 'Poland' and the Polish eagle symbol into the cave walls.

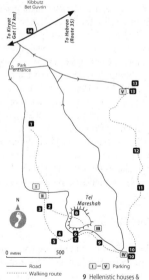

Bet Guvrin National Park

Columbarium (3)

A large number of columbaria have been found in this area, though this one is probably the finest example. Shaped like a double cross, this large columbarium still has over 2,000 niches for nesting pigeons, though initially it may have had many more. Although considered as something of a nuisance by some cultures, pigeons had significant uses in Byzantine times. A source of food, pigeons were also used for ritualistic purposes. Their droppings, which you may well encounter in this cave, were collected and used as fertilizer. After the third century this cave was probably used as a storehouse.

Bath Cave (4)

Hip baths from the third to second centuries BCE can be seen in two small chambers cut into the rock. The baths were filled by spouts linked to conduits bringing water from

---

Kibbutz Bet Guvrin

To Kiryat Gat (17 km)

To Hebron (Route 35)

Park entrance

0 metres   500

—— Road
------ Walking route

1 Mareshah's northern burial site
2 "Polish Cave"
3 Columbarium
4 Bath Cave
5 Olive Press Cave
6 Hellenistic House
7 The water cisterns
8 Northwestern tower of Tel Mareshah

[I] – [V] Parking

9 Hellenistic houses & underground complexes
10 The Sidonian burial caves
11 Crusader Church of St Anne
12 The "Bustan" Cave
13 The Bell Caves
14 Roman amphitheatre and Crusader castle

Tel Mareshah

outside. Decorated pottery braziers found nearby were almost certainly used to heat the water.

Olive trees contributed significantly to the local economy during the Hellenistic period, and 20 such oil presses have so far been discovered in the Mareshah vicinity. Assuming that there were 30 such oil presses in the area, it has been calculated that annual production would exceed 250,000 kilogrammes. To support this industry, substantial areas of olive groves would have occupied the surrounding area. In fact, such was the level of production that surplus was exported to Egypt and to the towns on the coast. A restored oil press is presented in this cave, along with a description of the production process.

Olive Press Cave (5)

Used primarily as a house, this partially reconstructed building may also have been used as a place of business during the third to second centuries BCE. Twenty-five silver coins were found in a juglet under the floor in one of the rooms, the latest dating to 113 BCE. This corresponds to the year in which John Hyrcanus conquered the city, so it is assumed that the house was destroyed then. All of the coins were minted at Ashqelon, each weighing around 14 grammes. Each coin featured an eagle on one side, and the image of the ruler(s) on the other. The oldest coin depicts Cleopatra Thea and Antiochus VIII (c. 122 BCE).

Hellenistic House (6)

The design of the house features rooms built around a central courtyard (4.7 metres by 3.5 metres), from where a spiral staircase led to the second floor. The second story has not survived, though extensive rubble from this part of the building was found. This debris included a number of column drums and four Ionic capitals, perhaps part of a decorative façade attached to the wall facing the courtyard. The upper floor probably contained living quarters. On the ground floor was found a kitchen, with an oven *in situ*. Also on the ground floor is a reception room and a pantry in which numerous *amphorae* (two-handled ceramic jars used for transporting grains and liquids) of the Mediterranean, Aegean and Italian-North African type were found. Below the house is located a system of connecting water cisterns.

Rain water was collected from the roof of the house, the yard, and the surrounding lanes by a series of channels and clay pipes, and then funnelled down into the water cisterns below the house. A steep staircase descends into these beautifully cool underground storage systems, and then ascends via the neighbouring house's cistern.

The Water Cisterns (7)

A path leads up to the 'tel' upon which stood the upper city of Mareshah. The mound is about 152 metres in diameter, and was first excavated in 1900 by the British Palestine Exploration Fund. The upper city probably covered an area of 2.5 hectares, with a square grid plan surrounded by a wall with towers. Three major levels of strata were identified; two from the Hellenistic period (332-37 BCE), and one from the Israelite period (Iron Age, 1200-586 BCE).

Northwestern Tower of Tel Mareshah (8)

Little remains to be seen of the upper city, bar the square tower at the northwest corner, and this is probably best seen from the road below the hill. The first stage of the tower was built c. 300 BCE, on top of rubble from earlier periods. The second phase of building dates to the first half of the second century BCE, when the tower rose to some 12 metres high.

The lower city of Mareshah, also surrounded by a low wall, was an underground city of several hundred caves below a network of streets, houses and public buildings (see page 507).

Mediterranean Coastal Strip

Hellenistic Houses and Underground Complexes (9) To the southeast of Tel Mareshah there are further Hellenistic houses, using the same pattern of rooms arranged around a central courtyard, with a staircase leading to the upper floor. Beneath each house is a water cistern, and a passage has now been cut so that you can pass from one cistern to the next. There are also a number of underground chambers, a columbarium, and an oil press.

The Sidonian Burial Caves (10) The dead of Mareshah were buried in three groups of necropolis that ringed the city, to the east, north, and southwest. Two of the tombs from the eastern necropolis, known as the 'Sidonian burial caves', are currently open for viewing.

Though tombs I and II had already been excavated, their subsequent discovery by grave robbers in 1902 apparently brought fanatic Muslims from the Arab village of Bet Jibrin with the intention of effacing the figures in the wall paintings. The initial excavators, Peters and Thiersch, dashed to the site, and within three days had succeeded in copying the paintings and inscriptions from tombs I-IV. These copies were used recently in the work that has restored tombs I and II to their former glory.

Tomb I is the most impressive, and an outstanding example of how the people of Mareshah buried their dead. It is entered through the large bush (!), from where you emerge into an entrance hall. This large tomb (22 metres by 17.5 metres) comprises three burial chambers, of which the middle chamber is the most impressive. It features fourteen *loculi* (rectangular, shelf-like burial niches), seven on either side. A recess in the far wall leads to a further three burial rooms. The decorative friezes have been well restored, and mainly depict hunting scenes and animals. A number of Greek inscriptions were found in the tomb, the most important of which is probably the epitaph of **Apollophanes**, the head of the Sidonian community in Mareshah for 33 years (hence the 'Sidonian burial caves'). Many of the family members were buried in this tomb (the three chambers have a total of 32 *loculi*), and the epigraphic references provide much information on the social and family structure of Mareshah. For example, the fact that the names of the fathers are generally Semitic, whilst those of the sons tend to be Greek, reflect the assimilation of the Sidonian community amongst the population of Mareshah.

Tomb II, sometimes referred to as the '**Musicians' Cave**', is also open for viewing. Constructed on a similar plan to tomb I, though smaller (and darker), the decorated walls feature a musician in a striped tunic playing a flute, with a woman behind playing a harp. Inscriptions in the tomb are dated between 188 and 135 BCE.

NB From parking lot IV outside the Sidonian Burial Caves, it is possible to drive the 2.4 kilometres to parking lot V outside the Bell Caves. Alternatively, you can walk there (only 1.5 kilometres) via sites 11 and 12.

Crusader Church of St Anne (11) The remains of the apse of a 12th-century Crusader church dedicated to St Anne stands on the earlier site of a Byzantine church. Small portions of elaborately worked mosaics, featuring birds and flowers, were uncovered here, though sadly they are incomplete. The Crusader church is often referred to by its Arabic name of '**Santahanna**' (or 'Sandahanna/Sandachana'), and is located 500 metres north of the Sidonian Burial Caves.

The 'Bustan' Cave (12) This is a complex of bell-shaped caves and a columbarium, though the caves are not as spectacular as those further north (see below).

The Bell Caves (13) Originally it was thought that these caves were dug to be used as dwelling places, water holes and storage installations. However, it is now clear that these bell-shaped caves are essentially quarries dug to provide building materials, and that the uses suggested above came only after the quarries were exhausted. The caves in this vicinity date not to the city of Mareshah, but to the later city of Bet Guvrin, and most of the quarrying here was done in the 7th-10th centuries CE. There is a 10th-century reference to the quarries here by Mohammad ibn Ahmad al-Muqadasi, the Arab geographer/historian, who commented about Bet Guvrin: "it is a land of riches and abundance and has many marble quarries … ". (**NB** The "marble" referred to is chalk.)

The quarrying techniques involved here are remarkably advanced, taking full advantage of the local geological structure. The quarriers begun by digging a hole through the surface crust (*nari*; 1.5 to 3 metres thick) until the softer chalky rock below was reached. The rock below was then gradually scooped out, eventually forming the large 'bell-shaped' quarries. The bell shape provides structural support, maintaining the security of the quarriers below.

In many of the caves there are crucifixes and altars carved into the walls, along with Arabic inscriptions; the two combining to suggest that most of the quarrying was carried out by Christian Arabs. Connoisseurs of cheesy films may recognize the caves from scenes in *Rambo III* – a film that was set in Afghanistan! Unfortunately, due to structural instability, the Northern Bell Caves complex is closed, though the southern complex remains open. ■ *Sunday-Thursday 0800-1700, Friday 0800-1600. Adult 18 NIS, student 14 NIS.*

A number of interesting archaeological finds were discovered on, or near, the lands of Kibbutz Bet Guvrin (opposite the National Park). Permission must be sought before visiting sites within the kibbutz's land. These include the remains of a **Roman amphitheatre (14)** and **Roman inn**; the Byzantine **church at Mahat el-Urd** and **mosaics at el-Maqerqesh**; plus sections of a **Crusader church** and **fortress**.

Other attractions outside the National Park

Lachish (Tel Lakhish)

Colour map 2, grid C3

Tel Lakhish is the mound site of the ancient city of Lachish. The city's strategic location has brought triumph and tragedy to Lachish's population. The city enjoyed the status of being the largest city in Canaan and, in later periods, as the second city of the kings of Judah. Unfortunately, Lachish's importance as a fortified town has also been its downfall. Almost all historical sources, including numerous biblical references, have one reoccuring theme – the city's capture and destruction. Lachish has been destroyed on at least five occasions, and was finally abandoned when the nearby sites of Mareshah and Bet Guvrin rose to prominence (see page 507). Those who have already visited Mareshah and Bet Guvrin may be disappointed by the neglected state of this site.

Mediterranean Coastal Strip

Ins and outs

To reach Tel Lakhish by public transport is not easy. You can take any of the Hebron-bound buses from Kiryat Gat that go via Route 35 (plus bus 011 to Kibbutz Bet Guvrin: see page 507), and get off at the junction for Lachish 8 km out of town (marked by an orange sign). From here it is 2.5 km to the site. If travelling by your own transport, turn off Route 35 (Kiryat Gat to Hebron road) 8 km southeast of Kiryat Gat on to Route 3415 (Amazya road). Continue for 2.4 km until a small white sign at the junction points right. The tel is 300 m on the left, opposite a large house with a red-tiled roof.

Getting there and getting around

Unfortunately, the site of Tel Lakhish itself does not live up to its billing as one of the most important excavations in the area. Today, the site probably looks pretty much as it did after one of its many sackings – totally abandoned. Inside the inner walls you are likely to be confronted by waist high grass, obscuring all the remaining building and explanatory signs. Given the number of underground passages and tunnel shafts, it is probably not wise to stray off the main footpath.

History

The Canaanite city Although there is evidence of much earlier occupation, it was by the Middle Bronze Age IIB (1750-1550) that one of the major cities of southern Canaan had developed on this site. Remains from this era include fortifications (with the *glacis* of particular note), a palace, a cult place, plus residential quarters. Most of the Middle Bronze Age city was destroyed in a major conflagration, though precise details of this conflict are unknown.

The city on the mound here slowly recovered, and by the end of the Late Bronze Age (1550-1200 BCE) it may well have been the largest city in **Canaan**. A number of important buildings from this period remain today, including the **Fosse Temple** and **Acropolis Temple**. The Late Bronze Age Canaanite city was under Egyptian surezeinty during this period; a fact reflected in both architectural style and a number of surviving letters sent between the rulers of Lachish and the Pharaohs (including the 'Hermitage Papyrus 1116A', dated c. 1427-1402 BCE).

The reasons for the city's demise c. 1130 BCE are not entirely clear, though at least two theories are suggested. Some suggest that Lachish became a victim of the 'Sea Peoples' (including the Philistines), whilst others believe the Israelites were the conquerors. This latter theory rather depends upon accepting the Bible (*Joshua 10:1-35*) as a work of history, although archaeological evidence does to a certain extent support the biblical account. It has been suggested that it would be unlikely that a city on a raised mound could be captured so quickly (Joshua mentions a campaign lasting just two days), yet archaeologists have now proved that the Canaanite city was in fact unfortified at this time.

Kingdom of Judah The mound site was unoccupied for a long period, though at some stage, either during the United Monarchy or early in the time of the kings of Judah, Lachish was rebuilt as a fortified city. Lachish is mentioned as one of the cities that **Rehoboam** (928-911 BCE) built "for the defence of Judah" (*II Chronicles 11:5, 9*), though it could be that Rehoboam was only responsible for beginning the fortification work. Important structures from this period that remain today include the **city walls**, **outer gate**, **inner gate**, **palace-fort** and '**Great Shaft**'.

The cause of the destruction of the city is not clear. The earthquake c. 760 BCE, as mentioned in the Books of Zechariah and Amos (*Zechariah 14:5; Amos 1:1*), may have been a possible cause, or perhaps the aftermath of the rebellion against **Amaziah** (798-769). The fact that the king of Judah selected Lachish as his place of refuge from the rebels in Jerusalem indicates the importance of the city. Unfortunately for Amaziah, "they sent after him to Lachish, and slew him there" (*II Kings 14:19; II Chronicles 25:27*).

Assyrian conquest In 701 BCE Lachish was conquered by **Sennacherib**, the king of Assyria, during his invasion of Judah. There are numerous biblical references to Sennacherib's assaults on the fortified cities of Judah (*II Kings 18:14, 17; Isaiah 36:2, 37:8, 11; II Chronicles 32:1*), plus evidence that "he himself laid siege against Lachish, and all his power with him" (*II Chronicles 32:9*).

The Assyrians attacked from the southwest by building a large siege ramp

The Sacking of Lachish: the evidence

Part of the significance of Lachish as a major archaeological site is the fact that there are so many different sources of evidence corroborating the historical events. One such example is the sacking of Lachish in 701 BCE by the Assyrian king Sennacherib.

When John L Starkey excavated the site in 1932-36, the discovery of over 1,500 skeletons in a pit dating to the exact period confirmed the story of the sacking of Lachish as told in the Bible (2 Kings 18:13-17). However, the most graphic description of the sacking is seen in the bas-relief that Sennacherib commissioned for his palace in Nineveh. The Israeli author Amos Elon says of the bas-relief: "Viewing it, we seem to occupy a ringside seat overlooking the battlefield – some five hundred feet from the southwest corner of the city – on a spot where Sennacherib might have stood supervising the advance of his troops" (Amos Elon, Jerusalem – City of Mirrors, 1989).

In three scenes, the bas-relief tells the story of the battle and its aftermath. Sennacherib's infantry advance on Lachish's fortified walls, the attackers manouvring their ladders, battering rams and great siege trains under a hail of arrows and burning torches from the defenders above. The moat and battlefield is littered with corpses. The final scene shows a victorious Sennacherib, seating on a throne viewing his booty. Prisoners are led before him, whilst others are being tortured or executed. The inscription reads "Sennacherib, king of the world, king of Assyria, sat on his throne and the spoil from Lakisu (Lachish) passed in review before him." In the background, the surviving civilian population are being led off into slavery and exile. The original bas-relief from Nineveh can be seen in the British Museum in London, though there is a copy in the Israel Museum in Jerusalem.

(70-75 metres wide, 50-60 metress long). Though parts of the siege ramp remain to the northeast of the parking lot, much of it was removed by early British excavators who failed to identify its true purpose. The defenders of Lachish, meanwhile, constructed a defensive counter-ramp opposite the siege ramp with the purpose of creating a secondary, higher line of defence within the city walls. Numerous remains of arms and ammunition were discovered at this place, reflecting the intensity of battle.

Lachish declined rapidly after Sennacherib's murderous assault, and by the time of Josiah's reign over Judah (639-609 BCE) the site had been abandoned. However, within a remarkably short period of time the city had been rebuilt, though on a smaller scale than before. The fortified city of Lachish is mentioned as one of the cities that **Nebuchadnezzar** attacked during the Babylonian invasion that brought to an end the rule of the kings of Judah in 586 BCE (*Jeremiah 34:7*). **Babylonian conquest**

A number of important artefacts dating to the period of the last king of Judah, Zedekiah (596-586), were found amongst the burnt ruins of a room in the outer gate. Known as the **Lachish letters**, they are possibly letters exchanged between the military commanders of Lachish and Jerusalem, or signals sent by a subordinate stationed near Lachish "to my lord Yaush", commander of the city's garrison.

Lachish may have been abandoned for a period after Nebuchadnezzar's assault, though a seal found on the mound that bears the words "belonging to Gedaliah, who is over the house" ties in with biblical evidence that "for the people that remained in the land of Judah, whom Nebuchadnezzar king of Babylon had left, even over them he made Gedaliah the son of Ahikam, the son **Babylonian, Persian and Hellenistic periods** of Shaphan, the ruler" (*II Kings 25:22*). The Book of Nehemiah also refers to people settling in Lachish following the Babylonian exile.

A number of interesting buildings, including the '**Solar Shrine**', were built in the Persian period (586-332 BCE), and many continued in use during the Early Hellenistic period (332-167 BCE). Lachish was finally abandoned in the Late Hellenistic period (167-37 BCE), when Mareshah and Bet Guvrin (see page 507) became the dominant cities of the region.

Sights

Fosse Temple   The path up to Tel Lakhish passes the site of the Fosse Temple, to the north-west of the mound. Three successive temples were built on this site during the Late Bronze Age (1550-1200 BCE), though each in turn was destroyed. A rich assemblage of temple-related artefacts were found in the immediate vicinity, and the third Fosse Temple is reasonably well preserved despite being destroyed by fire in the late 13th century BCE. Today, the excavated remains are barely visible.

Outer   The entrance to the fortified city is via the outer gate, having ascended a ramp
fortifications   that lies adjacent to Sennacherib's **siege ramp**. The outer gate uses the defensive principle of indirect access, with the orientation of the entrance also meaning that anyone approaching the gate would have to expose their unprotected flank to the city's defenders; swords were carried in the right hand, protective shields in the left.

The **gate area** that you see today is a modern restoration of the city fortifications that were built by the early kings of Judah, possibly Rehoboam (928-911 BCE). At the time of construction it was the largest city gate in Israel, exceeding similar examples at Megiddo, Hazor, Gezer and Ashdod. It was subsequently destroyed by Sennacherib (701 BCE) and later reconstructions were on a far less grand scale. The modern restoration used debris found in the immediate vicinity. The outer gate opens into a courtyard, from where you pass through the **inner gate** into the city. It was in one of the small chambers in the gate area that the **Lachish letters** were found.

Immediately to your right, inside the enclosed mound, are the remains of the counter ramp, built in an ultimately futile attempt to repel the Assyrian army. To the left, a path leads to the expansive podium area where important city structures were built.

Tel Lakhish / Lachish

Acropolis   This was built on the site as part of the
Temple   Late Bronze Age (1550-1200 BCE) Canaanite city. Though the Acropolis Temple yielded few finds, the temple's plan is well defined. Egyptian hegemony over the region during this period is reflected in the design of the temple, with similar structures having been identified in a number of places in Egypt.

'Palace-forts'   On the east side of the podium-platform lie the superimposed remains of a series of 'palace-forts'. The initial palace-fort,

■ Large house with red tiled roof

1 Fosse Temple	6 Counter Ramp
2 Assyrian Siege Ramp	7 Acropolis Temple
3 Ramp Entrance	8 Palace Forts
4 Outer Gate	9 'Great Shaft'
5 Inner Gate	10 Solar Shrine

0 m   30

referred to by the site's excavators as **palace A**, was quite possibly built by Rehoboam (928-911), with a later building on the same site, **palace B**, serving as the headquarters of the royal-appointed governor. A third palace, **palace C**, was built upon the foundations of the earlier buildings during the Persian period (586-332 BCE). Though smaller than its predecessors, the Persian-period palace was impressively built, with imposing porticos giving way to a large inner court-yard, The palace is a synthesis of building styles, borrowing from Achaemenid and classic Greek architecture.

To the east of the podium area a deep shaft was located. Hewn from the rock, the 'Great Shaft' measures almost 25 metres by 25 metres, and is over 20 metres deep. Several theories have been put forward to explain its purpose, with early consensus of opinion suggesting that it was built as an alternative water supply to the 45-metre-deep **well** in the northeast corner of the mound. However, it is more likely that it is in fact a quarry dug to supply building stone for the city of the early kings of Judah. **Great Shaft**

To the northwest of the Great Shaft is a building that was labelled 'The Solar Shrine' when the site was first excavated. However, the exact function and date of construction has not been finally determined. It has been suggested that the temple/shrine was built in the Hellenistic (332-37 BCE) and not Persian period (586-332 BCE), and may well have been a Jewish cultic site. **The Solar Shrine**

Bet Guvrin to Jerusalem

From Bet Guvrin there is an interesting route (largely along Route 38) to Jerusalem that takes in a number of minor places of interest on the journey through the Shephelah into the Judean Hills. Refer to colour map 2 for orientation. Public transport to these sights is not good.

The Elah Valley is the traditional site of the battle between **David and Goliath**, with the biblical passage (*I Samuel 17:1-58*) rather matching the setting on Route 38 just north of Ha'Ela Junction. A little way to the south of this junction is **Mitzpe Massu**, an attractive forest watchtower set in an appealing picnic spot, whilst nearby on Route 39 are some **Roman milestones** dating to around 210 CE. **Elah Valley**

A little to the north of Ha'Ela Junction (near the turn off on Route 383) is a low bald mound that is now generally accepted as the site of the biblical city of **Azekah** (see *Joshua 10:10-11; Jeremiah 34:7*). The site is sometimes referred to as Tell Zakariya, though there is little to see.

The name of this development town recalls the Israelite city of Beth-Shemesh that stood at the head of the route between the Philistine city of Ashdod and Jerusalem. Remains of the Israelite city can be seen at **Tel Beth-Shemesh**, signposted just to the west of the modern town. Though there is not a great deal of interest to see at the site, it does have a long and well-documented history. It was to Beth-Shemesh that the Philistines returned the Ark of Covenant after finding that it brought nothing but ill fortune to them (*I Samuel 6:8-9*). Beth-Shemesh was the scene of a battle between Joash, king of Israel, and Amaziah, king of Judah (*II Kings 14:11-13; II Chronicles 25:21-23*), and was later captured by the Philistines (*II Chronicles 28:18*). **Beth-Shemesh**

A little to the south of Beth-Shemesh, at **Beit Jemal**, is the **Monastery Our Lady of the Assumption**, built on the site of a Byzantine church that suppos-edly marked the burial place of St Stephen, the first Christian martyr (*Acts*

Mediterranean Coastal Strip

6-7). The monastery is renowned for its excellent handmade pottery (there is a small shop). ■ *T02-9911889, F9911880. There are regular buses from Jerusalem and Tel Aviv to Beth-Shemesh, although you'll probably have to walk from the town to reach the nearby attractions.*

Avshalom Reserve and Soreq Stalactite Cave

The Soreq Stalactite Cave is another of Israel's natural wonders. The cave was discovered during quarrying in 1968, and comprises an awe-inspiring collection of stalactites (growing down) and stalagmites (growing up) condensed into what appears to be a naturally formed auditorium. The whole 'show' began some five million years ago and is an extremely complex process of chemical and physical weathering. Water permeated with carbon dioxide acts as an acid, slowly dissolving the limestone and dolomite rock. The water becomes satured with the dissolved rock, but as it 'drips' from the ceiling the carbon dioxide is released, causing the dissolved rock to precipitate. Each drop of water leaves behind a hollow ring of stone the same diameter as the drop, and as these build up they form the stalactites. Should the hollow core of the stalactite become blocked, the dripping water runs down the outside, creating even more outrageous shapes. If the water manages to drip before the carbon dioxide is released, the gas is released at the point where it hits the floor. The action of the rock precipitating here causes stalagmites to form, which ultimately 'grow' up. The splash effect of the water hitting the floor can also lead to imaginative formations. The overall effect is far more spectacular than the science suggests, particularly at points where stalagmites 'grow' up to meet descending stalactites.

Tours are generally conducted when there are enough people to form a group. Tours are given in Hebrew unless there are a majority of English-speakers. A slide show explains the science, with a series of out-of-focus slides showing the more spectacular or amusing formations. A walkway passes around the cave, with the guide pointing out the key sites with a torch. Various points are dramatically lit, though lighting is kept to a minimum since it enourages a destructive algae to grow on the formations. ■ *T02-9911117. Sunday-Thursday and Saturday 0830-1545, Friday 0830-1245. Admission 18 NIS. No tours on Friday. **NB** Photography is only permitted at certain times (usually Friday, but call ahead). Smoking is prohibited. Note also that the 300-metre stepped path down to the cave is fairly steep. Unfortunately there is no public transport to the site. Bus 184 goes to Nes Harim from Jerusalem, though it's a seven-kilometre walk from there. Alternatively, it's a 10-kilometre uphill walk from Beth-Shemesh along Route 3855. If you don't have your own transport it may be possible to join an organized tour (try Egged Tours in Jerusalem).*

The Tel Aviv to Jerusalem Road

*There are a number of points of interest on or around the **Ajalon freeway** (Route 1), which provides the main road between Tel Aviv and Jerusalem. Many of these sights have come to be associated with the gospel account of Jesus' resurrection appearance on the road to Emmaus (see box on page 518), or with battles between the Arabs and Israelis during the 1948 war. If you are relying upon public transport, most of these sights are best visited as an excursion from Jerusalem.*

The Ajalon Valley

The **Ajalon Valley**, through which the modern Tel Aviv to Jerusalem road largely runs, is the route through which the tribes of Dan pushed down to the sea; following the exile, the Jews also used this route to expand their settlements down to the coast; Joshua swept down Ajalon, driving the Canaanites before him; Benjamin and Ephraim used this route to raid the Philistines, whilst the Philistines came right back up this route, disarmed the Israelites, and subsequently forced them to come down to the mouth of the valley to get their tools sharpened (hence the name, Valley of the Smiths); David's armies swarmed down this valley when he "smote the Philistines", with the Romans suffering a similar rout here in 66 CE when Cestius Gallus led the assault on Jerusalem; the Egyptians, Maccabees and Crusaders all battled their way along the Ajalon Valley, with Richard Coeur de Lion gaining nothing but a brief glimpse of Jerusalem before Salah al-Din's armies drove him back to the coast.

During the war that accompanied Israel's independence in 1948, the Ajalon Valley was the scene of some of the bloodiest battles between the Israelis and the Arabs, notably for the control of Latrun and Kastel. The valley was the main supply route for the beleagured Israeli forces in West Jerusalem, with the rapidly built so-called '**Burma Road**' running largely to the south of the modern Route 1.

Latrun area

The area around Latrun occupies a historically important strategic position on the road from the coastal plain up to Jerusalem. The 'Latrun area' lies roughly on either side of the main Jerusalem to Tel Aviv highway (Route 1) at the main northwest to southeast bend in the road.

To the west of the road lie the Crusader fortress of **Le Toron des Chevaliers**, with the Cistercian 'Monastery of the Silent', **Latrun Monastery**, nearby. To the east of Route 1 lies the former site of the Arab village of 'Imwas, identified in some sources as the site of the biblical village of **Emmaus**. A number of remains from different periods can be seen in **Canada Park**, a recently developed recreational area. Close to the entrance to the park are the remains of an extensive **Roman/Byzantine bathhouse**, plus the **Churches of Emmaus-Nicopolis** that mark the traditional Byzantine and then Crusader location of Emmaus.

Ins and outs

Getting there Regular buses run to Latrun from Jerusalem's Central Bus Station, though you can in fact take almost any one of the Jerusalem to Tel Aviv buses that pass along Route 1 and ask to be let off at the junction. As soon as you board the bus, make sure that you

Around Latrun

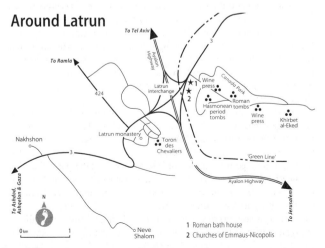

1 Roman bath house
2 Churches of Emmaus-Nicopolis

Jesus' Resurrection appearance on the road to Emmaus

Luke's gospel (Luke 24:13-35) recalls that on the day of the Resurrection, two of the disciples were making their way on foot to the village of Emmaus, some seven miles from Jerusalem. As they discussed the events of this first Easter, "Jesus himself came up and walked with them; but something prevented them from recognizing him." The two disciples and the 'stranger' discussed what had happened in Jerusalem, with Jesus explaining how Christ's martyrdom had been prophesied in the Bible. On reaching their destination the disciples, one of whom was called Cleopas, persuaded the 'stranger' to dine with them. It was only when the 'stranger' broke the bread and said the blessing that they recognized him as Jesus. He subsequently disappeared, leaving the two disciples to rush back to Jerusalem to explain the 'Good News' of the Resurrection to the other disciples.

*The location of the gospel Emmaus is unknown, though since the fourth century CE four different sites have been suggested: **Abu Ghosh**, **Latrun** ('Imwas), **el-Qubeibeh** and **Qalunieh**.*

Discrepancies in different gospel manuscripts have led to this confusion, with some reading that Emmaus was located 60 stadia from Jerusalem, whilst others mention 160 stadia. The 60 stadia (11.5 kilometres) criteria certainly fits both Abu Ghosh and el-Qubeibeh (and would have been sufficiently close for the two disciples to reach Emmaus and return to Jerusalem in one day). Both these identifications, however, are relatively late, dating to the Crusader period. The identification with Latrun is comparatively early, and is mentioned in Eusebius' Onomasticon (c 330 CE). The former Arab village of Qalunieh (abandoned in 1948, located on the ridge above the Jerusalem-Tel Aviv highway below Motza) is the probable site of a village established in the first century CE for 800 Roman veterans of the First Jewish Revolt (see Josephus, Jewish War, VII, 217), and named Emmaus. Apart from the fact that it is 30 stadia from Jerusalem, and thus within 'day-trip' range of Jerusalem, this is the only connection with the gospel Emmaus.

inform the driver that you want to get off at Latrun, and remind him as the bus approaches the junction.

History

A capital of one of the Roman toparchies of Judaea by the first century BCE, it was during the third century CE that the fortunes of **Emmaus** changed dramatically. Emmaus was granted the status of a city by the emperor Elagabalus (218-222 CE), subsequently becoming known as Nicopolis. This favour was largely the result of petitioning at the emperor's court by the soldier-diplomat turned scholar, Julius Africanus, who had settled in Emmaus. It is thought that the Roman bathhouse here was first built after the granting of this imperial charter (see below).

Earliest Christian associations with Emmaus are hard to fix accurately, though it is known that Julius Africanus was a member of the early church. The first Christian basilica found at Emmaus dates to the third century CE, and can be seen as part of the 'Churches of Emmaus-Nicopolis' complex (see below). It is not clear if the gospel event had been localized here at this point, though it certainly had by the time Eusebius had compiled his *Onomasticon* in 330 CE. A further church, plus a baptistry, was constructed on the site in the sixth century CE, though events shortly after the Arab conquest of Palestine were soon to erase the identification of Emmaus from the collective memory. An outbreak of plague here in 639 CE claimed many thousands of lives, with many Arab sources suggesting that Emmaus was the source of the subsequent plague epidemic that swept through the entire Middle East. Though the Crusaders settled in the area in the 12th century CE, building a small church within the existing Byzantine basilica, it is not thought that the site was associated with the gospel tradition of Emmaus. In fact, the Crusaders appeared to prefer the association of Emmaus with Abu Ghosh or el-Qubeibeh (see box on page 518), and the church here may have been built merely to serve the community that developed around the Le Toron des Chevaliers fortress. The name Emmaus is preserved in the name of the Arab village of 'Imwas.

Sights

Excavation of the church complex here has revealed remains of five structures. Little remains of the recesses hewn out of rock and foundations of walls that date to the second and first centuries BCE, though some remnants of a second century CE **Roman villa** are clearly discernible. In particular, the remains of the mosaic floor can be identified and include scenes of a lion devouring a bull, a panther attacking a gazelle and a number of birds perched on lotus flowers. In the third century CE a large Christian **basilica** was built here, and in the sixth century CE a second **basilica** was built, possibly because the original basilica was damaged or destroyed in the Samaritan revolt of 529 CE. The second basilica also featured a **baptistery** in which was found a trefoil-shaped stone baptismal font, plus a smaller font for baptising children. During the 12th century CE the Crusaders built a Romanesque style **church**, reusing the central apse of the third-century church and adding their own vaulted hall.

Churches of Emmaus-Nicopolis

A source of the name Emmaus is Hamat or Hamata, with Jewish sources referring to a place of "fine water and a fine dwelling" (*Eccles. Rab. 7:15*), ie a place of rest and of baths. However, Emmaus was renowned not just for its thermal springs, but for the quality and quantity of its ordinary water. Gichon, who led the major excavation of the 'southern baths' here, suggests that the bathhouse complex that can be seen today near the entrance to Canada Park is probably just one part of the bath installations at Emmaus, with others yet to be discovered and excavated.

Roman/ Byzantine bathhouse

First built as part of the imperial charter that granted Emmaus-Nicopolis city status (after 221 CE, but before the early fourth century CE), the present remains comprise just four rooms preserved to their original ceiling height. They appear to have been damaged in, but survived, the major earthquakes of 498, 502 and 507 CE. In fact, the bathhouse's survival at all is attributed to an unusual series of events. The commander of the Arab armies in Palestine, Abu 'Ubeideh, is believed to have died in the plague epidemic that struck Emmaus in 639 CE. In the 13th century CE, the Mamluks sought to reinforce the site's link with Islam, partially in an attempt to counter the nearby site venerated by the Christians and partially as a means of establishing a religious cause at this strategic crossroads. The baths subsequently became a holy place linked to the memory of Abu 'Ubeideh (with some sources still referring to the baths as Maqam esh-Sheikh 'Ubeid).

A rather attractive landscaped park, complete with wooded areas, walking trails and picnic tables, Canada Park features a number a remains from the Hellenistic, Roman, Byzantine and Crusader periods. Of particular note are the sophisticated **Roman aqueduct system**, the **Hasmonean grave complex**, a number of **wine-presses** from the Byzantine period, plus the site of the **Crusader fortress** of Castellum Arnaldi.

Canada Park

Mediterranean Coastal Strip

Le Toron des Chevaliers This fortress was one of several established along this road by the Order of the Templars some time after 1132. It is in fact claimed that the name 'Latrun' is derived from the original Crusader name Le Toron des Chevaliers (Tower of the Knights), though a counter-claim suggests that Latrun comes from the title *castellum boni latronis*, or 'fortress of the good thief' (since it marked the birthplace of the 'good thief' who was crucified with Jesus). Situated as it is close to the main theatre of confrontation between the Crusaders and the Muslims, the fortress changed hands on a number of occasions, with its guest list including Salah al-Din, Richard Coeur de Lion and the Mamluk sultan Baibars. By 1283 the fortress was in ruins, though a large caravanserai was built nearby in the 14th century CE. Today the fortress is rather forlorn and overgrown. It is reached through the grounds of the adjacent Latrun Monastery.

Latrun Monastery The monastery was established here in 1890 by the Trappist Order, subsequently becoming known as the Monastery of the Silent. Though expelled by the Turks during WW1, the monks returned in 1926, building the present monastery. The Latrun Monastery, as it is more commonly known, has a good reputation for the quality of the wine it produces, and this is available (along with a number of other locally produced items) from the small shop that the monks run. It is also possible to visit the monastery gardens. ■ *Shop open Monday-Saturday 0830-1130 1430-1630.*

Abu Ghosh The present name of this small Arab village just north of the main Jerusalem to Tel Aviv highway (Route 1, 13 kilometres from Jerusalem) preserves the name of a 19th-century CE sheikh who used to levy tolls on pilgrims using this route to reach Jerusalem. The former Arabic name for the village, Qaryet el-Enab, in turn preserves the biblical name, Kirjath-jearim (modern Hebrew name: Qiryat Yearim). A small hill village on the border of the tribes of Judah and Benjamin, it was at Kirjath-jearim that the Ark of the Covenant was kept during the twenty-year period between its restoration by the Philistines (*I Samuel 6:21-7:2*) and its removal to Jerusalem by David (*II Samuel 6; I Chronicles 13:5-14*). The village from this period occupied the hill-top area (Deir el-Azhar) and is now marked by a large statue of the Virgin Mary and the infant Jesus in the grounds of the Notre Dame de l'Arche d'Alliance. This modern church (1924) stands on the site of a Byzantine chapel that was built to mark the traditional site of the house of Abinadab, where the Ark was kept (*I Samuel 7:1*). Parts of the chapel's fifth century CE mosaic floor can still be seen. ■ *Open daily 0800-1130 1330-1800; admission free, donations accepted; ring the bell if locked.*

At an as yet undetermined date, the settlement here moved down to a new site on the valley floor. Murphy-O'Connor (*The Holy Land*, 1993) suggests two preconditions for this move: relative political stability and a sufficient amount of traffic along the road between Jerusalem and the coast to sustain the settlement. Thus he suggests a second century CE date when the Romans built a reservoir over the spring here. The reservoir was entered via two stepped passages hewn from the rock (and now incorporated into the Crusader church, see below). It was almost certainly built by a detachment of the Roman Tenth Legion Fretensis who were stationed on the old Roman road up to Aelia Capitolina (Jerusalem). The event is marked by an inscription on the walls of the Roman reservoir. In the mid-ninth century CE, a **caravanserai** was built east of and tangential to the Roman reservoir. Water from the Roman reservoir supplied a pool beneath a pavilion at the centre of the caravanserai's courtyard, whilst a large reservoir was built on the east side. The caravanserai continued in use up until the Crusader period, and was later restored by the Mamluks some time between 1350 and 1400.

During the Crusader period, the village here became associated with the gospel story of the resurrected Christ's appearance to two disciples on the road to Emmaus (*Luke 24:13-35*, see box on page 518). The reason for the Crusaders locating the biblical Emmaus here was based largely on circumstantial evidence; they simply selected the nearest village that was located the necessary 60 stadia (11.5 kilometres) from Jerusalem, believing that the spring and reservoir would have been a suitable place for Jesus and the disciples to stop for their meal. In 1142, the village and all its land were granted to the Order of the Hospitallers, and a large **Crusader church** was built above the reservoir. The former eastern reservoir built in the ninth century CE was turned into a great vaulted hall, whilst the Early Arab period caravanserai was considered to be the place where the meal took place. In latter years the Crusaders located Emmaus at el-Qubeibeh (see below). The Crusader church is very well preserved, particularly the crypt over the Roman reservoir, thanks in part to extensive renovations carried out at the end of the 19th century CE. The church was presented to Napoleon III at the conclusion of the Crimean War, and subsequently entrusted to the French Benedictine Lazarus Fathers. To find the church in the village head for the tall minaret of the adjacent mosque. ■ *T02-6342798. 0830-1100 1430-1700, closed Thursday and Saturday. Admission free, donations accepted. The church is marked by the sign "Eglise de Croisse – Crusaders' Church". Buses 185/186 both run to Abu Ghosh from Jerusalem's Central Bus Station.*

El-Qubeibeh Though el-Qubeibeh lies the necessary distance from Jerusalem to qualify as Emmaus (see box on page 518), the association with the gospel tradition is rather nebulous. Located on the **Roman road** to Jerusalem (parts of which can still be seen), in the eighth or ninth century CE a number of **houses** (still visible) were built here by Arab settlers, who thus founded a village. Some time in the first half of the 12th century CE the Canons of the Holy Sepulchre in Jerusalem acquired the land, ostensibly for tax farming purposes. The village probably took its name, Parva Mahomeria, from the small Muslim shrine that stood in the village (el-Qebeibeh means 'little cupola'). A small fortress and hospice were built to service the needs of Christian pilgrims using this route to Jerusalem. It is now widely believed that later Christians became confused as to why a church had been established here; the only tradition that seemed to fit the location was the gospel story of Christ's resurrection appearance at Emmaus, and given that the distance matched certain versions of Luke's gospel, the tradition stuck. The present Franciscan church here was consecrated in 1902, though the foundations of the Crusader-period church are still visible. Visitors are shown a wood panel in the floor to the left of the nave, which is claimed to be part of the house of Cleopas (though this is highly unlikely). The church at el-Qubeibeh (to the northwest of Abu Ghosh) is the venue of a popular pilgrimage on Easter Monday. ■ *T02-952495 extn 4. 0800-1145 1400-1700. Admission free, donations accepted.*

Ein Hemed Just to the south of Route 1 (at Qiryat Anavim Junction) are the insubstantial remains of the Crusader monastery of Aqua Bella (known locally as Ein Hemed).

Kastel Also south of Route 1, just to the west of Jerusalem, is Kastel, site of a Roman fortress. Most visitors, however, come here to see the scene of one of the major battles in the war that accompanied Israel's independence. The story of the battle is told in gushing detail in Collins and Lapierre's *O Jerusalem* (1972), with the actual battlefield laid out with explanation boards and models. Some

Mediterranean Coastal Strip

argue that the death here of the leader of the Arab forces, Abdul al-Qader al-Husseini, changed the course of the entire war. ■ *Saturday-Thursday 0800-1600, Friday 0800-1500. Adult 9 NIS. Best reached by bus 183 from Jerusalem.*

North of Tel Aviv

Herzliya/Herzliya Pituach

Phone code: 09
Colour map 2, grid A2

Established as an agricultural settlement in 1924 and named after the 'founder' of modern Zionism Theodor Herzl, the town is now Israel's most up-market beach resort. With a beautiful stretch of fine white sand, yet just 15 kilometres and a 20-minute drive north of Tel Aviv (barring inevitable traffic jams), Herzliya has also become one of the country's more salubrious residential neighbourhoods, favoured by foreign diplomats and the affluent classes.

Ins and outs

Getting there
There are actually two parts to the town. The older part of the town, Herzliya itself, is further inland, to the east of the main road (Route 2) that connects Tel Aviv to Haifa. Visitors will be more concerned with Herzliya Pituach ('Herzliya-on-Sea'), the resort area on the coast. The Central Bus Station (which is served by Egged and Dan buses from Tel Aviv's Central Bus Station) is located on Wolfson, in Herzliya itself. Some, but not all, Egged buses continue on to Kikar Shalit in Herzliya Pituach. Thus, the most convenient way to get to Herzliya Pituach is to take the *United Tours* bus 90 from Tel Aviv (see 'Transport' on page 524). This bus will drop you on Kikar Shalit or Kikar Ha-Ziyyonit in Herzliya Pituach. Note that this bus also runs on Shabbat. If you are coming by bus from the north, ask to be let down at Accadia Junction (the turn-off from Route 2). The train station is also located in Herzliya.

Getting around
If you arrive in Herzliya itself, note that bus 13 runs from the Central Bus Station, past the Municipality, railway station, then along Ramat Yam (past the hotels) to Kikar Shalit, then north to Sidna Ali Beach (every 35-60 mins, 0730-2130). Bus 29 runs from the Central Bus Station, via the railway station, to the *Sharon Hotel* (every 8-20 mins, 0600-1900).

Sights

Beaches
Herzliya's prime attractions are the beaches, though you must pay to use them. Non-residents pay 12 NIS per visit (8 NIS child), whilst residents pay for a season ticket, the price of which depends upon how far from Herzliya they live! Facilities are good, with showers, changing rooms and toilets, plus a wide (but expensive) choice of restaurants and cafés. The most popular beaches are **Zevulun-Daniel Beach**, opposite the *Holiday Inn Hotel*, and the **Sharon** and **Accadia** beaches, near to the hotels of the same name. The remote **Shefayim Beach**, five kilometres to the north, is favoured by nudists. **Warning** There is danger from the strong undercurrents, and bathers should only swim where life-guards are on duty.

Sidna Ali Beach and Sidna Ali Mosque
There is a free beach, **Sidna Ali**, to the north of Herzliya Pituach, though take care not to get cut off at high tide, and should not attempt to climb the crumbling cliffs. Toilets, showers, changing rooms and parking are provided.

Mediterranean Coastal Strip

A number of features make Sidna Ali Beach interesting. Besides the ruins of the Crusader fortifications that dot the beach (see below), there is the extraordinary beach house of an eccentric known as the '**Caveman**'. A lesson in recycling, the 'house' is built primarily from materials found washed up on the beach below, and features a number of extravagant sculptures. In the summer the owner operates a small café. Further north along the beach is another small community of people living close to nature.

The beach takes its name from a Muslim holy man who died fighting the Crusaders. His shrine is housed within the **Sidna Ali Mosque** above the beach (though it's not generally open to the public).

Above the beach, to the north of the Sidna Ali Mosque, is the ancient site of Tel Arsuf. Over a thousand years ago this was an important port, though today there's little more left than a pile of rubble, a large fence, and signs proclaiming 'danger'. **NB** Having recently visited the site and declared it on a parallel to that of Caesarea, the Mayor of Herzliya has announced a 1.5 million NIS plan to prepare the site for visitors by Pesach in the year 2000.

Tel Arsuf/ Apollonia

Herzliya Pituach

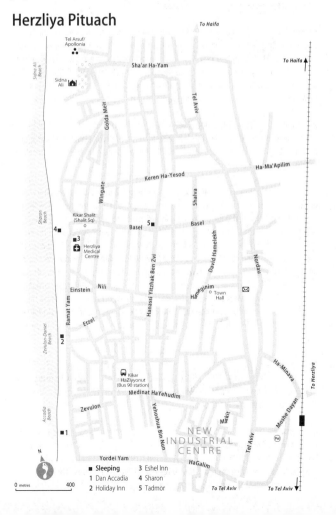

Mediterranean Coastal Strip

■ **Sleeping**
1 Dan Accadia
2 Holiday Inn
3 Eshel Inn
4 Sharon
5 Tadmor

The city was founded in the Persian period (586-332 BCE) as Arshof (derived from the Phoenician god Reshef), though it became known as Apollonia during the Hellenistic period (332-37 BCE). The city was captured by the Persians in 614 CE, and shortly after by the Arabs (since when it has been known by the Arab corrupt form, Arsuf). Under the Arabs it developed as one of the major port towns of Palestine, but was captured by the Crusaders in 1101 (when it became known by the Crusader corrupt form, Arsur). It was near here, in 1191, that Richard Coeur de Lion defeated the army of Salah al-Din. The Crusaders were eventually defeated in battle in 1265 by the Mamluk Baibars, and the city was razed.

Essentials

Sleeping
■ *on map;*
Price codes:
see inside front cover

L2 *Dan Accadia*, Ramat Yam, T9597070, F9597090. Popular luxury hotel billing itself as having a 'country club' atmosphere, has standard rooms facing the patio or tennis courts, deluxe rooms facing the pool and sea (extra $60), plus a choice of more expensive chalets and suites. Leisure facilities include tennis, pool, kid's pool, health club, plus choice of restaurants. Recommended.

L3 *Holiday Inn*, 60 Ramat Yam, T9544444, F9544675. Formerly the *Daniel*, this recent acquisition to the chain is lavish and ornate throughout, perhaps even somewhat over the top. There's no getting away from the fact that you are in a luxury hotel, with full facilities that you would expect. **L3** *Sharon*, 5 Ramat Yam, T9525777, F9572448. Best rooms have sea-facing balconies, all with a/c, cable TV, some family rooms in *Bella Vista* wing, full sports and dining options plus supervised child activities.

A-B *Tadmor*, 38 Basel, T9525000, F9574560. Used for training hotel employees, so hence the service is very keen, though price is a little high for a place so far from the beach. **B-C** *Eshel Inn*, 3 Ramat Yam, T9568208. Cheapest place in town with small a/c rooms, though rather run down.

Eating

Of the hotel restaurants, the *Al Bustan* at the *Dan Accadia* is the pick. There are a number of attractive café/restaurants on Ramat Yam where 'being seen' is as important as the quality of the food; *Dabush* and *Picasso* are popular choices. There is a selection of restaurants down on the beachfront, though Herzliya Pituach's main dining area is for some reason found in the 'New Industrial Centre'. *Churrascaria Brasileira*, 29 Maskit, T9512313, and *Dona Flor*, 22 HaGalim, T9509669, are two recommended Brazilian restaurants where a full meal costs around 90-120 NIS per head. *El Gaucho*, 60 Medinat Ha-Yehudim, T9555037, and *Whitehouse Steakhall*, Mercazim Building, Maskit, T9580402, both offer meals on the 'giant steak' theme. *Tandoori*, Mercazim Building, Maskit, T9546702, offers high-quality North Indian cuisine, main dishes 35-72 NIS. There are several reasonably priced restaurants on Kikar Shalit.

Entertainment

Art galleries *Herzliya Museum of Art*, Wolfson, Herzliya, T9551011, Sunday-Thursday 1700-2000, Friday-Saturday 1000-1400, free. **Cinemas** *Star*, T9589068. **Museums** *Founders' Museum*, 8 HaNadiv, Herzliya, Monday-Thursday 0900-1300, Friday 0900-1230, free.

Transport

Air Herzliya's airport (T9502373) is used primarily by companies offering sight-seeing tours ovar Israel, private charters, or flying lessons. *Chim-Nir Aviation Service*, T9520520, F9508708; *F.N. Aviation*, T9548525, F9548691; *Moon Air*, T9587280, F9509696; *Nesher Aviation & Tourism*, T9505054. **Buses** The Central Bus Station is on Wolfson, in Herzliya, and is served by Dan and Egged buses. However, for those travelling to or from **Tel Aviv**, it is far more convenient to use *United Tours* Bus 90, which connects Tel Aviv with **Herzliya Pituach**. The bus starts outside the *Dan Panorama Hotel* in Tel Aviv,running through HaYarkon – Allenby – Ben Yehuda – Bograshov – Dizengoff Sq – Reines – Adam HaCohen – Arlozorov – Weizmann – Jabotinsky – Namir, before heading north to Herzliya Pituach. **NB** This bus also **runs on Shabbat** (Sunday-Friday 0655-0110, Saturday 0745-0110, peak every 35 mins, off-peak every 30-45 mins, night every 45-60 mins, 11 NIS. Egged Bus 425 runs a mornings-only service to **Jerusalem** from opposite the *Sharon Hotel*. **Train** The train station is not particularly conveniently located. Trains run twice an hour to **Tel Aviv** (first around 0615, last around 2100), with reduced services on Friday and Saturday. To **Haifa** via **Netanya** they run twice per hour during peak, every 2 hours off-peak, with reduced services on Friday-Saturday.

Communications Phone code: T09. **Post offices** The main post office is just off Route 2, the main Tel Aviv to Haifa road. **Hospitals and medical services** *Herzliya Medical Centre*, 7 Ramat Yam, T9592555.

Directory

Netanya

By general consensus Netanya is an unpretentious town, perhaps drawing more comfort from comparisons with the English seaside resort of Brighton than more lofty talk of a 'Miami-on-the Med'. Its prime attraction is over 10 kilometres of sandy beach, with a Mediterranean climate that remains pleasant throughout the year. The town also prides itself on the variety of activities and entertainment that it sponsors, most of it free. Netanya has a wide selection of hotels and restaurants, and can serve as a good base from which to explore the rest of the Sharon Plain and Mediterranean coastal strip.

Phone code: 09
Colour map 2, grid A3

Ins and outs

Netanya is easily accessible from most parts of the country, notably from Tel Aviv and Haifa. The train station is some distance from the town centre (and even further from the beaches), thus making the bus the best way to arrive.

Getting there

The town centre is fairly compact, with the bus station being less than 20 minutes walk from the beach (or you can take Bus 12 during July/August). Buses 5/5a run from the train station to the bus station. The main tourist activity (sleeping, eating, drinking, shopping) is centred around Kikar Ha'Atzma'ut and the pedestrianized section of Herzl.

Getting around

Mediterranean Coastal Strip

History

Founded as an agricultural settlement specializing in citrus production in the 1920s, the town takes its name from the Jewish-American philanthropist Nathan Strauss. The Second World War saw two new industries spring up in Netanya that continue to sustain the town to this day. The use of Netanya as a convalescent centre for British officers founded the beginnings of the tourism industry, whilst the setting up of diamond-cutting workshops by immigrants from Antwerp led to the establishment in Netanya of this multi-million-dollar business.

Prior to the redrawing of Israel's border that followed the 1967 war, Netanya was located at one of Israel's narrowest spots, just 15 kilometres from the Jordanian military outpost of Tulkarm. In the words of one native of

Netanya in Thomas Friedman's *From Beirut to Jerusalem*, "In Netanya before the '67 war, if you put your car in fifth gear you could find yourself across the border"!

Sights

Beaches Netanya has a number of fine white sand beaches that are clean, with facilities such as sun-chairs (10 NIS per day), showers, changing rooms and toilets. There are also plenty of restaurants and snack-bars, plus water-slides, basketball courts, children's playgrounds and an outdoor gym for poseur men with large muscles and small swim-suits. Life-guards are on duty most of the year, and it is important to adhere to the warning flags set out for swimmers (see under 'Tel Aviv, beaches' on page 460). Those who want quieter and less crowded beaches should head further north or south from the main town beach area.

Diamond An interesting diversion from the beach is a visit to Netanya's National Dia-
factories and mond Centre (NDC). Over 10,000 people are employed directly and indirectly
showrooms in the diamond trade in Netanya, and at the NDC you will get a chance to see some of them in action. If easily tempted, leave your credit card at home, because those people that you will see in action include sales staff, as well as diamond cutters and polishers! A short ten-minute video is followed by a quick tour of the factory floor where you see the artisans at work, from where you emerge into the sales showroom. ■ *90 Herzl, T6427790, F8615106. Sunday-Thursday 0800-1900, Friday 0800-1400, Saturday closed. Admission and tour free. NB There are other factory/showrooms in town.*

Yemenite Located just off Kikar Ha'Atzma'ut is a small museum tracing the history and
Folklore Centre culture of the Yemenite Jewish community (in both Yemen and Israel). ■ *11/4 Kikar Ha'Atzma'ut, T8331325. Sunday-Thursday 0830-1600.*

Mediterranean Coastal Strip

Netanya

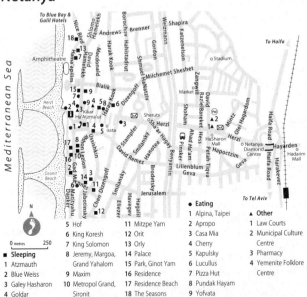

■ Sleeping		
1 Atzmauth	5 Hof	11 Mitzpe Yam
2 Blue Weiss	6 King Koresh	12 Orit
3 Galey Hasharon	7 King Solomon	13 Orly
4 Goldar	8 Jeremy, Margoa, Grand Yahalom	14 Palace
	9 Maxim	15 Park, Ginot Yam
	10 Metropol Grand, Sironit	16 Residence
		17 Residence Beach
		18 The Seasons

● Eating	▲ Other
1 Alpina, Taipei	1 Law Courts
2 Apropo	2 Municipal Culture Centre
3 Casa Mia	3 Pharmacy
4 Cherry	4 Yemenite Folklore Centre
5 Kapulsky	
6 Lucullus	
7 Pizza Hut	
8 Pundak Hayam	
9 Yofvata	

Excursions from Netanya

There are a number of attractions in the Sharon Plain around Netanya, although some are not readily accessible by public transport.

The Poleg Nature Reserve stands on land reclaimed from the swamps by the early Zionist pioneer settlers. There are any number of pleasant picnic sites on the banks of the Poleg River. Many visitors combine a visit here (eight kilometres south of Netanya) with a trip to the superb **beach** at Kibbutz Ga'ash, a couple of kilometres further south. In addition to the attraction of being quiet and uncrowded, the beach is backed by spectacular cliffs rising to over 60 metres. ■ *T9524411. For details of how to get there, see 'Netanya, Transport' on page 530.*

Poleg Nature Reserve and Kibbutz Ga'ash

There are a couple of places of interest in the **Tel Mond** area, to the southeast of Netanya. The **Kfar Hess Parrot Farm** offers guided tours of its breeding and petting farm, and its collection of rare parrots. **Moshav Mishmeret** offers guided tours of its bee-hives and honey production farm. ■ *Call ahead for both sites: Kfarr Hess T7961773; Moshav Mishmeret T7961260.*

Tel Mond

At the moshav of Aviha'li, three kilometres to the north of Netanya, a small museum records the role of the Jewish Legion within the British Army, in particular during the First World War. ■ *Beit Hagdudim, Moshav Aviha'li, T8822212. Sunday-Thursday 0800-1400. For buses, see 'Netanya, Transport' on page 530.*

Jewish Legion Museum

Just north of Aviha'li is the Bitan Aharon Nature Reserve, a small reserve featuring a number of Roman and Byzantine caverns. At the centre, on top of a low hill, is a 19th-century stonehouse that now houses a small museum describing the lifestyle of the pioneering Zionist settlers. The complex also features an art workshop, a children's activity centre and a restaurant. Visitors should call ahead for a guided tour. ■ *T8663777. The reserve is 100 metres north of the Havatselet Hasharon intersection, five kilometres north of Netanya.*

Bitan Aharon Nature Reserve

At the moshav of Kfar Vitkin, six kilometres north of Netanya, is the beautifully situated *IYHA Emek Hefer Youth Hostel* (see 'Sleeping' below). There is a supermarket, plus the popular *Kfar Vitkin Pancake House* (see 'Eating' on page 529). The attraction of staying at Kfar Vitkin, beside the tranquil location, is the beautiful sandy **beach** nearby. ■ *The Youth Hostel can be reached by Bus 029 from* **Netanya**, *or directly from* **Tel Aviv** *(702, 852, 901) and* **Haifa** *(901, 921).*

Kfar Vitkin and Nahal Alexander National Park

Just to the north of Kfar Vitkin, on the road to Mikhmoret, is the attractive **Nahal Alexander National Park**, renowned locally for its turtle population.

Essentials

There's no lack of hotels in Netanya, though most fall into the mid-price range. Price categories below are for the 'regular' season; note that during the 'high' season and Jewish holidays rates can double.

Sleeping
■ *on map;*
Price codes:
see inside front cover

L2 *The Seasons*, 1 Nice Blvd, T8601555, F8623022. Very ugly exterior belies the rather luxurious interior, features 'oversized' studios and suites, full leisure, business and dining facilities, though much better value out of season.

Mediterranean Coastal Strip

L3 *Blue Weiss*, 22 Gad Machnes, T8603939, F8603940. Part of *Zyvotel* chain, this new-ish apartment hotel has a real feeling of opulence with panoramic views, a/c, cable TV, and a luxurious spa and health centre in the basement. Minimum stay 1 week, pretty good value. Recommended. **L3** *Mercure Blue Bay*, 37 Hamelachim, T8603603, F8337475. Quiet location on semi-private beach several kilometres to north of town, good range of leisure facilities, rooms a reasonable size, better deal out of season.

A *Galil*, 26 Nice Blvd, T/F8624455. Sea-facing rooms (most with balconies) can accommodate up to 5, a/c, cable TV, pool, sauna and fitness room, restaurant, night-club, part of *Zyvotel* chain. **A** *Goldar*, 1 Ussishkin, T8338188, F8620680. Now part of *Zyvotel* chain, has recently had a long overdue refurbishment. 145 a/c rooms, cable TV, small balconies, central location, pool, bar, restaurant. **A** *King Solomon*, 18 Hamapilim, T8338444, F8611397. Friendly hotel with high percentage of returning guests, though a little expensive for what it is. Sea-facing balconies, a/c, TV, pool, fitness centre, children's activity room, restaurant.

B *Metropol Grand*, 17 Gad Machnes, T8624777, F8611556. Box-like rooms with tiny balconies, a/c, TV, all very old fashioned, pool, bar, restaurant. Very hard to justify these prices. **B** *Park*, 7 David HaMelekh, T8623344, F8624029. All 90 rooms have private balcony, a/c, TV, phone, though whole set-up is showing signs of age (though price is reasonable). Panoramic restaurant, bar, swimming pool, sauna, fitness room, good beach access. **B** *Residence Beach*, 16 Gad Machnes, T8623777, F8623711. Part of *Zyvotel* chain, excellent location, choice of studios or suites, all with kitchenette, a/c, cable TV, plus 'hydroelectro physiotherapy' spa complex. Good value out of season, but price doubles during the high season.

C *Ginot Yam*, 9 David HaMelekh, T8341007, F8615722. Busy hotel recently renovated, though rooms a little box-like, restaurant, bar, terrace. **C** *Grand Yahalom*, 15 Gad Machnes, T8624888, F8624890. Simple but light rooms, a/c, TV, reasonable value with discounts for longer stays. **C** *Jeremy*, 11 Gad Machnes, T8622651, F8626450. 48 old-fashioned rooms, a/c, no balconies, terrace bar, restaurant. **C** *King Koresh*, 6 Harav Hook, T8613555, F8613444. Comfortable a/c rooms but rather old-fashioned, though a little expensive considering the lack of sea views. **C** *Margoa*, 9 Gad Machnes, T8624434, F8623430. Friendly family-run place, small shared balconies (though sea-view obscured), a/c, TV, pub, restaurant. **C** *Maxim*, 8 David HaMelekh, T8621062, F8620190. Rooms not huge but nicely furnished, some with sea-view balconies, all with a/c, TV, suite rooms are good value out of season. One of the better choices in this category. **C** *Mizpe Yam*, 1 Jabotinsky/4 Carlebach, T/F8623730. 35-room friendly and quiet family-run hotel, a/c, TV, restaurant, pleasant roof-top terrace, not a bad deal. **C** *Orly*, 20 Hamapilim, T8333091, F8625453. Rooms rather small and balconies tiny, but hotel is well located and reasonably priced. One of the better deals in this category. **C** *Palace*, 33 Gad Machnes, T8620222, F8620224. Recently refurbished, motel-like rooms, a/c, TV, restaurant, conference hall. **C** *Residence*, 18 Gad Machnes, T8623777, F8623711. Part of *Zyvotel* chain, this 96-room hotel has a good location, and though nothing special it is pretty good value by Netanya standards. Most rooms have balconies, all with a/c, cable TV, bar, restaurant. Recommended. **C** *Sironit*, 19 Gad Machnes, T8840688, F8623139. Recently taken over by *Zyvotel* chain: let's hope they spend some money on it soon (even its sign is falling down). Currently poor value, can use facilities at *Galil Hotel*.

D *Galey Hasharon*, 42 Ussishkin, T8825125, T8338128. Very friendly family-run place, breakfast included, cheapest deal in the mid-price categories. **D** *Hof*, 9 Kikar Ha'Atzma'ut, T8624422. Rather grim-looking place with not-very-private balconies overlooking square. **D** *Orit*, 21 Chen, T8616818. Small, simple, Swedish-run hotel, very clean, rooms with attached bath, communal lounge and fridge, quiet neighbourhood, reservations recommended. Not a bad deal. **D-E** *IYHA Emek Hefer Youth Hostel*, T/F09-8666032. There are dorms (6-8 beds), doubles and family rooms, including some cottages and bungalows (**D**), all with a/c and private bath.

F *Atzmauth Hostel*, 2 Ussishkin, T8621315, F8822562. Excellent value hostel, all dorms (5-6 beds) a/c with attached bath, fridge, very clean. For $30 dorms can be hired as a private room. Very friendly owner. Highly recommended.

Apartment rental and B&Bs An option for longer-stay visitors is to rent an apartment or private rooms in Netanya. If considering this option, it is best to do so either through a recognized agent (who will charge a fixed fee at 10% of the rental), or through the Tourist Information Office (see page 531 for details). A 1-bedroom flat (can sleep 4) generally costs around $700-$800 per month, whilst a 2-bedroom flat (sleeps 6) costs $850+ per month. Larger flats are also available, and deals are negotiable for longer lets. With costs shared, these can work out at fairly good value. Many of these apartments are located on the plush Nice Blvd. Rooms in private houses are best organized through the Tourist Information Office.

Several kibbutzim around Netanya offer 'countryside' accommodation (**C**) in their *Guesthouses*, including Kibbutz Bachan, T8763351, F8763350; Kibbutz Ga'ash, T9521253; Kibbutz Yad Chana, T8765433.

Most of Netanya's restaurants are crowded around Kikar Ha'Atzma'ut and the **Eating** pedestrianized section of Herzl. Touts outside battle for custom, and discounts and deals can be struck. The best guide is often the number of diners sat there eating, although the food is often fairly bland. Most offer pizza, pasta dishes, schnitzel, burgers, etc, with chips and salad for around 25-45 NIS. Most of the cheaper falafel and shwarma places are further inland along Herzl and Sha'ar Hagay towards the Central Bus Station. A number of places that have been recommended follow. *Alexander*, 1 David HaMelekh, T8841539. Imaginative mixed menu and splendid views. *Alpina*, Gad Machness. Swiss-French menu in central location, main courses 40-70 NIS. *Apropo*, Gan HaMelekh, near Kikar Ha'Atzma'ut, T8624482. Excellent location, coffee shop plus good Thai dishes. *Ha-Nassi President*, 5 Herzl, T8617147. Traditional Jewish Shabbat meals (must be ordered and paid for in advance), main dishes 30-50 NIS. *Kapulsky*, 12 Kikar Ha'Atzma'ut, T8628883. Popular coffee shop chain with light dairy meals and diet-busting cakes. *Kfar Vitkin Pancake House*, Kfar Vitkin (see page 527), a roadside restaurant serving pancakes (18-32 NIS), beer and Mexican food. *Lucullus*, junction of Gad machnes/Jabotinsky, T8619502. Very nice Italian-French restaurant specializing in seafood, good value business lunch 65 NIS. Recommended. *Pundak Hayam*, 1 Harav Kook, T8615780. No-nonsense Middle Eastern dishes for under $10. *Yotvata*, Kikar Ha'Atzma'ut, T8627576. Very busy branch of kibbutz dairy vegetarian chain.

Bars There are a number of bars along Herzl and around Kikar Ha'Atzma'ut; the language their signs are written in is a clue to the clientele they are aiming at. It is also possible to arrange tasting trips to the *Tempo Brewery*, HaMalekha, Poleg Industrial Estate, call ahead (T8630630), Bus 48 or 601 from Central Bus Station. **Nightclubs** *No1*, 4 Kikar Ha'Atzma'ut; *Plaisance*, 7 Kikar Ha'Atzma'ut; *The Place*, 11 Kikar Ha'Atzma'ut; *The Dream* 13 Echad Ha'am; *Hotel Galil Club*, 37 Nice Blvd; *Blue Bay Club*, 37 Hamelachim. **Bars & nightclubs**

Art galleries *Abecassis Gallery*, 4 Raziel, T8623528; *Gallery on the Cliff*, Shaked Promenade, Hama'apilim, T8335423; *Gosher Gallery*, T8331384; *Kad Café*, T7967535; *Municipal Gallery*, 4 Raziel, T8842506. **Cinemas** *GG Gil*, Hadarim Mall, T8628452; **Entertainment**

Mediterranean Coastal Strip

Rav Chen, 58 Herzl, HaSharon Mall, T8618570/8841133. **Concerts** These often take place in the modern **amphitheatre** in Gan Hamelekh (park), on the cliff-side. Check the Tourist Information Office for upcoming events. For details of the **Herzliya Chamber Orchestra's** programme, T9500761.

Special events Netanya prides itself on the range of public activities and special events that is organized in the town. Most of these activities are listed in the monthly "Kan Netanya", a kind of "What's on in Netanya", available from the Tourist Information Office. Regular special events include: '**Oriental Evening**', every Sunday 1900, telephone Beit Harishonim Rachel T8663176 for details; '**Cabaret Show and Dance Music**', every Friday, *Galil Hotel* , T8624455; '**Israeli Songs & Songs of the 60s**', every Friday, lobby of *Park Hotel*, T8623344; **Noon-time concert**, every Monday 1200-1300, Kikar Ha'Atzma'ut; **Folk dancing**, every Saturday 2000, Kikar Ha'Atzma'ut; **Bingo**, every Sunday 2000, at American and Canadian Association (see Directory on page 531); **Bridge Club**, every Monday and Thursday 2000, at Women's League House, 5 MacDonald; **Chess Club**, every Monday 1900-2200, at Municipal Library (see Directory on page 531).

Shopping Unless you are in the market for diamonds (see page 526), Netanya is not particularly renowned as a shopping centre. The main shopping districts are on Herzl, Benjamin and Raziel. There is a large open market on Zangwill, near to one of the main diamond workshop areas.

Sports **Bowling (Crown Green)** *Wingate Institute*, T8650193. **Bowling (Ten-pin)** *Bowling Netanya*, T8625514. Open 1000-0200; *National Bowling*, T8852853. **Fishing** *Burgata Fishing Park*, T8688075. **Golf** See *Dan Hotel* at Caesarea (page 543), T06-6269122/6361172. **Gym and Fitness Centres** *Elitzur Sports Centre*, Radak, T8652931. Sunday-Thursday 0600-2200, Friday 0600-1600 (Bus 8 from Central Bus Station). Also facilities at *Blue Bay Hotel* and *King Solomon Hotel* (see 'Sleeping', page 527.) **Hiking** *Society for the Protection of Nature in Israel (SPNI)*, 59 Smilansky, T8827884. **Horse riding** *Cactus Ranch*, T8651239. Daily 0800-sunset, pub/restaurant. *The Ranch*, 2 km north of *Blue Bay Hotel*, T8663525; lessons, plus moonlight riding, about 50 NIS per hr, (Bus 17 or 29 from Central Bus Station). **Karting** 1 Harakevet, T8611874. Sunday-Thursday 1100-2400, weekends 1000-2400. **Paragliding and Flying** *Ariba*, T8840010. Paragliding flights, instruction, equipment hire. *Omni Horizon*, T8686188. 'Ultra-lite' flights. **Petanque** 4 Ichilov, T8341814. Daily. **Swimming** *Elitzur Sports Centre*, Radak, T8652931. May-September, Sunday-Thursday 0600-1800, heated pool. Also available at some of the hotels. **Tennis** *Maccabi Tennis Centre*, Zangwill, T8824054; *Elitzur Sports Centre*, Radak, T8652931 (also **squash**); also at *Blue Bay Hotel* (see 'Sleeping', page 527). **Volleyball/Basketball** Courts are available (free) on Sironit, Herzl and Green beaches.

Transport **Local Car hire** *Avis*, 1 Ussishkin, T8331619; *Budget*, 2 Gad Machnes, T8620454; *Eldan*, 12 Ha'Atzma'ut, T8616982; *Hertz*, 8 Ha'Atzma'ut, T8828890; *Reliable*, 2 Gad Machnes, T8620567; *Suntours*, 1 Ussishkin, T8629611; *Tamir*, 8 Ha'Atzma'ut, T8331831; *Traffic*, 1 Ussishkin, T8330618. **Taxis** *Hashahar*, 1 Hameyasdim, T8614444; *HaSharon*, 15 Smilansky, T8822323; *Hen*, Sha'ar Hagaay, T8333333; *Netanya*, 8 Raziel, T8344443.

Long distance Buses **Central Bus Station**, 3 Benyamin, T8606202. **Aviha'il** (for Jewish Legion Museum), 1a, 0645, 0715, 0840, 1040, 1200, 1300, 1400, 1700, 1940, 2030; **Be'er Sheva**, 995, 4 per day, 2½ hrs; **Eilat**, 991, 1 daily plus extra services in summer, 5½ hrs; **Hadera** (for **Caesarea**), 705/706, 1-2 per hr, 11 NIS, 30 mins; **Haifa**, 946/947/992/995, every 30 mins, 18 NIS, 1 ½ hrs; **Jerusalem** (via **Ben-Gurion**

Airport), 428/947, every 30 mins, 22 NIS, 1 ¾ hrs; **Kfar Vitkin** and **Mikhmoret** (for Nahal Alexander NP), 029, about 1 every 2 hrs; **Poleg Nature Reserve** (continuing to **Kibbutz Ga'ash**), 601, every 30 mins; **Tel Aviv**, 650 direct, 600/602/605 via Herzliya, every 10 mins, 15 NIS, 1 hr (with traffic). **Sherut/service taxi** Sheruts to **Tel Aviv** leave from the junction of Herzl/HaNatziv. **Train** Train station, T8823470. There are 2-4 trains hourly to **Tel Aviv**, at least 1 per hour to **Haifa** with some services continuing to **Akko** and **Nahariya**.

Banks There are a number of banks with ATM machines on Kikar Ha'Atzma'ut (check rates and commission charges if changing cash/TCs). **Money changers**: *Changespot*, junction of Kikar Ha'Atzma'ut and Dizengoff (daily 0900-1900, commission-free at good rates), plus several others around Kikar Ha'Atzma'ut. **Communications Phone code**: T09. **Post offices**: Central Post Office, 57 Herzl, T8621577 (Sun, Mon, Tue, Thu 0800-1230 1530-1800, Wed 0800-1330, Fri 0800-1200); branch post office at 2 Herzl, T8627797. **Telephones**: *Solan Communications*, 8 Kikar Ha'Atzma'ut, T8622131, daily 0800-2300, Europe/North America 2 NIS per min, cellular phone rental. **Cultural centres** *American and Canadian Association*, 28 Shmuel HaNaziv, T8330950; *British Olim Society*, 7 HaMatmid; *Israel Pearl Tribes (Pninat Shivtei Israel)*, 11/4 Kikar Ha'Atzma'ut, T8331325. Yemenite folklore centre, Sun-Thu 0900-1100, 5 NIS; *Municipal Cultural Centre*, 4 Raziel, T8603392; *WIZO*, Wizo House, 13 MacDonald, T8823192. **Hospitals and medical services** Chemists: *Centerpharm*, 1 David HaMelekh, T8831533; *Hadassa*, 24 Herzl, T8822243; *Merkaz*, 36 Herzl, T8822739; *Trufa*, Kikar Ha'Atzma'ut, T8828656, (Sun-Thu 0800-1300 1600-1900, Tues 0800-1300, Fri 0800-1345), plus numerous others around town. **Hospitals**: *Laniado*, (to north of city centre), T8604666. **Libraries** *Municipal Library*, 60 Benyamin, T8860250. **Places of worship** Synagogues: *Beit Israel*, 11 Kikar Ha'Atzma'ut, T8340557; *Central Synagogue*, 'Shone Halachot', Herzl; *Zehor Yosef*, 18 Lilinbloom, T8341468. **Tour companies and travel agents** *issta*, 2 Herzl, just south of Kikar Ha'Atzma'ut, T8320002, (Sun-Thu 0900-1800, Fri 0830-1300); *Peltours*, Dizengoff. **Tourist offices** *Tourist Information Office*, Kikar Ha'Atzma'ut, T8827286. Open Sun-Thu 0800-1600, Fri 0900-1200, can help with booking long and short-term apartment lets, plus plenty of brochures detailing events in and around Netanya. They also have a web-site: www.insite.co.il/netanya/netanya/htm **Useful addresses and phone numbers** **Police**: T100, or T8604444. **Ambulance**: Magen David Adom T101, or T8623333. **Fire**: T102, or T8622222.

Directory

Hadera

Hadera is a pleasant small town famed for the fragrant orange blossom perfume that is said to saturate the air every spring. Hadera has an interesting historical museum, telling the story of the early Zionist pioneers' struggle to turn malaria-infested swamps into productive agricultural land. It is also an important transport junction for visitors to Caesarea.

Phone code: 06
Colour map 1, grid C2

Hadera's massive factory chimneys are a prominent landmark on the main Tel Aviv to Haifa road (Route 2). The bus station (see map) has regular connections to Tel Aviv and Haifa, as well as being the main public transport junction for Caesarea (see 'Transport' on page 532). The train station is located about 2km west of the town centre (15 minutes walk or Bus 015), and has regular connections south to Tel Aviv and north to Haifa.

Ins and outs

Hadera is compact enough to get around on foot, though Buses 1/3/7/75 run from the bus station to the town centre.

Hadera

To Haifa
Shimoni
Frank
Burger
King
Ahad Ha'am
To Tel Aviv
N
Rambam
Six Day War St
Hanasi
Herbert Samuel
Hillel
Yaffe
Herzl
Rothschild
Zabutinsky
Bialik
Hagibborim
Soldiers' Memorial
Founders Monument
K'han Historical Museum
0 km   1

The modern history of the town dates to the end of the 19th century. In 1891, a delegation representing 178 Zionist families in Russia arrived in Palestine seeking land. The delegation eventually purchased a large

History

Mediterranean Coastal Strip

estate of some 30,000 dunams (3,000 hectares) near Caesarea, giving it the name of the old Arab village of Hudaira ('green'), and quickly encouraged their brethren to sell their property in Russia and begin a new life here. The families were heartened by descriptions of abundant land, a plentiful water supply, and by the possibility of raising fish in the "lakes".

It soon transpired that the "vast, open stretch of land flooded with water and rich in greenery" was little more than a swamp; a perfect breeding ground for malarial mosquitoes. As yet, the world had not identified the cause of malaria, and within the first 20 years of settling at Hadera 210 out of the 540 residents died. It soon became apparent that the "lakes" around Hadera, rather than supporting the community were harbouring disease and death, and thus they had to be drained. This was to be no small task since the swamps comprised almost 15 percent of the land area (although the role of Palestinian and Egyptian paid labourers in this endeavour is understated in the 'official' history presented at the town's museum).

As the swamps were slowly drained and brought under control, and the community learned how to farm the land, there were further influxes of settlers. These included not only idealistic Zionists from Poland and Russia, but also 40 families from Yemen. Today, Hadera retains its agricultural base, though the linking of the town to the country's rail network has brought additional industrial employment.

K'han Historical Museum The town's early history is well presented in the K'han Historical Museum; certainly worth a visit, particularly if you have time on your hands whilst awaiting a transport connection to Caesarea. ■ *74 Hagiborim, T06- 3223300. Sunday-Thursday 0800-1300, plus Sunday and Tuesday 1600-1800. Free, guided tours by prior appointment.*

Kibbutz Ein Shemer Just to the northeast of Hadera along Route 65, the kibbutz here has a reconstruction of an early pioneers' settlements. ■ *T06-8374327. Sunday- Thursday 0800-1600, Friday 0800-1300.*

Transport The bus station is on Ahad Ha'am to the west of the town centre. It has an information office, cleanish toilets (1 NIS), cafés, and an inspector who's a dead ringer for Blakey! **Tel Aviv**, 921, every 15 mins until 2240 (restricted services on Friday/Saturday), 19 NIS, 1 hr 20 mins. **Haifa**, 921, every 15 mins until 2130 (restricted services on Friday/Saturday), 16 NIS, 1 hr. For **Caesarea** take Bus 76, Sunday-Thursday 0600 0635 0900 1100 1345 1445 1740 1930, Friday 0600 0635 0840 1100 1240 1500, Saturday 2030, 10 NIS, 45 mins (this bus passes Hadera hospital, Dan Caesarea Hotel, then goes right 'round the houses' to Caesarea and Kibbutz Sdot Yam). Bus 76 returns from Caesarea to **Hadera** Sunday-Thursday 0635 0730 0940 1140 1435 1525 1830 2010, Friday 0635 0730 0930 1135 1310 1535, Saturday 2116.

K'han Historical Museum

Not to scale

1 Office
2 Museum Archives
3 Lecture Hall
4 Archaeological site
5 "The Beginning" wing
6 Diorama Room
7 Family Room of the 1930s
8 Hadera Photos
9 Workshop (Former Stable)
10 Central Synagogue of Hadera
11 Oil Press
12 Gate
13 Section of early agricultural implements
14 Remains of K'han Warehouse
15 Village Bell
16 Remains of Oil Press (2nd cent CE)

Caesarea

Caesarea is one of Israel's most important historical sites and certainly the pre-
mier archaeological attraction on the Mediterranean coast. Stretching for 3.5
kilometres along the sea-shore, and covering some 94 hectares, Caesarea is a large
site comprising numerous restored and semi-restored structures from the Helle-
nistic, Herodian, Roman, Byzantine, Arab and Crusader periods. Most of the
*highlights are contained within the **Caesarea National Park**, and are well pre-*
sented for public viewing. A visit to Caesarea is highly recommended.

Phone code: 06
Colour map 1, grid C2

Ins and outs

There are two options for getting to Caesarea by public transport. One option is to take any of the Haifa to Tel Aviv buses that use the **old Haifa to Hadera to Tel Aviv road** (Route 4), get off at the junction for Caesarea (or Akiva Junction), and walk the 4km to the site. (**NB** When you get on the bus, make sure that it uses the **old** road, and not the quicker Route 2 highway). A far better way to reach Caesarea is to take a bus direct to the bus station in **Hadera**, and from there take Bus 076 directly to the site (45 mins, 10 NIS). Although there are only 8 buses to Caesarea per day, you can either plan your journey to Hadera so that you connect with Bus 076, or kill time in Hadera by visiting the museum. To return from Caesarea, take Bus 076 from the stops outside either of the main entrances. For full timetable, see 'Transport', above.

Getting there

The key attractions are located within the **Caesarea National Park**. Ticket offices (**1**) are located next to the Roman theatre, south of the Crusader city wall and at the east gate of the fortified medieval city. All other sites are free. **NB** Retain your ticket since this allows access to all sites. There is no one fixed route for seeing the attractions, though most visitors tend to start at the Roman theatre and work their way from south to north. A tour of the major attractions takes 1-2 hrs, a longer tour that takes in more distant sites (eg the high-level aqueduct) can take 2-3 hrs, whilst the grand tour, including all the outlying places of interest, can take 4-6 hrs.

Getting around

History

Between 22 and 9 BCE, **Herod the Great** built a magnificent new city on the site of the old Phoenician port town of Straton's Tower, naming it after his patron Caesar Augustus: Caesarea. The new harbour that was constructed, **Sebastos**, remains one of the greatest engineering feats of the era, although the question is often asked why Herod didn't simply choose the easier option of refurbishing the more natural port at Jaffa (Joppa). In fact, Herod shrewdly judged that the Jewish population in Jaffa were more nationalistic in their political outlook, whereas at Straton's Tower he could virtually start from scratch in building a truly Herodian city.

Herodian period

Herod's attempt to win over the hearts and minds of his subjects manifested itself in the grandiose scale of the building projects undertaken, and Josephus provides a graphic description of this "exceptional" new city (*The Jewish War, I, 407-21*). It is interesting to note that, although Jews did settle in Caesarea, the city was distinctly pagan, greatly resembling in its municipal functioning the earlier Greek city-states of the Hellenistic period.

Following the annexation of Judaea in 6 CE by the Romans, Caesarea became the seat of the provincial governor and the *de facto* capital of Judaea (later called *Palaestina*). One of the more famous Roman prefects of Judaea,

Roman rule

Mediterranean Coastal Strip

Pontius Pilate (26-36 CE), dedicated a temple to the emperor Tiberius during his residence in Caesarea.

It appears that discrimination against the Jewish population of Caesarea in favour of the Greco-Syrian citizens was a continual source of tension between the two communities. Interestingly, both communities claimed the city as their own, the Jews "on the ground that it had been built by a Jew, King Herod" and the Greco-Syrians on the assumption that, although the founder was a Jew, "Herod would not have set up statues and temples if he had meant it for the Jews" (*The Jewish War, II, 264*). When the First Jewish Revolt erupted in 66 CE, "the people of Caesarea had massacred the Jewish colony, in less than an hour slaughtering more than 20,000 and emptying Caesarea of the last Jew"(*The Jewish War, II, 467*). The destruction of the temple in Jerusalem (70 CE) was celebrated by "special games" in the Caesarea amphitheatre in which, according to Josephus, over 2,500 Jews "perished in combats with wild beasts or in fighting each other or by being burnt alive" (*The Jewish War, VII, 44*).

During the next couple of centuries of Roman rule, increased trade with the rest of the Roman empire led to a thriving economy in Caesarea, though Jewish leaders continued to shun the city. Rabbis referred to Caesarea as 'daughter of Edom' (ie 'daughter of Rome'), leading to a saying that "If you hear that Caesarea thrives and Jerusalem suffers, then believe it. If you hear that Jerusalem thrives whilst Caesarea suffers, believe it. But if you hear that both Jerusalem and Caesarea are thriving, don't believe it."

Byzantine period

There is an early Christian association with Caesarea, with "a certain man in Caesarea called Cornelius, a centurion" (*Acts 10;1*) perhaps being the first gentile that **Peter** converted to Christianity. **Paul** was imprisoned in Caesarea for two years, before being sent to Rome (*Acts 23-27*). Like the Jewish population of Caesarea, most of the Christian community is presumed to have been massacred by the city's pagan majority on the eve of the First Jewish Revolt (66 CE).

By the end of the second century CE, however, Christians and Jews had begun to return in number to Caesarea, and by 250 CE celebrated rabbinical academies and Christian theological and scholarly centres had been established here. Christian scholarship was centred around the great theologian **Origen**, who assembled a magnificent library and compiled the hexapla text of the Bible. His manuscript collection was added to by Pamphilius, who's own pupil **Eusebius**, (the 'first biblical geographer'), compiled the *Onomasticon*. This classic text has enabled many biblical sites in the Holy Land to be located and identified.

Renovation of the harbour at the beginning of the sixth century CE looked set to add to Caesarea's prosperity. However, the Samaritan revolt of 529-530 CE (and subsequent death, enslavement or banishment of

Roman & Byzantine street system, Caesarea

Medieval/Crusader City Walls

Harbour

Street I

Street II

Street III

Byzantine Street- 'Statues' Square'

Street I

Street 2

Street 3

Street 4

Street 5

N

0 metres   200

Promontory 'Palace'

Byzantine Fortified Walls

Roman Theatre

After Holum & Raban

the Samaritan community) destroyed the agricultural base upon which Caesarea was dependent.

Having passed through the hands of the Persians (614 CE) and the Romans again (628 CE), Caesarea fell to the Arabs in 641 or 642. Many commentators seem keen to denigrate the Arabs, suggesting that they "allowed the port to silt up", thus bringing about Caesarea's decline. Though the population declined and older parts of the city began to collapse, the Arab geographer el-Muqaddasi, visiting in the 10th century, describes a flourishing town at the heart of a rich agricultural region.

Early Arab period

With the return of seafarers, Caesarea's port was rebuilt once more. **Baldwin I** captured the town in 1101 after a brief siege and formed a Crusader principality. A Christian church replaced the Arab mosque on Herod's pagan temple platform. Amongst the booty that Baldwin captured was a hexagonal green glass, believed to be the Holy Grail used by Jesus at the Last Supper. The object is now preserved in the church of San Lorenzo in Genoa (where it has been found to be a glass dish from the Roman period).

Arrival of the Crusaders

Though Caesarea was captured by **Salah al-Din** in 1187 and much of it razed, it was recaptured by **Richard Coeur de Lion** in 1191. Most of the Crusader ruins that you see today date from the reign of the French king **Louis IX**, who, between 1251 and 1252, is said to have "laboured on the fortifications with his own hands, as an act of penance".

The Mamluk sultan **Baibars** captured the city in 1265, though the Crusaders apparently managed to slip away by sea at night to Acre (Akko) whilst surrender negotiations were underway. To prevent reoccupation the Mamluks dismantled many of the fortifications and, perhaps following the precedent set by Louis IX, Baibars is said to have "pick in hand, assisted at its demolition". In 1291 his successors levelled the site.

Sights

Many parts of the complex within the Caesarea National Park remain closed whilst further excavation and restoration takes places (notably the promontory 'palace'), though much more of the Roman/Byzantine street system (between the Roman theatre and the medieval city) is now revealing its true glory. ■ *T06-6361358/6361010, F6262056. Saturday-Thursday 0800-1700, Friday 0800-1600. 20 NIS. Restaurants, clean toilets, souvenir shops.*

The Roman theatre is probably Caesarea's best-known attraction. Herod built the original theatre and can be said to have introduced this form of entertainment into the region. The theatre that you see today was modified and added to throughout the centuries. At its peak it could seat up to 4,000 spectators, with a special box in the central *cuneus* (wedge-shaped block of seating) for the provincial governor.

Roman theatre (2)

Remains from Herod's theatre include the *cavea* (spectators' section) and stairways, *euripus* (channel for removing water from the orchestra), and the concentric gangways. The floor of the orchestra was decorated with painted plaster, depicting floral, fish-scale and geometric patterns. Behind the stage stood the *scaenae frons*, a wall three storeys high that provided the stage backdrop. Built in Hellenistic style, it had a central square *exedra* (recess) flanked by smaller concave niches. The front of the stage facing the audience (*pulpitum*) was painted to match the plasterwork in the niches. Some time in the second century CE the *exedra* in the *scaenae frons* was made semi-circular,

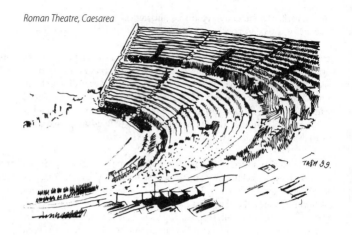

Roman Theatre, Caesarea

Caesarea

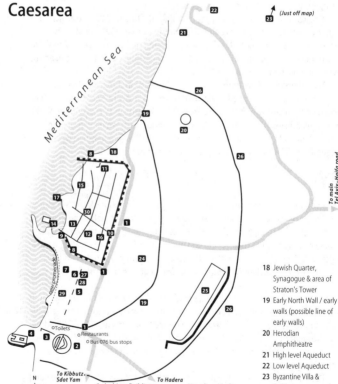

Mediterranean Sea

To main Tel Aviv–Haifa road

(Just off map)

To Kibbutz Sdot Yam

To Hadera

N

0 metres 200

1 Ticket Offices
2 Roman Theatre
3 Byzantine Fortified Walls
4 Promontory 'Palace'
5 Byzantine Street
6 Archives Buildings
7 Mithraeum
8 Medieval/Crusader City Walls
9 South Gate
10 East Gate
11 North Gate
12 Temple Podium (Roman Temple, Crusader Church,

Herodium Vaults
13 Site of former inner basin of harbour
14 Harbour Fortress
15 Western part of Medieval City
16 Crusader Streets and House
17 Sebastos (Herodian Harbour)

18 Jewish Quarter, Synagogue & area of Straton's Tower
19 Early North Wall / early walls (possible line of early walls)
20 Herodian Amphitheatre
21 High level Aqueduct
22 Low level Aqueduct
23 Byzantine Villa & Bathhouse
24 'Statues Square'
25 Hippodrome (Circus)
26 Possible line of Byzantine city walls
27 Mosaic floor
28 Byzantine bathhouse complex
29 Herodian amphitheatre
30 Nymphaeum

Mediterranean Coastal Strip

and the *pulpitum* was rebuilt. Changes were also made to the orchestra and *cavea*, with a greater use of marble and stone rather than the Herodian conglomerate.

In the third century CE a semi-circular platform was added behind the stage, and a century later the orchestra area was converted into a large basin that could be flooded (*columbetra*), suitable for nautical games (*tetimimi*) and mock naval battles.

Numerous fragments of statues, reliefs and inscriptions were found in the theatre area, including a statue of Diana of Ephesus. A stone being used as a step in the theatre from the third to fourth centuries was found to bear an inscription mentioning Pontius Pilate as prefect of Judea, and the temple in Caesarea that he dedicated to the emperor Tiberius. A replica of the stone, plus a selection of the statues, reliefs and inscriptions found nearby, greet the visitor between the National Park ticket office and the theatre.

In the Byzantine period (324-638 CE) the theatre is thought to have become a victim of the puritanical church elders who disapproved of lascivious and bloody entertainment, and it fell out of use. It subsequently became part of the **Byzantine fortress**, or *kastron*, that is referred to in some texts from the period. Remains of the Byzantine fortifications (**3**) can be seen continuing west from the theatre.

Early visitors to Caesarea mention a set of ruins on the promontory just to the west of the Roman theatre. Though wave action has severely eroded the rock upon which these ruins stand, there is just enough remaining to discern that a large complex, perhaps a spacious villa, once stood on this promontory. Some archaeologists surmise that this could be Herod's palace, as mentioned by Josephus. **Promontory 'palace' (4)**

Of further confusion is the large (35 metres by 18 metres) pool at the west end of the promontory. The pool is connected to the sea by a series of open channels and pools, leading some to believe that the complex was a *piscina*, serving as part of the city's fish market. However, it appears that these channels and connecting pools were apparently cut from the rock *after* the buildings around the pool were destroyed, and thus what was originally a decorative or swimming pool had a different function in later years.

The best-preserved part of the promontory complex, to the east of the pool furthest from the sea, contains a number of rooms with mosaic floors. Though some of the floors have been damaged in a conflagration that may have destroyed the entire complex, the mosaic carpet in the middle room is preserved in entirety. The mosaic, comprising geometric patterns in red, black, yellow and white, is almost identical to one found in the *triclinium* (dining room) at Herod's winter palace in Jericho.

NB The true function of this structure built on the promontory may be determined by further excavation, though unfortunately this means that the area is currently closed to visitors.

Excavations in this area continue (much currently closed to the public), though a number of places of interest have been identified. Numerous sections of the Byzantine system of streets (**5**) have been discovered in this area, with *kurkar* (fossilized dune sandstone) paving slabs laid above both ceramic water pipes and stone-built sewers. Though no sections of Herod's grid-plan city have been uncovered (as described by Josephus), its plan can almost certainly be deduced from the remains of the Roman and Byzantine streets that were laid out on the same grid. 'Street II' (see map page 534) was flanked by colonnades on either side, covering mosaic pavements. Since this work was a **Excavations between the Roman theatre and medieval city** sixth-century addition to the original street plan, the archaeologists who excavated this area suggest that such urban renewal indicates a period of prosperity in the city's history.

Just to the south of the medieval city walls lies the Byzantine commercial and administrative area. Among the structures excavated here is the **Archives Building (6)**. The building opens eastwards onto 'Street II', and consists of seven rooms positioned around a central court. Greek inscriptions on the mosaic floor include one that reads 'Christ help Ampelios, the keeper of the archives, and Musonius, the financial secretary, and the other archivists of the same depository'. With further references to *chartoularioi* (secretaries), *noumerarios* (accountants) and a *skrinion* (bureau), it is almost certain that this building was a government building, probably attached to the palace of the imperial governor of Palestine. The building was destroyed in the early Arab period (and the mosaic is now in the Sdot Yam Museum, see page 543). A building with a well-preserved **mosaic floor (27)** has recently been uncovered just to the east.

Along the sea-front, for a long time concealed by a sand dune, stands a complex of barrel-vaulted *horrea* (warehouses) dating to the Herodian period. Artefacts and containers used for shipping wine, oil and other commodities were found here, suggesting strong trade links with North Africa, Spain, Italy, Greece and Gaul. The northernmost *horreum* was converted into a **Mithraeum (7)** in the first century CE, and used as a sanctuary in the cult worship of the god Mithras. A hole was cut into the roof of the *horreum*, allowing a shaft of light to illuminate the altar near the eastern end. Frescoes depicted Mithraic scenes on the walls, whilst a marble medallion found in the vault shows Mithras slaying the sacred bull. Few Mithraeums were built in the Middle East, and this is the only one that has been found in Israel.

To the southeast of the Archives Building and the Mithraeum lie the remains of a **Byzantine bathhouse complex (28)**, whilst the 10,000-seater **Herodian amphitheatre (29)** has now been extensively excavated.

Medieval city walls and gates Of all the towns built at Caesarea the Crusader city is the smallest, covering less than nine hectares. The city was originally walled on all four sides but almost the entire seaward wall has been lost, though the defensive walls on all other sides remain impressive (**8**). The architectural features suggest that the majority of the medieval city walls were built by Louis IX.

Though the fortifications still look formidable, most of what you see today is just the *glacis*, the sloping base of the defensive wall. The *glacis* was previously surmounted by a 10-metre-high wall, parts of which remain only along the south wall. A seven-metre-wide *fosse* (ditch or trench) provided extra security.

The **south wall** is approximately 275 metres long, with four towers providing additional strength. Though the Crusader city walls are at their most complete here, with parts of the main defensive wall rising above the *glacis*, it seems that the **South Gate (9)** was never completely finished and only the outer gateway was constructed in full.

The **east wall** is 650 metres long and is fortified by nine towers that project seven to eight metres beyond the wall. The **East Gate (10)** was the main entrance to the city and was entered via a bridge over the *fosse*. The supporting pillars and arches are still in place. For added defensive purposes the doorway of the gatehouse looks north rather than east, and is further protected by loopholes and gaps through which burning oil could be poured. The hall of the gatehouse contains a well and a basin, a stone bench, and a doorway in the west wall leading to the town. All of these features were added by Louis IX when he modified the existing fortifications. 30 metres north of the East Gate is a secret passage leading from the town into the *fosse*.

Parts of the **Crusader city street plan** remain, particularly around the East Gate area, though much of the street paving is recycled material from the Roman era. A section of street near to the east wall has a cross vault roof, plus holes in the pillars for tying horses. A large **Crusader house (16)** is located nearby, though the foundations date to the Early Arab period (638-1099 CE). A large treasure of 10th-century gold and silver coins was found under the floor.

The north wall is approximately 275 metres long, and is protected by three towers. The square **North Gate (11)** stands in the centre of the north wall, and again follows the principal of indirect access with the actual doorway facing to the west. The four pillars that supported the cross vault ceiling are decorated with floral motifs. Another secret passage opening into the *glacis* is located near to the northeast tower.

When excavations within the medieval city walls begun in earnest in the 1960s, it was soon realized that the mound to the east of the harbour was not a natural hill, but a raised podium. Thus, it fitted in with Josephus' description of a temple mounted on a podium dominating the inner harbour. Further excavation has in fact revealed that this raised podium is not entirely artificial; Herod's engineers took advantage of the topography and extended the natural bedrock ridge with a series of barrel-vaulted chambers. The west face comprises twelve barrel vaults running east to west. At the centre of the west face, a monumental staircase led down from the podium to the harbour quay. The podium (105 metres north to south, 90 metres east to west) is now raised 15 metres above the surrounding area, though in Herod's day it may have been considerably higher. Few remains of the temple itself have been found, and those that could possibly have been part of the temple foundations are just as likely to pre-date Herod's building process to the time of Straton's Tower.

Temple podium (12)

In Byzantine times, a large **Octagonal Church** was built on the former temple podium, though only the foundations remain today. The inner octagon measured 22.1 metres in diameter and comprised a continuous row of columns (*stylobate*) supporting a wooden roof. The octagonal foundations of the outer wall measure 38.8 metres in diameter, and would have provided side chapels and rooms for clergy and pilgrims. A **Grand Mosque** stood on the temple podium following the Arab conquest of Caesarea, though there is little evidence of its presence.

The most visible remains on the podium today are of the unfinished 13th-century **Crusader church**. The initial plan involved building the west half of the nave and the north aisle above the podium's southern vaults. Strong buttresses were built to support the west side of the podium, and three apses of well-dressed sandstone were completed before two of the vaults collapsed. The builders seemed to have lost heart after this set-back, and the subsequent attempts to construct the church according to an alternative plan were not realized with any real finesse.

It was from the Harbour Fortress, located on the southern breakwater of Herod's harbour, that the Crusaders were alleged to have slipped away in the dead of night to Acre (Akko), from the besieging forces of sultan Baibars. The citadel's defences were strong, with a 20-metre channel separating it from the town and four strong towers protecting the land access. Only the two to the east are visible today, next to the row of souvenir shops. Baibars is said to have been incensed by the Crusaders' moonlight flit in 1265.

Harbour Fortress (14)

Mediterranean Coastal Strip

Sebastos (Herodian harbour) (17)

Prior to the advent of systematic marine archaeology, it was not unreasonable to assume that Josephus' triumphant adoration of Herod's harbour-building efforts is somewhat over-done (*Jewish War I, 408-415*). However, subsequent underwater exploration, coupled with the use of aerial photography, now suggests that Sebastos was indeed a miracle of marine engineering.

The Herodian harbour comprises three basins, one inside the other. The inner harbour (**13**) may well be part of the original Phoenician harbour of Straton's Tower. Archaeologists believe that they can identify a stretch of the original quay 30 metres by 5 metres, though only the foundations remain of the sea wall. The **middle basin** was part of a natural bay, protected to the north and south by rocky promontories. The **outer basin**, formed by building two long breakwaters thus enclosing a large expanse of open sea, is Herod's construction miracle.

Some of Josephus' descriptions of the construction process are rather inaccurate, though this may be attributed to his over-enthusiasm and lack of knowledge as an engineer. However, a contemporary of Herod, **Vitruvius** (*De Architectura, V, 12*), provides detailed technical construction data on what was an engineering first. It must have been an impressive sight, sailing into Sebastos! The main body of the breakwater was in fact made of conglomerate blocks poured into a wooden frame and then lowered on to a bed of rubble. The average size of these blocks was 1.8 metres by 3.9 metres by 3.9 metres, with the outer edge of the breakwater resting on 5-metre-long ashlar blocks. Not quite the dimensions that Josephus refers to, but evidence from the sea-bed does confirm the overall scale of the harbour and the existence of the huge towers that he describes. Near the main entrance to the harbour huge ashlar slabs on the sea-bed, 2 metres by 3 metres by 5 metres, may well belong to Josephus' Drusium (a massive tower).

Tectonic faulting has caused the sea-bed to subside five to seven metres, causing the outer harbour constructions to sink several metres below their original level. As a result Herod's breakwater became a major danger to shipping and the remains of several ships have been found that floundered attempting to sail over this sunken obstacle. Though it is not entirely clear when the final submergence of the Herodian harbour took place, dating of samples from the ships wrecked attempting to sail over the sunken breakwater suggest a date early in the fourth century CE. Carbon-14 tests of wooden beams found near the northern breakwater suggests that serious attempts to rebuild the sunken harbour were undertaken by the Byzantine emperor Anastasius (491-518 CE).

The **Crusader harbour** was built in part of the middle basin of the Herodian harbour, and was dominated by the Harbour Fortress (see above).

Western part of medieval city (15)

Extensive excavation in the western part of the medieval city revealed remains that pre-date the Crusader occupation. The second stratum of the dig contained evidence of a flourishing settlement dating to the middle and late **Arab period** (9th to 10th centuries CE). Large houses built around private courtyards, with numerous alleys and culs-de-sac, conform to classic Islamic city design. Water delivery and storage systems are technologically advanced, though archaeologists were disappointed by the paucity of artefacts found.

The lower, fourth stratum revealed extensive remains from the **Byzantine period** (324-638 CE), including an eight-metre-wide paved street. An unidentified large public building was also uncovered, complete with sections of mosaic floor and two marble pillars; one has the Hebrew word *shalom* carved into it.

Excavations to the north of the medieval city walls have provided evidence that this area was almost certainly the main Jewish quarter of the Herodian, Early Roman, and later, Byzantine period cities. Finds from the Hellenistic period in lower levels of stratum also suggest that the site of **Straton's Tower** was centred here, though the lack of pottery finds seems to confirm Josephus' assertion that the town was in decline when Herod chose the site for his new city.

Jewish quarter (18)

Talmudic sources mention a synagogue in Caesarea near to the sea, and in the 1920s a *capital* carved with a seven-branched menorah was found on the sea-shore. Subsequent excavations revealed parts of the walls of a building that possibly served as a synagogue in the Herodian period and after. It is speculated that this is the **synagogue *Knestha d'Meredth*** (Synagogue of the Revolt) that is mentioned in Talmudic sources, and whose desecration was one of the sparks that lit the First Jewish Revolt (66 CE).

A number of synagogues from different periods are superimposed upon one another, reflecting periods of persecution and then tolerance of the Jewish community. The best-preserved Jewish remain is a **fifth-century synagogue**, paved with a mosaic floor bearing the inscription: "Beryllus, archisynagogue and administrator, son of Ju[s]tus, made the pavement work of the hall from his own money". One of the marble columns in the building refers to "The gift of Theodorus son of Olympus for the salvation of his daughter Matrons", whilst other columns bear the seven-branched menorah.

To the north of the synagogue/Straton's Tower area is a segment of perimeter wall. The wall includes two round towers and one that is polygonal, similar to those found at Samaria that date from the Hellenistic period (332-37 BCE). Their drafted sandstone block construction is similar to work found in the vault excavated at the southwest corner of the temple podium, and it is suggested that this early north wall formed part of the city walls of Straton's Tower. Other sources, however, date the wall to the Herodian period with Roman period additions, noting how well it fits in with the Roman and Byzantine street pattern (see map).

Early north wall (19)

Little remains of the Herodian amphitheatre that Josephus describes (*Jewish War I, 415*), bar an oval imprint (95 metres north to south, 62 metres east to west) to the southeast of the early north wall.

Herodian amphitheatre (20)

The water supply system that served Caesarea was one of the most technically advanced and efficient in the country, and the Roman aqueducts here are the best preserved in Israel. Caesarea was fortunate in that it had two sources of water. The high-level aqueduct (**21**) brought water from the springs on the southern slopes of Mount Carmel, possibly providing the town's source of drinking water. The low-level aqueduct (**22**) brought water from a dam on the Zarqa River (Nahal Tanninim), possibly for use in irrigation.

High-level aqueduct and low-level aqueduct

There is some dispute as to who built the nine-kilometre-long high-level aqueduct, with some sources claiming that it was built by Herod, and later repaired by the Roman Second Legion (Traina Fortis) and the Tenth Legion (Fretensis) during Hadrian's reign (117-138 CE). There is certainly evidence that the Roman legions worked on the aqueduct, with at least eight Latin inscriptions set in the masonry referring to their work. Others suggest that the plaster-lined 'channel A' furthest from the sea was built by Herod, whilst the western 'channel B' was built circa 130 CE by Hadrian. With channel A delivering 900 cubic metres per hour, more than enough for a city of over 50,000, there is some question as to why the additional 1,600 cubic metres per hour provided by channel B was necessary. The date and builder of the low-level aqueduct are not known.

Tel Mevorakh Beyond the high-level aqueduct (just to the north of Moshav Beit Hananya on the old coastal road) lies the site of Tel Mevorakh. Standing on the south bank of the Nahal Tanninim, this small mound has provided a number of interesting finds from almost all periods from around 2200 BCE until 1516 CE. The most famous finds are the marble sarcophagi that are now housed in Jerusalem's Rockefeller Museum. There is not much to be seen at the tel, although parts of the high-level and low-level aqueducts can be seen nearby, including an inscription on the high-level aqueduct referring to the building work done by the Roman Tenth Legion.

Other excavations There are a number of other excavations located to the north and northeast of the medieval city, though some can be difficult to locate. To the northeast of the medieval city the remains of a Byzantine building have been excavated. The fact that there were no traces of roofing columns found have led some to suggest that this was a *basilica discoperta*, a sort of open church used for pre-burial ceremonies. Later opinion suggests that this may well be a **Byzantine villa (23)**, complete with a large mosaic pavement. Nearby, also on the same ridge, is a small **Byzantine bathhouse**, perhaps belonging to one of the nearby villas. Both of these attractions are located in the modern residential area of Caesarea, and can be difficult to locate without assistance. The bathhouse can be reached on foot along the dirt road to the east of the low-level aqueduct.

Byzantine street and square Just to the east of the medieval city's East Gate excavations have revealed a large public square dating to the Byzantine period (324-638 CE). Paved with large marble slabs, the square contains a number of large statues, giving it the popular name **'Statues Square' (24)**. The porphyry statue features a man seated on a green granite throne, perhaps the emperor Hadrian, whilst the subject of the white marble statue, also a man seated on a throne, has not been identified. It is clear, however, that the upper and lower parts of the two statues do not match, suggesting that the second- or third-century statues were moved to this square at a later date in the Byzantine period. The most significant find in this square was a large, incomplete marble statue of **Tyche** (the city's goddess), depicting her as an Amazon with her right foot resting on the prow of a ship and a ceremonial sword on her left hip. A small figure stands at her right ankle. The statue dates to c. 125 CE but was moved to the square in the Byzantine period. Minus the head, lower right leg, left ankle and arms, the statue now stands in the Louvre in Paris.

A large tripartite gate to the north of the square leads via a rectangular room to a flight of ten steps. At the foot of the steps, an inscription refers to an unidentified Byzantine governor and the sixth-century city mayor Flavius Strategius under whose authority "the wall, the apse, and the stairway" were refurbished. A street continues north of the Statues Square, and the large number of buildings in and around the square and street has led some to assume that this was the main Byzantine city marketplace.

Hippodrome (circus) To the southeast of the medieval city it is still possible to make out the outline of the second-century hippodrome (**25**), or circus. At its peak, this huge racetrack stadium (450 metres north to south, 90 metres east to west) could seat over 30,000 spectators, and became renowned for the quality of its racing. The centre of the racetrack (*spina*) was marked by a row of columns, the mightiest of which (a porphyry obelisk 27 metres high) now rests where it fell. The hippodrome has not been reconstructed and now appears somewhat neglected, set amidst the cultivated land. The entrance is marked by a modern arch beside the road.

Many items found in the Caesarea area are now on display in the small museum in the grounds of the adjacent Kibbutz Sdot Yam. The kibbutzniks have been responsible for a large number of chance finds over the years; the Byzantine street and square ('Statues Square') was accidently discovered in 1951 when a kibbutz tractor struck a colossal porphyry statue! ■ *T06-6364367. Saturday-Thursday 1000-1600, Friday 0800-1400. 9 NIS.*

Sdot Yam Museum of Caesarea Antiquities

There are three beaches in the vicinity of Caesarea, though sadly they are often badly polluted by the nearby kibbutz factory. The Old City beach is set within the Herodian harbour, and has facilities including chairs, umbrellas, showers and toilets (but swimming is not allowed). Facilities are run by the *Caesarea Beach Club* (T06-6361441) and admission is 15 NIS. A free beach is available to the north, with the high-level aqueduct providing a superb backdrop. Life-guards operate in season. To the south of Caesarea is the sandy Shonit beach, with life-guards, showers, toilets, and a small snack-bar/restaurant. The beach is free, though there is a fee for parking. **NB** As per anywhere on Israel's Mediterranean coast, beware of strong currents and undertows. Swim only in marked areas and observe warning flags.

Beaches

Essentials

L2 *Dan Caesarea*, Caesarea 30600, T06-6269111, F6269122. Luxury 'country-club' style resort set in extensive grounds. Full facilities include choice of retaurants, pool, floodlit tennis, health club, fitness centre, plus a range of activities also available. Recommended. The hotel is also noted for having Israel's only 18-hole **golf course** (closed Monday). Note that this activity is **not cheap** (hotel guests pay $83 for a mid-week round, $97 at weekends, plus $25 for club hire!).

Sleeping

D-E *Kef-Yam Guesthouse*, Kibbutz Sdot Yam, T06-6364470, F6362211. Dorm beds (**E**) as well as a/c holiday apartments (**D**) with attached bath, TV, fridge. The kibbutz offers glass-bottom boat tours, sailing, speed boat rides and jeep tours.

There are a number of restaurants located not just in the Caesarea National Park, but as part of it. *Herod's Kosher Restaurant* (or *Herod's Palace*), T6361103, actually sits atop the Crusader walls. Although the food is quite good (main course 30-70 NIS), and the view is excellent, you cannot but help wondering if this sort of development is appropriate. *Charly's*, T6363050, is similarly located. Both remain open in the evening, after the National Park has shut. A poor value snack-bar/restaurant is located next to the National Park ticket office by the Roman theatre, whilst Kibbutz Sdot Yam has a reasonable value cafeteria.

Eating

Mediterranean Coastal Strip

Caesarea to Haifa: the coastal route

Colour map 1, grid B/C 2

Heading north from Caesaerea, there are two options for continuing on to Haifa. The coastal route takes in some idyllic beaches and important archaeological sites and is probably the most popular of the two.

Ins and outs

Getting there and around Most of the sights along this route are located on or just off the two main roads connecting Tel Aviv and Haifa (Route 2 and Route 4). Buses running along these two roads should be able to drop you off at the turnings for the various sights, and you will rarely have to walk for more than 15-20 minutes to reach them. With your own transport, access provides no such problems. Even using public transport, all these spots on the coastal route can be visited as excursions from Haifa (or from Tel Aviv with an early start).

Ma'agan Mikha'el In 1985, a member of Kibbutz Ma'agan Mikha'el discovered the wreck of a ship complete with cargo lying in 1.5 metres of water just 75 metres from the beach. Subsequent investigations suggest that the ship was a fifth-century BCE merchantman, and the '**Ma'agan Mikha'el Shipwreck**' is now recognized as one of the most important marine archaeological discoveries along the Israeli coast.

Many of the ship's timbers were recovered in a remarkable state of preservation, and almost the entire lower part of the hull was salvaged intact. The preserved part of the hull measures 13 metres long and 4 metres wide, and was made largely of Aleppo pine. The other fittings that were recovered, including the maststep, were made from the same wood. The 8-metre keel is pine, with a false keel of oak. The hull of the ship also supplied a large number of utensils used by the crew, including storage jars, oil lamps, cooking pot, jugs, and even the shipwright's tool kit. A model of the boat stands in the foyer of the Reuben and Edith Hecht Museum, at the University of Haifa.

The kibbutz's land forms part of the **Beit Safer Sadeh Nature Preserve**, and is a popular destination for bird-watchers. Accommodation is provided in the **C** *Kibbutz Guesthouse*.

Dor

Phone code: 06 Colour map 1, grid C2

A little over 12 kilometres north of Caesarea (and 22 kilometres south of Haifa), is one of the Mediterranean coast's loveliest spots. In addition to an important archaeological site that has yielded many superb finds from the Iron Age, Persian, Hellenistic, Roman and Byzantine periods, the beach at Dor is considered by many to be Israel's finest.

Ins and outs There is no direct transport all the way to the beach/site (though this perhaps keeps it quieter). The Tel Aviv to Haifa Buses 921 and 922 pass the turn-off for Dor ('Dor Junction', look for the **Kibbutz Nahsholim** sign), from where it is a half-hour walk to the beach. The Haifa to Zichron Ya'akov Bus 202 also passes this junction. **NB** Make sure you inform the driver in advance where you wish to get off.

History A 13th century BCE Nubian inscription lists Dor as one of the major cities of the *Via Maris*, with further references in the biblical description of the Israelite conquest of Canaan (*Joshua 12:1, 23*). Excavations now suggest that the maritime site was first inhabited in the Middle Bronze Age IIA (2000-1750 BCE), and was continually occupied until at least the third century BCE. Though Dor was abandoned in the Late Roman period (132-324 CE), evidence suggests that shipping continued to use the natural anchorage here until the end of the nineteenth century CE. In fact, it was on the beaches of Dor (Tantura) that Napoleon's army awaited in vain for the arrival of the French evacuation fleet following defeat at Acre (Akko) in 1799. Large quantities of French ordnance, including cannons, rifles and daggers have been found on the sea-bed.

Tel Dor

The Tel Dor mound has been extensively excavated. A massive wall 3 metres high and 2.5 metres wide, presumably built in the 12th-11th century BCE by the Sikil (one of the tribes of the Sea Peoples/Philistines), is considered to be the most impressive Philistine fortification yet discovered in Israel. The tel has provided a large number of cult objects from the Persian period (586-332 BCE), including clay figurines and masks. The Hellenistic period (332-37 BCE) is also well represented, with numerous examples of pottery vessels. The Roman period (37 BCE-132 CE) has provided extensive remains of a medium-sized town, with several large piazzas, streets, drainage channels, and part of the aqueduct that brought water from the springs in the Mt Carmel range. Portable items found include moulded drinking vessels in the shape of a Negroid head and a dog. A number of artefacts from Dor are displayed at the Reuben and Edith Hecht Museum, University of Haifa.

Byzantine church

To the east of the Tel Dor mound, close to Kibbutz Nahsholim, stand the remains of a Byzantine church (324-638 CE). The church was probably built during two separate periods, possibly on the site of a Hellenistic cult worship temple. The original church was probably destroyed in the late fourth or early fifth century CE, rebuilt, then destroyed again in the seventh century CE.

Dor

Purple dye factory

The purple dye factory to the north of the mound is considered to be the best-preserved example in the eastern Mediterranean. The dye was extracted from the murex sea snail, and subsequently used to produce the purple garments that symbolized royal and religious authority in Hellenistic, Roman and Byzantine times (see *The Jewish War VII, 149*).

Nahsholim Museum

The Nahsholim Museum is the home of the **Centre for Nautical and Regional Archaeology**, and features an impressive collection of local finds. A visit is highly recommended prior to exploring the remains of ancient Dor. The building was originally intended for use as a glass factory, established by Baron Edmond de Rothschild to supply the wineries at Zichron Ya'akov. Unfortunately, the project failed due to the poor quality of the sand. ◼ *Kibbutz Nahsholim, T06-6390950. Sunday-Friday 0830-1400, Saturday 1030-1500. 10 NIS.*

Maritime Dor Maritime Dor owes its significance to the off-shore reefs and rocky islands that act as natural breakwaters, providing one of the few natural anchorages along Israel's Mediterranean coast. It was in the Middle Bronze Age IIA that the harbour city was first established. Ironically, the instability of the underwater sand dunes at the entrance to the main port claimed many victims, and it is through the cargoes of these wrecks that much of the information about maritime Dor has been gathered. Major finds include 140 stone anchors dating from 1900 BCE to the sixth century BCE, a complete Persian war helmet dating to the fifth century BCE, a number of sixth- or seventh-century bronze steelyards inscribed with crosses and bearing the words (in Greek) "Jesus Christ the Saviour", plus a number of less important finds dating to the period when the Crusaders established the stronghold of Merle on the summit of the mound. Because of changes in sea-level, it is difficult to picture maritime Dor at its peak, though parts of the **Later Bronze Age** quay are still visible as are **three long-boat slipways** from the Persian period (586-332 BCE) in the central anchorage.

Beaches Variously referred to as **Dor Beach**, **Tantura Beach** or **Nahsholim Beach**, the stretch of fine white sand here is clean, uncrowded, and an excellent place to relax. Four small, rocky islands just off-shore act as breakwaters and form natural lagoons. Each island also functions as a bird sanctuary. A three-kilometre walk north along the beach leads you to the archaeological site of Tel Dor (see page 545).

Sleeping The nearby Kibbutz Nahsholim operates a **A-B** *Holiday Village*, T06-6399533, F6397614, with 80 a/c rooms with attached bath. Guests have full access to facilities, including tennis courts and children's play activities. Substantial discounts are offered in winter, though prices can soar on Jewish holidays. Half-board (using the kibbutz's excellent dining hall) is required in summer. A cheaper option is to camp at the campsite in the nearby Moshav Dor (T/F6397180), camp on the beach (though this may be risky), or visit as a day trip from Haifa.

Nahal Me'arat Nature Reserve ('Carmel Caves')

Colour map 1, grid C2 The Mt Carmel range comprises mainly hard limestone and dolomites and is extensively pitted with caves, many providing evidence of habitation dating back to Prehistoric times. Four main caves here have been excavated and are open to visitors.

Ins and outs The 'Carmel Caves' are located within the Nahal Me'arat Nature Reserve, roughly equidistant from Dor and Haifa (just east of Route 4, the Hadera to Haifa road). Buses 921, 922 and 222 will drop you on Route 4 about one kilometre away (make sure the driver knows where you want to get off). Although the caves are well labelled, it is worth phoning ahead to arrange an English-speaking guide. A well-marked trail (blue and white) leads through the Nature Reserve, with numerous attractive picnic spots. ■ *T04-9841750. Sunday-Thursday 0800-1600, Friday 0800-1300. Adults 15 NIS, students 12 NIS.*

Tabun Cave This cave (Cave of the Oven) has revealed remains from the Lower and Middle Palaeolithic periods, with radio-carbon (carbon-14) dating suggesting that the cave was abandoned around 40,000 years ago. It is speculated that the cave may have been first occupied around 500,000 years BP, though there is insufficient evidence to confirm a continual sequence of occupation. The discovery of the body of a woman of the Neanderthal type, perhaps over 120,000 years old, has suggested that both Neanderthal (*Homo erectus*) and Cro-Magnon

(*Homo sapiens sapiens*) may have coexisted for a while in this region, since the woman's body antedates numerous specimens of *Homo sapiens sapiens* found in the nearby Skhul Cave (see below).

During Tabun Cave's period of occupation sea-level was considerably higher, though subsequent environmental change led to a substantial drop in sea-level and an expansion of the coastal plain in front of the cave. Tabun Cave was probably abandoned when the chimney at the rear of the cave opened up, though this in turn provided an ideal trap into which animals could be driven.

This cave has so far failed to provide any substantial remains, though it is thought certain that the cave was occupied. The cave now contains a representation of the daily life from the Early-Late Mousterian period (c. 100,000-40,000 BP). **Jamal Cave**

This cave (Cave of the Valley) is approximately 90 metres long and comprises two large chambers and a corridor. Though the site had been mentioned in the writings of 19th-century travellers, it was not until stone quarrying began in 1928 for use in Haifa harbour that the archaeological wealth of the site was uncovered. The site was probably first occupied in the Upper Palaeolithic (45,000-30,000 BP), though it is the finds from the Natufian period (12,950-10,300 BP) that are considered to be the most interesting. A number of attractive necklaces, made of dentalium and bone pendants, have been found, in addition to Natufian burials with skulls decorated with necklaces of dentalia. **El-Wad (Nahal) Cave**

Skhul Cave (Cave of the Kid) was almost certainly used as a burial place of the Mousterian culture, and has revealed fourteen skeletons, of which three are complete. All have been identified as *Homo sapiens sapiens*, thus providing possible evidence of a brief co-existence with Neanderthal man (see Tabun Cave, above). **Skhul Cave**

'Atlit (Athlit)

Standing on this promontory jutting out into the Mediterranean are the remains of one of the most important Crusader castles in the Holy Land. It was one of the last strongholds to be abandoned after the fall of Acre in 1291, and the Mamluks were so impressed by the fortifications they ordered much of it to be dismantled for fear that it may be reoccupied. The ancient site around the castle is rich with remains from both ancient and medieval periods. *Colour map 1, grid C2*

There is no public transport direct to the site. The train between Haifa and Tel Aviv runs to the modern settlement of 'Atlit, though this is still a 30-min walk away. Alternatively, take any of the buses that run along Route 4 (old Haifa to Hadera to Tel Aviv road) and ask the driver to let you down at the 'Atlit turn-off ('Oren Junction' on Route 4, 'Atlit Interchange on Route 2; look out for the castle, the camp, or signs idicating 'Apilim). From here it's a 15-20 min walk. **Ins and outs**

The Crusader castle was completed during the Fifth Crusade in 1218, largely in order to control the coastal road as a first step in the attempt to regain Jerusalem. The castle takes its name from the Crusaders ('pilgrims' or 'peregrini') who assisted the Knights Templar and Teutonic Knights in its construction: Castrum Peregrinorum or Château des Pèlerins (Castle of the Pilgrims). **Castle of the Pilgrims**

The fortress comprises two concentric rings of fortifications, the inner line of defence commanding the outer. Additional fortifications were introduced in stages, generally following a successful repulsion of an attack. A second east

Mediterranean Coastal Strip

wall (complete with three towers) further strengthened the landward approach, and security was enhanced by a low wall along the outer edge of the fosse. The outer walls were faced with rusticated sandstone blocks, providing additional strength. Further defensive measures included the construction of passages and bridges connecting the various tiers, plus the introduction of portcullis above the gateways and numerous loopholes that could accommodate the firepower of three crossbowmen at a time. The fortress also had the advantage that, being at sea-level, there was no danger of undermining; a fate that had befallen many of the seemingly impregnable castles inland (eg Belvoir). The castle was twice successfully defended whilst under construction, and then again during October 1220. Such was the reputation of the fortress that it was never seriously threatened again (though the Mamluk sultan Baibars sacked the town in 1265, he did not dare attack the castle). The fortress was finally abandoned in August 1291 when the Templars decided to return to France. Subsequently the castle was stripped of its defences by the Mamluks, then the Turkish governors of the Ottoman empire removed large blocks of masonry for use in the construction of the new sea wall at Akko (Acre). Finally, a severe earthquake in 1837 reduced it to its present state.

NB The site is now a closed military area and access is not possible. The fortress can, however, still be admired from a distance, though you should ask permission before taking any photographs in the vicinity.

Other excavations in the vicinity The Crusaders were certainly not the first to occupy this strategic point. Excavations around castle have proved evidence of occupation in the Middle to Late Bronze ages (2200-1200 BCE), Persian period (586-332 BCE), Early Hellenistic period (332-167 BCE), as well as numerous remains from the Crusader period. Even more exciting to archaeologists has been the recovery of artefacts from the sea-floor around 'Atlit, and, in particular, the discovery of a Pre-Pottery Neolithic settlement (8300-5500 BCE) now located on the sea-floor some 400 metres north of the Crusader fortress.

Underwater surveys of the coastal area around 'Atlit have revealed a number of interesting discoveries. More important finds include the **wreck of a wooden ship** that provided a cargo containing many copper and bronze objects, parts of a throne, a horse's bit, bracelets, and the winged foot of a chair,

Castle of the Pilgrims, 'Atlit

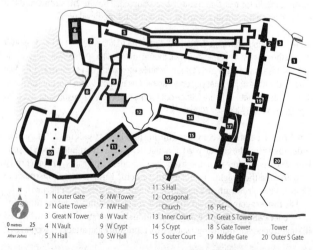

N

0 metres 25

After Johns

1 N outer Gate	6 NW Tower	11 S Hall
2 N Gate Tower	7 NW Hall	12 Octagonal Church
3 Great N Tower	8 W Vault	13 Inner Court
4 N Vault	9 W Crypt	14 S Crypt
5 N Hall	10 SW Hall	15 S outer Court
		16 Pier
		17 Great S Tower
		18 S Gate Tower
		19 Middle Gate
		20 Outer S Gate

Tower

plus, in less than 4 metres of water 100 metres north of the Crusader castle, part of the bow of a **classical Greek warship** complete with a decorated 500-kilogramme bronze-cast battering ram. Carbon-14 dating of the wooden hull suggest a fourth century BCE date. Excavations have also allowed archaeologists mentally to reconstruct plans of the ancient Phoenician harbour, as well as the much later Crusader harbour.

A **cemetery** on the rocky ridge to the southeast of the Crusader castle has revealed burials from the seventh to the second century BCE. Remains of outer fortifications, and parts of the Crusader town can be seen outside the main castle walls. These include a **small church**, **stables** capable of housing 50 horses and 250 head of cattle, and a **bathhouse**. Of most interest is the 13th-century **Crusader cemetery**, containing some 1,700 Christian graves. The tombs are typical of the period, with a simple carved cross and an emblem revealing the man's status or occupation rather than his name.

A number of artefacts from 'Atlit are displayed at the Reuben and Edith Hecht Museum, University of Haifa.

During the British Mandate period, 'Atlit was the site of a detention camp used for holding illegal Jewish immigrants. A number of the original camp structures remain and the camp is now used as a museum. Models, photographs, reconstructions and a short audio-visual presentation give some idea of conditions inside the camp. On 10th October 1945, three units of the Palmach (the proactive wing of the underground Jewish self-defence organisation, the Haganah) successfully attacked the camp, freeing a large number of detainees.

Ma'apilim 'Atlit Camp

'Atlit

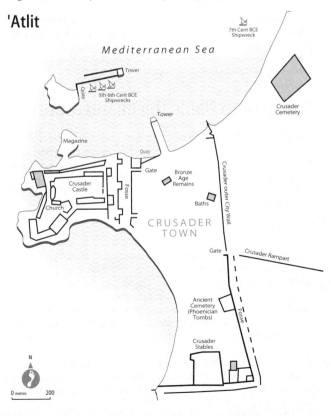

Mediterranean Coastal Strip

One of the three units was led by Yitzhak Rabin, future Prime Minister of Israel. ■ *T04-8841980. Sunday-Thursday 0900-1530, Friday 0900-1230, Saturday 0900-1500. 15 NIS. Caters mainly for tour groups, though individuals are welcome: best to call ahead.*

Ein Hod A popular excursion from Haifa (15 kilometres south of Haifa, 5 kilometres inland of 'Atlit), Ein Hod is an attractively located artists' colony. The colony was established in 1953 by the one of the founders of the Dadaist movement, **Marcel Janco** (1895-1984), on the site of an Arab village that had been abandoned during the 1948 war. There are a number of attractions, beside the use of bronzes and sculptures in open spaces. The **Ein Hod Artists' Gallery** features exhibitions of the village artist's work. ■ *T04-8842548. Saturday-Friday 0930-1600. 4 NIS.* The **Janco-Dada Museum** contains works by Janco, contemporary Israeli Dadaists, and a short audio-visual show explaining the movement ■ *T04-9842350. Same hours. 10 NIS.* There is also the **Art and Wear Gallery** (*same opening hours. Free*). A small **amphitheatre** hosts evening concerts. ■ *T04-9842029, or check listings at Haifa tourist office.* The *Ein Hod Restaurant*, Main Square, T04-9842016, is a popular dining spot.

Sleeping There is no accommodation in Ein Hod itself, though it is possible to stay at the **C** *Kibbutz Nir Etzion Hotel*, T04-9842541, F9843344, several kilometres further inland at Nir Etzion. Kosher meals, synagogue, pool and children's playground are available, though the emphasis is very much on (Jewish) families. It is also rather expensive, though all rooms have a/c, TV and bath.

Transport Take Buses 202, 921 or 922 from Haifa that follow the **old Haifa to Hadera road** (Route 4) and get off at the Ein Hod Junction (20 mins, 6 NIS). From here it is a 2km walk (uphill) to the village. **NB** There is no transport here on Shabbat, and generally no public transport back to Haifa after the concerts. Those with own vehicles should note that they must be parked outside the village.

Caesarea to Haifa: the inland route

Colour map 1, grid B/C 2 *Though the majority of visitors take the coastal route between Caesarea and Haifa, this inland route is a very pleasant alternative, passing through the beautiful undulating scenery of Israel's wine country and taking in a number of fascinating places of interest. Many of the settlements on this route were founded with the financial assistance of Baron Edmond de Rothschild (1845-1934) and bear the name of his family members.*

Ins and outs

Getting there and around This route is undoubtedly at its best if you have the flexibility of your own transport. Having said that, it is certainly possible to appreciate this area using public transport. The places of interest to the north (**Daliyat el-Carmel**, **Isfiya**, **Mukhraka**) can easily be visited by a combination of bus and walking as an excursion from Haifa. Bearing in mind that the southernmost places of interest, (**Shuni**, **Ramat HaNadiv** and **Zichron Ya'akov**) are less than 8km apart, it is perfectly feasible, and very pleasant, to walk between the main sites.

Binyamina This small agricultural settlement was founded in 1922, and bears the Hebrew version of Rothschild's name (Benjamin/Binyamin = Edmond). Observing the simple village pattern, the vineyards laden with grapes and the architectural style of single-storey houses with red terracotta roofs, you could be forgiven for thinking that you are travelling through Provence. (Binyamina is served by a number of trains on the Tel Aviv–Haifa line.)

Shuni

Shuni (Miyamas) stands on a gently sloping hill at the southern end of the Carmel Range, and the key attractions have now been incorporated within **Jabotinsky Park**. The park takes its name from the leader of the Irgun Zvai Leumi (Irgun) underground/terrorist organisation, Ze'ev Jabotinsky (1880-1940), whose units used this remote area as a base for attacks. The park is an excellent site for a picnic, with the *Shuni Castle Restaurant*, (T06-6380227, reservations recommended) one of the most highly recommended restaurants in Israel's north.

The key attraction is the partially restored **Roman theatre**. The theatre is reasonably large, with 20 rows of seats divided in two by a narrower row of seats, and two lines of steps separating the audience from the orchestra. The floor of the orchestra was paved with smooth slabs of limestone quarried nearby on Mt Carmel, with the remains of what is thought to be an altar to Dionysus or Asclepius (see below) at its centre. The theatre was destroyed by an earthquake in the fourth century CE.

In the Byzantine period (324-638 CE), remains from the Roman theatre were reused, though the standard of workmanship on the subsequent Byzantine theatre was not high. Later in the Byzantine period, and continuing into the Early Arab period, the theatre area was used as an oil press and threshing floor.

The **springs** at Shuni were also the source of water that fed the high-level aqueduct to Caesarea (see page 541). A marble statue of **Asclepius** (the god of healing) was found near to the high-level aqueduct, providing a link with a reference in the writings of the Bordeaux Pilgrim (333 CE), who refers to a mountain called Mons Syna close to Caesarea from which a miraculous spring enabled barren women to become pregnant. Ritualistic bathing was an important element of this cult, and a system of small pools fed by an aqueduct (dating to the Early Byzantine period) were found to the south of the Roman theatre. Other pools to the west of this aqueduct were decorated with intricate mosaic floors. The statue of Asclepius now resides in the Rockefeller Museum in Jerusalem. ■ *T06-6389730. Sunday-Thursday 0900-1600, Friday 0900-1230. 10 NIS. Call ahead for a guided tour. Shuni is best reached by bus from Haifa.*

Jabotinsky Park

Ramat HaNadiv

Located on a southern ridge of Mt Carmel, Ramat HaNadiv, literally 'the Benefactor's Heights', has been developed into a beautiful park containing the family tomb of Baron Edmond de Rothschild. Also lying within the park are a number of important archaeological sites.

Colour map 1, grid C2

The centre-piece of the 450-hectare parkland is the Rothschild Memorial Gardens, two kilometres along the unpaved road from the park entrance. The gardens are beautifully maintained and feature separate rose, palm and fragrance gardens set between manicured lawns shaded by Cedars of Lebanon. The bodies of Baron Rothschild and his wife, Baroness Adelaide, were brought here from France in 1954 aboard an Israeli warship and placed in the crypt beneath a single slab of black marble. It's a fine place to be buried, whilst the living can appreciate a magnificent view of the Sharon Plain and the Mediterranean coast from Dor to Caesarea. The Rothschild family's small winery nearby, (**Baron's**

Rothschild Memorial Gardens & Tomb

Mediterranean Coastal Strip

Winery, T06-6380434), offers tours and tastings.

Kebara Cave The prehistoric Kebara Cave is one of several such sites on Mount Carmel. The cave entrance opens on to a spacious chamber 26 metres by 20 metres. Excavations have revealed at least ten layers of occupation, dating back to the end of the Middle Palaeolithic period (c. 45,000 BP). The most significant finds date to the Natufian culture (Late Mesolithic, c. 12,950-10,300 BP), and include a large number of bone implements and tools. Also of great interest to archaeologists was the discovery of skeletons belonging to a baby and a young Neanderthal male, similar to those found at Tabun Cave (see page 546). ■ *Follow the marked trail from the main parking lot. NB Further excavation means that the cave is not always open to visitors.*

Second Temple period & Byzantine period remains, Ramat Hanadiv

Outer wall of Second Temple period Farm

Byzantine period Villa

0 metres 100

Storerooms & Livestock enclosures

1 Second Temple period bathtub
2 Second Temple period stepped Mikveh (Ritual Bath)
3 Oil Press
4 Byzantine period Cistern
5 Wine Press
6 Wine Press
7 Threshing floor area
8 Byzantine period Wine Press

Second Temple period farm A large agricultural estate dating to the end of the Second Temple period has been excavated at Ramat HaNadiv. The farm was owned by a Jewish family, though the reason for its eventual abandonment remain unclear. Dating of pottery remains found at the site suggest that it was not abandoned during the First Jewish Revolt (66-70 CE), when the Jewish population at nearby Caesarea suffered greatly (see page 534). A more likely date for the abandonment of the estate would be the Bar Kokhba Revolt (Second Jewish Revolt) of 132-135 CE.

The L-shaped estate covers less than a third of a hectare and is surrounded by a wall one metre thick. A large (defensive?) tower has been identified at the northern part of the compound, with storerooms and livestock enclosures to the south. The residential area of the compound has revealed an oval bathtub and a stepped *mikveh* (Jewish ritual bath). Winepresses are located to the west of the residential area, and to the east, just outside the eastern wall.

Byzantine period villa Some time at the beginning of the sixth century CE, a Byzantine villa was built on the site of the abandoned estate (see plan). The villa's design, with the eastern wing roofed by three parallel vaults and numerous windows in the supporting walls, is common in Roman-Byzantine buildings throughout other parts of Israel but almost unique to this area. Water was supplied by the cistern just to the south. A large Byzantine winepress is also located nearby.

The villa was abandoned at the beginning of the Early Arab period (638 CE), but remained in fairly good condition up until the beginning of this century. In fact the vaulted structures were still standing when Conder and Kitchener visited the site on behalf of the British Palestine Exploration Fund in 1873. ■ *Ramat HaNadiv/Rothschild Memorial Gardens, T06-3697821. Sunday-Thursday 0800-1600, Friday 0800-1400, Saturday 0800-1600. Free. Ramat HaNadiv can be reached by sherut taxi on the Zichron Ya'akov-Binyamina route. Alternatively, it is not far to walk from either Zirchon Ya'akov (two kilometres) or Binyamina and Shuni (see page 551)..*

Zichron Ya'akov

This small hill-top town sits at the heart of arguably Israel's best wine-producing country. A tasting session at the Carmel Oriental Wine Cellars is top of most visitors' priorities here, though there are a couple of other attractions.

Phone code: 06
Colour map 1, grid C2

Ins and outs

A very limited number of trains on the Tel Aviv to Haifa line serve Zichron Ya'akov (see 'Transport' on page 554). Alternatively, there are good bus connections with Tel Aviv and Haifa (and most points in between).

Getting there

History

The settlement here was founded in 1882 by Jewish immigrants from Romania. The early pioneers, however, fell into immediate difficulty with high mortality rates compounded by little experience in farming such land. The population of this early settlement, along with others in the immediate area, were saved from ruin by a wealthy benefactor, Baron Edmond de Rothschild. He purchased the entire valley (subsequently HaNadiv, or Benefactor's Heights), with the pioneers becoming salaried employees. The settlement was named Zichron Ya'akov, 'In Memory of Jacob', after Rothschild's father.

A telling contribution of Rothschild was his decision to bring expert agronomists into the area for an assessment of the land's productive potential. The soil and climate were found to be suitable for vine cultivation, and so began Israel's wine producing industry.

Sights

Not surprisingly, one of Zichron Ya'akov's main attractions is a tour of the Carmel Oriental (Carmel Mizrachi) Winery. 'Carmel' is often translated as 'God's Vineyard' (Kerem El), and some fine wines are produced here (connoisseurs, however, will tell you that the wines from the Golan are the nation's best). The tour finishes with a tasting and the opportunity to make purchases at discount prices. The winery also produces a selection of spirits. ■ *HaNadiv, T06-6341241/6639241, F6347739. Sunday-Thursday 0900-1400, Friday 0900-1230, except August and September. Adult 15 NIS, student 12 NIS. Best to call ahead for a tour.*

Carmel Oriental Wine Cellars

The Aaronson Museum serves a dual function. Part of the exhibits emphasize the work of **Aaron Aaronson** (1876-1919) as a leading botanist and agronomist, with a small natural history museum displaying examples of Palestinian flora. The rest of Aaronson's former home is devoted to his role as a spy-master, controlling a spy-ring (that included his sisters), dedicated to the termination of Ottoman rule in Palestine. Working closely with British intelligence, Aaronson and his sisters Sarah and Rebecca led an organisation called NILI (an acronym for "The Eternal One of Israel will not prove false", a quote from the *Book of Samuel*) in spying operations against the Turks. Sarah was later imprisoned and tortured by the Turkish police before committing suicide. Aaron survived the British victory in Palestine, but was presumed killed when his plane disappeared on the way to the Paris Peace Conference. ■ *Beit Aaronson, 40 Hameyasdim, T6390120. Sunday-Thursday 0830-1300. 10 NIS.*

Aaronson Museum

Mediterranean Coastal Strip

Old town   Much of the original town still remains, and recent refurbishment has provided attractive cobbled streets lined with old-fashioned lamp-posts. The
original synagogue, **Beit Ya'akov**, built in 1885 still remains, as does the old
town's water-tower, **Binyamin Pool**, and the old **Town Hall**.

Beit Daniel   In 1938, following the suicide of her 18-year-old son Daniel (a former child
prodigy), Lillian Friedlander built this 'artists' retreat' on the western edge of
Zichron Ya'akov overlooking the Carmel coast. Amongst those who stayed
here are Leonard Bernstein and Toscanini. This small complex of buildings is
now a museum, featuring Daniel's Steinway piano, and is also the venue for a
chamber music festival held twice yearly on the Jewish Pesach and Sukkot holidays. ■ *Habroshim, T6399001.*

Essentials

Sleeping   **L3** *Radisson Moriah Gardens Hotel*, 1 Etzion, T6300111, F6397030. Top of the range
accommodation, with full luxury features, views, pool, several function suites and
conference centres. **A** *Baron's Heights*, Box 332, Zichron Ya'akov, T6300333,
F6300310. A beautifully furnished modern hotel, with 100 suites with balconies on 14
levels of a terraced hill. Indoor and outdoor pool, health club and full restaurant services. **A** *Beit Maimon*, 4 Zahal, T6390212, F6396547. Small, family run hotel, with
highly recommended terrace restaurant. **A** *Eden Inn*, T6393900, F6393930. Modern
hotel and conference centre, with 112 rooms, lawns and pool. Part of chain that owns
the *Sporton Zichron Country Club*, T6397787. **B** *Beit Daniel*, Habroshim, Box 13,
T6399001, F6397007. This modest, yet tranquil retreat offers boarding with breakfast,
half or full board. Reserve well in advance for the music festival.

Eating   The most highly recommended food in town comes in the form of Middle Eastern and
Eastern European fare at *Casa Barone*, (T6390212), the terrace restaurant at the *Beit
Maimon Hotel* (see above). A short drive away there is also the *Shuni Castle*,
(T6380227), at Shuni (see page 551).

Transport   **Bus** From **Tel Aviv** Bus 872 (20 NIS), from **Haifa** Buses 202, 921 (14 NIS). **Train** A
very limited number of trains serve Zichron Ya'akov (usually 1 morning and 1 after-
noon train from both Tel Aviv and Haifa). **Sherut** Shared taxis run between Zichron
Ya'akov and Binyamina.

Directory   **Tourist office** 12 Hameyasdim, just behind the Central Bus Station, T6398811/6398892. Open
Sun-Thu 0830-1300, Fri 0830-1200.

NB There are a number of attractions between Zichron Ya'akov and Haifa (Route
70/672) that are detailed in 'Around Haifa' (see page 580). These include **Mukhraka**,
Daliyat el-Carmel, **Isfiya** and **Mount Carmel National Park**.

Haifa & the North Coast

10

Haifa & the North Coast

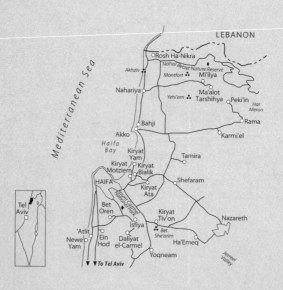

This chapter deals with the port city of Haifa, the short stretch of Mediterranean coast up to the border with Lebanon, and a few places of interest in Western Galilee just inland from the coast. Opinions of Haifa, Israel's key port facility, are varied. It has the potential to be an attractive city, sprawling as it does down the western slopes of Mount Carmel to the sea. However, its development, whether residential neighbourhoods or industrial parks, has not been particularly attractive and the whole sweeping scene of Haifa Bay is perhaps best seen from Mt Carmel at night, when the twinkling lights disguise what lies beneath them; from this viewpoint the whole is certainly more attractive than the component parts. Nevertheless, there are many points of interest within the city itself, notably in the broad selection of galleries and museums. For those not endeared to the urban environment there is the opportunity to walk your socks off in the nearby Mount Carmel National Park.

Another fine attraction to the north of Haifa is the labyrinth-like quarter of Old Akko (Acre), the last bastion of Crusader rule in the Holy Land.

Nahariya is a modest seaside resort on the coast, whilst further north at Rosh Ha-Niksa are the cliffs referred to in the Bible as the 'Ladders of Tyre'. Inland of here are a number of archaeological sites of some interest, as well as the remains of an idyllically-situated Crusader castle.

Background

The section of coastline between Haifa and the Israeli border with Lebanon is dominated by **Mt Carmel**. Though geologically part of the limestone and dolomite Central Range, Mt Carmel is actually separated from the rest of the ridge by a number of lower, softer hills. Mt Carmel has played an important role in the cultural/religious life of Israel (see under 'Haifa, History' on page 559). It has a history of occupation dating back to the Middle Palaeolithic (120,000-45,000 years BP) and has featured heavily in the three great monotheistic faiths: Judaism, Christianity and Islam. It is most noted as the scene of Elijah's battle with the 450 priests of Baal (*I Kings 18:17-40*).

The hills that separate Mt Carmel from the Central Range have historically allowed access to one of the most important routes in Palestine/Israel: the **Plain of Esdraelon** and the **Jezreel Valley**. This has represented an important trading and invasion route since antiquity. Even the Philistines, based on the coast far to the south, marched this far north in order to follow the easy passage of the Plain of Esdraelon to fight the Israelites at Gilboa. Likewise, the Egyptians used this route to reach the Euphrates (see 'Galilee and Golan' chapter on page 633 for full details of the Jezreel Valley).

The stretch of coastline to the north of Mt Carmel (Haifa) has been known since antiquity as the **Phoenician coast**, after the great sea-faring peoples who settled here and further north in modern-day Lebanon. The Bay of Akko (Acre) is the only real sheltered gulf on the whole of Israel's Mediterranean coast, and it can be little wonder that major harbours have been established at its northerly and southerly headlands (Akko and Haifa). The coastal strip north of Haifa has also served as an important contact point between the peoples of the eastern and western Mediterranean. Though there are ancient sites along this coast, such as Akhziv (Achziv) to the north of Nahariya, perhaps this history of contact with the Western world is best seen at Akko (Acre), the last bastion of Crusader power in the Holy Land.

Haifa

Phone code: 04
Colour map 1, grid B2

Haifa is a city of sweeping panoramic views, with a number of places of interest and fine museums, easy access to nearby beaches, as well as being a good base from which to explore the surrounding area.

Haifa may not quite be San Francisco, but there is some justification for the comparison. Physically, the city resembles its Californian counterpart by sprawling down the slopes of the wooded Mount Carmel in a series of switchbacks and winding roads, to the sandy coastline below. In terms of temperament, the allusion also works. Despite Haifa's reputation for being a city of hard work, the town does have a laid-back atmosphere where all are welcome. Despite some set-backs, there is a relatively stable relationship between the Jewish and Arab communities, plus the city has become home to two formerly persecuted groups, the Baha'is and the Ahmadies. The current 'Miss Israel', an Israeli-Arab, comes from Haifa!

Ins and outs

Getting there Haifa has good transport links with the rest of the country, and indeed the wider world. Many visitors arrive and depart Israel on the regular ferry services that connect Haifa with Limassol (Cyprus), Rhodes and Piraeus (for Athens). These boat services run year round and have tickets to suit all budgets.

For those travelling up and down the Mediterranean coast, the train service argu-ably offers the most enjoyable way of getting around. Haifa has several train stations, though most visitors will only use Haifa Bat Galim. Southbound, there are direct ser-vices to Tel Aviv every 2 hours, plus 1-3 slower services per hour that also stop at 'Atlit, Binyamina, Hadera, Netanya and Herzliya. Northbound, trains go to Nahariya via Akko about once per hour.

'Express' and 'regular' buses run from the Central Bus Station on HaHaganah to just about anywhere you could wish to go in Israel. Although the bus station itself is closed on Shabbat, some services still run on the sabbath (from the western end of HeHaluz). There are also a number of sherut companies that operate on Shabbat (see 'Transport' on page 577 for full details).

Getting around

Haifa is stratified into three main levels, with affluence increasing as you ascend. The lower town area around the port is the poorest and seediest. Above this stands the **Hadar HaCarmel** ('Glory of the Carmel', or Hadar for short). This is the main business, shopping and commercial centre. Standing proudly on the upper slopes of Mount Carmel, looking down physically and metaphorically on the rest of the city, is the **Carmel Centre** district, home of the upper classes, the upmarket hotels and the trendier shops, cafés and bars.

Due to the hilly nature of Haifa, seeing all of the town's attractions on foot can be rather hard work unless you limit yourself to viewing groups of places of interest that are on the same level. Buses around town are numerous, though the system does take some getting used to due to the city's unusual one-way system. Many of the attrac-tions are, however, within reach of a Carmelite stop (underground rail system, though really a funicular, Sunday-Thursday 0600-2200, Friday 0600-1500, Saturday 1900-2400). The Carmelite does not run on Shabbat, though many of the buses around town do (starting from Herzl, not the bus station).

The Tourist Information Office has put together a number of walks, "The Thousand Steps Way", that use the numerous flights of stairs that link Haifa's different levels. Unfortunately, these tours are not as successful as, say, Tel Aviv's 'Orange Routes', and the tendency here is to see a lot of steps, but not so many places of interest. A free walking tour provided by the Municipal Tourist Office leaves from Carmel Centre (junction of Yefe Nof and Sha'ar HaLebanon) each Saturday at 1000 (approx 2½ hrs). There is also 'The Little Haifa Train', which drives the scenic route between the Pan-orama Centre and Stella Maris (T050-264795). NB Purchasing the colour **map** of Haifa from the Tourist Office (4 NIS) is recommended. The *Haifa Guide*, free from the Haifa Tourist Board and many hotels, has discount vouchers for admission to many sights.

History

In comparison with many other cities in Israel, the name Haifa is not particularly ancient; there is, however, a long history of occupation of the site, with **Mt Car-mel** featuring as a symbol throughout Old Testament writing (usually as both a symbol of God's munificence, and as a sanctuary, eg *Songs of Solomon 7:5; Isaiah 35:2*). The karstic caves on Mt Carmel's escarpment were used as far back as the Middle Palaeolithic period (120,000-45,000 BP), and have revealed evidence of occupation by *Homo sapiens sapiens* and *Homo erectus*.

Mt Carmel

Carmel's status as a sanctuary comes primarily from the Old Testament story of the prophet **Elijah**'s battle with the priests of **Baal** (see box on page 561). The cave on Mt Carmel in which the prophet is said to have sought sanc-tuary (Elijah's Cave, see page 569) is today venerated as a place of worship by Jews, Christians and Muslims alike.

Ancient history   Remains pre-dating Elijah's exploits have been found at **Tel Shiqmona**, just over one kilometre southwest of Carmel Cape (near to the present day National Institute of Marine Research). Almost all periods from the beginning of the Late Bronze Age I (c. 1550 BCE) through to the reign of Hoshea (724 BCE) are represented. However, there is little to see today and the *Jerusalem Post* recently described the site as "inaccessible, largely ignored, garbage-strewn … accumulating rubbish that has obviously not been cleared up in modern history" (2/4/99)!

Elijah's defeat of Baalism, however, was short-lived, and the cult worship of Baal was reintroduced following the **Assyrian** conquest in 732 BCE. During the **Persian period** (586-332 BCE) a Phoenician town occupied the site at Shiqmona. The Greeks also occupied this site during the **Hellenistic period** (332-37 BCE), identifying the cult of Baal with the worship of Zeus, whilst the **Romans** (37 BCE-324 CE) celebrated the derived forms of Deus Carmelus and Jupitor of Heliopolis at this site. A series of fortresses stood at Shiqmona during the latter three periods.

In the fourth century BCE, the settlement at Shiqmona is referred to by Eusebius (in his *Onomasticon*) as **Hefa** – subsequently **Haifa**. The origin of the name is unclear, though it may be derived from the Hebrew *hof yafe*, or 'beautiful coast'. The name may, alternatively, have come from Caiphas, a high priest in the Temple at Jerusalem who was born in the city.

Crusaders, Mamluks and Ottomans   There is a large gap in the recorded history of Haifa during the Early Arab period (638-1099 CE). The implication is that the city entered into an era of relative decline, having been bypassed in favour of Acre, 'Atlit and Caesarea. The **Crusaders** captured Haifa ('Cayfe') in 1099/1100, but also preferred to develop alternative sites. **Salah al-Din** recaptured the city in 1187, though it subsequently fell again to **Richard Coeur de Lion** in 1191. It was around this time that the early forebears of the Carmelite Order began to settle on Mount Carmel.

The Mamluk **Sultan Baibars** razed the city in 1265, expelling first the Crusaders and then the Carmelites. The town was rebuilt and refortified in 1740 by the rebel Arab chief, the self-declared Lord of Galilee **Dahr el-Omar**. His successor, the great **Ahmed el-Jazzar**, further developed the town and was in turn responsible for expelling **Napoleon's** invading troops in 1799.

Haifa at the turn of the 20th century   Preceded by years of prolonged stagnation and periodic conflagration, the approach of the 20th century marked an important new era in Haifa's development. Jewish immigration into Haifa began to increase steadily, augmented by the arrival of the German Templars (see 'German Colony', below). The early 20th century also saw two other religious reform groups, the Baha'is and the Ahmadies, settle in Haifa.

The port facilities were expanded to enable steamships to dock, whilst the connection of the city to the Hejaz Railway (via a branch line to Damascus) proved to be the major catalyst in the town's development.

British Mandate   British forces finally captured the city from the Ottoman Turks in September 1918, after a prolonged and bloody battle. With the British awarded the Mandate over Palestine at the conclusion of the First World War, Haifa was further developed to suit British strategic interests. A new rail line linking Haifa to Egypt was completed, and in 1933 a major new port was constructed. Two years later, the British finished laying a pipe that connected their oil-fields in northern Iraq to the port facility at Haifa. In June 1940, the oil refinery in Haifa was largely sustaining the British war effort in North Africa and the Mediterranean.

Elijah versus the priests of Baal

Though Carmel was incorporated within David's United Monarchy (1004-965 BCE) by the time of the eighth King of Israel, **Ahab** *(871-852 BCE)* and his infamous wife Jezebel, worship of the cult of Baal was widespread throughout the kingdom. The First Book of Kings *tells the story of Elijah's epic battle on Mount Carmel with the 450 high priests of Baal.*

"And it came to pass, when Ahab saw Elijah, that Ahab said unto him, 'Art thou he that troubleth Israel?' And he answered, 'I have not troubled Israel; but thou, and thy father's house, in that ye have forsaken the commandments of the Lord, and thou hast followed Baalim. Now therefore send, and gather to me all Israel unto Mount Carmel, and the prophets of Baal four hundred and fifty ... '

" ... So Ahab sent unto all the children of Israel, and gathered the prophets together unto Mount Carmel ... Then said Elijah unto the people, 'I, even I only, remain a prophet of the Lord; but Baal's prophets are four hundred and fifty men. Let them therefore give us two bullocks; and let them choose

one bullock for themselves, and cut it in pieces, and lay it on wood, and put no fire under: and I will dress the other bullock, and lay it on wood, and put no fire under. And call ye on the name of your gods, and I will call on the name of the Lord: and the God that answereth by fire, let him be God.'

" ... And it came to pass at the time of the offering of the evening sacrifice, that Elijah the prophet came near, and said, 'Lord God of Abraham, Isaac, and of Israel, let it be known this day that I am thy servant, and that I have done all these things at thy word.'

" ... Then the fire of the Lord fell, and consumed the burnt sacrifice ... And when all the people saw it, they fell on their faces; and they said, 'The Lord, he is the God; the Lord, he is the God.'

" ... And Elijah said unto them, 'Take the prophets of Baal; let not one of them escape.' And they took them: and Elijah brought them down to the brook Kishon, and slew them there."

(I Kings 18:17-40).

The late 1920s and early 1930s saw increasing antagonism between **Jews** and **Arabs** all across Palestine, as Jewish immigration expanded rapidly. Haifa did not escape this rivalry, and the tensions across Palestine that culminated in the **Arab Revolt** of 1938 were felt in Haifa, where Arab attacks on Jews were reciprocated with equal ferocity.

Rather than discouraging **Jewish immigration**, Britain's '1939 White Paper' actually encouraged 'illegal/clandestine' immigrants to attempt to beat the British blockade. Many of the major, and most tragic, scenes of these attempts were seen in and around Haifa.

Following Israel's declaration of independent statehood, and the subsequent **The 1948 War** war between the Arab armies and the fledgling Jewish state, Haifa fell to the Haganah after just 24 hours of intense fighting. Much of the Arab population of Haifa fled, though the circumstances surrounding this flight remain controversial. Israel has maintained that the civilian population was ordered to leave by Arab radio broadcasts, so as to make way for the all-conquering Arab armies. Evidence of this has remained elusive, suggesting that a climate of fear had been installed instead, by stories of the massacre at Deir Yassin (see page 781). Most families, however, left expecting to return shortly in the wake of the victorious Arab forces. There is evidence, though, that in Haifa attempts were made by the Jewish community to reassure the Arabs of the town that it was safe to stay. Collins and Lapierre (1978, *O Jerusalem*) claim that special permission was granted by the Chief Rabbi for the city's Jewish bakers to break the Sabbath, and bake bread for the Arab community in the quarter captured by the Haganah.

Modern town Haifa is now Israel's third largest city with a population approaching a quarter of a million people. With the country's number one port and the major concentration of oil, chemical, textile, glass, cement and other heavy industrial plants, the city makes a major contribution to the economy of Israel. With two universities, including the leading technology institute at the Technion (see page 572), it is also one of the country's key educational centres.

Sights

For convenience, the sights below have been divided into the following five sections: Central Haifa, Lower town/port area, Western Haifa, Carmel Centre and Outskirts/suburbs of Haifa.

Central Haifa

German Colony The 'German Colony' was founded in 1868 by the German religious reform movement, the Pietist Society of the Temple. Many of the Templars' fine stone buildings still stand today, particularly on Ben-Gurion Avenue, and the whole street has recently been subject to a very appealing restoration programme. Some buildings have received a new lease of life as up-market restaurants, whilst others still retain the original Germanic family names on the door lintels. Prior to substantial land reclamation, the former sea-shore extended to what is now the junction of Ben-Gurion and Ha'Atzma'ut. It was at this point in 1898 that the German Kaiser Wilhelm II disembarked for his tour of the Holy Land. Most of the German community in Haifa were expelled during the Second World War.

Wadi Nisnas neighbourhood Not all of Haifa's Arab population fled or were expelled during the 1948 war, and a number still live in the Wadi Nisnas neighbourhood (see map). This is certainly no Cairo, Damascus, or even East Jerusalem, but you can still feel

Haifa & the North Coast

Related map:
A. Haifa Centre,
page 564

■ Sleeping	4 Mount Carmel	2 Elijah's Cave	4 National Maritime
1 Carmel Beach	5 Dan Panorama	3 Museum of	Museum
2 IYHA Carmel Youth		Clandestine	5 Jewish Cemetery
Hostel	▲ Other	Immigration & Naval	6 Christian Cemetery
3 Marom	1 Cable Car	Museum	7 Muslim Cemetery

something of the Arab world in its narrow, twisting streets. Particularly pleasant is St John Street, with its fruit and veg markets, and cheap restaurants.

Another attractive neighbourhood to the east of Wadi Nisnas is the Wadi Salib/old city district (see map). Most of these magnificent three- and four-storey buildings appear to have been abandoned, and wandering down the stepped paths between them is like entering a ghost town. This must surely be a prime piece of real estate awaiting gentrification. A number of pubs and clubs have already moved into the former warehouses. At the centre of Wadi Salib is the **el-Istakal Mosque**, one of Haifa's main Muslim places of worship, and nearby is the **Hejaz Railway Monument** (commemorating the completion of the Damascus to Mecca rail line in 1904).

Wadi Salib/old city district

Hadar (or Hadar HaCarmel) is Haifa's midtown area, with most of the key shopping and business districts, plus several hotels and sights. A number of recommended restaurants are located on the pedestrianized **Nordau Mall**, though for a pedestrian precinct, there seem to be an awful lot of cars using it.

Hadar district

The magnificent **Shrine of the Bab** is without doubt Haifa's most beautiful building, dominating all others, not in size, but in style. It is a subtle synthesis of classical European and Eastern styles, culminating in a golden dome glistening under 12,000 gold leaf tiles. The mausoleum is built of Italian-cut Chiampo stone, with supporting columns of Rose Baveno granite. Floodlit at night, it is an inspiring sight.

Baha'i Shrine and Persian Gardens

The mausoleum contains the remains of the **Bab**, the Martyr-Herald who foretold the coming of **Baha'ullah**, the founder of the Baha'i movement (see box on page 567). The Bab was martyred in Tabriz in 1850 and his mortal remains kept hidden until a suitably splendid place of burial could be found. In 1909, followers of the Baha'i secretly brought his remains to Palestine and constructed this shrine. The site is said to have been selected as the place where Baha'ullah pitched his tent, following his enforced exile from Persia. The shrine was completed in 1953 by the addition of the monumental dome. The interior of the tomb is a place of tranquil contemplation, comprising two small rooms. The first is a simple carpeted prayer chamber, from which you look

Shrine of the Bab

through the low arch to the second chamber containing the shrine. The tomb is located beneath the red carpet under the chandelier. The candles and flowers have no religious significance and are merely a means of beautification. (The tomb of Baha'ullah can be seen at **Bahji**, three kilometres north of Akko, see page 595.) **NB** This is a place of worship so it is important to act with decorum in your behaviour and dress. Do not wear shorts, short sleeves, or revealing tops (both men and women). Remove shoes before entering the Shrine, and remain quiet once inside.

Haifa & the North Coast

Haifa centre

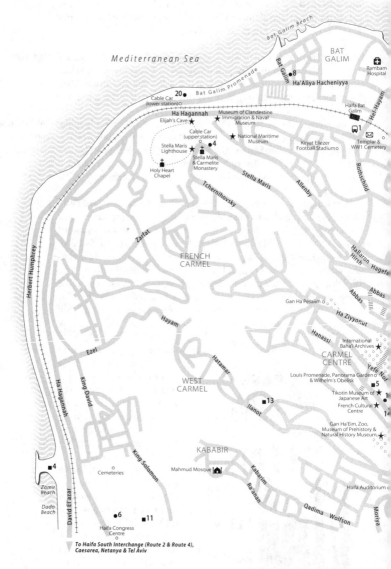

N

0 metres   500

Mediterranean Sea

BAT GALIM

Rambam Hospital

Bat Galim Beach

Bat Galim Promenade

●8
Ha'Aliya Hacheniyya

Haifa Bat Galim

20 ●
Cable Car (lower station)○

Ha Hagannah

Elijah's Cave ★

Cable Car (upper station)

Museum of Clandestine Immigration & Naval Museum

National Maritime Museum ★

Kiryat Eliezer Football Stadium○

Templar & WW1 Cemetery

Rothschild

Hel Hayam

Stella Maris Lighthouse ★

■●4

Holy Heart Chapel ✝

Stella Maris & Carmelite Monastery

Stella Maris

Allenby

Tchernihovsky

Zarfat

FRENCH CARMEL

HaBaron Hirsh

Hagefe

Abbas

Herbert Humphrey

Gan Ha Pesalim ○

Ha Ziyyonut

Hanassi

Hayam

International Baha'i Archives ★

CARMEL CENTRE

Yefe Nof

Ezel

Haramar

WEST CARMEL

Ilanot

■13

Louis Promenade, Panorama Garden & Wilhelm's Obelisk ○

Tikotin Museum of Japanese Art ★

■5

★ 1

French Cultural Centre ★

1■

Gan Ha'Eim, Zoo, Museum of Prehistory & Natural History Museum ○ ★

Ha Hagannah

King David

KABABIR

Mahmud Mosque 🕌

Katarin

Ra'anan

Haifa Auditorium

■4

Zamir Beach

Dado Beach

David El'azar

Cemeteries ○

King Solomon

●6

■11

Haifa Congress Centre ○

Qadima   Wolfson

Moriya

To Haifa South Interchange (Route 2 & Route 4), Caesarea, Netanya & Tel Aviv

Haifa & the North Coast

■ Sleeping
1 Aliya
2 Bethel Hostel
3 Beth Shalom
4 Carmel Beach
5 Dan Carmel
6 Dan Panorama
7 Dvir
8 Eden
9 Haifa Tower
10 Holiday Inn Haifa
   Bayview
11 IYHA Carmel Youth
   Hostel
12 Lev Haifa & Nesher
13 Mount Carmel
14 Nof

● Eating
1 Abu Yusuf
2 Avraham King of
   Falafel
3 Casa Ristorante
   Italiano, Dr Lek,
   La Trattoria,
   McDonalds, The Bank
   & Zampa Bar
4 China Ribs
5 Chin Lung, New York
   New York &
   Supermarket
6 Cowboy Steakhouse
7 Crispy
8 Dolphin
9 Eclipse & Sea Waves
10 El Gaucho, Back
   Door Pub, Tweety
   Club, 120 Club
11 Falafel & shwarma
   places (cheap)
12 Gratar Leon Yoji
   Rominesc
13 Kapulsky
14 La Chaumiere
15 Little Haifa Pub,
   Pizza Panorama
   & USO Office
16 Paradise Pub
17 Prego
18 Taiwan
19 Voila
20 Yotvata in Town
21 1873

ⓒ Carmelite subway
1 Kikar Paris
2 Solel-Boneh
3 HaNevi'im
4 Masada
5 Golomb
6 Gan Ha'Em
   (Carmel Centre)

Haifa & the North Coast

🚍 **Buses**   2 To Akko & Nahariya
1 Central Bus Station   (on Shabbat)

Do not attempt to visit the Shrine after noon (though the gardens remain open).

The shrine is set in the immaculate **Persian Gardens**, currently the scene of a $200 million revamp and expansion. In time, the manicured, geometrically planned lawns and cypress trees will stretch down via 19 terraces from Carmel Centre to the German Colony.

Above the Shrine of the Bab, on the other side of HaZiyyonut, are two other splendid Baha'i buildings, though neither is open to the general public. The **Universal House of Justice** is the home of the co-ordinating body of the Baha'i faith's worldwide activities; a marvellous white, neoclassical building supported by a colonnade of 58 Corinthian columns. Nearby stands the **International Baha'i Archives** building, the administrative headquarters of the faith, built in classic Ionic style and modelled on the Parthenon. ■ *HaZiyyonut (though entrance is on Shiphrah), T8358358. Shrine of the Bab is open daily 0900-1200, admission free. Persian Gardens open daily 0900-1700, admission free. Baha'i Archives and Universal House of Justice not open to general public. Buses 22, 23, 25, 26.*

Gan HaPesalim (Ursula Malbin Sculpture Garden) Located just to the west of the Baha'i Shrine is the Sculpture Garden; a small, pleasant garden overlooking the Bay of Haifa, and enhanced by 22 bronze sculptures by Ursula Malbin, a former refugee from Nazi Germany. ■ *135 HaZiyyonut. Free. Buses 22, 23, 25, 26.*

New Haifa Museum/Museum of Art The Haifa Museum has recently been revamped, hence the addition of the word 'New' to its title. The museum still comprises three museums in one, with separate sections dedicated to 'Ancient Art', 'Modern Art' and 'Music and Ethnology'. ■ *26 Shabbtai Levi, T8523255. Sunday, Monday, Wednesday, Thursday 1000-1600, Tuesday 1600-1900, Friday 1000-1300, Saturday 1000-1400. Adult 16 NIS, student 12 NIS, keep ticket for access to Tikotin and Maritime museums. Buses 10, 12, 21, 28, 41.*

Beit HaGefen Arab-Jewish Cultural Centre A unique institution in Israel, this cultural centre seeks to promote greater understanding between the two communities. Various cultural interchanges are promoted by the centre, with regular exhibitions by Arab and Jewish artists on display in the gallery. Call ahead for forthcoming programme. ■ *2 HaGefen, T8525251. Gallery open Sunday-Thursday 0800-1300, 1600-2000, Friday 0800-1300, Saturday 1000-1300. Free. Buses 10, 12, 22, 41, 42.*

Artists' House/Chagall House Features a selection of temporary exhibits, and is used primarily as a show-case for contemporary artists to sell their work. ■ *24 HaZiyyonut, T8522355. Sunday-Thursday 1000-1300, 1600-1900, Friday closed, Saturday 1000-1300. Free.*

City Hall and Gan HaZikkaron A small park on Hassan Shuqri, opposite the City Hall, serves as a memorial garden to those (presumably Jewish, and not Arab) who died in the 1948 'liberation' of Haifa, as well as those of "Haifa's citizens who fell in the line of duty in the Israel Defence Forces".

National Museum of Science, Design and Technology Forget notions of trudging around boring exhibits at traditional museums; this is hands-on science in action. Housed in the Old Technion building, this is less of a museum and more of a 'science activity centre'. Seemingly complex principles of physics and chemistry are explained through interactive displays, suitable for old and young alike. The museum also works hard to emphasize technological advances in Israeli industry. ■ *Old Technion Building, Balfour,*

The Baha'i Faith

Described as a Universalist world religion, the Baha'i faith claims around four million adherents worldwide. Presenting a syncretist view of world religions, its basic ethos is that all religions are essentially the same, merely differing in unimportant aspects of dogma. Thus, Baha'ism is the logical progression since it encompasses them all. God is manifested to men and women by divine revelation through a succession of prophets (Moses, Jesus and Mohammad included), of which Baha'ullah is the latest. The Baha'i look forward to a single world government, language and faith. For further details (in the UK) call T0171-5842566/9402.

Hadar, T8628111. Sunday, Monday, Wednesday, Thursday 0900-1800, Tuesday 0900-1900, Friday 1000-1500, Saturday 1000-1700. Adult 18 NIS, student/child 12 NIS. Buses 12, 21, 24, 28, 37.

Lower town/port area

Harbour/port area

Approaching the coast at Haifa by sea, there are magnificent views of Mt Carmel and the whole sweep of the bay up to Akko. As you get closer, the view becomes dominated by the unattractive port installations and the massive Dagon grain silo (see below). The modern harbour was finished by the British in 1933, built primarily to ship oil from the British controlled fields in Iran and Iraq without having to use the Suez Canal.

The harbour area is like any other port in the world; seedy and unattractive. Palmer Gate seems to be the centre of dubious activity, with numerous touts offering black market money (steer clear), or a range of other 'services'. Boat tours of the harbour are available (try the 'Carmelit' boat from Kishon Port), though photography of the port installations is strictly forbidden.

Dagon grain silo

Whilst the Baha'i Shrine dominates the middle level of Haifa, and the twin towers of the Dan Panorama Hotel in Carmel dominate the sky-line above the city, the Dagon grain silo is the most conspicuous building in the lower town/port area. With a capacity of over 100,000 tonnes and standing almost 70 metres high, this is the largest industrial building in the country. Guided tours are available, including the small museum that examines the history of grain production and processing in the region. ■ *Palmer Square, T8664221. Guided tours at 1030 only, or by appointment. Free.*

Railway Museum

Train enthusiasts can enjoy this collection of railway paraphernalia and rolling stock dating primarily to Britain's construction of the Damascus-Cairo railway. ■ *Old Haifa East Station, Hativat Golani, near Kikar Feisal, T8564293. Sunday, Tuesday, Thursday 0900-1200. Free. Buses 17, 41, 42.*

Israel Edible Oil Museum

Probably not the world's most exciting attraction, this museum examines the region's important edible oil industry, with some exhibits dating back 2,000 years. ■ *2 Tuvim, Haifa Bay, T8654237. Sunday-Thursday 0800-1430. Bus 2.*

Templar and WWI cemetery

On Yafo, just to the east of the Central Bus Station, lies the Templar and the WWI cemeteries. The latter honours those killed in the Palestine campaign of 1917-18, and is superbly maintained by the Commonwealth War Graves Commission. The Commonwealth Regiments are represented in some number here, with two separate compounds for Hindu and Muslim soldiers of the Indian Army. Behind the WWI cemetery is the Templarfriedof, since 1869 the

Haifa & the North Coast

graveyard of Haifa's Templar community (see 'German Colony' on page 562). First impression suggests that this cemetery is very overgrown, particularly when compared with the manicured lawn of the WWI cemetery. However, closer inspection actually suggests that this cemetery is a living, thriving garden, with graves located between shady trees and beautiful flowering plants.

Beaches/Bat Galim Promenade There are a number of beaches in and around Haifa, though the most pleasant ones are a bus ride away. **HaShaqel Beach**, or 'Quiet Beach', is closest to the town centre, located behind the Rambam Hospital. This is a 'religious beach', with separate bathing days for men and women. Though free, with showers, changing rooms and restaurants, it's most unattractive. It's only about 100 metres long, with a hospital directly behind, a large car-park to the left, and the main port to the right.

Bat Galim Beach is a 10-minute walk from the Central Bus Station and, due to its small size, it can become very crowded. It's free, with life-guards, showers, changing rooms, children's playground, and cafés. On the down side, the sand is similar to that found on building sites and it is enclosed on one side by a closed military area complete with machine-gun towers! The **Bat Galim Promenade** extends for several hundred metres along the sea-shore, with several pleasant sea-food restaurants and a number of noisy pubs.

Haifa's more attractive beaches are at the base of the western slopes of Mt Carmel, near to the main highway south to Caesarea and Tel Aviv. These include the **HaCarmel**, **Zamir** and **Dado Beaches** that are, in reality, just the beginning of the long stretch of sand south to 'Atlit and Dor. These beaches have a number of facilities, though the further south you go the more it is just sea and sand. Take buses 41, 42, 43, 44a, 45 (plus additional services in summer).

Western Haifa

Cable car This unexciting and over-priced cable car runs from the lower station on the Bat Galim Promenade up to the Carmelite Monastery on the western slopes of Mount Carmel. A commentary (Hebrew/English) gives sparse details on sites seen during the brief ride, though the view from the cable car is no better than the view from the upper station platform. ■ *Lower Station Bat Galim Promenade, Upper Station Carmelite Monastery, T8335970. Sunday-Saturday 1000-1800, Friday 0900-1400. Adult 16 NIS, child 12 NIS per one-way trip.*

Stella Maris Lighthouse, Stella Maris Church and Carmelite Monastery The Stella Maris Church, belonging to the Carmelite Order on Mt Carmel, is a small, circular chapel with a beautifully executed painted dome. It illustrates Elijah elevated to Heaven in his chariot, David playing the harp, the saints of the Carmelite order, plus the prophets Isaiah, Ezekiel, Daniel, and the Holy Family, and was completed in the late 1920s by a member of the order. Beneath the altar is a small grotto, believed to be the dwelling place or tomb of Elijah. Above the altar is a magnificent statue of Our Lady of Mount Carmel. The head was carved by Caraventa of Genoa in 1820, and crowned three years later in the Vatican in the presence of Pope Pious VII. The body is a century younger and is carved from Cedar of Lebanon.

A small **museum** is attached to the church, containing a bizarre collection of artefacts. There is a model of the grotto of the Nativity, some fossil shells, Crusader coins and ceramics found nearby, plus marble and stone fragments of the Byzantine church and ancient lighthouse that previously stood on the site.

The Carmelite Monastery now houses the International College of Theology of the Carmelites in Rome, plus a Pilgrims' Hospice, though neither is

The Carmelite Order at Mount Carmel

The Catholic Carmelite Order have a long, though not continuous, history of occupation on the mountain from which they draw their name. Imitation of the life of the prophet Elijah first brought Crusaders to this site in the 12th century, and early in the next century, under the tutelage of their Prior Brocard (later St Berthold), the Carmelite Order was born.

The spread of the order throughout Europe was contemporary with the withdrawal of the Carmelites from the Holy Land, following the Crusaders' defeat at Acre (Akko) in 1291. The Discalced ('barefoot') Carmelites returned to Mount Carmel in 1631 and built a small monastery on the site near to the ancient Stella Maris lighthouse. Once again the Carmelites were driven out, this time by the Muslim Dahr el-Omar in 1767, though they returned shortly after, building a large church and monastery over

a grotto where Elijah is said to have lived. A previous Byzantine (324-638 CE) chapel and the medieval Greek Abbey of St Margaret had occupied this site.

During Napoleon's ill-fated Palestine campaign in 1799, wounded French soldiers were left at the monastery, though they were massacred by the Turks once the main body of French soldiery had withdrawn. A small memorial to the fallen French, in the form of a forged iron cross atop a pyramid, stands outside the main entrance today. Twenty-one years after the massacre, Abdallah Pasha of Akko had the ruined monastery completely destroyed. The present church and monastery dates to 1836 and was granted the status of 'Minor Basilica' by Pope Gregory XVI three years later.

open to the public.

The present Stella Maris Lighthouse ('Star of the Sea') was built in 1821 as Abdallah Pasha's summer palace, using masonry from the Carmelite monastery that he had ordered destroyed (see box on page 569). After two years, however, the building was passed to the Carmelite order who subsequently used it as a pilgrims' hostel. The British Army took it over in 1927, ever since which it has remained in military hands. It is now occupied by the Israeli military and photography is forbidden. Outside the lighthouse stands a statue of the Virgin Mary, known as Our Lady of Mt Carmel.

Behind the lighthouse, a winding path leads down past the **Holy Heart Chapel** (formerly a windmill, but converted into a chapel in the 1960s), and down to Elijah's Cave. **NB** Though the path is quite long and steep, there is plenty of shade, with benches to rest on, plus some panoramic viewing platforms near to the top. ■ *T8337758. 0800-1300, 1500-1800 daily. Free. Buses 25, 26, 27, 30, 31.*

Though some cities in Israel are holy to more than one faith, and indeed some sites within those cities are revered by different faiths, there are few places in Israel where you are likely to see Jews, Muslims and Christians worshipping in the same place, at the same time. Elijah's Cave, however, is one such place where you may seen this phenomenon. **Elijah's Cave**

Ascending some steps above Allenby, opposite the National Maritime Museum, a small path leads to an enlarged chamber cut from the rock. Jews and Christians believe that the prophet Elijah sheltered in this cave from King Ahab, having slain the prophets of Baal on Mount Carmel (*I Kings 18:20-46; 19:9-13*). Later Christian tradition suggests that the Holy Family rested here on their return from Egypt. Muslims revere the site as the Cave of el-Khader, the 'green prophet' (Elijah).

A mihrab (prayer niche) is located behind a curtain at one end of the cave, towards which praying Muslims turn. In an adjacent wall, Jews turn towards a larger hollow, praying for Elijah's return as the harbinger of the Messiah. Christians make do anywhere. The cave is ascribed with miraculous healing powers and has served as a place of pilgrimage for generations. The sight of Jews, Christians and Muslims worshipping here, not necessarily together but at least in the same room, is extraordinary.

From the picnic area beneath the cave, a steep but shady path leads up to the Stella Maris Lighthouse and Carmelite Monastery. **NB** This is a religious site: modest dress and behaviour is essential. ■ *Corner of Allenby and HaHaganah, T8527430. Summer Sunday-Thursday 0800-1800, Winter Sunday-Thursday 0800-1730, Friday 0800-1300, Saturday closed. Free. Buses 3, 5, 43, 44, 45.*

Museum of Clandestine Immigration and Naval Museum During the period of the British Mandate, quotas were placed on the number of Jewish immigrants who were allowed to enter and settle in Palestine. This museum tells the story of those Jews who attempted to bypass the British blockade and enter illegally/clandestinely. The museum may be considered by some to be controversial – it tells one version of history – but the exhibits are well presented, with labels and commentaries in Hebrew and English. More importantly, the courage of the refugees on board the ships and in the detention camps is not diminished by the need to make a political point. A visit is recommended.

The tour of the museum usually begins with a short audio-visual presentation detailing the clandestine immigration operations, chronicling the number of ships and refugees attempting to run the blockade, and describing the fate of those who were unsuccessful. Exhibits from the clandestine operations are displayed in an area under the keel of an old tank landing craft, the *Af-Al-Pi*, that was itself used to bring illegal Jewish immigrants ashore. Further displays and reconstructions give some idea of the fate of those immigrants who were unsuccessful, and found themselves interred in camps in Cyprus, having just fled from the Holocaust in Europe. Inside the hull of the *Af-Al-Pi* is a reconstruction of immigrants' quarters on board ship.

The rest of the exhibits form part of the **Naval Museum**, telling the story of the foundation and development of the Israeli Navy. Pride of place goes to items from the *Ibrahim el-Awal*, an Egyptian destroyer captured intact by the Israeli Navy during the 1956 war. ■ *204 Allenby, T8536249. Sunday-Thursday 0900-1600, Friday 0900-1300. 8 NIS. Buses 3, 5, 43, 44, 45. Note that the road layout has changed significantly here.*

National Maritime Museum The permanent maritime exhibits here are superb, certainly reaching Israel's high standard of museum presentation. The basement features a permanent exhibition titled 'The Sea and its Ancient Treasures', most of which was discovered during dredging operations along Israel's northern Mediterranean coast. Pottery, statues and bronzes, along with model ships, ancient maps, and globes maintain the museum's nautical theme.

The upper floor is particularly educational, with exhibition themes including 'The Age of Maritime Discovery', plus a selection of old and new navigational aids such as maps, compasses and sextons. Special features detail the maritime exploits of the Phoenicians, Greeks, Romans and Crusaders, plus sea-going peoples from other regions, such as the Vikings. ■ *198 Allenby, T8536622. Sunday, Monday, Wednesday, Thursday 1000-1600, Tuesday 1600-1900, Friday 1000-1300, Saturday 1000-1400. Adult 16 NIS, student 12 NIS, keep ticket for Tikotin and New Haifa museums. Buses 3, 5, 43, 44, 45.*

Carmel Centre

The social and economic stratification of Haifa is in evidence up on Carmel Centre, from where you can gaze down upon the poorer folk down the hill. The top hotels, restaurants and up-market shops are generally located on these upper slopes of Mount Carmel, along with the better residential neighbourhoods. The whole sweep of Haifa Bay (and up to Lebanon) can be seen from the Louis Promenade and Panorama Garden on Yefe Nof, with the beautiful Baha'i Shrine, and the not so beautiful Dagon grain silo, in the foreground. This is an ideal spot at any time of the day, though the view is particularly attractive at sunset.

Louis Promenade, Panorama Garden and Wilhelm's Obelisk

In the corner of the Panorama Garden stands a small obelisk, known as 'Wilhelm's Obelisk', built to commemorate the visit of Kaiser Wilhelm II of Germany on 25 October, 1898. The Kaiser, along with his wife the Kaiserin Augusta Victoria, landed in Haifa at the beginning of their tour of the Holy Land, and came to this spot to view the German Colony (see page 562).

This elevated position was used by the Turkish artillery against the British forces during the First World War, with the **cannon** displayed here forming part of the Turkish defences. ■ *Numerous buses reach Carmel from the downtown area, including 21, 22, 23, 24, 27, 28, 37, though the Carmelit is equally convenient. Also, many of Haifa's 'Thousand Steps' paths lead up to Carmel, though it is certainly easier to descend than ascend.*

The Ukranian-born Expressionist painter Mane Katz (1894-1962) lived and worked in this house during the latter years of his life. This attractive building is now a museum that houses a permanent collection of Katz's work, with its emphasis on Jewish life in Eastern Europe, plus his private collection of carpets, antiques and Judaica objects. ■ *89 Yefe Nof, T8383482. Sunday, Monday, Wednesday, Thursday 1000-1600, Tuesday 1400-1800, Friday 1000-1300, Saturday/holidays 1000-1400. Free, except special exhibitions.*

Mane Katz Museum

This museum has developed far beyond the private collection of Japanese art that Felix Tikotin gifted to the city almost 40 years ago. It now features regularly changing exhibits of Japanese art, both ancient and contemporary, that are said to adhere to the Japanese tradition of displaying beautiful objects in harmony with the season. ■ *89 Hanassi, Carmel Centre, T8383554. Sunday, Monday, Wednesday, Thursday 1000-1600, Tuesday 1600-1900, Friday 1000-1300, Saturday 1000-1400. 16 NIS, keep ticket for Maritime and New Haifa museums. Buses 21, 22, 23, 27, 30, 31, Carmelit-Carmel.*

Tikotin Museum of Japanese Art

Gan Ha'Eim, or 'Mothers' Park', features entertainment for children (playground, etc), plus entertainment for adults (cafés, bars, nightclub, etc) at the heart of Carmel Centre. On the north side of the park are the zoological gardens, focusing primarily on animals indigenous to Israel, plus the **M. Stekelis Museum of Prehistory**, featuring archaeological finds from Mt Carmel and illustrating prehistoric life in the region. The **Natural History Museum** and **Biological Institute** present the flora and fauna of Israel. ■ *Zoological and Botanical Gardens, plus M. Stekelis Museum of Prehistory etc, Gan Ha'Eim, Hanassi, Carmel Centre, T8372886/8371833. Sunday-Thursday 0800-1600, Friday 0800-1300, Saturday 0900-1600, July and Aug until 1800. Adults 25 NIS, students 18 NIS, children 15 NIS. Buses 21, 22, 23, 27, 28, 37, Carmelit-Carmel.*

Gan Ha'Eim, zoo and museums

Haifa & the North Coast

Outskirts/suburbs of Haifa

Technion, Israel Institute of Technology

Israel's leading institute of technology moved to its present campus in the 1980s, having outgrown its previous site in the Old Technion Building in downtown Hadar. Many of Israel's engineers, architects (70 percent) and town planners have graduated from here, with faculties for medicine and life sciences having been added in recent years. Research is particularly strong in areas such as laser technology, fibre optics and weaponry, with companies involved in such work able to locate nearby in order to share in the research.

Funding such research is not cheap; the Technion's annual budget was $100 million in 1990. Much of the money is raised by private contributions from the diaspora; $25 million comes from private donations from the USA alone. The work and achievements of the various departments is presented in the **Coler-California Visitors' Centre**, including an English language film narrated by Kirk Douglas and Jack Lemmon. ■ *Kiryat HaTechnion, T8320664. Sunday-Thursday 0830-1500. Free. Call ahead for information and tour details. Buses 17, 19, 31.*

University of Haifa/Eshkol Tower

Serving as the centre for higher education in the north, the University of Haifa offers a broad range of studies, including a unit that looks at the socio-economic function of the kibbutz, plus a special centre studying interaction between Jews and Arabs.

Most visitors to the university come to admire the stunning views from the **observatory** at the top of the 30-storey Eshkol Tower. On clear days, the view extends up to the Lebanese coast and sometimes to the snowy peak of Mt Hermon. The building was designed by Oscar Niemeier, who was also responsible for the United Nations building. The university is also the site of the **Reubin and Edith Hecht Museum of the Archaeology of the Land of Israel** (see separate entry on page 572). ■ *Abba Khushi, Mt Carmel, T8240097. Eshkol Tower Observatory, T8240007. Sunday-Thursday 1000-1600. Buses 24, 36, 37, 93, 191, 192.*

Reubin and Edith Hecht Museum of the Archaeology of the Land of Israel

Not only does this museum contain a remarkable array of artefacts from the 'Land of Israel', many of which were found locally, the exhibits are beautifully presented in a light and airy setting. A visit is certainly recommended. The small art wing is less impressive. ■ *University of Haifa, T8257773. Open Sunday-Thursday 1000-1600, Tuesday until 1900, Friday, Saturday 1000-1300. Free. Transport as per University of Haifa, page 572.*

Mahmud Mosque, Kababir

The Druze and the Baha'i are not the only religious sects found within Haifa. In the suburb of Kababir, several kilometres to the west of Carmel Centre, lives a community of a thousand or so **Ahmadies**; a religious reform movement that may be best described as a messianic sect of Islam (see box on opposite page).

The Ahmadiyyat was first established in Kababir in 1929 by Jalaludin Shams, an early missionary of the movement, with the foundation stone of the first Ahmadiyya mosque in the Middle East being laid here in 1931. Several years ago, the beautiful **Mahmud Mosque** was built in Kababir using funds raised by the local Ahmadiyya community. The mosque has handsome, twin minarets and a grand white dome. The interior is simply furnished in plain white, and very light. Casual callers are well received (if modestly dressed), with adherents willing to explain the beliefs of the movement. ■ *Ra'anan, Kababir, T8385002. Open to casual callers, though not during Friday prayers. Bus 034.*

Ahmadiyyat

The Ahmadiyyat is a religious reform movement founded in Qadian, India, by **Mirza Ghulam Ahmad** (1835-1908). A devout and pious Muslim scholar, Mirza Ghulam Ahmad announced in 1889 that he was Mahdi, the promised Messiah foretold in the Qu'ran (Koran) and the Bible. To many Muslims such a statement is heretical and many subsequent followers of the Ahmadiyyat have faced discrimination and persecution (see below).

However, the Ahmadiyyat is not a new religion and the founder was quick to point out that he was a follower of the Prophet Mohammad and the basic tenets of the Qu'ran. "Ahmad was a prophet, not the Prophet; the Qu'ran, the book, not a book among many; Islam, the original religion whose recovery Ahmad sponsored" (Hammann L.J., 1985). Thus, the purpose of the movement is to "reestablish the true Islamic values and carry the message of Islam with practical emphasis on its application to the present age." In effect, Ahmad offered a fresh, modern commentary on the Muslim holy book, the Qu'ran.

Another interesting aspect of Ahmad's teaching was revealed in one of his eighty published books, Jesus in India: being an account of Jesus' escape from death on the cross and his journey to India. Ahmadis reject the Christian account of the crucifixion, insisting that Jesus ('Yus Asaf') escaped from the cross, settled in Kashmir, married, had children, continued his prophetic vocation, and died at the age of 120. He was buried in Srinagar, where his 65th generation of decendents still live. That is not to say that Ahmad saw a contradiction between the Ahmadiyyat and other revealed religions such as Christianity; rather he emphasized what he saw as wrongly perceived interpretations by man.

Today, the movement has some 10 million adherents spread across the world, with the institutional structure centred in the Pakistani town of Rabwah. However, the current leader of the movement, Mirza Tahir Ahmad, a grandson of the founder, has had to flee Pakistan where the Ahmadi community faces considerable persecution. Ordinance XX of 1984, dating to the martial law government of General Zia ul-Haq, is still in force today. According to the Annual Report of the Human Rights Commission of Pakistan, the bill in effect prohibits the Ahmadis from "adopting any of the religious forms and observances associated with the Muslims. Thus they could not call their place of worship 'masjid' (mosque), could not recite the formal call to prayers, could not display the Kalim-i-Tayyaba, the formal declaration of faith in the oneness of God. There was even a demand raised that the Ahmadis should be obliged by law to change the architecture of their places of worship so as not to resemble a Muslim mosque." Pressure on the Ahmadi community in Pakistan seems generally to be mounted by fundamentalist sections, though the government frequently acquiesces. The Ahmadi community in Israel (which has no formal diplomatic relations with Pakistan) faces no such persecution.

Finally, note should be taken of the source of the name of the movement. It is not a reflection of the ego of Mirza Ghulam Ahmad; it is in fact the Prophet Mohammad's second name.

Essentials

Haifa does not have a huge number of hotels, though, with the exception of the budget end, there is a fairly good spread. Those looking for budget accommodation will find it much cheaper (and more plentiful) in Akko (a 13 NIS, 45-min bus ride to the north).

Sleeping
■ *on maps; price codes see inside front cover*

L2 *Dan Carmel*, 85-87 Hanassi, T8306306, F8387504. Considered the best in town, though it's looking a little dated and not as luxurious as other hotels in the *Dan* chain.

Worth paying the extra $20 for a bay-view, or further $20-40 for the deluxe rooms. Pool, health club, tennis, squash, choice of restaurants including panoramic *Rondo Grill*. Tentatively recommended. **L2** *Dan Panorama*, 107 Hanassi, T8352222, F8352235. As far as 'more expensive' hotels go, this is pretty good value. Standard rooms are not huge so it's worth an extra $20 for the spacious 'superior' rooms, and if you're paying this much definitely go for the 'superior bay-view' rooms. Pool, fitness centre, shopping mall plus choice of restaurants (see 'Eating' on page 575). Recommended. **L2** *Holiday Inn Haifa Bayview*, 111 Yefe Nof, T8350835, F8350836. Opened early in 1999, huge 100-room hotel features 'executive' rooms, non-smoking rooms, disabled rooms, indoor pool, sauna and health centre, business centre, choice of restaurants including 'health bar', commanding views.

L3 *Carmel Beach*, Ha-Carmel Beach, southern approach to Haifa, T8508888. Recently built luxury beach-front hotel. **L3** *Nof*, 101 Hanassi, T8354311, F8388810. Seems quite expensive for what looks like quite an 'old' hotel, though rooms are quite large and service is reported to be 'keen' and 'intimate'. Has a recommended kosher *Chinese* restaurant.

A *Dvir*, 124 Yefe Nof, T8389131, F8381068. Used as training hotel for *Dan* chain so service is keen, can use facilities at other *Dan* hotels, rooms are spacious though not all have the great views. **A** *Haifa Tower*, 63 Herzl, T8677111, F8621863. Resembles an office block at the heart of Hadar; it's really hard to see how they justify these prices. **A** *Mount Carmel*, 103 Hayam, T8381413, F8381763. Isolated though pleasant location on western rise of Mt Carmel, 60 attractive a/c rooms with full facilities. **A** *Shulamit*, 15 Kiryat Sefer, T8342811, F8255206. In remote residential neighbourhood (Shambur), good service but still rather overpriced.

B *Beth-Shalom*, 110 Hanassi, T8377481, F8372443. Clean, functional a/c rooms in this Christian-run hotel, advance reservation for 3 nights minimum essential, reasonable value. **B** *Marom*, 51 Palmach, T8255545, F8254358. Peaceful if remote location out in Romena, 45 a/c rooms, terrace restaurant.

C *Aliya*, 35 HaHalutz, T8623918. Rather unappealing location, rooms overpriced. **C** *Lev Haifa*, 61 Herzl, T8673753. Formerly the *Talpiot*, very basic bare rooms, attached primitive shower and toilet (no seats), whole place smells of cabbage, mainly Eastern Europeans (looks as if you can rent rooms by the hour).

D *Eden*, 8 Shemaryahu Levin, junction with HaHalutz, T8664816. Basic rooms with a/c, shower, central (noisy) location, rather overpriced for what you get. **D** *Nesher*, 53 Herzl, T8620644. Basic but adequate rooms with attached bath, those at back a little quieter, TV room.

E *Bethel Hostel*, 40 HaGefen, 8521110. Haifa's only real budget option (lower end of **E** category), and consequently a little noisier and busier than it used to be (especially in summer around ferry arrivals/departures). Very well run hostel set in pleasant garden, very clean single-sex dorms with attached showers, breakfast included. There's a 2300 curfew (so you should get a good night's sleep), and you must be out of the dorms between 0900 and 1700. If you arrive during the 'lock-out' period there is a secure room to store baggage (check-in 1700-2200), and you can while away the day in the garden or lounge area (free tea/coffee). The staff are very friendly (free BBQ on Monday and Friday) and though this is a Christian-run establishment there is no attempt to 'preach'. The hostel is an uphill 30-min walk from the bus/train station, with Bus 22 going nearest until 1800; after that try 18 (any bus from HaGefen except 10, 12, 45 will take you to the Central Bus Station). Recommended (though people arriving from Tel Aviv or Jerusalem view it as being rather 'expensive' for a dorm bed). **E** *IYHA Carmel Youth Hostel*, Kfar Zamir NP, Hof HaCarmel, T8531944, F8532516. Great location for the beach and tennis centre, though restaurant-wise you're restricted to what's on offer at nearby Haifa Mall, (Buses 3, 3a, 43, 43a). Very peaceful out here, recently refurbished 6-bed dorms plus a/c private rooms (**D**). Good choice if you can cope with the remoteness.

There's a good range and choice of restaurants in Haifa, though you must be aware that some pride themselves on their views and ambience as much as their food. Popular dining areas include the German Colony, Nordau Mall, Carmel Centre, the sea-front promenade, plus the Arab quarters of town (notably Wadi Nisnas).

Eating

Budget Eating cheaply and well in Haifa is not difficult. Many of the restaurants mentioned below offer good value meals, particularly at lunch-time. For falafel and shwarma, head to the junction of HaNevi'im and Hehalutz for some of Israel's cheapest. There are also a number of similar establishments near the junction of Allenby and HaZiyyonut, including *Avraham, King of Falafel*, one of Israel's oldest and best. Kikar Paris (Paris Square) and the Wadi Nisnas neighbourhood have many cheap Middle Eastern restaurants, which can be very good value if you stick to hummus and fuul. Fruit and veg can be bought in the market here also. If you head out to Haifa University, in addition to fine views, there is a very cheap self-service cafeteria. There are snack places in the Central Bus Station, though they're not particularly good value.

Café/bars *Crispy*, HaNevi'im. 24-hr shop and snack place; *Eclipse*, 99 Yefe Nof. Nicely located café/bar. *Kapulsky*, 11 Nordau Mall, T8645633, and Panorama Centre, 109 Hanassi, T8361757. Popular for pastries and light meals. *The Bank*, 119 Hanassi, T8389623. Popular with 'oldies' during the day and the 'trendy' crowd at night, coffee 8 NIS, 'frappuchino' 15 NIS, toasts 33 NIS, salads 40 NIS, pasta 30-40 NIS. *Zampa*, 125 Hanassi. Pleasant café/bar, pizza 35 NIS.

Central/North/South American *Cowboy Steakhouse*, 1 K'dushei Yasei, near Haifa Congress Centre, T8501111. *El Gaucho*, 120 Yefe Nof, T8370997. Part of the Argentinian steakhouse chain. *New York New York*, 122 Hanassi, near Carmel Centre Carmelite stop, T8361501. American style steakhouse.

Chinese/Southeast Asian *China Ribs*, Stella Maris (upper cable-car station), T8330323. Interesting Chinese dishes. *Chin Lung*, 126 Hanassi, T8381305. Recommended but expensive Chinese restaurant. *Sea Waves*, 99 Yefe Nof, T8383025. Recommended Chinese restaurant, fairly pricey though business lunch (Sunday-Friday 1200-1500) is good value. *Taiwan*, 59 Ben Gurion, T8532082. One of Haifa's oldest and best Chinese restaurants, main dishes 30-50 NIS, good value business lunch 49 NIS.

Fast food/chain *Dr Lek*, 119 Hanassi. Ice cream parlour. *McDonald's*, 119 Hanassi, T8360823, and at the Central Bus Station. *Yotvata in Town*, Bat Galim Promenade, near cable-car station, T8526853. Part of kibbutz chain of popular dairy restaurants.

French *La Chaumière*, 40 Ben Gurion, T8538563. Long established family-run establishment is continually recommended as one of Haifa's best restaurants. 3-course meal approx 150 NIS, reservations recommended. Recommended. *Oh! La La!*, 5 Haim, T8662520. Good value business lunch. *Voilà*, 21a Nordau Mall, T8664529. Famed for its intimacy as well as its French-Swiss food, main courses 40-85 NIS plus good value midday business lunch, reservations recommended. Recommended. *1873*, 102 Yafo, German Colony, T8532211. Mixture of French and Italian dishes served in a charmingly restored building.

Haifa & the North Coast

Hotel restaurants *Rondo Grill*, *Dan Carmel Hotel*, 85-87 Hanassi, T8306306. Popular for its splendid views as much as its high quality (but expensive) food, window seats are in high demand, 3-course meal 150 NIS, reservations recommended. Recommended. The *Dekel & Alon*, *Deli Dan Gourmet* and *Old Tel Aviv Dairy* restaurants at the *Dan Panorama Hotel* are all highly spoken of.

Italian *Casa Ristorante Italiano*, 119 Hanassi, T8381336. Top location, famous clientele, but very reasonable prices with main dishes 25-30 NIS. Recommended. *Palermo Pizza*, Panorama Centre, T107 Hanassi, T8389129. More Italian than American, excellent thin-crust pizza from 30 NIS plus toppings. *Prego*, 97 Hanassi, T8373455. Good value business lunch 59 NIS (Sunday-Thursday 1200-1600).

Jewish (traditional) *Gratar Leon Yoji Rominesc*, 31 HaNevi'im, T8675073. Small and easy to miss but considered the best Romanian restaurant in Israel, full and generous meals for 30-50 NIS. Recommended. *Kosher Veta'im*, 40 Herzl, T8645976. Popular lunch-time self-service kosher restaurant, main dishes under 20 NIS, no English sign. *Hamoshava Haktana*, 56 Allenby, T8515152. Eastern European style, advance reservation essential. *HaTzimhonia*, 30 Herzl, T8674667. Popular lunch-time venue serving traditional Eastern European kosher veg, fish and dairy lunches.

Middle Eastern There are numerous places serving fine, and often very cheap, Middle Eastern fare in the port and Wadi Nisnas areas. Of those located around Kikar Paris, *Abu Yusuf*, 1 HaMeginim, T8663723, is particularly recommended. *La Trattoria*, 119 Hanassi, T8382020. Fine Tunisian couscous (50 NIS) as well as Italian and French dishes. *Salah Brothers*, 5 HaMeginim, T8640763. Good variety at reasonable prices.

Seafood *Dolphin*, 13 Bat Galim, T8523837. Noted seafood menu, fish main course 50-75 NIS. *Grilldag*, 1 Bat Galim, T8526779. Kosher seafood. *Shimon Hadayag*, 4 Mahanayim, T8382862.

Bars & nightclubs

Bars Those who like their bars seedy, full of sailors and prostitutes, will be attracted to the various drinking establishments around Palmer Gate (near the docks). More salubrious watering holes are found up in Carmel Centre, notably *Little Haifa* on Sha'ar Lebanon. There are also a number of lively places down on Bat Galim Promenade. Note that none really get going before 2300. Other pubs include: *Back Door Pub*, 120 Yefe Nof; *Berale*, 99 Ha'Atzma'ut, T8531794; *Hasandak (The Godfather)*, 30 Kdoshei Bagdad, Palmer Gate, T8671888; *Paradise Pub*, Gan Ha'Em, T8371964. 'Welcome to the US Navy'!. *The Bear*, 135 Hanassi, T8381703.

Nightclubs A new generation of clubs tends to come and go in the semi-derelict area of Wadi Salib, though you'll have to ask around as to what is 'in'. Locals tend to head to the nightspots out in the residential neighbourhoods of Romena and Danya, and when the US Fleet is in the places around Gan Ha'Em are the spots to be (or not!). During July/August there are a lot of events organized on the various beaches. Other nightclubs include: *Chaplin*, *Dan Panorama Hotel*, T8352222; *120 Club*, 120 Yefe Nof; *Tweety Club*, 120 Yefe Nof.

Entertainment

Bridge Sunday, Tuesday, Thursday 2000, Beit Goldblum, 124 Hanassi, T8382104. **Chess** Sunday-Thursday 1000-2100, Friday-Saturday 1000-1900, 11 Nordau, T8673508. **Cinemas** *Atzmon 1-5*, T8673003. *Cinematheque*, 142 Hanassi, T8383424, Buses 21, 22, 23, 28, 37. *Cinema Café Amani*, T8325755. *Orly*, T8381868. *Panorama*, T8382020. *Rav-Chen*, T8500055. *Rav-Gat 1-2*, T8674311. *Rav-Mor 1-7*, T8416898. *Rav-Or 1-3*, T8246553. **Concert halls** *Haifa Auditorium*, 138 Hanassi, T8380013, Buses 21, 22, 23, 28, 37. *Haifa Symphony Orchestra*, 50 Pevzner, T8620741.

Israeli folkdancing Classes and displays: Sunday, Tuesday, Wednesday at 2030, Thursday 2100, Saturday 2200 Beit Hastudent, Technion; Monday 2030, Haifa University. **Theatres** *Haifa Municipal Theatre*, 50 Pevzner, T8620670, Buses 8, 21, 23, 24, 28, 37, 42.

For further details check with the Haifa Tourist Board, T8535606. **April**: Children's Theatre Festival (usually during Pesach). **May**: Haifa marathon; Haifa triathlon; Haifa swimming championships. **June**: International Fencing Competition. **June/July**: International Festival of Folklore. **July/August**: 'Fun at the Beach'; 'Dado Beach Promenade' events; 'The Island at the Bat Galim Promenade'; Concerts at Gan Ha'Em. **October**: 'Neighbours' International Film Festival; National Sprint and Triathlon Championship. **December**: Festival of Festivals in Wadi Nisnas. **Festivals**

Books *Steimatzky* have branches in the Central Bus Station, HaNevi'im Tower, 82 Ha'Atzma'ut, and the Carmel Centre. **Jewellery** *Caprice*, 2 Keren Hayesod, T8572121. For all your diamond needs. **Shopping Malls** *Haifa Mall*, 4 Fliman, near Haifa Congress Centre, T8550360; *Horev Centre*, 15 Horev, T8246164; *Hutzot Hamifratz*, Volcan Junction, Haifa Bay, T8723261; *Lev Hamifratz*, 55 Hahistadrut, Haifa Bay, T8416090; *Panorama Centre*, 109 Hanassi, T8375011. **Shopping**

Bowling (ten-pin) *Bowling Ltd*, 251 Hahistadrut, Kiryat Ata, T8720529. **Cycling** *Beyond Biking*, 4/10 Ramban, T8679796. *Gideon's Bikes*, T8221288. Bicycle rental; **Mountain bikes** can be bought for around 500 NIS at the shop at 14 Yafo, T8532093, opposite the WWI cemetery. **Diving** *Val-Tal*, 47 Pinhas Margolin, T8514809. Introductory dives, equipment rental, etc. *Yamit Haifa Centre*, 2 Ben-Gurion, T8512418. Offers one-day dives off Carmel coast for around $100, including equipment hire. **Flying** *Kanfei Paz (Golden Wings)*, T8724474. School and fun flights over Haifa. **Football** Two of Israel's top clubs, Maccabee Haifa and current league champions (1998-99) Hapoel Haifa, play at the *Kiryat Eliezer Stadium*, opposite the Central Bus Station. Matches usually take place late Saturday afternoons (check Tourist Office for fixtures). **Golf** See under 'Caesarea' on page 543. **Hiking** *Carmel Field School*, T8664159. *Haifa Ramblers Club*, T8665825. *Society for the Protection of Nature in Israel (SPNI)*, 18 Hillel, T8664135/6 or T8529557 (Open 0700-1900, location shown on colour Haifa map available from the Tourist Information is wrong). **Horse riding** *Riders Experience*, Beit Oren, just south of Haifa, T8307242. **Ice-skating** *Lev Hamifratz Shopping Centre*, T8415388. **Sailing** *Israel Marine Centre*, T8556505, F8510563. *Ma'agan Shachaf*, Kishon Port, T8418765. **Shooting** *Northern Shooting*, Lev Hamifratz Mall, 55 Hahistadrut, T8412635 and 38 HaNamal, T8640318. **Squash** *Squash Centre*, Kfar Zamir, T8539160. **Swimming** *Neve Sha'anan Sports Centre*, Ya'acov Dori, T8211028. *Maccabi Centre*, Bikkurim, T8388341. **Tennis** *Tennis Centre*, Kfar Zamir, T8522721, has 20 or so floodlit courts (book in advance). **Sports**

Local Bus Urban lines information T8549131. Buses used to reach the different sights within Haifa are mentioned under the relevant entry. Single fare around town is 5 NIS. **Car hire** *Budget*, 186 Yafo, T8512847. *Eldan*, 12 Hahistadrut, T8410910. *Europcar*, 90 HaMeginim, T8517839. *Hertz*, 90 Ha'Atzma'ut, T8523239. *Reliable*, 33 Hahistadrut, T8422832. *Thrifty*, 10 Hahistadrut, T8725525. *Traffic*, 28 Natanzon, T8621330. **Carmelit Subway** The subway runs from Kikar Paris (port area), via Solel-Boneh (Hassan Shukri), Ha Nevi'im (Hadar area), Masada, Golomb to Gan Ha'Em (Carmel Centre). Open Sunday-Thursday 0600-2400, Friday 0600-1500, Saturday 1 hr after sundown-2400. Information office 122 Hanassi, T8381703, 5 NIS single ride. Good way of getting from downtown area up to Carmel district. **Taxis** *Hamoni*, HaNevi'im, T8664343. *2525*, Balfour, T8662525. **Transport**

Haifa & the North Coast

Air Haifa's airport is located to the east of the city (T8722220, Buses 58 and 58a from the Central Bus Station). There are daily flights with *Arkia* to Eilat (1 hr 15 mins), several weekly to **Jerusalem** (30 mins), and daily to **Tel Aviv** (30 mins). There are also plans to develop direct flights to various resorts in **Turkey**.

Buses Haifa's **Central Bus Station** (T8549133) is on HaHaganah, at the junction with Yafo and Rothschild. The terminus has three levels: inter-city Egged buses leave from the ground floor, inter- and intra-city buses arrive on the upper level, and intra-city buses depart from the front (south side) of the bus station. **Egged Bus Information Office** (T8549555) is on the upper floor, plus **left luggage** and **lost property** on the ground floor. Tickets should be bought from the **ticket office** on the ground floor, though most people seem to buy them on the bus. Student discount tickets (10% with ISIC cards) should be bought from the ticket office.

NB Below are a selection of services to other towns. Though exact departure times may change during the lifespan of this book, you will still have a good idea of the frequency of the service. Timetables shown are for Sunday-Thursday only. The bus station is closed during Shabbat, so check at the information desk for details of buses on early Friday and late Saturday. Reg = regular, exp = express, pl = departure platform number.

Afula: Bus 302, 0605 0630 0655 0955 1230, pl 8; Bus 301, 0540-2330, pl 22; Bus 434 (via **Bet Shean**), 0740 1120 1420 1600, pl 22. **Akko**: Bus 251 (reg), 0824-2115, 2 per hr, pl 13; also buses 251/261/270/271/272, pl 14/15, 13 NIS, 45 mins, or from stop on Daniel, off HaNevi'im (see map). '**Atlit**: Buses 121/122, every 2 hrs, pl 44; Buses 921/922, 0540-2230, pl 31, ask to be let off at 'Oren Junction'. **Be'er Sheva** (via Petah Tiqva and Netanya): Bus 995, pl 33. **Ben-Gurion Airport**: Buses 945, 947, (see under Jerusalem, below). **Bet Shean**: Bus 434, 0740 1120 1420 1600, pl 22. **Bet She'arim**: Various, including bus 301, 0540-2330, pl 22. **Daliyat el-Carmel and Isfiya**: Bus 192, 1215 1400 1530 1630, pl 42. **Dor**: Bus 921/922, 0540-2230, pl 31, ask to be let off at 'Dor Junction'. **Hadera** (for **Caesarea**): Bus 945, 8 per day, pl 30. **Jerusalem**: Bus 940 (direct), 0550-2000, every 15 mins, pl 29; bus 947 (via **Netanya** and **Ben-Gurion Airport**), 0550-2020, every 15 mins, pl 30; Bus 945 (via **Hadera** and **Ben-Gurion**), 0535 0640 0725 0800 0910 1050 1210 1600, pl 30. **Kiryat Shemona**: Bus 500 (direct), 0550-1815, pl 23; via **Karmi'el** and **Tzfat/Safed**, bus 501, 4 per day, pl 23. **Nahariya**: Bus 271 (reg), 0510-2330, every 15 mins, pl 14; Bus 272 (exp), 0645-2030, every 15 mins, pl 15; bus 270 (direct), 0930 1340 1410 1437 1500 1524 1548 1612 1640 1710, pl 15, 17 NIS, 1 hr; also from bus stop on Daniel (see map). **Nazareth** (via **Shefaram**): Bus 341, 1300 1510 1620, pl 18; **Nazareth** (direct): Bus 431, 0550-2030, 12 per day, pl 21, 19 NIS, 1 hr 10 mins. **Netanya**: Bus 947, 0550-2020, every 15 mins, pl 30. **Tel Aviv**: Bus 900 (direct), 0535-2020, every 15 mins, pl 26; bus 901, 0535-2305, 1 per hr, pl 28, 26 NIS, 1 hr 40 mins. **Tiberias** (via Nazareth): Bus 431, 0550-2030, 12 per day, pl 21; Bus 430, 0655-1915, hourly, pl 21, 24 NIS, 1 hr 15 mins. **Tzfat/Safed** (via **Karmiel**): Bus 361 (reg), 0550-1900, pl 24; Bus 362 (exp), 7 per day, all early morning, pl 24. **Zichron Ya'akov**: Bus 202, 0605-2130, 1 per hr, pl 32.

Sherut/service taxi Taxi to Ben-Gurion Airport, T8664444/8237240. *Amal*, T8662324 (junction of HeHalutz/HaNevi'im, see map, and from outside the Central Bus Station) offer a sherut/shared taxi service to **Tel Aviv**, including Shabbat. Sheruts to **Akko** from Zidon, off HaNevi'im (see map). *Aviv*, T8666333, offer sherut/taxi services to **Tel Aviv**; *Kavei HaGalil*, T8664422, to **Akko**, **Nahariya**; *Taxi Carmelit*, T8664640, to **Isfiya and Daliyat el-Carmel** from Eliyahu HaNavi (near Kikar Paris) until 1700, thereafter from Shemerayahu Levin/Herzl until 2000. There are also sheruts to **Nazareth** from Kikar Paris.

Train Haifa has three railway stations, though most visitors will only use **Haifa Bat Galim** (T8515793). This station is located right behind the Central Bus Station, and is connected by a foot tunnel next to the bus station's platform 33. **Southbound**, there are direct services to **Tel Aviv** every 2 hours (1 hr journey time, 20 NIS), plus 1-3 slower services per hour (1 hr 30 mins to Tel Aviv) that also stop at '**Atlit**, **Binyamina**, **Hadera**, **Netanya** and **Herzliya**. There are also recently introduced once-daily services to **Ashdod** and **Be'er Sheva**. **Northbound**, trains go to **Nahariya** (43 mins journey time) via **Akko** (32 mins) about once per hour. **NB** Holders of ISIC student cards get a 20% discount, making train travel cheaper than the bus.

Sea/boat Haifa is also an international arrival/departure point for ferries and cruise ships (Haifa Port Passenger Terminal, T8518246; Haifa Port, T8518111). You should arrive at the port passenger terminal at least 4 hrs prior to sailing. There are several sailings per week to **Piraeus** (for Athens), **Rhodes** and **Limassol** (Cyprus). Fares vary between high season (HS = mid-June to mid-September) and low season (LS = January-June and September-December), and between levels of comfort/discomfort (from 'deck space' to 'luxury outside, with WC and shower'). As a rough guide, the fares listed below are for 'deck space' (DK), 'aircraft-type seat' (AS) and for sharing '4 berth inside with WC and shower' (AB4) for high season (HS) and low season (LS).

   Piraeus: DK, $106 HS, $96 LS; AS, $116 HS, $106 LS; AB4, $207 HS, $179 LS. **Rhodes**: DK, $101 HS, $91 LS; AS, $111 HS, $101 LS; AB4, $202 HS, $174 LS. **Limassol**: DK, $58 HS, $48 LS; AS, $72 HS, $53 LS; AB4, $106 HS, $92 LS. Add $22 port tax to fare. Tickets can be booked from the following agents, as well as from agents in Tel Aviv: *Allalouf*, 40 HaNamal, T8671743. *Ardo Shipping*, 1 Palmer Gate, T8673173. *Jacob Caspi*, 76 Ha'Atzma'ut, corner of 1 Natan, T8674444, F8674456. Main agent for *Poseidon Lines*. *Mano Seaways*, 2 Palmer Gate, T8667722. *Mayron Shipping*, 53 HaMeginim, T8517620. **NB** Those booking 'deck space' should be prepared for low night-time temperatures, even in summer. Food on board is fairly expensive (and shekels are not accepted).

Airline offices *Arkia*, 84 Ha'Atzma'ut, T8643371, and Haifa airport, T8722220. *British Airways*, 84 **Directory**
Ha'Atzma'ut, T8670756. *El Al*, 5 Palyam, T8612612. El Al also has an advance baggage check-in in Haifa at 6 HaNamal, T8677036. *Lufthansa*, 5 Palyam, T8679258. *Olympic*, 104 Ha'Atzma'ut, T8510221. *Tower*, 76 Ha'Atzma'ut, T8674485. *TWA*, 104 Ha'Atzma'ut, T8528266.

Banks As always, check exchange rates and commission charges before changing money at banks. Post offices offer commission-free foreign exchange (including TCs) at good rates. *Change Pot*, 5 Nordau Mall; *Hapoalim*, 15 Horev, T8244116; *Israel Discount Bank*, 47 Ha'Atzmaut, T8617111; *Leumi*, 21 Yafo, T8547111. There are numerous more banks around Haifa; those marked on the map have an ATM machine. Ignore the 'change money?' offers around the Palmer Gate/port area. **American Express** are represented by *Meditrad Rehov 'Azza*, 80 Ha'Atzma'ut (up the side alley), T8645609.

Communications Phone code: T04. **Post offices**: the main post office at the junction of Shabetai Levi and HaNevi'im offers full services, including foreign exchange and **international phone calls** (though it may be cheaper to buy phone cards and use public call boxes). Open Sunday-Thursday 0800-1900, Friday 0800-1200. Other branches are at 19 HaPalyam (for **poste restante**), 152 Yafo, and elsewhere in the city. **Internet/email**: *Active Communications*, 63 Herzl (in plaza below *Haifa Tower Hotel*), T8676115; *Aroma Café*, 140 Hanassi, T8370069; *Net Station*, 125 Hanassi.

Cultural centres *Centre Culturel Français*, 96 Hanassi; *Haifa Congress Centre*, 2 K'dushei Yasai, T8518000.

Embassies and consulates Though the USA (T8670616), France and others maintain consulates here, you will almost certainly be referred to Tel Aviv.

Hospitals and medical services Chemists:*Hehalutz*, 12 Hehalutz, T8662962; *Merkaz*, 130 Hanassi, T8381979; *Shomron*, 44 Yaffo, T8524171. Hospitals: *Bnei Zion Medical Centre*, 47

Haifa & the North Coast

Golomb, T8359359. *Rambam Medical Centre*, 8 Aliya, Bat Galim, T8543111. Haifa's main hospital. *Carmel Medical Centre*, 7 Michal, T8250211.

Libraries *Civic Library*, 50 Pevsner, T8667766. Open Sunday-Thursday 0900-2000, Friday 0900-1315.

Places of worship Baha'i: see page 567. **Christian**: *Elias Church*, Lutheran Community Centre, 43 Meir, T8523581; *Roman Catholic*, 80 HaMeginim, T8524346; *Carmelite Monastery*, Stella Maris, T8337758; *Greek Catholic*, 23 Ein Dor, T8523012; *St Luke's Church of England*, 4 St Luke's St, T8523370; *Scandinavian Seaman's Mission*, 43 HaGeffen, T8521422. **Muslim**: *El-Istakal*, Kikar Faisal, Wadi Salib; *Haj Abdallah*, Halisah; *Jareneh*, Ha'Atzma'ut; *Mahmud Mosque* (Ahmadiyya), 60 Ra'anan, Kababir, T8385002. **Jewish**: *Central*, 60 Herzl; *Moriah Conservative*, 7 Horev, T8251495; *Reform Congregation*, Or-Hadash, 55 Hantke, T8343905; *Sephardic 'Heichal Natanel'*, 43 Herzl, T8662204.

Tour companies and travel agents *Egged Tours*, 4 Nordau, T8623132. Country-wide tours. *issta*, 2 Balfour, T8670222. Offer discount student travel to holders of ISIC cards. *Mazada Tours*, 4 Kyat, T8624440. Daily buses to Cairo from Tel Aviv and Jerusalem. *Nazareth Tours*, Kikar Plumer, T8624871. Daily buses to Amman, Jordan. For details of booking ferries from Haifa to Greece and Cyprus, see 'Transport, sea', on page 579.

Tourist offices *Haifa Tourist Board*, 48 Ben Gurion, T8535606. New location in beautifully refurbished 'German Colony' house, Sun-Thu 0830-1800, Fri 0830-1300. Lots of maps and brochures: pick up the free *Haifa Guide* for details of local events and lots of discount coupons.

Useful addresses and phone numbers Police: T100 (28 Yafo Rd). Fire: T102. Ambulance: Magen David Adom T101 (6 Yitzhak Zadeh). Gay info hotline: T8525352 (Tue evenings). Hebrew lessons: *Ulpan*, Beit Erdstein, 20 YL Peretz, T8625840. USO: 2 HaLebanon, T8382057. Rape Crisis Centre: T8660111 (24 hrs). Visa extensions: 11 Hassan Shukri, T8667781. Sun-Thu 0900-1300, arrive early.

Around Haifa

Mt Carmel National Park
The Mt Carmel National Park is the largest park in Israel, covering some 10,000 hectares of forest and woodland slopes. There are some well-marked trails through the pine, cypress and eucalyptus forest, of varying length and requiring differing degrees of fitness. Trail descriptions are marked at the park's main entrance, where the helpful staff can suggest walks suited to your ability. For those intending to follow the longer, more adventurous trails, it may well be worth purchasing the detailed map of the park from the **SPNI** office in Haifa (18 Hillel, T8529577). Though the map is only available in Hebrew, park staff can translate the relevant information. The scenery is beautiful here, and the sense of tranquillity certainly makes a visit worthwhile, even if just for a picnic. ■ *T9841750/8228983. Daily 0800-1700. Buses 37 or 192 from Haifa go to the main park entrance.*

Druze villages

Colour map 1, grid B2
Another popular short excursion from Haifa is a visit to the Druze community villages of 'Isfiya and Daliyat el Carmel. (**NB** For further details of Druze beliefs and practices, see the 'Religion' section on page 802). It is also possible to combine an excursion to these villages with a walk down to the monastery at Muhraka.

Ins and outs
Public bus services to 'Isfiya and Daliyat el Carmel are fairly limited. Bus 192 runs from Haifa's Central Bus Station at 1215, 1400, 1530 and 1630 (about 40 mins, 15 NIS),

though the service is not that reliable (and doesn't run on Saturday). **Sheruts** offer the better option, running from Eliyahu HaNavi, near Kikar Paris and Ha'Atzma'ut. Guided walks, during which you are hosted by members of the Druze community, can be arranged in advance (T8390125).

'Isfiya

This is the smaller of the two villages, though most people concur that it is less attractive than its neighbour further down the road, Daliyat el Carmel. However, it does have the advantage of being quieter and less commercialized. The village is associated with the former Jewish village of Husifah that dates to the Roman and Byzantine periods, and a fifth- or sixth-century CE synagogue was excavated here, though next to nothing remains in the village today.

It is possible to stay here at the **D-E** *Stella Carmel Hospice* (T04-8391692, F8390233). A quiet retreat run by the Anglican church, it has some dorms and private rooms (couples must be married in order to share a room), reservations are recommended. 'Isfiya has a very fine restaurant in the *Nof Carmel* (T04 8391718), where you can sample various Middle Eastern dishes whilst admiring the view down into the valley below. The *Druze Restaurant* has also been recommended.

Daliyat el Carmel

The village is located slightly further on from 'Isfiya, but has become such a popular day-trip from Haifa that some feel that what you see now is more of a Druze community theme-park. Many visitors are attracted by the clothes and handicrafts on display, but potential purchasers should be aware that not all the goods are made locally. The village is quieter, and more attractive on weekdays, away from the Shabbat crowds. **NB** Most of the shops in the bazaar are closed on Friday.

The best insight into the Druze community in Daliyat el Carmel is probably through the **Druze Heritage House**; a small, eclectic collection of artefacts and memorabilia in the back room of the *Mifqash Ha'Akhim Restaurant* (T04-8393169, admission 6 NIS) in the main bazaar.

Daliyat el Carmel was also the former home of **Sir Lawrence Oliphant**, a late 19th-century Christian Zionist. An unusual 'Christian mystic', Oliphant not only established close links with the Druze, he is also credited with sheltering both Arab and Jewish insurgents fighting to end the British Mandate rule. His former home, **Beit Oliphant** (ask for directions) has been renovated and turned into a memorial to Druze members of the Israeli Defence Forces.

Muhraka

Some four kilometres beyond Daliyat el Carmel is **Muhraka**. You may be able to take a taxi to the monastery from Daliyat el Carmel (20 NIS), though the chances are that if you don't have your own transport, you will have to walk. Make sure that you bear left at the only fork on the road from Daliyat to Muhraka.

This is believed by some to be the site where Elijah defeated the 450 priests of Baal (*I Kings 18:17-40*, see the box on page 561). Although open to conjecture, with no archaeological evidence to confirm either the story or its actual location, circumstantial evidence here does fit the biblical text. The site does stand at the entrance to the Jezreel Valley, as described in the *First Book of Kings* (*I Kings 18:46*); it is possible to see the sea (*I Kings 18:43*); and the Kishon Brook does run along the base of the hill (*I Kings 18:40*).

The Carmelite order built a **monastery** here in the late 19th century, from whose roof there is a superb panoramic view ■ *Mon-Sat 0800-1330, 1430-1700, Sun 0830-1330; Admission 3 NIS.*

Haifa & the North Coast

Longer excursions from Haifa

Haifa is a good base from which to make longer excursions. Details of the coastal route between Haifa and Caesarea (including **Ein Hod**, **'Atlit**, **Nahal Me'arat Nature Reserve**, **Dor** and **Caesarea**), and the inland route, (including **Zichron Ya'akov**, **Ramat HaNadiv**, **Shuni and Binyamina**), are found in the chapter **Mediterranean Coastal Strip: North of Tel Aviv**, starting on page 522. Further information on how to reach these sites by public transport from Haifa is included in the section 'Haifa, Transport', on page 577.

Day trips into Lower Galilee can also be made from Haifa, visiting such places as **Nazareth**, **Cana**, **Mount Tabor**, **Sepphoris**, as well as many places in the Jezreel Valley (such as **Bet She'arim** and **Megiddo**). Full details of these sites can be found in the **Galilee And The Golan: Lower Galilee** chapter starting on page 613. Further information on how to reach these sites by public transport from Haifa is also included in the section 'Haifa, Transport' on page 577.

North of Haifa

The 'Phoenician coast' to the north of Haifa has a number of attractions, as well as a few sights of interest lying a little inland in Western Galilee. Most of these places can be visited from Haifa as day-trips, although there is accommodation to suit the majority of budgets most of the way along this coast.

Akko (Acre)

Phone code: 04
Colour map 1, grid B2

The 'Old City' of Akko is one of the highlights of the Mediterranean coast. Although the town has a long and ancient history, it is the remains from the medieval period that delight most visitors. This was the last bastion of Crusader rule in the Holy Land, and many of the structures they built can be seen on a short walking tour of the labyrinth-like winding streets of 'Old Akko'. The Crusader buildings have been added to during the Fatimid and Mamluk periods, and again by the Ottomans, and the quarter continues to be a living-breathing Arab town. 'Old Akko' certainly fits that cliché of being a 'living museum'. Note that 'Acre' is the Crusader name; it's Akka in Arabic and Akko in Hebrew.

Ins and outs

Getting there   There are two parts to the city: most of the attractions are confined to the Old City area (Acre/Akka), whilst the transport connections are found in the New City (Akko). Akko's tiny railway station is located one block behind the bus station, with fairly regular services north to Nahariya and south to Haifa (continuing via Netanya to Tel Aviv). The Central Bus Station is on Ha-Arba'a, and offers more regular services both north- and southbound. For longer distances, it makes sense to go to Haifa and change (services are more frequent from here). Many services also run on Shabbat.

Getting around   The Old City is less than 15 mins walk from the main bus station in the new city. The Old City area is fairly small, making it pleasant to just wander around at will. Most people enter the Old City along Weizmann, beginning their tour at the el-Jazzar Mosque and Subterranean Crusader city. The subsequent sights below are listed in a more or less clockwise tour of the Old City, though the twisting lanes and culs-de-sac mean that some backtracking is inevitable. Visitors should note that substantial restoration work is in progress around the Subterranean Crusader city and the Citadel, and subsequently the entrances and exits to these sites may now have changed.

History

Though dominated by buildings from the Crusader, Late Arab and Ottoman periods, the ancient city of Akko (Acco) was established as a major coastal settlement as early as the beginning of the second millennium BCE. The original settlement was located on a mound to the east of the present city, referred to as **Tel Akko** (Tell el-Fukhar, or the Mound of Potsherds), although there is precious little to see at the site today.

Early history

Just about anybody who was anybody in history passed through Akko at some stage, including the **Egyptian** pharaohs, the **Israelites** (*Judges 1:31-33; II Samuel 24:7; I Kings 9:11-13*), the **Phoenicians** (who developed a major port city here), the **Assyrian** king Sennacherib, the **Greeks** (Alexander the Great founded a coin mint here in 332 BCE that was to remain in operation for almost 600 years), the **Seleucids** (who renamed it Antiochia Ptolemais), **and** the **Romans** (who annexed Akko in 63 BCE). Subsequent important visitors to Akko included **Julius Caesar** in 47 BCE, **King Herod** in 39 BCE (who began his process of legitimating the lands granted to him by the Romans from here), **Paul** (who passed through 'Ptolemais' on his third voyage; *Acts 21:7*), and finally the future emperor **Vespasian**, who used Akko as his base from which to suppress Galilee during the First Jewish War (66-73 CE). Akko continued to prosper under the Romans and under the subsequent **Byzantine empire** (324-638 CE).

With the arrival of the Arabs in 636 CE, the city reverted to its former name Akko, and saw its harbour facilities expand rapidly as it became the main port of the Umayyad capital at Damascus. The decline of Caesarea's harbour further south along the coast made Akko the key port in the Holy Land, and an obvious target for the sea-faring Crusaders. However, it was not until 1104, five years after the conquest of Jerusalem, that the Crusaders were able to take Akko. **Baldwin I** was assisted by the Genoese fleet in capturing Akko, with the key European maritime powers and city-states instrumental in the town's development (Genoese, Venetian, Amalfi and Pisan quarters all developed within the city). The various military-religious orders all established headquarters here, including the Order of the Knights of St John (Hospitallers), the Knights Templar, the Teutonic Knights and the Order of St Lazarus. The city was renamed after St Jean d'Acre and became known as **Acre**.

Arab and Crusader periods

Following the loss of Jerusalem, Acre briefly became the capital of the Latin kingdom in the Holy Land, though the Crusaders were obliged to surrender the city without a fight to **Salah al-Din** in 1187. The town was recaptured in 1191 by **Richard Coeur de Lion** and **Philip Augustus of France**, and restored to its position as the capital of the Latin Kingdom (the Crusaders being excluded from Jerusalem). **St Francis of Assisi** and **Marco Polo** both visited Acre.

However, disputes soon arose between the various merchant communities of Acre, and between the various military-religious orders. The Venetian and Genoese fleets even fought a sea battle off the coast of Acre in 1259, despite the fact that the invading Mongol army were at the city walls. The warring factions managed to unite long enough to repel the Mongols, and the Mamluks who attacked in 1265, but perhaps the writing was on the wall for the Crusader city. Despite the efforts of **Henry II of Cyprus** to unite the city under his claim to the throne in 1285, Acre's defences were ill prepared to repel the numerically superior forces of the Mamluk forces in 1291. Nevertheless, despite being out-numbered by ten to one, the Crusaders held the city for two months before it finally fell to the sultan **el-Malik el-Ashraf**. Though between 30,000 and 40,000 of the city's inhabitants managed to flee to Cyprus, the Mamluks took a bloody revenge on the remaining Christian population, who a year previously had slaughtered a large number of the city's Muslims. The town was razed, and left uninhabited for over 300 years.

Recent history It was the self-declared ruler of Galilee **Dahr el-Amr** who initiated the city's revival. Between 1750 and 1775, he substantially rebuilt the city's defences (what is now the city's inner wall), making Akko one of the key towns in the fiefdom that he carved out of the Ottoman empire. He was succeeded in 1775 by **Ahmed el-Jazzar** ('The Butcher'), who engineered his succession by mur-dering his predecessor! Restoration of the town continued, despite a brief interlude in 1799 in which the British fleet intervened on el-Jazzar's behalf and repelled **Napoleon's** attempts to conquer the city. El-Jazzar's building programme continued, and he is responsible for restoring much of the har-bour, and for building the Great Mosque and the Turkish baths.

Ibrahim Pasha took the city from the Turks in 1832 with his Egyptian army, though within eight years the British had pressurized him into retiring back to Egypt. The **British** themselves captured the city from the Turks in 1918, and continued to rule Akko throughout the Mandate period. The former Citadel was converted into a prison and used to house Jewish underground fighters (or 'terrorists', according to your viewpoint). Arab opposition to

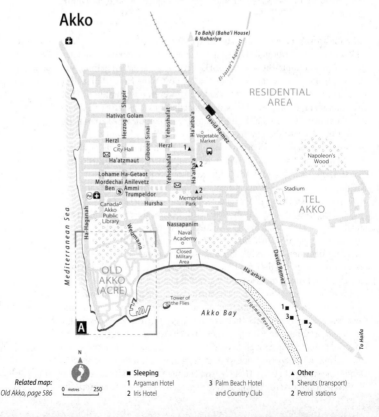

Akko

■ Sleeping
1 Argaman Hotel
2 Iris Hotel
3 Palm Beach Hotel and Country Club

▲ Other
1 Sheruts (transport)
2 Petrol stations

Zionism was vociferous locally, and the prison was also used to hold those involved in the Arab revolt of the 1930s. In May 1948 the **Israelis** captured the city.

Warning Though the people of Akko are generally friendly, there are numerous reports by foreign women of sexual harassment in and around the Old City. Despite generally just being verbal harassment, it is worth bearing this situation in mind whilst exploring the area, particularly after dark. The problem may be reduced by dressing modestly, though you may encounter a large number of idiots in the Old City who seem to exist solely to hassle foreigners.

Sights

The stout city walls surrounding Akko today, together with the deep fosse and counterscarp, were built mainly by el-Jazzar, following the defeat of Napoleon's forces in 1799. Very small portions of the original Crusader city walls can be seen on Weizmann as you approach the Old City. The city enclosed by the Crusader city walls was considerably larger than el-Jazzar's fortified town, and possibly extended as far north as Ben Ammi Street and as far east as the present Naval Academy. The 'Accursed Tower' of the Crusader city, from where Richard Coeur de Lion pulled down the banner of the Duke of Austria in 1191, probably stood near to where the Memorial Park is located today (see map).

City walls and gates

By climbing up the ramparts to the '**Land Wall Promenade**' behind the **Moat Garden** (see map), it is possible to walk along a section of the city walls. In the late afternoon this is a popular location for newly-weds to be photographed.

Occupying the former site of a Crusader church, the Ahmed el-Jazzar Mosque (or Great Mosque) is a fine example of Ottoman period building style. A short flight of steps leads into the mosque's pleasant courtyard, enhanced by palms, flower beds and shady trees. Many of the columns in the courtyard were 'recycled' from Caesarea. The arcade around three sides of the courtyard opens on to small rooms used to accommodate pilgrims and religious students. To the right of the mosque is a simple domed mausoleum containing the sarcophagi of Ahmed el-Jazzar (died 1804) and his adopted son and successor, Suleiman (died 1819).

Ahmed el-Jazzar Mosque/Great Mosque

To the east side of the courtyard is the entrance to an underground reservoir. The mosque is built on the quarter of the city occupied in the Crusader period by the Order of the Knights of St John (Hospitallers), and it is believed that this structure was part of the original Crusader church of St John. When el-Jazzar built the mosque in 1781, he turned the former church into an emergency water cistern and reservoir. Water was supplied from the Pasha Gardens via ceramic pipes, and from rainfall, and was integrated within the city's main water supply system. It still fills with rain water. A lighted walkway has been built around the cistern.

In front of the entrance to the mosque is the ritual ablutions fountain, resembling an elegant pavilion with a green copper roof supported by slim columns. The interior of the mosque is fairly simple, with a plain white dome supported by brown, black and white stone decorated with verses from the Qu'ran on a blue background. Galleries on three sides above the main prayer floor are reserved for women. ■ *Daily 0800-1230, 1330-1600, 1645-1830, though closed during prayers. 4 NIS. Remove shoes before entering, and wear modest dress (though the doorkeeper may provide you with additional coverings if he feels that*

Haifa & the North Coast

your dress is not modest enough). Guides may offer their services though they are highly variable in ability.

Subterranean Crusader city The moniker of 'subterranean' or 'underground' to describe this part of the former Crusader city is something of a misnomer; what was street level during the 12th and 13th centuries is now up to eight metres below the present surface level. Successive occupiers of the site simply found it easier to fill in the Crusader halls with rock and earth filler, and build over them. Now that these 'subterranean' structures have been largely excavated, the fact that much of the site still remains underground makes it even more interesting to visit.

NB Plans are underway to double the area currently open to the public, and to introduce all sorts of interactive displays and exhibitions. Thus, the whole complex may have changed considerably from the description here, including the location of entrances and exits. It is certainly worth picking up the 'easyguide' (pre-recorded tour description played through headphones) at the entrance.

Old Akko / Acre

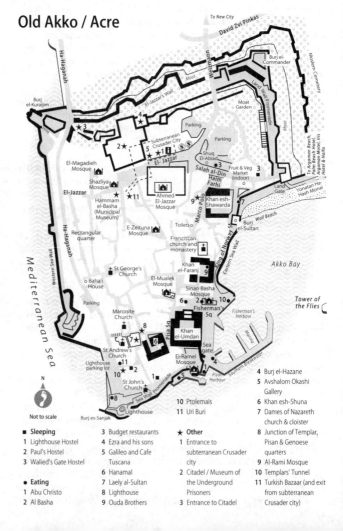

■ Sleeping
1 Lighthouse Hostel
2 Paul's Hostel
3 Walied's Gate Hostel

● Eating
1 Abu Christo
2 Al Basha

3 Budget restaurants
4 Ezra and his sons
5 Galileo and Cafe Tuscana
6 Hanamal
7 Laely al-Sultan
8 Lighthouse
9 Ouda Brothers

10 Ptolemais
11 Uri Buri

★ Other
1 Entrance to subterranean Crusader city
2 Citadel / Museum of the Underground Prisoners
3 Entrance to Citadel

4 Burj el-Hazane
5 Avshalom Okashi Gallery
6 Khan esh-Shuna
7 Dames of Nazareth church & cloister
8 Junction of Templar, Pisan & Genoese quarters
9 Al-Rami Mosque
10 Templars' Tunnel
11 Turkish Bazaar (and exit from subterranean Crusader city)

Haifa & the North Coast

Tour of the complex: The current entrance to the Subterranean Crusader city is diagonally opposite the el-Jazzar Mosque. The **entrance hall (1)** is supported by a number of massive columns, though what you see here dates to two distinct periods. The lower section of the hall is part of the original Crusader structure, whilst the upper parts are an Ottoman period addition. Crusader embellishments include carved fleurs-de-lis, whilst Turkish decorations tend towards the abstract. The entrance hall contains the ticket office and the desk where you pick up your 'easyguide'.

Descending some steps you pass into an **intermediate hall (2)**. The upper arches of the Crusader columns protrude from the floor, suggesting that the original Crusader level is some four metres or so below the current one. The printed visitor's guide to the complex makes much of the fact that an illegal wine-press was operated by Muslims in this hall during the Ottoman prohibition.

As you pass from the intermediate hall into the **courtyard (3)**, the Citadel built by Dahr el-Amr and el-Jazzar looms up above you. Substantial restoration work is currently underway in this area, as attempts are made to excavate the Crusader city further without disrupting the foundations of the Citadel.

The entrance to the fortress of the Order of the Knights of St John (Hospitallers), and the Knights' Halls, is through a large **Ottoman Gate**. The original Crusader gate is probably located some metres below the surface. It is said that the Turkish rulers used to hang the condemned from the main beam of this gateway. The **Knights' Halls (4)** is a series of seven barrel-vaulted chambers, though only four have been fully excavated for fear of undermining the Citadel built directly above them. Their exact function is unclear, though it is generally suggested that the seven chambers reflect the seven 'tongues', or national groups, that comprised the Order of the Knights of St John (Auvergne, England, France, Germany, Italy, Provence, Spain). The halls have been used recently for theatre and concert performances, and are now air-conditioned!

An interesting story relates to the patch of modern concrete that is still visible in the ceiling of one of the chambers. During a jailbreak from the British-run prison in the Citadel, a number of prisoners tunnelled out through the floor of their cells. To their surprise, they emerged into these rubble-strewn halls. However, the rubble fill was so dense, they could make no further progress, and were forced to return to their cells. Their escape tunnel was only discovered when the halls were being excavated, and has only recently been filled by the concrete patch that you see.

At the time of going to press, the route of the tour emerges from the most westerly of the excavated Knights' Halls into the **Citadel courtyard (9)**, since it is currently not possible to visit the complex of halls known as the **Grand Maneir (5)**. It is thought that this was the administrative centre of the city, though it has also been identified as a dormitory for the soldier-monks of the Order. This area is only partially excavated, and it is hoped that more light will be thrown on the complex's function some time in the near future. What is clear, however, is that the principal architectural style is very different to that of the Knights' Halls. This suggests that the Grand Maneir was built during a different period, with the vaults of the Knights' Halls probably dating to the Ottoman period.

From the Citadel courtyard the current route descends down into the **Refectory (6)**, often erroneously referred to as 'The Crypt'. The most impressive of all the halls thus far excavated, the refectory is built two metres above the bedrock, possibly on the remains of a Hellenistic-Roman structure. Two carved fleurs-de-lis, one in the northeast corner and one in the southeast corner, suggest that the hall was built around 1148, when Louis VII (leader of the

Second Crusade) established the lily as the emblem of the French kingdom. The architectural style of the refectory is interesting, marking a transition from Romanesque to Gothic. The Crusader's stone-masons cut the stone on the spot, evidenced by the discovery of a quarry on the west side of the refectory. As its name suggests, the refectory was used as a grand dining room and guest hall, though the suggestion that Marco Polo was entertained here is pure conjecture.

Some 350 metres of underground passages have so far been excavated, some leading north to the city walls, others leading south towards the port. A section of the **underground passageway (7)** has been lit, and leads to the final section of the tour. The exact function of the 'secret tunnel' is unclear. Some speculate that it was part of an elaborate Crusader sewerage system, though it was probably intended as part of a secret escape route; that's certainly what el-Jazzar had in mind when Napoleon was attacking the city.

The underground passage opens into the **el-Bosta (8)**, sometimes referred to as 'The Post'. The el-Bosta comprises a series of six parallel halls opening on to a courtyard, and is probably part of a large khan (caravanserai) dating to the Fatimid period (11th-12th century). During the Crusader period the el-Bosta was probably used as an infirmary by the Order of the Knights of St John (hence 'Hospitallers'), and is shown as such on Marino Sanuto's map. (**NB** The terms 'el-Bosta' and 'The Post' derive from the French 'Poste' referring to a 'guard' or 'position', and have nothing to do with the Turkish post-office.)

Displayed in the el-Bosta is a Crusader tombstone dated 1290, and a carved

Subterranean Crusader City

Not to scale

≡ Staircase

a Ticket office
b 'Easyguide'
c Toilets
1 Entrance Hall
2 Intermediate Hall
3 Courtyard
4 Knights' Halls

5 Grand Maneir
6 Refectory
7 Underground
   passageway
8 el-Bosta
9 Citadel courtyard

walkway

Entrance

Exit

marble tablet with a Latin text that was found nearby. It reads: "In the year 1242 after the incarnation of our lord, the XVII of October, past [*sic*] away brother Pierre de Vieille Brioude, 8th Grand Master of the Hospitallers, after the capture of the Holy Land. Let his soul remain in peace, Amen. In his time, the Duc of Montfort and other French Barons were released from Egyptian captivity, and Richard Duc of Cornwall re-erected the fortress of Ascalon."

At present, the tour finishes here, though the exit may move as the complex is further developed. **NB** The current exit from the Subterranean Crusader city is some distance away from the current entrance (in the heart of the Old City, close to E-Zeituna Mosque: see map). ■ *T9911764. Sunday-Thursday 0800-1700, Friday 0800-1400, Saturday 0900-1800. Adult 15 NIS, student 12 NIS. Map 3 NIS, film shows for groups over 15, or at 1100 1400 1600, tours available in English, French, German, Spanish. Same entrance ticket covers Turkish baths. It is worth taking the 'easyguide' machine that describes the route through a pair of headphones (there are currently no written descriptions).*

Hammam el-Basha (Turkish bath)

Constructed by el-Jazzar in the style of a Cairo public baths, the Hammam el-Basha previously housed the **Municipal Museum**. The artefacts held here, displaying aspects of the last 2,000 years of Akko's history, are apparently now in storage, awaiting a new permanent site within the revamped Subterranean Crusader city complex.

However, the Hammam el-Basha is still worth a visit since it has been restored as … an 18th-century Cairo public baths. The 'cold room', 'luke-warm room' and 'steam room' are elegantly presented, with original platforms and ablutions fountains in place. ■ *Admission on same ticket as Subterranean Crusader city.*

Citadel/Museum of the Underground Prisoners

Built initially upon the foundations of the Crusader city by Dahr el-Amr, and added to by his successor el-Jazzar in the late 18th century, the Citadel at Akko has had an interesting and varied history. It is perhaps a good place to begin a tour of the city since the 40-metre-high Burj el-Hazane (Tower of the Treasury) provides the best possible view of 'Old Akko'.

The Ottoman rulers of Akko simultaneously used the Citadel as a residential palace, a barracks, an armoury and as a prison. Amongst the political prisoners held with the common criminals was **Baha'ullah**, the founder of the Baha'i faith (see page 595).

The British also made use of the jail facilities, eventually developing it into the largest prison in Palestine. Amongst the first Jewish prisoners held here was Ze'ev Jabotinsky, in 1920, who later went on to found the Irgun 'terrorist/freedom fighters' organization. At its peak, the prison was holding political prisoners from both the Jewish and Arab communities, common criminals from both communities, and clandestine Jewish immigrants who had been captured by the British. On 4th May, 1947, the prison was the scene of a spectacular prison breakout that saw 41 Jewish and 214 Arab detainees initially escape. The breakout featured prominently in Leon Uris' book *Exodus* (with the film scene shot on location here).

Tour of the museum The current route of the tour around the museum begins at the British-built bridge at the entrance to the fortress. A staircase descends to the moat, from where you make your way along the base of the Citadel's walls. The large blocks at the base are Crusader foundations, whilst the smaller blocks date to the fortress's 18th-century construction.

An iron staircase ascends into the museum, located in the Burj el-Hazane (Tower of the Treasury). The first floor exhibitions trace the chronology of

Haifa & the North Coast

events in Akko's history. The second floor exhibits give an idea of conditions inside the British Mandate prison. Apparently, the hospital had two types of medicine; quinine was used to lower temperatures, whilst 'shorba' was used to treat all other illness!

Emerging on to the roof of the tower, there are spectacular views not just of the Old City, but of the whole surrounding area. Clearly visible in the distance are Haifa's leading landmarks, the Dagon grain silo, the Dan Panorama Hotel and the Eshkol Tower.

Exiting through the west gate of the tower, the tour heads towards the northwest wing of the Citadel. (**NB** This route may be disrupted by current excavations in the Subterranean Crusader city: follow the sign-posts.) The northwest wing houses a number of interesting items, including a room dedicated to the 1947 prison breakout; maps, a model and newspaper cuttings attempt to recreate the event. The northwest part of the prison courtyard houses the cells where Jabotinsky and Baha'ullah were held, the latter becoming a place of pilgrimage for Baha'is. It is also possible to visit the gallows where a number of Jewish prisoners were executed. ■ *T9918264. Sunday-Thursday 0900-1600, Friday 0900-1300. Adult 8 NIS, Student 4 NIS. Parts of museum are currently closed whilst excavations are underway. Current entrance is opposite the Burj el-Kuraijim.*

Avshalom Okashi Gallery
This gallery displays the work of the Jewish abstract painter Avshalom Okashi (1916-1980). He was a resident of Old Akko from 1948 until his death, and many of his paintings feature scenes from the city. ■ *Sunday-Thursday 0830-1600, Friday 0830-1400, Saturday 0900-1630. 5 NIS.*

The following tour of Akko follows a more or less clockwise route around the Old City, beginning from the el-Jazzar Mosque and Subterranean Crusader city.

Shuq el-Abiad
Built by Dahr el-Amr in the mid- to late 18th century, this low arcade stands at the entrance to the main bazaar. Today, the Shuq el-Abiad (White Market) houses a number of cheap foodstalls.

Land Gate
Though now standing as the eastern entrance to el-Jazzar's fortified city, it should be remembered that the original Crusader walls extended considerably further east, possibly as far as the Naval Academy. However, until the breach in the wall was made to accommodate Weizmann Street in 1910, this gate provided the only land access to the fortified town.

Khan esh-Shawarda
Built on the site of the Franciscan Convent of St Clare, whose nuns are said to have preferred suicide to dishonour when Acre fell to the Mamluks in 1291, only parts of the Khan esh-Shawarda (Merchants' Inn) remain today. It is also believed that, in Crusader times, an inner anchorage penetrated the city here, perhaps related to the fact that the arsenal was located here.

Burj el-Sultan
The Burj el-Sultan (Sultan's Tower) is the last Crusader city tower that still stands to its full height. The tower is shown on Marino Sanuto's map of the Crusader city as being at the edge of the Venetian Quarter, and, until its incorporation into the 18th-century Turkish sea-wall, it was enclosed by water on three sides. Inside the tower is a guardroom and a subterranean dungeon.

Khan el-Faranj
Directly to the south of the 18th-century **Franciscan church and monastery** is the Khan el-Faranj, or 'Inn of the Franks'. This was initially the heart of the

Venetian Quarter during the Crusader period, though European ('Franks') traders established themselves on this site at the beginning of the Ottoman period (1516). The caravanserai (khan) was built by the Druze emir Fakhr ed-Din around 1600 and, as such, is the oldest khan in Akko.

Khan el-Umdan

Old Akko's best preserved caravanserai, Khan el-Umdan (Khan of the Pillars), was built by el-Jazzar in 1785 on the site of a former Crusader period Dominican order monastery. It takes its name from the splendid row of granite and porphyry columns that el-Jazzar 'recycled' from Caesarea. The tall clock-tower above was built in 1906 to mark the 30th year of the rule of the Ottoman Sultan, Abdul Hamid II. A similar clock-tower in Jaffa marks the same event.

Fisherman's Harbour and Marina

Since Persian times at least (586-332 BCE), Akko's ancient harbour has been located where the Fisherman's Harbour and Marina now lie. During dredging work on the harbour in 1983, ancient cargo from two boats sunk in the fourth

Citadel / Former British Prison, Akko

Haifa & the North Coast

Not to scale — - - - Route taken by escapees

A Points where wall was breached from outside
B Points where armoured doors where broken by prisoners inside
C Place where diversionary fire was set
D Turkish bathhouse
E Gathering points for escaping prisoners
F Prison workshop
G Sewing & shoe repair workshop
H Warehouses
K Prisoners' reception room
L Ze'ev Jabotinsky's cell
M Cells of prisoners condemned to death
N Gallows
O Memorial hall to executed prisoners
P Solitary confinement cells
1 Guardhouse block
2 Moat
3 British era bridge (& current entrance)
4 Prisoner governor
5 Burj el-Hazane (Tower of the Treasury)
6 Shower block
7 Prison courtyard
8 Arab prisoners' block
9 Jewish prisoners' block
10 Current ticket office

or fifth century BCE and the first century CE respectively, was discovered. The foundations of the southern breakwater in use today were probably laid during the late sixth or early fifth centuries BCE, though the Romans raised its height, perhaps reflecting a change in sea-level.

The Tower of the Flies   The Tower of the Flies stands on an artificially created island 70 metres east of the tip of the breakwater. Its function is unknown, though it may have served as 'a kind of emporium or free port for foreign trading vessels' (Raban, 1993). During early Arab rule, a 400-metre-long eastern breakwater probably connected the Tower of the Flies to the shore to the north (near to the Naval Academy). The Crusaders also made alterations to the harbour plan, again perhaps reflecting a considerable drop in sea-level (possibly 1.5 metres). There may well have been an inner basin, possibly an anchorage for the Genoese fleet, as well as the separate anchorage that the Pisans built (see page 592).

Dhar el-Amr and Ahmed el-Jazzar both substantially repaired the harbour, the latter again 'recycling' marble and porphyry columns from Caesarea.

Today, the harbour is filled with fishing boats and pleasure craft, with a number of attractive seafood restaurants lining the quay.

Sea Gate   This gate, which dates to the Crusader period, is thought to stand at the point where a nine-metre-wide channel used to extend from the Crusader harbour in to what may have been an inner basin used by the Genoese.

Pisan Harbour   This inner anchorage, though outside the main harbour, was created by the Pisans on the site of the former western anchorage of the Phoenician port. It allowed small vessels to sail up to the commercial centre of the Pisan Quarter around the Khan esh-Shuna. A couple of restaurants now sit on the quay of the Pisan harbour.

Khan esh-Shuna   Formerly the 'Inn of the Pisans', the Khan esh-Shuna is now used as a workshop area. Just to its north is the former site of a Templar tower that controlled the **junction** of the Templar, Pisan and Genoese quarters.

Sea wall promenade   At the southern tip of the mini peninsula on which Akko stands, it is possible to take a short walk along the ramparts. At the centre of the sea wall promenade is **St John's Church**, built by the Franciscans in 1737. Marino Sanuto's map of Crusader Acre suggests that this was formerly the site of the Crusader church of St Andrew. The **Lighthouse** is thought to mark the former site of the Burj es-Sanjak (Flag Tower) Crusader tower.

The section of 18th-century sea wall to the north of the lighthouse was destroyed in an earthquake in 1837. This whole area, now the 'lighthouse parking lot', was formerly occupied by the Templars' fortress. Renowned for its beauty as much as for its strength, it was destroyed by the Mamluks following the Crusader departure in 1291 to ensure that the Christians would not return. No trace remains today.

Western section of Old Akko   The western section of Old Akko has a number of interesting features, most notably the Crusader street plan. Continuing north from the lighthouse, take the steps to your right opposite the viewpoint to the north of the 'lighthouse parking lot'. Located here is the **Dames of Nazareth Church and Cloister** and a **Maronite Church**, though the former is generally closed up and the latter looks as if someone is living in it. Behind these buildings is the former **junction** of the Templar, Pisan and Genoese quarters. The narrow street that heads north from here has a number of interesting Crusader houses to the left.

The street leads to Genoa Square, where the fortified gate at the entrance to the Genoese Quarter used to stand. On the west (sea) side of the square, at the junction of HaHaganah, is the **Baha'i House** where Baha'ullah spent twelve years of his exile. The large house – identifiable by its whitewashed walls, blue doors and frames, and red tiled roof – is not open to the public.

At the east side of the square is the Greek Orthodox **St George's Church**. Built on medieval foundations, the church is usually dated to the 17th century, though the carving over the door lintel of St George slaying what appears to be people, as opposed to a dragon, is dated 1845. Behind the church a tablet bears dedications to a number of British officers who fell in action here.

The two small streets lead north from behind the Baha'i House into the so-called 'Rectangular quarter'. Much of the original Crusader street pattern is retained, with houses set forward every 50 metres or so in order to make the city more defensible. Likewise, the sharp turns at the north and south ends of the street prevent the enemy from having a clear line of fire. The street to the east (right) was a 'neutral street', dividing the Genoese quarter from the area controlled by the Dominicans. It has Crusader buildings on both sides, though the lower storeys to the west are the best preserved.

There are several beaches around Akko, though none is particularly nice and foreign women often receive a fair amount of unwanted attention. **Wall Beach** next to the Land Gate is for watersports only and bathing is forbidden. **Argaman** or **Purple Beach** is to the east, where the *Argaman Motel* and *Palm Beach Hotel and Country Club* are located. It's about a 15- to 20-minute walk from the Land Gate. There are much nicer beaches along Israel's northern Mediterranean coast than here.

Beaches

Essentials

A *Palm Beach Hotel and Country Club*, Argaman Beach, T9815815, F9910434. Excellent facilities include pool, indoor pool, Jacuzzi, health club, tennis, squash, volleyball, basketball, nightclub, beach access, plus very comfortable rooms.

Sleeping
■ *on map;*
price codes see inside
front cover

B *Argaman Motel*, Argaman Beach, T9916691, F9916690. On the beach, modern rooms most with private balconies, a/c, TV, restaurant, but poor value when compared with *Palm Beach Hotel*. B *Iris*, Argaman Beach, on road to Haifa, T9916190, F9911734. Newly built hotel close to beach, 25 a/c rooms, TV, radio, phone, terrace restaurant.

F-G *Lighthouse Hostel*, 11/175 HaHagana, T9911982, F9815530. Formerly the *IYHA Youth Hostel*, this is probably one of the best deals in Israel. Now run as a private hostel by the same friendly family that own *Walied's Gate Hostel*, this former Ottoman period mansion features spacious high-ceilinged rooms with plenty of light and ventilation – the sitting area is particularly charming. Dorms are spacious and not overcrowded, with 4-10 beds, single-sex or mixed, plus a number of private rooms (**D-E**). Free use of kitchen, pleasant dining hall, clean toilets and showers, free pick-up from station possible, tours, bicycle rental. Very friendly, excellent value. Recommended. **F-G** *Walied's Gate Hostel*, Salah al-Din, near Land Gate, T9910410, F9815530. For some reason 2 other guidebooks really slag this place off, though it's hard to see why. Run by a very friendly family, we've had nothing but praise for this hostel from readers. The cheap mixed and single-sex dorms are currently being refurbished, and there are now some very cheap private rooms with shared bathrooms (**E**), plus 6 nice large modern doubles with a/c, attached bath (**D**). Free use of kitchen, roof terrace, tours to the Golan (including Safed, Nimrod Castle, Mt Hermon etc, 150 NIS) and to Rosh Ha-Nikra (40 NIS). Recommended.

Haifa & the North Coast

G *Paul's Hostel*, T9912857. Up alleyway beside *Uri Buri* restaurant (ask for owner at nearby shop). It's hard to see why other guidebooks recommend this place since it's just everybody dumped together in one cavernous room. If you want a private room (**D**) the owner and his wife will shift out of their room! Not good value.

Eating   **Budget** There are numerous falafel and shwarma stands on Salah al-Din, near to the el-Jazzar Mosque. Some good value meals (hummus, pita, etc) can be had in the friendly restaurants opposite Haim Farhi Sq, near to *Walied's Gate Hostel* (see map). A cheap fruit and veg market is diagonally opposite *Walied's Gate Hostel*, with a small supermarket further along.

Fast food/chain For coffee, pizza, fast food and people-watching, try the pedestrianized section of Ben Ammi, in the new city.

Mixed menus *Ezra and his sons*, Fisherman's Harbour. Usual 'catch of the day' and selections from the grill. *HaNamal*, Fisherman's Square. Simple good value food, omlette and chips 15 NIS, hummus 10 NIS, steak or fish and chips 40 NIS. *Lighthouse*, HaHagana, T9917640. Formerly the site of *Migdal Or*, pleasantly situated terrace, choice of fish, lamb, salads, Middle Eastern dishes, main courses 30-70 NIS. *Ouda Brothers*, Khan el-Faranj, T9912013. Middle Eastern salads, shashliks and hummus are specialities here in this friendly dining hall, main courses 25-65 NIS.

Seafood *Abu Christo*, Pisan Harbour, T9910065. An Akko institution, charming location on the quay, excellent selection from the daily catch, main dishes 40-75 NIS, wine 50-120 NIS, reservations recommended. Recommended. *Galileo & Café Tuscana*, Pisan Harbour, T9914610. Bar/café upstairs and good fish restaurant downstairs (right on the water's edge), main fish dishes from 50 NIS. *Ptolemais*, Fisherman's Harbour, T9916112. Another good location, fish heavily featured, grills also available 35-40 NIS. *Uri Buri*, near to the lighthouse. Fish restaurant, but not as well placed as others.

Sports Though primarily for use by residents, there are a number of sports facilities available at the Palm Beach Hotel and Country Club (see 'Sleeping' on page 593). **Boating** *TELM Ltd/Venus Tour Boat*, Acre Marina, T9724667. Boat hire for fishing, diving, cruises. Short boat tours are also available from Fisherman's Harbour (about 15 NIS for 30 mins). **Diving** *Ramy's Diving Centre*, Fisherman's Harbour, T9918990. **Fishing** There is a fishing tackle shop close to El-Mualek Mosque (see map).

Transport **Buses** Akko's small Central Bus Station is on Ha-Arba'a (T9916333). Southbound, there are buses every 15 mins or so to **Haifa** (13 NIS, 45 mins). Buses 270/272 are express services whilst 251/261/271 stop at all points along the way. For destinations further south change at Haifa. Northbound, Buses 270/272 go direct to **Nahariya** (8 NIS, 30 mins), whilst local (*me'asef*) Buses 251/271 stop *en route* at **Bahji** and **Beit Lohamei Ha-Geta'ot**. There are also less regular buses from Akko to **Karmi'el**, **Safed** and **Tiberias**.

Sherut/service taxi The main sherut stand for services to **Haifa**, **Nahariya** and sometimes **Safed** is opposite the bus station (including Shabbat).

Train Akko's tiny train station is one block behind the bus station (T9549555). **Nahariya**: Sunday-Thursday 10 trains per day, 0550-1900, Friday 4 per day 0630-1330, Saturday no service, 15 mins. **Haifa**: Sunday-Thursday 10 trains per day, 0600-1830, Friday 5 per day, 0600-1430, Saturday no service, 40 mins. All trains south to Haifa continue on to **Netanya** and **Tel Aviv**.

Directory

Banks Most of the banks (with ATM machines also) are located along Weizmann and Ben Ammi. Beware of poor rates/high commission charges at banks near the el-Jazzar Mosque. Post offices offer good value foreign exchange. **Communications** Phone code: T04. **Post offices**: the main post office is at 11 Ha'Atzma'ut, and offers **post restante**, **foreign exchange** and international **phone calls** (Sun, Tue, Thu 0800-1230 1600-1800, Mon, Wed 0800-1400, Fri 0830-1230, Sat closed). There are branch offices on Ben Ammi and inside the 'Subterranean Crusader City'. **Hospitals and medical services** Chemists: several on Ben Ammi. **Hospitals**: the main hospital is north of the New City (see map), though there is a first-aid post at the junction of Ben Ammi and HaHaganah (T9912333). **Libraries** *Canadian-Akko Public Library*, 13 Weizmann, T9910860. Sun-Thu 0900-1200 1500-1900. **Tourist offices** Limited information, as well as a worthwhile 5 NIS map of Akko, is available from the small Tourist Information Office by the entrance to the 'Subterranean Crusader City' (T9910251). **Useful addresses and phone numbers** Police: 16 HaHaganah, T9910244 (or T100). Ambulance: Magen David Adom T9912333 (or T101). **Fire**: T9912222 (or T102). **Akko Municipality**: T9910250.

Yodfat (Jotapata)

Though little remains to see today, this is the former location of Jotapata, site of a key battle in the First Jewish Revolt (66-73 CE), and scene of one of the historian **Josephus**' greatest moments (in his eyes at least). This is one of those sites in Israel where it really pays to stand with a copy of Josephus' *The Jewish War* in your hand, and read the relevant passages of text (III, 158; III, 383).

Ins and outs

Yodfat is located a little over 20km southeast of Akko. You really need your own transport to reach the site. Take Route 85 and head east from Akko. Turn right at Akhihud Junction (about 8km) and then left at Yavor Junction (3km) on to Route 805. Continue for around 9km, then turn left at the sign for Yodfat.

Jotapata

Jotapata was perhaps the strongest of the fortified Galilean villages controlled by Josephus, prior to his switch of allegiance to the Romans. Such was the strength of Jotapata that it took 47 days of bitter fighting before the Romans finally overran the town. Josephus estimates that 40,000 were killed in the battle, with many of the defenders preferring suicide to surrender.

Josephus himself managed to escape this grisly end, hiding in a cave with some 40 others. Against Josephus' wishes, his 40 companions entered a suicide pact, rather than submit to the Romans. In an excellent passage that sums up the author, Josephus describes how lots were drawn to establish who would kill whom (so that nobody would have to die by their own hand). Miraculously, by 'divine providence', it was Josephus who was left as last man alive! It is interesting to note that an early Slavonic translation dispels this notion of 'divine providence' interceding on Josephus' behalf. Referring to the lottery, it says of Josephus, "he counted the numbers cunningly and so managed to deceive the others"!

Bahji

To the east of the Akko–Nahariya road, about three kilometres north of Akko, is Bahji, holiest pilgrimage site to followers of the Baha'i faith. **Baha'ullah**, founder of the religion, lived here under house arrest in the red-tile roofed **Bahji House** following his release from Akko prison. He died here in 1892 and is buried in a small shrine in the beautiful **Persian Gardens**. Laid out in the 1950s, these fabulous gardens are open daily to the public. For more information on the Baha'i faith, see page 567. ■ *T04-9811569. Shrine open Sunday, Monday, Friday, Saturday 0900-1200; Persian Gardens open daily 0900-1600. Free. Take the 271 local (me'asef) bus between Akko and Nahariya. Don't take 270/272 because they won't stop. NB Main entrance gate is for Baha'is only: other visitors must enter through the side gate 500 metres beyond the military base. This is a holy religious shrine and visitors must be modestly dressed.*

Accommodation can be found nearby at the **B-C** *Shomrat Country Lodging*, Kibbutz Shomrat, DN Asherat, 25218, T04-9854897, F9854828. There are spacious, well-furnished air-conditioned rooms – including two that are equipped for disabled people – with kitchenette and TV. There is also a pool, mini zoo and playground and pleasant gardens. Food is available in the kibbutz dining hall. Recommended.

Beit Lohamei Ha-Geta'ot and El-Jazzar's aqueduct
Several kilometres north of Bahji is the kibbutz of Lohamei Ha-Geta'ot (Hebrew for 'fighters of the ghetto'), founded in 1949 by survivors of the Nazi Holocaust. A small museum has been set up to commemorate those who died in the camps and ghettoes. The museum contains the booth in which Adolf Eichmann sat during his 1961 trial in Jerusalem. ■ *T04-9958080. Sunday-Thursday 0900-1600, Friday 0900-1300, Saturday 1000-1700. Free but donations accepted.*

Standing just to the south of the museum is a superbly preserved section of **Ahmed el-Jazzar's aqueduct**, built in 1780 to supply Akko with water from the Kabri spring to the north. Large sections of the aqueduct can be seen almost the whole way from Akko to Nahariya.

North and inland of Akko

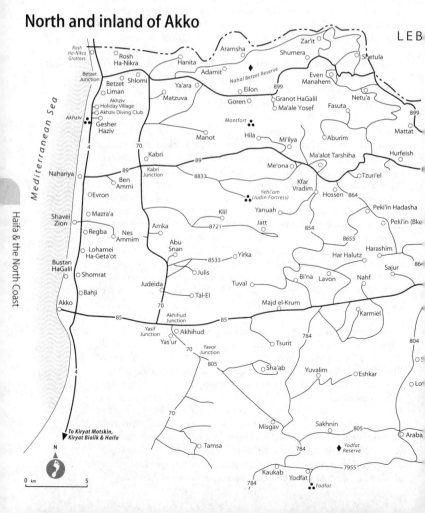

The kibbutz offers B&B accommodation in its **B-C** *Bait ve Kait Country Lodging*. Rooms have air-conditioning, phone and TV; facilities include a pool, tennis and basketball in a tranquil atmosphere. ■ *T04-9933271, F9933218. Take the 271 local (me'asef) bus between Akko and Nahariya. Don't take 270/272 because they won't stop.*

Shavei Zion

This settlement has a beautiful setting, amongst orange groves and avocado orchards, fronting on to an uncrowded stretch of Mediterranean beach (fee paying). This part of the coastline has been a rich hunting ground for marine archaeologists, with the wreck of a fifth century CE ship off the coast of Shavei Zion giving up an interesting cargo.

In 1955 a **Byzantine church** was discovered amongst the groves of Shavei Zion, complete with an extensive **mosaic pavement**. The designs are reasonably simple, featuring crosses, pomegranates and fish, though they are quite well executed. A ten-line Greek inscription in the *narthex* (antechamber to the nave) mentions the name of the donor, and the date 485-486 CE. ■ *Seven kilometres north of Akko; couple of trains daily to and from* **Nahariya**, **Haifa** *and on to* **Tel Aviv**. *Bus 271 (local bus, me'asef) stops at the turning for Shavei Zion, from where it's a short walk. Accommodation available at the* **B-C** *Beit Hava Hotel, Shavei Zion, T04-9820391, F9820519.*

Nes Ammin

This Christian kibbutz was founded in the 1960s with the twin aims of Jewish-Christian reconciliation, and to show Christian support for the State of Israel. Visitors are welcomed (call in advance), or you can stay in the tranquil rural setting of the (**B-C**) guesthouse. ■ *DN Asherat, 25225, T04-9950000, F9950098. Beautiful setting, doubles with air-conditioning and phone, plus 2- and 3-bed apartments, pool, cycles for hire, children's playground and kindergarten, and conference facilities.*

Nahariya

There are few reminders of Nahariya's ancient past (the biblical Helbah/Heleph), with the modern town presenting itself as a laid-back beach resort that is a popular destination for honeymooning Israeli couples. It's a pleasant enough place, although the beach isn't quite nice enough, nor the range of accommodation quite broad enough, to make it a really outstanding holiday spot.

Phone code: 04
Colour map 1, grid B2

Haifa & the North Coast

Ins and outs

Getting there and around

The whole town is compact enough to get around on foot. The train station is at the eastern end of the main road, Ha Ga'Aton, with all trains running to Akko, Haifa, Netanya and Tel Aviv. The Central Bus Station, also on Ha Ga'Aton, has regular connections to Akko and Haifa, and is also the transport hub for excursion to Akhziv, Montfort, Peki'in, Rosh Ha-Nikra and Yehi'am.

History

Nahariya's Canaanite origins, plus its Persian/Hellenistic remains, are largely buried beneath the modern town, and there are few remains from its Roman and Byzantine periods. The modern town takes its name from the Nahal Ga'Aton (river) that still flows along the centre of the main street (Ha Ga'Aton).

The town was the first Jewish settlement in Western Galilee, and was founded in 1933 by German Jews fleeing Hitler. Attempts at agriculture were not particularly successful and thus, taking advantage of Nahariya's clean beaches and rural setting, the idea was born of turning the town into a tourist resort. The rest, as they say, is history, though the tourism industry was hit badly in the 1970s and early 1980s when the town became the occasional target for Katyusha rockets fired from inside Lebanon. Tourism now forms a major sector of the town's economy, though the role of light industry (employing 45 percent of the population) is probably more important. About 35,000 people now live in Nahariya.

Sights

Beaches on northern coast Nahariya's prime attraction is its beaches, though it must be said there are better beaches on Israel's northern coast. The main strip of sand, **Galei Galil**

Nahariya

■ Sleeping	'Rooms for rent'	16 Motel Ariela	6 Maxim's	13 Big John Bar
1 Astar	8 Beit Amigo	17 Motel Charley	7 McDonald's	
2 Carlton	9 Beit Goldfarb		8 Mister Pizza,	▲ Other
3 Erna	10 Beit Gaviazda	● Eating	Burger Beach	1 Supermarket
4 Frank	11 Beit Milgram	1 Abu Bulus	9 Pacific	2 Dentist
5 Kalman	12 Beit Reiss	2 Cafe Misha	10 Pinguin, El	3 Steimatzky
6 Panorama	13 Beit Rotman	3 Domino Pizza	Pancho	(bookshop)
7 Rosenblatt	14 Beit Sarah	4 Golden River	11 Pizza Mario	
	15 Beit Sirtash	5 Kapulsky	12 Singapore	

Beach, has showers, an occasional life-guard and a breakwater just off shore, but the sand is not particularly nice and the other facilities such as the outdoor pool and kids' playground are looking a bit run down (15 NIS). A new indoor pool here has recently been completed (0600-2200 daily, 30 NIS). Free beaches north and south of Galei Galil, but take care in the heavy surf.

The scant remains of a Canaanite temple and *bamah* (cultic high place or altar platform) are located 20 minutes walk north of Galei Galil Beach. Most remains date to the Middle Bronze Age IIB (1750-1550 BCE), though some are older. When the earlier temple fell into disuse, the *bamah* was constructed, with offerings brought to honour the goddess of the sea, Asherah. A second temple was then erected to the north of the *bamah*. There is little to see today, though some artefacts from the site are displayed in the Municipal Museum.

Canaanite temple

This small museum has four themes: 'archaeology of Western Galilee', 'art', 'malacology' and 'history of Nahariya', with the collection of sea-shells (malacology) and artefacts from the surrounding area (archaeology) being the most interesting exhibits. ■ *fifth/sixth/seventh floors, Municipality Building, Ha Ga'Aton, T9879863. Sunday-Thursday 1000-1200, Sunday and Wednesday 1600-1800. Free.*

Municipal Museum

In the early 1970s, the remains of a Byzantine basilical triapsidal church were excavated in the Giv'at Katzenelson neighbourhood. The church has a beautiful mosaic pavement, and is certainly worth the effort of arranging a visit. ■ *Near Giv'at Katzenelson School: see map. You must call ahead for a prior appointment, T9823070, ask for Mr Manfred. 4 NIS.*

Byzantine church mosaic pavement

Phoenician burial caves from the second to fifth centuries CE excavated to the east of Nahariya have revealed a quantity of elaborate glass vessels. A modern version of this 'Nahariya Glass' is manufactured in the workshops of Andreas Meyer Ltd. Tours of the workshop are available by prior arrangement, where you can see the glass cut, decorated and fired. ■ *100 Herzl, T9920066.*

Nahariya glass workshop

Essentials

For a town billing itself as a seaside resort there are suprisingly few hotels, and a pretty poor spread across the price categories (virtually nothing for budget travellers). Note that prices sky-rocket during weekends and Jewish holidays, especially the 'honeymoon season' that follows *Lag Ba'Omer*.

Sleeping
■ *on map;
price codes see inside
front cover*

A *Carlton*, 23 Ha Ga'Aton, T9005555, F9823771. Best in town, rooms simple but spacious, some suites, a/c, cable TV, large pool (covered and heated in winter), kids' pool, health club and sauna, supervised children's activities, restaurant, cheesy nightclub, reputation for good service.

B *Frank*, 4 HaAliya, T9920278, F9925535. Rooms are quite large with picture windows, a/c, TV, but it's a little old-fashioned and rather expensive for what you get. If swimming is your thing ascertain before booking as to whether there's any water in the pool.

C *Astar*, 27 Ha Ga'Aton, T9923431, F9923411. Reasonably good value 26-room hotel (especially out of season), a/c, cable TV, noted *Lachmi* restaurant downstairs. **C** *Erna*, 29 Jabotinsky, T9929852, F9928917. Quiet residential neighbourhood, rather 70s décor but clean with good service, a/c, TV. **C** *Motel Charley*, 34 Hama'Apilim, T9928132. 15 clean and modern a/c rooms, cable TV, double beds, book in advance, discounts for longer stays, pretty good value. **C** *Panorama*, 8 Hama'Apilim, T9920555.

Haifa & the North Coast

Room prices vary according to size and view, good beach access, rooftop terrace. **C** *Rosenblatt*, 59 Weizmann, T9920051, F9928121. Family-orientated a/c chalet rooms around pool, popular with returning guests, restaurant, reasonable value.

D *Kalman*, 27 Jabotinsky, T9920355, F9926539. Quiet, family-run place that welcomes disabled visitors, simple and old-fashioned a/c rooms with TV, restaurant, garden, friendly, pretty good value.

Apartment rental and B&Bs With no budget accommodation in Nahariya, the only cheap alternative is to rent a room. Signs advertising 'rooms for rent' (*Tzimerrim*) can be found all over town, though your best bet is to go to the Municipal Tourist Office and obtain their list of registered places. Most places have 8 to 12 double rooms with private bathroom, and sharing a common kitchen. Prices vary, though $30-$40 per room per night is average. Discounts are available for longer stays, and bargaining may be in order. The following are registered with the Municipality (all have attached toilets): *Beit Amigo*, 41 Kaplan, T9926116, 11 units, common kitchen, 2 family units. *Beit Goldfarb*, 38 Hama'Apilim, T9921103, 8 units, a/c, common kitchen. *Beit Gaviazda*, 12 Jabotinsky, T9921049, 8 units, a/c, shared kitchen. *Beit Milgram*, 36 Balfour, T9924331, F9925269, 10 units, fridge, a/c, phone, 4 family units, a/c, kitchen, phone. *Beit Reis*, 12 units, a/c, shared kitchen. *Beit Rehayim*, 6 Wolfson, T9920557, probably cheapest of all with dorm beds, kitchen, bike rental. *Beit Rotman*, 17 Remez, T9921017, 8 units, TV, fridge, kitchen. *Beit Sarah*, 77 Weizman, T9921549, 9 units, a/c, kitchenette. *Beit Sirtash*, 22 Jabotinsky, T9922586, 8 units, a/c, kitchen, garden. Recommended. *Motel Arieli*, 1 Jabotinsky, T9921076, 7 units, a/c, common kitchen.

Eating **Budget** The usual collection of falafel, shwarma and pizza places are located along Ha Ga'Aton. There are a couple of supermarkets opposite the bus station.

Café/bars *Café Misha*, Ha Ga'Aton, next to *El Poncho*. Coffee (10 NIS), shakes, pastries, light meals. *Kapulsky* have a restaurant offering cakes and light meals on the promenade at the end of Ha Ga'Aton. *Pinguin*, 31 Ha Ga'Aton, T9920027. Popular informal café atmosphere, schnitzels, blintzes, light meals, salads etc.

Central/North/South American *El Poncho*, Ha Ga'Aton, next to *Pinguin*. Argentinian grill offering big lunch-time feed for 40 NIS.

Chinese/Southeast Asian *Golden River*, 43 Weizmann, T9921088. Good reputation but currently looks closed. *Maxim's*, Galei Galil Beach Complex, T9921088. New location, receives rave reviews from locals, main dishes 25-55 NIS. *Pacific*, Ha Ga'Aton, T9510877. Set lunch 40 NIS, set dinner 55 NIS, take-away lunch 30 NIS. *Singapore*, corner of Jabotinsky and Hameyasdim, T9929209. A close second to *Maxim's*, similar prices though set menu and business lunch are good value.

Fast food/chain *Burger Ranch*, 41 Ha Ga'Aton, T9822674. *McDonald's*, Central Bus Station (the 'Egged restaurant' here as described in some guidebooks closed years ago). *Mister Pizza*, Ha Ga'Aton. *Pizza Mario* and *Domino Pizza* are both on Ha Ga'Aton, opposite the Municipality.

Indian *Salaam Bombay*, 17 Jabotinsky, T9924952. Passable Indian cuisine.

Seafood *Abu Bulus*, western end of Ha Ga'Aton. Reasonably priced fish restaurant.

Vegetarian There's a health-food shop on Ha Ga'aton, next to the *Carlton Hotel*. *Lachmi*, *Astar Hotel*, 27 Ha Ga'Aton. Highly recommended veggie restaurant noted for its salads and breakfasts.

Bars & nightclubs There are a number of bars in the blocks opposite the bus station and the Municipality, plus several places on the seafront at the western end of Ha Ga'Aton. The *La Scala* nightclub at the *Carlton Hotel* is described in their brochure as the "most magnificent and happening nightclub in the north", though I dare say there's not much competition (Open 2200, Admission 50 NIS).

Cinemas *Hechal Hatarbut*, Ha'Atzma'ut, T9927935; *Hod*, Herzl, T9920502. **Entertainment**
Folkdancing Takes place at the amphitheatre every Tuesday and Saturday at 1930 in July and August.

Diving *Achziv Diving Club*, at Akhziv, T9823671, also **sailing** and **jeep tours**. **Sports**
Cycling *Rosen and Meents*, 46 Ha Ga'Aton, T9829333 sell *mountain bikes* for around 500 NIS. **Mini-golf** Really exert yourself at Mini-golf, near to Kibbutz Evron, 'opposite the vegetable man', on the road south to Akko, T9857859.
Swimming New, heated (29°C) indoor pool at Galei Galil Beach, adult 30 NIS, children 15 NIS, under 3 free, daily 0600-2200.

Car hire *Budget*, 35 Lohamei Ha-Geta'ot, T9929252; *Eurodollar*, 66 Weizmann, **Transport**
T9921614; *Europcar*, 63 Weizmann, T9826005.

Long-distance buses Nahariya's Central Bus Station is at 3 Ha Ga'Aton, T9923444, with the main bus services being the 270/271/272 to **Haifa** (every 15-20 mins, 0600-2300, 45-60 mins, 17 NIS) via **Akko** (30 mins, 8 NIS).
   Nahariya is also the transport junction for visiting a number of places inland and to the north: **Akhziv:** Bus 022, gate 5, 0930 1130 1430, 15 mins. **Montfort:** Buses 039, 040, 041, 044 to **Mi'ilya** (then walk), approximately hourly, gate 9, 15 mins, 10 NIS, or irregular Bus 025 to **Goren Park** (then longer walk). **Peki'in:** Bus 044, platform 9, 0545 0705 1100 1230 1400 1435 1700 2030, 1 hr, 15 NIS. **Rosh Ha-Nikra:** Bus 022 direct to the site, gate 5, 0930 1130 1430, 20 mins, 9 NIS, or more regular buses 020, 024, 028, 032, 033 to Rosh Ha-Nikra junction (Bezet junction), 3km uphill walk from the site. **Yehi'am:** Buse 039 at 1200 2000, Bus 042 at 0535 1700, or take one of the more regular Mi'ilya buses (see above) to the junction of routes 89 and 8833, and walk the remaining 6.5km. **NB** Some services pull out from platform 6 then pull in to platform 9 to pick up more passengers. Actual departure times may vary during the life-span of this book, though frequencies rarely change. There are clean toilets at the bus station (1 NIS).

Sherut/service taxi Shared taxis run from outside the Central Bus Station, and from the junction of Ha Ga'Aton and Ha'Atzma'ut, north to **Bezet junction** (via Akhziv), and south to **Akko**.

Train Nahariya's train station is at 1 Ha Ga'Aton, at the junction with Ha'Atzma'ut, T9546446. All trains run to **Akko** (10 mins), **Haifa** (45 mins), **Netanya** (1 hr 45 mins) and **Tel Aviv** (2 hrs 15 mins): Sunday-Thursday 10 per day, 0545-1830; Friday 4 trains, last at 1300, Saturday no service.

Banks There are branches of *Bank Leumi* T9925631, *Israel Discount* T9928881 and *Mercantile* **Directory**
Discount on Ha Ga'Aton, though you should check commission charges and exchange rates. The main **Post Office** offers commission-free foreign exchange. **Communications** Phone code: T04. Post offices: The main branch is at 40 Ha Ga'Aton, T9920180, and offers **poste restante**, **international calls** and **foreign exchange** (Sun-Thu 0800-1230 1530-1800, Wed 0800-1330, Fri 0800-1200). **Hospitals and medical services** Chemists: *Szabo Pharmacy*, 3 Ha Ga'Aton, T9920454. **Hospital:** the *Municipal Hospital* is on Ben Zvi Hanassi (T9850505) to the east of town, across from the main Rosh Ha-Nikra to Akko road (Ha'Atzma'ut). **Dentists:** 44 Ha Ga'Aton, T9511595. **Tourist offices** The *Municipal Tourist Office*, Ground Floor, Municipality Building, T9879800 (Sun-Thu 0800-1300, 1600-1900, Fri 0800-1300) has lots of free maps, brochures on events and places in and around Nahariya, as well as advice on renting rooms. **Useful addresses and phone numbers** Police: T100 emergency; (5 Ben Zvi Hanassi, T9920344). Ambulance: Magen David Adom T101 emergency (or T9823333). **Nahariya Municipality:** T9879811.

Montfort

Though not the most spectacular Crusader castle in the Holy Land, Montfort has a very picturesque setting, and a visit can be combined with a short hike through an attractive nature reserve.

Ins and outs

Getting there and around

There are two ways of getting to Montfort – from the north or the south – both of which involve some very pleasant walking. The easiest approach is via the Christian Arab village of **Mi'ilya** to the south, which can be reached from Nahariya by taking any of the buses bound for Ma'alot Tarshiha (039/040/041/044) and asking to be set down at Mi'ilya (15 mins, 10 NIS). (It is easy to flag down a return bus on Route 89 from Mi'ilya back to Nahariya.) From the sign-post (and bus stop) announcing Mi'ilya, head uphill, following the main road through the village, and out and down the other side. Beyond Mi'ilya the paved road takes a sharp 90-degree bend to the right (20 minutes walk). From here you have two choices. If you follow the paved road turning right at the 90-degree bend, after 200 metres on your left is a **lookout point** and car-park. From here it is possible to make a 4-hour walking loop down to the castle and back up to Mi'ilya. Follow the black-and-white marked trail down to **Nahal Keziv**, then take the green-and-white trail along the river (Nahal Keziv/Wadi Qurein), before joining the red-and-white trail up to the castle and back to Mi'ilya. There is plenty of shade *en route*, though you should make sure that you have a hat/sunblock and plenty of drinking water.

The alternative approach from Mi'ilya is by turning left at the 90-degree bend after the village, and heading along the dirt track. About 100 metres down the track the path forks. The left fork is part of the black-and-white trail to **Horbat Bilton** and **Nahal Sha'ar**, whilst the right fork follows the red-and-white trail down to **Nahal Keziv** and **Montfort**. Following the red-and-white trail down hill, it branches to the right after ten minutes walking. Follow this path down into **Nahal Keziv Nature Reserve**, where the trail becomes lined on either side by trees. After walking through this avenue of trees for ten minutes, a set of stone steps leads off to your right. You can either take the steps or walk for another 100 metres and scramble up the rocks marked by the red-and-white trail. Both routes lead to a narrow path, before you get your first glimpse of the castle ruins ahead. You approach the castle close to the smaller, additional moat from where you can scramble up the castle walls to the keep. Return to Mi'ilya by the same route (though it's now uphill all the way), or continue along the red-and-white trail to **Goren Park**.

The approach to Montfort from the north is via **Goren Park**, though transport to here is less regular: from Nahariya take one of the irregular buses going to Goren (025) and ask to be set down at Goren Park (30 mins, 14 NIS). The red-and-white trail descends from Goren Park, and after $1\frac{1}{2}$ hours of walking you reach Montfort. From here you can continue onto Mi'ilya.

Return buses from Goren to Nahariya are not regular, and stop running quite early. If you wish to arrive at the castle by one route and leave by another, it is recommended that you arrive via Goren Park and leave through Mi'ilya.

History

Today, much of Montfort lies in ruins following its surrender to the Mamluk sultan **Baibars** in 1271 after a brief siege in which the Muslim forces breached the outer walls and much of the inner western defences. The Crusaders were permitted to surrender and retreat to Acre, though without their arms. Baibars dismantled much of Montfort to prevent its reoccupation.

Montfort Castle

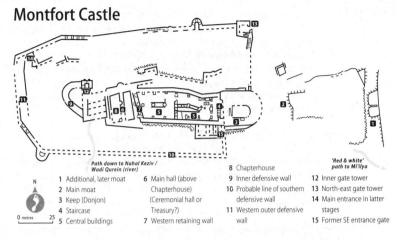

Path down to Nahal Keziv / Wadi Qurein (river)

'Red & white' path to Mi'ilya

N

0 metres   25

1 Additional, later moat
2 Main moat
3 Keep (Donjon)
4 Staircase
5 Central buildings
6 Main hall (above Chapterhouse) (Ceremonial hall or Treasury?)
7 Western retaining wall
8 Chapterhouse
9 Inner defensive wall
10 Probable line of southern defensive wall
11 Western outer defensive wall
12 Inner gate tower
13 North-east gate tower
14 Main entrance in latter stages
15 Former SE entrance gate

However, when constructed in 1226 it was the main Crusader fortress in Palestine of the **Knights of the Teutonic Order** (Teutonic Knights). The castle stands on a narrow ridge running east to west above the Nahal Keziv (Arabic: Wadi Qurein). The literal meaning of the French name Montfort is 'strong mountain', with its Latin (Mons fortis) and German (Starkenberg) names meaning the same. The fortress was part of a defensive chain protecting the Plain of Acre (Akko) that included the Chateau du Roi (formerly at Mi'ilya) and the Judin Fortress (at Yehi'am, see below). Roads were cut linking the fortresses, and connecting Montfort to Acre via the Nahal Keziv.

Sights

Only parts of the outer defensive walls remain, though the best preserved parts to the north and west can be seen almost in their entirety. The wall is about two metres thick, and, like the rest of the fortress, is built with stone quarried and cut less than one kilometre from here. A path runs along the top of the wall from where the Crusaders could fire arrows through loopholes in the wall. The western fortifications look particularly impressive, though according to the Arab writer Ibn Furat (who may have witnessed the battle and describes the siege in some detail), the Muslims breached this area in some strength.

The main moat, 20 metres wide and 11 metres deep, protects the east flank of the fortress. About 50 metres further east, a narrow, deep depression was expanded to form a second moat. A number of modern ladders and walkways allow you to get a better view of this additional moat.

Montfort had three main gates, and possibly a number of secondary entrances. The **main entrance gate** in the latter stages of the castle's

Walls, gates and moats

Haifa & the North Coast

Montfort Castle cross-section

(looking from south to north)

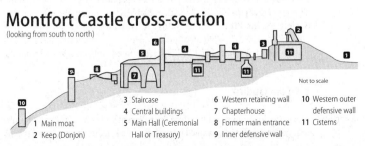

Not to scale

1 Main moat
2 Keep (Donjon)
3 Staircase
4 Central buildings
5 Main Hall (Ceremonial Hall or Treasury)
6 Western retaining wall
7 Chapterhouse
8 Former main entrance
9 Inner defensive wall
10 Western outer defensive wall
11 Cisterns

occupation is well preserved, standing to the northwest. The path from this entrance leads to the **inner gate tower**, also well preserved. The inner gate tower is 17 metres high and comprises three storeys. A gallery at the top allowed a free arc of fire for the Crusaders, whilst the bowmen could also fire through the loopholes in the storey below. The gate's entrance formed the lower floor. It is thought that this was formerly the main entrance prior to the later construction of the northwest entrance gate. Little remains of the **southeast entrance gate**, though parts of the northeast gate tower still stand.

Keep The strongest part of the fortress, the **keep** (or 'donjon', as it is described when referring to Crusader architecture) is on the east side. By climbing up here you can get great views of the rest of the fortress, and the surrounding wooded hills. The keep is about 25 metres square, though the destruction of the outer rooms means that its original plan cannot be determined. The keep's cellar forms a large cistern.

Central buildings Only sections of the central buildings remain, though archaeologists have been able to make guesses as to the various buildings' functions. The situation is confused, however, because several stages of construction are discernible. A row of seven Gothic columns probably supported a Gothic roof on a two-storey building. A large section of the **western retaining wall** still stands. Some sources identify this area as containing 'knights' houses', with the discovery of pieces from a stained-glass window suggesting that a church also stood here. A wine-press was discovered, with other artefacts indicating workrooms and a kitchen.

Prior to the construction of the outer walls, this was the western defensive position, with the original fortress just comprising the keep and central buildings. Located amongst the later fortifications to the immediate west are two halls, preserved in entirety (including ceilings). Labelled by some as the **chapterhouse**, above them stood the fortress's **main hall**. This may have been a ceremonial hall or possibly the treasury.

Cisterns A number of rock-cut cisterns for water storage have been found throughout the fortress, in addition to cellars used as reservoirs.

Outlying building A stepped path leads down to the Nahal Keziv from the southwest side of Montfort (this is how you will arrive if coming via the Goren Park or Nahal Keziv hike routes). A two-storey building on the river bank originally served the Crusaders as a flour mill, though, when the splendid Gothic ribbed-vault roofed upper storey was added, it probably served as a pilgrims' hostel.

Nahal Betzet Nature Reserve North of Goren is the beautiful Nahal Betzet Nature Reserve. There are several trails marked through the reserve, taking in giant maple forests, bathing pools, and a number of ancient ruins. The red-and-white trail leads to the hanging **Bow Cave**, a natural arch that provides stupendous views of rural Galilee. Those intending to hike in the park are advised to contact the offices of the **Society for the Protection of Nature in Israel** (SPNI) in either Haifa (18 Hillel, T04-8529577, 0700-1900), or at the field school located just north of Akhziv Holiday Village (T04-9823762). **NB** Public transport to and from the nature reserve is limited.

Yehi'am (Judin)

Judin Fortress The Judin Fortress was built early in the 13th century by the Templars and subsequently bought and occupied by the Teutonic Knights. It formed part of the defensive line of fortresses protecting the Plain of Acre (Akko). Following its capture by the Mamluk sultan **Baibars** in 1265, most of the fortress was destroyed. The most impressive Crusader ruins visible today are parts of the walls and the **eastern tower**.

In the 18th century, the site was occupied by a local sheik, **Mahd el-Hussein**, who rebuilt some of the fortress and turned it into his stronghold. In 1738, the stronghold was captured by **Dahr el-Amr**, who substantially rebuilt the fortress, with most of the main structures visible today due to his building efforts. These include the **mosque**, **bathhouse** and **main hall**.

In 1946 **Kibbutz Yehi'am** was established near to the Judin Fortress. Initially occupying parts of the fortress, the kibbutz took its name from Yehi'am Weitz, one of the members of the Palmach unit killed during the 'Night of the Bridges' (see Akhziv Bridge, page 607). The Judin Fortress once again saw action during the 1948 war, when the kibbutz was besieged by the Arabs. A memorial has been erected on the road to Yehi'am to the members of a relief convoy who were killed in an attack near to Kabri.

Kibbutz Yehi'am offers accommodation close to the Judin Fortress, as well as having opened a restaurant within the fortress that offers theme 'Renaissance Nights' (see under 'Sleeping' below). The Judin Fortress has been designated as **Yehi'am National Park**. ■ *T04-9856040. Sunday-Thursday 0800-1700, Friday 0800-1600. Adult 11 NIS, student 8 NIS.*

Nahal Yehi'am Nature Reserve

The area around the Judin Fortress is part of the Nahal Yehi'am Nature Reserve, with a number of attractive trails marked through the Yehi'am forest. Staff at the Yehi'am National Park can advise you on suitable walks. The nearby village of **Klil** was founded by Israeli environmentalists "on the philosophy of mutual co-existence between nature and humans".

Sleeping

Kibbutz Yehi'am offers **B-C** B&B accommodation in its *Teva B'Yehi'am Guesthouse*, T04-9856057, F9856085. Spacious family rooms, a/c, kettle, pool, tennis, basketball, clubhouse with TV, children's zoo and playground. The Guesthouse also has a fully equipped (**F**) campsite. For details of the 'Renaissance Night' experience, T04-9856059.

Transport

There are limited bus services to and from Yehi'am. From **Nahariya**, take Bus 042 at 0535 and 1700, or Bus 039 at 1200 and 2000 (25 mins). The other alternative is to take a bus bound for Ma'alot Tarshiha on Route 89 (039/040/041/044), get off at the junction for Yehi'am, and walk the remaining 6.5km along Route 8833.

Haifa & the North Coast

Yehi'am (Judin) Fortress

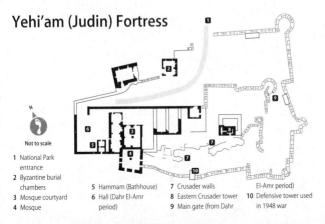

Not to scale

1 National Park entrance
2 Byzantine burial chambers
3 Mosque courtyard
4 Mosque
5 Hammam (Bathhouse)
6 Hall (Dahr El-Amr period)
7 Crusader walls
8 Eastern Crusader tower
9 Main gate (from Dahr El-Amr period)
10 Defensive tower used in 1948 war

Peki'in (Bke'ah)

Colour map 1, Grid B3 Peki'in (Arabic: Bke'ah) is an attractive hillside village in the heart of rural Galilee. Jewish sources claim that it is the only village in Israel with an uninterrupted Jewish presence since the time of the Second Temple (destroyed 70 CE). Today, the village has a mixed population (though predominantly Druze), with the diversity of beliefs reflected in the range of religious institutions; a Druze Hilwes (House of Prayer), a Greek Catholic church, a Greek Orthodox church (built in 1894 on the ruins of the ancient church of St Gregory), several mosques, and a 19th-century synagogue.

The village is particularly important to Jews as it is believed to be the spot where **Rabbi Shimon Bar Yochai**, and his son **Eliezer**, fled from Roman persecution during the second century CE. A Roman decree banned the study of the Torah, but for 12 years the pair hid in a small cave in the hillside and continued their study. It was during this period of contemplation that the rabbi produced a number of thoughts and teachings that later found their way into the *Zohar*, the treatise on Jewish mysticism first written down in the 1280s CE.

The **Cave of Rabbi Shimon Bar Yochai** is the village's main attraction today, though it can be a little hard to find, and is sure to disappoint. Despite signs announcing that the cave is a holy religious site, it is poorly cared for.

Though the key site in Peki'in is rather unexciting, this is a pleasant village to visit, with none of the commercial trappings of Druze villages such as Isfiya and Daliyat el-Carmel (see 'Around Haifa' section on page 580). There are a couple of friendly café/restaurants at the western entrance to the village.

Transport Bus 044 from **Nahariya**, 0545 0700 1050 1230 1355 1435 1640 2030, Friday last bus 1400. The bus really 'goes round the houses', taking 1hr to reach Peki'in (16 NIS). **NB** Do not get off at the new settlement of Peki'in Hadasha, 3km before Peki'in.

Akhziv National Park

Colour map 1, grid B2 The Akhziv National Park is an excellent place to come for a picnic, with a small stretch of beach that must rank as one of the most attractive along this stretch of coastline. A natural breakwater shelters the beach, forming a shallow wading pool and a deeper 'natural' swimming pool. As a backdrop to the beach there are a number of 'antiquities' that hint at Akhziv's long and

Peki'in

historical past, plus modern facilities such as showers, toilets, changing rooms, picnic tables, cafés and a small stage/amphitheatre.

Ancient Akhziv (Achziv) dates back to the beginning of the Middle Bronze Age (c. 2200 BCE), and was settled continuously until the Crusader period, though none of the 'antiquities' in the park is labelled.

Just to the north of the National Park, an old Arab mansion stands at the centre of a plot of land. An eccentric by the name of Eli Avivi settled here in 1952, making a unilateral declaration of independence! Now you can visit the 'state' of **Akhzivland**, even getting a stamp in your passport if you wish. A small collection of finds from the local area are displayed in Eli's home (admission 10 NIS). It's possible to stay here overnight, though some horror stories exist concerning lone females who have stopped here. ■ *T04-9823263. Summer 0800-1900, winter 0800-1600. Adult 12 NIS, student 9 NIS.*

Sleeping C *Achziv Holiday Village*, just north of National Park, T04-9823602, F9826030. Attractive a/c cabins and a/c caravans, plus cheaper (**F**) camping area, restaurant, children's pool, pub, prices drop in winter. **E** *Yad Le Yad Youth Hostel*, just north of *Holiday Village*, T04-9823345, F9820632. Dorms or private rooms, a/c. **E** *SPNI Field School*, T04-9823762, F9823015. Dorms, dining hall.

Sports Between the National Park and the Achziv Holiday Village is the *Achziv Diving Club*, T04-9823671, which can organize introductory dives and dive courses.

Transport Buses 022/025/028/032/033 from Nahariya all pass Akhziv National Park, as do sheruts from Nahariya.

Akhziv Bridge and Yad Le-Yad Memorial Just to the north of Akhziv is the Yad Le-Yad Memorial, a monument to a bizarre incident dating to the British Mandate period. On the night of 17th June, 1946, in an attempt to disrupt the communication lines of the British, a unit of the Palmach (the striking arm of the Jewish resistance) attempted to blow up the railway bridge at Akhziv. The 14 members of the demolition team were spotted by a British sentry, who then fired a flare to illuminate the scene. By bizarre chance the flare ignited the team's explosives, blowing up the bridge but also killing all the members of the Palmach unit. The Yad Le-Yad

Akhziv National Park

To Rosh Ha-Nikra

Mediterranean Sea

'Akhzivland'

Beach

To Nahariya

'Club Med'

N
Not to scale

1 Parking
2 Entrance & Ticket office
3 Toilets
4 Showers
5 Playgrounds
6 Drinking water fountain
7 Lifeguard station
8 Café
9 Stage
10 'Antiquities'

Haifa & the North Coast

Memorial ('memorial to the fourteen') stands near to the site of the incident that became known as 'The Night of the Bridges'.

The nearby **Kibbutz Gesher Haziv**, named after the incident, offers accommodation at its (**B**) *Guesthouse* ■ *T04-9958568/9825715, F9958652/9825718. All rooms a/c, with TV, plus discount diving through the kibbutz's dive centre.*

Rosh Ha-Nikra

Straddling Israel's border with Lebanon are spectacular chalk cliffs from which thousands of years of wave action have cut a series of grottoes and blow-holes. Referred to in antiquity as the 'Ladders of Tyre', the wave-cut caverns are said to have been expanded by **Alexander the Great** in 323 BCE to allow passage for his army during the siege of Tyre (31 kilometres north). Following the Arab conquest, the site became known as *A-Nawakir* ('the grottoes') and subsequently *Ras-A-Nakura*. The present name is the Hebraicized version.

During World War I the tunnels were widened by the **British** to allow the passage of motor vehicles, and during the Second World War further tunnels were dug to accommodate the Beirut to Haifa railway.

The **sea grottoes** are now marketed as a tourist attraction, with a very brief (but extortionately priced) cable-car ride providing access. A walk through the grottoes takes no more than 5-10 minutes, though it can be an exhilarating experience, particularly if the sea is rough. **NB** Swimming here is both illegal and highly dangerous. Also included in the price of your entrance ticket is a short 3D audio-visual presentation in the **Peace Train**, in one of the old tunnels. The scratched plastic 3D glasses are enough to make you go blind, and you'll learn nothing from the film (alternatively Hebrew and English). For example, "it's only a matter of time until the train runs between Israel, Lebanon, Syria and Turkey"! There is a snack-bar down by the grottoes, and a restaurant above the cliff, by the Israel/Lebanon border. **NB** Photography is not permitted at the border, except in front of the "Jerusalem 205km, Beirut 120km" sign. ■ *T04-9857109, F9857107. Summer Saturday-Thursday 0830-1800, Friday 0830-1600, winter Saturday-Friday 0830-1600. Adult 25 NIS, student 22 NIS, family rates available.*

Sleeping **D-E** *Rosh Haniqra Youth Hostel and Guesthouse*, 5 mins from grottoes, T04-9825169, F9821330. Dorms (5 per room, **E**) or a/c rooms with bath and kitchenette (**D**) set in large spacious grounds, kosher dining hall, pool, close to public beach, reservations recommended, wheelchair access. Recommended. **E** *Shlomi Youth Hostel and Guesthouse*, POB 2120, Shlomi, T04-9808975, F9809163. Located a couple of kilometres inland from Betzet Junction, has 4-person a/c rooms, breakfast included, kosher dining hall, cafeteria, TV room. Take buses 022/023 from **Nahariya**.

Transport Bus 022 from Nahariya goes directly to the site, but only 3 times per day, 0915 1130 1430 (20 mins, 9 NIS). The bus only waits for 15 mins. More regular buses (020/022/023/024/025/028/032/033) go to Betzet Junction, from where it is a 3km uphill walk to the site.

Rural accommodation in Western Galilee In addition to the accommodation listed in the places mentioned above, there are a number of alternative options for those who wish to experience something of rural Western Galilee. Most of the accommodation is run by rural kibbutzim and moshavs, the rest by private individuals, and falls within the **C**, **D**, **E** price categories. Some also provide cheaper camping or dormitory facilities. Contact the tourist office in Haifa for details, or the "Kibbutz Hotels Reservation Centre", PO Box 3194, 90 Ben Yehuda, Tel Aviv, T03-5246161, F5278088.

609

Galilee & The Golan

11

Galilee & The Golan

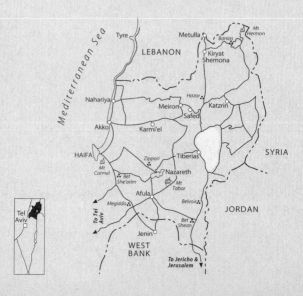

With the possible exception of Jerusalem, there are probably more 'unmissable' places of interest in Galilee and Golan than in any other part of Israel. This is not just a function of the region's long and eventful human history and importance within Judaism and Christianity, but also a reflection of Galilee and Golan's supreme natural beauty. Places where Jesus preached and Jewish sages compiled central texts and treatises on the Law compete for attention with lush waterscapes, rolling hills and rugged plateaux. Those who like their history can choose from the Bronze Age, Iron Age, Hellenistic, Roman, Byzantine or medieval periods, with some sites conveniently providing remains from all six. This is another area that deserves extensive exploration.

This chapter of the Handbook *is divided into four sections: 'Lower Galilee', 'Tiberias and the Sea of Galilee', 'Upper Galilee' and 'The Golan'. Though a hired car is undoubtedly the way to explore this region fully, the key attractions in the first two sections are all more or less available by public transport. It's not impossible to explore Upper Galilee and The Golan by bus, though having your own transport will certainly make things easier.*

Background

Geography The Galilee has clearly defined geographical boundaries. To the south is the Jezreel Valley (or Plain of Esdraelon), forming the boundary with the northern hills of Samaria (West Bank), whilst to the west is the former Phoenician coast of the Mediterranean (see 'Haifa and the North Coast' chapter beginning on page 555). The geographical boundary to the north is formed by the Litani River, though the political boundary is the border with Lebanon. And in the east the Syrian-African Rift Valley through which the Jordan River flows forms both a physical and political boundary.

Galilee is characterized by a number of low mountain ranges, with rolling hills interspersed by fertile valleys that afford easy passage. Most of the bedrock is chalk, limestone and dolomite, with basalt-covered areas to the east and into Golan. The western region (included in the 'Haifa and the North Coast' chapter) is relatively flat, and is drained by a series of wadis running east to west. Upper Galilee is more mountainous, dominated by the chalk and limestone Meiron range to the west of Safed. The rest of Upper Galilee comprises the 'Galilee Finger' of the Hula Valley running from the Sea of Galilee up to the Lebanese border at Metulla. Terrain has dictated the pattern of human settlement and movement throughout the Galilee, with the most densely populated areas being the plains of Lower Galilee, and the Jezreel Valley in particular. The Sea of Galilee has also been a major focus of the region.

Climate Galilee has a Mediterranean climate, moderated by altitude. Average temperatures are higher and levels of rainfall lower in Lower Galilee when compared with Upper Galilee. Lower Galilee receives around 600 millimetres of rain per year, as opposed to 800 millimetres in Upper Galilee and 1,000 millimetres on the higher slopes of the Meiron range. The **best time to visit** is in spring and autumn, thus avoiding the winter rains (60 days per year in Upper Galilee, mainly in January and February), and the excesses of summer heat in the lower areas (Tiberias is particularly muggy in summer).

Vegetation The abundant water (both precipitation and ground water), plus the relatively low levels of population density (particularly when compared to the Mediterranean coast), has allowed the Galilee to retain the country's richest diversity of vegetation. The natural vegetation is Mediterranean forest, a surprising amount of which has been preserved by the establishment of protected nature reserves. The Jezreel Valley provides the country's richest agricultural land. The impression of the Galilee that most people take away with them is one of green valleys dividing wooded rolling hills.

History Galilee's long and rich history has been largely influenced by its physical geography. In particular, wide valleys such as the Jezreel became integral parts of international trading routes such as the *Via Maris*, connecting Egypt to Babylonia via the Galilee. It has also become a major theatre of war with the first written account of a military battle (Pharaoh Thutmose III's defeat of the Canaanites in 1468 BCE) taking place in the Jezreel Valley before Megiddo. The Israelites' return to the Promised Land saw the tribes of Naphtali, Zebulun and Asher settled in the Galilee (*Joshua 19*), with the tribe of Dan arriving later (*Judges 18*). However, despite Deborah's victory in 1125 BCE, many of the fortified cities still remained under the control of the Canaanites. The first king of the United Monarchy, Saul, also suffered defeat in Lower Galilee before his successors David and Solomon conquered the region. Israelite control was short-lived, however, with the Assyrian king Tiglath-pileser III sweeping through the region in 733-32 BCE, with no new significant Jewish settlement in the region until the Hasmonean era of Alexander Jannaeus (103-76 BCE).

The Early Roman period saw much of Galilee controlled by Herod the Great, and subsequently his successors, and witnessed the establishment of predominantly Jewish towns such as Sepphoris and Tiberias. Peace in the Galilee was short-lived, however, the region being the scene of many key events in the early stages of the Jewish Revolt (66-67 CE) against Rome that Josephus describes so colourfully. A number of ancient synagogues that have been found across the Galilee hint at the conscious separation of the Jewish and pagan communities from the mid-third century onwards. This is a reflection of the growing importance of Galilee to the Jews following the destruction of the Temple at Jerusalem in the first century CE, with the shifting of the Sanhedrin to Bet She'aram, and then Sepphoris and Tiberias.

The Byzantine period (324-638 CE) was a time of great prosperity in the Galilee, with the expansion of existing settlements and the founding of new ones. It also saw the development of religious and economic competition, as Christianity became established in the Galilee. In Upper Galilee Christianity does not appear to have encroached into Jewish areas, though in Lower Galilee it certainly did. The bitter rivalry between the competing communities is perhaps best reflected in the Persian invasion of 613-14 CE, when the Galilee's Jews assisted the invading army in persecuting the region's Christian community. Roles were reversed when the Byzantine army reasserted its authority 15 years later.

The Arab invasion of 638 CE dealt a serious blow to the Christians, though the Jewish communities appear to have been left unmolested. Subsequent Christian-Muslim rivalries, in particular the Crusades, dominate the medieval history of the Galilee. Many great battles were fought here (most notably the crushing defeat of the Crusaders by the army of Salah al-Din at the Horns of Hittim in 1187) and have left a legacy of spectacular fortresses perched on high mountain tops. The Galilee was subsequently in Muslim hands for the next six centuries until the final defeat of the Ottoman Turks during the Palestine campaign of the First World War (1918). The British ruled Galilee for the next 30 years or so until the expiry of their Mandate for Palestine. The United Nations Partition Recommendation (1947) envisaged a divided Galilee, with the eastern and western blocks apportioned to the Jews, and a wide swathe through the centre from Nazareth to Lebanon to be part of a future Arab state. The Arab rejection of this plan, and the subsequent war, saw the whole of the Galilee fall into Israeli hands. The Galilee is now home to 17 percent of Israel's population, including a sizeable Arab minority, with an economy based largely upon agriculture, tourism and light industry.

Lower Galilee

Nazareth

The large Arab town of Nazareth is one of the most important Christian pilgrimage destinations in the Holy Land. Though the place of Jesus' childhood, plus later scenes in his life (including an appearance before his disciples following his resurrection), Nazareth is most revered as the site of the Annunciation: the Archangel Gabriel's appearance before the Virgin Mary at which he announced the

Phone code: *06*
Colour map *1, grid B3*

Galilee & The Golan

impending birth of Jesus. A number of churches mark the traditional sites of the key Christian events in Nazareth.

At the time of going to press, Nazareth was one of the pilgrimage centres gearing up for a huge influx of visitors expected in the year 2000. It has been suggested that Pope John-Paul II will celebrate mass here on the Feast of the Annunciation at the end of March 2000.

Ins and outs

Getting there The majority of visitors to Nazareth arrive as part of an organized group, with tour buses regularly blocking all routes in and out of town (though in fairness to tour groups, just a couple of buses can bring complete traffic gridlock). Nazareth is easy to visit independently, however, and can be visited as a day trip from either Haifa or Tiberias (both just 1 hour away on the bus).

Getting around Most of Nazareth's key attractions are within walking distance of each other, though visitors should be prepared for some steep climbs if they wish to visit all the various churches and monasteries on the hillside above the town centre. The view from the top is certainly worth the exertion. The focus of the downtown area is the Basilica of the Annunciation; also Nazareth's most prominent landmark. The twisting alleyways of the old Arab souq just to the north can be initially confusing, and it may take some wandering back and forth to find the various sites located in this area (the map is vastly over-simplified). It can also be a little frustrating if you are attempting to find the right path/flight of steps up to the various sites on the hillside above the town; you can often see the church/monastery but can't find the path leading there. Shop-keepers will generally point you in the right direction. **NB** Remember, you will be denied access to most sites unless you are suitably dressed (no shorts for either sex, no bare shoulders, etc). **Warning** A number of women have complained of harassment whilst visiting Nazareth. Dressing conservatively may go some way towards reducing this unwanted attention (and is pretty much essential if you wish to visit the holy sites). Some recommend that women only visit Nazareth in pairs, or with a male escort, and all sexes should avoid the bazaar area at night. This may be overstating things a little, but it is probably best to err on the side of caution.

History

The first written references to Nazareth appear in the New Testament, though the history of settlement of the site is considerably longer. Excavations in the vicinity of the Basilica of the Annunciation have unearthed at least one cave containing a number of artefacts dating to the Middle Bronze Age II (2000-1550 BCE), whilst a second cave shows remarkable similarity to the Bronze Age caves at nearby Megiddo. Pottery from the Israelite period (1200-586 BCE) has also been found in the granary caves beneath the Basilica. A fairly large necropolis from the Roman/Byzantine periods has been discovered, mainly across the hill to the west of the Basilica of the Annunciation.

Despite Nazareth's importance within Christianity, the picture of the early Christian community here is rather confused. **Eusebius** suggests that until the sixth century CE Nazareth was a small village inhabited solely by Jews, though some sources point to the existence of a Judaeo-Christian community in the second and possibly third centuries CE. The settlement became a minor pilgrimage site in Byzantine times, with **Egeria** noting in his visit c. 380 CE that the cave (later the 'Grotto of the Annunciation') had been consecrated with an altar, and the **Pilgrim of Piacenza** mentioning the presence of two churches in his visit of c. 570 CE. It is unclear whether Nazareth was particularly affected by the Persian invasion of 614 CE, when the Jews of Galilee sided with the Muslims against the Christians, though the Pilgrim of Piacenza had previously mentioned the particularly good relations between the Jews and Christians of Nazareth.

Our first detailed reference to Nazareth following the **Arab** conquest of the Holy Land (c. 638 CE) comes from the pilgrim Arculf, who describes two substantial churches during his visit c. 670 CE, though later visitors during the Early Arab period (638-1099 CE) claim that the Christian community had frequently to pay bribes to the Muslims not to destroy the early Church of the Annunciation. The **Crusader** conquest of the Holy Land saw Nazareth become a major pilgrimage site, with a proliferation of church construction marking the holy places and the establishment in the town of several European monastic orders. A major church was built on the site of the Annunciation and the rapidly growing town became the seat of an archbishop.

The defeat of the Crusader Latin Kingdom at the Horns of Hittim in 1187 saw the expulsion of the Christian population of Nazareth, though a

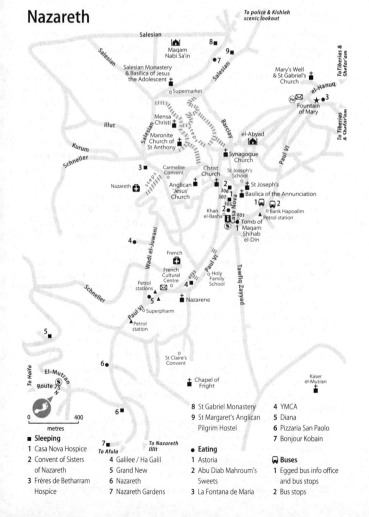

Nazareth

■ Sleeping
1 Casa Nova Hospice
2 Convent of Sisters of Nazareth
3 Frères de Betharram Hospice
4 Galilee / Ha Galil
5 Grand New
6 Nazareth
7 Nazareth Gardens

● Eating
1 Astoria
2 Abu Diab Mahroum's Sweets
3 La Fontana de Maria
4 YMCA
5 Diana
6 Pizzaria San Paolo
7 Bonjour Kobain

8 St Gabriel Monastery
9 St Margaret's Anglican Pilgrim Hostel

🚌 Buses
1 Egged bus info office and bus stops
2 Bus stops

Galilee & The Golan

Jesus of ... Nazareth?

Christian scholars are still divided as to whether Joseph and Mary actually lived in Nazareth prior to the birth of Jesus. It is suggested that were Nazareth their home town, they would be more likely to have fled there, rather than Egypt, when Herod began to implement his infanticide. With Joseph being of a Judean family, and Egypt being a common refuge for fleeing Judeans, circumstantial evidence could be said to support the interpretation of Matthew's gospel (Matthew 2) that the couple were from Bethlehem. The family could well have moved north to Nazareth to escape the potentially murderous

attentions of Herod's successor, his son Archelaus (4 BCE-6 CE). Murphy-O'Connor (The Holy Land, 1992) also suggests that Joseph may well have been encouraged north by Herod Antipas' recruitment drive for artisans to work on his new capital at Sepphoris (Zippori, see page 627). Luke's clear assertion that the family were originally from Nazareth (Luke 2:4) may have been based on the premise that since Jesus was brought up there as a child (Matthew 13:54; Luke 4:16), and had relatives there (Matthew 13:55-56), his parents were actually born there.

subsequent treaty between Emperor Frederick II and el-Malik el-Kamil allowed access to the city for pilgrims, and a return for a part of the permanent Christian population. When the Crusaders finally left the Holy Land in 1291 Nazareth went into a seemingly terminal decline, with one early 14th-century source describing the Muslim population of the town as being "wicked of heart, cruel and fanatical, who wreaked havoc upon all the Christian churches".

The **Ottoman** conquest of Palestine saw little change in the status of Nazareth until the Druze emir **Fakhr ed-Din** allowed a significant Christian population to return to the town. In 1620 the Franciscans established a monastery and began the reconstruction of a church on the traditional site of the Annunciation. The respite was short lived, however, and following the execution of the emir a period of persecution and discrimination resumed.

The first half of the 18th century saw the Bedouin sheikh **Dahr el-Amr** carve out a semi-independent fiefdom in the Galilee, and being reasonably well disposed towards Christians he allowed considerable construction of churches and monasteries within Nazareth. The church that the Franciscans built over the site of the Annunciation stood until work on the present basilica began in 1955. Despite persecution and the threat of genocide under **Ahmed el-Jazzar** ('The Butcher') towards the end of the 18th century, Nazareth continued to grow. Greater stability in the mid-19th century saw a major increase in the volume of visitors from Europe, notably Russia, and a return to the status of a major pilgrimage site that it occupied in the Crusader period.

The Allied forces under General Allenby captured Nazareth in September 1918 as part of the campaign that saw the rout of the German-Turkish forces across the Plain of Esdraelon. The **British** made Nazareth their Galilean administrative headquarters, and, following their withdrawal from Palestine at the end of the Mandate period, the **Israelis** captured the town on 16th July, 1948.

Today, Nazareth (En-Nasra) is one of the largest Arab towns in Israel with a population evenly split between Christianity and Islam. This has led to some friction in recent years. The local council's plan to build a large piazza on land just below the Basilica of the Annunciation to receive the huge numbers of visitors expected in the year 2000 has been scuppered by a Muslim group who have occupied the land, claiming a mosque once stood here and demanding that it should be rebuilt. The scene turned particularly ugly over Easter 1999, when a Muslim mob attacked Christian worshippers leaving the Basilica. At the time of going to press an uneasy stand-off remained, and there is currently talk of a compromise involving the construction of a temporary piazza in time for 2000, followed by the building of a mosque at a later date.

A large Jewish town, **Nazareth Illit** (Nasrat Illit, or Upper Nazareth), has developed on the hills above the Arab town; the combined population of the two towns is around 60,000. Though there is substantial industry within Nazareth, and the surrounding area is an important agricultural region, tourism remains a major sector of the local economy. Most visitors agree, however, that Christian holy places apart, Nazareth is a distinctly unattractive town with high levels of traffic and low levels of urban planning.

Sights

Dominating the lower town, the modern Basilica is built over the reputed site of the home of the Virgin Mary; the scene of the Annunciation (*Luke 1:26-38*). Consecrated in 1969, the current Basilica is said to be the largest church built in the Holy Land for the best part of 800 years. The exterior design is not to everybody's liking, with the Basilica being variously likened to a giant lantern or a lighthouse ('Light unto the World'). This is more than compensated for inside, however, by the skill of the architects in incorporating parts of the earlier places of worship that stood on this site into the bold and modern structure seen today.

Basilica of the Annunciation

Extensive excavations were undertaken on this site in 1955 by the Franciscan Institute for Biblical Research, unearthing a network of granaries, caves

Grotto of the Annunciation

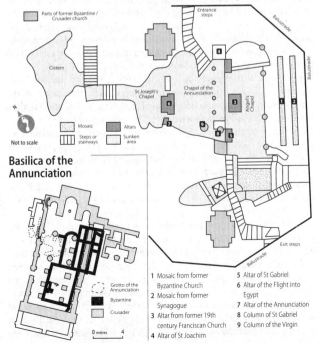

Parts of former Byzantine / Crusader church

Cistern

Entrance steps

Balustrade

Balustrade

St Joseph's Chapel

Chapel of the Annunciation

Angel's Chapel

Mosaic

Altars

Steps or stairways

Sunken area

Not to scale

Exit steps

Balustrade

Basilica of the Annunciation

Grotto of the Annunciation

Byzantine

Crusader

0 metres 4

1 Mosaic from former Byzantine Church
2 Mosaic from former Synagogue
3 Altar from former 19th century Franciscan Church
4 Altar of St Joachim
5 Altar of St Gabriel
6 Altar of the Flight into Egypt
7 Altar of the Annunciation
8 Column of St Gabriel
9 Column of the Virgin

Galilee & The Golan

and vaulted storage cells dating to the Roman period at least. One such granary cave has subsequently been venerated as the Grotto of the Annunciation. The 1955 investigations also revealed the plan of a large three-wing Byzantine church, probably fourth or fifth century CE, that incorporated the Grotto within its design. Several mosaic floors have survived from the Byzantine church, and have subsequently been relaid.

The basilica that the Crusaders built on this site in the late 12th century is considered to have been one of the most magnificent structures that they built in the Holy Land. Built on the ruins of the Byzantine church, and incorporating the Grotto and crypt to its north, the interior was elaborately decorated by French masons as well as local craftsmen. Work was probably not yet complete when the Christian community was expelled from Nazareth following Salah al-Din's victory at Hittim in 1187. The present basilica largely follows the line of the Crusader church.

The main entrance is on Casa Nova Street, from where it is possible to admire the superb **west façade**. At the apex stands a statue of Jesus, below which in bas-relief is a representation of the angel Gabriel bringing the message to Mary. Matthew, Mark, Luke and John, together with their traditional symbols (man, lion, bull and eagle), are depicted below, along with quotations from Genesis (*3:14-15*) and Isaiah (*7:14*). Above the door is a line from the New Testament: "The Word was made flesh, and dwelt among us" (*John 1:14*). The huge central door features six key events in the life of Jesus depicted in bronze, with ten further incidents detailed in copper.

The Basilica is built on two levels with the main entrance leading to the **Grotto of the Annunciation**. A low balustrade surrounds the sunken enclosure that contains the Grotto, though access to this chapel is generally only granted to pilgrim groups who have made a prior appointment to hold a brief mass. Parts of the Byzantine and Crusader churches are clearly visible. Of the two parallel strips of **mosaic** opposite the cavern, the one nearest the balustrade is thought to belong to a synagogue that previously stood on this site. The second strip is from the Byzantine church. The **central altar** in this chapel comes from the 18th-century Franciscan church that previously occupied the site. The octagonal opening above the sunken enclosure allows worshippers in the nave of the Basilica to look down into the Grotto.

Passing the attractive coloured glass windows that spread shafts and patterns of brightly coloured light across the lower level of the Basilica, ascend the spiral staircase into the main body of the church. Note the fine **stained-glass window** in the southwest wall of the nave. The **cupola** of the Basilica measures 16 metres in circumference, 55 metres above the nave, and represents an inverted lily, it roots stretching up to heaven and its petals enveloping the site of the Annunciation. The floral association is derived from the Semitic name 'Nazareth', meaning flower. Above the high altar is a huge **mosaic** depicting Jesus, arms outstretched, flanked by St Peter and a seated Virgin Mary. The two small **chapels** either side of the altar are dedicated to St Francis and the Holy Ghost respectively.

Leaving the Basilica through a small side door, you come to the **Baptistry**; traditionally separated from the Basilica by a custom that forbade those who were not baptized from entering the church. The bronze-cast font is encased with amethyst and green glass panels. Below can be seen some of the **network of caves**, oil presses, dwellings, cisterns and granaries that were discovered during the excavations of 1955. Some contained potsherds dating to the Israelite period (Iron Age: 1200-586 BCE), though most of the remnants found are from the Roman and Byzantine periods. To the north of the Basilica, within the same compound, is St Joseph's Church. ■ T6572501. *1st April-30th*

September Monday-Saturday 0830-1200 1400-1745, Sunday 1400-1730, 1st October-31st March Monday-Saturday 0900-1200 1400-1630, Sunday 1400-1630; admission free; toilets available.

Identification of this site with Joseph's carpentry shop is thought to be a 17th-century tradition, though it is not clear whether the triapsidal Crusader church that previously occupied this site claimed any such association. The present church, built on the lines of the Crusader structure, dates to 1914. The rock-hewn water reservoir can be viewed through metal grilles in the floor of the crypt. Lower levels have revealed a granary cave and a pit. Artefacts from this site have been dated to Israelite (1200-586 BCE), Hellenistic (332-37 BCE), Roman (37 BCE-324 CE), Byzantine (324-638 CE) and medieval periods. To the rear of the crypt, behind the iron guard, a two metres by two metres basin has been cut into the floor, accessible by seven steps. Similar in style to an early baptistry found beneath the Basilica of the Annunciation, it is tentatively identified as an early baptismal pool, possibly pre-Constantine (ie prior to the fourth century CE). ■ *Open same hours as the Basilica of the Annunciation.* **St Joseph's Church**

Those staying at the Sisters of Nazareth Convent (see 'Sleeping', page 621) will already appreciate the tranquil confines of the convent's walled courtyard. By making a prior appointment it may also be possible to view sections of the first- to fourth-century Jewish necropolis located beneath the convent. Archaeologists suggest that the necropolis has one of the best examples in the country of a tomb sealed by a rolling stone. It is thought that the burial chamber was used as a storeroom during the medieval times, with remains of a Crusader monastery or convent on this site clearly visible. ■ *No 3, Street 306, T6554304, F6460741.* **Sisters of Nazareth Convent**

Despite its narrow winding streets and labyrinth-like properties, Nazareth's 'old' bazaar area is certainly not the stuff of "1001 Nights". Most of the produce is the simple everyday essentials of a modern town; fruit and vegetables, clothing and household utensils, with the odd smattering of mass-produced junk for the pilgrim/tourist market. The whole area has recently been re-paved, resulting in the disappearance of the open sewer that used to feature so prominently. Beware, however, of opening your nostrils wide to inhale that rich aroma of fresh coffee; the open sewer has not disappeared completely. **Bazaar area**

Located within the bazaar area is a small church run by the Greek Catholics referred to as the 'Synagogue Church'. Tradition has it that this is the site of the synagogue in Nazareth where the young Jesus was taught, and to where, as an adult, he returned to read from the scriptures, thus fulfilling their prophesy (*Luke 4:16-21*). Such a site is first mentioned in the writings of the Pilgrim of Piacenza around 570 CE, though the simple barrel-vaulted room that you see inside the courtyard to the left of the church dates only to Crusader times. Indeed, the Pilgrim of Piacenza was even shown the bench upon which Jesus sat learning the scriptures as a child, and notes that whilst Christians were able to lift it and move it about, Jews were unable to budge it at all! **Synagogue Church**

To reach the Synagogue Church, head up Casa Nova Street from the Basilica. Where the road bears right, head left through the new stone arch into the paved old bazaar. About 100 metres on your left take the first left turn. Walk to the end of the street, turn right, and the pillar-flanked archway leading into the Synagogue Church's courtyard is 20 metres on your right. ■ *T6568488. 0830-1800, or ring bell. A small donation is expected.*

Galilee & The Golan

Mensa Christi Church A large slab of stone measuring 3.6 metres by 3 metres, reputed to be the table at which Jesus is said to have dined with his disciples shortly after his resurrection, is the centrepiece of the small Mensa Christi (*Latin*: 'Table of Christ') Church. The 'table' is scored by the graffiti of centuries of pilgrims. Built by the Franciscans in 1861, the church is located to the northwest of the bazaar area (though it is not always open to the public; ask at the Basilica of the Annunciation). Close by is the 18th-century **Maronite Church of St Anthony**, whilst to the south is the 19th-century **Anglican ('Jesus') Church**, built in the shape of a cross. ■ *Church of St Anthony: T6554256, open Sunday 0800-1200; Anglican Church: T6456348, open 0800-1230 1600-1800.*

Salesian Monastery and Basilica of Jesus the Adolescent Dominating the hillside above Nazareth is the monastery belonging to the French Salesian order. This Gothic-style basilica, built in 1918, features a large statue above the high altar of Jesus as an adolescent. Although it is a fairly steep and winding climb up to the monastery from the bazaar area, and the basilica is not always open for visitors, it is worth making the effort to get up here in order to enjoy the view across Nazareth. ■ *T6468954, open 0830-1145 1400-1700.*

The hill in the middle distance, just beyond the edge of town, is the '**Mount of Precipitation**' ('Mount of the Leap of the Lord') from which the people of Nazareth are reputed to have attempted to throw Jesus, having rejected his teachings (see 'Chapel of Fright/Notre Dame de l'Effroi', on page 620). Above the Salesian Monastery, beyond the *St Gabriel Monastery Hotel*, you can make out the rocket-like minaret of the **Maqam Nabi Sa'in Mosque**.

Mary's Well and St Gabriel's Church Greek Orthodox tradition holds that the Archangel Gabriel's first appearance to Mary took place at the village well or fountain (see the second-century *Protoevangelium of James*, or *Apocryphal Gospel of St James*). This mid-18th-century church is built over the site of Nazareth's fresh-water spring ('Mary's Well'), though the site has been revered since Byzantine times; the Pilgrim of Piacenza visited around 570 CE the spring from which Mary is said to have drawn water, whilst the pilgrim Arculf mentions a church on this site during his visit around 670 CE.

Like most Greek Orthodox churches, St Gabriel's has a lavishly decorated interior, with painted screens (iconostasis), icons and hanging lamps. Seven steps descend into a vaulted chamber built by the Crusaders, where, on the left, you can draw water from the shaft with a metal cup. The spring can be seen two metres below the metal balustrade at the far end of the chamber.

Close to St Gabriel's Church, just off the traffic roundabout, is the unattractive **Fountain of Mary**; a modern outlet for the waters of the ancient spring. Both church and fountain are located about 500 metres northeast of the Basilica of the Annunciation, along Paul VI Street. ■ *T6574566/6576437/6554914. 0800-1145 1500-1800, closes half-hour earlier in winter. A small donation is expected.*

Chapel of Fright (Notre Dame de l'Effroi) Following Jesus' preaching in the synagogue at Nazareth (see *Luke 4:16-21*, and details of the Synagogue Church on page 619), the people of the town grew agitated, "rose up, and thrust him out of the city, and led him unto the brow of the hill whereon their city was built, that they might cast him down headlong. But he passing through the midst of them went his way" (*Luke 4:29-30*). The hill mentioned in Luke's narrative, the '**Mount of Precipitation**' (or 'Mount of the Leap of the Lord'), is supposedly located just to the south of Nazareth, on the edge of the modern town. The Franciscan's **Chapel of Fright**, or Notre Dame de l'Effroi, is built on the site from which Mary is said to have witnessed this scene. The Orthodox community have their own chapel, **Kaser**

el-Mutran, on a different site (see map). A wealthy Russian pilgrim is said to have donated the funds for the chapel's construction in 1862.

The Franciscan's Chapel of Fright can be reached by heading south on the road opposite the *Galilee/HaGalil Hotel* on Paul VI Street (next to the Nazarene Church), and continuing beyond St Claire's Convent. The 'Mount of Precipitation' is about two kilometres outside the town centre. Visitors hoping for a few moments of thoughtful contemplation should note that the nearby 'Swiss Mountain' is the proposed site of a tourist hotel and leisure complex, possibly linked to the 'Mount of Precipitation' by cable-car!

There are a number of other sites in Nazareth, though they are of limited interest or appeal. The **el-Abyad (White) Mosque**, on the edge of the bazaar area to the north of the Basilica, was built in 1812 and is Nazareth's oldest. The unimpressive **Khan el-Basha**, just up from the Tourist Information Office, is a caravanserai renovated by Abdullah Pasha in the same year. Along a narrow alley just up from, and opposite, the Tourist Information Office is the small white domed **Tomb of Maqam Shihab el-Din**, a Muslim leader and nephew of Salah al-Din. This is next to the contested site for the new piazza/mosque (see 'History' on page 614). There are numerous other churches in Nazareth, though few are particularly worth a visit. Architecturally, the old wing of the **French Hospital** is rather attractive. ■ *White Mosque T6569061, daily 0900-1700.*

Other sites

Essentials

Nazareth has a reasonable range of accommodation, though there is often a severe shortage of bed space. Advance reservation is recommended at all times, and essential around the main Christian festivals. Group discounts are available at most places.

Sleeping
■ *on map;*
Price codes:
see inside front cover

A *Nazareth Gardens*, outskirts of town, T6468686, F6573008. Fabulously ugly building though serene location amidst parkland on the edge of town, renovated rooms are well equipped (some with private gardens). Facilities include pool, fitness centre, children's play area, panoramic-view dining area.

B *Galilee/HaGalil*, Paul VI, T6571311, F6556827. Catering mainly to (Italian) pilgrim groups, central location, recently renovated with huge new extension. 400-seat self-service restaurant, souvenir shop, tours organized. Busy and not very intimate. **B** *Grand New*, Hamotran, T6573020, F6576281. Recently refurbished 'tourist class' hotel in quiet location to the west of the town centre. **B** *St Gabriel Monastery*, PO Box 2448, off Salesian, T6572133, F6554071. Excellent location above town, large picture windows (so make sure you get a front-facing room), a/c not necessary in this stone building, pleasant rooms, good restaurant, attractive terrace and gardens. Recommended. **B** *St Margaret's Anglican Pilgrim Hostel*, Orfaneg, T6573507, F6567166. Formerly a 19th-century orphanage for girls, this is a beautiful white-façaded building set around a charming courtyard. Rooms are quite large and well furnished, views are fabulous, and staff are friendly. Recommended, especially at discounted tour group prices.

C *Casa Nova Hospice*, Casa Nova, T6456660, F6579630. Reasonably good value doubles and triples with ensuite bath, a/c, phone, price includes half-board (or $4 extra per person for full board), advance booking essential, check-out 0930, curfew 2230. **C** *Nazareth*, Paul VI, T6577777, F6578511. Recently renovated (though nothing special), on rather noisy road.

Galilee & The Golan

E *Frères de Betharram Hospice*, 85 Rd 5050, Eilout, T6570046. Simple pilgrim accommodation in (non-English speaking) monastery grounds. **E** *Sisters of Nazareth Guest House and Youth Hostel*, PO Box 274, No 3, St 306, T6554304, F6460741. An excellent choice. The *Guest House* features 30 centrally heated private rooms with good half- and full-board options, plus there are very cheap single-sex dorms (**F**) with shared kitchenette and living room in the *Youth Hostel*, all set around a tranquil cloistered courtyard. Check-in 1600, check-out 1000, strict 2100 curfew.

Eating Many visitors staying in Nazareth will be offered full and half-board terms at their hotels, and these can be reasonably good value. Casa Nova St and Paul VI St are lined with restaurants selling hummus, falafel, shwarma, grilled chicken, etc, though none is exceptional. *Astoria*, T6573497, at the junction of Casa Nova and Paul VI, is probably the pick of the bunch. *La Fontana de Maria*, 3 Paul VI St, just to the east of Mary's Well, has received some reasonable reviews. The *YMCA* restaurant, off Wadi el-Juwani (opposite French Hospital), T6465680, is quite good value. *Abu Diab Mahroum's Sweets*, T6571802, offers excellent sweets and Middle Eastern desserts with coffee, though it is best to go to the original, adjacent to the Basilica, rather than one of the imitation *Mahroum's Sweets* that also line Casa Nova St.

Entertainment **Cinemas** *GG Gil*, Nazareth Illit, T6561332. **Festivals** Easter Week is marked by a Sacred Music Festival, with similar musical perfomances over the Christmas period (tickets for church services should be arranged in advance through the tourist office). The **Feast of the Annunciation** (23rd March 2000) is the most exciting (and busiest) time to visit Nazareth. The **Nazareth Festival of Arab Folklore** is held towards the end of summer.

Transport **Local Car hire**: Most hotels can arrange car (and driver) hire, notably for excursions to Mt Tabor (see page 625). *Europcar*, T6554129; *Hertz*, T6575313. **Taxis**: *Abu el-Assal*, near junction of Paul VI and Casa Nova, T6554745.

Buses There is no bus station in Nazareth; simply a series of bus stops on either side of Paul VI. Those on the north side (close to the Egged information office, T6549555) run to destinations to the south and west (Haifa, Tel Aviv, Afula), whilst those on the south side (close to the Hamishbir department store) run east and northwest (Tiberias, Cana, Akko, Zippori, Shefar'am). **Afula**: see Tel Aviv. **Akko**: Bus 343, Sunday-Thursday 1 per hr until about 1700, Friday last at 1600, Saturday limited morning service, 45 mins, 20 NIS. **Cana (Kafr Kana)**: Bus 022, hourly, or Bus 431 (see Tiberias bus) passes through the village, 15 mins. **Haifa**: numerous services, including 331, 336, 341, 343 (via **Akko**), 351, 431, leaving at least every 20-40 mins, 1 hr, 20 NIS. **Megiddo**: Bus 823 (see Tel Aviv below) passes the site, though this is not a designated stop. Best to change at Afula. **Shefar'am**: Buses 341/343 pass turn-off for the town (see Haifa, below, and Akko, above). **Tel Aviv** via **Afula** and **coastal road**: Bus 824, Sunday-Thursday hourly until 2030, Friday last at 1600, Saturday limited service from sundown, 1½-2 hrs, 34 NIS. **Tel Aviv** via **Afula** and **Petah Tiqva**: Bus 823, Sunday-Thursday 1 per hour until about 1900, Friday limited service until 1630, Saturday several services after sundown. **Tiberias**: Bus 431, Sunday-Thursday 1 per hour until early evening, Friday hourly until late afternoon, Saturday limited service after sundown, 45 mins, 18 NIS. **Zippori**: Buses 341/343 (see Haifa and Akko, above) pass the intersection, 4km from the site. **Sherut/service taxi** There are sheruts to **Haifa**, **Tel Aviv** and **Tiberias** from close to the Hamishbir department store on Paul VI.

Directory **Banks** *Bank HaPoalim*, Paul VI St, T6570923; *Bank Leumi*, Paul VI St, T6570282; *Israel Discount Bank*, Casa Nova: all change money, though beware of commission charges or poor rates. *Change-Spot*, 81 Paul VI St, offers quick, commission-free exchange. **Communications** Phone

Galilee & The Golan

code: T06. **NB** If you have an old 6-digit number, try prefacing it with a '6'. **Post offices**: *Central Post Office* (including poste restante) is a couple of blocks to the west of Mary's Well (Open Mon, Tue, Thu, Fri 0800-1230 and 1530-1800, Wed 0800-1330, Sat 0800-1200). There's also a small post office on Paul VI, close to the *Galilee Hotel*. **Cultural centres** French Cultural Centre, Paul VI St, T6560954, F6571508. **Hospitals and medical services** Chemists: Concentrated at lower end of Wadi el-Juwani (see map), or try *Farah*, T6554018, close to bus information office. **Hospitals**: *Nazareth*, Wadi el-Juwani, T6571501; *French*, off Wadi el-Juwani, T6574530 (very attractive!); *Holy Family*, northeast of town, T6574535. **Tourist offices** *Tourist Information Office*, Casa Nova St, T6573003/6570555, F6573078. Open Mon-Fri 0830-1700, Sat 0830-1400. Quite helpful, reasonable map, will also book tickets for church services during the main Christian festivals. **Useful addresses and phone numbers** Police: T100 (emergency), T6574444 (close to Mary's Well). **Fire**: T102. **Ambulance**: Magen David Adom T101.

Around Nazareth

Cana

The small Arab village of Kafr Kanna some nine kilometres northeast of Naza- *Phone code: 06* reth is claimed as the site of the biblical town of Cana, where Jesus performed *Colour map 1, grid B3* his first miracle by turning water into wine at a wedding feast (*John 2:1-11*). There is no archaeological evidence to sustain this belief, though there is a long tradition dating back to the early Christian era of associating this site with the miracle. Sceptics might like to note that another village in Western Galilee is also called Kafr Kanna (near to Yodfat) and claims the same distinction, whilst cynics will enjoy the numerous souvenir shops in this village selling 'Cana wedding wine'. Further, two different factions of the Christian church compete to claim the event as their own.

Around Nazareth

Ins and outs Cana is best reached by bus from Nazareth. Bus 022 runs at least once an hour from Nazareth, while it is also possible to take the Haifa to Tiberias bus (431), and ask to be let off as it passes through Cana. Most of Nazareth's hotels will arrange taxi tours to Cana, usually also including a visit to Mt Tabor (see page 625).

Franciscan Church of the Wedding Feast This Roman Catholic church is located in the centre of the village. Though it was built in the late 19th century, parts of earlier Crusader and Byzantine churches can be seen within the crypt. The church's red dome and twin bell-towers are the village's main landmark. The interior of the church is fairly simple, with the main points of interest being in the crypt. Before descending the twelve steps note the section of third or fourth century CE mosaic beneath the grille to the right. A translation of the Aramaic inscription reads "Memory of the pious Joseph son of Canhourn son of Bota and of his children who made this table, may it be for them a blessing. Amen." It is suggested that the inscription was originally part of a synagogue bench, with the Joseph mentioned being a Christian convert and founder of several new churches in Galilee during the early Byzantine period.

Franciscan Church of the Wedding Feast, Cana

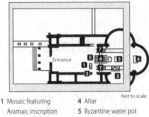

Not to scale

1 Mosaic featuring Aramaic inscription
2 Translation of inscription
3 Well
4 Altar
5 Byzantine water pot
6 Steps to crypt
7 Stairs to upper floor

The crypt contains a Byzantine fountain and water pot, plus the remains of ancient cisterns. Some claim that this crypt is the actual site of the miracle, with an altar commemorating the spot and a pictorial representation of Jesus blessing the wine. The numerous jars and pots just off the passageway to the left are not claimed to be the original vessels used at the wedding; simply replicas. Exiting the crypt to the left you emerge via a room dedicated to the act of worldwide Christian marriage. Numerous banners and pennants proclaim "World Marriage Day", and "Marriage Encounter Australia – with love from Down Under", etc. ■ *Monday-Friday 0800-1200 1400-1700, Saturday 0800-1200, Sunday closed. Free, donations accepted.*

Cana Greek Orthodox Wedding Church Close to the Roman Catholic church is the Greek Orthodox version. Built around the end of the 19th century in the shape of a Greek cross, this small church features a grand central chandelier, a large number of icons, and church benches that seem to have been ordered from the latest IKEA catalogue. The most important artefacts are two stone jars that are rather improbably claimed to have featured in the miracle itself. It's tempting to suggest that they came from the same source as the benches, though they are more likely to be around 300 years old (though not 2,000!). ■ *0830-1830. Free, donations accepted.*

Nathanael Chapel Cana was also the home of Nathanael, a man whose initial suspicions of Jesus led to his oft-quoted expression "Can there be anything good come out of Nazareth?" (*John 1:46*), but who later became one of the early disciples of Jesus (*John 1:49*) and was present when the resurrected Christ appeared to his disciples at the Sea of Galilee (*John 21:2*). To the north of the village of Cana the Franciscans have built a small chapel (Nathanael Chapel) over the supposed site of his former home.

Mt Tabor

Since the fourth century CE, Mt Tabor has been identified with the "high mountain apart" *(Matthew 17:1; Mark 9:2)*; the scene of Christ's **Transfiguration**. Rising above the surrounding countryside to a height of 588 metres, Tabor is a suitable location for such an important event in the Christian tradition: "Jesus took Peter, John and James and went up a mountain to pray. And while he was praying the appearance of his face changed and his clothes became a brilliant white. Suddenly there were two men talking with him – Moses and Elijah – who appeared in glory and spoke of his departure, and the destiny he was to fulfil in Jerusalem … there came a cloud which cast its shadow over them; they were afraid as they entered the cloud, and from it a voice spoke: 'This is my son, my chosen; listen to him.' After the voice had spoken, Jesus was seen to be alone. The disciples kept silence and did not at that time say a word to anyone of what they had seen." *(Luke 9:28-36).*

Phone code: 06
Colour map 1, grid C3

Ins and outs

Public transport to Mt Tabor is not particularly good. From **Tiberias**, the buses bound for Afula or Tel Aviv travelling along Route 65 pass the base of the mountain. From **Nazareth** it is possible to take Bus 357 via **Afula** to the village of Daburiya at the base of the hill. This bus only runs thrice a day (twice early in the morning and once mid-afternoon). Either way, it is a very steep climb to the top of Mt Tabor (8km if you get off at the junction with Route 65 on the main Afula to Tiberias road). Most visitors to Mt Tabor arrive on tour buses, particularly those visiting from Nazareth. These tend to park on the north side of Mt Tabor, close to the village of Shibli, where white stretch Mercedes taxis ferry the multitudes to the summit.

History

Early Christian scholars vacillated in their placement of the scene of the Transfiguration, with Eusebius unable to decide between Tabor and Mt Hermon and the Pilgrim of Bordeaux (c. 333 CE) suggesting the Mount of Olives as the true site. Mt Tabor finally installed itself as the first choice after Cyril, Bishop of Jerusalem, decided in its favour in 348 CE. By the late sixth century the Pilgrim of Piacenza described three basilicas built on the site. Currently two churches on the summit commemorate the event.

The appeal of Mount Tabor as a "high mountain apart" was recognized as long ago as the second millennium BCE, when the **Canaanites** created a 'high place' here for the worship of Baal. It was also from the top of Mt Tabor c. 1125 BCE that **Deborah** and Barak swept down upon the 900 iron chariots of Sisera, general of the king of Hazor, and vanquished the Canaanite army *(Judges 4:4-24)*. A similar feat was achieved by Antiochus III of Syria in 218 BCE, who lured the Egyptian garrison down from their position of strength atop the mountain and slaughtered them to a man.

Mount Tabor

N
Not to scale

1 Church of St Elias
2 Church of the Transfiguration
3 Chapel
4 Gate of the Wind
5 Graveyard
6 Parking

Mt Tabor remained a stronghold in Roman times with the Jewish commander of the Galilee **Josephus** fortifying the mountain-top prior to the advance of Vespasian's army (although he later embraced the Roman cause). Josephus describes how the huge defensive rampart around the summit was built within just 40 days, though he also describes Mt Tabor as being "no less than 20,000 feet high" *(Jewish War, IV, 55)*! Nevertheless, parts of a large

Galilee & The Golan

defensive wall dating to this period can still be seen. Josephus' account of the subsequent battle is an excellent lesson in duplicity; the Roman commander Placidus, with an army of 600 horsemen, found the ascent too steep and thus offered the Jewish garrison surrender terms with the intent of slaughtering them once they left their mountain stronghold. The Jewish garrison, in turn, feinted a surrender and then attacked the Roman army. The superior organization of the professional Roman army won the day with most of the Jewish army killed or captured and the rest fleeing to Jerusalem (*Jewish War, IV, 56*).

The **Crusaders** built new churches and monasteries on the Byzantine ruins following their conquest of the Holy Land in 1099, though the small community of Benedictine monks that they installed were murdered by the Turks in 1113. Subsequent Crusader-built places of worship on Mt Tabor were more akin to fortresses, withstanding Salah al-Din's attack in 1183. Following their defeat at the Horns of Hittim four years later, the Crusaders abandoned Mt Tabor, though the threat of their return (the Fourth Crusade, 1202-04) forced the sultan of Damascus **Melek el-Adel** to re-fortify the site. Many of the defences still visible today were built by the sultan and his son **Melek el-Moudzam**.

The presence of this Muslim-built stronghold on the site of the Transfiguration inspired the Fifth Crusade, and though the Crusaders failed to capture the mountain, Melek el-Adel dismantled much of his fortress in order to placate the Christians. Pilgrims and monastic orders were permitted a presence on the mountain-top, though they were subsequently banished by the sultan Baibars in 1263.

The Druze emir Fakhr ed-Din allowed the Franciscans to build a monastery on Mt Tabor in 1631 and they have remained ever since. In 1911 the Greek Orthodox built a church dedicated to St Elias (Elijah) on the north side of the summit.

Sights An extremely steep and winding road climbs up from the base of the mountain. Close to the top the road forks, with the path to the left leading to the Greek sector and the right to the Franciscan-owned area. The right fork leads through the **Gate of the Wind**; part of Melek el-Adel's medieval fortress (ignore the no-entry sign). It is possible to trace the line of the 13th-century defensive walls (with their twelve towers) around the summit of Mount Tabor, though they are generally unremarkable. Parts of ancient walls, possibly Josephus', can also be seen about 50 metres to the right. Continuing along the tree-lined avenue of the Franciscans' estate, a medieval graveyard lays to the left of the path whilst a small **chapel** stands to the right. Little is known about the Byzantine structure that forms the building's foundations though the chapel itself is a Crusader commemoration of the conversation between Jesus and his disciples following his Transfiguration. The graveyard dates to the first century CE whilst the surrounding ruins are probably part of the Benedictine monastery complex destroyed by the Turks in 1113.

Beyond the car-park, behind the wrought-iron gates, is the piazza of the Franciscans' complex. A modern monastery and hospice stands opposite the 12th-century ruins of the Benedictine monastery. At the end of the path is the splendid **Church of the Transfiguration**. Completed in 1924, the Italian architect Antonio Barluzzi incorporated the monumental building style of the early Christian church in Syria into the design. Everything is on a grand scale including the twin projecting towers marking the façade, whilst the nave is separated from the aisles by wide arches and is at a middle level between the altar and crypt. A large mosaic in the vaulting depicts the Transfiguration of Christ. The colourful crypt reveals parts of the earlier Crusader and Byzantine churches as well as evidence of the Canaanite occupation of the summit. Two chapels in the west towers are dedicated to Elijah and Moses respectively, the latter containing a mosaic floor dating to before 422 CE (after that date the Emperor Theodosius II banned the representation of crosses on church floors).

On leaving the church turn sharp left up the stairs to the **viewpoint**. From here there are unprecedented views north across the Galilee, east to the Jordan Valley, and south across the Jezreel Valley to Samaria.

Leaving the Franciscans' property, head over to the Greek Orthodox sites on the north side of the summit. These include the **Church of St Elias** (Elijah), built in 1911 upon the ruins of a Crusader church. The church stands above the '**Cave of Melchisedek**' (enter through small iron door outside); dubiously supposed to be the site where Melchisedek, king of Salem, received Abraham (*Genesis 14:18-20*). ■ *T6767489. 0800-1200 1400-1800, closes 1700 in winter. Free. Modest dress essential.*

There are a number of minor places of interest in the vicinity of Mt Tabor, though none really merits a special trip. The Arab village of **Daburiya** at the western foot of Mt Tabor is named after the Israelite Prophetess and Judge, Deborah. Tradition holds that upon coming down from the mountain, after the Transfiguration, Jesus healed an epileptic boy here (*Luke 9:37-42*). The small Bedouin village of **Shibli** just to the north of Mt Tabor has a recently opened *Galilee Bedouin Heritage Centre*. Several kilometres to the northeast of Mt Tabor is the village of **Kafr Kama**; a small settlement established by Circassians in 1880 who were escaping the persecution of Muslims in Russia. **Ein Dor**, (to the southeast of Mt Tabor, just off the Afula to Tiberias road, Route 65), is the reputed site of the biblical city of En-dor where, prior to his fateful battle on Mt Gilboa, Saul consulted with a witch in order to communicate with the the spirit of the prophet Samuel (*I Samuel 28:7-25*). There's nothing to see here now though the kibbutz has an attractive guesthouse complete with swimming pool. Further south still, closer to Afula along Route 65, is **Nain**, supposed site of the miracle at which Jesus restored to life the only son of a widow (*Luke 7:11-17*). A small church marks the site. ■ *Galilee Bedouin Heritage Centre: Saturday-Thursday 0900-1600, 10 NIS.*

Sights around Mt Tabor
Phone code: 06

Sepphoris (Zippori)

The city of Sepphoris was a major Jewish town in Galilee during the Roman and Byzantine periods. Known by its Hebrew name of Zippori (sometimes Tzipori), the site here is now a National Park with a well-marked trail leading you through the substantial remains of the successive cities built on the mound. Zippori National Park is noteworthy for two particular factors; its superbly preserved Roman and Byzantine mosaics and its excellent standard of dynamic presentation.

Phone code: 06
Colour map 1, grid C3

Ins and outs

Zippori is not the easiest place to get to by public transport. Bus 016 leaves once a day from Nazareth (at 1310) though there is no return connection. Bus 343 between Nazareth and Akko and Bus 341 between Tiberias, Nazareth and Haifa travel along Route 79, and there is a bus stop at the turn-off for the site. From this junction it is a four-kilometre walk. See 'Around Nazareth' map on page 623 for orientation.

Getting there

History

Roman rule The ancient city of Sepphoris has played a major role in the history of Roman Galilee. During the Hasmonean period (152-37 BCE) Sepphoris was probably the administrative centre of the whole of Galilee, with Josephus mentioning the town during the reign of Alexander Jannaeus (103-76 BCE). Eight years after the Roman conquest of Palestine in 63 BCE, the proconsul **Gabinius** instituted a number of administrative reforms and declared Sepphoris the capital of the district of Galilee, perhaps suggesting that it was already the most important city in the region. **Herod the Great** took the city without opposition as one of his first acts after gaining power in 37 BCE (Josephus, *Jewish War I, 304*).

Following Herod's death the townspeople rose up and attempted to sever links with Rome. The rebellion was short lived and under the command of Varus, governor of Syria, Sepphoris was razed and its inhabitants enslaved (*Jewish War II, 68*). Thus, when Herod the Great's kingdom was partitioned, the Sepphoris that his son **Herod Antipas** inherited was an uninhabited ruin. Some scholars argue that the ambitious reconstruction plan that Herod Antipas initiated drew artisans and craftsmen from far and wide, including a certain Joseph who chose to settle in nearby Nazareth (see page 616). Herod Antipas' city became known as Autocratoris, though it soon receded in importance around 20 CE when the capital was shifted to the new city of Tiberias.

The picture of Sepphoris during the **First Jewish Revolt** against Rome (66-73 CE) is rather confused. As Governor of Galilee, **Josephus** oversaw the fortification of much of the province pending the imminent Roman attack. He writes that "Only in Sepphoris were the citizens invited to build a wall on their own responsibility: Josephus saw that they had ample means and that their enthusiasm for war needed no stimulus" (*Jewish War II, 566*). However, when the Roman army arrived, the population of Sepphoris surrendered their city without a fight, Josephus now noting that the inhabitants of Sepphoris were "the only people in Galilee who desired peace" (*ibid, III, 33*). It could be that the people of Sepphoris had learnt their lesson during the build up to the war with Rome, when their dalliance with Josephus' rival John had forced the former to subdue the town. Josephus decided to "give the citizens a sharp lesson by pillaging it, then by giving back their possessions to recover their good will" (*ibid, II, 647*)!

Relations with the Romans following the First Jewish Revolt appear to have been relatively stable, with the Jewish local government even minting coins in honour of the Roman emperor Trajan (98-117 CE). But though there are no records of events in Sepphoris during the Bar Kokhba Uprising (132-135 CE), the resulting fate of Sepphoris suggests that the Romans did not enjoy the support of the local people; the Jewish local government was abolished and replaced with a gentile one, and the city was given the Roman name Diocaesarea.

Jewish renaissance Sepphoris' Jewish renaissance really dates to the second and third centuries CE. Towards the end of the second century CE **Rabbi Judah I ha-Nasi** shifted the **Sanhedrin** (highest judicial and ecclesiastical council of the ancient Jewish nation) from Bet She'arim to Sepphoris (or **Zippori**), and it was here c. 200 CE that the codification of Jewish law, *Mishnah*, was completed. With the restoration of local government, Jewish life in Zippori flourished and the town is subsequently mentioned many times in Talmudic literature. Indeed, the Hebrew name of Zippori is explained in the *Babylonian Talmud*: "Because it is perched on the top of a mountain like a bird [zippor]" (*Megillah 6:a*). The Sanhedrin continued to sit in Zippori until the middle of the third century, when it was shifted to Tiberias by Rabbi Yohanan.

Byzantine period

With Christianity becoming the state religion of the Roman empire, a Jewish convert named Joseph received permission from the emperor to build Sepphoris' first church, though it was probably never completed and the town remained almost exclusively Jewish. A brief insurrection against Gallus Caesar, Roman governor of the Syrian Province, broke out in Sepphoris in 351 CE, though the uprising was quickly suppressed and recriminations were not catastrophic for the town. However, the massive **earthquake** that hit Palestine in 363 CE was, totally destroying the town. The subsequent rapid reconstruction of Sepphoris saw an influx of Christians, but though the town became the seat of a bishop it remained a predominantly Jewish town until the mid-sixth century at least.

Later history

Sepphoris' history during the Early Arab period (638-1099) is unremarkable, and even the Crusader fortress built here (Le Sephorie) would be little remembered if it were not from the spring near here (Ein Zippori) that the Crusader army set out on 3rd July, 1187 for their fateful battle at the Horns of Hittim (see page 677).

In the 18th century, the Bedouin ruler of Galilee, Dahr el-Amr, fortified the Arab village of Saffuriyyeh at the site; it later became an Arab base during the 1936-39 revolt and the 1948 War of Independence. A year after its capture by the Israelis a moshav was founded here, taking the ancient Hebrew name of Zippori. Though the British had undertaken some excavations in the 1930s, a series of major digs in the 1970s, 80s and 90s revealed most of what is visible today. In 1992 **Zippori National Park** was opened.

Sights

The tour of the site begins from the plan/explanation of the site in the **'plaza'** **(1)** just above the car-park. Because excavation work is continuing, the route of the walking tour around the site is liable to minor change. The tour takes about two hours, excluding the reservoir/water supply system.

Passing the remains of a **Byzantine house (2)**, still being excavated, you come to the theatre.

Theatre (3)

Of traditional Roman design, the theatre was originally built at the beginning of the first century CE, possibly as part of Herod Antipas' building programme. Since it remained in use until the Late Roman or Early Byzantine period (fourth century CE) it underwent a certain degree of modification and refurbishment during its life-span. Most of the *cavea* (spectator seating area) is cut out of the bed-rock and it would probably have seated 4-5,000 people, though much of the limestone slab seating has been looted. The large stone stage (6 metres by 31 metres) had a wooden cover, with the actors' dressing rooms located beneath it. Remains of the *scaenae frons* (stage back-drop) were found in the vicinity. The presence of the pagan institution of theatre in an essentially Jewish city did not go unnoticed, with contemporary commentators criticizing theatre-goers in the Babylonian Talmud (*Avoda Zara, 18:b*).

The path leaves the theatre, climbing gently uphill through large cacti and pomegranate trees. The latter are praised on sign-boards quoting the *Song of Songs, VIII:2*. Follow the arrows to the observation point.

Galilee & The Golan

Observation point (4)
A number of interesting points can be noted from the observation point. In the foreground is the **Convent of the Sisters of Santa Anna (15)**, with parts of a 12th-century **Crusader church (13)** incorporated into its west side. The Pilgrim of Piacenza, visiting Sepphoris in 570 CE, was shown a chair that the Virgin Mary was supposedly seated in when she received her visit from the Archangel Gabriel, and thus begun the medieval tradition that Mary was born in Sepphoris. The Crusader church is supposedly built on the site of the home of Anne and Joachim: the Virgin Mary's parents. The area beyond the Convent is dotted with burial caves from the Roman and Byzantine period, including the presumed **tomb of Rabbi Yodan Nessiya**. This can be visited as you leave Zippori National Park, immediately to the right of the road that heads back towards Route 79.

The tour continues across the summit of the mound, heading towards the large square-block Citadel. The path passes through a large residential area.

Residential area (5)
Most of the buildings in this area date from the Roman period (37 BCE-324 CE), though parts of some structures date to the Hasmonean era (152-37 BCE) of the Late Hellenistic period (167-37 BCE). A paved street 2.2 metres wide runs southeast to northwest through the area, with buildings and courtyards adjoining on both sides, most having rock-cut cisterns or storehouses below. The large number of *mikvehs* (ritual baths) attests to the Jewish character of the town. The buildings appear to have been in use until the fourth century CE.

Citadel (6)
The dominant building on the mound, the Citadel, was probably built by the Crusaders as a watch-tower, though they used materials from earlier structures in its construction. Note, for example, the rubble-filled Roman sarcophagus incorporated as the southwest corner-stone. Dahr el-Amr added an additional storey in the 18th century and at one time it was used as a school for the Arab children of Saffuriyyeh.

The ground floor features an excellent video presentation (English or Hebrew) detailing the history of the area. The **museum** on the first floor features touch-screen computers, explaining features of the superb mosaics found here (see page 631), as well as a detailed feature on Sepphoris' water-supply system. Highlights from the surrounding district are also explained and replicas of items excavated at the site are displayed. There is also a comprehensive explanation of the *Mishnah* (compilation of oral law) that was completed at Sepphoris (Zippori).

The **viewpoint** on the roof should not be missed. Picture boards describe the key sites in all directions. There are a number of highlights. The **Eshkol Reservoir** to the northwest (beyond the Convent in the foreground) is part of the National Water Carrier that carries irrigation water from the north to

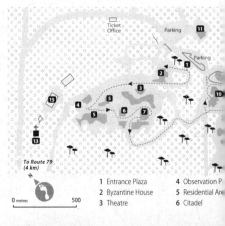

Zippori National Park

To Route 79 (4 km)

0 metres — 500

1 Entrance Plaza
2 Byzantine House
3 Theatre
4 Observation P[oint]
5 Residential Are[a]
6 Citadel

semi-arid regions in the south of the country. From here, after treatment, the water is carried in a closed pipeline. The village beyond the Eshkol Reservoir, **Kafr Manda**, is said to be the burial place of Moses' wife Zipporah. The village of **Rumana** to the northeast could be the Shihin of the Talmudic and Mishnaic periods, recalled in the Babylonian Talmud by the story of the rain putting out a catastrophic fire there, whilst the **Rimmon Valley** to the east may be the "field of corn" of the Gospels (*Matthew 12:1; Luke 6:1*).

From the Citadel, follow the arrows east to the 'luxurious residence'.

'Luxurious residence' (7)

The prime location of this third-century CE palatial mansion on the summit of the mound suggests that the occupier was a person of some means. The pagan nature of the mosaic pavements suggests that it housed a gentile, possibly the city governor, though the possibility of the owner being a wealthy Jewish citizen has not been ruled out. The building was apparently destroyed in the earthquake of 363 CE.

The most remarkable features of this 'luxurious residence' are the superb **mosaic floors** found *in situ*. The central hall served as a *triclinium*, or dining hall, and is embellished with one of the best mosaic pavements thus far found in Israel. Comprising 1.5 million tesserae (tiles) in 28 hues, the central mosaic features scenes from the life of the Greco-Roman god **Dionysus**. Eleven of the original central panels are completely preserved, whilst the one partially preserved panel and the three destroyed panels are being restored. Though all aspects of Dionysus' life are depicted, including his victory procession to India and his marriage to Ariadne, it is his revelry that is best celebrated. Scenes include his drinking competition with Hercules, and are labelled with Greek inscriptions such as "Dionysus' drunkenness", "drinking competition", "Procession of Merrymakers", "Merriment", etc. Another fine panel has the head of an attractive woman, subsequently known as the "Mona Lisa of the Galilee", and featured on countless Israeli Ministry of Tourism posters. A modern building has been built to protect the mosaic floors, with a raised walkway allowing an excellent vantage point for viewing. Illuminated cut-out panels explain the various scenes.

From the 'luxurious residence' the tour heads across the wooden bridge towards the Citadel, turning south down the steps through the cactus beds. Following the path past the Muslim cemetery the route divides. Head right first, following the sign for the colonnaded street and the Nile mosaic building.

Colonnaded street (8)

Much of the lower market of Zippori that is mentioned in the Talmud can be seen here. Two colonnaded streets bisected the town, forming a cross. Parts of the transom (*decumanus*, or east to west axis) can be seen, whilst a large section of the upright (*cardo*, forming the north to south axis) is well preserved. The limestone pavement slabs of the street still bear the ruts

Galilee & The Golan

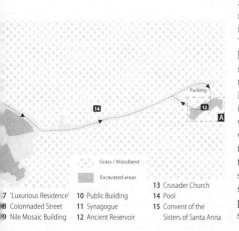

Grass / Woodland

Excavated areas

Parking

7 'Luxurious Residence'
8 Colonnaded Street
9 Nile Mosaic Building
10 Public Building
11 Synagogue
12 Ancient Reservoir
13 Crusader Church
14 Pool
15 Convent of the Sisters of Santa Anna

made by wagon wheels, though the mosaics from the colonnaded walkways (*stoae*) on either side have disappeared.

Ancient reservoir, Sephho

a Plastered aqueduct e Layers of pla
b Sedimentary shaft,   on reservoir f
c&d Layers of plaster f Support wall
  on reservoir walls g Maintenance

Nile mosaic building (9) To the east of the colonnaded street, near to the south end of the preserved section, is a large Byzantine building that occupies almost an entire *insula*, or city block. The mosaic floors of this building are of exceptional workmanship, though one in particular stands out.

The mosaic in the largest room features the unusual combination of the Nile festival illustrated alongside hunting scenes. The central image depicts the Nile River flowing from the mouth of a Nilotic beast. Above the river is a nilometer, bearing the numbers IE, IS, and I2 (referring to 15, 16 and 17 cubits). A man standing on a woman's back engraves the number I2, indicating the river's level that year. The reclining female form in the upper left corner personifies Egypt, one arm resting on a fruit-laden basket with her other hand holding a fruit-filled cornucopia. The male personification of the Nile sits astride an animal from whose mouth the river flows. He is beckoning towards him two naked figures bearing offerings. The lower section of the mosaic deals with the annual celebration of the rise of the Nile and features what appears to be the Pharos lighthouse of Alexandria. Other panels depict hunting scenes.

Back-tracking to the fork in the path, head left to the public building.

Public building (10) This large (40 metres by 60 metres) building was located at the intersection of two of the town's main thoroughfares. Comprising a central pillared courtyard surrounded by rooms of various sizes, it is speculated that this may have served as the market place from the first to fourth centuries CE.

Synagogue (11) In recalling the funeral of Rabbi Judah I ha-Nasi, the Talmud speaks of eighteen synagogues in Zippori. Until very recently, though fragments have been found scattered across the site, not one single complete synagogue had been discovered. The first has now been excavated, just below the modern car-park area. The central hall features a mosaic with a Zodiac motif with a number of Greek and Aramaic inscriptions.

It is also possible to visit Sepphoris' ancient water-supply system, several kilometres southwest of the main site. For those with their own transport, a paved road leads all the way from the main car-park.

Ancient reservoir (12) The town's water came from three main sources. The spring at Ein Zippori (2.4 kilometres south of the mound), though plentiful in supply, is located below the level of the city and consequently would not flow to the populated area. Water from this source had to be carried by donkeys. The town's main water supply came from springs located in the hills around Nazareth, with water being brought on two aqueducts built in the first and second centuries CE. The two aqueducts merge into a single conduit before splitting again close to the city. The northern one leads to a pool (**14**), whilst the southern one leads to the subterranean reservoir (**12**) that has been excavated here.

The reservoir is carved out of the soft chalk, taking advantage of a natural fault line. It measures 260 metres long, between 2 and 4 metres wide, is up to 10 metres deep, and has a storage capacity of some 4,300 cubic metres. The

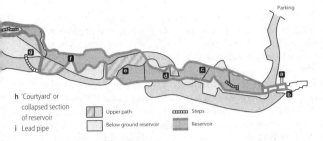

Parking

h 'Courtyard' or collapsed section of reservoir
i Lead pipe

Upper path   Steps

Below ground reservoir   Reservoir

plastered aqueduct (**a**) brings the water from the spring to the east, entering the reservoir via a sedimentary shaft (**b**). As you enter the reservoir at the top of the 36 steps, note the layers of plaster over the walls (**c** & **d**), in places up to several layers thick. The north wall here is of hard limestone whilst the south wall is softer. When you reach the bottom of the steps note how the floor is also plastered to prevent seepage (**e**). It is up to 60 centimetres thick here, including a layer of asphalt. Passing the support walls hewn out of the rock (**f**) you come to a flight of steps (**g**) that allowed maintenance engineers access to the reservoir. Through the narrow 'doorway' a flight of 52 steps leads you up to a section of the reservoir that has collapsed and has not been excavated (**h**). At the west end you can see the lead pipe (**i**) through which the water exited the reservoir. Flow was controlled by a valve and ran through a 240-metre-long man-made tunnel towards the city. An above-ground stone aqueduct then fed water into the municipal water system, though it should be noted that houses on the summit were dependent upon rainwater filling their rock-cut cisterns. A short flight of stairs leads up from the west end of the aqueduct. ■ *T6568272. 0800-1600 daily. 17 NIS adult, 14 NIS student.*

Shefar'am

Briefly the home of the **Sanhedrin** (highest judicial and ecclesiastical council of the ancient Jewish nation) for a short period of the second century CE, there are few reminders today of this town's former importance. Located 13 kilometres northwest of Sepphoris (Zippori) along Route 79, the most prominent feature of the town today is the crumbling citadel built in the 18th century by the Bedouin ruler of Galilee, Dahr el-Amr. It's possible to drive right up to the citadel, though it is rather dilapidated inside. Parts of the outer buildings are still used as homes by the townspeople of Shefar'am. The citadel doesn't merit a special journey, and is probably best admired from a distance (eg the window of Bus 343 as it passes the town along Route 79).

Galilee & The Golan

Jezreel Valley/Plain of Esdraelon

Phone code: 06
Colour map 1, grid C3-4

The Jezreel Valley (Hebrew: Ha'Emeq Yizre'el) is a series of several plains that run broadly northwest to southeast from Mt Carmel on the coast to the Jordan Valley, dividing the hills of Samaria from those of Galilee. Known in the Bible as the Plain of Esdraelon, such has been this region's importance in history that the great biblical geographer George Adam Smith was moved to call this plain "the classic battle ground of Scripture" (Historical Geography of the Holy Land, 1894). Smith is not far from the truth in describing Esdraelon as a "vast theatre" for the "spectacle of war" since its flatness presents a "clearly-defined stage" and the strategic passes that enter the plain act as "exits and entrances".

The topography of the valley provides the easiest passage between the

Esdraelon: battleground of the famous

The cast of characters who have performed their acts of warfare upon this stage reads like a Who's Who of the Middle East. The earliest written evidence of a battle refers to the confrontation between the Pharaoh Thutmose III and an alliance of Canaanite and Syrian cities that took place on the Plain of Esdraelon in 1468 BCE. The Israelites fought one of their first great battles here during the time of the Judges, the divinely inspired Deborah and Barak defeating the Canaanites. Gideon drove the Midianites from the valley, whilst Saul was less successful with the Philistines; his head and body parted company c. 1004 BCE. David and Solomon regained the valley for the Israelites, but the Egyptians were back in 925 BCE in the all-conquering form of the Pharaoh Shishak. The Assyrians came and captured in the eighth century BCE, whilst the Bible's last righteous king descended from David, Josiah, was killed here in the seventh century BCE.

In later years, the Roman legions of Pompey, Mark Anthony, Vespasian and Titus marched this way, whilst later still the Christian armies of the Crusaders fought the Muslim Arabs in a series of great battles. Many an ambitious emperor or general came a cropper here, with Napoleon suffering the first great retreat of his career here in 1799. And to prove that the Plain of Esdraelon has retained its strategic importance up until contemporary times, it formed one of General Allenby's major military objectives during the 1918 Palestine campaign.

Smith's summary is no over-statement: "What a Plain! Upon which not only the greatest empires, races, and faiths, east and west, have contended, but each has come to judgement – on which with all its splendour of human battle, men felt there was fighting from heaven, the stars in their courses were fighting" (Historical Geography of the Holy Land, 1894). Little wonder then that the final battle between the forces of good and evil that will herald the second coming (Revelation 16:16) is scheduled to take place in this valley, at a site known as 'Armageddon'.

Mediterranean coast and the east, and thus Esdraelon fell naturally into the great trading route, the Via Maris (Way of the Sea). Coupled with the plain's great fertility, little wonder that Esdraelon was so regularly fought over.

The valley is the largest in Israel and today is a major contributor to the agricultural economy of the country. For the tourist, there are several major places of interest, most notably the ancient city of Megiddo to the west and the country's best-preserved Roman-Byzantine city, Bet Shean, to the southeast. Those with time to explore should not miss the Crusader castle of Belvoir, or may like to consider taking time out at the delightful Gan HaShlosha Park.

Bet She'arim

Colour map 1, grid B3 Located at the western end of the Jezreel Valley, Bet She'arim was formerly the seat of the highest Jewish religious and judicial body in the country, and as such was the spiritual centre of Jewry. At the time when the Romans had closed Jerusalem to Jews, Bet She'arim became the most desirous alternative burial site and today it is possible to visit the impressive rock-cut tombs of the necropolis within Bet She'arim National Park. Part of this vast subterranean network of catacombs is open to the public, including one tomb that has been converted into a museum containing a number of Jewish burial artefacts. There are also several points of interest located just outside the National Park.

Ins and outs

Getting there

Bet She'arim is best reached by public transport as an excursion from Haifa (19km to the northwest), though some walking is necessary. Most Nazareth-bound buses from Haifa (301, 331, 332, 336, 338, 351, 431, 432, 434) pass the town of Kiryat Tiv'on along Route 75. As Route 75 passes Kiryat Tiv'on (10 NIS, 35 mins), it goes straight on at the roundabout (the road to the town centre turns right), and begins to descend a steep winding hill. Almost immediately an orange sign points right, indicating Bet She'arim. Get off the bus at the stop here (if you continue to the main junction to Jenin you've gone too far). Follow the orange sign pointing down Yizre'el St and walk for about 15-20 mins. Another orange sign for Bet She'arim indicates the right fork, and after 300m a further orange sign directs you to the right. To return to Haifa you must walk back up to Route 75. (**NB** An irregular bus service, 10, connects Bet She'arim National Park to Kiryat Tiv'on town centre, from where you can take a bus to Haifa).

Getting around

The various tombs that are accessible to visitors are fairly close together, so there is no fixed route for viewing the site. However, display boards in the car-park outside the kiosk do provide some background information on Bet She'arim, so it may be worth beginning here and working your way back towards the National Park entrance. Bet She'arim comprises a huge area, with not all of the burial sites confined within the National Park. In addition, there are a number of other places of interest just outside Bet She'arim National Park.

History

Following the failure of the First Jewish Revolt (66-73) and the destruction of the Temple in Jerusalem, the focus of Jewish life gravitated first to Yavne in the southern maritime plain then subsequently to Lower Galilee. By the second century CE Bet She'arim was already home to many important Jewish scholars, and its status was further enhanced by the arrival of the Jewish patriarch **Judah I ha-Nasi** (c. 135-217), leader of the Sanhedrin and teacher in the celebrated rabbinical academy. With Jews totally excluded from Jerusalem following Hadrian's suppression of the Second Jewish (Bar Kochba) Revolt (135 CE), Bet She'arim expanded rapidly under ha-Nasi's influence. It was here

Bet She'arim

that he compiled much of the *Mishnah* (the written code of 'Oral Law' that is central to Judaism).

Though ha-Nasi moved to Sepphoris during the illness of his latter years, following his death (c. 217 CE) he was brought for burial to Bet She'arim. Whilst Jerusalem remained forbidden, Bet She'arim became the central Jewish necropolis with communities from all over Palestine and the diaspora wishing to have their dead interred here.

Bet She'arim was largely destroyed by Gallus Caesar in 351 CE during the suppression of a third Jewish uprising. Excavations began at the site in 1871 under the auspices of the Palestine Exploration Fund, though most progress was made in a series of digs between 1936 and 1959 led primarily by Mazar and Avigad.

Sights

All of the tombs have been cut from the rock, with most of them fronted by a wide entrance courtyard. Others have been cut directly into the hillside and are approached by a long central passageway. Such catacombs tend to contain a larger number of burial places, though the reason for this is not entirely clear. The inference is that the popularity of Bet She'arim as a Jewish final resting place eventually led to further burial space being at a premium as the necropolis reached saturation point. Another theory suggests that the more crowded burial places reflect the socio-economic status of those buried there, with only the wealthy and prominent able to afford the more spacious burial chambers.

Inscriptions have been found in Aramaic, Hebrew, Palmyrene and Greek, and generally mention the name and lineage of the deceased plus a sentiment such as "good luck in your resurrection". A wide range of professions are mentioned in these inscriptions, with those interred including rabbis, heads of synagogues, physicians, bankers, textile merchants, perfume merchants and goldsmiths.

Many of the tombs fell victim to grave robbers who smashed the sarcophagi in search of plunder. Some remained intact, however, and revealed objects such as jewellery, coins, pottery and vessels. This enabled archaeologists to reconstruct burial practices of the period.

Museum One of the main chambers of **Catacomb 20** houses a small museum of finds associated with Bet She'arim. These include descriptions of the varying forms of carved menorahs found here, details of Jewish burial practices, a model of a tomb and accompanying mausoleum, plus translations and interpretations of inscriptions and symbols found in the burial chambers here. In the centre of the museum is a large slab of glass, considered to be the biggest single glass object to have been made in ancient times (over 8,000 kilogrammes).

Catacomb 20 Sometimes referred to as the 'Catacomb of the Sarcophagi', this catacomb is one of the most important at this site. The façade has been restored and it is one of the few tombs that you can enter. Over 130 limestone sarcophagi were found in this catacomb, though like all others at Bet She'arim grave robbers had preceded the archaeologists. However, many coffins remain intact, with the Hebrew inscriptions and decorations providing some clue as to who was buried in this tomb. Common features include menorahs, heraldic eagles, hanging wreaths and *tabulae ansatae* (a tablet with triangular handles, intended to carry an inscription), with the quality of workmanship suggesting that this catacomb contains the tombs of Jewish notables. Avigad and Mazar point to a number of sarcophagi decorations that seemingly depict likeness to

Greek gods, suggesting that this is an indication of the tolerant attitude of Jewish leaders of the day, interpreting potentially idolatrous themes as simply sculpture and decorative art.

The best preserved sarcophagi are all lit, with low-key lighting illuminating the rest of the catacomb. There are also translations of the more interesting Hebrew inscriptions.

Catacomb 14

This tomb is one of the most important at Bet She'arim, featuring the common architectural form of a three-arch façade fronting on to a large courtyard. The importance of Catacomb 14 lies in the Hebrew inscriptions that mention **Rabbi Simon**, **Rabbi Gamaliel** and **Rabbi Anina**. Avigad and Mazar suggest that these could be the men referred to by Patriarch Judah I ha-Nasi: "Simon my son shall be *hakham* [president of the Sanhedrin], Gamaliel my son Patriarch, hanina bar Hama shall preside over the great court". It has also been suggested that this is the burial vault of ha-Nasi's family, with the tomb built to the rear of the chamber being that of Patriarch Judah I ha-Nasi himself.

Above both Catacombs 20 and 14 there are remains of open-air structures that were surrounded by benches. These are thought to have been used as places of assembly for prayer and sermons during burial and mourning, and were so designed to add aesthetic beauty to the necropolis.

Other catacombs

The entrance to **Catacomb 23** has collapsed, though this enables us to see one form of the burial patterns at Bet She'arim. A passage entrance to the left gives some indication as to the extent of 'burrowing' into the hillside. It is also possible to enter the interior of **Catacomb 15**. A central passageway leads into the hillside with burial chambers cut at head height to the left and right. Each contains places for three bodies, with eight alcoves in all.

Just inside the main entrance to the National Park is the 'Staircase Catacomb', or **Catacomb 13**. By descending 30 or so steps it is possible to peer through the small one-metre-square doorways that are hewn from the rock-face. Inscriptions inside declare that "This is the resting place of Yudan, son of Levi, forever in peace. May his resting place be [set] in peace." Like many other chambers here, Catacomb 13 is the site of multi-burials, with this catacomb actually being carved into two storeys. ■ *Sunday-Thursday 0800-1700, Friday 0800-1300. Adult 12 NIS, student 9 NIS.*

Other attractions outside the National Park

Catacombs 1-4 and 11

Just before the entrance to Bet She'arim National Park, at the hairpin bend in the road, a dirt track leads southwest towards a number of other catacombs. Amongst these are Catacombs 1-4 and 11. Though walkways have been built to aid viewing, the site is now surrounded by a large fence and a sign warning "Danger of collapse". This is a pity since some of these catacombs are particularly important. Catacombs 1-4 are particularly rich in wall inscriptions, reliefs and carvings, though most are poorly executed. They feature depictions of men and animals, architectural designs, plus Jewish symbols such as menorahs, shofars, ritual objects and images of the Ark of the Law.

A large, elaborate mausoleum previously stood above Catacomb 11, probably dating to the third century. Sections of the frieze above the arch, featuring scenes of lions hunting, wolves fighting, and an eagle, are all that remain. A Greek epitaph inscribed on a marble tablet was found near Catacomb 11.

Basilica

From Catacombs 1-4 a dirt path leads to the top of the hill above Bet She'arim (though there is an alternative route up: see map). At the top of the hill stands a

Galilee & The Golan

large **basilica** (40 metres by 15 metres) dating to Byzantine times (324-638 CE). There are remains beneath the basilica, however, that suggest an almost continuous occupation of the site from the ninth century BCE until the Late Arab period (1291-1516 CE). The basilica was constructed of large ashlars (hewn stone laid in horizontal courses) and was divided by rows of columns into a nave and two aisles. It was probably destroyed around 351 CE when Gallus Caesar razed the city.

Statue of Alexander Zaid Near to the basilica is a **statue of Alexander Zaid**, one of the founders of 'The Shomer' and a guardian of the Jewish settlers living in this area. He was killed by Arabs during the uprising of the late 1930s. He is featured in the statue sitting on his horse, gazing into the distance: you can't blame him, for it is a fine view.

Tomb of Sheik Abreik A little further down the hill is the small, twin-domed **mausoleum of Sheik Abreik**; the man who gave his name to the Arab village formerly on this site. The tomb is in a very poor state of repair and it is not particularly pleasant to enter inside to view the green cloth-shrouded sarcophagi.

Synagogue At the foot of the hill on the road leading to the National Park (see map) you pass the remains of an **ancient synagogue** dating to the third or fourth century CE. The synagogue resembles somewhat a basilica, with a central nave and two aisles divided by rows of columns. The façade features three monumental doorways aligned towards Jerusalem. The walls of the synagogue were previously decorated with marble tablets and inscriptions in plaster honouring those who contributed towards the construction. The synagogue and surrounding buildings were destroyed by the major conflagration that consumed the city in 351 CE. The precise dating of the city's destruction is provided by a hoard of some 1,200 coins discovered in the area. All the coins date to the reigns of Constantine I and Constantius II, with none minted later than 351 CE. Near to the synagogue are the remains of a two-room **oil press**.

Megiddo

Phone code: 06
Colour map 1, grid C3

One of the most important archaeological sites in the north of the country, Megiddo owes its long and violent history to its strategic position on that great trade route between Egypt, Asia Minor and Babylon, the Via Maris *(Way of the Sea). The earliest written record of a major military encounter refers to a battle that took place here, whilst history is replete with the names of armies who fought on the Plain of Esdraelon (Jezreel Valley) before Megiddo. Consequently, Megiddo has come to symbolize the apocalyptic battle to end all battles: 'Armageddon' (Revelation 16:16). Thus, this is a site that is expecting a lot of visitors in the year 2000.*

The tel (mound) upon which Megiddo stands is now a well presented National Park, though the complexity of the site can make it somewhat confusing.

Ins and outs

Getting there Megiddo is located approximately 35km southeast of Haifa, on Route 66 (Haifa to Jenin road) close to the junction with the Tiberias – Afula – Hadera – Tel Aviv (Route 65) road (Megiddo Junction, 2km southeast). Public transport poses few problems though you have to be on the look-out for the sign so that you can request the driver to stop. From **Haifa**: Bus 302 direct, 4 morning services, plus local Bus 248 (that

'Armageddon' and the 'End of Days'

Despite the extensive archaeological record of Megiddo's antiquity there is nothing seemingly Christian to bring pilgrims to the site; it was after all completely abandoned four centuries prior to the birth of Jesus. However, just one single line in the Revelation of St John the Divine (Revelation) has given Megiddo worldwide fame and ensured a constant flow of Christian pilgrims to the site. Indeed, such is the importance of the site to Christians that during the only visit to the Holy Land by a pontiff (in 1964), Pope Paul VI chose to meet the Israeli prime minister Levi Eshkol at Megiddo.

Revelation is a visionary description of the apocalypse; the 'End of Days' that leads to the second coming. Attributed to the apostle John (though some scholars claim it to be a composite work written c. 90 CE), Revelation describes the army of righteousness of God Almighty as it prepares to meet the forces of evil in battle: "And he gathered them together into a place called in the Hebrew tongue Armageddon" (Revelation 16:16). Subsequently 'Armageddon', a corruption of the Hebrew 'Mount (Har) of Megiddo', has come to represent this final conflagration.

Whether this line in Revelation is to be taken literally or not is a considerable point of dispute within Christian theology. Many evangelical groups follow the 'premillennialist' argument, believing that the actual final battle will take place at Megiddo. The 'amillennialists', on the other hand, see Revelation as an allegorical work drawing attention to the seemingly endless succession of battles fought at Megiddo throughout its history, and pointing out the symbolism of line 16:16 in much the same way as there are symbolic references to 'Babylon' and 'Rome'.

Those who are particularly interested in Megiddo may like to contact Pennsylvania State University, which leads digs to the site (Prof. Baruch Halperm, The Megiddo Expedition, Pennsylvania State University, 103 Weaver Building, University Park, PA 16803-5500, Fax 814 8656204, email Megiddo@psu.edu, or visit their web site at http://squash.la. psu.edu/jst/megiddo/welcome.html) Tel Aviv University also has a 'Megiddo web site' (http://www.tau.ac.il/ ~archpubs/index.html)

continues to the West Bank town of Umm el-Fahem). From **Nazareth** via **Afula**: Bus 823, every 30-60 mins until 1930 to Megiddo Junction, 2km from site. From **Tiberias** via **Afula**: Buses 830, 840, 841, 842 all pass Megiddo Junction, 2km from the site, *en route* to Tel Aviv – you have to remind the driver to stop. To return, if in doubt head to **Afula** from where connections are pretty good.

History

Such is the complex nature of Megiddo's history that archaeologists have identified 25 levels of occupation on the tel (mound). Whilst lowest levels of stratum suggest settlement in the Chalcolithic period (4500-3300 BCE) or earlier, it is in the period between the Late Bronze Age (c. 1550 BCE) and the latter stages of the Iron Age IIC (700-586 BCE) that the city experienced the key events in its history.

The first written reference to Megiddo dates to the 15th century BCE, though excavations confirm that major fortified cities occupied the tel at points during the Early Bronze (c. 3300-2200 BCE) and Middle Bronze (2200-1550 BCE) periods. **Thutmose III** describes in his inscription at the Temple of Karnak a detailed account of the crushing blow that he dealt the Canaanites on the plain below Megiddo in May 1468 BCE. This testimony represents the

Bronze Age (Canaanite period)

Galilee & The Golan

earliest-known record of a military engagement.

Megiddo subsequently became a vassal state of Egypt, with the high quality of buildings and artefacts excavated from this period confirming that it was the pharaoh's major base in the Jezreel Valley. The city is mentioned in a number of documents from this period, including the *Taanach letters*, the *el-Amarna letters*, and the *Papyrus Anastasi I*, the latter including a detailed description of the *Via Maris* route as it passes Megiddo.

Iron Age Megiddo was one of the major **Canaanite** cities in the Jezreel Valley during the
(Israelite period of the Judges, but how and when the city passed into Israelite hands is
period) still unclear; the various biblical accounts give a confusing picture of the political set-up at the time (compare *Judges 5:19; Judges 1:27-28; Joshua 17:11-13; Joshua 12:7 and 21; I Chronicles 7:29*).

Most commentators conclude that Megiddo was taken by the **Israelites** during the early stages of the United Monarchy (c. 1020-928 BCE), probably by **David** (1004-965 BCE). Excavations across the mound have revealed a rich assemblage of pottery from stratum VIA (11th century BCE). The violent conflagration that totally destroyed the city at this level is concomitant with David's campaign in the region. What is sure is that Megiddo became one of **Solomon**'s fortified northern cities (*I Kings 9:15*), with a large defensive casement wall enclosing a rich complex of public structures built during his reign (965-928 BCE).

Having been conquered and largely destroyed by the pharaoh Shishak c. 925 BCE, a completely new city was built on the mound by the Israelite king

Megiddo

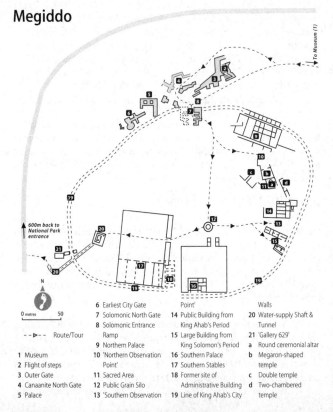

To Museum (1)

600m back to
National Park
entrance

N

0 metres   50

- - -▷- - - Route/Tour

1 Museum
2 Flight of steps
3 Outer Gate
4 Canaanite North Gate
5 Palace
6 Earliest City Gate
7 Solomonic North Gate
8 Solomonic Entrance Ramp
9 Northern Palace
10 'Northern Observation Point'
11 Sacred Area
12 Public Grain Silo
13 'Southern Observation Point'
14 Public Building from King Ahab's Period
15 Large Building from King Solomon's Period
16 Southern Palace
17 Southern Stables
18 Former site of Administrative Building
19 Line of King Ahab's City Walls
20 Water-supply Shaft & Tunnel
21 'Gallery 629'
a Round ceremonial altar
b Megaron-shaped temple
c Double temple
d Two-chambered temple

Ahab (871-852 BCE). Retaining just the previous main north gate, a new city wall 820 metres long and 3.6 metres thick was built to encircle the mound, and a extensive complex of new buildings was constructed. This included a new stable compound to the north (which can be seen superimposed on 'palace 6000'), an extension of the residential district, and the large southern stable complex ('building 1576'). The construction of these two stables complex have led some scholars to suggest that Ahab turned Megiddo into a "chariot city", though this assumption has been challenged (see page 643).

Ahab's new city survived for a century or more until the arrival of the Assyrian king **Tiglath-pileser III** in 733-732 BCE (*II Kings 15:29*). Having conquered the whole of Galilee and the Jezreel Valley, Tiglath-pileser III made Megiddo the administrative capital of the Assyrian province of Magiddu, building his own city on the site on a revolutionary new plan. The best preserved buildings of this era can be seen to the right (west) as you enter the main north gate.

The death of the Judean king Josiah at the hands of the Pharaoh Necho at Megiddo in 609 BCE (*II Kings 23:29; II Chronicles 35:20-24*) suggests that the city may have passed into Judean hands, though the archaeological evidence suggests an unfortified city clearly in decline. The site may have been partially occupied during the Babylonian/Persian period (586-332 BCE), though from the fourth century BCE Megiddo was abandoned.

Whilst the precise locations of many biblical cities remain in doubt, the same **Later events** cannot be said for Megiddo; Estori ha-Parhi identified the site here as early as the 14th century CE. Robinson also noted the location in the 19th century, with the first extensive excavations here being undertaken in 1903 by Schumacher on behalf of the German Society for Oriental Research. **General Allenby** based the British forces here during the latter stages of the Palestine campaign of the First World War, later taking the title of Viscount Allenby of Megiddo and Felixstowe! Interestingly, Smith notes how closely Allenby's advance north from Gaza to do battle at the Plains of Esdraelon with the Turks and Germans corresponds with Thutmose III's campaign of 1468 BCE (*Historical Geography of the Holy Land*, 1931 edition). It is also said that Allenby consulted Smith's 1896 edition of this classic work on a daily basis during the 1917-18 campaign.

The Oriental Institute of Chicago undertook extensive digging at the site in the 1920s and 30s (though some of their conclusions have been challenged). Israel's greatest archaeologist Yigael Yadin oversaw the major excavation of Megiddo in the 1960s and early 70s, and the site has subsequently been turned into a National Park.

Sights

Because Megiddo has so many strata of occupation (25) it is a somewhat confusing site. It is highly recommended that you begin your tour in the **museum** **Museum** (1). A short video presentation in the foyer sets the scene well. The centrepiece of the museum is the large model of the tel. Different points of interest can be illuminated and identified by touch-buttons, whilst levels of strata that are hidden can be revealed by operating the hydraulic lifts built into the model.

From the museum follow the marked trail along the right fork of the path. The **North Gate area** flight of **steps** (2) that you pass to your left are part of an **outer gate** (3) built into the northern wall during the Solomonic period (965-928 BCE), whilst the path above it (which you would be walking along if you took the left fork from

Galilee & The Golan

the museum) is part of the Solomonic **entrance ramp (8)**.

Continuing up the path you arrive at the Canaanite **North Gate (4)**, probably built sometime between 1650-1550 BCE. Typical of a Middle to Late Bronze Age city gate, it comprises a straight passageway with a series of three piers projecting from the inner walls, still allowing passage for chariots but reducing the speed at which any traffic could pass through. This gate remained in use for some four centuries.

Immediately inside the gate to the right are the indistinct remains of a **palace (5)** built during the same period. It was enlarged during the following century (c. 1550-1479 BCE), reaching its peak between c. 1479-1350 BCE. The building has been identified as a palace by the rich treasure of jewellery and carved ivories found there, many of which can now be seen in the Rockefeller Museum in Jerusalem.

Beyond the remains of this palace to the right (west) stands what is left of the city's **earliest gate (6)**, dated tentatively c. 1800-1750 BCE. Built of mud-brick on stone foundations, it comprises two narrow entrances set at right angles and was only large enough to accommodate pedestrians.

Having passed through the Canaanite North Gate, you are greeted on your left by the **Solomonic North Gate (7)**. A raised wooden walkway enables you to get a better idea of the gate's form, though only the east side has been preserved. The picture is further confused by the fact that the six-chambered gateway was reduced to four chambers during the ninth-eighth centuries BCE, and further modified by the Assyrians following their conquest in 732 BCE.

Northern observation point

From the Solomonic North Gate follow the marked path left (east) towards the northern observation point. On your left you pass the **northern palace (9)** (referred to by the excavators as 'palace 6000'), built during the 10th century BCE as part of Solomon's expansion programme. Constructed using thick ashlars, the plan is typical of the rulers' residences found in the northern Syrian cities of this period and is identical to the other palaces that Solomon built at his fortified cities of Hazor and Gezer. Rich pottery remains were found in the Solomonic stratum excavated here. The remains that you see here today are rather confused by the fact that the palace was destroyed during Pharaoh Shishak's campaign of 926 BCE, and by the construction on the same site of the **northern stables (9)** by King Ahab in the second quarter of the ninth century BCE.

The **northern observation point (10)** looks down into the **Sacred Area (11)** where the remains of temples from several periods can still be seen. It is thought that the temples were built to serve the deities of El, his wife Ishtar and Dagan. The oldest temple is to the left (east), and appears to be a two-chambered temple (**d**) from the end of the Chalcolithic period/beginning of the Early Bronze Age I (c. 3300-3000 BCE). The temple is similar to the Chalcolithic temple at Ein Gedi. The large round ceremonial altar (**a**) (over 8 metres in diameter and 1.4 metres high) was built in the Early Bronze Age (c. 2500 BCE) and was surrounded by a *temenos* wall that was used to form a sacred precinct. Evidence of numerous sacrifices was found in this area in the form of scattered animal bones and potsherds. The altar is built of small rubble stones and ascended by steps on the east side. The altar was probably raised in height in a later period, coupled with the construction of three new temples in its vicinity. A new temenos wall joined the round altar complex to the temple to the north. Because this temple resembles in form the Aegean megaron (the most basic and simplest architectural form of a Greek temple, such as the megaron buildings of Troy II) it is sometimes labelled the megaron-shaped temple (**b**). This was a complicated area to excavate and the archaeologists have had some problems accurately dating the various levels here. The most recent suggestion is that the megaron-shaped temple dates c.

2000-1850 BCE, though some sources date it to a far earlier period (c. 27th century BCE). The presence of a fenestrated bronze axehead found in the rebuilt north wall of the megaron-shaped temple is characteristic of those in use from the Middle Bronze Age I to the early Middle Bronze Age IIA, thus suggesting this later date for construction. The two temples just to the west, sometimes referred to as the double temple (c), were almost certainly built before the megaron-shaped temple and may already have been in ruins by the time the latter was built. They probably date to the Middle Bronze Age I (c. 2200-2000 BCE). The recently provided isometric drawings at the 'northern observation point' allow a better appreciation of how the 'sacred area' looked during various stages of its history.

From the northern observation point, retrace your steps to the crossroads and then follow the path south towards the **public grain silo** (**12**). Approximately eight metres deep, the silo is thought to date to the period of Jeroboam (784-748 BCE). From the grain silo you can explore in three directions. To the left (east) is the southern observation point, behind (south) is the southern palace, and to the right (west) are the southern stables and city water-supply system.

Southern observation point (13)

Heading east (left) from the public grain silo the path divides. The left fork leads to the **southern observation point** (**13**) from where you can again look down into the Sacred Area (see above). Close to the southern observation point is a **public building from King Ahab's period** (**14**) (871-852 BCE), known to the excavators as 'building 338' and sometimes incorrectly labelled as "residence of the commander of King Solomon's chariots". It is fairly safe to assume that this building replaced the northern and southern palaces of the previous levels of stratum, though on a less grand scale. It is referred to as the governor's palace.

The right fork on the path from the public grain silo to the southern observation point leads to a **large building** (**15**) from the Solomonic period (965-928 BCE), though it was initially thought to date to his predecessor David. Some fine portico pillars are still standing.

Behind (to the south) of the public grain silo (**12**) is the rather overgrown **southern palace** (16) complex, built during Solomon's period of reconstruction (965-928 BCE). Built with thick walls of ashlar masonry, the palace stood within a large enclosure protected by a gate tower to the north. The adjacent **administrative building** (**18**) (known to the excavators as 'building 1482') to the west now lies beneath the southern stables complex (see below).

Southern palace

There is still some debate amongst scholars as to the true nature of this large walled compound to the west of the public grain silo and southern palace. Most agree that the presence of stone troughs, tethering holes in the stone pillars, as well as the paved halls and courtyards, confirm that these buildings were the **southern stables** (**17**) of the "chariot city" of Megiddo. Others suggest that they are merely storehouses and point out that if these buildings were indeed stables, they could only have housed fairly small ponies. However, what is clear is the dating of construction. Despite what you may read in some guides, including the sign-posts here at the site, this cannot be "Solomon's chariot city" since this complex was clearly built by Ahab in the ninth century BCE. Indeed, if anything, Megiddo was "Ahab's chariot city". This fact is further confirmed by the fact that the Solomon-built administrative building ('building 1482') lies beneath the southern stables. Beyond the southern stables can be seen a section of the **city walls** (**19**) built during Ahab's reign.

Southern stables

City water-supply system

For a city attacked and besieged as many times as Megiddo, a reliable **water-supply (20)** was essential. The city's main source was a spring just to the west of the mound and several attempts have been made to secure this supply. Some time in the 11th-10th century BCE a long narrow passageway built of well-dressed stone (referred to by the excavators as '**gallery 629' (21)**) was built from the mound towards the spring, allowing concealed access. Its remains can be clearly seen today.

The gallery was blocked by Ahab's new city wall in the ninth century BCE when work on a new secure access route began. This involved the cutting of a 30-metre-deep square shaft into the bedrock within the city's secure walls connected to an 80-metre-long horizontal **tunnel (20)** leading to the spring. It's still possible to walk through the cool but clammy tunnel, though this involves a descent of 183 steps followed by an ascent of 80 steps. You should also note that the tunnel deposits you on a road outside the National Park from where it's a 600-metre walk back to the site entrance. Tour groups often arrange to be met by their transport outside the tunnel exit. ■ *T6522167. 0800-1700 daily, winter 1600. Adult 20 NIS, student 17 NIS. Cafeteria, toilets.*

Tel Kedesh

A low mound (about six metres high) just to the north of Route 66 about mid-way between Megiddo and Taanach has tentatively been linked with the **Kedesh** where Heber the Kenite pitched his tent (*Judges 4:11*), with the minimal 12th-century BCE remains at the site being associated with Deborah's campaign in the area. This is the locality of the battle on the Kishon fought between the Canaanites and the Israelites (*Judges 5:19*). In reality, there is little to see here.

Taanach

The history of Taanach is very closely linked with that of Megiddo, just eight kilometres to the northwest. This was the scene of the battle between the Israelites, led by Deborah and Barak, and Sisera's Canaanite army (*Judges 5:19*). Though seemingly conquered by Joshua (*Joshua 12:21*) and later assigned to Manasseh, it appears that the **Canaanite** city was too strong to conquer (*Judges 1:27-28; Joshua 17:11-13*), though tribute was exacted. Like Megiddo, Taanach was also conquered during the campaigns of Thutmose III (1468 BCE) and Pharaoh Shishak I (918 BCE). As recently as the third century CE Taanach was described by Eusebius (*Onomasticon*) as a "very large village".

Taanach is located on a low mound (40 metres high, 340 metres north to south, 110 metres east to west) just to the west of the modern village that bears the same name, off Route 66 between Megiddo Junction and Jenin. In truth there is not a great deal to see at the site and there are no information markings. Some important discoveries have been made here though, most notably an archive of 12 Akkadian cuneiform tablets (dating to the 15th-14th centuries BCE) and an elaborate 10th-century cult stand. The dominant structure visible on the mound today is the comparatively recent Late Abbasid palace from the 10th-11th century CE. **NB** Some caution must be exercised when visiting Taanach since it is located just within the 'Green Line' that marks the boundary of the West Bank. ■ *Bus 302 between Haifa and Jenin, via Megiddo, passes along the main road fairly close to both Tel Kedesh and Taanach. You'll specifically have to ask the driver to stop when you see the tel.*

Afula

Though there is nothing much to see in this small town in the centre of the Jezreel Valley, it does serve as an important transport junction for the surrounding area. Excavations have revealed evidence of interrupted occupation from the Ghassulian culture of the Chalcolithic period (c. 4500-3300 BCE) through the Bronze and Early Iron Ages, as well as some use in the Crusader and Ayyubid periods of the 11th-13th centuries CE, though almost all these remains have been consumed by the construction of the modern town.

Transport Many of the buses from here serve the Jezreel Valley sites between Afula and Bet Shean. **Beit Alpha Synagogue**: see Bus 953 Jerusalem via Jordan Valley, Bus 412 to Bet Shean, or Bus 434 to Tiberias via Bet Shean. **Bet Shean**: Bus 412, Sunday-Thursday 20 per day first 0605 last 2210, Friday 18 per day last 1535, Saturday 7 per day first 1630; also Bus 434, see Tiberias. **Daburiya** for **Mt Tabor**: Bus 357, Sunday-Friday 3 per day. **Gan HaShlosha**: see Bus 412 to Bet Shean. **Haifa** via **Route 66**: Bus 302, Sunday-Thursday 7 per day, Friday last at 1345, Saturday no service. **Haifa via Nahalal**: Bus 301, every 10-20 mins, last bus 2130 Sunday-Thursday 1630 Friday, first bus 1620 Saturday. **Jerusalem** via **Bet Shean** and **Jordan Valley**: Bus 952/953, Sunday-Thursday 0530 0700 0730, Friday-Saturday 0730. **Ma'ayan Harod Park**: see Bus 434 to Tiberias via Bet Shean. **Megiddo**: Bus 302 direct, see Haifa via Route 66 timetable. **Megiddo Junction**: see Tel Aviv Buses 823 830 840 841 842. **Nazareth**: numerous, including 249 355 357 823 824 955. **Tel Aviv**: Buses 820 821 823 824 828 829 830 833 834 840 841 842, at least 1-2 per hour, last bus Sunday-Thursday 2210, last on Friday 1700, first on Saturday 1555. **Tiberias** via **Bet Shean**: Bus 434, Sunday-Thursday 0540 0900 1240 1540 1725, Friday 0540 0910 1230 1630 1725, Saturday no service. **Tiberias** via **Golani Junction**: Bus 830/831, 1-2 per hour until 2045, last on Friday 1700, first on Saturday 1900.

Jezreel/Yizre'el

The kibbutz of Yizre'el (Jezreel), midway between Afula and Jenin, is built on the site of the ancient city of Jezreel where **King Ahab** (871-852 BCE) and his wife **Jezebel** had their palace. The town was best known for the biblical story of Naboth the Jezreelite, whose vineyard Ahab so desired (*I Kings 21:1-29*). When Naboth refused to even sell his vineyard to Ahab, Jezebel had him falsely accused of blasphemy then stoned to death. When the prophet Elijah heard of this he threatened to "cut off from Ahab him that pisseth against the wall" (*I Kings 21:21*)! The wicked Jezebel later got her comeuppance in Jezreel at the hands of Jehu; or rather at his feet: he "trod her under foot" (*II Kings 9:33*) declaring "the carcase of Jezebel shall be as dung upon the face of the field in the portion of Jezreel" (*II Kings 9:37*). The Persians destroyed Ahab's palace and there is little of interest to justify a visit today. The remains of the Crusader castle that was built at the site, Le Petit Gérin, are not particularly inspiring.

Ma'ayan Harod National Park
Phone code: 06

Located on the northern slopes of Mt Gilboa (see page 647) is the attractive Ma'ayan Harod National Park. Source of the Harod river at a point sometimes referred to as the **Well of Harod**, the 120-hectare National Park features a number of amenities including a large open-air swimming pool. The spring is generally associated with the days of the Judges, when Gideon camped beside the "well of Harod" prior to driving the raiding Midianites back across the Jordan, and defeating them there. ■ T6532211. *0800-1600 daily. Adult 20 NIS, hostel guests 10 NIS. Buses 412, 415, 434 between Afula and Bet Shean lead to a junction one kilometre from National Park.*

Sleeping D-E *IYHA Ma'ayan Harod Youth Hostel*, T6531660, offers attractive a/c chalets, check-in 0800-1200 1600-1900, meals available, call ahead for reservations.

Ein Harod

The kibbutz of Ein Harod (located two kilometres north of the Afula to Bet Shean road (Route 71) and about 12 kilometres southeast of Afula) features the Bet Sturman Regional Museum (T06/6531605); a collection of archaeological and natural history exhibits related to the local area. The Museum of Art (T06/6531670) here features work by Chagall, amongst others.

Galilee & The Golan

Beit Alpha Synagogue

Phone code: 06
Colour map 1, grid C4

The kibbutzim of Beit Alpha and Hefzi-ba were part of the early 20th-century pioneering Jewish settlement of the Jordan Valley region. Whilst digging a new irrigation channel in 1928, members of the kibbutzim stumbled upon the remains of a sixth-century CE synagogue. Though little of the structure of the **Beit Alpha Synagogue** remains, the splendid mosaic floor is almost entirely preserved and is considered to be one of the best examples from this period in the country.

Ins and outs   Beit Alpha Synagogue is located at Kibbutz Hafzi-ba (and not Kibbutz Beit Alpha; make sure you get off at the right stop if coming by bus). These kibbutzim are both on Route 669, just south of the Hashitta Junction with Route 71. The site is served by almost all the buses that run between Afula (11 NIS) and Bet Shean (9 NIS), including 409, 412, 415, 434, 828 and 829.

Beit Alpha Synagogue   Aligned to face Jerusalem, the synagogue probably stood in a residential area of narrow streets and comprised a rectangular hall flanked by two aisles, an **atrium** (**1**) (courtyard) and a **narthex** (**2**) (vestibule). Though no direct evidence has been found, it is assumed that the narthex supported a second-storey gallery, possibly for use by women (see box on page 647). The walls of the synagogue were built of undressed stone and plastered on the inside and out. Little remains of the geometric designs that adorned the floors of the atrium and narthex, though it is the floor of the main hall that visitors come to see.

The hall is divided into a **central nave** (**4**) (5.4 metres wide) and two **aisles** (**3**) (2.75 metres and 3.1 metres) by two rows of plastered stone pillars. On the southern wall an **apse** (**5**) (raised a little above the level of the nave) housed the Ark of the Covenant. A shallow depression in the floor of the apse, the **genizah** (**9**) that is usually used as a depository for sacred texts, revealed a hoard of 36 Byzantine coins.

A wooden walkway built above the hall now allows visitors to walk around and view the mosaic carpet. While the geometric designs in the western aisle are well executed, it is the ornate scenes in the **nave** (**4**) that catch the eye. Three panels dominate the floor of the nave. To the north, nearest you as you enter through the modern doorway, is a panel depicting the **Offering of Isaac** (**6**). Abraham is shown bearing the child Isaac in one hand and a sword in the other, with the names 'Abraham' and 'Isaac' inscribed above the figures. An inscription in Aramaic at the base of the mosaic mentions the artists who laid the floor, dating it to the reign of Emperor Justin, though crucially the floor is broken where the year of his reign is mentioned. Scholars agree that this must be Justin I (518-527

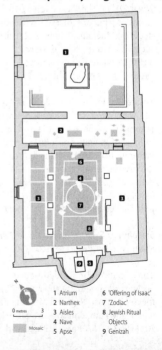

Beit Alpha synagogue

0 metres   3

Mosaic

1 Atrium
2 Narthex
3 Aisles
4 Nave
5 Apse
6 'Offering of Isaac'
7 'Zodiac'
8 Jewish Ritual Objects
9 Genizah

Synagogue design: the myth of the women's gallery?

Any area that is partitioned from the main hall of an ancient synagogue, for example a balcony, is often described by excavators as being reserved for women. However, an increasing number of scholars are challenging such assumptions. Lee I. Levine, writing in the New Encyclopedia of Archaeological Excavations in the Holy Land *(1993, p. 1423)*, points out that though there are plenty of examples that attest to women's participation at the synagogue *(Acts 16:12-13; 17:1-4, 10-12; I Corinthians 14-34; Tosefta, Meg. 3:11; J.T. Sot. 1, 4, 16d),* there is no mention in rabbinical literature of any physical separation or specific seating area such as a 'women's gallery'. Instead, he argues, the identification of specific areas in ancient synagogues as being designated for women is "purely speculative", adding that the separation of men and women in the synagogue probably only dates to the Middle Ages, perhaps evolving within the influence of Christianity or Islam.

BCE), though the building itself is probably older (possibly late fifth century CE).

The central panel is the most intriguing, depicting the cycle of the **zodiac** (7) around an image of the sun god Helios driving his chariot across the sky. At the four corners the busts of winged women represent the seasons. For the record, the twelve signs are (proceeding anti-clockwise from the '3 o'clock' position): *Taleh*, Aries; *Shor*, Taurus; *Teomin*, Gemini; *Sartan*, Cancer; *Aryeh*, Leo; *Betulah*, Virgo; *Meoznayim*, Libra; *Aqrab*, Scorpio; *Kashat*, Sagittarius; *Gedi*, Capricorn; *Deli*, Aquarius; *Dagim*, Pisces. This representation of pagan-influenced symbols in a synagogue is perhaps surprising, particularly adjacent to the image of the Offering of Isaac where the message is surely that the future is divinely ordained and not 'in the stars'. It has been suggested by some scholars that by the sixth century CE the connection in the Jewish consciousness between the zodiac and idol worship had long since disappeared, and that this design was therefore used solely for decorative purposes. However, others are not so sure and Murphy- O'Connor argues that "the very human desire to look into the future was too strong, and they [the rabbis] were forced to find ways to make the zodiac acceptable" (*The Holy Land*, 1992). One such means was to link the symbolism of the *twelve* tribes of Israel to the *twelve* signs of the zodiac.

The upper panel, closest to the apse, features **Jewish ritual objects (8)**, such as the Ark, a lighted menorah, shofar, etc, flanked by guarding lions. ■ *T6532004. Saturday-Thursday 0800-1700, closes one hour earlier on Friday and in winter. Adult 8 NIS, student 6 NIS.*

Mt Gilboa Dividing the Plain of Esdraelon from the biblical land of Samaria to the south is a line of low basalt hills that includes the 508-metre **Mt Gilboa**. What sets this particular rise apart from the rest of this chain is that this was the site of **Saul's** disastrous battle against the **Philistines**, c. 1004 BCE. Having consulted the witch at En-dor (who foresaw his grisly fate, see *I Samuel 28:7-25*), Saul's Israelite army was resoundingly defeated with his three sons Jonathon, Abinadab and Malchi-shua all being killed (*I Samuel 28-31*). Such was the watching Saul's despair that he fell upon his own sword, whilst the jubilant Philistines hung his headless body from the walls of Bet Shean (*I Samuel 31:10*). David's famous lament over Saul's death (*II Samuel 1:17-27*) is the source of the expression "how the mighty have fallen".

A number of biblical geographers have attempted to locate precisely the scene of the battle by examining the biblical passages *in situ*. Smith (1894) asserts that the battle took place on the slopes of the hill, rather than the plain before it, favouring the south side opposite Jenin. There are no archaeological remains to be seen though the 22-kilometre **Gilboa Scenic Route** provides pleasant views as it snakes its way along the top of the line of hills. The route begins at the Ma'ale Gilboa (Ascent of Gilboa) Junction on Route 669, and terminates at a point opposite Jezreel (Yizre'el). The summit of the hill is part of the **Gilboa Nature Reserve** and features several attractive picnic spots in the forest planted by the Jewish National Fund. Each spring there is the 'Annual Gilboa Popular Walk' (T6533242, F6533362 for details).

Gan HaShlosha (Sachne) Park   A great favourite with weekend-ing Israelis and local *kibbutzniks*, this beautiful park features landscaped lawns leading down to a series of natural pools connected by waterfalls that combine to form a beautiful swimming environment. The water is deliciously refreshing in summer, but still remains inviting during cooler months. Visibility is good though you must be prepared to share your bathing experience with millions of tiny fish. Other facilities include water-slides, an indoor pool, children's pool, changing rooms and toilets, restaurant and coffee shop, children's playground, picnic tables and a first-aid station. Other attractions here include a Museum of Regional and Mediterranean Archaeology, and a restored tower and stockade, though they don't seem to drag many people away from the water. After a hard day of sight-seeing in the Jezreel Valley, the park here makes a highly recommended break. **Warning** The water in the main pools is deep so children should be supervised. Take care with your possessions whilst swimming since theft is not unknown. The park may become too overcrowded for some during weekends and holidays. ■ *T06/6586219. Saturday-Thursday 0800-1800, Friday 0800-1700, closes one hour earlier in winter. Adults 25 NIS. The park is served by Buses 412 and 415 running between Afula and Bet Shean, as well as Bus 409 between Haifa and Bet Shean.*

Bet Shean

Phone code:T06
Colour map 1, grid C4

With a history spanning almost 6,000 years, the excavations at Bet Shean have provided an important window to the region's past. Long before digging at the site began it was noted by a visitor in 1894 that "few sites promise richer spoil to the first happy explorer with permission to excavate" (Smith, Historical Geography of the Holy Land). When excavation work did begin in 1926, the Field-Director was able to write to Smith that "the wonderful truth of your forecast about the richness of the antiquities … has been amply proved".

Today, Bet Shean National Park attracts a large number of tourists to see the best-preserved Roman-Byzantine town in Israel, and the site is very well presented. But though Bet Shean does live up to its billing, and is definitely worth visiting, those who have visited Jerash (in Jordan) may feel something of an anti-climax here.

Ins and outs

Getting there   Bet Shean can be reached from a number of places. From **Tiberias** (50 mins, 18 NIS) there are several options, including Jerusalem-bound buses (961/963/964, hourly), certain Haifa-bound buses (434, four per day), and one Tel Aviv-bound bus (832, at 0510). From **Afula** (35 mins, 12 NIS) take Bus 412, Sunday-Thursday 20 per day first 0605 last 2210, Friday 18 per day last 1535, Saturday 7 per day first 1630, or Bus 434,

Sunday-Thursday 0540 0900 1240 1540 1725, Friday 0540 0910 1230 1630 1725, Saturday no service. There is also a service from **Haifa** (Bus 434, four per day via Afula, 1 hr 20 mins, 27 NIS). To reach the site from the bus station turn left onto Shaul Hamelekh and then turn right at the Bank Leumi.

The tour of the site begins at the theatre, and follows a roughly clockwise route. Excavations remain in progress so some areas may be sealed off and the route is subject to change. Some of the less impressive attractions are located outside the National Park (see 'General Plan'). **Getting around**

History

Such has been the strategic importance of the site here that it has been more or less continuously occupied from the Late Neolithic period (c. 5000 BCE) until the Early Arab period (638-1099 CE). Bet Shean lies at the junction of two important routes: the *Via Maris* (Way of the Sea) linking Egypt and the Mediterranean coast to Babylon and the east, and the Jordan Valley road, connecting the Sea of Galilee to the Dead Sea and on to Eilat. The desirability of thiss location was enhanced by the abundance of the water supply and the fertility of the surrounding land. Bet Shean's history, and subsequently its archaeology, can be divided into two distinct periods: during its early history, the superimposed settlements occupied the four-hectare mound – **Tel Bet Shean** (*Arabic*: Tell el-Husn) – at the north of the site. Some time in the third century BCE the city moved down to the plain to the south and west of the mound, with very limited building taking place on the mound itself.

From finds excavated on Tel Bet Shean it appears that the site was first settled **Early history** in the Pottery Neolithic period of the fifth millennium BCE, with numerous finds dating from the later Chalcolithic period (fourth millennium BCE). The occupation of the site from the Early Bronze Age (c. 3300 BCE) to the end of the Middle Bronze Age (c. 1550 BCE) appears to be intermittent, perhaps seasonal, with a surprising lack of fortifications discovered on the tel. By the middle of the Late Bronze Age (c. 1550-1200 BCE), however, Bet Shean was firmly established as an **Egyptian** administrative centre following **Thutmose III**'s successful campaign in the region (see 'Megiddo', on page 638). The town is subsequently mentioned in several New Kingdom sources, including Thutmose III's list of cities at the Karnak Temple.

Following the **Israelite** conquest of the region in the 13th century BCE, Bet Shean is mentioned as one of the Canaanite cities that was perhaps too strong to be taken (*Joshua 17:11; Judges 1:27*). The town later became infamous as the place where the **Philistines** hung the headless torso of Saul from the city walls after the Israelite defeat on Mount Gilboa in 1004 BCE (*I Samuel 31:9-10*). Bet Shean came under Israelite control probably during the reign of David (1004-965 BCE) and is listed as one of **Solomon**'s (965-928 BCE) administrative districts (*I Kings 4:12*), though it was also one of the cities captured during Pharaoh **Shishak**'s campaign of 925 BCE.

A substantial gap now appears in the recorded history of Bet Shean. The name **Later history** does not appear in the lists of cities captured during the Assyrian or Babylonian conquests, though it must surely have featured in these campaigns. In fact, it is not until the third century BCE that Bet Shean reappears, this time under the name of **Scythopolis** and now located at the foot of the tel. It is still unclear how it came to be known as 'City of the Scythians' and few of the explanations offered seem particularly plausible. The picture is further confused by references to the town as 'Nysa', the supposed place where Dionysus (Bacchus) was nursed by the nymphs. References to the town are numerous during the reign of Antiochus IV (175-164 BCE), when it was given the status of a polis.

The situation in the city during the early years of the **Maccabean (Hasmonean) Revolt** (166-63 BCE) is unclear, though Jewish control over the city was firmly established c. 107 BCE by the uncompromising **John Hyrcanus** (third son of Simon, last of the Maccabee brothers). He offered the citizens of the town the choice of conversion and circumcision, or exile; most chose the latter. During the reign of John's son and successor, the despotic **Alexander Jannaeus** (103-76 BCE), an ageing **Cleopatra** paid a visit to Scythopolis following the conclusion of their peace treaty.

Many of the exiled citizens of Scythopolis returned when the city fell into **Roman** hands following Pompey's conquest of Palestine, and a period of sustained growth ensued. The development of the town was briefly interrupted by outbreak of the Jewish revolt against Rome (66-73 CE). Josephus records the tragic experience of the Jewish population of Scythopolis during the early days of the revolt. Rather than supporting their compatriots, the Jews "lined up with the Scythopolitans, and treating their own safety as of more importance than the ties of blood, they joined the battle with their countrymen" (*Jewish War, II: 466-8*). However, the Scythopolitans became suspicious of the excessive zeal of their Jewish allies, and in a remarkable display of treachery lured them to a

Roman & Byzantine remains, Bet Shean

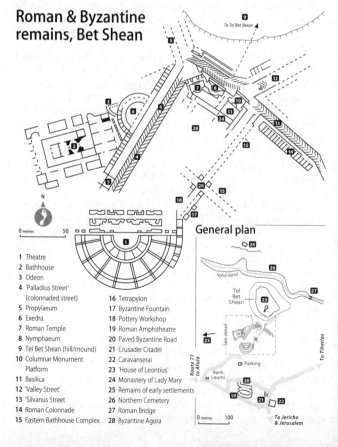

1 Theatre
2 Bathhouse
3 Odeon
4 'Palladius Street' (colonnaded street)
5 Propylaeum
6 Exedra
7 Roman Temple
8 Nymphaeum
9 Tel Bet Shean (hill/mound)
10 Columnar Monument Platform
11 Basilica
12 'Valley Street'
13 'Silvanus Street'
14 Roman Colonnade
15 Eastern Bathhouse Complex
16 Tetrapylon
17 Byzantine Fountain
18 Pottery Workshop
19 Roman Amphitheatre
20 Paved Byzantine Road
21 Crusader Citadel
22 Caravanserai
23 'House of Leontius'
24 Monastery of Lady Mary
25 Remains of early settlements
26 Northern Cemetery
27 Roman Bridge
28 Byzantine Agora

General plan

grove and slaughtered all 13,000 of them.

Following the suppression of the Jewish Revolt by Vespasian, Scythopolis experienced something of a boom, with Josephus describing it as the largest city of the **Decapolis** (the league of ten cities established by Pompey to serve as the bastion of Graeco-Roman influence). By the end of the third century CE Scythopolis was one of the leading textile producing centres in the Roman Empire, famed for its quality linen. The Christianization of the Roman Empire saw an influx of Christians, with the 'biblical geographer' Eusebius later referring to Scythopolis as "a noble city" (*Onomasticon*). The city also produced the sixth-century CE Christian historian Cyril of Scythopolis. Inevitably, the decay of the **Byzantine Empire** saw a decline in the city's fortunes, most notably after the exodus of the skilled linen workers. Those who feel that history is cyclical will note the current plight of Bet Shean. A development town almost totally dependent on the textile industry, the recent closure of the Kitan clothing factory has pushed unemployment levels in the town well above the national average.

In 634 CE the town fell to the **Arabs** following a major tactical blunder by the Byzantine army. Having fallen back upon Scythopolis, the Byzantines took advantage of the plentiful local water supply to flood the surrounding plain, making it an impenetrable marshland. However, as the Arab army prepared for a long and potentially futile siege, the Byzantine army rashly attacked, suffering a complete defeat. The victorious Arabs revived the old Semitic version of city's name (*Arabic*: Besian), with this battle celebrated in the annals of Islam as the 'Day of Besian'. Though the name was revived the city's fortunes were not, and this once great urban centre's fate was sealed by the devastating **earthquake** of 749 CE.

The **Crusaders** briefly occupied Bet Shean, though they preferred to concentrate their fortifications at Belvoir, to the north (see page 655). This was to prove a fateful mistake, ignoring the glaringly obvious strategic location of Bet Shean in favour of a remote, and thus ineffectual, position. Smith suggests that "when the Crusaders left Bet Shean to its fate, they sealed their own".

Sights

Bet Shean's Roman **theatre** (1) is spectacular, despite the fact that only one of three tiers of seating is preserved; at its peak, it could probably accommodate in the region of 5,000 spectators. Built of cement mixed with basalt, its state of preservation is remarkable. Eight vaulted entrances (*vomitoria*) provided access to the spectator's seating area (*cavea*), with a six-metre-broad staircase added in the Byzantine period providing access directly to the city centre to the east. One of the theatre's most remarkable features is the ornately decorated *scaenae frons* (several-storey-high stage back-drop), built with imported marble and granite. The style is unusual and may have reflected the fashion of the day. It is in the process of being restored. The date of construction is placed tentatively within the reign of the Roman Emperor Septimius Severus (193-211 CE), though an earlier theatre could well have stood on this site. Alterations and repairs were made throughout the Roman and Byzantine periods, indicating that the theatre remained in use throughout these periods. It was largely destroyed in the great earthquake of 749 CE.

Theatre

Though built upon Roman foundations, the **bathhouse** (2) standing today was built over several periods of the fifth and sixth centuries CE and is the largest bathhouse building as yet excavated in the country. The plan of the central complex is in the shape of a T, with four halls on an east to west axis joined to

Byzantine bathhouse

Galilee & The Golan

five rooms on a north to south axis. The heating system (*hypocaust*) that provided hot air to the *caldaria* (hot rooms) and *tepidaria* (tepid rooms) can be clearly seen from the recently completed walkway.

Odeon The remains of an **odeon** (**3**) or bouleuterion were found just to the northeast, between the bathhouse and the *exedra* of the colonnaded street (see below). Sections of seating from the auditorium as well as remains of the orchestra were identified, though most of the building was destroyed when the rooms adjoining the *exedra* were built.

Palladius Street This 180-metre-long **colonnaded street** (**4**) running from the foot of the tel (mound) to the theatre takes its name from an inscription discovered in the *stoa* (roofed portico that served as a sidewalk) that mentions the city's governor, Flavius Palladius, who had the *stoa* built and paved. This street was probably first laid in the mid-fourth century CE though it was repaired several times subsequently. The street plan of Bet Shean is largely orthogonal (ie parallel streets that intersect at right angles), though modifications had to be made to account for the local topography. The street is paved with basalt slabs in a herring-bone pattern with a two-metre-deep sewage channel running down the centre, and is generally between 7.2 and 7.5 metres wide. The west side of the street was flanked by a raised *stoa* approximately seven metres wide, with a roof supported by columns topped by Ionic capitals. The floor of the *stoa* was paved with mosaics. Beyond the *stoa* stood a row of around 20 shops, about half of which have been excavated. The east side of Palladius Street has not been completely excavated, though it's not thought that the portico along this side was roofed.

About half-way along the street, to the west, is a semi-circular **exedra** (**6**), or plaza. Some of the buildings that open on to the *exedra* have their original mosaic floors. A viewpoint just above the *exedra* provides a good perspective from which to appreciate the colonnaded street area.

At either end of 'Palladius Street' stands a **propylaeum** (**5**), (gateway to a sanctuary that is usually marked by a monumental structure), though neither here is particularly well preserved.

Roman temple At the northeast end of Palladius Street stands a **Roman temple** (**7**) that is speculatively associated with dedication to the worship of Dionysus or Tyche (though there is no firm evidence to support this theory). The façade of the temple faces northwest onto a paved plaza containing a statue-less pedestal, though a Greek inscription suggests that the figure of the Roman Emperor Marcus Aurelius (161-180 CE) once looked down from here. A 20-metre-wide monumental stairway rises to the *prostyle* (columned façade of the temple) where four 15-metre-high columns once stood on high pedestals. The two collapsed columns laying broken on the ground are a dramatic reminder of the 749 CE earthquake.

Nymphaeum Just to the east of the temple is the **nymphaeum** (**8**) (monumental structure featuring a public fountain), though this was also a major victim of the earthquake. A Greek inscription on one of the beams attributes construction to a Flavius Artemidorus in the fourth century CE, though much of the building is quite obviously two centuries older. A conduit brought water from the rear of the nymphaeum to a small pool at the front. Archaeologists plan to rebuild this structure eventually. A viewing platform above the 'Valley Street' provides a detailed explanation of the nymphaeum's plan. Just south of the nymphaeum is the **Byzantine agora** (**28**), which is undergoing further excavation.

A steep path above the nymphaeum viewing platform now takes you back several thousand years, to the site of Bet Shean's early history. Though thoroughly
excavated there is little of great visual impact on the top of **Tel Bet Shean (9)**,
but it is certainly worth the climb for the view alone (not least of which is the
panorama over the Roman-Byzantine city). However, the meagre **remains of
the early settlements (25)** belie the rich treasure troves from the Nineteenth
and Twentieth Egyptian dynasties discovered here: the most important such
finds in Israel. They can now be seen in the Israel Museum in Jerusalem.

Tel Bet Shean

The low rise to the north of the tel forms part of the **northern cemetery (26)**
that revealed over 50 sizeable fragments of anthropoid coffins from the Late
Bronze to the Early Iron Age (c. 1300-1150 BCE), possibly belonging to the
Egyptian garrison at Bet Shean. On the next hill slightly further north stands
the **Monastery of Lady Mary (24)** (Tell Istaba, see page 654).

Returning to the Roman-Byzantine city at the foot of the hill, next to the
nymphaeum stands a **stone platform** that originally supported a **decorative
columnar monument (10)**. The platform stands about four metres high and
has been partially restored and though the exact plan of the monument is
unclear, the varied debris found here suggests Corinthian columns supporting
an elaborate *entablature* (cornice or frieze) with scattered statues standing on
marble pedestals. Damn that earthquake.

**Columnar
monument
platform**

Adjoining the columnar monument platform to the rear and sharing its southwest wall is a large **basilica (11)** (28 metres by 65 metres), only parts of which
have been excavated. It is suggested that it was the main public building of the
Roman town, serving as a public meeting place. A hexagonal altar dedicated to
Dionysus with an inscription dating it to 142 CE was excavated from the
basilica.

Basilica

Opposite the columnar monument platform a Roman colonnaded street
('**Valley Street**' **(12)**) runs northeast towards a **Roman bridge (27)** over the
Nahal Harod. The basalt paved street is an impressive 11 metres wide, though
including the colonnaded sidewalks on either side it measures 24 metres
across in places. A plaza was formed in front of the columnar monument platform where the three roads join from the west, northeast and southeast. The
road running southeast is sometimes referred to as '**Silvanus Street**' **(13)**.

Valley Street

Running southeast from the columnar monument platform and the basilica is
a 56-metre-long **Roman colonnade (14)** comprising 18 limestone columns
standing on pedestals and topped with Ionic capitals. Part of a second-century
stoa whose rear wall is yet to be excavated, this was yet another victim of the
earthquake. A superb marble statue of Dionysus (now housed in the Israel
Museum, Jerusalem) was found in the debris of the *stoa*. An **ornamental
stepped pool** (50 metres by 7.5 metres) once reflected the columns fronting
the *stoa*, but was filled in and topped by a **row of shops** in the Byzantine
period. At the east end of the *stoa* are a number of artist's reconstructions of
'Silvanus Street' in the Roman (second to fourth centuries CE) and Early Arab
(seventh to eighth centuries CE) periods.

**Roman
colonnade and
row of shops**

Returning towards the theatre, recent excavations have now revealed the full
glory of the **eastern bathhouse complex (15)**. It appears that this structure
was built during the Roman period and later renovated in Byzantine times. It is
possible to make out the *caldarium* to the north and the *frigidarium* to the
south.

**Eastern
bathhouse
complex**

Galilee & The Golan

Tetrapylon The **tetrapylon** (16) is an elaborate structure comprising four column- or statue-bearing piers that marks the intersection of the Roman city's main streets. This building was rebuilt during the Byzantine period and later converted into an industrial unit, possibly connected with the textile industry during the Early Arab period. Access to the **Byzantine fountain** (17) and Early Arab period **pottery workshop** (18) is currently restricted.

Other sites outside the National Park There are several other places of interest related to Bet Shean that are not enclosed within the boundaries of the National Park. The **Roman amphitheatre** (19) is located to the south of the National Park, on the southern fringes of the Roman town. You pass it within a small park as you enter/exit the National Park. Its external measurements are 102 metres by 67 metres, though only three out of perhaps twelve rows of stone seats remain. Dating construction is not precise though it may well have been built whilst the Sixth Legion (Ferrata) were stationed here in the second century CE. It fell out of use in the fourth century with the decline in support of gladiatorial conquests between man and beast, and man and man, amongst the increasingly Christian population.

Alongside the amphitheatre to the north runs a section of **paved Byzantine road** (20) (c. 522 CE according to an inscription) lined with shops, suggesting that this was a densely populated residential area by the Byzantine period. Many gold coins, including some dating to the succeeding Early Arab period, were found in the ruins of the buildings destroyed by the earthquake.

The **Crusader citadel** (21) and the **caravanserai** (22) near the centre of the modern town are hardly worth visiting, though the 'House of Leontius' and the Monastery of Lady Mary certainly are. Before setting out to visit them, ensure at the National Park ticket office that they are open. The '**House of Leontius**' (23) is a Byzantine-period synagogue located several hundred metres west of the Byzantine bathhouse. The floor of the building features some particularly fine mosaics, with some cryptic Greek inscriptions suggesting that the synagogue may have been part of an inn.

A particularly fine calendar mosaic can be seen in the floor of the **Monastery of Lady Mary** (24) (*Arabic*: Tell Istaba), built to the north of Bet Shean (and visible from the tel) in 567 CE. ■ *T6587189, F6581899. 0800-1800 daily, closes one hour earlier on Friday. Adult 18 NIS. Cafeteria, toilets.*

Border crossing into Jordan

There is a recognized land border crossing between Israel and Jordan just six kilometres east of Bet Shean. It is known as the **Jordan River Border Crossing** or **Jisr Sheikh Hussein** (Sheikh Hussein Bridge) according to which side of the border you are on, and unlike the crossing point closest to Jerusalem (Allenby/King Hussein Bridge), **it is possible to get a Jordanian visa on the border**. This crossing point is closer to Jerusalem than the Arava crossing point near Eilat.

Bus 016 from Bet Shean runs four times per day to the border (11 NIS), or you can take a taxi (15 NIS). From the Jordanian side irregular minibuses run to Irbid (0.50 JD) from where regular buses run to the capital Amman. (For further details see Footprint's *Jordan, Syria and Lebanon Handbook*). Aim to cross the border as early in the day as possible. Information on this border crossing can be found on T06-6586442. For full details on border crossing formalities (departure tax, visas, opening times, etc) see the 'Getting there, overland' section on page 32.

Belvoir

Belvoir remains one of the best-preserved Crusader castles in Israel, though as the name suggests the splendour of the setting is part of the attraction. It was built to defend a number of important routes, most notably the Jordan Valley road, the route via Mount Tabor and Nazareth to Acre (Akko), and the ancient Via Maris through the Jezreel Valley. However, as we shall see, the fortress was probably too isolated to fulfil this role.

Phone code: 06
Colour map 1, grid C4

Though Belvoir was partially dismantled in the 13th century, the substantial remains still standing give a good idea of the plan of a concentric ring castle, making it well worth the effort of getting here. If nothing else you can appreciate the superb view of the Jordan Valley some 500 metres below you, and across to Mount Gilead in Jordan. On a clear day you can see north across the Sea of Galilee to the snowy peaks of Mt Hermon and southwest to the hills of Samaria.

Ins and outs

Belvoir is not easy to get to by public transport. It is located about midway between the southern end of the Sea of Galilee and Bet Shean, just off Route 90 that runs between Tiberias and Bet Shean. (NB Belvoir is within **Kokhav HaYarden National Park**, with all directional signs using this name.) Buses that run between Tiberias and Jerusalem via Bet Shean (961/963/964, 1 per hr) pass the turn-off for the site (Kokhav HaYarden Junction), and though there is a bus stop here you'll have to remind the driver to pull over (look for the orange sign). From here it is a very steep 6.5km twisting

Getting there

Belvoir

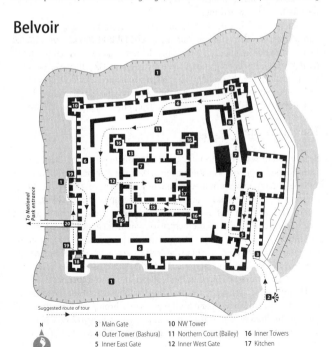

Suggested route of tour

0 metres   30

N

1 Moat
2 Viewpoint

3 Main Gate
4 Outer Tower (Bashura)
5 Inner East Gate
6 Outer Fortress Vaults
7 Water Cistern
8 Workshop Installations
9 NE Tower

10 NW Tower
11 Northern Court (Bailey)
12 Inner West Gate
13 Vaults of Inner Fortress
(Donjon)
14 Inner Courtyard
15 Refectory

16 Inner Towers
17 Kitchen
18 SW Tower and Entrance
to Sally Port
19 Sally Port
20 Modern Drawbridge

Galilee & The Golan

climb up Route 717 to Belvoir. I cannot emphasize enough how steep and long this climb is. Take plenty of water. An alternative route approaches along Route 717 from the west, via Ein Harod and Moledet, though the quality of this road is very poor and officially this is private.

History

The **Order of the Knights Hospitaller** constructed the castle here in 1168 on the site of a fortified farm established some 30 years earlier. Its name Belvoir ("fine view") requires no explanation. In 1182-83 the superbly constructed fortress easily withstood **Salah al-Din**'s assault, yet four years later the garrison stood by impotently as Salah al-Din's troops by-passed Belvoir on their way to defeating the Crusader army at the Horns of Hittim, just 25 kilometres to the north (see page 677). One of Belvoir's strengths, its remoteness, became a weakness, succinctly put by Smith: "The Christian banner at Belvoir waved a mere signal, remote, ineffectual above the Arab flood that speedily covered the land" (*Historical Geography of the Holy Land*, 1894).

Following the defeat of the Latin Kingdom at the Horns of Hittim, Salah al-Din's army laid siege to Belvoir. A testament to the resolution of the garrison and the fortress's superb construction, the Crusaders held out for 18 months. The Crusaders were eventually forced to sue for peace when the Arab army, having tunnelled under the outer fortification wall, undermined the east tower and brought about its collapse. In recognition of the garrison's courage, and an indication of the integrity of Salah al-Din, the Crusaders were allowed free passage to Tyre. Though the Arab army dismantled the church, the fortress itself was left largely intact.

It was not until the early 13th century when, fearing the return of the Christian armies, the then ruler of Damascus, **el-Malik el-Mu'azzam**, ordered Belvoir to be dismantled. In effect only the upper storey was removed, but though the Crusaders regained Belvoir by treaty in 1241 their stay was too short to effect any restoration. The fortress remained abandoned until the early 19th century when Bedouins established the village of Kaukab el-Hawa ("Star of the Winds") amongst the ruins. This too was abandoned in 1948.

Tour of the site

Belvoir comprises two concentric rings; a building style common in the late Latin Kingdom period. The knights, including the commander of the order and the priesthood, were housed within the inner keep (or *donjon*), whilst the ordinary soldiery, auxiliaries and mercenaries occupied the area between the *donjon* and the outer fortification wall. This was seen as a safeguard against treachery when the loyalty of the mercenaries could not be guaranteed, though as Murphy-O'Connor points out, this was "bad psychology; no one in the outer ward was prepared to fight to the death. Mercenaries were tempted to go over to the enemy, and knights to retreat to the central keep" (*The Holy Land*, 1992). In the case of Belvoir, this does not appear to have happened.

The tour of the site usually begins at the viewpoint just outside the southeast tower, and is adequately explained on sign-boards throughout the fortress and through the free brochure from the ticket office. ■ *T6581766. 0800-1600 daily, closes one hour earlier on Friday. Adult 11 NIS. Cafeteria, toilets.*

Tiberias and the Sea of Galilee

Not only is the Sea of Galilee central to the physical geography of Galilee, regulating the micro-climate and providing a source of drinking water, irrigation and food, it is also central to the cultural and religious geography of the region. Most visitors use the Jewish holy city of Tiberias as a base from which to explore the beautiful surrounding countryside and numerous archaeological sites, most notably the locations associated with the Galilean Ministry of Jesus.

Geography

Located in the Jordan Valley some 209 metres below sea level, the Sea of Galilee is the largest reservoir of fresh water in Israel, and second only in the Middle East to Lake Nasser. As such it is a vital component of the water economy of Israel, supplying around 25 percent of the country's water requirement through the National Water Carrier. At its widest points it is 21 kilometres north to south and 12 kilometres east to west, with a maximum depth of 46 metres. The salinization of the lake is an ever-present threat, with several salt water springs flowing into the lake close to Tabgha and other subterranean springs located beneath the lake bed. Steps taken to reduce this threat include piping salt water from Tabgha along the western shore of the lake, and then into the Jordan River to the south, as well as ensuring that the level of the lake does not drop below the critical 213 metres below sea-level mark. Currently, the pressure of the volume of fresh water in the Sea of Galilee suppresses the saline aquifers beneath the floor of the lake, preventing them from penetrating the lake itself. It is feared that should the level of the lake drop too far the saline streams may be able to break through. The drought at the end of the 1980s-early 1990s (and again in 1999) saw water conservation measures introduced as the surface of the lake dropped perilously close to the minus 213 metres level. In addition to providing water for agriculture and municipal functions, the Sea of Galilee generates income through tourism and fishing, the latter revolving mainly around an indigenous species of perch known locally as St Peter's fish.

Physically, the basin in which the lake lies is said to remind some of a poorly wooded Scottish loch (Smith, 1894), though Mark Twain was less impressed. Visiting the Holy Land in 1867 on a trip that the American wit P.J. O'Rourke describes as an opportunity for "making the world's first fun of package tourism" (*Holidays in Hell*, 1988), Twain describes the Sea of Galilee region as "an unobtrusive basin of water, some mountainous desolation, and one tree" (*The Innocents Abroad*, 1911). It's remarkable how Twain's derogatory remarks have been used by Zionists to forward their argument that the land was unoccupied and uncared for. He came to mock, not make a political statement.

Biblical history

It is for its biblical history that most people know the Sea of Galilee. In the 'Fourth Book of Moses, called Numbers' (*Numbers 34:11*) the 'Sea of Chinnereth' (or 'Kinnereth') is first mentioned in the account of the distribution of land amongst the tribes of Israel (see also *Deuteronomy 3:17; Joshua 13:27*). The name 'Kinnereth' is said to be derived from the Hebrew word

Galilee & The Golan

kinnor, or harp, which the shape of the lake is said to resemble. Tiberias, the only one of the large cities built around the lake that still exists, became a great centre of Jewish learning and remains one of the four holy cities of the Jews.

For Christians also there is a deep attachment to the Sea of Galilee as the theatre in which so many events in the life of Jesus were acted out. Capernaum, on the northwest shore, became Jesus' "own city" where he performed several miracles. It was also the place at which he called Matthew, Peter, Andrew, James and John to follow him, the latter four of whom made their living as fishermen on the lake. Indeed, it was for these fishermen that he "stilled the storm" (*Matthew 8:23-27; Mark 4:35-41; Luke 8:22-25*), and walked on the water to give them faith (*Matthew 14:22-32; Mark 6:47-51; John 6:16-21*). The "Sermon on the Mount", delivered on the Mt of Beatitudes just above the northwest shore, has become one of the basic tenets of Jesus' teachings.

Tiberias and the Sea of Galilee

Tiberias

The largest town on the shores of the Sea of Galilee, Tiberias is a natural base from which to explore the Galilee and Golan region. To Jews it is one of the four holy cities (with Jerusalem, Safed and Hebron) and features several important pilgrimage sites, whilst the modern town is pitching itself as a holiday resort with a more than lively nightlife. The hot sulphur pools of Hammath-Tiberias have remained a major attraction since Roman times.

Phone code: 06
Colour map 1, grid B4

Ins and outs

Tiberias has good transport connections with the rest of the country, and also acts as a base from which to visit much of the Galilee and Golan region. The nearest airfield is 27km north at Rosh Pinna, from where there are flights to and from Tel Aviv, Haifa and Jerusalem. Buses connect Tiberias to Tel Aviv (2½ hrs), Jerusalem (2½ hrs), Nazareth (45 mins) and Haifa (1 hr 15 mins), as well as all the major sites in Upper Galilee and the Golan. There are numerous car hire firms based in Tiberias, with a rented car being easily the most convenient way to explore the Sea of Galilee, Upper Galilee and the Golan. However, demand is high and it pays to reserve your vehicle in advance if possible (especially cheaper cars). During Pesach (and other Jewish hoildays) prices soar and all classes of vehicle become scarce.

Getting there

The town centre is compact enough to get around on foot, and even the sites to the south can easily be reached by walking (though Buses 5/5a run as far as the hot springs). You may like to consider taking a bus (also 5/5a) if heading up the steep hill to the new suburb of Kiryat Shmuel above Tiberias, though you'd only need to come here if your hotel is located in this suburb.

Getting around

History

Many visitors to Tiberias seem to assume that there is a strong link between the city's history and Christianity, perhaps influenced by the references in the Gospels to Jesus' Ministry in the Sea of Galilee region. Though Tiberias is mentioned in the New Testament (*John 6:1, 23*), there is no evidence that Jesus ever visited here. In fact, it is within **Judaism**, and not Christianity, that Tiberias finds its significance.

Founding of the city

The city was founded between 17 and 20 CE by a son of Herod the Great, **Herod Antipas**, and named after his patron Tiberias Caesar. The new city, which soon replaced Sepphoris as the district capital of Galilee, was built by Herod Antipas primarily to revive the process begun by his father; namely creating a progressive, Hellenized version of the Jewish state. Ironically, the new city had difficulty attracting Jewish residents since it was built on the site of an ancient cemetery and thus violated Jewish law. Josephus suggests that Herod Antipas attracted new settlers by "equipping houses at his own expense and adding new gifts of land" (*Antiquities XVIII, 36-38*), though the truth is that force and coercion were more likely inducements to settle here. Tax exemptions were offered and even the poor and runaway slaves were given citizenship, though many Jews living in the surrounding area were forced off their land and relocated to Tiberias.

Josephus presents a picture of a magnificent city built in the Roman style with a large royal palace, baths, cardo and a large synagogue "capable of accommodating a large crowd" (*Life, 277*). Ironically, by the middle of the first century CE Herod Antipas' new Graeco-Roman city had a Jewish majority,

Galilee & The Golan

though the king's Judaism was often questioned. Not only did he decorate his palace and the gates of the city with idolatrous images, he also broke Mosaic law by marrying his brother's wife. It was John the Baptist's condemnation of such marriage practices that had led to his beheading.

Roman Tiberias and Jewish Renaissance
Upon the death c. 44 CE of Herod Antipas' successor Agrippa I, the city came under the direct control of the Roman procurator of Judea. Tiberias remained the district capital of Galilee until 61 CE, when the city was annexed by **Agrippa II**, whose capital was already established at Caesarea-Philippi (Banias, see page 743).

In the build-up to the Roman advance into Galilee during the **First Jewish Revolt** (66-73 CE), Tiberias was a pawn in the struggle for control of the opposition armies between Josephus, Governor of Galilee, and his rival John (though it should be noted that the main source of detail of this rivalry is Josephus himself!). When the city revolted against his command, Josephus felt himself compelled to hand it over to his soldiers to pillage, though he later "collected all the plunder and gave it back to the townspeople to … give the citizens a sharp lesson by pillaging it, and then giving back their possessions to recover their good will" (*Jewish War, II, 647*; see also Sepphoris, page 627). Perhaps fearing that the Roman commander would not be so magnanimous, Tiberias surrendered to Vespasian without incident, the town's zealots fleeing to Tarichaeae (see Migdal, on page 684). Tiberias continued to be ruled by Agrippa II until his death c. 96 CE, after which the city came under direct Roman rule. A period of economic prosperity followed, notwithstanding the Jewish Bar Kokhba Uprising of 132-35 CE, though Tiberias' role in this revolt is unclear.

Despite the construction early in the second century CE of a large pagan temple honouring the Roman Emperor Hadrian, the city was 'cleansed' of ritual impurity by **Rabbi Simeon Bar Yochai** (c. 145 CE), thus making it acceptable for Jews to settle here in numbers. When the city was granted the status of Roman colony by the Emperor Elagabalus (218-222 CE), Tiberias became the centre of Jewish life in Israel (Jerusalem still being designated off-limits to Jews). **Rabbi Yohanan ben Nappaha** (c. 180-279 CE) established the Great Study House (*Beth HaMidrash HaGadol*) in Tiberias c. 220 CE, where he continued his study of the oral code of law (*Mishnah*) that had been compiled by his teacher and mentor, Rabbi Judah I ha-Nasi. The work that Yohanan began in testing the logical consistency of the *Mishnah* manifested itself in the *Gemara*, finally completed by his disciples c. 400 CE. With the *Mishnah*, the *Gemara* forms the Palestinian (Jerusalem) Talmud, with the system of Hebrew punctuation developed in Tiberias becoming the accepted standard for the Torah. The Jewish renaissance in Tiberias was highlighted by the shifting here from Sepphoris (Zippori) of the **Sanhedrin**, (the highest judicial and ecclesiastical council of the ancient Jewish nation), c. 235 CE.

Byzantine period
Tiberias flourished as the Jewish capital, with major expansion of the city limits, including a new suburb around the hot springs of Hammath-Tiberias to the south. Substantial remains from this grand building period can still be seen, though excavations are still not complete and restoration work is yet to begin.

Despite the adoption of **Christianity** by the Roman empire, Galilee remained predominantly Jewish during the early years of the Byzantine period (324-638 CE). However, the gradual conversion of the pagan population to Christianity brought them into conflict with the Jewish population. The Persian invasion of Palestine in 614 CE saw the Jews support the invaders, with many Christians massacred and their churches destroyed. When the Roman

Byzantine army retook the region in 628 CE, the massacres were reciprocated. Despite this, Tiberias remained for a time the seat of Jewish study, with the Academy (Yeshiva) of Eretz-Israel that succeeded the Sanhedrin continuing to function here well into the 10th century CE.

When the **Arabs** defeated the Byzantine army at Yarmuk River in 636 CE, they established Tiberias as their northern capital, though later shifted it to Bet Shean. The importance of Tiberias to the Jews declined, not due to Muslim persecution, but due to the Arab decision to allow Jews to re-occupy Jerusalem. The earthquake that destroyed Bet Shean in 749 CE effectively revitalized Tiberias, establishing it again as the Arab capital of the province of Jordan. Ironically, a major earthquake in 1033 largely destroyed Tiberias.

> **Early Arab and Crusader periods**

When Tancred conquered the Galilee for the **Crusaders** in 1099 a new city was built at Tiberias, just to the north of the original site. The city was encircled by **Salah al-Din** in 1187 and it was on the way to relieving the city that the forces of the Latin Kingdom were defeated at the Horns of Hittim 10 kilometres to the west (see page 677), thus bringing to an end Crusader rule in the Holy Land. Though the Crusaders returned to the Galilee, they were finally expelled by the **Mamluks** in 1265.

Turkish rule was established in Palestine following the defeat of the Mamluks in 1516. Keen to attract Jewish entrepreneurial skill, the early Ottoman sultans encouraged the Jews recently expelled from Spain and Portugal to settle in Palestine. In 1562 Suliman the Magnificent granted tax collection rights in Tiberias to **Joseph Nasi**, a Marrano Jew from Portugal, and his mother-in-law **Donna Gracia**. They were permitted to rebuild the city walls and to establish a silk industry, with a view towards establishing a safe haven for Jews that may later become an independent Jewish enclave. Their plans were thwarted by the failure of the Ottomans to retain effective control over this part of their empire.

> **Ottoman period**

Tiberias became a relative backwater once more until the Druze war-lord **Fakhr al-Din** briefly revived the city's fortunes when he established his capital here between 1595 and 1635. After another period of Ottoman rule, Tiberias once again became semi-autonomous under the rule of the Bedouin sheikh **Dahr el-Amr**. Relative stability was brought to Tiberias under Dahr el-Amr, though in 1742, just two years into his period of rule, annoyed by his refortification of the city the Turkish army marched from Damascus to teach him a lesson. After a siege lasting 85 days the Turks captured Tiberias, and having admonished Dahr el-Amr marched directly back to Damascus. He didn't seem to learn from this example and 33 years later the Turks assassinated this 'upstart'.

The subsequent Turkish governor of the Galilee, **Ahmed el-Jazzar**, known affectionately as 'The Butcher', ruled with an iron fist, though fear of his excesses served to bring peace to the region. He was succeeded briefly by the invading Egyptians, headed by Ibrahim Pasha. In 1837 Tiberias was once again levelled by a major earthquake.

At the conclusion of World War I Britain assumed the Mandate for Palestine. Relations between the Jewish and Arab communities seem to have been relatively good, with few incidents reported during the Arab uprising of 1929. The Arab riots of 1936-38 were considerably more bloody.

> **British rule and the War of Independence**

The UN Partition Plan of 1947 envisaged Tiberias as being part of the Jewish state. This decision was partially influenced by the pattern of Jewish landholding in the region that had resulted from the establishment here of pioneering Jewish agricultural communities in the late 18th and early 19th

Galilee & The Golan

centuries. The population of Tiberias was approximately 52.5 percent Jewish and 47.5 percent Arab. Following a series of battles in and around the town, the Golani Brigade successfully entered the city in mid-April 1948, cutting the city in two. Under the protection of the British Army, most of the Arab population were evacuated east to Jordan. A mounted "Davidka" (home-produced mortar) outside the Post Office on HaYarden now tells the story of how Tiberias was the first mixed town to be "liberated" by the Israelis.

Modern Tiberias The modern town, with a population of around 36,000, has expanded rapidly since independence. It now markets itself as a seaside resort and holiday centre, though it has to be said that much of the development has been particularly unattractive. Many of the hotels, and the promenade area in particular, are showing their age and are in desperate need of a face-lift. Many of Tiberias' historical sites are badly neglected and as yet the cash has not been found to renovate and restore the Roman/Byzantine city remains. There are, however, several sites of particular note related to Tiberias' rich Jewish history. Tiberias also remains a good base from which to explore the Galilee and Golan areas. **NB** In the months of July and August, the town can become unpleasantly hot and sweaty.

City centre

Archaeological Garden The 'Archaeological Garden' that now stands in the heart of the modern town is located on the site of the northern residential quarter of Byzantine Tiberias,

Tiberias

To Golani Junction, Afula, Nazareth & Route 7717 to Horns of Hittim & Arbel

7 ■ To Tabgha, Capernaum, clockwise circuit of Sea of Galilee & Upper Galilee

Sea of Galilee

Garden of Kisses

Yeshiva

City Hall

Panorama beach

Blue beach

Quiet beach

Nelson Beach
Lido

Ancient Cemetery (Tomb of Maimonides)

Religious beach

Tomb of Rabbi Akiva

0 metres   500

Ha Yarden

Bibas

To Roman/Byzantine city, Hammath-Tiberias & Route 90 to Bet Shean

Related map:
A. City Centre, Tiberias, see next page.

■ **Sleeping**
1 Ariston
2 Astoria
3 Bet Berzik
4 Brighton (closed)
5 Caesar
6 Carmel Jordan River
7 Club
8 Continental
9 Eden
10 Eshel

11 Genossar (ruins)
12 Golan
13 Hartman
14 Hod
15 Kolton-Inn
16 Mercure Quiet Beach

17 Meytal
18 Prima Tiberias
19 Radisson Moriah Plaza
20 Ron
21 Ron Beach
22 Tiberias

23 Tiberias Gardens
24 Washington

● **Eating**
1 Deck's
2 Domino Pizza

3 Liquid Beach Bar
4 Pagoda Chinese
5 Take-away Pizza
6 The House

Chinese

▲ **Other**
1 Sixt Car Rental
2 Petrol station
3 Cemetery

and in the centre of the Crusader period city. The construction of the *Carmel Jordan River Hotel* and the *Radisson Moriah Plaza* uncovered remnants from both periods, although little was preserved to be seen today. Insubstantial remains of the '**northern synagogue**', probably one of Tiberias' 13 synagogues mentioned in the Talmud, can still be seen, most notably parts of a mosaic containing an inscription in Greek to "Procolus son of Crispus". It's not clear whether this refers to the synagogue's founder or the mosaic's craftsman.

The Archaeological Garden also contains a **Crusader/Mamluk-period building** that now houses the helpful **Tourist Information Centre**, some small sections of the **Byzantine residential quarter** and a modern open-air theatre. In the grounds of the *Carmel Jordan River Hotel*, close to the pool, are traces of a **Crusader church**.

Greek Orthodox Monastery of the Apostles

To the southeast of the Archaeological Garden, at the south end of the *Tayyelet* (promenade), is the 19th-century **Greek Orthodox Monastery of the Apostles**. The fourth-century church and monastery here was destroyed during the Persian invasion of 614 CE and has subsequently been rebuilt several times; the most recent renovations were just 20 years ago. The monks may admit you

City centre, Tiberias

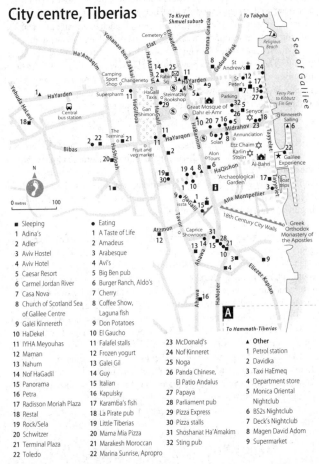

■ Sleeping	● Eating		▲ Other
1 Adina's	1 A Taste of Life	23 McDonald's	1 Petrol station
2 Adler	2 Amadeus	24 Nof Kinneret	2 Davidka
3 Aviv Hostel	3 Arabesque	25 Noga	3 Taxi HaEmeq
4 Aviv Hotel	4 Avi's	26 Panda Chinese,	4 Department store
5 Caesar Resort	5 Big Ben pub	El Patio Andalus	5 Monica Oriental
6 Carmel Jordan River	6 Burger Ranch, Aldo's	27 Papaya	Nightclub
7 Casa Nova	7 Cherry	28 Parliament pub	6 BS2s Nightclub
8 Church of Scotland Sea	8 Coffee Show,	29 Pizza Express	7 Deck's Nightclub
of Galilee Centre	Laguna fish	30 Pizza stalls	8 Magen David Adom
9 Galei Kinnereth	9 Don Potatoes	31 Shoshanat Ha'Amakim	9 Supermarket
10 HaDekel	10 El Gaucho	32 Sting pub	
11 IYHA Meyouhas	11 Falafel stalls		*Related map:*
12 Maman	12 Frozen yogurt		**A.** *Roman/Byzantine*
13 Nahum	13 Galei Gil		*city and Hammath-*
14 Nof HaGadil	14 Guy		*Tiberias, page 667.*
15 Panorama	15 Italian		
16 Petra	16 Kapulsky		
17 Radisson Moriah Plaza	17 Karamba's fish		
18 Restal	18 La Pirate pub		
19 Rock/Sela	19 Little Tiberias		
20 Schwitzer	20 Mama Mia Pizza		
21 Terminal Plaza	21 Marakesh Moroccan		
22 Toledo	22 Marina Sunrise, Apropro		

Galilee & The Golan

if you ring the bell. There are four small chapels within the walled courtyard dedicated to St Peter, St Nicholas, Mary Magdalene and the disciples. The foundations of St Nicholas' chapel, also visible to the east outside the court-yard, are thought to belong to a Crusader period tower.

Running between the monastery and HaBannim is a short stretch of the black basalt **city walls** built by Dahr el-Amr in the mid-18th century.

Tayyelet and Midrahov The foci of the Tiberias entertainment scene are the *Tayyelet* (sea-front prom-enade) and the *Midrahov* (pedestrianized area). This area features most of the restaurants and cafés, pubs and night-spots, plus several places of interest (see below). In actual fact, the *Tayyelet* is now pretty tatty; an unattractive concrete strip along the water's edge that is in serious need of beautification. The view across the Sea of Galilee is very attractive, but the foreground, with its semi-submerged shopping trolleys and empty beer cans, is not.

The Galilee Experience This is probably not a bad place to start a tour of this northern region. A 36-minute show that features 2,000 slides illuminated by 27 com-puter-sequenced projectors claims to make "4,000 years of Galilee history come alive before your eyes". The commentary is a bit cheesy, and the Zionist element is blatant propaganda (with no mention of the Arabs, who comprise 50 percent of the region's population), but overall it's worth a look. Shows are in ten languages, including English, Hebrew, French, German and Spanish, with the medium seemingly decided by the majority vote. Viewers wishing to listen in languages other than English or Hebrew are advised to call ahead for timings. The 'Galilee Experience' is located halfway along the *Tayyelet*, where the promenade projects out into the lake to form the marina. The complex fea-tures souvenir shops, amusement arcade, several water-front restaurants, and a couple of bars that tend to be a bit quieter than those at the north end of the *Tayyelet*. ■ T6723620. 0800-2200 except Shabbat. Adult 20 NIS.

Al-Bahri Mosque Tucked away between the *Radisson Moriah Plaza* and the Galilee Experience complex is the small late 19th-century **al-Bahri Mosque**, complete with a short stubby minaret and two low white domes. It is adjoined by a barrel vaulted hall. For years the tourist literature has suggested that this is shortly to become the new **Municipal Museum**, though work doesn't appear to have begun on its transformation from an empty shell.

Synagogues There are three synagogues situated in the city centre area. The **Karlin-Stolin Syna-gogue**, just inland of the al-Bahri Mosque, is built on the site of the former home of Rabbi Menachen Mendel of Vitebsk (d. 1788), who is buried in the cemetery to the south of the city centre (see page 667). It is named after two towns in Lithuania where the rabbi was active and where the Hassidic sect of Rabbi Aaron ben Jacob was founded. The **Etz Chaim** ('tree of life') **Synagogue**, located close by (and marked on some maps as the "Rambam Synagogue") is named after a book by the Hebron-born Rabbi Chaim Abulafia (d. 1744, and buried in the same cemetery). It was Rabbi Abulafia whom Dahr el-Amr invited to re-establish the Jewish presence in Tiberias. The present synagogue dates to 1950 and stands on the site of several previous buildings. The mid-19th-century **Senyor Synagogue**, on the *Midrahov,* just west of the *Caesar Resort Hotel*, is now in a pretty similar state to the al-Bahri Mosque, proving that there's nothing racist or sectarian in the neglect of the city's older buildings!

A church was established here by the Crusaders in the 12th or 13th century, almost certainly to commemorate the ministry of Jesus in the Galilee. The nave of the Crusader church, designed in the shape of an upturned fishing boat to symbolize Peter relinquishing his profession to follow Jesus, forms part of the current church seen today. The lack of Crusader churches on long-established sites of Christian worship around the Sea of Galilee (eg Tabgha, Capernaum) suggests that these places of pilgrimage were not identified by the Crusaders, and hence the decision to celebrate Jesus' ministry in a city that he probably never visited. The church has had a mixed history. A *mihrab* (niche indicating the direction of Mecca) in the south wall suggests that the church was converted into a mosque, whilst the Turks later used it as a caravanserai. In addition to the Crusader sections, parts of the church date to 1870, 1903 and 1944 respectively. The monument in the courtyard was built by Polish soldiers billeted in Tiberias during World War Two. ■ *T6720516. Daily 0800-1145 1400-1700. Entrance from Tayyelet next to Galei Gil restaurant.*

St Peter's Catholic Church

St Andrew's Church at the north end of the *Tayyelet* is linked to the Sea of Galilee Centre just to the northwest. The latter was founded in 1885 as the region's first hospital by the Scottish missionary **Dr David Torrance**. Jewish critics of Torrance claim that he was on a proselytizing mission, though the fact that he converted only two Jews and several Muslims whilst treating thousands of people of all denominations suggests that his motives were humanist. In fact, upon his death in 1923, Tiberias' chief rabbi was moved to say that "Tiberias was blest with three things: the Sea of Galilee, the hot springs and Dr Torrance". In 1959 the hospital was converted into a pilgrim hostel, with major renovations in 1992 making it one of the most attractive places in town to stay (see 'Sleeping' on page 671). The Centre is jointly run by the Church of Scotland and the Episcopal Church in Jerusalem and the Middle East.

St Andrew's Church and Sea of Galilee Centre

Another 19th-century building with historic interest in Tiberias is the former Hotel Tiberias (now the *Menyous Youth Hostel*, see 'Sleeping' on page 671). Formerly a luxurious hotel serving the sea planes landing on the Sea of Galilee, it later became the British HQ in Tiberias and was the subject of bitter fighting between Jews and Arabs in the 1948 War of Independence.

Hotel Tiberias

This was obviously once a splendid building, now in a shameful state of repair and located rather incongruously at the centre of a run-down shopping plaza. Dahr el-Amr, the Bedouin sheikh who carved a semi-autonomous fiefdom out of the Ottoman empire in Galilee in the mid-18th century, encouraged Jews to resettle in Tiberias and it is suggested that in gratitude they funded the construction of this mosque.

Great Mosque of Dahr el-Amr

Erroneously referred to on some maps as a 'Crusader castle', the citadel just to the north of the city centre was built during the reign of Dahr el-Amr (though it is usually attributed to his son Chulabi). It is now owned and run by a local artist, Rivka Ganun, who has converted it into a studio/gallery (T6721375, 10 NIS for a look around).

The Citadel

Whilst some of Tiberias' later rabbis are buried in the 'new' cemetery just to the south of the city centre, several important Jewish figures from an earlier period now rest in the **Ancient Cemetery** on Ben Zakkai Street, just to the northwest of the city centre. **NB** Modest dress is required.

Ancient Cemetery

  The key attraction here is the **Tomb of Rabbi Moses ben Maimon** (known commonly as **Rambam** or **Maimonides**). Born in Spain in 1135, Maimonides

Galilee & The Golan

fled persecution to Morocco at an early age, passing briefly through Israel before settling in Egypt. In addition to being one of the leading Jewish sages of the 12th century (as well as a noted Aristotelian philosopher), he was also the personal physician to Salah al-Din's vizier Al-Fadi al-Baisami, and later Salah al-Din's son who became sultan in 1198. It is also said that such was his reputation as a doctor, that he was offered the position as court physician to the 'Frankish King' (either England's Richard Coeur de Lion, or Amalric, King of Jerusalem), though he declined the invitation. Upon his death in 1204 it is said that an unled camel brought him from Egypt to this spot for burial. His major life's work was the 14 books of the *Mishne Torah*, represented by the 14 black stones that line the path to his tomb. A tall, red iron structure stands above the cenotaph (marking the position of the cemetery from some distance away).

The camel that brought Maimonides' body here selected a place of burial next to the first century CE leader of the Sanhedrin, **Rabbi Yohanan ben Zakkai**. During the siege of Jerusalem in the Second Jewish Revolt (66-73 CE), ben Zakkai is said to have approached the commander of the besieging forces, Vespasian, and addressed him as Caesar (Emperor). As Vespasian ordered the rabbi killed, a messenger from Rome announced the death of Caesar and declared Vespasian's succession. A stunned Vespasian, believing ben Zakkai to be a prophet, spared his life and granted the rabbi's request that the Jews be allowed to continue Torah study at Yavne. Interestingly, the Jewish historian Josephus tells us a similar story, though the version of this event that he tells takes place at Jotapata and the prophet is … Josephus! Ben Zakkai temporarily took charge of the Sanhedrin, but took to his grave the terrible doubt as to whether he should have been more ambitious in his request to Vespasian and asked for the Temple in Jerusalem to be spared, but at the risk of losing everything.

Amongst others buried in the ancient cemetery is Rabbi Isaiah ben Abraham haLevi Horowitz (d. 1630), author of the *Shnei Luchot haBrit*, and former head of Jerusalem's Ashkenazi Jewish community.

Tomb of Rabbi Akiva Another important figure from the rabbinical tradition is also buried in Tiberias, **Rabbi Akiva**. An illiterate shepherd until the age of 40, Rabbi Akiva (c. 50-135 CE) went on to become one of the most knowledgeable Torah scholars of the age, and teacher and mentor to Rabbi Me'ir Ba'al Ha-nes (see page 670). During the Bar Kokhba Revolt against Rome of 132-35, Rabbi Akiva proclaimed Bar Kokhba as the messiah and was executed by the Romans for his trouble. His cave-like grave is covered by a small white dome. ■ *To reach the tomb, head northwest along Elhadeff, bearing left where it turns into Yehuda haNasi. Take the fifth left on to Trumpeldor just before the police station/government offices and head southwest. At the loop in the road take the third left along HaGevura and continue straight until the Hebrew sign points to the tomb; Bus 4 goes as far as the police station/government offices, otherwise it's a hell of a walk.*

Beaches If the definition of a beach is where water meets land, then yes, Tiberias does have beaches. Sand is totally absent and the rocky shoreline can make getting in and out of the water rather difficult. Tiberias' best beaches are all privately run and admission fees charged, though facilities generally include showers and changing rooms, chairs and umbrellas, and cafés/restaurants. **Lido Beach** (*T6721538, open 0800-1700*), just north of the city centre, is one of the better private beaches, charging 15 NIS for use of the facilities. The *Lido Kinnereth Sailing Co*, (*T6721538*), runs cruises on the lake, including trips to Capernaum. **Nelson Beach** (open 24 hrs) offers a similar deal, in addition to allowing you almost to replicate Jesus' trick of walking on the water (*Matthew 14:22-32; Mark 6:47-51; John 6:16-21*) by being towed behind a motor-boat on an inflatable banana (*30 NIS for 15 mins*)! **Blue Beach** (*T6720105, open 0900-1700, 20 NIS*) and **Quiet Beach** (*T6790125, open 0800-1700, 30 NIS*), owned by the hotel of the same name, are a little further north. The **Religious Beach** opposite the Sea of Galilee Centre (*T6791509, open 0800-1700*) offers segregated bathing (*women Sunday, Tuesday, Thursday; men Monday, Wednesday, Friday*).

To the south of the city centre, **Gai Beach** (*T6700713, open 0900-1700, 50 NIS, kids under three free*) is a water-park featuring giant water-slides and a variety of pools. **Sironit Beach** (*T6721449, open 0900-1600, 15 NIS*) is not particularly impressive, whilst the **Municipal Beach** (*T6720709*) is a dump.

If you have your own transport, or are prepared to wait around for buses, there are quieter and more attractive beaches dotted around the Sea of Galilee. The **Luna Gal** water park (*T6731750*) across the lake near Moshav Ramot is far more impressive than Tiberias' effort.

Southern part of the city

Roman/Byzantine city and Hammath-Tiberias

■ Sleeping
1 Gai Beach
2 Ganei Menara
3 Holiday Inn
4 Park Inn
5 Royal Plaza

★ Sights
1 Bathhouse
2 Municipal Market Place
3 Cardo
4 Southern Gate
5 Basilica Complex
6 Sewage Treatment Plant
7 Possible Beth HaMidrash HaGadol of Yohanan ben Nappaha

The southern boundaries of the modern town centre are marked by a small Muslim cemetery and a larger **Jewish cemetery** (just northwest of the *Gai Beach Hotel*). Several 18th- and 19th-century rabbis who led Jewish followers to Tiberias to precipitate the arrival of the messiah are buried here. The most notable are Rabbi Chaim Abulafia (d. 1744), Rabbi Nachman of Horodenka (d. 1780), Rabbi Menachem Mendel of Vitebsk (d. 1788) and Rabbi Yisrael ben Shmuel of Shklov (d. 1839).

Graves of 18th- and 19th-century rabbis

The small hill that stands above and to the west of the Roman/Byzantine city area is known by popular tradition as Mt Berenice (Bereniki), after the sister of Agrippa II. However, during Agrippa's period of rule over Galilee (c. 61-96 CE) it seems clear that Berenice remained at his court in Caesarea-Philippi (Banias) and thus there is no archaeological evidence to connect her with this hill. The detailed excavation of the Mt Berenice has yet to locate the magnificent palace of Herod Antipas that Josephus describes in such detail. Excavations have revealed the remains of a **Byzantine church**, however, built on the site of a former Canaanite *bimah* (high place). Though there are good views, the

Byzantine church at Mt Berenice

Galilee & The Golan

effort of getting here is not really compensated for by the remains of the triapsidal basilica. ■ *Head south on Ahawa, turning right on to the winding Toledano, before turning left on to the dirt road that leads 1.5 kilometres to the site.*

Yohanan ben Nappaha's Beth HaMidrash HaGadol

The site of Tiberias' new sewerage treatment plant ((**6**) on map) would not at first seem much of an attraction to visitors. However, considerable interest has been aroused by a discovery made by contractors during expansion work on the site; so much so that there is talk of relocating the sewerage treatment plant. A large **public building** (**7**) dating to the Roman period has been excavated, with its location at the foot of Mt Berenice (Bereniki) and the presence of an adjoining stepped pool (probably a *mikveh*, or Jewish ritual bath) suggesting to some that this may be the Great Study Centre (**Beth HaMidrash HaGadol**) that **Rabbi Yohanan ben Nappaha** established in Tiberias c. 220 CE for the study of the *Mishnah*, and culminated in the writing of the *Gemara*. If so, this is a significant find, though there is not really a great deal to see. ■ *To reach the site take the small road opposite the Gai Beach Water Park, turn left at the first fork, continue through the treatment plant before exiting to the right. The site is marked by a sign in Hebrew only.*

Roman/ Byzantine city

The substantial remains from Tiberias' Roman and Byzantine city lay predominantly in the stretch of land between the *Holiday Inn Hotel* and the southern end of the modern city (marked roughly by the two cemeteries opposite the *Gai Beach Hotel*). As yet, however, this is an untapped tourist resource with excavations far from complete and restoration not yet underway. In fact, despite plans to restore the ancient city there seems to be precious little activity at the site; it's largely fenced off with signs reading "Tiberias Archaeological Excavations – no entry". When funds become available and the remains are properly restored, this will be a leading attraction. The 'keep out' notices are not rigorously enforced, though prospective visitors should be careful when visiting the remains; not just for your own safety but for the preservation of the site.

The most substantial remains are from a large **bathhouse** (**1**) (42 metres by 31 metres) adjacent to the *cardo* (main north to south street) and the marketplace. Built in the fourth century CE and remaining in use until the 11th century CE, its size and location suggest that it is the central Tiberias bathhouse that is mentioned in Talmudic literature. The east wing contains dressing rooms, with a large hall possibly used for social or ceremonial functions, whilst the west wing housed the bathing rooms. Both wings feature mosaic floors, though those in the west wing are particularly fine and in a good state of preservation. A colonnaded pool was located three metres below the west wing (crawl in through the narrow hole next to the palm tree; bring a torch), though because such a feature is rare in bathhouses of this period its exact function is unknown. Hirschfeld, who is directing excavations at the site, speculates that its construction "may well be connected with the laws of purity as practised by the city's Jewish population" (*New Encyclopedia of Archaeological Excavations in the Holy Land*, 1993). The bathhouse is protected by a modern (but crumbling) roof.

The municipal **marketplace** (**2**), a sixth century CE columned structure covering some 800 square metres, is located just to the north. Adjoining both the bathhouse and the marketplace to the west is the **cardo** (**3**), the 12-metre-wide paved main street flanked on both sides by a colonnaded sidewalk five metres wide. Probably initially paved in the second century CE, short stretches still remain. The street originally ran 370 metres south, down to the **southern gate** (**4**). This gate, protected by two round towers (diameter seven metres) whose bases are clearly visible, may well date to the foundation of the city at the beginning of the first century CE. The picture is confused somewhat by the addition of further building during later periods.

Also visible to the east of the marketplace, (close to the road, roughly between Sironit and Municipal Beaches), are the insubstantial remains of a second century CE **basilica complex (5)** that was converted for Christian use in the fifth to sixth centuries CE.

Graves of Rabbi Jeremiah ben Abba and Rabbi Kahana

Two revered rabbis are buried in what are now the grounds of the *Holiday Inn*! **Rabbi Jeremiah ben Abba** (enter grounds, bear left behind large hall and look for small white dome) sounds a most entertaining, and slightly mischievous, character. One story about him explains how he came to be suspended from one particular Talmud discussion session. A group of learned rabbis were contemplating a subject that Rabbi Jeremiah ben Abba obviously found rather trivial; the question of ownership of a dove found far from its cote. After lengthy debate it was agreed by the wise men that if a dove is found within 50 cubits of the cote it belongs to the cote owner. If, however, it is found more than 50 cubits from the cote, it can be claimed by the finder. Rabbi Jeremiah ben Abba was thrown out of the meeting when he asked "If the bird is found with one foot within and the other foot beyond 50 cubits, what is the law?"!

The second tomb (enter grounds, continue up driveway to top of the hill, climb the steps, turn right, then head up the cliff-face, aiming towards the small white dome) belongs to **Rabbi Kahana**, one of the most important Babylonian rabbis of the third century CE. There's not a great deal to see at either tomb.

Tiberias Hot Springs (Hamme Teverya)

Legend has it that King Solomon created the hot springs here by ordering demons to bring the water up to the surface from the bowels of the earth. Because he then made the demons deaf it appears that the demons have not heard the news that Solomon died in 928 BCE, so they're still working away like mad. You can come and appreciate their industrious efforts at the **Tiberias Hot Springs Health Spa** and **Tiberias Hot Springs Recreation Centre** located on either side of Route 90/Eliezer Kaplan Boulevard adjacent to Hammath-Tiberias National Park. The former (sometimes known as 'Old Mineral Hot Springs') specializes in therapeutic treatments such as the Piluma mud pack, whilst the latter (sometimes the 'Young Mineral Hot Springs') is more of a recreation resort (mineral pools, massage rooms, cosmetic treatments, health and fitness centre). A selection from the price list follows.

Mineral pool complex (including pools, sauna, shape-up club, beach) $14, with discounts available through the Tourist Information Centre; 'Ethereal bubble bath' $26; 'Regular massage' $31; 'Piluma mud pack' $30; 'thallosotherapy pleasure' ('seaweeds pampering treatment') $122; 'Exotic pleasure' ('massage + cosmetic mud pack + mineral bath') $81; 'Shiatzu' $60; 'Thai massage' $60. The brochure features photos of young, nubile Israelis, whilst most visitors seem to be old and wrinkly. ■ *T6791967. 'Old' Sunday-Thursday 0700-1600, Friday 0700-1330, Saturday closed. 'Young' Sunday, Monday, Tuesday, Thursday 0800-2300, Wednesday 0800-2000, Friday 0800-1700. Bus 1 or 05 from Central Bus Station via HaGalil every five minutes.*

Hammath-Tiberias National Park

Though initially developing as a separate walled town, Hammath-Tiberias eventually merged with Tiberias sometime in the first century CE. Its independent development can perhaps be explained by the reluctance of the priestly order to settle in Tiberias itself since it was built on the site of an ancient cemetery. The presence of the **hot springs**, almost certainly a deciding factor in Herod Antipas' decision to build his new city here, has supported the

Galilee & The Golan

economy of the city from Roman times right through to today.

The **Hammath-Tiberias National Park**, approximately two kilometres south of the modern city centre, features a number of points of interest from the ancient city, most notably the **synagogue**. Originally dated to the Early Roman period (37 BCE-132 CE), it is now clear that the Hammath-Tiberias synagogue was built during a later period, most probably the fourth to fifth centuries CE, with alterations and repairs continuing into the eighth century CE. It was most likely destroyed in the earthquake that hit the region in 749 CE. Its plan is unique, comprising a broadhouse (15 metres by 13 metres) orientated southeast to northwest, with an entrance facing Jerusalem. Three rows of columns divide the hall into four rooms. A separate room outside the main hall provided a permanent platform for the Ark of the Law, and is one of the earliest synagogues in Israel that had such a form. Subsequent synagogues housed the Ark in an apse on the main hall (see, for example, Beit Alpha Synagogue).

The most remarkable feature is the well-preserved **mosaic pavement**, now protected by a modern canopy roof. The central panel has a representation of the zodiac, pre-dating the one at Beit Alpha and better executed. For the details of the symbols see under Beit Alpha Synagogue (page 646), though the sequence here begins at '12 o'clock' as opposed to '3 o'clock'. The busts of four women (representing the seasons) appear in the corners of the panel, whilst the central image of the sun god Helios riding in his chariot has been partially destroyed. The top panel depicts two flaming menorahs flanking the Ark of the Law, whilst the bottom panel features a long dedicatory inscription flanked by two lions. The Greek inscription, mentioning a Severus as the builder of the synagogue, is the first to mention the patriarchs of the Sanhedrin. (For a discussion on the incongruity of the representation of the pagan zodiac in a synagogue, refer once more to Beit Alpha Synagogue on page 646).

To the south and west of the synagogue are insubstantial remains of the **Byzantine city walls**, including parts of the southern city gate and tower. The remnants here only hint at the size of the Byzantine city, when Hammath-Tiberias covered almost 20 hectares. A **museum** located within the former Ottoman period bathhouse traces the history of the hot springs here.

■ *Route 90/Eliezer Kaplan, two kilometres south of city centre, T6725287. Sunday-Thursday 0800-1700, Friday 0800-1500. Adult 10 NIS, student 7 NIS. Bus 5a from the Central Bus Station is the most regular service, though 015, 017, 018, 019, 021, 023, 024, 026, 028, 030 and 032 all pass.*

Tomb of Rabbi Me'ir Ba'al Ha-nes Standing just above the Hammath-Tiberias National Park, accessible by the link road just to the north, is the **Tomb of Rabbi Me'ir Ba'al Ha-nes**. The Rabbi Me'ir ("he who brings light") Ba'al Ha-nes ("the miracle worker") was a second century CE Jewish sage who is attributed with producing the *Mishnah's* anonymous rulings: a commentary on the code of the oral law. A Jewish patriot, the Rabbi was forced to flee Israel following the Bar Kokhba Revolt of 132-35 CE when Roman prohibitions banned Torah study. His tutor and mentor, Rabbi Akiva, was executed by the Romans and is also buried in Tiberias (see page 666). Rabbi Me'ir Ba'al Ha-nes later returned to Tiberias to complete his work.

The tomb is marked by two domes; the blue-domed building (c.1898) belongs to the Ashkenazi community, whilst the white-domed building (c.1873) is the domain of Sephardic Jews. Both are said to be built over the burial cave where the Rabbi was apparently buried standing up, anticipating the arrival of the Messiah. Though one of Judaism's most important sites, the plaza in front of the tomb has been the victim of a particularly ugly restoration programme. There's a gift shop outside and a stall selling kosher snacks, whilst out back is a rather incongruous coke machine. Although there's not much to see, the tomb is fascinating on the anniversary of the Rabbi's death (14th Iyar), when thousands of pilgrims come to pray. Lag B'Omer (18th Iyar) is also an excellent time to visit. Visitors must be modestly dressed (cardboard yarmulkes and headscarfs for women are provided).

Essentials

Tiberias has a broad spread of hotels and hostels. However, at the upper end of the scale the majority of hotels hold themselves in too high esteem and some are grossly over-priced. A good lick of paint wouldn't do most of Tiberias' hotels any harm. Because prices rise dramatically at weekends, in the summer, and during Jewish holidays, it has been necessary to spread some individual hotels between two categories. Finding accommodation here during Pesach can be a nightmare; hotels double or treble their prices whilst hostels cram all their backpackers into spare rooms (including storerooms!) and then rent the dorms out to young Israelis for astronomical prices.

Sleeping

■ *on maps;*
price codes
see inside front cover

There is also plenty of 'rural accommodation' in the Sea of Galilee and Galilee area. For a good listing, pick up the *Israel Tourism Guide: Galilee* brochure at the tourist office.

L2 *Galei Kinnereth*, 1 Eliezer Kaplan, T6728888, F6790260. Tiberias' original hotel (older than the State of Israel itself) and now part of the *Howard Johnson* chain, though you cannot help feeling that despite the new annexe this place is showing its age and is somewhat trading on reputation. Some would argue that you can't put a price on class, but facilities just don't match the price (compare with what you get for this price in Eilat). **L2** *Radisson Moriah Plaza*, Tayyelet, T6792233, F6792320. Ugly building dominating town centre and rooms nothing special, but good facilities including pool, health club, choice of restaurants, lobby bar.

L3 *Caesar Resort*, Tayyelet/Midrahov, T6727272, F6791013. One of the best in town, some disabled rooms, non-smoking floors, some suites, facilities including outdoor pool, children's pool, heated indoor pool, health and fitness centre, restaurant, coffee bar, *Le Pirate* pub. One of the few upmarket hotels in Tiberias that reflect their price tag. **L3** *Carmel Jordan River*, HaBannim, T6714444, F6722111. Though doing nothing for Tiberias' skyline this modern hotel has a good range of facilities, including good views from small private balconies, indoor and outdoor pools, health and fitness centre, baby-sitting service, children's activities, restaurant, bar. **L3** *Club*, Ahad Ha'am, T6791887. Built as time-share apartments, has recently undergone a $7.5 million refit, large suites feature kitchenette, lounge, 2 TVs, great views, large pool and play area, tennis, beauty treatments, good value buffet breakfast and dinner, snack-bar, lots of children's entertainment, 'disco', good service, though can be noisy when full of kids. Recommended. **L3** *Four Points Paradise Tiberias*, 7 Hashomer, T6791281, F6791484. *Sheraton*-run hotel, quiet location above the town, quite large rooms, good facilities, nice pool and health spa set in large gardens, good service. **L3** *Gai Beach*, Gai Beach, Eliezer Kaplan, T6700700, F6792776. By Tiberias' standards this is pretty good value. Well-equipped rooms with balconies (upper floors more private) opening on to huge pool/park/beach leisure area, choice of restaurants, attractive lobby bar/café. Recommended. **L3** *Holiday Inn*, Eliezer Kaplan, T6728555, F6724443. The former *Ganné Hammat Hotel* tower-block is a candidate for the ugliest building in town, though the new wing is far more appealing (extra $25 per night), good facilities, pool, health and hot spa centre, choice of restaurants, recently spruced up gardens, private beach.

A *Ariston*, 19 Herzl, T6790244, F6722002. Sea-facing room would be a huge advantage, but the price is still a joke for what is little more than a motel. **A** *Golan*, 14 Ahad

Ha'am, T6791901, F6721905. No real balconies but large picture windows (great views), modern a/c rooms, restaurant, pool, nice terrace area, reasonable. **A** *Hartman*, 3 Ahad Ha'am, T6791555, F6791556. Great views (though not all rooms have balconies), a/c, TV, fridge, rooftop pool and sauna. **A** *Mercure Quiet Beach*, Gedud Barak, T6790125, F6790261. Two buildings divided by bridge over road (block on sea side is 15% cheaper because it has a 'star' less), looking rather old fashioned, views not great (and few rooms have balconies), private beach, evening entertainment. **A** *Ron Beach*, Gedud Barak, T6791350, F6791351. Nice waterfront location to the north of town, fairly spacious rooms with balconies (upper floor more private, with plans for a further floor?), a/c, cable TV, pool, sundeck, friendly staff. Not a bad choice at all. **A** *Royal Plaza*, Ganei Menora Blvd, off Eliezer Kaplan (to south of town), T6700000, F6700001. Formerly the *Days Inn*, deals mainly with tour groups, rooms are a reasonable size (plus some suites) but there isn't really the feeling of luxury (except perhaps in the bathrooms), 2 restaurants, *Red Lion* pub, spa. **A** *Tiberias*, 19 Ohel Ya'akov, T6792270, F6792211. Part of *Holiday Inn* chain (so hence free entry to hot springs), sunny lobby patio, though rather old fashioned and hard to justify these prices.

B *Church of Scotland Sea of Galilee Centre*, corner of HaYarden/Gedud Barak, T6723769, F6790145. This completely renovated 19th-century building makes a real change from the modern concrete disasters that blight Tiberias, all rooms a/c with attached bath, spotlessly clean, set in tranquil garden, private beach, meals available ($12), check-in after 1400, check-out 1000, advance reservations essential. Recommended. **B** *Eden*, 4 Ohel Ya'akov, T6790070, F6722461. Popular with groups though not a great location, reasonably sized rooms, a/c, TV, kosher restaurant. **B** *Hod*, Usishkin, T6792261, F6724484. Formerly the *Daphna*, recently modernized and refitted, large rooms with picture windows, some family rooms, lobby bar, restaurant, pool, health centre, not a bad deal. Recommended. **B** *Kolton-Inn*, 2 Ohel Ya'akov, T6791641, F6720633. Popular with groups, large a/c rooms, some with balconies, cable TV, fridge, sauna, jacuzzi, kosher restaurant, lobby bar, 'disco', not a great location. **B** *Park Inn*, Ganei Menora Blvd, off Eliezer Kaplan (to south of town), T6724424, F6724450. Unpretentious hotel, smallish rooms, a/c, cable TV, bar, restaurant. **B** *Restal*, Yehuda HaLevi, T6790555, F6720006. Ugly building with views of the bus station that only 'bus-spotters' would appreciate, rooms rather box-like and cramped, a/c, cable TV, fridge, pool, bar. **B** *Terminal Palace*, The Terminal, HaShiloah, T6717176, F6717175. New hotel built above a shopping centre, 27 a/c rooms, cable TV, phone, choice of restaurants. **B** *Washington*, Zeidel, T6791861, F6721860. Modern spacious rooms, light and airy, a/c, pool (summer only), restaurant.

C *Astoria*, Ohel Ya'akov, T6722351, F6725108. Long established family-run hotel, modest but spacious rooms, some with balconies, kosher restaurant, nice pool area. **C** *Continental*, Elhadeff, T6720018, F6791870. Old-fashioned place, exterior rather shabby, rooms simple but clean, home-cooking, but where do these prices come from? **C** *Ganei Menora*, Ganei Menora Blvd, off Eliezer Kaplan (to south of town), T6717330, F6717114. Formerly *Kinneret Gardens*, very much aimed at religious Jewish families, friendly welcome. **C** *Meytal*, corner of Bialik/Neiberg, T6724660. Rooms not particularly light and airy but reasonable value, a/c, cable TV. Not a bad deal. **C** *Nof HaGalil*, Rabin Sq, HaYarden, T6712880, F6712890. New, simple rooms, box-like but clean, phone, TV, small modern attached bath. **C** *Prima Tiberias*, Elhadeff, T6791166, F6722994. Formerly the *Galilee*, reasonably sized a/c rooms, TV, restaurant, not a great location. **C** *Tiberias Gardens*, Bruria, off Ohel Ya'akov, T6726736, F6790780. Quiet, very old fashioned, but at cheaper end of this price category.

D *Adina's*, 15 HaShiloah, T6722507. Sign says 'hostel' but this is more of a family 'guesthouse', good-value rooms (if you can negotiate a good price), kosher kitchen, nice terrace, some dorms (**F**). **D** *Aviv Hotel*, HaNoter, T6712272, F6712275. Owned by same people as the *Aviv Hostel*, recently built, a/c rooms with kitchenette and cable TV, some with Jacuzzi, rarely busy so haggle hard for a good deal. **D** *Bet Berzik*, corner of Elhadeff/Tabbur HaArez, T6720127. Sign just says 'motel', cheap simple a/c rooms, friendly. Pretty good value. **D** *Eshel*, corner of Tabbur HaArez/Kiach, T6790562. Quiet, family-run place aimed primarily at Jewish families, kosher kitchen. **D** *HaDekel*, HaGalil/1 HaNoter, T/F6725318. All rooms a/c, attached bath, TV. Basic but reasonable. **D** *Mezuman*, HaYarkon, T6723767. Small family pension, rather run down, balconies have great views of the street-scenes below, but what a smell from the fish market! **D** *Motel Toledo*, Bibas, T6721649. Rooms very basic and old fashioned, but hotel is clean and friendly, dining hall. **D** *Panorama*, HaGalil, T6720963, F6790146. Simple, pleasant family-style hotel, a/c rooms with balconies are the better option, roof-top terrace has attractive views. Tentatively recommended. **D** *Ron*, Ahad Ha'am, T6790760. Claims to be "the hotel which is your home", though my home doesn't smell of cabbage. Rooms a/c with cable TV but it's pretty run down and disorganized, real 70s décor.

E *Adler*, HaGalil, T6720031. Rather run-down and depressing place occupied mainly by 'oldies' who are here for the hot springs, not much English spoken. **E** *IYHA Meyouhas Youth Hostel and Guesthouse*, HaYarden, T6721775, F6720372. Huge, superbly maintained hostel, 30 a/c dorms (4-6 beds), plus 24 private rooms (2-4 beds, **C**), no curfew, check-in after 1400, check-out 1000, hot dinner $7, TV room, lockers, reservations recommended. **E** *Schwitzer*, 14 HaShiloah, T6721991. Currently closed.

F *Aviv Hostel*, HaGalil, T6720007. This place has gone downhill rapidly, with the owners keen to cram backpackers in and pack the foyer with prostitutes. A/c dorms of varying sizes, attached bath, those without balconies are rather dark. **F** *Casa Nova*, off Tayyelet, T6712281, F6712278. Simple pilgrim accommodation. **F** *Maman*, HaShiloah/Atzmon, T6792986. Popular backpacker place, spacious a/c dorms (4-8 beds), clean attached bath, kitchen, bar, Moroccan restaurant, small cold pool, no curfew, tours, bike rental. Recommended. **F** *Nahum*, Tavor, T6721545. Very clean and spacious dorms with a/c, fridge, kitchenette, attached bath (24 hrs hot water guaranteed), some good-value private rooms (**E**, prices negotiable), plus some cheaper and more basic dorms downstairs at the back (**G**). Kitchen, rooftop bar/TV lounge, tours, bike rental. Recommended. **F** *Petra*, Ahawa, T05-2669942. Formerly *Minilon*, rather disorganized with little English spoken, run-down dorms and cheap doubles. **F** *Rock/Sela*, HaGalil. Used mainly as an overspill from the *Nahum* (check there for details), a little run down, popular with long-stay Israelis.

Budget Those on a tight budget, and hence on a diet of falafel and shwarma, are **Eating** well served by the numerous stalls along HaGalil, along HaYarden towards the bus station, and at the junction of HaBannim and the Midrahov. There's a large **supermarket** on HaYarden, behind the Bank Leumi.

Café/bars *Apropo*, 'Galilee Experience' block, T6722681. Bright and breezy interior, or sit on the terrace, themed business lunches (35-45 NIS 1200-1600) such as 'light', 'New York', 'Paris', 'Thai', pasta 45 NIS, pizza 42 NIS, fish 60-75 NIS, breakfasts 30-45 NIS.

Chinese/Southeast Asian *Panda*, just off Midrahov, T6790221. Well reviewed, good-value business lunch. *The House*, T6720226, and *The Pagoda*, T6792564, are located on either side of Gedud Barak Street in the Lido Beach area. Run by the same people, both are consistently recommended amongst the best Chinese/SE Asian restaurants in Israel. *The Pagoda* is kosher and closes on Shabbat, though *The House* opens whilst the former is closed. The setting is particularly attractive, and the food is excellent, prepared by Bangkok-hotel trained staff. Expect to pay around 30-70 NIS for main course. Reservations recommended, credit cards. Recommended.

Fast food/chain *Burger Ranch*, Midrahov. *Don Potatoes*, HaGalil. Jacket spuds with choice of filling, 14 NIS. *McDonald's*, Tayyelet.

French *Au Bord du Lac*, *Galei Kinnereth Hotel*, 1 Eliezer Kaplan, T6728888. This long-standing hotel restaurant has a fine reputation for French cuisine, served in a picturesque setting. Main dishes 40-80 NIS. Evenings only, closed Friday, reservations recommended, credit cards.

Italian *Aldo's*, Midrahov. You could row across the Sea of Galilee on the pizzas served here, though it's fairly cheap (7-9 NIS per slice). *Mama Mia*, Midrahov. More 'American' than 'Italian', but not too expensive.

Jewish (traditional) *Guy Restaurant*, HaGalil, T6721973. One of the best value places in town serving simple home-cooked Sephardic ('Oriental Jewish') meals of generous proportions. Try the stuffed eggplant (23 NIS), spicy meat balls (10 NIS), 'cigars' (4 NIS), stuffed vine leaves (7 NIS) or grilled shishlik (38 NIS for 2 skewers). Closed Shabbat. Recommended.

Middle Eastern *Arabesque*, Tayyelet. New upmarket Middle Eastern restaurant, house menu 69/85/95 NIS, main dishes 40-70 NIS. *Marakesh Moroccan*, HaGalil, T6726825. Busy (usually a good recommendation), main dishes 30-55 NIS. *Shoshanat Ha'Amakim*, 56 HaGalil, T6790441. Authentic Moroccan cuisine, main dishes 40-45 NIS.

Miscellaneous *El Patio Andaluz*, next to *Panda*, just off Midrahov. Tapas, light meals, not bad value. *Marina Sunrise*, 'Galilee Experience' block. Pub/restaurant, grill 60 NIS, fish 45-50 NIS. *Little Tiberias*, HaQishon. Popular taverna in quiet setting.

Seafood One of the most popular dishes served in Tiberias is St Peter's Fish. If you're part of a pilgrim/tour group visiting the Sea of Galilee, it's inevitable that you will be brought to a restaurant on Tiberias' Tayyelet and made to try the dish. Tastes like bass, though it's of the perch family. Expect to pay around 45 NIS. *Galei Gil*, Tayyelet. St Peter's Fish 42 NIS, grilled meats 42 NIS. *Karamba's Fish*, Tayyelet, T6724505. Rather pushy staff, fixed St Peter's dish meal 55 NIS. This used to be one of the best vegetarian places in town (with great veggie pies), but now seems to be just another 'St Peter's Fish' place. *Lagona*, Midrahov. Standard grilled fish, 33-39 NIS fixed menu. *Nof Kinneret*, Tayyelet. Usual fish fayre.

South American *El Gaucho*, HaQishon. Part of Argentinian steakhouse chain, good value business lunch (250g steak 49 NIS).

Vegetarian *A Taste of Life*, HaQishon, T6712133. A "vegetarian's paradise", eat in or take-away, tofu main dishes 40 NIS, eggplant medley 40 NIS, steamed veggies 10 NIS. *Cherry*, Midrahov. Excellent Italian vegetarian dishes, salads 40 NIS, quiche 35 NIS, pasta 40 NIS, sauté veg 50 NIS, plus diet-busting cakes.

Bars & nightclubs **Bars** Tiberias' night-life revolves around three main bars. *Big Ben*, on the Midrahov, is a popular meeting place, with an English-style pub inside and floodlit waitress-service tables outside. Carlsberg 14 NIS for a half-litre. Of the three main bars this is the only one that stays open throughout the winter. *La Pirate Pub*, at the junction of the Midrahov

Galilee & The Golan

and Tayyelet (promenade), features a large expanse of outdoor tables and loud music, though the atmosphere is a little flat unless it's crowded. *Papaya*, on the Tayyelet, has been the main scene for the past couple of summers, with loud music, a small dance floor, hard-drinking backpackers (Carlsberg 15 NIS per half-litre), and the 'beautiful people' of the young Israeli crowd. None gets going much before 2230, and they don't close until 0200-0400. The bar on the roof of the *Nahum Hostel* (open 1800 until demand expires, Goldstar 7 NIS) is a good place for 'starters'. There are several other bars on the Tayyelet, plus quieter ones in the marina complex (see 'Galilee Experience' on map). *Parliament Pub*, HaGalil, has opened recently and can get quite lively.

Nightclubs Deck's, Lido Beach. *Monica Oriental Nightclub*, on square next to Great Mosque of Dahr el-Amr, T6712943. Wednesday-Saturday 2230 onwards. *Kibbutz Yardennit*, to the south of Tiberias, runs a disco most nights (about 30 NIS by taxi, or cheaper sherut, cheap drinks and entry). Some of the more expensive hotels have 'nightclubs'.

Art galleries *Caffein*, Donna Gracia, T6721087. Sunday-Thursday 1100-2200, Friday 1100-1500, Saturday 1900-2200. *Rivka's*, Citadel, Donna Gracia, T6721375. Sunday-Thursday 1000-1300 1700-1900, Friday-Saturday 1000-1300. **Folk-dancing** Carmel Jordan River Hotel, T6714444. Hosts 'Israeli Folklore Evenings' every Monday at 2100.   **Entertainment**

Books Steimatzky, 3 HaGalil, T6791288. **Camping** *Camping HaGalil*, HaGalil, T6723350. *Camping Sport*, 38 HaYarden, T6721406. **Jewellery** *Adipaz Golan Israel Diamond Experience*, next to *Holiday Inn Hotel*. Sunday-Thursday 0900-2100, Friday 0900-1400, diamond-polishing process explained, and then you can buy! *Caprice*, Tavor, T6792616. Centre includes a "history of diamonds" display, "Diamonds are Forever" multi-media presentation, tour of cutting and polishing plant, and then the opportunity to spend in the showroom. **Photography** *Photo Golan*, 1 Elhadeff, T6726785. **Souvenirs** *Sea of Galilee Treasures*, 'Galilee Experience' block, T6725610. For all your souvenir needs (including junk you never knew you needed).   **Shopping**

Boating/sailing *Holyland Sailing*, T6723006. Aimed at pilgrim groups who want to sail on boats called 'Matthew', 'Peter', etc. *Jordan Boat*, Marina Building, T6720671. *Kinnereth Sailing*, Tayyelet, T6658007/6721831. Offers short boat rides on the Sea of Galilee. *Lido Kinnereth Sailing Company*, T6721538. *Tiberias Rowing Club*, south end of Tayyelet, T6733348. Boat hire, waterskiing, banana boat. **Gliding** *Machanayim Airfield*, Rosh Pinna, T6939148. **Hiking** *SPNI*, 38 HaYarden, T6723972. Essential hiking information (office is at the *Camping Sport* shop). **Tennis** *Tennis Centre*, off Ohel Ya'akov, T6731564. **Waterskiing** *Water Ski Club*, Lido Beach, T6792353.   **Sports**

Local Bicycle hire: *Danny's bikes*, c/o Nahum Hostel, T051-543444. Most reliable place to hire bikes for tour around the Sea of Galilee, 40 NIS per day, bikes have racks, water-bottle holder, free call-out service. Recommended. *HaDekel*, HaGalil/HaNoter, T6725318. *Imperial*, 1 Ha'Amaqim, T6726775. Most of the hostels can arrange bicycle hire. **Car hire:** *Avis*, Central Bus Station, T6722766. *City Car*, Elhadeff, T6792766. Waives minimum age requirement. *Eldan*, Carmel Jordan River Hotel, T6720316/6720385. *Eurodollar*, T6790999. *Europcar*, T6724191. *Hertz*, Carmel Jordan River Hotel, T6723939. *Sixt*, Elhadeff.   **Ferry:** A thrice-daily ferry service runs during the summer between Tiberias and **Kibbutz Ein Gev** directly to the east across the Sea of Galilee (1130 1330 1600, 15 NIS one-way, 28 NIS return, bicycles carried free). **Taxis:** *Alon*, T6716969. *HaEmeq*, HaYarden, T6720131. *HaGalil*, HaYarden, T6720353. *Kinneret*, T6792505.   **Transport**

Galilee & The Golan

Air The nearest airport is the **Machanayim Airfield** at Rosh Pinna, 27km to the north (T6935302). *Arkia* offer flights here from Tel Aviv, Haifa and Jerusalem.

Buses The **Central Bus Station**, T6729222, occupies a city block on HaYarden. There's an electronic departure board and an unhelpful information office. **NB** During the life-span of this book, exact departure times are bound to change. However, the times given here will at least give an idea of frequency of services. Double-check exact times for yourself. **Afula**: see Bus 434 to Haifa, or Buses 830/840/841/442 to Tel Aviv. **Bet Shean**: served by Jerusalem-bound Buses 961/963/964 and Haifa-bound Bus 434 (40 mins, 20 NIS). **Capernaum**: Buses 459/541/841/963 to Kfar Nahum Junction ('Tabgha Junction') and walk (4km), 20 mins, 12 NIS. **Haifa**: via Bet Shean, Bus 434, Sunday-Thursday 4 per day, Friday last at 1205; via Nazareth, Bus 431, Sunday-Thursday every hr until 2000, Friday reduced service last at 1630, Saturday 1700 1830 2000 2100 (1 hr 15 mins, 24 NIS). **Hammat Gader**: Bus 024, daily 0900 1030 (30 mins, 12 NIS). **Jerusalem**: Buses 961/963/964, Sunday-Thursday at least 1 per hr last at 1700, Friday reduced service last at 1330, Saturday 1530 1930 (2½ hrs, 40 NIS). **Kiryat Shemona**: Buses 840/841/963/998, Sunday-Thursday at least 1 per hr until 2330, Friday last at 1730. **Nazareth**: Bus 431, Sunday-Thursday almost hourly 0530-2000, Friday reduced service last at 1630, Saturday 1700 1830 2000 2100 (45 mins, 18 NIS). **Safed**: Bus 459, Sunday-Thursday hourly until 1900, Friday last around 1500, Saturday first around 1700 (1 hr, 18 NIS). **Sea of Galilee** circuit: a number of irregular local buses make a circuit of the lake, generally clockwise via Ein Gev. These include 015/017/018/019/021/022. **Tabgha**: Buses 459/541/841/963 to Kfar Nahum Junction ('Tabgha Junction') and walk (2km), 20 mins, 12 NIS. **Tel Aviv**: via Afula, Hadera and coast road, Buses 830/840, Monday-Thursday every 30 mins, Friday every 30 mins until 1545, Saturday 1730-2030, (2-2½ hrs, 40 NIS); via Afula, Hadera and Petah Tiqva Bus 841; via Golani Junction and Afula Bus 442; via Bet Shean Bus 832.

Sherut/service taxi *Aviv*, Elhadeff, near Central Post Office, T6720098. Sheruts to **Tel Aviv**, Sunday-Friday, 35 NIS. **Blue Line Tours**, T6722234. 24-hr transfer service to **Ben-Gurion airport**. Other sheruts run to **Nazareth** from outside the Central Bus Station.

Directory **Banks** Bank HaPoalim, HaBannim, T6798411 and Bank Leumi, corner of HaYarden/HaBannim, T6727111 both offer foreign exchange, though check commission/exchange rates. Both have an ATM cashpoint offering cash advances on credit cards. Banking hours Sun, Tue, Thu 0830-1230 1600-1800, Mon, Wed 0830-1230, Fri 0830-1200. The **post office** (see below) offers commission-free foreign exchange. Speedy, commission-free foreign exchange of cash and travellers' cheques, at good rates, is available at: *ChangeNet*, junction of HaYarden/Ha'Atzma'ut; *Changepoint*, junction of HaYarden/HaGalil, T6716770; *MoneyNet*, Midrahov, T6724048. Sun-Thu 0800-1900, Fri 0800-1230. **Communications** Phone code: T06. **NB** Tiberias numbers are now 7-digit, beginning with a '6'. **Post offices**: Central Post Office, corner of HaYarden/Elhadeff, T6720019, (open Sun, Tue, Thu 0800-1230 1530-1800, Wed 0800-1330, Fri 0800-1230), offers poste restante, foreign exchange and international calls. **Telephones**: *Solan*, Midrahov, T6726470. Discount international phone calls and faxes, cellular phone rental, open daily 0800-2400. **Hospitals and medical services** Chemists: *Netanel*, Bibas/HaGalil, T6790613; *Pharma*, T6791170; *Rasco*, T6790871; *Schwartz*, HaGalil, T6720994; *Superpharm*, HaYarden. Hospitals: *Poriya Hospital*, (just off map) T6738211/6738311; *Tiberias Medical Centre (Lev HaGalil Centre)*, T6723077. **Laundries** *Akoveset*, HaMisgad Sq, T6790038; *American Express*, Rasco, T6722186; *Panorama*, HaGalil, T6724324. **Places of worship** Synagogues: *Great Synagogue Ohel Nachum*, Herzl (Ashkenazi); *Great Synagogue Ohel Ya'akov*, Ohel Ya'akov (Ashkenazi); *Gur Arye*, HaMaginim (Sephardi). Churches: *St Peter's*, Seashore, T6720516 (Catholic, services: Sat 1800 winter 1900 summer, Sun 0830, Mon-Thu 0700); *St Andrew's*, Tayyelet, T6721001 (Protestant Church of Scotland, services: Sun 0730 1800, Mon-Sat 0745 in guesthouse); *YMCA*, Route 90, 3km north of Tiberias, T6720685 (interdenominational). **Tour companies and travel agents** *Alon Tours*, 1 HaBannim, T6722982; *Egged Tlalim*, Central Bus Station, T6712160,

F6712258. Runs a 1-day tour to Upper Galilee and Golan Heights (including Capernaum, Tabgha, Qasrin, Kuneitra viewpoint, Banias, "good fence" at Metulla) $38, every Tue and Sat (plus Thu in Apr-Oct). If you can only spare 1 day, then this is reasonable value, though you should note that some of these places are just 'photo-stops' and don't allow enough time for proper exploration. Two or more people can do this tour themselves (and cheaper) by hiring a car. *Egged* also run a tour around the Sea of Galilee, stopping at all the main sites incl Hammat Gader ($36, every Mon, plus Wed in Apr-Nov). Most of the hostels can book these tours for you (sometimes at a discount). *issta*, HaGalil. Tours to Upper Galilee and Golan ($38) and round the Sea of Galilee ($36). *SPNI*, 38 HaYarden, T6720474. Every Tue leads a 3-day hiking tour of Galilee and Golan for 'moderately good hikers', advance booking essential. **Tourist offices** Tourist Information Office, 'Archaeological Garden', HaBannim, T6725666. Open Sun-Thu 0800-1200 1300-1700, Fri 0800-1200, Sat closed. Good for brochures and possibly discount vouchers for hot springs, though little else. A local archaeologist, Edna Amos, conducts a free walking tour of 'Old Tiberias' every Sat at 1000 from the *Radisson Moriah Plaza Hotel* (English/Hebrew). Aviva Minoff (licensed tour guide) runs a walking tour of Safed (leaving from Tiberias, T6920901). **Useful addresses and phone numbers** Police: T100 (T6792444). Ambulance: Magen David Adom T101 (T6790111). Fire: T102 (T6791222). **Working** Though most skint backpackers find themselves working in Tel Aviv, Eilat or Jerusalem, an increasing number are seeking work in Tiberias. Most work is seasonal, dependent upon the summer holiday season. Girls (particularly attractive ones!) have the advantage when it comes to bar and restaurant work. But beware: the main pubs/nightclubs pay no salary, and your reward is entirely dependent on tips! It's still possible to make at least 100 NIS a day, rising in the high season. Other options include hostel work, particularly 'running' (meeting people at the bus station and convincing them to go to the hostel that's paying you).

Excursions from Tiberias

Horns of Hittim/Qarne Hittim

From a distance, particularly through the window of a bus speeding along Route 77 between Tiberias and Nazareth, it does not really look much; just a line of low, grassy hills with the peaks at either end vaguely resembling a pair of horns. Yet this is the scene of the most decisive battle of the Crusades, with the crushing defeat of the Crusader army at the hands of the Muslims bringing an end to the Latin Kingdom in the Holy Land.

The Horns of Hittim are located just to the north of the Tiberias to Nazareth road (Route **Ins and outs** 77), approximately 8km west of Tiberias. You could take any bus that passes along this road and ask to be let off about 2km east of the turn-off to Kibbutz Lavi. Alternatively, to get closer to the battle site and the Grave of Nabi Shu'eib, take Bus 042 from Tiberias (0645 1000 1415) along Route 7717 towards Moshav Kfar Zeitim, and follow the orange signs. (See 'Tiberias & the Sea of Galilee' map on page 658).

Having encircled the Crusader garrison at Tiberias, **Salah al-Din** encamped **History** most of his 12,000-strong army of mounted bowmen at Ein Sabt (close to the modern-day moshav of Sde Ilan). This provocative gesture was designed to lure the Crusader army into battle, but on the Muslim commander's terms. All Salah al-Din needed now was for the Christians to accept the bait.

Meeting at Ein Zippori close to Sepphoris, **Raymond of Tripoli**, lord of Tiberias, urged restraint, whilst the Grand Master of the Templars, **Gerard of Ridfort**, egged on by the reckless **Reynald of Châtillon**, had the scent of battle in his nostrils. The king, **Guy de Lusignan**, by all accounts a weak-willed man, ruled against the procrastinators and ordered the troops to ready themselves to march the next morning. It was to be a fateful decision, though, in fairness to the king, the threat of withdrawal of the Templars' support left him with little option. At 4 a.m. the following morning 1,200 mounted knights, protected by

Galilee & The Golan

16,000 infantry, set out for Tiberias, 22km to the east.

Almost as soon as they began their march the Crusader army came under attack. The Muslim troops took care not to become embroiled in a full-scale confrontation, preferring to severely harass the Crusader rearguard with lightning strikes on their swift, manoeuvrable ponies. By midday the Crusader army, dressed in full armour and toiling under the heat of a scorching July sun, had covered little over half the distance to Tiberias. Having passed no water sources on their march, the desperate Crusader army diverted north to the spring at **Hittim** but found their path blocked by one of Salah al-Din's regiments. By mid-afternoon the commander of the rearguard, **Balian of Ibelin**, having borne the brunt of Salah al-Din's deadly sorties, told the king that they could proceed no further. The Crusader army, still water-less, set their camp for the night and prepared for one last defiant stand.

Contrary to Crusader expectations, Salah al-Din failed to attack at dawn. Instead, he waited until the July sun was high in the sky, then set fire to the scrub around the besieged army. Then he attacked. The first assault was beaten off, but sustained charges against the bewildered and disorientated knights, without water for over 24 hours and still in full armour, soon turned the tide in Salah al-Din's favour. A final desperate attempt by Raymond of Tripoli's mounted knights to break out to the spring was foiled by the tactics of Salah al-Din's horsemen, who wheeled their ponies out of the way of the Crusader charge, side-stepping all contact. Faced by the inevitability of defeat, the remaining knights made a last stand around the red tent of the king. They were swiftly overrun, and the 'True Cross' was captured from the hands of the dead Bishop of Acre. As Smith describes it, "A militant and truculent Christianity, as false as the relics of the 'True Cross' round which it rallied, met its judicial end within view of the scenes where Christ proclaimed the Gospel of Peace, and went about doing good" (*Historical Geography of the Holy Land*, 1894). The chivalrous Salah al-Din spared the king, though many of the knights (most notably Reynald of Châtillon) were executed for past misdeeds.

Sights   The area takes the name **Horns of Hittim** (*Arabic*: Qarne Hittim, sometimes Hattim) from the form of the hills created by the collapse of an extinct volcanic crater. Though there are remains here of a Late Bronze Age fortress (c. 1550-1200 BCE) and an Iron Age II city (c.1000 to its destruction at the hands of Tiglath-pileser in 733-732 BCE), the area is best known as the scene of Salah al-Din's victory over the Crusader army on 4th July, 1187 (see page 677). Though there are no physical reminders of the battle, the views of the Galilee from the top of the hill can be inspiring, particularly if you are holding in your hand a copy of Beha ed-Din's *Life of Saladin*, open at the page that describes the battle.

The Horns of Hittim is also the site of the most sacred **Druze** shrine in the country: the **Grave of Nabi Shu'eib**. The Druze sect identify Nabi Shu'eib with Jethro, father-in-law of Moses, and each year on his *Urs* (death anniversary, 25th April) they hold an elaborate feast here. The small shrine is marked by the green, yellow, white, blue and red Druze flag.

Arbel

The ancient Jewish settlement of Arbel (biblical 'Beth-Arbel', *Hosea 10:14*) stands at the top of a cliff about six kilometres northwest of Tiberias, looking down on the Ginnosar plain below, with the Sea of Galilee to the east. The caves that riddle the cliff below the village have been the site of two significant battles in Jewish history, the latter being colourfully recorded by the Jewish historian Josephus.

For those with their own transport, it is possible to explore Arbel and the Horns of Hittim (see page 677) in the same day, though this would be more difficult if dependent on public transport. To reach the synagogue and cliff above the fortress, head west out of Tiberias on Route 77, turning right (northwest) on to Route 7717 shortly after clearing the city limits. Pass the turning for Kfar Hittim, taking the next right (north) turn for Moshav Arbel (if you carried on you would arrive at the Grave of Nebi Shu'eib). Continue through the moshav grounds and follow the signs for the synagogue and old town. A little way further on, from near to the highest point at the top of the cliff, red-and-white trail markers indicate the descent. To reach the foot of the cliff (and the end of the hiking trail) by car, drive north from Tiberias on Route 90, turning left (west) after 5.6km at Migdal Junction onto Route 807. Take the first left after about 1km (marked Hamam), and the foot of the cliff trail is a further 1km or so on your left. To reach Arbel by public transport take Bus 042 from Tiberias (0645 1000 1415) to Moshav Arbel. To return to Tiberias from the foot of the cliff trail you will have to walk to Migdal Junction (2km) and stop a bus there.

Ins and outs

The settlement was probably founded by the **Hasmoneans** (Maccabees) in the second century CE, with its 10-hectare size suggesting a population later rising to around 2,500. The caves in the cliff-face below the village were fortified by the Hasmoneans, though the Syrian commander Bacchides captured them during his campaign of 161 CE (*I Maccabees 9:2*). When **Herod the Great** first attempted to exercise his newly acquired power during the early years of his reign (c. 38 BCE), the Hasmoneans once again returned to their fortified caves. Josephus vividly describes Herod flushing them out: "These caves opened out on to almost vertical slopes and could not be reached from any direction except by winding, steep and very narrow paths; the cliff in front stretched right down into ravines of immense depth dropping straight into a torrent bed. So for a long time the king was defeated by the appalling difficulty of the ground, finally resorting to a plan fraught with the utmost danger. He lowered the toughest of his soldiers in cradles till they reached the mouths of the caves; then they slaughtered the bandits with their families and threw firebrands at those who proved awkward ... Not a man voluntarily surrendered, and of those who were brought out forcibly many preferred death to captivity" (*Jewish War I, 303-313*, though Josephus' description in *Antiquities 14: 423-6* is even more gruesome). The settlement overcame this set-back and later flourished as a centre of Jewish learning. A *Beth Midrash*, or 'house of study', was built in Arbel, whilst the Rabbi Nittai, a member of the Sanhedrin, resided here.

History

The remains of the fourth-century limestone-built **synagogue** stand out in sharp relief against the dark basalt walls of the other village buildings. A hoard of 140 coins, some dating back to the second century CE, was found on the floor of the synagogue, though scholars are now largely agreed on the later date as the period of construction. Design changes were made in subsequent years. The significant features of this synagogue include its easterly as opposed to a southerly entrance (a rare feature in synagogues in the Galilees), plus its unique main entrance, with threshold, door jambs and lintel carved from a single stone. The village and synagogue were probably destroyed in the earthquake of 749 CE.

Sights

From the top of the cliff a red-and-white marked **hiking trail** descends past the **caves** and the **Arbel Fortress** to the Nahal Arbel (Wadi Hamam) below. The views are excellent. The caves, containing carved cisterns and *mikvehs* (ritual baths), have been incorporated into a fortress built by the Bedouin sheikh Fakhr al-Din in the late 16th-early 17th century CE. **NB** The path is very

Galilee & The Golan

steep and can be rather tricky in places. Once you reach the bottom it's a real bitch to climb back up to the top, so if you have your own transport it's advisable to get someone to drive to the base of the cliff to pick you up. Those on 'shank's pony' will have to continue on foot to Migdal Junction.

Hammat Gader

Phone code: 06
Colour map 1, grid B5

A visit to Hammat Gader is one of the most enjoyable ways of spending a day/half-day in Galilee; it just about has a bit of everything. In addition to the hot springs and sulphur pool which first attracted the Romans, this large park also features a fascinating alligator farm and mini zoo, as well as the remains of the best-preserved Roman baths in the country. There are children's pools, a playground, trampolines and some water-slides, plus picnic facilities.

Ins and outs   Hammat Gader is about 17km southeast of Tiberias as the crow flies. Head south on Route 90 around the shore of the lake, and when Route 90 bears south (right) at Zemiah Junction, continue round the lake on Route 92. Take the first right on to Route 98 and follow the winding road above the Yarmuk River (and international border) to the park. Bus 024 runs to Hammat Gader from Tiberias only twice per day (0900 1030) and not at all on Saturday (30 mins, 12 NIS). **NB** Though Bus 024 is scheduled to return from Hammat Gader at 1300 and 1500, it often leaves early if the driver feels like it. Arrive at least 15 mins early. If you do get stuck, it's often possible to hitch a lift with an Israeli family. Hammat Gader gets impossibly crowded during Jewish holidays.

History

The history of Hammat Gader is really the history of the baths here. They were built to serve the Roman town of **Gadara** (one of the cities of the Decapolis),

Hammat Gader

1 Entrance / Ticket Office
2 Souvenir Shop
3 Alligator / Crocodile / Caiman Cages
4 Alligator Pool
5 Raised Walkway
6 Aviary
7 'Alligator Show'
8 Roman Theatre
9 Restaurant
10 Waterslides
11 Trampolines
12 'Photo Crocodile'
13 Playground
14 Children's Pools
15 Mosque
16 Showers, Changing Rooms & Lockers
17 Siam Thai Restaurant
18 Private Pool
19 Pool
20 Covered Pool
21 First Aid & Kiosk
22 Cold Water Pool
23 Snack Bar
24 Synagogue
25 Observation Point

Galilee & The Golan

just across the Yarmuk River. The baths and the city are now divided by the international border between Israel and Jordan, so the remains of Gadara (Umm Qais) can only be visited from the Jordanian side (for full details see the *Jordan, Syria and Lebanon Handbook*). The ancient geographer Strabo mentions the hot springs close to Gadara at the end of the first century BCE, though he doesn't refer to Hammat Gader by name. The historian Origen, writing in the mid-third century CE, also mentions the baths here, suggesting that visitors came from as far away as Athens to be treated. The fact that an Eudocia inscription found in the baths mentions the emperor Antoninus Pius (138-161 CE) suggests that the original baths may well have been constructed in the late second/early third century CE. Eusebius also refers to the baths in his early fourth-century *Onomasticon*.

By the end of the fourth century CE the baths were being described by the Greek writer Eunapius as being second only in beauty to those at the imperial resort at Baia, on the Bay of Naples, though his contemporary Epiphanius is more critical in his assessment, with acerbic references to the fact that men and women bathed together. There are also several mentions of the baths in Talmudic literature, and it seems that many of the learned rabbis of Tiberias (including Rabbi Me'ir Ba'al ha-Nes, Judah I ha-Nasi and Judah ha-Nasi II) visited the baths, though the inference is that they were not here for recreational purposes, but rather to discuss the Sabbath boundary between the baths and Gadara town!

The baths were at the height of their fame during the fifth-seventh centuries CE, as attested to by a number of inscriptions in the Hall of Fountains, though the period of uncertainty that accompanied the collapse of the Byzantine empire may have seen considerable damage inflicted on the building. The Umayyad Caliph Mu'awiya (661-680 CE) instituted a refurbishment of the complex, with an inscription in the Hall of Fountains announcing the baths' reopening in 662 CE. Less than a century later, however, they had entered a terminal decline, possibly another victim of the great earthquake of 749 CE. Though their existence has always been known, and it seems certain that sick people continued to bathe in the ruins here throughout the centuries, it was not until 1979 that the Roman baths were systematically excavated.

Sights

Roman baths, Hammat Gader

N

| 0 metres | 10 |

1 Modern entrance
2 Entrance corridor
3 Hall of Pillars
4 Hall of Inscriptions
5 Passage corridor
6 Leper's Pool
7 Oval Hall
8 Stone Drainage Pipe
9 Service Hall
10 Hot Spring
11 Spring Pool
12 Hall of Fountains

Roman baths

The bathhouse complex at Hammat Gader is particularly large, covering an area in excess of 5,000 square metres. It was built using coarsely dressed basalt stones, with the exception of the Hall of Fountains where finer limestone blocks were used. The long, high retaining wall to the southwest featured a line of windows that supplied both light and ventilation. Water was channelled to the bathing pools via conduits and an intricate system of lead pipe plumbing, examples of which can be clearly seen. Seven main bathing halls have been identified, with the temperature of the water generally regulated by the distance from the hot spring source.

Galilee & The Golan

Lead and clay pipes carrying cooler water were also used to moderate temperatures. It is suggested that visitors to the baths would enter through the **Entrance Corridor** (2) to the northwest, then move from one bathing hall to the next, eventually reaching the hotter water closest to the spring.

The Entrance Corridor leads to a large hall known as the **Hall of Pillars** (3). A 1.5-metre-deep stepped pool in the centre of the hall remained in use until the mid-fifth century CE, when it was filled in and covered with a marble floor. The hall was subsequently used as some form of a 'games room'. The hall takes its name from the two rows of pillars along its east and west sides that helped to support the vaulted ceiling some 18 metres above. Three smaller pools are located between the pillars on the west side.

Adjacent to the Hall of Pillars is the **Hall of Inscriptions** (4), taking its name from the 40 or so dedicatory inscriptions found in the floor. Most are in Greek and are probably the legacy of wealthy patrons who wished their visit to be commemorated. All date to the latter period of the baths' usage (late fifth century CE), when the main pool in this hall had been filled in and paved with marble.

Between the Hall of Inscriptions, Hall of Pillars and the Oval Hall is a narrow space divided into two chambers. The northern chamber of this **Passage Corridor** (5) served as a connecting passageway, whilst the antechamber to the south housed a small pool 1.25 metres deep. The fact that this pool was seemingly sealed off from the rest of the complex, and that the remains of numerous clay oil lamps dating to the fourth and fifth centuries CE were found here, has led some commentators to suggest that this is the **'leper's pool'** (6) as described by Antoninus of Placentia. It appears that lepers were encouraged to fall asleep in the pool, whilst the one that saw a vision would be cured. There are a few discrepancies in his description of the position of the leper's pool, however, since this chamber is not located directly in front of the hot spring as described.

The **Oval Hall** (7) features a large, stepped bathing pool (20.3 metres by 8.1 metres by 1.15 metres deep) in an excellent state of preservation. Being so close to the hot spring source the water in this pool would have been particularly warm. The water was moderated by a flow of cool water via lead pipes from the four small baths in the semi-circular alcoves in each of the hall's corners. Large decorative windows provided the light. The **Service Area** (9) to the west and south of the Oval Hall and Hall of Pillars contained the drainage channels and pools that took away the waste water. A nine-metre-long stone drainage pipe, with an external diameter of 80 centimetres (internal 40 centimetres), was found *in situ*.

The **Hot Spring** (10) fed water to all parts of the complex, with water from this source being in the region of 50°C. The **Spring Pool** (11) close by was probably the ultimate destination of visitors to the baths. The pool was originally rectangular but was altered to its present shape in the late fifth century. A dedicatory Greek inscription at its centre mentions a "Petrus son of Romanus". The five marble fountains around the pool fed in cooler water. Because of its position close to the spring, some argue that this may have been the leper's pool described by Antoninus. However, substantial changes have been made over the years around the spring, possibly to rectify earthquake damage, and hence the discrepancies in Antoninus' description.

The large pool in the **Hall of Fountains** (12) served as the *frigidarium*, or cold room, with a large cold-water pool (1.3 metres deep) at its centre. The pool was fed by a network of lead pipes, with the water emerging from 32 carved marble fountains. The figures that decorated these fountains were seemingly defaced during the Muslim period. This hall was almost certainly open to the sky, in keeping with other such baths of the period. To the east and south of the Hall of Fountains, only partially excavated, are several other small bathing chambers, and possibly a number of dressing rooms.

Bathing in the pools of the Roman bathhouse is now forbidden for fear of damaging them, though potential bathers are more than compensated for by the modern facilities. There is a large, warm bathing pool, particularly welcome when air temperatures drop significantly in winter, plus hot and cold pools. Take advice from staff on the maximum length of time that you should remain in the water. There is also a 'massage waterfall', a covered pool, plus various health and beauty treatments available. The springs/pools are particularly popular with elderly eastern Europeans, and any budding Henri Cartier-Bressons/Martin Parrs are advised to bring plenty of film.

Hot springs/sulphur pool

The original residents of this farm were imported from Florida some years ago as a tourist attraction, but such has been the success of the breeding programme that alligators are now being exported. When it's warm, and the beasts come out to sun themselves, it's a fantastic (though slightly terrifying) sight. A wooden walkway runs through the main enclosure, though the fact that it's only three metres or so above the pool, and the railings are not particularly high, makes it a rather unnerving experience. (**NB** Children need to be closely supervised.) A number of crocodiles and caimans are to be found in the caged areas, and several times a day there is a show featuring an alligator and a parrot (1100 1300 1500)! The mini zoo nearby features ostrich, ibex and turkeys, amongst other creatures.

Alligator farm

On the tel, or mound, above Hammat Gader lie the remains of an early fifth-century **synagogue**, standing on the site of two earlier buildings. There is not a great deal to be seen, with the impressive mosaic floors having been removed to the museum at nearby Degania (see page 703). Also within the park area stand the insubstantial remains of Hammat Gader's 2,000-seater **Roman theatre**. ■ *T6659911. Monday-Thursday 0700-2130, Friday 0700-2400, Saturday-Sunday 0700-2300. Adult 51 NIS, evening entry 40 NIS, children under one metre free. Snackbars, toilets, 'Siam' Thai restaurant (main dishes 40-70 NIS, fixed menu 70 NIS).*

Other features

Sea of Galilee (Lake Kinneret)

Tour around the Sea of Galilee

The description below describes a **clockwise** circumnavigation of the lake beginning at Tiberias (since this seems to be the most popular route). See map on page 658 for orientation. It should be noted that it is impossible to see and appreciate all the sites described below in one day, even if you have your own transport and make an early start. One option, particularly for those cycling, is to spend more than one day exploring the region. A ferry runs thrice daily in summer between Tiberias and Kibbutz Ein Gev on the east shore, meaning that the lake can be divided into two sections. For those who only have one day to spare, it is a matter of deciding what it is you want to see. The key sites, and also the most crowded, are the ones with the major Christian interest, on the northwest shores: Tabgha, Mt of Beatitudes and Capernaum. That said, the east side of the lake is blissfully traffic-free, and a fine place for cycling.

Phone code: 06
Colour map 1, grid B 4-5

Ins and outs The easiest way to tour the lake is by car. The most enjoyable way, despite the high levels of traffic in places, is by **bicycle**. For details of bike hire see the 'Tiberias' section on page 675. Cyclists should note that one lap is nearer to 65km, and not 55km as you may be told (8-9 hrs). It's generally pretty flat, though there are a few killer hills around Tabgha. Traffic (especially tourist coaches) can be heavy in the region around Tabgha to Capernaum, and again in the 'home-stretch' from Zemiah Junction to Tiberias. Don't forget that once you get half-way round the lake, you can get a ferry back to Tiberias from Kibbutz Ein Gev. Take protection against the sun and plenty of drinking water. You should not drink the water in the lake. **NB** Although shorts may seem like a good idea for cycling, they are not suitable for visiting any holy sites, where modest dress is required. Irregular **bus** services (015/017/018/019/021/022) also run around the lake, though you should be prepared for some long waits. Almost all of the settlements around the Sea of Galilee offer some form of 'country accommodation' (pick up brochures in the tourist office in Tiberias).

Routes Head north from Tiberias on Route 90, passing Dekel Beach (1.6km), Panorama Beach (1.7km) and the YMCA (2.9km). At 5.6km you arrive at **Migdal Junction**. The left turn (Route 807) leads northwest, with the left fork after 1km leading to the base of the cliff below Arbel (see 'Excursions from Tiberias', page 677). Also just off Route 807 is the moshav of Migdal and Migdal Holiday Village. The right turn at Migdal Junction leads to Hawaii Beach and Migdala Beach (20 NIS). Also on the sea-shore is the site of ancient **Migdal**.

Migdal

The ancient settlement of Migdal (as opposed to the modern moshav of the same name to the west of Route 90) is located down on the lakeside. Sometimes referred to as either **Magdala**, or by its Greek name of **Tarichaeae**, this is the reputed birthplace of **Mary Magdalene**; one of the New Testament's most famous repentant sinners, who washed Jesus' feet with her tears and wiped them with her hair (*Luke 7:37-50*). A small fenced-off area belonging to the Franciscans is associated with the tradition, though it's not generally open.

Josephus describes Tarichaeae during the Roman period as being a city of some 40,000 people, and describes in some detail the battle between the Jewish zealots who had fled Tiberias during the Second Jewish Revolt (66-73 CE), and Vespasian's Roman army. The zealots on the land were swiftly defeated, whilst others put out in their boats on to the lake. The Roman army built rafts and followed, routing the Jewish navy: "A fearful sight met the eyes – the entire lake stained with blood and crammed with corpses; for there was not a single survivor. During the days that followed a horrible stench hung over the region. The beaches were thick with wrecks and swollen bodies which, hot and steaming in the sun, made the air so foul that the calamity not only horrified the Jews but revolted even those who had brought it about … The dead, including those who had earlier perished in the town, totalled 6,700" (*Jewish War, III, 532*). Parts of the key and harbour ('Migdal Nunya') were excavated in the 1970s, though there's little to see today.

Route Continuing north on Route 90 from Migdal Junction, the road passes several turnings right for various beaches (Nirvana Holiday Village, Ilanot, Tamar) before arriving at **Ginnosar** (2.2km).

Kibbutz Ginnosar

Founded originally as an agricultural community, Kibbutz Ginnosar (Ginosar) now makes a sizeable amount of its income from tourism. As well as a beach and luxury accommodation, there is an interesting museum/education centre featuring a fishing boat that is around 2,000 years old.

Phone code: 06
Colour map 1, grid B4

This museum details the history of 'Man in the Galilee', and has a number of notable exhibits. Of great interest is the interactive audio-visual programme that allows you to determine historical events from a certain period, with the computer displaying the consequences of your actions. Writing your own version of history? Just the country to play this game. ■ *T6721495. Sunday-Thursday 0900-1700, Friday 0900-1300, Saturday closed. Adult 15 NIS.*

Beit Yigal Allon Museum

During the major drought that the region suffered in 1986, the level of the Sea of Galilee dropped considerably, revealing the frame of an old fishing boat lying on its port side in the mud just to the south of Kibbutz Ginnosar's beach. Using innovative techniques a rescue excavation was undertaken and the boat placed in a special tank built at the Beit Yigal Allon Museum. After a number of treatments the boat is now drying out.

Ancient boat

Carbon-14 dating, as well as analysis of the construction technique and style, has suggested that the boat was built some time between 100 BCE and 70 CE. Because of this date all sorts of insinuations are made about its ownership and former life. Subtle hints are banded about, pointing out that Jesus and his disciples (some of whom were fishermen) were active in this area during this time span, but there is absolutely no proof to suggest any such link. Other insinuations, perhaps seen to be more credible, suggest that the boat may have been involved in the great naval battle of 67 CE between the Jews and the Romans that Josephus describes in such gory detail (see 'Migdal' on page 684). Unfortunately, the truth is more mundane. Two of the boat's excavators, Wachsmann and Raveh, write that after a long work life and numerous repairs, "its usable timber –– including the mast step, stempost, and the sternpost – were removed; the remaining hull, old and now useless, was then pushed out into the lake, where it sank into the silt" (*New Encyclopedia of Archaeological Excavations in the Holy Land*, 1993). Appreciate it for what it is: a well-preserved 2,000-year-old boat. ■ *T6721495. Sunday-Thursday 0800-1700, Friday 0800-1600, Saturday 0900-1600. Adult 10 NIS.*

The beach here is about as good as you get on the Sea of Galilee, with nice pool and seating area. Sailing, wind-surfing and kayaking is available, as well as fishing trips. Admission is 25 NIS adult, 20 NIS child (more at weekends), open 0800-1800. At the entrance to the kibbutz is a camel farm that arranges rides (you're even encouraged to don "biblical garments" before mounting the camels!). ■ *T6723007, F6790262, winter 0900-1700, summer 0900-2030, adult 20 NIS, child 15 NIS.*

Nof Ginnosar (beach)

B *Nof Ginosar Hotel*, Kibbutz Ginnosar, T6792161, F6792170. All rooms a/c, comfortable though not that large, kosher restaurant, bar/cafeteria, function halls, pool, private beach, tennis, breakfast included.

Sleeping & eating

Continuing north on Route 90 from Kibbutz Ginnosar, after 3km a road to the left (Route 8077) heads up Ammud Creek towards Kibbutz Huqoq (Bus 052 from Tiberias).

Route

Galilee & The Golan

There is a nice hiking excursion off this road, following black-and-white trail markers along the seasonal Ammud Creek all the way to Mt Meron, 15km to the north (see page 723). The first 5km of this hike (until you hit Route 85) are particularly attractive. This hike actually forms part of the 3-day 'Yam L'Yam' (Mediterranean Sea to Sea of Galilee) hike.

A further 500m along Route 90 is **Sapir**. On the low natural hill adjacent to Sapir, and sloping down to the shore of the lake, is **Tel Kinneret**. To the right of Route 90, a track leads down to Karei Deshe Beach (cars 50 NIS, pedestrians 15 NIS) and **Horvat Minnim**. The (**E**) *Karei Deshe Youth Hostel*, Karei Deshe Beach, T6720601, F6724818, is an excellent place to stay, with a/c dorms, some family rooms, a kosher dining hall, TV room, nice views and a private beach.

Sapir From the road 'Sapir Site' looks rather like an electricity generating plant, though it is actually the starting point of Israel's **National Water Carrier**. Israel has a major regional imbalance in water availability: most of the water is in the north, whilst the population centre is in the centre, and the only land not yet fully exploited is in the semi-arid south. The National Water Carrier is the main artery in Israel's freshwater supply network. Its importance was perhaps best underlined in the major drought of 1991, when it was said to be providing close to 100 percent of Israel's drinking water. It was built to counter Israel's regional imbalance in water by supplying freshwater through a network of pipes, aquaducts, open canals, reservoirs and tunnels (some up to 6.5 kilometres long) from the north to the semi-arid south. In fact, pumping water consumes an estimated 12 percent of Israel's electricity consumption. Running for 130 kilometres, the National Water Carrier took 11 years to build and was completed in 1964.

The visit to 'Sapir Site' includes an introductory video and explanation of Israel's water management, followed by a tour of the pumping station. It's really for enthusiasts only. **NB** Non-Israelis must arrange their visit with Mekorot's Public Relations Department, 9 Lincoln, Tel Aviv, T03-6208705, F6208833, giving full details of all members of the group, including passport numbers. These will be checked when you arrive. If you're Syrian, Iranian, etcetera, you will probably have to give it a miss. Israelis can phone 'Sapir Site' directly to arrange a visit, T6721399, but must bring their ID cards.

Tel Kinneret The first thing to say about Tel Kinneret (Tel Chinnereth) is that there is not much to see; in fact you may have difficulty finding it at all. It comprises a small tel on top of the low hill adjacent to Sapir Site, with the remains of the lower city extending down the slope towards the lake. The paltry remains from the Early Bronze Age (c. 3300-2700 BCE) and the Middle Bronze Age II-Iron Age II (c. 2000-586 BCE) belie the site's former importance as the city that gave its name to the lake (Lake Kinneret, *Numbers 34:11; Deuteronomy 3:17; Joshua 13:27*). Unfortunately, it's hardly worth getting off your bike for.

Horvat Minnim Another site that won't divert you from your tour of the lake for long is Horvat Minnim, just off the track that leads to Karei Deshe Beach. For a long time this site was identified as Capernaum, until that town's true location further northeast was finally established. The rather overgrown remains here are in fact a palace and mosque dating to the Umayyad period of Arab rule, possibly initially built during the time of Caliph el-Walid I (705-715 CE). It probably belonged to a wealthy princely landowner, though it may later have been used as a caravanserai in the Mamluk period (c. 13th-15th centuries CE). The plan of the structure is almost square (73 metres by 67 metres), with round towers at each corner and semi-circular towers in the middle of the north, west and south walls. The main section that you can make out today, via the rather dodgy-looking wooden walkway, is the monumental domed gateway that stood in the centre of the east wall.

Returning to Route 90, after 1.6km the road leads to **Kfar Nahum Junction** (Tabgha   **Route** Junction'). There are several options here. The tour around the lake continues on the road to the right, now Route 87. The road to the left, Route 90, heads directly north as far as Metulla in Upper Galilee (near the Lebanese border). The majority of visitors who are touring the lake take a short excursion up Route 90 to the **Mt of Beatitudes** (3.4km), possibly also to **Chorazin/Korazim National Park** (9km), before returning to Route 87 to visit **Tabgha** (2km) and **Capernaum** (4km). The route described here firstly details the attractions on Route 87 (Tabgha and Capernaum), before returning to the loop that includes Mt of Beatitudes and Chorazin, then back again to Route 87. Confused? Look at the 'Tiberias & Sea of Galilee' map on page 658 and all will become clear.

Tabgha

Tabgha is the reputed site of Jesus' miracle of the multiplication of the loaves and   *Phone code: 06*
fishes: "the feeding of the 5,000" (Matthew 14:13-21; Mark 6:30-44; Luke   *Colour map 1, grid B4*
9:10-17; John 6:1-13). Matthew and Mark also report a second feeding – "the
feeding of the 4,000" (Matthew 15:32-39; Mark 8:1-10) – that took place at Tel
Hadar on the northeast shore of the lake, whilst Luke and John combine both
events into one. A church has stood on this site at Tabgha since the fourth century
CE, whilst another chapel at the water's edge marks the traditional site where
Jesus appeared to his disciples after his Resurrection (John 21:1-24). Tabgha is a
major Christian pilgrimage site and can become a little too busy for some, partic-
ularly when several coachloads of visitors arrive at the same time.

Ins and outs

Tabgha is located approximately 15km north of Tiberias along Route 90 (and Route 87   **Getting around** for the last 2km). Buses 459/541/841/963 go from Tiberias to Kfar Nahum Junction ('Tabgha Junction', 20 mins, 12 NIS), from where they continue north on Route 90. Get off at the junction and walk the last 2km. Alternatively, take one of the slower local buses that circumnavigate the lake.

Tabgha

To Kfar Nahum Junction

Route 87

To Church of the Beatitudes

Birket Ali el-Daher (Byzantine water-storage towers)

Parking

Church of the Multiplication (Heptapegon)

Byzantine water-storage tower

Entrance Gate

To Capernaum

Crusader Period Building

Chapel of the Primacy of St Peter

'Sower's Bay'

N

0 metres 50

History

The name 'Tabgha' is an Arabic derivative of the Greek "(Land of) the Seven Springs", or **Heptapegon** (*Hebrew*: Ein Sheva). The springs were described by the pilgrim Egeria in 383 CE, and can still be seen today to the east of the Chapel of the Primacy of St Peter. Their warmth and high sulphur and salt content are said to help sustain an environment suitable for the 'St Peter's fish' that live in the lake. Egeria mentions that the rock upon which Jesus placed the five loaves and two fish had become an altar within a small chapel, and subsequent archaeological investigations

Galilee & The Golan

have revealed the presence of such a structure built c. 350 CE. It is speculated that a Jewish convert from Tiberias, Joseph (St Josipos), may have been responsible for building it. Later visitors to Tabgha such as St Sabas (late fifth century CE), Theodosius (c. 530 CE) and Antoninus Placentinus (c. 570 CE) all mention the church that replaced the chapel, though by the time Bishop Arculf visited the site in 670 CE the church lay in ruins. This could have been as a result of the Persian invasion of 614 CE or the Arab invasion of 636 CE. It appears that the site then disappeared from view for the next 1,200 years or so, until initial exploration was carried out in 1892, and full excavations in 1932. Though there are Crusader remains in the vicinity, it is not certain that they managed to identify the site, perhaps explaining why aspects of Jesus' Galilean ministry are celebrated in churches in Tiberias.

Sights

Church of the Multiplication
The present church on the site was consecrated in 1982, replacing a more modest effort built in the mid-20th century. It is built on the same plan as the fifth-century Byzantine Church of Heptapegon and incorporated as many original features as possible. Notice from the plan how the original fourth-century chapel, measuring 15.5 metres by 9.5 metres with an apse 2.6 metres deep, was aligned 28 degrees more to the south. The later Byzantine church,

Tabhga mosaics

built c. 480 CE, had this alignment corrected to the east, thus requiring the venerated stone to be moved to its new position under the altar. Throughout the centuries the stone that Jesus is said to have laid the bread and fishes upon has shrunk in size as pilgrims chipped off pieces to take home. Modern visitors use a camera or video-recorder to take their souvenir home. The Byzantine structure was a basilica with north and south transepts, and built mainly of roughly dressed local basalt.

The key feature of the Church of Heptapegon is its **mosaics**, parts of which have been preserved in the current church. Though the two most complete floors are those in the transepts, it is the restored mosaic in the presbytery, in front of the altar, that is most famous. The image of the two fish flanking a basket carrying the loaves can be seen on postcards, t-shirts and all forms of souvenir throughout the Holy Land. Notice how the basket only contains four loaves; a real loaf is usually placed on the altar to complete the five. As pilgrims pray and sing, tourists jostle to photograph the mosaic. It's not very dignified. ■ *T6721061. Monday-Saturday 0830-1700, Sunday 0945-1700; Admission free, though donations welcome. Parking, toilets, snack-shop, souvenirs. **NB** modest dress required and guides are not permitted to give commentaries inside the church.*

Chapel of the Primacy of St Peter
Close to the Church of the Multiplication, down on the lake's shore, is the Chapel of the Primacy of St Peter. To reach it you have to go back out on to Route 87 and walk a couple of hundred metres along the road to the gate. There is a car-park opposite but it's usually full. Beware of the heavy traffic on this road.

Tradition has it that this was the site of Jesus' appearance to the disciples following his Resurrection (*John 21:1-24*), when he commissioned Peter to "feed my sheep". The large stone inside the present chapel is said to be 'Mensa Christi' ('Table of Christ') upon which Jesus prepared the breakfast for the disciples prior to commissioning Peter. The pilgrim nun Egeria described seeing some steps during her visit c. 383 CE upon which Jesus is said to have stood, and there are some rock-cut stairs close to the water's edge. Egeria did not mention a church on the site during her visit, though a later document suggests that a small chapel may have been built over the 'Mensa Christi' during the Byzantine period, and the large heart-shaped blocks that you can see down by the water's edge may have been part of the early Christian settlement here. Known as the **Twelve Thrones**, they may have been placed here to commemorate the Twelve Apostles. By the ninth century CE the site was known as the "place of burning coal", from the line in John that describes the breakfast meal (*John 21:9*). There is evidence of a church being here in the Crusader period, though it appears to have been destroyed, rebuilt, then destroyed again.

Chapel of the Primacy of St Peter

The present chapel was built by the Franciscans in 1933 and features commemorations of Pope Paul VI's visit in 1964. Outside is a communal prayer area and a bronze statue of Jesus commissioning Peter with his crook.

Some visitors claim that, whilst standing quietly at the water's edge, it is possible to imagine the shallow bay to the east as the '**Sower's Bay**', where Jesus preached the 'Parable of the Sower' (*Matthew 13:1-9, 18-23; Mark 4:1-9; Luke 8:4-8; John 13:18-23*) from a boat to the assembled multitude.

Within the grounds of the Chapel of the Primacy of St Peter, along the path between the entrance and the chapel, are the remains of Byzantine water-storage towers, some Crusader period buildings, and some later water mills.

A steep path from the car park opposite the entrance to the Chapel of the Primacy of St Peter leads up the hill to the Mt of the Beatitudes (traditional site of the 'Sermon on the Mount'), though those on tour coaches or with their own car generally return to Kfar Nahum Junction and drive up Route 90 (see below). ■ *T6724767. 0800-1200 1400-1700. Admission free, donations accepted. **NB** modest dress required.*

Route From Tabgha it is 2km along Route 87 to the turn-off for **Capernaum** (just beyond the 'St Peter's Fish Restaurant'). From the turn-off it is 500m to the site.

Capernaum

Phone code: 06
Colour map 1, grid B5

Though the references to Capernaum in the gospels are frequent, the origin of the name (Hebrew: Kfar Nahum, or Village of Nahum) is unclear. It is an important site of Christian pilgrimage as the scene of many events during the Galilean Ministry of Jesus; it became "his own city" (Matthew 9:1) when he was driven out of Nazareth, it was here that he called Peter, Andrew, James, John and Matthew to be his disciples, and he performed several miracles at Capernaum (see box on page 690). Parts of the first century CE town can still be seen, including a house that compelling evidence suggests was the home of St Peter. Capernaum is also renowned for the remains of one of the most splendid synagogues in Galilee.

Ins and outs

Getting there Unless you have your own transport, you'll have to follow the instructions for getting to Kfar Nahum Junction (see 'Tabgha' on page 687), and then walk the 4km from there (about 40 mins). An interesting way to reach Capernaum is by boat run by Lido Kinnereth Sailing Co from Lido Beach in Tiberias (T6721538 for details).

Galilee & The Golan

Capernaum: town of Jesus

After "leaving Nazareth, he [Jesus] came and dwelt in Capernaum, which is upon the sea coast, in the borders of Zabulon and Nephthalim" (Matthew 4:13). His subsequent time in the town for once justifies the tourist hype (and sign at the entrance to the site): "Capernaum: town of Jesus". The following gospel events are just some of those that took place here: Calling of Peter, Andrew, James and John (Matthew 4:18-22; Mark 1:16-20); Calling of Peter, James and John (Luke 5:1-11); Calling of Matthew (Matthew 9:9; Mark 2:13-14; Luke 5:27-28); Healing of the Centurion's servant (Matthew 8:5-13; Luke 7:1-10); Healing of Peter's mother-in-law (Matthew 8:14-15; Mark 1:29-34); Healing of many (Matthew 8:16-17); Healing of the Paralytic (Matthew 9:1-7; Mark 2:1-12); Raising of Jairus' daughter (Matthew 9:18-19 23-26; Mark 5:21-24 35-43; Luke 8:40-42 49-56); Healing of the woman with haemorrhage (Matthew 9:20-22; Mark 5:25-34; Luke 8:43-48); Healing of the demoniac (Mark 1:21-28).

History

Though there are numerous ancient literary references to Capernaum, there are still several aspects of the town's history that remain unexplained. There is no mention of Capernaum in the Old Testament, though archaeologists have discovered some evidence of occupation from the second millennium BCE. It was during the Early Roman period (37 BCE-132 CE) that the settlement really developed, almost certainly as a result of its position on the *Via Maris* trading route. The gospels confirm that Capernaum had a customs post, Matthew himself, "sitting at the receipt of custom" (*Matthew 9:9*). Yet despite its favourable position on the *Via Maris*, the inference is that this was such a poor community that it had to rely on a Gentile, the centurion commanding the garrison, to build the synagogue (*Luke 7:5*). What has yet to be satisfactorily explained is why the magnificent fourth century CE synagogue that you see today was built in this relatively poor community, particularly since the decline in importance of the *Via Maris* in later years must have hastened Capernaum's own decline.

Capernaum

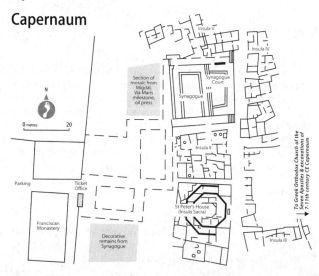

Galilee & The Golan

The structure of Capernaum's population in the centuries following Jesus' crucifixion also remains unclear. Epiphanius (writing in 374 CE) claims that until the fourth century CE the Jews of Capernaum forbade Christians, Samaritans and gentiles from living in their midst, yet the archaeological and written evidence attests to the permanent presence of Jesus' followers from the first century CE onwards. This small minority of converts would be more accurately described as a Judeo-Christian community, or *Minim* ('followers of Jesus'), and probably still considered themselves to be essentially Jewish. But as the Jewish and Christian faiths gradually moved farther apart, there may have developed considerable tension between the two groups. The acceptance of Christianity as the state religion by the Roman emperor Constantine at the beginning of the fourth century CE may have fuelled this tension, though both communities continued to exist in Capernaum. Indeed, rather than manifesting itself in a violent form, this rivalry between the two communities may have been the driving force behind the building efforts that produced an ornate synagogue that seems so out of place, and the expansion of Peter's house through the stage of *domus ecclesia* (house church) to a basilica.

Both the synagogue and church had been destroyed prior to the Arab conquest of Palestine in 636 CE, though how and by whom is not clear. It's not unlikely that the church was destroyed by the Jews during the Persian invasion of 614 CE, and the synagogue was razed by the Christians when the Byzantines retook the land fifteen years later. Perhaps this is what Jesus prophesied when he said "And thou, Capernaum, which art exalted unto heaven, shalt be brought down to hell" (*Matthew 11:23*). It was initially thought that this was the end for Capernaum, but recent excavations on land now owned by the Greek Orthodox Church to the east of the main site (towards the present-day Church of the Seven Apostles) shows that Capernaum was rebuilt. Not much is known about Capernaum's subsequent history, though the traveller Burchardus, writing in 1283, describes the town as being a poor village of just seven fishermen's houses. The lack of construction during the Crusader period on this important Christian site may be explained by the vulnerability to attack of this location. The site was first tentatively identified by the American explorer Robinson in 1838, though it wasn't until the Franciscans acquired the site in 1894 that extensive excavations began.

The plan to build a pier here just below the surface of the water, allowing pilgrims to recreate Jesus' act of walking on the water, appears to have been scrapped!

Sights

In 1990 the Franciscans built a modern church above the traditional site of the **House of St Peter**. The church serves as a Roman Catholic place of worship, as well a protection from the elements for the ancient site. The exterior is considered by some to be extremely unattractive, though the interior is rather nice and provides a fine view through the glass floor of the house below. (**NB** The church is not always open to visitors and is primarily reserved for pre-booked tour groups who wish to celebrate Catholic mass).

House of St Peter

The House of St Peter is characteristic of the other first century CE residencies that can be seen here, most notably **Insula II** between the House of St Peter and the synagogue. The term 'insula' (plural 'insulae') refers to the city block form containing multiple dwellings that was characteristic of this period. The houses at Capernaum were built of basalt and characterized by a large central court surrounded by small dwellings. Each block was occupied by up to 15 related families (as many as 100 persons), with the communal courtyard

Galilee & The Golan

serving as the centre of family life. The insula that contains St Peter's house is referred to as **insula sacra** (sacred quarter).

Sceptics who may doubt the authenticity of the claim that this is the actual house of St Peter would do well to bear in mind the compelling evidence that supports it. From as early as the first century CE, a small room (5.8 metres by 6.45 metres) at the centre of the 'insula sacra' has been accorded special treatment. Though artefacts found here (including fish-hooks) attest to general usage in the first half of the first century CE by the second half of the century the room was put to some kind of public use. It is the only one in the block that has plastered walls and floors, whilst 131 inscriptions in Greek, Aramaic, Syriac and Latin have been carved into the walls. Some of this graffiti mentions 'Jesus', 'Lord', 'Christ' and 'Peter', and suggests that Peter's house was used as a *domus ecclesia* (house church). By the fourth century CE an enclosure wall separated this house from the rest of the town, with a central arch supporting a more permanent roof structure (see *Mark 2:3-4*) and a polichrome pavement laid on the floor. The pilgrim nun Egeria, visiting c. 383, describes in some detail how the "house of the prince of Apostles was changed into a church", with some scholars speculating that this work was done by Joseph of Tiberias (St Josipos).

By the mid-fifth century a church had been built on the site. A small central octagon was built around the house, with an ornate mosaic carpet replacing the polichrome pavement. The peacock centrepiece of the mosaic symbolizes immortality. A larger concentric octagon and an outer semi-octagon enclosed the site, with a baptismal font added to the east apse. The church is described by the anonymous pilgrim of Placentia c. 570 CE. The church was destroyed at some stage in the seventh century. The early stage from which this site was venerated gives much credence to the suggestion that this was indeed St Peter's house.

The Synagogue The history behind the synagogue is more complex. The key question is why such a fine building, constructed of imported limestone as opposed to the locally found basalt used for residential quarters, was built in what by all accounts was a relatively poor town? It is also far from clear who built it, whilst its date of construction remains contentious. It is now generally agreed that the synagogue was built at the end of the fourth century CE, with the court to the east completed in the fifth century. A cache of 25,000 Late Roman period coins and some pottery finds buried in the foundations seem to support this date. However, the style of the building is very different to other synagogues built in Galilee during the same period. Whereas the synagogues at Hammath-Tiberias and Beit Alpha (albeit the latter belonging to the sixth century CE) have plain exteriors and elaborate mosaic floors inside, Capernaum's synagogue had an impressive ornamental façade and exterior, but a relatively plain stone floor inside. Further, the period when the synagogue was built was a time of considerable tension between the Jewish and Christian communities, and it would have been unusual for the Byzantine authorities to allow the construction of such a large synagogue so close to a church. More speculative theorists suggest that the synagogue was actually built by the Christian community in order to create a spectacular reminder of some of the scenes from Jesus' time in Capernaum.

The synagogue comprises three main sections: a large prayer hall, the court to the east, and the porch along the façade. Despite the wealth of remains discovered here it has not been possible to reconstruct the complete plan of the synagogue. For example, experts still disagree as to whether there was an upper gallery, possibly for use by women (see argument on page 647). The floor plan is that of a basilica, with the rectangular prayer hall (20.4 metres by 18.65

metres) divided by a *stylobate* into a wide nave and three aisles to the west, north and east. The prayer hall was joined to the east by a court which had roofed porticoes to the north, east and south. This would probably have served as some form of community centre/meeting place. The hall and court were both paved with stone slabs. The interior of the synagogue was plastered and decorated with reliefs.

The synagogue faces south, towards Jerusalem, and is entered by one of three doorways up a flight of steps. The reference to a synagogue where the "way in is up many steps, and it is made of dressed stone" by Egeria c. 383 has been one factor in the argument for dating the construction somewhat earlier. Sections of the intricately carved lintels, cornices, capitals and gables remain *in situ*, whilst fallen sections are displayed in the compound just inside the entrance to the site, to the right of the ticket office.

Excavations beneath the synagogue have revealed the remains of a large public building dating to the first century CE (you can see the lines of black basalt beneath the white limestone of the present synagogue). It has been suggested that this could be the synagogue where Jesus taught and performed some of his miracles. Against this argument is the fact that the lower remains here are at the same level as the first century CE Insula II buildings, and thus this cannot belong to the synagogue that "is up many steps", as described by Egeria. However, the counter-argument is that these lower remains are just the foundations of the first century CE synagogue, and the building itself would have been somewhat higher. ■ *T6721059. Daily 0830-1600. Adult 5 NIS. Souvenir shop, toilets, parking. **NB** modest dress essential.*

The land to the east of the Capernaum site is the property of the Greek Orthodox Church, and contains the remains of the town from around the late seventh century CE until the mid-11th century CE. The most notable finds have been the remains of a large square building that may have served as some form of fish storage facility and a long lakeside quay.

Greek Orthodox Church of the Seven Apostles

The **Greek Orthodox Church of the Seven Apostles**, just to the east of Capernaum, is one of the loveliest spots in the area. The small church, built in 1931, is distinguished by its two red domes which can be seen from some distance. The interior of the church is elaborately decorated in the Greek Orthodox tradition, with numerous icons and images of Jesus and the Apostles. You can reach the church by walking across the fields from the Franciscan-owned site, or by continuing for a further 1.7 kilometres along and then turning right on to an unmarked track. ■ *T6722282. Daily 1000-1600. Free. **NB** modest dress only.*

From Capernaum, Route 87 continues along the north shore of the Sea of Galilee to the junction with Route 8277. This is where the short excursion from the lakeside road via the **Mt of Beatitudes** and **Chorazin** rejoins Route 87 (see page 694).

Route

Mount of Beatitudes

The Mount of Beatitudes is the traditional site of the 'Sermon on the Mount' (*Matthew 5:1 to 7:27; Luke 6:17-49*), and though there is no archaeological evidence to support this claim, this is most surely an appropriate spot for one of Jesus' most important lessons.

Phone code: 06
Colour map 1, grid B4

The fact that the 'Sermon on the Mount' may have taken place here, and not "Judea AD 33, Saturday afternoon, about tea-time" confirms the historical inaccuracy of Monty Python's *Life of Brian* (with its "Blessed are the cheese-makers", and all that)!

Galilee & The Golan

Ins and outs Take bus 459/541/963 from Tiberias and get off at the second stop after Kfar Nahum Junction (give the driver plenty of warning, 20 mins, 12 NIS). On foot the church is reached either by taking the steep path from opposite the entrance to the Chapel of the Primacy of St Peter at Tabgha, or by car/bus in a short excursion away from the lakeside road (Route 87). To reach by road, take the steep, winding road (Route 90) heading upwards from Kfar Nahum Junction. After 2.4km of switchback turns, a road sign-posted "Hospice of the Beatitudes" heads off 1km to the right. There can be heavy coach jams on this road.

Church of the Beatitudes The original fourth century CE Monastery of the Sermon on the Mount was built close to Tabgha (near to the car-park opposite the Chapel of the Primacy of St Peter), but fell out of use in the seventh century CE. The modern **Church of the Beatitudes** is one of the more attractive churches in the Holy Land, set in one of the most attractive locations. Built in 1937, the church is constructed of local basalt, with white Nazareth stone used in the arches and columns. Designed by the renowned Italian architect Antonio Barluzzi, the eight sides of its octagonal plan represent the eight Beatitudes (which bless the poor in spirit, those that mourn, the meek, those that hunger and thirst after righteousness, the merciful, the pure in heart, the peacemakers, and those who are persecuted for righteousness), whilst the dome symbolizes Christ's promise of reward in heaven. There are excellent views of the area of Jesus' Ministry through the narrow horizontal windows, or from the arcaded ambulatory around the church. Despite the crowds, the landscaped gardens provide a fine setting for quiet contemplation. ■ *T6790978. Daily 0800-1200 1430-1700. Free. Parking, toilets, souvenir shop, though the battle for souvenirs can be brutal. **NB** modest dress required.*

Church of the Beatitudes

Route If you wish to continue on this excursion away from the lakeside, return to Route 90 and continue north. After 4.5km turn right at Korazim Junction onto Route 8277. Immediately on your left is **Vered HaGalil**. Proceeding east on Route 8277, passing the turn off on the left for the settlement of Korazim, continue for 2.5km until you come to **Korazim National Park (Chorazin)** on your right.

Beyond the National Park, Route 8277 continues east towards the kibbutz at **Almagor** (3.3km), site of a four-day battle between the Israelis and Syria in 1951. The road then bears south, after 5.7km rejoining the lake ring-road, Route 87.

Vered HaGalil The *Vered HaGalil Ranch and Guest Farm*, near Korazim Junction, T6935785, F6934964, provides very pleasant **B** category accommodation in chalets, or the choice of bunkhouse accommodation in the **C** price category. It may also be possible to camp in their grounds (call ahead). The restaurant here is highly recommended. Meaning the 'Rose of Galilee', the main attraction here is the stud farm and riding stables where you can hire horses to explore the surrounding countryside. Typical prices are 70 NIS per hour, 100 NIS for two hours, 250 NIS per day, plus the option of escorted full and half-day treks. On Thursday nights in summer there are 'western horse-shows', a barbeque and square-dancing.

Korazim National Park (Chorazin)

The fine remains of this ancient Jewish town, most notably the fourth-fifth century CE synagogue, stand on a low hill above the Sea of Galilee amongst a barren landscape littered with black basalt stones. Many dolmens (upright stones supporting a horizontal slab, used for burial) are located in the area around the town. Though the remains are not extensive, this must rate as one of the best presented sites in the region.

Phone code: 06

The ancient Jewish settlement of **Chorazin** (variously spelt Korazim, Chorozain, etc) is best known as one of the three towns (also Capernaum, Bethsaida) that Jesus cursed for rejecting his teachings (*Matthew 11:20-24*; *Luke 10:12-16*). Excavations suggest that the town was founded in the first or second century CE, and concentrated mainly on the upper, north side of the hill (north of Route 8277, labelled on map as '**Northern Quarter**'). The settlement expanded over the centuries and by the Talmudic period of the late third-early fourth centuries CE it extended over most of the hill.

History

Some time in the early fourth century CE the town was destroyed, and is described in Eusebius' *Onomasticon* as being "a village in Galilee, cursed by the messiah, [that] lives in ruins today". The causes of this calamity are unknown,

Korazim National Park (Chorazin)

Synagogue detail

Galilee & The Golan

a Entrance Court	**d** Aisles	2 Ticket Office	7 Open Square at
b Bedrock	**e** Site of Ark of the Law	3 Ritual Bath Complex	Entrance to Synagogue
c Central Hall	**f** 'Seat of Moses'	4 'Building A'	8 'House of Arches'
	1 Grave of Sheikh	5 'Building B'	9 Subterranean Chamber
	Ramadan	6 Synagogue	10 Oil Presses

though an earthquake is a more likely explanation than the sometimes mentioned theory of Christian-Jewish communal strife. The town, including the impressive synagogue, was swiftly rebuilt pretty much on the same plan as the earlier settlement. The site continued to be occupied for the next few hundred years, with alterations and repairs made to all the major buildings. The town began to decline in the eighth century CE and may even have been abandoned completely until the area was resettled (on a far smaller scale) in the 12th or 13th century CE. A small community of Jewish fishermen were still reported to be living here in the 16th century CE. Bedouins occupied the site intermittently until 1948.

The site was first identified in 1869, though early commentators (most notably St Jerome) confused Chorazin with Kursi on the east shore of the Sea of Galilee (see page 699). Systematic excavations took place in the 1920s, 1960s, and most recently in the mid 1980s when the site was turned over to the National Parks Authority.

Grave of Sheikh Ramadan (1) Before entering the National Park it is possible to examine the recently restored **Grave of Sheikh Ramadan** (**1**), located just behind the ticket office (**2**). Built originally during the Mamluk period, this is believed by the Bedouin to be the grave of one of Salah al-Din's generals. The Bedouin used to gather here to make vows and settle disputes, believing that guilt or innocence could be established beyond doubt.

Ritual bath complex (3) A well-labelled walking trail begins at the ticket office and heads south. To the right of the path is the **ritual bath complex** (**3**), enclosed within a walled courtyard paved with flagstones to the east and lime plaster to the west. Nine steps (two above ground, seven below) lead down into the *mikveh* (ritual bath) itself. The pool was fed by the subterranean cistern close by. Both are partly cut from the rock and partly built with stone. A central column in the cistern supported a stone roof. A series of rooms around a central hall were linked to the ritual bath complex to the south.

Central Quarter The blue and white arrows lead you south along the main north–south road of the town to the '**Central Quarter**' of the residential area, built on the wide natural platform on the top of the hill. This quarter comprises two main buildings ('A' and 'B'), both of which feature a central courtyard surrounded by a row of rooms. A large cistern in the courtyard of '**Building B**' probably served both residential units. The blue/white arrows lead you into this courtyard from where you can see the plan of '**Building A**' to the east. The main doorway to 'Building A' was via the courtyard of 'Building B' to the west (not to the east, as described on the information board at the site), though there are smaller exits to the east and south. Despite minor alterations to both buildings in the late sixth and eighth centuries CE, they pretty much conform to their original late fourth-early fifth century CE plan. The blue and white arrows lead you out from 'Building B's' main entrance in the south towards the synagogue.

Synagogue The **Synagogue** (**6**) is one of Chorazin's most impressive sights. In contrast to Capernaum's synagogue it is built of local black basalt, though the plan and design is similar. Notice how remnants of the large slab of rock to the northwest were left *in situ*. The synagogue appears to have been damaged early in the fourth century CE and substantially restored in the late fourth or early fifth century CE, and several changes made to its basic plan. In its original phase a monumental staircase led from the **large open square** (**7**) to the south up to the synagogue's three entrance doorways. These led into the central prayer hall, with a U-shaped arrangement of 12 columns dividing it into a central hall and two aisles. Just inside the entrance to the left, between the main doorway and the southwest doorway, stands a decorated column that may well have been part of a structure designed to hold the Ark of the Law. Inside the entrance to the right, between the main doorway and the southeast doorway, is an *aedicula* (small niche) in which was discovered a stone chair bearing the inscription "Seat (Cathedra) of Moses". There are also substantial remains from the decorative elements of the synagogue, including sections of friezes, cornices and capitals. A carved conch, possibly part of a window, is particularly fine.

Leaving the synagogue, the blue and white arrows head towards the '**Western Quarter**'. A large information board invites you to look through a hole cut in a small stone. A horizontal piece of metal suspended three metres away intersects with a vertical pole some 300 metres to the south to form the shape of a crucifix, floating above the Sea of Galilee. The tree behind the information board, *Zizyphus spina christi*, is traditionally the species from which Jesus' crown of thorns was made.

Western Quarter

Though fragments of earlier periods are visible, the houses in the 'Western Quarter', most notably the '**House of Arches**' (**8**), date from the medieval period. It is possible to see here how the double row of arches supported the stone beam roof. To the south of the 'House of Arches' is a **subterranean chamber** (**9**) that probably served as a storeroom or cistern in the Talmudic period (c. fourth century CE). To the west of the 'House of Arches' are the remains of several **oil presses** (**10**), one of which appears to have been in use from the fourth century CE until the 17th century CE. Sections of the '**Southern Quarter**' and '**Eastern Quarter**' can also be seen, though they are not open to the public. ■ *T6934982. Daily 0800-1600. Adult 14 NIS.*

Continuing northeast along the lakeside road (Route 87), from its junction with Route 8277, after 2km you come to the **Ariq Bridge**. Several km beyond here is the turning for the **Jordan River Park**.

Route

Jordan River Park

This short section of the Jordan River has been turned into a wonderful recreation site. In addition to the nature trails and bird-watching opportunities, and the archaeological remains of the ancient Jewish settlement of Bethsaida, the park's most notable attraction is the opportunity to paddle down the Jordan in a kayak or float down in an inner tube.

Jordan River Park

There is no public transport directly to the park, though buses that circumnavigate the lake may be able to drop you off at the junction just past the Ariq Bridge.

Ins and outs

This low tel (mound) to the east of the Jordan River Park is the remains of the ancient Jewish settlement of **Bethsaida** (Beth Zaida). It was founded by **Herod Philip** upon the territories inherited from his father Herod the Great and named **Julius-Bethsaida** after the wife of the Roman Emperor Augustus. Herod Philip was buried here upon his death

Tel Bethsaida

in 33 CE. Bethsaida is also the reputed birthplace of the Apostles **Peter** and **Andrew**, but was one of the towns (with Capernaum and Chorazin) that was upbraided by Jesus for rejecting his teachings (*Matthew 11:20-24; Luke 10:12-16*). The town was destroyed by the Romans during the First Jewish Revolt (66-73 CE), leaving little to be seen today. Because of this site's association with Jesus, there are plans in hand to develop it further in time for the year 2000. Tours of the site can be arranged in advance (T6791520). **NB** The eastern part of the tel has not been cleared of mines: obey the signs and stay safe.

Kayak/inner tube hire *ABU-Kayak*, T6921078, F6920622, rent out two- and three-seater inflatable kayaks, or inflated inner tubes, for a very enjoyable one-hour float along the Jordan. Hire fee includes transportation back to the starting point (daily 0900-1700).

Walking trails There are two marked hiking trails (blue and red), both of which begin at the restored flour mills. The short red trail involves walking through the streams and thickets, and takes around half an hour to complete. The blue trail takes about one hour, the highlight of which is a fine panoramic viewpoint over the Jordan River.

Route At 1.2km beyond the turning for the Jordan River Park, Route 87 bears left in a northeast direction at Yehudiye Junction towards the fabulous **Ya'ar Yehudiya Nature Reserve** (see page 755). Details of this, and other attractions in the region, are included in the 'Lower Golan' section. Beyond Yehudiye Junction, the road running along the east side of the Sea of Galilee becomes Route 92. About 1.5km south of Yehudiye Junction, between the 25 and 24km stones, a dirt road heads west into the **Beit Zaida Nature Reserve**.

Beit Zaida Nature Reserve The Beit Zaida Nature Reserve (also known as **Majrasse**) is a low, flat delta area where a number of streams flow into the northeast corner of the Sea of Galilee. Several lagoons have been created, the extent of which depends upon the seasonal variation of the Jordan River, Meshushim, Yehudiye, Daliyyot and Shfamnun streams. The area attracts migratory birds, and is also the home of many other creatures, including over 20 different types of fish. There is an excellent hike through part of the reserve, though for much of its length it involves swimming through deep water. (**NB** Do not drink the water.)

Beit Zaida Nature Reserve hike

1 Turn off	4 Olive grove
2 Right fork	5 Low dam
3 Cross Nahal Yehudiya	6 Turn back to start

To reach the start point, turn west off Route 92 on to the dirt road (**1**) about **Hike**
1.5km south of Yehudiye Junction. After about 800m take the fork to the right
(northwest) (**2**) for a further 800m, and where it bears left stop at the eucalyptus tree: the hike begins here. After a couple of minutes walking, the path
crosses the Nahal Yehudiye (**3**). The depth here depends upon the season.
Bear left towards the olive grove (about 100m) (**4**), then follow the trail markers. These soon lead you into the water, which you will now be in for the next
couple of hours. Though there are no trail markers in the water, it is just a matter of following the course of the stream. **NB** It is very deep in places.
Depending upon the season, the stream will open out into a number of deep
pools. Having walked and swum for over one kilometre through the water, you
reach a low dam (**5**). Beyond this point the Nature Reserve is a protected area,
and visitors are excluded. Leave the water and head left towards the eucalyptus
trees. A track to the left (**6**) heads back to the start point, running parallel to the
stream through which you hiked. The total length of the hike is less than four
kilometres, though it can take up to five hours, depending upon how much
time you spend resting/swimming.

A couple of km further south along Route 92, at Ma'ale Gamla Junction, Route 869 **Route**
heads northeast towards **Gamla** (see page 756). Route 92 continues south, passing
the turning (at 2.5km) on the left for Ramot Holiday Village and right for Kinar Holiday
Village and Duga Camping. A further 1.3km brings you to **Luna Gal Water Park**.

This recreational park features the Sea of Galilee's best beach, plus the added **Luna Gal Water**
attractions of giant water-slides, kayak hire, inner tube rides, several pools and **Park**
waterfalls, plus café/restaurants and picnic areas. ■ *T6731750. Daily*
0930-1800. Adult 50 NIS for whole day, kayak and inner tube hire extra. Irregu-
lar buses 015 022 843 from Tiberias pass the entrance.

Continuing south on Route 92, passing Zeelon Beach to the right, after 2.6km you **Route**
come to Kursi Junction. Turn left here on to Route 789, and then turn immediately
right into the car park of **Kursi National Park**. Continuing east up the steep and
winding Route 789 leads to **Mitzpe Ofir Observation Point** and the start of the
Mitzpe Ofir to Ein Gev hike (see page 700).

Kursi National Park

The Byzantine monastery and church complex stands on the traditional site of *Phone code: 06*
the Miracle of the Swine, where Jesus exorcised a man tormented by devils,
and transferred the evil spirits to a nearby herd of pigs who subsequently
rushed headlong down into the lake and drowned (*Matthew 8:28-33; Mark
5:1-20; Luke 8:26-39*).

The identification of the site has been problematic since each gospel refers to **Byzantine**
the place of the miracle by a different name: Matthew, Gadara; Mark, Gerasa; **church and**
Luke, Gergesa. All agree, however, that it took place on the "other side" (east) **monastery**
of the Sea of Galilee. The question of the name has led some to place the scene
at Jerash (in Jordan), or Gadara (Umm Qais, also in Jordan). The name '**Kursi**'
may have been derived from the Aramaic word *kursa*, meaning 'chair' (a reference to the rock formation above the church). 'Kursi' is also similar to the
Greek word for swine, as well as possibly being a derivative of Chorozain (see
page 694), which for a long time was mistakenly identified with this site. However, the excavations of the **square tower** and **small chapel** on the hillside
above the church have revealed the presence of a natural cave, thus closely

Galilee & The Golan

matching the topographical features mentioned in the gospel narrative.

It appears that construction began on the monastery and church complex at the end of the fifth to beginning of the sixth century CE, though major alterations were made to the church at the end of the sixth century CE. The entire complex was badly damaged in the Persian invasion of 614 CE, and all but destroyed in the earthquake of 741 CE. Though the church has been largely restored, little remains of the **monastery**, bar a large section of the dressed basalt stone wall (120 metres by 140 metres) that surrounded the complex.

The Byzantine **church** is one of the largest basilicas yet excavated in Israel (45 metres by 25 metres). As one passes through the large *atrium* (forecourt) and *narthex* (antechamber to the nave), the main hall is divided by two rows of eight columns into a nave and two aisles. The mosaic floors of the aisles have survived remarkably well, though the representations of living forms have been systematically obliterated. To the north of the apse is a *sacristy*, whilst to the south a Greek inscription tells us that this chamber was converted into a *baptistry* in 585 CE. An olive press was found in the room to the north of the central hall, whilst the two chambers to the south of the main hall were used as a chapel and a *diaconicon* (storage room) respectively. In the crypt below the latter were found a number of burial troughs containing the remains of 30 men, presumably the priests or monks attached to the complex.

A path leads east from the church up to the remains of a **square tower**, built around a natural rock pillar. The **small chapel** attached to the east was built by enlarging a natural cave. It appears to have been cut at the same time as the church was built. ■ *T6731983. Daily 0800-1700, closes one hour earlier in winter. Irregular buses 015, 017, 019, 021,022 from Tiberias.*

Byzantine Church, Kursi

Path to square tower & small chapel →
■ Preserved mosaics

1 Atrium
2 Cisterns
3 Narthex
4 Nave
5 Northern Aisle
6 Southern Aisle
7 Sacristy
8 Baptistry
9 Olive Press
10 Chapel
11 Diaconicon
12 Entrance to Crypt

0 metres 10

Route From Kursi National Park it is possible to continue up the steep and winding Route 789. At 8.9km on the right, an orange sign indicates a dirt road to **Mitzpe Ofir**. A further 1.2km leads to the car-park.

Mitzpe Ofir Observation Point Mitzpe Ofir must be the best vantage point from which to view the Sea of Galilee. Standing at this observation point some 400 metres above the Sea of Galilee serves as a most visual of reminders as to why Israel is so reluctant to enter into any negotiations that might see the Golan returned to Syrian control. Prior to the Six Day War in 1967, the border between Israel and Syria ran along the base of this cliff, with Israel occupying a narrow strip of land around the east side of the lake. In fact, Mitzpe Ofir was actually a Syrian gun position, and it's easy to see just how easy it was to drop a few shells into Kibbutz Ein Gev; you could almost throw them. A hiking trail leads down from Mitzpe Ofir to Kibbutz Ein Gev. **Warning** Keep to the trail because there are still uncleared mine fields in the area.

Mitzpe Ofir to Ein Gev hike The trail descends to the south of the viewpoint, through the grove of olive trees, passing an uncleared minefield beyond the fence to your left. Continue on to the dirt track, and follow the path to the **Bir e Shikum** (spring). This was the former site of the agricultural community of **B'nei Yehuda** (Sons of Judah) established by religious Jews from Safed and Tiberias in the late 19th century

CE. The settlement was not a success, and dwindled from 52 families in 1885 to just 1 by 1920. The marked trail continues along the ridge, before striking off down towards the lake. Ein Gev viewpoint provides a final place to rest before tackling the steep descent. Pass through the outer fields of Kibbutz Ein Gev, along a narrow wadi, until you hit the main road (Route 92). The whole hike normally takes three to four hours from the start point.

Route

Continuing south on Route 92 from Kursi Junction, the road passes a number of beaches to the right, before arriving at **Kibbutz Ein Gev** (3.2km).

Ein Gev

The modern history of Kibbutz Ein Gev begins in 1937, when the "tower and stockade" became the first Jewish settlement on the east side of the Sea of Galilee. One of its founders was Teddy Kollek, the famous long-time major of Jerusalem. Following the armistice at the end of the 1948 War of Independence, Ein Gev was included within a demilitarized strip of land along the east side of the lake controlled by Israel. The kibbutz was particularly vulnerable to attack from the Syrian positions on the heights above, and access to the outside world was by boat only.

Since the capture and occupation of the Golan by the Israelis in 1967, Kibbutz Ein Gev has diversified from fishing and agriculture to include tourism as part of its economy. The *Ein Gev Holiday Village*, T6659800, F6659818, about 1.5 kilometres to the south of the kibbutz entrance, offers **C** price category accommodation (**B** during holidays), plus a campground, set in a lawn area on the lakeside. Within the kibbutz itself is its renowned *Ein Gev Fish Restaurant* (T6658008, St Peter's Fish 50 NIS), a mini-train that tours the grounds (T6658008, 1130 1330, 10 NIS), the Fishing Museum (T6658998) and the **ferry-boat** that runs thrice daily between Ein Gev and Tiberias (call ahead for

Mitzpe Ofir to Ein Gev hike

Galilee & The Golan

schedule, T6658008, F6750011, single crossing 15 NIS, return 28 NIS). The 5,000-seater auditorium is also the venue for concerts and music festivals. In addition to the ferry, irregular buses 015/017/018/019/021/022 run to Ein Gev from Tiberias (every two hours or so).

Route Almost opposite the entrance to Kibbutz Ein Gev, just slightly further south on Route 92, an unmarked road heads off to the east. After a steep and winding climb of 3.7km, a small layby to the left of the road (marked by the tree symbol of the National Parks Authority) indicates the entrance to the site of **Sussita**.

Sussita

Phone code: 06 Founded by the Seleucids in the Early Hellenistic period (332-167 BCE), the town is best known by its Greek name **Antiochia Hippos**, or **Hippos**. The promontory upon which it stands is said to resemble the shape of a horse (*Greek*: 'hippos'), with its Aramaic name **Sussita** having the same meaning. Before exploring the site, there are two points that should be borne in mind. Firstly, there is not a great deal to see, nothing is labelled and the site is rather overgrown. Secondly, the area is littered with **mines** (a legacy of Israeli and Syrian military occupation between 1948 and 1967), so it is important to stick to the path and not to cross any fences.

History Despite its stout defensive wall around the summit, the city was captured by **Alexander Jannaeus** for the Maccabees c. 80 BCE, though **Pompey** subsequently recaptured it in 63 BCE. According to the writings of Pliny it became one of the cities of the Decapolis, though the decision by the Roman Emperor Augustus to grant the city to Herod of Great in c. 30 BCE was not one that went down well with the city's population. Following the death of Herod, the town once more became part of the Province of Syria. Despite considerable trade between Hippos and Tiberias, the towns were deadly enemies, and the Jews attacked Hippos during the **First Jewish Revolt** (66-73 CE).

The town here developed substantially during the second and third centuries CE, primarily due to its location on the road between Damascus and Scythopolis (Bet Shean, see page 648); at its peak its population may have reached 20,000. The town enjoyed a great deal of prosperity during the **Byzantine period**, becoming the seat of a bishop. It was peacefully occupied by the **Arabs** following their conquest of Palestine in 636 CE, though it had to be abandoned when the elaborate aqueduct system that brought the city its water from a point 25 kilometres to the south was destroyed in the earthquake of 749 CE.

Sights The tour begins at the east of the promontory, between the two fences that mark the minefields. You enter past the southern pier of the **east gate** from the Roman period (though it was rebuilt in the Byzantine period). The path that you follow here was the **cardo maximus** (main street) of the Roman period. Isolated patches of the paving stones remain. Passing a number of abandoned buildings dating to the recent military occupation, to the south of the cardo lay the best preserved remains on the site: the Byzantine **cathedral**. The two rows of nine columns that divided the basilica into a nave and two aisles were found lying on the floor, along with a number of pink and white marble Corinthian capitals; a victim of the earthquake. An inscription in the southern aisles mentions the two Syrian philanthropist brothers, St Damian and St Cosmas, whilst another inscription in the baptistry dates the construction of this room to 591 CE. Slightly further west along the cardo are the remains of a **nymphaeum**

(monumental Roman structure housing a public fountain) attached to a deep subterranean cistern, as well as the remains of a Byzantine **bathhouse**. To the west of here there are few structures worth investigating, though there is a fine view across the Sea of Galilee.

Returning to Route 92, heading south from Kibbutz Ein Gev there are a number of beaches along the shore of the lake, including Shittim, Rotem, and Shizaf. The *Ha'on Holiday Village* (T6757555, F6757557), at 7km south, offers camping (**F**), caravans (**D**) and some basic rooms (**C-D**), though there is little to do here except go to the beach or visit the ostrich farm (0900-1600, closes 1300 on Friday, 15 NIS). Slightly further south on Route 92 a road heads off left to **Kibbutz Tel Katzir** (1km). This was the site of considerable tension between the Israelis and Syrians during the period 1948-67, and a small museum here details life on the kibbutz during this period (call ahead on T6756809).

A further 1.7km south on Route 92, you come to a T-junction. The road left (Route 98) heads down to the excellent attractions at **Hammat Gader** (about 12km south-east, see page 680). The right fork continues around the lake, passing the very attractive (**C-B**) Ma'agan Holiday Village (T6753753, F6753707).

A further 1km brings you to the major intersection at the southern tip of the Sea of Galilee. From **Zemiah Junction,** one branch of Route 90 heads south down the Jordan Valley, passing Belvoir and Bet Shean on its way to Jericho. The other branch of Route 90 continues around the lake, passing **Kibbutz Degania Alef** (2.6km), **Yardenit** (400m), **Kinneret** (**Beth Yerah**), before continuing along the 'home straight' for the 11km back to **Tiberias**. **NB** Traffic along this final section can get quite heavy: cyclists beware.

Zemiah Junction

Located at Zemiah Junction (sometimes 'Tzemah') is the recently built **Beit Gabriel Cultural Centre** (T6751175, F6751187), which hosts performing arts, exhibitions and cultural events. There is also a noted café here. It has also been suggested that any future trilateral peace treaty between Israel, Jordan and Syria would be signed in a special room here (from where all three states are visible).

Kibbutz Degania

Phone code: 06

The two small kibbutzim here, Degania Alef (Degania A) and Degania Bet (Degania B), often simply referred to collectively (no pun intended) as Kibbutz Degania, played a pivotal role in the establishment of the kibbutz system. There are several exhibits here that recall Degania's past.

Ins and outs

The easiest way to get here is on one of the Jerusalem-bound buses from Tiberias that are heading down the Jordan Valley Road (Route 90). Alternatively, irregular buses 015/017/018/019/021/022/024 all pass Kibbutz Degania (about 1 bus every 2 hrs).

History

Most guidebooks claim that Kibbutz Degania was the world's first kibbutz, though this statement is not strictly true; rather, it was the first *kvutza*, the forerunner of the kibbutz system. This collective settlement had its origins in a labour dispute between Jewish agricultural workers in Kinneret and their manager. As a means of resolving the dispute the head of the Palestine Office, Dr Arthur Ruppin (considered by many to have been the great unsung hero of the Zionist colonization movement), gave the green light to what can best be described as "an experiment in self-management" (W. Laqueur, 1989, *A History of Zionism*). In 1905, five agricultural workers from Kinneret signed a contract with the Palestine Office (that administered land bought by the National

Galilee & The Golan

Fund) to farm the land of Um Juni, taking collective responsibility for their success or failure. In 1910 ten men and two women settled permanently on the land that became Degania. As Laqueur notes, "failure at this stage might have had fatal consequences for the development of settlements of this kind" (*ibid*).

Degania struggled through its early years, and it was against the advice of those such as Franz Oppenheimer that Ruppin persevered with the 'experiment', despite the settlement exceeding its budget by 40 percent. Even the members of Degania themselves had no clear idea of the direction in which their movement was heading, with disputes arising over marriage, child care, the role of women, the status of children, to name but a few. There were even members of Degania who wished to move on to a new pioneering settlement once Degania became 'established'.

Yet Degania's relative success became a role model for other collective settlements, perhaps too much so: the fact that Degania started with 12 members was merely an accident, but it became the conventional wisdom that the new settlements should mimic the experience on Degania in every detail, whether it was suitable or not. It was only the arrival of greater numbers of immigrants needing to be absorbed after 1919 that put paid to this dogma of the 12.

Amongst the new arrivals in Palestine from Eastern Europe during 1919-20 were members of the Hashomer Hatzair (Young Watchman). Their view of collective settlement was far more radical than that of the generation that had established Degania, most notably in the education, care and upkeep of children. The family unit was replaced by a system of collective responsibility, with children being educated as a group and even sleeping in a special children's house rather than with their parents. However, whilst Beit Alpha in the Jezreel Valley is really the first true kibbutz (see page 646), Degania is still considered to be the 'mother' of the movement.

Sights Points of interest within Degania Alef's grounds include **Beit Gordon**, a small museum dedicated to the memory of **Aaron David Gordon** (1856-1922, one of the pioneering fathers of the kibbutz system who spent his last days at Degania), containing one wing dedicated to the history of the region and a second wing featuring aspects of Galilee's natural history. ■ *T6750040. Sunday-Thursday 0930-1600, Friday 0830-1200, Saturday 0930-1200. Adult 7 NIS.*

Next door to the museum is the *SPNI Kinneret Field School*, T6752340, where you can get information on hiking in the region. The **tank** standing at the main entrance to the kibbutz is a reminder of the events of the 1948 war (see box on page 705). Degania's **cemetery** is the final resting place of some of the leading Zionists of the late 19th and early 20th centuries, most notably AD Gordon (1856-1922) and Arthur Ruppin (1876-1943).

Sleeping **C-D** *Degania Bet Guesthouse*, T6755758, F6755877, offers B&B accommodation, a/c, kitchenette, plus 'visit to the kibbutz cowshed'.

Yardenit Baptism Site

Phone code: 06 Just to the west of Kibbutz Degania, on land owned by Kibbutz Kinneret, the Jordan River exits the Sea of Galilee. With an eye on the pilgrim dollar, Kibbutz Kinneret have built the **Yardenit Baptism Site**. This is not the site where John the Baptist is reputed to have baptized Jesus (*Matthew 3:13-17; Mark 1:9-11; Luke 3:21-22*); tradition holds that this event occured at al-Maghtes, to the southeast of Jericho. Nor is this a site identified with John's baptisms in the Jordan River (*Matthew 3:1-12; Mark 1:2-8; Luke 3:2-17*). However, with al-Maghtes being on the sensitive border between Israel and Jordan, and thus

Degania's role in the 1948 War of Independence

The major battle that took place at Degania during May 1948 was not just important because it gave the Israelis strategic control of the head of the Jordan Valley: it had a symbolic value that deeply affected the people of the newly emerging Jewish state. As the former President of Israel Chaim Herzog wrote in his book The Arab-Israeli Wars *(1984): "The significance of the victory at Degania lay less in the fact that the main thrust of the Arab invasion in the Jordan Valley area had been blocked than in the electrifying effect it had on the whole of the Jewish population of the newborn State of Israel ... The fact that this first major battle against an invading army was taking place at Degania [the 'mother of the kibbutzim'] was seen in many ways as an omen ... The morale-boosting effect of this success was to be decisive in the desperate days that followed."*

Yet the struggle for Degania was not a conventional battle as most people imagine warfare between two states, though events here repeated themselves at isolated Jewish settlements all across the country. By mid-May 1948, the settlements of Degania A and Degania B had become the front line of Israeli defence against the rapidly advancing Syrian first Brigade. A delegation of settlers from the area had rushed to Tel Aviv to beg Ben-Gurion for arms and reinforcements, only to be told that the whole country was faced with the same situation. All the settlers were able to bring back to Degania was advice from the Haganah's Chief of Operations, General Yigael Yadin, that *"There is no alternative but to let them reach 20 to 30 yards from the gates of Degania and to engage them at point-blank range in close combat"!*

As the Syrian tanks and infantry advanced at dawn on 20th May, under cover of artillery bombardment, the defenders of Degania A numbered just 70 lightly armed men. The Syrians rapidly broke through the settlement's outer defences, and just as it seemed that Degania A would be overrun, the Israelis had the morale-boosting success of stopping the leading Syrian tank in its tracks with a series of Molotov cocktails. The tank still stands at this spot today as a memorial to Degania's defenders. The Syrian forces subsequently withdrew, instead concentrating their attack on Degania B, until the arrival of Israeli artillery on 21st May forced the Syrians into retreat.

being out of bounds to visitors except on one day per year, Yardenit provides a convenient alternative. Though the setting is attractive and steps have been built to make the approach to the water easy, the presence of souvenir shops, snackbars and canoe-hire makes Yardenit just too commercialized for some; what is intended to be a religious experience becomes a day out at the river. Still, thousands come here each year to submerge themselves symbolically in the Jordan River. ■ *T6759111, F6759129. Sunday-Thursday 0800-1800, baptismal service until 1700, Friday 0800-1700, baptismal service until 1600. Changing facilities 5 NIS, or free with towel and white robe rental. Canoe-hire from* Rob Roy, *T6750333.*

Slightly further along the road from Yardenit is the **Kinneret cemetery**, where many of the leading lights of Zionism are buried: Moses Hess (1812-75), Ber Borokhov (1881-1917), Nahman Syrkin (1867-1924), and Berl Katznelson (1887-1944). The popular Hebrew poet Rachel Bluwstein (the "poet Rachel", 1890-1931) is also buried here. The tel (or mound) just above the cemetery to the south is the archaeological site of Beth Yerah.

Located on a low hill just to the north of the Jordan River's present exit from the Sea of Galilee is the site of **Tel Beth Yerah**. Excavation has revealed that the site was occupied in the Early Bronze Age (c. 3300-2200 BCE), and then again

Beth Yerah

Galilee & The Golan

from the Early Hellenistic period until the Early Arab period (c. 332 BCE-638 CE). At this point, the Jordan River flowed out of the Sea of Galilee slightly further north than its present course, with the west side of the mound being formed by the former bed of the river.

There are several identifications associated with Beth Yerah, most notably with Khirbet el-Kerak. The distinctive pottery ware from the Early Bronze Age III (c. 2700-2200 BCE) that was excavated here has given its name, Khirbet Kerak ware, to this style of pottery (typically red and black burnish with incised decoration) now found all across Israel and northern Syria. The site has also been identified with the city of Philoteria built by Ptolemy II Philadelphus (285-246 BCE), and with the town of Sennabris where Vespasian's army camped in 66-67 CE. Beth Yerah is also mentioned frequently in Talmudic sources.

Although excavations have revealed, amongst other things, a large **Roman fort** (60 metres by 60 metres) containing a **synagogue**, a **Roman bathhouse**, a **Byzantine church**, and what appears to be a large **public granary** from the Early Bronze Age III (and referred to as the 'building with circles'), the site is poorly kept with no labelling and next to nothing to see.

Upper Galilee

An increasing number of people are taking the opportunity to explore the regions of Upper Galilee and the Golan (Golan Heights). In addition to some diverse and dramatic scenery, these two regions have a rich history, which is presented in a number of sites that should not be missed. This section of the 'Galilee and Golan' chapter of the Handbook has been divided into two, with separate segments on Upper Galilee and the Golan (see page 741). The attractions in Western Galilee are included in the 'Haifa and the North Coast' chapter.

The highlights of Upper Galilee include the mystical Jewish holy city of Safed, the lush green Hula Valley and Hula Nature Reserve, and the ancient settlement of Tel Dan.

Ins and outs

Getting there and around Despite significant improvements in recent years, accommodation options in Upper Galilee still remain limited, particularly in the budget price bracket. For this reason, many visitors still choose to use Tiberias as a base, touring the region in a series of extended day trips. The majority of towns and sites of Upper Galilee detailed below lie on, or close to, the main highway that heads directly north from the Sea of Galilee (Route 90). Yet, in spite of this, transport is not straightforward. Though there are plenty of buses up and down Route 90, it is more difficult to access the sites not directly on this main highway, and visits to these places may require considerable amounts of walking, plus long waits for transport connections. This in turn means that you cover less ground per day. For this reason, many visitors choose to hire a car in Tiberias; a sensible option, particularly when the expense is shared between a group. That said, don't let these minor obstacles deter you from exploring Upper Galilee.

Safed (Tzfat)

Of the four holy Jewish cities that represent the principal elements of creation –
Jerusalem (fire), Hebron (Earth), Tiberias (water) and Safed (air) – it is Safed
that perhaps has the most appropriate association. At 834 metres it is Israel's
highest city, with the clean air, cooling climate and tranquil atmosphere making
Safed somewhat reminiscent of an Indian hill-station. Many of the visitors to
Safed are religious Jews making a 'pilgrimage' to the spiritual capital of Jewish
mysticism, though the town is equally attractive to the secular and gentile, who
come to admire the views, wander around the narrow streets of the Old City, or
browse amongst the galleries and workshops of the Artists' Colony.

Phone code: 06
Colour map 1, grid B4

Ins and outs

Safed is located just to the northwest of the Sea of Galilee, and though connected by
bus to the coast at Akko and Haifa, it is usually reached from Tiberias. In fact, given its
limited accommodation options it is often visited as a day-trip from Tiberias.

Getting there

It can be a little difficult to orientate yourself when you first arrive in Safed. The centre
of the town is the low hill (834m above sea-level) with the remains of the Citadel
perched on the top. The town's main road, Jerusalem St, runs around the hill in a continuous loop. The Central Bus Station is located at the east base of the hill, with the
suburb of Mt Cana'an (also called Ben-Gurion) further east. The Old Jewish Quarter
cascades down the west side of the hill, towards the various cemeteries. Adjoining the
Old Jewish Quarter to the south is the Artists' Colony, and to the south of here is
Southern Safed. The sights listed below have been grouped by neighbourhood.

Getting around

Safed is a religious city, and visitors must be modestly dressed (no shorts or bare
shoulders, and women are recommended to wear a long skirt as opposed to trousers). Head coverings (cardboard yarmulkes and scarfs) are provided at most sites,
though it may be as well to bring your own. It is requested that you refrain from smoking in the Old Jewish Quarter during Shabbat. Photography is permitted, except on
Shabbat, though it is generally recommended that you seek permission before pho-
tographing people. Visitors to Safed should also note that its relatively high altitude
can make it chilly at night, even in summer, so it may be an idea to bring some light
woollen clothing.

History

Safed has its origins in the Second Temple period (c. 520 BCE-70 CE) as one of
the chain of *masu'ot*, or beacon villages, that spread all across the land from
Jerusalem to Babylonia. This chain of hill-top bonfires was used to announce
the beginning of the new month or religious holidays (the Jewish religious calendar is lunar-solar), as decided by the Sanhedrin at Jerusalem.

Safed's location at 834 metres was also instrumental in Josephus' decision to
fortify the settlement in anticipation of the Roman legions' advance into Galilee (though no reference to the city is made in Josephus' account of the campaign), and in the Crusader choice of the site for a citadel some 1,100 years
later. The Crusader citadel was surrendered to Salah al-Din in 1188, regained
by treaty and rebuilt in 1240, and subsequently surrendered again in 1266, this
time to the Mamluks.

However, it is in the 16th century that Safed really reached its zenith, when
the city became the recognized centre of Jewish mysticism: **kabbalah** (see box
on page 709). Persecution of European Jewry, followed by expulsion from

Safed/Tsfat/Tzfat/Zefat: what's in a name?

It will soon become clear that there are several different ways of transliterating the Hebrew name for the city. The most common spelling amongst those with a mother-tongue of English is 'Safed', though most Israelis transliterate the Hebrew name as 'Tzfat' (including most electronic timetables at the bus stations). However, it is not unusual to see the name written as 'Zefat' or even 'Cfat'.

Pronunciation of the name can also be difficult. It is certainly not 'Saf-ed' as the

'English' spelling suggests. The best tip is to think of a bad wartime movie and imagine a British actor playing a German interrogator, pronouncing the first word of the line "Zwat iz your name?" with a heavy German accent! The word Safed has been translated as "overlook", referring to the fine views from the city, though the root of the Hebrew name is also derived from the word "anticipation": a reflection of the city's Messianic expectation.

Spain in 1492 and uncertainty in North Africa thereafter, saw an influx of Jews into Safed, many of whom were attracted by the growing school of kabbalistic thought emerging from here. **David ben Solomon ibn abi Zimra**, known as Radbaz, was perhaps the first notable mystic to establish himself in Safed, though he was quickly followed by **Moses ben Jacob Cordovero** (1522-70), who is credited with compiling the first systematic codification of the kabbalah. A subsequent arrival from Egypt, **Isaac ben Solomon Luria ('the Ari')**, was the rabbi who turned the kabbalah into a mass movement whilst based in Safed.

The 18th century saw a major influx of Hasidic Jews from eastern Europe, though the 19th century was more catastrophic, with a violent Arab attack in 1834, a devastating earthquake in 1837 that killed up to 5,000, and a sacking by the Druze three years later. The first half of the 20th century was equally violent, with Safed being deeply affected by the nationwide riots of 1929 and the Arab revolt of 1936-39. On both occasions the Old Jewish Quarter was sacked.

Safed was also the scene of a pivotal battle in the 1948 War of Independence. In a surprise move, the **British** forces withdrew from Safed at very short notice one month before the termination of the Mandate. The main military positions in the town – the police fortress on Mt Cana'an, the Citadel, Shalva House, and the police post overlooking the Jewish and Arab quarters – were all taken over by the majority **Arab** population (some 90 percent of Safed's occupants). Realizing that leaving Safed in Arab hands could jeopardize Israeli operations all across Galilee, the commander of the Jewish Palmach, Yigal Allon (a military hero from World War Two, who later went on to hold the civilian posts of Deputy Prime Minister and Foreign Minister), launched 'Operation Yiftah' to capture Safed. Following several failed attacks, by the morning of 10th May, 1948 the Jewish forces had captured all the strategic sites after a series of bloody battles. The entire Arab population fled and Safed has been a **Jewish** city ever since.

Recent years has seen a further influx of Jews into Safed from Ethiopia, eastern Europe, and the former Soviet Union, who now account for around a quarter of the city's population of just over 22,000.

Kabbalah

In the Talmud, the term kabbalah simply means 'received doctrine' or 'tradition', referring to the later books of the Bible (ie after the Torah, or first five books) and the oral teachings. However, the term subsequently came to mean "esoteric teaching, enabling the privileged few either to make direct communication with God or to acquire knowledge of God through non-rational means" (Johnson, A History of the Jews, 1987). The most interesting feature of kabbalah is the code used to unlock these 'secrets'. Kabbalists argue that since the Torah is holy, the words and numbers contained within it must be holy also, and thus once the 'key' could be found, the secret knowledge contained within the text could be unravelled. Each letter and accent of every word in the holy books has a numerical value, with calculations based on these values revealing things such as secret names for God. These 'passwords' in turn facilitate access to the secrets of the universe.

Kabbalah has become 'fashionable' in US showbiz circles in recent years, with Madonna, Sandra Bernhard and Roseanne Barr all expressing a deep interest in the subject (the latter declaring on a recent visit that she felt very Israeli with her "big mouth" and "horribly opinionated nature"!).

Citadel Park (Gan HaMetzuda) area

There are several minor points of interest in and around the Citadel Park area that occupies the hill at the centre of Safed (refer to the map for orientation).

Beit Busel Located at the junction of Jerusalem Street and Ha'Ari, this fine stone building was constructed at the turn of the century as part of a hospital complex established by Scottish missionaries. It is reported that Jews boycotted the hospital for fear of forced baptism, eventually persuading the Jewish financier Baron Rothschild to fund a Jewish hospital in Safed. Following its use by the Turkish army during World War One, the missionaries returned at the end of the war, converting the building into a college of higher education. Again war intervened, with this time the British using the building as their military headquarters. Towards the end of World War Two, the building was purchased by the Jewish Labour Union's Sick Fund ostensibly for use as a hotel, but in reality to act as a base for the Jewish underground. More recently the building has served as an absorption centre for Ethiopian immigrants, though it is currently standing empty.

Safed Regional College These buildings formerly served as part of the Jewish Hadassah Hospital complex (built 1912), but were also used by the Jewish underground for storing weapons and hiding members. This is ironic in the light of the moral outrage that the State of Israel expresses when Palestinians in camps in Lebanon have done the same thing. Opposite the main building of Safed Regional College is the War Memorial Garden that honours Safed's Jewish war dead.

Israel Bible Museum Located on Hativat Yiftah, the road that leads up to the citadel on the summit of the hill, is the Israel Bible Museum. The former residence of the Ottoman governor, the museum houses numerous sculptures and paintings depicting biblical scenes, most notably by the Jewish-American artist **Philip Ratner**, whose work can also be seen on permanent display at the White House, US Supreme Court and the Statue of Liberty. ■ T6973472. *Summer Sunday-Thursday 1000-1800, Saturday 1000-1400, winter Sunday-Thursday 1000-1400. Free*

Galilee & The Golan

Citadel   Though the setting and the view from the top of the hill is impressive, precious little remains of the Citadel. Its foundations are said to be solid and well preserved, but have been hidden from view since the British sealed them off to use as reservoirs for the city's water supply. The first **Crusader** fortress was built here in 1102 and managed to withstand **Salah al-Din**'s siege of 1188, though the garrison eventually agreed to surrender it in exchange for free passage to the coast at Tyre. The Crusaders regained the site by treaty in 1240, with the **French Templars** constructing a formidable new citadel on the hill. It comprised three concentric walls around a central *donjon*, or keep. The outer wall would have roughly followed the line of the current Jerusalem Street, whilst parts of the **second wall** and a **tower** can still be seen close to the Israel Bible Museum. Once again the citadel withstood a lengthy siege, this time by the Mamluk sultan **Baibars** in 1266, though again it had to be surrendered in exchange for safe passage to the coast. It is suggested that Baibars did not keep to his word and slaughtered all but two of the garrison after they had surrendered. Whilst appreciating the view across to Mt Meiron (west), Mt Tabor (south), and the Sea of Galilee (southeast), it is easy to see why this hill-top was used as part of the chain of *masu'ot* (beacon) villages, from which the lighted bonfires announced the beginning of the Jewish month. There is now a small park on the summit of the hill.

British Mandate period police station   There are several former **British police stations** scattered around Safed (including one close to Beit Busel; see page 709), all of which saw a great deal of action in 1948. When the British withdrew from Safed in April of that year, some weeks before the Mandate expired, the police station was handed over to the Arabs; a fact that still rankles with the Jews. It's not easy to look impartially at events surrounding the creation of the State of Israel and Safed's experiences are no exception. The British decision to hand over all the key military installations to the Arabs may have been based on the fact that the Jews comprised just 11 percent of the town's population, making Safed in British eyes an Arab town. This, however, ignores Safed's ancient Jewish history, but perhaps more seriously ignores the fact that advance British intelligence reports warned that the British withdrawal would be a signal for an Arab attack. Safed highlights the dilemma facing the British all across Palestine in 1948. Their offer of safe passage out of the city for the Jewish population was not surprisingly rejected by a community that had existed here for many generations. The building still bears the bullet pock-marks of the subsequent battle. Outside the former police station is a **Davidka**, a homemade mortar used extensively by the Jews during the 1948 War of Independence, that now serves as a war memorial.

    The monumental staircase opposite the police station, **Ma'alot Olei HaGardom**, was built by the British after the riots of 1929 to keep the two communities apart, dividing the Jewish Quarter from the Arab Quarter (the current Artists' Colony area).

Cave of Shem and Ever   Located in the garden behind the bridge that carries HaPalmach over Jerusalem Street (see map), this is the reputed place where Noah's son (**Shem**) and grandson (**Ever**) either: a) studied the Torah (though it was written generations later by Moses!); b) lie buried; c) established a yeshiva where Jacob studied. The cave is holy to Jews, Christians and Muslims alike, with the latter group referring to the cave as the 'Place of Mourning' since they believe that it is here that Jacob learnt of the death of his son Joseph.

The Old Jewish Quarter

The Old Jewish Quarter is the most attractive feature of Safed; a densely packed area of winding streets, narrow alleyways and simple, attractive housing. Its sheer number of synagogues has led some to dub it '**Synagogue Quarter**'. Getting lost is a certainty, though its small size means that you will soon find your way out again. Most pedestrians enter either via the Ma'alot Olei HaGardom staircase, or via the stairs next to the Tourist Information Office.

In the 16th century this location was on the very edge of town, so the synagogue is built on the reputed site where **Ari** and the other Kabbalists used to hold the *Kabbalat Shabbat* service to greet the Sabbath. The original synagogue, built after Ari's death, was destroyed by an earthquake in the mid-19th century, and was subsequently replaced with the building that you see today. The key features of the synagogue include the central *bimah*, or platform, where the Torah is read. The small hole in the *bimah* (facing the door) was

Ari Ashkenazi Synagogue

Old Jewish quarter & artists' colony, Safed

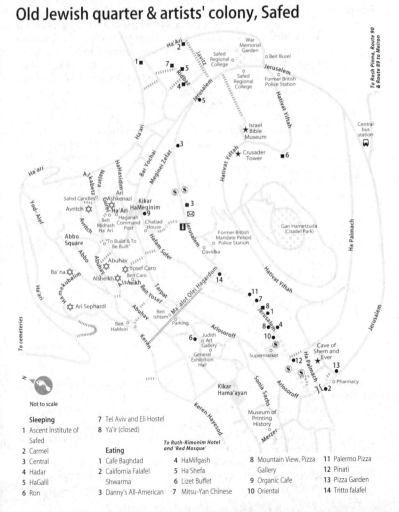

Sleeping
1 Ascent Institute of Safed
2 Carmel
3 Central
4 Hadar
5 HaGalil
6 Ron
7 Tel Aviv and Eli Hostel
8 Ya'ir (closed)

Eating
1 Cafe Baghdad
2 California Falafel Shwarma
3 Danny's All-American
4 HaMifgash
5 Ha Shefa
6 Lizet Buffet
7 Mitsu-Yan Chinese
8 Mountain View, Pizza Gallery
9 Organic Cafe
10 Oriental
11 Palermo Pizza
12 Pinati
13 Pizza Garden
14 Tritto falafel

caused by a piece of flying shrapnel during the 1948 war. Fortuitously, the assembled congregation had their heads bent in prayer at this moment, thus narrowly avoiding any injuries. The 100-year-old hand-carved Ark of the Law is also notable. In a room at the back of the synagogue is 'Elijah's Chair', used during the circumcision ceremony. Legend has it that couples who sit on this chair will produce a baby boy within a year.

Close to the Ari Ashkenazi Synagogue are a couple of buildings of some interest. One of them, marked by a small plaque, served as the **Haganah Command Post** during the 1948 war. The building next door is on the reputed site of the **Beit Midrash Ha'Ari**, where study of the Pentateuch took place during Ari's time, in order to make clear points of law. The **Avritch Synagogue** is also close by (marked by a blue door halfway down a flight of steps, though the synagogue is not open to tourists). In 1840, the Avritch rabbi was instrumental in persuading Sir Moses Montifiore to buy land in the Galilee to establish Jewish agricultural settlements.

Yosef Caro Synagogue This synagogue is located along Beit Yosef, a street lined with art and craft shops and stalls. The Yosef Caro Synagogue has a number of features not usually found in a synagogue, suggesting that its original function was as a house of study (*beit midrash*), as opposed to a house of worship. In particular, the windows are not placed high in the wall as at most synagogues (where they prevent worshippers being distracted by goings-on outside as well as permitting a glimpse up to the heavens). In fact, the first Chief Ashkenazi Rabbi of Israel, Rabbi Kook, went so far as to suggest that this was a welcome feature since it allowed the praying congregation to be brought into contact with their fellow man outside.

The building was restored around 1847 by an Italian Jew by the name of Guetta, following the destruction caused by the earthquake 10 years earlier. The three **Torah scrolls** in the Ark of the Law are of considerable antiquity: the scroll on the left, from Spain, is said to be over 500 years old; the central scroll, from Iraq, is around 300 years old; and the Persian scroll to the left dates from the 18th century.

The nearby **Beit Caro** (Beit Karo) is the recently restored former home of Rabbi Yosef Caro, and probably the place where much of the *Shulhan Arukh* was written. It now serves as an information centre. ◼ *7 Alsheikh, T6921336, F6920852.*

Alsheikh Synagogue This is the only original 16th-century building still standing in Safed (though it is only open to tourists in July and August). **Rabbi Moses Alsheikh** was a student under Yosef Caro and went on to become a leading Torah authority, though he was deemed by the Ari as not being suitable for the study of the Kabbalah. The walls on either side of the street on which the synagogue stands are painted a very attractive shade of light blue; said to suggest the heavens and concentrate your mind on God.

Abuhav Synagogue There are several traditions surrounding the Abuhav Synagogue. One has it that the synagogue was designed in Spain by the 15th-century Spanish rabbi Yitzhak Abuhav, and built in Safed the following century by his followers. Another suggests that it was originally built in Spain, then miraculously moved to Safed when the Jews were expelled *en masse*. It was largely destroyed in the earthquakes of 1759 and 1837.

The synagogue was designed to incorporate a number of Kabbalistic symbols, most notably the four supporting pillars that represent the four elements of creation: fire, water, earth and air. The six steps up to the *bimah* represent

Noted Safed Rabbis

Rabbi Isaac (Yitzhak) ben Solomon Luria: The Ari

The son of an Ashkenazi from east-central Europe, Isaac ben Solomon Luria (1534-72) was brought up by a tax-farmer uncle in Egypt. Though conducting a successful business in spice trading, as a young man Luria was recognized as an expert in orthodox non-mystic halakhah, though he also thoroughly absorbed the kabbalah legends. Just three years before his death he moved to Safed, though the impact that he had there in such a short time was staggering. He was not a prolific writer (there is only one book attributed to him), but his students assiduously memorized his teachings so that they later became a written form. The Lurianic kabbalah message that he spread was, according to Johnson, "a description of how ordinary Jews, by their prayers and piety, could precipitate the Messianic Age" (A History of the Jews, 1987). He was referred to by his followers as the 'Ari'; an acronym of the words "our master Rabbi Isaac (Yitzhak)", but also meaning 'lion' in Hebrew.

Rabbi Yosef Caro (1488-1575)

Born in Spain shortly before the expulsion, Rabbi Yosef Caro spent 32 years of his life compiling the Shulhan Arukh ('The Set Table'); the condensed version of which has become the standard guide on how to live your everyday life according to Jewish law. With Rabbi AlKabetz, Rabbi Yosef Caro helped develop the tradition of studying the Torah all night on Shavuot; the holiday when Jews celebrate the giving of the Torah.

the six days of the week, whilst the ultimate, the Sabbath, is where the Torah is read. The painting of the Dome of the Rock is not just a reminder of the destruction of the Temple, but also a call to tolerance.

The three Arks of the Law stand against the only original 16th-century wall. One of the Torah scrolls in the ark to the right was written by Rabbi Abuhav. The picture of the Western ('Wailing') Wall between the arks has something of the 'Laughing Cavalier' quality about it; from whichever side of the picture you view it, the street at the bottom is always facing you. On the pillar next to the 'Elijah's Chair' is a small plaque commemorating the Holocaust victims.

The Artists' Colony

The 'Artists' Colony' occupies much of the former Arab quarter of Safed. As its current name suggests, this is the area to browse amongst Safed's numerous galleries and studios. The quarter's former mosque now houses the **General Exhibition Hall;** a gallery featuring work by members of the Artists' Colony Association and an information centre.

The **Museum of Printing History** describes the development of Hebrew printing techniques from the arrival of the first printing press in Safed in 1576, until the industry declined in 1834. ■ *Merzer, off Tet-zayin, T6923022. Sunday-Thursday 1000-1200 1600-1800, Friday, Saturday 1000-1200. Free.*

The **Ruth-Rimonim,** currently Safed's top hotel, was built as a station of the postal network linking Cairo to the Euphrates during the Mameluke period. A little further along the same road is a **mausoleum** belonging to a former Mamluk governor of the town. Unfortunately it is in a very poor state of repair. Just beyond, criminally neglected, is the '**Red Mosque**' built by Sultan Baibars c. 1276. Classic Mamluk architecture, the restoration of this building

Galilee & The Golan

should be a major priority. The entrance is generally locked, though there are a few places you can scramble up to from where you get a peek inside the pleasant arched cloisters.

The Cemeteries The tour through Safed's cemeteries begins at the **Beit HaMeiri**, close to the bottom of the Ma'alot Olei HaGardom staircase. Established by a fifth-generation Safed Jew, the museum depicts Jewish life, and its struggles, throughout the last hundred years or so. ■ *T6971307. Sunday-Thursday 0900-1400, Friday 0900-1300. 5 NIS.*

Leaving the museum, turn right, taking the next set of stairs down on the left. A right turn at the bottom leads to the **Ari Sephardi Synagogue**. This synagogue serves the Sephardic community; descendants of the Jews expelled from Spain into North Africa and the Middle East in 1492, and sometimes referred to erroneously as 'Oriental Jews'. The Ari is said to have prayed here to demonstrate the equality of all traditions of worship, and legend suggests that he once studied here with the prophet Elijah. In fact, whilst his father had an Ashkenazi background, the Ari's mother was a Sephardic Jew from Jerusalem, perhaps partially explaining why his teachings were so readily accepted by both communities.

From the steps a path leads down into Safed's **Military Cemetery**. The most notable monument here is the shrine to the seven members of the *Irgun* (IZL: a Jewish underground movement that blurs the line somewhat between 'freedom-fighters' and 'terrorists') who were hanged by the British Mandatory government in Akko Citadel Prison. The monument is designed to resemble a gallows. Just below the platform is the **Grave of Rabbi Leib Ba'al HaYisurim**, a disciple of the first Lubavitcher Rebbe.

A path from the Military Cemetery leads to the **Ancient Cemetery** where many of Safed's Kabbalists are buried. These include the following: Rabbi Isaac (Yitzhak) ben Solomon Luria (the Ari) (whose *mikveh*, or ritual bath is located a little further up the hill); Rabbi Moses ben Jacob Cordovero (1522-70), known as 'Remak', and probably the provider of the first complete and systematic theology of the kabbalah; Rabbi Shlomo AlKabetz, whose hymn *L'cha Dodi* forms part of the *Kabbalat Shabbat*; and Rabbi Yosef Caro.

The domed tomb in the cemetery was built by the Karaites of Damascus, and is said to mark the **grave of the prophet Hosea**. Also buried on the hill, legend tells, is Hannah and her Seven Sons, whose martyrdom is recounted in the *Apocrypha* (two books of the Maccabees). The victims of the terrorist atrocities at Ma'alot in 1974 and Avivim in 1970 are also buried here.

Southern Safed

There are several sites of minor interest in the area of Southern Safed. The **Saraya** was originally built as a caravanserai in the Ottoman period, though it was later used by both the Turks and the British as an administrative building. Members of the Jewish community took refuge here during the riots of 1929. It now serves as the **Wolfson Community Centre**. Nearby is a tall sculpture by Victor Halvani titled 'Chariot of Fire' and depicting Elijah's ascent into heaven (*II Kings 2:11*). Nearby is the **Yigal Allon Theatre and Cultural Centre**, and opposite the **Memorial Museum of Hungarian Speaking Jewry**, featuring artefacts depicting aspects of the life of the Hungarian Jewish community. Also to the south of the town centre is the **Grave of Rabbi Nahum Ish Gamzu**, one-time teacher to the Rabbi Akiva (see Tiberias, page 658). ■ *Memorial Museum of Hungarian Speaking Jewry, T6971222. Sunday-Friday 0900-1300. 5 NIS.*

Essentials

Safed accommodation options are fairly limited, with just one good top-range hotel, several overpriced intermediate hotels, and a good budget hostel that is reserved for Jewish guests only. An alternative to the hotels and hostels are the private guest rooms in flats and apartments around the town. They are generally run by families, and can provide the best value (and sometimes the only) accommodation in the high season. It's best to contact them through the Tourist Information Centre and use ones that are registered there. Alternatively, call ahead, though most don't answer the phone on Shabbat. You may also be approached at the bus station. Don't pay until you have seen the room (then bargain) and be sure of what the deal is with regard to heating and blankets. The official summertime prices are 50 NIS single, 100 NIS double, though these are flexible, particularly in the off season.

Sleeping

■ *on maps;*
price codes
see inside front cover

L2 *Ruth-Rimonim*, Artists' Colony, T6994666, F6920456. Formerly the post house and then caravanserai, and now taken over by the *Howard Johnson* chain, retains the period charm with stone walls and high ceilings but with modern amenities such as a/c, heating, cable TV, pool, *Khan* restaurant. The deluxe rooms (with the best views) are worth the extra $40. Recommended.

B *Central*, Jerusalem St, T6972336, F6972366. Central location with views, but hugely overpriced for quality of room on offer. **B** *Tel Aviv/Eli Hostel*, Berenson House, off Ha'Ari/Ridbaz, T6972382, F6972555. Fine stone building built in 1858 to house the Austrian Consulate, now converted into a functional, though rather overpriced, hotel. A/c, TV, small gym, garden, dining room, breakfast included. The same building also holds the *Eli Hostel*, offering 4-bed dorms (50 NIS per person), or you can have the same room as a double (150 NIS) or a single (100 NIS).

C *Ron*, Hativat Yiftah, T6972590, F6972363. Functional rooms, swimming pool, though on the first occasion I visited the manager was extremely rude, and on the second occasion the service could only be described as 'indifferent' at best. Do you really want to stay at a place like this?

D *Hadar*, Ridbaz, T6920068. Not much English spoken (run by a little old lady), doubles with attached hot bath, good rooftop views, meals not available, old fashioned but very peaceful. **D** *HaGalil*, Ridbaz, T6921247. More basic than nearby *Hadar*, upper rooms with verandah more airy, those in the courtyard rather dingy, pay per bed.

E *Ascent Institute of Safed*, 2 Ha'Ari, T6771407, F6921942. Jews only (secular or otherwise), very attractive and well-run hostel, dorms (4-6 beds), private rooms (**D**), breakfast and free guided walking tours included, check-in 1600-1900, 5 NIS rebate for attending classes on Jewish mysticism, Shabbat dinners, reservations advised. Recommended. **E** *Carmel*, 8 Javitz, T6920053. Appears to be little more than a crash pad for young Jewish men, though it's an attractive building. **E** *Eli Hostel*, see under *Tel Aviv Hotel* in **B** category. **E** *IYHA Beit Binyamin Youth Hostel*, 1 Lohamei HaGeta'ot, near Amal Trade School, South Safed, T6921086, F6973514. Fairly long walk from the Central Bus Station (25 mins, or Bus 6 or 7), reception open 0900-1400 1700-1900, Saturday 1700-1900, dorms (4-6 beds) or private rooms (**D**), clean and well maintained.

Apartment rental and B&Bs *Ephraim family*, T6920221. Very attractive apartment with kitchen, bath, TV, excellent views. *Lifschitz family*, off HaPalmach (see map), T6974710. Another basic, yet friendly, favourite (call ahead). *Maman House*, pedestrianized section of Jerusalem St, T6970477. *Rado family*, T6921276. Very nice

Galilee & The Golan

villa accommodation. *Shoshan family*, T6923144. *Shoshana's apartments*, off HaPalmach (see map), T6973939. Long-term favourite with budget travellers (but call ahead). *Spiers family*, T6974701. Quiet flat in Artists' Colony, with kitchenette and garden.

Eating It is worth remembering that many restaurants close for most of Shabbat (particularly the Friday night), and at others Shabbat meals must be ordered in advance. The pedestrianized section of Jerusalem St (*midrahov*) is the main dining area, though it's largely a diet of falafel and shwarma. Almost all the places here are kosher. There is little in the way of night-time entertainment in Safed, and those after bars and nightclubs should head for Tiberias.

Budget *California Falafel and Shwarma*, 92 Jerusalem St. Probably the best place on the strip to eat this backpacker staple. There is a **supermarket** in the mall next to the Bank HaPoalim (opposite HaMifgash restaurant) on Jerusalem St (open Sunday-Thursday 0900-2000, Friday 0700-1400).

Café/bars *Mountain View*, Jerusalem St. Nice views, diet- and wallet-busting cakes (20 NIS), pasta 32 NIS, St Peter's Fish 55 NIS, salads 40 NIS, coffee 9-14 NIS. There are numerous other cafés offering light meals on the pedestrianized section of Jerusalem St.

Jewish (traditional) *HaMifgash*, 75 Jerusalem St, T6974734. Stands out as a continually recommended spot, with snacks and large portions of home-cooking style dinners, plus a wine cellar. Recommended. *HaShefa*, 23 Jerusalem St, T6920184 and *Eshel*, corner of Jerusalem St/Bar Yochai, T6920948, are two family-style restaurants that are recommended by Safed residents for their home-cooking. *Pinati*, 81 Jerusalem St, T6920855. One of the few places open on Shabbat, the walls are dominated by Elvis posters but there's not a cheeseburger in sight; goulash is the speciality.

Vegetarian *Café Baghdad*, Jerusalem St. Dairy vegetarian, blintzes, pizza, salads.

Entertainment **Art galleries** There are more art galleries in Safed than you can shake a paint brush at. Unsurprisingly, they're located in the Artists' Colony. A former mosque now houses the **General Exhibition Hall**, T6920087 (open Sunday-Thursday 0900-1700, Friday 0900-1400, Saturday 1000-1400), and a permanent exhibition of work. The staff here can direct you to the galleries of members of the Artists' Colony Association, or you could just wander in this area. Artists here work in mediums such as oils, water colours, copper relief, ceramics, woodcuts, pen and ink, bronze, etc. There's some beautiful items, but some real rubbish also. **Other** For details of theatres and concert halls, see under 'Cultural centres' on page 717.

Festivals There are two annual festivals in Safed that should not be missed if possible (though accommodation becomes near impossible and there are major traffic jams in and out of the city). **Lag b'Omer** (usually May-June) is possibly Israel's best-attended annual event, with several hundred thousand Jews making the pilgrimage from Safed to Rabbi Shimon bar Yochai's grave at nearby Meiron, where they dance with the Torah scrolls (see page 718). **Klezmer Festival**, held in July or August, attracts thousands for a series of concerts of Eastern European Jewish soul music. Accommodation in Safed is scarce during both events (though you could always commute from Tiberias).

Shopping **Books** *Greenbaum's Books*, Jerusalem St, has some good Safed references, most notably Yisrael Shalem's excellent *Safed: Six Self-Guided Tours In and Around the Mystical City*. 1991 (30 NIS). **Other** *Safed Candles*, Najara, near Ashkenazi Ari synagogue, T6921093, F6922557. Offers tours of its workshop and sells its famous (in

Safed) beeswax candles (Sunday-Thursday 0830-1800, Friday 0830-1300). *Jerusalem Wind Chimes*, Sonya Sachs, Artists' Colony, T6920867.

Swimming *Blue Valley Pool and Leisure Centre*, off Jabotinsky (downhill from bus station, on left) T6920217 offers a pool and other facilities. *Heated Indoor Pool*, New Industrial Zone, T6974294, has indoor pool, sauna and steam room, tennis courts. **Sports**

Air The nearest airport is the **Machanayim Airfield** at Rosh Pinna, just to the east (T6935302). *Arkia* offer flights here from Tel Aviv, Haifa and Jerusalem. **Long-distance buses** Central Bus Station, Ha'Atzma'ut Sq, T6921122 (toilets, cafeteria). **Akko**: Bus 362 via Karmi'el, every hour, Sunday-Thursday 0700-2045, last on Friday 1700, first on Saturday 2100, 45 mins, 20 NIS. **Alma** (and Rehania): Bus 045, 0845, 1315, 1600, 12 NIS. **Bar'am**: Bus 043, 0645 1230 1700, 13 NIS. **Haifa**: Buses 361/362 via Karmi'el, every 1 hr, Sunday-Thursday 0700-2045, last on Friday 1700, first on Saturday 2100, 1 hr, 26 NIS. **Jerusalem**: Bus 964 via Tiberias and Jordan Valley, 0700, 3½ hrs, 50 NIS, or go to Rosh Pinna for more regular services. **Kiryat Shemona**: Bus 501/511 via Rosh Pinna, every 2 hrs. **Meiron**: Bus 361/362 (see Haifa), every hour, Sunday-Thursday 0700-2045, last on Friday 1700, first on Saturday 2100, 10 NIS. **Rosh Pinna**: All Tiberias and Kiryat Shemona buses go through Rosh Pinna, from where some transport connections are better. **Sasa**: Bus 043 (see Bar'am). **Tel Aviv**: Bus 846 express via Karmi'el and coast road, 3 per day, or go to Haifa for more regular service. **Tiberias**: Bus 459, Sunday-Thursday hourly until 1900, Friday last around 1500, Saturday first around 1700, 1 hr, 18 NIS. **Sherut** *Edan Hasa'ot*, T6989536, offers shared taxis service to Jerusalem, Ben-Gurion Airport, B'nei Brak. **Transport**

Banks *Bank Leumi*, 33 Jerusalem St. *Bank HaPoalim*, 72 Jerusalem St. *Israel Discount*, 83 Jerusalem St (open Sun Tue Thu 0830-1230 1600-1800, Mon Wed 0830-1230, Fri 0830-1200). *First International*, 34 Jerusalem St (open Sun Tue Thu 0800-1400, Mon Wed 0800-1400 1600-1900, Fri 0830-1200). All offer foreign exchange (check rates and commission), as does Central Post Office (see below). **Directory**

Communications Phone code: T06. **NB** Safed numbers are 7-digit. If you have an old 6-digit number try prefacing it with a '6'. *Post offices*: Central Post Office, HeHalutz (look for communications tower to southwest of town), T6920405, offers poste restante and commission-free foreign exchange; there is also a more convenient *branch post office* at 37 Jerusalem St (both open Sun Mon Tue Thu 0800-1230 1530-1800, Wed 0800-1330, Fri 0800-1200).

Cultural centres *Yigal Allon Theatre and Cultural Centre*, HeHalutz, near Kikar Ha'Atzma'ut, T6971990. Features theatre, concerts, cinema (Sat night). *Wolfson Community Centre*, HaPalmach, T6971222. The former Turkish khan, hosts concerts. *Ascent Institute*, 2 Ha'Ari, T6771407, F6921942, www.ascent.org.il Offers English language lectures on Kabbalah and Hasidism. *Pardes Rimonim Institute for Tzefat Heritage in Halacha and Kabbala*, T6972946. Features lectures and study programmes on Judaism and Safed's Jewish heritage. *Machon Alte*, 33 Jerusalem St, T6974306, F6921412. An academic programme for "young Jewish women seeking to discover and establish their Jewish roots". *To Build and To Be Built*, Avritch, T6970311, F6921848, www.livnot.org.il An English-medium study programme that features community service and restoration work in Safed's Old Jewish Quarter.

Hospitals and medical services *Rebecca Ziev Hospital*, Henrietta Szold, Ammami, T6978811.

Tour companies and travel agents An organized guided tour of Safed is a good investment, and probably the best way to appreciate fully all the city's attractions. *Aviva Minoff*, T6920901, F6973116, mobile 050-409187, leads tours of Safed daily, meeting at the Tourist Information Centre or Rimon Inn at 0930 (30 NIS per person, 2-3 hrs). This tour also leaves from Tiberias. A highly recommended aid to your tour of Safed is Yisrael Shalem's *Safed: Six Self-Guided Tours In and Around the Mystical City* (1991). It should be available from most branches of *Steimatsky's*,

Galilee & The Golan

Greenbaum's Books on the pedestrianized section of Jerusalem St (*midrahov*), the *Central Hotel* reception desk, or the author himself at Sprinzak 329/27, Safed 13351, T6971870 (price 30 NIS).

Tourist offices *Tourist Information Office*, City Hall, 50 Jerusalem St, T6920961. Can help arrange accommodation, and may give you a map, but that's about it (Sun-Thu 0800-1600, Fri 0800-1200). *Beit Caro*, 7 Alsheikh, T6921336, F6920852. Former home of Rabbi Yosef Caro, now serves as an information centre offering guided tours and greater insight into kabbalah. *Luba Pinson Chabad House*, Hafam Sofer, also acts as an informal tourist information centre, particularly for those interested in kabbalah.

Useful addresses and phone numbers Police: T100 (emergency), T6920444. **First Aid**: T101 (emergency), Magen David Adom, near Central Bus Station, T6920333.

Around Safed

Safed to Meiron There are several minor points of interest on the road west from Safed to Meiron (Route 89). Shortly after leaving Safed you pass on your left a small white dome. This is the **tomb of Rabbi Yehuda bar Ilai**, one of the spiritual leaders of the Jewish people following the Roman response to the Bar Kokhba Revolt (132-135 CE) whose work led to the re-establishment of the Sanhedrin. The tomb nearby is that of **Rabbi Yossi Saragossi**, one of the 16th-century CE rabbis whose presence in Safed led to it becoming such a major centre of Jewish learning.

Route 89 continues west, passing the former Jewish settlement of Ein Zeitim, abandoned since the Arab riots of 1929. Route 886 (to Alma and Rehania, see page 725) heads north from Ein Zeitim Junction here, passing the Ein Zeitim recreation park. Continuing west on Route 89, the large red sculpture on the top of the hill to your right (north) is the **Armoured Corps Memorial**; a war memorial to the tank brigade that formed up here in preparation for the assault on the Golan Heights in the 1967 war. Just beyond this point, on the left (south), a marked path leads off towards the Nahal Ammud Nature Reserve. There are a number of attractive hikes through here, most notably a leg on the Yam L'Yam (Mediterranean to Sea of Galilee) three-day hike. The main entrance to the Nature Reserve is actually off Route 866, south of Moshav Meiron, and details are included below. Route 89 continues on to the T-junction opposite Meiron. Route 89 bears right (north) to Jish, Sasa, Bar'am and Avivim, whilst the road left (south) heads via Nahal Ammud Nature Reserve towards Karmi'el and the coast.

Meiron (Meron)

Standing on the eastern foothills of Mt Meiron, this small Orthodox Jewish settlement lies close to the site of an ancient Jewish settlement that flourished during the third to fourth century CE. Parts of the lower city have been excavated, as has a splendid synagogue from this period. However, most visitors to Meiron come as pilgrims, to visit the graves of a number of important rabbis who are buried here.

Ins and outs

Getting there Buses 361/362 between Safed and Haifa, (every 1 hrs, Sunday-Thursday 0700-2045, last on Friday 1700, first on Saturday 2100, 10 NIS) pass Meiron. The less regular Bus 043 from Safed also stops at Meiron. See colour map 1 for orientation.

History

Excavations at Meiron suggest that settlement here dates to the Late Hellenistic period (167-37 CE), though it is not until the two major Jewish revolts against Rome (66-73 CE and 132-135 CE) were concluded that the village expanded significantly, to the size of a town. The settlement of Khirbet Shema' (known as Tekoa of Galilee) just to the south probably formed one of the suburbs of Meiron. There are many references to Meiron in rabbinic sources, generally connected with the ministry of **Rabbi Shimon bar Yochai**. Meiron reached its peak during the third and fourth centuries CE when it was a noted centre of olive oil production, though the town's economic orientation was probably to the north, towards the port at Tyre. Meiron was seemingly abandoned in 363 CE following the devastating earthquake of that year, though a process of systematic abandonment seems to have preceded this catastrophe in response to harsh taxes imposed under the Roman Emperor Constantius II (337-361 CE).

It was not until the late medieval period that occupation of Meiron began again in earnest, following the publication of the *Sefer-ha-Zofar*, or *Zohar*. Compiled by the leading Spanish kabbalist **Moses ben Shem Tov of Guadalajara** in the 1280s, this treatise on kabbalistic lore contained many of the sayings and teachings of Rabbi Shimon bar Yochai and his colleagues, and led to a revival in interest in the second century CE sage. In fact, it is not uncommon to still find claims that the *Zohar* was written by bar Yochai. His grave at Meiron subsequently became a major centre of pilgrimage, and was also a deciding factor in the decision of the leading kabbalist thinkers to settle in nearby Safed.

Sights

Rabbi Shimon bar Yochai was one of the leading Jewish opinion-makers during the period immediately following the Roman crushing of the Bar Kokhba Revolt (132-135 CE). In fact, his vocal opposition to Roman rule led to a death warrant being issued against him, and he was forced to seek refuge for 12 years in a cave in the village of Peki'in, on the western side of Mt Meiron). This period of contemplation resulted in the series of teachings that found their way into print over 1,100 years later, in the form of the *Zohar*: the central text of kabbalah. Each year his death is commemorated on the holiday of *Lag b'Omer*, when hundreds of thousands of Jews from all over the world congregate at the tomb for three days of celebrations. A procession carrying the Torah scrolls dances its way from Safed to Meiron, and though it becomes packed with people and cars, this is an excellent time to visit Meiron. It is also traditional for three-year-old boys to have their first haircut at Meiron during *Lag b'Omer*, in the style specified by *Leviticus 19:27*: "Ye shall not round the corners of your heads, neither shalt thou mar the corners of thy beard". Bar Yochai's son Ele'azar, who also hid for 12 years in the cave at Peki'in, is also buried here.

Tomb of Rabbi Shimon bar Yochai

Leaving bar Yochai's tomb and turning right, a path leads down to the burial cave of **Rabbi Hillel the Elder**. A famous teacher during the first century CE, Hillel preached a message of humility and humanity that later found an outlet in the teachings of Jesus; in fact some scholars believe that Jesus may have been a pupil of Rabbi Hillel (Johnson, *A History of the Jews*, 1987). Hillel's more humane and universalistic interpretation of the Torah is perhaps best summarized in Johnson's assessment that to Hillel "the essence of the Torah was its spirit; if you get the spirit right, the detail could take care of itself" (*ibid*). This is

Tomb of Rabbi Hillel the Elder

in direct contrast to the rigorous orthodoxy preached by Hillel's comtemporary, Rabbi Shammai the Elder, who is reputedly buried nearby (see Khirbet Shema', below).

Lower city Two major insulae, or settlement-blocks, from the settlement at Meiron have been excavated, located on either side of the dirt track leading from the car-park. On the east (right) side of the road lies a well preserved section of the **lower city**. Of particular interest is the former two-storey building, which served as a **cooperage** during Meiron's peak (c. 250-363 CE). This was a major centre of olive oil production, and Josephus describes how his rival, John of Gischala (see nearby 'Jish/Gush Halav', page 724), cornered the market in this trade, making an eight-fold profit on the supplies he appropriated. The barrels produced in the cooperage would almost certainly have been used in this trade. A *mikveh*, or ritual bath, was also discovered in the courtyard here, linked to an elaborate system of rock-cut cisterns. There is also evidence of a sophisticated sewerage system serving the settlement.

On the opposite (west) side of the dirt track excavations have revealed several finely constructed houses that suggest that this was the wealthy or upper class district of the town. One house, labelled the '**Patrician House**' by the excavators, is particularly well built and contains a number of interesting features. The room in the northwest corner of the house had no visible means of access (except perhaps a trap-door in the roof). A number of finds from this room included storage jars containing food remains (nuts, wheat, barley and beans) that had been charred so as to make them inedible. One jar was inscribed with the words "fire" and another with "belonging to Julia [or Julian]". Nearby was found a small bell minus its clapper and a handle-less sickle. It has been speculated that the room was used as a repository by the pious family occupying the house, with these items found here being consecrated offerings. All had been deliberately rendered unusable. The '**Lintel House**' just to the east shares its foundations with the 'Patrician House', and is noted for its fine lintel above the door in the north wall.

Synagogue Little of the late third century CE **synagogue** remains, it becoming a victim of the 363 CE earthquake less than a hundred years after it was built. Most of the façade is reasonably well preserved. A tradition based on mysticism and numerology claims that the collapse of this gate will herald the Messianic era; perhaps the reason why the visitors on *Lag b'Omer* stomp and dance so vigorously! Stylistically, the synagogue is very different to the one just one kilometre away at Khirbet Shema' (see below).

Khirbet Shema' (Tekoa of Galilee)

Excavations suggest that this site was settled mainly between the mid-second and early fifth centuries CE, and it is most likely that it developed from a suburb of Meiron into an isolated village. Its most notable features are the synagogue and the mausoleum. It has been identified as **Tekoa** (of Galilee, as distinct from the ancient settlement of the same name in the Judean Desert, close to Chariton).

Ins and outs The small settlement at Khirbet Shema' on the foothills of Mt Meiron is separated from Meiron, 1km to the north, by the Nahal Meiron. To reach the site walk from Meiron along Route 866 (towards Karmi'el), and then take the steep uphill path to the right (west) at the first hairpin bend in the road.

The ancient **synagogue** at Khirbet Shema' has a number of interesting features, not least of which is the fact that several aspects of its construction seem to contradict *halachah* (Jewish religious law). Whether this is deliberate or just a reflection of the nature of the terrain dictating a number of constraints on the construction is not clear. For example, it is not built on the highest point of the settlement, as was the custom, but was in fact entered through a number of steps leading down into the sanctuary. Further, it is located unusually close to the mausoleum and a number of rock-cut caves, the latter of which would almost certainly have been used for burial. It appears that the builders have gone to great lengths, however, to make sure that the synagogue is orientated towards Jerusalem. The remains that you see today represent two distinct phases of construction, though exact dating is uncertain. It is assumed that the *mikveh* (ritual bath) beneath the northeast corner pre-dates the synagogue and was built some time after 180 CE. The first phase of the synagogue was destroyed by an earthquake in 306 CE and though the second phase began shortly afterwards, it is not certain when exactly. It is known, however, that the second phase synagogue was damaged by the earthquake of 363 CE and destroyed by another earthquake in 419 CE. Though the latter phase synagogue appears to have had the addition of a *bema* (raised platform), it is thought that the worsening socio-economic conditions in the area led to the decline in the quality of workmanship of the later synagogue.

Synagogue

Excavation of the mausoleum has produced next to no evidence to indicate for whom it was built, or indeed when it was built, though some circumstantial evidence suggests the fourth century CE. However, since medieval times, it has been venerated as the **Tomb of Rabbi Shammai the Elder**. This creates a certain amount of symmetry since Shammai's great rival, Hillel the Elder, is reputedly buried on the opposite hillside in Meiron. Whilst Hillel preached humility and humanity and was renowned for his gentle demeanour, Shammai is portrayed as an impatient man who did not suffer fools gladly and who preached a rigorous interpretation of the law. Johnson suggests that this rigorism, particularly when concerned with matters of cleanliness and ritual purity, "militated strongly against the ability of ordinary, poor people to achieve holiness", and may explain why the Shammai school took "his decendants and followers out of the rabbinical-Judaic tradition altogether, and they vanished like the Sadducees themselves" (Johnson, *A History of the Jews*, 1987). On the hillside above the tomb is the **Messiah's Chair/Rock**; traditionally the site where the Messiah will sit whilst the prophet Elijah announces the arrival with a blast on the trumpet.

Mausoleum

Mount Meiron

The peak of Mount (Har) Meiron is just to the west of the village of that name, and at 1,208 metres it is the highest mountain in the Galilee. Much of the mountain lies within the Har Meiron Reserve and there are a number of hikes of various lengths that can be made in this area.

Ins and outs

From Safed take the early Bus 043 to Kibbutz Sasa (departs 0645 1230 1700, returns 0750 1350 1805, 10 NIS). From Kibbutz Sasa, where the bus terminates, follow the signs to the left for 1km and then take the road to the right for 1km up to the Mt Meiron Field Study Centre (T6980023). You can get advice on the hikes here as well as a copy of the (Hebrew only) trail map of the area (44 NIS).

Getting there

Galilee & The Golan

Getting around The sh ortest hike is the Summit Trail, which follows red-and-white trail markers around the summit of Mt Meiron. The steep path leading up from Meiron village can take you there. You must stick to the trail since the top of the mountain itself is a closed military area. The best, though longest, hike takes in much of the Har Meiron range, though if you do not want to complete the entire 18km hike it is possible just to walk certain sections. The starting point for both hikes listed below is the Mt Meiron Field Study Centre, close to Kibbutz Sasa (to the northwest of Meiron).

Har Meiron Reserve hike This eight-hour, 18-kilometre hike begins at the parking lot behind the **Mt Meiron Field Study Centre (1)**. Follow the black-and-white trail markers heading southeast from the parking lot. This is part of a hiking route that stretches from Mt Hermon to Eilat! The trail leads to the look-out point on **Har Nerriya (2)**, from where there are fine views to the north and northeast. Continuing northeast, passing the small Iron Age look-out tower at the beginning of the forest, the trail soon meets up with the red-and-white Summit Trail around **Mt Meiron (3)**. Follow the trail in a clockwise direction around the summit, past the **Lebanon (4)** and then **Safed (5)** look-out points. The trail descends towards the picnic area, then follows the paved road towards Har bar Yochai. Follow the road until a trail marked blue-and-white heads off to the right. Continue along the blue-and-white trail (ignoring the green-and-white trail that heads off towards the Druze settlement of Beit Jann), passing through **Khirbet Bek (6)**. This former Druze village (Germak) was later selected as the site of a Jewish settlement, following the destruction of most of Safed in the 1837 earthquake. The settlement only lasted four years. The blue-and-white trail continues west, reaching a wadi and dirt road that cross the trail after one kilometre. If you follow the dirt road down to the left you will come across one of the best examples of the **karst sink-holes (7)** that are a feature of this region. This landscape is created by the process of carbonic acid eroding the limestone, creating spectacular and unusual rock formations. It is claimed that the Druze residents of Germak used to dispose of Ottoman tax collectors down this particular hole!

Returning to the blue-and-white trail, and following it down through the forest, you pass the first of a number of ancient wine presses. Eventually you

Har Meiron Reserve hikes

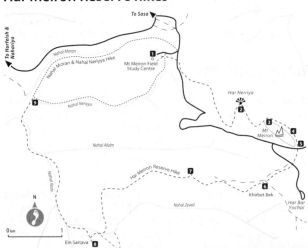

reach the Nahal Zeved, where you turn right towards the bed of the Nahal Keziv. Cross to the west bank of the Nahal Keziv towards the spring at **Ein Sartava** (**8**). The trail heads northwest along the course of the Nahal Keziv, following black-and-white trail markers. As the river bed becomes narrower (after about two kilometres), continue along the east bank. You soon come to a point where the route of the Har Meiron Reserve hike intersects with the final leg of the Nahal Moran and Nahal Neriyya hike (see below) (**9**). Follow the green-and-white trail to the right (east), and then join the red-and-white trail that heads east along the course of the Nahal Neriyya. After three kilometres of walking through pleasant shady forest, the trail hits the road just below the Mt Meiron Field Study Centre.

This shorter, four-hour hike begins at the turn-off to the **Mt Meiron Field Study Centre** (**1**). The trail marked green-and-white heads off northwest, then west, into the forest, before following the course of the Nahal Moran along its south bank. This is a particularly pleasant route, most notably in spring when the flowers are in bloom. Look out especially for the marjoram plant and wild garlic. The trail eventually begins to bear southwest and then meets up with the final section of the **Har Meiron Reserve hike** (**9**). Turn left (east) and follow the red-and-white trail along Nahal Neriyya through this lovely forest. After three kilometres the trail hits the road just below the Mt Meiron Field Study Centre.

Nahal Moran and Nahal Neriyya hike

This pleasant, easy-going hike begins 2.5 kilometres south of Meiron on Route 866 (that heads towards Karmi'el). There is the option of a four-kilometre loop that leads you back to where you started, or a five-kilometre trail leading all the way to Safed. There is also the far longer alternative of following the course of the Nahal Ammud all the way down to the Sea of Galilee (20 kilometres or more).

South of Meiron on Route 866 an orange sign indicates **Nahal Ammud Nature Reserve** to the left (east) (**1**). Follow the track across the cattle-grid and through the forest to the **parking lot** (**2**). From here follow the red-and-white trail along the water-pipe for 500 metres, as far as the **former British police station** (**3**). The station was built to protect the pumping station at **Ein Yakim** (*Arabic*: Ein a Tina) below (**4**). Follow the path down to the pumping station and then proceed along the trail that follows the water carrier along the south bank of the Nahal Meron. After 100 metres cross the stream over the bridge to the north bank, re-crossing the stream again shortly afterwards. Slightly further on a **tributary** joins from the north (**5**). Follow the blue-and-white trail markers in a southerly direction along the east bank of the stream. At the next bridge over the stream you meet the **trail junction** (**6**). The

Nahal Ammud Nature Reserve

Upper Nahal Ammud hike

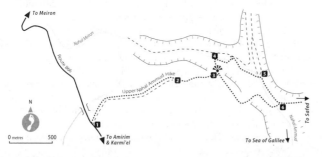

easterly route heads towards Safed, emerging close to the cemeteries. The black-and-white trail heads south along the course of the Nahal Ammud all the way to the Sea of Galilee. Many hikers continue a short distance along the black-and-white trail as far as the flour mill and the Sekhvee pools. This makes an ideal spot for a dip on a hot day. To return back to the starting point on the loop trail, head west from the trail intersection, following the black-and-white trail across the Nahal Ammud alongside the water channel as far as Tahunet el-Batan, the old wool factory. From here the trail leads you back to the deserted police station, and then back to the start point.

Amirim

Phone code: T06

The moshav at **Amirim**, located some five kilometres south of Meiron along Route 866, represents an unusual living experience. Seventeen different families here offer **B-C** price category lodgings focused on 'back-to-nature' in a very tranquil setting. All 300 members of the moshav are vegetarians, and there are six veggie restaurants from which to choose. For further details call T6989571.

Jish/Gush Halav

The settlement of Jish, some four kilometres north of Meiron along Route 89, is mentioned in ancient texts as the site of the city of **Gush Halav**, transliterated into Greek as **Gischala**. The *Mishnah* refers to Gush Halav as one of Joshua's fortified cities, though more is known about the settlement from the early Roman period when the town was fortified in preparation of the Roman advance (Josephus, *Jewish War, II, 575*). Though **Josephus**, as Governor of Galilee, was responsible for preparing many of the defences against the Romans in the north, it was his great rival **John of Gischala** who built the defences here. John was later to survive the Roman conquest of Jerusalem, though he ended up as a chained prisoner in Titus' victory parade. This did not stop Josephus from doing a complete hatchet job on John, describing him as "the most unprincipled trickster that ever won ill fame by such vicious habits … a ready liar and clever at winning the trust of his victims, he made a virtue of deceit and practised it on his closest friends, and while parading his humanity was prepared to murder anyone for his money" (*Jewish War, II, 585-587*)! Jerome was later to claim that Gush Halav was the home town of Paul's parents, though his suspect grasp of the geography of the Holy Land means that this assertion should be treated with extreme caution. Gush Halav was famed for its silk and olive oil production, and like Meiron saw most of its trade linking it with Tyre to the northwest.

The main attraction at Jish/Gush Halav is the remains of the **ancient synagogue**. Archaeologists are unable precisely to place the date of construction, though it is now widely assumed that there were four main phases of construction (250-306 CE; 306-63 CE; 363-460 CE; 460-550 CE). Those familiar with the history of the Galilee will note that the final dates of at least two phases (306 and 363 CE) coincide with the dates of two major earthquakes that hit the region. Further, the date of the synagogue's destruction is just one year before the devastating earthquake of 551 CE, suggesting that the building was destroyed in one of the shocks that preceded the major quake. Construction techniques employed, most notably the particularly strong foundations at the four corners, suggest that the builders knew that Gush Halav was located on the fault line of the Safed epicentre but were still unable to build a structure that could completely withstand the tremors. It is still possible to make out the ground plan of the synagogue today, the most unusual features of which are the two storage rooms to the east of the main hall and the long corridor along the west side.

Also of note in Jish/Gush Halav is the **mausoleum**, with its well-built ante-chamber at the entrance to the rock-cut burial cave. It is part of the huge Gush Halav necropolis of the Mishnaic and Talmudic period. To reach Jish/Gush Halav take Bus 043 from Safed (see page 717 for details).

Bar'am synagogues

The synagogues at Bar'am are located about 2km north of Hiram Junction (Route 89 meets Route 899), and about 1km south of Moshav Dorev (and not at Kibbutz Bar'am slightly further north). Take Bus 043 from Safed (see page 717 for details). **Ins and outs**

The remains of the two **synagogues** at the site of the former third-century CE Jewish settlement of Bar'am suggest that in its day this must have been a wealthy and flourishing community. Though little remains of the **small synagogue** (it was described in some detail in the 16th, and again in the 19th centuries CE, and decorative parts of it can be seen in the Louvre in Paris), the **large synagogue** is in a particularly fine state of repair and gives some idea of how the similar Galilean synagogues at Capernaum and Chorazin must have looked at their peak. **The site**

The most notable feature is its much-photographed façade, largely intact. Facing south towards Jerusalem, like its contemporaries at Capernaum and Chorazin it has a large central doorway flanked by two smaller entrances. The lintel of the central doorway featured the figure of a winged Nike bearing a wreath, though at some stage it has been deliberately defaced. A frieze above the lintel features a twisting vine branch above which is a cornice and an arched window. The sill of the east window of the façade has a Hebrew inscription that reads "Built by El'eazar son of Yudan", though the exact dating of the synagogue is unsure. Several medieval visitors ascribed the synagogue to the second century CE Rabbi Shimon bar Yochai (see 'Meiron' on page 718), though this is far from certain.

The unique feature of the synagogue is the porch that ran the length of the façade. The porch was supported by six columns at the front and one on either side between the corner column and the building. A triangular pediment with an arch at the centre almost certainly rested above the porch. The interior of the synagogue is divided into a nave and two narrow aisles by a U-shaped row of 14 columns, with a floor paved using heavy flagstones. A number of sections of the decorative frieze have also been discovered. The building remains close to the synagogue belong to a former Maronite Christian village abandoned in 1948.

Alma Cave

One of the few attractions in the area around Safed that does not involve a visit to an ancient synagogue is a trip down into the **Alma Cave**. What it does involve is getting very wet, muddy and sweaty. The cave is part of the chain of caverns and tunnels that have been carved out of the chalk and limestone by the sustained processes of chemical and physical erosion. The trip involves a steep descent (slide) into the subterranean chambers, followed by several hours of walking and crawling through narrow, muddy passages up to 100 metres below the surface. The tour finishes with a steep and slippery climb back up to the surface.

Obviously, there are a number of safety precautions that should be borne in mind. 1) You should never attempt this alone (three is a good number to have in your party); 2) You should inform somebody of your plans, including what time you expect to return, and should make sure that you 'check-in' with them when you have completed the trip; 3) You should be confident that you are not going to freak out at the prospect of being in a small, dark, muddy tunnel 100 metres below ground for several hours; 4) One reliable torch per person is the minimum (head-torches are ideal); 5) Bring drinking water, but not much else; 6) Do not deviate from the marked trail (white leads you in, red leads you out); 7) Do not leave any litter, or touch the stalagmites and stalactites; 8) You will have to be reasonably fit and supple – the climb out is particularly challenging when you're tired; 9) You will get very, very muddy.

Tour The cave is located between the villages of **Alma** and **Rehania**, to the north of Safed. Take Bus 045 from Safed (0845 1315 1600, returning at 0915 1345 1630, 12 NIS) and get off at the entrance to Rehania. The path to the caves can be a little tricky to find (ask around). You head along the dirt paths opposite the entrance to Rehania village (some of them disappear) for about 1.5 kilometres until you come to a large rock with a crack down the centre. The white markers lead you down into the hole in the ground at its base. Slide down the slope, keeping to the right. About halfway down the slope, two large rock columns mark the entrance to the cave complex. Follow the white trail markers in and don't lose sight of them. Towards the end of the trip the caverns are full of stunning stalagmite and stalactite formations. (An old English joke explains the difference: tites/'tights' come down). The subsequent climb out is steep, slippery and quite tiring (though the metal hand-rails assist your progress).

North of Safed

The majority of sites in Upper Galilee lie either on, or very close to, the main Route 90 road that heads due north from the Sea of Galilee, all the way to Metulla on the Lebanese border.

Rosh Pinna

Rosh Pinna is one of the oldest settlements established in Palestine in the 19th century by the Zionist pioneers. It has a number of reminders from its past, some appealing restaurants, as well as being an important transport junction.

Ins and outs Rosh Pinna stands as an important transport junction on Route 90 between Tiberias (27km) and Metulla (38km), and Route 89 that heads west to Safed (5km) and on to the coast at Akko. Rosh Pinna is on the bus route between Tel Aviv and Kiryat Shemona (Bus 842), Haifa and Kiryat Shemona (Bus 500), Tiberias and Safed (Bus 459/964), with further connections to Katzrin (55/56/57) and Kiryat Shemona (480/500/501/511/842/845/969/998). Note that most of these buses will drop you at the roundabout at the bottom of the hill that leads to the old part of town, as well as calling at the modern bus terminal. The Machanayim Airfield at Rosh Pinna (T6935302) has Arkia flights here to and from Tel Aviv, Haifa and Jerusalem.

History The original settlement here of Gai Oni was founded by religious Jews from Safed in 1878, though their project aimed at Torah study combined with agricultural work collapsed just three years later. The land was subsequently sold to Romanian Jews escaping persecution in Europe and renamed 'Rosh Pinna'; 'cornerstone' in Hebrew. This settlement too would have floundered were it not for financial support from the Jewish philanthropist **Baron Edmond de Rothschild**.

Though there is not a great deal to see, the **Rosh Pinna Pioneer Settlement Site** (T6936603), just up the hill from the modern town, has preserved a number of original buildings, most notably the **Schwartz Hotel** and the **synagogue**. Staff at the Old Rosh Pinna office, next to the 'Baron's Stables' pub on Ha'Elyon Street, may be able to give more information, or show you around.

Sights

A *Sea View Hotel and Health Farm*, Route 89, T6937014, F6937191. Very comfortable accommodation, particularly in the new wing, specializes in 1-week breaks that are designed to get you back into shape via special diet, massage, shiatsu, etc, no smoking, veg food only. Restaurant recommended. **E** *IYHA Rosh Pinna /Nature Friends Youth Hostel*, HeHalutzim, T6937086. Dorms (4-6 beds), plus private rooms (**D**), breakfast included, very clean and very quiet. There are a number of attractive pubs and restaurants on Ha'Elyon Street in the old part of town, as well as fast food places in the modern bus terminal.

Sleeping and eating

Hazor

The ancient 'tel' (mound) of Hazor is the largest and most important archaeological site in Upper Galilee, though it is not necessarily the most visually impressive.

Ins and outs

Tel Hazor is located 7km north of Rosh Pinna. Note that the turning left into the site is particularly tight, and located right on the bend. Buses 501/511 between Safed and Kiryat Shemona, and buses 840/841/963/998 between Tiberias and Kiryat Shemona stop at the entrance to Kibbutz Ayelet HaShahar, 500m north of the site on Route 90.

Getting there

The fact that there are at least 21 separate strata of occupation has necessitated some considerable detective work on the part of the site's excavators in determining the historical sequence of Hazor, and consequently the site may be somewhat confusing to visitors. However, site-plans and labels attempt to bring some order to the chaos, and for those with an interest in archaeology, Hazor is certainly worth some time. The site comprises two main areas, the upper city and the lower city, though only the former is open to the public. The tour of Hazor begins at the ticket office. The site is divided into lettered areas (eg. 'Area A', 'Area L'), as designated by the archaeologists who made the excavations.

Getting around

It is highly recommended that you visit the museum at Kibbutz Ayelet HaShahar (500m further north) that features finds from the site (see page 730).

Tel Hazor

A-M: excavation areas

0 metres   200

History

The first recorded reference to Hazor is in the Egyptian Execration texts of the 19th to 18th centuries BCE, though excavations here have revealed evidence of occupation by the Khirbet Kerak culture of the 29th-28th centuries BCE. It was in the **18th century BCE** that Hazor reached its first peak, when the large lower city was founded. Why the city expanded so rapidly at this point is

Galilee & The Golan

still not clear, though it is obvious that Hazor must have experienced a sudden and dramatic influx of settlers (up to 30,000) who could not be accommodated in the upper city. Hazor's position on the great *Via Maris* trade route between Babylon and Egypt explains the city's importance, as attested to in the city lists of pharaoh Thutmose III's conquered cities, and the city lists of Amenhotep II and Seti I.

During the Late Bronze period (c. 1550-1200 BCE) Hazor was repeatedly destroyed and rebuilt, though its peak was undoubtedly in the **14th century BCE**, when it was the largest city in the whole of Canaan. Documents from this period, most notably the '**el-Amarna letters**', suggest that the king of Hazor was one of the few Canaanite rulers who was justified in proclaiming himself 'king'. A major conflagration destroyed Hazor in the mid-13th century BCE; an event evidenced in both archaeological and written sources. The thick layer of ash in stratum XIII of both the upper and lower cities is a result of the conquest of Hazor by the **Israelites**, described in vivid detail in the *Book of Joshua* (*11:10-13*). The special emphasis in this passage on the burning of Hazor suggests the importance of this Canaanite city.

The Israelite rebuilding of Hazor was not immediate, with most remains from the 12th and 11th centuries BCE suggesting a limited, perhaps semi-nomadic settlement of the site. However, in the mid-10th century BCE **Solomon** used some of the levy of "six score talents of gold" sent from Hiram, king of Tyre, to rebuild Hazor along with Megiddo and Gezer (*I Kings 9:14-15*). The Solomonic city was considerably smaller than Canaanite Hazor, occupying perhaps just the western half of the upper city area. **Omri** (c. 882-871 BCE) and **Ahab** (871-852 BCE) both considerably expanded Hazor, though still within the confines of the upper city mound. In 732 BCE Hazor was captured and destroyed by the Assyrian king **Tiglath-pileser III** (*II Kings 15:29*), and with very few minor exceptions has been unoccupied ever since.

Sights

Lower city   As mentioned earlier, only the upper city is open to visitors, though some mention should first be made of the **lower city**. The conclusion of the initial excavation of the lower city by Garstang (1928) was that it was merely an enclosure or camping ground for the infantry and chariotry, as opposed to a permanent dwelling area. However, subsequent excavations have revealed the true picture. Five strata of permanent occupation (18th century BCE; 17th-16th century BCE; 15th century BCE; 14th century BCE; 13th century BCE) have been identified across the entire area. The lower city covers somewhere in the region of 170 acres and is clearly defined on all four sides. To the south a **deep fosse** (ditch) separates it from the upper city, whilst to the west there is a **great earthen rampart** with a brick core, protected by another deep fosse. The earthen rampart (alone) continues around the north side, whilst the east side is protected by a **steep slope** reinforced with a **high wall and glacis**. Some notable features of the lower city include: the **temples** located in Area H, the **city gates** in Area K, and the **graves** in Area F.

Area G   Most of Area G comprises fortifications built by the kings Omri and Ahab (9th century BCE) and the defences hurriedly prepared in the face of Tiglath-pileser III's attack (732 BCE). The former include the **casement wall** (**1**) and **towers** (**2**) and the **small postern gate** (**3**) that led down into the lower city. This was later filled in with mud-brick during preparations for the Assyrian king's final assault. A further **defensive wall** (**4**) provided greater security. The **glacis and fosse** (**5**) below are part of the original 18th century BCE fortifications.

'Area G', Hazor

1 Casement wall   3 Postern gate   5 18th century
2 Tower   4 Defensive wall   BCE fosse

'Area A', Hazor

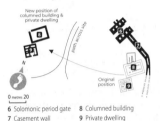

6 Solomonic period gate   8 Columned building
7 Casement wall   9 Private dwelling

Continuing west along the mound of **Area A** the upper city, to the left of the trees is Area A. Because so many levels are superimposed upon each other here, it can be fairly confusing. However, in order to make the picture clearer some of the buildings excavated here have been physically removed to a new position some 60 metres to the west. Still visible here are the foundations of the **Solomonic period city gate (6)** (10th century BCE). Visitors to Megiddo will immediately recognize the plan. Parts of the **casement wall (7)** to which it was attached are still visible. The gate was built over the site of the entrance to a Late Canaanite period temple, which confuses the plan somewhat, though a diagram of the two structures on the sign-board here clarifies their respective positions. A raised platform provides a good viewing point.

Within the confines of the casement wall, to the south of the Solomonic period gate, were excavated the two buildings that have subsequently been moved 60 metres to the west across the main path. The diagram of Area A shows their position *in situ*. The fine **columned building (8)** is in fact a storehouse dating to the Omrid period (9th century BCE) and was probably destroyed during the earthquake in Jeroboam II's reign (784-48 BCE). The adjacent building served as **private dwelling (9)** from the same period. Some inscriptions found on various sherds have even provided the names of some of the occupants of this dwelling.

'Area L', Hazor

10 4-roomed house   Not to scale
11 Entrance structure   13 Tunnel
12 Vertical shaft   14 Underground pool

Continuing west along the mound **Area L** you reach Area L, the later city's **water-supply system**. This is one of the most exciting discoveries made at Hazor, with the **four-roomed house (10)**, **entrance structure (11)**, **vertical shaft (12)** and tunnel taking a full year to excavate. Clues to the source of the city's water-supply were suggested by the large dip in the ground on the south side of the tel, opposite the point at the foot of the mound where the Wadi Waqqas springs were located. However, it was not until the system was fully excavated that the technical ability of the engineers became apparent. A four-room building stood at the entrance to the shaft. Steps have been built to allow visitors to descend into the complex, though the original access was via two ramps of crushed limestone and then a series of five flights of rock-cut steps. The shaft is 30 metres deep, with the top half supported by retaining walls (still visible) and the lower section hewn directly from the rock. A 25-metre-long, 4-metre-high vaulted tunnel slopes down gently to the **underground pool (14)**. The genius of the engineers is that they dug the tunnel into the aquifer itself, rather than the

Galilee & The Golan

springs, thus saving the need to dig an additional 75 metres through the rock, and thereby managing to enclose the water-source within the mound itself (unlike Megiddo). The entire complex is dated to the period of king Ahab (871-852 BCE).

Area B Most of the western end of the mound, Area B, is occupied by the **large citadel** (**19**) built in the early ninth century BCE. The preserved plan that is visible from the raised viewpoint is of the lower level cellars, and, though the staircase to the upper storeys has remained intact, the upper levels themselves have not survived. The **buildings** (**15**) to the north side probably had some administrative function and were divided from the citadel by an open area with a **monumental entrance** (**16**). Parts of the Solomonic casement walls can be seen, though at a later date sections have been filled in to form a **solid wall** (**18**). The citadel was destroyed by Tiglath-pileser III. ■ *T6937290. Daily 0800-1600. Adult 14 NIS, same ticket for museum at Kibbutz Ayelet HaShahar.*

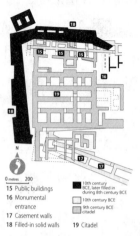

'Area B', Hazor

0 metres 200

15 Public buildings
16 Monumental entrance
17 Casement walls
18 Filled-in solid walls

10th century BCE, later filled in during 8th century BCE
10th century BCE
9th century BCE citadel

19 Citadel

Kibbutz Ayelet HaShahar

Phone code: 06

A large number of finds from the site at Hazor, plus copies of pieces that have been removed to the major museums in Jerusalem and Tel Aviv, are on display at the small **Hazor Museum** just inside the entrance gate to Kibbutz Ayelet HaShahar. The displays are well presented and superbly labelled, and will increase your understanding of the site at Hazor by 200 percent. ■ *T6934855. Daily 1000-1600. Adult 14 NIS, same ticket for Hazor National Park.*

Sleeping and eating

C *Hotel Ayelet HaShahar*, Kibbutz Ayelet HaShahar, T6932611. Very attractive setting, good facilities including pool, tennis, TV room, dining hall, breakfast included. Recommended.

Hula Nature Reserve

Phone code: 06
Colour map 1, grid A5

The Hula Nature Reserve (Huleh) is one of the last remaining areas of natural wilderness in the north of the country, and serves as a fitting reminder of how much of Palestine must have looked when the early Zionist pioneers arrived in the late 19th century. The marshland and swamps that formerly occupied most of the Mediterranean coast have long since been drained, as has all of the Hula Valley bar this small pocket. Declared a protected area in 1964, the Hula Nature Reserve is a delightful place to visit. In fact, this is still a nice reserve to visit even if you manage to miss all the wildlife (early morning is best).

Ins and outs

Getting there

Around 6km north of Tel Hazor along Route 60 a road is sign-posted right (east) to HaHula. Buses 441/500/501/502/511/842/845/846/963/998 all stop at this turn off.

Follow the road for 2km until you come to the fork; left for Hula Nature Reserve and right 750m for Dubrovin Farm.

A Visitors' Centre introduces you to the flora and fauna before a 1.5km marked trail leads you through the reserve. Sections of the walk, dubbed the 'swamp trail', are along a raised wooden walkway through the heart of the swamp's papyrus thickets. It's not unusual to come across furry critters (all harmless) sharing the path with you. A covered section extends out over the lake, providing an excellent 'hide' from which to observe the bird-life. A high observation tower further along the trail fulfils a similar function.

Getting around

Background

The Palestinian (Jerusalem) Talmud describes seven ancient seas that surround the Land of Israel. Included amongst these is the '**Sea of Hula**' (Lake Semechonitis); a reference to the huge body of water that once occupied the Hula Valley roughly between the modern day settlements of Kiryat Shemona and Rosh Pinna. The Hula Valley is in fact part of the Upper Jordan Valley. Some 20,000 years ago a basalt spill from the Golan Heights blocked the valley to the south, creating the huge lake that became known as the 'Sea of Hula'. Eventually the excess of water cut a narrow passage through the basalt allowing the flow of water south into the Sea of Galilee, though a large body of water remained on the surface here.

By the turn of this century this swamp and marshland covered somewhere in the region of 6,000 hectares, representing an almost untouched wetlands ecosystem. However, draining the swamps became a priority for the Jewish settlers who arrived in Palestine in the late 19th and early 20th centuries. Though several schemes were drawn up they were rejected for a variety of reasons by both the Ottomans, and then the British. The reasons for wanting to drain the Hula Valley were twofold; in addition to the desire to employ the land for agricultural purposes, there was also a pressing need to eliminate the malaria that was endemic in the swamps. Cynics may argue that there was also a political motive behind this programme; an agriculturally productive Hula Valley would show how the newly founded Jewish state "cared" for the land, "rescuing" it from the neglected state perpetuated by the ambivalence of its previous occupants. Three years after Israel became independent, the Jewish National Fund implemented a massive eight-year programme to drain the Hula Valley.

In terms of eradicating malaria and establishing productive agricultural land, the drainage programme was remarkably successful. However, there was a high price to pay. Many migratory birds ceased nesting and feeding here, and some such as the darter have never returned. Several mammal species moved out altogether, whilst others 'invaded' in disastrous numbers. The same process also occurred in the plant world. Even the small pocket of the 'Sea of Hula' that scientists and conservationists had managed to exempt from the drainage programme was affected as fertilizers and pesticides from the agricultural sector seeped into the reserve, whilst over-use of water resources caused sections to dry up.

Fearing the total disappearance of this unique wetlands ecosystem, the remaining area was declared a protected reserve in 1964 (the first in Israel) and a long-term management plan was drawn up. New pools connected by a network of drainage channels were constructed, and constant monitoring of water levels and quality was introduced. To help finance the programme the reserve was opened to tourists in 1978. To the relief of the scientists and

Galilee & The Golan

conservationists many, though not all, of the migratory birds have returned. Unfortunately, the battle does not appear to be over. There is still talk of building a tourist hotel and water-sports centre on or close to the reserve's lake. If built, the consequences do not bear thinking about.

The inherent dynamism of the ecosystem means that nature is not static, so it is foolish to suggest that the original form of the 'Sea of Hula' has been 'recreated' here. However, the Hula Nature Reserve has been a remarkable exercise in conservation (as opposed to 'preservation'): long may it continue. ■ *T6937069. Daily 0800-1700, no admission after 1600. Adult 14 NIS. Visitors' Centre, snack-bar, toilets, picnic area.*

Dubrovin farm Located just to the southeast of the Hula Nature Reserve is Dubrovin farm; a reconstruction of an early 20th-century agricultural estate. This particular farm was established in 1904 by the Christian **Dubrovin** family from Russia who converted to Judaism and moved to the Holy Land. The small museum in the farmhouse tells the Dubrovin family's story and displays many of the agricultural implements that they used. Presentation is aided by a short audio-visual programme, whilst the *Farmyard Restaurant*, T6934495 (run independently), receives very good reviews. Entrance to the museum is deducted from the price of the main course. Expect to pay around $30 for three courses (reservations recommended, credit cards). ■ *T6937371. Sunday-Thursday 0900-1700, Friday 0900-1500. Adult 12 NIS.*

Hula Nature Reserve to Kiryat Shemona: alternative route Route 90 continues due north along the Hula Valley to Kiryat Shemona (14 kilometres). However, those with their own transport may like to make a short diversion along a road that runs parallel to Route 90, just to the west. At **Koah Junction**, six kilometres north of the turning to Hula Nature Reserve, turn left on to Route 899. The road climbs steeply for 4.2 kilometres to Yesha' Junction where you turn sharp right into the car-park of the military base. This is the **Nebi Yusha Fortress** (*Hebrew*: Metzudat Koach) located on the strategic heights of the Hills of Naftali. During the 1948 war in the prelude to the operation to capture Safed, attacks on the Arab held Nebi Yusha Fortress by both the Palmach and Haganah were repulsed with heavy loss of life. The fortress was finally captured by the 'Yiftach' Palmach Brigade under Colonel 'Mula' Cohen on the night of 16th May, and was subsequently used in the defence of the

Hula Nature Reserve

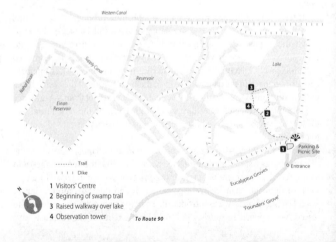

```
Western Canal
Supply Canal
Nahal Einan
Einan Reservoir
Reservoir
Lake
3
4          2
1  Parking & Picnic Site
Entrance
Eucalyptus Groves
'Founders' Grove'
To Route 90
```

········ Trail
ı ı ı ı Dike

1 Visitors' Centre
2 Beginning of swamp trail
3 Raised walkway over lake
4 Observation tower

Galilee 'finger'. A path leads round behind the current IDF base to a war memorial, and though there is not a great deal to see here the viewpoint down to the Hula Valley is superb.

Continuing west along Route 899, after 700 metres take the road to your right, heading due north (Route 886). You are now running parallel to the Lebanese border to the west and to Route 90 to the east. At Margaliot (14 kilometres) you come to the former site of the Crusader fortress of **Chateauneuf**, built in 1107 by Hugh of St Omer. The fortress has subsequently been destroyed and rebuilt a number of times, and most of what you see today dates from the Mamluk period.

Having passed Margaliot, take the winding road down to the right (sign-posted 'Kiryat Shemona', 'Metulla', 'Tel Hai'). This is Route 9977, though it is shown on some maps as a continuation of Route 886. As it continues down to the junction with Route 90 (just to the north of Kiryat Shemona) it passes several places of interest, including Kibbutz Kfar Gil'adi, with its Beit Hashomer Museum, and then the settlement of Tel Hai.

The **Beit Hashomer Museum** was established at Kfar Gil'adi to tell the story of the '*Hashomer*'; an organization of 'watchmen' or 'guardians' whose purpose was the defence of the early Jewish pioneers who were settling in remote places all across Palestine. Its members comprised refugees from pogroms in Russia and eastern Europe who formed the Second Aliyah (mass immigration) of Jews into Palestine at the turn of the century. The Hashomer evolved from the clandestine Bar-Giora organization founded in Jaffa in 1907, though its roots were in the self-defence associations founded in eastern Europe. Many members of the Hashomer were instrumental in founding the Haganah, the forerunner of the Israeli army (IDF). The museum at Kibbutz Kfar Gil'adi has an interesting collection of exhibits, though not all are labelled in English. Make sure that you pick up the free explanatory brochure. ■ *T6941565. Sunday-Thursday 0800-1200 1400-1600, Friday 0830-1200. Free.*

Kibbutz Kfar Gil'adi

Sleeping and eating **B-C** *Kibbutz Kfar Gil'adi Guesthouse*, T6941414, F6951248, features a/c rooms, kosher dining hall, pool, tennis.

Tel Hai

Following the withdrawal of the British from the region towards the end of the First World War, the military outpost of Tel Hai sitting on the low promontory just above the Hula Valley, along with the settlements at Kfar Gil'adi and Metulla, seemingly lapsed into the sphere of control of French-administered Syria and Lebanon. In 1920 a group of Arab farmers gathered here to protest that the Jewish settlers were aiding and abetting the French in expropriating their land. There are several versions of what happened next. One version tells how the leader of Tel Hai, **Yosef Trumpeldor,** allowed a delegation of Arabs inside the compound at Tel Hai to search for French agents, only for them to turn on the settlers, killing eight. A second version suggests that the Arabs simply over-ran Tel Hai, killing six men and two women, Trumpeldor included. Whatever the truth of events, Trumpeldor's alleged last words, "It is good to die for your country", became a rallying cry of the early Zionists. The eight victims (whose sacrifice is commemorated at the nearby town of Kiryat Shemona, or 'Town of Eight' in Hebrew) are buried in the military cemetery just up the road from the hostel. A statue of the 'Lion of Judah', a nickname for Trumpeldor, inscribed with his last words looks down into the Hula Valley. The settler's original tower and stockade has been turned into a small **museum** telling the story of

Phone code: 06
Colour map 1, grid A5

Galilee & The Golan

Tel Hai and Yosef Trumpeldor. ■ *T6951333. Sunday-Thursday 0800-1600, Friday 0800-1300, Saturday 0900-1400. 8 NIS. Buses 20/21/23 run the three kilometres from Kiryat Shemona to Tel Hai.*

A further attraction in the Tel Hai Industrial Park, opposite Tel Hai on the east side of Route 90, is the **Museum of Photography**, featuring some excellent temporary exhibitions from Israel and around the world**.** *T6950769. Sunday-Thursday 0900-1600, Friday closed, Saturday 1000-1700. Adult 10 NIS).*

Sleeping and   **E** *IYHA Tel Hai Youth Hostel*, T6940043, F6941743. Located 300m up the road to Tel
eating   Hai from Route 90, features 6-bed dorms, a/c, breakfast included, check-in 1600-1900, check-out 0900, reservations recommended in summer.

Kiryat Shemona

Though Kiryat Shemona (spelt with any combination of the words Kiryat, Qiryat, Shemona, Shmona, Shmonah) is a relatively obscure town, with no real attractions or places of interest, many people who have never even visited Israel appear to have heard of it. Kiryat Shemona's fame, or infamy, is a direct by-product of its position close to the border with Lebanon. No doubt this small town of around 20,000 people would prefer to be referred to as the gateway to Upper Galilee and the Golan, with its administrative and transport functions, though most visitors only know it by its troubled past.

Ins and outs   Kiryat Shemona stands at a major crossroads. Immediately north Route 99 heads east (then northeast) via Horshat Tal National Park and Tel Dan (see page 738) into the Golan Heights (see page 741). Continuing north from Kiryat Shemona on Route 90 leads to Nahal Ayoun Nature Reserve (4km), and then to Metulla (right) and the 'Good Fence' (left).

Buses run to Kiryat Shemona from all the major cities, though they're often packed to bursting point with young soldiers.

History   During the 1970s, 1980s, and indeed the 1990s, the town has been a victim of persistent **terrorist attacks**. In 1974, Palestinian terrorists infiltrating from Lebanon murdered 18 Israeli civilians here. Attacks in subsequent years generally came in the form of *katyusha* rockets fired from southern Lebanon (so much so that the town became nicknamed Kiryat Katyusha!). The prolonged attacks of 1981, when Kiryat Shemona was bombed for 12 days solid, caused 80 percent of the population to flee and resulted in the establishment here of a pioneering Community Stress Prevention Centre. Such rocket attacks were Israel's justification for launching its bloody invasion of southern Lebanon in 1982 ('Operation Peace for Galilee'), though as many commentators point out early 1982 was one of the quietest years for cross-border rocket attacks.

More recent Hizbollah rocket attacks nearby led to the Israeli 'Operation Grapes of Wrath' offensive in Lebanon that culminated in the massacre at the UN camp at Qana in early 1996. The subsequent US-brokered ceasefire understanding has introduced new rules of engagement in which Hizbollah can only attack Israeli troops in occupied southern Lebanon, whilst Israel is only allowed to bomb guerrilla positions, so in theory Kiryat Shemona should remain safe.

Sleeping   **C** *North Hotel*, Tel Hai Blvd, opposite Bus Station, T6944705. Modern a/c rooms, TV, phone, though a little expensive.

Transport   **Air** Kiryat Shemona's airport has limited *Arkia* flights to **Haifa**, **Jerusalem** and **Tel**

Yosef Trumpeldor (1880-1920)

Yosef Trumpeldor was an extraordinary character. Born in Russia in 1880, he lost an arm serving in the Czar's army during the Russo-Japanese war and was subsequently decorated for gallantry by the Russian empress. A committed Zionist, Trumpeldor believed that young Jewish pioneers should receive training in the diaspora in preparation for a life of manual work in Palestine. His experiences upon his arrival in Palestine in 1912 convinced him even more that advance preparation was essential, and the conversations that he had with Jabotinsky during the First World War led to the formation of such an organization, Hehalutz, in Russia towards the end of the war.

Despite his handicap, Trumpeldor served the Allies with distinction during the First World War, helping in the creation of several specifically Jewish units including the Zion Mule Corps and three battalions of the Royal Fusiliers (38th, London East End; 39th, American volunteers; 40th, drawn from the Yishuv). Amongst the places where he saw action was the disastrous Allied landings at Gallipoli. Following the war he helped to establish the settlement at Tel Hai, as well as being instrumental in the formation of his pre-war pet project, the Gdud Ha'avoda or 'Legion of Labour'. Tragically, Trumpeldor was killed before the 'Legion of Labour' officially came into being, and though it only survived for six years it was at the vanguard of the pioneer movement. Thus, Trumpeldor fully deserves his place in the annals of Labour Zionism.

Aviv, T6959901. **Buses** The Central Bus Station is on the main road, Tel Hai Blvd, T6940740. Because bus travel in Upper Galilee and Golan is limited, check departure and return times carefully. **Banias**: Bus 055 goes closest, 2 per day, 11 NIS. **Hazor**: take a Tel Aviv, Tiberias, Rosh Pinna or Safed bus. **Horshat Tal**: Buses 026/027/036 run infrequently, 8 NIS. **Katzrin**: Bus 055 runs twice a day in a long loop via Upper Golan, 22 NIS. **Metulla**: Bus 020, 8 per day, 7 NIS. **Neve Ativ**: Bus 014, but only 1 per day. **Nimrod's Fortress**: Buses 055 and 014 pass within 1 hr walking distance! **Rosh Pinna**: take a Tiberias or Tel Aviv bus. **Safed**: Bus 501/502, every 2 hrs, or change at Rosh Pinna. **Tel Aviv**: Buses 840/841/842/845, hourly, 42 NIS. **Tel Dan**: Buses 026/035, limited service, 8 NIS. **Tel Hai**: Buses 20/2123, 8 per day, 4 NIS. **Tiberias**: Buses 840/841/963/998 head via Rosh Pinna, regular, 19 NIS.

Most of Kiryat Shemona's other 'necessities', such as post office, **restaurants**, **supermarkets**, **banks** are located in the area just south of the Central Bus Station. The shopping mall here even has a fully equipped bomb shelter! **Directory**

Kibbutz Kfar Blum, about five kilometres southeast of Kiryat Shemona, was established by members of a Zionist youth movement, *Habonim*, that was founded in London's East End in the early 1930s and later spread to like-minded communities in Sweden and Holland as well as other English-speaking countries. The (C) *Kibbutz Kfar Blum Guesthouse*, T6836666, F6836600, offers 109 attractive rooms with good service and facilities including pool, sauna, tennis, playground. Its position on the Jordan River means that there is opportunity for bird-watching, fishing and **kayak hire** ■ *T6902616, F6948440, daily 0900-1700 April-October).* **Kibbutz Kfar Blum** *Phone code: 06*

Nahal Ayoun Nature Reserve

The Nahal Ayoun Nature Reserve provides the opportunity for a very pleasant two- to three-hour walk along the course of the Ayoun Valley. Though there is lush green vegetation all year round, the reserve comes into its own out of the

Galilee & The Golan

summer season when the full streams produce a number of spectacular waterfalls. The area is teeming with bird life and you may be lucky enough to spot kingfishers, wallcreepers, long-tailed wagtails, rock doves and kestrels (winter and spring are best for bird-watching).

Ins and outs There are 2 entrances to the reserve: one just off Route 90 some 4km north of Kiryat Shemona, and one just to the southeast of Metulla (see page 736). The once-hourly (8 per day) Bus 020 from Kiryat Shemona to Metulla can drop you at the southern trailhead, or in Metulla town itself from where the northern trailhead is a short sign-posted walk. Alternatively, you can walk to the southern trailhead from Kiryat Shemona. The brief route description here follows a south to north course.

South to north hike A 10-minute walk from the southern entrance to the reserve brings you to the 30-metre-high **Tanur Falls**. This is the reserve's best known landmark, with some sources referring to the park as the Tanur Nature Reserve. The name is a corruption of 'Tabor', the chimney-like oven that Arab peasants used to use, and the falls are said to resemble. A different school of thought suggests that the falls resemble the long skirt, 'Tanura', that Arab women wear. The falls are a spectacular sight when gushing but rather an anti-climax in summer when bone dry.

Crossing to the west bank of the river you can see how the canyon begins to narrow. There are several waterfalls along this section with the two biggest examples, the **Cascade Falls** at 10 and 5 metres respectively, being about one hour's walk away. Continuing north you come to an old flour mill at the base of the 21-metre-high **Mill Falls**. The mill was purchased early in this century by Baron Edmond de Rothschild and continued serving the local Jewish settlers until it was abandoned following the fighting at Tel Hai in 1920 (see page 733).

The path continues north along the course of the Nahal Ayoun, crossing several times depending upon the season until reaching **Ayoun Falls**. The wall built by the British above the nine-metre falls was used to create a reservoir that could supply the troops based here. There is a camping and picnic ground at the northern entrance to the reserve, from where it is possible to continue on foot to Metulla (though this isn't much good if you have parked your car at the southern entrance). ■ T6951519. Daily 0800-1600. Adult 8 NIS.

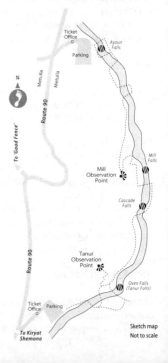

Nahal Ayoun Nature Reserve

Ticket Office

Ayoun Falls

Parking

Metulla

Metulla

Route 90

N

To 'Good Fence'

Mill Falls

Mill Observation Point

Cascade Falls

Tanur Observation Point

Oven Falls (Tanur Falls)

Route 90

Ticket Office Parking

To Kiryat Shemona

Sketch map
Not to scale

Metulla

Phone code: 06
Colour map 1, grid A4

Israel's most northerly town (though 'large village' may be a more apt description), Metulla was one of the string of settlements that Jewish pioneers established in Upper Galilee at the end of the last century. Like so

Galilee & The Golan

many others, it owed its continued existence to financial support from Baron Edmond de Rothschild. Sometimes referred to as 'Israel's Little Switzerland', it is best known today for the 'Good Fence' just to the west of town.

Ins and outs

The town of Metulla itself is rather attractive. Though little more than one main street (HaRishonim), it features some very pleasant hotels and pensions and is a very relaxing place to unwind. Bus 020 runs to and from Kiryat Shemona 8 times per day (7 NIS).

The 'Good Fence'

This is merely a border crossing point between Lebanon and Israel that an excellent PR job has somehow turned into a tourist attraction (*Hebrew*: HaGader HaTova). It takes its name from the fact that villagers from southern Lebanon are allowed to pass through in order to seek free medical services in Israel, as well as visiting relatives and commuting to jobs in the Galilee. It has also been reported that this only applies to Christians and Druze, and not Muslims, so perhaps the 'Partially Good Fence' would be a better description. There's not a great deal to see at the border bar lots of barbed wire, some entwined Lebanese and Israeli flags, and lines from Isaiah about "beating swords into plough-shares". There are several snack bars and falafel stands that will also sell you some Lebanese currency if you wish. Photography does not appear to be a problem here.

Canada Centre

Those with excess energy to burn should head for the Canada Centre (*T6950370, F6950970*), one of the best sports centres in the country. It features Israel's best skating rink, a pool plus slides, Jacuzzi, sauna, gym, shooting range (*T6951514, daily 1000-1900*), squash (*12 NIS per hour*) and table-tennis (*8 NIS per 45 minutes*). Admission (*adult 35 NIS, student 24 NIS*) includes skate-hire and free use of most facilities (*daily 1000-2200*). The *Galileo* restaurant (*T6950112*) on the top floor serves some excellent, healthy Italian food and is probably the best place in town to eat.

Sleeping and eating

Although there are only 4 or so 'proper' hotels in Metulla, there are at least 50 guest houses ('zimmers'), with almost every house having a 'rooms for rent' sign outside. For a full listing either consult the information centre at the Municipality (T6941364, Sunday-Thursday 0900-1600), or pick up the latest 'Israel Tourism Guide': Galilee brochure from any main tourist office. Most of the hotels and zimmers can provide meals, although there are half-a-dozen café/restaurants in the town centre. **B** *Sheleg HaLevanon*, T6997111, F6997118. A very nice hotel with well-furnished rooms, attractive dining area and facilities including tennis, pool, children's pool. **C** *Cohen Galila*, T6997349. In very quiet side road opposite *Sheleg HaLevanon*, pleasant B&B pension. **C** *Pension Arazim*, T6997145. Attractive pension, rooms have TV and central heating, restaurant, bar, pool, tennis. **C-D** *Hamawri*, T6997337. One of the best deals in town, the rooms with balconies are particularly attractive.

Horshat Tal National Park

This large National Park is one of Upper Galilee's most popular recreational spots. The Dan River has been diverted to create a number of (ice-cold) swimming pools, whilst the picnic lawn is shaded by a forest of ancient oaks. Legend has it that 10 companions of the prophet Mohammed (PBUH) rested here, and finding neither shade nor posts to tether their horses they drove their staffs into the ground. When they awoke the following morning their staffs had sprouted into a forest of magnificent oaks. ■ *T6942360. Saturday-Thursday 0800-1700, closes one hour earlier on Friday and in winter. Adult 25 NIS. The park is located six kilometres east of Kiryat Shemona on Route 99, and can be reached from there on Buses 26, 27 and 36.*

There are a couple of places to stay in the area. The (**B-C**) *Kibbutz Hagoshrim Guesthouse* (Kibbutz Hagoshrim (next to park), T6816000, F6816002) is nicely located, with modern rooms, a kosher dining hall, pool, tennis, children's playground, and TV room. The kibbutz's *Pub Gosh* is particularly recommended for its vegetarian meals, fish, soups and salads, as well as its location for an end-of-day beer (or 10). Female visitors to Kibbutz Hagoshrim who are considering using the swimming facilities at the National Park next door, but are concerned about their 'bikini line' or unwanted body hair, may or may not be interested to know that the 'Epilady', a highly innovative depilatory appliance, is a product of Hagoshrim's workshops! The (**F**) *Horshat Tal Camping Ground* (next to park, T6942360) allows you to pitch a tent (30 NIS per person), or take a space in the 4-person bungalows (**D**). Prices rise 50 percent on Shabbat and Jewish holidays.

Kibbutz Daphna and Moshav Yishuv   About 3.5 kilometres northeast of Horshat Tal National Park along Route 99 is **Kibbutz Daphna**, which features a charming **B-C** *Guesthouse*, T6945795, F6945794. Moshav She'ar Yishuv opposite was the scene in February 1997 of Israel's worst ever military aviation accident, when two helicopters ferrying troops to Israel's self-declared security zone in southern Lebanon collided and crashed in poor weather, killing over 70.

Tel Dan

Colour map 1, grid A5   *Tel Dan Nature Reserve compares favourably for beauty with any of Israel's other nature reserves. The perennial Dan River, the major source of the Jordan River, flows through the reserve supporting a dense mix of vegetation that is unrivalled in the rest of the country. Four different marked trails traverse this small reserve, taking in the floral and faunal highlights as well as exploring the evidence of mankind's sojourn in the area. Dan is most commonly known through the numerous biblical references used to express the boundaries of the ancient Land of Israel: "from Dan to Be'er Sheva" (I Samuel 3:20; II Samuel 3:10, 17:11, 24:15; I Chronicles 21:2). The ancient site, built upon the Canaanite city of Laish (Leshem), is now a minor attraction within an area most appreciated for its natural charms.*

Ins and outs

Getting there   Just beyond Kibbutz Daphna along Route 99 is Kibbutz Dan, and immediately after this kibbutz there is a difficult turning left (across the traffic and on a slight bend) towards the Tel Dan Nature Reserve. The site is 1.5km down this road, passing Beit Ussishkin (see page 741) on the way. Buses 026/036 from Kiryat Shemona run to Kibbutz Dan, from where it's a 1.5km walk.

Getting around   There are four marked walking routes around the reserve, the shortest of which is accessible by wheelchair: 'Short trail' (1 hr, red markers); 'Long trail' (1½ hrs, green markers); 'Ancient Dan trail' (2 hrs, yellow); 'Combined trail' (2½ hrs, yellow-and-green markers). If the weather is good, and time allows, the 'combined trail' is the best option. Armed with the map a detailed route description is not necessary, though some details of the natural and man-made sites are included below. You are reminded that it is illegal to pick any plants or flowers or disturb the wildlife. You must stick to the paths and note that swimming/paddling is allowed at one marked spot only. The flour mill has been restored to working order but operation must be supervised by staff.

History

It is not difficult to see why this site was selected for human habitation. Two groupings of springs, **Ein Dan** and **Ein Leshem**, feed the **Dan River**, themselves drawing water from a deep aquifer that collects snow-melt from Mt Hermon. The water is extremely potable with a remarkably low mineral content. This water source was able to support the large Canaanite city of **Laish** (or Leshem) that was established at the junction of the major north to south and east to west trade routes. The city of Laish is mentioned in the Egyptian Execration texts of the 18th century BCE, and in the lists of cities captured by the pharaoh Thutmose III in the 15th century BCE. Its defining moment came following the conquest and subsequent division of the Land of Israel by Joshua. Unable to hold the coastal plain against the Philistines, the tribe of the children of Dan headed north: "[they] went up to fight against Lesham, and took it, and smote it with the edge of the sword, and possessed it, and dwelt therein, and called Lesham, Dan, after the name of Dan their father" (*Joshua 19:47*, see also *Judges 18:29*, where the Canaanite city is referred to as Laish).

During the period of the United Monarchy (c. 1020-928 BCE) Dan marked the northern boundary of the kingdom (*I Samuel 3:20; II Samuel 3:10, 17:11, 24:15; I Chronicles 21:2*). However, the death of Solomon saw the splitting of the kingdom between Judah in the south and Israel in the north. In a direct challenge to the first King of Judah Rehoboam (928-911 BCE), who was custodian of the Temple at Jerusalem, the first King of Israel **Jeroboam I** (928-907 BCE) built his own "house of high places" in Dan, staffing it with "priests of the lowest of the people, which were not of the sons of Levi" (*I Kings 12:31*). He even set a golden calf there and offered sacrifices to it (*I Kings 12:28-33*). One of the cultic high places built by Jeroboam I can be seen on the tour of the reserve (note that it is the one closest to the southern gate; the other cultic high place was built later by Ahab).

To protect his city Jeroboam strengthened the southern gate and built new defensive walls. These appear to have been breached when a subsequent King of Judah, Asa (908-867 BCE) encouraged Ben-Hadd of Damascus to attack the King of Israel, Baasha (906-883 BCE) at Dan and other Galilean cities (see *I Kings 15:20; II Chronicles 16:4*).

Dan was rebuilt by Omri (882-871 BCE) and Ahab (871-852 BCE), and during the reign of Jehu (842-814 BCE) we have a description of the golden calf still standing at Dan (*II Kings 10:29*). Dan also appears to have been the administrative and military centre of Jeroboam II's northern kingdom (784-748 BCE). The city's subsequent history is not entirely clear. The inference is that Dan was captured by the Assyrian king Tiglath-pileser III in 732 BCE, though it may not have been destroyed (*II Kings 15:29*) since there are later references to Dan during the rule of Hezekiah (King of Judah 727-698 BCE, see *II Chronicles 30:5*) and Josiah (King of Judah 639-609 BCE, see *Jeremiah 4:15, 8:16*). Archaeological evidence suggests that the mound was occupied in the Hellenistic period (332-37 BCE) and also in the Roman period, before finally being abandoned in the fourth century CE.

Flora and fauna

If it is rainy, do not despair. This greatly enhances your chances of seeing the bright yellow and black spotted salamander (*Salamandra salamandra*). If you are very lucky you may spot an otter or mongoose, an Indian crested porcupine, or a marbled polecat. There is also a wide variety of birdlife and butterflies, including the famous Death's Head Hawk Moth (*Acherontia atropos*).

Galilee & The Golan

However, you are far more likely to see stuffed examples of all these creatures at Beit Ussishkin (see page 741) than live ones here. Notable tree species include the Syrian Ash, at the southernmost margins of its distribution, tall Laurels, magnificent Tabor Oaks, plus several Atlantic Pistachios, one 2,000-year-old example of which has been sadly burnt to death.

Sights

Southern gate The fortifications along the southern side of the tel (mound) are generally attributed to Jeroboam I (10th century BCE), who may have been keen to protect his golden calf. The following century saw the construction of the gate complex. The gate (29.5 m by 17.8 m) comprises two towers with two guard rooms on either side. The large paved square outside resembles the description of the one in which Hezekiah assembled his "captains of war" at Jerusalem (*II Chronicles 32: 6*). Considerable changes were made to the gate in the 8th century BCE.

Canaanite gate This gate is extremely well preserved, perhaps to its full height of 47 courses. It is built of sun-baked bricks and comprises three arches (the outer one of which is the only one that you can see beneath the modern protective roof). Ceramic finds have dated its construction to the Middle Bronze Age IIA-IIB (c. 2000-1550 BCE), though the fact that it was only used for 50 years or so and then filled in with earth has ensured its excellent state of preservation. Parts of the great earthen rampart, preserved up to a height of 10 metres though originally higher, can also be seen in this area. At its base the rampart is up to 50 metres wide, with a six-metre-thick stone core running through its centre.

Cultic site There are two cultic high places thus far excavated at Tel Dan. The one closest to the southern gate appears to have been constructed by Jeroboam I, perhaps the one referred to in *I Kings 12:31*. The charred stones are possibly the result of its destruction at the hands of Ben-Hadd (see page 739). The site appears to have been recycled as a high place in later years, with some of the construction here being Hellenistic. The second cultic site to the north of the mound closer to Ein Leshem, appears to be an Iron Age cult precinct from the ninth century

Galilee & The Golan

Tel Dan Nature Reserve

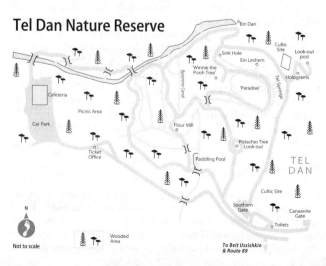

Ein Dan

Cultic Site
Look-out post

Sink Hole
Ein Leshem

Byzantine Canal

'Winnie the Pooh Tree'

Holograms

'Paradise'

Tel Springs

Cafeteria

Picnic Area

Car Park

Flour Mill

Pistachio Tree Look-out

TEL DAN

Ticket Office

Paddling Pool

Cultic Site

Southern Gate

Canaanite Gate

N

Not to scale

Wooded Area

Toilets

To Beit Ussishkin & Route 89

BCE, possibly built by Ahab. By sticking your head into the upright tubes just above the precinct, you get a holographic representation of the presumed cultic ritual. Bizarre.

When Britain and France divided up the Levant between them at the end of the First World War, Dan was right on the border between the two spheres of influence. In fact in 1964 the Syrians, as successors to the French, used the thickness of the pencil-drawn line on the map that accompanied the 1923 treaty as a justification for drawing water from the Dan. Continued disputes over the boundaries of the respective states escalated into a major battle in November 1964, which Israel won. ■ *T6951579. Saturday-Thursday 0800-1700, Friday 0800-1600. Adult 17 NIS, keep ticket for discount entry to Beit Ussishkin. Self-service restaurant, snack-bar, toilets.*

Look-out post

This attractive building one kilometre to the south of Tel Dan houses a museum that presents in great detail the biogeography and geomorphology of the area. Upstairs mainly comprises stuffed creatures (all well labelled), whilst downstairs the botany of the Hula Valley and the geology of the Golan are explained. ■ *T6941704, F6902755. Sunday-Thursday 0830-1630, Friday 0830-1530, Saturday 0930-1630. Adult 12 NIS, or 7 NIS with ticket from Tel Dan. Same buses as Tel Dan, though it's only 500 metres from main road.*

Beit Ussishkin

The Golan

The Golan (or Golan Heights) is a high basalt plateau extending from Mt Hermon in the north, to the Yarmuk River in the south, bounded on the west by the Hula Valley/Sea of Galilee of the Jordan Rift Valley and on the east by the Raqqad River. Captured from the Syrians by Israel in 1967, the status of the Golan dominates bilateral relations between the two states. Though the fate of the Golan is uncertain, it is clear that it will not be returned to Syria in the immediate future.

In the mean time, a growing number of visitors, Israelis and foreigners alike, are ignoring the transport and accommodation shortfalls and exploring the Golan's many attractions. The region has a rugged, almost desolate beauty, coupled with a number of exceptional historical sites. Highlights of the Golan include the rich waterscape at Banias, the superbly preserved medieval Nimrod Fortress, some challenging hiking opportunities in the Ya'ar Yehudiya Nature Reserve and the combination of stunning views and enthralling history at Gamla. This is a region not to be missed.

Ins and outs

There are three main points of access into the Golan Heights: (a) travelling east on Route 99 from Kiryat Shemona in Upper Galilee into Upper Golan; (b) travelling east on Route 91 across the B'not Ya'akov Bridge, roughly to the northeast of Safed; (c) travelling northeast on Route 87 from the northeast corner of the Sea of Galilee.

Getting there

With the possible exception of the ski resort in the Upper Golan and the various kibbutz guesthouses, accommodation options in the Golan Heights region are extremely limited (and virtually non-existent in the budget price range). As a further constraint on tourism, transport connections to the Golan's relatively isolated sites are also poor. For these reasons, many visitors choose to base themselves in Tiberias and either hire a car or book themselves on organized tours (see 'Tiberias, Essentials' on page 671). Though

Getting around

Galilee & The Golan

organized tours are useful to non-drivers, or those with limited time or budgets, they do tend to be rather rushed. Renting a car and sharing the expense between a group of people is undoubtedly the best way to get the most out of the Golan.

Warning Syrian and Israeli land mines still litter the Golan Heights, and whilst the slightest prospect remains that any part of the Golan is to be handed back to Syria there is understandably little incentive on the part of the Israelis to clear them. Most suspect areas are fenced off, with a yellow and red sign warning of the danger in English, Hebrew and Arabic. However, the best advice is not to cross any fences whether sign-posted or not. It should also be noted that it is a legal requirement that any proposed trek in the Golan must be first cleared with the SPNI (see Katzrin or Nahal Hermon Reserve).

Geography

Though the Golan is part of a larger area of volcanic basalt fields that stretch north and east, the 1,200 square kilometres of the Golan Heights plateau that Israel controls has distinct geographical boundaries. In the north the limestone bedrock of Mt Hermon is separated from the basalt of the Golan by the Nahal Sa'ar that runs through Banias. At its western margins the plateau slopes down to the Jordan Rift Valley, falling away steeply at the Sea of Galilee. The southern margins, known in the Bible as the land of Geshur, are bounded by the Yarmuk River and the biblical lands of Gilead, the latter now part of Jordan. The eastern boundary is formed by the Raqqad River, still controlled by Syria.

The basalt that covers most of the Golan was created in a series of volcanic eruptions that began almost four million years ago; a relatively recent process that is still continuing. Notable features in the eastern Golan, particularly prominent from the 'Kuneitra Viewpoint' (see page 750), are the small volcanic cones and 'tuffs', or volcanic particles, created by violent eruptions. Those in the south have been largely eroded into a series of low hills. The younger basalt cover in the northeast has developed into layers of red and brown Mediterranean soils, whilst the soils elsewhere are somewhat older. With the moderating effects of climate, this has influenced the pattern of vegetation and human settlement.

Climate

The Golan experiences a Mediterranean climate that is considerably moderated by altitude. The Mt Hermon range heavily influences levels of precipitation in the north, with the peak levels of 1,200 millimetres per annum being double the levels received in the southern Golan, less than 50 kilometres away. Heavy snowfall is often recorded in Upper Golan. Likewise, temperatures are influenced by the changes in altitude, averaging around 9°C in the north but almost 20°C in the south. **NB** Visitors to the Golan should be aware of the climatic differences between the Golan and, say, Tiberias (particularly in autumn and winter). It may be sunny with clear skies when you leave Tiberias in the morning, but a one-hour drive up to the Golan can leave you amongst low cloud with rain, and a very noticeable drop in temperature. Take appropriate clothing.

Vegetation

In antiquity, the Golan was covered by thick Mediterranean vegetation, with considerable forested areas. Today, just three percent of the Golan is forested, concentrated in a number of reserves such as Odem and Yehudiya. Most of the vegetation cover is now scattered grasslands, with extensive cultivation of the more fertile plain to the south.

The political future of the Golan Heights

Standing on the edge of the Golan plateau looking west into the Hula Valley and Upper Galilee or down upon the Sea of Galilee, it is easy to see the strategic advantage of occupying the high ground, and why Israel is so reluctant to enter into any negotiations on the Golan's future. Throughout the 1960s the Syrian army took advantage of this elevated position randomly to shell Israeli settlements in Upper Galilee and the Sea of Galilee region, but since the Israelis captured the Golan in 1967, as former Israeli prime minister Benjamin Netanyahu puts it, "Israel has looked down at the Syrians, rather than the other way around" (*A Place Among the Nations*, 1993). In fact, whilst many Israelis are willing to concede the Gaza Strip and parts of the West Bank to the Palestinians, you meet few who advocate a return of the Golan Heights to Syria.

However, the Syrian government have a similar argument. Not only does the Golan provide a buffer for the Israeli population centres of Galilee, "strategic depth" as Netanyahu calls it, it also serves a similar function for Syria. During the Yom Kippur War of 1973 armoured Syrian divisions initially broke through Israeli defences on the Golan, almost reaching the bridges across the Jordan into Upper Galilee. In a campaign graphically described in Chaim Herzog's *The Arab-Israeli Wars* (1982), the Israeli counter-attack reached within 40 kilometres of the Syrian capital at Damascus before the Israeli Military High Command felt that they had made their point and withdrew. Thus, the Golan is also seen by the Syrians as crucial to the defence of their capital.

Yet it is clear that the issue of the Golan must be resolved if there is to be any normalization of relations between Israel and Syria. In fact, the Syrian regime of President Assad has claimed that the late Israeli Prime Minister Yitzhak Rabin made a verbal agreement to return the Golan to Syria as a pre-condition for peace. This seems unlikely, even in light of Rabin's efforts to conclude peace treaties with his neighbours just prior to his assassination.

The election of Ehud Barak as Prime Minister in 1999 has seen a series of encouraging statements emanating out of Jerusalem about a peace deal with Syria. That said, it does rather suit Israel to prolong the status quo and it seems unlikely that any progress will be made on the issue in the near future. Israel's stated minimum requirement, forward monitoring and listening bases, is totally rejected by Syria, whilst Damascus' call for a unilateral Israeli withdrawal as a pre-condition for any future peace deal is unthinkable for Israel. Thus, the Golan Heights remain in Israeli hands, annexed by Begin's Likud government in December 1981 in a move not recognized by the international community.

Upper Golan

Banias (Nahal Hermon Nature Reserve)

Now enclosed within the Nahal Hermon Nature Reserve, at the southwest foot of Colour map 1, grid A5
Mt Hermon, is an area of supreme natural beauty that is also of considerable historical and archaeological interest. The site of one of the sources of the Jordan River, and the point where several streams collecting snow melt from Mt Hermon converge, the reserve is an area of running water, cascading waterfalls and a dense mix of vegetation types. Several marked walking trails wind their way through the natural wonders of the reserve, passing en route *an ancient cultic cave site dedicated to the worship of the god Pan, remains of a city established in*

Galilee & The Golan

'Banias': Etymology of a name

The name Banias (sometimes spelt Banyas) is a corruption of the ancient Greek and Latin name Panias (or Paneas, Paneias); an obvious reference to the cult worship here of Pan. The change from a 'P' to a 'B' can be dated to the arrival of the Arabs and has stuck ever since (the French Crusaders using the 'B' in their version, Belinas). However, Banias has had a variety of names throughout its long history. The polis built here in 2 BCE by Herod the Great's son Philip was named Caesarea, in honour of the emperor

Augustus, with 'of Philip' being added to distinguish it from the city of the same name on the Mediterranean coast. Although the Gospels refer to the city as Caesarea Philippi (Matthew 16:13-20; Mark 8:27-30), the name does not appear to have been in common usage. Neither did Agrippa II's attempt to rename the city after the emperor Nero (Neronias) have much lasting impact. Most second- and third-century sources refer to the city as Caesarea Panias, and subsequently as simply Panias then Banias.

the first century BCE, plus medieval fortifications dating to the period of the Crusades. Banias also receives a significant number of Christian visitors since tradition holds that it is here that Jesus referred to Peter as the "rock" upon which he would build his church.

Ins and outs

Getting there Transport to Banias is not that regular. Bus 055 runs there twice a day from Kiryat Shemona, but the last bus back leaves at noon. If you walk the 5km back to Kibbutz Dan, you can get a later bus (035/036, last at 1930). There are two entrances to the reserve: the first is about 3km to the northeast of Tel Dan along Route 99 and is sign-posted as "Banias Waterfalls"; the second entrance is 2km further east along Route 99 and is sign-posted "Banias".

Getting around A walking trail links the two entrances to the reserve, with a variety of diversions available *en route*. Trail A follows a roughly circular route beginning at the more easterly entrance and taking in the Banias Cave (Sanctuary of Pan area), the Grave of Nebi Khader, Herod's Palace, plus most of the remaining medieval Crusader buildings. The complete circuit takes about 2 hrs. About half-way round the circuit, Trail B leads off in a southwesterly direction via the Officers' Pool and Banias Waterfall to the westerly entrance. This walk takes about 1 hr. As can be seen from the map, completing both trails will require a certain degree of back-tracking, particularly if you have parked a car at one of the entrances.

Perhaps the best route, if you have the time, is to begin at the westerly entrance, passing the very attractive Banias Waterfalls (10 mins walk) and continuing up to the Officers' Pool (Breichat Haketzinim, 25 mins). This is a large concrete pool built for the Syrian officers formerly stationed here, and fed by the warmer waters of Ein Khilo (spring). Officially it is forbidden to bathe here, though this order is frequently ignored. If time is short, and you have your own transport, return to the westerly entrance and drive up to the second entrance to see the cave and spring. Otherwise continue along the trail. Shortly after crossing the Nahal Nimrod (stream), the path divides. The shorter but more picturesque route is to the left, via the Druze bakery, the flour mill, Crusader tower and Roman bridge. The longer, more interesting route is to the right, via the Crusader fortifications and the Grave of Sheikh Sidi Ibrahim. Both routes end up at the Banias Cave (1-2 hrs walking). Note that there is an excellent, but tiring walking route from the main parking lot via Banias Observation Point up to Nimrod Fortress (2 hrs+).

In 200 BCE, the defeat of the Ptolemy forces of Egypt here by the army of **History** Antiochus III brought the whole of Palestine under the control of the **Seleucids** of Syria. A subsequent reference to the battle by Polybius mentions a grotto dedicated to *Paneion*, suggesting that a cult place dedicated to Pan as part of the Ptolemaic dynastic cult of Dionysus had been established here as early as the third century BCE. Pan worship was common throughout Ptolemic Egypt and the Pan site may have been built here as a rival to the Semitic cult site at nearby Dan (see 'Tel Dan', page 738). The Ptolemies returned to this area, though the subsequent conquest of the entire region by Pompey saw the district of Panias divided into smaller and smaller units. In 20 BCE the land was granted to Herod the Great, who built a temple close to the Pan cave in honour of his patron Augustus.

Following the death of Herod in 4 BCE, Panias and its territory passed to his son **Philip**. A new polis was built to serve as the capital of Philip's tetrarchy, **Caesarea Philippi**, with Gospel sources claiming that Jesus and his disciples visited here (*Matthew 16:13-20; Mark 8:27-30*). After a brief period of uncertainty following Philip's death in 34 CE the city eventually came under the control of Agrippa II, though his attempts to refound the city in 61 CE as Neronias do not appear to have caught on. The First Jewish Revolt (66-73 CE) saw the small Jewish community of Caesarea Philippi imprisoned and subsequently murdered. The city during this period must have been fairly extensive with impressive amenities since **Titus** rested here for some time with his troops following the capture of Jerusalem in 70 CE. From Josephus' account it appears that Titus' R&R comprised "shows of every kind" in which "many of the prisoners perished … some thrown to wild beasts, others forced to meet each other in full-scale battles" (*Jewish War, VII, 23-24*).

Following Agrippa II's death in 93 CE, Caesarea Philippi came under Roman control. Its subsequent history is sketchy, with evidence from coins, inscriptions and the few written references suggesting a predominantly pagan population, but with Jewish and later Christian minorities. By the fourth century CE a small Christian community was well established here, as attested to by Eusebius. The name Caesarea Philippi appears to have disappeared completely by this stage, with most references being to Panias.

The Early Arab period (638-1099 CE) saw Banias as capital of a district within the province of Damascus, though the town appears to have been devastated by the earthquake of 1033 CE. By 1126 Banias was in the hands of an Isma'ili sect known as the **Assassins**. Though they heavily fortified Banias in anticipation of an attack from Damascus, the Assassins instead chose to offer the city to the Crusader king **Baldwin II** in exchange for asylum. The offer was accepted in 1129 and Banias and its domain was conferred upon Rainier of Brus. Despite considerable fortification Shams el-Mulk captured it for Damascus in 1132, though the local ruler installed here by Damascus, Ibrahim ibn Turghut, subsequently rebelled and offered Banias to Zengi, ruler of Mosul. This action resulted in an extraordinary turn of events. Now given a common cause, the Christian and Muslim armies combined to retake Banias in 1140, the town then becoming a place for Frankish and Muslim nobles to meet for hunting and sport.

Seventeen years later Zengi's son **Nur ed-Din** laid siege to Banias, succeeding in breaking through the outer fortifications and forcing the Crusader garrison to retreat into the inner fortress. The precise location of this inner fortress is still unknown, though it is now clear that it was not the castle now known as Nimrod's Fortress (see page 747). Reinforcements sent by Baldwin II forced Nur ed-Din's army to withdraw temporarily and though much of the defensive fortifications was rapidly rebuilt, Nur ed-Din succeeded in capturing Banias in 1164. The subsequent history of Banias saw the city captured,

Banias (Nahal Hermon Nature Reserve)

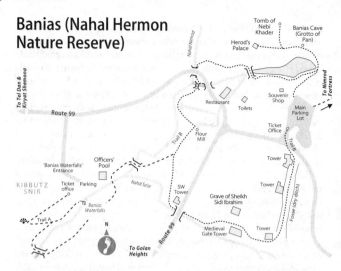

destroyed, and rebuilt a number of times, until it eventually drifted into insignificance. When the Israelis captured the Golan from Syria in 1967 Banias was just a poor village occupied by some 200 inhabitants.

Sanctuary of Pan

The centrepiece of the sanctuary dedicated to honouring Pan is a small, rectangular artificial cave (*operosum antrum*) quarried out of the rock face. This '**grotto of Pan**' was formerly plastered, with a small niche in the rear wall housing a statue of Pan playing the flute to three goats that share a single head. The statue has never been found and this description has been determined by images found on third century CE coins. Three other decorated niches have been cut into the rock face with Greek inscriptions dating some of the work to 148-49 CE. Some of the work may be from the previous century, executed on a site used for the Pan cult since the third century BCE. A number of architectural fragments such as Attic bases and Corinthian columns were found in the area in front of the cave (and can still be seen today), though the exact plan of any temple or building here is not known.

Close to the grotto is a large **cavern**, part of a phreatic cave (created below water level). Josephus describes how the source of the Jordan River flowed from the cave. Subsequent seismic action has now forced the water from the underground springs to emerge from a crack below the cave. The collapse of the cave's roof in the 1837 earthquake has prevented the excavation of the Hellenistic and Roman remains inside.

A path above the cave leads to the small white domed **Tomb of Nebi Khader**; a Druze holy place said to be the burial site of St George (el-Khader). Further up the hill limited excavations have revealed the ground plan of a man-made terrace upon which a building attributed to Herod the Great stands (referred to as **Herod's Palace**). Though archaeologists are fairly sure that it was built by Italian masons presented to Herod by Marcus Agrippa, it is still not entirely clear whether this is a palace or some form of temple.

Nimrod Fortress

1 Western Gate
2 SW Tower
3 Cisterns

0 metres 30

To Route 989

Galilee & The Golan

Both the Crusader and Muslim towns followed the plan of the ancient town. Thus to the south and the west the fortifications followed the natural lines of defence provided by the Nahal Nimrod, Nahal Hermon and Nahal Sa'ar. The **curtain wall** to the west and south can be seen in a number of places, as can the dry ditch that defended the east side. The exact line of the north wall can only be guessed at, though it probably stood around 200 metres (and thus out of weapons range) from the cliff. The best preserved of the medieval buildings is probably the **Gate Tower** to the south, which is preserved to a height of around 25 metres. Some Roman columns and blocks are incorporated in secondary use in the gate's construction, with recent research suggesting that the Frankish masonry may be of secondary use too. This, along with the fact that the overall fortification plan is somewhat irregular, have led some of the site's main excavators to suggest that the defences seen here are not Crusader at all, but instead belong to the Ayyubid or Fatimid Arabs (see Ma'oz in *New Encyclopedia of Archaeological Excavations in the Holy Land*, 1993). ■ *T6950272. Daily 0800-1700, closes one hour earlier on Friday and in winter. Adult 17 NIS, one ticket valid for both entrances. Toilets, café, souvenir shop available at both entrances.*

Medieval buildings

E *SPNI Hermon Field Study Centre*, T6941091, F6951480. Located close to Kibbutz Snir (about 2km west of the 'Banias Waterfalls' entrance to the Nahal Hermon Nature Reserve), the *Field School* provides dorm and private room (**D**) accommodation, though it is essential to book in advance. Anyone contemplating hiking anywhere in the Golan region should call here first.

Sleeping and eating

Nimrod Fortress

Less well-informed guidebooks and tourist brochures refer to Nimrod Fortress as the "best-preserved of Israel's Crusader castles". Perhaps a far more accurate description would be the "best-preserved castle in Israel", particularly when you bear in mind that all the historical and architectural evidence now suggests that not only was the fortress not built by the Crusaders, but that they never occupied it. Historical inaccuracies aside, not only are the sweeping views from here the best in the whole of the north of the country, but the thrill of being in such a dramatic setting is enough to bring out the Errol Flyn in those who are old enough to know better.

Unfortunately, Nimrod Fortress is not easy to get to without your own transport. Bus

Ins and outs

Galilee & The Golan

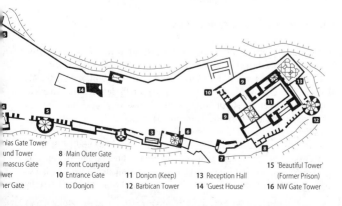

nias Gate Tower	8 Main Outer Gate	
und Tower	9 Front Courtyard	15 'Beautiful Tower'
mascus Gate	10 Entrance Gate	(Former Prison)
wer	to Donjon	11 Donjon (Keep)	13 Reception Hall
er Gate	12 Barbican Tower	14 'Guest House'	16 NW Gate Tower

014 that runs once a day from Kiryat Shemona to Neve Ativ passes the bottom of the road leading up to the fortress (1-hr walk). Bus 055 runs from Kiryat Shemona to Banias, from where it is a steep 2-hr climb (very hot, no shade, take plenty of water). Alternatively, it is 11 km by the steep and very winding Route 998. If it's wet, snowy or cloudy, this road is a real bugger. Note that the last bus back from Banias leaves at noon, with the only later option being to walk to Kibbutz Dan (4km from Banias). You should also note that many of the 1-day tours of the Golan (usually from Tiberias) often only feature Nimrod Fortress as a "photo-stop".

History The controversy in identifying the builder of this monumental work and assigning a date lies in the fact that the Crusader fortress at Banias (see page 743) has yet to be located. Thus references to the "Banias Fortress" have mistakenly been applied to Nimrod Fortress. The mistake is understandable in so far as no systematic excavation has been undertaken at the fortress, but it should also be noted that Nimrod features many characteristic Arab styles whilst key features of the Crusader style of construction are entirely absent. The current school of thought suggests that the castle that you see today was initially built at the beginning of the 13th century CE, though all references dated before 1228 CE should be treated with caution since there is the possibility of confusion between Nimrod and "Banias Fortress".

What is known for sure about Nimrod Fortress is that **el-Malik el-'Aziz 'Uthman** carried out substantial rebuilding work here between 1228 and 1230. A number of Arabic inscriptions, very well preserved, list building work completed by him and others. It seems likely that the previous fortress had been largely dismantled in 1219 by **el-Malik el'Mu'azzim** following the success of the Fifth Crusade. Further restoration work during the period 1239-40 is confirmed by inscriptions found *in situ*. It appears that the Crusaders attempted to take the fortress in 1253 but were unsuccessful. An account of this campaign refers to the fortress as **Qal'at es-Subeiba**; almost certainly a name derived from the Arabic word for 'cliff' (*subeib*). The name Nimrod (Nimrud) evolved later from the Arab legend that the "mighty hunter" Nimrod (*Genesis 10:8-9*) used to sit on the mountain here, 815 metres above sea level, and cup his hand to draw water from the Banias spring below.

The Mamluk sultan **Baibars** carried out rebuilding work at Nimrod between 1260 and 1277, but the final departure of the Crusaders from the Holy Land after the fall of Acre in 1291 reduced the strategic importance of the castle. It was subsequently used as a jail for political prisoners before being finally abandoned. ■ *T6942360. Daily 0800-1700, closes one hour earlier on Friday and in winter. Adult 13 NIS. Toilets, snack-bar. **NB** you are strongly advised to keep to the marked path, and supervise children closely.*

Mt Hermon Ski Centre/Neve Ativ

Phone code: 06 From Nimrod Fortress, Route 989 winds northeast to the town of **Neve Ativ**. The moshav established here shortly after the Israelis captured the Golan from Syria in 1967 has developed itself into something of a resort, serving the **Mt Hermon Ski Centre**. The skiing facilities here, on the less than 10 percent of Mt Hermon that Israel controls, get mixed reviews though they remain extremely popular with Israelis. There are 25 kilometres of ski runs, though the sensitive nature of the setting means that there is no facility for skiing off-piste (the Israelis and Syrians fought major battles here in 1967 and 1973, and it remains a strategic military position). There are three beginners' runs, six graded as 'easy', five 'difficult' and two 'extremely difficult'. A chair-lift is also provided for non-skiers to visit the viewing point (40 NIS return). **NB** It really is best to avoid this place on Shabbat or holidays if possible. The season lasts from December until late April. For details on snow conditions, T6981337 or T03-5656040. Calling ahead is a good idea: lack of snow meant that no skiing was possible during the winter of 1998-99!

Though the ski centre has 2,000 sets of skis and boots, most Israelis prefer to hire rather than own their equipment and thus it's not unusual to find all the equipment rented out at weekends. Arrive early to avoid disappointment and to ensure that you get a pair of boots that fit properly. A day's skiing costs 150 NIS for an adult, with equipment rental adding another 100 NIS. There are a number of package deals available that are worth considering. A ski pass for 2 days costs 240 NIS, 3 days 310 NIS, 4 days 360 NIS (includes use of lifts but not equipment rental or accommodation). Equipment rental costs 180 NIS for 2 days, 220 NIS for 3 days, 300 NIS for 4 days. **Ski passes and equipment rental**

A *Hermon Heights*, T6985888, F6985666. This is a real sign of the times: the moshav's 'holiday village' has been taken over by the *Howard Johnson* chain! Features 44 stylish wooden chalets with bath, shower, cable TV, phone, and views. Other facilities include health club, pool, restaurant and lobby bar. There are a number of cheaper accommodation options, such as the friendly B *Hermon Hotel – Alimi's*, T6981345, as well as numerous 'rooms for rent' let out by moshav members (T6981333, F6984280, or pick up a free copy of the *Galilee & Golan Guide*). There are also a number of package deals that are worth considering, with or without equipment rental (price including equipment rental is in brackets): 2 days skiing, 1 night accommodation 350 NIS (520 NIS); 2 days skiing, 2 nights accommodation 540 NIS (750 NIS); 3 days skiing, 2 nights accommodation 750 NIS (975 NIS). If you are a non-skier but take one of these packages, free skiing lessons are provided. **Sleeping and eating**

Bus 055 runs twice a day from Kiryat Shemona to Neve Ativ (and on to Katzrin). Drivers should note that at weekends it is obligatory to park several kilometres away and take the free shuttle bus to the ski centre. There are a number of transport packages available. Arkia will fly you from Tel Aviv's Sde Dov Airport to Kiryat Shemona, from where you pick up a hire car. The 1-day package costs 375 NIS (or 450 NIS with equipment rental); 2-day package costs 525 NIS including ski rental and basic accommodation for 1 night. To book a package T6981333. **Transport**

From Neve Ativ Route 989 continues east to **Majdal Shams**, the largest of several Druze villages in the area. On a cold and wet winter's day this is a bleak town indeed. The Druze are a fiercely independent people (for details of the Druze religion see page 802), and unlike their brethren in the villages around Haifa they consider the Israelis as an army of occupation. Heavily armed IDF units patrol the streets in a manner that has recently disappeared from the Palestinian Authority-controlled parts of the Gaza Strip and West Bank. It is usually written that the Druze villagers here would prefer to be part of Syria, though this is only true to a certain extent. Many wish to be reunited with family and friends across the disengagement zone in Syria, though they would prefer to be left to their own devices under the broad umbrella of nominal Syrian authority. A white UN building on the opposite hillside marks the border, acting as an observation point. Many a foreign journalist has come up here in order to by-line their story *Givat Ha-Tza'akot*, or "Shouting Valley", where each Friday and Saturday Majdal Shams' Druze come to shout across to their relatives and co-religionists on the Syrian controlled side of the border. **Druze villages**

Smaller Druze villages in the area include **Mas'ada** to the south, though the most attractive is easily **Ein Kuniya** to the south of Nimrod Fortress. The Druze are in fact the largest single community on the Golan plateau,

Galilee & The Golan

numbering some 16,000 as opposed to 10,000 Jews. Most kibbutzim and moshavs in the area offer **B-C** price category accommodation (check in your free *Israel Tourism Guide: Galilee* or *Galilee & Golan Guide*).

Birket Ram From Madjal Shams Route 98 heads south, passing another Druze settlement at **Mas'ada**. Just to the east of the settlement is the lake of **Birket Ram**. The perfectly round shape of the lake suggests volcanic origins, though it was in fact formed by the action of underground springs breaking through the surface stratum. It was believed for a long time that the lake was the source of the Jordan River, after Philip, founder of Caesarea Philippi (Banias, see page 743) "proved" this fact in the first century CE. Josephus recounts how chaff was thrown into "Phiale", or "the Bowl" here, later appearing at Caesarea Philippi (Josephus, *Jewish War III, 512-13*). What Josephus does not explain is that this was a trick; a courtier dropped more chaff in at Caesarea Philippi so as not to disappoint his patron.

It's possible to hire paddle-boats (30 NIS per hour) or wind-surfers (50 NIS per hour) for a trip on the lake. The *Birket Ram Restaurant* is also recommended. Cheaper snacks are available at the kiosk.

Kuneitra/ The viewpoint here looks down upon the deserted town of **Kuneitra**
Quneitra (Quneitra), located in the Disengagement Zone between Israel and Syria. This
Viewpoint is a good spot to stand with a detailed map of the Golan and to take out a copy of Chaim Herzog's *The Arab-Israeli Wars* (1984). The former President of Israel describes in great detail the major battles that took place here in 1967 and 1973. Prior to the Six Day War (1967), Kuneitra was a modest-sized Syrian town inhabited largely by Circassians. It was captured without a fight by the Israelis on 10th June, 1967, though the armoured brigade that rolled in under the command of Col. Albert Mandler had been involved in some of the heaviest fighting for the Golan Heights, as they fought their way down from the northwest. The ceasefire that concluded the Six Day War left Kuneitra on the Israeli side of the 'Purple Line'.

In October 1973 (the Yom Kippur War), Syrian tanks and artillery crossed the 'Purple Line', concentrating their attack at Rafid 20 kilometres to the southeast of Kuneitra. After initial early gains the Syrian forces were routed. Herzog estimates that of the 1,400 Syrian tanks that crossed the 'Purple Line' on 6th October, not a single one remained in fighting condition to the west of that line four days later. The subsequent ceasefire and the disengagement agreement negotiated the following year saw Kuneitra returned to Syrian control, but located in a demilitarized zone between the two states. The Syrians have made no attempt to redevelop Kuneitra, and today it stands as a ghost-town. It can only be visited from the Syrian side (see *Jordan, Syria & Lebanon Handbook* for further details).

B'not Ya'akov This bridge on the Jordan River is a major communications junction, effec-
Bridge tively marking the boundary between Upper Golan and Lower Golan. This has been a strategic crossing point of the Jordan for several thousand years, with the indistinct remains of the fort of 'Ateret being identified with the Antiochia that the Seleucids built following their victory over the Ptolemies at Banias in 200 BCE. In fact the name of this crossing point, meaning 'Daughters of Jacob', is far older, referring to the crossing of the Jordan into Canaan by the family of Jacob. There have subsequently been battles to control this crossing point between the Crusaders and the Arabs, Napoleon and the Ottoman Turks (1799), the Turks and the British (1918), and the Israelis and the Syrians (1948, 1967).

From the bridge Route 91 heads west towards Route 90 (which provides access either north to Upper Galilee or south to the Sea of Galilee). Alternatively, you can head northeast from the bridge along Route 91 as far as Zivan Junction, from where Route 98 leads you to the sights of Upper Golan. And finally, by heading northeast from B'not Ya'akov Bridge for seven kilometres you come to Katzrin North Junction, where Route 9088 leads to the town of Katzrin and the attractions of Lower Golan.

Lower Golan

Katzrin/Qasrin

Katzrin (Qasrin, Qazrin) is a modern settlement established around 20 years ago in order to project an impression of permanence on the Israeli occupation of the Golan Heights. It now has a population of around 3,000, though generous government resettlement grants should eventually help the town to 'fill out' to the planned size of around 10,000. It has already established itself as the *de facto* administrative 'capital' of the Golan Heights. Recent excavations, however, confirm that Jewish settlement on the Golan doesn't just date to post-1967: just to the east of the new town, Ancient Qasrin Park displays the reconstructed remains of a Talmudic (fourth to eighth century CE) village.

Phone code: 06
Colour map 1, grid B5

There are three main approaches to Katzrin: (a) from the west via Route 90, then Route 91 across the B'not Ya'akov Bridge; (b) from the northeast, via Routes 98/91 from Upper Golan; (c) from the south, via Route 87 from the northeast corner of the Sea of Galilee. All three routes are served by a very limited bus route. Buses 055/056/057 connect Katzrin to Rosh Pinna (approach 'a', 35 mins, 11 NIS); Bus 055 runs twice daily in a huge loop from Kiryat Shemona, via Banias and Mas'ada to Katzrin (approach 'b'); Buses 015/016/019 run to Katzrin from Tiberias (approach 'c', 50 mins, 17 NIS). All the buses pull in to the Commercial Centre area.

Ins and outs

Katzrin/Qasrin

Talmudic Village & Synagogue, Ancient Qasrin Park

0 metres 5

1 'House of Uzi'
2 'House of Rabbi Abun'
3 Viewpoint
4 Spring
5 Synagogue

Though the site of the ancient village here was identified in 1913, it was not until the Israelis established control over the Golan Heights in 1967 that Qasrin was systematically excavated. Approximately 10 percent of the village has been cleared, including a finely preserved synagogue. Village life during the Talmudic period (fourth to eighth centuries CE) has been recreated by placing models and replicas of everyday utensils, tools and furniture in two of the restored houses. A free brochure from the ticket office gives details of the articles displayed in the **'House of Uzi'** and **'House of Rabbi Abun'**.

The pattern of the village follows the *insulae* form, with separate extended family units divided from neighbours by narrow paths. The

Ancient Qasrin Park

Galilee & The Golan

basic nuclear family unit comprises a large multi-purpose room, or *triclinium*, divided from a large storage room by a 'window wall', above which stands a sleeping loft. The rooms open on to a courtyard, with additional extended family units joined on to form a self-contained *insula*. The village seen today was probably established in the fourth to fifth centuries CE and continued in use until the mid-eighth century CE earthquake that struck the region. The site was resettled during the Mamluk period (13th-15th centuries CE) and a mosque built on the ruins of the synagogue. There is also evidence of Bedouin settlement in the 20th century CE.

The **synagogue** is the best-preserved example in the Golan. It appears to have gone through three stages of construction, four different architectural phases, and five floors. Most of what you see today dates from the second synagogue (sixth to seventh century CE) and hints at the economic prosperity of a village economy based upon olive oil production. Many of the artefacts found at the site are displayed in the Golan Archaeological Museum in the new town. ■ *T6962412. Sunday-Thursday 0800-1700, Friday 0800-1300, Saturday 1000-1600. Admission 12 NIS, or 18 NIS with combined ticket to Gamla, also includes entrance to Golan Archaeological Museum. Site is located just to the east of the modern town of Katzrin, off Route 9088.*

Golan Heights Winery   Located close to Ancient Qasrin Park, on the Industrial Estate to the east of the new town, is the Golan Heights Winery. It is generally agreed that Israel's best wines are produced here, most notably Hermon Red and Yarden cabernet sauvignon. Tasting tours can be arranged in advance. The Eden Springs nearby produce high-quality bottled mineral water. ■ *T6961646. Sunday-Thursday 0800-1600, Friday 0800-1300. Admission, including tour and tasting 15 NIS. **NB** wines bought at the shop here are not necessarily cheaper than they are throughout the rest of the country.*

Golan Archaeological Museum   Many of Ancient Qasrin's finds are displayed at the museum in the heart of the new town's commercial centre. There is also an audio-visual show on the "story of Gamla" (in English, Hebrew, French, Russian, Spanish, German and Italian). Note that the same ticket gains you admission to both sites. ■ *T6969636. Sunday-Thursday 0800-1700, Friday 0800-1500, Saturday 1000-1600. Admission 12 NIS, includes Ancient Qasrin Park.*

Dolls Museum   The Dolls Museum in the Commercial Centre features "a trip into the past and present of the Jewish people. Heroes, heritage and legends presented in eighty excitingly accurate dioramas (*sic*) and almost one thousand lifelike models". ■ *Sunday-Thursday 0900-1700, Friday 0900-1400, Saturday 0900-1700. Adults 14 NIS.*

Sleeping and eating   **D/E** *SPNI Golan Field School, Katzrin*, Zavithan, T6961352/6961234, F6961233. A/c dorms (**E**) plus some single rooms (**D**). There is also space to pitch a tent. Advance reservations are highly recommended. This is also an indispensable source of hiking information for the Golan region. Most of the places to eat, including a supermarket, are located in the Commercial Centre.

Tourist information   There is a helpful information office in the Commercial Centre (T6962885).

Ya'ar Yehudiya Nature Reserve

At the risk of repetition, it is fair to say that the Ya'ar Yehudiya Nature Reserve offers some of the best hiking possibilities in Israel. There are several options, all of which are fairly challenging, but offering sweeping views, spectacular rock formations, waterfalls and attractive waterscapes. Details of the three best hikes are included here, plus information on how to reach the amazing Brekhat HaMeshushim, or Hexagon Pools.

Ins and outs

Getting there The reserve is located on Route 87, about half-way between Yehudiye Junction on the northeast corner of the Sea of Galilee, and Katzrin Junction South, close to Katzrin and the boundary between Lower and Upper Golan.

Getting to the reserve by public transport is a hassle since the only buses that pass the site (015/016/019) do not leave Tiberias early enough. One option is to camp at the Yehudiya Campground overnight, and hike the next day. It costs 12 NIS per person to pitch a tent in the designated campground, with bathroom facilities, a snack-bar, and storage lockers (7 NIS) available. Other alternatives are to get to Yehudiye Junction or Katzrin, and walk/hitch. Those with their own transport have no such problems. **NB** Note that there is separate travel information for taking the short route to Brekhat HaMeshushim (see page 755).

Getting around **NB** It is strongly recommended that you consult with the helpful staff before commencing any hikes. They are able to provide up-to-date information on local conditions, as well as tips on routes and journey times. The map in this *Handbook* should be

Ya'ar Yehudiya Nature Reserve hikes

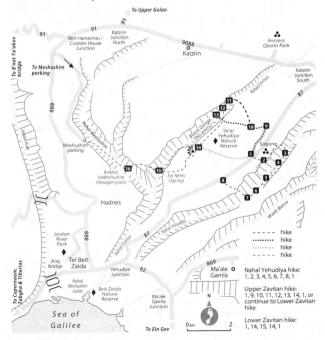

Galilee & The Golan

suitable for all the hikes, though you will get a better idea of the topography of the land if you buy the relevant SPNI Golan Hiking Map. Unfortunately this is only available in Hebrew, though the staff here should be able to translate the relevant points. Likewise, the free map given out when you enter the park should be good enough, though again it may only be available in Hebrew. An English translation is posted on the notice-board outside the main information office. On most of the hikes there is no drinking water *en route* so you should make sure that you are carrying an adequate supply (1-2 litres per person). On some of these hikes you will get wet, and in some places you need to be able to swim.

Nahal Yehudiya hike

This excellent hike takes around four to five hours, with the option of extending it into a loop trail that adds another two to three hours. **NB** This hike involves a very steep nine-metre descent down a ladder, plus swimming across pools of deep water. You will need a swimming costume plus waterproof bags for valuables/maps, etc.

The hike begins at the entrance to Ya'ar Yehudiya Nature Reserve (**1**). Cross to the east side of Route 87, following the red trail markers (away from the main entrance). Almost immediately you come to the ruins of an ancient town identified as **Sogane** (Tell Khushniyye). It is described by Josephus as one of the towns that he fortified against the approaching Romans (*Jewish War II, 572*), though it appears that unlike Gamla (see page 756), Sogane surrendered to Rome's representative Agrippa II at the beginning of the revolt (66 CE). Its subsequent history is not entirely clear, though it is known that Turcomans from Central Asia settled here in the 19th century CE.

As you skirt the site to the south the trail divides (**2**), with the red trail heading northeast and the green trail heading southwest. Take the red trail to the left, along the top of the canyon. After a kilometre or so the trail descends into the Nahal Yehudiya at the foot of the waterfall (**3**). You can stop for a swim here, though there is plenty of opportunity for getting wet later! Follow the red trail along the river. After 500 metres you reach a second waterfall (**4**). Climb down to the pool nine metres below using the steep ladder. Officially it is not permitted to jump from the top of the ladder into the pool, though many hikers ignore this rule. Swim across the (deep) pool. Several further pools have to be negotiated as you follow the course of the Nahal Yehudiya towards the Sea of Galilee. The trail crosses the stream from bank to bank a number of times. About a kilometre below the pools, a green trail heads off to the right (northwest) (**5**). This trail returns to Sogane (**2**), completing the shorter circuit.

If you want to complete the longer circuit, continue to follow the red trail along the course of the Nahal Yehudiya. The trail encounters a series of waterfalls and pools, though you pass these to your left . The final deep pool (**6**) you have to swim across. About a kilometre further on look out for the red trail markers as the path climbs the bank to the right (**7**). Once you reach the plateau it can be a little difficult to follow the red trail markers through the Yehudiya Forest of Tabor oaks, though if you head in a northwest direction after less than a kilometre you should hit Route 87 (**8**). From here it should not be more than one or two kilometres back to the Nature Reserve entrance (**1**).

Upper Zavitan hike

This hike takes around three to four hours, though it can be extended if you combine it with the Lower Zavitan hike (add four hours). It's a fairly easy walk, with one tricky descent, and features some interesting rock formations, a waterfall, and a swimming pool.

The hike begins at the reserve entrance (**1**). Head north through the gate along the old semi-paved road for 1.5 kilometres. If you have a car you can drive this section. At the foot of the lava flow, near the electricity pole (**9**), head to the left (west) along the blue marked trail. After one kilometre the trail divides (**10**). Take the black trail to the right and head northwest for 1.5 kilometres. When the trail meets the Nahal Zavitan (**11**) descend to the west bank and follow the canyon downstream. After a short walk you arrive at two small pools (**12**). The unusual rock formations here were created some three million years ago by the rapid cooling of the lava flow, with the basalt cracking into these hexagonal shapes. The red trail continues along the canyon, crossing the Nahal Zavitan several times, in part following the course of the old abandoned Arab-built aqueduct. You reach another pool featuring hexagonal rock formations above the 25-metre-high Zavitan Waterfall (**13**). The red trail bypasses the waterfall by turning to the left. After a few minutes walking, a treacherous blue trail descends to the swimming pool below the waterfall. From here, there are two options. It's possible retrace your footsteps back up the blue trail, and follow it back to the intersection with the black trail (**10**), and the starting point (**9**). Alternatively, you can continue on to the Lower Zavitan hike.

NB If you continue on to the Lower Zavitan hike, note that it is illegal to enter the dangerous 'Black Gorge' that leads down from the swimming hole at the end of the Upper Zavitan hike (**13**). Instead you must follow the red trail along the southeast side of the Black Gorge. After a kilometre or so it meets the green trail that marks the beginning of the Lower Zavitan hike (**14**) (see below).

Lower Zavitan hike

The Lower Zavitan hike takes around four hours and can be started either from the entrance to the reserve (**1**), or from the finish of the Upper Zavitan hike (**14**). If you begin your hike from the reserve entrance, head west on the green trail through the Tabor oaks and cattle grazing area. After 1.5 kilometres the green trail meets the red trail at a cliff viewpoint above the Nahal Zavitan (**14**). Follow the red trail for a very short distance to the right, then look out for the black trail markers that lead left down the stepped path into the canyon. Turn left into the stream bed and follow its course. Passing one attractive pool, the trail leads to a deep circular swimming pool at Ein Netef (spring) (**15**). This is a great stop for a break.

If you are continuing on to Brekhat HaMeshushim (**16**), cross the river bed and follow the red trail in a westerly direction (see page 755). Note that these hexagonal pools are another two hours away at least. To complete the Lower Zavitan hike cross to the southeast side of Nahal Zavitan, then follow the red trail to the northeast above the canyon. After a short distance you will reach the intersection with the green trail (**14**), from where you return to the reserve entrance (**1**).

Brekhat HaMeshushim (Hexagon Pools)

The Brekhat HaMeshushim, or Hexagon Pools, are located on the Nahal Meshushim shortly before it meets the Nahal Zavitan (**16**). Though these rock formations are found elsewhere in this area, they are their most spectacular here as perfectly formed six-sided basalt columns, three to five metres high, line either side of the stream. It's certainly worth the effort of getting here.

If you have your own transport the Hexagon Pools can be reached after just 2 ½ hours walking (plus the same time back again). At Beit Hameches/Custom House Junction, between Katzrin and B'not Ya'akov Bridge, Route 888 runs south towards the Jordan River Park. Just to the south of this junction a road heads southeast to the Meshushim parking lot. (Alternatively, Custom House Junction can be reached by heading north along Route 888 from the Jordan River Park and the Sea of Galilee). From the parking lot it takes 2½ hours to reach the pools along the red trail along the southwest bank of the Nahal Meshushim.

The longer approach to the Hexagon Pools is by continuing along the red trail from Ein Netef (**15**) on the Lower Zavitan hike. **NB** It is six hours one-way from the Nature Reserve entrance (1) to Brekhat HaMeshushim (16). ■ *T6962817. 0800-1700, closes one hour earlier on Friday, Saturday, and in winter. Adult 17 NIS.*

Gamla

Phone code: 06
Colour map 1, grid B5

Most scholars agree that this magnificent site is the ancient town of Gamla (Gamala), scene of one of the most dramatic battles in Josephus' account of the First Jewish Revolt against the Romans (66-73 CE). Though certain aspects of the terrain do not entirely match Josephus' description (see box opposite), it is a set-ting worthy of the human tragedy that unfolded at Gamla. Whether viewed from the Sea of Galilee looking due east, or from the cliff above with the Sea of Galilee in the background to the west, Gamla is an impressive sight. The remains of the town and citadel stand on a hump-shaped hill ('gamal' is Hebrew for camel) that divides a wide valley between the Nahal Daliyyot to the south and its tributary Nahal Gamla to the north. The hill is connected to the higher Golan plateau by a narrow saddle. The cliff face above Gamla is a major breeding ground for birds of prey, so as you look down on an amazing panoramic vista towards the Sea of Gal-ilee, huge vultures effortlessly glide pass you in the foreground, soaring and swooping on the air currents. And if all that were not enough, there are walking trails that will take you to dramatic waterfalls where the Nahal Gamla and Daliyyot drop down from the Golan plateau into the valley and down to the Sea of Galilee. Though Gamla is difficult to reach without your own transport, it is rec-ommended that you make every effort to get here.

Ins and outs

Getting there Unfortunately there is no public transport to Gamla, with the nearest bus stops being quite some distance away. Buses 018/019 from Tiberias go as far as Ramat Magshimim 8km to the southeast, whilst 022 goes to Ma'ale Gamla, a similar distance to the west. Another alternative could be to go to Katzrin and hitch, though there's no guarantee of success. If you cannot get hold of your own transport it may be worth

Ancient Gamla

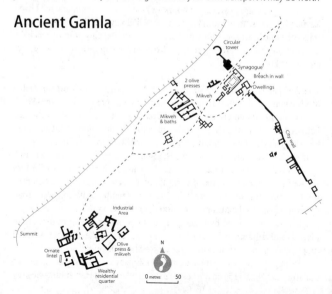

Circular tower

Synagogue

2 olive presses

Breach in wall

Dwellings

Mikveh

Mikveh & baths

City wall

Industrial Area

Summit

Olive press & mikveh

Ornate lintel

Wealthy residential quarter

N

0 metres   50

Identifying Gamla

The identification of Gamla with the camel-hump hill here was first proposed by Gal in 1968 and confirmed two years later by Gutman, who is said to have worked with a copy of Josephus in his hand. Certainly the setting matches Josephus' description: *"Sloping down from a towering peak is a spur like a long shaggy neck, behind which rises a symmetrical hump, so that the outline resembles that of a camel ... On the face and both sides it is cut off by impassable ravines. Near the tail it is rather more accessible, where it is detached from the hill; but here too, by digging a trench across, the inhabitants made access very difficult. Built against the almost vertical flank the houses were piled on top of one another, and the town seemed to be hung in mid-air and on the point of tumbling on top of itself from its very steepness"* (Jewish War IV, 4-7).

However, there is one crucial line in Josephus' account that throws doubt upon this identification. He describes how *"It faced south and its southern crest, which rose to an immense height, served as a citadel, resting on an unwalled precipice that went straight* down into the deepest ravine" (ibid, IV, 8). In actual fact, the citadel here is actually to the west of the hump.

So, is this just a simple typographic error in Josephus' narrative, or is he describing somewhere else? Scholarly opinion is divided on this one, with some suggesting that the description applies much more accurately to Tell ed-Dara', near the village of Jamle on the Syrian side of the ceasefire line. Yet it is difficult to ignore the substantial evidence that suggests that this is Gamla. Not only does Josephus' description fit superbly, bar one small point, but the discovery of numerous Roman period iron arrowheads and spearheads plus numerous ballista stones from the Roman catapults suggests that a major battle took place here during the First Jewish Revolt. Given the numerous inconsistencies and inaccuracies in Josephus' works, it's very tempting to give him the benefit of the doubt here.

trying to get on an organized tour. Try contacting the SPNI Field School in Katzrin (T6961352/6961234, F6961233), the Tourist Information Centre in Tiberias (T6725666, F6725062), Egged Tours in Tiberias (T6712160), or enquire about group trips at the large hotels in Tiberias. A hire-car from Tiberias is the best option.

Gamla's fine attractions have been divided into three marked walking trails. The **Getting around** Ancient Trail leads down from the viewpoint on the plateau to explore the ancient town on the camel-shaped hill below. The Vultures Trail follows the line of the cliff face to the north, passing through the bird of prey nesting areas and up to Israel's highest perennial waterfall. The Daliyyot Waterfalls Trail heads southeast along the cliff face, offering sweeping views and also passing some memorable waterfalls. Making an early start it's not impossible to complete all three walks in one day.

History

The bulk of Gamla's history has been gleaned from the writings of **Josephus**, though almost all points are backed up by archaeology. The town is first mentioned in the context of Alexander Jannaeus' campaign in the region c. 83-80 BCE, though Talmudic sources refer to a walled city here dating back to the time of Joshua. The earliest coins found here date only to 280 BCE, but excavations on the east side of the hill have unearthed remnants from the Early Bronze Age (c. 3300-2200 BCE).

The Hellenistic settlement that Alexander Jannaeus captured appears to have been populated by Jews during the reign of Herod the Great in the first

The Roman capture of Gamla

Gamla was the last of the major fortified towns in the north to fall to Vespasian's all-conquering Roman army, and given the town's formidable natural defences, coupled with the defensive walls, trenches and underground passages that the inhabitants had built, it is easy to see why the occupants were reluctant to surrender. In fact it was to take three legions of the Roman army, and a stunning setback, before the Roman might eventually prevailed. After the siege-engines had battered the walls, the Romans "poured in through the breaches with a great blare of trumpets and din of weapons, and shouting themselves hoarse flung themselves upon the defenders of the town." With the scent of victory (and blood) in their nostrils the usually disciplined Roman army surged forwards, pursuing the defenders towards the upper part of the town. As Vespasian was to concede later the Romans should have withdrawn at this point and consolidated their hold on the lower town. Instead they pushed on, falling into the trap set for them. The Jewish defenders "swung round and counter-attacked vigorously. Swept down the slope and jammed inextricably in the narrow alleys, the Romans suffered fearful casualties ... they climbed on to the roofs of the houses ... [but] crowded with men and unequal to the weight these quickly collapsed ... many were buried under the debris, many while trying to escape found one limb or another pinned down ... the debris furnished them [the Jews] with any number of great stones, and the bodies of the enemy with cold steel: they wrenched the swords from the fallen and used them to finish off those who were slow to die ... unacquainted with the roads and choked

with the dust, they [the Romans] could not even recognize their friends, but in utter confusion attacked each other." Even Vespasian himself had succumbed to the excitement of the assault and only a disciplined retreat had prevented his capture.

The demoralized Roman army withdrew and regrouped outside the town. Morale was boosted by Vespasian's pep-talk, who sought not to apportion blame for the ill-discipline that had precipitated the disaster (himself not being wholly blameless). Instead he pointed out how Roman victories were attained by adhering to a tactical battle-plan. Some days later, when the walls had been breached by three members of the Fifteenth Legion undermining a projecting tower, Vespasian's son Titus led an ordered advance into the town at the head of 200 cavalry. The Romans pressed forward relentlessly "as men were slaughtered on every side, and the whole town was deluged with the blood that poured down the slopes." Mindful that the Roman army would be in no mood to take prisoners, those trapped in the citadel "despairing of escape and hemmed in every way, they flung their wives and children and themselves too into the immensely deep artificial ravine that yawned under the citadel"; a scene that was to be repeated several years later at Masada. In fact, as at Masada just two women survived, with Josephus succinctly pointing out that "the fury of the victors seemed less destructive than the suicidal frenzy of the trapped men; 4,000 fell by Roman swords, but those who plunged to destruction proved to be over 5,000." (Josephus, The Jewish War, IV, 27-83)

century BCE. At the beginning of the **First Jewish Revolt** (66 CE) it was within the kingdom of Agrippa II and appears to have kept its allegiance to Rome. However, it switched allegiance during the struggle against the Romans and became one of the northern cities that the Jewish commander Josephus fortified (before he too switched allegiance). Agrippa II's seven-month siege of Gamla failed to break the town and it is was only after a severe setback that **Vespasian**'s legions were able to capture the town in late 67 CE (see box on page 758). The site does not appear to have been occupied after the Roman conquest.

The Ancient Trail

Though it is only about 500 metres down to the ancient town on the hill below the plateau, it's a killer climb on the way back so you should allow around two hours for this walk. The black marked trail begins just behind the remains of the Byzantine settlement of Deir Quruh, just beyond the car-park. At the top of the descent a diagram illustrates the phases of the battle for Gamla, whilst quotes from Josephus are stuck on rocks throughout the site. Descending to the defensive city walls, it is possible to see the breach made by the Romans during the first assault on Gamla. The walls extend for around 350 metres on the east side, whilst the other approaches are protected by natural steep cliffs.

Close to the point where the walls were breached is a large rectangular structure (25.5 metres by 17 metres) built on a northeast to southwest axis. It is usually identified as a **synagogue** dating to the period of Herod the Great, though some commentators challenge this viewpoint. Murphy-O'Connor, whilst conceding that the stepped benches around the four walls are a feature that can also be found at the synagogues at Herodium and Masada, suggests that there are "no specifically Jewish features either in design or decoration" (*Holy Land*, 1992). Gutman, who largely excavated the site, is certain that it is a synagogue, pointing out that its unusual orientation (not facing Jerusalem) is determined by the topography of the ground. If it is indeed a synagogue, it is one of the oldest ones found in the Holy Land and the only one built within city limits whilst the Temple at Jerusalem was still standing. The synagogue is adjoined by a *mikveh* (ritual bath), a study room and a courtyard, and would have been the centre of community life.

From the synagogue it is possible to wander through the remains of the town to the **wealthy residential area** at the western tip. Many of the buildings in the town are labelled, including several well-preserved oil presses.

The Vultures' Trail

This red marked trail is a simple one-hour stroll along the cliff top and back, and should not be missed. Passing above the main breeding grounds of the Griffon vultures, Egyptian vultures, Bonelli's eagle, long-legged buzzard, kestrels and short-toed eagles, soaring **birds of prey** are your constant companions above the ravine of the Nahal Gamla to your left, as they "flap lazily overhead, then plunge into the ravine in search of lunch" (Stephen Brook,

Galilee & The Golan

Gamla Nature Reserve

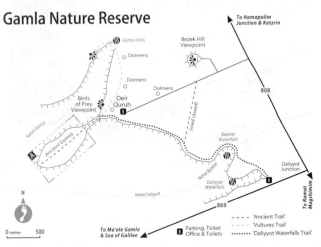

To Hamapalim Junction & Katzrin

Gamla Falls

Dolmens

Bezek Hill Viewpoint

Dolmens

Dolmens

Birds of Prey Viewpoint

Deir Quruh

808

(road closed)

Nahal Gamla

Ancient Gamla

Bazelet Waterfalls

Nahal Bazelet

Daliyyot Junction

Daliyyot Waterfalls

Nahal Daliyyot

To Ramat Magshimim

869

N

0 metres   500

To Ma'ale Gamla & Sea of Galilee

Parking, Ticket Office & Toilets

- - - - 'Ancient Trail'
– – – 'Vultures' Trail'
.... 'Daliyyot Waterfalls Trail'

Winner Takes All, 1990). With the camel-hump hill of Gamla in the foreground, the waterscape of the Beit Zaida Nature Reserve beyond, and the Sea of Galilee in the distance, the planing birds complete the scene nicely. To the right (east) of the trail are scattered a field of **dolmens**; 4,000-year-old megalithic blocks stacked together to serve as burial sites. The trail crosses the Nahal Gamla just above **Gamla Falls**, at 51 metres Israel's highest perennial waterfall. A smaller waterfall is also seen slightly further on. The trail finishes at a viewpoint from where it is possible to look back at the nesting sites in the cliff face. **NB** It is illegal to descend the cliffs or to the river-bed, or to disturb the birds in any way. Keep to the paths. Do not proceed beyond the final viewpoint because an IDF firing zone begins here. Return by the same route.

The Daliyyot Waterfalls Trail This red-and-white trail can be completed in either direction, beginning at either the main entrance to Gamla Nature Reserve, or at the southerly entrance on Route 869 (road down to Sea of Galilee at Ma'ale Gamla Junction) close to Daliyyot Junction. The walk takes about two hours in either direction (four hours return). The highlights of this walk are the stunning views down towards Gamla and beyond, and the waterfalls on the Nahal Daliyyot and its tributary, Nahal Bazelet. ■ *T6963721. Summer 0800-1700, closes one hour earlier in winter. The reserve sometimes closes on weekdays for military exercises, so it is best to call ahead to make sure it is open. Adult 18 NIS, adult in a group 15 NIS. Keep ticket for 25 percent discount at Ancient Qasrin Park. Toilets, kiosk, picnic area.*

The Basilica of the Annunciation, Nazareth

Background

12

Background

History

It is very difficult to present the history of this land (whether you call it Israel, Palestine, the Holy Land, or whatever title suits your viewpoint) in just 25 pages. Events that took place here some 4,000 years ago, and would be considered 'pre-history' elsewhere, are as fresh in the collective memory as the defining moments of the 20th century. Thus, the history of Israel begins not with the establishment of the State of Israel in 1948, but with the beginning of Jewish history around 1650 BCE.

Likewise, there are different interpretations of history; not so much truth, but versions. The author of this *Handbook* has attempted to be impartial in the following presentation of history, striving to present together dichotomous views of the same events. Yet the history of Israel/Palestine, even the nomenclature, is a veritable minefield of contrary positions and interpretations, and it is inevitable that a few explosions will be set off in attempting to guide readers through it. For this reason, at the end of each section a small selection of further reading is included that may help provide a greater understanding of the opposing viewpoints.

Ancient Israel

Early settlement

Though Jewish history can be said to have begun some 4,000 years ago when Abraham made the purchase of the Cave of Machpelah at Hebron, the Patriarchs and their descendants the Israelites were by no means the first peoples to settle the land here. The move from food-gatherers to food-producers by members of a Pre-Pottery Neolithic culture some time in the ninth millennium BCE, and the subsequent construction of a defensive wall around their settlement, gives rise to Jericho's claim as the oldest city in the world.

At some point in the Early Bronze Age, around 3300 BCE, a civilization known ass **Canaanite** established itself on the coastal strip that now roughly corresponds to the present-day Israel, sandwiched between the more highly advanced civilizations of Egypt and Mesopotamia. The Canaanites belonged to the northwest Semitic peoples of northern Mesopotamia and Syria; a region that was also to produce the group subsequently known as Jews. The land that became known as Canaan was in fact a series of city-states, all subject to the power and influence of generally stronger neighbouring civilizations. At some point in the Middle Bronze Age (circa 18th or 17th century BCE) other groups began to settle in Canaan, notably the **Philistines** on the coast, and in the hills a nomadic people known as the **Habiru**.

The Patriarchs

The Habiru, including the 'early Hebrews', were led into Canaan by the patriarch of the tribe, **Abraham** of Ur (in present day Iraq). The Bible/Torah recalls how God made a covenant with Abraham, calling upon him to lead God's chosen people, and telling him that "I will give unto thee, and to thy seed after thee, the land wherein thou art a stranger, all the land of Canaan, for an everlasting possession" (*Genesis 17:8*). Abraham is thus the first true believer in the one God, with this belief in a single god evolving into the monotheism that underlies Judaism, Christianity and Islam. Abraham's tribe called themselves 'B'nei Israel' (the people or tribe of Israel), subsequently known as the **Israelites** and now the **Jews**. Archaeology, plus various

A note on dating

*Whilst Christians date history from the birth of Christ, and Muslims from the departure of the prophet Mohammed from Medina, Jews date history from the Creation. Thus, the year that this Handbook is published is 1999 in the Christian chronology, 1419 in the Islamic calendar, and 5760 in the Jewish calender. The conventional system of writing dates is to use the formulation BC ('before Christ') and AD (meaning 'after Christ'). To avoid a Christian gloss, the editor of this Israel Handbook has chosen to use **BCE** ('before the common era') and **CE** ('common era'). Though this formulation may be less well known to an English-speaking audience, it is the system used at almost all archaeological and historical sites in the country. Remember, BCE = BC and CE = AD. Refer to the glossary in the 'Footnotes' section at the end of this Handbook.*

literary archives that have emerged from Bronze-Age Syria and Mesopotamia, has allowed a rough dating of the Patriarchs (Abraham, his son Isaac, and grandson Jacob) to the first half of the second millennium BCE, with Abraham's purchase of the Cave of Machpelah in Hebron usually dated to around 1650 BCE.

Exodus

The spread of famine throughout Canaan saw Abraham's grandson Jacob and his twelve sons and their families establish themselves to the east of the Nile delta in Egypt. The reproductive rate of the Israelite community in Egypt was such that the new pharaoh, fearing that they may soon out-number his own subjects, had the Israelite community enslaved and pressed into forced labour. There is considerable evidence of a historical-archaeological nature, however, that suggests that a sizeable Israelite population remained in Canaan during the period of their brethren's Egyptian bondage.

After some 400 years of enslavement in Egypt, according to the biblical narrative, **Moses** was called upon by God to lead his people out of slavery and back to the "promised land": the **Exodus**. It was during the 40 years of wandering in the Sinai desert that the Israelites received the Law of Moses (including the Ten Commandments), and though the sojourn in Egypt and then the desert involved

Genealogy of the Patriarchs

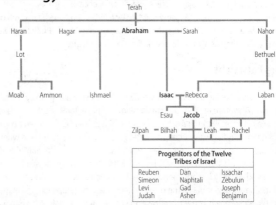

only part of the Israelite community, it effectively forged them into a nation. As Johnson observes, "Before they went to Egypt, the Israelites were a small folk almost like any other, though they had a cherished promise of greatness. After they returned, they were a people with a purpose, a programme and a message to the world" (*A History of the Jews*, 1987).

In the 200 years or so that followed the Exodus, the various tribes of the Israelites abandoned their nomadic ways and set about conquering much of Canaan. The tribes functioned through an institution dating back to Abraham and Moses, prophetship, an essential part of the Israelite theocracy since this was the medium through which God communicated with his "chosen people". The role of the prophets stretched beyond mediating between man and God, or mere prophesy; they became political and military leaders as well as **'judges'** on spiritual matters.

United Monarchy

Though the Israelites continued to have significant military success in dispossessing the Canaanites, the **Philistines** proved to be far more formidable opponents. In fact, it was in response to the threat of Philistine power that the Israelites turned to a new institution: kingship. This significant change in social organization was in fact engineered through the existing institution of prophetship (the 'judges'). Before agreeing to anoint **Saul** as leader of the Israelites, the prophet/judge **Samuel** went to great lengths to explain the implications of kingship, even going as far as to suggest that the abandonment of the theocracy was a rejection of rule of God (*I Samuel 10:18-19; 12:1-25*). Eventually Samuel bent to the will of God (*I Samuel 8:22*) and the popular mandate of the people, anointing Saul as king. The loose confederation of Israelite tribes now became joined under the **United Monarchy**.

Despite early successes against the Canaanites, Saul's period of kingship can hardly be considered a success. Samuel and the rest of the clergy appear to have lost confidence in him and within a year of his anointment Saul's Israelite army was comprehensively defeated by the Philistines at Mount Gilboa (and Saul himself killed). However, for all his shortcomings Saul's lasting legacy to the Israelites was a mercenary that he had recruited to their cause: **David**. It is beyond the scope of this brief introduction to delve exhaustively into David's background, though suffice to say the popular image of King David encountered today appears a long way from reality. As Johnson notes, though David's reign (1004-965 BCE) has been regarded by Jews as the 'golden age' for more than 2,000 years now, "At the time … his rule was always precarious … His most dependable forces were not Israelites at all but his personal guards of foreign mercenaries … The tribes [of Israel] were still separatist by instinct … They resented the cost of David's campaigns … and the apparatus of oriental kinship he introduced" (*ibid*).

Despite the revolts against his regime and the successional dispute that continued all through his reign, he was still a great king, carving out a huge empire through a combination of conquests and alliances. One of his conquests included Jerusalem, where David effectively legitimated the concept of kingship. It should perhaps be noted, however, that the question of the relationship between religion and temporal power that arose with the acceptance of the kingship formula remains unresolved today, famously resurrected in the 'religious versus secular state' argument that still plagues Israeli society.

Significantly, David designated his son **Solomon** to be his successor; not a warrior or a general but a scholar-judge. Perhaps this was a result of David's realization that in order for the balance between kingship and theocracy to continue, it was essential that the Israelites were ruled by someone capable of discharging the religious as well as temporal duties. David recognized that a degree of centralization was necessary to defend the Israelites from outside attack, though

Background

turning Israel into a royal temple-state was beyond the remit granted to the Israelites by God.

Solomon appears to be much more of a pragmatist than his father, with one of his first acts upon assuming the throne, building the Temple at Jerusalem, effectively being a means of instituting royal absolutism "in which the king controls the sole shrine where God could be effectively worshipped" (Johnson, *ibid*). During his lifetime Solomon consolidated the territorial gains made by his father, expanded the trading networks with neighbouring economies, and raised the profile of the nation to the status of an equal with the other great regional powers.

Divided Monarchy

Despite notable successes, Solomon's reign was hardly an unqualified success. Towards its end there was considerable discontent amongst the populace over a number of issues, particularly the high levels of taxation necessary to finance his ambitious foreign policy and domestic building programme, and the preferential treatment that he showed the members of his own tribe. Upon his death in 928 BCE, the northern tribes rejected the principle of hereditary succession through the family of David, and the monarchy divided on regional lines: a northern kingdom of **Israel** and a southern kingdom of **Judah**.

The Kingdom of Israel, comprising the ten northern tribes, survived a little over 200 years before being crushed by the expanding **Assyrian** empire in 722 BCE. Though many refugees fled from Israel to Judah, notably to Jerusalem, the majority of the ten tribes were sent into exile (and subsequent oblivion).

The Kingdom of Judah, based upon the tribes of Benjamin and Judah, fared a little better, lasting until 586 BCE when the invading **Babylonian** army (led by Nebuchadnezzar II) captured Jerusalem, razed the Temple, and sent the population into exile. This conquest marked the end of the First Jewish Commonwealth (and the end of the 'First Temple Period').

The Exile and Return

Though relatively brief (less than 50 years), the **Babylonian Exile** represents one of the most significant events in Jewish history. Though pro-Israeli histories are prone to refer to the Exile as a time in which the Jews never forgot their connection to the homeland, usually quoting Psalm 137:5-6 ("If I forget you, O Jerusalem", etc), there are far more important aspects of the Exile to consider. Two themes that require further consideration are the questions of the evolution of Judaism as a religion and the formation of a diaspora mentality amongst Jews.

Space does not permit a comprehensive analysis of these themes in this *Handbook*, though those with an interest may care to refer to Paul Johnson's *A History of the Jews* (1987) for a very thorough examination of these issues. However, to paraphrase Johnson's thesis, the Exile saw the Jews first become disciplined into the regular practice of the given laws of their religion (for example circumcision; rules of purity and diet; the Sabbath, holidays and festivals; and the study of the Law). It was not that these practices were ignored prior to the Exile, more that the system of laws and practices that comprise what we now call Judaism were more rigorously enforced in Exile as the Jews sought to preserve their unique spiritual identity. The voluntary nature of the submission to the Law is significant.

The defeat of the Babylonian empire by the Persian Achaemenid dynasty in 539 BCE saw Cyrus the Great deliver a proclamation that allowed the Jews to return to their historic homeland. Though work began almost straight away on building a new Temple (and thus ushering in the **'Second Temple period'**), it took fully four waves of returnees before Jewish recolonization could be said to be successful. The

Kings of Judah and Israel

THE UNITED MONARCHY

Saul   c.1020-1004 BCE
David   1004-965
Solomon   965-928

JUDAH		ISRAEL	
Rehoboam	928-911	Jeroboam	928-907
Abijam	911-908	Nadab	907-906
Asa	908-867	Baasha	906-883
Jehoshaphat	867-846	Elah	883-882
Jehoram	846-843	Zimri	882
Ahaziah	843-842	Tibni	882-878
Athaliah	842-836	Omri	882-871
Joash	836-798	Ahab	871-852
Amaziah	798-769	Ahaziah	852-851
Uzziah	769-733	Jehoram	851-842
Jotham	758-743	Jehu	842-814
Ahaz	733-727	Jehoahaz	814-800
Hezekiah	727-698	Jehoash	800-784
Manasseh	698-642	Jeroboam	784-748
Amon	641-640	Zechariah	748/747
Josiah	639-609	Shallum	748/747
Jehoahaz	609	Menahem	747-737
Jehoiakim	608-598	Pekahiah	737-735
Jehoiachin	597	Pekah	735-733
Zedekiah	596-586	Hoshea	733-724

fourth wave was led by Ezra the Scribe and the prominent Persian official Nehemiah in 445 BCE, and saw the re-emergence once more of Jerusalem as a major city. This time, however, it represented the centre of a new version of the Israelite faith that had evolved during the exile: **Judaism**. In the centuries subsequent to the Return, this new 'religion' recieved a legal and official sanction in the form of a written document: the Old Testament.

Further reading: Paul Johnson, *A History of the Jews*

Hellenistic and Hasmonean periods

Alexander the Great's successful foreign campaigns of the early fourth century BCE saw Greek colonists arrive in great number in West Asia, bringing with them the concept of the *polis*, or Greek city-state. The effect on the population of the land that is now Israel ranged between two extremes. On the one hand, the process of Hellenization saw fundamentalist groups emerge within Judaism, often retreating into isolated communities to preserve their spiritual purity. On the other hand, many Jews embraced the Greek culture, seeking to rush through Hellenizing reforms. Perhaps such a reaction is inevitable when one race is preaching a message of universal monotheism and the other the notion of universalist culture. It was not so much that the two concepts are totally incompatible; after all, Abraham and Moses could both be reinvented as 'great citizens of the world'. However, any attempt to reform the Law was seen as an attack on the Law itself. Inevitably, the two competing cultures were to clash.

Early Hellenistic period

Background

Hasmoneans

Jonathon 152-142 BCE	Salome Alexandra 76-67
Simeon 142-134	Aristobulus II 67-63
John Hyrcanus 134-104	Hyrcanus II 63-40
Aristobulus 104-103	Matthias Antigonus 40-37
Alexander Jannaeus 103-76	

Hasmonean Dynasty

The emerging conflict was brought to a head during the reign of the Seleucid king Antiochus IV Epiphanes (the **Seleucids** being Alexander's Syrian-based successors, as opposed to the Egypt-based successors, the **Ptolemies**). His Hellenizing reforms effectively sought to abolish Mosaic law and turn the Temple into an interdenominational place of worship. The spark that lit the fire of revolt occurred in Modi'im, a small town in the Judean foothills, with members of the priestly Hasmonean family leading what became known as the **Maccabean Revolt**. The success of the uprising must be seen within the context of the growing pressure on the Seleucid empire through the rising power of Rome; in 161 BCE the Hasmonean family had signed an alliance with Rome that effectively recognized them as the ruling family of an independent state. By 152 BCE the Seleucids had all but abandoned their programme of forced Hellenization, recognizing the head of the Hasmonean family, Jonathon, as high priest. His successor, Simeon (Simon Maccabee) became both high priest and ruler; the Jews were once more ruled by a Jew.

Summarizing the **Hasmonean** dynasty, Johnson suggests that "They began as the avengers of martyrs; they ended as religious oppressors themselves. They came to power at the head of an eager guerilla band; they ended surrounded by mercenaries. Their kingdom, founded on faith, dissolved in impiety" (*ibid*). So what went wrong? In many ways the Hasmoneans raised many of the old dichotomies that had been a feature of David's rule; notably the question of religion and temporal power. Indeed, this was perhaps inevitable when John Hyrcanus revived the concept of rule through kingship. He was also on a mission, divinely inspired as he believed, to restore the Davidic kingdom, and like his role model he did it by creating a large mercenary army. His son Alexander Jannaeus continued the policy of expansion and forced conversion, though unlike his father whose reputation remained relatively untarnished, Alexander Jannaeus is remembered as a bully and despot who split rather than united the Jewish people.

By the time of Alexander Jannaeus' death, the **Romans** had established themselves as the successors to the Seleucid empire in the region, and following the successful campaign of the Roman governor of Syria **Pompey** in 63 BCE, Judaea effectively became a Roman client-state. Jewish efforts to reassert their independence under Hyrcanus II were ultimately futile, and by 37 BCE the Romans had appointed a new King of Judaea to rule the latest vassal state of the Roman Empire: **Herod the Great**. The Jews were not to become fully independent again in the Land of Israel for another 2,000 years.

Roman period

Early Roman period

In many respects the Early Roman period (37 BCE-132 CE) is the most interesting era in the history of this land. It saw the Temple rebuilt and destroyed, the coming of a

Herodian Dynasty

Herod (the Great) 37-4 BCE	*Philip 4 BCE-34 CE*
Archelaus 4 BCE-6 CE	*Herod Agrippa I 37-44 CE*
Herod Antipas 4 BCE-39 CE	*Agrippa II 53-100 CE (?)*

man known as Jesus Christ who would change the course of world history irreversibly, and it saw two major Jewish revolts against Roman rule.

Despite rebuilding the Temple in Jerusalem into one of the most magnificent structures of its time, Herod's Idumean background and admiration for Greco-Roman culture meant that his Jewishness was always open to question amongst his subjects. Yet despite being a puppet-king of the Romans, Herod enjoyed real executive power in domestic affairs and was effectively one of the most powerful monarchs in the region. A summary of his rule produces many contradictions; a ruthless barbarian but brilliant politician; an admirer of Solomon (his idol) but an instigator of Hellenizing reforms; the consummate diplomat with more than a touch of insanity. Herod's successors generally proved incapable of following his act (perhaps unsurprisingly), and by 44 CE the province was under direct Roman rule.

First Jewish Revolt

In 66 CE the Jews rose up in open revolt against Rome. The causes of this uprising were many and complex, and it is misleading to suggest that it was a popular revolt against "increasingly harsh and insensitive Roman rule" (*Facts About Israel*, Israel Information Center, 1995). Johnson suggests that the roots of the conflict lie far deeper, and that the revolt "should be seen not just as a rising by a colonized people, inspired by religious nationalism, but as a racial and cultural conflict between Jews and Greeks" (*ibid*). Though the Greeks had submitted physically to the Roman military machine, they had in fact taken it over intellectually, with Greek culture effectively being the cornerstone of the Roman empire. Thus, the First Jewish Revolt was effectively a re-run of the Maccabean uprising that had begun two centuries earlier.

The story of the First Jewish Revolt is graphically told through the writings of Josephus, despite the numerous contradictions and his thorough unreliability as a historian (see 'Further Reading' section below). Though the revolt lasted the best part of seven years, only concluding with the mass suicide of the Jewish Zealots holding out at Masada, it was effectively over in 70 CE when the Romans took Jerusalem and destroyed the Temple.

Bar Kokhba Revolt

The Second Jewish Revolt against Rome took place in 132-135 CE, led by the charismatic **Simon bar Kokhba**. Inevitably the might of the Roman empire prevailed and recriminations were harsh. Jerusalem was effectively levelled and refounded as '**Aelia Capitolina**' along the lines of a Greek *polis*, standing as the capital of the new Roman province of *Filistina* ('Palestine', derived from the word 'Philistine').

Late Roman period

Many of the Jews who survived the revolt were either sold or forced into exile, marking another key stage in the diaspora experience. The failure of the revolts of 66-73 CE and 132-135 CE had two significant consequences: firstly it led to the the final separation from Judaism of a nascent reform movement that ultimately manifested itself in the doctrine of Christianity; and secondly it led to a fundamental change in the nature and practice of Judaism itself. In fact, it was this period of introspection, in which study of the religious texts replaced attempts to assert Jewish independence through nationalist uprisings, that perhaps ensured the survival of the Jews as a distinct race. The next couple of hundred years saw the formation of the *Sanhedrin*, or supreme legislative and judicial body of the Jews, the completion of the *Mishnah* (the first written compilation of the Oral Law) and the *Talmud* (the commentary on Jewish law and lore), thus effectively enlarging the Torah from a religious text into a logical and consistent code of moral theology and community law.

Further reading: Josephus, *The Jewish War*; Paul Johnson, *A History of the Jews*

Byzantine period

Byzantine rule

The conversion of the Roman emperor **Constantine the Great** to Christianity in 313 CE, and his unification of the West and East empires in 324 CE, brought Christian Byzantine rule to Palestine. Churches were established on the key holy sites, notably in Jerusalem, Bethlehem and the Galilee, accompanied by a phenomenon that has continued to sustain the economy to this day: religious tourism. Large Christian communities developed primarily as a result of pagan converts, and the population of the land may well have become predominantly Christian. Christian rule saw Jewish communities have many of their privileges withdrawn, such as the right to hold state office, serve in the army, proselytize or inter-marry with Christians. Such discriminations had their origin in the charge of deicide levelled against the Jewish people as a whole (for having crucified Jesus), though the idea that the Jews were somehow part of 'God's great plan' prevented them being ethnically cleansed. Instead their communities were marginalized from mainstream life, left to decay slowly as the ultimate symbol of the truth of Christianity: the victory of church over synagogue.

By the early seventh century CE, the Byzantine empire was in an advanced state of decline, exacerbated by early splits within the Church. The Persians, assisted by the Jews, invaded in 614 CE, destroying numerous Christian places of worship and massacring Christian communities. Though the Byzantine army rallied to expel the Persians in 629 CE (and take their revenge on the Jews), the empire was tottering precariously on its last legs.

The Arabs and the spread of Islam

Early Arab period

Significantly, the same year that the Byzantine army expelled the Persians, **Mohammad** conquered Mecca. Just two years after his death, the Arab army comprehensively defeated the Byzantines at the Battle of Yarmuk and by 638 CE the whole of Palestine was in Muslim hands.

The status of the non-Muslim communities in Palestine were determined by the Islamic concept of *dhimmis*, whereby Jews and Christians were considered to be inferior, having received but failed to adhere to God's law, but nevertheless entitled to protection upon payment of a special tax known as *jizya*. Jews in particular were treated better by the Muslims than they had been under the Byzantine Christians, whilst the Christians felt particularly aggrieved at having been 'reduced' to the same status as Jews. As a general rule, the treatment of *dhimmis* reflected the external threats posed to Muslim rule.

As with the Christian church before it, Islam became riven by disputes, in this case over the succession of the Caliphate. The four Orthodox Caliphs were succeeded in 661 CE by the **Umayyads**, who in turn were succeeded by the **Abbasids**, with the capital being shifted from Damascus to Baghdad. Around 975 CE the **Fatimids**, who had conquered Egypt some six years earlier, came to power in Palestine. Christian pilgrims continued to visit the Holy Land throughout this period, though this all changed under the second Fatimid Caliph **al-Hakim**, who systematically persecuted the non-Muslim population of Palestine, particularly the Christians. This persecution culminated in his destruction of the central shrine in Christendom, the Church of the Holy Sepulchre. The **Seljuk Turks**, who had come to power in the region in 1055, continued where al-Hakim had left off, generally harassing Christian pilgrims to the Holy Land and eventually slamming the gates of Jerusalem firmly shut. Such a provocation put the Muslim world on a collision course with Christian Europe. Although the Seljuk Turks were defeated by the Fatimids, it was too late; the Christian armies were on their way.

Battle for the Holy Land

The Crusades

In 1095 at the Council of Clermont, Pope Urban II called upon all Christians to take up arms to recover the holy places from the infidels. Four years later, at midday on 15th July, 1099, the **Crusaders** eventually captured Jerusalem, slaughtering most of its Muslim and Jewish inhabitants in the process. Godfrey de Bouillon, who led the campaign, declared himself 'Protector of the Holy Sepulchre', to be replaced upon his death 1 year later by his brother Baldwin who crowned himself king of Jerusalem.

Though the 12th century CE was marked by Crusader expansion across the Holy Land, they can hardly be said to have established a Christian kingdom since their power was mainly confined to a series of isolated castles and fortified cities. The securing of main routes, however, allowed the Christian pilgrimage trade to flourish in a way that Jerusalem hoteliers can only dream about today.

Of course the Crusader kingdom was in reality a house of cards, riven by internal factional fighting, and it can be little surprise that the Crusaders were eventually defeated and driven from the Holy Land. The fact that their adversary, **Salah al-Din**, was such a worthy opponent made their defeat at the Horns of Hittim in 1187 an inevitability (see page 667). A series of Crusades throughout the rest of the 12th and 13th centuries saw the Crusaders regain a measure of control over the Holy Land (partly through conquest and partly through treaty), though again their influence was confined to a network of fortified castles. Eventually, in 1291, the Crusaders were finally driven from the Holy Land by the Mamluks.

Mamluk period

A dynasty arising from freed slaves of Turkish or Circassian origin, the **Mamluks** (variously Mameluks or Mamlukes) came to power in Egypt in 1250, though a rival élite based itself in Damascus. Palestine was effectively a province administered from the latter, though Jerusalem was considered to be a separate entity under the jurisdiction of Cairo, where the sultan was charged with protecting the Islamic holy places. A notable feature of the Mamluk period was a large influx of Jewish immigrants, ostensibly a result of their mass expulsion from Spain and Portugal in 1492.

The Crusades

First Crusade 1095-1099
Second Crusade 1147-1149
Third Crusade 1189-1192
Fourth Crusade 1202-1204

Fifth Crusade 1217-1221
Sixth Crusade 1288-1229
Seventh Crusade 1248-1254
Eighth Crusade 1270

Ottoman Empire

Ottoman rule

The defeat of the Mamluks in 1516 by the **Ottoman Turks** saw Palestine come under Ottoman rule for the next four centuries. Palestine never constituted a political administrative unit in its own right, but was divided into districts known as *sanjaks* and incorporated into a province (*vilayet*) of greater Syria that was ruled from Damascus. After 1841 it was further divided, with the northern section going to the *vilayet* of Beirut. The *sanjak* of Jerusalem remained important as a source of revenue through levying taxes on pilgrims. The Islamic *dhimmis* system applied to non-Muslims, and it is fairly safe to say that Jews in particular were afforded better protection by the Ottomans than their brethren in medieval and early modern Europe.

Unsupervised Ottoman officials tended to have more local power than the imperial government in Istanbul, and often lined their own pockets with exorbitant tax demands. Indeed, the Ottomans gradually came to rely on prominent local families (such as the Nusaybas, Husaynis, Nashshashibis) to perform local government functions such as tax collection, *waqf* administration, etc. The *Tanzimat* laws passed by a reformist administration in Istanbul in 1858 allowed land in Palestine to pass into private ownership, though the result appears to be far from what the land reform movement intended. With agriculture moving from subsistence farming to a market economy, wealthy families acquired huge properties in Palestine with the result that tenant farmers now became share-croppers, and heavily indebted to absentee landlords.

Palestine in the 19th century

The importance of finding an accurate picture of Palestine under the Ottomans

Ottoman Palestine & Syria, 1910

Background

(and in the 19th century in particular) will soon become apparent. Pick up any pro-Israeli or Zionist account of history and a familiar pattern emerges. The references are to a land "brought to a state of widespread neglect", bedevilled by "capricious" taxation and "absentee landlords", with the land "denuded of trees" and where "swamp and desert encroached on agricultural land" (*Facts About Israel*, Israel Information Center, 1995). Accounts of travels in the region are trotted out (Chateaubriand, Mark Twain, Lamartine, Nerval, Disraeli, etc), all seeming to confirm this picture of a land in decline. The purpose of course is to present an image that fits the popular Zionist slogan of the time, "A land without people for a people without a land." This sentiment is perhaps best summarized in the words of one right-wing Israeli, Samuel Katz: "The land, unloved by its rulers and uncared for by most of its handful of inhabitants, whose silences Lamartine had likened to those of ruined Pompeii, and which Mark Twain had compassionately consigned to the world of dreams, began to come to life again with the blossoming of Jewish restoration in the 19th century" (*Battleground: Facts and Fantasy in Palestine*, 1985 edition).

   Of course, such a sentiment ignores one indisputable point: the land here was already home to a significant Arab population. As the Palestinian intellectual Edward W. Said observes, "No matter how backward, uncivilized, and silent they were, the Palestinian Arabs *were* on the land" (*The Question of Palestine*, 1979), with Said also pointing out that the 19th-century travellers that are so often quoted by the Zionists (such as Lamartine and Twain) all carry accounts of the Arab inhabitants here. The question of whether the 19th-century Arabs had any sense of national identity, whether they thought of themselves as Palestinians, is also a starting point for debate. As late as 1969 Israeli Prime Minister Golda Meir was asserting that the Palestinians "did not exist", whilst Yitzhak Rabin's usual expression was "the so-called Palestinians". In many ways the argument is irrelevant as long as it is recognized that the land (whether you call it 'Palestine' or not) was overwhelmingly occupied by Arabs when the early Jewish Zionists began to arrive in the late 19th century. In fact, it would not be far from the truth to suggest that Palestinian Arab nationalism and identity were direct products of the perceived threat of Jewish immigration (with many of the nationalist/political organizations that they formed being on the Zionist model). But, as Johnson observes, the Arabs rather missed the boat: "the Arabs were developing a nationalist spirit just like the Jews. The chief difference was that they started to organize themselves two decades later. Jewish nationalism, or Zionism, was part of the European nationalist movement, which was a 19th-century phenomenon. The Arabs, by contrast, were part of the Afro-Asian nationalism of the 20th century" (*A History of the Jews*, 1987). The Jews' head start was to prove catastrophic for the Palestinians.

Further reading   Edward W. Said, *The Question of Palestine*; Samuel Katz, Battle-ground: Facts and Fantasy in Palestine

Zionism

European Jewry and the rise of Zionism

Whilst Palestinian Arab nationalism may be seen as a response to increased Jewish immigration, political Zionism emerged in the context of continued anti-Semitism and persecution of Jews in Europe. To suggest that political Zionism was founded by **Theodor Herzl** in 1897 is a bit like saying Karl Marx invented socialism in 1848 (Laqueur, *A History of Zionism*, 1989), though without doubt it was Herzl who gave the movement the impetus it needed. The infamous Dreyfus trial in France convinced Herzl that despite the Enlightenment and attempts to integrate into European society, Jews would always be discriminated against and persecuted

Zionism

The term 'Zionism' derives from the word 'Zion', a synonym for the Land of Israel that acknowledges Jewish attachment to this particular piece of land. Whilst Zionism implies the redemption of the Jewish people in their ancestral homeland, some identify a distinction between **spiritual Zionism** and **political Zionism**. The former is seen as an inherent part of Jewish existence that has underpinned the Jewish Diaspora experience since the Babylonian Exile (586 BCE). On the other hand, political Zionism is seen as blending "elements of contemporary [19th-century] European nationalism and secular liberalism with the older religious strain" (Joffe, Keesing's Guide to the Middle-East Peace Process, 1996).

unless they had their own state or homeland. The founding of the World Zionist Organization at the Zionist Congress (1897) largely changed the way in which a 'return to Zion' was approached. The system of relying on Jewish philanthropists such as the Rothschilds to support fledgling Jewish agricultural settlements in Palestine was supplemented by political lobbying that sought international backing for the Zionist cause. Following Herzl's untimely death in 1904, this task fell chiefly to **Chaim Weizmann**.

Away from the capitals of Europe, increasing waves of Jewish immigrants were making *Aliyah* (literally 'going up') to Palestine. The *First Aliyah* (1882-1903) comprised mainly poor farmers from Russia and eastern Europe escaping pogroms and persecution, whilst the *Second Aliyah* (1904-14) were much more ideological and secular in outlook, inspired by political Zionism. By the outbreak of the Second World War, the Jewish population in Palestine had risen to around 85,000 from just 24,000 in 1880 and as little as 5,000 at the beginning of Ottoman rule. The Arab population in 1914 was around 500,000 as opposed to 470,000 in 1880 (though all figures concerning the Arab:Jew ratio remain controversial). Not surprisingly these Jewish immigrants soon came into conflict with the Arab population already living in Palestine. The words of the Maronite Catholic Naguib Azoury in his 1905 book *Le Réveil de la Nation Arabe* were to be prophetic: "The reawakening of the Arab nation, and the growing Jewish efforts at rebuilding the ancient monarchy of Israel on a very large scale – these two movements are destined to fight each other continually, until one of them triumphs over the other."

First World War and the peace settlements

No sooner had the First World War begun than the Allied powers, notably France and Britain, began planning on how they were going to carve up the Middle East between them at the conclusion of the war. For example, the **Sykes-Picot Agreement** that was ratified in May 1916 defined the proposed spheres of direct and indirect British and French influence in Arab lands and in southeast Turkey. At the same time, the British were conducting negotiations with other interest groups as they sought not just to maintain the war effort, but to be in a better position to pick over the bones of the Ottoman Empire when its inevitable defeat came. For example, the **Husayn-McMahon Correspondence** between the British High Commissioner in Cairo, Sir Henry McMahon, and Husayn, Sharif of Mecca, seemed to offer some degree of 'independence' to the Arabs (under British tutelage) in return for Arab support against the Ottomans. McMahon's failure to be specific in his promises is now seen as means by which the British could avoid contradicting pledges given to the French in the Sykes-Picot Agreement.

Meantime, in London, Chaim Weizmann was lobbying hard on behalf of the Zionists. The eventual outcome was the **Balfour Declaration** of 2nd November, 1917. The

Background

The Balfour Declaration: Bob's your uncle

Here's one for trivia fans and pub-quiz buffs: Arthur Balfour (he of the 'Declaration') is the source of the English expression "Bob's your uncle" (implying that a simple action can achieve something rather easily). The saying originated in 1886 when British Prime

Minister Lord Salisbury (first name Robert, or Bob) appointed Balfour to a senior government post. Popular lore suggests that Balfour received this post because he was Salisbury's nephew; ie 'Bob was his uncle'!

original draft requested British recognition of the whole of Palestine as the national home of the Jews, unrestricted Jewish immigration, and Jewish internal autonomy, but was rejected in favour of the following declaration: "His Majesty's Government view with favour the establishment in Palestine of a national home for Jewish people, and will use their best endeavours to facilitate the achievement of this object, it being clearly understood that nothing shall be done which may prejudice the civil and religious rights of existing non-Jewish communities in Palestine, or the rights and political status enjoyed by Jews in any other country." Whole books have been written about the Balfour Declaration, with some suggesting that it was just another example of British wartime expediency: it was seen as an attempt to keep post-revolutionary Russia in the war (with Jews seen as being influential amongst the Bolsheviks), or as an appeal to American Jewry to back US involvement in the First World War. Zionists saw the Balfour Declaration as a recognition of Britain's moral obligation to the Jews, thus enabling them to claim betrayal when the British reversed their policy on Palestine with the issue of the 1939 White Paper (see page 776). It is interesting to note that pro-Zionist commentators concentrate on the first half of the Declaration, whilst pro-Palestinians emphasize the part about the rights of "existing non-Jewish communities in Palestine". Perhaps the best summary of the Sykes-Picot Agreement, Husayn-McMahon Correspondence and the Balfour Declaration can be left to Johnson: "The Allies, for their part, issued during the war a lot of post-dated cheques to countless nationalities whose support they needed. When the peace came some of the cheques bounced and the Arabs, in particular, found that they had been handed a stumer" (*A History of the Jews*, 1987). Though the 'cheque' to the Jews initially bounced, they were eventually able to re-present it, and this time it turned out to be good.

Further reading Walter Laquer, *A History of Zionism*; Edward W. Said, *The Question of Palestine*; Charles D. Smith, *Palestine and the Arab-Israeli Conflict*; Shlomo Avineri, *The Making of Modern Zionism: The Intellectual Origins of the Jewish State*; Ibrahim Abu-Lughod, *Transformation of Palestine*; Walid Khalidi, *From Haven to Conquest: Readings in Zionism and the Palestine Problem until 1948*; Maxime Rodinson, *Israel: A Colonial-Settler State?*

British Mandate

Jewish and Arab resistance to the British Mandate

Ottoman rule in Palestine was effectively brought to an end in December 1917 when General Edmund Allenby, at the head of the British forces, marched into Jerusalem. The conclusion of the First World War saw a whole host of conferences (Versailles, London, San Remo, Sèvres) at which the post-war territorial carve-up began. The San Remo Conference of 1920 granted the British the 'Mandate' for Palestine (confirmed by the League of Nations in 1922), but though the **Mandate for Palestine** included the Balfour Declaration in its preamble, it was open to interpretation and seemed to promise the same thing to Jews and Arabs alike. Later that same year the area of Transjordan to the east of the Jordan River (now Jordan) was exempted from the provisions given in the Balfour Declaration, making it a separate entity within the Mandate and effectively banning Jewish settlement there.

The period between the two world wars saw three further major influxes of Jews into Palestine. The *Third Aliyah* (1919-23) saw some 35,000 or so Jews arrive from eastern Europe (notably Russia), inspired by Zionism and socialism, many of whom went on to establish the kibbutz and moshav communal system. The *Fourth Aliyah* (1924-28) brought around 60,000 new immigrants mainly from Poland, though many from this influx were artisans and middle-class immigrants and thus chose to settle in towns where they established small businesses and light industry. The *Fifth Aliyah* (1929-39) reflected sinister developments in Europe, with some 165,000 immigrants, mainly from the academic and professional classes, escaping the rise of Hitler and Nazi power.

Fears amongst the Arab majority of the 'Jews taking over' were manifested in a number of ways, though an increasingly common feature of the 1920s was the series of physical attacks on individual Jews or isolated Jewish communities. These attacks culminated in the 'riots' of 1929, when the attacks on the Jewish communities of Safed, Jerusalem and notably Hebron can be described as effectively being pogroms. The immediate effect of the 1929 'riots' upon the Arabs was the lost chance to be represented politically in the Mandate structure (in which they were already discriminated against, in spite of their numerical superiority). Despite the clear sympathies towards the Palestinian Arabs of the British military officials in Palestine (who resented the Zionist's abrasiveness in demanding Jewish rights immediately, and then going behind their backs to London if they didn't get their way), Arabs were not represented in government posts in ratio to their population size, Jewish salaries were higher for identical posts and Jews had greater access to officials in high places who were either sympathetic to or fully supportive of Zionism. In the public works sector the Jewish Agency had obtained British agreement to distribute work between Jews and Arabs on a 50-50 basis instead of on the population ratio (which would have favoured Arabs by a margin of 70:30). This was justified by the fact that Jews contributed 50 percent of the tax burden, though this was more a reflection of the European-style economy that had been installed in Palestine by the Jews. Arab unemployment was also exacerbated by the problem of a growing landless class, resulting from Arab land sales and Jewish land purchases. The classic colonial-style exploitation of Palestine worked totally to the disadvantage of Arab smallholders, who had to sell increasing amounts of their land just to survive.

Peel Partition Plan and the 1939 White Paper

Arab opposition to Jewish expansion in Palestine led in 1936 to a call to 'revolt' by the Higher Arab Committee. This 'revolt' took many forms including a general strike by all Arab workers and government officials (not particularly effective since Arab labour was simply replaced by Jewish labour), a boycott of Jewish goods and sales to Jews, plus attacks on Jews and Jewish settlements and British forces.

In many ways the 'revolt' was a failure, even counter-productive, though it did force the British to face the unpalatable truth that the mandate was not working. The British response was the **Peel Commission**, which in 1937 presented a partition plan that envisaged an Arab State, a Jewish State and a (British) Mandated Sphere that would include Jerusalem and a corridor to the port at Jaffa (see map below). Perhaps more interesting than the response to this proposal is the way in which the response has been presented through the years. For example, the Israel Information Center's *Facts About Israel* (1995) states that "The Jewish leadership accepted the idea of partition and empowered the Jewish Agency to negotiate with

Peel Commission Partition Plan (1937)

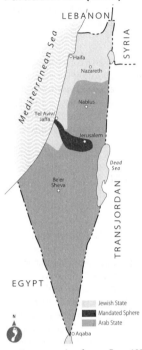

LEBANON

Mediterranean Sea

SYRIA

Haifa
Nazareth
Nablus
Tel Aviv/ Jaffa
Jerusalem

Dead Sea

Be'er Sheva

TRANSJORDAN

EGYPT

Jewish State
Mandated Sphere
Arab State

N

Aqaba

the British government in an effort to reformulate aspects of the proposal. The Arabs were uncompromisingly opposed to any partition plan." There can be little doubt that the Jewish acceptance of the partition plan was based upon the assumption that the borders of the Jewish state would be expanded at some later date (as Ben-Gurion's speech to the World Zionist Congress that year makes clear). However, it is important to examine the reasons for the Arab rejection of partition, rather than merely dismiss them as being "uncompromisingly opposed to any partition plan". Though the Jewish state would only be alloted 20 percent of Palestine (and excluding the huge area 'lopped off' in 1922 to form Transjordan), it effectively included almost all of the most fertile agricultural land, and would require the 'evacuation' of some 250,000 Arabs from Galilee. And whilst the Arab state would be 90 percent Arab in ethnic composition, the proposed Jewish state would still feature a roughly 50-50 Arab-Jew population split.

The partition plan, however, was swiftly overtaken by events in Europe as the continent geared up for war. From 1939 onwards British policy in Palestine became inextricably linked to the strategic importance of the Middle East to the war effort. Thus, as Smith so succinctly puts it, "Resolving the Palestinian crisis in a manner favourable to the Arab population came to be seen as a means of acquiring the cooperation of the Arab world once the war began" (*ibid*). This was done by issuing a **White Paper** on 17th May, 1939 that outlined future British policy on Palestine. Restrictions were to be placed upon Jewish immigration, whilst there was the promise of some sort of independent Arab Palestine within which a 'Jewish National Home' could be established. Not surprisingly, the Jews were devastated by this betrayal of the promises made in the Balfour Declaration (and subsequently the principles of the Mandate), and ever since the White Paper has been presented as "denying European Jewry a place of refuge from Nazi persecution" (*Facts About Israel*, 1995). Other commentators go further. Former Israeli Prime Minister Benjamin Netanyahu declares that the British "made themselves accomplices in the destruction of European Jewry" (*A Place Amongst the Nations*, 1993), though he conveniently forgets to mention Britain's not insignificant role in the war effort and the fight against fascism, or the reluctance of other countries (notably US, Canada and Australia) to take increased numbers of Jewish refugees during this period. The reaction of the Jewish community in Palestine was perhaps best summed up by David Ben-Gurion, who declared that "We will fight the war as if there were no White Paper, and the White Paper as if there were no war."

Second World War and the Holocaust

The Second World War saw Nazi Germany's systematic attempt to destroy European Jewry. Some six million Jews, or two-thirds of the pre-war European Jews, were victims of the **Holocaust**, reducing the world's largest and most vibrant Jewish community to a remnant. (**NB** It is very difficult in the space given here to do justice to the Holocaust, the memory of its victims and survivors, and its impact on world Jewry, so it is highly recommended that you conduct some further reading of your own. See below for some recommended sources).

Further reading   Paul Johnson, *A History of the Jews*; Martin Gilbert, *The Holocaust: The Jewish Tragedy; Auschwitz and the Allies; Atlas of the Holocaust*; Daniel Goldhagen, *Hitler's Willing Executioners*; Charles D. Smith, *Palestine and the Arab-Israeli Conflict*; **NB** the pack recently produced by the Holocaust Educational Trust and The Spiro Institute for the Study of Jewish History and Culture for Key Stage 3 of the History discipline of the British National Curriculum provides an excellent review of the subject.

Birth of the State of Israel

End of the Mandate

British policy in Palestine at the conclusion of the Second World War continued as before, with quantative restrictions on Jewish immigration. Jewish underground groups continued with their clandestine efforts to smuggle Jewish immigrants into the country whilst the British navy mounted a blockade. Some 85,000 Jews were brought into Palestine by these clandestine efforts in the period 1945-48, though British immigration policy resulted in the ridiculous (and tragic) situation in which those caught trying to enter Palestine were interned in camps. In addition to being inhumane, such a policy was a propaganda and public relations disaster since many of those interned were Holocaust survivors (and former prisoners in Nazi death camps).

The British administration was also deeply affected by the increasingly violent opposition that it was meeting from the Jewish underground groups that had been established in the 1930s. Whilst a *modus vivendi* appears to have been worked out between the British and the *Haganah* (the Jewish self-defence organization), smaller Jewish groups were less restrained. Some restricted their targets to military personnel and positions, though others were less discriminating. A corollary today would perhaps be between Palestinian groups that targetted Israeli soldiers only, and those that targetted Israelis in general. Of course both groups are branded "terrorists" by Israel, though attempts to brand the Jewish underground groups of the 1930s and 1940s as terrorists gets the Israeli right-wingers crying "foul".

Nevertheless, the general failure of British policy in Palestine, coupled with the inability to reconcile the conflicting demands of the two communities, led to Britain placing the problem before the newly created United Nations.

Partition

The 11-member United Nations Special Committee on Palestine (UNSCOP) toured Palestine for five weeks in 1947, being fêted by the Zionists and boycotted by the Palestinian Arab leadership. Their conclusion was that the British Mandate should end, with the committee voting by a majority of eight to three for partition of Palestine into a Jewish State and an Arab State, with Jerusalem being internationalized (see map). The British did not wait for the debate scheduled for November 1947, instead unilaterally ending the mandate and handing the matter to the UN. At the time of the partition recommendation Arabs outnumbered Jews by two to one, with Jews owning 20 percent of the cultivable land and 6 percent of the total land area.

UN Partition Recommendation (Resolution 181) 1947

Jewish State
International Zone
Arab State

The UN vote on the future of Palestine was taken on 29th November, 1947, with the General Assembly voting by 33 to 13 in favour of the UNSCOP partition plan (with 10 abstentions). It is interesting to note how in the 'Cold War' years the Soviet-backed Arab bloc repeatedly referred to the creation of Israel as the work of a capitalist-imperialist conspiracy. In fact, during the 1947 UN vote the entire Soviet bloc voted for partition, and when Israel later declared itself independent in May 1948, Stalin recognized this *de jure* independence just three days later. Further, it was in fact two of the greatest 'capitalist-imperialist' powers, the US and Britain, who were most concerned at the creation of a Jewish state, with the US State Department's Secretary James Forrestal denouncing the machinations of the Jewish lobby in swaying the US vote: "No group in this country should be permitted to influence our policy to the point where it could endanger our national security" (*The Forrestal Diaries*, 1951).

In the light of the subsequent Cold War, the timing of Israel's push for independence was remarkable. As Johnson observes, "If British evacuation had been postponed another year, the United States would have been far less anxious to see Israel created and Russia would almost certainly have been hostile. Hence the effect of the terror campaign on British policy was perhaps decisive to the entire enterprise. Israel slipped into existence through a fortuitous window in history which briefly opened for a few months in 1947-48. That too was luck: or providence" (*ibid*).

Arab-Israeli War 1948-49

Of course, the UN vote on partition did not guarantee the creation of the Jewish state; instead it triggered an increase in armed conflict as the Palestinian Arabs (aided by 'irregulars' from sympathetic Arab states) attempted to prevent the Jewish state coming into being, whilst Jews sought to consolidate their hold on the land allocated to them. It is difficult to find impartial sources on events that followed the partition vote, though Smith summarizes as follows: "Terror and atrocities were committed by both sides, with little regard for non-combatants or women and children when avenging an attack … The British were accused by both sides of favouring the other. They were attacked by both sides, and their forces intervened on occasion to relieve sieges against either Arab or Jewish communities" (*ibid*).

On the eve of the termination of the British Mandate, on 14th May, 1948, David Ben-Gurion proclaimed the **State of Israel**. The declaration brought *de facto*

Background

recognition from the US, *de jure* recognition from the Soviet Union, and prompted the regular armies of Egypt, Syria, Jordan, Lebanon and Iraq to invade with the invowed intent of "driving the Jews into the sea". For full details of the war, see the recommended 'Further reading' at the end of this section. However, as a brief summary, the war fell into two distinct phases. From May 1948 until mid-June 1948 the Israelis tenaciously (but precariously) hung on to the areas granted to them under the UN partition plan, though the millennia-old Jewish presence in the Old City of Jerusalem was to end. The brief truce between 11th June and 6th July, despite the supposed arms embargo, saw the Israelis receive huge new stockpiles of heavy weaponry (notably from Czechoslovakia, eager for hard currency). Despite considerable numerical reinforcements to the Arab armies, the tide of the war had been turned and the Israelis made considerable advances before an Armistice was agreed in the second half of 1949. The West Bank (including part of Jerusalem) was subsequently annexed by King Abdullah of Jordan in a move recognized only by Britain and Pakistan.

Of course one of the key unresolved consequences of Israel's independence is the fate that befell the Palestinian Arabs: what they term as *Al-Naqba* or 'The Catastrophe'. Indeed, one of the most controversial aspects of the war was the way in which somewhere in the region of 500,000 to 725,000 (the figures are disputed) Arabs left or were driven out of the land that became the State of Israel (see 'Deir Yassin' box on page 781, for example). Once again, space does not permit a full assessment of the Palestinian and Israeli perspectives on the creation of the State of Israel, though readers may like to compare the case presented in Edward W Said's *The Question of Palestine* with the Israeli viewpoint in Benjamin Netanyahu's *A Place Among the Nations* or Samuel Katz's *Battleground: Facts and Fantasy in Palestine*. If nothing else, it will show just how far apart the two positions are.

Armistice line after 1948–49 War

■ Israel
■ Occupied by Jordan (West Bank)

Further reading   Collins and Lapierre, *O Jerusalem*; Chaim Herzog, *The Arab-Israeli Wars*; Paul Johnson, *A History of the Jews*; Edward Tivnan, *The Lobby: Jewish Political Power and American Foreign Policy*; John Snetsinger, *Truman, The Jewish Vote and the Creation of Israel*; Edward W Said, *The Question of Palestine*

Israel's early years

Nation building

Israel's process of Nation and State building must be seen within the context of its birth. Jewish immigration remained (as today) a priority, formalized in the passing of the Law of Return in 1950 (see page 813). Many of these new arrivals (up to 600,000) arrived in Israel as a result of mounting discrimination and insecurity in Muslim countries in which they had resided for generations. Infrastructural development was a major challenge, as was the expansion of the agricultural and industrial base, though all these projects had to be realized within the constraints of

Deir Yassin

A key event in the fighting of 1947-49 occurred at Deir Yassin, a small Arab village strategically located on the road to Tel Aviv to the west of Jerusalem. The attack on the village was undertaken by the Irgun and Stern Gang, though such was the resistance from the villagers that 'regular' Palmach forces had to be summoned. What happened next is a source of considerable controversy. The consensus of opinion is that the Jewish forces subsequently massacred up to 250 Arab villagers (the figures are still disputed), engaging in acts of rape and torture during the process (see for example Collins and Lapierre, O Jerusalem, *Paul Johnson,* A History of the Jews, *both of whom include detailed accounts that they say were exhaustively researched). An alternative view is presented in Samuel Katz's* Battleground: Facts and Fantasy in Palestine. *He claims that: "The Arabs leaders seized on the opportunity to tell an utterly fantastic story*

of a 'massacre', which was disseminated throughout the world by all the arms of British propaganda. The accepted 'orthodox' version to this day, it has served enemies of Israel and anti-Semites faithfully." Katz's message is clear: to criticize Israel is to be anti-Israel, and to be anti-Israel is to be anti-Semitic.

The significance of Deir Yassin is the impact it had on the war. Whether the massacre happened or not, the threat of 'further Deir Yassins' was no doubt a major factor in the resulting flow of Palestinian refugees into neighbouring states. Again, whether the refugees were encouraged to flee by the Jews or by Arab leaders remains a bitter point of debate.

For further information about Deir Yassin (on the internet) see the box on page 50 of the Essentials chapter.

bellicose and belligerent neighbours. There was also the not unimportant question of what sort of state Israel should be: a state for Jews or a Jewish state? (See the 'Immigration: the continued ingathering' and 'Unity in diversity?' headings in the 'Modern Israel' section on pages 804 and 805).

The Suez Crisis

One of the first challenges to the fledgling Israeli state came in the so-called Suez Crisis of 1956. Of the four states participating in the events following Nasser's nationalizing of the Suez Canal, there were two winners and two losers. Britain confirmed that it was no longer a dominant imperial power in the Middle East (or anywhere else for that matter), with the French invasion ending in fiasco (for which they blamed the British). Ironically, despite the military defeat, Nasser emerged as a hero in the Arab world (though this was to be short-lived). The greatest beneficiary of the Suez Crisis was Israel. It is now claimed that Israel was acting in response to Egyptian provocation in closing the Straits of Tiran to Israeli shipping (a technical act of war), though Ben-Gurion's comments to the French and British during the planning stages of the operation suggest that he had greater designs involving Israeli territorial gains in Lebanon, the West Bank and the Sinai (see Michael Bar Zohar's 1978 biography *Ben-Gurion*). By the end of the Suez campaign Israel controlled the entire Sinai peninsula and Gaza Strip, though they were forced to withdraw under US pressure (though a UN observer force was positioned along the border, and Israel obtained a commitment from Egypt to allow free navigation in the Gulf of Aqaba/Eilat).

Six Day War of 1967

Two decades after Israel became independent, the Arab world once more felt in a position to match its anti-Israel rhetoric with deeds. The **Six Day War** of 1967 is

Background

often depicted as an act of Israeli aggression since they technically 'fired the first shot', though this is stretching the truth somewhat. With Egypt having ordered the UN observers out of Sinai and massed their troops on the border (and then closed the Straits of Tiran to Israeli shipping), they may be said to have already been in a state of war with Israel. However, it must be said that the Israeli politicians and military planners appear to have looked favourably upon the prospects of war.

Israel opted to make a pre-emptive strike against Egypt. At 0745 on 5th June, 1967 the Israeli air-force undertook a mission that was to decide the course of the war. Within 3 hours, 309 out of Egypt's 340 serviceable combat aircraft had been destroyed, largely on the ground. Syria, Jordan and Iraq, meanwhile, believing the reports of crushing victories for Egypt emanating out of Cairo, launched their own attacks on Israel's eastern flank. By the end of 5th June, the entire Jordanian air force had been wiped out, along with two-thirds of Syria's military aircraft.

Ceasefire lines after Six-Day War

1 Golan Heights
2 West Bank
3 Gaza

Though a series of bitter infantry, artillery and tank battles were to follow, the outcome of the war was almost certainly settled by Israel's early attainment of complete aerial supremacy. Within six days Israel had defeated the combined might of the Arab armies, with the joke in the West being that they had the arms on a seven-day free trial! By the time the UN-brokered ceasefire was imposed on 10th June, Israeli controlled the whole of the Sinai peninsula, the Gaza Strip, the entire West Bank (including Jerusalem) and the Golan Heights.

Further reading   Chaim Herzog, *The Arab-Israeli Wars*

Israel after the Six Day War

After the Six Day War

Perhaps more important than the military details of the war itself is the effect that the war had not just on Israel and her Middle East neighbours, but on world Jewry. To appreciate the euphoria that the victory created in the Jewish world it is necessary to recall the mood in Israel prior to the war, when many were privately preparing for another Holocaust. Indeed, such was the 'intoxication' that this transformation from vulnerability to strength brought, that many considered it to be divinely inspired. A new, radical nationalist variant of religious Zionism emerged after Israel's acquisition of the West Bank, the heart of the biblical Land of Israel, with groups claiming that it was an obligation to settle there if the Jews were to strive for redemption. The new territories that Israel now occupied afforded increased security against future attack – 'strategic depth' as it is now called – though they came with a price: a large and resentful Palestinian population, many of whom were themselves refugees from the earlier war of 1947-49. Israel once again found herself facing the question of what sort of state it wished to be (see page 807), with the physical and political suppression of Palestinian rights in Gaza and the West Bank eroding Israel's image as the progressive democratic state that it claimed to be.

Subsequent negotiations on the status of territories occupied by Israel since 1967 must be seen within the context of US-Soviet superpower rivalries. The

UN-drafted resolution that sought to resolve this question is notoriously vague and open to interpretation. Nevertheless, it has remained the basis for negotiations ever since. Israel tends to quote the lines from **UN Security Council Resolution 242** that refer to the "right to live in peace within secure and recognized boundaries free from threats or acts of force", whilst Palestinians emphasize the illegality under international law of conquering and settling territory through acts of war, highlighted in the resolutions call for "all parties to the conflict to withdraw from territories occupied by them after June 4, 1967." It should also be noted that the draft version of this resolution referred to "the territories", with "the" being withdrawn from the final resolution at Israel's request. It has subsequently allowed a completely new interpretation of the resolution.

War of Attrition

The ceasefire that concluded the Six Day War of 1967 effectively inaugurated a 'war of attrition' against Israel, with Arab countries maintaining their stance of "no recognition of Israel". In 1969 the **Palestinian Liberation Organization** (PLO), (founded some five years earlier as a puppet organization through which Nasser sought to control the Palestinians), was relaunched under a charismatic new chairman, **Yasir Arafat**. The Palestinian National Charter was amended, calling for "armed struggle" to liberate Palestine and "liquidate the Zionist and imperialist presence", and guerrilla attacks were launched on Israel from neighbouring countries. Such attacks soon spread beyond the Middle East, with Palestinian groups bringing their campaign against Israel to Europe and the rest of the world. Perhaps the most infamous terrorist incident of this period was the attack on Israeli athletes at the 1972 Munich Olympics, in which 11 Israelis died in the subsequent shoot-out.

Yom Kippur War of 1973

The fragile ceasefire brokered between Israel and her Arab neighbours in 1967 was broken on 6th October, 1973, when Egypt and Syria launched a surprise attack on Israel. The fact that the attack was timed to take place on Yom Kippur, the holiest day of the Jewish year, is usually presented as a double-blow to Israel since most reservists were off-duty and thus at home (or synagogue). However, Israel's lack of preparedness is often attributed to the over-cockiness that emerged from the stunning victory of six years earlier. Chaim Herzog suggests that not only was Israeli intelligence assessment poor, but the Israeli military stubbornly assumed that "the unrealistic and unfavourable ratio of forces along the borders was adequate to hold any Egyptian or Syrian attack" (*The Arab-Israeli Wars*, 1984).

It is also important to see the Yom Kippur War in the light of the strategic aims of Egypt and Syria. Unlike the Six Day War of 1967, it was not an attempt to destroy the State of Israel (though had the opportunity arisen, there is no doubt that Syria and Egypt would have taken it). The 1973 war was in fact an attempt to break the deadlock in the Arab-Israeli conflict before proceeding to a peace conference at which, it was hoped, the superpowers would pressurize Israel to return to her pre-1967 borders. Such a scenario would avoid forcing any Arab country to sign a formal peace treaty with Israel, (thus granting her any recognition of legitimacy). Egypt and Syria's early successes in the 1973 war allowed them to claim victory, thus partially erasing the memory of the humiliation that they had suffered six years earlier, though both Arab states were relieved at the opportunity to accept the UN's ceasefire proposals on 22nd October as the Israelis had fought back to make a series of major gains. The subsequent **UN Security Council Resolution 338** called for direct talks based upon the principles of the earlier Resolution 242.

Camp David Accords

There were many political heavyweight casualties of the Yom Kippur War, and the growing disillusionment with the ruling Labour coalition (that had ruled Israel since its independence in 1948) saw the Likud bloc returned to power at the 1977 elections. It is suggested that Likud's victory was largely as a result of Sephardi and Mizrachi dissatisfaction with the Ashkenazi dominated establishment (see 'Modern Israel' section, page 802). What is perhaps most remarkable is that a party leader who had lost eight consecutive elections, **Menachem Begin**, was still head of the Likud bloc at this stage!

It is ironic that the first full peace treaty signed between an Arab state and Israel should take place during the term of office of Israel's most reactionary prime minister. The **Camp David Accords** that US President Carter hosted in 1978 were perhaps more an indication of Egyptian President Sadat's desperation to sign a deal, and the American willingness to facilitate it, than Begin's desire for peace. Begin brought a new interpretation to Resolution 242, suggesting that it did not apply to the West Bank, and continually reminded anyone who would listen that the PLO was a Nazi organization, and even if they accepted 242 he would never deal with them. All references to 242's application to the West Bank were withdrawn, and thus Begin was able to sign a document that included the term "the legitimate rights of the Palestinian people" because he considered it to be meaningless in the light of Israel's guaranteed occupation of the region (Smith, *ibid*). Having been excluded from the negotiating process, the PLO (since 1974 recognized by the Arab world as the "sole legitimate representatives of the Palestinian people") rejected the plans for their future that were included within the Israel-Egypt deal. Thus, when the peace treaty between Egypt and Israel was finally signed on 26th March, 1979, only the proposals related to bilateral relations were implemented. The treaty worked on the principle of relinquishing territory for peace, with Israel agreeing to a phased withdrawal from the Sinai in return for Egypt's commitment to peace and the recognition of Israel's "right to exist". Whilst Begin and Sadat received the Nobel Peace Prize for their efforts, Egypt was expelled from the Arab League and Sadat subsequently assassinated (in 1981).

Israel after the Camp David Accords (present de facto borders)

Israel
1 Golan Heights
2 West Bank
3 Gaza

Israeli invasion of Lebanon, 1982

If the Six Day War of 1967 radically altered the way the world viewed Israel (and the way Israelis viewed themselves), then the Israeli invasion of Lebanon polarized opinion even more. Yet to criticize Israel's actions in Lebanon in 1982 is to lay yourself open to charges of at best being a victim of Arab propaganda, at worst being an anti-Semite. Compare for example these two accounts of Israeli operations in Beirut: "only West Beirut, the last PLO stronghold, remained, and the Israeli army was selectively bombing PLO strongholds in the hope of forcing a surrender and preventing the higher casualties that would be involved in a direct assault" (Benjamin Netanyahu, *A Place Among the Nations*, 1993); "If Adolf Hitler were hiding out in a building along with 20 innocent civilians, wouldn't you bomb the building?" (Menachem Begin, Israeli prime minister at the time); "The Israeli bombardment of 4 August was, we realized, later, *discriminate*. It targeted every civilian area, every institution, in west Beirut – hospitals, schools, apartments, shops, newspaper offices, hotels, the prime minister's office and the parks. Incredibly, the Israeli shells even blew part of the roof off the city's synagogue in Wadi Abu Jamil where the remnants of Beirut's tiny Jewish community still lived" (Robert Fisk, *Pity the Nation*, 1990).

Israel presents its 1982 invasion of Lebanon as 'Operation Peace for Galilee', claiming that its desired aim was to stop once and for all the shelling and rocket attacks on Israel from PLO bases in southern Lebanon (where the PLO had effectively created a mini-state). Ironically, early 1982 was a relatively quiet year for PLO rocket attacks across the border, and thus Israel used the attempted murder of their ambassador to London on 3rd June, 1982 as the 'excuse' to invade three days later. Such was the scale of the invasion, however, that its planning must have begun long before the shooting in London. Israel was always to claim that 'Operation Peace for Galilee' was "not directed against the Lebanese or Palestinian peoples ... The terrorists are responsible for any civilian casualties since they were the ones who had placed their headquarters and installations in populated civilian areas" (Israeli press release, 21st June, 1982). Yet, on 4th July the Israeli army cut off water and power supplies to West Beirut, ostensibly to put pressure on the PLO. When the UN Security Council condemned this action, Israel denied it had cut off the water and power to West Beirut, though it was later forced to retract this denial.

Most objective historians now believe that the purpose of 'Operation Peace for Galilee' was to terminate the PLO once and for all, and to install a pro-Israeli Christian government in Lebanon. Thus, the invasion did not stop at the Litani River (as had a similar incursion in 1978), but instead proceeded all the way to Beirut. Begin's attempts to get some sort of peace treaty with Lebanon to secure Israel's northern border ignored one crucial point: there was no person or group in Lebanon capable of signing and implementing any such agreement. As Thomas Friedman describes it, "Begin reminded me of a man determined to get a check [cheque] from another man for an unpaid bill – even though everyone else knew the man had no money" (*From Beirut to Jerusalem*, 1989).

Like many foreign armies before them (and after them), the Israelis found that it was easier to get into Lebanon than to get out. Indeed, it was not until 1985 that the Israeli army substantively withdrew, though they still maintain a unilaterally declared 'security zone' of 1,550 square kilometres in southern Lebanon that is occupied by an undisclosed number of Israeli troops and the SLA, a proxy army. In many ways, the invasion of Lebanon changed fundamentally the way many Israelis saw themselves, and the way diaspora Jews viewed Israel. Between September 1982 and June 1983, 60 Israeli soldiers were imprisoned for refusing to do reserve duty in Lebanon, whilst the Peace Now movement was able to bring between 200,000 and 400,000 people on to the streets in opposition to the war in Lebanon. In the wider world many diaspora Jews began to make a distinction between the wars that Israel had been forced to fight (1947-49, 1967, 1973) and this war that Israel had 'chosen' to fight. As Friedman puts it, "In 'mopping up' Lebanon, Israel lost its luster" (*ibid*).

Intifada

It is all too easy to ignore the significant strides that Israel made in the late 1980s in bringing the economy under control. However, Israel's rapid GDP growth and mastery of run-away hyper-inflation in this period is overshadowed by the next phase in her conflict with the Palestinians: the *intifada*. The *intifada* (literally 'shaking off' in Arabic) was in fact a "spontaneous eruption of hatred and frustration incited by a specific incident" (Smith, *ibid*); that is, a traffic accident in Gaza on 8th December, 1987 that killed four Palestinians. However, the protest that followed

The Sabra and Chatila massacres

*Perhaps the most controversial of all the episodes in the 1982 invasion occurred after the PLO had been escorted out of Beirut: the massacres at the **Sabra** and **Chatila** camps. Ironically, as Fisk observes, most of the civilians of west Beirut, including these camp's residents, "would have been as happy as the Israelis to see the PLO leave, providing the guerrillas were not replaced by Phalangist militiamen from east Beirut" (ibid). Yet this is exactly what happened.*

Again, compare the reporting of this atrocity: "This horrifying massacre was not perpetrated by Israeli forces but by Arabs … Israeli forces did not participate in the massacre, did not enable it, did not even know about it" (Netanyahu, ibid); "The guilty were certainly Christian militiamen … but the Israelis were also guilty. If the Israelis had not taken part in the killings, they had certainly sent the militia into the camp. They had trained them, given them uniforms, handed them US army rations and Israeli medical equipment. Then they had watched the murderers in the camps,

they had given them military assistance – the Israeli air force had dropped all those flares to help the men who were murdering the inhabitants of Sabra and Chatila – and they had established military liaison with the murderers in the camps" (Fisk, ibid); "The goyim are killing the goyim and they want to hang the Jews for it" (Menachem Begin to his Cabinet); "The Israeli soldiers did not see innocent civilians being massacred and they did not hear the screams of innocent children going to their graves. What they saw was a 'terrorist infestation' being 'mopped up' and 'terrorist nurses' scurrying about and 'terrorist teenagers' trying to defend them, and what they heard were 'terrorist women' screaming. In the Israeli psyche you don't come to the rescue of 'terrorists'. There is no such thing as 'terrorists' being massacred" (Thomas Friedman, who won a Pulitzer Prize for his reporting of the Sabra and Chatila massacres).

soon took on a life force of its own, fuelled by the anger and frustration of years under Israeli military rule, rapidly developing into a general uprising against Israel. As Joffe observes, "what distinguished the *intifada* from previous Palestinian protests was its ability to generate itself, and involve most sections of the community" (*Keesing's Guide to the Middle-East Peace Process*, 1996). Ironically, it took the PLO (now based in Tunis) as much by surprise as it did Israel, and though they were unable to take credit for starting it they worked hard to harness its potential.

The effects of the *intifada* were manifold. Not only did it bring the Palestinian struggle back onto the world stage, it fundamentally altered the world's perception of the Palestinians. No longer were they seen as the plane-hijacking terrorists of the 1970s (as the Israeli right continues to present them), but now they were the victims; stone-throwing children being shot by Israeli soldiers (though in the period 1987-91 nearly as many Palestinians were killed by other Palestinians as 'collaborators' as were killed by the Israeli army). The more the Israelis imposed the 'iron fist' to crack down on the *intifada*, the more the image of Israel suffered. It was not just the international community who were bringing pressure on Israel to resolve the 'Palestinian issue'; Israelis themselves (notably on the 'left') began to question the price of holding on to the territories. The Israeli right, notably the settler movements, became more vocal in their determination to retain all of Eretz Yisrael whatever the cost, thus polarizing Israeli society even more.

Though it was difficult to see it as such at the time, the *intifada* was in fact the catalyst for change that made the current peace process possible. One of the first people to recognize the need to come to some sort of accommodation with the Palestinians of the West Bank and Gaza Strip was Yitzhak Rabin; the man who as

Minister of Defence at the height of the *intifada* was widely credited with ordering soldiers to 'break the bones' of Palestinian demonstrators.

Algiers Declaration, 1988

The seemingly moribund PLO was revitalized by the *intifada*, and thus sought to initiate a new policy that would reflect the changing set of realities in the region. The Algiers Declaration of Nov 1988 represented a declaration of Palestinian statehood that envisaged a bi-national state, with negotiations to take place on the basis of Resolutions 242 and 338; effectively the PLO were going back to the 1947 UN partition plan (Resolution 181). Although recognition of Israel was implicit in this declaration it was not specified, and so Arafat was forced explicitly to renounce terrorism and recognize Israel at the United Nations. The whole event actually turned into something of a farce. Contrary to their contractual obligations to the UN, the US State Department refused Arafat a visa to visit the US, and thus the entire UN General Assembly had to shift to Geneva to hear Arafat's speech. Yet, with the world waiting to hear Arafat renounce violence and recognize Israel, he choked. At the last minute he had changed the speech that had been 'approved' by the Americans, and what he offered certainly did not meet US conditions for an opening of dialogue with the PLO. Fortunately for Arafat he got a second chance, with a hastily convened press conference the following evening (14th December, 1988). This time he read from a speech 'approved' by the US, recognizing "the right of all parties in the Middle East conflict to exist in peace and security", and emphasizing that "we totally and absolutely renounce all forms of terrorism". In their biography of Arafat, Gowers and Walker suggest that "his stage fright was such that the word [terrorism] came out sounding like 'tourism'" (*Yasser Arafat and the Palestinian Revolution*, 1990)!

The US subsequently put pressure on Israel to negotiate with the Palestinians (but not necessarily the PLO), though many in Israel doubted the PLO's commitment to peace (pointing out how they were unable to control various splinter groups and how their National Covenant still called for the destruction of Israel). Nevertheless, Israeli prime minister Yitzhak Shamir put forward his own peace plan in April 1989, though it must be certain that he knew it would be unacceptable to the Palestinians. Thus, Israel would be able to claim that they were striving for peace, yet the Palestinians were rejecting the offer. Indeed, after Shamir formulated a second plan (after Labour had left the coalition government), US Secretary of State James Baker denounced the Shamir government as "not being serious about peace". However, the opportunity to break the log-jam in the Arab-Israeli conflict was brought about by the perceived 'New World Order' that emerged from the Gulf War of 1991.

The Gulf War

Though diplomatically and morally on the side of the US-led coalition, Israel was requested to refrain from taking a proactive role in the military action against Iraq for fear of splitting the coalition. Thus, Israel had to sit by silently as Iraq rained Scud missiles down on its cities. Nobody was fooled by Saddam Hussein's assertion that the invasion of Kuwait was linked to the Arab-Israeli conflict and the status of Palestinians. In fact, the PLO appeared to have shot itself in the foot somewhat with Yasir Arafat seemingly supporting Iraq's stance, with the effect that most of Kuwait's Palestinian migrant worker population were expelled in the wake of the 'Allied' victory.

Further reading Robert Fisk, *Pity the Nation: Lebanon at War*; Thomas Friedman, *From Beirut to Jerusalem*; Chaim Herzog, *The Arab-Israeli Wars*; Andrew Gowers and Tony Walker, *Yasser Arafat and the Palestinian Revolution*; Zachary Lockman and Joel

Background

Beinin (editors), *Intifada: The Palestinian Uprising Against Israeli Occupation*; Don Peretz, *Intifada: The Palestinian Uprising*; Ze'ev Schiff and Ehud Ya'ari, *Intifada: The Palestinian Uprising – Israel's Third Front*; Robert Hunter, *The Palestinian Uprising: A War by Other Means*

The peace process

Madrid, Oslo and the Middle East peace process

In outlining his perception of the 'New World Order' at the conclusion of the Gulf War in 1991, US President Bush highlighted the need to resolve the Israeli-Palestinian question. US Secretary of State James Baker subsequently began a prolonged bout of 'shuttle diplomacy' between the various capitals of the Middle East, eventually persuading all interested parties to attend a regional conference in Madrid. The price of Israeli participation appears to have been an agreement to allow them to 'vet' the Palestinian delegation, with no members of the PLO being admitted and the Palestinian delegation effectively coming under the 'umbrella' of the Jordanian team. As Joffe observes, although Madrid bore all the hallmarks of earlier peace proposals, it "also has some new elements, which arguably forced the process onto a new quantum level, and would lead to something irreversible" (*Keesing's Guide to the Middle-East Peace Process*, 1996). The most notable of these "new elements" was of course direct negotiations between Israel and the Palestinians, as well as various confidence-building measures.

Though there was some progress in the talks, the deadlock was broken in June 1992 by the election of a Labour government in Israel that had campaigned largely on a 'peace ticket'. In fact, the outgoing Likud prime minister Shamir was to admit in a post-election interview that he intended to drag out the Madrid talks indefinitely, thus maintaining the status quo that deprived the Palestinians of any degree of autonomy. Although the Madrid conference progressed through 10 round of talks (November 1991-July 1993), the newly elected Labour government realized that a new approach was needed. It was obvious that, despite the pretence, the Palestinian delegation at Madrid were in fact taking orders direct from the PLO in Tunis. Thus, despite contacts with the PLO still being a criminal offence in Israel, a direct channel of talks was initiated. The facilitator of this 'secret track' was Terje Larsen, a Norwegian social scientist who was conducting research in Gaza. The secret talks began in January 1993 in a town close to Oslo, eventually 'going public' on 30th August, 1993. These talks resulted in the **Declaration of Principles On Interim Self-Government Arrangements** (DOP, or 'Oslo I'), signed in Washington on 13th September, 1993 following the now famous handshake between Rabin and Arafat on the White House lawn. The DOP envisaged a three-stage process: i) immediate self-rule in Jericho and Gaza, ii) 'early empowerment' for Palestinians in the rest of the West Bank, and iii) an Interim Agreement on the West Bank and Gaza.

Reaction to the deal was mixed (with the Palestinian delegation at Madrid feeling particularly annoyed about having been excluded from the process). Many Palestinians rejected the proposals as a sell-out, though others pointed out that Israel's development had been based on the principle of accepting part of the land it wanted, and then expanding its frontiers at later stages. The DOP was in turn ratified by the UN, the PLO Central Council, and eventually the Israeli Knesset, though opposition remained strong. In February 1994 a right-wing Israeli extremist massacred Muslim worshippers in Hebron in attempt to sabotage the fragile peace process, whilst *Hamas* responded with a series of suicide bomb attacks within Israel. The irony of extremist Israeli and Palestinian groups uniting in their methods to de-rail the 'peace process' was not lost on many Middle East commentators.

The **Israeli-Palestinian Interim Agreement on the West Bank and Gaza Strip** ('Oslo II') that had been envisaged in the DOP agreement was eventually thrashed out and signed in Washington on 28th September, 1995. 'Oslo II' covered a multitude of issues (it included seven annexes), though its key issues were Israeli troop withdrawal, elections to a Palestinian Council, preventing terrorism, economic cooperation, plus other matters such as water, education, human rights, religious sites and the special status of Hebron. However, all the key sticking points (and potential flashpoints) were deferred to **Final Status Talks**. Such issues included the seemingly unreconcilable questions of refugees, settlers, water, borders and the future status of Jerusalem.

Further reading   Lawrence Joffe, *Keesing's Guide to the Middle-East Peace Process*; Edward W Said, *Peace and Its Discontents; The Politics of Dispossession*.

Recent events

Post-Oslo

With the ink barely dry on the 'Oslo II' deal, the whole peace process came to a shuddering halt with the murder of Yitzhak Rabin at the hands of a right-wing Jewish extremist. Whilst not killing the peace process outright, the bullets fired by Rabin's assassin mortally wounded it, with many commentators feeling that the final *coup de grâce* was not far off. At the general election that followed Rabin's murder the Israeli electorate indicated their doubts about the peace process by narrowly returning the Likud bloc to power. Israel's first direct election for prime minister saw Likud leader **Benjamin Netanyahu** become the youngest person to hold this post.

Netanyahu had always stressed his dissatisfaction with 'Oslo II', and sought to bring a very narrow interpretation to the agreements already signed. With his government constantly under great pressure from the various right-wing groups who supported his fragile coalition, the Jewish settlement programme in East Jerusalem and the West Bank went on largely unabated. Netanyahu, in turn, accused the Palestinian Authority of failing to fulfil its 'Oslo II' commitments, most notably with regard to preventing terrorist actions. Meantime, the Clinton administration in the US, generally perceived to be the most pro-Israeli US government in history, perpetuated the charade of acting as the 'honest broker' in the 'peace process'.

In effect, the so-called 'peace process', deeply flawed in the first place, appeared effectively to be dead even before the thorny issues due to be tackled in the final status talks came before the negotiating parties. Many commentators likened Netanyahu's attitude to that of Yitzhak Shamir: drawing out negotiations indefinitely in an attempt to maintain the status quo, or offering the Palestinians deals that they know are unacceptable, then decrying Arafat's intransigence in refusing these initiatives.

Elections of 1999

Having called early elections for May 1999, Netanyahu was the main casualty in a particularly vicious election campaign. The three contenders for the post of prime minister were Netanyahu, his former Defence Minister Yitzhak Mordechai (who had left the government to join the new Center Party), and Labour's **Ehud Barak** (running under a 'One Israel' coalition ticket). Eventually, Mordechai dropped out, recommending that his supporters vote against Netanyahu, and Barak won a landslide. The vote for Knesset members was less clear cut: both Labour and Likud actually lost seats whilst most of the parties with a 'special interest' base (for

Background

example Yisrael B'Aliyah for Russian immigrants and Shas for orthodox Sephardi/Mizrachi Jews) gained seats. When Barak eventually named his ruling coalition it contained 77 members from seven different parties.

Barak's early pronouncements *vis-à-vis* the peace process seem encouraging; significantly he travelled to Egypt, Jordan and met with Arafat before presenting his credentials in Washington. There is even hope of a reopening of negotiations with Syria. However, he is keen to move straight to 'final status' negotiations with the Palestinians whilst Arafat is determined that Israel first implements the next stage of phased withdrawal from the West Bank (as agreed in the so-called 'Wye River Memorandum' signed by his predecessor); this could be his first real test.

Some commentators see Barak's sweeping victory in the direct elections for prime minister as a mandate for change; a vote for the peace process and a vote against the increasing influence of the religious parties. However, in selecting his cabinet it is suggested that he has had to sacrifice the latter for the sake of the former; the Ministry of Religious Affairs portfolio, for example, is in the hands of the orthodox Shas party. In reality, things are a little less clear cut: the direct vote for prime minister may have been a mandate for change, though the separate vote for Knesset members suggests that the Israeli electorate continues to vote along narrow factional lines. The National Religious Party and Ashkenazi ultra-Orthodox United Torah Judaism each won five seats, whilst Shinui won six seats with an uncompromising message of curbing ultra-Orthodox power and priviliges.

Land and environment

Boundaries and borders

Israel is a small country, measuring some 470 kilometres north to south and 116 kilometres at its widest east to west point. Within its present *de facto* boundaries it occupies 28,230 square kilometres (this figure includes East Jerusalem, 5,860 square kilometres of the West Bank, 360 square kilometres of Gaza and 1,240 square kilometres of the Golan Heights). Within its *de jure* boundaries Israel occupies just 20,770 square kilometres, and in places is less than 15 kilometres wide. It has a recognized land border with Egypt to the southwest, a recently recognized land border with Jordan to the southeast and east, a disputed border with Syria to the northeast (demarcated by a ceasefire line) and a recognized land border with Lebanon to the north (though Israel presently occupies a unilaterally declared 'security zone' of 1,550 square kilometres in southern Lebanon).

Topography

Israel is characterized by four broad topographical features: a large arid and semi-arid zone to the south (the Negev), with three parallel strips running north to south above it (Coastal plain, mountain spine, and the Jordan rift valley). More details of the regional landscape are given in the relevant chapters of this *Handbook*.

Coastal plain   Israel's Mediterranean coast stretches for some 270 kilometres in a gently curving arc, comprising mainly sandy shorelines and dunes (though there are cliffs in places, notably to the north). The coastal plain that borders the shoreline is between just 16 kilometres and 40 kilometres in depth, though it has subsequently become home to some 50 percent of Israel's population, most of its industry and a sizeable proportion of its agriculture. For further details see the 'Mediterranean Coastal Strip' and 'Haifa and the North Coast' chapters.

Mountain spine

Israel's mountain ranges broadly run in a north to south direction, effectively forming the backbone of the country. In places tectonic fault-lines have produced broad transverse valleys, the most notable of which is the Jezreel Valley (see 'Lower Galilee' section on page 613). The mountain areas in the north comprise the rolling hills and wide valleys of Galilee, consisting primarily of limestone and dolomite and rising to a maximum height of 1,208 metres. A separate upland area in the northeast is the high basalt plateau of the Golan; a geologically young feature. The mountain spine of Israel is formed by the central ranges of the hills of Samaria in the north (maximum height 1,108 metres) and the Judean Hills in the south (maximum elevation 1,020 metres). For further details see the 'Galilee and Golan' and 'West Bank' chapters.

Jordan rift valley

Israel's eastern border is largely defined by the Jordan River, running through a section of the Great Syrian-African Rift Valley. The Jordan River rises in the Mt Hermon area to the north, with its northern reaches for many years passing through the swamp land of the Hula Valley. This area has now been extensively drained (see 'Upper Galilee' section on page 706). It then enters the rift valley as it exits the Sea of Galilee. This upper section of the rift valley between the Sea of Galilee and the Dead Sea is often referred to as the Ghor (literally "hollowed out"). The topography of the rift valley has a profound effect upon the microclimate, most notably because of its great depth **below** sea-level. The Dead Sea is in fact the lowest point on earth, at some 395 metres below sea level (for further details see the 'Dead Sea Region' chapter). To the south of the Dead Sea the rift valley continues through the Wadi Arava depression all the way to the Red Sea.

Topography

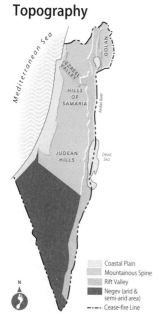

Coastal Plain
Mountainous Spine
Rift Valley
Negev (arid & semi-arid area)
-·-·- Cease-fire Line

Negev

The arid and semi-arid triangular wedge that occupies the southern half of Israel is referred to as the Negev. Home to just 7 percent of the population of Israel (but occupying about 50 percent of the land area), the Negev is usually classified as desert, though the reality is a little more complicated. The northwest section is more of a steppe climatic zone, allowing significant agricultural activity through careful use of irrigation. The wide swathe through the centre of the Negev is closer to desert, also featuring examples of a spectacular geological feature known as a *makhtesh* (erosion crater). An extremely arid zone subject to catastrophic flash-flooding borders the Wadi Arava area and the southern section of the Negev. Outcrops of Nubian sandstone create a number of extraordinary landscapes. For full details see the 'Negev' chapter.

Background

Rivers and water

Israel's principal river (and water source) is the **Jordan River**, which winds for some 330 kilometres in a 700-metre descent from its source near Mt Hermon to the Dead Sea. Three streams form its source (Banias, Dan, Hazbani) and it is joined by several tributaries, notably the **Yarmuk**. Because of the long dry summers that Israel experiences (and the high rate of evaporation) many of the rivers are in fact seasonal streams (*nahal* in Hebrew, *wadi* in Arabic), flowing for only part of the year. Spectacular but catastrophic flash-floods are often a winter and spring feature of these streams.

Israel's principal freshwater reservoir is the **Sea of Galilee**; perhaps the most graphic illustration of the country's regional water imbalance. As a means of countering the imbalance between the well-watered north and the semi-arid south, Israel has constructed the **National Water Carrier**, completed in 1964 (see page 683). A more recent proposal envisages bringing water from the Red Sea or Mediterranean to the Dead Sea in order to take advantage of the power-generating potential of water dropping into the rift valley (thus providing cheap power to run desalinization plants).

Despite leading the world in arid and semi-arid irrigation techniques, Israel still faces a potential chronic water deficit. This point was perhaps brought most sharply into focus in November 1964 when the Israeli air-force bombed a joint Lebanese-Syrian-Jordanian project that sought to divert the sources of the Jordan River, with the Israelis claiming that such a project was effectively an act of war. In fact, many commentators suggest that the next major confrontation in the Middle East will be over the question of water. The Palestinians regularly claim that the Israelis are stealing their water in the West Bank, with a glance at the map accompanying the current Interim Agreement between the two sides perhaps reflecting the position of aquifers and groundwater reservoirs as much as population distribution. Israel has naturally interpreted the 'security' aspects of the agreement as including the need to secure water supplies. In the matter of water, it appears that the Jordanians have gained much more from the current 'peace process' than the Palestinians, with their 'reward' for signing a peace treaty with Israel improving their access to waters from the Jordan, Yarmuk and Arava groundwaters by some 30 percent. Israel presently controls some 1.6 billion cubic metres of annual renewable water resources, 75 percent of which is used for agriculture. For further details on water issues in the region you could do worse than consult *Water, Peace and the Middle East: negotiating resources in the Jordan Basin* (edited by J.A. Allen, Tauris Academic Studies, London, 1996).

Climate

Israel has four broad climatic zones, though there are local and micro-variations influenced by factors such as proximity to the coast, altitude, aspect, topography and season. As a very general classification, Israel marks a transition zone between Mediterranean and Desert climate.

Much of the country falls within a **Mediterranean climate** zone, characterized by hot, dry summers (April-October) and mild, wet winters (November-March). Proximity to the coast has a marked moderating effect on this zone, as does the change in altitude as you move inland. Much of the Northern Negev comprises a **desert climate**, with this zone extending in a narrow finger along the Jordan Valley largely as a result of the rift valley's great depth below sea-level. Bordering the desert climate zone to the southeast is a region of **extreme Desert climate**, where rainfall is negligible, daytime temperatures are very high, and where there is a wide

Climatic zones

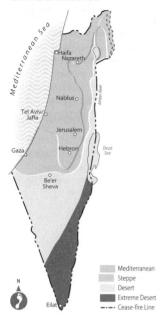

- Mediterranean
- Steppe
- Desert
- Extreme Desert
- –·–·– Cease-fire Line

Vegetation zones

- Mediterranean Zone
- Dune Vegetation
- Sudano-Deccanian Enclaves
- Saharo-Sindinian Zone
- Irano-Turanian Zone
- –·–·– Cease-fire Line

diurnal temperature range. The Mediterranean and desert zones are bordered by a species of transition zone that may effectively be described as a **steppe climate**. For details of the climatic influence upon the best time to visit and a brief weather sketch, see the 'Planning your trip' section (page 21).

Vegetation

Israel's wide range of plant and animal life is a direct function of its location at the junction of three continents (Europe, Asia, Africa), and its status as a transition zone between the Mediterranean and desert climatic zones. Over 2,800 types of plants have been identified, located in four broad vegetation zones. A comparison of the 'Climatic zones' and 'Vegetation zones' maps will indicate how inter-related these factors are. In many areas the natural vegetation has been radically modified by human action, some of which has been very recent. Medieval accounts of the Mediterranean coastal plain, for example, describe a thickly wooded area, though subsequent deforestation led to much of this area becoming swampland. This was in turn drained and turned into rich agricultural land, thanks mainly to the efforts of the early Zionist pioneers (late 19th and the 20th century). The same is also true of the Hula Valley in Upper Galilee.

Mediterranean zone

Though remnants of Tabor oak (*Quercus ithaburensis*) can still be found in parts of the Mediterranean vegetation zone (notably Lower Galilee), much of the vegetation is secondary, particularly the scrub forests of calliprinos oaks and pistacios. Other species of oaks, laurels, cypresses, Aleppo pines and a number of evergreens occupy more upland areas. Most of the lower areas in this zone have been given over to agriculture.

Irano-Turanian zone

A transition zone occupying much of the north and northwest Negev, and bordering the drier climatic zones to the south and east, this zone comprises a savannah-like mix of grasses, low-growing trees and bushes, plus a number of dwarf species.

Background

Saharo-Sindinian zone This vegetation zone occupies the desert regions of the Negev, Arava depression, Jordan rift valley and the Judean Desert, and reflects the constraints imposed by low levels of rainfall. Many species here have developed sophisticated methods of reducing water loss through surface evaporation (such as leaf shape and size, waxy leaf texture, deep roots, etc). The Tamarisk tree, for example, secretes a salty residue on to the ground surrounding it, thus discouraging other plants from competing with its roots for the water resource. Many species are found in seasonally dry wadi beds, flowering only after the stream is in flow. In some areas, remnants such as the Atlantic Terebinth (*Pistacia atlantica*) and Mesopotamian poplars (*Populas euphratica*) serve as living reminders of the process of environmental change.

Sudano-Deccanian zone There are a number of oases in Israel's arid and semi-arid zone where favourable groundwater reserves, coupled with high temperatures, allow the growth of certain tropical and sub-tropical species (such as date palms). These oases represent pockets of the Sudano-Deccanian vegetation zone, the two most notable of which are 'En Gedi and Jericho.

Wildlife

Israel has an extremely diverse collection of wildlife, again reflecting its geographical position as a European-African-Asian transition zone.

Birds Over 380 different species of birds can be seen in Israel, though the vast majority are just temporary visitors. Israel stands on the main migratory flight-path between Europe and Africa, with notable 'twitching' spots being in the Eilat region and around the Hula Nature Reserve in Upper Galilee. Gamla National Park in Lower Golan provides a spectacular back-drop for a key nesting area for birds of prey.

Mammals Some 60 mammal species can be found in Israel, though many are elusive due to nocturnal habits and the need to retreat to more remote locations away from predatory man. The Negev is the best area to see larger mammals such as the Nubian ibex (*Capra ibex*), striped hyena (*Hyaena hyaena*) and the ubiquitous rock hyrax (*Procavia capensis*), though your chances of seeing one of Israel's 15 or so remaining leopards (*Panthera pardus jarvisi*) are slim indeed. Wild pigs (*Sus scrofa*) are occasionally encountered in the Galilee.

Reptiles There are 80 different reptile species native to Israel, including lizards, snakes, scorpions and chameleons. Few are dangerous and they are rarely encountered, though the Palestinian viper (*Vipera palaestinensis*) should be avoided. You are much more likely to encounter a gecko in your hotel room, though.

Marine life Visitors to Israel should make every effort to view the spectacular marine life that lives on the coral bed of the Red Sea. An underwater observatory and glass-bottomed boats mean that visitors to Eilat need not get their feet wet in the process, though snorkelling and scuba-diving remain more adventurous options. In addition to the vivid colours of the smaller fish, it is also possible to see larger creatures such as sharks, dolphins and rays. Encounters with freshwater fish are likely to be confined to eating 'St Peter's Fish' caught in the Sea of Galilee (or bred on nearby fish farms).

La cage aux folles

A pair of Israel's endangered griffon vultures in Jerusalem zoo made the news recently, when they successfully reared a surrogate chick after the egg had been slipped into their nest. Raising orphaned chicks in such a way is not particularly unusual, though what makes Dashik and Yehuda (as zoo staff have named the pair) unique is the fact that they *are both males. The pair set up home together last year, and according to some reports, "openly and energetically mated" (*Independent, 2/8/99*) though unsurprisingly they failed to produce an egg! Nevertheless, according to zoo staff, they make excellent parents.*

Religion

Judaism

Jewish beliefs

Judaism is the first great revealed religion of the Middle East, arguably the world. The Judaic tradition grew up from the teachings of the prophets in the belief that God was the God of the Jews. Later, Jews came to the belief that God was more than a tribal god; instead God had a universal and supreme role. Judaism is seen to be founded on five great principles:

(1) that God needs no intermediary in the form of an incarnation of himself in his dealings with man;

(2) that all Jews have equal rights and responsibilities before God and that the rabbis are teachers only – not a priesthood (**NB** the concept of man's equality before the law is arguably the Jews' greatest legacy to mankind);

(3) that justice and living by the law are obligations for all Jews;

(4) that learning and reason (and in some societies mystical powers) are great virtues and the scholar is to be respected in Jewish society;

(5) that the honourable and upright will be rewarded in this world, with the implication that there is no life after death (the body instead returning to God to await physical resurrection on the Day of Judgement, so hence no cremation and the reluctance to submit a body for autopsy).

Written texts

The sacred Jewish texts are based upon the **Torah**; the five books of Moses (*Genesis, Exodus, Leviticus, Numbers , Deuteronomy*) that in the Christian tradition are known as the first five books of the Old Testament (the Greek *Pentateuch*). The Torah contains God's laws as laid down to **Moses**, including guidelines and regulations that determine how Jews must behave in their everyday life, and forms the basic text upon which all else rests. In its written form, the Torah was almost certainly completed before the Babylonian Exile (586 BCE), though some subsequent editing appears to have taken place.

However, the Torah is just the foundation stone of Jewish sacred literature, with Jewish sacred scholarship comprising a series of layers built one upon another, but each dependent upon its predecessor. The second layer comprises the books of the prophets, the psalms and the wisdom literature, which appears to have been

Background

canonized by **Rabbi Yohanan ben Zakkai** between 70 and 132 CE (see under 'Yavne' and 'Tiberias'). A third, non-canonical layer aids in the study of Jewish religion and history and comprises works such as the *Septuagint* (Greek translation of the Bible), the Apocrypha, and even records such as Josephus.

The next layer represents an attempt to codify the Oral Law that has accumulated through countless generations of study and commentary. Such a practice is referred to as *Mishnah* , literally 'repeat' or 'study' since the Oral Law was learnt by rote, memorized, and then repeated verbally to future generations. *Mishnah* comprises three distinct elements: *midrash*, which involves making clear points of law through study of the Torah; *halacha* (or *halakhah*), which is the body of accepted legal decisions on individual points; and *aggadah*, which is an anecdotal system of conveying the technical points of law in everyday terms to ordinary people. By about 210 CE the code of Oral Law had found a written form in a work known as the **Mishnah**, largely completed through the efforts of Rabbi Judah Ha-Nasi.

Whilst the Mishnah provided the written codification of Oral Law, later scholars sought to provide a commentary on it based largely upon judgements in actual legal cases: the result was the **Talmud** (meaning 'learning' or 'study'). Two main schools of commentary evolved, reflecting both the Jews continued presence in Israel and the diaspora experience, thus producing two versions of the Talmud. The **Jerusalem (Palestine) Talmud** was produced in Israel around 390 CE, with the **Babylonian Talmud** being produced around a century later.

In subsequent centuries, further great scholars have produced additional commentaries aimed primarily at simplifying the sheer mass of material accumulated. Johnson suggests that the great strength of such a body of material is that it "gave to the Jews a moral and social world-view which is civilized and practical and extremely durable", adding that there is "no system in the history of the world which has sought for so long to combine moral and ethical teaching with the practical exercise of civil and criminal jurisprudence" (*A History of the Jews*, 1987).

Branches of Judaism

In a faith as ancient as Judaism, and one that has been subject to so much scholarly study, it is unsurprising that a number of reformist streams have emerged. Whilst the majority of Jews belong to the **Orthodox** stream (with others being considered ultra-Orthodox, see page 803), a sizeable proportion of Jews are choosing to affiliate with more liberal streams, particularly in the Diaspora (notably the US). **Reform (Reconstructionist and Progressive)** Judaism emerged in Germany in the 19th century, almost certainly in light of the European emancipation and enlightenment. It soon became established in the US (by 1880 some 90 percent of America's 200 or so synagogues were Reform), with the **Conservative (Masorati)** stream also rising to prominence. In recent years, the split between Orthodox, Reform and Conservative streams, and the relationship between Israel and the Diaspora, has been brought sharply into focus, most notably in the question of the Law of Return (see page 813).

There are also a number of sub-sects within Judaism that reflect less a desire to reform the faith, and more the historical experience of the Jews. Such groups include the **Samaritans**, who regard themselves as descendants of the tribes of Joseph and his sons Menasseh and Ephraim. Another faction within Judaism are the **Karaites**, who emerged in the eighth century and profess adherence to the Torah alone as the source of religious law. Today they number around 15,000, living mainly in Ramla, Ashdod and Be'er Sheva.

For details of **kabbalah**, or Jewish mysticism, see page 709.

Everyday practices

Formal worship is conducted in a **synagogue**, though there is an argument that this institution plays a far greater role in community life in the diaspora than in Israel itself. A quorum of 10 adult males is required for traditional Orthodox worship. Prayers are conducted three times a day, generally led by a **rabbi** (who is considered a teacher and not a priest or intermediary with God). Men and women are seated separately and their heads are covered (see also box on page 647). The Holy Ark containing the Torah scrolls is the focal point of the synagogue, with a prescribed Torah portion being read cyclically throughout the Jewish year. It is not uncommon to see prayers being conducted in public places (notably the Western Wall, but sometimes in shopping precincts) where men strap a small leather box to their head, with leather straps wrapped around their arms. These implements are known collectively as **tefillin**, with the box containing a prescribed portion of the Torah. The purpose is to remind Jews that the heart, mind and body has been given to perform good, not evil, with the straps and box symbolically binding the mind and body.

The Torah prescribes that male children should be **circumcised** on the eighth day after birth. Jewish males reach adulthood at 13, at which age they become subject to Jewish law. On the first Shabbat after his 13th birthday, a Jewish male reads from a portion of the Torah in the synagogue for the first time. This rite of passage is known as **bar mitzvah**, and is generally an occasion for family celebration (particularly exuberant when held at the Western Wall). Further details on Jewish **dietary** practices can be found in the 'Food and drink' section. For details of Jewish **festivals** and **holidays** see page 56.

Christianity

Christian beliefs

Christian theology has its roots in Judaism, with its belief in one God, the eternal Creator of the universe. Judaism saw the Jewish people as the vehicle for God's salvation, the 'chosen people of God', and pointed to a time when God would send his Saviour, or Messiah. **Jesus**, whom Christians believe was 'the Christ' or Messiah, was born in the village of Bethlehem some 20 kilometres south of Jerusalem. Very little is known of his early life except that he was brought up in a devout Jewish family. At the age of 29 or 30 he gathered a small group of followers and began to preach in the region between the Dead Sea and the Sea of Galilee. Two years later he was crucified in Jerusalem by the authorities on the charge of blasphemy that he claimed to be the son of God.

Christians believe that all people live in a state of sin, in the sense that they are separated from God and fail to do his will. They believe that God is personal, 'like a father'. As God's son, Jesus accepted the cost of that separation and sinfulness himself through his death on the cross. Christians believe that Jesus was raised from the dead on the third day after he was crucified, and that he appeared to his closest followers. They believe that his spirit continues to live today, and that he makes it possible for people to come back to God.

The New Testament of the Bible, alongside the Old Testament, is the text to which Christians refer as the ultimate scriptural authority. It consists of four 'Gospels' (meaning 'good news') and a series of letters by several early Christians referring to the nature of the Christian life.

☞ *Main branches of the Christian Church in the Holy Land*

The four main branches of the Church operating in the Holy Land today are the **Eastern Orthodoxy** (Greek, Russian, Serbian, Bulgarian Orthodox); **Oriental Orthodoxy** (Armenian, Coptic, Ethiopian, Syrian Orthodox); **Catholicism** (Roman/Latin, Maronite, Greek Catholic); and **Protestantism** (various denominations).

Eastern Orthodoxy The dominant Eastern Orthodox church (and the main ecclesiastical body in Israel) is probably the **Greek Orthodox Church**, despite the fact that its worldwide constituents are few in number and drawn from a limited geographical area. The Greek Orthodox Church established a Patriarchate in Jerusalem in 451 CE, and now 'owns' the major portions of the Church of the Holy Sepulchre in Jerusalem and the Church of the Nativity in Bethlehem. The priesthood is almost exclusively Greek-speaking despite the fact that the vast majority of its congregation are Arabs (around 32% of all Christian Arabs). The **Russian Orthodox Church** also has a notable presence in the Holy Land, though again this mission is divided in two by competing claims as to who is the legitimate successor to the 19th-century Russian government mission.

Oriental Orthodoxy The main 'Oriental Orthodox' churches include the **Armenian Orthodox Church**, which established a presence in Jerusalem in the 4th century CE and whose continuity in the Holy Land has far from reflected the

experiences of the Armenian state. The **Syrian Orthodox Church** (sometimes referred to as the Jacobites) also have a significant presence in the Holy Land, with the seat of an archbishop in Jerusalem. The **Copts** (Egyptian Christians) are also represented in Israel. Their long-time rivals are the **Ethiopians**, who claim a line of descent through Solomon's union with the Queen of Sheba.

Catholicism The **Latin (Catholic) Church** became established in the Holy Land only in the medieval period, as a result of the Crusades. Thus papal influence on Christians in Israel nowhere near reflects the global influence of the Pontiff. In fact, relations between the Holy See and the State of Israel have always been rather strained, with full diplomatic links only being established in 1994. Only one serving Pope has ever visited the Holy Land (in 1965 when the charge against the Jews of deicide was formally dropped), though a papal visit is anticipated in March 2000. The **Greek Catholic (Melkite) Church** still observes the Greek rite, though it has been united with Rome since 1709 and recognizes the Pope as head of the church.

Protestantism Another late arrival in the Holy Land was the **Protestant Church**, whose ministry began largely in the 19th century. Numerous sub-sects of the Protestant church are active in Israel, with the largest one possibly being the Anglicans (comprised mainly of Arabs).

Christian worship

Although Christians are encouraged to worship individually as well as together, most forms of Christian worship centre on the gathering of the church congregation for praise, prayer and the preaching of God's word, which usually takes verses from the Bible as its starting point. Different denominations place varying emphases on the main elements of worship, but in most church services today the congregation will take part in singing hymns (songs of praise), prayers will be led by the minister, priest or a member of the congregation, readings from the Bible will be given and a sermon preached. For many Christians the most important service is the act of Holy Communion (Protestant) or Mass (Catholic) which celebrates the death and resurrection of Jesus in sharing bread and wine, which are held to represent Christ's body and blood given to save people from their sin.

Christian sects in the Holy Land

Numerous sects and sub-sects of Christianity operate in the Holy Land, largely reflecting the theological, political and physical separation of the Eastern and Western churches. Though international power politics in the 18th and 19th centuries have played a role in this inter-denominational rivalry, the first split was considerably earlier (451 CE in fact), arising primarily out of the condemnation of Monophysitism as heresy at the Fourth Ecumenical Council held in Chalcedon. Almost all the sects are nationalistic in outlook, yet the balance of power between the various denominations in the Holy Land do not reflect global realities. The rivalry between the various sects is often bitter, sometimes violent, and seriously calls into question the concept of Christian brotherhood.

Islam

Islamic beliefs and practices

The word Islam translates roughly as 'submission to God'. The two central tenets of Islam are embodied in the creed "There is no god but Allah and Mohammad is his Prophet" ("*Lah Illaha illa 'Ilah Mohammad Rasulu 'Ilah*") which affirms the belief in the oneness of God and recognizes Mohammad as the divinely appointed messenger of God.

The *Qur'an* (generally referred to as the Koran in English) is Islam's holiest book. The word translates literally as 'recitation', and unlike the Bible is considered to be the *uncreated* (ie direct) word of God, as revealed to **Mohammad** through *Jibril* (the angel Gabriel). The text consists of 114 chapters, each known as a *sura*. Each sura is classified as Meccan or Medinan, according to whether it was revealed to Mohammad in Mecca or Medina. Most of the text is written in a kind of rhymed prose known as *saj*, and is considered by Muslims to be inimitable. Each chapter of the Koran begins with the words "*Bismillah al-Rahman al-Rahim*" ("In the name of Allah, the Merciful, the Compassionate"), an invocation which can also be heard being uttered by Muslims in numerous everyday situations; when boarding a bus or before eating food for example.

In addition to the Qur'an, there is the *Hadith* body of literature; a record of the sayings and doings of Mohammad and his followers that forms the basis of Islamic laws (*Shariat*) and precepts. Unlike the Qur'an, the Hadiths are recognized to have been written by men and are therefore potentially flawed and open to interpretation. Thus they are commonly classified into four major categories according to their trustworthiness: *Sahih* (sound, true, authentic), *Hasan* (fair, good), *Da'if* (weak) and *Saqim* (infirm). The two most revered compilations of Hadiths are those of *al-Bukhari* and *Muslim*. It is in the interpretation of the Hadiths that most of the controversy surrounding certain Islamic laws and their application originates.

While Mohammad is recognized as the founder of the Islamic faith and the principle messenger of God, Muslims also regard him as having been the last in a long line of Prophets, starting with Adam and including Moses, Abraham and Jesus. They do not, however, accept Jesus as the son of God, but simply another of God's Prophets. Both Jews and Christians are considered *Ahl-e-Kitab* ('People of the Book'), the Torah and the Gospels being completed in Islamic belief by the Qur'an.

Nearly all Muslims accept six basic articles of the Islamic faith: belief in one God, in his angels, in his revealed books, in his Apostles, in the Resurrection and Day of Judgement, and in his predestination of good and evil. Heaven is portrayed in Muslim belief as a Paradise filled with sensuous delights and pleasures. The idea of heaven as paradise predates Islam: Alexander the Great is believed to have brought the word into Greek from Persia, where he used it to describe the walled Persian gardens that were found even before the birth of Christ. Hell, on the other hand, is portrayed as a place of eternal terror and torture, which is the certain fate of all who deny the unity of God.

Islam has no ordained priesthood or clergy. The authority of religious scholars, learned men, Imams, judges, etc derives from their authority to interpret the scriptures, rather than from any defined status within the Islamic community.

The development of Islam

Mohammad, the founder of the Islamic faith, was born around 570 CE in the city of **Mecca** in present-day Saudi Arabia. His family were of noble descent, members of the house of **Hashim**, belonging to the **Abd Manaf** clan and part of the **Quraish** tribal confederacy of Mecca. The Abd Manaf clan had a semi-priestly status, being responsible for certain functions during the annual pilgrimage to the *Ka'ba* in Mecca (the Ka'ba, the cube-shaped building to which Muslims face when praying, predates Islam; Muslims believe that it was established by Adam and revere it as a sanctuary where closeness to God can be achieved).

At the age of 40 Mohammad received his first revelations of the *Qur'an* and began preaching his message. He encountered stiff opposition from the powerful Quaish leaders, the temple guardians and the rich traders, and was eventually forced to flee to **Medina**, known then as Yathrib (the famous *Hijra*, or 'flight', which marks the beginning of the Islamic calendar). There he established himself and achieved a position of power, fighting three major battles with the Meccans before finally returning there in triumph two years before his death in 632 CE.

In his lifetime he had become recognized as a prophet and founded the Islamic faith. Part of his success was in incorporating many aspects of the ancient Arabian religion, such as the pilgrimage to Ka'ba, as well as aspects of Judaism and Christianity. But his success was not purely in religious terms. He was also an accomplished statesman who laid the foundations for what would later become a great Islamic empire.

Islamic sects

In the century following Mohammad's death, Islam divided into two major sects. Mohammad left no sons and therefore no obvious heir, and gave no instructions as to who should succeed him. There were two main contenders: **Abu Bakr**, the father of Mohammad's wife, and **Ali**, the husband of Mohammad's daughter Fatimah, and his cousin. In the event Abu Bakr assumed the title of *Caliph* (vice-regent). He died two years later in 634 CE and was succeeded by **Omar** who was killed in 644. **Uthman**, a member of the powerful **Umayyad** family, was chosen to succeed him but proved to be a weak leader and was murdered in 656.

At this point the aggrieved Ali managed to assume the title of Caliph, thus ousting the Umayyads. However, **Muawiya**, the governor of Syria and a member of the Umayyad family, soon rose up in revolt. He managed to gain the upper hand; in 661 Ali was murdered (by one of his own supporters) and Muawiya proclaimed himself Caliph. Ali's eldest son **Hassan** set up a rival Caliph in Iraq, but was soon persuaded to abdicate. However, the seeds of the schism in Islam had already been sown; between the **Sunnis** (those who accepted the legitimacy of the first three Caliphs) and the **Shias** (those who recognized only Ali as the first legitimate Caliph). Later, when Muawiya died in 680, Ali's second son Hussain attempted to revolt against the Umayyads, but was defeated and killed in 681 at Karbala, providing the Shias with their greatest martyr.

Followers of the **Sunni** sect, generally termed 'Orthodox', account for around

The Five Pillars of Islam

There are five practices or Akran, known as the Five Pillars of Islam, which are generally accepted as being obligatory to Muslims.

*   ***Shahada*** *The profession of faith ("There is no god but Allah … "), which also forms the basis of the call to prayer made by the muezzin of the mosque.*

*   ***Salat*** *The ritual of prayers, carried out 5 times a day at prescribed times; in the early morning before the sun has risen above the horizon, in the early afternoon when the sun has passed its zenith, later when the sun is halfway towards setting, immediately after sunset and in the evening before retiring to bed. Prayers can be carried out anywhere, whether it be in a mosque or by the roadside, and involves facing towards the Ka'ba in Mecca and prostrating before God while reciting verses of the Qur'an.*

*   ***Zakat*** *The compulsory payment of alms. In early times this was collected by officials of the Islamic state, and was devoted to the relief of the poor, debtors, aid to travellers and other charitable purposes. In many Muslim communities, the fulfilment of this religious obligation is nowadays left to the conscience of the individual.*

*   ***Sawm*** *The 30 days of fasting during the month of Ramadan, the 9th month of the Muslim lunar calendar. It is observed as a fast from sunrise to sunset each day by all Muslims, although there are provisions for special circumstances.*

*   ***Hajj*** *The pilgrimage to Mecca. Every Muslim, circumstances permitting, is obliged to perform this pilgrimage at least once in their lifetime and having accomplished it may assume the title of Hajji. The lack of diplomatic relations between Israel and Saudi Arabia makes performing the Hajj all but impossible.*

80 percent of Muslims globally, but almost all Muslims in Israel/Palestine. They base their *Sunna* (path, or practice) on the 'Six Books' of traditions. They are organized into four orthodox schools or rites named after their founders, each having equal standing. The *Hanafi* is the most moderate. The others are the *Shafii*, *Maliki* and *Hanbali*, the latter being the strictest. Many Muslims today prefer to avoid identification with a particular school, preferring to call themselves simply Sunni.

The other main Islamic group is the **Shia** sect, and though important in southern Lebanon, they have next to no presence in Israel/Palestine. Aside from the dispute over the succession of Mohammad, Sunnis and Shias do not generally differ on fundamental issues since they draw from the same ultimate sources. However, there are important differences of interpretation, which partly derive from the practice of *ijtihad* ('the exercise of independent judgement') amongst Shias, as oppose to *taqlid* (the following of ancient models) as adhered to by Sunnis. Thus Shias divest far more power in their *Imams*, accepting their role as an intermediary between God and man and basing their law and practice on the teachings of the Imams. (**NB** The term Imam is also used more generally by both Shias and Sunnis to refer to the prayer leader of a mosque.) The majority of Shias are known as *Ithna asharis* or 'Twelvers', since they recognize a succession of 12 Imams. They believe that the last Imam, who disappeared in 878 CE, is still alive and will reappear soon before the Day of Judgement as the *Mahdi* (one who is rightly guided), who will rule by divine right.

A further sect of Islam found within Israel is the **Ahmadiyyat**, though many Muslims believe that this group is heretical (see page 573 for full details).

Background

Other faiths

Druze

Very few details are known about the true nature of the Druze faith, largely because not all Druze are initiated into the precepts of the faith themselves. Those who are aware of the doctrines are referred to as *uqqal* ('intelligent'), whilst the 'ignorant' members are *juhhal*. Some of the basic dogma is known, however, and is related to a Western audience as a form of Gnostic mysticism. The key point of the doctrine involves 'the oneness of God', reflecting the Druze roots in Islam from which it split in the reign of the Caliph al-Hakim (996-1021 CE). God is believed to reveal himself through a number of human incarnations, the last of whom was al-Hakim himself. For some further details see under 'Minority communities in a Jewish state' in the 'Modern Israel' section, on page 803.

Baha'i

Israel is also home of the Universalist Baha'i faith. For further details see the 'Haifa' section on page 567.

Modern Israel

Population and society

Israeli society

Seeking to examine the different components that make up Israeli society is a little more complicated than dividing the population into 'Jews' and 'non-Jews'. For example, despite having the common bond of Judaism, the Jewish faith does have a number of different streams (see under 'Religion' on page 795), whilst Israel's Jewish society can be divided into three broad groupings.

Ashkenazi Jews This group comprises mainly Jews of European origin (Ashkenaz deriving from the Hebrew word for Germany), though in Israel it often includes those who arrived from Europe via North and South America, South Africa and Australia. The early Zionist movement and the early years of the State of Israel were largely shaped by the Ashkenazi community.

Sephardi Jews The term 'Sephardi' is frequently wrongly applied to describe all Middle Eastern and North African Jews. The word Sephard does in fact refer to the ancient Hebrew word for Spain, and when correctly applied refers to those descended from the 200,000-strong Jewish community expelled from Spain (and Portugal) by King Ferdinand of Aragon and Queen Isabella of Castile in 1492. They eventually settled in such places as Turkey, Holland, Italy, Bulgaria, Greece, and in parts of North Africa, with the latter group probably being the reason for the continued misuse of the term Sephardi. Most appear to have made their way to Israel in a series of individual and collective immigrations.

Mizrachi Jews This is the grouping that is usually wrongly referred to as 'Sephardi'. Mizrachi Jews are in fact the 'Oriental' or 'Eastern' Jews that originate from the very ancient Jewish

Basics

Capital Jerusalem (though this is not recognized by the UN or most nations, with most retaining embassies in Tel Aviv).

Flag White backround with pale blue horizontal band at top and bottom (to symbolize the tallit, or Jewish prayer shawl) and a pale blue Star of David at the centre.

National Anthem "Hatikva" ("The Hope").

Population 5.57 million (including East Jerusalem and Golan, but excluding areas under Palestinian Authority control).

Language Hebrew; Arabic (around 15%); European languages.

Ethnic divisions Jews 81% (50% born in Israel; 38% in Europe, Americas or Oceania; 7% in Africa; 5% in Asia); non-Jews 19% (mainly Arab).

Religion Judaism 81%; Islam 14.4%; Christianity 2.9%; Other 1.7% (mainly Druze).

communities in the Islamic countries of North Africa and the Middle East. The term may also be applied to the Jewish community from Cochin in India, since this group actually arrived on the sub-continent from the Middle East. Though many arrived in Palestine during the late 19th and early 20th centuries, the majority arrived in Israel in the period 1948-72 having left (or been expelled from) Islamic countries that became enemies of Israel following the latter's independence. A number, such as the Ethiopian Jews, arrived in a series of spectacular airlifts/rescue operations (for example 'Operation Moses' in 1984 that brought 15,000 and 'Operation Solomon' in 1991 that brought the rest of the community). Such operations had their precedent in 'Operation Magic Carpet' that brought some 46,000 Jews out of Yemen in the years 1949-50. For details on the struggle of the Sephardi and Mizrachi groups to adapt to life in Israel, see 'Unity in diversity?' on page 805.

Other groups

There are a number of other communities that perhaps need to be mentioned here. Amongst the most visible of the Jewish communities in Israel (and the world in general) are the **Haredim**, or ultra-Orthodox Jews. The word *haredim* literally means 'those who fear heaven', and is the usual designation given to those belonging to the stream of strict ('ultra') orthodox Judaism that opposes accommodation with both the non-Orthodox trends within Judaism (Reform, Conservative) and secularism. Their attitudes to Zionism and the State of Israel in general range from outright hostility to ambivalence. A small but volatile sector of the community believe that Jewish sovereignty in the Land of Israel, even a state founded according to Jewish religious law (*halacha*), cannot be established before the coming of the Messiah. Thus, they oppose, and refuse to participate in, the State of Israel. Other groups are more pragmatic, using their considerable voting potential to win concessions and benefits for their community.

Other branches, or sub-sects, of Judaism found in Israel are the small communities of **Samaritans** and **Karaites**, though numerically they are insignificant.

Minority communities in a Jewish State

Approximately 19 percent of the population of Israel (excluding the territories occupied by Israel since 1967 and the Palestinian Authority areas) is non-Jewish; around one million people. They are generally referred to collectively as **Israeli Arabs**, though this is a gross over-simplification. Whilst standards and access to education and healthcare have improved since this group became included within the State of Israel, and the status of women in society has undergone a number of liberalizing trends, it is widely accepted that Israeli Arabs have faced considerable discrimination when compared to their Jewish Israeli counterparts. On the other hand, Israel would argue with some justification that Israeli Arabs have far greater democratic and legal rights than most of their brethren in

Background

neighbouring Arab states. This issue is further explored in 'Pluralism and segregation' on page 807.

Muslim Arabs account for around three-quarters of Israel's non-Jewish population, almost all of whom belong to the Sunni branch of Islam. **Christian Arabs** are Israel's second largest minority group, comprising about 150,000 people. They are concentrated mainly in the Nazareth, Shefar'am and Haifa area, plus smaller communities in Jerusalem. Christian Arabs belong mainly to the Greek Catholic (42 percent), Greek Orthodox (32 percent) and Roman Catholic (16 percent) denominations of Christianity, though there is often a feeling of resentment in the lack of representation of Christian Arabs amongst the higher echelons of the clergy.

Bedouins represent around 10 percent of the Muslim Arab population of Israel (around 70,000 people). In common with nomadic groups across the world, the 30 or so bedouin tribes in Israel are under considerable pressure to adopt a sedentary lifestyle. Permanent settlements complete with education and healthcare facilities are being built, though such towns tend to be located in peripheral areas of the country where a secure economic base is uncertain. Some tribes, such as the Jahalin, have been forcibly removed from their traditional homes, only to be subsequently evicted a second time to accommodate the expansion of Israeli settlements.

Druze communities number approximately 80,000 members, mainly in the Haifa and Upper Golan regions. Those concentrated in the Haifa and Western Galilee region tend to participate fully in Israeli society (including the army), whilst those in the Golan look more to their co-religionists in neighbouring Lebanon and Syria.

Circassians belong to a distinct ethnic group that migrated to Palestine in the 19th century from the Caucasus region of Central Asia. They number around 3,000, living in two small villages in Upper Galilee. They are Sunni Muslim and tend to use Arabic as their everyday language. In keeping with the request of their community leaders, their young men are liable for the Israeli military draft. Other small religious communities in Israel include the **Ahmadies** (see page 573) and members of the **Bahai** faith (see page 567).

Studying the figures of the 'ethnic division' of Israel, it is immediately apparent that, including the territories occupied since 1967, Israel has a significant non-Jewish population within its borders. This is sometimes referred to as Israel's "demographic demon", implying that because of their higher birth rate, Arabs will become a majority in Israel in the next 30 years or so. However, there is more to Israel's demographic future than just high birth rates; population change is in fact governed by four factors, of which birth rate must be considered alongside death rate, emigration and immigration. The latter, of course, is the key. Former prime minister Benjamin Netanyahu argues that "The history of Zionism has been the history of Jewish immigration. Israel's demographic future hinges on this one factor … The struggle for immigration is thus the struggle for the existence of Israel" (*A Place Among the Nations*, 1993). Thus, Israel does all that it can to facilitate the immigration of Jews from the Diaspora; it is one of very few countries that encourages a species normally turned away by other nations – the 'economic migrant' (see page 804).

Immigration: the continued ingathering

The whole *raison d'être* of the creation of the modern State of Israel is the "ingathering of the exiles" (*Genesis 15:13-16*), to provide a homeland and refuge for the Jewish people. This concept is the essence of the Zionism founding philosophy, and is enshrined within the Law of Return (see page 813).

Within a space of less than 50 years Israel has absorbed around 2.4 million immigrants, around three times the size of its population at independence. In this regard, Israel is perhaps unique in relying on substantial immigration to increase its population. The number of Palestinians who left or were forced out during the war that accompanied Israel's independence in 1948 (a contentious figure that is placed at anywhere between 550,000 and 725,000) is roughly matched by the number of Jewish immigrants into Israel who left or were forced out of Arab countries during the period 1948-72 (around 570,000 *Mizrachi* or 'Oriental' Jews, see page 802).

At independence, the majority of Jews living in the newly created State of Israel came from three main sources: the *Yishuv*, or ancient Jewish community of Palestine; the early Zionist pioneers, who were predominantly *Ashkenazi* Jews (see page 802) from eastern and central Europe; and refugees from the Nazi Holocaust in Europe, mainly Ashkenazi, but also a sizeable portion of *Sephardi* Jews (see page 802). Such a rapid influx of *Mizrachi* Jews in the period 1948-72 drastically altered the nature of the state within just one generation of its independence.

The continued ingathering perpetuates the process of social change in Israeli Jewish society. Since 1990 Israel has absorbed somewhere in the region of 600,000 new immigrants from the **former Soviet Union**. This large, and highly visible, community has had a major impact on contemporary life in Israel. The economic impact alone of providing housing, jobs and social security has been immense, though Israel has perhaps learnt that it is not unique, and that when it comes to prejudices facing immigrants, it is pretty much like every other country in the world (see 'Unity in diversity?' on page 805). The key attacks are on the 'Jewishness' (or lack of it) of these immigrants, though links to the Russian mafia and other criminal groups is another cause for concern. The voting power of this constituency should not be underestimated; they are largely credited with determining the outcome of the direct vote for prime minister in both the 1996 and 1999 elections. Significantly, the leader of the party (Yisrael B'Aliyah) that represents their interests (Natan Sharansky, former Soviet 'refusenik') now heads the all-important Ministry of the Interior in Ehud Barak's ruling coalition.

Unity in diversity?

Although around 81 percent of Israel's population are Jews, this figure actually represents a community drawn from some 80 countries around the world, and not surprisingly represents a very broad collection of ethnic, cultural and social backgrounds. Israel has many anomalies, such as "a vibrant multi-party democracy, but also a strong military establishment; a socialist state structure, married to a highly entrepreneurial industrial sector; strongly secular political mores, but a solid religious political grouping always in the wings" (Joffe, 1996).

It is easy to identify very broad and very bitter divisions in Israeli society, though the fact is often ignored that Israel is not just a Jewish homeland, but also a multi-cultural, multi-ethnic and multi-lingual society. In the words of one government mouthpiece, "Israel is not a melting-pot society, but rather more of a mosaic made up of different sectors" (*Facts About Israel*, Israel Information Centre, 1995). Palestinians and Israeli Arabs would perhaps argue that they have been deliberately excluded from this mosaic.

Divisions in Israeli society are over many things. The most obvious of course is the relationship with the Palestinians, and notably the idea of withdrawing from the West Bank and Gaza Strip, or the concept of exchanging land for peace. Perhaps of greater threat to Israel as a cohesive unit, however, are the divisions within Jewish society itself. Many such divisions are a direct result of the way in which Israel came into being, and the means by which this 'New Society' was created.

As mentioned in the section on 'Immigration' above, at independence the population of Israeli comprised mainly Ashkenazi and Sephardi Jews. Their tastes and customs reflected their European origins, with the early ideals of these

Background

👉 *Shop around the clock: the "culture war"*

A graphic illustration of the widening gulf between 'religious' and 'secular' Jews can be seen in the continuing struggle over a supermarket in Jerusalem's New City. The '2000 Drugstore' on Shamai Street is just a regular corner convenience store – except of course that it offers the opportunity to shop 24 hours a day, 7 days a week.

Opening on Shabbat in Jerusalem (apart from in predominantly Arab areas) is unheard of, and possibly against the Municipality's laws. In fact, the Municipality even employ Druze inspectors specifically for the task of implementing these rules on Shabbat (since Jewish inspectors are unable to work on the Sabbath). However, the owner of '2000 Drugstore' has an ingenious method for avoiding prosecution for opening a Jewish business on Shabbat; just before sundown each Friday he sells the business (for one shekel) to a Muslim Arab, before buying it back (presumably for the same price) at the end of Shabbat on Saturday!

The courts are still deciding as to whether such a practice is indeed legal, though more radical members of the 'religious' community prefer to take matters into their own hands – almost every Shabbat the '2000 Drugstore' gets all its windows smashed!

immigrants – "belief in the benefits of scientific rationalism, secularism, socialist notions, democratic assemblies" (Joffe, *ibid*) – dictating the way in which Israel developed. The sudden arrival within the first 25 years or so of Israel's existence of over half a million Mizrachi Jews ('Oriental' or 'Eastern' Jews, though often mistakenly referred to as 'Sephardi'), presented a grave challenge to the new Jewish State. On the whole, the Mizrachi Jews were more patriarchal in their social organization, unfamiliar with the 'Western' ideals through which the state functioned, with their generally lower levels of education acting as a constraint upon employment opportunities and political advancement. In effect, Israel's early years were characterized by an Ashkenazi Israel and a Mizrachi Israel.

Mizrachi rejection of their 'second-class' status was soon manifested at the ballot box, with the Likud victory in the 1977 election largely attributed to the 'Oriental' vote. Here, perhaps, is another example of anomaly in Israel; an under-class voting out a socialist government in favour of a party dedicated to economic liberalization. A further irony is that the Mizrachi community are now largely integrated within Israeli society, being well represented in government, military and business spheres, whilst the most recent Ashkenazi influx (from the former Soviet Union) have struggled to become acculturated and accepted. The issue has also been raised of the treatment of Israel's 60,000 Ethiopian Jews, who feel that their 'Jewishness' is often questioned, whilst they also complain that efforts to integrate them have not produced the generous grants and welfare programmes that the later Russian *émigrés* have enjoyed.

A further division within Israeli society is often classified under the heading of 'religious versus secular Jew'. This issue has largely risen out of the diaspora experience, where some communities chose to integrate with their host societies at large whilst other chose to (or were forced to) turn in upon themselves (notably in the ghettos of eastern Europe). Thus, nowadays in Israel, Jewish society comprises observant, non-observant and secular Jews. It is rather difficult to put figures to the categories of 'religious' and 'secular' Jews, though it is widely accepted that 20 percent of the Jewish population of Israel fulfil all religious precepts, 60 percent follow some combination of Jewish religious laws and practices, whilst 20 percent are totally non-observant (*chilonim*). These divisions come into sharp focus when the nature of the State of Israel is discussed. Though religion and state are effectively separated, there is no formal basis to this separation; just a *modus vivendi* that has

What sort of country?

The New York Times' foreign-affairs columnist Thomas Friedman believes that to "fully appreciate the reason's for Israel's paralysis one must go way back to the birth of the nation" (From Beirut to Jerusalem, 1989). His thesis is that the Zionist Jews who brought the State of Israel into being had three basic objectives in mind: a) a Jewish state, b) a democratic state, and c) a state located in the historical homeland of the Jewish people. When independence became possible, only options a) and b) were available, so the Zionists took them. The Six Day War of 1967 brought a new set of realities. Israel now had all the land of the historic homeland, option c), though in order to remain a Jewish state, Israeli democracy would have to be curtailed, thus only fulfilling options a) and c). Alternatively, Israel could annex the West Bank and Gaza, give democratic rights to the Palestinian population there, but at the risk of losing the Jewish character of the state, thus only keeping options b) and c). The final choice was to remain a Jewish and democratic state by returning the territory captured in the Six Day War, but once again surrendering option c). "So, on the seventh day of the Six-Day War, amid the jubilation and flag waving, a huge question once again hung over the Israelis: Who were they? A nation of Jews living in all the land of Israel, but not democratic? A democratic nation in all the land of Israel, but not Jewish? Or a Jewish and democratic nation, but not in all the land of Israel?" (Friedman, ibid). It is a rather simplistic analysis, though it does go some way towards posing questions that have still not been answered.

operated since Israel's inception. In some quarters there is the call for a *halacha* state based upon the precepts of Jewish religious law. Currently, *halacha* is binding in the areas of marriage, divorce and the personal status of Jews, whilst the law of the state applies to all other fields (though the courts may, at their discretion, take account of *halacha* where no secular legislation is applicable). It is often said that most of Israel wants to live in a Jewish Sweden, whilst the rest want to live in a Jewish Iran.

Pluralism and segregation

The true test of Israel's pluralist credentials is the way in which it deals with minorities. Can a state, for example, be considered truly democratic when a large number of the people living within its borders are disenfranchised or discriminated against? For example, Muslim and Christian Arabs, plus Bedouins, who live in the areas that became part of Israel after 1948 constitute almost one million people. Although they are granted Israeli citizenship (and can thus vote in elections, and have some of their own parties and Knesset members) it is widely accepted that they are discriminated against, with their commitment as Israeli citizens often questioned. On the other hand, it may be argued that levels of education, women's rights, and general economic conditions have improved significantly amongst most Arab Israeli communities. The subject is far more complex (and controversial) when discussing the Palestinian residents of areas that Israel has occupied (or 'administered', according to your viewpoint) since 1967.

The extent of segregation within Israeli society is another topic of hot debate. Many communities choose to segregate voluntarily in order to maintain their cultural, religious and ethnic identity. Notable amongst this group are the ultra-Orthodox Jews and the recent immigrants from the Soviet Union, though the latter group may eventually follow the same process of full or partial integration that the Mizrachi Jewish community followed. Other groups that may consider their segregation as being of a somewhat less voluntary nature are Israeli Arabs and

Background

Ethiopian Jews. Both groups make claims about not being fully accepted by their fellow Israelis.

Of course the most public and controversial segregation concerns the Palestinians of the West Bank and Gaza Strip. The very nature of producing areas with varying degrees of autonomy (that underlines the current 'peace process') quite naturally produces a degree of segregation. But critics of the deal signed between the Israelis and Palestinians claim that what is in fact evolving is a kind of apartheid based upon the creation of 'bantustans', with Palestinian autonomous areas becoming ringed by Jewish settlements connected by Jewish roads. Of particular concern to Palestinians is the way in which Jerusalem is being ringed by new Jewish suburbs, effectively disconnecting 'Arab' East Jerusalem from its Arab hinterland.

The kibbutz and moshav system

Though the concept of collective, communal settlement is not unique to Israel, the wider economic and social framework that it represents, as well as the impact that it has had on national life, most certainly is. Growing out of the pioneering Zionist programme that saw Jewish redemption through working the land, the *kibbutz* and *moshav* system had a disproportionately larger impact on Israel's early development than the number of kibbutzniks (kibbutz members) suggested. The percentage of Israelis living on a kibbutz has never risen above 8 percent, and has tended to settle at the present figure of around 3.8 percent, but, as Stephen Brook points out, kibbutzniks' impact on civil life has been immense: "One third of the young state's first constituent assembly in 1948 was composed of kibbutzniks. For the first twenty years of Israel's existence, a third of all cabinet members were kibbutzniks. The number of kibbutznik officers in the IDF is six times greater than their proportion of the population would lead one to expect, and during the Six Day War, one quarter of the casualties were kibbutzniks" (*Winner Takes All*, 1990).

The picture of the kibbutz system today is very different indeed, and is often labelled as an institution in crisis. The decline in the contribution to the national economy of the agricultural sector has seen many kibbutzim turn to light industry and tourism as a means of survival. Meanwhile, the transfer to the government and Israeli mainstream of functions such as immigration, settlement, defence and agriculture has seen the kibbutz movement become marginalized to the fringes of society.

There are divisions within the kibbutz movement today, with many suggesting that the eroding of the collective ethos is shifting the institution away from its founding principles, whilst other argue the need to be pragmatic and make fundamental changes if the kibbutz is to survive. (**NB** For details of working on a kibbutz or moshav, see page 62).

The role of the military in Israeli society

Another key Israeli institution is the **Israeli Defence Forces**, or IDF. Israel's standing army is in the region of 175,000 men and women, though the nature of compulsory service and reserve duty makes being an Israeli and being a soldier very much one and the same thing. All eligible men and women are drafted at the age of 18, with men serving three years and women serving two (including Druze and Circassian men). Women are eligible for over half of the job categories in the services, including a recently formed combat unit, though the image of women soldiers that most visitors to Israel take away with them is of soldiers wearing lipstick, make-up and nail varnish!

Upon completion of service, all soldiers are assigned to a reserve unit, with 30 days being the average amount of reserve duty expected each year (though this can be increased when necessary). Men serve reserve duty up to the age of 51, with unmarried women liable to the draft up to 24. National service conscription is in fact considered to be an essential rite of passage and national unifying factor. Israeli Arabs and Bedouins are exempt from national service, though there are options for them to join if they wish. Ultra-Orthodox Jews, notably men involved in Torah and religious study, are also exempt, though there is considerable animosity about this amongst many sectors of Israeli society, who resent the political and economic benefits that the ultra-Orthodox community enjoy without sending their sons to the army.

David Eliazar, IDF Chief of Staff during the Yom Kippur war of 1973, once suggested that "The qualitative level of an army is a direct function of the level of the people, their sense of national identity, and their cultural and technological sophistication." However, as Joffe observes, "the 1982 Lebanon War and the 'iron fist' reaction to the *intifada* severely tested this belief, undermined the formerly unanimous unity behind Israel's military policy, and sparked a national debate which still rages today. Indeed, the issue has played a large role in shaping the timing and nature of the current peace process" (*Keesing's Guide to the Middle-East Peace Process*, 1996).

Career soldiers may retire after 20 years of service, with many entering the field of politics. Former military men are often far more pragmatic about the need to make concessions to achieve peace than their 'civilian' counterparts. The irony of this situation should not be lost. The recently elected prime minister Ehud Barak is Israel's most decorated soldier, yet is seen as the man to push through the peace process. Yet, as Palestinian intellectual Edward Said has pointed out, Israeli soldiers are decorated for fighting wars against (ie killing) Arabs.

Government, politics and institutions

Israeli is a parliamentary democracy that comprises three main bodies: the legislature (the Knesset, or parliament); the executive (the elected government); and the judiciary (the court system). The structure is based upon the separation of powers, with a number of checks and balances built into the system. Despite the number of political parties with a religious platform, Israel follows the liberal model used in the West of separating Church (or rather, Synagogue) and State.

The political system

Israel has a multi-party political system that is probably the most democratic in the Middle East. The legislative assembly is the **Knesset**, a unicameral assembly (ie no upper house such as the House of Lords in Britain), whose function is to legislate and oversee the workings of the government. The Knesset is elected every four years, though it may dissolve itself and call new elections before the end of its term. It takes its name from the *Knesset Hagedolah* (Great Assembly of the Jewish Commonwealth) that Ezra and Nehemiah convened in Jerusalem in the 5th century BCE.

The system by which the Knesset functions draws on a number of models from around the world, noticeably the British and American legislative systems. Like the British model, the elected prime minister enjoys real executive authority at the head of a Cabinet of his or her choice. The prime minister must be a Knesset member (MK), though ministers in the Cabinet need not be. Ministers are either assigned a specific portfolio and head a ministry (for example, defence, foreign affairs, etc), or serve without portfolio. There is no set number of ministers in a Cabinet, and it varies from government to government. The President is largely a titular head of state, though, unlike the monarchy system in Britain, the Israeli president is elected every five years by popular mandate. Similarities with the US system include the powerful Committee system.

Background

The Knesset operates in plenary sessions and through the 10 standing committees that deal with specific areas of the country's affairs. To become law a new bill must pass its first reading in the Knesset before being referred to the appropriate committee for discussion. It is then reviewed in plenary session before a final vote is cast after the third reading. It is then signed into law by the minister concerned, the prime minister, and the president.

Checks and balances

The government is responsible to the Knesset and may be dismissed if it fails a vote of no-confidence. At least 61 votes are required to dismiss the government. Checks and balances on the Israeli democratic process include a strong independent Judiciary, whose independence is guaranteed by law (see page 814), plus a State Comptroller and Ombudsman who oversee public services and deal with any complaints. They are answerable to the Knesset.

Election process

Israel's election process uses the system of **proportional representation** in its very purest form. Individual parties submit a list of candidates, with the names of the most important potential MKs at the head of the list (for example, Labour's list would have Ehud Barak at number one). There is no constituency system, and thus Knesset seats are assigned in proportion to each party's percentage of the total national vote. The Knesset's 120 seats are then assigned to individual candidates according to the sequence upon which they appear on their party's list. To date, no party has ever received enough (ie 61) seats to allow it to form a government on its own, and thus all Israeli governments have been a coalition of groups often representing very different viewpoints.

The unsavoury 'horse-trading' that has traditionally accompanied any dominant party's attempt to patch together enough seats to form a coalition government left such a bad taste in the mouth after the 1992 elections that a new system was introduced for the 1996 elections. In addition to the one-person one-vote system that elects the country's 120 MKs, there are now direct elections for prime minister, with the winner being able to appoint half the government ministers of his choice. In practice, however, nothing seems to have changed, with the Cabinets appointed by both Netanyahu (1996) and Barak (1999) comprising a familiar collection of competing and rival parties each pursuing their own aims according to the views of the interest group that they represent.

Another potential by-product of these electoral reforms is a situation where a prime minister of one party presides over a government of another. For example, although Barak won a landslide victory in the direct vote for prime minister in 1999, his party actually lost seats in the separate vote for MKs.

A further electoral reform that came into effect in 1996 was the introduction of a threshold designed to exclude extremely small extremist groups from enjoying access to power (such as the neo-fascist *Kach*). The only problem with this commendable measure is that there are in fact some extremely large extremist groups who continue to enjoy power in Israel (parties need only win 1.5 percent of the vote to enter the Knesset).

Political parties

There is a very broad spectrum of issues occupying the minds of Israeli voters. As such, there has been a proliferation of political parties (and pressure groups) that reflect this wide range of viewpoints, and seek to look after the interests of their

Israel's Prime Ministers and political groupings

David Ben-Gurion (1948-54) – Labour	*Menachem Begin (1977-83) – Likud*
Moshe Sharett (1954-55) – Labour	*Yitzhak Shamir (1983-84) – Likud*
David Ben-Gurion (1955-63) – Labour	*Shimon Peres (1984-86) – Labour*
Levi Eshkol (1963-69) – Labour	*Yitzhak Shamir (1986-92) – Likud*
Yigael Allon (1969 acting) – Labour	*Yitzhak Rabin (1992-95) – Labour*
Golda Meir (1969-74) – Labour	*Shimon Peres (1995-96) – Labour*
Yitzhak Rabin (1974-77) – Labour	*Benjamin Netanyahu (1996-99) – Likud*
Shimon Peres (1977 acting) – Labour	*Ehud Barak (1999-) – Labour ('One*

constituent base. In some cases these interests are extremely narrow. The origins of the main political parties lie in the political groupings found in Zionist circles in east and central Europe at the beginning of the 20th century, with political Zionism dividing into three main trends by the 1930s: "Labour Zionism, essentially nationalist but with a strong socialist component; Revisionist Zionism, which originated as a revolt against the former, and which stressed free market values and strong defence; and finally Religious Zionism, which combined Jewish faith with an acceptance of the renaissance of a Jewish secular state" (Joffe, 1996, *ibid*).

Newer elements represent Israeli Arabs as well as ultra-orthodox Jewish groups that reject the secular State of Israel (believing that the revival of the Jewish nation can only be divinely ordained), but participate in politics in order to win benefits and concessions for its constituents. The latter really wind up their secular colleagues in the Knesset when they refuse to sing the national anthem! An even more recent development has seen the establishment of parties to represent ethnic groupings, like Sephardi/Mizrachi (or 'Oriental') Jews, or communities such as recent Russian immigrants.

A glance at the list of Israel's prime ministers indicates how politics in this country has been dominated by two main political groupings; **Labour** and **Likud**. To define either Labour or Likud as a political party is over-simplistic; an "alignment of factions" is probably a far more accurate description (Joffe, 1996, *ibid*). **Labour** has traditionally been a myriad of socialist groups from the Labour Zionism trend, with recent initiatives being the support for a "land for peace" compromise with the Palestinians and Israel's Arab neighbours. **Likud** is the direct successor to the Revisionist Zionism movement, favouring free-market economics and being 'hawkish' on defence and security issues.

A number of smaller parties have traditionally acted as power-brokers during the unseemingly struggle to form coalition governments, with parties and individual members regularly changing alliances; nearly one in four Knesset members who took office in 1996 ran on a different ticket in the 1999 election.

Other main parties

Yisrael B'Aliyah, headed by renowned former 'refusenik' Natan Sharansky, represents Israel's large Russian immigrant community. This is now one of Israel's key vote-blocks, with Sharansky being rewarded in 1999 with the all-important Ministry of the Interior portfolio. The **Center Party** attracted a number of heavyweight members (Yitzhak Mordechai, Dan Meridor) in its run up to the 1999 election, as it seeks to occupy the 'middle ground' in Israeli politics. The **Arab Democratic Party** campaigns for increased rights for Israel's Arabs, and is in favour of a Palestinian state. **Meretz** is a largely secular party, strong on women's rights and curbing religious privileges, and in favour of an accommodation with the Palestinians. **Moledet** is a far-right party popular with settlers, and campaigns for a 'transfer' of Palestinians from the West Bank and Gaza Strip. **National Religious Party** (NRP) represents the Religious Zionism trend, supporting the settler movement and pressing the 'Greater Israel' theme. **Meimad** is seen as a more pragmatic and

Background

Israel's Presidents

Chaim Weizmann (1949-52)
Yitzhak Ben-Zvi (1952-63)
Zalman Shazar (1963-73)
Ephraim Katzir (1973-78)

Yitzhak Navon (1978-83)
Chaim Herzog (1983-93)
Ezer Weizman (1993-)

moderate off-shoot of the NRP, running on the 'One Israel' ticket with Labour in the 1999 elections. **Shas** is an extremely important party, having largely come to represent the Sephardi/Mizrachi voting block. It made significant gains at the 1999 election despite its charismatic Moroccan-born leader Aryeh Deri being convicted in a number of financial and political scandals shortly before voting began. It has dominated the Ministry of the Interior for some time, but has recently lost this portfolio (though has been given the important Ministry of Religious Affairs as a 'consolation prize'). Deri's resignation as party chief was seen as the 'price' for entering Barak's ruling coalition. Its position on peace is said to be "ambiguous". **Shinui** ('Change') has been revitalized by the arrival of Tommy Lapid: formerly Israel's most controversial journalist, and now Israel's most controversial politician. The Shinui platform in the 1999 election was clear: "exposing the untenability of the ultra-Orthodox relationship with mainstream Israel – a relationship based on privileges without responsibilities" (*Jerusalem Report*, 19th July, 1999). In one pre-election interview 'Tommy' is said to have referred to the ultra-Orthodox as "the sickness" and himself as "the doctor" (*ibid*). Shinui won six seats in the 1999 election and have tabled 30 bills aimed at limiting Orthodox control. **Third Way** seeks to occupy middle ground between Labour and Likud, and is in favour of accommodation with Palestinians but against withdrawal to pre-1967 lines. The ultra-Orthodox Ashkenazi **United Torah Judaism** campaigns for more rigorous interpretation of Israel as a Jewish state, though is less militant on settler issues than other groups. For a comprehensive breakdown of all the political parties and groupings in Israel, see *Keesings Guide to the Middle-East Peace Process* (Lawrence Joffe, 1996, Cartermill, London).

Pressure groups

The Israeli political scene is also notable for the high number of pressure groups that lobby on a number of platforms. Perhaps best known is the **Peace Now** group; organizers of the pro-peace demonstration in Tel Aviv at which Yitzhak Rabin was assassinated. The group has its origins in a group of army officers who sought to keep alive the prospect of peace with Egypt that arose from the Camp David deals, though it really rose to prominence in its opposition to Israel's 1982 invasion of Lebanon. It is now mainly involved in promoting some sort of equitable deal with the Palestinians, though members are divided as to whether this involves a full or partial withdrawal from territory that Israel has occupied since 1967. Peace Now has strong links to other like-minded groups in the US and UK, but is generally despised by the Israeli right.

Eyal is a group that is totally opposed to the current 'peace process' between Israel and the Palestinians, coming to prominence lately as the organization to which Yitzhak Rabin's assassin belonged. Another right-wing group that has been linked with extremist elements is **Gush Emunim** (Bloc of the Faithful); a religious settlers' group that sees settlement in the whole of biblical Eretz Yisrael (notably the West Bank and Gaza Strip) as being a religiously ordained duty. There are numerous other pressure groups supporting a number of issues.

The Law of Return (1950) and the Law of State Lands (1960)

The Law of Return, passed in 1950, is one of the cornerstones of the State of Israel, and in fact underlies the very concept of the "ingathering of the exiles". Under this law every Jew is granted the right to return to Israel, and, upon entry, automatically to acquire citizenship (subject to a number of checks that seek to deter criminals and undesirables). The 1960 Law of State Lands determines the status of the land in Israel. Both laws frequently come under attack, though for completely different reasons.

One case against these laws is perhaps most eloquently argued by the Palestinian intellectual Edward W. Said: "Whereas the moral and political right of a person to return to his place of uninterrupted residence is acknowledged everywhere, Israel has negated the possibility of return, first by a series of laws declaring Arab-owned land in Palestine absentee property, and hence liable to expropriation by the Jewish National Fund (which legally owns the land in Israel 'for the whole Jewish people', a formula without analogy in any other state or quasi state), and second by the Law of Return, by whose provision any Jew born anywhere is able to claim immediate Israeli citizenship and residence (but no Arab can, even if his

residence and that of his family for numerous generations in Palestine can be proved). These two exclusionary categories systematically and juridically make it impossible, on any grounds whatever, for the Arab Palestinians to return, be compensated for his property, or live in Israel as a citizen equal before the law with a Jewish Israeli" (The Question of Palestine, 1979).

A further attack on the Law of Return comes from the Orthodox community inside Israel, who are seen as wanting to discriminate against converts to Reform or Conservative Judaism (dominant streams in the US) who wish to emigrate to Israel by imposing a stricter interpretation of who is, or isn't, a Jew (see 'Religious courts' below). It has been argued that such a move could divide Israeli society over an issue that is largely irrelevant, since the number of American Reform and Conservative Jews now seeking to come to Israel is negligible. However, it would have major implications for the non-Jewish or Jewish convert former Gentile spouses of recent former Soviet immigrants.

The presidency

The President of Israel performs mainly ceremonial and formal duties, acting as a titular head of state. The president is elected every five years by the Knesset from candidates selected for their stature and contribution to the state. Previous presidents have included scientists, historians and writers, former military leaders, career diplomats and prominent businessmen (with some having careers that encompassed all these roles). A president may serve two consecutive terms.

Local government

Municipal and local councils are chosen in a manner identical to the Knesset election process, whilst mayors and council leaders are elected by a direct vote. Local government bodies are responsible for healthcare, social security, education and municipal functions such as road maintenance, water supply and sanitation. They are funded in part by central government grants, and by means of direct tax raising through municipal taxes. Permanent residents who are not Israeli citizens (ie Palestinian residents of Jerusalem, West Bank and the Gaza Strip) are eligible to vote in municipal elections, though in the past they have widely boycotted this process. For example, most Palestinian residents of Jerusalem do not recognize the

Background

jurisdiction of the Municipality of Jerusalem, with fewer than seven percent of them voting in the 1993 municipal elections. Currently no Palestinian residents of Jerusalem sit on the city council.

Legal system and judiciary

Basic laws

Israel does not have a written Constitution, though an operative constitution has evolved via a series of **Basic Laws**. These provide a framework within which Israel's main structures – the legislature, the executive and the judiciary – can work. The key Basic Laws are: Law of Return (1950); The Knesset (1958); State Lands (1960); The President (1964); The Government (1968); The State Economy (1975); Israel Defence Forces (1976); Jerusalem (1980); The Judiciary (1984); The State Comptroller (1988); Human Dignity and Liberty (1992); Freedom of Occupation (1992).

In addition, when Israel became independent, it passed the Law and Administration Ordinance (1948) that saw all prevailing laws prior to independence remain in force as long as they did not contradict the principles embodied in the Declaration of the Establishment of the State of Israel. The irony of this is that laws created during the British Mandate period (1922-48) to suppress Jewish and Arab resistance (armed or otherwise) to British rule, and against which Jews fought because they were deemed unjust and illegal, have in turn been used to deal with Palestinians in the West Bank and Gaza Strip.

The judicial process

The judiciary is designed to be entirely independent of the political system. Judges are appointed by a special committee, with confirmation of appointments coming through the president. The legal system works through a hierarchy of Magistrates' Courts, District Courts and a Supreme Court, with certain matters referred to Special Courts, Military Courts and Religious Courts (see below). The chief legal adviser to the government is the **Attorney-General**. This is considered to be a post totally independent of the political system, despite the fact that the Attorney-General is actually appointed by the government.

Religious courts

Jurisdiction in matters of marriage and divorce have been delegated to the religious courts: rabbinical courts for Jews, sharia courts for Muslims, and ecclesiastical courts for Christians.

The rabbinical courts have become a considerable source of controversy in recent years, dominated as they are by the Orthodox and ultra-Orthodox streams of Judaism. In particular the matter of the "conversion law" and its relevance to the Law of Return (see page 813) has seen a return of the 'who is a Jew?' debate that first surfaced in the 1980s. If passed, the so-called "conversion law" will see the Orthodox establishment effectively hold a veto over conversions to Judaism performed by their rival Reform and Conservative movements. Effectively this will demote Reform and Conservative community leaders to the status of second-class rabbis, also casting doubts on eligibility of converted Reform and Conservative Jews (and particularly, their converted formerly Gentile partners) to become Israeli citizens under the Law of Return. The issue has already brought Israel into conflict with the large US Jewish community, much of which is Conservative or Reform. Currently the Law of Return determines that someone is Jewish if they have at least one Jewish grandparent, though *halacha* (Jewish religious law) defines Jewishness as coming exclusively from a Jewish mother. At the time of going to press, the "conversion law" has been put on hold whilst a *modus vivendi* is worked out.

Human rights

The question of Israel's human rights record is a very thorny issue, inside and outside of the country. One the one hand, there are a large number of monitoring organizations, both international and indigenous, that are allowed to operate relatively freely within the country (unlike Israel's neighbours, for example). On the other hand, however, almost all produce damning testimony and put paid to the Israeli claim of 'enlightened' occupation in the West Bank and Gaza Strip. The annual US State Department report released by the Bureau of Democracy, Human Rights, and Labor, as well as Amnesty International's annual country profile of "Israel and the Occupied Territories" make rather grim reading.

In his book *From Beirut to Jerusalem* (1993), the American journalist Thomas Friedman examines the way in which Israel appears to be judged by a different standard from other countries (particularly those in the Middle East) on issues such as human rights. He quotes Israeli statesman Abba Eban, who was charged with presenting Israel's claim for statehood to the United Nations in 1947: "It was not easy to make our case … We had to make ourselves exceptional. So we based our claim on the exceptionality of Israel … We knew we were basically appealing to a Christian world for whom the biblical story was familiar and attractive, and we played it to the hilt. We are still victims of our own rhapsodic rhetoric, and our own rhapsodic defence … Some Israelis now complain about being judged by a different standard. But the world is only comparing us to the standard we set for ourselves. You can't go out and declare that we are the descendants of kings and prophets and then come and say, 'Why does the world demand that we behave differently from Syria?'" Others may argue that the continued criticism of Israel for failing to live up to its promise as a "light unto the nations" is a means by which other states can absolve themselves of guilt for their complicity in the Holocaust, or lead attention away from their own poor record on issues such as human rights.

Economy

Key characteristics

There are a number of key features that dominate Israel's economic performance. A major drain on the economy is the high level of **defence spending**, though given Israel's situation this is seen as a necessary evil. In fact, election pledges to increase defence spending are seen as something of a vote winner. Whilst most 'Western' countries spend around 3-5 percent of GDP on defence, Israel spends 10-15 percent (currently about $6.5 billion annually). This actually marks a huge drop from the 'cold war' of the 1970s when defence spending accounted for around 25 percent of the annual budget.

A second major drain on the economy is Israel's huge **external (foreign) debt** (currently standing at around $28 billion), which along with defence spending accounts for between 50 and 60 percent of the country's budget. The bulk of Israel's foreign debt is governmental and very long term. The total value of foreign aid that Israel has received since its inception is in the region of $90 billion (in current figures), and has come in a variety of forms. Foreign government grants and loans, (mainly from the US), form a large proportion of this aid, though Israel has also received aid in the form of funds brought by immigrants, restitution payments to victims of the Nazis, donations from Jewish fund-raising organizations abroad, plus other unilateral transfers.

Israel's external debt problem is exacerbated by the growing **balance of payments** deficit that it has been running since it became independent in 1948. Though the value of exports has risen significantly (from $43 million in 1949 to $23 billion in 1994 at current dollar rates), value of imports has followed the same pattern, increasing the deficit from $220 million in 1949 to $10 billion in 1994 (at current dollar rates). Israel's rapid GDP growth and increased value of exports has, in recent years, meant that exports are now financing a greater share of imports, though there is a long way to go before the problem gets even close to being solved.

In addition to high levels of defence spending, a number of other crucial factors have largely determined the way in which Israel's economy has performed. One such factor has been the need to absorb large scale **immigration**, put somewhere in the region of 2.4 million people in the last 50 years. This challenge was brought sharply into focus once again in the 1990s, when some 600,000 immigrants arrived from the Soviet Union. The need to provide jobs, housing, healthcare and education has been a further drain on Israel's delicately poised economy. Though the standard of Israel's public services (such as healthcare, social security, education, housing) is probably the envy of the region, it is not without its economic cost. Vast resources have also been spent on providing a modern economic infrastructure of roads, water, sanitation, power and communications, much of which was inadequate at independence. The state is also Israel's largest single employer, and hence public sector wage settlements have a major impact on the nation's economy.

Given the nature of Israeli politics, whereby the government usually comprises a precarious coalition of competing interest groups, economic policy is often determined by political and not economic thinking.

Recent performance

The key characteristic of the Israeli economy in the 1980s was three-digit **inflation**, reaching 445 percent per annum in 1984 and threatening to go four-digit the following year. Emergency measures introduced by the government, including the introduction of the New Israeli Shekel (NIS), slashed annual rates to around 14 percent, with the rate currently just in single digits. However, it should be noted that even in the 1980s heyday of hyper-inflation, despite the damage it did to the national economy, individual Israelis were largely untouched by the phenomenon since items such as salaries, rent, income tax brackets and the like were all linked to a fixed value (for example foreign currency or consumer price index).

The key feature of the 1990s has been an economy running at full speed, with Israel achieving the highest **GDP growth rate** of all Organization for Economic Co-operation and Development (OECD) countries. In fact, Israel's GDP growth in the 1990s has been likened to the 'tiger' economies of Southeast Asia. However, like these 'tiger' economies, there is an ever-present danger of the economy over-heating. Both Likud and Labour now seem keen to reduce the state control over the economy and introduce a process of economic liberalization. **Unemployment** stood at just over 200,000 in April 1999.

Foreign trade

Israel's trading economy is constrained by two key factors: the relatively small size of the domestic market, and the difficulty in penetrating the markets of its regional neighbours. It remains to be seen whether the current 'peace process' sees these markets opening up to Israel (they haven't yet, with many Arab governments making noises about Israel wanting to dominate the region economically), though even if they do penetrate these markets, their relative immaturity compared with the Israeli economy makes it uncertain as to just how much business Israel could do there. Thus, most of Israel's foreign trade has been conducted with long-distance markets. Europe accounts for around 38 percent of Israel's exports, with goods being able to enter the EC market tariff free. Israel is also a member of the GATT agreement, and has a free trade deal with the US and Canada (accounting for 34 percent of exports). Asia (16 percent), Africa (2 percent) and 'others' (10 percent) account for the rest of Israel's exports.

Agriculture

It is easy to think of Israel as being a country dominated by agriculture; after all, the process of "turning the desert green" is one of the key claims made by Zionism. Dramatic advancements have been made in agriculture in Israel since its independence some 50 years ago, with the total area under cultivation increasing by a factor of 2.6 to 440,000 hectares, and land under irrigation rising by an astonishing factor of 8. However, although the absolute value of agricultural production and exports has risen dramatically, its share of GDP, exports and employment have all decreased.

Israel meets most of its domestic food needs, with its main food import needs (grain, oilseeds, meat, coffee and sugar) easily financed by agricultural exports. Such exports include winter fruit, vegetables and flowers (northern hemisphere winter), plus dairy and poultry exports. Israel invests heavily in agricultural research and development (R&D) and may be said to lead the world in arid and semi-arid agriculture R&D.

Industry

A lack of natural resources has forced Israel to concentrate industrial output on manufactured products with high added value (though natural gas has recently been found some 40 kilometres off the coast at Ashqelon, and British Gas are exploring for oil and gas in Israel's Mediterranean waters). Israel is the world leader in the field of diamond polishing (producing 40 percent of the world's polished diamonds) despite the fact that no diamonds are actually mined in the country! Israel's investment in **research and development** (R&D) sees it now rank amongst the world's leading players in the field of **high technology**. Notable advances in the world of **electronics**, electro-, laser- and fibre-**optics**, **computer technology**, **aeronautics**, **robotics**, plus **medical**, **energy** and agricultural R&D can be attributed to Israeli scientists and researchers. Much of the foreign investment in Israel is in the high-tech sector. Israel is ranked twelfth in the world in **conventional-weapons** exports (1998, Stockholm International Peace Research Institute).

Tourism

Israel markets itself very aggressively around the world as a major tourist destination, with tourism now comprising a significant source of foreign exchange earnings. In fact, tourism is often seen as Israel's saviour in reducing its chronic external debt, though it can be a very fickle friend indeed (recent security concerns have served to scare potential visitors away, although over the past few decades the general trend has been upwards). Record tourist arrivals in recent years (2.2 million in 1996) have prompted the construction of additional hotel rooms to a figure now pushing 40,000. Tourism contributes around three percent to GNP, comprises about

Background

nine percent of exports, and directly employs around 70,000 people. The prediction for the number of tourist arrivals in the all-important year 2000 range from four million to six million, though it's still unsure as to whether this figure will be realized.

Around 75-80 percent of foreign tourists to Israel come from North America and Western Europe, with USA (20 percent), UK (14 percent), Germany (10 percent), France (8 percent) and Italy (4 percent) being the main sources.

International relations

United States

It would perhaps seem logical to begin a brief review of Israel's international relations with an account of her relationship with her Arab neighbours; Israel is after all located in the Middle East. Yet Israel's relationship with the United States is of such significance that it fully deserves its place at the head of the list. It is in fact an extraordinary relationship, full of contradictions, subject to numerous 'lover's tiffs' and rocky patches, though incredibly enduring. Israel is the largest beneficiary of US overseas aid (receiving about $3 billion per year), and also the recipient of substantial US loan guarantees that allow Israel to secure loans for projects such as absorbing immigrants (notably from the former Soviet Union). The US is also Israel's greatest champion in the outside world and defender at the United Nations (see page 821).

Defining the basis of the relationship is not straightforward. Some argue that though approximately one-quarter of the world's Jewish population lives in Israel, one-third of world Jewry lives in the United States, and thus it is little surprise that the US is Israel's champion in the outside world. Others suggest that both states are vibrant democracies whose "political and legal systems are anchored in liberal traditions; both were pioneer societies; and both are still receiving and integrating new immigrants" (*Facts About Israel*, Israel Information Center, 1995). The real answer probably lies at some point between the two, though the relationship should also be seen in the context of US-Soviet superpower rivalries in the region.

The relationship has had its ups and downs over the years, though in the view of many commentators the present Clinton administration is the most pro-Israeli in history. This unwavering support goes beyond the White House, allowing journalists to resurrect another old joke about Israeli-occupied territory including the West Bank, Gaza, the Golan, and Congress. This rather calls into question the plausibility of the US's description of itself as the 'honest broker' in the current peace process.

Arab neighbours

Israel's relationship with her neighbours is of course tempered by the memory not just of five major wars and numerous terrorist attacks launched from within their borders, but also by the long-standing Arab rejection of Israel's right to exist, very presence at all, and by the economic and political boycott sponsored by the Muslim world. Developing any sort of relationship at all has been a long and arduous business.

Egypt The turning point came in 1977 when Egyptian President Anwar Sadat made a ground-breaking visit to Jerusalem. This event led to the Camp David Accords signed between the two states in September 1978, and the subsequent peace treaty signed in March of the next year. Israel completed its withdrawal from the Sinai in April 1982 in a deal based upon the principle of exchanging land for peace. As a result of signing this treaty Egypt was expelled from the Arab league, and Sadat subsequently assassinated. The impact of this treaty on relations between the two

The 'Jewish lobby' in the USA

Israel divides public opinion on many issues, though few as bitterly as the question of the 'Jewish lobby' in the United States. Opinions on the matter range from those who believe that Jews determine the outcome of US elections and US foreign policy, to those who deny that any such lobby exists. For example, in his book A Place Among the Nations (1993), the future Prime Minister of Israel, Benjamin Netanyahu, effectively argues for the establishment of a Jewish worldwide lobby and propaganda campaign: "Support among the nations, especially in the great democracies of the West, can be bolstered, cultivated, and protected by an incessant campaign to win over the public. If the Jewish people had understood this principle during the course of this century, it could have activated others to assist it in times of peril rather than having the very opposite happen. And had Israel understood this principle, it certainly would not have allowed Arab propaganda … [to capture] the high ground of international opinion."
Netanyahu's selective memory is astounding. It is not unreasonable to argue that the State of Israel came into being partly through the very lobbying that Netanyahu proposes! Earlier in his book, Netanyahu himself describes the lobbying efforts of Theodor Herzl and Chaim Weizmann in the capitals of Europe, and even calls one of the book's chapters 'The Betrayal' when dealing with the British decision not to fulfil its commitments made in the Balfour Declaration: itself perhaps the greatest achievement of Jewish lobbying this century.

Having established that such a thing as the 'Jewish lobby' does exist, just how effective is it, particularly in the US? Firstly, it can be quite clearly stated that the Jewish vote in the US does not determine who becomes US President; its constituency is just too small and, what's more, America's Jews have traditionally voted Democrat anyway.

However, there is considerable evidence to suggest that financial pressure is brought to bear on potential political candidates to make pro-Israeli statements and policy. There have in fact been instances where the 'Jewish lobby' has actually taken credit for certain senator's de-selection (eg Paul Findley). Further, the main Jewish lobbying groups in the US – eg American Israel Public Affairs Committee (AIPAC, often described as the most effective lobbying group in the US), the Anti-Defamation League of B'nai B'rith (ADL), and the Conference of Presidents of Major American Jewish Organizations – have all sought through a variety of means to influence US foreign policy, particularly in areas related to Israel and the Arab world. One vital point that is often forgotten is that this is surely the whole point of the lobbying process: to direct public opinion and government policy towards the aims of the constituency that you are representing. It is the means that the 'Jewish lobby' uses that is so objectionable to some commentators.

It is beyond the scope of this Handbook to attempt to explore this issue fully, though there are any number of books on the subject. Whether you agree with the authors' conclusions or not, such books never fail to make an absorbing read. Try: John Snetsinger, Truman, The Jewish Vote and the Creation of Israel, 1974, Hoover Institution Press; Edward Tivnan, The Lobby: Jewish Political Power and American Foreign Policy, 1987, Simon & Schuster; Paul Findley, They Dare To Speak Out: People and Institutions Confront Israel's Lobby, 1985, Lawrence Hill.

states has been mixed. Whilst the threat of war has subsided, a legacy of decades of mutual distrust and hostility still needs to be overcome, and the goals of economic and cultural integration still remain a long way off. In many regards, the description of relations between Israel and Egypt as a 'cold peace' is remarkably apt.

Jordan Though outwardly enemies, secret talks remained a major feature of Israeli-Jordanian relations throughout the period of the Arab boycott of Israel. These talks were perhaps the results of King Hussein's pragmatism, though any agreements reached between the negotiating teams were usually scuppered by domestic opposition. The Israeli-PLO Declaration of Principles signed in 1993 effectively "broke the log-jam between Jordan and Israel" (Joffe, 1996), allowing the two states to sign a mutually beneficial peace treaty in 1994. Both sides stand to gain significantly from the treaty: Israel through increased security on her eastern border, plus improved access to the regional economic market; and Jordan, through a larger share of water resources of the Yarmuk and Jordan rivers, plus the financial incentive to sign given by the United States (that saw Jordan's $480 million debt to the US wiped off at the stroke of a pen). There is widespread opposition to a normalization of ties with Israel within Jordan, not least amongst the considerable Palestinian refugee population, though this treaty does look particularly secure.

Syria The peace treaty signed between Egypt and Israel in 1978 saw Syria assume the mantle of the leader of the Arab opposition to Israel; a role it has relished. However, the collapse of the Soviet Union, Syria's long-time patron, has seen a new set of global realities imposed on the region. Though there is now a far better relationship between Damascus and Washington, Syria has deliberately refrained from beginning a process of normalization of relations with Israel. President Assad is a very shrewd operator and appears to be following a 'wait and see' policy *vis-à-vis* the on-going negotiations between the Israelis and Palestinians; initial observations that Syria feared being 'left out' of the peace process appear to have been false.

Of course relations between Israel and Syria are dominated by the issue of the Golan Heights. Syria is maintaining its stance that Israel must withdraw completely before the two states can even begin negotiating a peace treaty, whilst Israel believes that it needs either the Golan Heights or a satisfactory peace treaty (or both) to secure its safety from the Syrian military threat. Even if Israel did agree to withdraw from the Golan, its demands for early warning stations on Mt Hermon, plus a demilitarized zone complete with UN or US observers on the Golan itself remain unacceptable to Syria. At the time of going to press both Assad and Barak were making positive noises about some sort of deal, though it's hard to see Syria accepting anything less than a full Israeli withdrawl.

Lebanon At the time of going to press, Israel continues to occupy a narrow strip of southern Lebanon (7-11 kilometres wide, 120 kilometres long, covering 1,550 square kilometres and home to around 180,000 Lebanese) as a self-declared 'security zone'. It is manned by an undisclosed number of Israeli troops plus around 2,500 members of a proxy militia, the South Lebanon Army (SLA), with a stated purpose of protecting Israel's northern regions from terrorist and rocket attack. Increasing military setbacks, and public pressure at home, has brought the subject of this occupation to the top of the Israeli domestic agenda, and it appears that prime minister Barak is keen to withdraw Israeli troops as soon as possible. However, Lebanon's dependence on Syria, and the proxy war with Israel that Syria can pursue through various groups in southern Lebanon, reduces the prospects for an immediate equitable peace settlement.

Europe

Israel maintains reasonably good links with the like-minded 'Western' democracies of Europe, with the collapse of the Soviet Union seeing new relationships develop between Israel and the states of eastern Europe. For many years now the EC has been Israel's key trading partner (38 percent of exports heading there), with a free trade agreement being signed by the two sides back in 1975.

The EC has been seeking a greater mediating role in the peace process, perhaps hoping to counter the seemingly pro-Israeli bias of that 'honest broker', the United States. An official EC special envoy to the peace process has now been appointed, though equal status with the US as guarantors of the process has been rejected by both Israel and Washington as an 'unnecessary complication'. The EC remains the largest donor to the Palestinian Authority.

United Nations

Israel has had a fractious relationship with the United Nations, largely as a result of the 'automatic majority' of Arab and Muslim nations, the non-aligned movement and the former Soviet bloc guaranteeing the adoption of resolutions condemning Israel. However, it should be noted that not all resolutions condemning Israel are passed solely because of this bloc (many such resolutions are opposed by just three nations: Israel, USA, and the USA-dependent Micronesia).

Perhaps the most famous (or infamous) such incident at the United Nations concerning Israel occurred on the 10th November, 1975, when the General Assembly voted by a majority of 72-35 (with 32 abstentions) to condemn Zionism as "a form of racism and racial discrimination". Benjamin Netanyahu suggests that "Such an achievement had eluded even the great anti-Semitic propagandists of our millennium like Torquemada and Joseph Goebbels" (*A Place Among the Nations*, 1993), adding that "for the first time in history, a world body had given its stamp of approval to the libelling of an entire people", whilst the US Ambassador to the UN at the time, Daniel Moynihan, declared "The US will not abide by, it will not acquiesce in, this infamous act. A great evil has been loosed upon the world. The abomination of antisemitism [sic] has been given the appearance of international sanction". Others disagree. Edward W. Said, whilst suggesting that "Israel's Jewish achievements … are considerable achievements, and it is right that they not sloppily be tarnished with the sweeping rhetorical denunciation associated with 'racism' … " declares that "*Racism* is too vague a term: Zionism is Zionism. For the Arab Palestinian, this tautology has a sense that is perfectly congruent with, but exactly the opposite of, what it says to Jews" (*The Question of Palestine*, 1979). Said also goes out of his way to explain that "To write critically about Zionism in Palestine has therefore never meant, and does not mean now, being anti-Semitic … all liberals and even most 'radicals' have been unable to overcome the Zionist habit of equating anti-Zionism with anti-Semitism". A 'free' vote took place on the resolution in the UN in December 1991, with the General Assembly voting to revoke the equation by a margin of 111-25 (with 13 abstentions).

Other important relationships

A significant step was taken in 1994 when diplomatic relations were formally established between Israel and the **Holy See** (Vatican). It is remarkable to think that it was only in 1965 that Pope Paul VI issued *Nostra Aetate*, which formally dropped the charge of deicide against the Jewish people.

A somewhat surprising burgeoning diplomatic relationship is that between Israel and **Turkey** (particularly when you bear in mind that it largely developed under Turkey's first, though short-lived, Islamic government). Israel already had an arrangement to use Turkish airspace for training flights (by the time you've gone supersonic over Israel you're out of its airspace), though the decision to hold joint manoeuvres between Turkey, Israel and the US in late 1997 surprised (and dismayed) many in the Arab world. Trade between the two states is now said to stand at $500 million per year. Perhaps the best indication of how this relationship

Background

should be viewed is by studying the way the Palestinians have reacted to it. During a visit in 1999, Turkish President Suleyman Demirel had to be ushered out of al-Aqsa Mosque after "angry Palestinians called him a traitor and an agent of Israel. The protesters said they did not want to see him at al-Aqsa as a visitor, but as a liberator" (*Independent*, 15/7/99).

Israel currently has full diplomatic relations with 153 states, of which over half were established or renewed following the signing of the Declaration of Principles between Israel and the PLO in 1993. Two notable additions to this list are **China** and **India**. As Joffe points out, "At the beginning of 1991, there were only two Israeli embassies (in Romania and Nepal) and one consulate (in Bombay) in the territory extending from former East Germany in the west to Vladivostok in the east and India in the south. Today, Israel has embassies in all but five countries in this swathe of land – North Korea, Pakistan, Afghanistan, Bangladesh and Bhutan" (1996, *ibid*).

Palestinian Authority

The role of the Palestinian Authority

The Palestinian Authority (PA) was created by the 'Oslo I' agreement of 1993 to administer the areas granted limited autonomy under that deal (Gaza and Jericho), and to act as a mechanism through which the Israelis and Palestinians could negotiate future and final issues. (**NB** The PA is sometimes referred to as the Palestinian National Authority (PNA) though Israeli references prefer to drop the 'National' component. This *Handbook* uses the term found in the 'Oslo I and II' documents, ie PA).

In effect, the PA is a temporary institution designed to bridge the gap between early self-rule and final status, though what the ultimate nature of the Palestinian entity will be (autonomy, confederation, statehood) is yet to be negotiated. According to the terms of the agreements signed between Israel and the Palestinians, the PA is due to hand over its powers to its elected successor body, the **Palestinian Legislative Council**, which will ultimately look after the well-being of Palestinians in the area under its remit. However, despite the election of members to the Council by Palestinians in self-rule areas in 1996, the Council claims that it has been prevented in executing its duties by the Palestinian Authority. The PA, it appears, has taken on a life force of its own, and though it is still required in its role as mediator with the Israelis on final status talks, it has effectively taken over all legislative and governmental responsibilities in the self-rule areas.

The timetable for 'Oslo II' envisaged 'final status' negotiations being concluded by May 1999; in fact this date came and went without them having even begun. Indeed, at one stage Arafat was threatening to declare an independent Palestinian state on 4th May, 1999, although he eventually backed down when it was realized that such a move would almost certainly serve to re-elect the right-wing Netanyahu government at the general election later that month. It is even suggested that Netanyahu chose the date of elections with this in mind.

Newly elected prime minister Barak is keen to move swiftly to 'final status' negotiations, though the Palestinians have been pressing for the next agreed stage of Israeli withdrawl from the West Bank ('Wye Accords') to be implemented first. This was done in late 1999.

The performance of the PA

In assessing the performance of the PA it is important to bear a number of factors in mind. Firstly, it should be remembered the constraints within which the PA must operate. Critics of the current 'peace process' suggest that the flawed agreement that Arafat signed effectively makes the PA "the Israeli enforcer of the military occupation by other means" (Edward W. Said, *The Guardian*, 23/8/96). Indeed, the 'Oslo II' agreement prohibits the PA or Legislative Council from passing legislation "which amends or abrogates existing Laws" (Article XVIII), most of which have been inherited from the Israeli military courts. As Ghassan Abu Sitteh observes, "Hence the PA is only able to administer the laws of occupation, not change them" (*Middle East International*, No 549, 2/5/97). He also points out that "the Oslo Accords have denied the PA those powers (for example sovereignty) to mobilize people around a state-building project by maintaining effective control of the economy and pursuing unrestricted access to international markets. Yet the PA was given all the powers and resources needed to physically punish its people" (*ibid*). And whilst far from condoning the human rights abuses that the PA has committed against its people, organizations such as Amnesty International (AI) recognize the pressures that the PA is under: "AI recognizes that the PA has been under external political pressure, in particular from Israel and the USA, to clamp down on those who have organized violent attacks on Israeli citizens. Time and again wide-ranging measures to prevent violent attacks on Israeli targets have been made a prerequisite for the implementation of what has been already agreed, or in order to progress to the next stage in the peace process. Such pressure has undoubtedly been a factor in encouraging the PA to carry out large-scale arbitrary arrests ... leading to the detention of hundreds without charge or trial, and the summary, unfair and often secret trials of those suspected of participating in violent attacks against Israelis or other politically-motivated offences" (AI Index: MDE 15/68/96).

Secondly, the PA's powerlessness to challenge Israeli hegemony cannot be overstated. This fact is perhaps most evident in Israel's ability to close its 'border' with PA areas, or impose 'internal closures' at will. As AI comments, "While the Israeli Government states that this is done in an attempt to avoid such attacks [terrorist attacks inside Israel], it is widely perceived as a form of collective punishment" (*ibid*). AI continues "The Israeli policy of closure is said to have cost the PA, in lost trade and remittances, from $4.5–$6 million a day. Unemployment in Gaza in mid-1996 was estimated at about 39.2 percent and in the West Bank at 24.3 percent. There has been a striking fall of 22 percent in real incomes in the West Bank and Gaza Strip" (*ibid*).

Nevertheless, the PA's performance on **human rights** issues has been abysmal (see Amnesty International's report into "Palestinian Authority: Prolonged political detention, torture and unfair trials", AI Index: MDE 15/68/96, December 1996 for some very grim reading), and it is unreasonable to lay all the ills of the PA's performance at Israel's door. The renowned Palestinian intellectual Edward W. Said, a major critic of the agreement signed with the Israelis, places much of the blame for conditions in Gaza and the West Bank at the door of Yasir Arafat: "I regarded him [Arafat], therefore, as a Pétain figure who has taken advantage of his people's exhaustion and kept himself in power by conceding virtually everything significant about our basic political and human rights. What he did after he came to Gaza in July 1994 has in my opinion worsened the effects of the 29-year-old occupation (which still continues), and over the months I have single-mindedly reminded my readers, of whom he seems to be one, that cronyism, a huge security apparatus, kowtowing to the Israelis, buying people off, torturing or imprisoning dissidents at will, are not the way to establish a new polity for our people" (*Guardian*, 23/8/96).

Background

☞ *Police and security forces in PA areas*

National Security Service (al-'amn al-watani) *In theory in charge of all the security services, but effectively one body among others.*
Civil Police (al-shurta) *Main law-enforcement body.*
Public Security (al-'amn al-'ammi) *General security service.*
Palestinian Preventative Security Service (al-'amn al-wiqa'i) *Main coordinating body with Israeli security services.*
Criminal Investigation Department (al-bahth al-jina'i) *Charged with investigating offences after they have been committed.*
Intelligence (mukhabarat) *Charged with arresting political detainees.*
Military Intelligence (istikhbarat) *Particularly concerned with surveillance over members of security services.*

Force 17 (quwa sab 'a 'asher) *Sometimes described as the Presidential Guard* (al-haras al-ri'asi), *evolved in Lebanon as force designed to protect Arafat as PLO chairman.*
Naval Police (bahriyya) *Marines or Coastal Police, have particularly bad reputation for abuses in Gaza.*
Special Forces (al-quwat al-khassa) *Remit to oversee operation of other branches of security forces.*
Civil Defence (al-difa' al-madani) *emergency services and rescue.*
University Security System (jihaz ;amn al-jami'a) *Founded in 1996 to 'monitor' and probably oppress student activity; widespread opposition has forced it to remain in abeyance.*

Source and comments: Amnesty International, 1996.

It is not just the PA's human rights record that is under scrutiny; the PA has an unenviable record in **financial mismanagement and corruption**. A recently leaked report from the PA's General Auditing Office makes shocking reading. It suggests that in the region of $323 million, or 40 percent of the PA's annual budget, has been misused or wasted by the various PA ministries. It is also highly critical of the various PA ministers and their deputies, accusing them of directing donor funds into personal accounts and squandering resources on luxury items (for example $400,000 was spent on ministerial "furniture").

The annual PA budget for 1997 (published six months late) also made alarming reading. Expenditure was set at $866 million and revenues at $814 million, with the deficit due to be met by the donor community. However, some 12.5 percent of this total budget was allocated to the "President's Office", presumably to meet commitments to the PLO apparatus (even though this is beyond the remit of the PA). A further $248 million was earmarked for the "myriad" security services, with revenues from these expected to be generated by a dozen or so monopolies in Gaza that are controlled by various PA and PLO cronies. As Graham Usher observed, "at a time of widespread poverty and unemployment in the occupied territories, it was how and where money was spent that caused the real furore [when the report/budget were released]" (*Middle East International*, No 551, 30/5/97).

Footnotes

13

Footnotes

13

Glossary of archaeological and architectural terms

A

acropolis fortified part of upper city, usually containing political, administrative, religious centre

AD Anno Domini ('after Christ', see *CE*)

agora marketplace, place of assembly

alabaster generally white or translucent form of gypsum used for statues, vessels, etc

ambo freestanding church pulpit

ambulatory usually covered passageway around sanctuary or church nave

amphitheatre oval shaped building used for shows or spectacles, with seating facing central arena

amphora(-ae) two-handled ceramic jug

Apocrypha books included in the Septuagint (Greek) and Vulgate (Latin) versions of Hebrew Bible, but excluded from Jewish and Protestant versions

apodyterium(-ia) changing room in Roman baths

apse, apsidal semi-circular niche at narrow end(s) of basilica or at eastern end of a church

architrave horizontal beam resting above an entrance, beam spanning space between two columns, mouldings decorating exterior of an arch

arcosolium(-ia) rock-cut arched recess or bench for burial

ashlar square or rectangular hewn stone laid in regular horizontal courses

assemblage collection of archaeological finds

atrium central court in Roman house, forecourt of Christian church

attic upper horizontal piece above a cornice

B

bab gate (Arabic)

bamah/bimah cultic high place, synagogue platform for reading Torah

barbican outer fortification

basilica church with nave and lateral (colonnaded) aisles, rectangular structure with two or more internal colonnades, often ending in an apse

BC/BCE Before Christ/Before the Common Era

beth midrash Jewish house of study (Hebrew)

bir well (Arabic)

birkat pool or reservoir (Arabic)

bouleuterion council building in Greek polis

BP Before Present

broadhouse rectangular building with entrance in one of the long walls

C

caldarium(-ia) hot room in Roman baths

capital topping of column or pier

caravanserai see *khan*

carbon-14 dating technique used to determine age by calculating degree of disintegration of carbon-14 element

cardo main street of Roman/Byzantine city, generally running N-S and intersecting main E-W street (*decumanus*) at right-angles

casement wall double fortification wall with partitioned compartments between

cavea spectator seating area in theatre or amphitheatre

CE Common Era (*AD*)

corbel projecting or overlapping stone blocks supporting a vault

cornice projecting upper section of *entablature*

crenellations battlements

cupola dome

D

dado column pedestal or lower panel of wall

decumanus(-i) main E-W street in Roman/Byzantine city (see *cardo*)

deir monastery (Arabic)

derekh street (Hebrew)

Dionysus Greek god of wine (equivalent to Roman god Bacchus)

dolmen megalithic (burial) monument comprising two upright stones supporting a horizontal stone

donjon keep or strongest part of Crusader fortress

Doric austere Greek architectural style

E

entablature collective architectural term to describe *architrave*, *frieze* and *cornice*

epigraphy study of ancient inscriptions

Execration texts figurines or tablets from 20-19th century BCE Egypt, generally inscribed with names of actual or potential enemies (in Syria/Palestine), rather like the voodoo doll principle

exedra semi-circular or rectangular recess

F

fosse ditch or trench outside city walls

frieze central section of *entablature*, generally a carved relief

frigidarium cold room in Roman baths

G

gadrooned voussoirs *voussoirs* decorated with sets of convex curves at right-angles to the *architrave*

Gemara rabbinic commentary of the *Mishnah*

genizah repository for discarded books and sacred objects in a synagogue

glacis sloping defensive fortification wall

H

hamman/hammam bath house (Arabic)

har mountain (Hebrew)

Haram sanctuary (Arabic)

holy of holies innermost chamber of temple or sanctuary

Homo erectus human type from Lower Palaeolithic (cranial capacity 1,000-1,200 cc)

Homo sapiens modern human type (cranial capacity 1,400 cc)

hypocaust space beneath floor of Roman house or bath house through which hot air is passed

I

iconostasis screen (upon which icons are generally hung) in Orthodox church separating sanctuary from main body of church

insula(-ae) quadrangular city block featuring multiple dwellings

Ionic Greek architectural style

J

Jami' Masjid Friday congregational mosque (Arabic)

jebel/jabal hill (Arabic)

juglet one-handled vessel for liquids

joggled voussoirs joined by notches and corresponding projections

K

khan accommodation for caravans featuring single-gated courtyard, surrounded by rooms and stables; see *caravanserai*

khanqah monastery for Sufi mystics (Arabic)

khirbet ruin (Arabic)

kokhim rock-cut Roman period burial place

Kufic script early angular form of Arabic script (named after Kufa in southern Iraq)

L

loculus(-i) rectangular, shelf-like burial niche in tomb

M

madrasa/madrassa Islamic religious school

Malaki fine limestone found in Jerusalem area, used widely in building there

Mar Christian saint (Arabic)

martyrium chapel, church or repository dedicated to a martyr

masseba(-ot) ritual standing stone (Hebrew)

mazar shrine of (Muslim) pilgrimage (Arabic)

menorah seven-branched candelabrum used in Jewish ritual

mezad fort (Hebrew)

mihrab niche in mosque, indicating direction of prayer (Mecca)

mikveh/miqveh Jewish ritual bath

minaret tower used for Muslim call to prayer

minbar freestanding pulpit in mosque

Mishnah collection of oral Jewish law and traditions, forming a basic part of the *Talmud*

monoapsidal church church with single apse

murex shells mollusc (snail) used to produce purple dye

N

nahal river (Hebrew)

narthex antechamber to nave of church (after 5th century CE)

nave elongated central hall in basilica or church

necropolis extensive or important cemetery (from Greek for `city of the dead')

nephesh/nefesh memorial monument above or next to shrine

Nike Greek goddess of victory

nilometer indicator of height of Nile

nymphaeum(-a) monumental structure in Roman city, generally a public fountain

O

onomasticon alphabetical list of identified sites from the Bible, most famous version written by Eusebius, bishop of Caesarea, in 4th century CE

orchestra circular place in front of stage in Greek theatre, semi-circular in Roman theatre

orthogonal plan town plan of streets intersecting at right-angles

ossuary receptacle used for secondary burial of bones once flesh has decayed

P

palaeography study of ancient alphabets and writing styles

pediment triangular space beneath a gabled roof in Greek and Roman architecture

peristyle open courtyard surrounded by columns

pier vertical roof support

pilaster engaged pier or column projecting slightly from a wall

portico colonnade or covered ambulatory at entrance to a building

postern small opening in fortification wall

propylaeum(-a) monumental structure marking entrance to a sanctuary

proto-Aeolic capital common in Israelite/Judean architecture, a decorated stone capital

Q

qanatir arcade (often stepped), eg Dome of the Rock platform

qibla marking direction of prayer (Arabic)

qubba/qubbat dome (Arabic)

R

rehov street (Hebrew)

ribat medieval (Muslim) pilgrim hostel (Arabic)

rotunda circular structure

S

sabil public fountain (Arabic)

Sanhedrin highest court and supreme council of Jews (1st century BCE-6th century CE)

saray palace (Arabic)

sarcophagus(-i) stone coffin

scaena(-ae) stage building in Roman theatre

scaenae frons façade of Roman stage building used as backdrop

sederot boulevard or avenue (Hebrew)

Septuagint pre-Christian Greek translation of Hebrew Bible, supposedly written simultaneously by 70 scholars in 70 days, c. 3rd-2nd century BCE

sha'ar gate (Hebrew)

shari'a street (Arabic)

sherd broken piece of pottery (potsherd)

spandrel triangular space between two arches or between arch and wall

springer support on wall from which arch springs

stela(-ae) upright slab of pillar, usually with an inscription

stoa roofed portico, or Greek free-standing 1-storey building with long rear wall and row of columns bearing a sloping roof at the front

stucco high-quality plaster coating

stylobate continuous base supporting a row or rows of columns

suq market or bazaar (Arabic)

T

Tabula Peutingeriana 4th century CE road map of Roman provinces showing roads, cities, towns, and distances, drawn by Castorius c.365 CE

Talmud interpretation of *Mishnah* and *Gemarah*

tariq road (Arabic)

tel/tell artificial mound (Hebrew/Arabic)

tepidarium warm room in Roman baths

tessera(-ae) small square pieces used to form a mosaic

tetrapylon structure of four piers supporting columns at intersection of Roman streets

Tosefta supplement to the *Mishnah*

transept space between nave and apse of a church

triclinium(-ia) Roman dining room

turba mausoleum (Arabic)

tympanum triangular wall above a cornice

V

Via Maris Way of the Sea, one of the two main routes linking Egypt and Mesopotamia, via Canaan/Israel coast

vomitorium(-ia) entrance/exit to theatre and amphitheatre

voussoir wedge-shaped stone blocks forming an arch

W

wadi seasonal stream(bed) (Arabic)

wali Muslim saint or holy man

waqf Islamic endowment

Y

yad memorial (Hebrew)

yeshiva rabbinical seminary

Yishuv pre-20th century CE Jewish population of Palestine

Z

zawiya Muslim religious dwelling, place of devotion or burial (Arabic)

zuqaq alley

Principal source: *New Encyclopaedia of Archaeological Excavations in the Holy Land*, 1993, Simon and Schuster

Shorts

Special interest pieces on and about Israel

Maps

Index

Will you help us?

We try as hard as we can to make each Footprint Handbook as up-to-date and accurate as possible but, of course, things always change. Many people write to us - with corrections, new information, or simply comments.

If you want to let us know about an experience or adventure - hair-raising or mundane, good or bad, exciting or boring or simply something rather special - we would be delighted to hear from you. Please give us as precise information as possible, quoting the edition number (you'll find it on the front cover) and page number of the Handbook you are using.

Your help will be greatly appreciated, especially by other travellers. In return we will send you details about our special guidebook offer.

Write to Elizabeth Taylor
Footprint Handbooks
6 Riverside Court
Lower Bristol Road
Bath
BA2 3DZ
England
or email info@footprintbooks.com

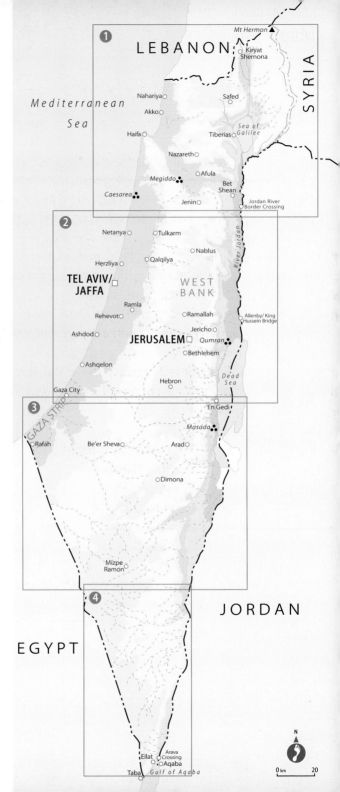

Israel

Altitude in metres
- 1000
- 500
- 200
- 100
- 0
- Below sea level
- -200

Neighbouring Country

- Motorways
- Primary Routes
- Major Roads
- Minor Roads
- Tracks
- Railway
- ◆ National Park
- International Border
- Cease-fire Line
- 'Green Line'
- Seasonal Rivers

1

LEBANON

Mt Hermon ▲

Kiryat Shemona

SYRIA

Mediterranean Sea

Nahariya ○

Safed ○

Akko ○

Haifa ○

Tiberias ○

Sea of Galilee

Nazareth ○

Afula ○

Megiddo ◆◆

Bet Shean

Caesarea ◆◆

Jenin ○

Jordan River Border Crossing

2

Netanya ○

Tulkarm ○

Nablus ○

Herzliya ○

Qalqilya ○

WEST BANK

River Jordan

TEL AVIV/ JAFFA ☐

Ramla ○

Rehevot ○

Ramallah ○

Allenby/ King Hussein Bridge

Ashdod ○

JERUSALEM ☐

Jericho ○

Qumran ◆◆

Bethlehem ○

Ashqelon ○

Dead Sea

Hebron ○

Gaza City ○

'En Gedi

3

GAZA STRIP

Masada ◆◆

Rafah ○

Be'er Sheva ○

Arad ○

Dimona ○

Mizpe Ramon ○

4

JORDAN

EGYPT

Eilat ○

Arava Crossing

Taba ○

Aqaba ○

Gulf of Aqaba

N

0 km   20

Map 1

A

N

0 km ——————— 10

Mediterranean Sea

Rosh Ha-Nikra Grottoes
Rosh Ha-Nikra
Hanita
Zar'it
Shumeru
Sh
Aramsha Eilon
Betzet
Liman
Shlomi
Goren
Nahal Betzet Nature Rese
Akhziv
Gesher Haziv
Montfort
Ma'ila
Tarshih
Kabri
89
Mi'ilya
Nahariya
89
Kabri jctn
8833
Yanuah
Hosser
Ben Ammi
Yehi'am
Shavei Zion
Jatt
Ha
Lave
Regba
Abu Snan
Julis
Na
Bustan HaGalil
Shomrat
Tal-El
Akko
Bahji
85
Ahihud jctn
Ahihud
Tzurit
K
70
Sha'ab
Yu
805
Kabul
Haifa Bay
Kiryat Yam
70
Shehanya
Sac
4
Tamira
Kaukabo
Yoc
Kiryat Motziem
Kiryat Bialik
Shefaram
Kfar
Ru
Haifa
Kiryat Ata
79
Eshkol Reservoir
Haifa south interchange
672
781
4
4
75
Sepphori (Zippori)
Tirat Carmel
672
Kiryat Tiv'on
77
79
Mt. Carmel
Mt Carmel National Park
Nazaret
'Atlit Beach Reserve
Ma'apilim
'Atlit Camp
'Atlit Interchange
Bet Oren
Oren jctn
672
Isfiya
75
Nahalal
Castle of the Pilgrims
7111
Daliyat-El-Carmel
Bet She'arim
Migdal Ha'Emeq
75
'Atlit
722
Ein Hod
Neve Yam
7110
Ein Kamel
Mukhraka
Yokneam
Afu
Mishmar Ha'Emeq
Aful
4
Nahal Me'arat Nature Reserve (Carmel caves)
Hazore'a
672
Ofer jctn
70
Tel Dor
Nahsholim
Dor/Tantura/Nahsholim Beach
7011
Ofer
Dor
Bat Shlomo
Megiddo
Megiddo jctn
Fureidis
Zichron Ya'akov
Tel Kedesh
Kibbutz Ma'agan Micha'el
Ramat HaNadiv
Giv'at Nill
Ma'agan Micha'el Beach
652
654
Shuni
Jabotinsky Park
Regavim
Jizr e-Zarka
Binyamina
653
Umm el-Fahm
Taanach
Caesarea
65
Je
66
Caesarea
Or Akiva
652
Kibbutz Sdot Yam
Pardes Khana
Mishmarot
2
651
Caesarea interchange
Karkur
650
Ein Shemer
Rehan
574
WEST BA
65
Hadera
581
Mikhmoret
Nahal Alexander Nature Reserve
Kfar Vitkim
Arraba

Map 3

Mediterranean
Sea

Gaza City
Nezarim
Deir el-Balah
GAZA STRIP
Kisufim
242
Khan
Darom
Khan
Yunis
240
Gush-Katif
Rafah
Rafah
Border
Crossing

Netivot
334
293
Beit Kama
jctn
232
Shokeda
25
Shuval
Dvira jctn
Dvira
Laha
Fores
31

Tidhar
Brosho
Ta'ashur
Rahat
232
234
Patish
Ranen
Bitha
Gilat jctn
Maslul
Gilat
Hanasi jctn
Ofakim
Tifrah
Urm
241
A
Nie Oz
Magen
Eshkol
National Park
Ofakim
Reserve
Nahal HaBesor
Scenic Route
25
Hazerim
2357
Be'er
Sheva
Omer
Tel Be
She
35
Sufa
Yesha
Nir
Yizhak
Holit
Pri Gan
Talmei
Eliyahu
Kerem
Shalom
Dekul
Sde Nizan
Gvulot
Ze'elim
Yevul
Talmei
Yosef

Haluza Dunes
222
Golda
Meir Park
Haluza
(Elusa)
Mizpe Tau
Ha Negev
jctn
Retamin
Revivim
Rehovot-in-
the-Negev
222
Ramat Negev
Exp Station
Mash'abbe
Sade jctn
B
10
Shunera Dunes
French
Commando
Viewpoint
Tlalim
jctn
Tlalim
211
Ashalim
40

EGYPT
1948
Horvat
Halukim
Halukim
jctn
Sde Bo
(Ben Guri
Desert Ho
Nizzana
Checkpoint
Nizzana
Tel Nizzana
(Nessana)
Shivta
(Sobata)
Ben Gurion's
Grave Site
Ben Gurion
of 2
Havarim
Cistern
Upper Parking Lo
Ein Avdat
National Park
Lower Parking Lot
Wilder
10
Avdat
(Oboda)
40

C
Ezuz
Haruhot
jctn
Mizpe
Ramon
171
Makhtesh Ram
Kadesh Barnea
Borot Lotz

1   2   3

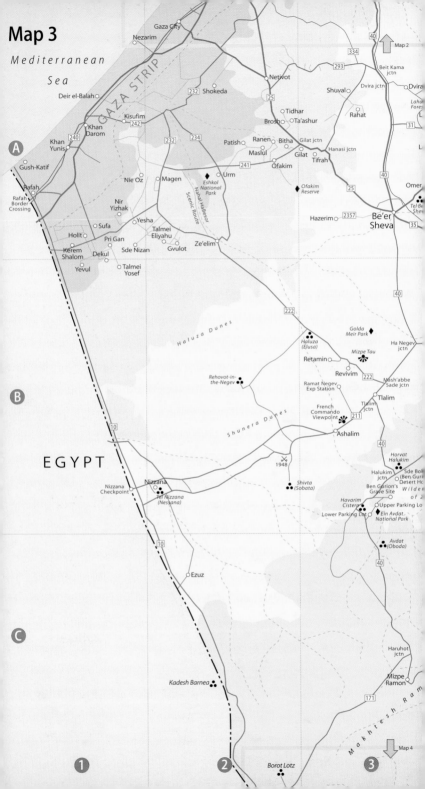

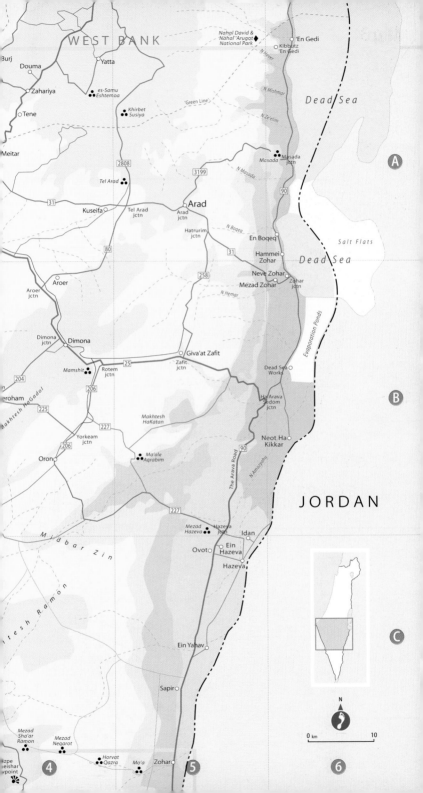

Map 4

Boror Lotz

Mezad Sha'ar Ramon
Mezad Neqarot
Horvat Qazra
Mo'a
Zohar

Map 3

Mizpe Hameishar Viewpoint

A

Paran
Kushi Rimon
Kilometre 101
Be'er Menuha
Menuha Jctn

Mizpe Paran Viewpoint

13

Zihor jctn

Midbar Paran

Nahal Shitim

40

B

Shizzafon
Yahel

Shizafon jctn

90

12   40

Kibbutz Lotan
Qetura Jctn

10

Qetura
Gerofit

Yeʼelim Holiday Village

'Uvda (Ovda) Airport

Shaharut
Yotvata

EGYPT

12

Hai-Bar Yotvata Wildlife Reserve

Samar

Elifaz

Sayarim jctn

Timna National Park

90

JORDA

Red Canyon

Be'er Ora

C

Mt Hizqiyyahu Observation Point

'Hidden Valley'

'Amram's Pillars'

'Black Canyon' (Nahal Shehoret)

Aqaba Airport

Netafim Crossing
Ein Netafim

Eilot
Arava Crossing

12

Mt Yoash
Mt Shlomo

Eilat

Aqaba

Mt TzʼFahot

Gulf of Aqaba

N

0 km   10

1   **2**   **3**

Complete listing

Latin America
Argentina Handbook 1st
1 900949 10 5 £11.99
Bolivia Handbook 1st
1 900949 09 1 £11.99
Bolivia Handbook 2nd
1 900949 49 0 £12.99
Brazil Handbook 1st
0 900751 84 3 £12.99
Brazil Handbook 2nd
1 900949 50 4 £13.99
Caribbean Islands Handbook 2000
1 900949 40 7 £14.99
Chile Handbook 2nd
1 900949 28 8 £11.99
Colombia Handbook 1st
1 900949 11 3 £10.99
Cuba Handbook 1st
1 900949 12 1 £10.99
Cuba Handbook 2nd
1 900949 54 7 £10.99
Ecuador & Galápagos Handbook 2nd
1 900949 29 6 £11.99
Mexico Handbook 1st
1 900949 53 9 £13.99
Mexico & Central America Handbook 2000
1 900949 39 3 £15.99
Peru Handbook 2nd
1 900949 31 8 £11.99
South American Handbook 2000
1 900949 38 5 £19.99
Venezuela Handbook 1st
1 900949 13 X £10.99
Venezuela Handbook 2nd
1 900949 58 X £11.99

Africa
East Africa Handbook 2000
1 900949 42 3 £14.99
Morocco Handbook 2nd
1 900949 35 0 £11.99
Namibia Handbook 2nd
1 900949 30 X £10.99
South Africa Handbook 2000
1 900949 43 1 £14.99
Tunisia Handbook 2nd
1 900949 34 2 £10.99
Zimbabwe Handbook 1st
0 900751 93 2 £11.99

Wexas
Traveller's Handbook
0 905802 08 X £14.99
Traveller's Healthbook
0 905802 09 8 £9.99

Asia
Cambodia Handbook 2nd
1 900949 47 4 £9.99
Goa Handbook 1st
1 900949 17 2 £9.99
Goa Handbook 2nd
1 900949 45 8 £9.99
India Handbook 2000
1 900949 41 5 £15.99
Indonesia Handbook 2nd
1 900949 15 6 £14.99
Indonesia Handbook 3rd
1 900949 51 2 £15.99
Laos Handbook 2nd
1 900949 46 6 £9.99
Malaysia & Singapore Handbook 2nd
1 900949 16 4 £12.99
Malaysia Handbook 3rd
1 900949 52 0 £12.99
Myanmar (Burma) Handbook 1st
0 900751 87 8 £9.99
Nepal Handbook 2nd
1 900949 44 X £11.99
Pakistan Handbook 2nd
1 900949 37 7 £12.99
Singapore Handbook 1st
1 900949 19 9 £9.99
Sri Lanka Handbook 2nd
1 900949 18 0 £11.99
Sumatra Handbook 1st
1 900949 59 8 £9.99
Thailand Handbook 2nd
1 900949 32 6 £12.99
Tibet Handbook 2nd
1 900949 33 4 £12.99
Vietnam Handbook 2nd
1 900949 36 9 £10.99

Europe
Andalucía Handbook 2nd
1 900949 27 X £9.99
Ireland Handbook 1st
1 900949 55 5 £11.99
Scotland Handbook 1st
1 900949 56 3 £10.99

Middle East
Egypt Handbook 2nd
1 900949 20 2 £12.99
Israel Handbook 2nd
1 900949 48 2 £12.99
Jordan, Syria & Lebanon Handbook 1st
1 900949 14 8 £12.99

What the papers say

"I carried the South American Handbook in my bag from Cape Horn to Cartagena and consulted it every night for two and a half months. And I wouldn't do that for anything else except my hip flask."

Michael Palin

"Footprint's India Handbook told me everything fro[m] the history of the region to where to get the best cur[r]

Jennie Bond, BBC correspondent

"Of all the main guidebook series this is genuinely th[e] only one we have never received a complaint about.

The Bookseller

"All in all, the Footprint Handbook series is the best thing that has happened to travel guidebooks in years. They are different and take you off the beaten track away from all the others clutching the competitors' guidebooks."

The Business Times, Singapore

Mail order

Available worldwide in good bookstores, Footprint Handbooks can also be ordered directly from us in Bath, via our website or from the address on the back cover.

Website

www.footprintbooks.com
Take a look for the latest news, to order a book or to join our mailing list.

Acknowledgements

Thanks to all who bought the first edition of the *Israel Handbook*, especially those who took the time to write and email with their comments and corrections. Particular thanks go to: Haskell Askin, USA; Seb Ballard, UK and Southern Africa; Allan Chapman, UK; Danan family, email; Dr Tim Dowley, UK; Rev. GR Fisher, email; JA Harari, Israel; Lawrence Joffe, UK; Monika Leech and John McGlade, email; Clare, Charlie and Beryl Leeke, Northern Ireland; Rudolf Eliot Lockhart, UK; Ivan Mannheim, editor of Footprint's *Jordan, Syria & Lebanon Handbook*; Rachel Parkinson, email; John Raley, USA; Dr Stefan Raueiser, Germany; Ben and Ann Robinson, UK; John Sitzia, UK; Mike Truman, email.

I would also like to thank all those who have been such great company during my various trips to Israel, notably: Sharon Biffin, Australia; Charlie and Alex, Sheff Wednesday; Darren Corrigan, USA; Scott 'join the military' Debie, USA; Richard 'Natchwey' Donovan, Canada; Lyse Doucet, BBC, Israel; Grethe Eneberg, Norway; Julie Goodwin, UK; Siobhan McGrath, Rep. of Ireland; Father Jerome Murphy-O'Connor, École Biblique et Archéologique Française, Jerusalem; Monique, Ash and Yassin, Jerusalem; Naomi Rosenberg, UK; Kath Ryan, New Zealand; Duncan 'oh, another bloody continental', UK. The superb line drawings are courtesy of Sahra Carter and Gareth (Tash) Courage. Most of all I would like to thank my wife Laurence for her continued love and support.